SCHEIN
BÜCHER

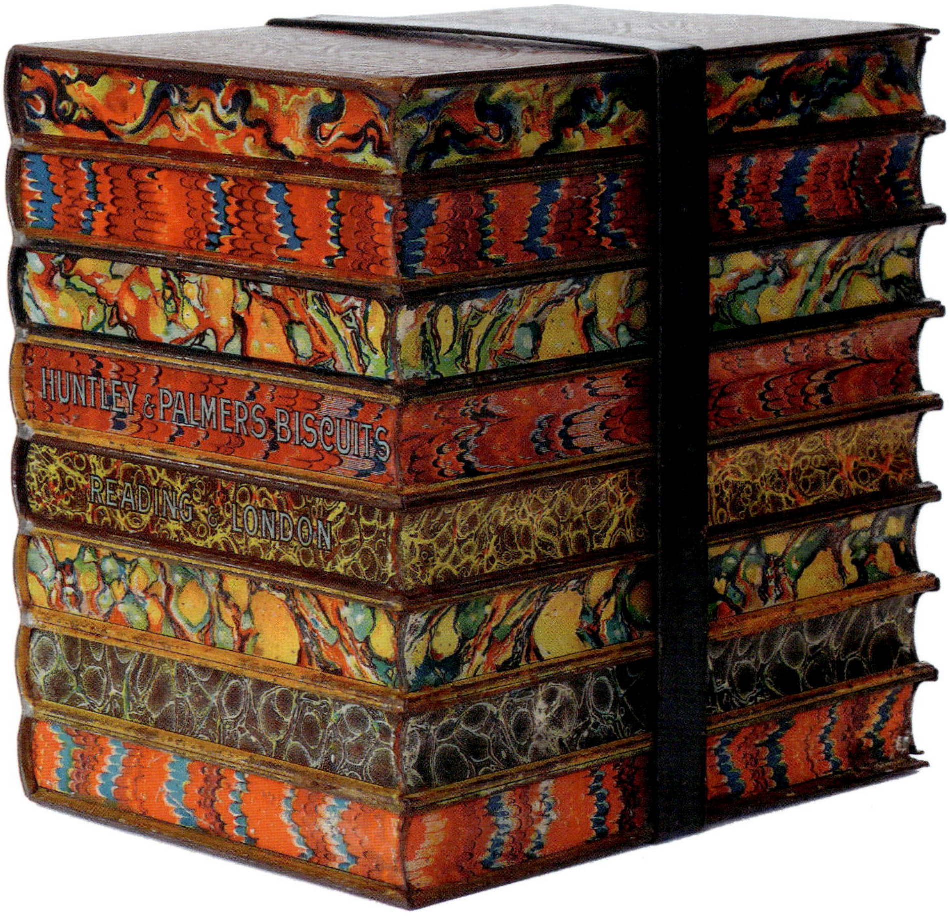

FAKE
BOOKS

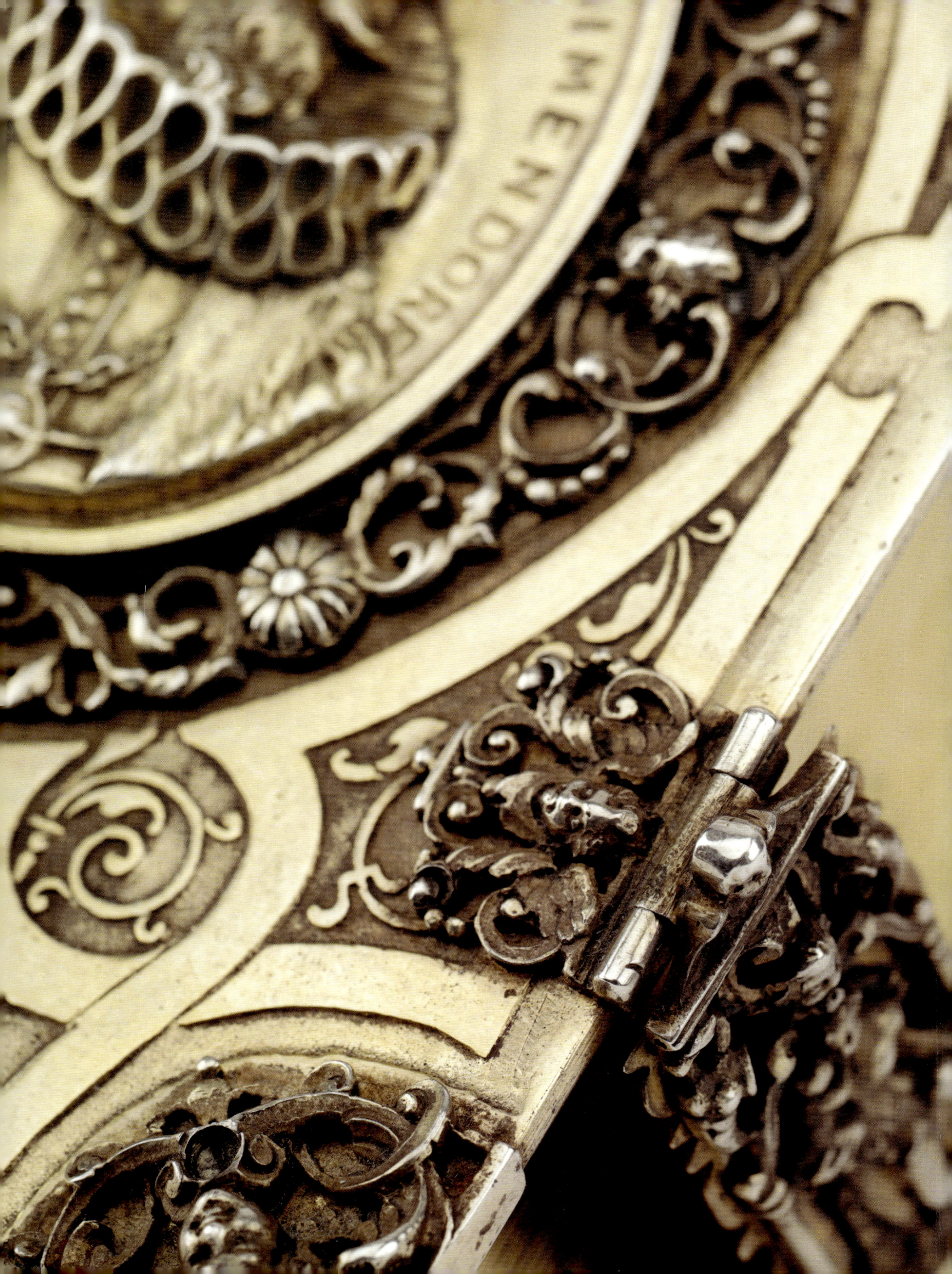

SCHEIN BÜCHER

Die Kunst der bibliophilen Täuschung

Die Sammlung Armin Müller Winterthur

FAKE BOOKS

The art of bibliophilic deceit

The collection Armin Müller Winterthur

BENTELI

Inhalt / *Contents*

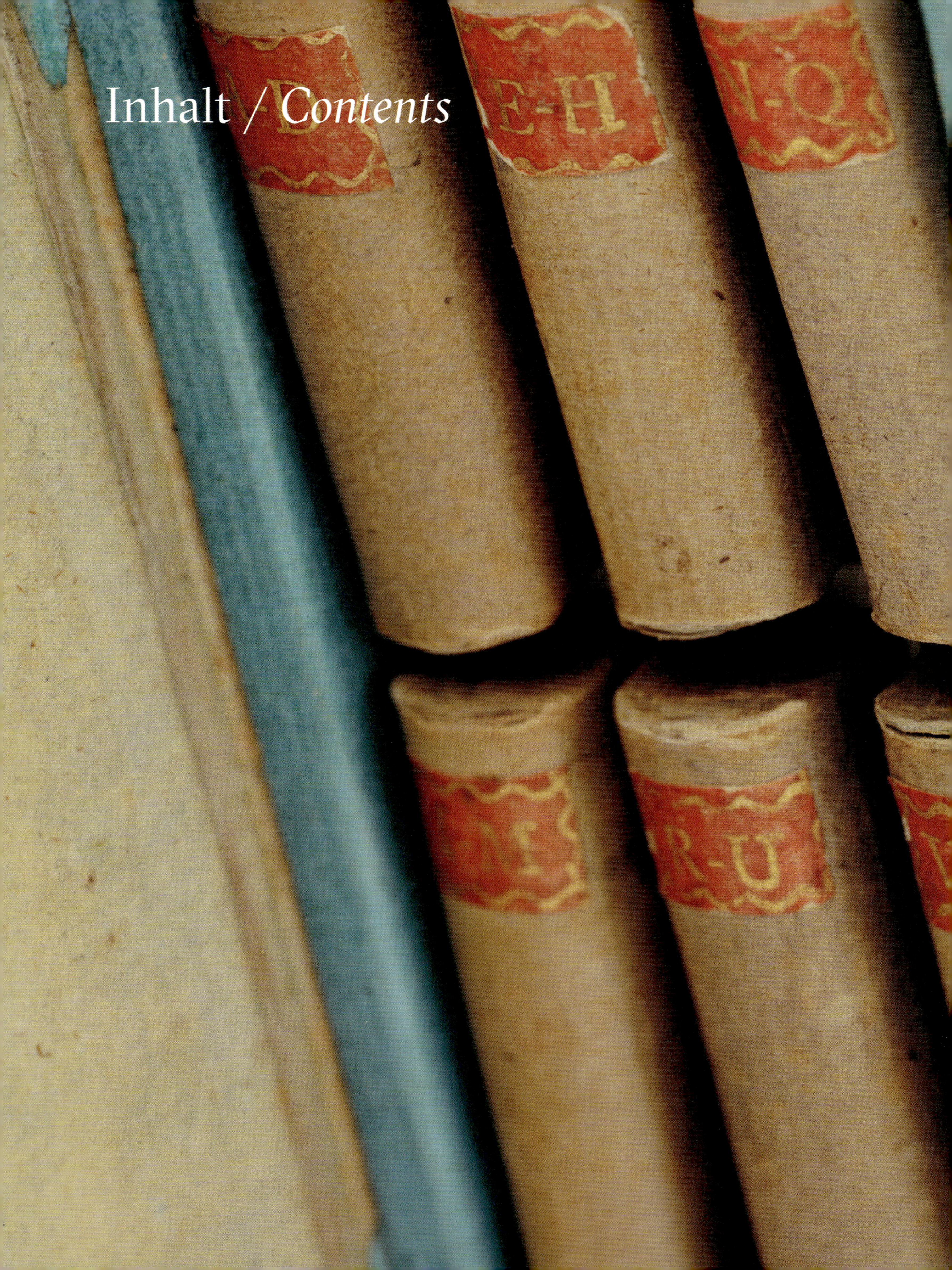

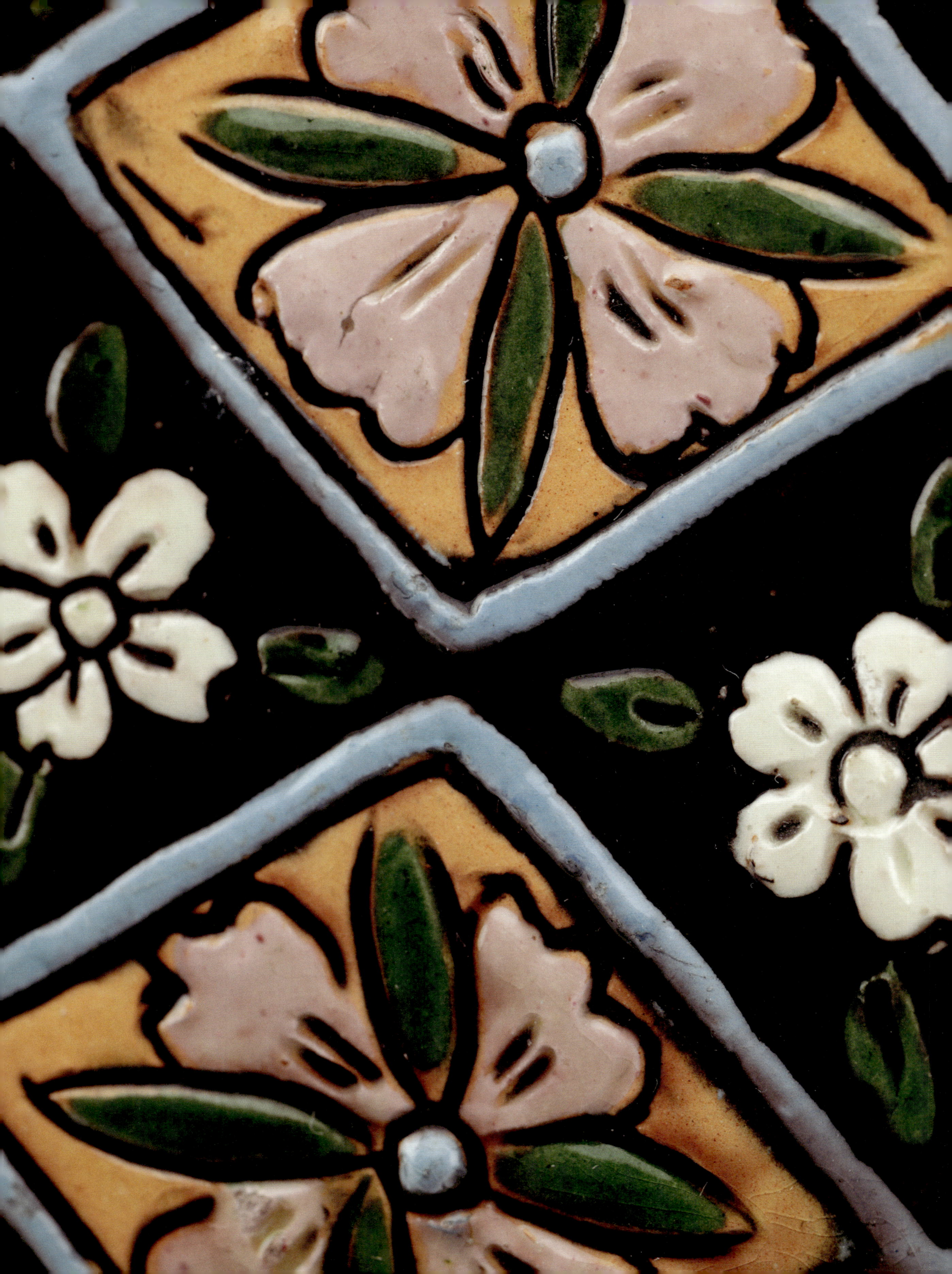

Umriss meiner Sammlung

Armin Müller, Winterthur

In meiner Kollektion von Scheinbüchern und Buchattrappen sind bis Anfang 2020 über 1500 Objekte zusammengetragen worden. An meine erste Buchattrappe kann ich mich nicht mehr genau erinnern. Vermutlich handelt es sich um ein bescheidenes Kartonschächtelchen in Buchform. In der Sammlung befinden sich wertvolle, kunsthistorisch und handwerklich interessante Stücke bis hin zum Kitsch. Zu finden sind sie auf Flohmärkten, Antiquitätenmessen und Auktionen. In meiner über fünfzigjährigen Sammlertätigkeit bin ich immer wieder überrascht vom Reichtum, den das Gebiet der Buchattrappen mit fantasievollen und kreativen Scheinbüchern hervorbringt. Kaum ist ein Objekt erstanden, setzt das Suchen und Aufspüren von neuem ein.

Buchattrappen sind echten Büchern nachempfunden: Sie simulieren richtige Bücher. Die geheimen Sammelbehälter sind entweder hohle oder massive Nachbildungen. Oft werden auch echte Bücher für Wertgegenstände, Liebesbriefe, Pistolen und vieles mehr ausgeschnitten und die Hohlräume mit Buntpapier ausgefüttert. Meistens sind die ersten paar Seiten erhalten, damit wird der Anschein eines echten Buches vorgetäuscht. Sehr wenige Bibliotheken und Sammler beschäftigen sich mit dieser Materie. Öffentliche Bestände sind im Deutschen Literaturarchiv Marbach und in der Zentralbibliothek Zürich vorhanden. Private Sammler gibt es kaum. Ebenso existiert kaum Literatur über das spezielle Thema. Die verwendeten Materialien sind äußerst vielfältig: Karton, Papier, Leder, Holz, Blech, Messing, Silber, Gold, Zinn, Elfenbein, Horn, Glas, Porzellan, Steingut, Stein, Wachs, Gewebe, Plüsch, Seide, Stroh, Bakelit und Kunststoff. Den Formaten sind ebenfalls keine Grenzen gesetzt. Sie reichen von Minibüchern bis hin zu großen Folianten.

Im Deutschen wird der Ausdruck mit Buchattrappe, Scheinbuch, Buchsimulant, falsche Bücher, oder Bücher, die keine sind, bezeichnet. Im Französischen spricht man von livres feints, livres simulés oder faux livres, im Englischen von counterfeit books, faux books, dummy books, book replicas oder fake books.

Wenn Gelehrsamkeit zur Attrappe wird, gibt sich der Besitzer eines Scheinbuches einerseits den Anschein des Belesenen, Gebildeten, andererseits ist das Buch, das keines ist, praktisch nutzbar. Funktionswandel heißt das Zauberwort, welches das Symbol von Bildung und Zivilisation für den, der das Geheimnis kennt, banalisiert.

In der Sammlung fehlen die sogenannten Bücher mit der Thematik Buch als Kunstwerk. Die Gattung würde den Rahmen sprengen. Eine umfassende Ausstellung dieser neuen künstlerischen Auseinandersetzungen mit dem altbekannten Buch als Objekt“ wurde 1977 in Kassel im Rahmen der documenta 6 unter dem Titel Metamorphose des Buches, Künstlerbücher der documenta 6“ gezeigt. Das Buchobjekt wendet sich gegen die sprachlich verstellte Wirklichkeit, schafft durch das Schweigen der Schrift Sprachfreiraum. Mitte der 1930er-Jahre taucht der Begriff Buchobjekt im Zusammenhang mit den Arbeiten des surrealistischen Künstlers und Buchbinders Georges Hugnet, 1906–1974, auf. Hugnet interpretierte mit der äußeren Gestaltung den Inhalt der Bücher, der durch ihn künstlerisch unangetastet bleibt.

Das Sammeln von Blechdosen ist weit verbreitet und sehr beliebt. Die Blütezeit der Blechverpackung liegt in den Anfängen des letzten Jahrhunderts. Die Biskuitdosen der 1841 gegründeten Firma Huntley & Palmer aus England, manche in Buchform, zählen zu den Inkunabeln aus der Geschichte der industriell gefertigten Behältnisse. Die Blechverpackung konnte im Laufe der Jahre ihren Zweck als Verpackung, die den Inhalt vor Bruch und Verderb schützen soll, beibehalten und hat zusätzlich die Funktion der visuellen Kommunikation angenommen. Dabei wurden alle grafischen und künstlerischen Register gezogen. Die Blechdose eignete sich ideal für direkte Werbebotschaften, da sie sich im Gegensatz zu Karton und Papier beliebig formen ließ. Das Bedrucken in großen Serien auf Blech war mit der Technik der Lithografie möglich. Im Allgemeinen wurde das Blech nach dem Druck noch mit Glanzlack überzogen, bevor die weitere Verarbeitung zur dreidimensionalen Dose erfolgte.

Wiener Bronzen, die eine auf einem offenen, die andere auf einem geschlossenen Buch sitzend, farbig gefasst
Viennese bronzes, one sitting on an open, the other one on a closed book, colored setting
Um / *Around* 1900 | 4 x 3,5 x 2,7 cm

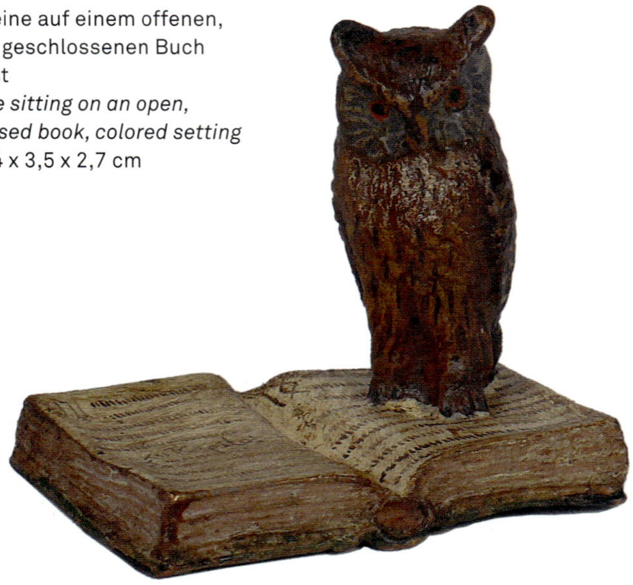

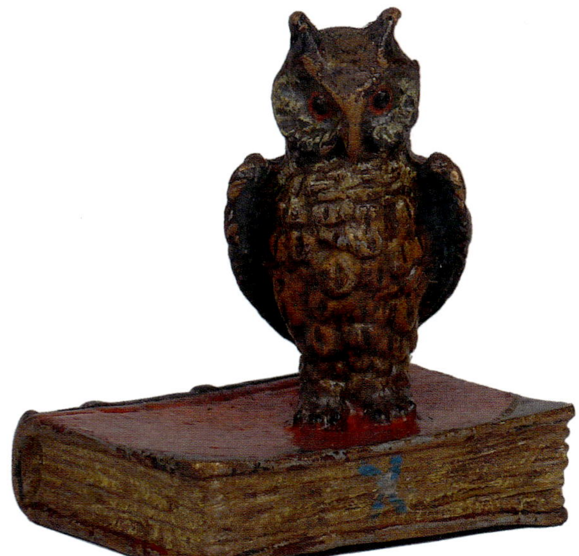

Von nachgeahmten Trinkgefäßen in Buchform sprach man im 16. und 17. Jahrhundert auch von Schnapsbibeln und Teufelsgebetbüchern. Oft werden sie auch mit den sogenannten Körperwärmeflaschen und Handwärmern verwechselt. Hervorzuheben ist ein Scherztrinkgefäß in der Form eines Buches aus Fayence, datiert 1584, in der Sammlung des Schweizerischen Landesmuseums in Zürich, hergestellt vom ersten tätigen Hafner und Maler Ludwig I. Pfau aus Winterthur, geboren um 1547, gestorben am 7. August 1597. Die Herstellung der Trinkgefäße reichten von edlen Materialien bis hin zum Kunststoff.

Sehr behütet werden die sogenannten Holzbibliotheken, auch Xylotheken genannt. Berühmt sind die Ebensberger Bestände aus Deutschland, die zwischen 1790 und 1804 vom ehemaligen Niederaltaicher Benediktinermönch, späteren Pfarrer zu Ebensberg und Forstbotaniker Candid Huber (1747–1813) aus dem Kloster Ebensberg in Bayern angefertigt wurden. Eine Holzbibliothek ist eine Sammlung von Holz und anderen Bestandteilen verschiedener Baumarten und Sträuchern in Buchform. Die kastenförmigen Behälter dienten der Aufnahme von Zweigen, Blättern, Samen, Früchten und gelegentlich auch von Schädlingen des jeweiligen Baumes, die dreidimensional vorgestellt werden. Die Außenseiten dieser Holzbücher zeigen den Längsschnitt des Holzes, die Buchrücken bestehen aus der Rinde des Baumes. Titelschilder auf den Buchrücken sind in lateinischer, deutscher, französischer und englischer Sprache angebracht. Lederscharniere und Lederbänder halten die Holzbücher zusammen. Aufgestellt sind die Bände in sieben unterschiedlichen, nach „Höhenklassen" der Gewächse abgestuften Formaten von Bauholz bis hinab zu rankenden Sträuchern und kriechendem Erdholz. Die Bände der wertvollsten, zum Bauen geeigneten Hölzer sind mit 23 cm am höchsten. Die kleinsten, nur 10 cm hohen Bände stellen Sträucher wie z. B. die Preiselbeere dar. Das Anfassen der Bände erlaubt die Erfahrung des Gewichts sowie die Härte und Struktur des Holzes mit den Händen. Candid Hubers Holzbibliotheken waren der Mühe und dem Aufwand bei Materialsammlung entsprechend kostspielig. Die 100-bändige von 1792 kostete 50 Gulden, damals den halben Jahreslohn eines einfachen Handwerkers. Die Abnehmer waren im Wesentlichen adelige Waldbesitzer, Klöster und Forstleute. Für Akademien war der Besitz solcher Sammlungen eine Prestigeangelegenheit.

Eine beachtliche Sammlung von Candid Huber kam als Schenkung vom Bergwerksdirektor und Salinenkommissar Sebastian Clais 1795 an die Stadtbibliothek Winterthur. Clais stammte aus dem Badischen, wo er beim Markgrafen hohes Ansehen genoss. In Winterthur wurde er zum „Schweizer Pionier der Wirtschaft und Technik", und ließ sich das herrschaftliche „Lindengut" bauen. Die Stadtoberen hatten mit der Konservierung des kuriosen Geschenks ihre liebe Mühe, sodass sich bald einmal „allerley Würmer und zehnfingrige Insekten verderblich" darüber hermachten. 1813 wurde deshalb kurzerhand beschlossen, das hölzerne Buchwerk einem Liebhaber gegen „anständige" Bücher einzutauschen. Auf diesem Umweg gelangte die Kostbarkeit 1950 von 93 Bändchen schließlich in den Besitz der Naturwissenschaftlichen Sammlung in Winterthur. Das Naturmuseum Frauenfeld besitzt ebenfalls 135 Holzbücher von Huber. Die Kollektion wurde erst kürzlich in einem vergessenen Kasten auf dem Dachboden wiederentdeckt. Berühmt und wertvoll ist die Sammlung von Holzarten von Carl Schildbach (1730–1817) im Naturkundemuseum Kassel. Die Sammlung ist mit ihren 530 Bändchen, spätestens ab 1780 von Hölzern und Pflanzenteilen angefertigt, die kunstvollste ihrer Art.

Die umfangreichste Holzbibliothek in Moskau, wohl einzigartig weltweit, ist vor rund 100 Jahren vom russischen Holzforscher Professor Turski in die Abteilung für Forstwirtschaft an der Timirjazev-Akademie für Landwirtschaft gegründet worden. Sie enthält Muster von über 600 Baum- und Buschhölzern, die wie Bücher auf Gestellen aufgereiht und mit russischen und lateinischen Namen beschriftet sind. Es handelt sich hier nicht nur um ein interessantes Kuriosum,

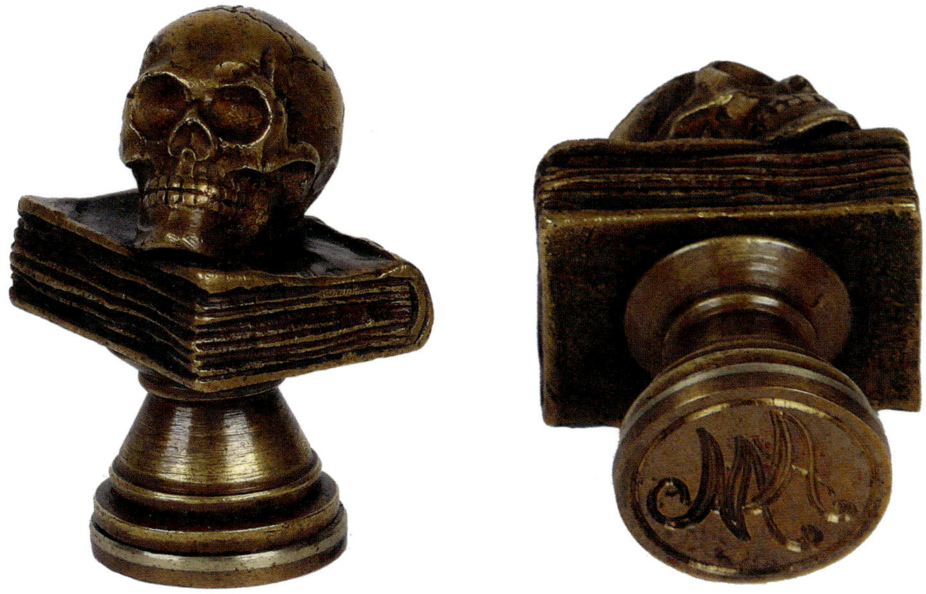

Bronzepetschaft mit Totenkopf auf einem geschlossenem Buch, graviertes Monogramm „AM“
Signet in bronze with skull on a closed book, engraved monogram “AM”
Um / *Around* 1900 | 4,5 x 2,8 x 2,2 cm

sondern auch um ein nützliches Instrumentarium für wissenschaftliche Arbeit.

Buchtäuschungen im großen Stil verdanken wir dem Barock und Rokoko. Fiktive Bibliotheken sind nicht nur auf Wände, sondern auch auf Schränke, Regale und Türen gemalt. Bibliotheksbesitzer wollten oft nicht zugeben, dass sie gar nicht so viele Bücher hatten, so wurden Scheinbuchbestände errichtet. Die falschen Buchrücken wurden einfach auf den Verputz gemalt, in mehr oder weniger aufwändiger buchbinderischer Ausführung, aus vergoldetem Leder, auf Wände, Türen und Möbelstücke geklebt. Später sind auch Buchtapeten verwendet worden, wie sie die Trompe-l'œil-Malerei herstellt.

Der Wachsstock, ein typisches Produkt volkstümlicher Frömmigkeit, ist als spezielle Form der Kerze anzusehen. Unter der Vielfalt der möglichen Formen finden sich häufig Nachbildungen von Gebetsbüchern, teilweise mit buchartig zu öffnenden Deckeln und detailfreudig gestalteten Frontispizen. Meist ist der Wachsdraht um einen Holzkern gewickelt. Vom 16. bis 19. Jahrhundert war der unverzierte Wachsstock ein einfaches, aber wertvolles Leuchtmittel. Als der Wachsstock im 19. Jahrhundert und vor allem im 20. Jahrhundert seine Funktion als Beleuchtungsmittel verlor, begann er zu einem kostbaren, in Ehren gehaltenen Erinnerungsstück zu werden. Reich verziert und aufwändig geformt waren diese Wachsstöcke zu schade und zu schön zum Abbrennen. Umgeben sind sie von Rahmenwerk und floralem Dekor in farbiger Wachsbossierung. Der Rücken ist leicht gewölbt, die Schnitte sind vergoldet, und den Vorderschnitt überspannen zwei „Schließen“. Noch heute gibt es mancherorts ein reiches Angebot von solchen schnurförmigen Kerzen. Vor allem im katholisch geprägten süddeutschen und österreichischen Raum gab es früher den Brauch, an Mariä Lichtmess (2. Februar) der Braut, den Töchtern und auch den Dienstmädchen Wachsstöcke zu schenken.

Das Stammbuch ist eine frühe Form des Poesiealbums. Zu kaum einer anderen Zeit nahm der Freundschaftskult einen solchen Stellenwert ein wie in der Epoche des Biedermeier. Bestand die frühe Form eines gebundenen Bändchens aus leeren Blättern, so machte sich zum Ende des 18. Jahrhunderts eine Veränderung bemerkbar. Es entstanden kleine Kästchen, im Oktavformat richtigen Büchern nachempfunden. Die losen Blätter konnten nun einzeln zum Beschriften aus der Hand gegeben werden, und nicht mehr das ganze Buch, was sicher ein großer Vorteil war. Der Ausstattung der Kassetten waren kaum mehr Grenzen gesetzt. Imitierte, handvergoldete Halb- und Ganzlederbände, geprägte Kaliko-Einbände im Kathedralstil, Papiereinbände mit Farb-, Gold- und Silberprägung waren zu dieser Zeit in Mode. Im 19. Jahrhundert wird die bildliche und gotische Gestaltung des Einbandes als Kirchenarchitektur optisch zum Abbild der Kathedrale. Das Innenleben ist meistens mit farbigem Glanzpapier ausgefüttert, und die losen Blätter sind mit einem Goldschnitt versehen, die mittels eines Seidenbändchens aus der Kassette herausgezogen werden konnten. Die Vorsatzblätter sind oft mit einem kolorierten Kupferstich oder mit einer Stickerei versehen. Ganz gleich wie luxuriös oder schlicht die Aufmachung und die inhaltliche Gestaltung auch waren, letztlich erfüllten sie nur einen Zweck: Erinnerung und Freundschaft sind die Zauberworte, die Seele dieser entzückenden Kästchen: „Ewig soll die Freundschaft blüh'n“.

Den meisten sind die Buchattrappen von Möbelhäusern geläufig. Sie sind ein Element der Raumgestaltung, die den Käufer täuschen und beeindrucken sollen. Sie werden auch Buchimitate und Platzhalter genannt, und suggerieren einen dekorativen und imponierenden Wissensraum. Ältere Produkte sind aus massiven gerundeten Holzbrettchen gefertigt und mit Leder überzogen, die Buchrücken handvergoldet. Das Ziel ist auch hier, den Besucher und Betrachter zu täuschen.

Die Vielfältigkeit und Palette der Scheinbücher scheinen unerschöpflich zu sein. So finden sich immer wieder noch nie entdeckte, kuriose und interessante Stücke. Oft sind die Objekte der Verwendung, der Herkunft und dem Alter nach nur schwer zuzuordnen.

Outline of my collection

Armin Müller, Winterthur

In my collection of bogus books and book dummies, I have more than 1500 objects collected until the beginning of 2020. I cannot remember exactly my first book dummy. Presumably it was a modest cardboard box in book form. The collection varies from art historical and
artisanal pieces of interest to kitsch. They can be found at flea markets, antique fairs and auctions. In my collecting activity of more than 50 years, I have always been surprised by the imaginative and creative richness in the field of book dummies. As soon as an object has been purchased, the search and hunt-up starts again.

Book dummies are based on real books; they give the impression of real books. The secret collection containers are either hollow or massive replicas. Often real books are cut out; the cavities are lined with colored paper and used for objects of value, love letters, pistols and much more. Mostly, the first few pages are preserved, so as to give the impression of a real book. Very few libraries and collectors deal with this matter. Public stock is available in the German Literature Archive Marbach and in the Zentralbibliothek Zürich. There are hardly any private collectors or any literature on the specific topic. The materials used are extremely diverse: cardboard, paper, leather, wood, tin, brass, silver, gold, tin, ivory, horn, glass, porcelain, stoneware, stone, wax, fabric, plush, silk, straw, Bakelite and plastic. The formats are also unlimited. They range from mini books to large folios.

In German, the terms used are Buchattrappe, Scheinbuch, Buchsimulant, falsche Bücher, Bücher, die keine sind. In French one speaks of livres feints, livres simulés or faux livres. In English, counterfeit books, faux books, dummy books, book replicas or fake books.

When eruditeness becomes a dummy, the owner of a bogus book gives on one side the appearance of the well-read, educated. On the other hand, the book, which is not really a book, is put to practical use. Functional change is the magic word which trivialises the symbol of education and civilization, for the one who knows the secret.

The collection lacks so-called books with the theme 'book as a work of art'. This genre would go beyond the scope. A comprehensive exhibition of these new artistic involvement with the well-known 'Book as an object', was shown in Kassel in 1977 as part of documenta 6 under the title 'Metamorphosis of the Book, artist books of documenta 6'. The book object turns against the linguistically distorted reality, creating a breathing space enabled through the absence of writing. In the mid-1930s, the term book object emerged in connection with the work of the surrealist artist and bookbinder Georges Hugnet, 1906–1974. Hugnet interpreted with the external design the content of the books, which remained artistically untouched by him.

Collecting tin cans is widespread and very popular. The heyday of tin packaging dates back to the beginning of the last century. The biscuit tins from England, Huntley & Palmer, founded in 1841, with some in book form, are among the incunabula from the history of industrially manufactured containers. Over the years, tin packaging has retained its purpose as packaging designed to protect the contents from breakage and spoil, and has additionally adopted the function of visual communication. All graphic and artistic stops were pulled out. The tin can was ideally suited for direct advertising messages, as it could be shaped as desired in contrast to cardboard and paper. The printing in large series was possible with the technology of lithography. In general, the sheet was coated with gloss paint after printing before further processing on the three-dimensional box.

In the 16th and 17th centuries, imitation drinking vessels in book form were also called schnapps bibles and devil prayer books. Often they are also mistaken for the so-called hot water bottles and hand warmers. Of particular note is a joke drinking vessel in the form of a faience book in the collection of the Swiss National Museum in Zurich, dated 1584, produced by the first active potter and painter Ludwig l. Pfau from Winterthur, born about 1547, died on August 7, 1597. The production of the drinking vessels ranged from noble materials to plastic.

Histoire de l'Eglise, Vol. 4
Ausgehöhlter, brauner, marmorierter Kalbsledereinband, Geheimfach ausgefüttert mit Schneckenmarmorpapier, Rücken- und Deckelvergoldung, Supralibros, zwei Titelschilder, dreiseitiger Sprengschnitt
Hollowed brown marbled calfskin binding, secret compartment lined with snail marbled paper, gilt spine and cover, supralibros, two title plates, all edges sprinkled
Toulouse, Frankreich / *France*
1809 | 21,3 x 13,6 x 4 cm

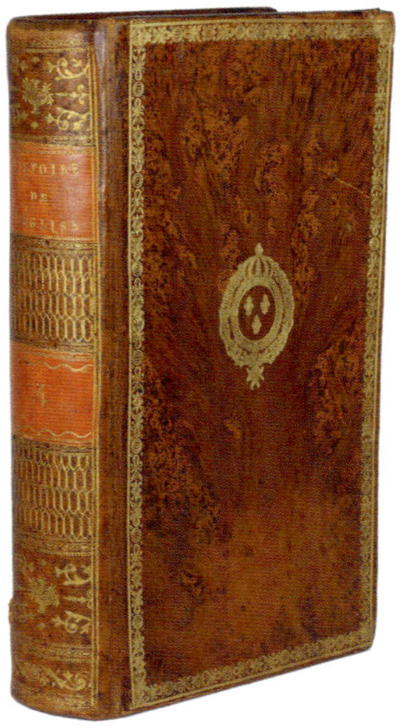

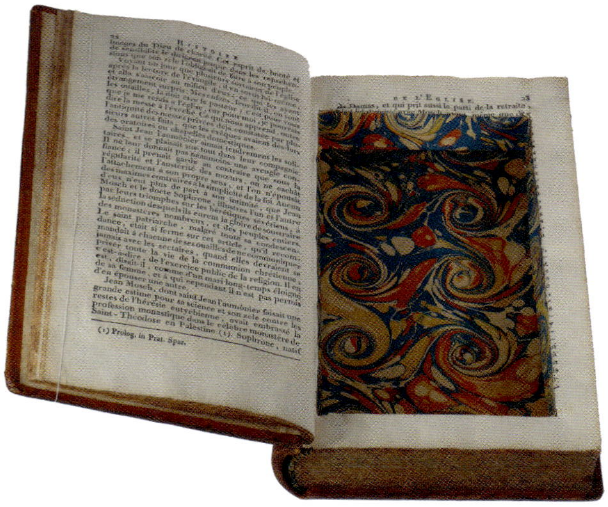

Very protected are the so-called wooden libraries, also called xylothecs. Famous are the Ebensberger stocks from Germany, which were made between 1790 and 1804 by the former Niederaltaicher Benedictine monks, and later by pastor Ebensberg and forest botanist Candid Huber (1747–1813), from the monastery Ebensberg in Bavaria. A wooden library is a collection of wood and other components of various tree species and shrubs in book form. The box shaped containers were used to hold branches, leaves, seeds, fruits and occasionally pests of the tree, which are presented three-dimensionally. The outsides of these wooden books show the longitudinal section of the wood, the spines are made of the bark of the tree with title plates in Latin, German, French and English language. Leather hinges and leather straps hold the wooden books together. The volumes are arranged in seven different formats, graded according to 'height classes' of the plants, from timber to shrubs and trailing wood. The highest volumes, at 23 cm high, are made of the most precious and valuable wood and most suitable for the construction of buildings. The smallest volumes, at only 10 cm high, depict shrubs such as cranberries. Touching the volumes allows the experience of the weight as well as the hardness and structure of the wood by hand. Candid Huber's wood libraries were the most expensive and as a result took time to collect. The 100-volume from 1792 cost 50 guilders, which was half the annual wage of a simple craftsman. The customers were essentially aristocratic forest owners, monasteries and foresters. For academies, the possession of such collections presented a prestigious opportunity.

A considerable collection of Candid Huber's has been given as a donation from the mine director and Salinenkommissar Sebastian Clais, 1795, to the city library Winterthur. Clais came from the Baden region, where he enjoyed high reputation of the margrave. In Winterthur he became a 'Swiss pioneer of the economy and technology', and had built the lordly 'Lindengut'. The city leaders had considerable trouble with the preservation of the curious gift, resulting in 'all kinds of worms and ten-fingered insects ruining it'. In 1813 it was decided without further ado that the wooden books would be given to a lover of such books and exchanged the collection for 'decent' books. In 1950, the treasure of 93 booklets finally came into the possession of the Natural History Collection in Winterthur. The Naturmuseum Frauenfeld also own 135 wooden books by Huber. The collection was recently rediscovered in a forgotten box in the attic of the museum. Famous and valuable is the collection of wood species by Carl Schildbach, 1730–1817, in the Natural History Museum, Kassel. The collection with its 530 booklets made of wood and plant parts of no later than 1780, is the most artful of its kind.

The largest wooden library in Moscow, probably the only one of its kind in the world, was founded around a 100 years ago by the Russian wood scientist Professor Turski in the Department of Forestry at the Timirjazev Academy of Agriculture. It contains patterns of more than 600 trees and shrubs that are lined up like books on racks and labelled with Russian and Latin names. This is not only an interesting curiosity, but also a useful tool for scientific work.

We owe much to Baroque and Rococo for book illusions. Fictional libraries are not only painted on walls, but also on cabinets, shelves and doors. Library owners often did not want to admit that they did not possess that many books, so bogus book stocks were established. The fake spines were simply painted on the plaster, or in more or less demanding bookbinding with gilded leather glued to walls, doors or furniture. Later, trompe-l'œil painting wallpapers were used.

The wax stick, as a special form of candle is to be regarded as a typical product of popular religiosity. Among the variety of possible forms are often replicas of prayer books, some with book-alike opening covers and detailed designed frontispieces. Mostly the wax wire is wound around a wooden core. From the 16th to the 19th century, the undecorated wax taper was a simple but valuable illuminant. In the 19th century, and especially in the 20th century, as wax

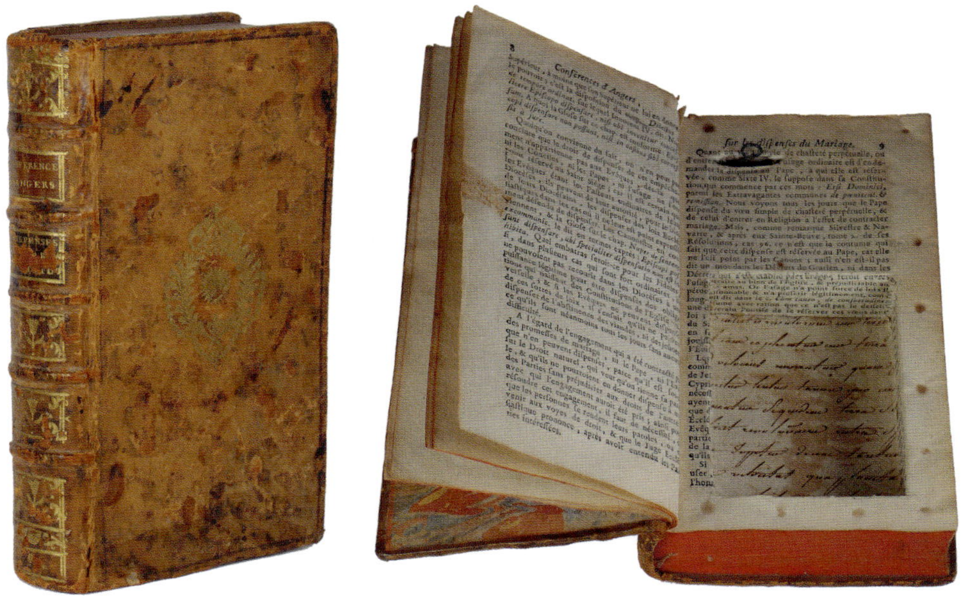

Conferences Dangers
Ausgehöhlter, brauner, marmorierter Kalbsledereinband, Geheimfach und Spieldose, fünf erhabene Bünde, Rückenvergoldung, zwei Titelschilder, Supralibros, dreiseitiger roter Farbschnitt, Schneckenmarmorpapiervorsatz
Hollowed brown marbled calfskin binding, secret compartment and music box, five raised bands, gilt spine, two title labels, supralibros, all edges in red color, scroll marbled endpapers
Paris, Frankreich / *France* 1778
17,5 x 10,8 x 3,7 cm

began to lose its function as an illuminant, it began to become a precious, cherished memento. Richly decorated and lavishly shaped, these wax sticks were too good and too beautiful to burn off. They are surrounded by framework and floral decor in colored wax embossing. The back is slightly arched, the cuts are gilded, and the front cut span had two 'clasps'. In some places, even today, a rich offering of such corded candles can be found. Especially in catholic South German and Austrian regions, there had been a custom of giving wax sticks to the bride, daughters and female servants on Assumption Day (2nd February).

The family book is an early form of the poetry album. At no other time did the cult of friendship take on such importance as in the epoch of Biedermeier. If the early form of a bound booklet consisted of empty leaves, then by the end of the 18th century there was a noticeable change. Small boxes in the octave format of real books were created. Instead of the whole book, the loose sheets could now be handed out individually for labelling, which was certainly advantageous. There were hardly any limits for the decor of the cassettes. Imitated hand-gilded, half-leather and leather volumes, embossed calico bindings in the cathedral style, paper-ober-boards with color gold and silver tooling were in fashion at the time. In the 19th century, the pictorial and gothic design of the binding as church architecture became a visual image of the cathedral. The interior is usually lined with colored glossy paper, and the loose sheets are provided with a gold section, which could be pulled out of the cassette by a silk ribbon. The endpaper is often provided with a colored copper engraving or with embroidery. No matter how luxurious or simple the presentation and the content were, they ultimately fulfilled only one purpose: memory and friendship are the magic words, the soul of these delightful little boxes: 'Friendship shall bloom forever'.

Most of the book dummies of furniture stores are familiar. They are an element of interior design that should deceive and impress the buyer. They are also called book imitations and placeholders, suggesting a decorative and impressive range of knowledge. Older products are made of solid rounded wooden boards and covered with leather, the spine hand gold-plated. The goal here too is to deceive the visitor and viewer.

The variety and palette of fake books seems to be inexhaustible. So you will find again and again never discovered, curious and interesting pieces. Often the objects are difficult to classify according to use, origin and age.

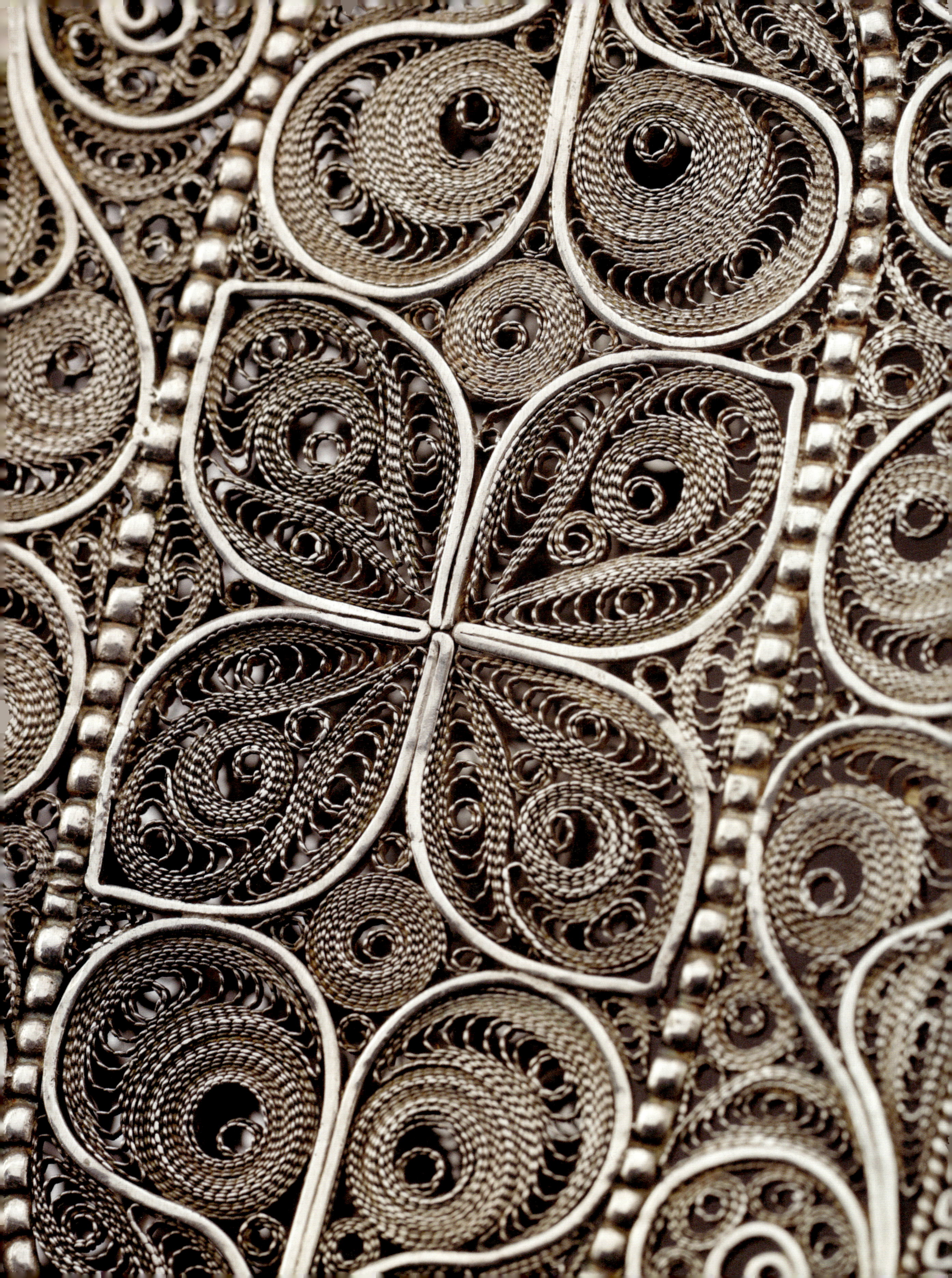

Besondere Schätze
Special Treasures

Das Aufstöbern von Raritäten und Kuriositäten auf Märkten ist sehr aufwändig, macht aber Spaß. Das Sprichwort „Die Konkurrenz schläft nicht" trifft hier ins Schwarze.

Flohmärkte gibt es in jeder Stadt und nahezu in jedem Dorf. In der Regel sind die Händler Privatpersonen, die sich überflüssiger gebrauchter Sachen entledigen wollen. Leider werden oft Ramsch von minderer Qualität und Neuwaren angeboten, gelegentlich auch „heiße Ware". Seinen Namen verdankt der Flohmarkt mutmaßlich der Vorstellung, dass in den angebotenen Textilien auch Flöhe sitzen. Der Begriff Brocante bezeichnet den Altwarenhandel und ist zwischen Trödel, Kunst- und Antiquitätenhandel anzusiedeln.

In der Schweiz finden Flohmärkte regelmäßig an Samstagen statt. In Zürich auf dem Bürkliplatz, in Winterthur in der Altstadt. Beliebt sind auch die Märkte in Genf, Basel, Tessin, die jährliche Veranstaltung in Le Landeron, die Weihnachtssammlerbörse in Zürich und neuerdings im Air Force Center in Dübendorf. Der Flohmarkt Kanzlei in Zürich ist wohl der größte schweizerische Ganzjahresflohmarkt.

Es lohnt sich, den sogenannten „Flohmarktknigge" oder die „goldenen Regeln" für Flohmarkt-Besucher zu befolgen: Je früher man auf dem Markt ist, desto größer und besser ist das Angebot. Je später man auf dem Platz ist, desto günstigere Schnäppchen sind möglich, da viele Händler ihre Ware lieber zu Spottpreisen verschleudern, als sie wieder mit nach Hause zu nehmen. Nie den geforderten Preis zahlen – feilschen ist in den meisten Fällen erlaubt! Der ausgehandelte Betrag liegt dann irgendwo in der Mitte.

Händlerinnen und Händler kennen im Laufe der Jahre die Sammelgebiete und Vorlieben ihrer Stammkunden. Sie bewahren Schätze und Raritäten oftmals separat unter dem Ladentisch. Um die besten Schnäppchen zu machen, muss man nicht frühmorgens anwesend sein. Jedoch kennen die Händler ihre Pappenheimer ganz genau, was sich manchmal im Preis bemerkbar macht.

Finding rarities and curiosities at markets is very time-consuming, but fun. The proverb "The competition doesn't sleep" hits the bull's eyes here. There are flea markets in every town and almost every village. Usually the traders are private individuals who want to get rid of superfluous used goods. Unfortunately, junk of inferior quality or new goods are often offered, occasionally also "hot stuff". The flea market owes its name probably to the idea that fleas reside in the textiles on offer. The term Brocante describes the old goods trade and is to be settled between second-hand goods, art and antiques trade.

In Switzerland, flea markets are held regularly on Saturdays. In Zurich on Bürkliplatz, in Winterthur in the old town. The markets in Geneva, Basel, Ticino, the annual event in Le Landeron and the Christmas collectors' fair in Zurich are also popular, as is the Air Force Center in Dübendorf. The flea market Kanzlei in Zurich is probably the largest all-year flea market in Switzerland.

It is worth to follow the so-called "flea market etiquette" or the "golden rules" for flea market visitors: The earlier you get to the market, the larger and better the offer. The later you are on the square, the better bargains are available, as many traders prefer to sell their goods at ridiculously low prices rather than take them home again. Never pay the required price - haggling is allowed in most cases! The negotiated amount is then somewhere in the middle.

Over the years, traders have become familiar with the collection areas and preferences of their regular customers. They often keep treasures and rarities separately under the counter. You don't have to be there early in the morning to get the best bargains. However, dealers know their customers inside out, which sometimes affects the price.

1.001
Schmuckschatulle aus Holz mit Spiegel und Stofffutter, Deckel mit Intarsien und Bemalung, zwei schwenkbare Einsätze
Wooden jewelry box with mirror and lining, lid with marquetry and painting, two pivotable compartments
1950er-Jahre / *1950s* | 13,5 x 24,5 x 2,7 cm

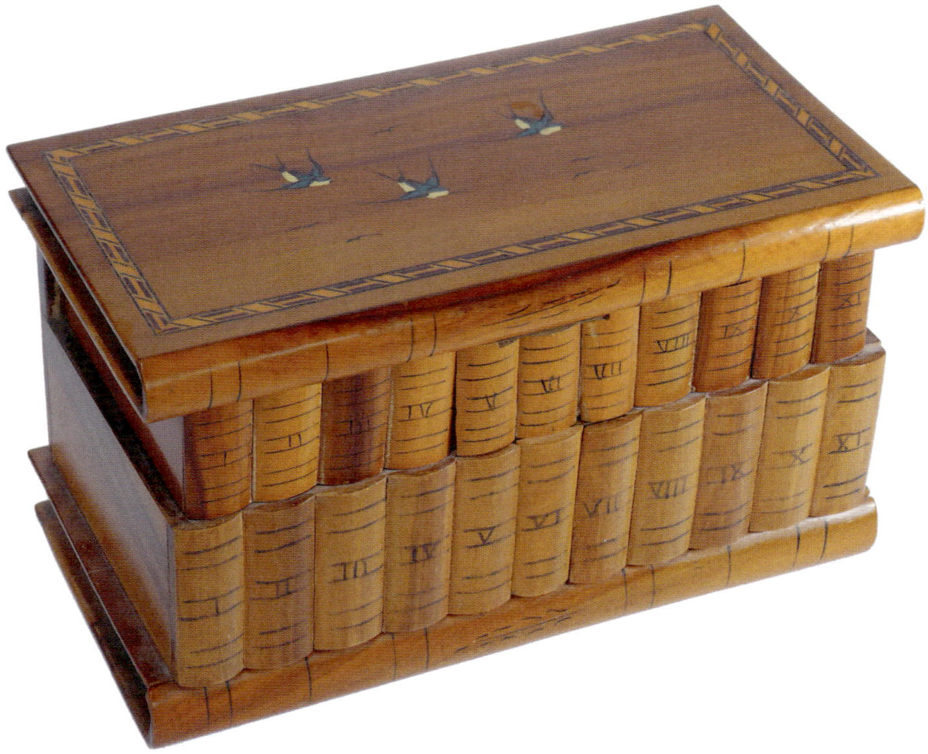

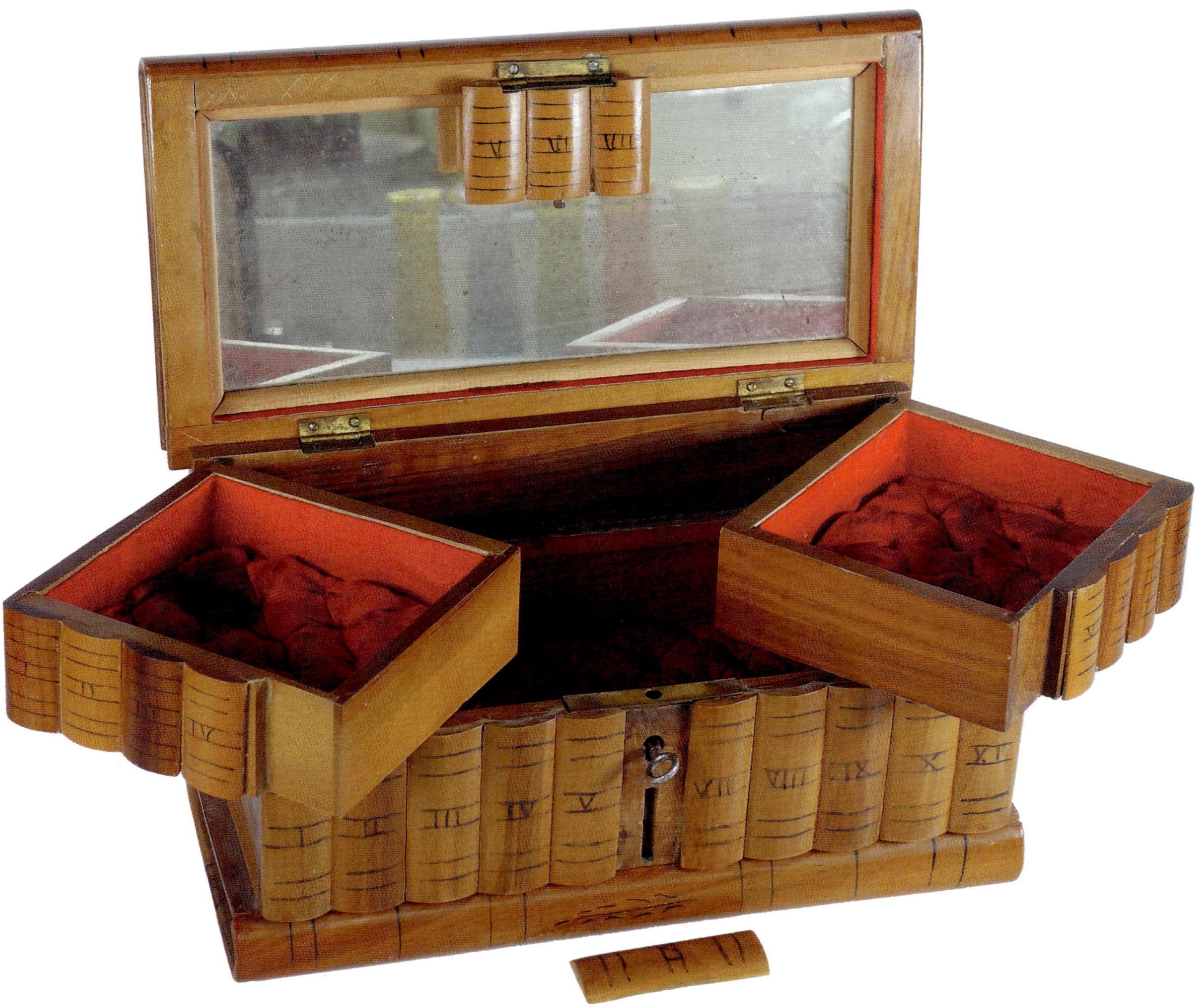

1.002
Schmuckschatulle aus Holz mit Stofffutter, Deckel mit Intarsien und Bemalung, Verschluss verschiebbarer Buchrücken
Wooden jewelry box with lining, lid with marquetry and an illustration, closure with a sliding spine
1950er-Jahre / *1950s* | 10,3 x 22,2 x 13,5 cm

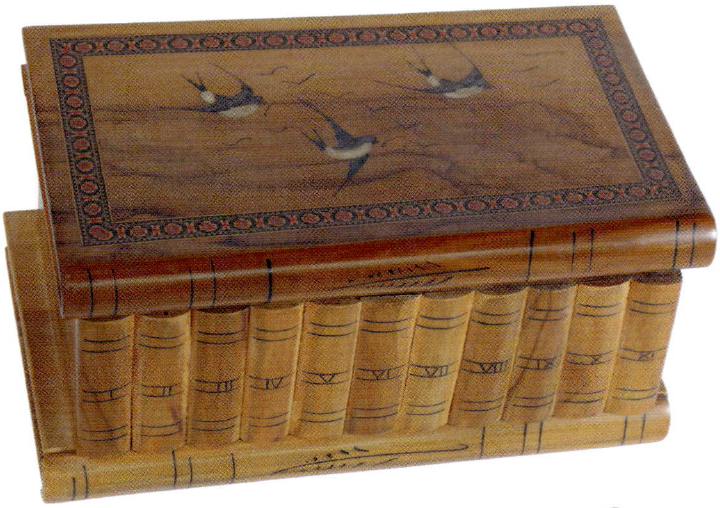

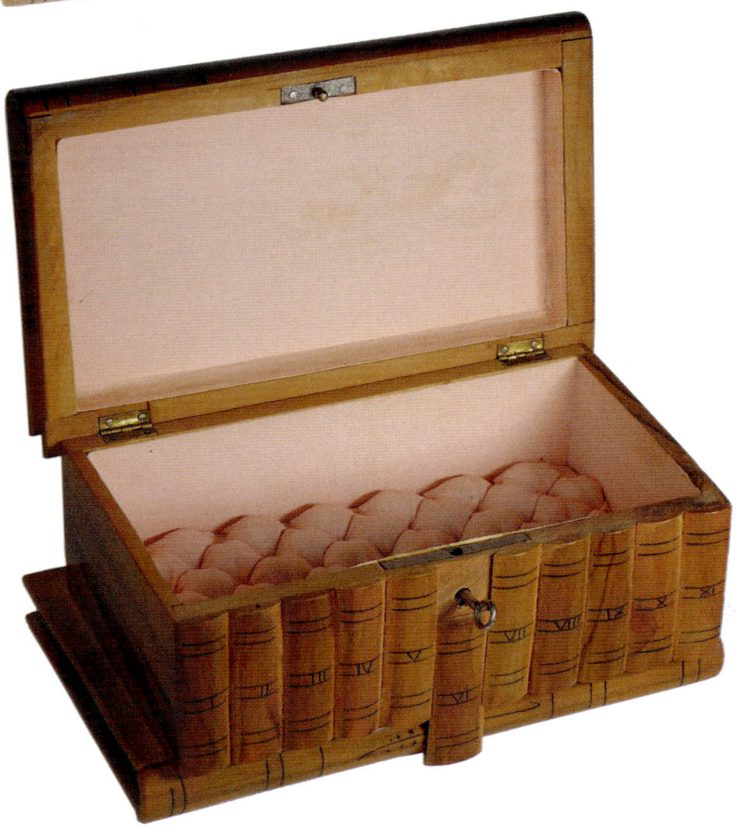

1.003
Souvenir of Naples
Schmuckschatulle aus Holz mit Stofffutter, Deckel mit Intarsien und Bemalung, Innendeckel verglast mit Damenbildnis, Verschluss verschiebbarer Buchrücken
Wooden jewelry box with lining, lid with marquetry and an illustration, inner board with a glazed portrait of a lady, closure with a sliding spine
1946 | 10,3 x 22,7 x 13,5 cm

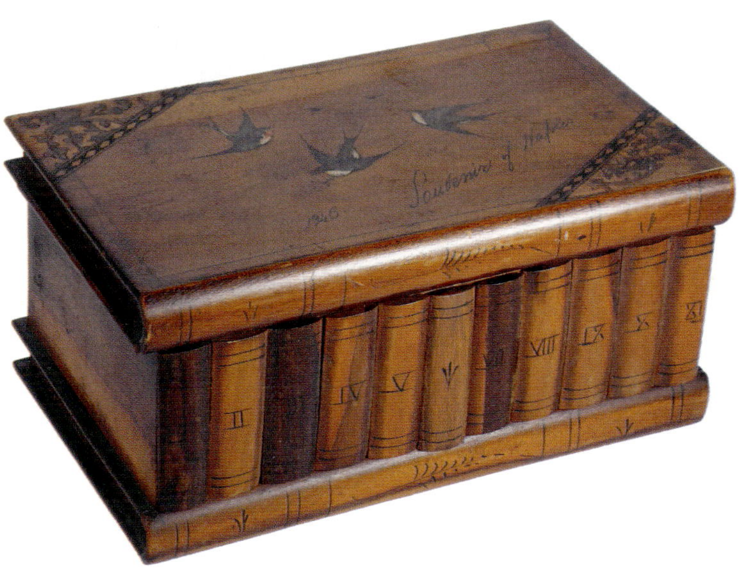

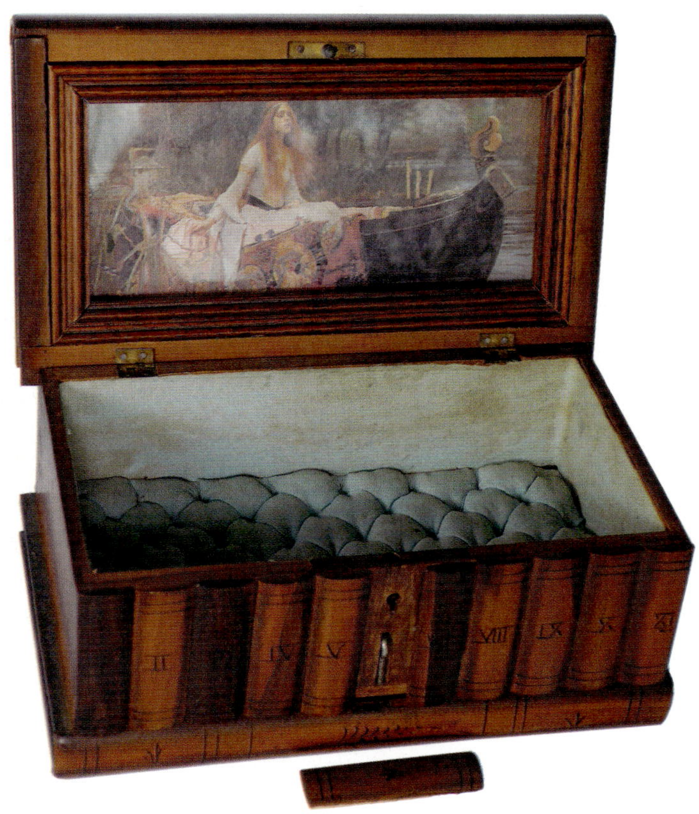

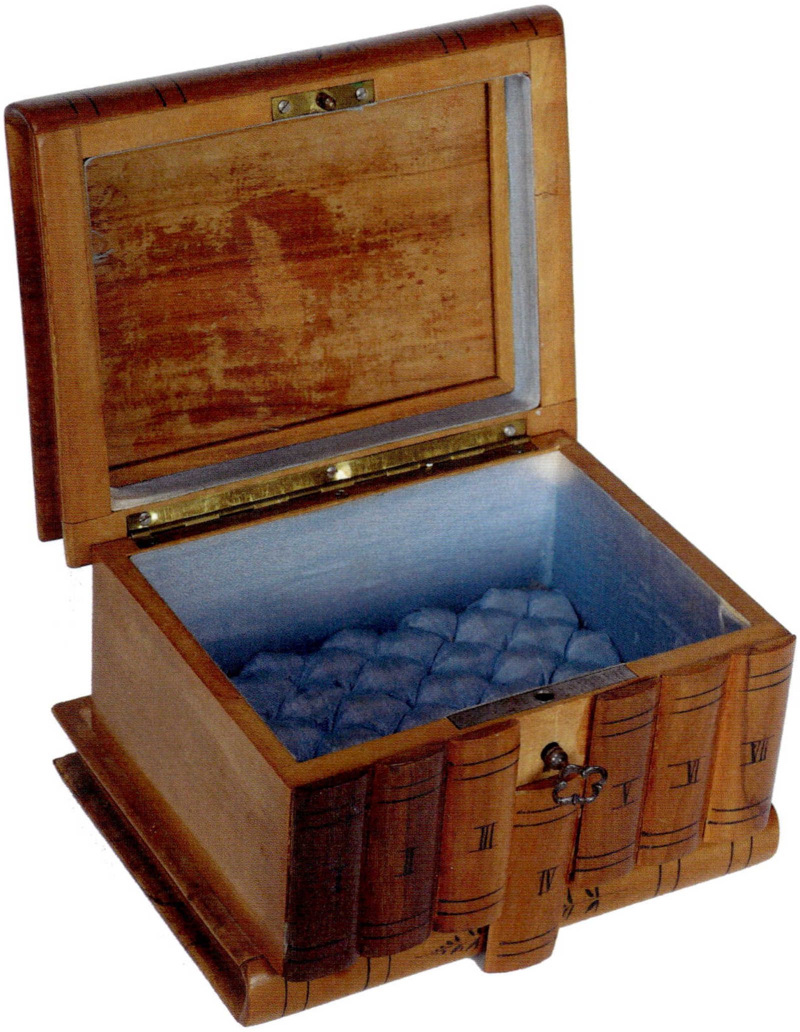

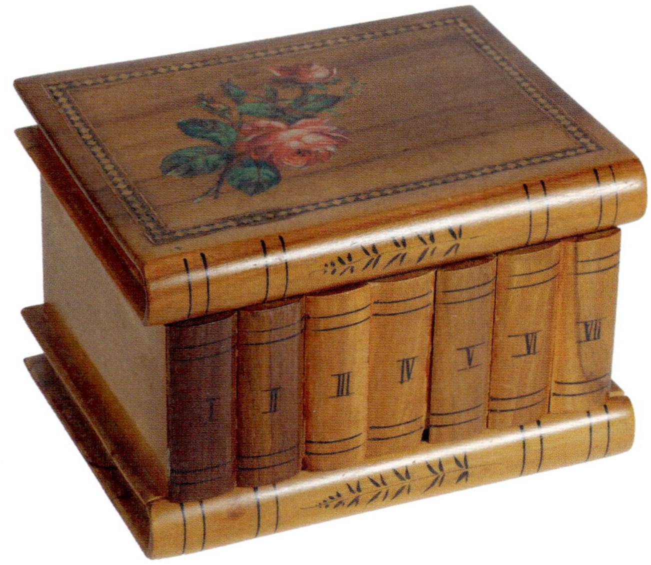

1.004
Schmuckschatulle aus Holz mit Stofffutter, Deckel mit Intarsien und Bemalung, Verschluss verschiebbarer Buchrücken
Wooden jewelry box with lining, lid with marquetry and painting, lock system with a sliding spine
1950er-Jahre / *1950s* | 10,2 x 15,6 x 12,2 cm

1.005
Schmuckschatulle aus Wurzelholz mit Seidenfutter, Einlegearbeiten auf beiden Deckeln und Rücken
Jewelry box made of burl wood with silk lining, marquetry on the lid, bottom and spines
Art Déco / *Art Deco* | 8,4 x 23,5 x 16 cm

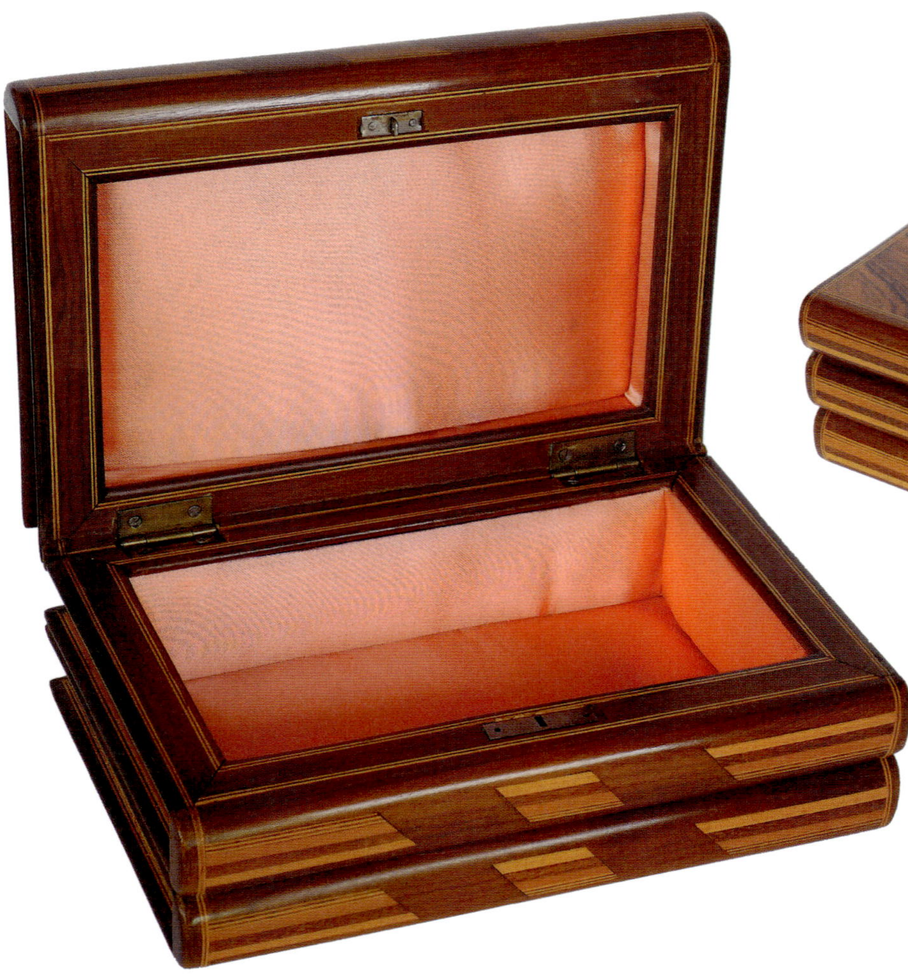

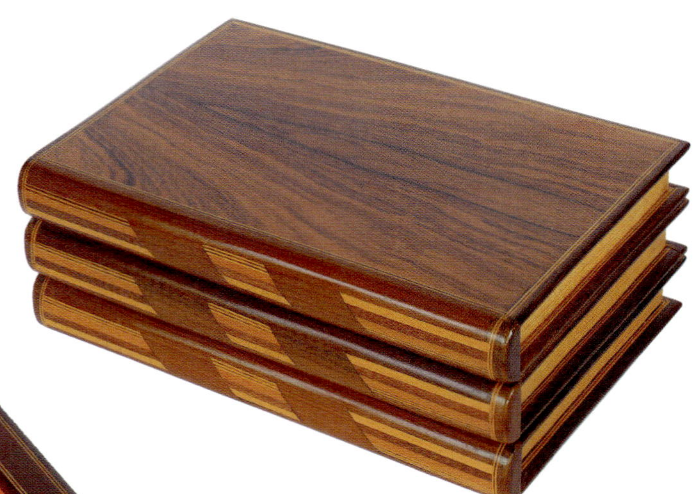

1.006
Holzschatulle für Schmuck mit Silberbeschlägen und Seidenfutter, facettierter Spiegel im Innendeckel, abschließbar
Wooden box for jewelry with silver fittings and silk lining, faceted mirror on the inner board, lockable
4,9 x 17,1 x 10,2 cm

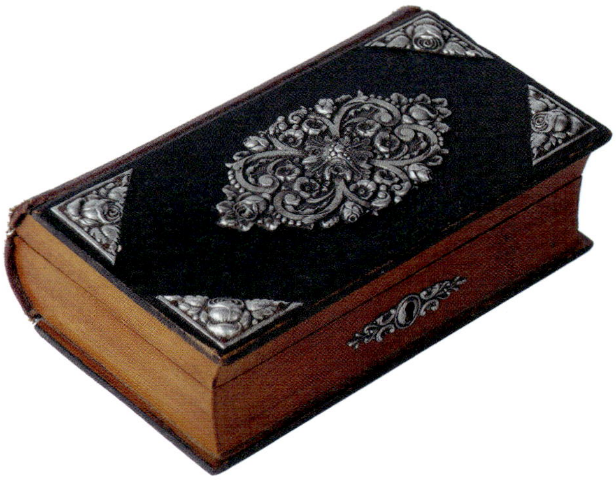

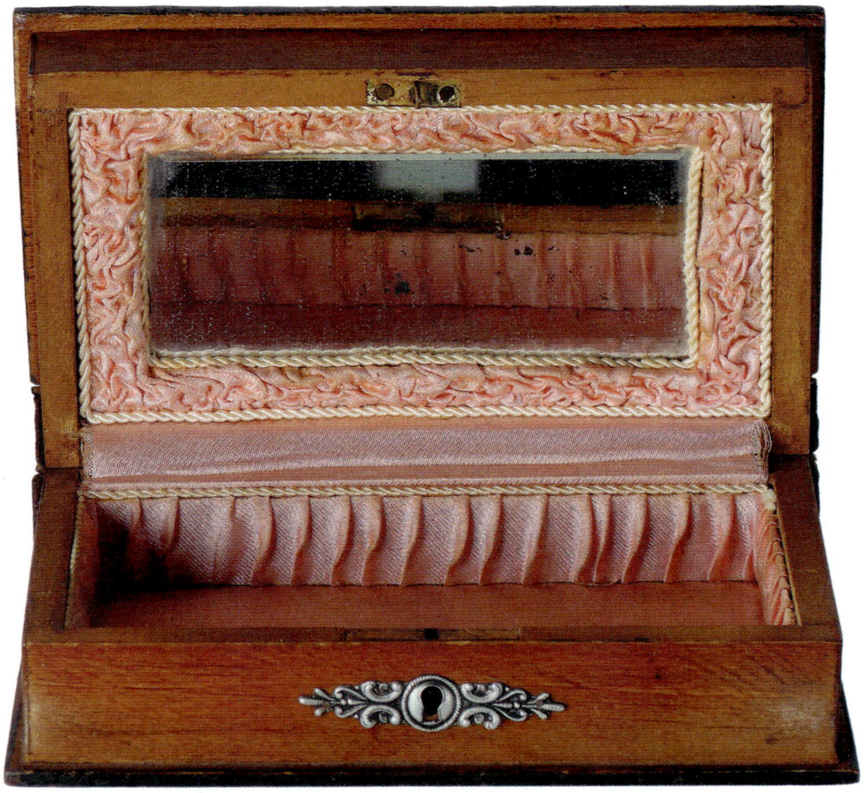

1.007
Samtschatulle ausgefüttert mit geknitterter Seide, zwei mit Plüsch eingerahmte Fotos im Innendeckel, Messingschließe, dreiseitiger Goldschnitt
Velvet Box lined with wrinkeld silk fabric, framed photographs on the inner board, messing buckle, all edges gilt
Um / *Around* 1900 | 3 x 21,4 x 16,2 cm

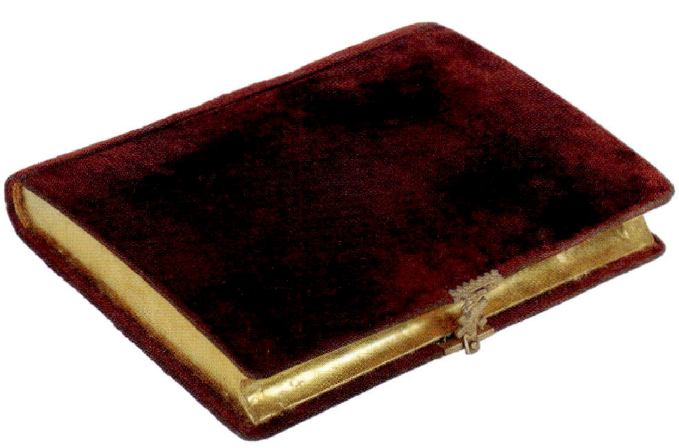

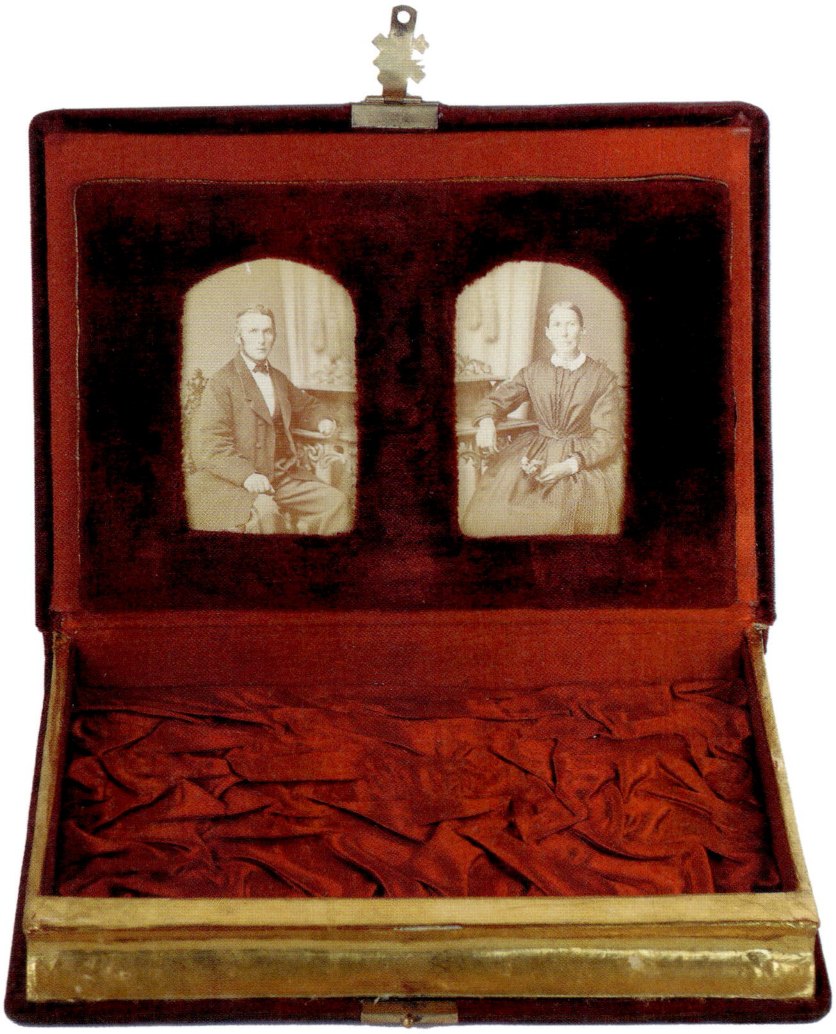

1.008
Kartondose für Eheringe mit Papierüberzug, zwei Fächer, dreiseitiger Goldschnitt
Cardboard box for wedding rings with paper-over-board, two compartments, all edges gilt
Gold Fuchs Singen, Germany
1,9 x 7,4 x 4,9 cm

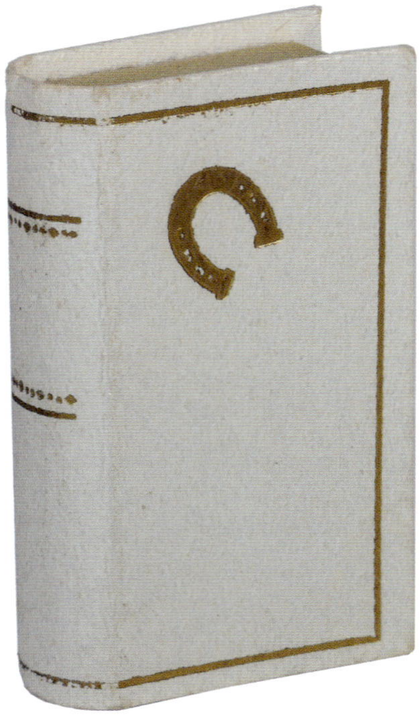

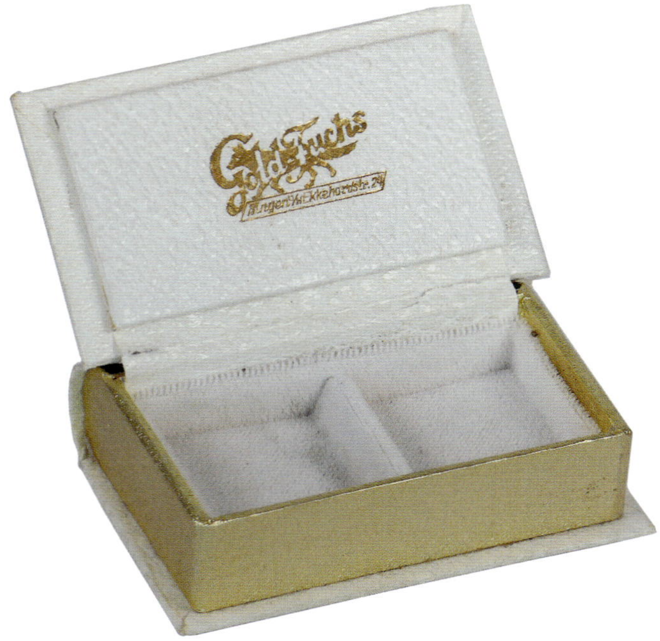

1.009
Viel Glück / *Good Luck*
Kartondose für Eheringe mit Gewebeüberzug, zwei Fächer, dreiseitiger Goldschnitt
Cardboard box for wedding rings, cloth binding, two compartments, all edges gilt
W. Bürki Goldschmied / *Jeweler*, Zurich, Switzerland
1,5 x 5,9 x 4,3 cm

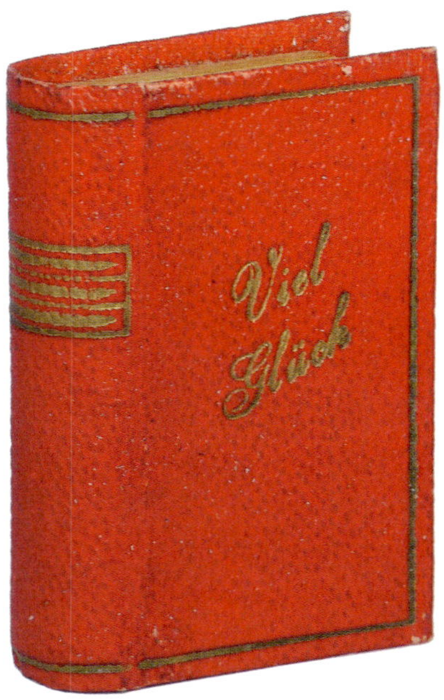

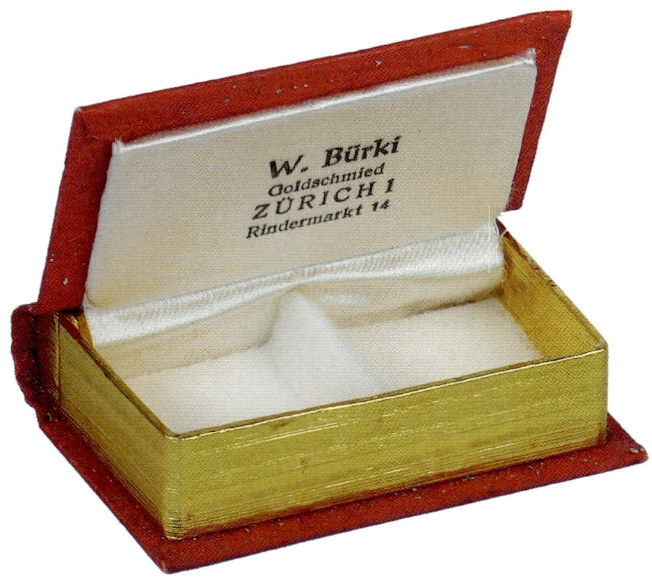

1.010
Nusbaum's Lucky Wedding Ring
Bakelitdose für einen Fingerring, Rücken- und Deckelverzierungen, Ringhalter
Bakelite box for a ring, ornaments on the spine and lid, ring holder
Um / *Around* 1900
1,8 x 3,2 x 3,8 cm

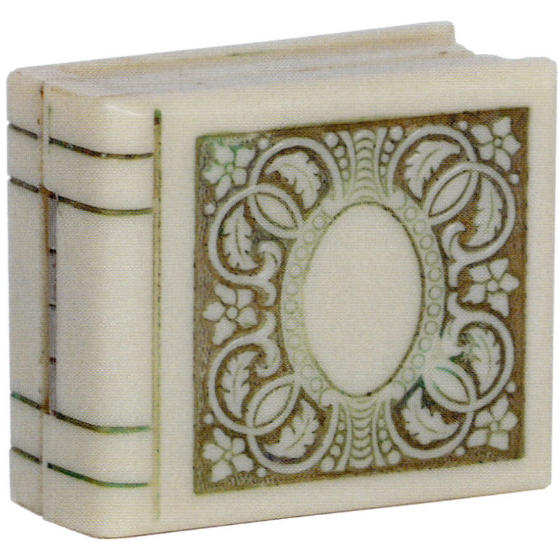

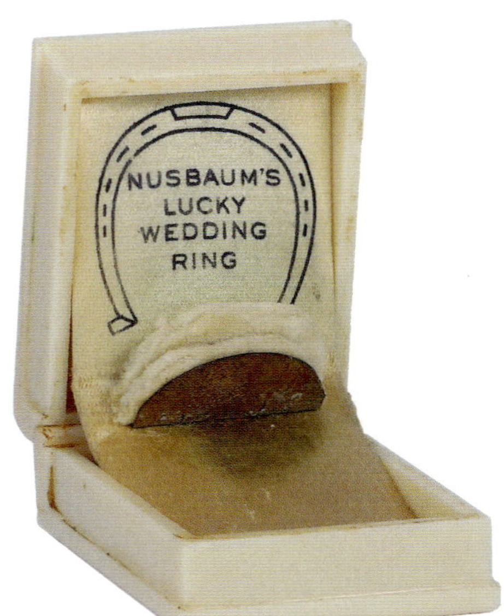

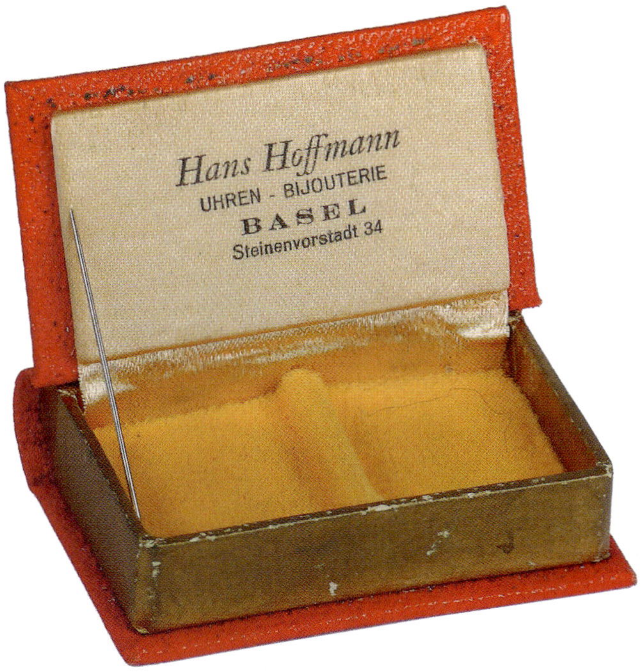

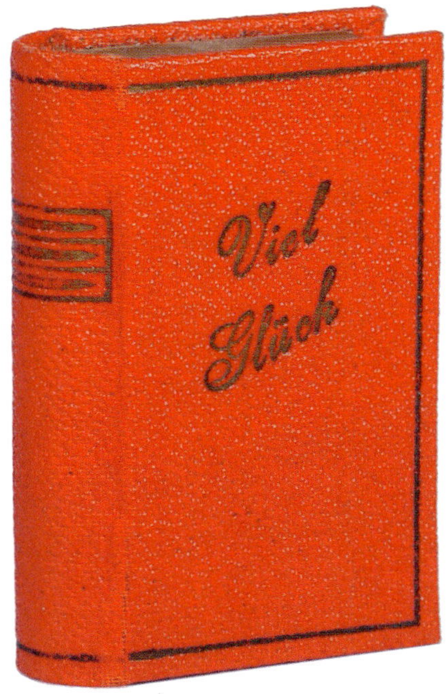

1.011
Viel Glück / *Good Luck*
Kartondose für Eheringe mit Gewebeüberzug, zwei Fächer, dreiseitiger Goldschnitt
Cardboard box for wedding rings with fabric cover, two compartments, all edges gilt
Hans Hoffmann Uhren-Bijouterie / Watches-Bijouterie, Basel, Switzerland
1,5 x 5,9 x 4,3 cm

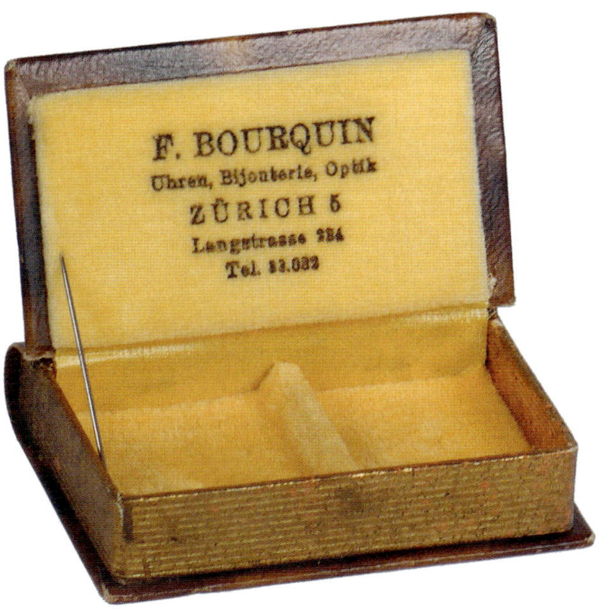

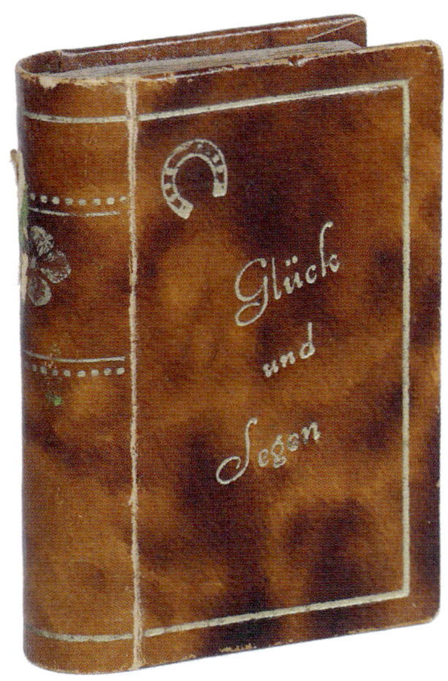

1.012
Glück und Segen / *Fortune and Blessings*
Kartondose für Eheringe mit Papierüberzug, zwei Fächer, dreiseitiger Goldschnitt,
Cardboard box for wedding rings with paper-over-board, two compartments, all edges gilt
F. Bourquin, Uhren, Bijouterie, Optik Watches, Jewelry, Optics, Zurich, Switzerland
1,3 x 5,9 x 4,3 cm

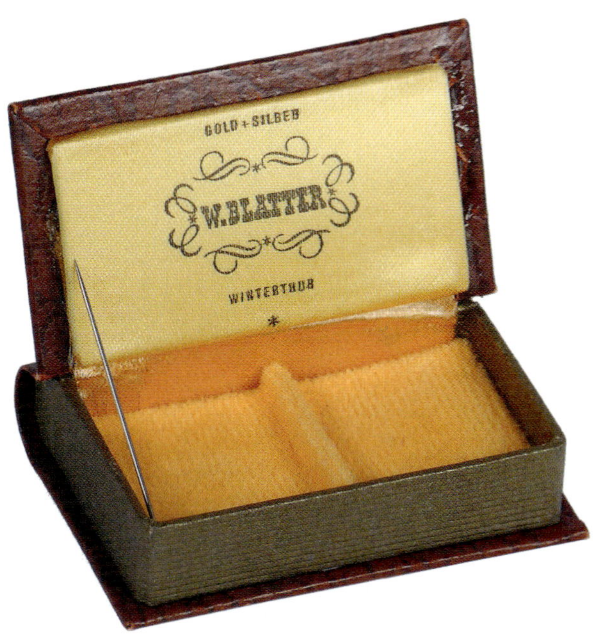

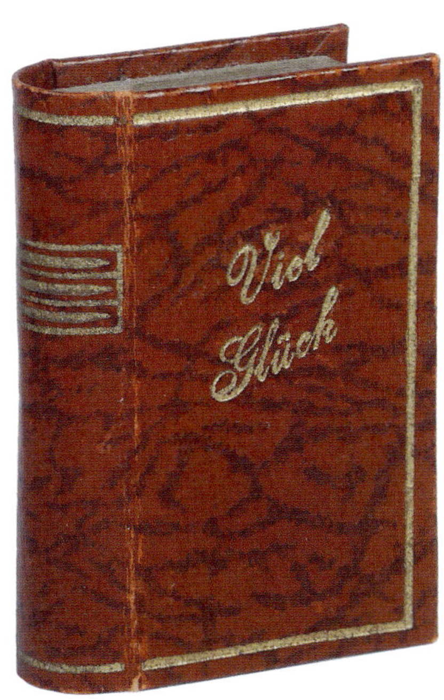

1.013
Viel Glück / *Good Luck*
Kartondose für Eheringe mit Papierüberzug, zwei Fächer, dreiseitiger Goldschnit, Gold + Silber
Cardboard box for wedding rings with-paper-over-board, two compartments, all edges gilt, gold + silver
W. Blatter, Winterthur, Switzerland
1,5 x 5,9 x 4,3 cm

1.014
Silberfingerring mit aufgesetztem Buchkorpus, aufklappbarer Vorderdeckel, Behältnis für ein Souvenir, Gravur auf dem Vorderdeckel, Ringgröße 56
Silver ring with book, hinged front board, container for a souvenir, engraving on the cover, size 56
Jugendstil / *Art Nouveau* | 0,5 x 1,8 x 1,3 cm

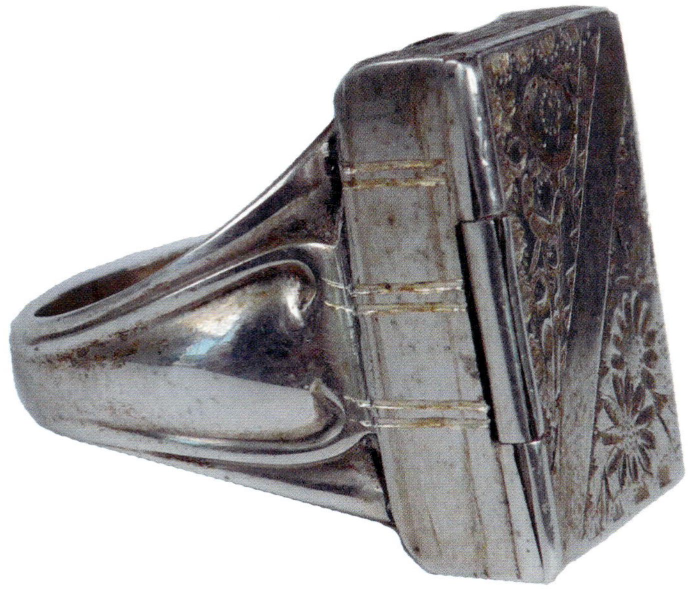

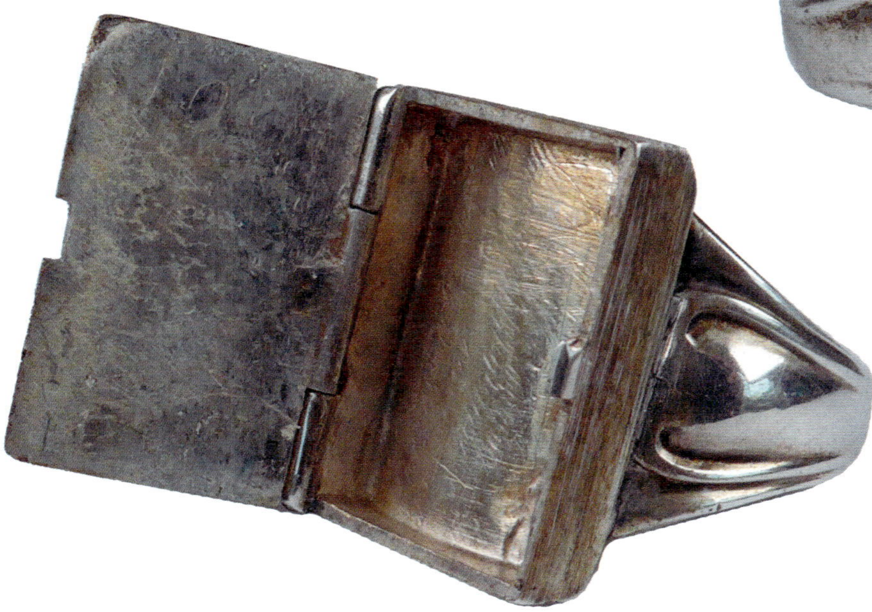

11.015
Kartondose mit Wattekissen für eine Kinderarmbandrassel, lithografiertes spielendes Mädchen mit ihren sieben Puppen, Goldpapiereinfassung, Blumenranke auf dem Innenspiegel
Cardboard box with wadding pad for a children's rattle, lithography of a playing girl with her seven dolls, gold paper edging, flower tendril on the inside cover
Anfang 20. Jh. / *Beginning of the 20th century*
1,8 x 8 x 6,4 cm

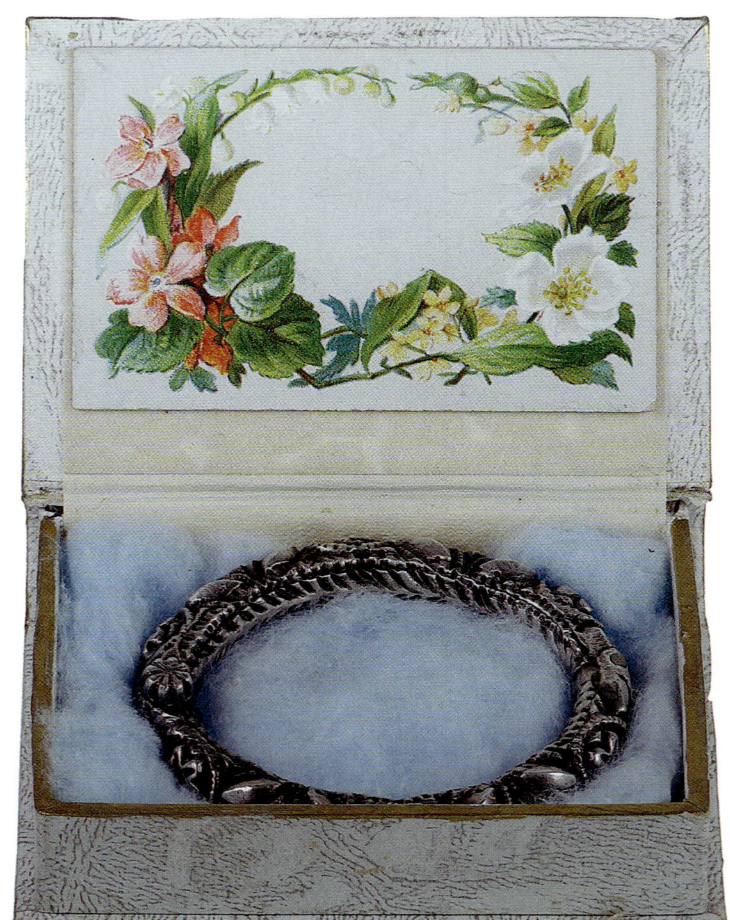

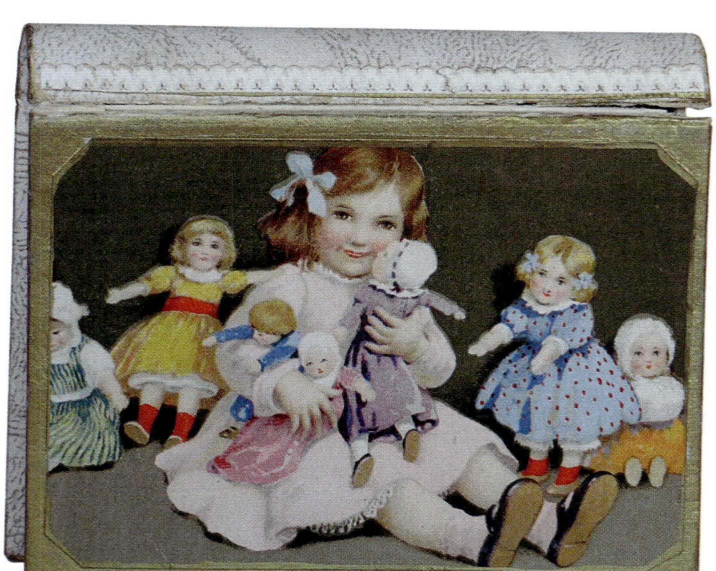

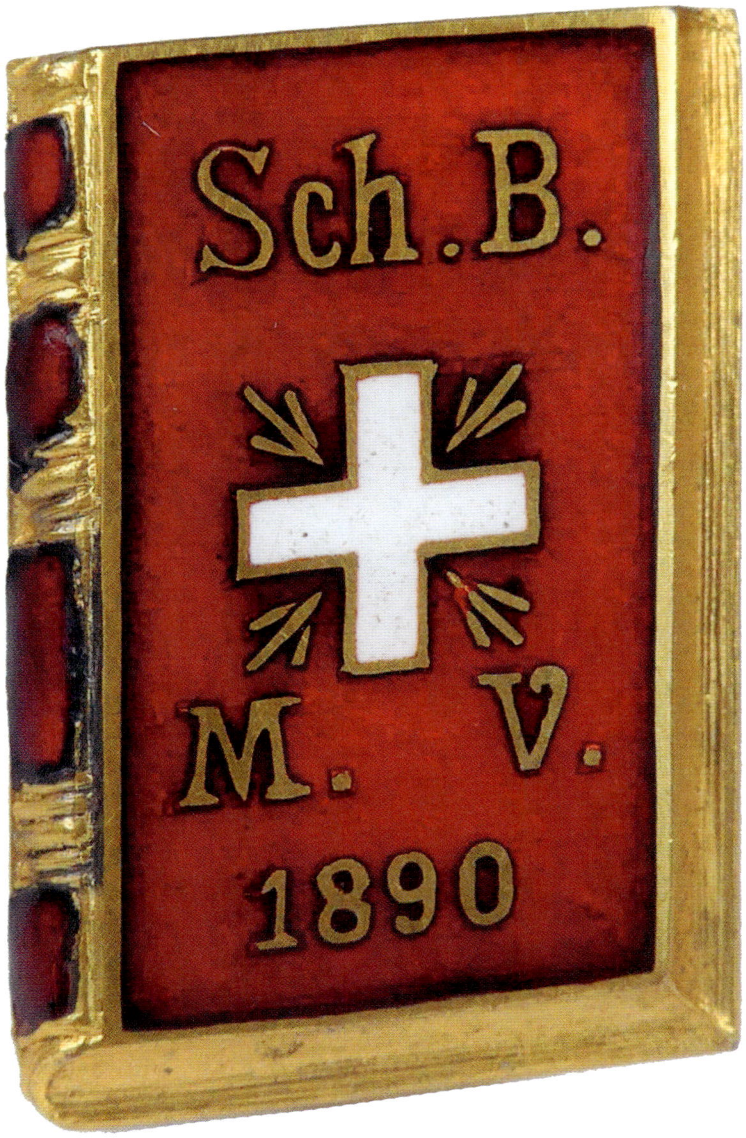

1.016
Sch. B.M.V. 1890
Pin mit Schweizerkreuz, Steckverschluss
Pin with the Swiss cross, buckle
2,2 x 1,6 x 0,1 cm

1.017
Buchbrosche aus buntem Celluloseacetat von Lea Stein Paris, Anstecknadel, signiert
Brooch made of multicolored cellulose acetate by Lea Stein Paris, pin, signed
Art Déco | 4,4 x 3 x 0,6 cm

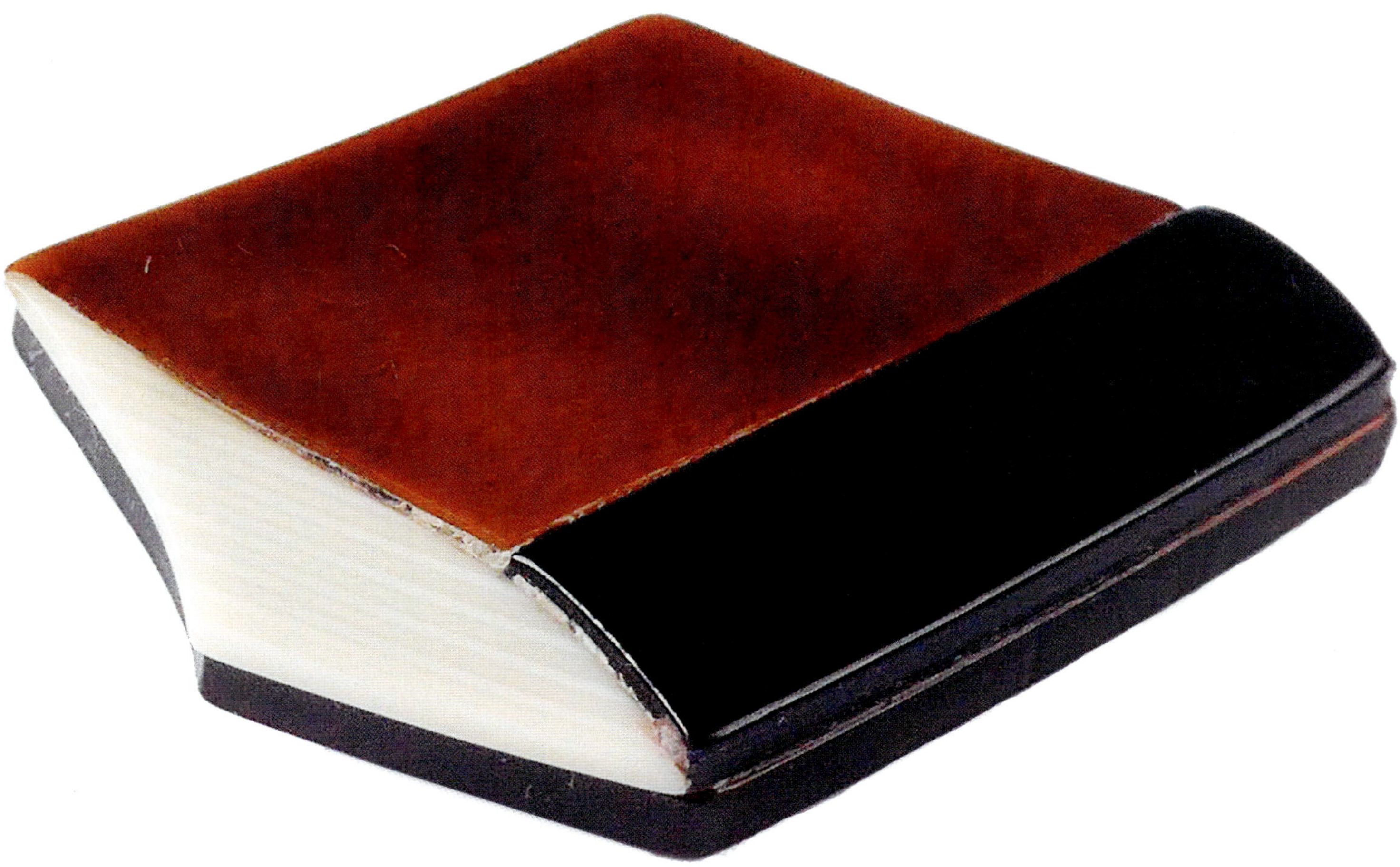

1.018
Silberdose für Pillen, aufgeschlagenes Buch mit getriebener Rose auf dem Buchblock
Silver box for pills, open book with embossed rose on the book block
1 x 2,8 x 2,5 cm

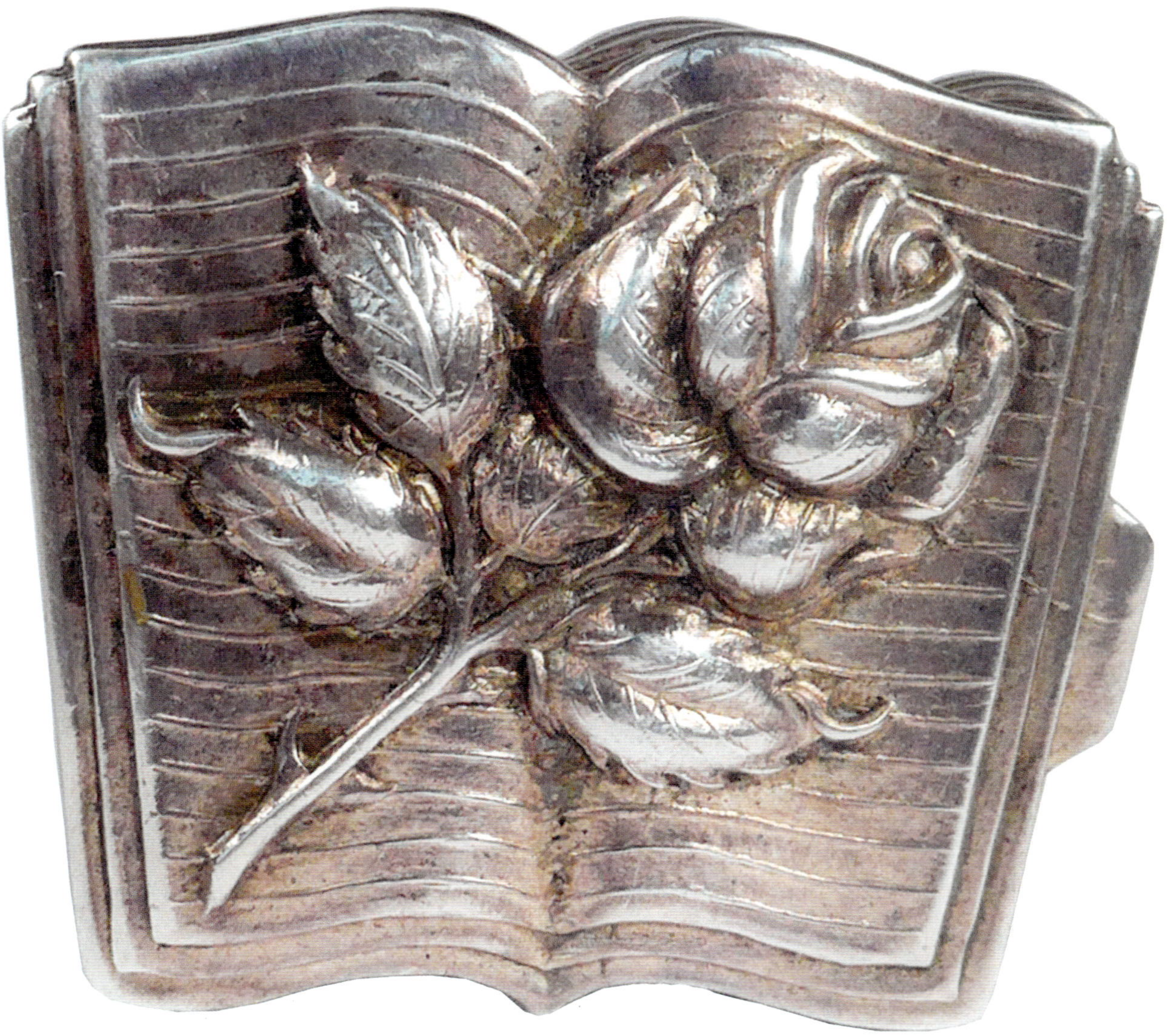

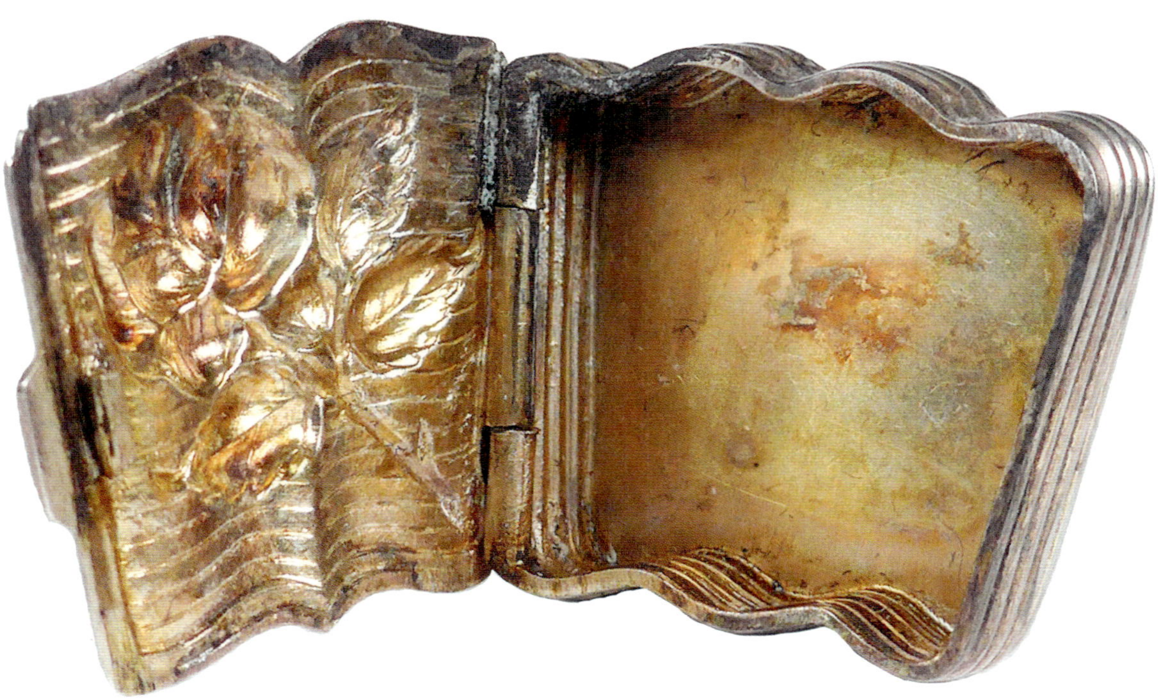

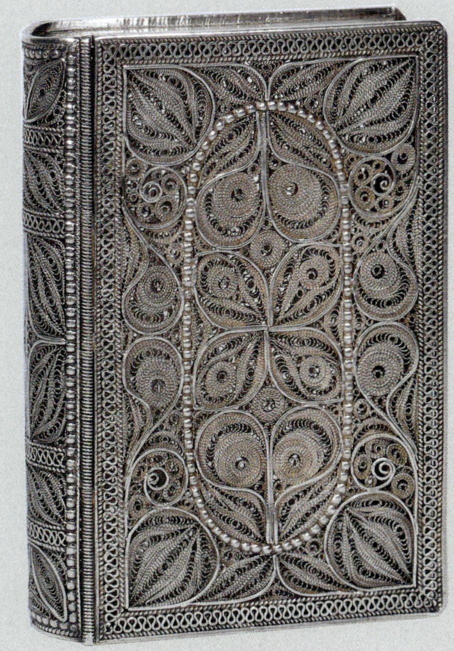

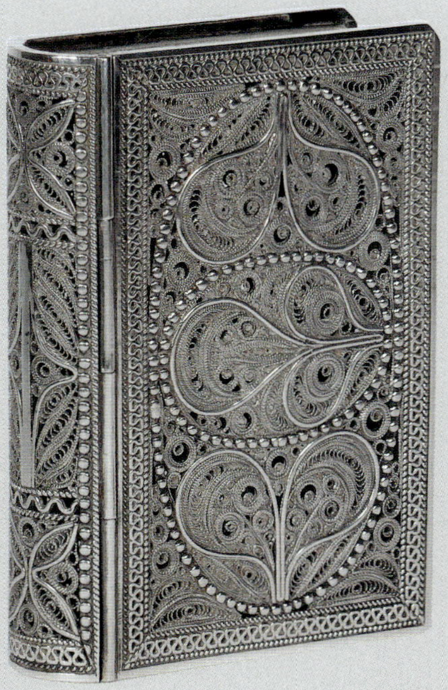

1.019
Filigrane Silberdose für Visitenkarten
Delicate silver box for business cards
Um / *Around* 1930
8,3 x 5,9 x 1,9 cm

1.020
Filigrane Silberdose für Visitenkarten
Delicate silver box for business cards
Um / *Around 1930*
8,6 x 6,2 x 2 cm

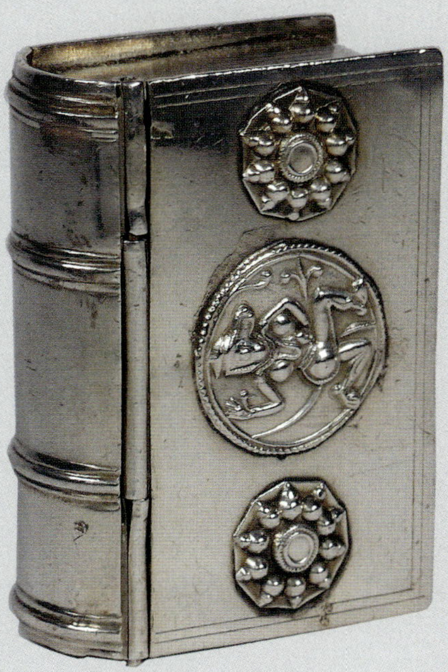

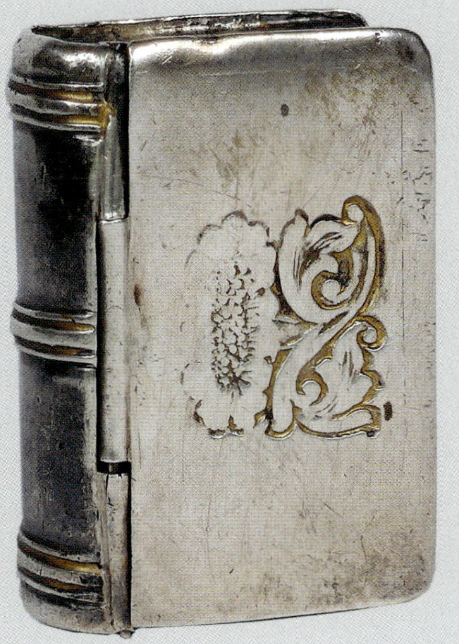

1.021
Silberdose mit kniender Figur und zwei Medaillons auf dem Vorderdeckel, Pillendose (?)
Silver box with a kneeling figure and two medallions on the front board, pill box (?)
Um / *Around* 1930
1,5 x 4,8 x 3,3 cm

1.022
Silberdose für Pillen mit Gravur auf dem Vorderdeckel
Silver box for pills with engraving on the front board
Jugendstil / *Art Nouveau* | 1,5 x 4 x 2,6 cm

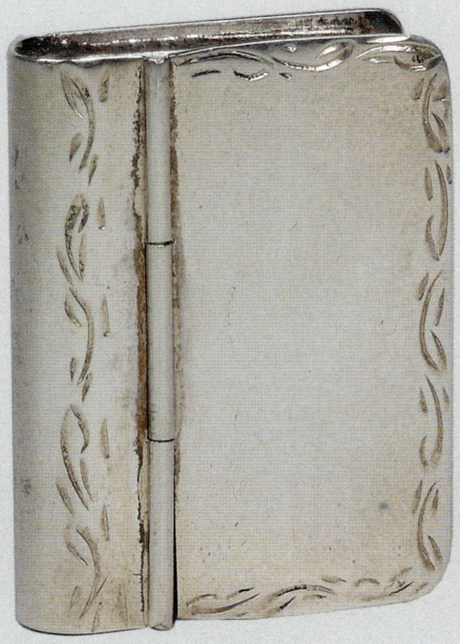

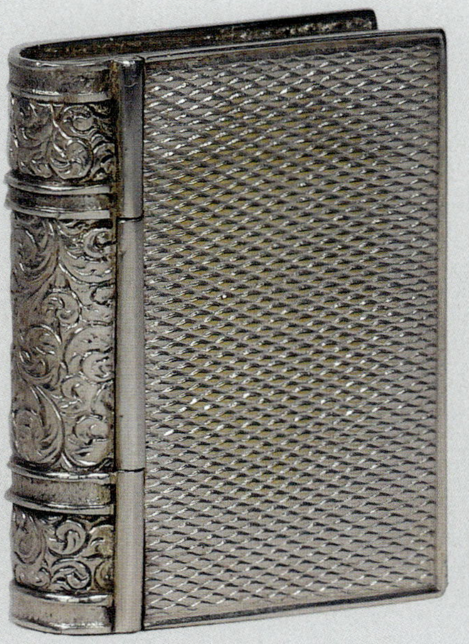

1.023
Silberdose mit graviertem Vorderdeckel, vermutlich für Pillen
Silver box with engraving on the front board, probably for pills
0,6 x 3,5 x 2,6 cm

1.024
Silberdose für Pillen mit Spitzkaroprägung auf beiden Deckeln, Rankenwerk auf dem Rücken
Silver box for pills with pointed checks on both boards, tendrils on the spine
Um / *Around* 1930
0,9 x 4 x 3,1 cm

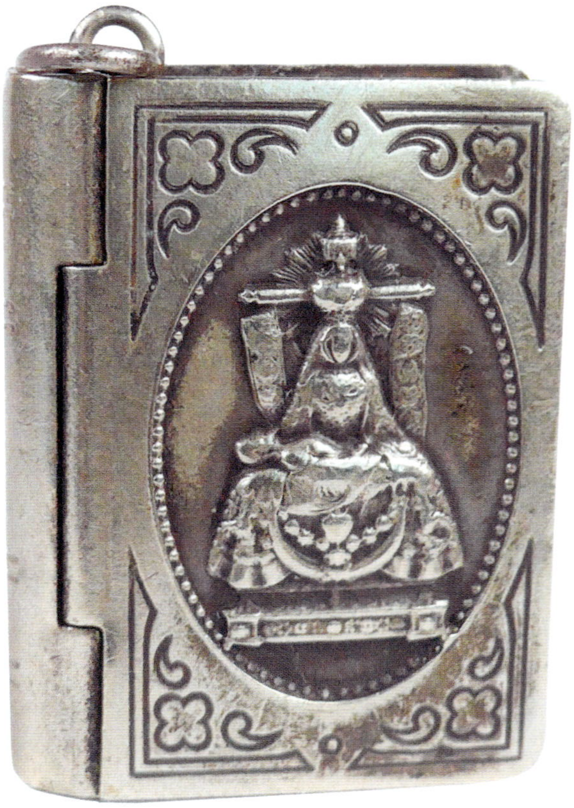

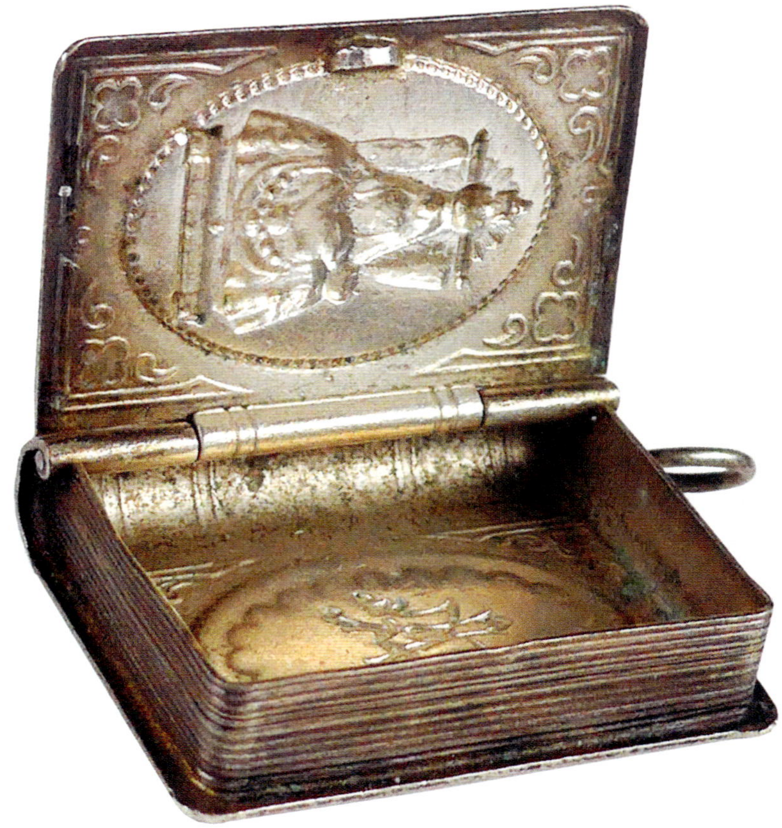

1.025
Alpacca-Rosenkranzdose mit getriebener Pietà, Gravur vorne auf beiden Deckeln
Alpacca rosary box with repoussé Pietà, engraving on both covers
Um / *Around* 1900 | 2,8 x 2,2 x 0,6 cm

1.026
Silbereinbanddecke mit geprägtem Mädchenportrait, drei Silberblätter zum Aufkleben von Fotos
Silver cover with embossed portrait of a girl, three silver leaves used for sticking on pictures
Um / *Around* 1900 | 2,5 x 1,9 x 0,3 cm

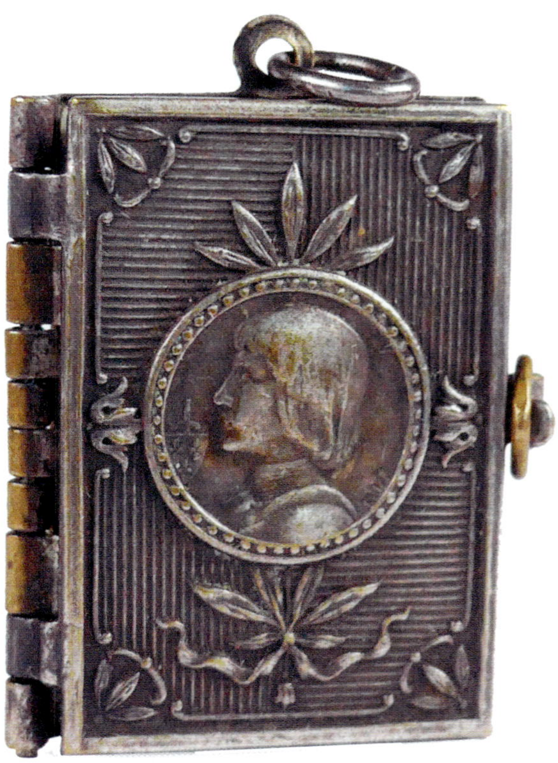

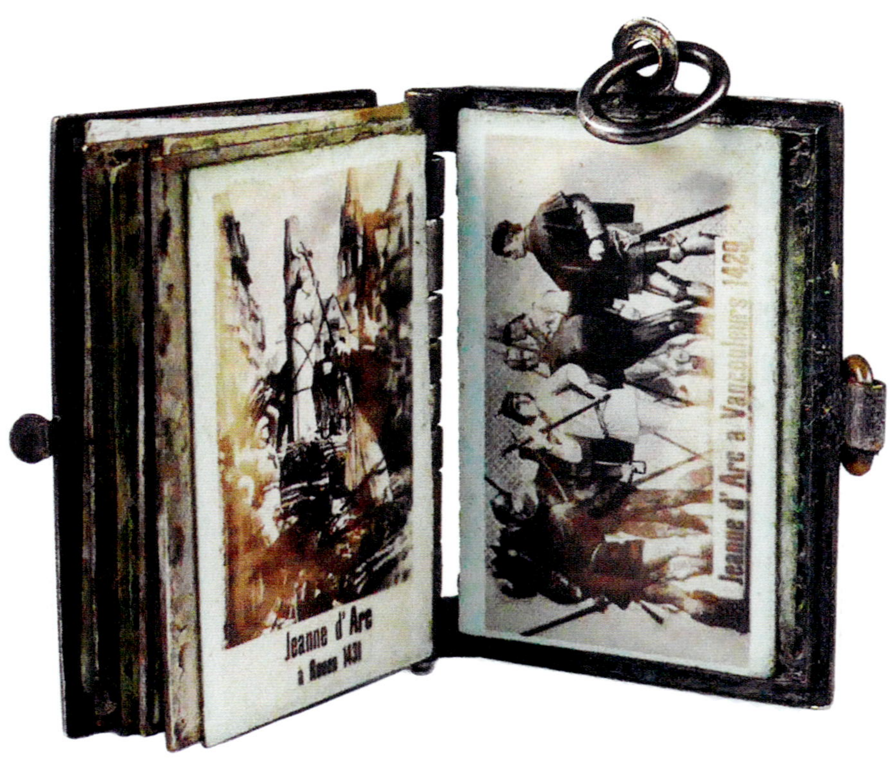

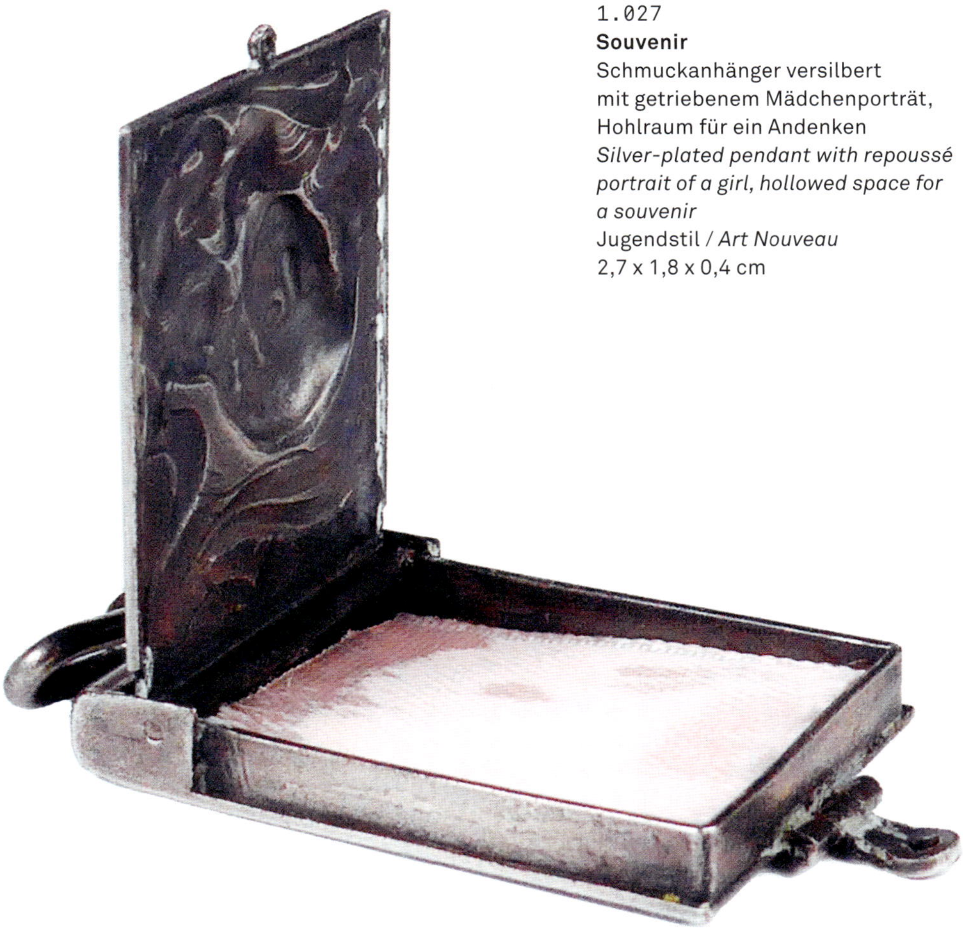

1.027
Souvenir
Schmuckanhänger versilbert
mit getriebenem Mädchenporträt,
Hohlraum für ein Andenken
Silver-plated pendant with repoussé portrait of a girl, hollowed space for a souvenir
Jugendstil / *Art Nouveau*
2,7 x 1,8 x 0,4 cm

1.028
Holy Bible
Schmuckanhänger aus Gold, offenes Buch
mit Titel und angedeutetem Text, kleinstes
Objekt der Sammlung
Gold pendant, open book with title and engraving simulating a text, smallest object of the fake book collection
Frühes 20. Jh. / *Early 20th century*
0,9 x 1 x 0,1 cm

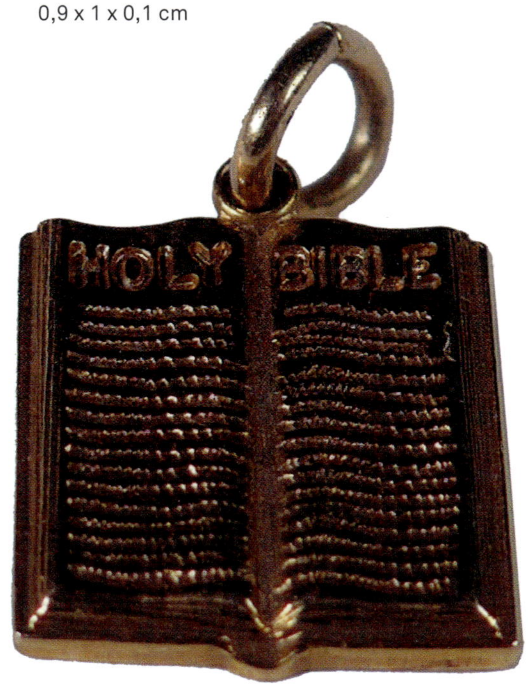

1.029
Elfenbeinanhänger beidseitig graviert
mit Löwenmotiv, Bohrung am Rücken und am
Kopf- und Fußschnitt, fünf erhabene Bünde
Pendant in ivory with a lion theme engraved on both sides, hole on the back and on the head and foot edge, five raised bands
3,1 x 2 x 0,8 cm

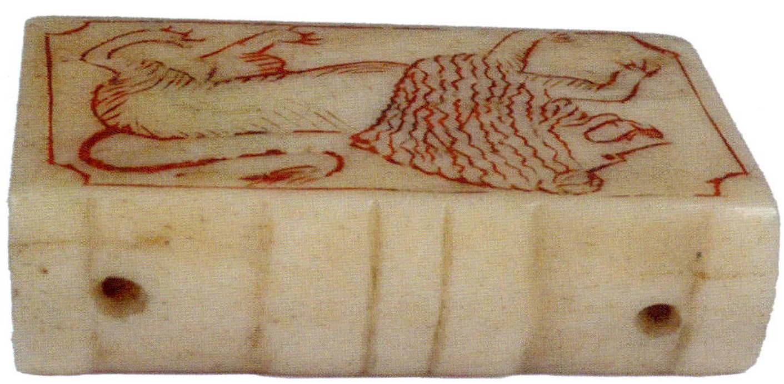

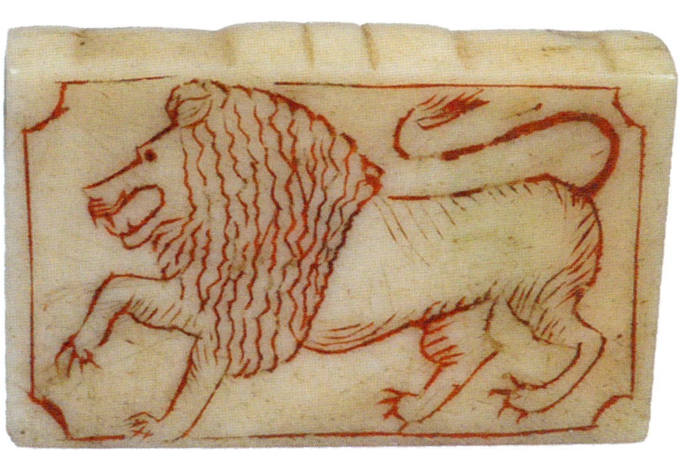

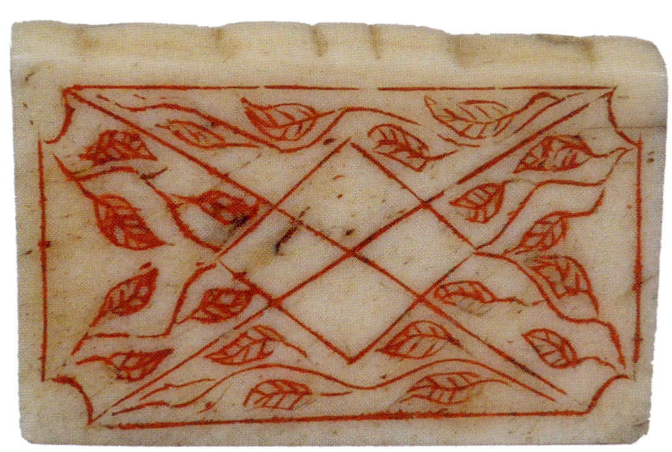

1.030
Schmuckanhänger, vergoldet, für vier Fotos, aufklappbare ovale Fotorahmen, gravierte Deckel, Ring für Kette, Metallverschluss
Gold-plated pendant for four pictures, hinged oval photo frames, engraved covers, ring for a chain, metal clasp
Um / *Around*1900
2,3 x 2,1 x 0,5 cm

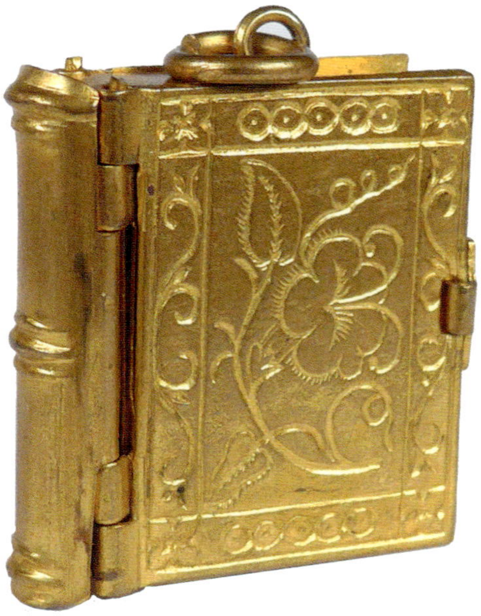

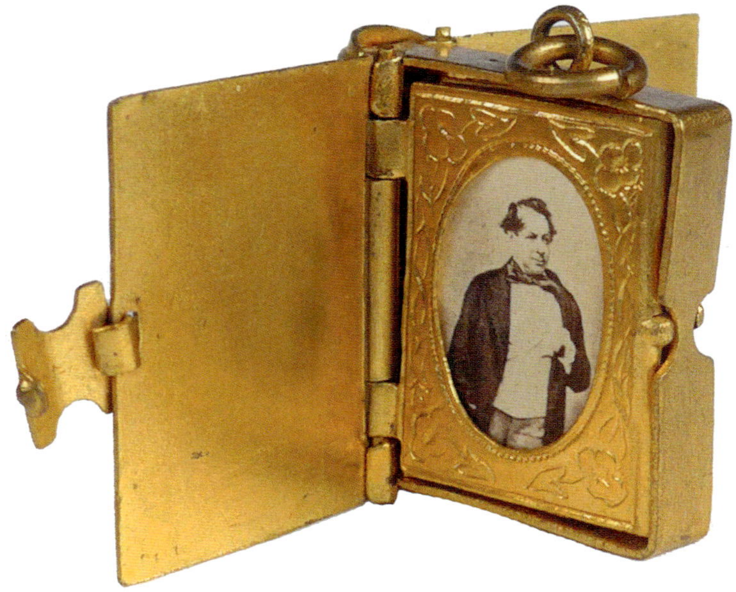

1.031
Schmuckanhänger vergoldet für vier Fotos, aufklappbare ovale Fotorähmchen, gravierter Rücken und Deckel, Ring für Kette, Metallverschluss
Gold-plated pendant with place for four pictures, hinged oval photo frames, engraved spine and cover, ring for a chain, metal clasp
Um / *Around* 1900
2,3 x 2,1 x 0,5 cm

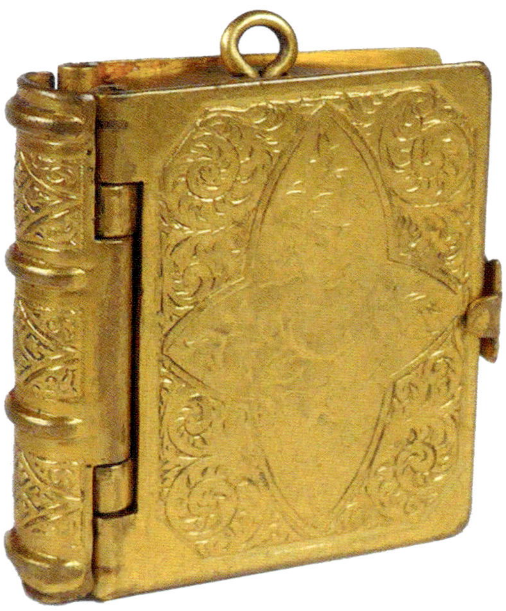

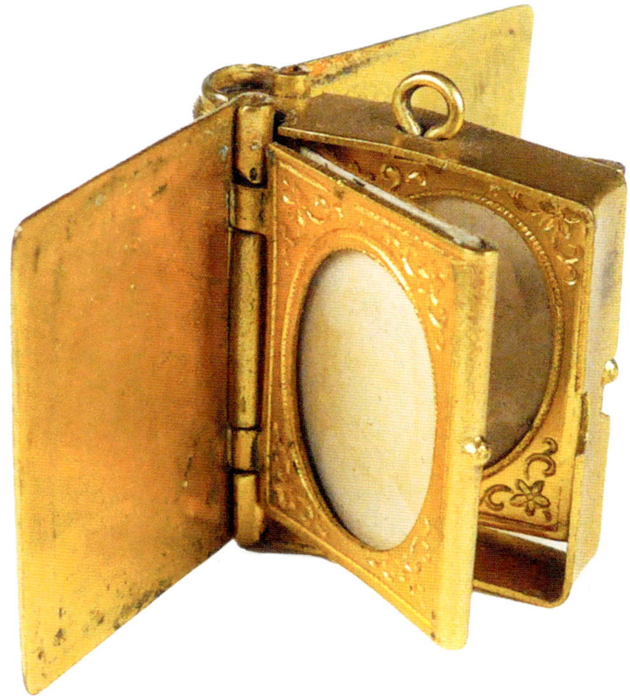

1.032
Schmuckanhänger versilbert mit zwei verglasten Medaillons auf den Innendeckeln, Außen- und Innengravur, Ring für Kette
Silver-plated pendant with two glazed medallions on the inside covers, engraving inside and outside, ring for a chain
Um / *Around* 1900
1,4 x 1,2 x 0,5 cm

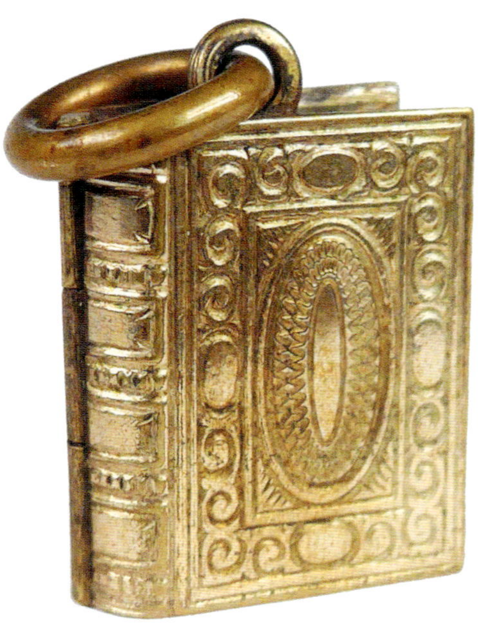

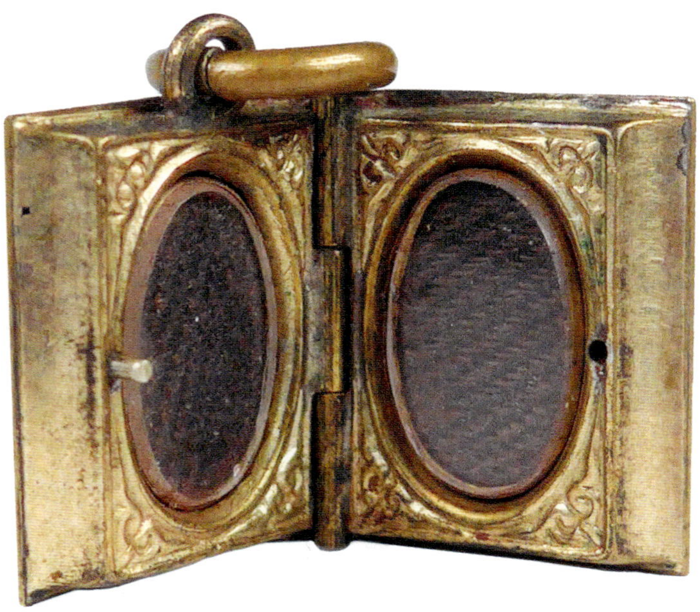

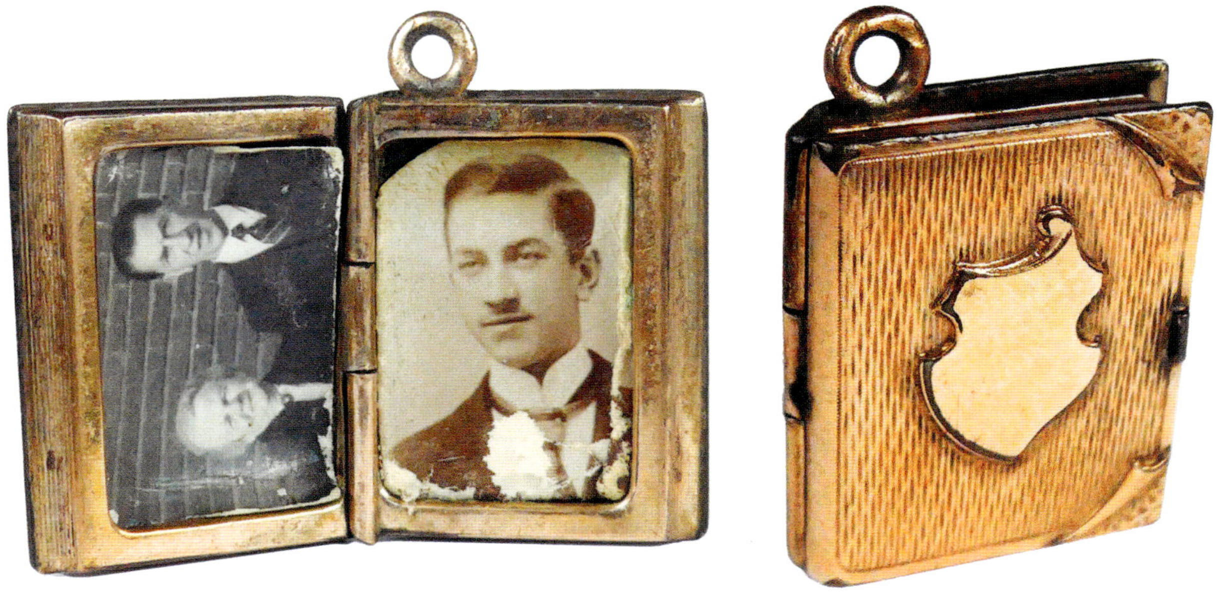

1.033
Schmuckanhänger vergoldet für zwei Fotos, erhabenes Wappen auf dem Vorderdeckel, Metallverschluss, Ring für Kette
Gold-plated pendant for two photos, raised emblem on the front cover, metal clasp, ring for a chain
Um / *Around* 1900
2,1 x 1,5 x 0,4 cm

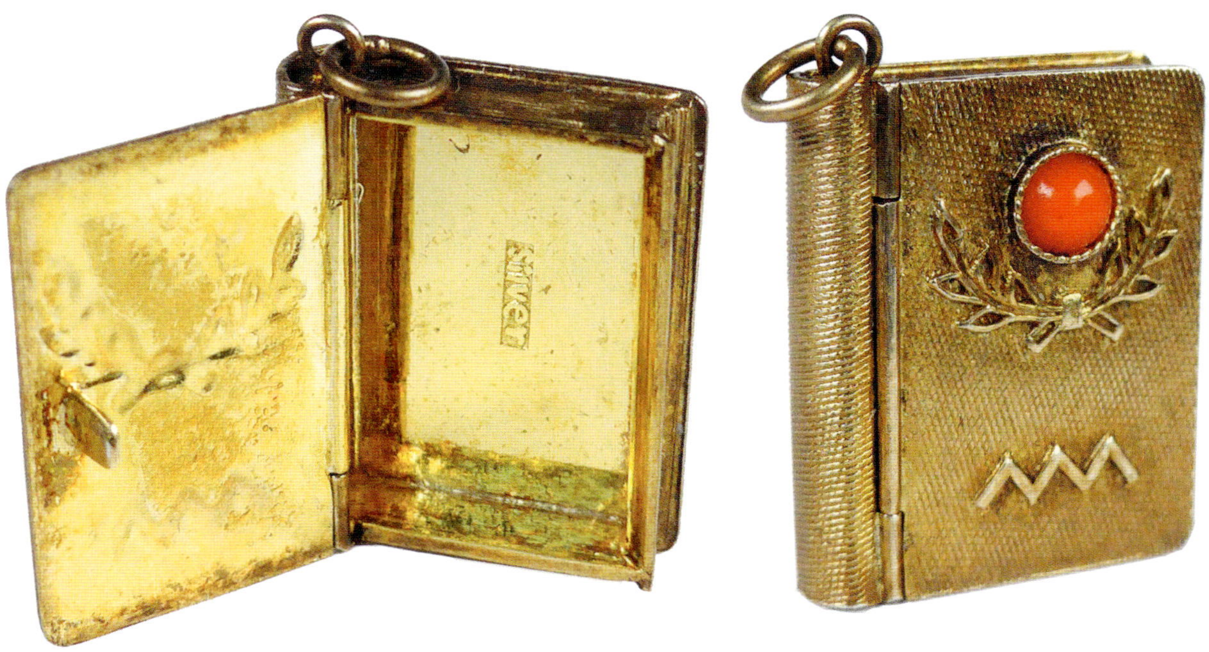

1.034
Schmuckanhänger aus Silber vergoldet mit Hohlraum für ein Andenken, aufgesetzte Koralle auf dem Vorderdeckel, Ring für Kette
Pendant in gold-plated silver with cavity for a souvenir, coral on the front cover, ring for a chain
Um / *Around* 1900
2,1 x 1,7 x 0,4 cm

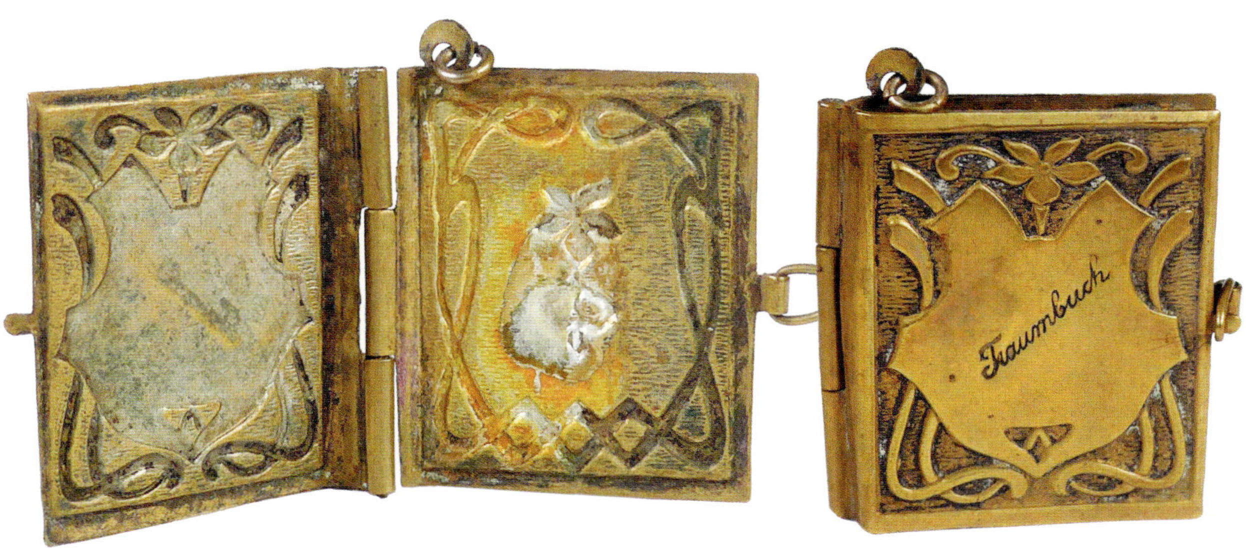

1.035
Traumbuch Messingeinbanddecke für ein Leporello, Deckelprägung mit Schild und Titel, Verschlussöse, Ring für Kette
Dream book brass book for a leporello, cover embossing with a titel plate, closing loop, ring for a chain
Jugendstil / *Art Nouveau*
3 x 2,7 x 0,5 cm

1.036
Livre d'heures
Aufklappbarer Reisewecker/Stundenbuch „Helveco" mit Lederfutter, Saffianeinband mit Handvergoldung, dreiseitiger Goldschnitt
Travel fold-up alarm clock/book of hours "Helveco" with leather lining, Saffian binding with gilding, all edges gilt
Made in Switzerland | 11 x 8,8 x 2,5 cm

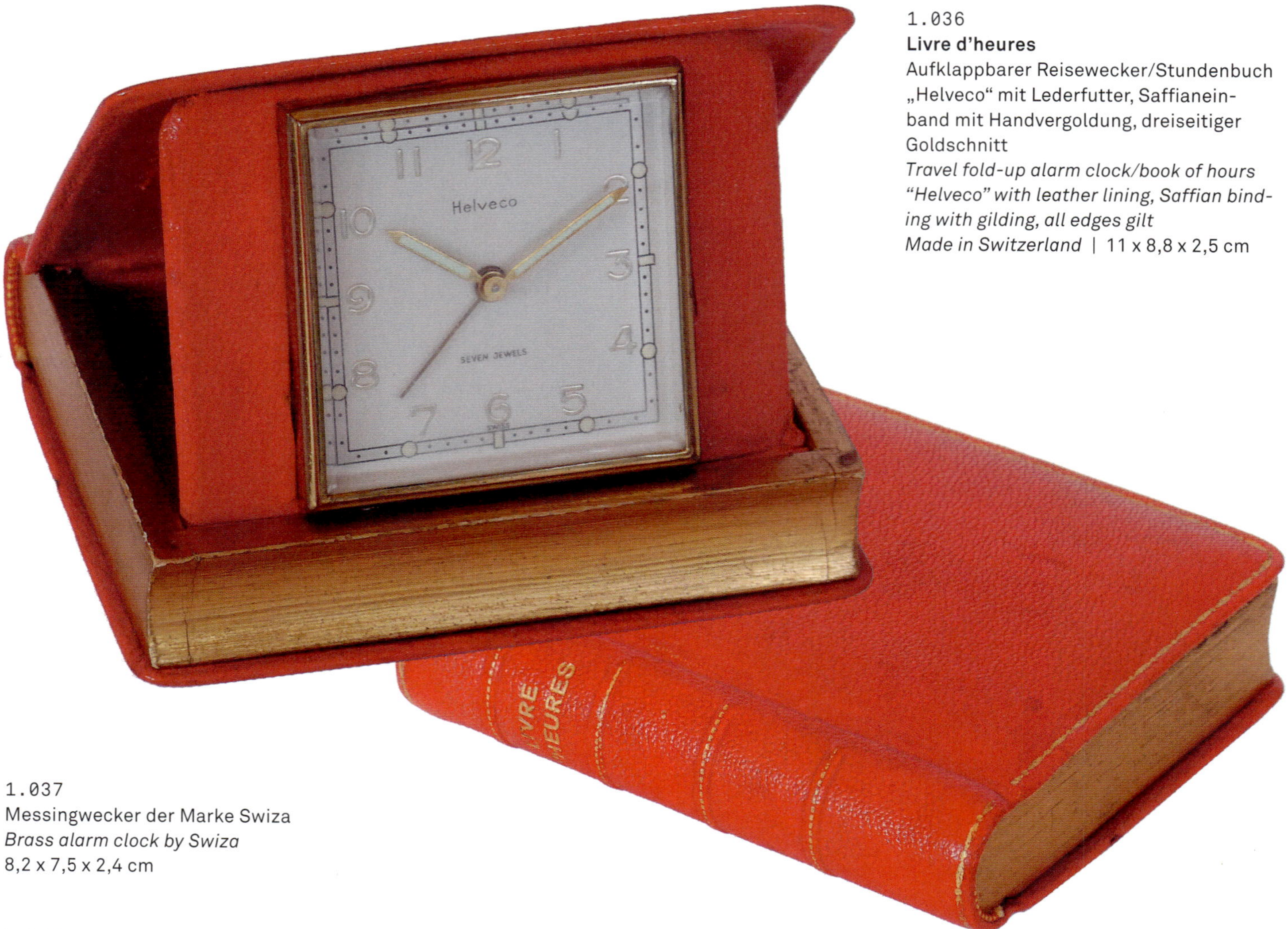

1.037
Messingwecker der Marke Swiza
Brass alarm clock by Swiza
8,2 x 7,5 x 2,4 cm

1.038
Charles Dickens, Oliver Twist, Swiss 8 Days
Reisewecker/Stundenbuch, Saffianeinband mit Handvergoldung, Schaflederfutter, Messingverschlüsse, Marmorschnitt
Alarm clock/book of hours with Saffian binding and sheepskin leather lining, brass clasps, manual gilding, marbled edges
15 x 11,4 x 3,1 cm

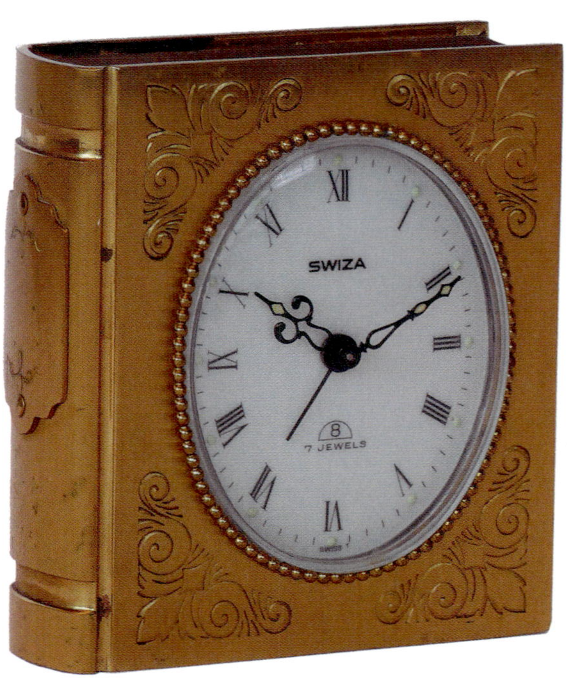

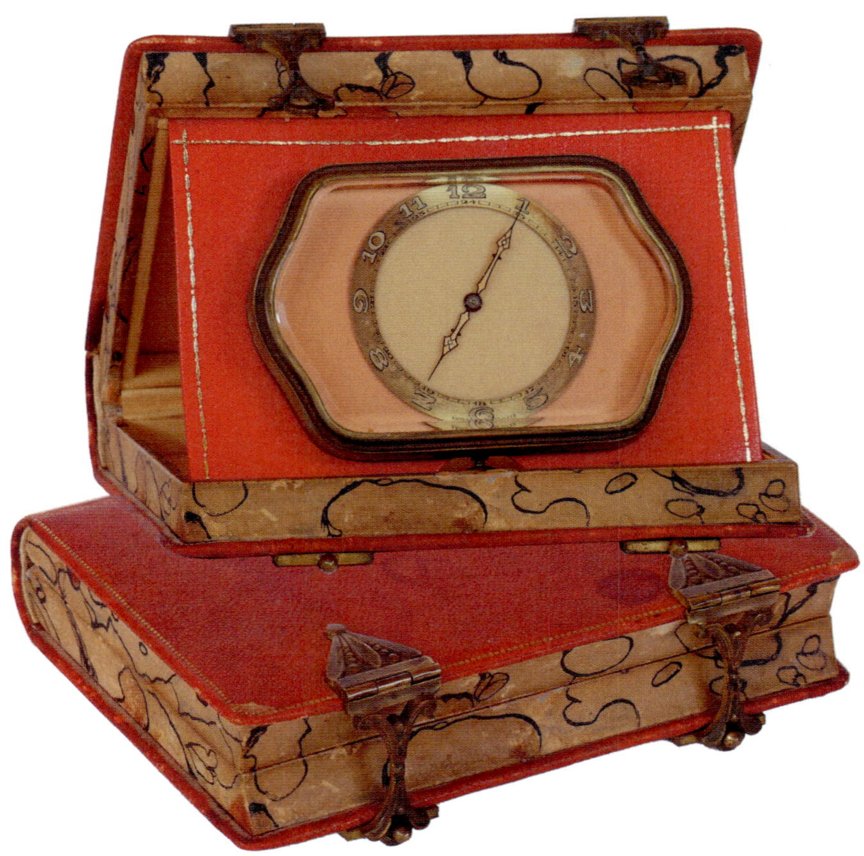

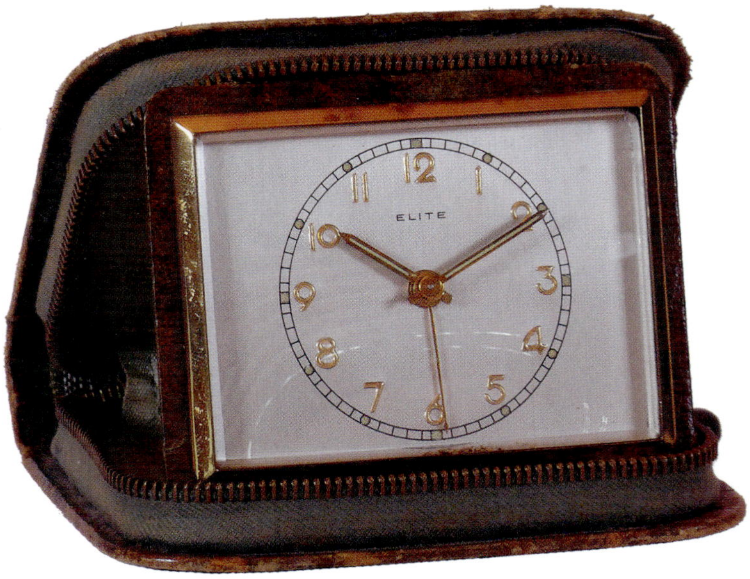

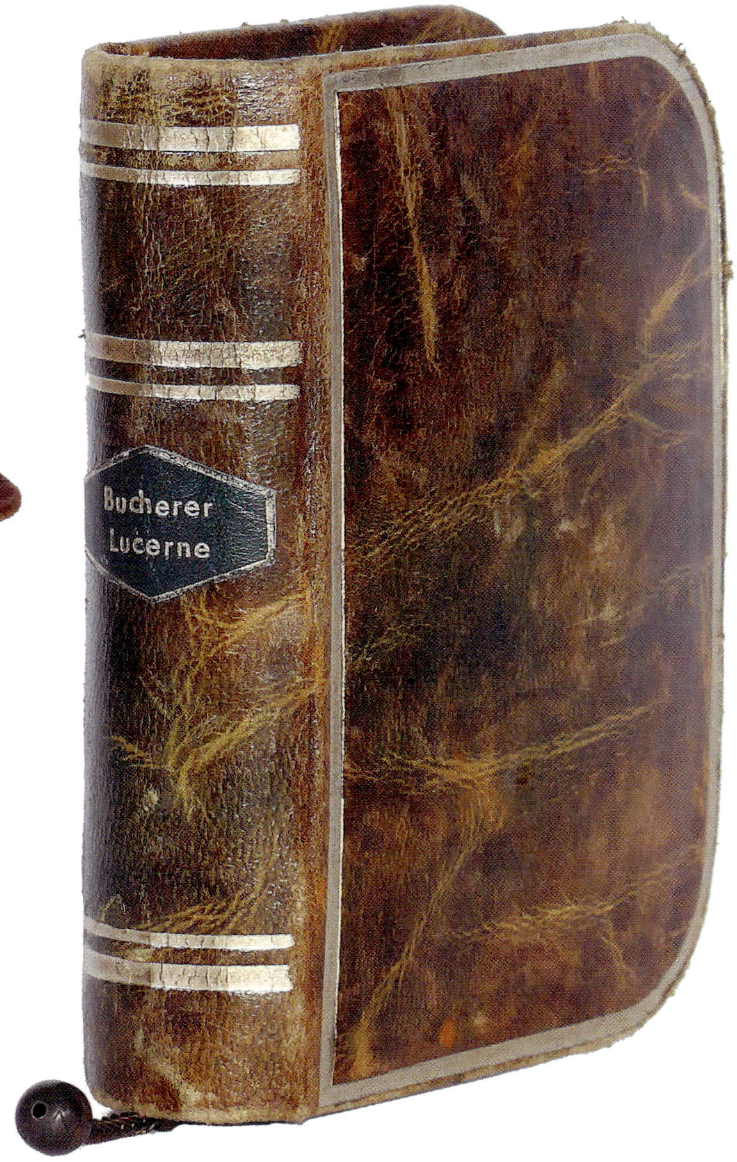

1.039
Bucherer Lucerne, „Elite“
Aufklappbarer Reisewecker/Stundenbuch, Grüner Ledereinband mit Reißverschluss
Fold-up travel alarm clock/book of hours, green leather binding with zipper
10,1 x 8,2 x 2,5 cm

1.040
Lexikon
Reisewecker/Stundenbuch, grüner Ledereinband mit Vergoldung, Schließe, aufklappbare Uhr und Thermometer der Marke „Kohler“
Travel alarm clock/book of hours, green leather binding with gilding, fold-up clock by “Kohler”
9,5 x 7,7 x 2,7 cm

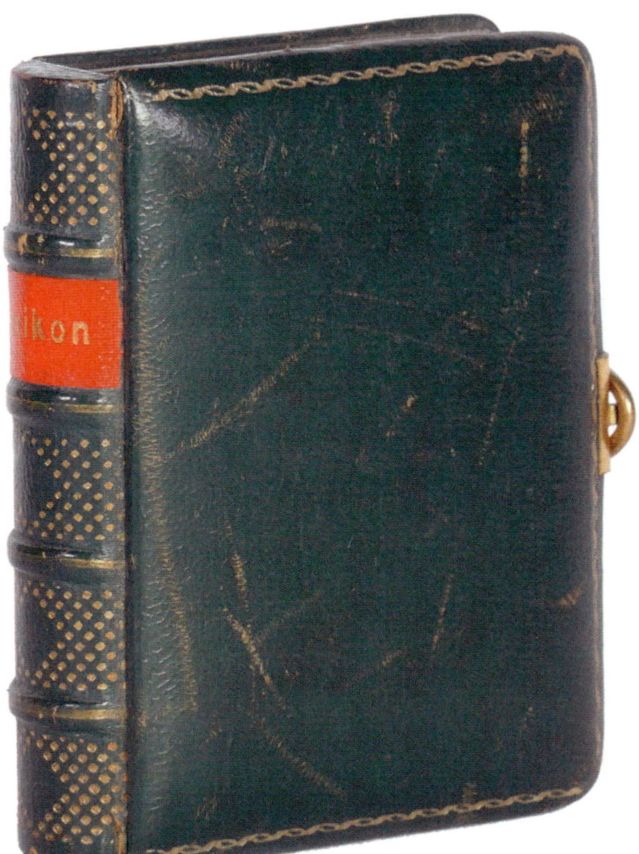

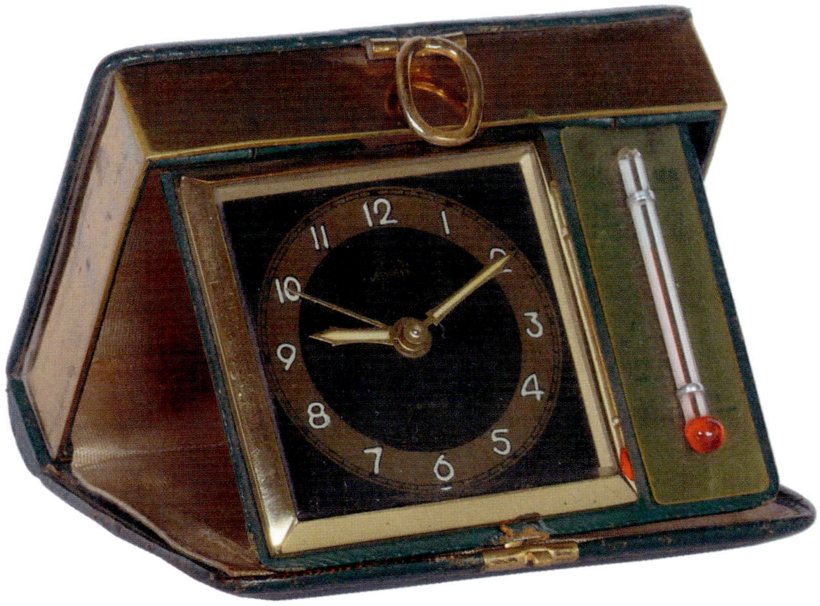

1.041
Livre d'heures, Ralco
Aufklappbare Taschenuhr in einem Ledereinband, dreiseitiger Goldschnitt
Fold-up pocket watch with leather binding, all edges gilt
Made in Switzerland
Um / *Around* 1900
6,4 x 5,5 x 1,4 cm

1.042
Livres d'Heures
Reisewecker „Coriolan" mit Prägung, dreiseitiger Messingbuchschnitt, Verschluss mit Druckknopf
Travel alarm clock „Coriolan" with embossing, brass edges, ribbon with snap closure
Made in France
3,5 x 10,5 x 9,6 cm

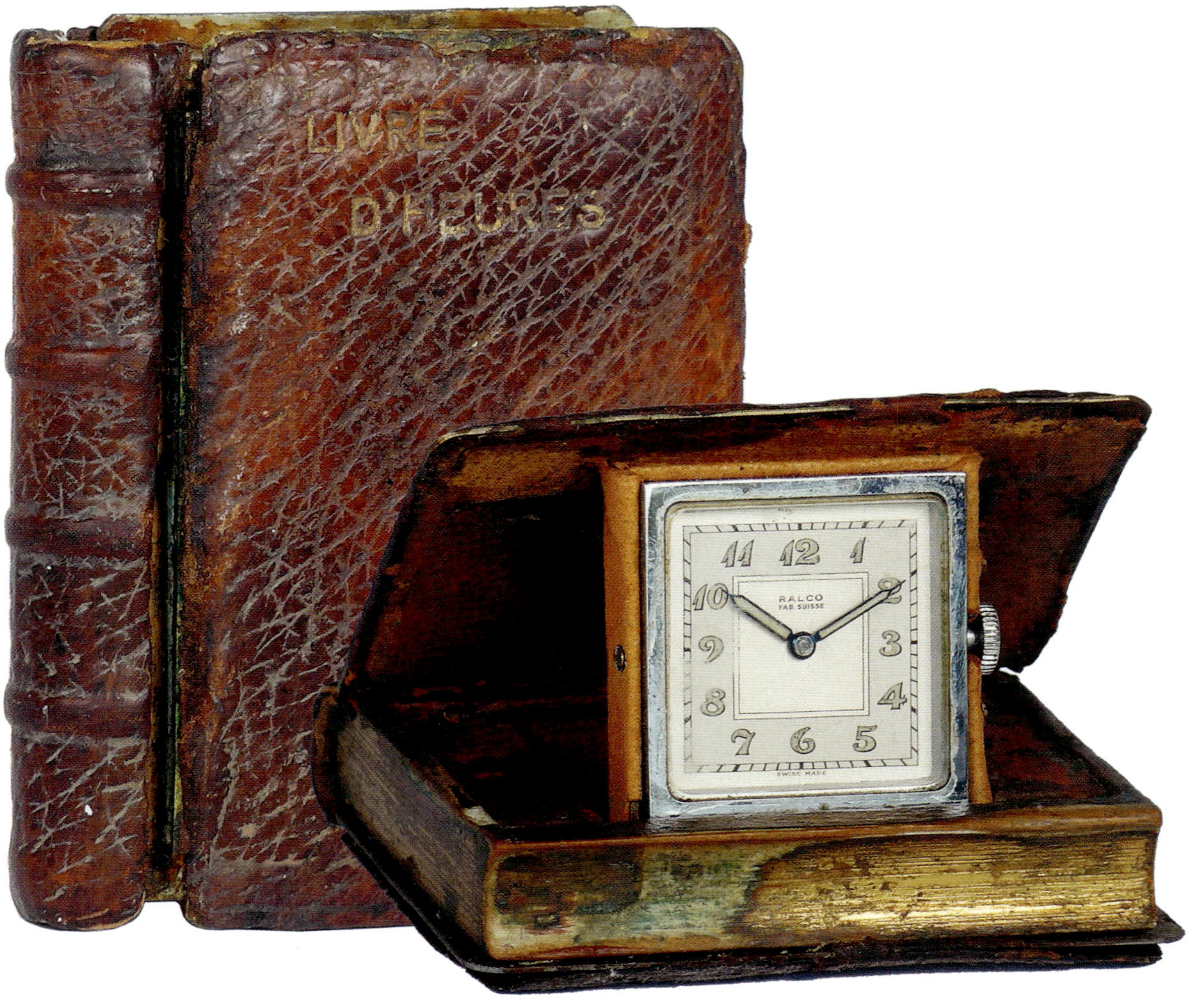

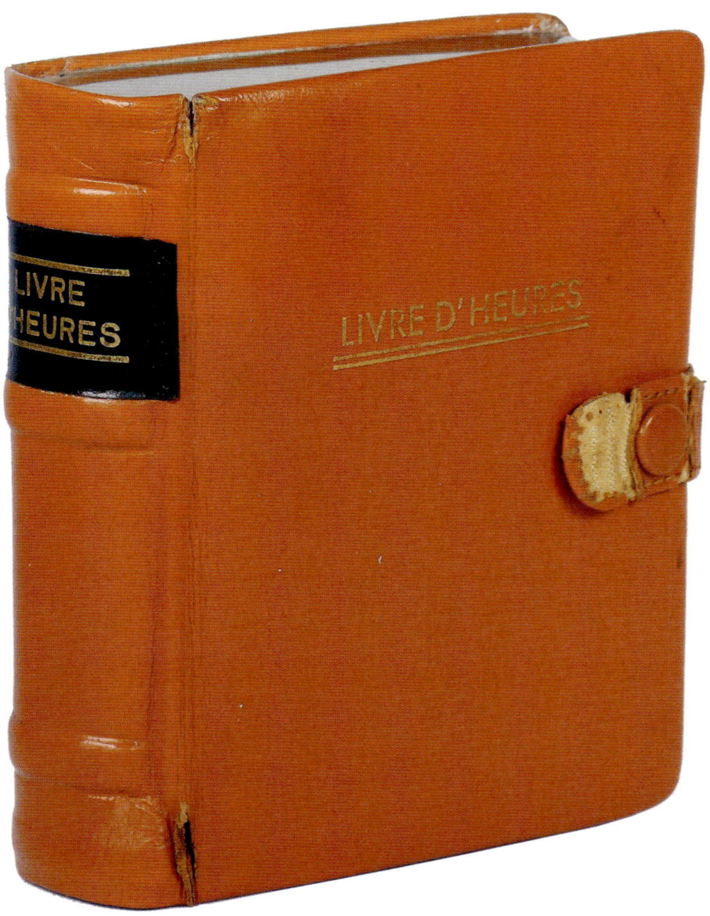

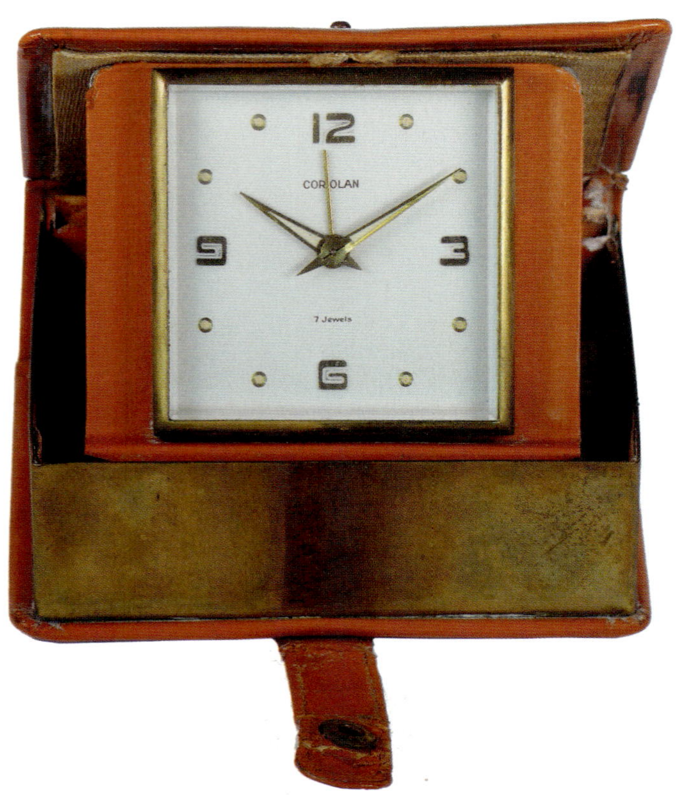

1.043
Reinh. Rose, Uhrmacher / *Watchmaker*, Delitzsch
Rote Samtkassette mit Messingbeschlägen, dreiseitigem Goldschnitt und einer Schließe für eine Taschenuhr.
Gilt-edged cassette with red velvet cover and brass fittings, buckle for a pocket watch
11,3 x 8,3 x 2,5 cm

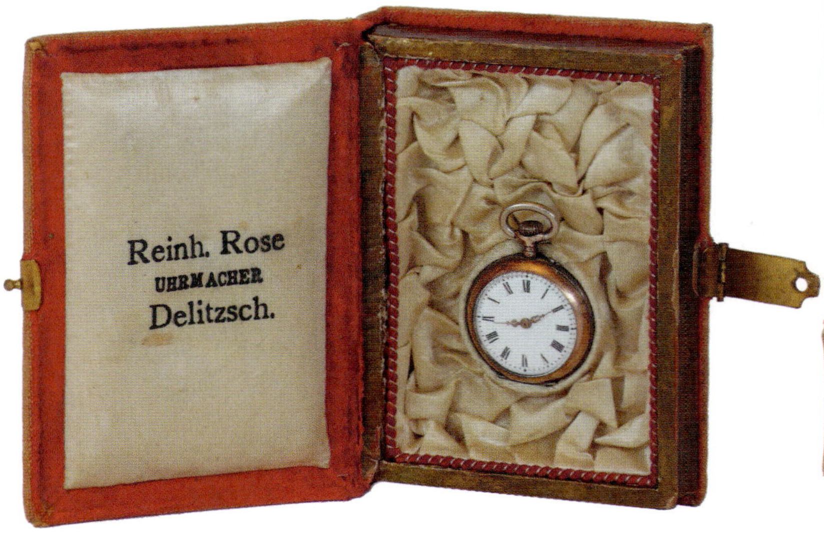

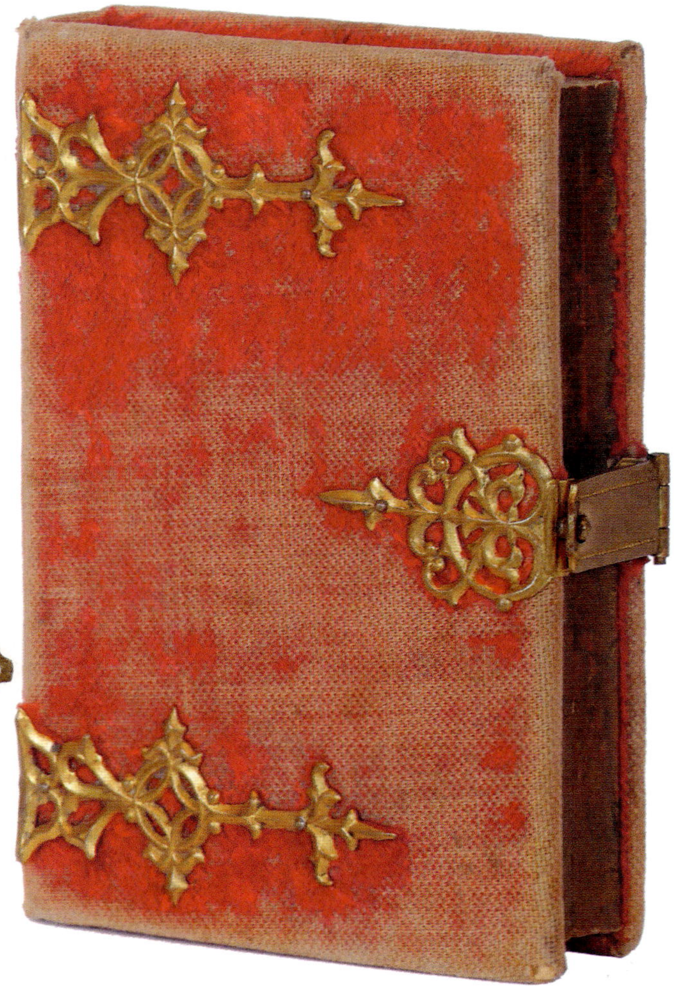

1.044
Tischuhr / *Table clock*, Gübelin, Luzern.
Vergoldetes Metallgehäuse mit Gravur, durchbrochener Deckel, Damengesellschaft der Renaissance im Hintergrund
Gilt metal case with engraving on the rear board, with perforated front, Renaissance lady's scene in the background
23,3 x 18 x 8,3 cm

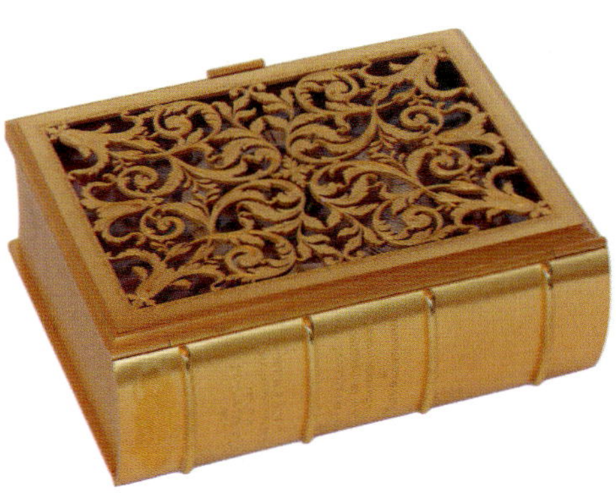

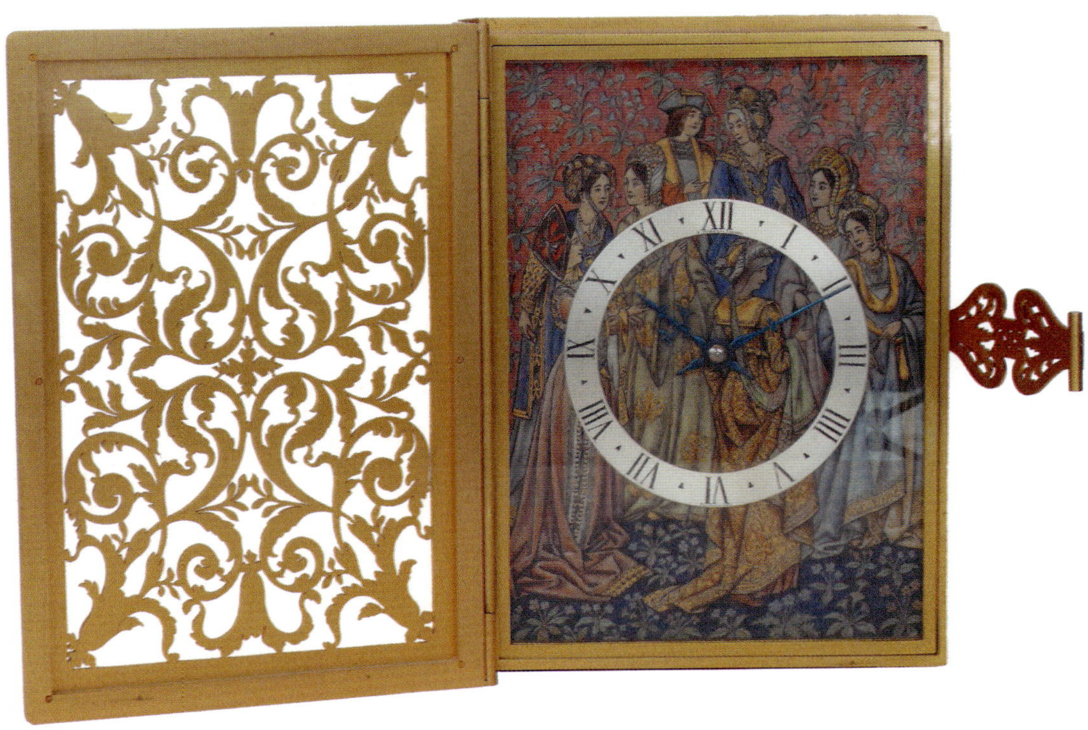

1.045
Zenith, „Dépose“
Kartonbehältnis mit Lederrücken
für eine Krankenschwesteruhr
Cardboard box with leather spine strip
containing a nurse's watch
14 x 5,5 x 5,4 cm

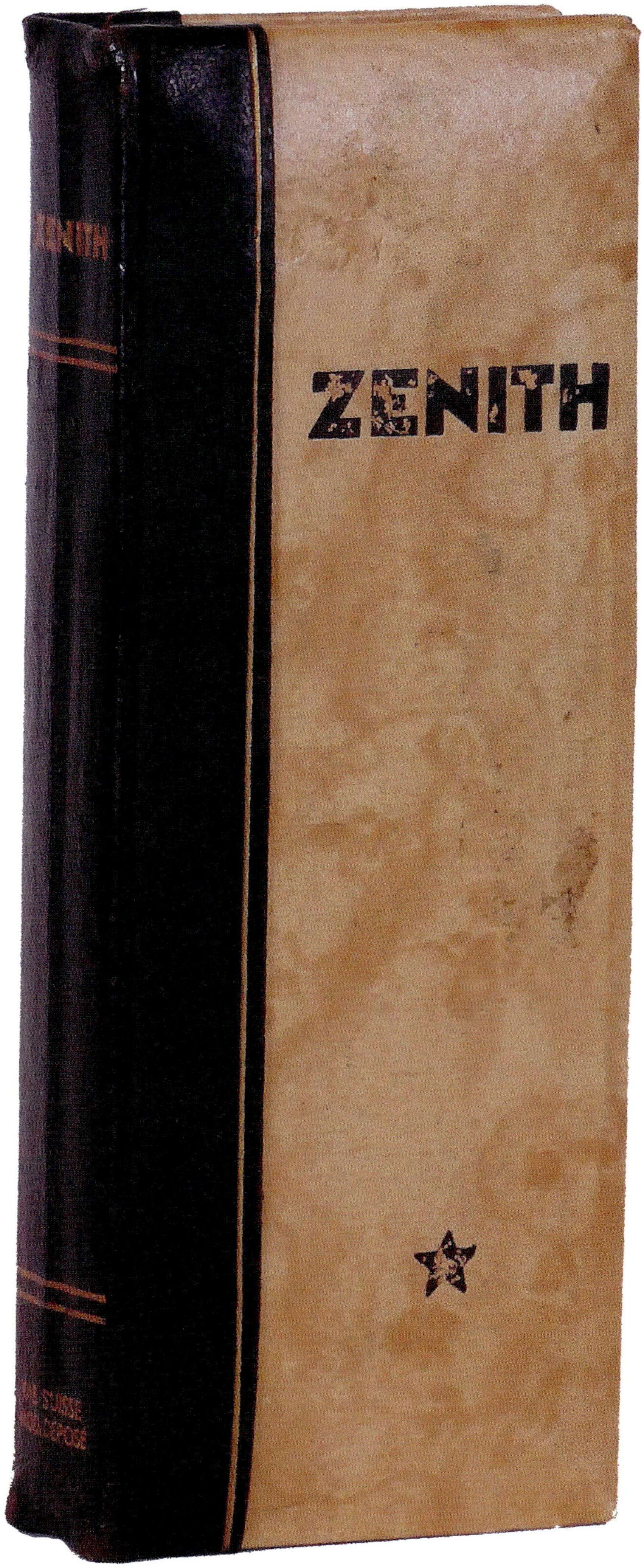

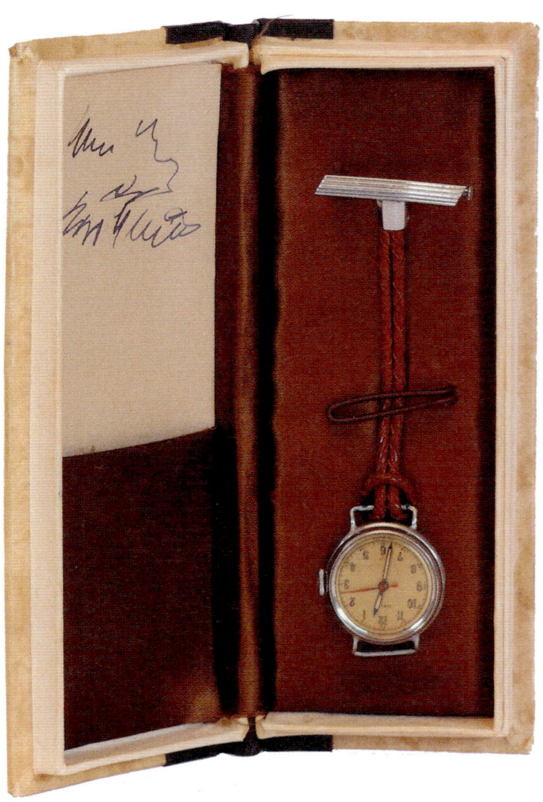

1.046
Jubilé JLC 1833–1958 (Jaeger LeCoultre), Pionniers de la haute précision
Ganzlederband mit Goldprägung, Lederfutter, dreiseitiger Goldschnitt, Schließe
Leather binding, gold tooling and leather lining, all edges gilt, clasp
15,8 x 12,3 x 4,2 cm

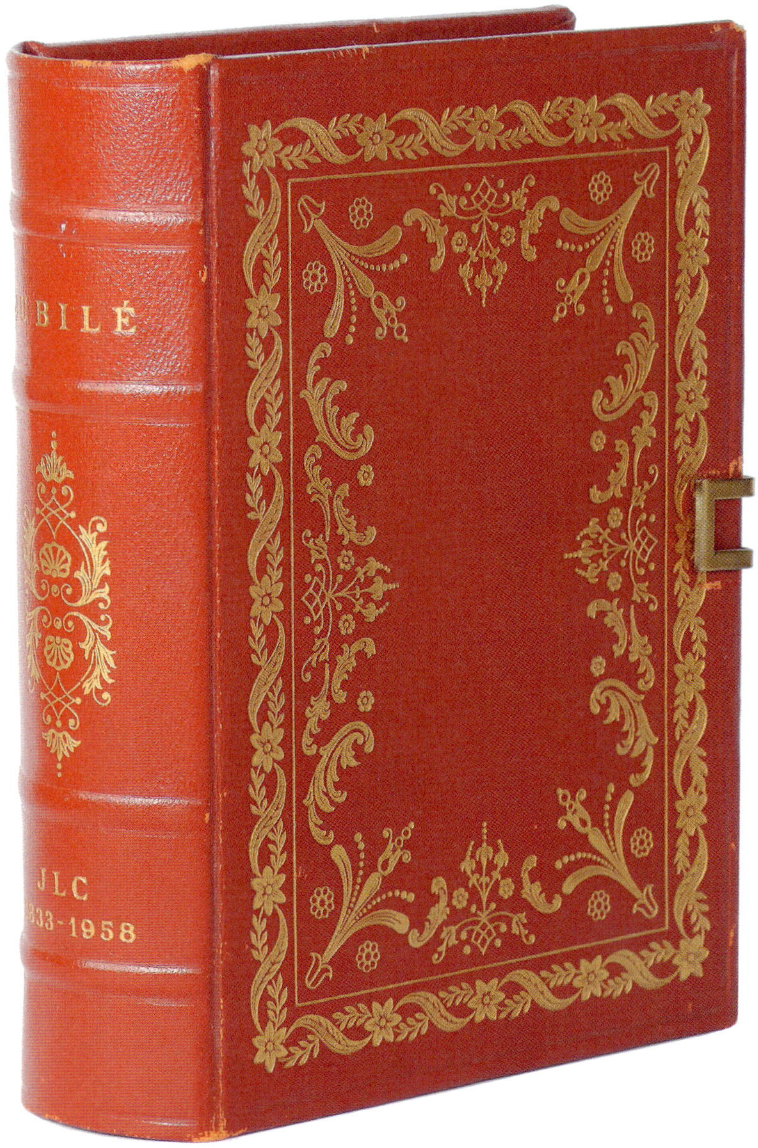

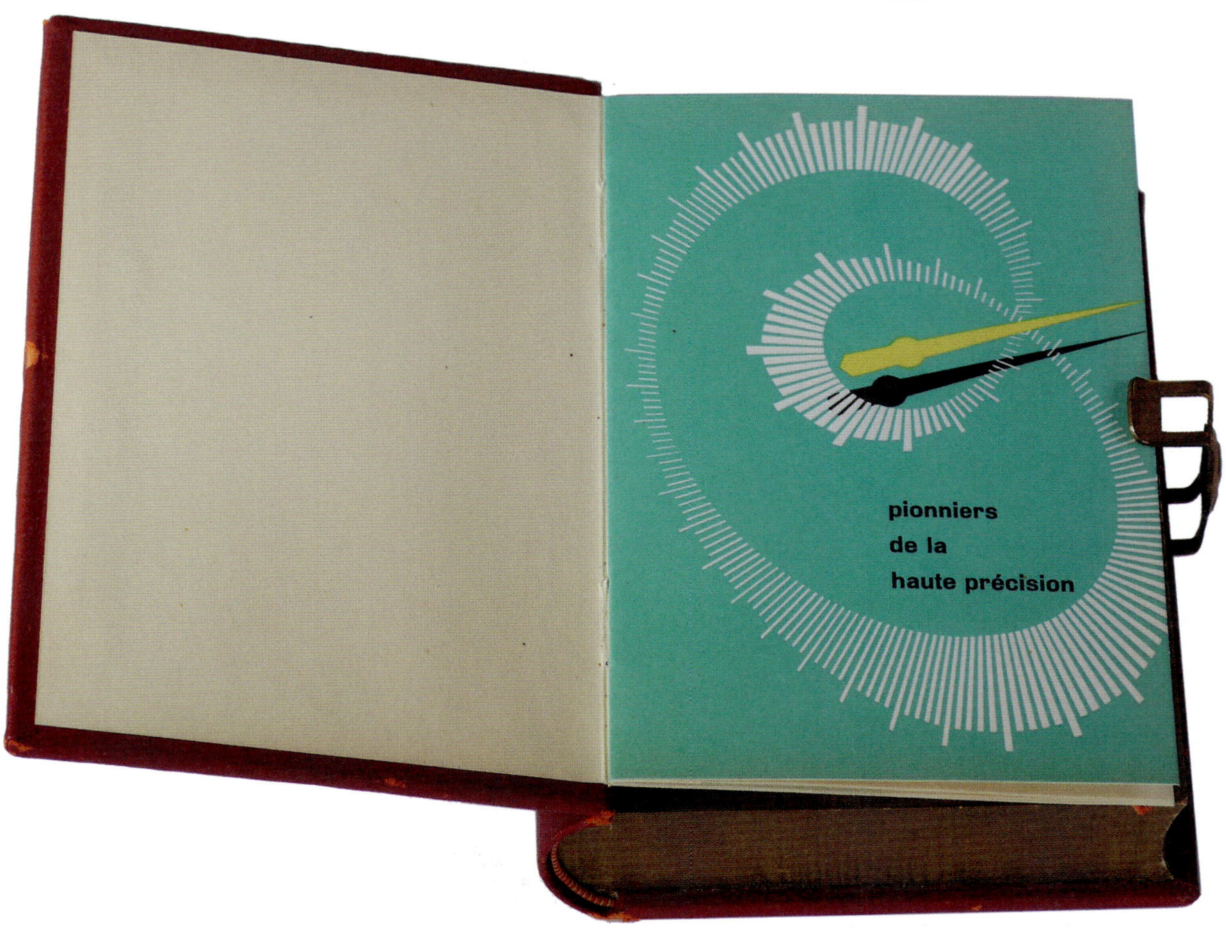

1.047
Schmuckschatulle aus Holz mit Stofffutter, Deckel mit Intarsien, Verschluss verschiebbarer Buchrücken
Wooden jewelry box with cloth lining, lid with marquetry, lock with a sliding spine
1950er-Jahre / *1950s* | 10,5 x 13,5 x 10,5 cm

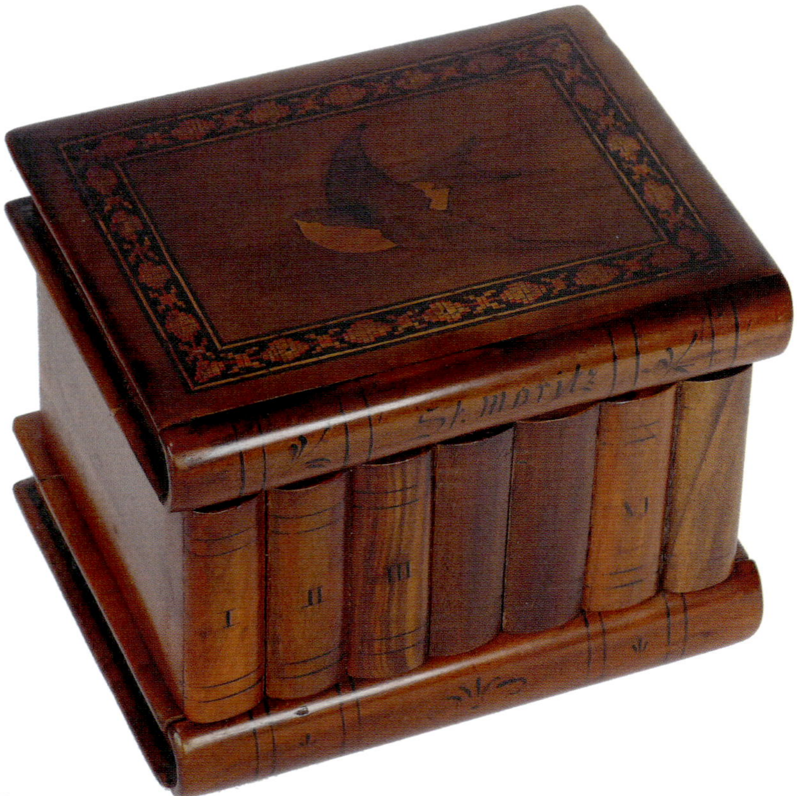

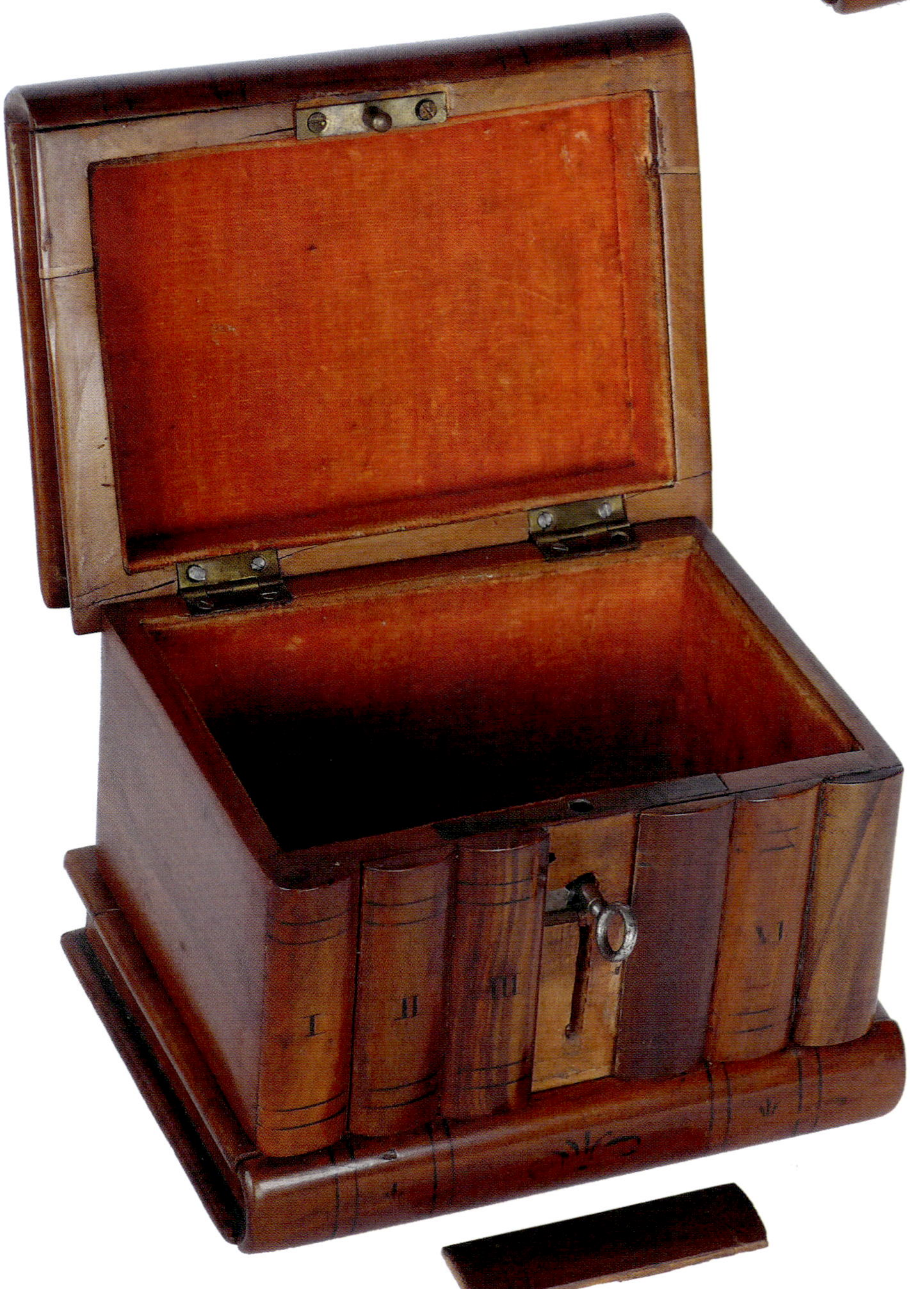

1.048
Souvenir-Holzschatulle, Front mit Buchrücken, bemalter Deckel mit Zigarettensujet
Wooden souvenir box, spines on the front part, a painted cigarette theme on the lid
1950er-Jahre / *1950s* | 4,8 x 10,8 x 8,5 cm

1.049
Souvenir-Holzschatulle, Front mit Buchrücken, Deckel mit Intarsien und Bemalung
Wooden souvenir box, spines on the front part, lid with marquetry and paintings
1950er-Jahre / *1950s* | 4,4 x 10 x 10,4 cm

1.050
Interlaken
Souvenir-Holzschatulle, Front mit Buchrücken, Deckel mit Intarsien und Bemalung
Wooden souvenir box, spines on the front part, lid with marquetry and paintings
1950er-Jahre / *1950s* | 3,1 x12,8 x 7,7 cm

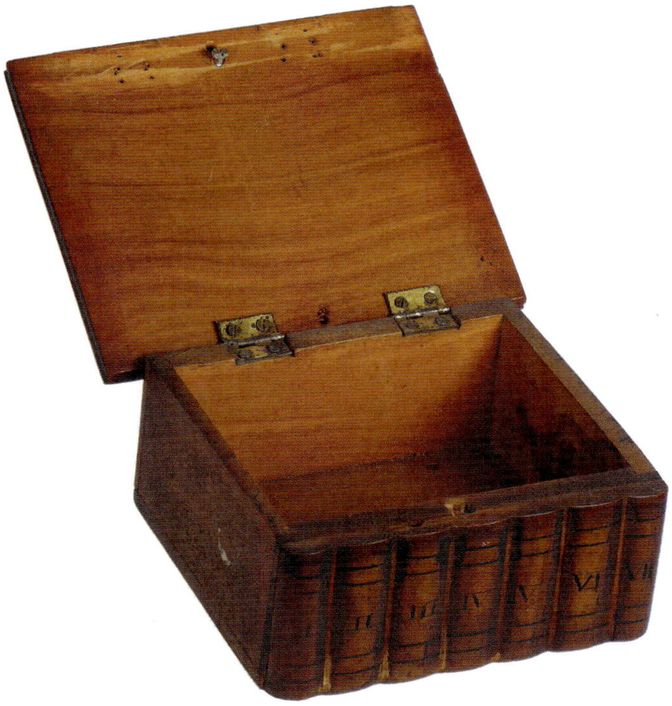

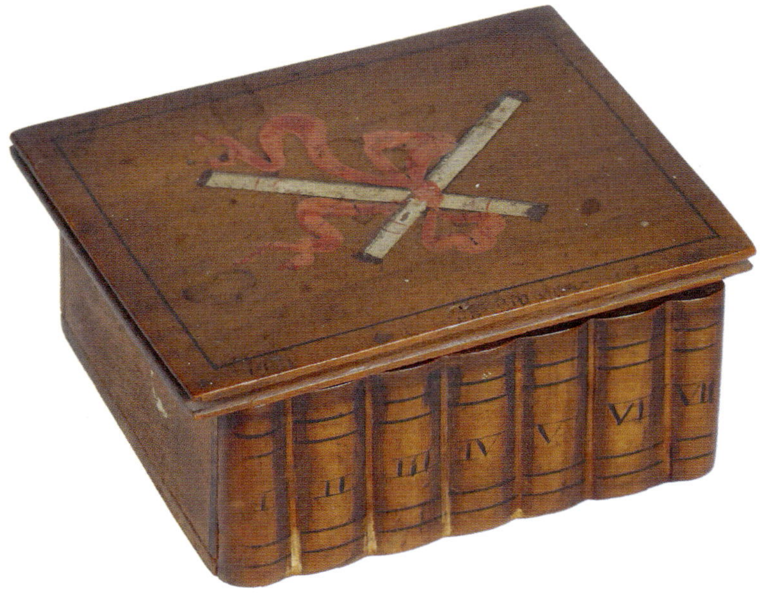

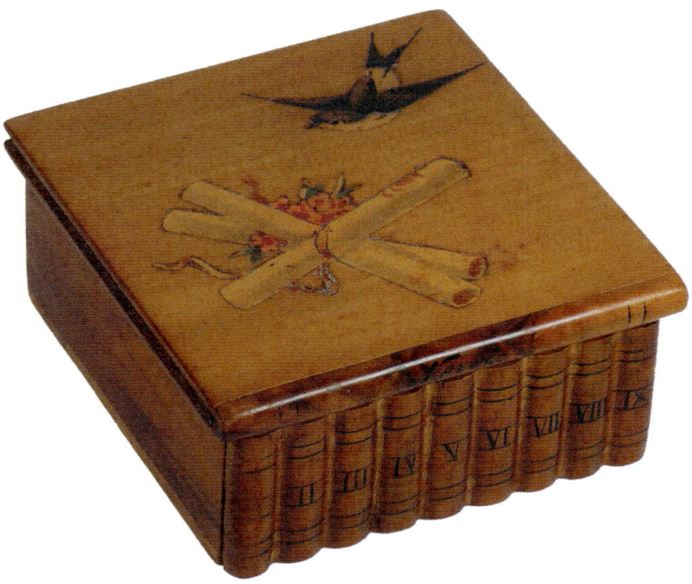

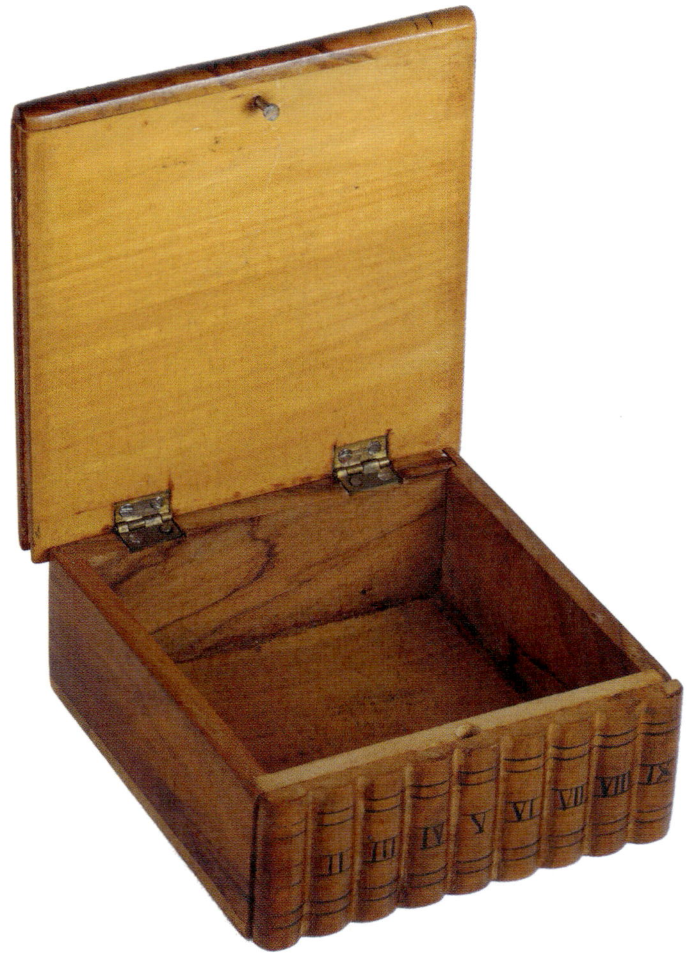

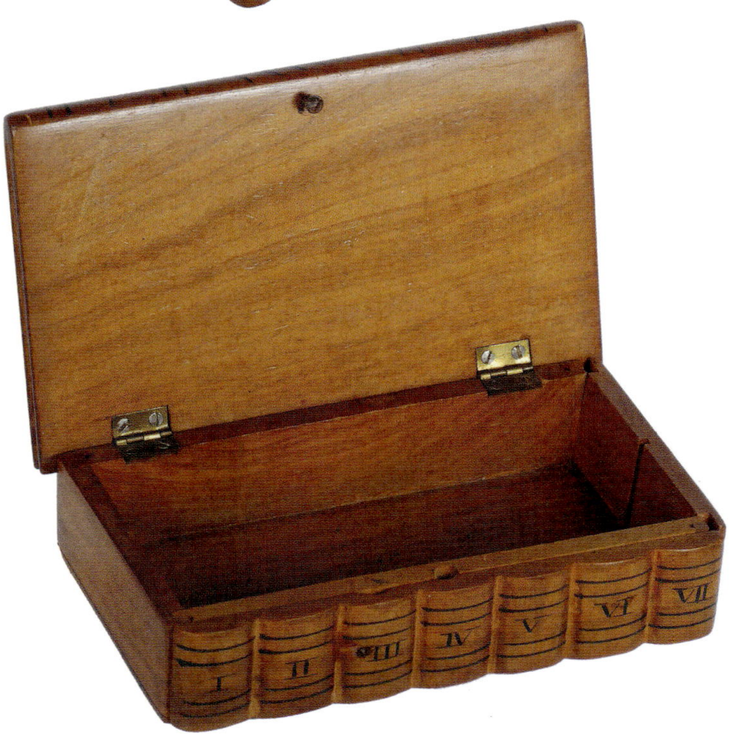

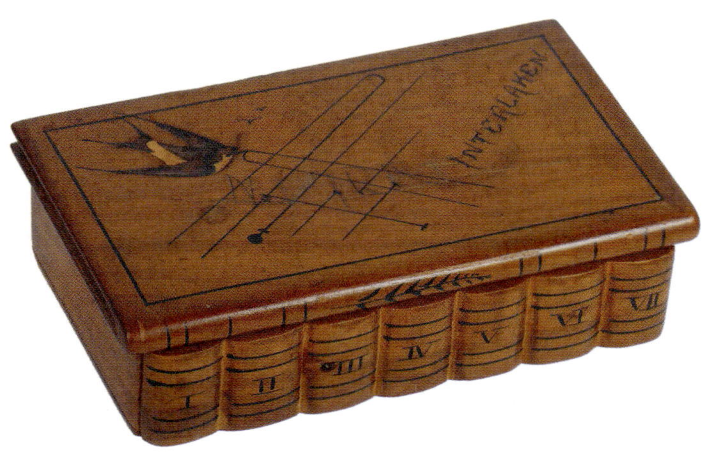
INTERLAKEN

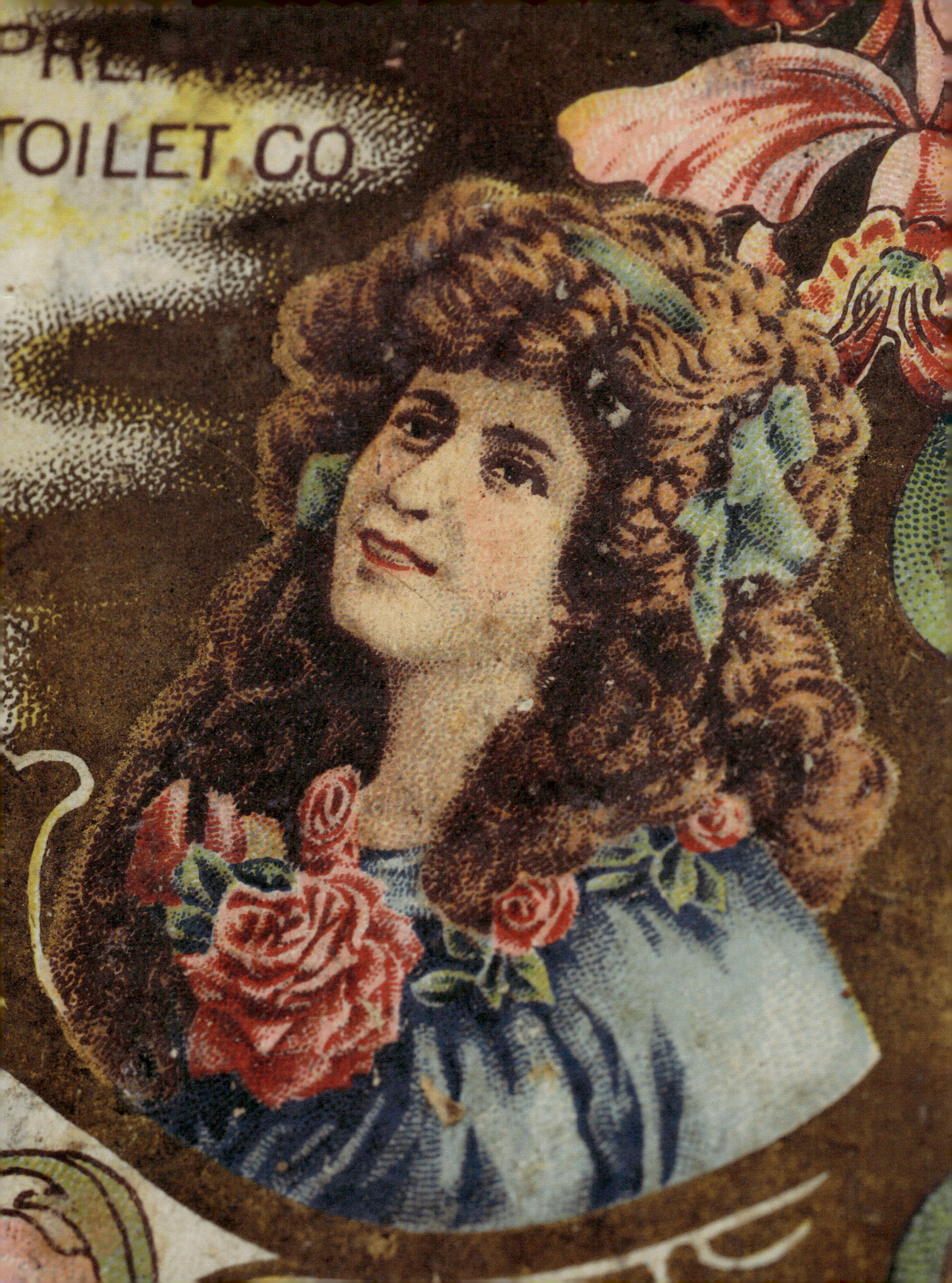
TOILET CO

Schönheit & Hygiene
Beauty & Hygiene

Der sehr geschätzte Sohn meiner Partnerin hatte das Glück, einige Zeit in London zu arbeiten. Selbstverständlich habe ich Thomas in Hampstead besucht, ein sehr bevorzugtes Wohnviertel der englischen Hauptstadt, wo er ein hübsches kleines Flat gemietet hatte.

Weil er tagsüber seinen Pflichten nachgehen musste, konnte ich die Zeit nutzen um meine Sammelleidenschaften zu frönen. An der King's Road, eine der populärsten Einkaufsstraßen Chelseas, hat es schicke und sehr gepflegte Geschäfte, auch gediegene Antiquitätenläden. In einer Schaufensterauslage ist mir sofort eine sehr hübsche Dose in Buchform aufgefallen. Nie zuvor habe ich ein Buchobjekt gesehen, das mit mehrfarbig geplätteten Strohgeflecht gearbeitet wurde. Das Innenleben ist verglast. Dreiseitig goldfarbenes Stroh imitiert einen Goldschnitt. Herstellungsort und Verwendungszweck sind unklar, trotzdem habe ich das tolle Objekt aus dem 19. Jahrhundert in die Kategorie Kosmetikdosen aufgenommen. Der Verkäufer ließ über den Preis nicht mit sich reden, gleichwohl habe ich das Highlight in die Sammlung aufgenommen.

The highly esteemed son of my partner was lucky enough to spend some time in London for work. Naturally, I visited Thomas in Hampstead, a very attractive residential area of the English capital, where he had rented a pretty little flat.

Because he had his duties during the day, I was able to use the time to pursue my collecting passions. On the King's Road, one of Chelsea's most popular shopping streets, there are chic and very well-maintained shops, including tastefully decorated antique stores. I quickly found a very pretty tin with a book design in one of the shop windows. Never before had I seen a book-like object that is decorated using multicolored,flattened straw netting. The inside is glazed. Golden straw on each of the three sides imitates a gilt edge. The location of origin and intended use are unclear, nevertheless I allocated this wonderful 19th-century object to the category of cosmetics boxes. The seller didn't want to negotiate the price, but I still added this gem to my collection.

2.001
Kunststoffdose für eine Parfümflasche, Vorderdeckel mit Relief
Plastic box for a perfume bottle, lid with relief Devon Violets by Manon
10,2 x 7,3 x 2,3 cm

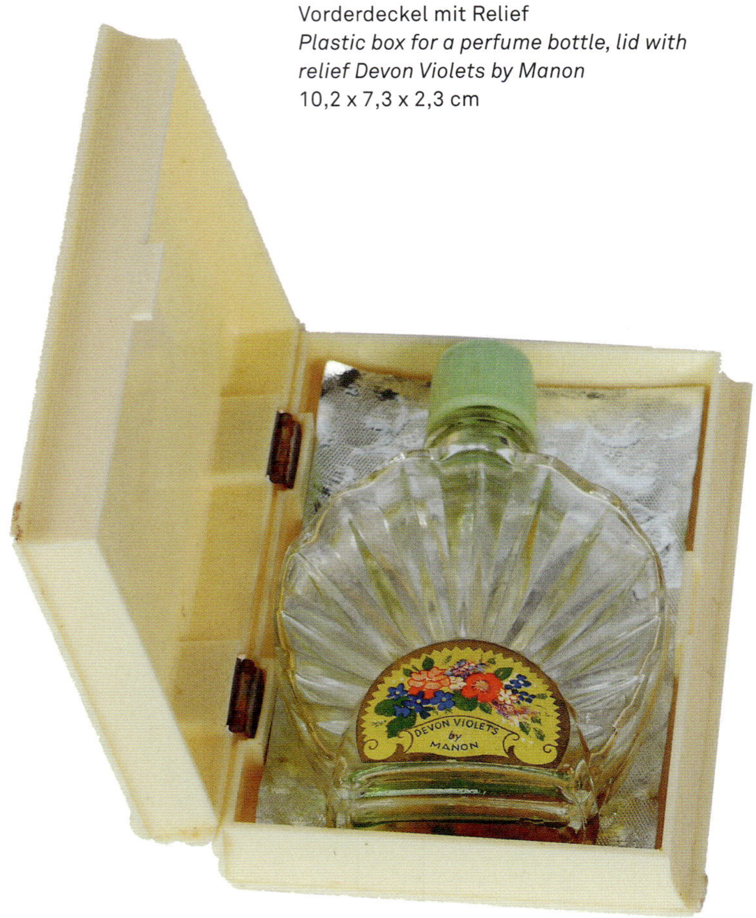

2.002
Griffonnage by Jacques Griffe (1909–1996)
Schachtel für eine Parfumflasche, Rücken- und Deckeltitel, dreiseitiger Goldschnitt
Box for a perfume bottle, title on the spine and lid, all edges gilt
Gefertigt in Paris / *Made in Paris* 1949
7 x 5 x 1,8 cm

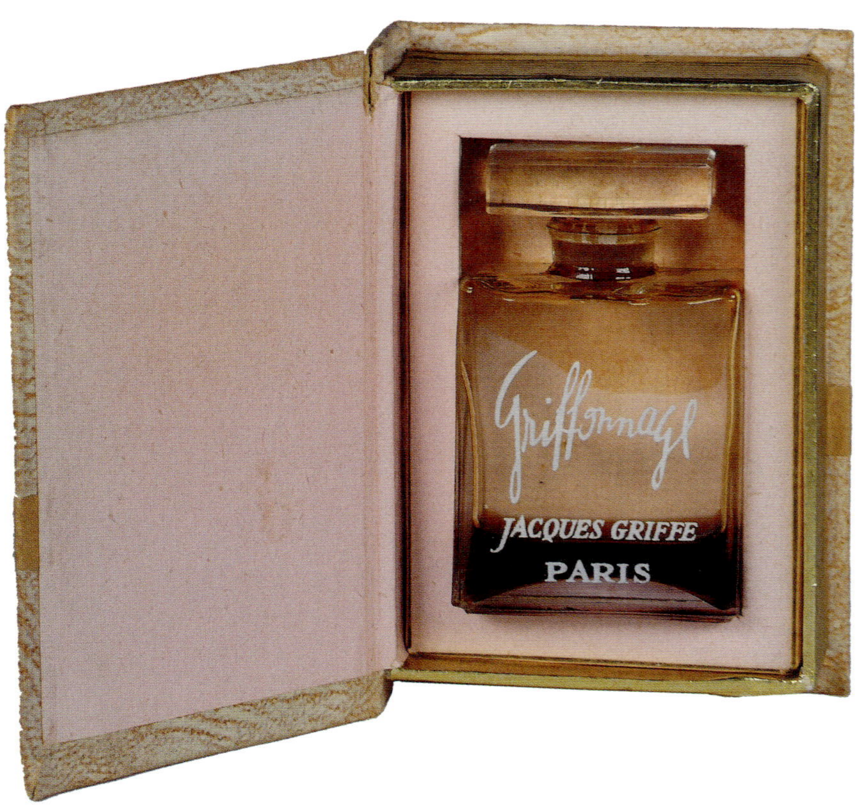

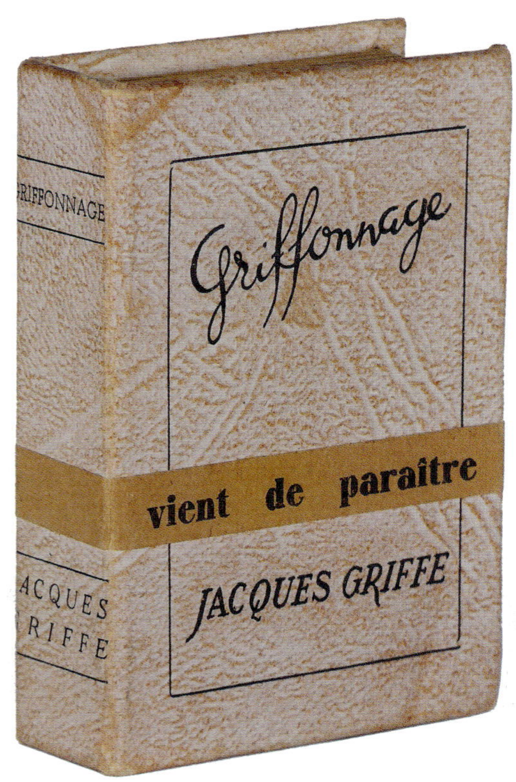

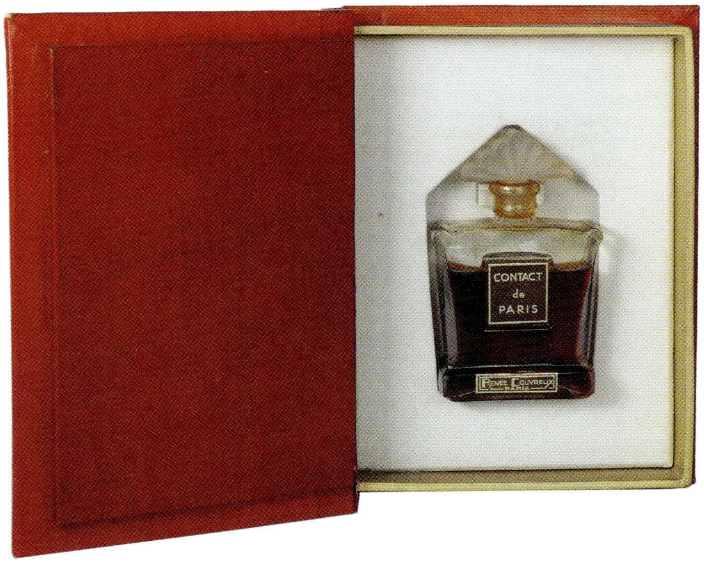

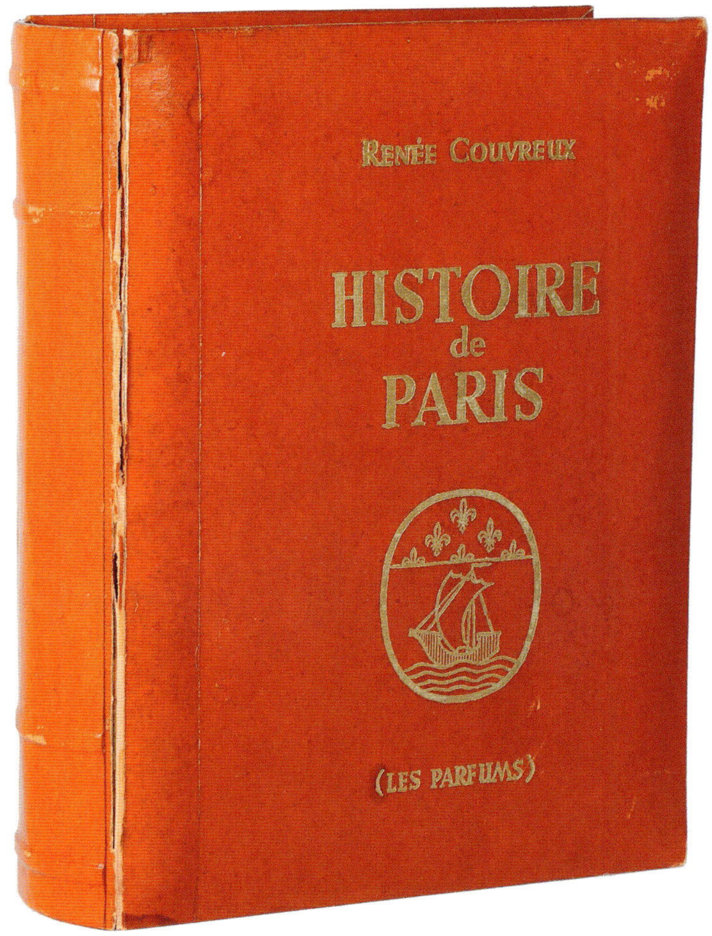

2.003
Renée Couvreux, Histoire de Paris (Les Parfums)
Schachtel für eine Parfümflasche, Goldprägung auf dem Vorderdeckel, dreiseitiger Goldschnitt
Box for a perfume bottle, gold tooling on the front cover, all edges gilt
4 x 16,4 x 13,2 cm

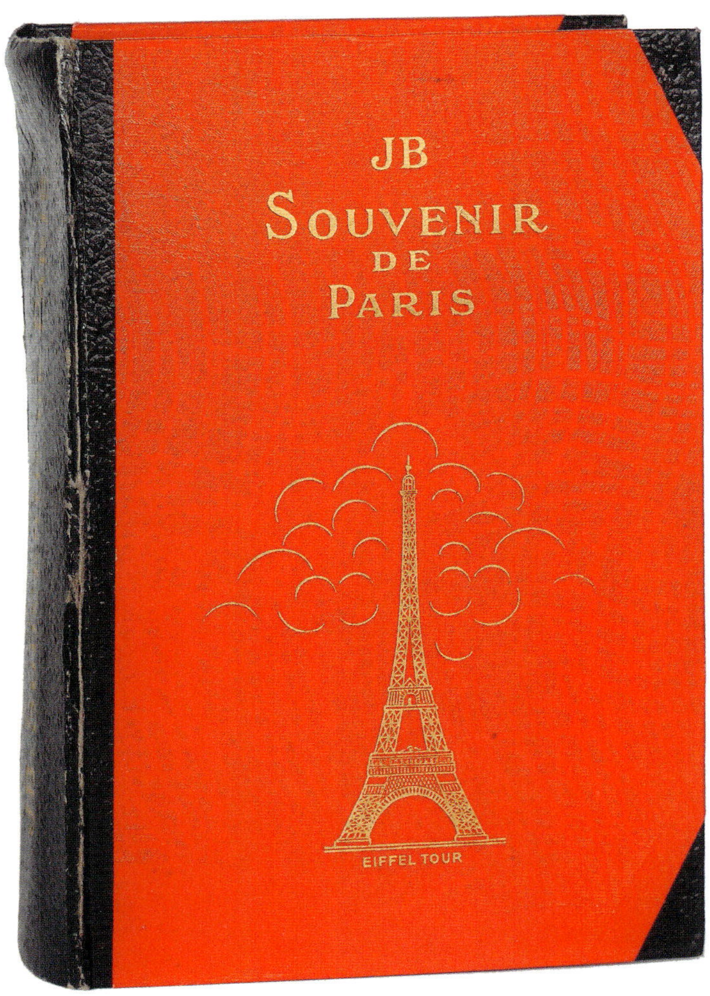

2.004
JB Souvenir de Paris
Schachtel für eine Parfümflasche im Schuber, Goldprägung auf dem Vorderdeckel
Box with slipcase for a perfume bottle, gold tooling on the front cover
Um / *Around* 1940 | 3 x 13,9 x 10,3 cm

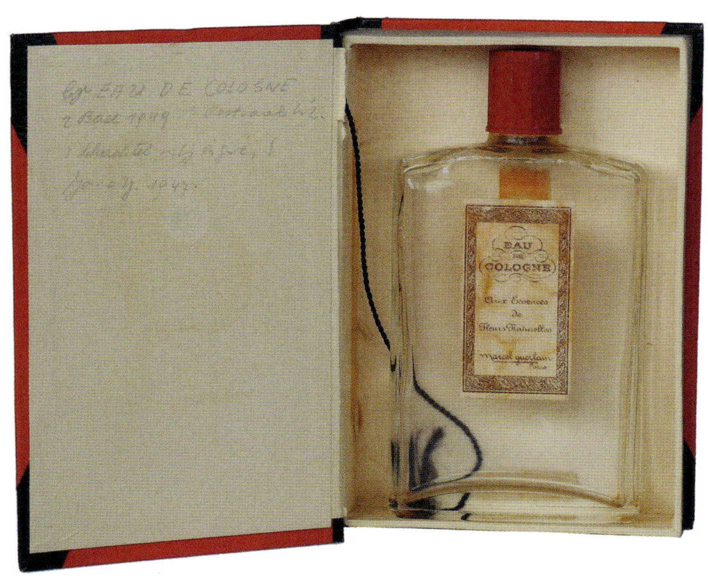

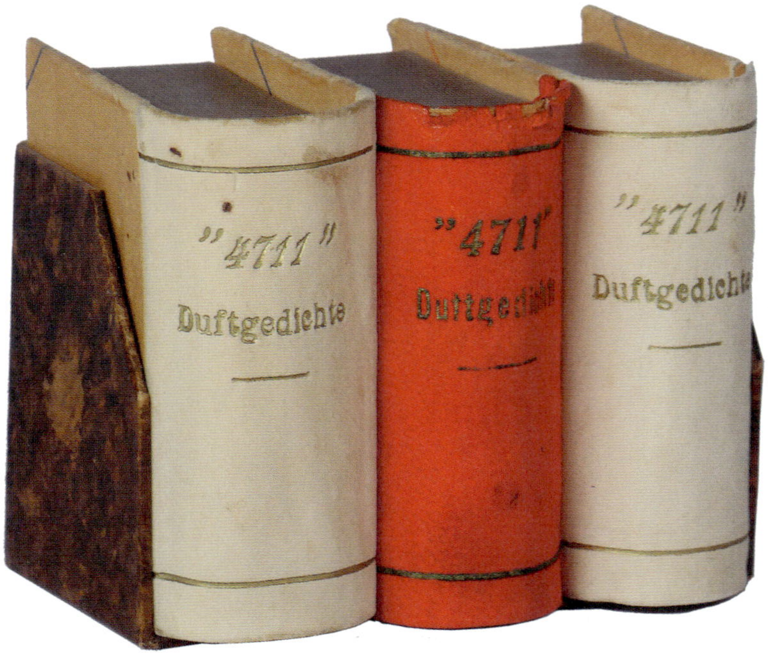

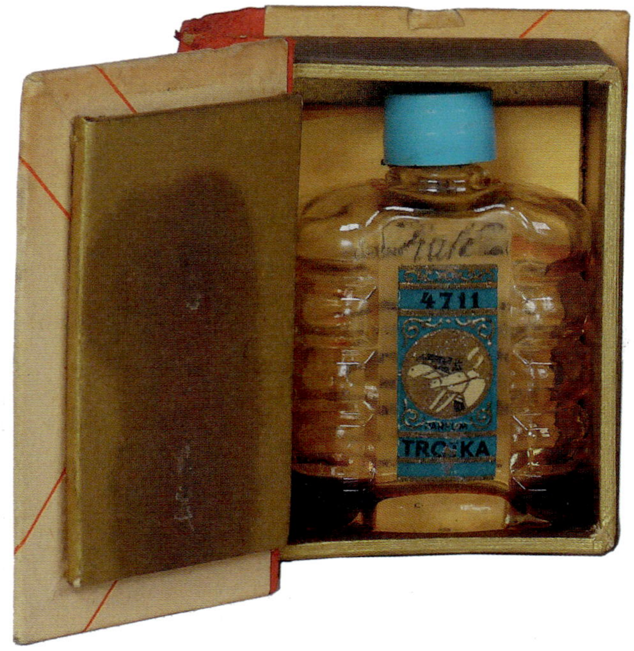

2.005
„4711" Duftgedichte / *Scent Poems*
Kleine Schachteln im Schuber mit Miniatur-Parfümfläschchen
Small boxes in a slipcase with miniature perfume bottles
Schindler Parfümerie Zürich, Switzerland
6,5 x 7,9 x 5,5 cm

2.006
„4711" Duft Gedichte / *Scent Poems*
Parfum-Halblederdosen mit Rückenvergoldung, drei Parfümfläschchen
Perfume half leather boxes with gilt spine, three perfume bottles
2,5 x 8 x 6,7 cm

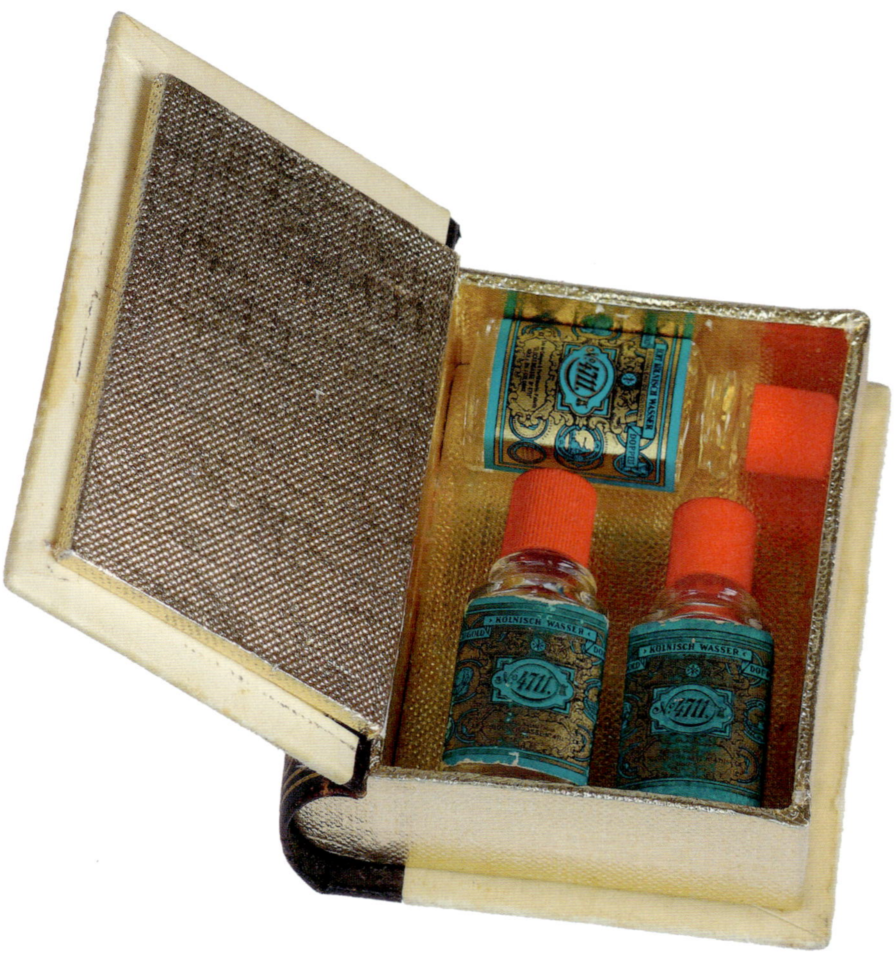

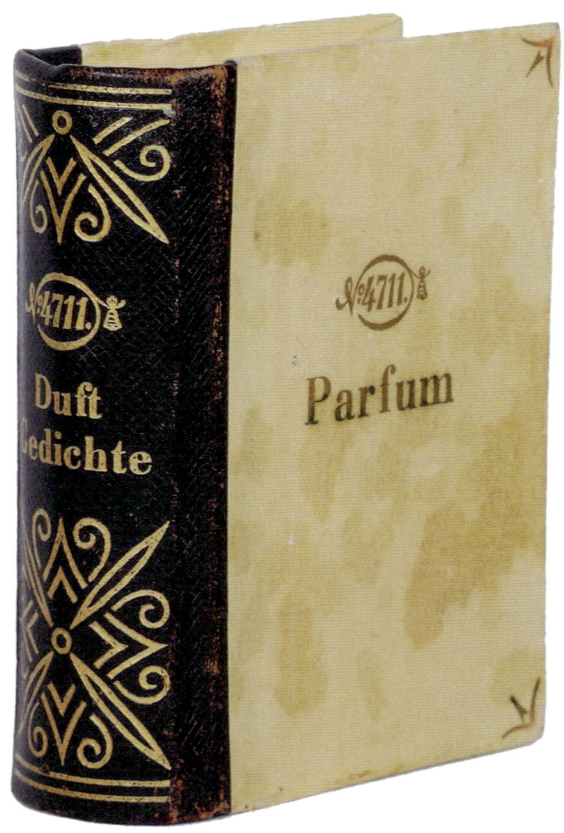

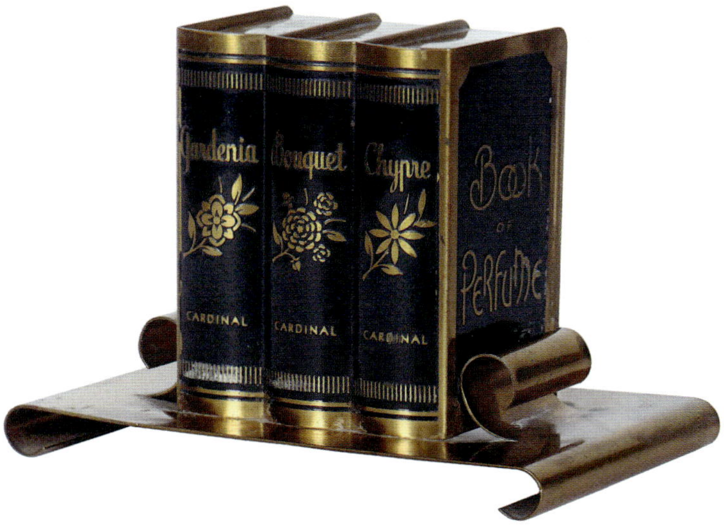

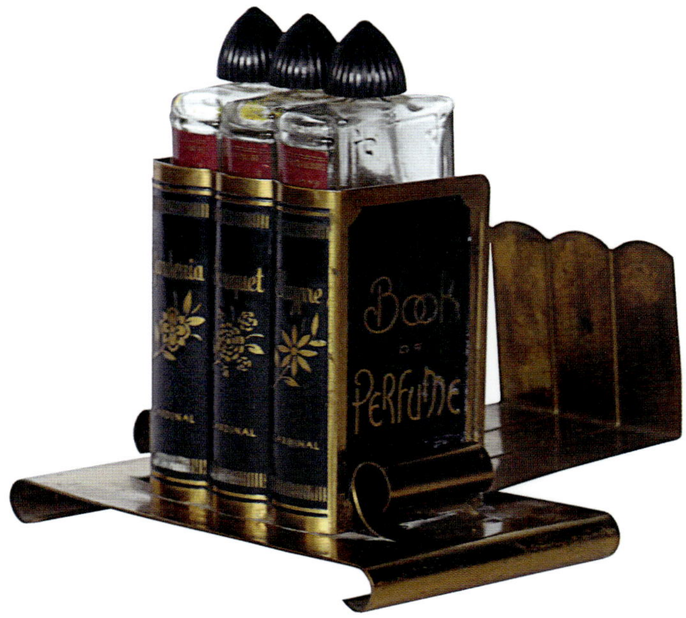

2.007
Gardenia, Bouquet, Chypre, by Cardinal Paris, Book of Perfume
Drei Messingbehältnisse auf Messingstand, Miniatur-Parfümfläschchen, goldene erhabene Beschriftungen
Three brass boxes on a brass base, miniature perfume bottles, gilt relief lettering
Um / *Around* 1940 | 7,2 x 9,9 x 6,2 cm

2.008
Parfumery Chiyotsubaki Prepared by Toilet Co. Japan
Lithografierte Blechdose für Parfüm, Schließe, lithografiertes Werbeschild auf dem Innendeckel
Lithographed tin box for perfume, clasp, lithographed advertising sign on the inner lid
1898 | 3,2 x 10,4 x 5,9 cm

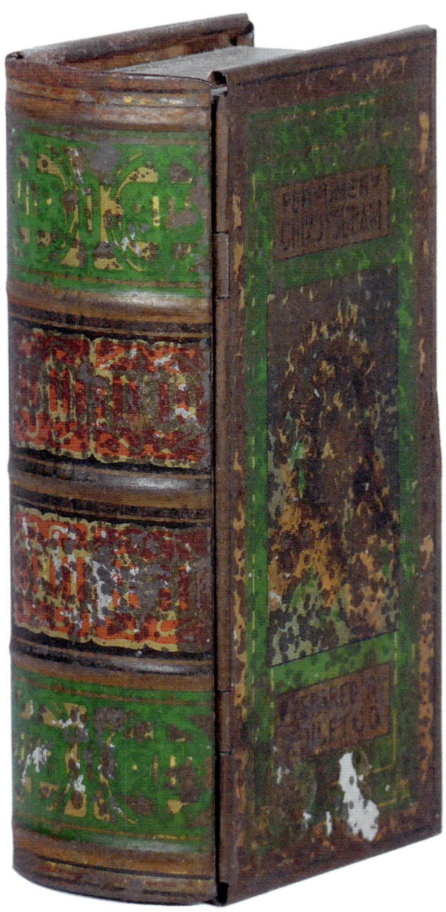

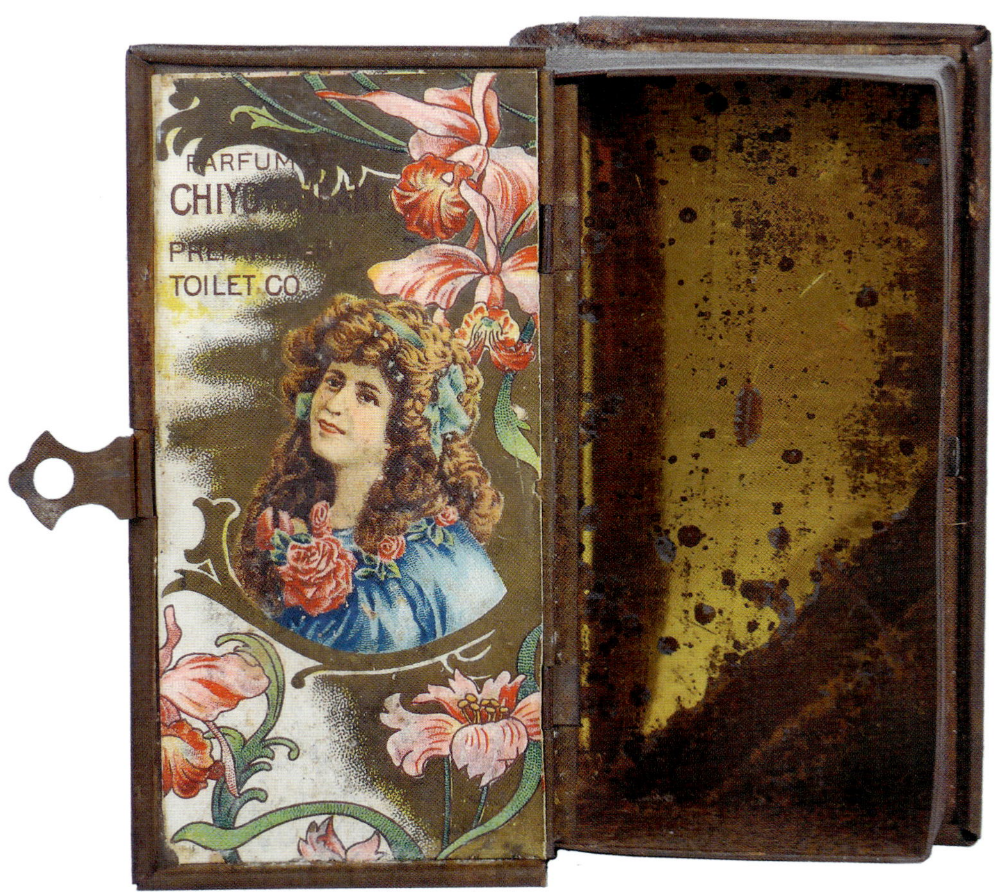

2.009
Messingpuderdose mit Innenspiegel und Puderfach
Powder box made of brass with a mirror and powder compartment
1,5 x 8 x 6,1 cm

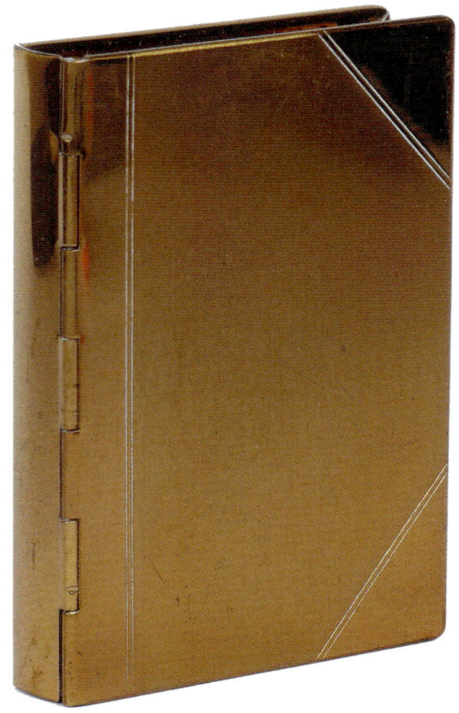

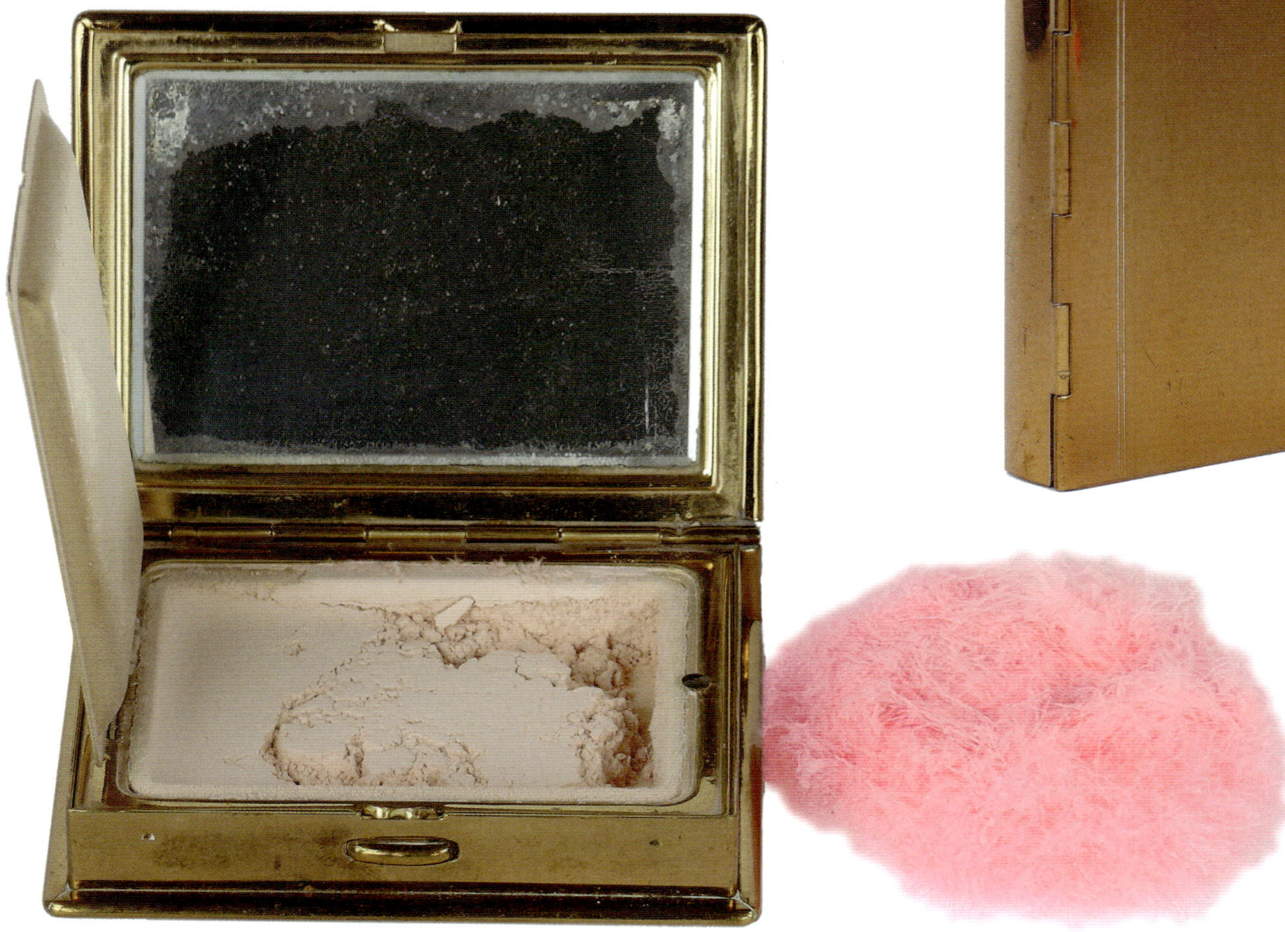

2.010
Ganzlederpuderdose der Firma Rothena mit facettiertem Spiegel und Puderfach, vergoldeter Vorderdeckel
Rothena leather powder box with faceted mirror and powder compartment, gilt lid
1,5 x 10,3 x 7,9 cm

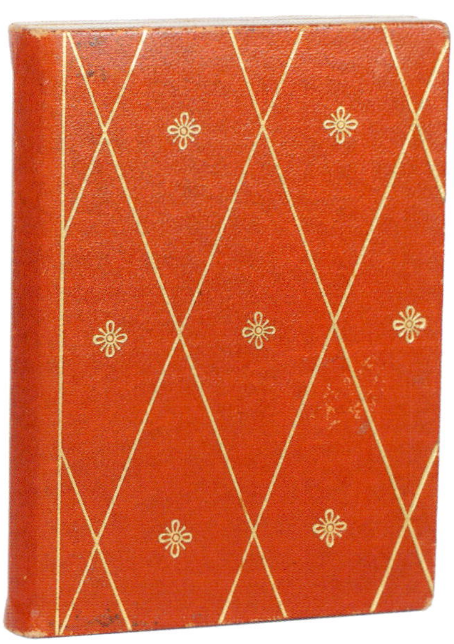

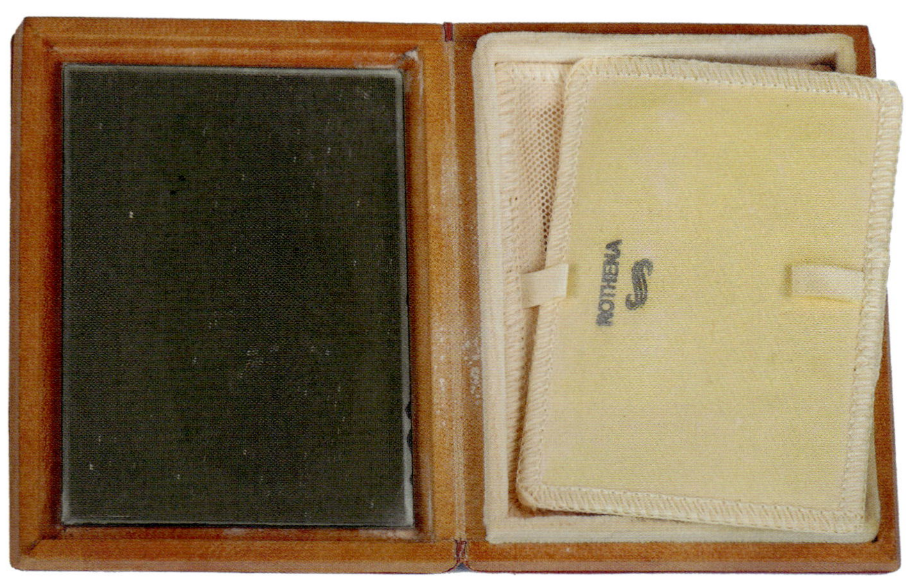

2.011
Messingpuderdose mit Lederüberzug, facettierter Spiegel, Puder- und Zigarettenfach
Brass powder box with leather cover, faceted pastedown, powder and cigarette compartment
Mondaine Cig.-Vannette, New York
Um / *Around* 1920 | 1,5 x 7,8 x 5,3 cm

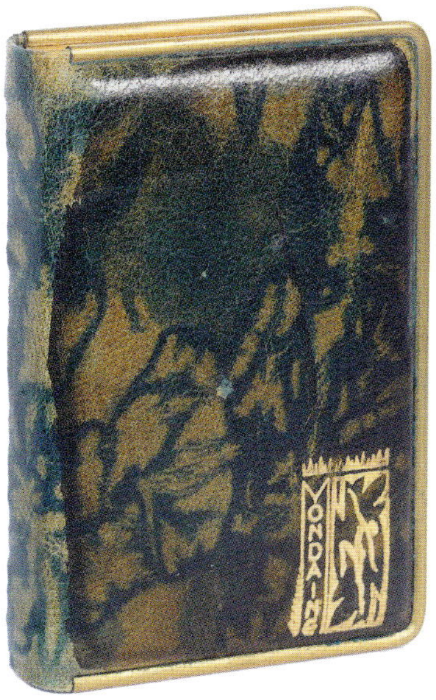

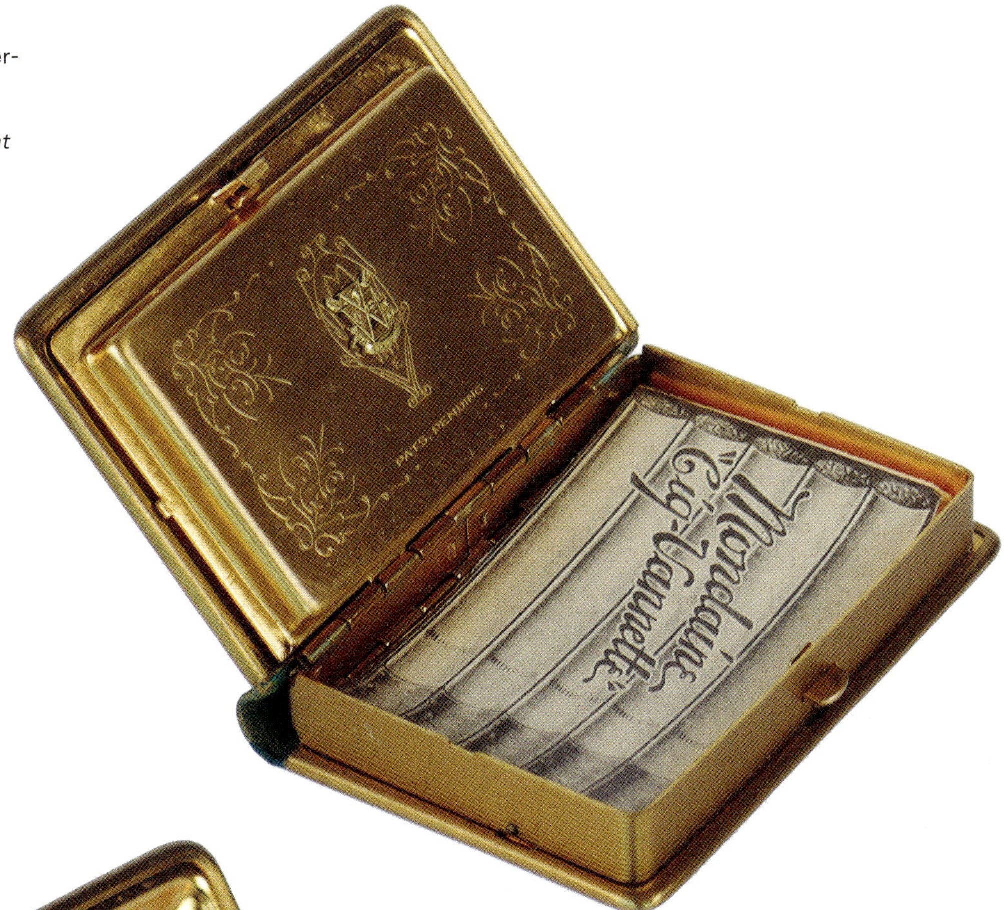

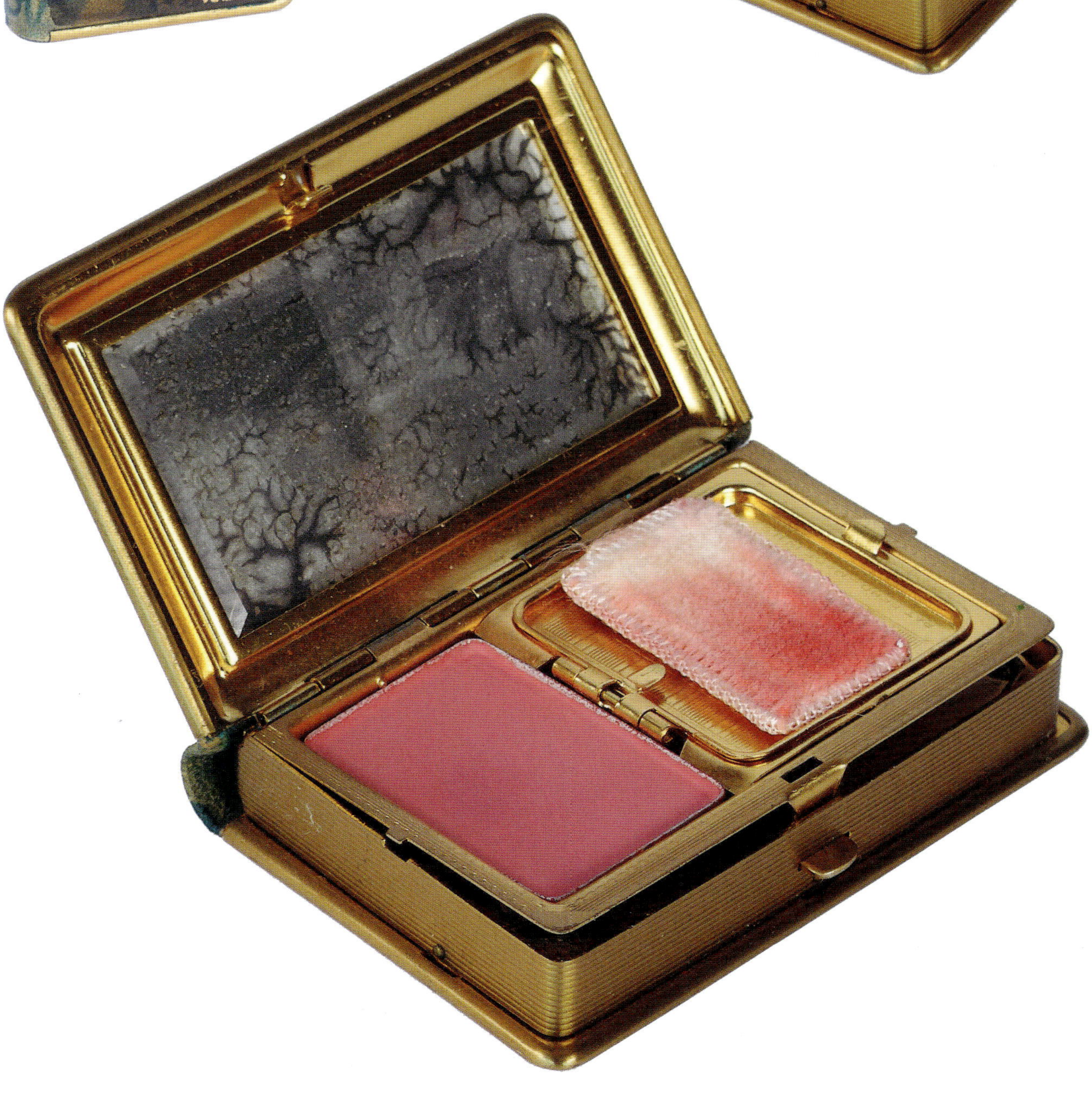

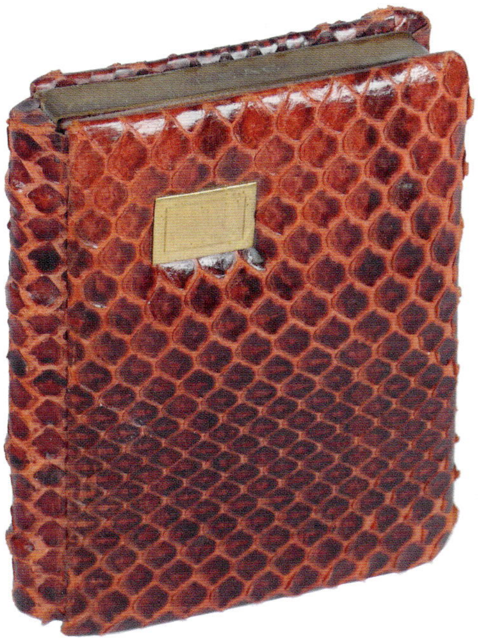

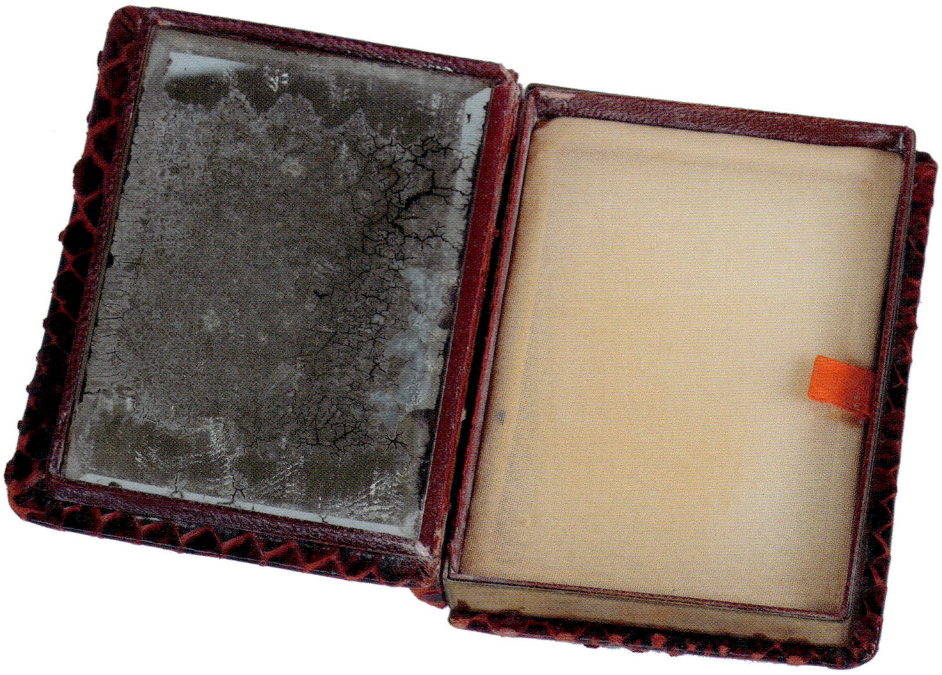

2.012
Schlangenlederpuderdose mit facettiertem Spiegel, Messingschnitt
Powder box made of snakeskin leather with faceted mirror, brass edges
Um / *Around* 1900 | 1,8 x 9,1 x 7,2 cm

2.013
„Remember Me“
Schachtel mit verglasten Deckeln, Innenspiegel und Lithografie, Einfassungen geprägtes Goldpapier
Box with glazed boards, interior mirror and a lithography, embossed gold paper edging
Mitte 19. Jh. / *Mid 19th century* | 1,7 x 7,6 x 5,2 cm

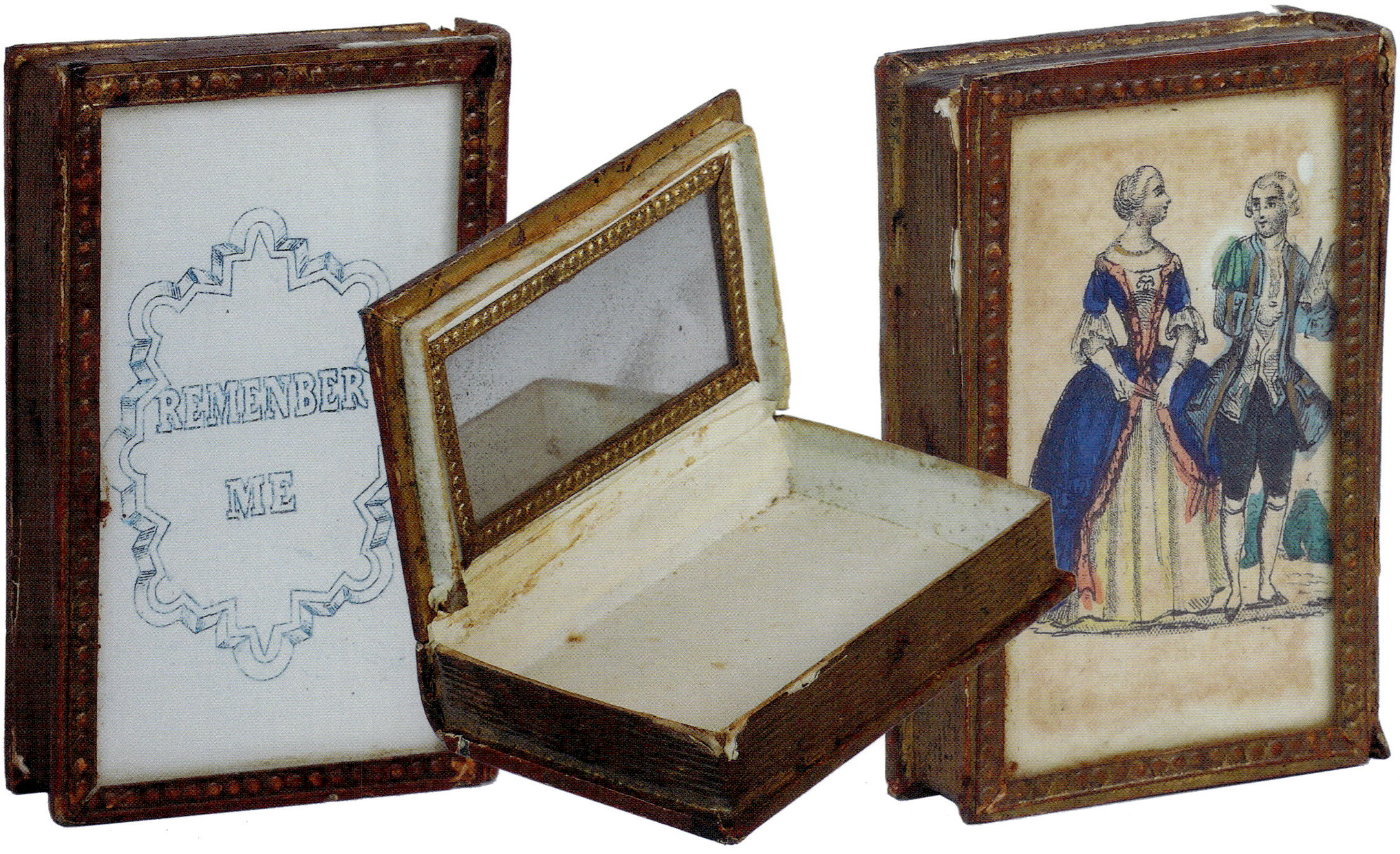

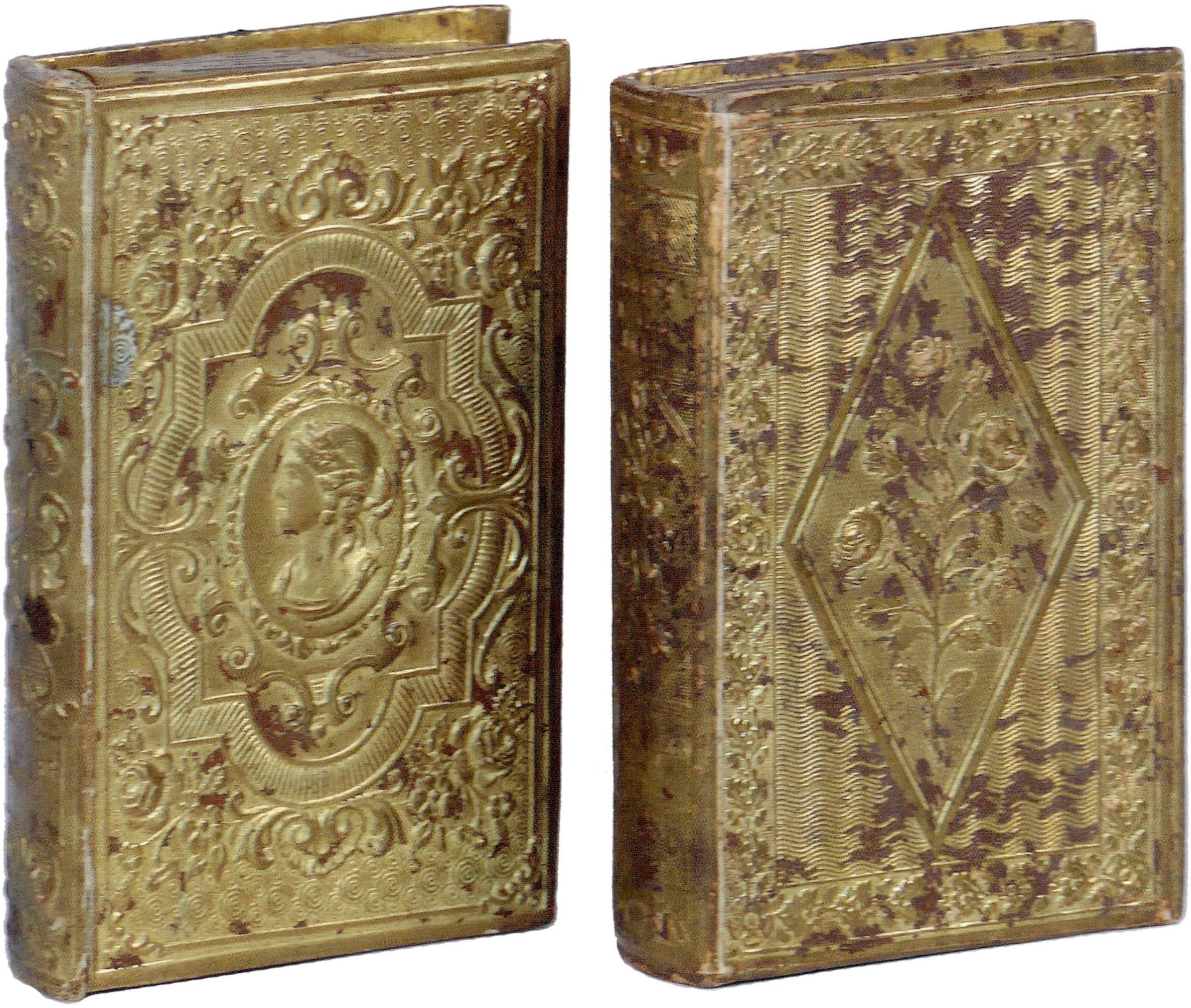

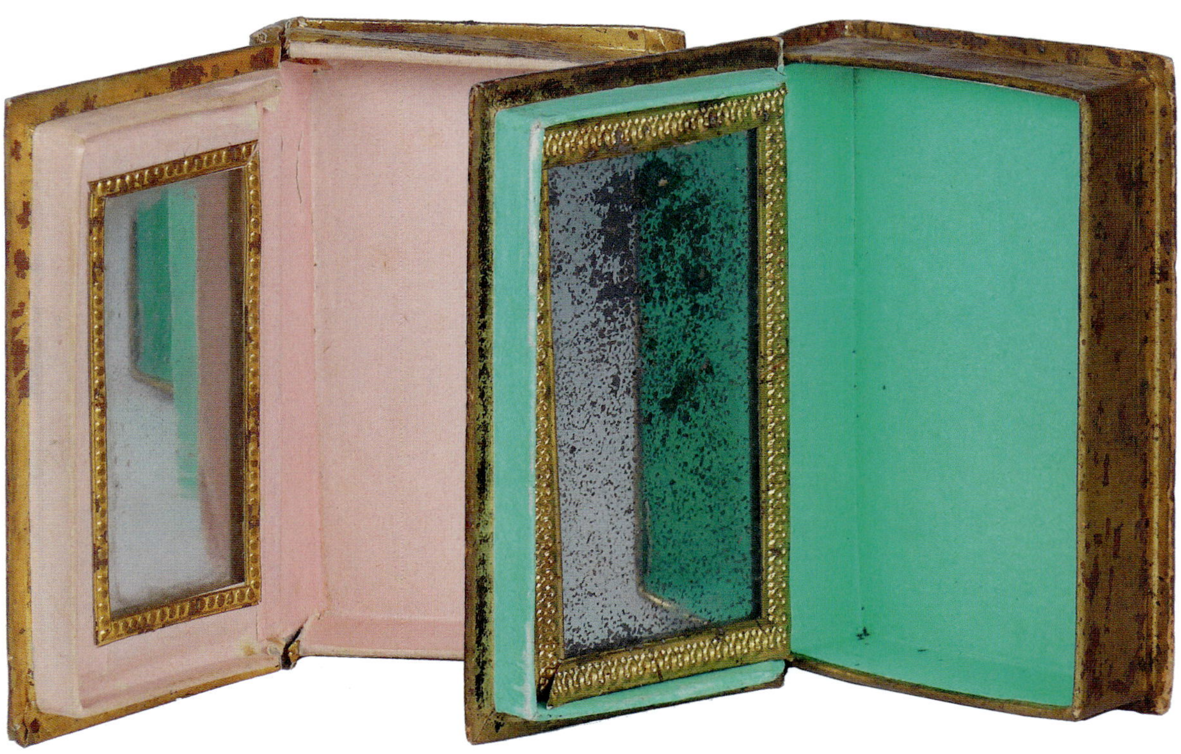

2.014
Contes a mes amis, Tome I
Schachteln mit geprägtem Goldpapierüberzug, Innenspiegel, geprägter Goldschnitt
Boxes covered with gold-tooled paper-over-board, mirror on the inner board, gold-tooled edges
19. Jh. / *19th century*
1,3 x 7 x 4,6 cm

2.015
Coute à mes petits amis, Tome l
Kartondose mit geprägtem Goldpapierüberzug, Innenspiegel, dreiseitiger Goldschnitt
Box with embossed gold paper-over-board, interior mirror, all edges gilt
1,5 x 6,5 x 4,5 cm

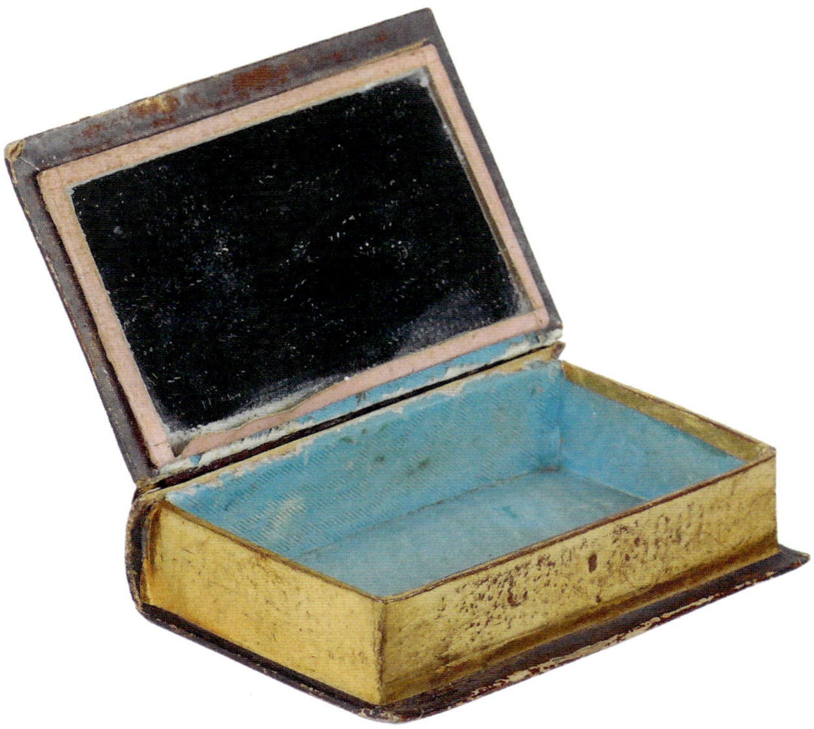

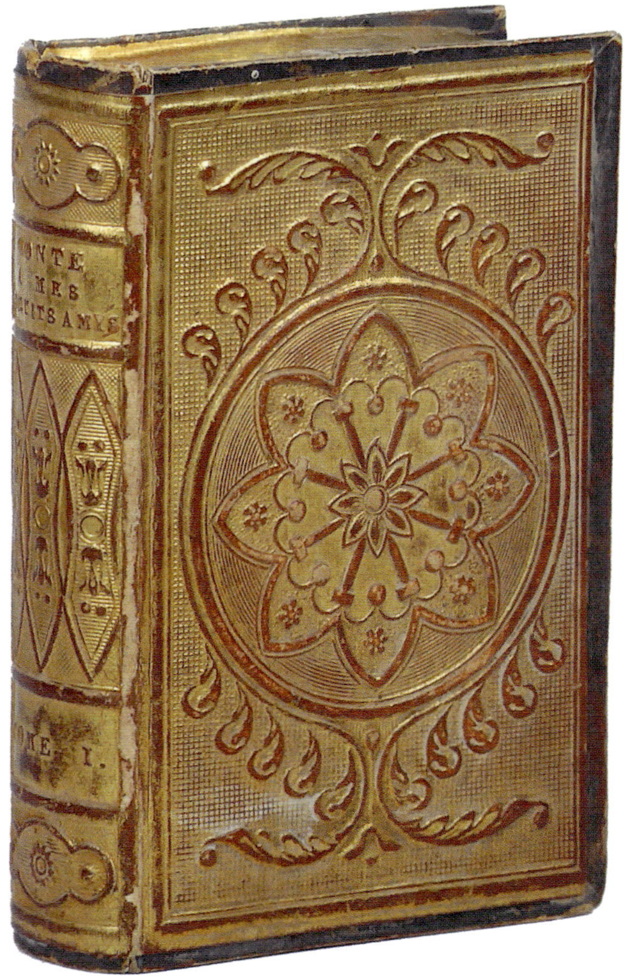

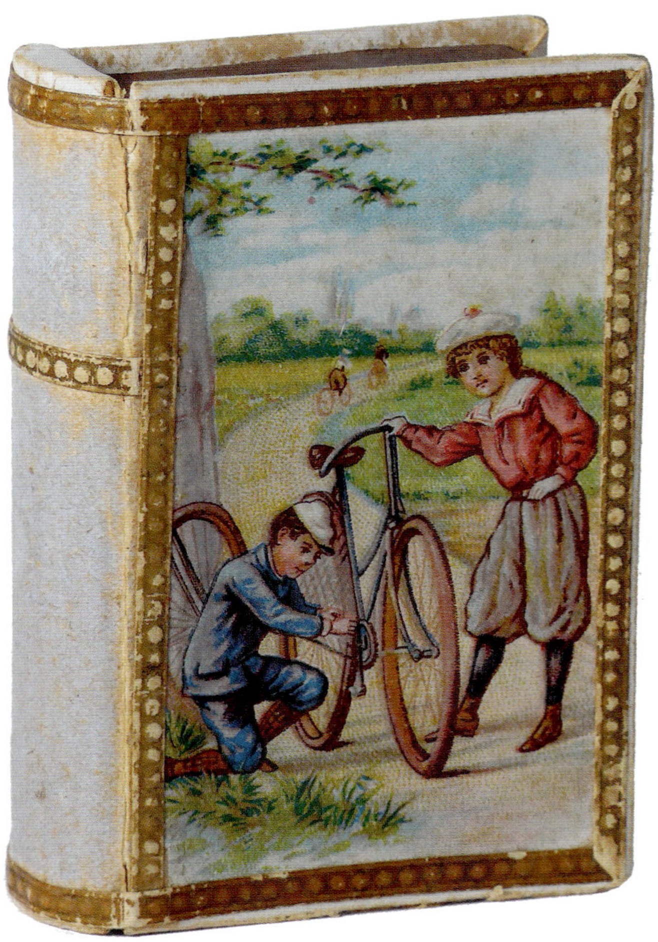

2.016
Kleine Schachtel mit Spiegel, Chromolithografie auf dem Vorderdeckel, Goldlitze, geprägter Goldschnitt
Small box with mirror, chromolithography on the lid, gold braid, gold-tooled edges
Spätes 19. Jh. / *Late 19th century*
8,5 x 6,2 x 2.3 cm

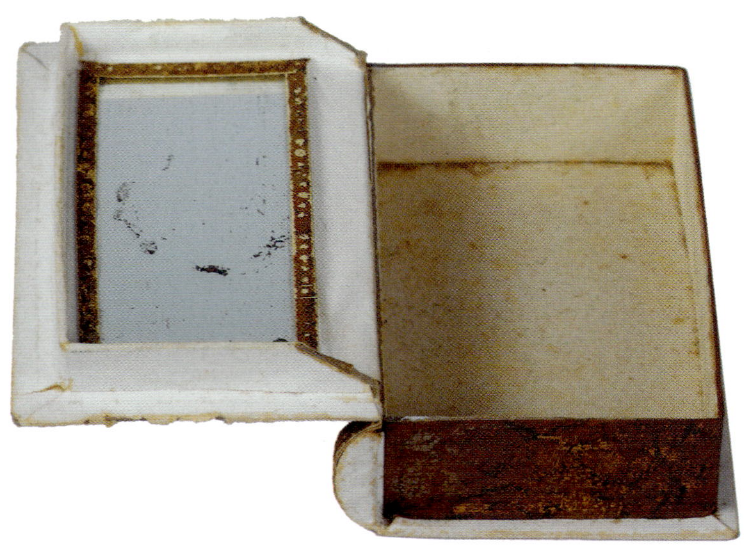

2.017
Oeuvres Diverses
Exklusives Behältnis mit Glasdeckel, geprägtem Goldpapierrücken und Kanteneinfassungen, Goldschnitt
Exclusive box with glass lid, gold-tooled paper on the spine and dentelle, gilt edges
19. Jh. / *19th century* | 9 x 6,5 x 1,6 cm

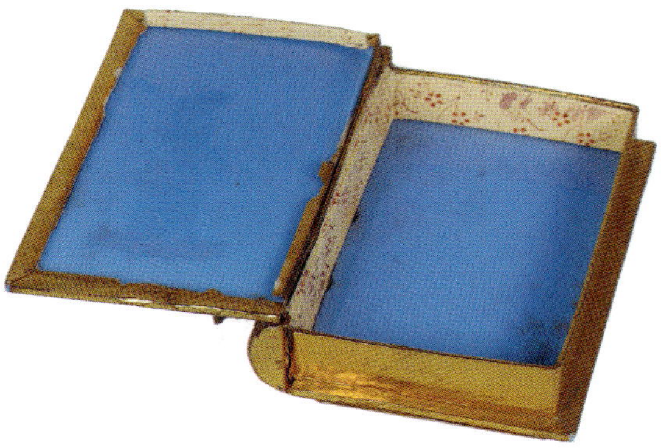

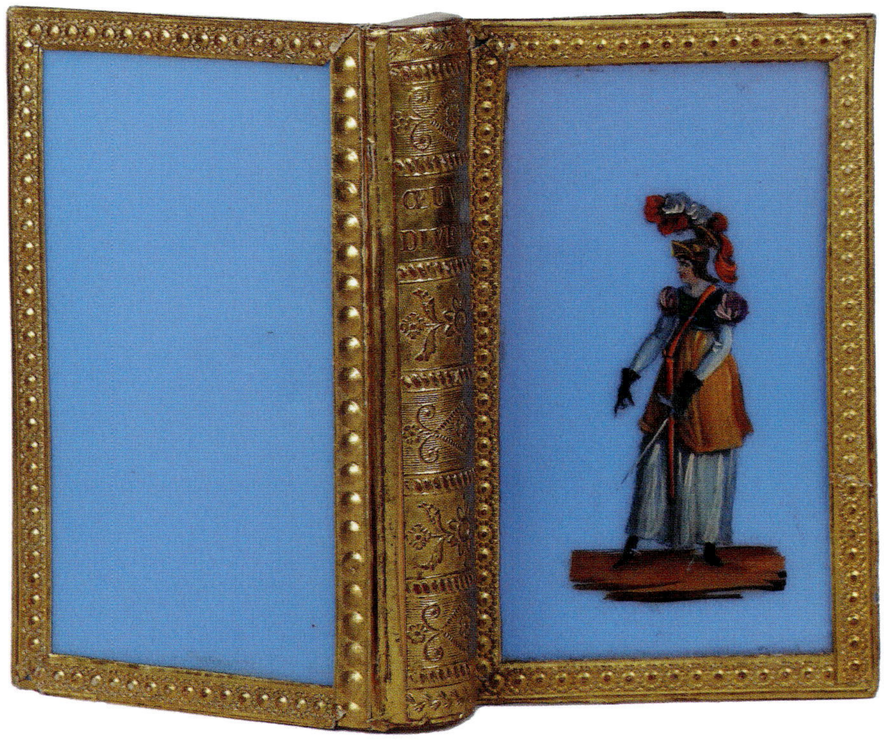

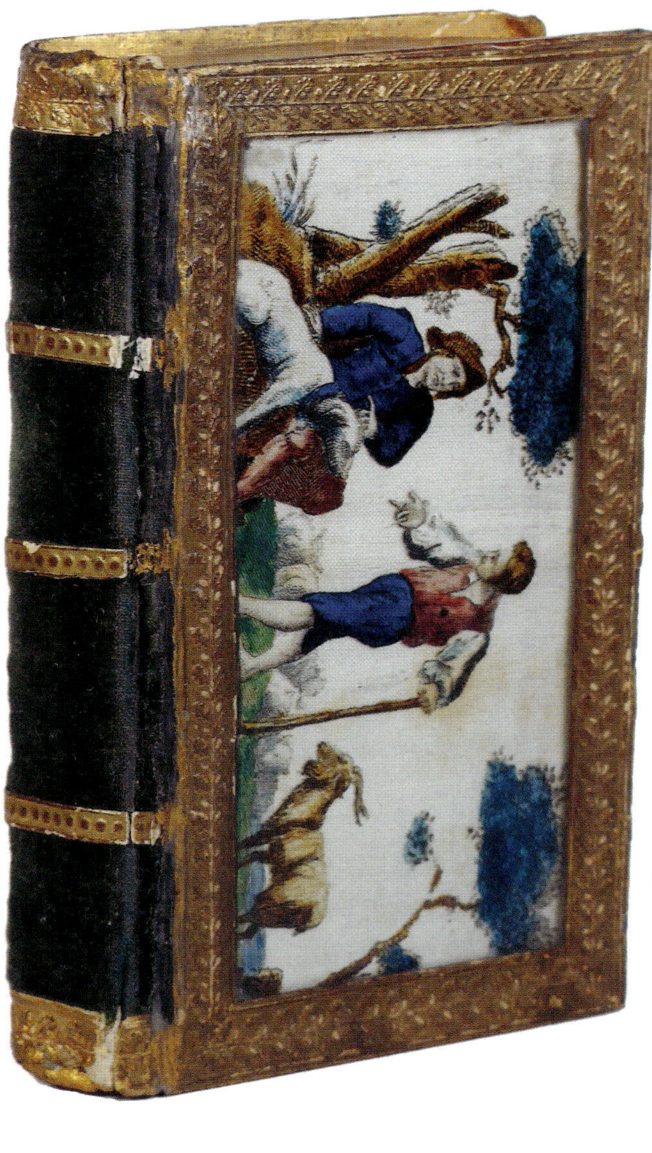

2.018
Samtdose mit Spiegel, Seidenbedruckte Schäferszene, Kanten und Bünde mit Goldlitze, Goldschnitt
Velvet box with mirror, decorated with a illustration of a sheper printed in silk, edges and bands with gold braid, gilt edges
Spätes 19. Jh. / *Late 19th century*
11,1 x 7,8 x 2 cm

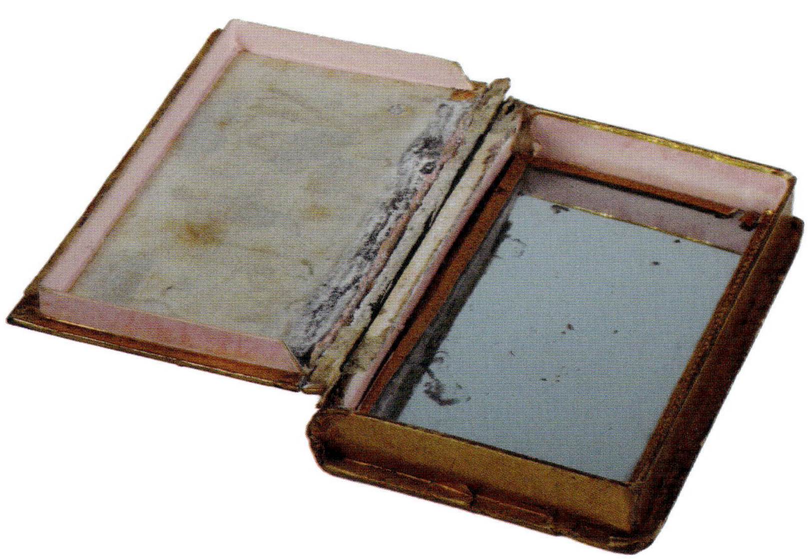

2.019
Box mit Einband aus Strohgeflecht, Goldschnittimitat durch Stroh, Innendeckel und Boden verglast
Box covered with braided straw, gilt edge imitation made of straw, glazed interior lid and bottom
19. Jh. / *19th century* | 9 x 6,2 x 2 cm

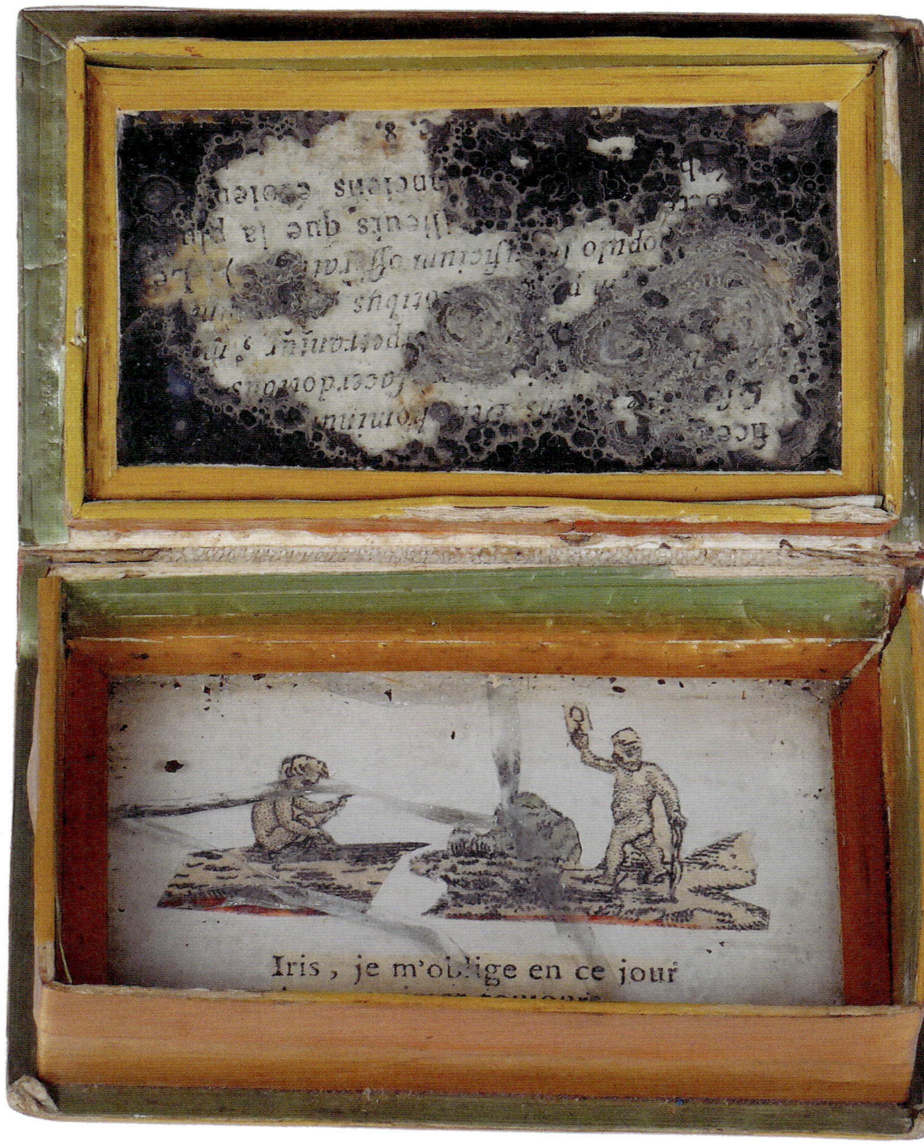

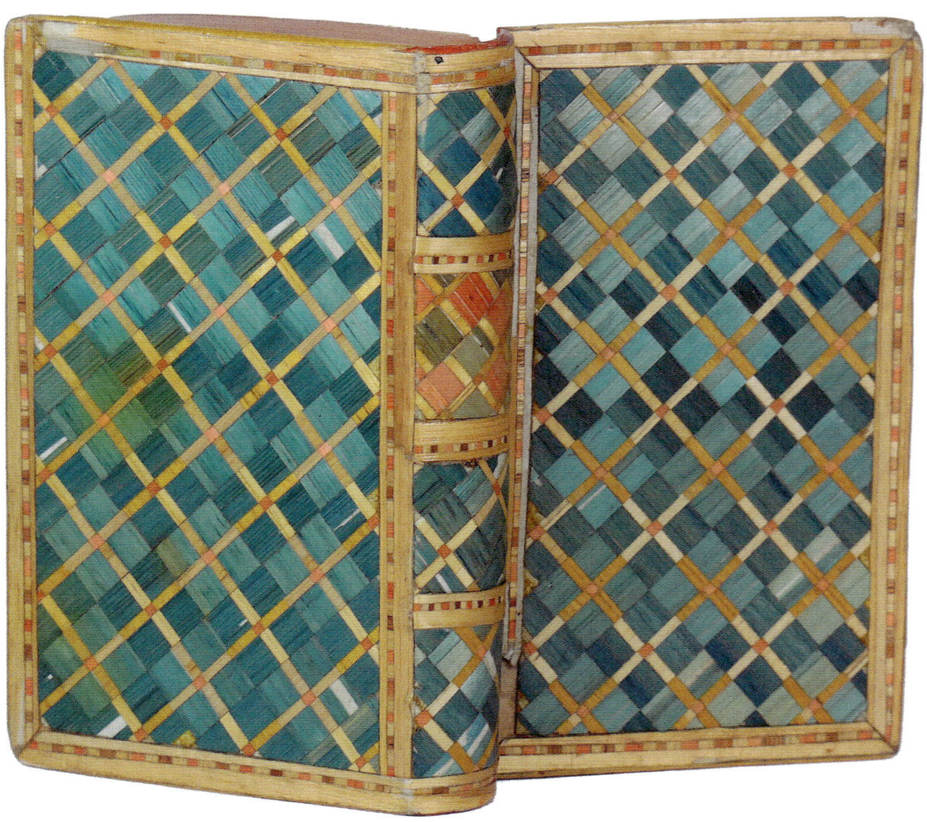

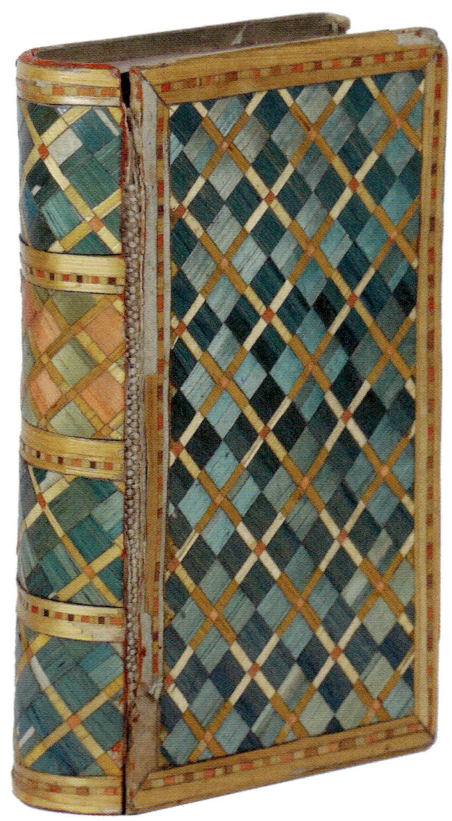

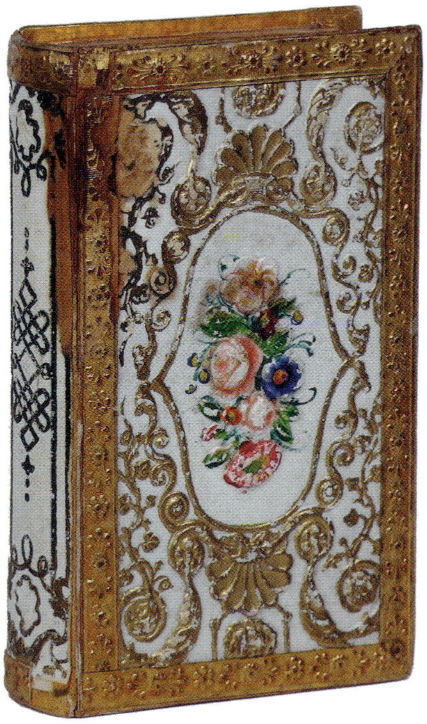

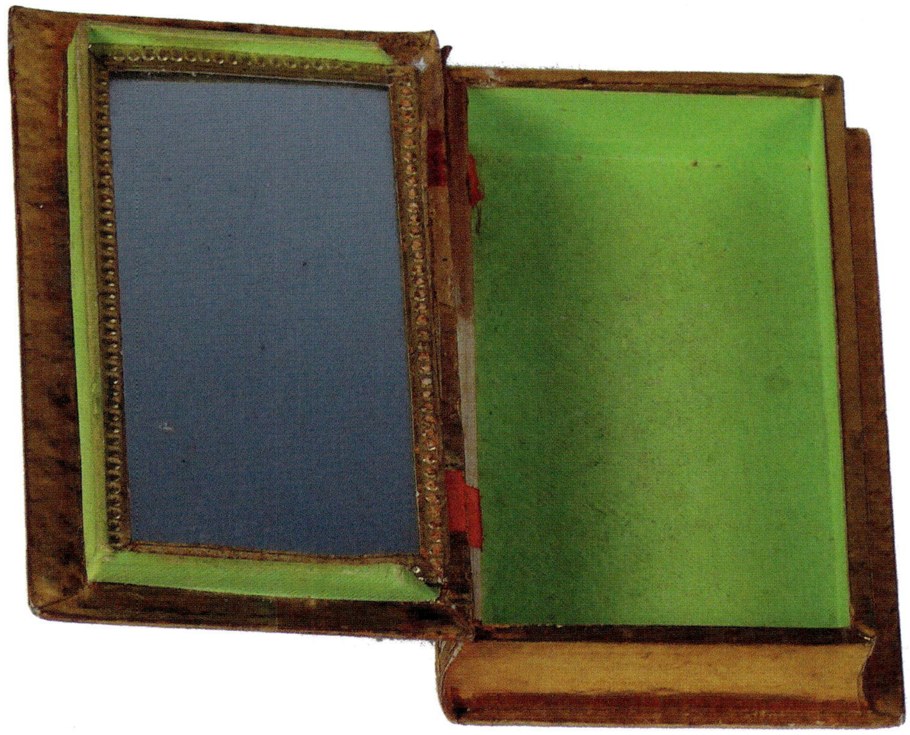

2.020
Kartondöschen mit Papierfutter und Spiegel, farbige und goldene Reliefprägung, dreiseitiger Goldschnitt
Small box with paper lining and mirror, reliefed color and gold tooling, all edges gilt
19. Jh. / *19th century* | 7,5 x 4,9 x 1,5 cm

2.021
Lederetui mit Innenspiegel und Textilfutter, farbig gedrucktes Blumenmotiv auf dem Vorderdeckel
Leather case with interior mirror and cloth lining, flowers printed in color on the front cover
1,5 x 11,1 x 5 cm

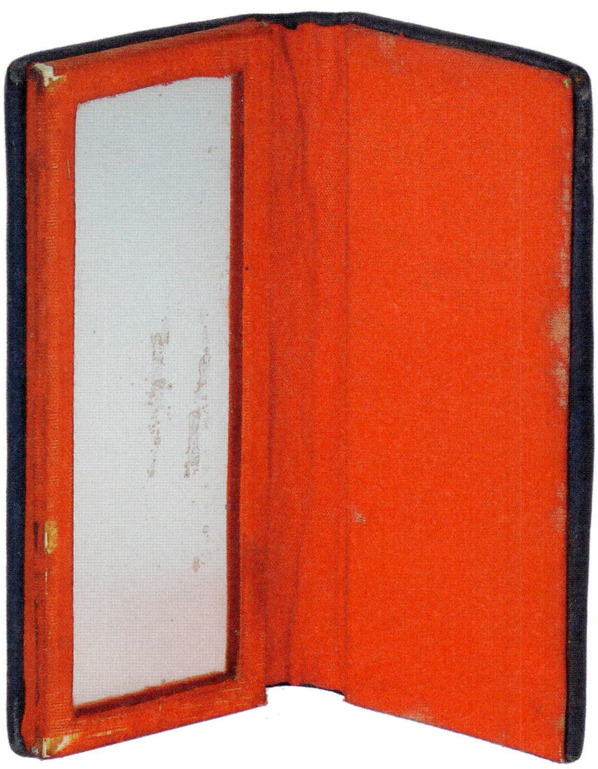

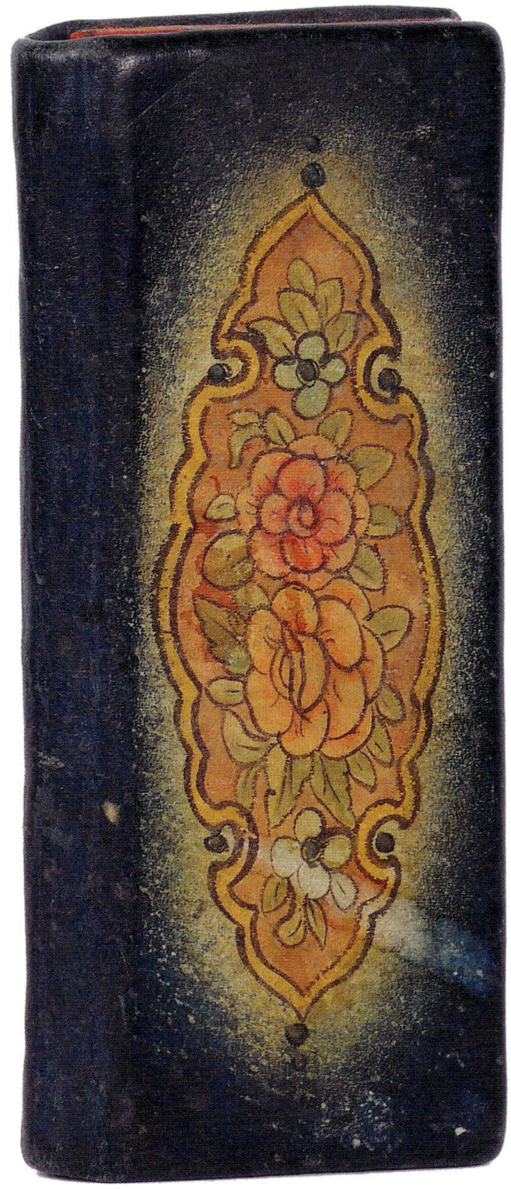

2.022
Lederdose für die Nagelpflege, schwenkbarer Buchschnitt, geprägter Goldschnitt
Leather box for nail care, pivotable edge, gold-tooled edges
Um / *Around* 1900 | 9,3 x 6,9 x 2,1 cm

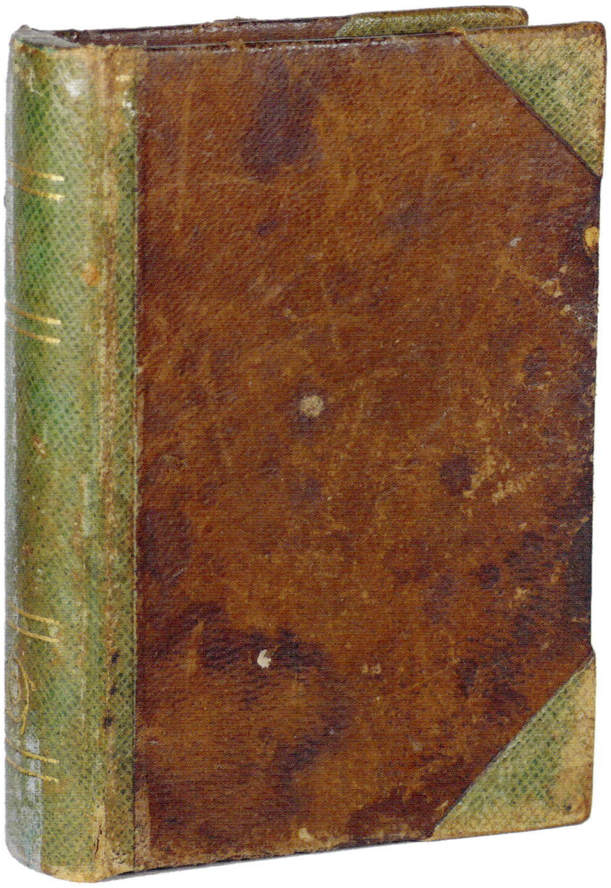

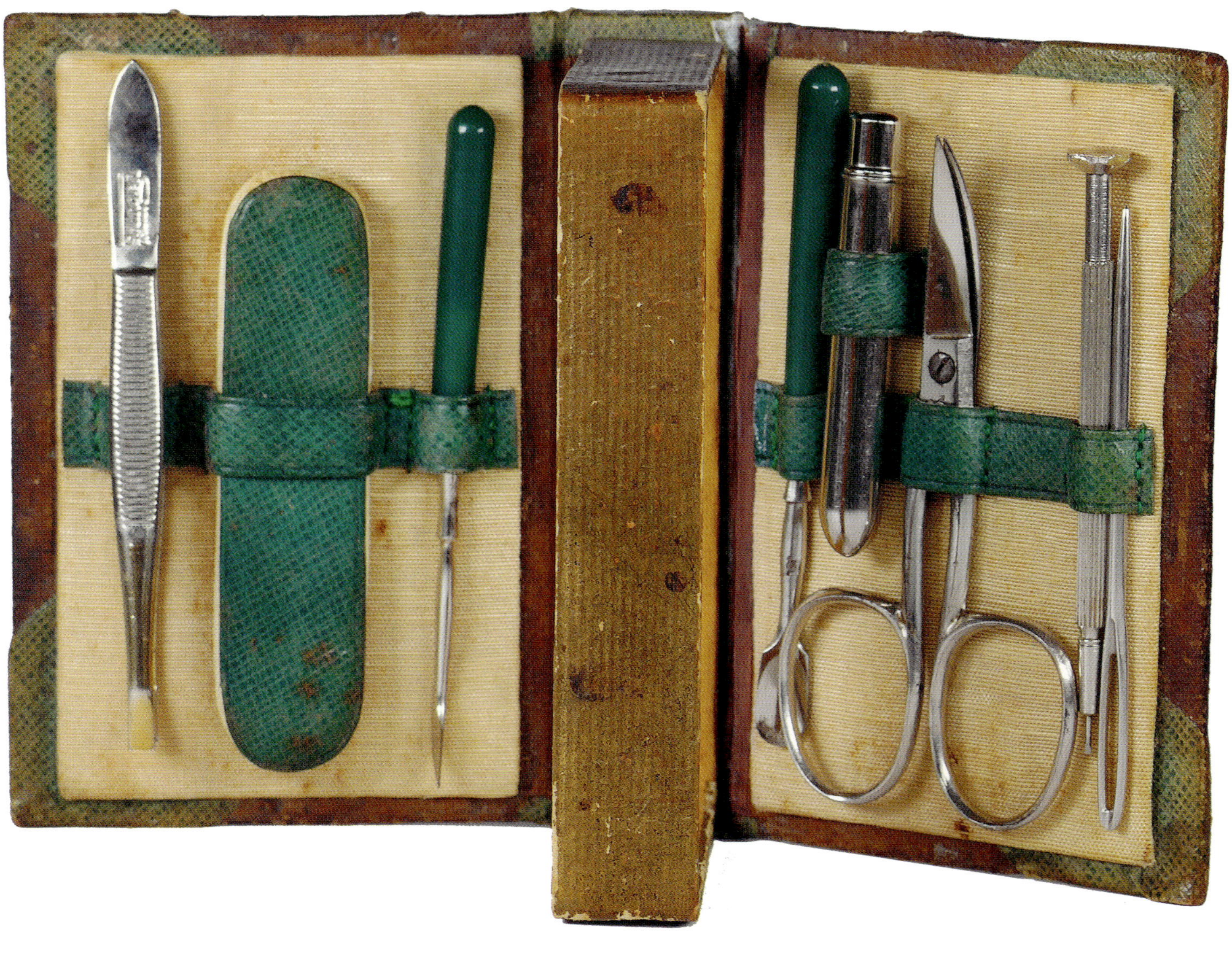

2.023
Ganzlederbox für die Nagelpflege, plastische Fingergestaltung aus Leder auf beiden Deckeln, Zugschließe, dreiseitiger Steinmarmorpapierschnitt, ausgefüttert mit Wildleder
Full leather box for nail care, leather finger applications on both covers, drawstring buckle, stone marbled paper edges, lined with suede
Sybille und August Wirz Winterthur, Switzerland
11,4 x 8,6 x 3 cm

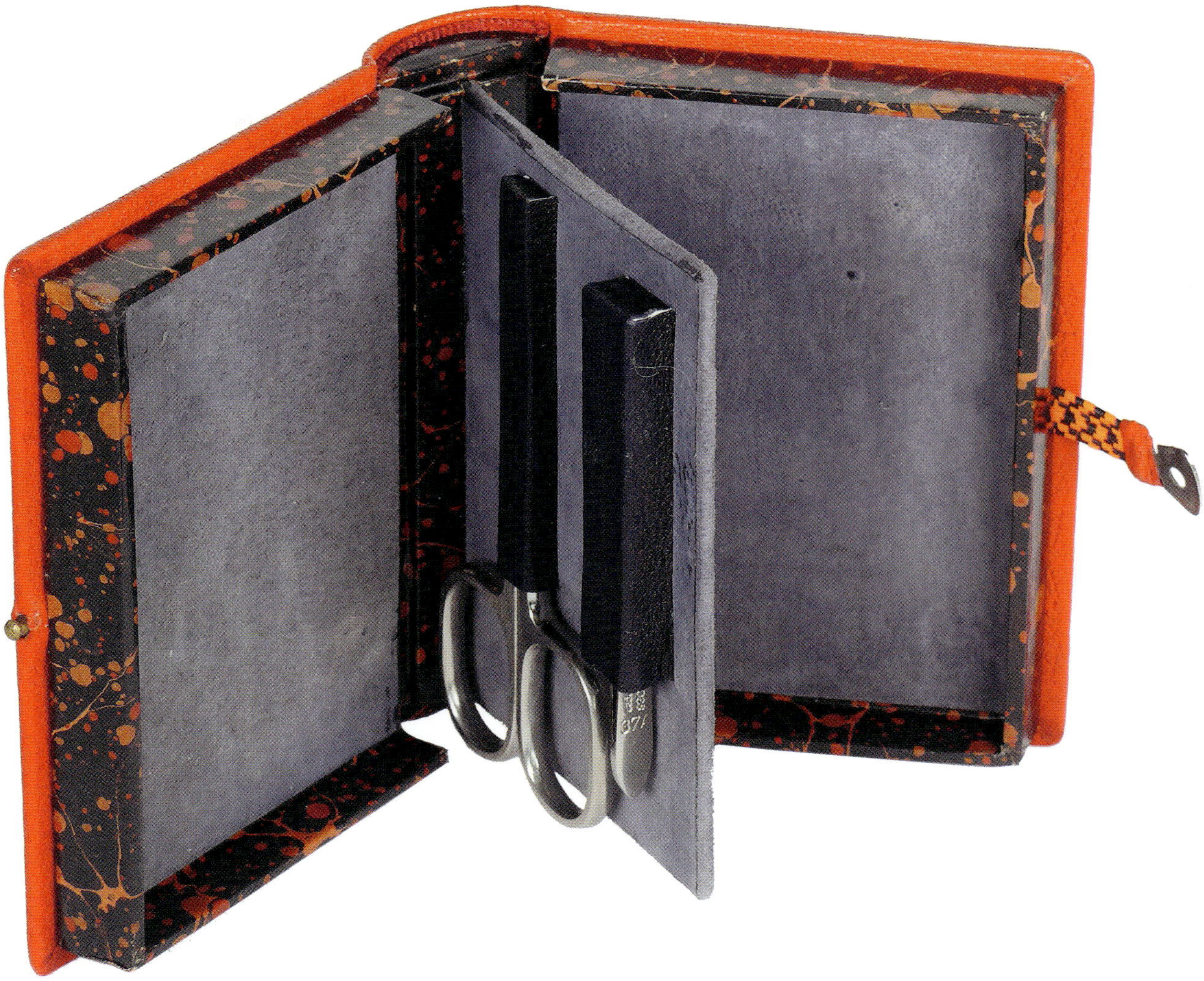

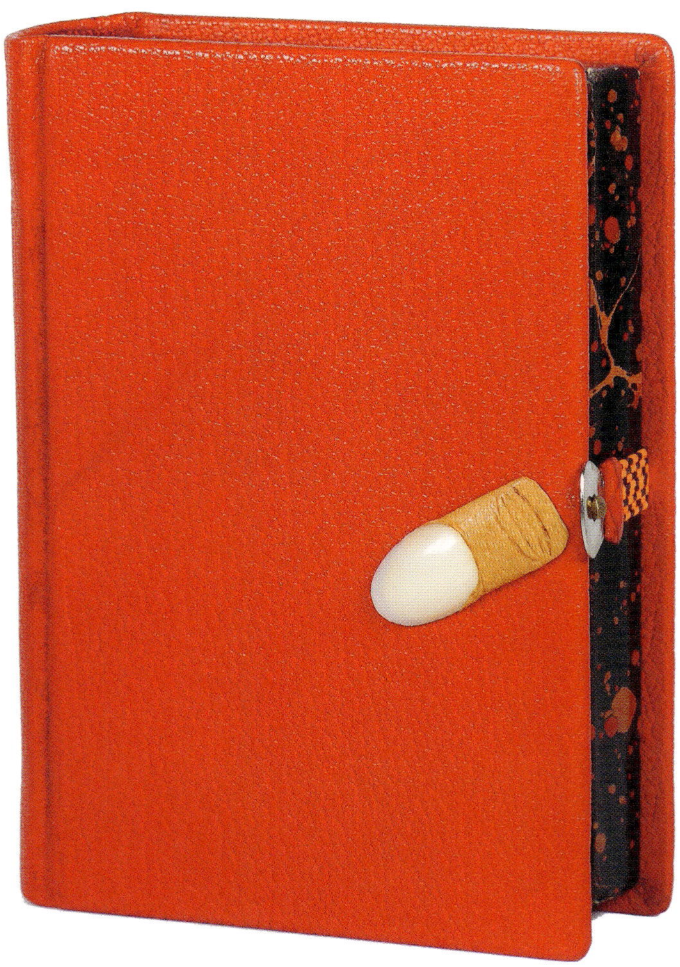

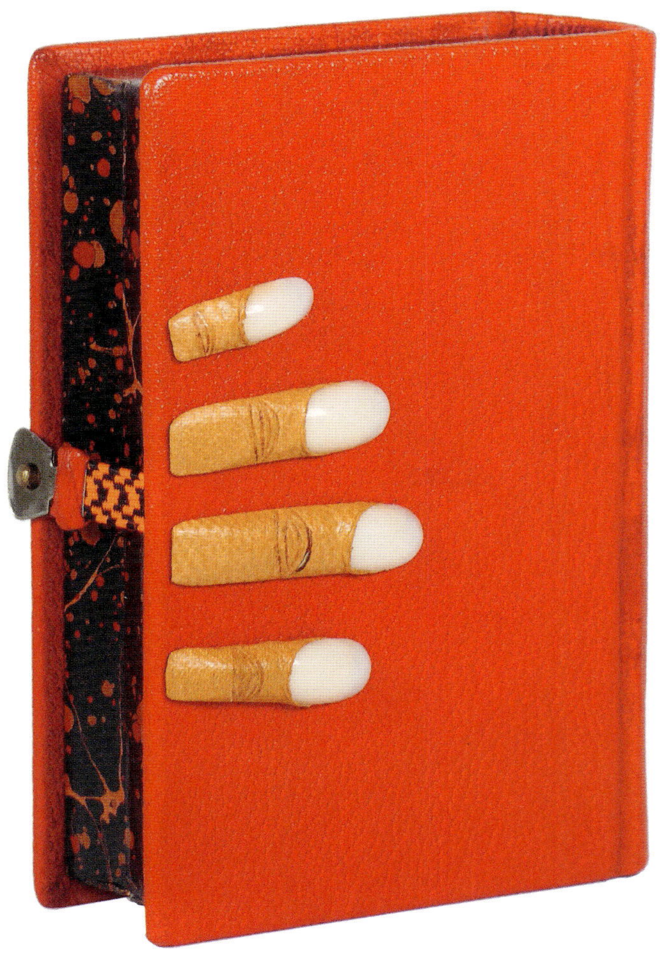

2.024
Handwärmer, Campania, Fayence bemalt in Mangan
Hand warmer, Campania, faience painted all in manganese
Wohl Ariano Irpino, Italien, 18. Jh. / *Probably Ariano Irpino, Italy, 18th century*
18,8 x 11 x 5,5 cm

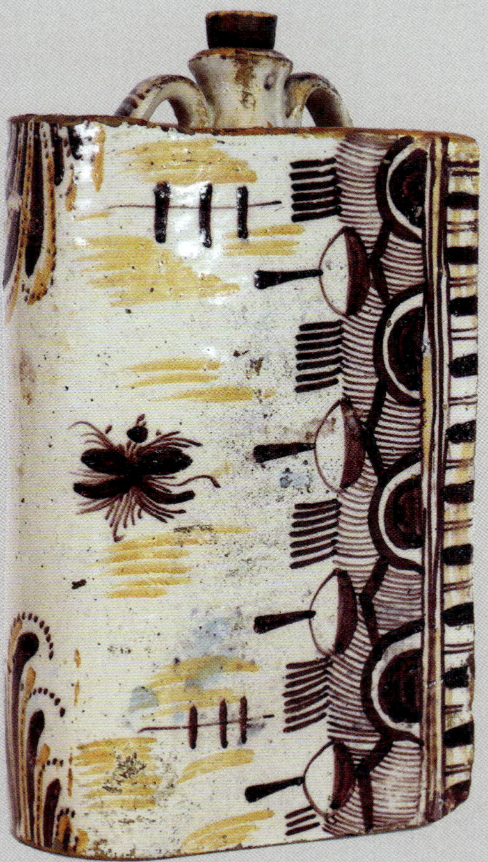

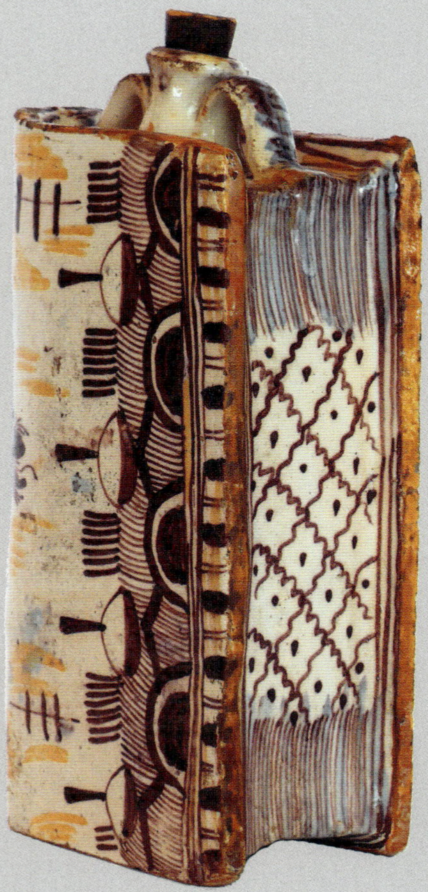

2.025
Handwärmer, Campania, Fayence bemalt in Mangan
Hand warmer, Campania, faience painted all in manganese
Wohl Ariano Irpino, Italien / *Probably Ariano Irpino, Italy*
18. Jh. | *18th century.*
17,5 x 10,4 x 5,8 cm

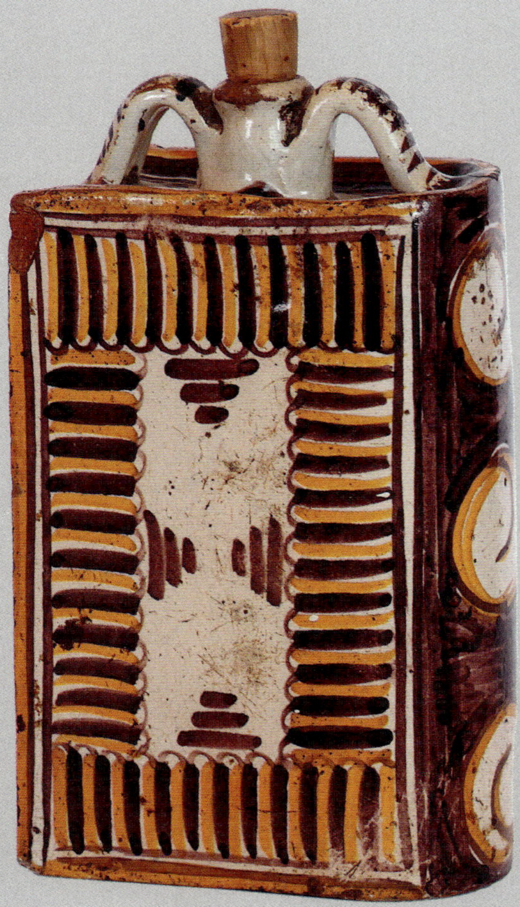

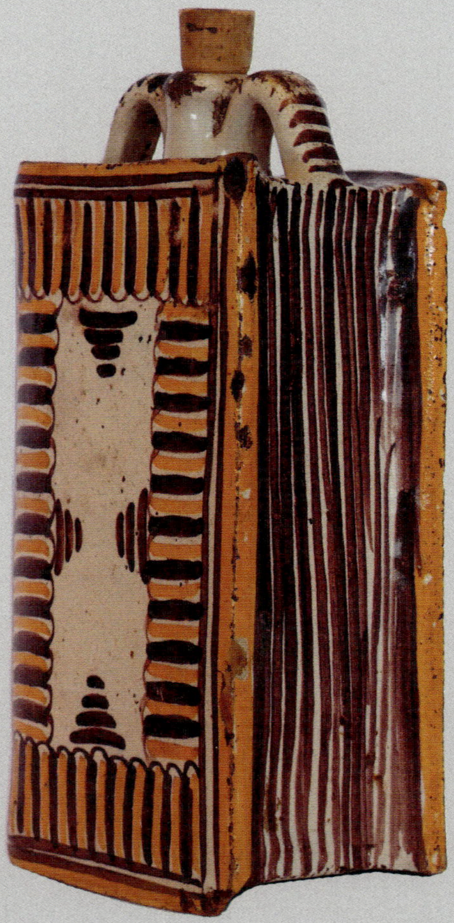

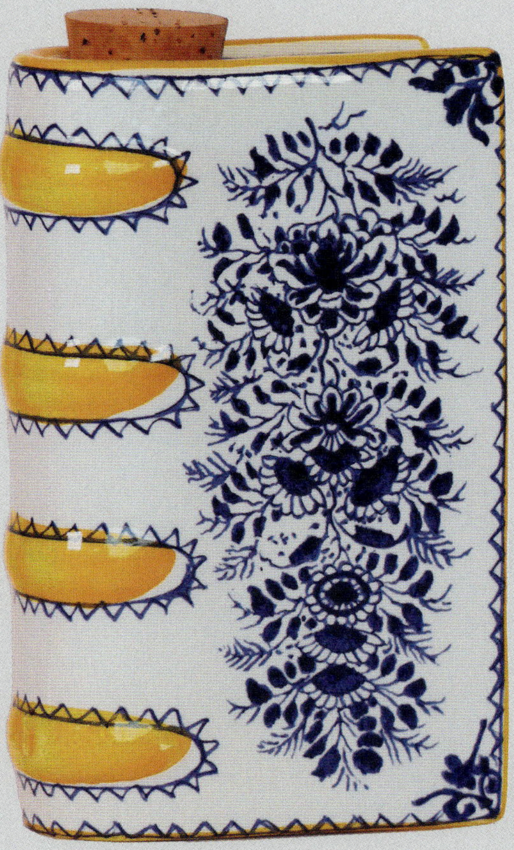
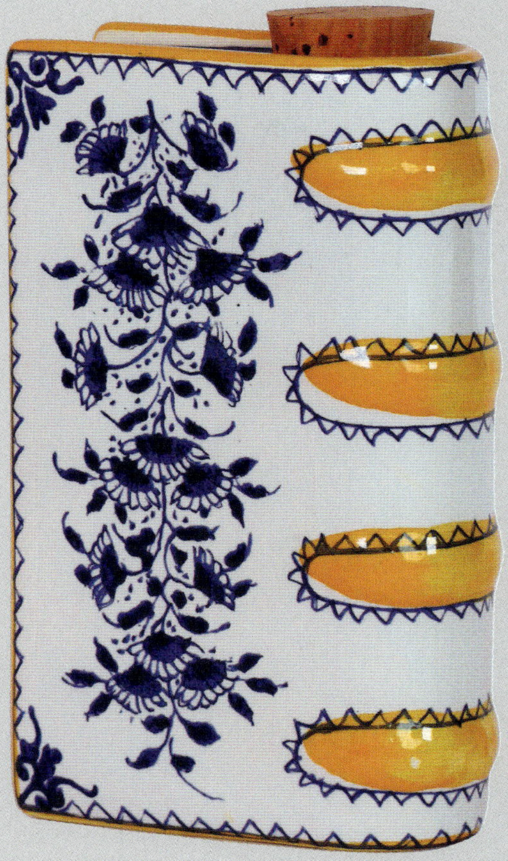

2.026
The gift is small good willisall
Keramik, farbig bemalt, Original im Metropolitan Museum of Art
Ceramic, painted in different colors, original at Metropolitan Museum of Art
Made in Portugal
Zeitgenössisch / *Contemporary*
12,9 x 8 x 3,7 cm

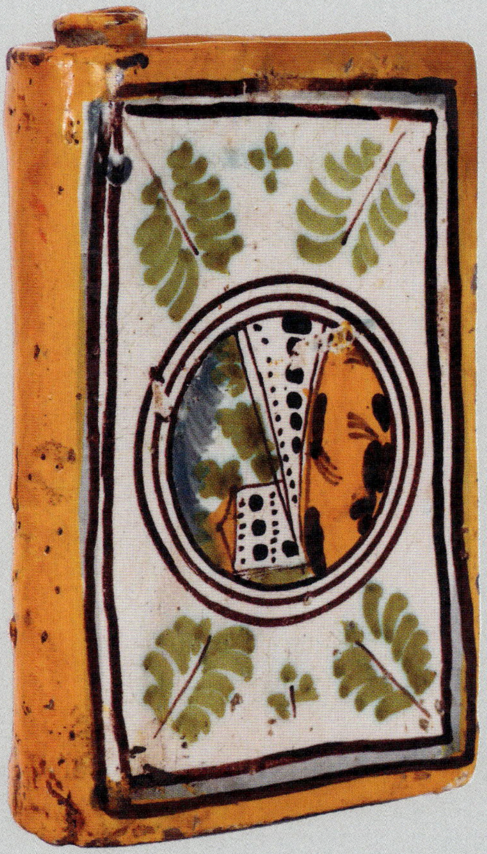
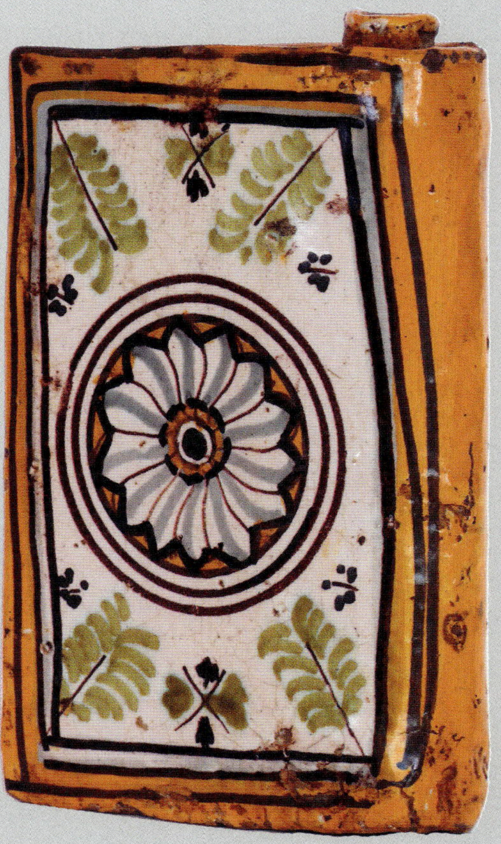

2.027
Handwärmer, Fayence farbig bemalt, Wohl Ariano Irpino
Hand warmer, colored faience, probably Ariano Irpino
Made in Italy
18. Jh. / *18th century*
17 x 10,8 x 3,7 cm

2.028
Keramik, farbig bemalt
Ceramic, painted in color
Malavoglia Caltagirone, Italien / *Italy*
Zeitgenössisch / *Contemporary*
10,7 x 7,1 x 2,7 cm

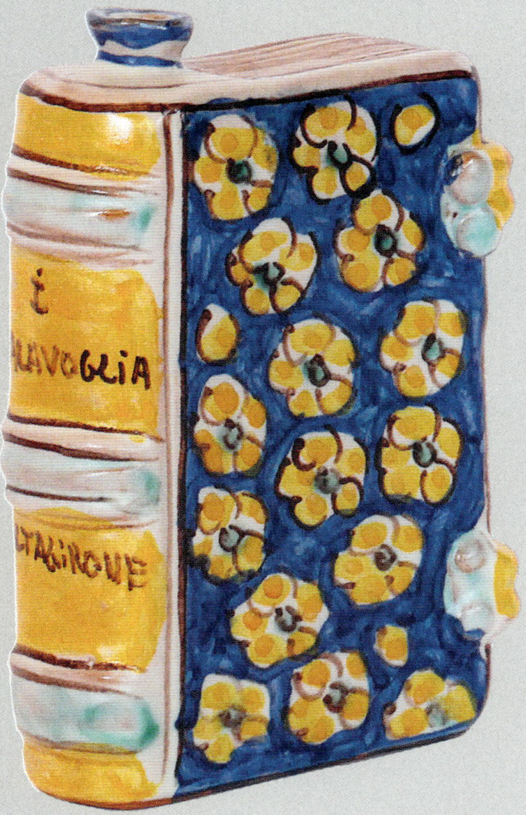

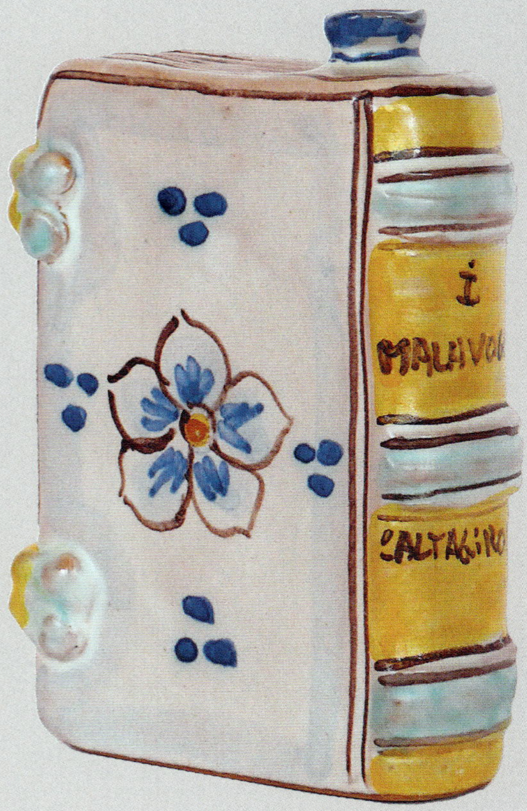

2.029
„Riechfläschchen“ oder „Parfümbrenner“ Fayence, farbig staffiert, Form eines „chauffe-mains“, möglicherweise ein „Riechfläschchen“ (durchlöcherte Oberfläche)
“Vinaigrette” or “perfume burner” Faience, painted in color, in the design of a „chauffe-mains”, probably a vinaigrette (perforations o the surface)
Nevers Frankreich / *France* | Um / *Around* 1800
9,7 x 7,2 x 2 cm

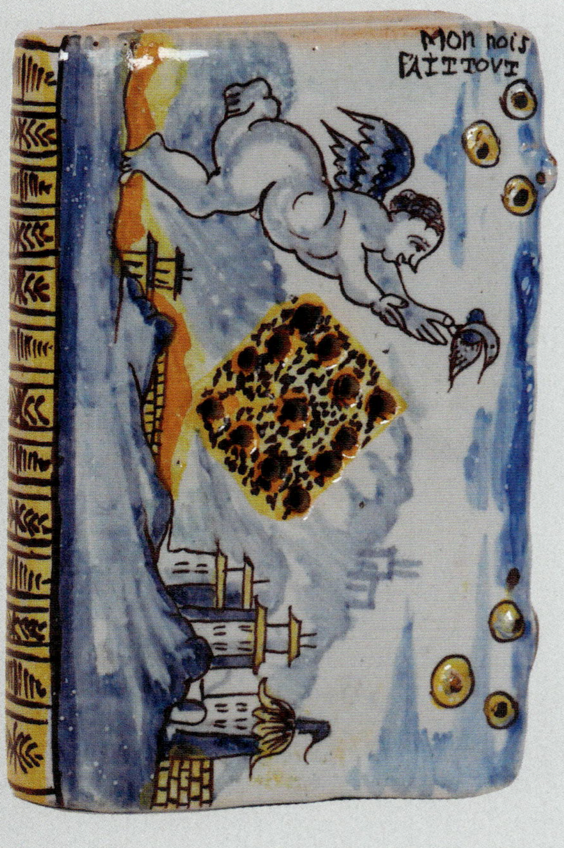

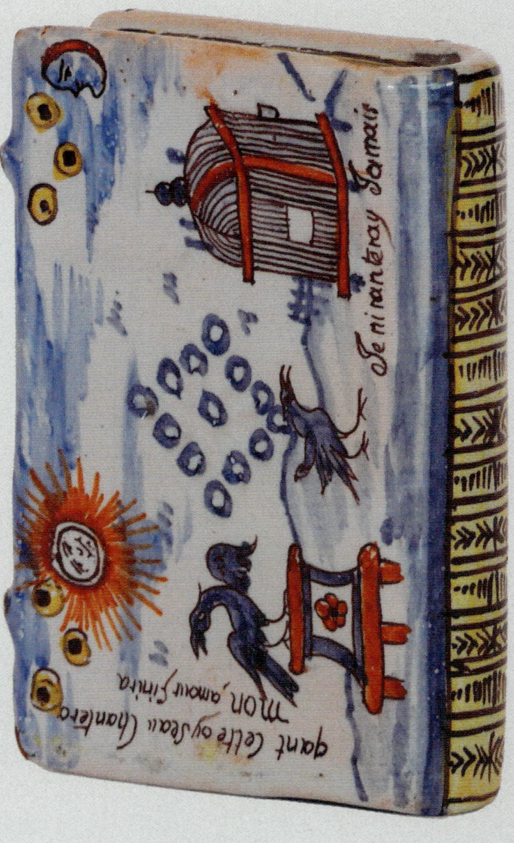

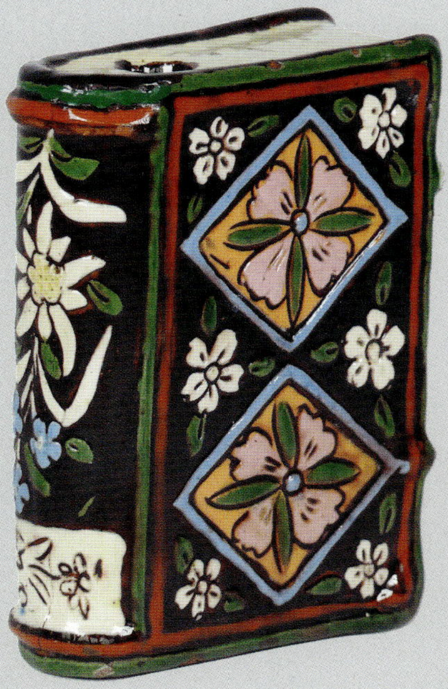

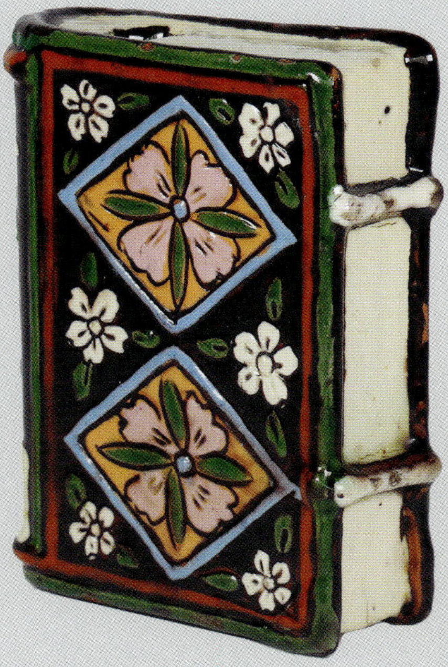

2.030
Keramik, florales Chrutmuster mit Edelweiß, zwei Schließen
Ceramic, Swiss Chrutmuster pattern with edelweiss flower, two clasps
Thun Majolica Belle Époque, Switzerland
Um / *Around* 1900
8,6 x 6,9 x 2,5 cm

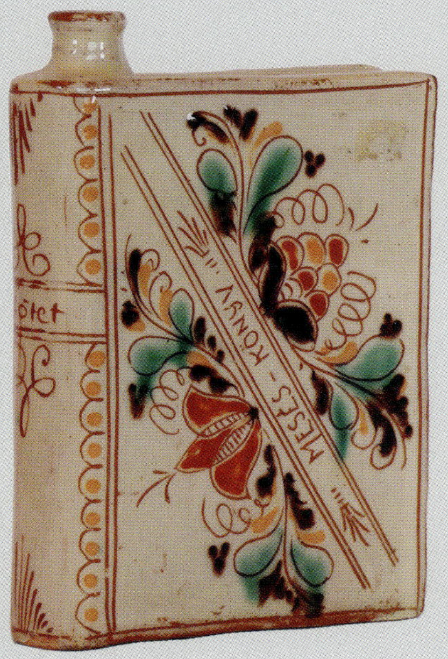

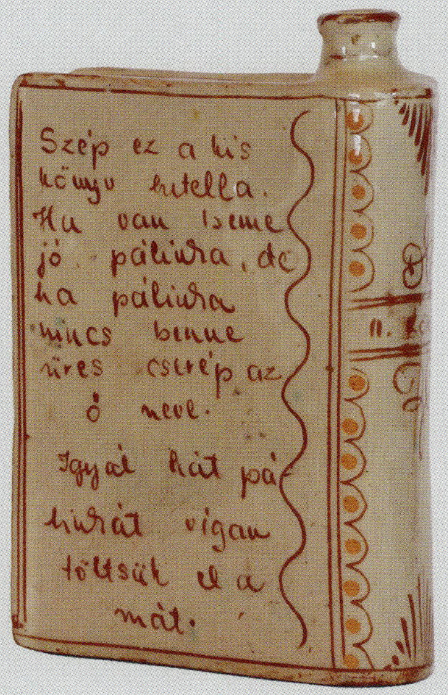

2.031
Keramik, farbig bemalt mit Sinnspruch
Ceramic, with a painted illustration and a saying
Wohl Ungarn / *Probably Hungary*
15,3 x 10,6 x 3,3 cm

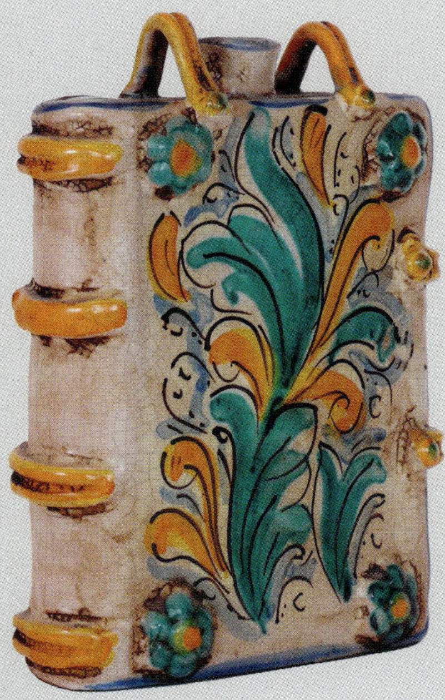

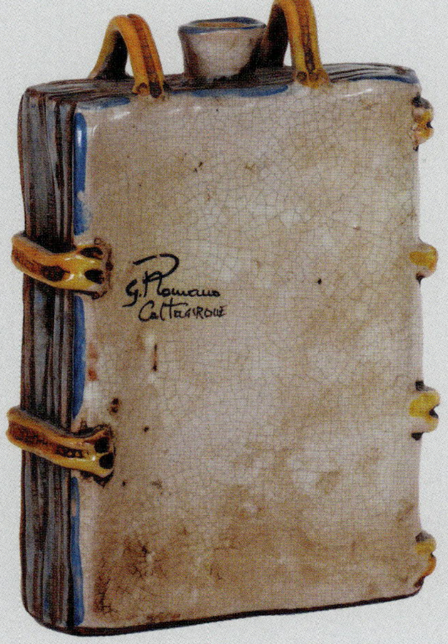

2.032
Keramik, farbig bemalt.
Ceramic painted in color.
Signiert / *Signed*: G.Romano, Caltagirone, Sicilia
Zeitgenössisch / *Contemporary*
16,6 x 12 x 4 cm

2.033

L. Bourgeat Lyon

Wärmeflasche aus Messing, Wärmeregulierung auf dem Deckel, Luftlöcher am Fuß- und Kopfschnitt, Traggriff, wird mit Tabletten aus chemischer Kohle von „Stocker" gefüllt

Heating bottle made of brass, temperature regulation on the lid, holes on the head and foot edges, handle, to be filled with chemical carbon tablet by Stocker

5,5 x 18 x 12,3 cm

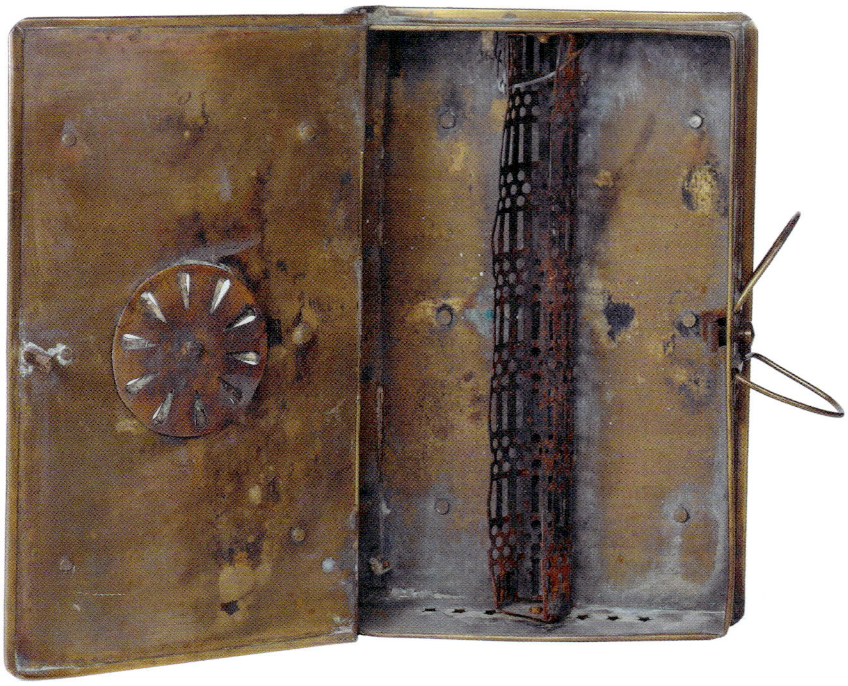

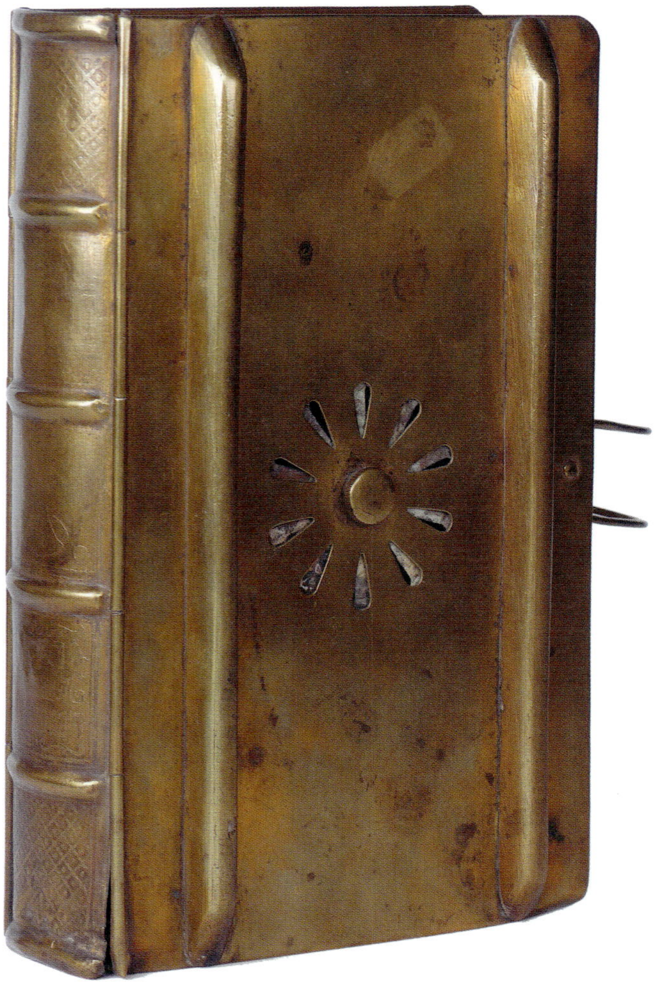

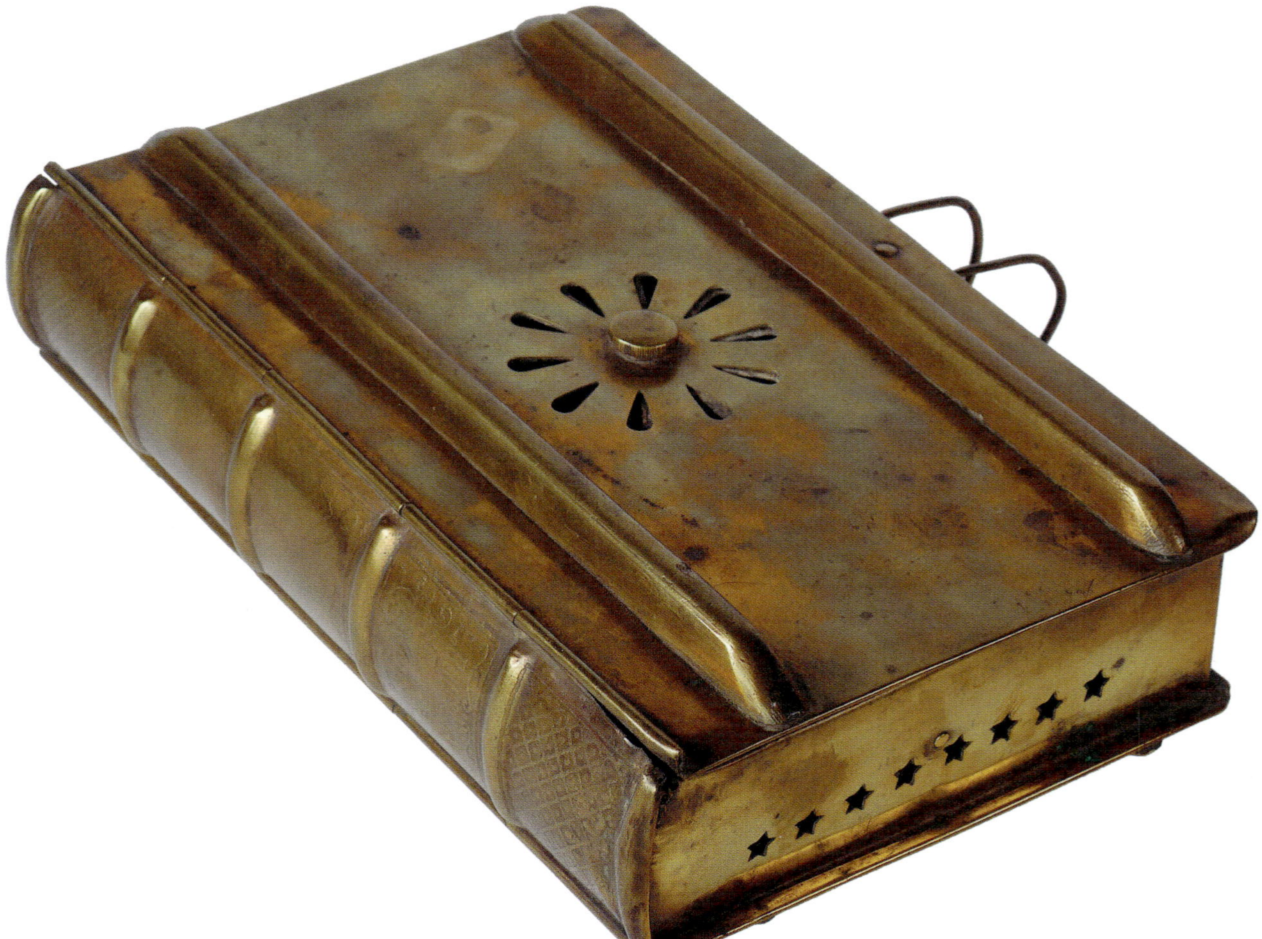

2.034
Zinnkanne mit Schraubverschluss, Kriegerszene, zwei Schließen,
Pewter jug with screw cap, warrior scene, two clasps
Zeitgenössisch / *Contemporary*
10,3 x 7,5 x 2,5 cm

2.035
Zinnkanne mit Schraubverschluss, erhabene Bünde auf Deckel übergreifend
Pewter jug with screw cap, raised bands embracing the covers
Zeitgenössisch / *Contemporary*
11,3 x 6,7 x 2,3 cm

2.036
Zinnkanne mit Schraubverschluss, 95% Zinn, Deckel mit heraldischen Szenen; Löwe und Ritterhelm
Pewter jug with screw cap, 95% pewter, covers with heraldic theme, lion and knights helmet
10,6 x 6,9 x 2,5 cm

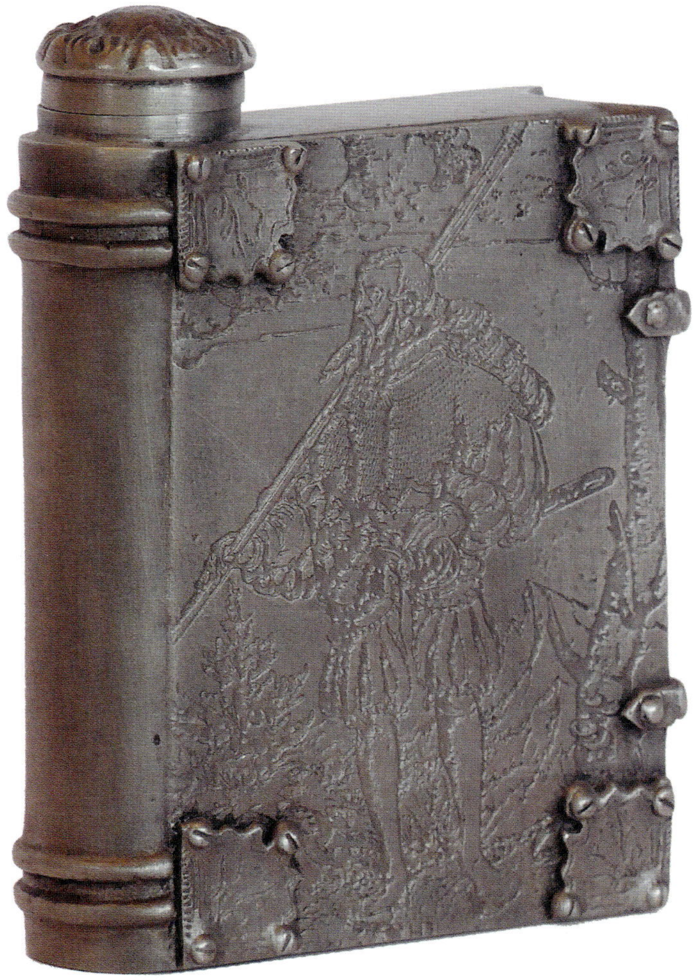

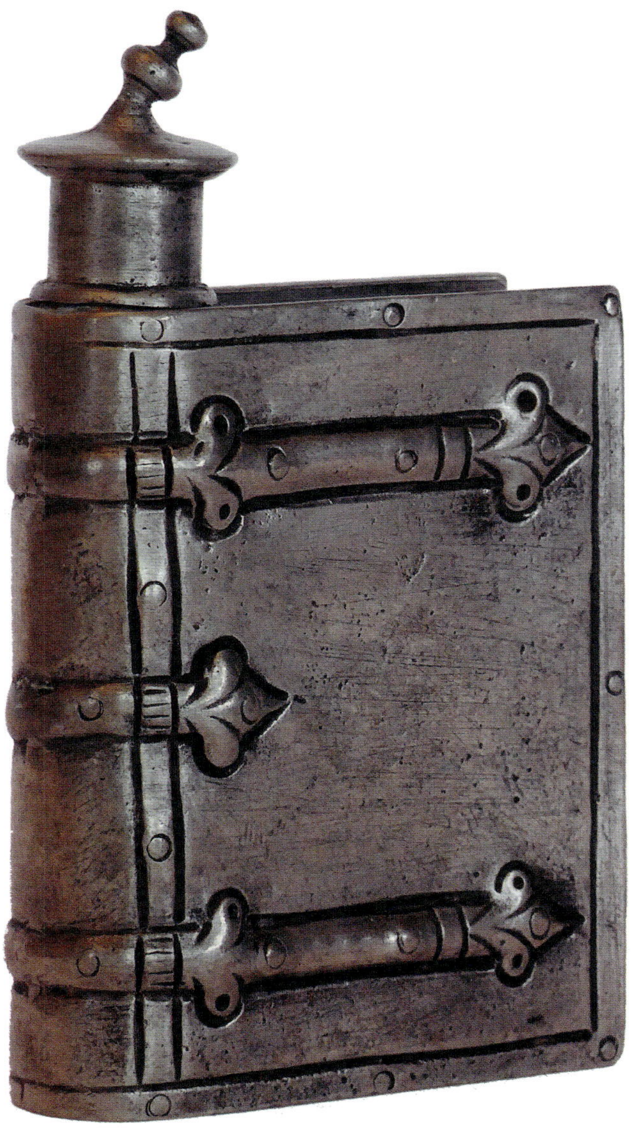

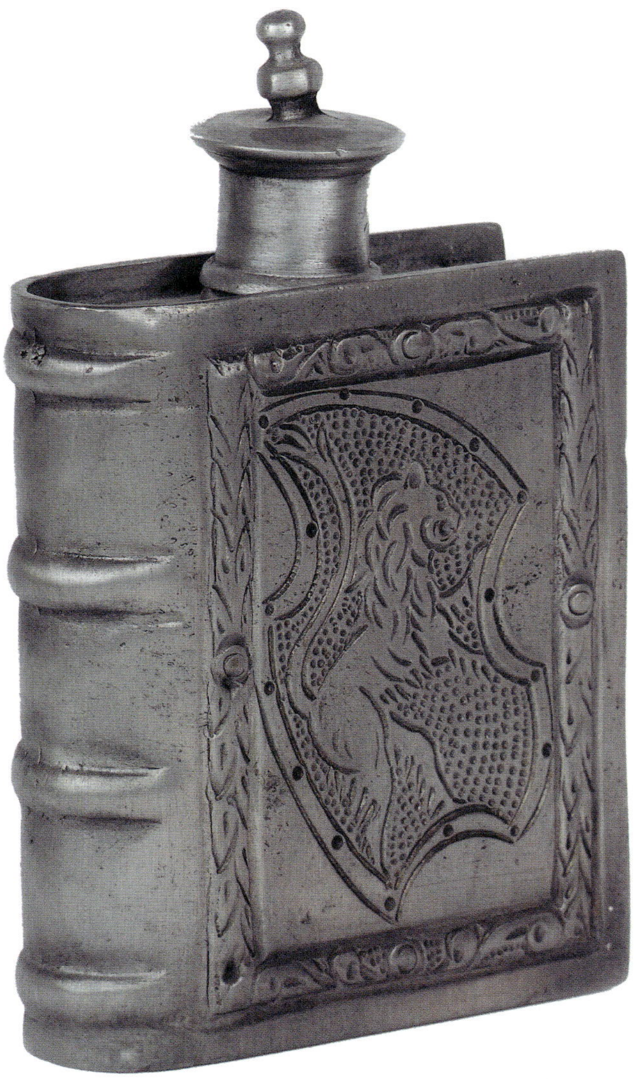

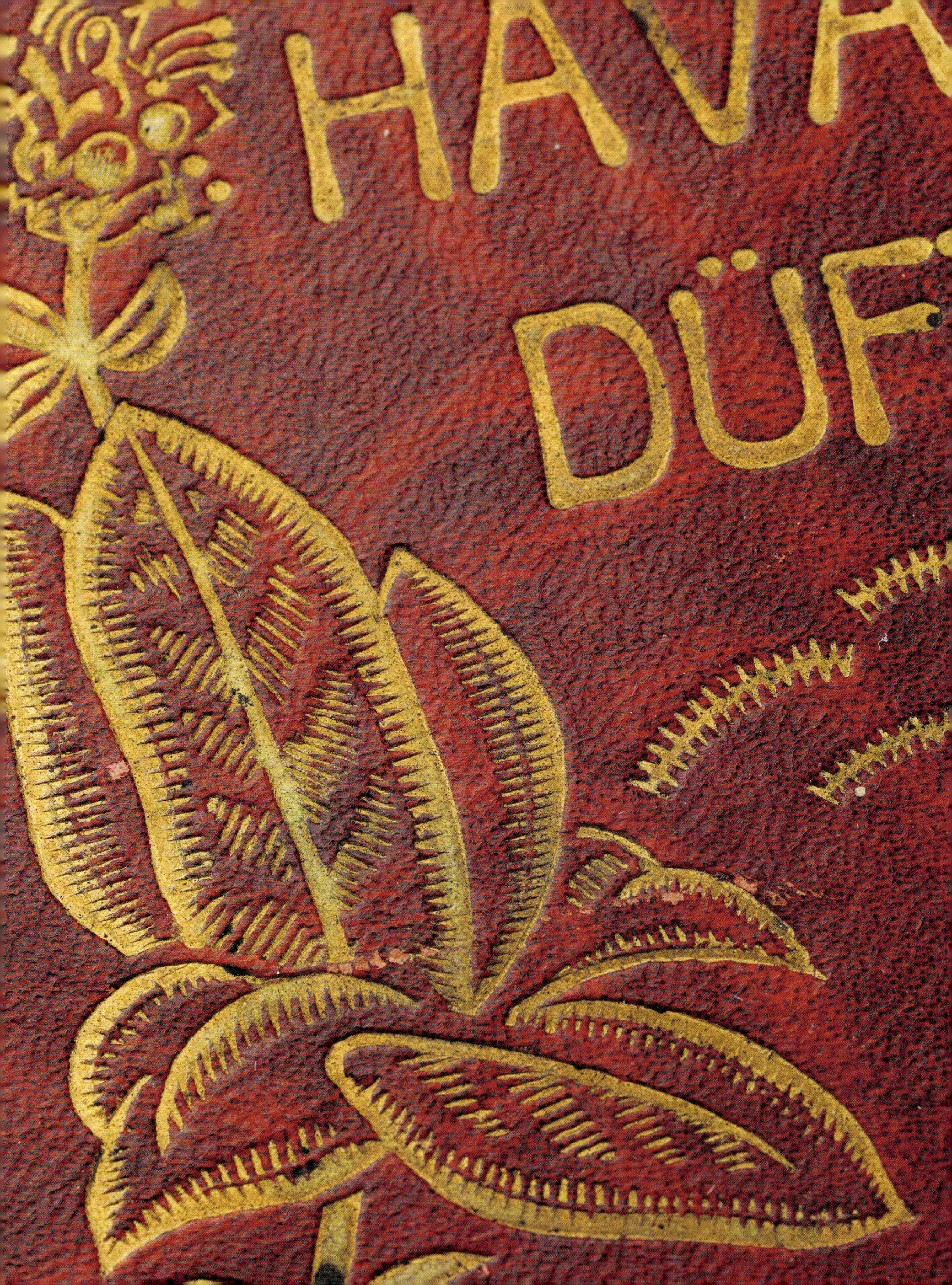
HAVA
DÜF

Rauchgenuss
Smoking Pleasure

Eine der größten Unterschiede zwischen Zigarette und Zigarre ist der Zeitfaktor. Die Zigarette ist etwas für Hektiker, für zwischendurch. Die Zigarre nimmt eine geraume Zeit in Anspruch. Dem Zigarrenrauchen nicht abgeneigt waren Bismarck, Winston Churchill, Fidel Castro, Alfred Hitchcock, Ernest Hemingway, Thomas Mann, Henry Ford und Katharina die Große. Christoph Columbus soll der erste Europäer gewesen sein, der 1492 auf Kuba mit Tabak in Kontakt kam.

Die Zigarre hat nicht nur mit Lifestyle, Genuss und Geschmack zu tun, sie ist zugleich ein Statussymbol für Macht und Wohlstand. Die Zeiten, in denen sie allein der Luxuswelt angehörte, sind vorbei. Heute sind es Gelegenheitsraucher, die die besten Zigarrenmarken am Leben erhalten. Tabakerzeugnisse können auch gekaut (Kautabak) oder geschnupft (Schnupftabak) werden.

Die besten Begleiter zur Zigarre sind Whisky oder Scotch, Rum, Cognac und Grappa. Die Zigarre mit einer Spirituose zu kombinieren hilft, die feinen Aromen hervorzuheben.

Meine Scheinbuchsammlung umfasst Zigarren- und Zigarettendosen, Feuerzeuge, Streichholzdosen und Streichholzschachtelhalter, Aschenbecher und Schnupftabakdosen. Bei Liebhabern ist das Sammeln von Zigarrenbändern oder Ringen, auch Bauchbinde oder Banderole genannt, weit verbreitet. Äußerst attraktiv sind die mit Farbe bedruckten und mit Gold geprägten Deckelbilder der Zigarrenkisten. Die Banderole ist auch 160 Jahre nach ihrer Erfindung eines der wichtigsten Marketinginstrumente des Zigarrenbusiness. Sie hat die große Aufgabe, den Raucher zu verführen und unverkennbar zu sein.

One of the greatest differences between a cigarette and a cigar is the time factor. The cigarette is something for hectic people, for in-between times. It takes a long time to smoke a cigar. Bismarck, Winston Churchill, Fidel Castro, Alfred Hitchcock, Ernest Hemingway, Thomas Mann, Henry Ford and Catherine the Great enjoyed smoking cigars. Christopher Columbus is said to have been the first European to smoke tobacco in Cuba in 1492.

Contact was made.

The cigar not only has to do with lifestyle, pleasure and taste, but is also a status symbol of power and prosperity. Gone are the days when they belonged exclusively to the world of luxury. Today, it is occasional smokers who keep the best cigar brands alive. Tobacco products can also be chewed (chewing tobacco) or snorted (snuff).

The best company for a cigar is whisky, scotch, rum, cognac, or grappa. Combining the cigar with a spirit helps release its fine aromas.

My fake book collection includes cigar and cigarette boxes, lighters, matchboxes, matchbox holders, ashtrays, and snuffboxes. Collecting cigar ribbons or rings, also known as belly bands or banderoles, is widespread among enthusiasts. Those printed in color and with gilt embossed illustrations on the lid of the cigar boxes are extremely attractive. Even 160 years after its invention, the banderole is still one of the most important marketing instruments in the cigar business. It has the great task of seducing the smoker and being distinctive.

3.001
Holzschachtel mit Schubfach für 28 Zigarillos, Blumenschnitzereien
Wooden box with pull-out compartment for 28 cigarillos, decorated with floral carvings
4,3 x 19 x 13,2 cm

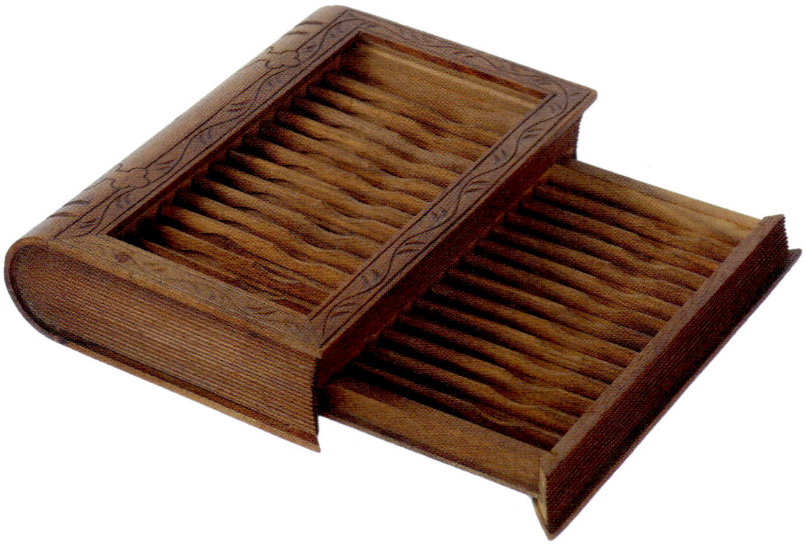

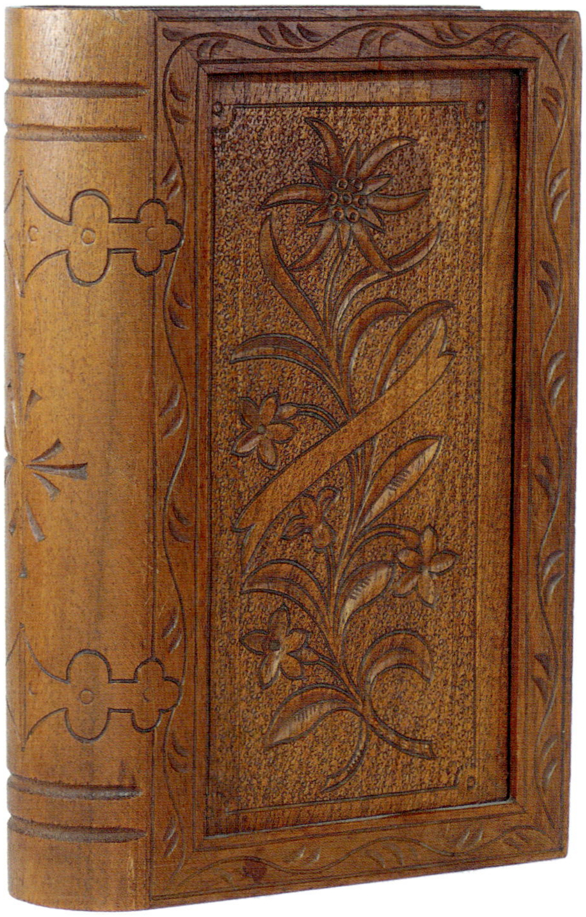

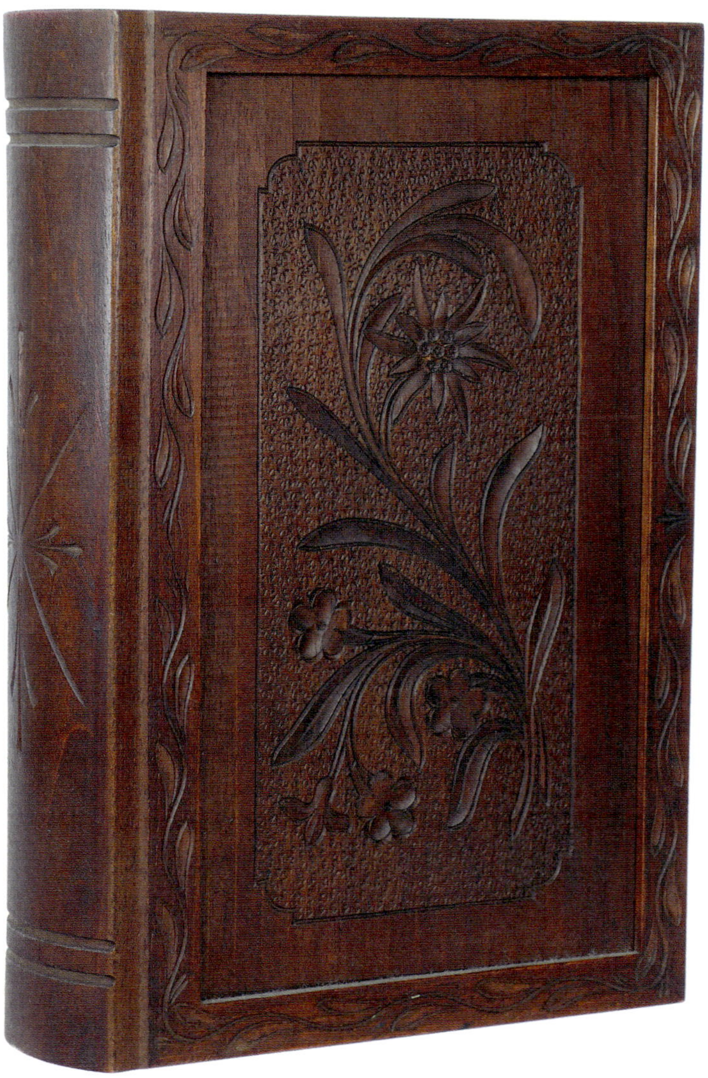

3.002
Holzschachtel mit Blumenschnitzereien, zweistöckig, Schubfach für 20 Zigarren
Two-storey wooden box with floral carvings, pull-out compartment for 20 cigars
6 x 25,6 x 18 cm

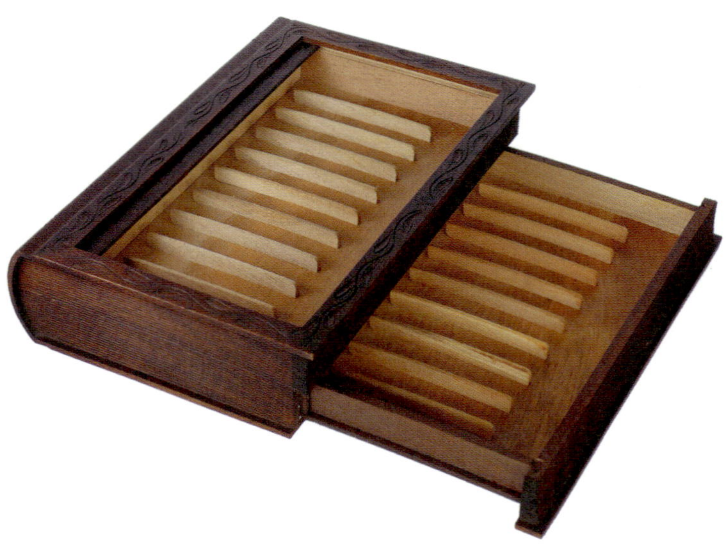

3.003
Don Quijote de la Mancha, Cervantes
Holzschachtel mit reliefgeprägtem Ledereinband und Lederfutter, Holzeinlagen
Wooden box with relief embossed leather binding, wooden marquetry
3,8 x 22 x 16,7 cm

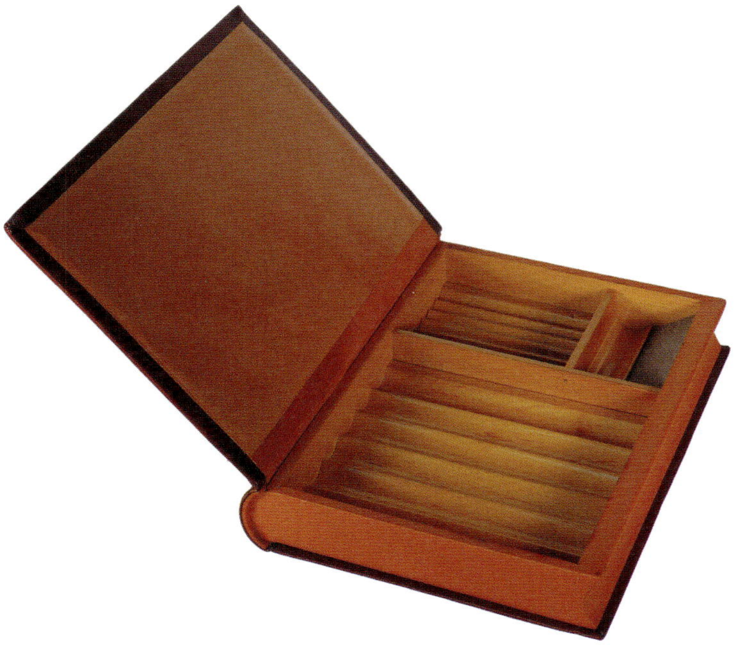

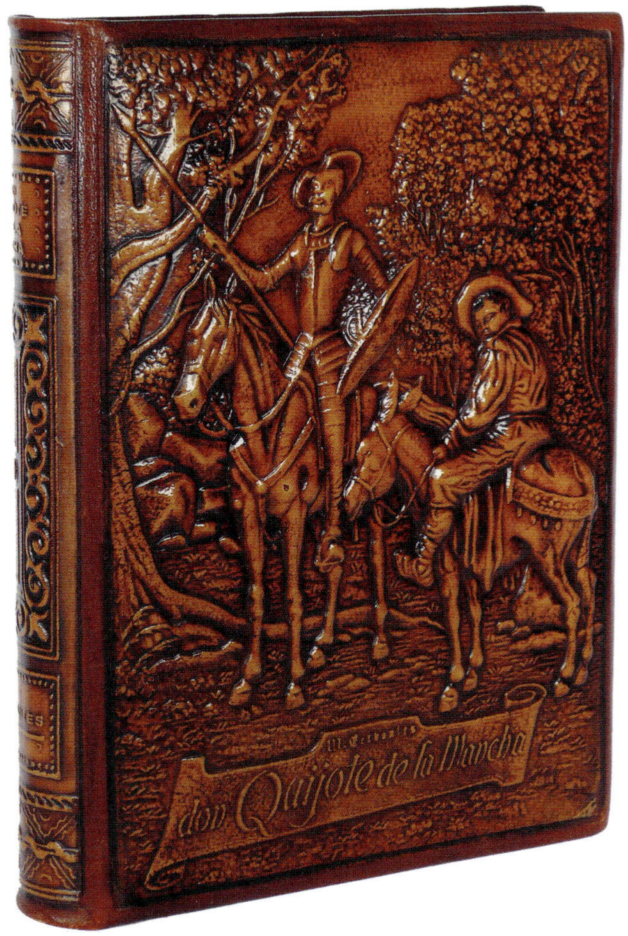

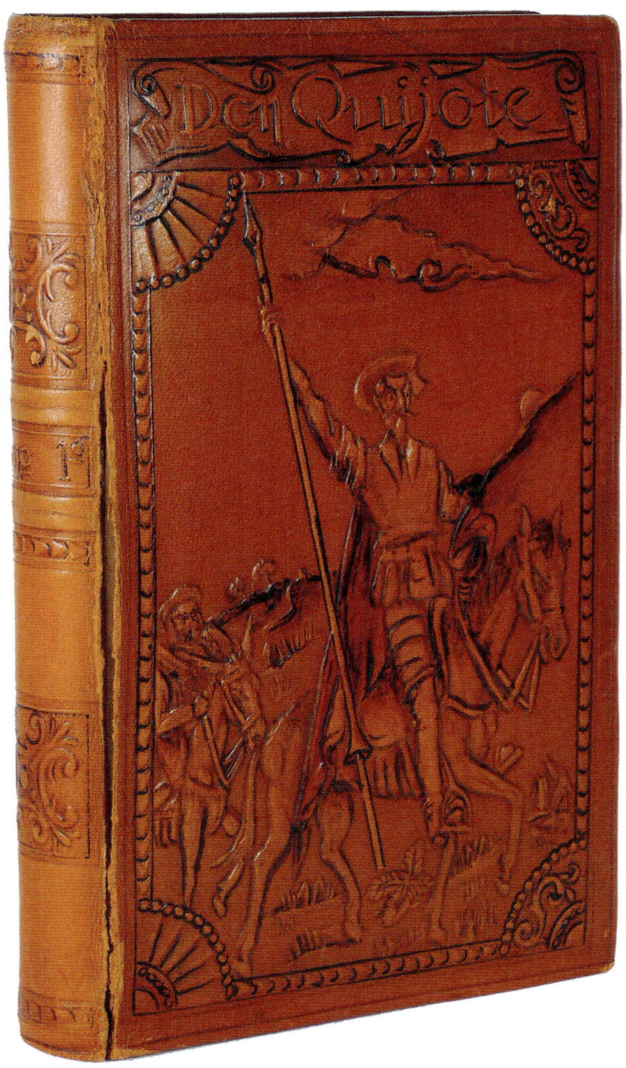

3.004
Don Quijote, Tome I
Holzschachtel mit reliefgeprägtem Ledereinband und Lederfutter, Holzeinlagen
Wooden box with embossed leather binding and leather lining, wooden marquetry
3,6 x 23 x 15,5 cm

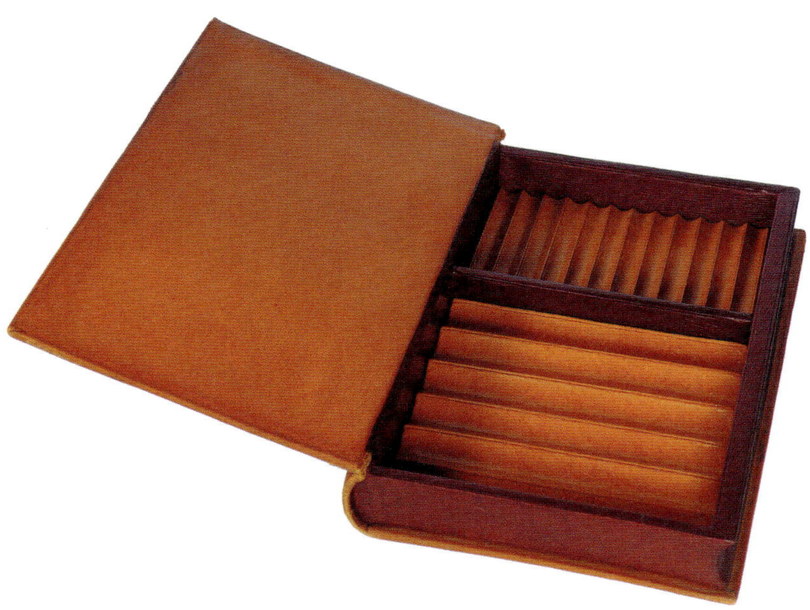

3.005
Doctor Qualm's Werke / *Works*
Schachtel mit Papierüberzug,Rücken- und Deckelvergoldung, Haarmarmorschnitt
Box with paper-over-board, gilt spine and cover, marbled edges
Jugendstil / *Art Nouveau* | 3 x 11,8 x 10,5 cm

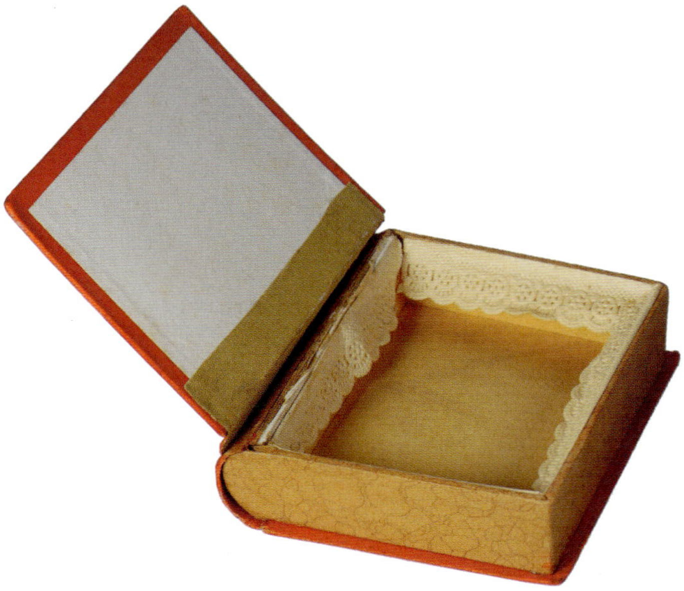

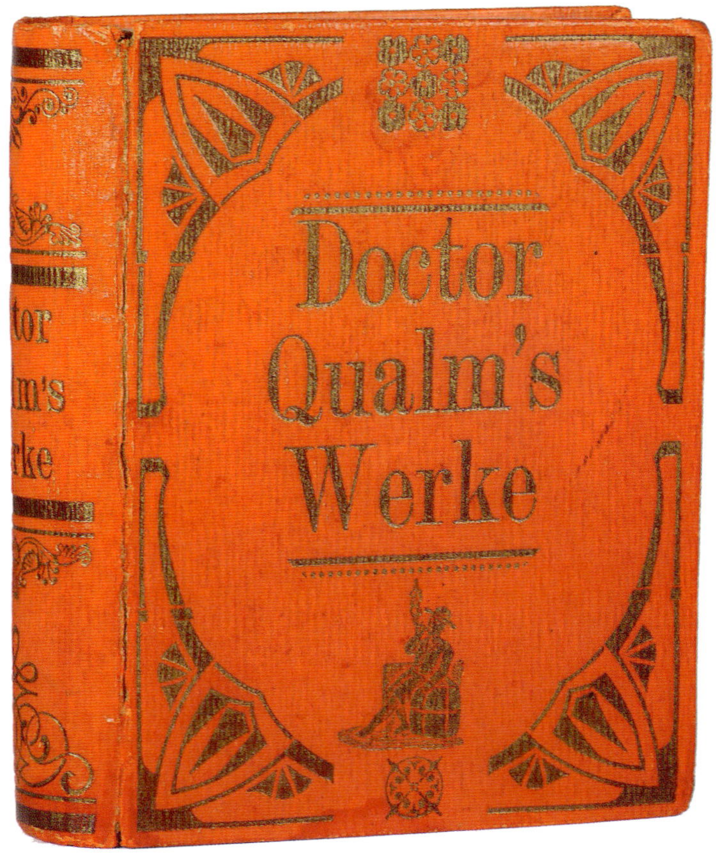

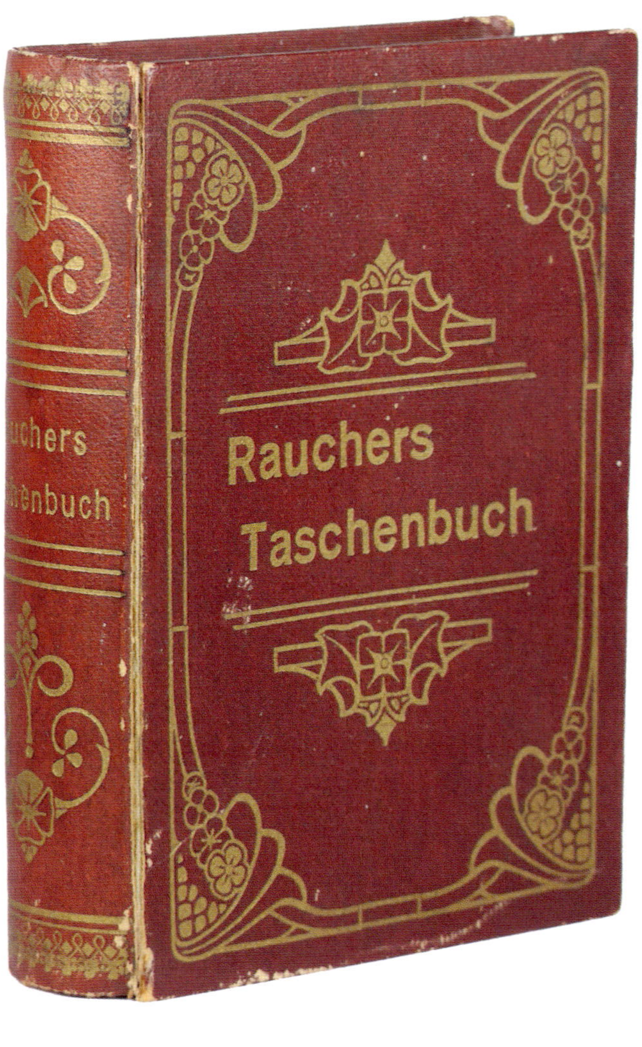

3.006
Rauchers Taschenbuch
Smoker's Paperback
Schachtel mit goldgeprägtem Rücken und Vorderdeckel, dreiseitiger Marmorschnitt
Box with gold embossing on the spine and front cover, marbled edges
Jugendstil / *Art Nouveau* | 3 x 12,2 x 3 cm

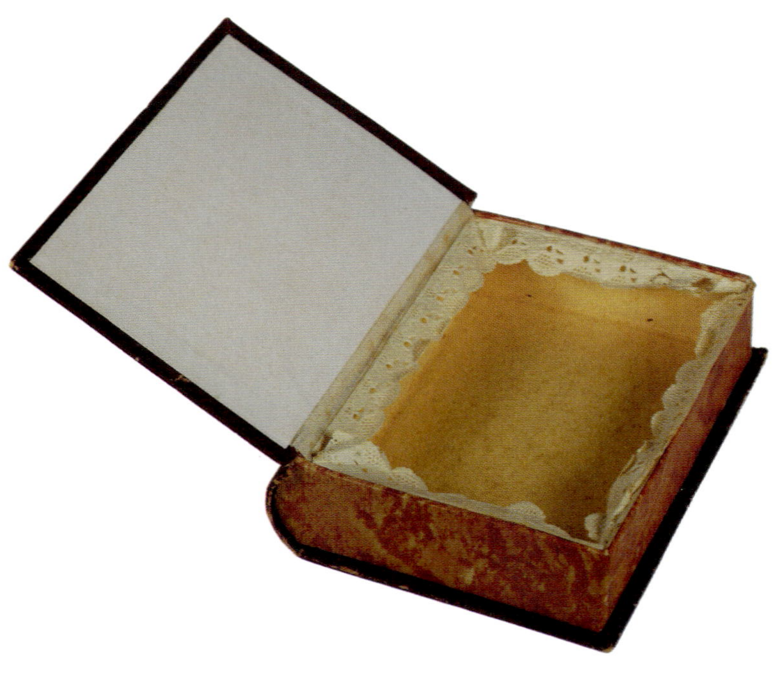

3.007
Doctor Qualm's Werke / *Works*
Kaliko-Schachtel, Papierüberzug Lederimitat mit Prägung, dreiseitiger Moiréepapierschnitt
Calico box, imitation leather over board with embossing, moiré paper edges
3,8 x 12,3 x 10,3 cm

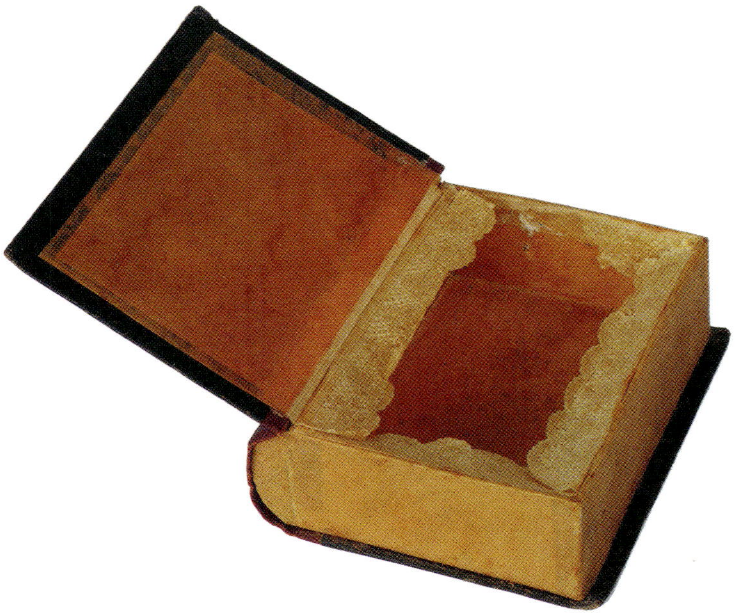

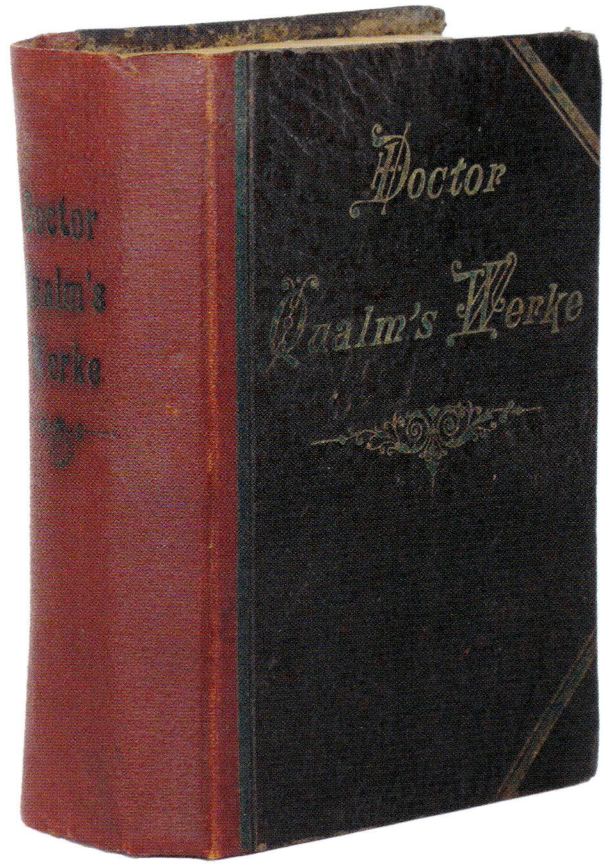

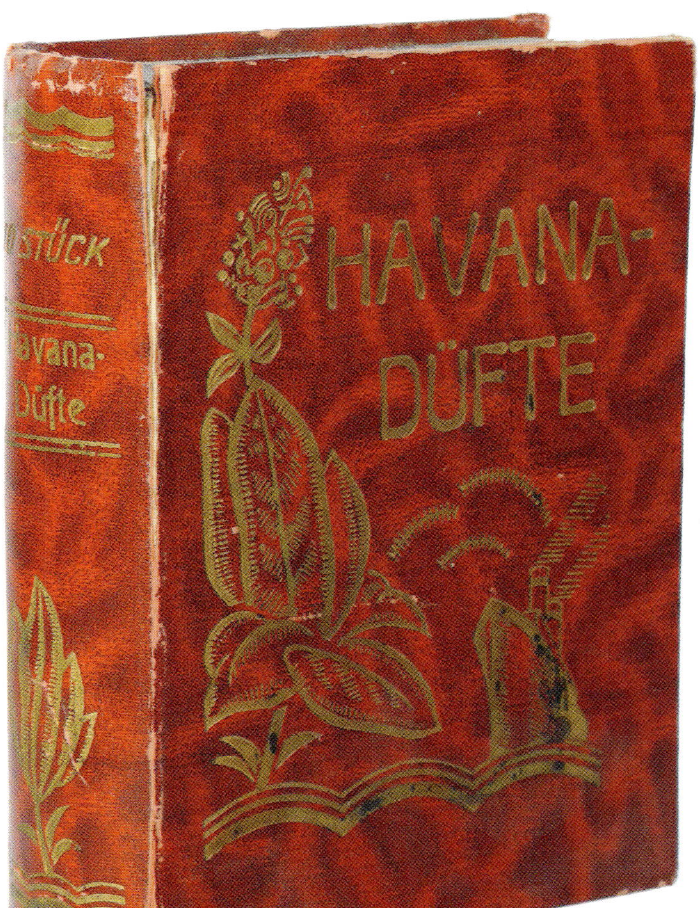

3.008
Havana flavors
Schachtel mit Papierüberzug, Rücken- und Deckelvergoldung, Marmorpapierschnitt
Box with paper-over-board, gilt spine and cover, marbled paper edges
3,7 x 13 x 11 cm

3.009
Schachtel mit Papierüberzug, Goldprägedruck, Messingschließe, geprägte Werbeschilder
Box with paper-over-board, gold tooling, brass clasp, embossed advertising labels
3,7 x 12,5 x 18,7 cm

3.010
Musset, Un Caprice
Messingdose mit Lederüberzug und Spaltlederfutter, Vergoldung auf Rücken und Vorderdeckel
Brass box with leather cover and leather lining, gold-plated spine and front cover
1,4 x 9,7 x 7,2 cm

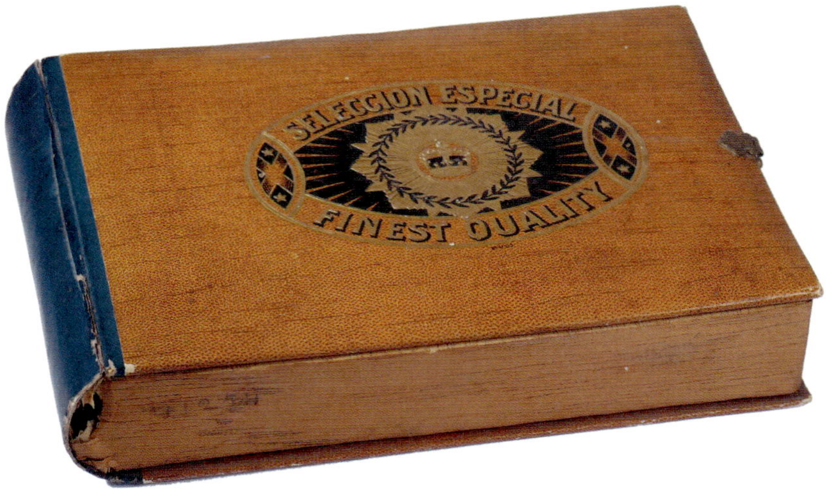

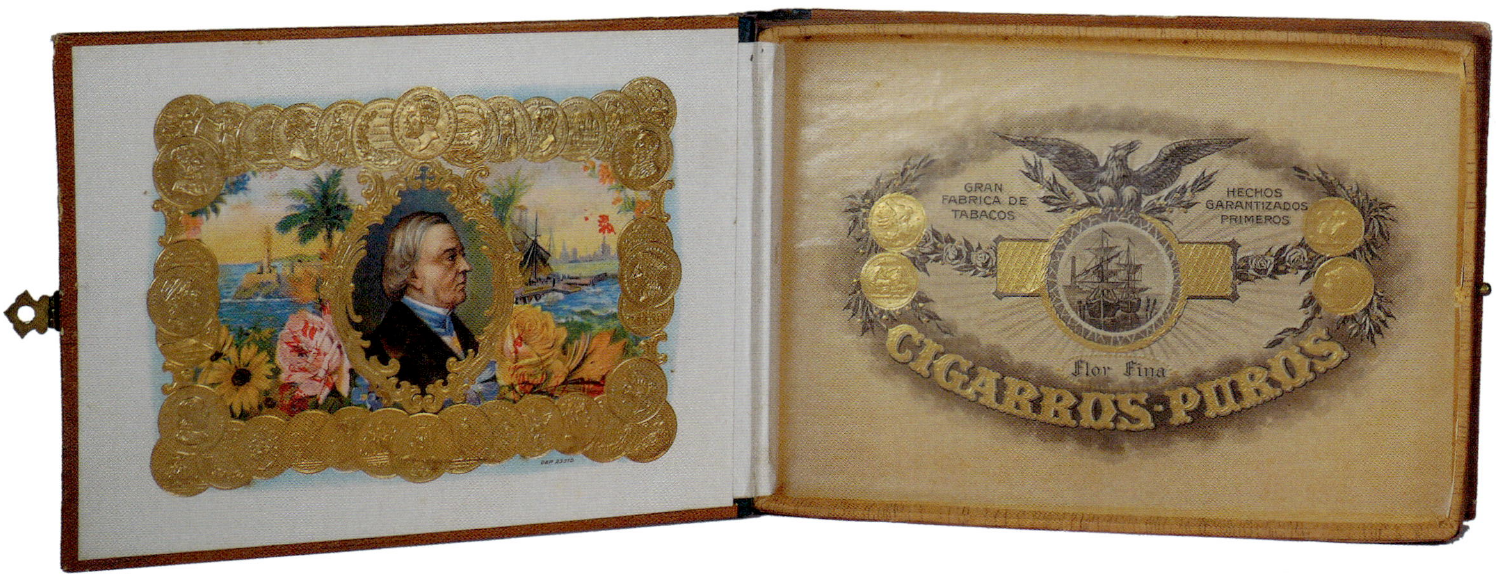

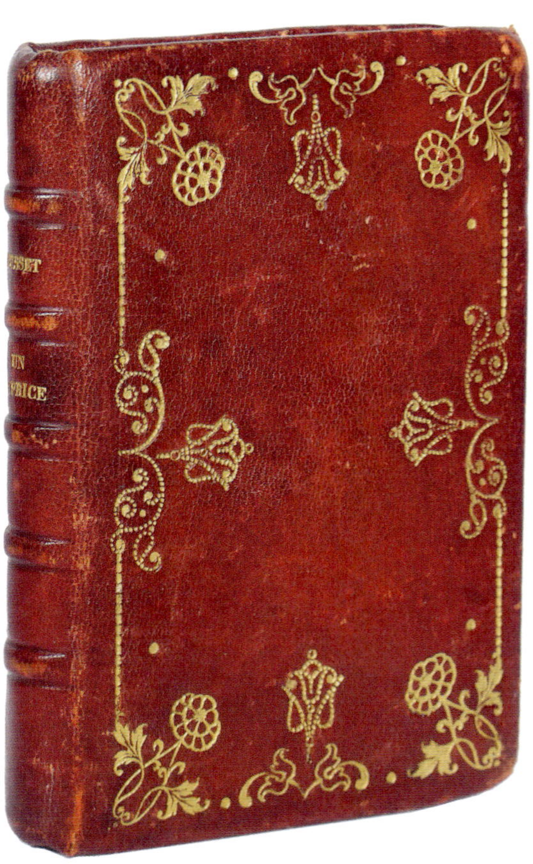

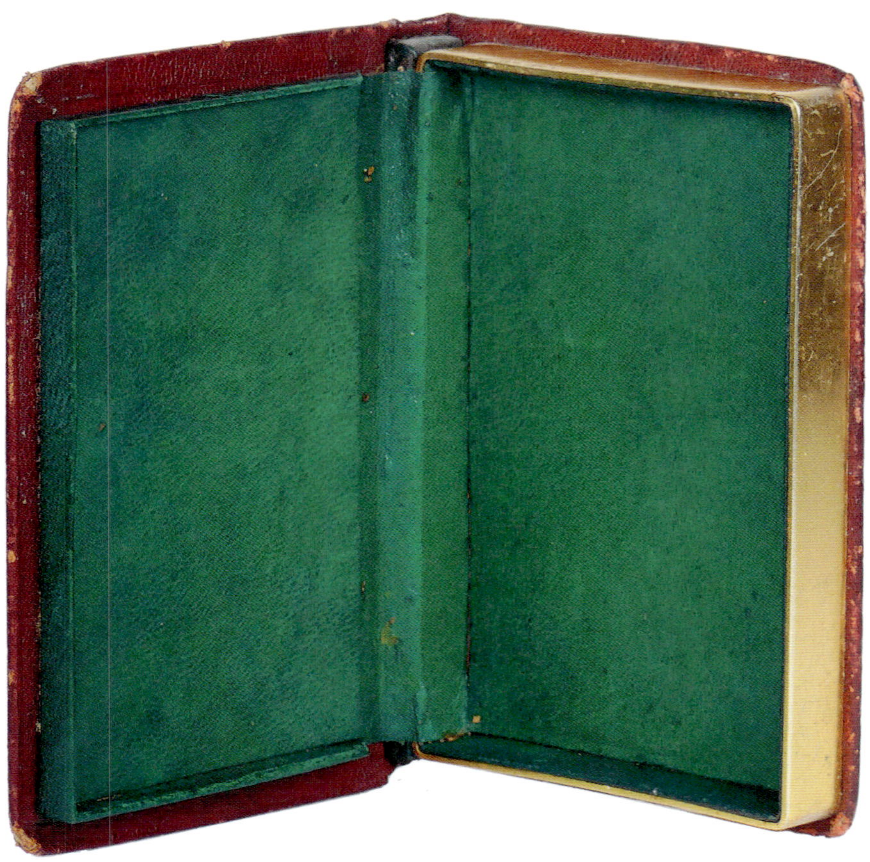

3.011

Auteur Professeur du bon goût.
Lecture intéressante pour fumeurs.
Cigarros de Buen Sabor, Flor Fina

Schachtel mit Goldprägung, dreiseitiger Haarmarmorschnitt, farbig- und goldgeprägtes Werbeschild

Box with gilt embossing, marbled edges, advertising label with color and gold tooling

3,1 x 20,8 x 13 cm

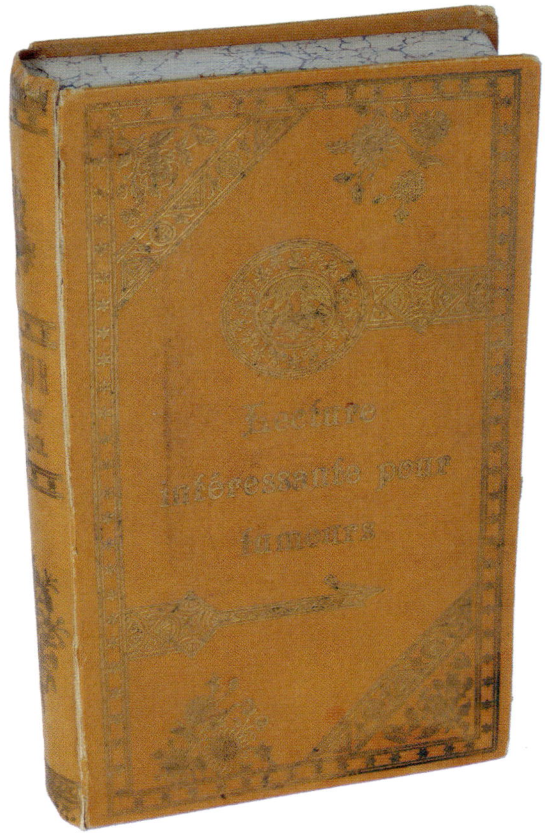

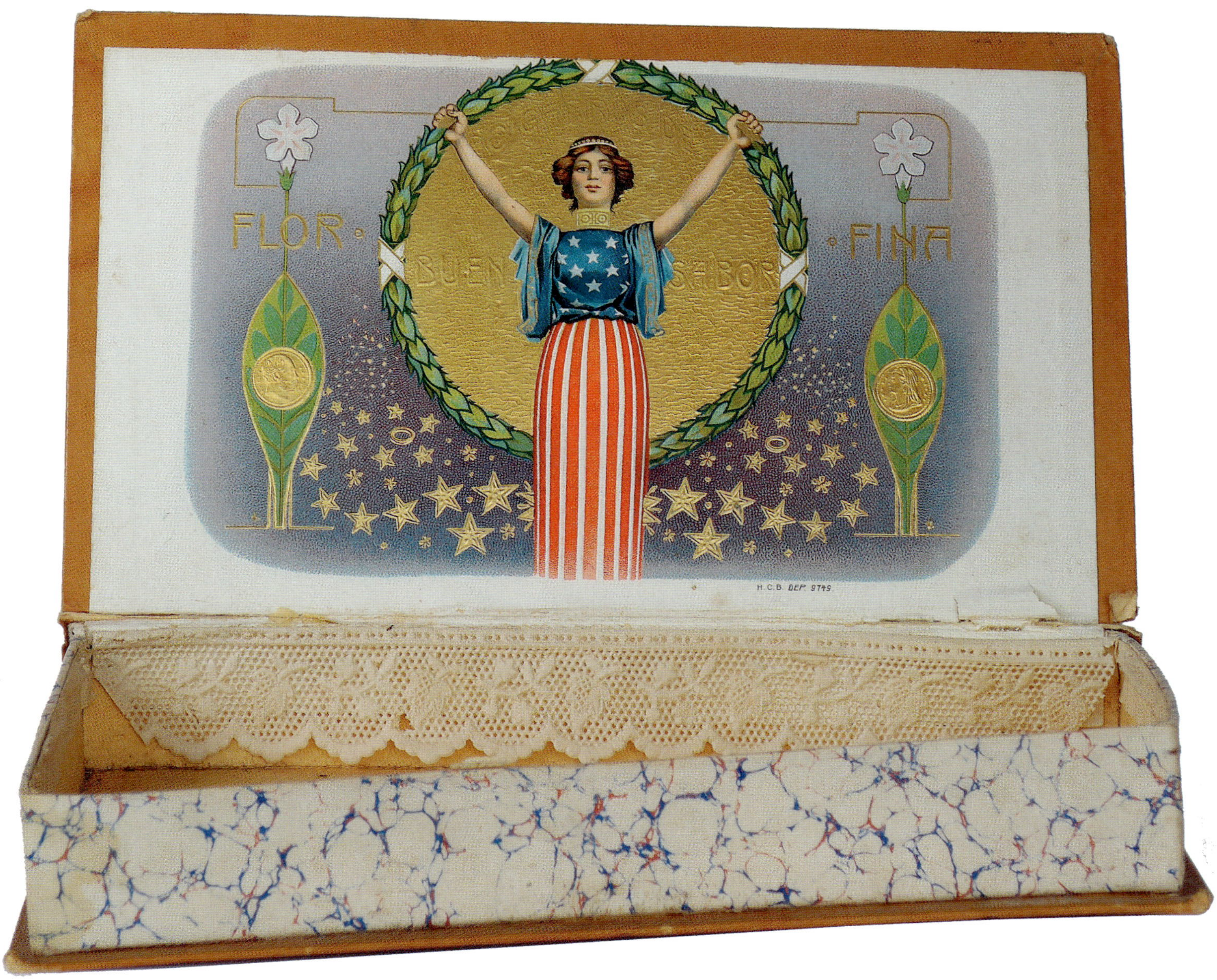

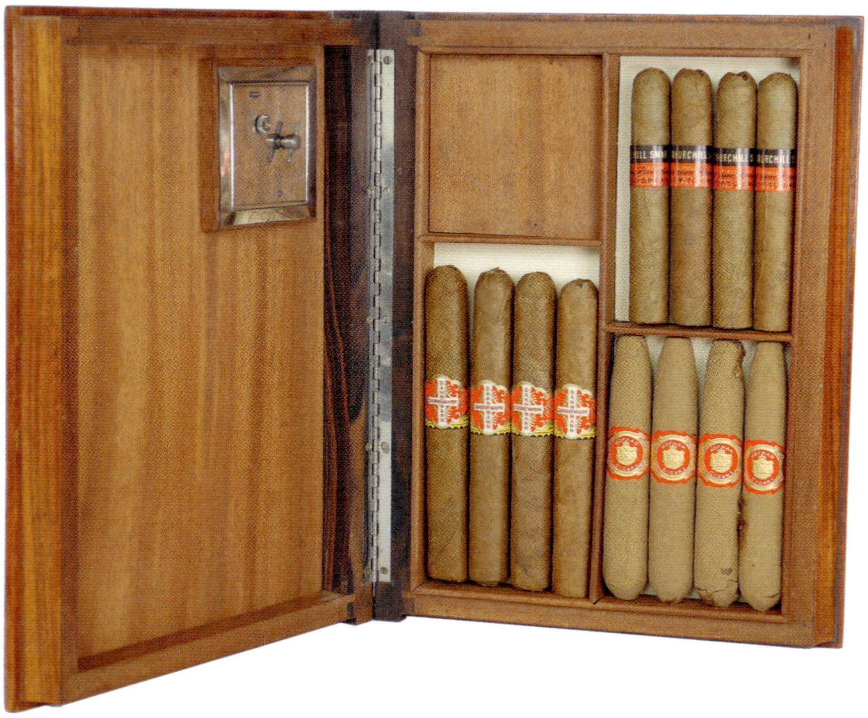

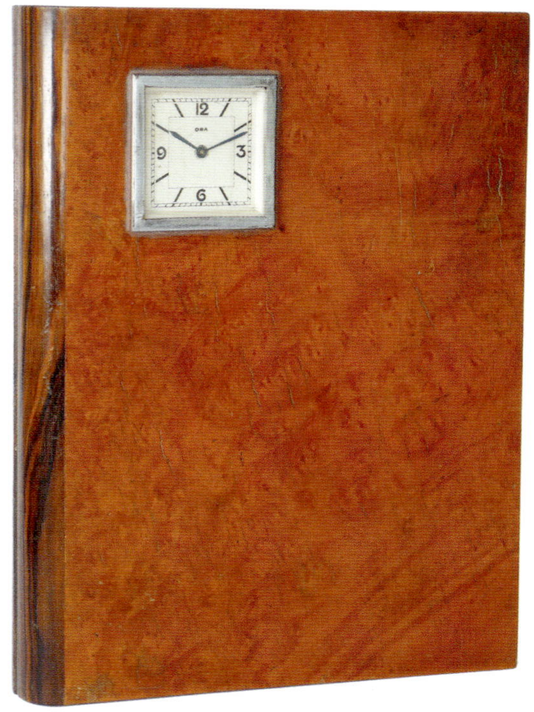

3.012
Wurzelholzschatulle mit Scharnier, eingelegte Uhr der Marke Ora Swiss
Box made of root wood with hinges, containing a clock by Ora Swiss
Art Déco | 4 x 25 x 19,7 cm

3.013
Libretto „El Pensador“,
Holzschatulle mit Messingverschluss, farbig- und goldgeprägtes Werbeschild
Wooden box with brass clasp, gold-tooled advertising sign with color embossing
4,3 x 26,4 x 17,5 cm

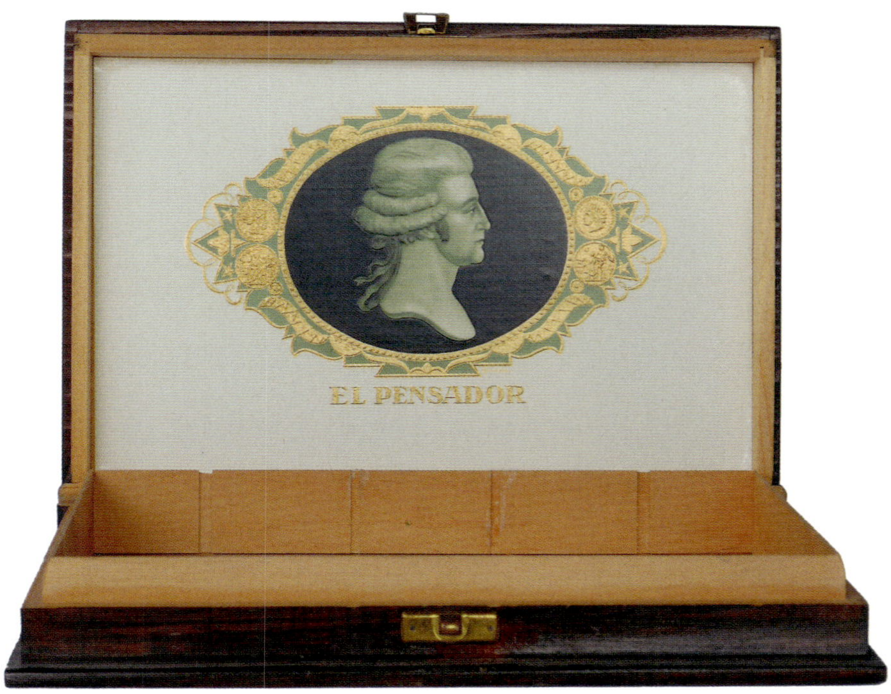

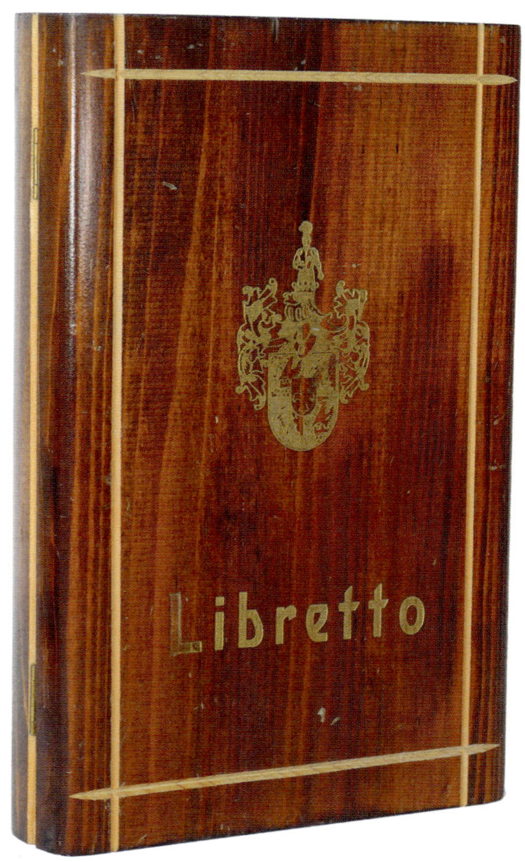

3.014
Habana
Holzschatulle mit Wurzelmarmorpapierüberzug, Goldprägung, wattierter Deckel
Wooden casket with marbled paper-over-board, gilt embossing, padded lid
10,7 x 14 x 11,8 cm

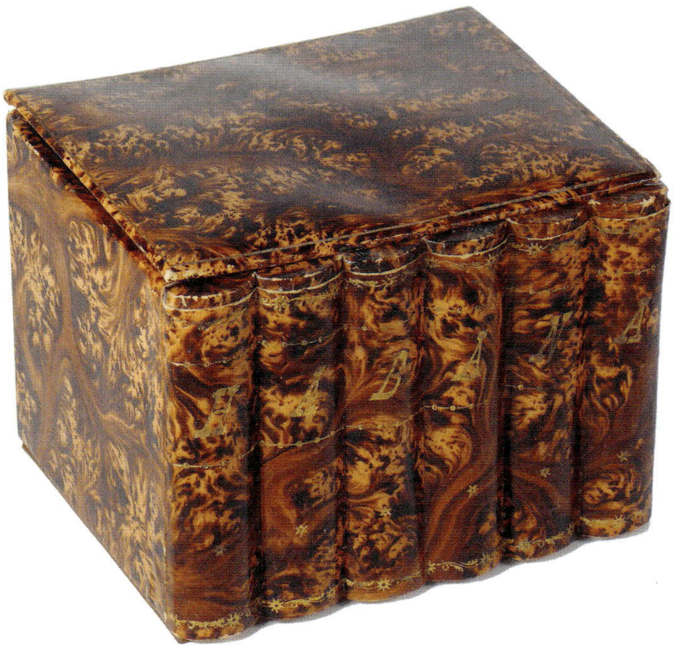

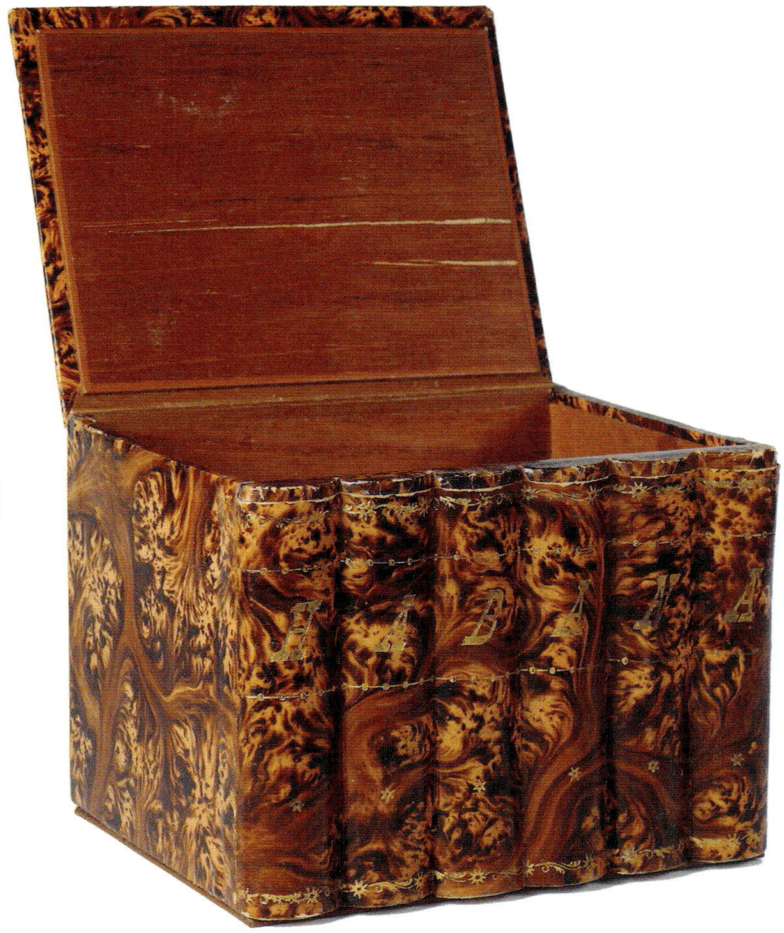

3.015
Holzbehälter mit Schieber am Kopfschnitt, Intarsien auf Vorder- und Hinterdeckel
Wooden box with slider at the head, marquetry on the front and rear board
Spätes 19. Jh. /
Late 19th century
13,6 x 9,5 x 1,9 cm

3.016
Holzbehälter mit aufklappbaren Kopfschnitt, Futter aus Buntpapier, Holzeinlegearbeiten, Monogramm „PK.Z"
Wooden box with fold-up head edge, colored paper lining, wooden marquetry, initials "PK.Z"
13,3 x 6,3 x 2,3 cm

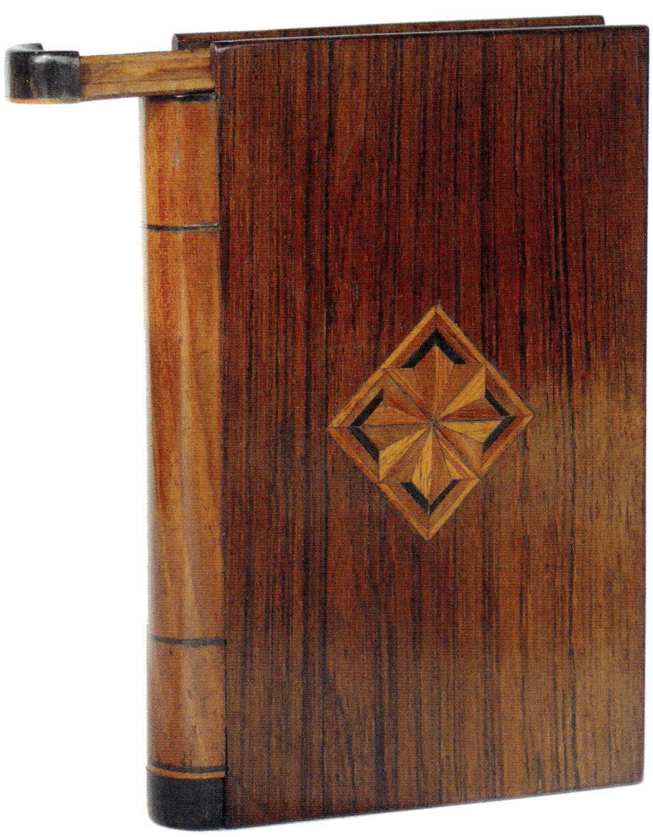

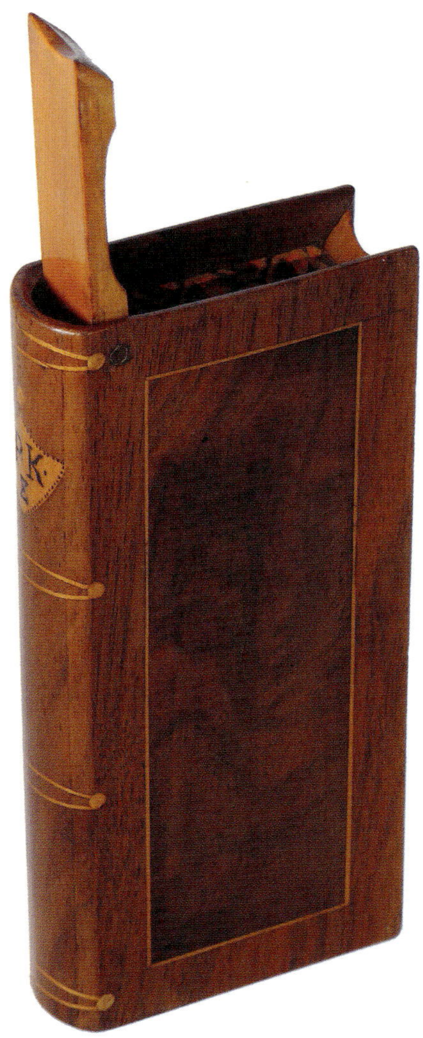

3.017
Raucherset aus Bakelit mit Quaste, Tragschlaufe, Vorderdeckelverzierung
Smoker kit made of bakelite with a tassel, sling and lid with ornaments
Um / *Around* 1900 | 2 x 7,7 x 5,5 cm

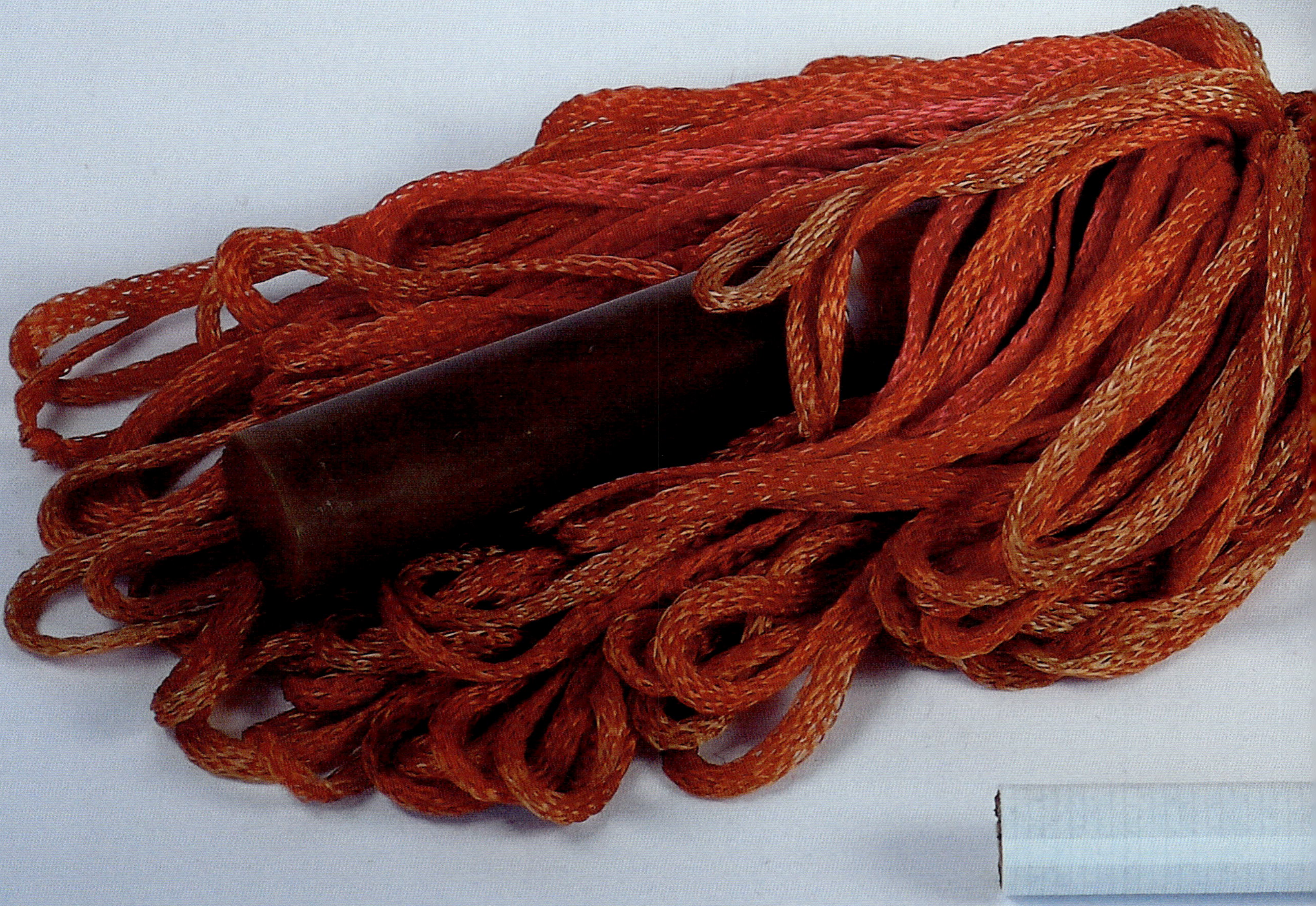

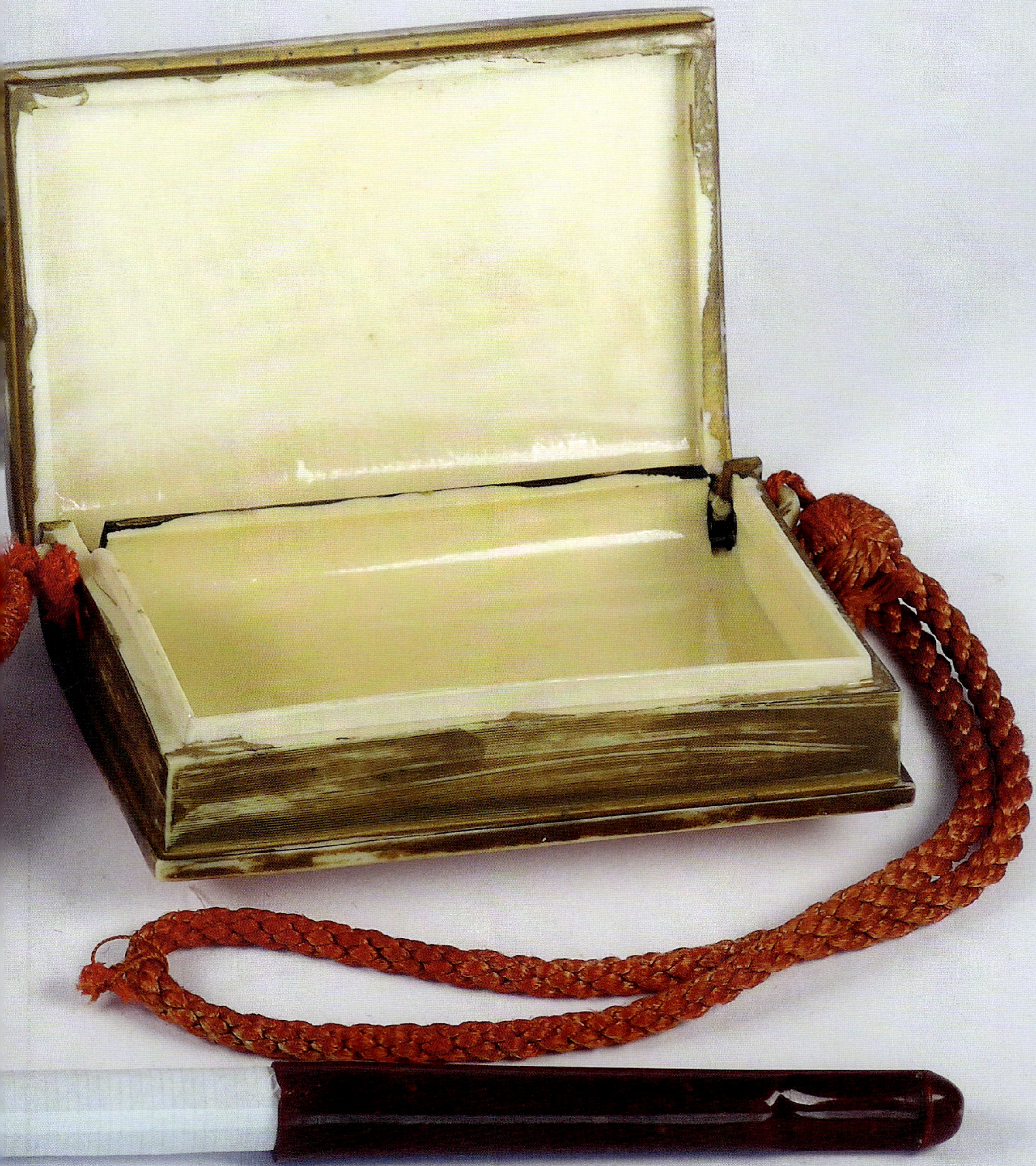

3.018
Silberdose mit graviertem Diagonalmuster auf beiden Deckeln
Silver box with engraved diagonal pattern on both lids
Anfang 20. Jh. / *Beginning of the 20th century* | 1,1 x 8,4 x 6,7 cm

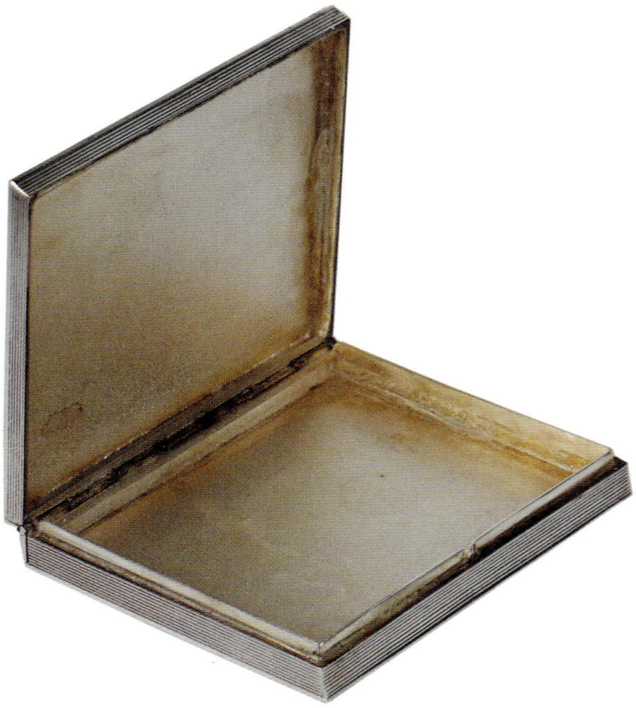

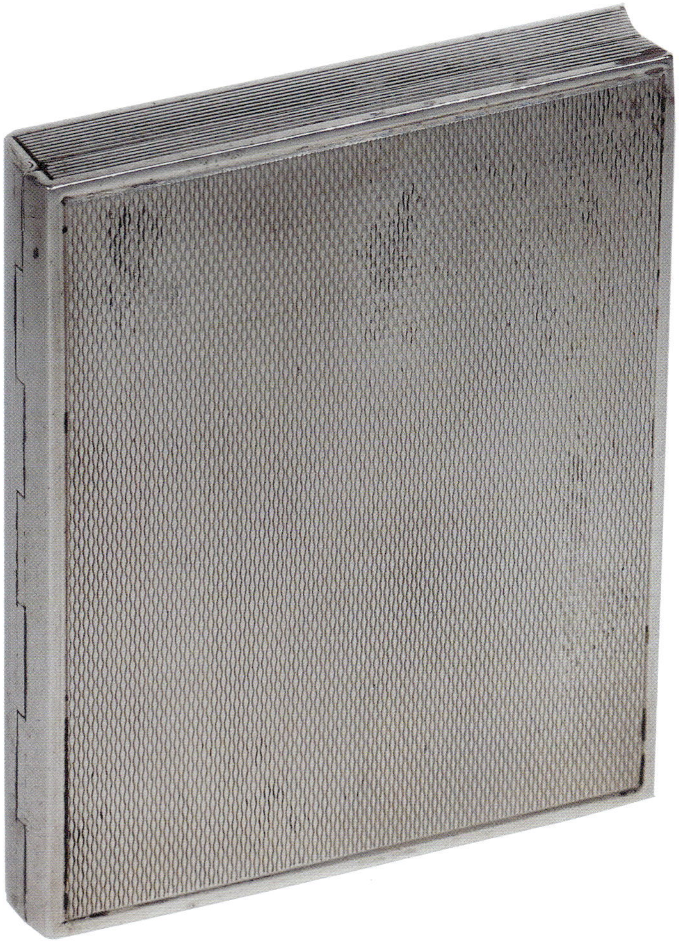

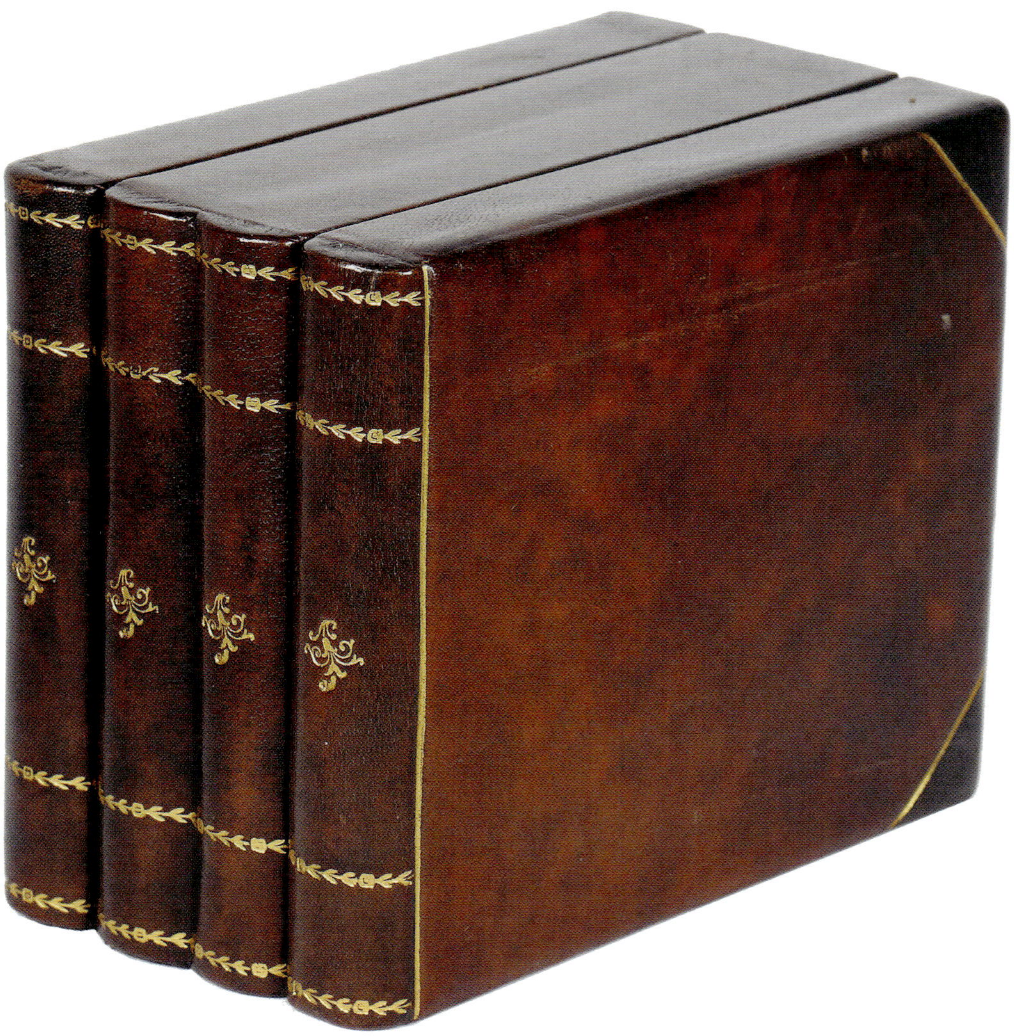

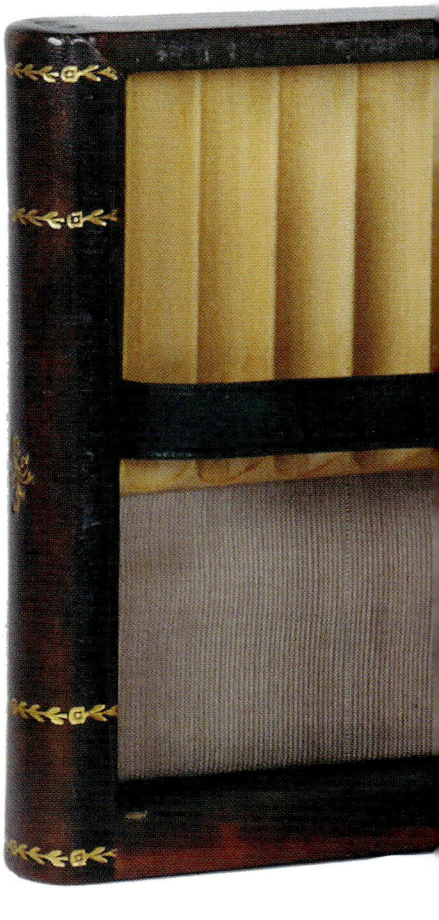

3.019
Rene, Geschichte des Tabaks / ***History of Tobacco***
Halbgewebedose für Zigaretten mit Papierüberzug, Illustration auf dem Vorderdeckel
Cigarette box made of half fabric and with paper-over-board, illustration on the front cover
3,7 x 10,4 x 9 cm

3.020
Schatulle aus Kalbleder mit Seidenfutter, beidseitig zu öffnen, Holzeinlage für 36 Zigaretten, Vergoldungen
Calfskin box with silk lining, openings on both sides, wooden marquetry, for 36 cigarettes, gilt ornaments
8,7 x 11 x 6,1 cm

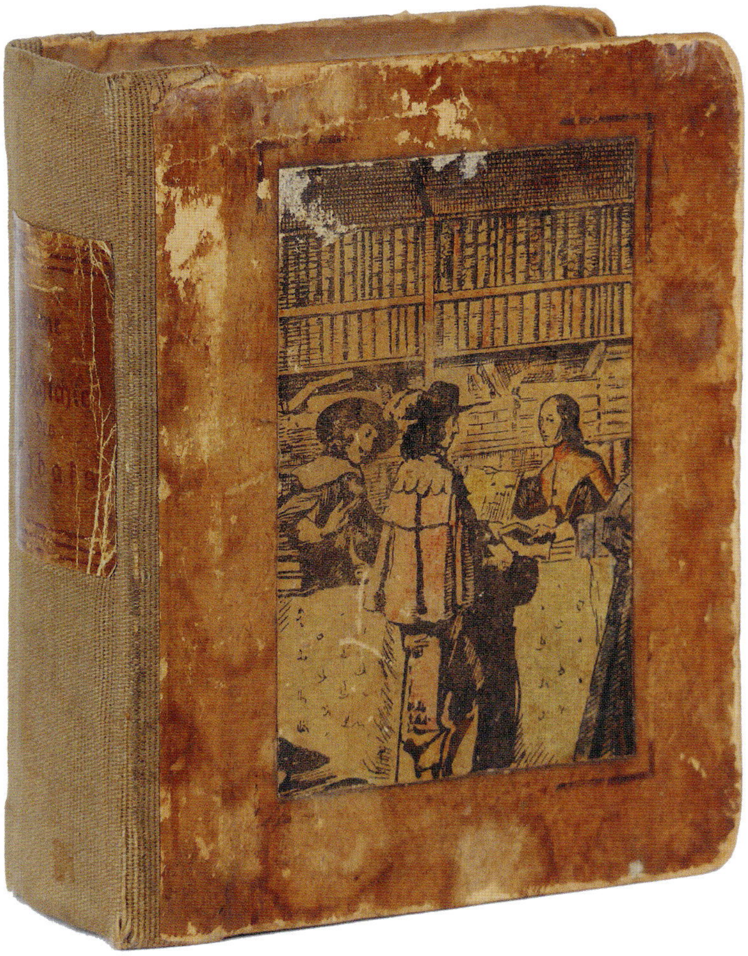

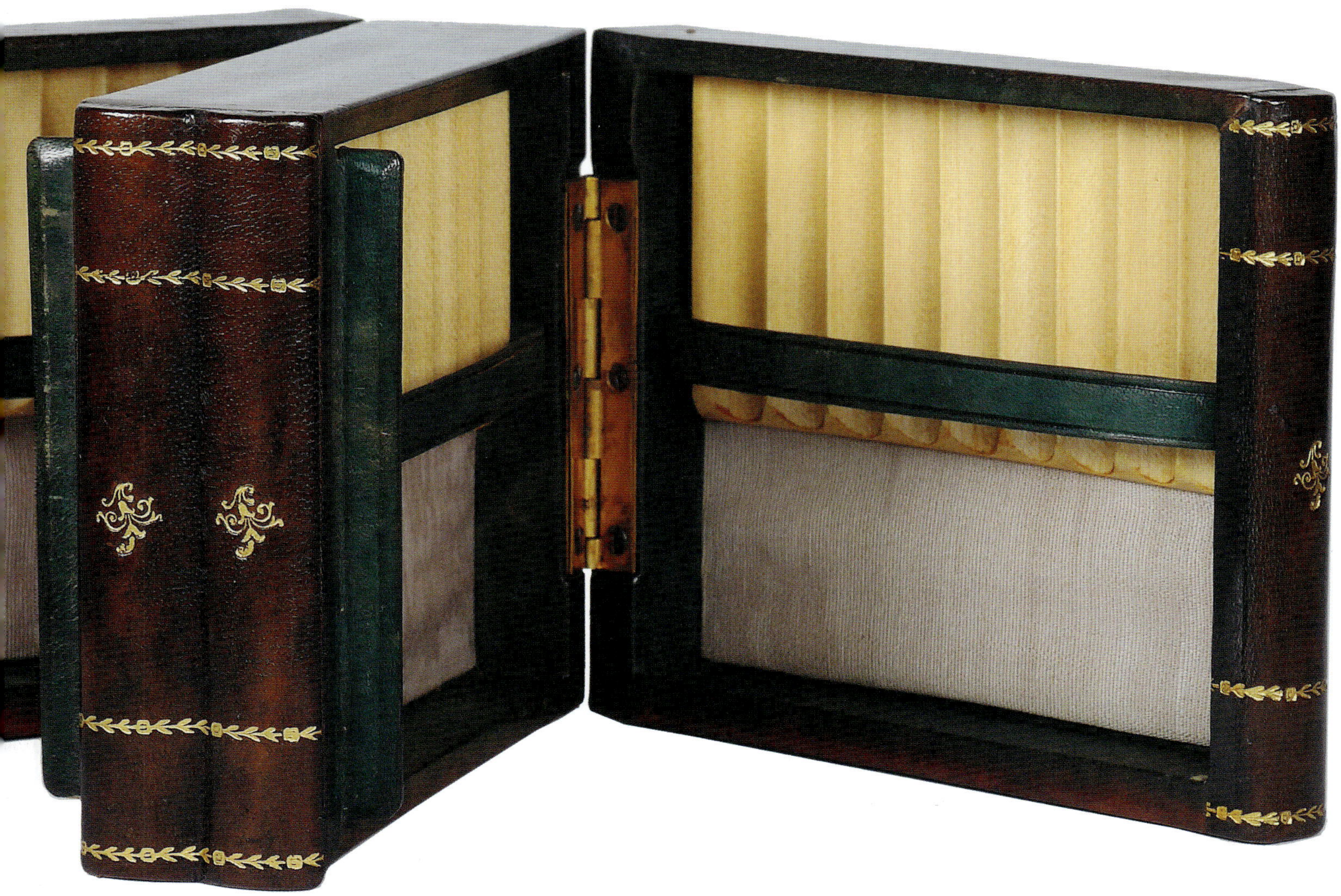

3.021
Zigarettenspender mit Spieluhr aus Blech
und Messing, Kunststoffstand
Cigarette dispenser with a music box made of sheet metal and brass, plastic base
Russland / *Russia* | Um / Around 1960
16 x 11,2 x 8,2 cm

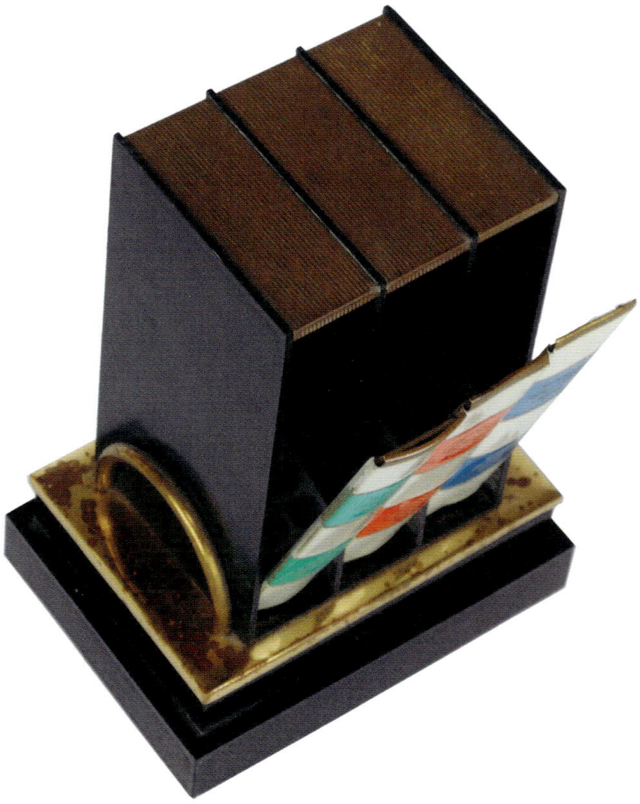

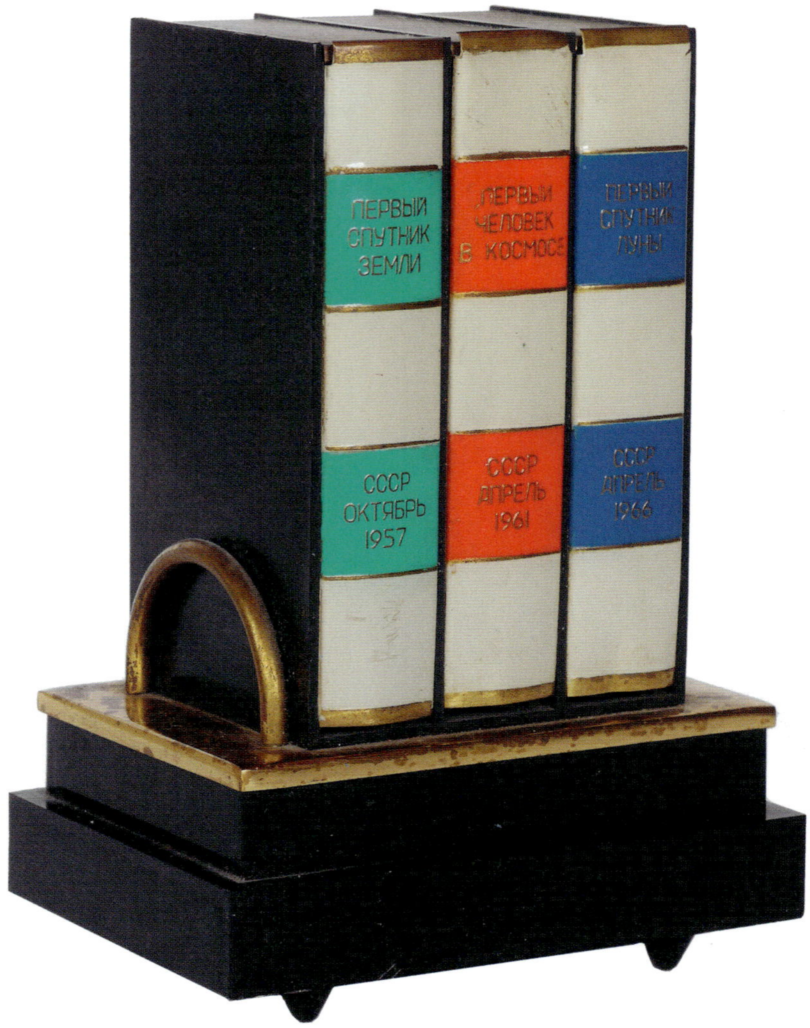

3.022
What is good and what is evil
Zigarettenspender mit Feuerzeug, zweiteiliges Buchbehältnis aus Kunststoff, Rücken- und Titelprägung, dreiseitiger Goldschnitt
Cigarette dispenser with lighter, two-piece plastic book container, embossed title and spine, all edges gilt
5,6 x 17,9 x 12,1 cm

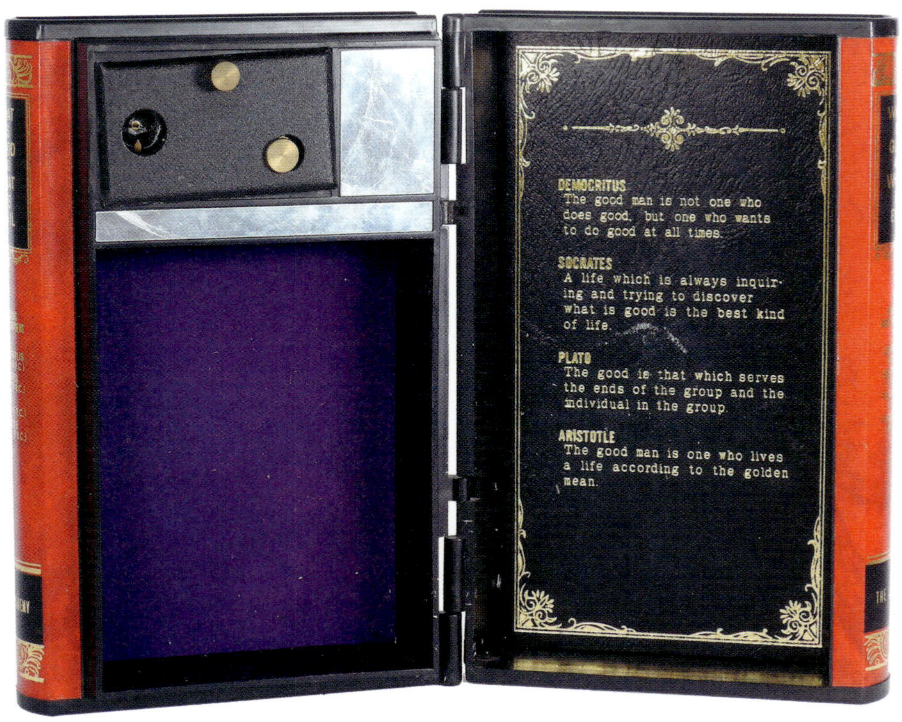

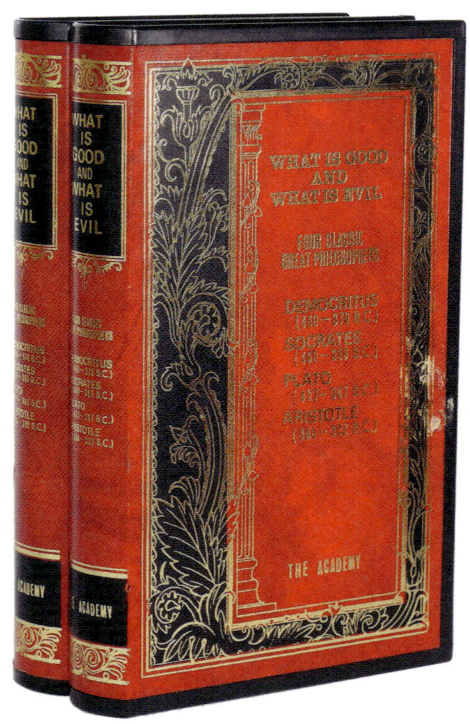

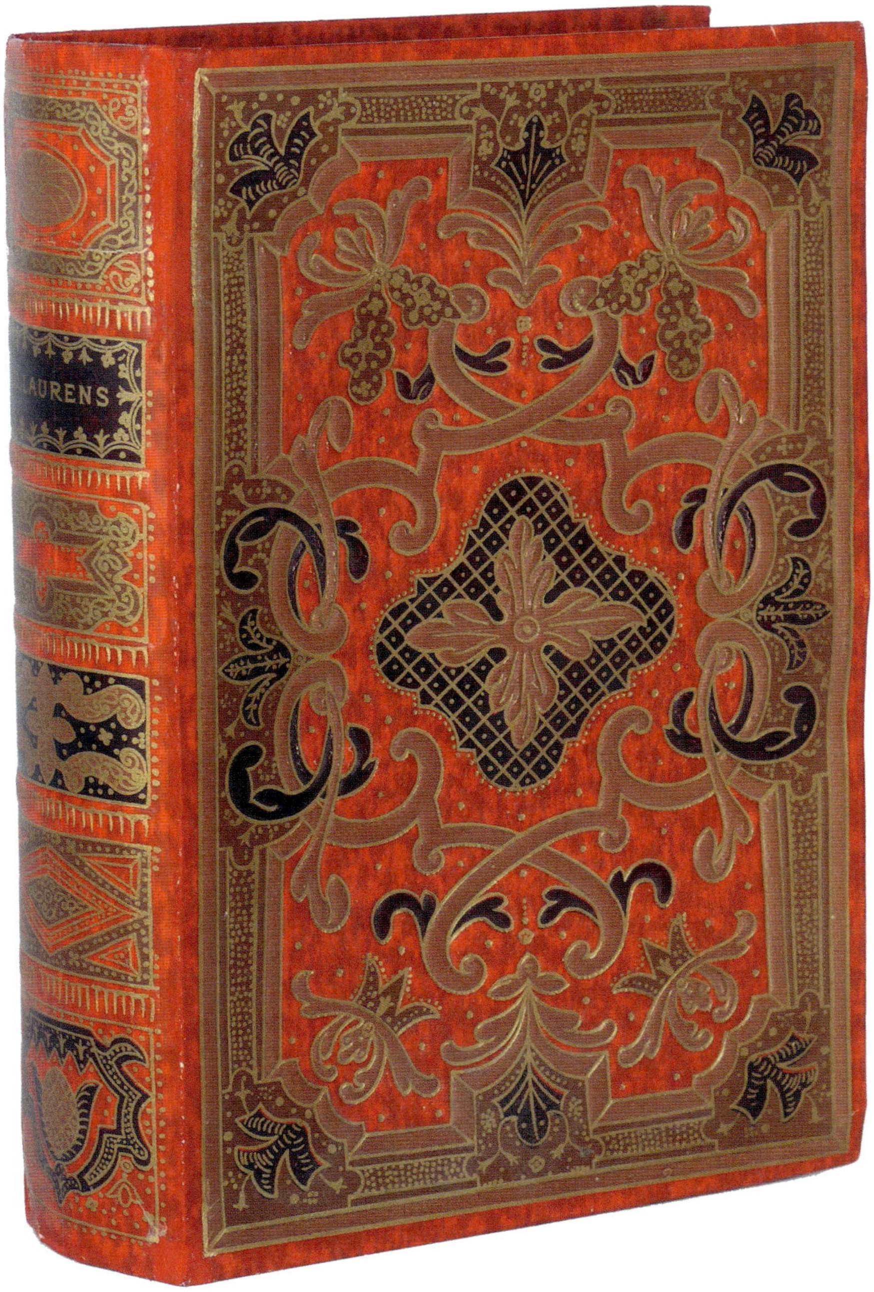

3.023
Ed Laurens: Reliure mosaiquée, style Padeloups Laurens
Schachtel mit farbigem Prägedruck, Goldschnitt
Box with relief embossing in color, gilt edges
Erste Hälfte 18. Jh. / *First half of the 18th century* | 4,5 x 16,3 x 12,4 cm

3.024
Vom Wunder des Tabaks, Zum Geburtstag
The Miracle of Tobacco, For Birthday
Holzkiste mit Papierrücken, Gold- und Blinddruck, Sinnspruch auf Innendeckel, geprägter Silberpapierschnitt
Wooden box with paper spine, gold and blind embossing, proverb on the inner lid, embossed silver paper edges
3,8 x 19,8 x 13,2 cm

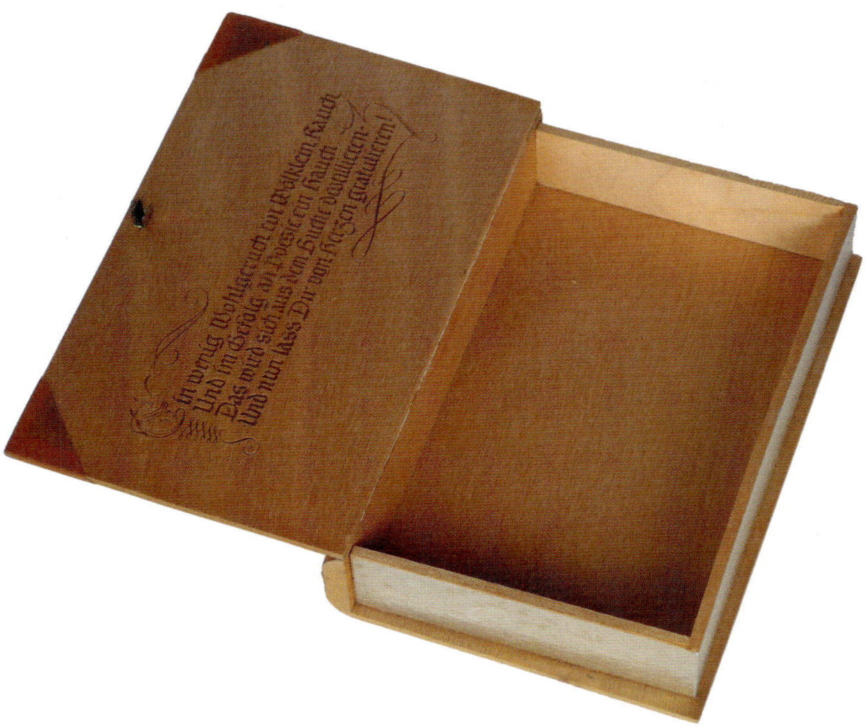

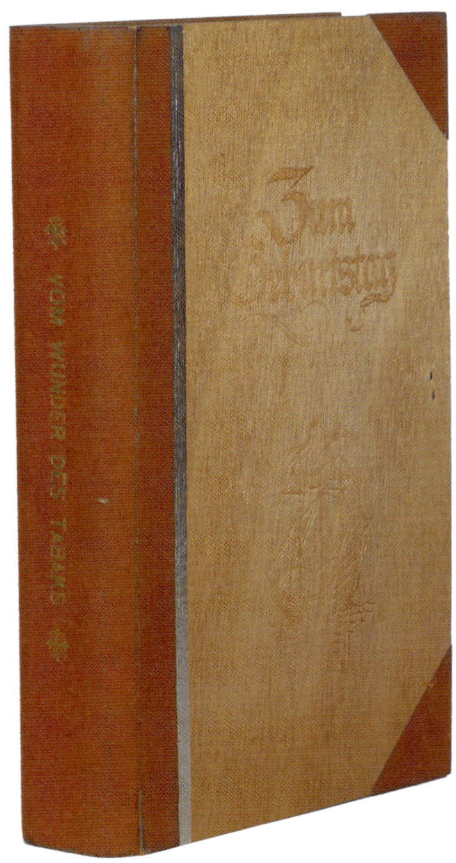

3.025
Messingfeuerzeug
mit ziseliertem
Deckel, aufklapp-
barer Vorderschnitt,
aufgesetztes De-
ckelschild
*Brass lighter with
chased covers,
hinged fore edge,
label on the cover*
Um / *Around* 1900
6,3 x 4 x 1,4 cm

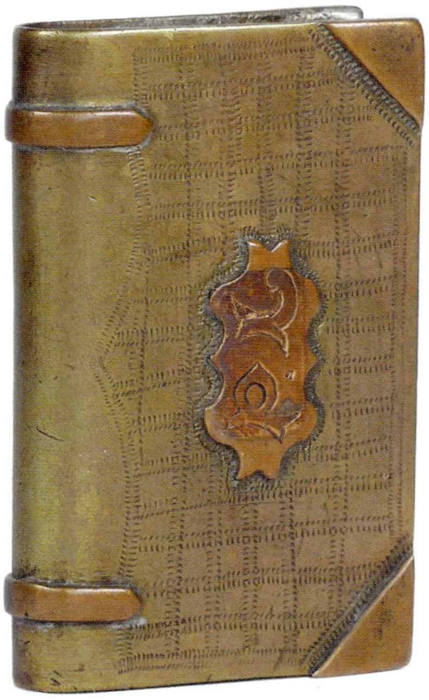

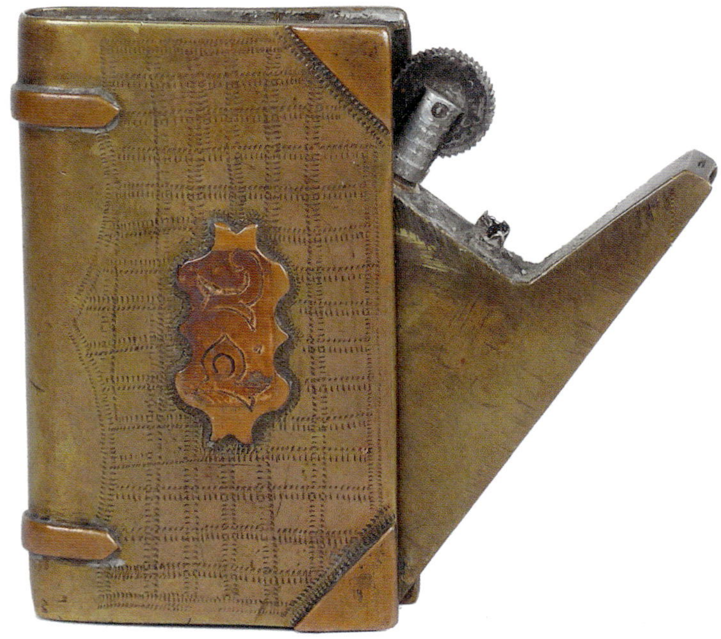

3.026
**Book of Smoking
Knowledge, Duber-
nard**
Batteriebetriebenes
Feuerzeug mit
Ganzledereinband,
Gold- und Blind-
prägung, Goldschnitt
*Battery-powered
lighter with full
leather binding, gold
and blind tooling,
gilt edges*
10,4 x 7,2 x 3 cm

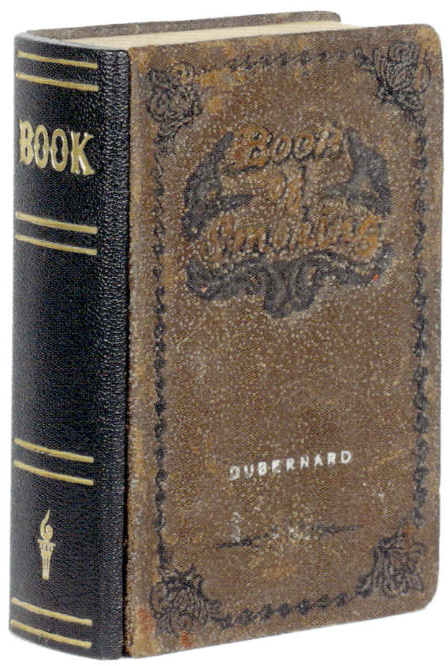

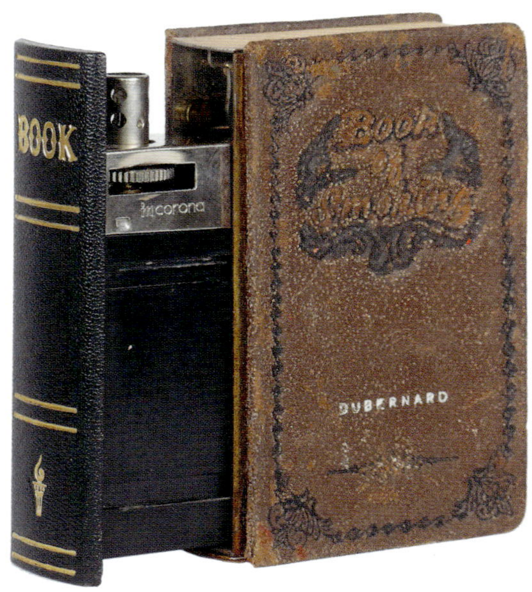

3.027
Metallfeuerzeug
mit aufklappbarem
Vorderschnitt, vier
große Messingecken
*Metal lighter with
hinged fore edge,
four large brass
corners*
Um / *Around* 1900
5,8 x 4,2 x 0,8 cm

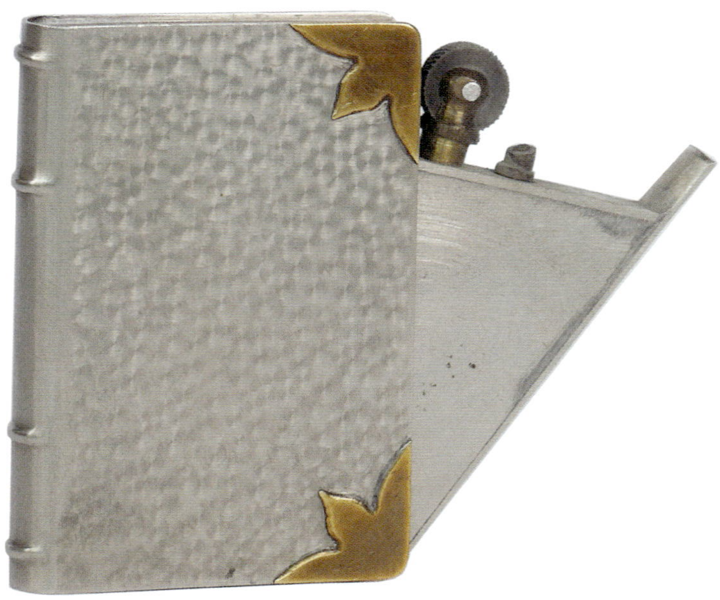

3.028
Messingfeuerzeug mit aufklappbarem Kupferrücken, vier Kupferecken
Brass lighter with hinged spine and edges made of copper
Um / *Around* 1900
5,8 x 4 x 1,3 cm

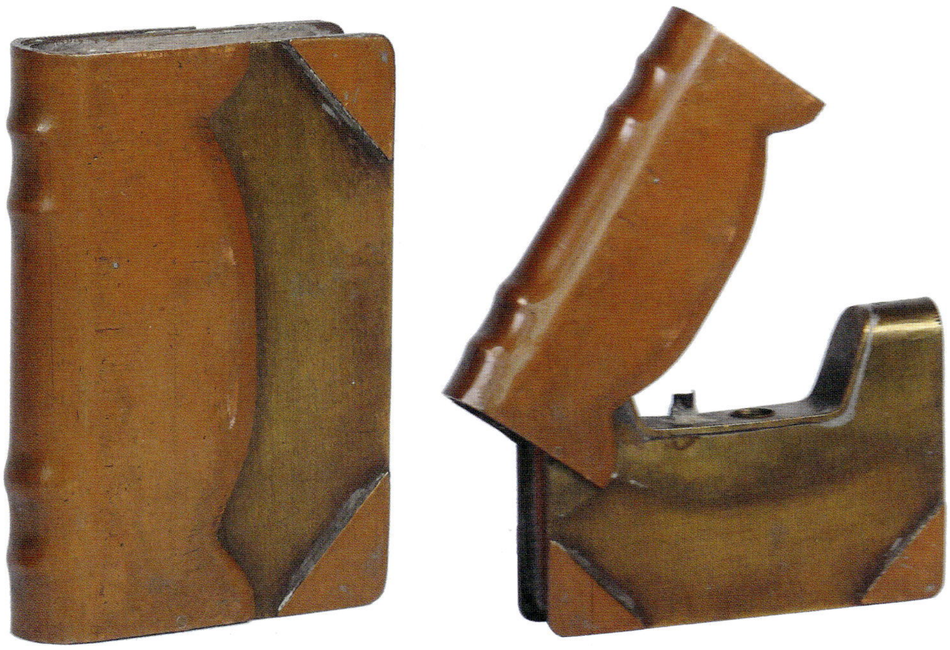

3.029
Messingfeuerzeug mit abnehmbarem Deckel, Lederüberzug, gravierte Zierlinien
Brass lighter with removable lid, leather cover, engraved ornamental lines
Um / *Around* 1900
5,6 x 4,3 x 1,1 cm

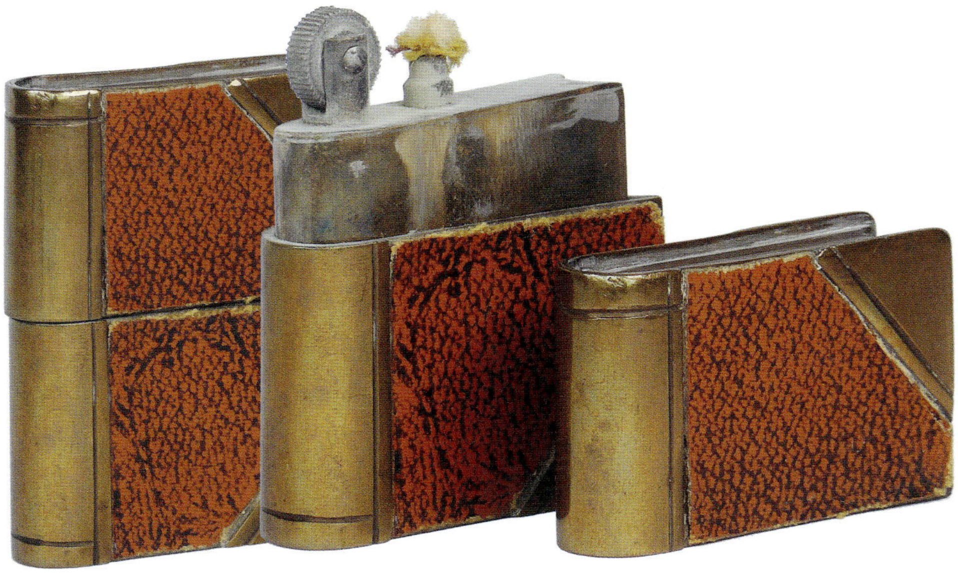

3.030
Messingfeuerzeug mit aufklappbarem Rücken, gravierte Deckel
Brass lighter with hinged spine, engraving on the front board
Um / *Around* 1900
5,3 x 3,6 x 0,9 cm

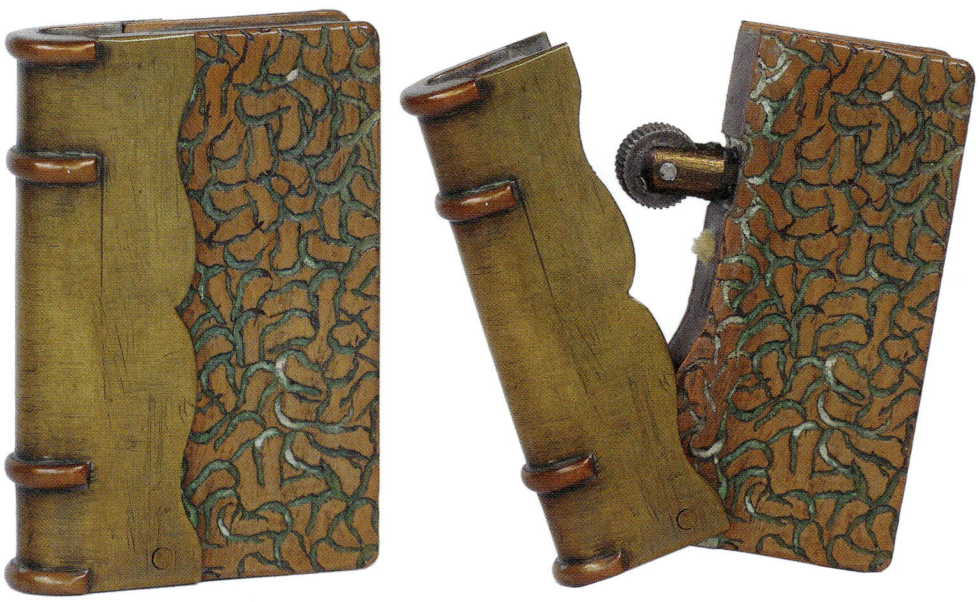

3.031
Messingfeuerzeug
mit abnehmbarem
Deckel, Deckelgravur
*Brass lighter with
removable lid, en-
graving on the cover*
Um / *Around* 1900
4,7 x 2,8 x 2,7 cm

3.032
Messingfeuerzeug
mit aufklappbarem
Vorderschnitt, Gra-
vierungen an Ecken
und Deckel sowie
Monogramm
*Brass lighter with
hinged fore edge,
engravings on the
corners and cover,
with monogram*
1918
5,1 x 3,5 x 1,2 cm

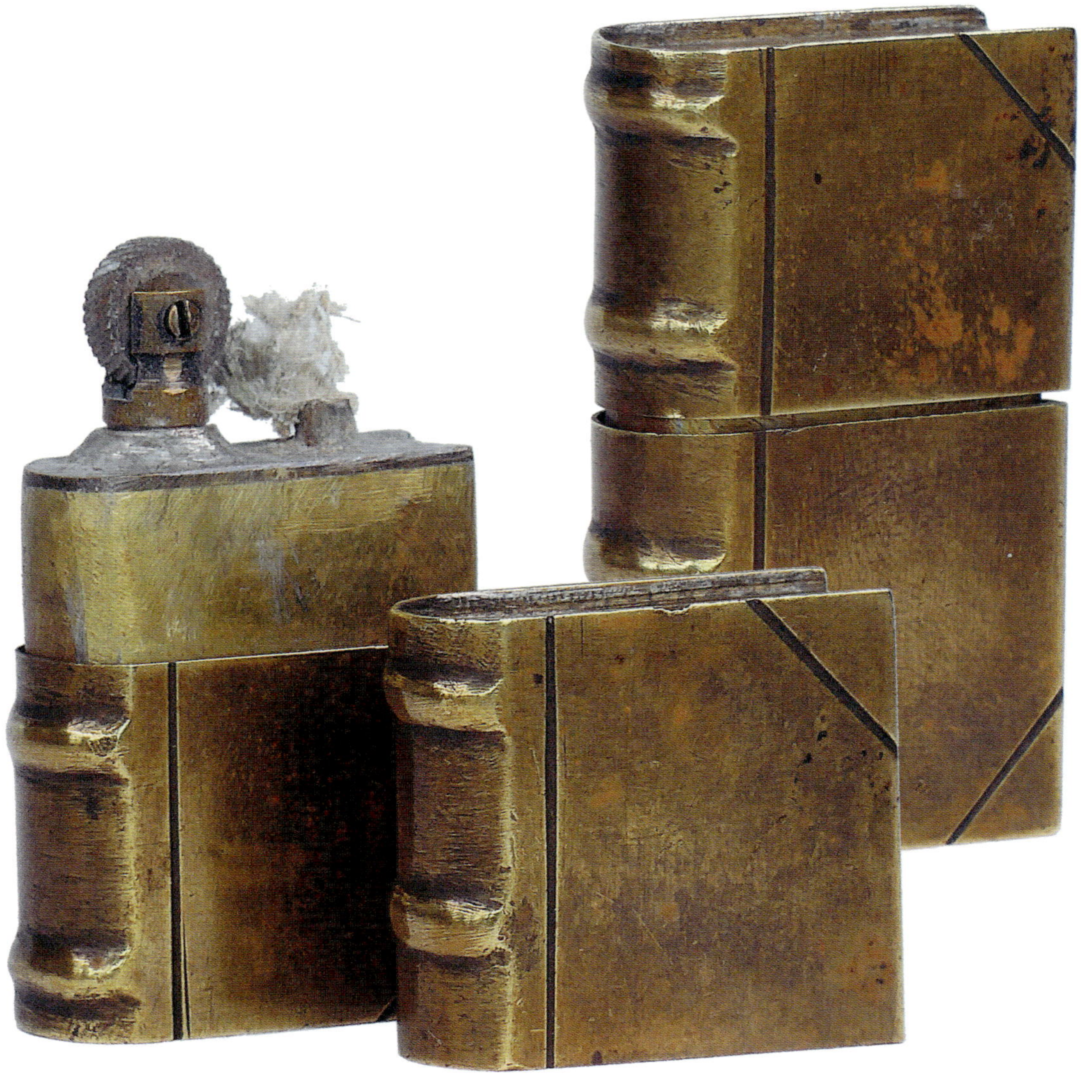

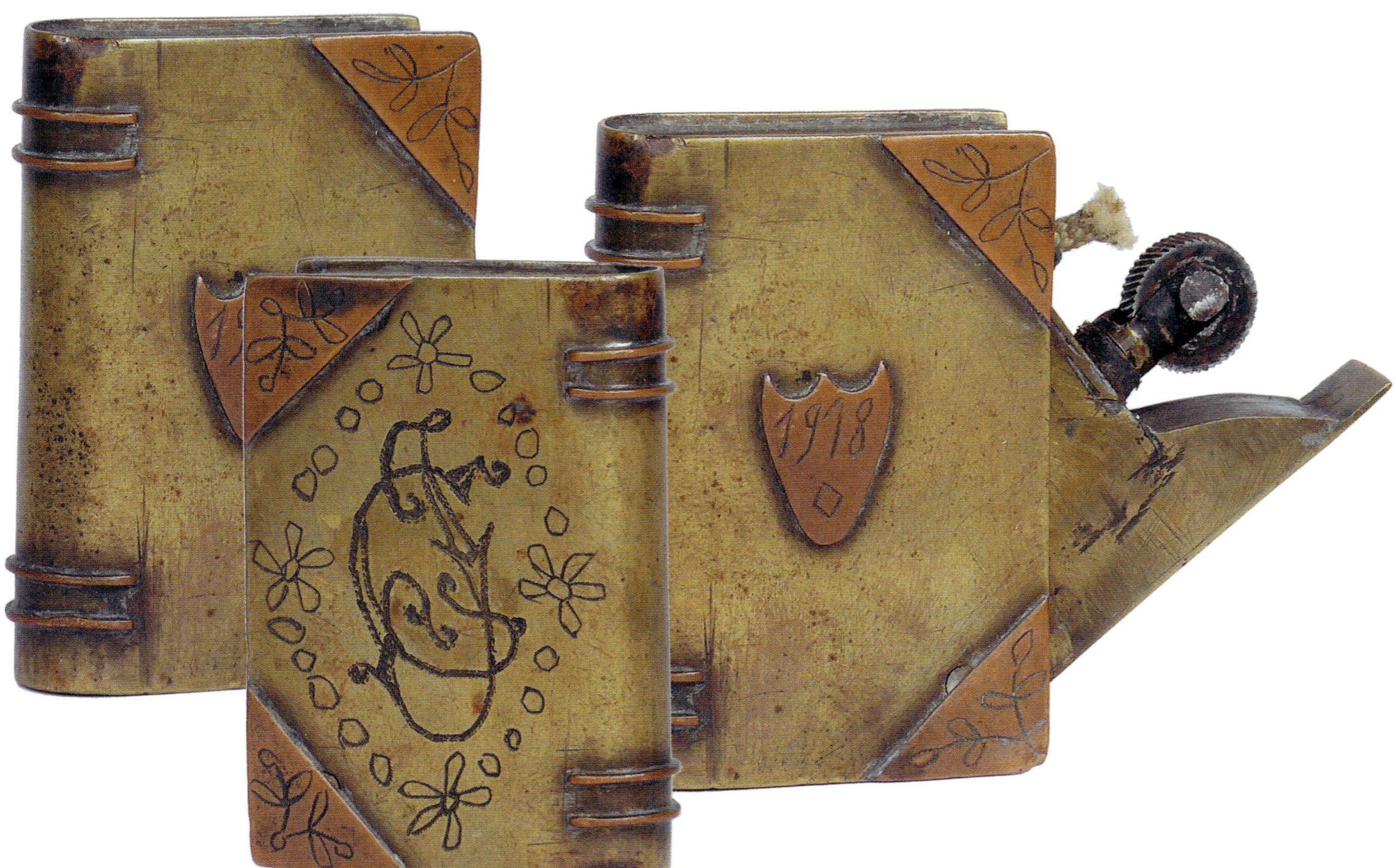

3.033
Messingfeuerzeug mit abnehmbarem Rücken, vier große Ecken
Brass lighter with removable spine, four large corners
Um / *Around* 1900
3,8 x 3,2 x 1,5 cm

3.034
Messingfeuerzeug mit abnehmbarem Deckel, vier große Ecken
Brass lighter with removable lid, four large corners
Um / *Around* 1900
6,5 x 4 x 1,1 cm

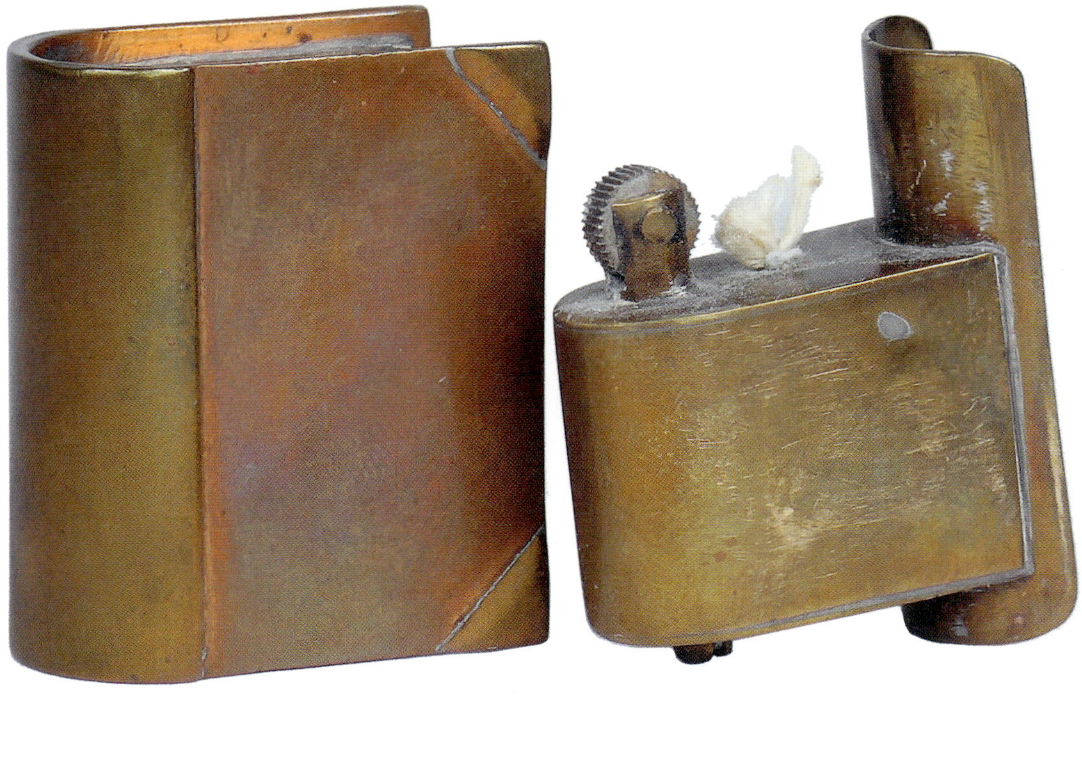

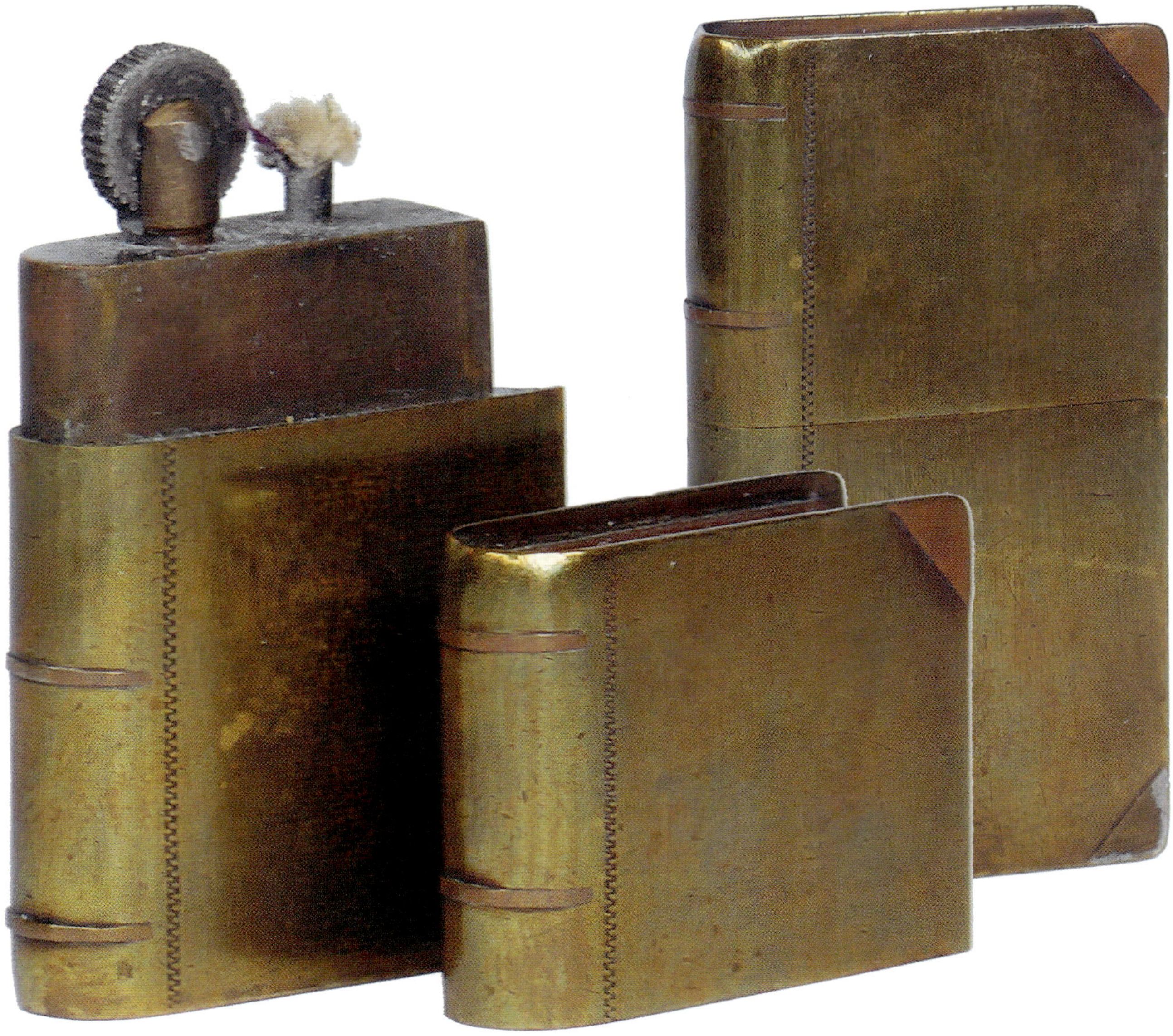

3.035
Brander Star
Lederdose mit Messingfeuerzeug, Vergoldung
Leather box with brass lighter, gilding
9 x 5,8 x 5,2 cm

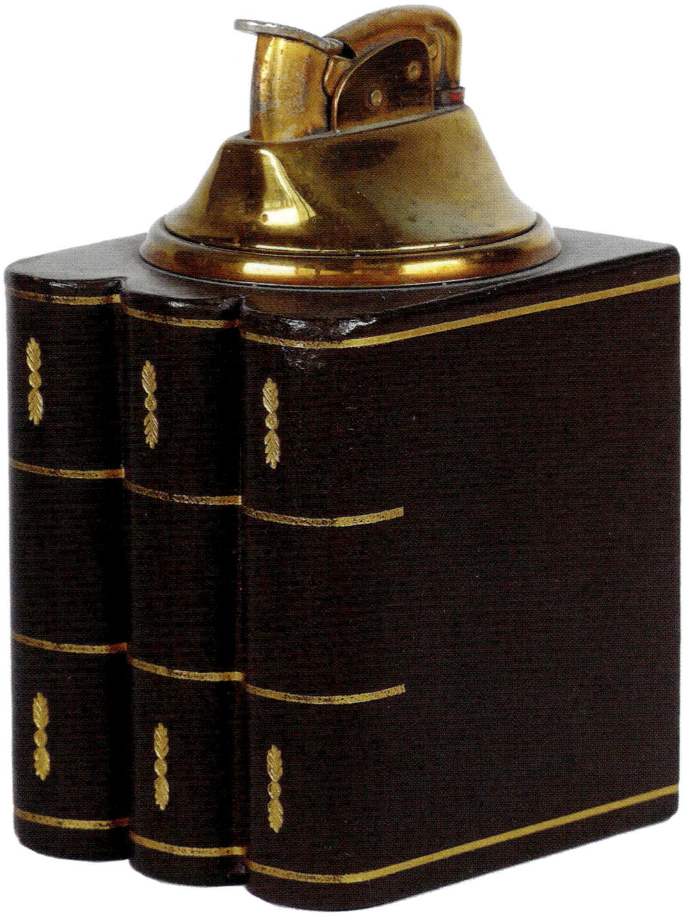

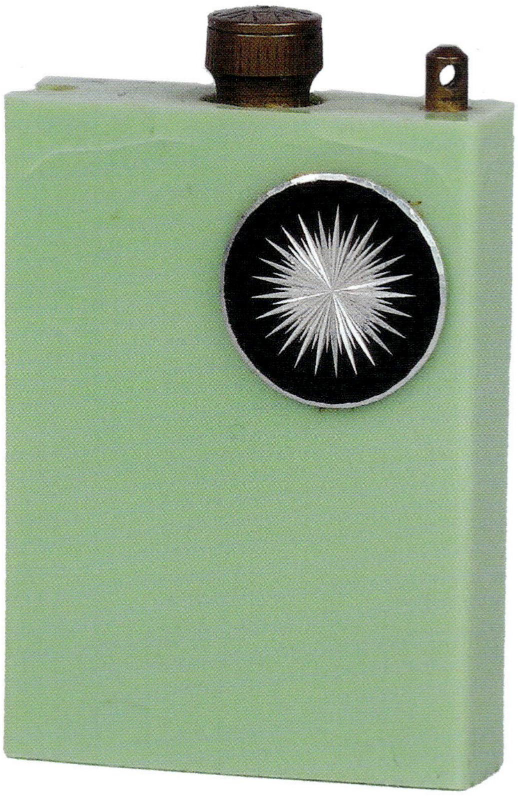

3.036
Permanent Match Feuerzeug, Kunststoff, Docht abschraubbar, Reibfläche am Vorderschnitt
Permanent Match lighter, plastic, detachable wick, friction surface on the fore edge
Zeitgenössisch / *Contemporary*
4,3 x 2,8 x 0,9 cm

3.037
Feuerzeug aus Bakelit mit abnehmbarem Rücken und Einlegearbeiten
Bakelite lighter with removable spine, with inlays
Art Déco | 4,8 x 4,2 x 1,7 cm

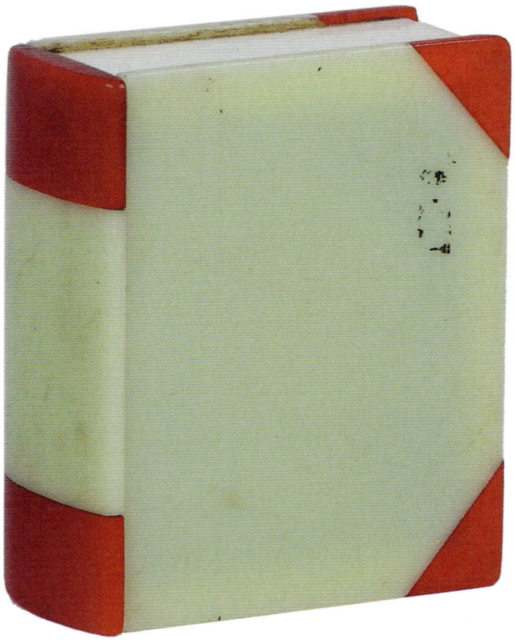

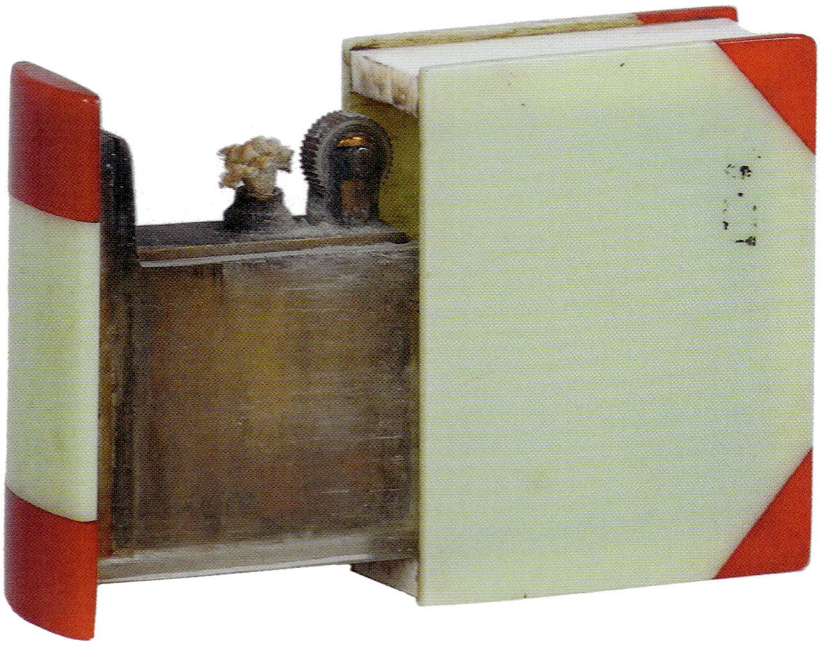

3.038
Permanent Match
Feuerzeug, Metall, abschraubbarer Docht, Reibfläche am Vorderschnitt
Permanent Match lighter, metal, detachable wick, friction surface on the fore edge.
Zeitgenössisch / *Contemporary*
4,8 x 2,9 x 1 cm

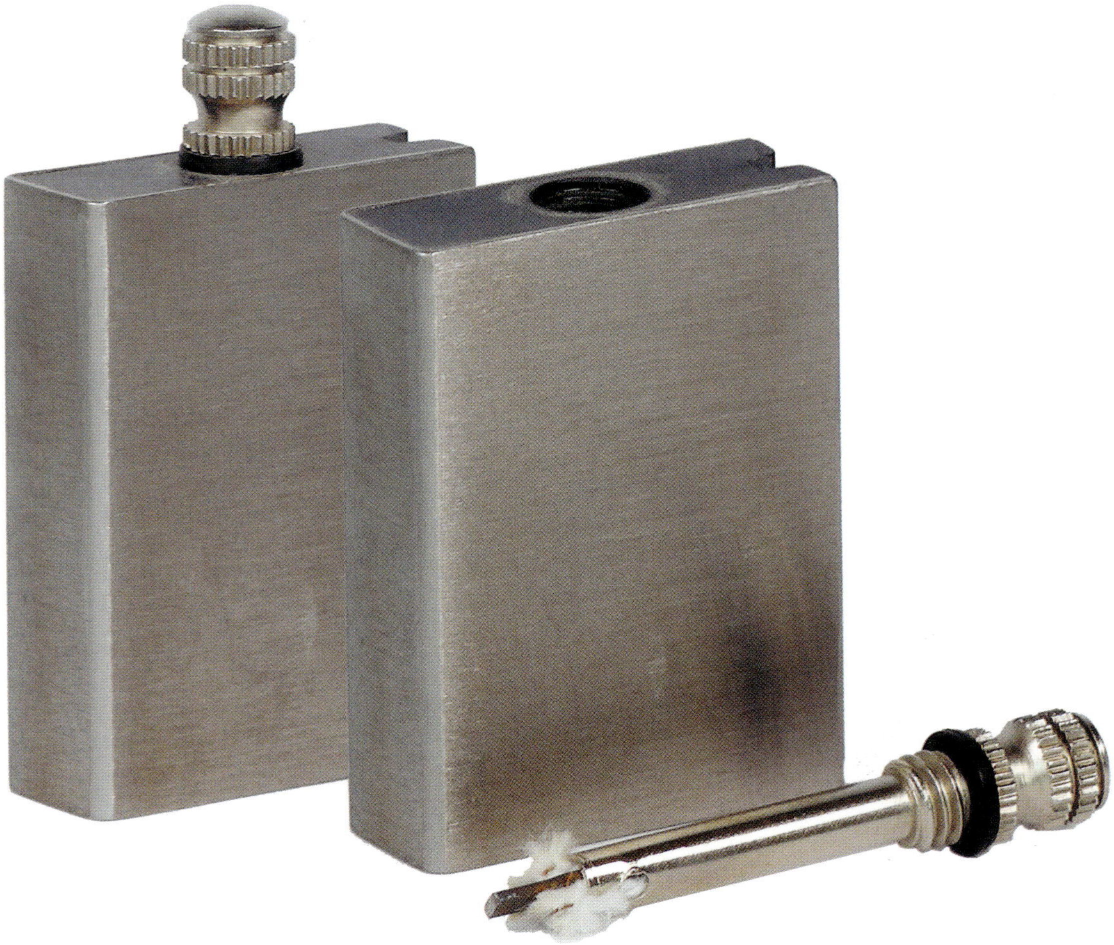

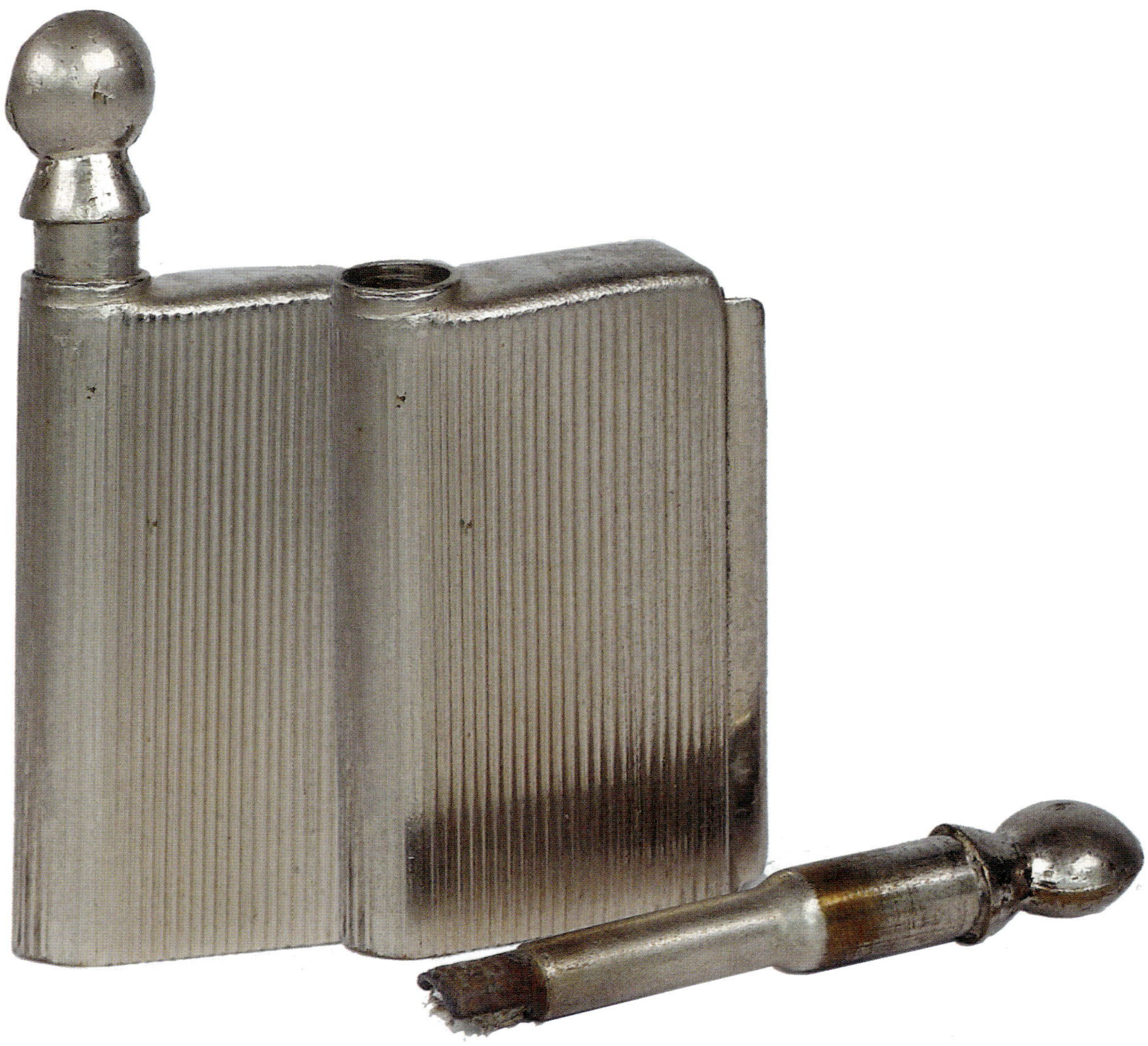

3.039
Permanent Match
Feuerzeug, versilbert, abnehmbarer Docht, Reibfläche am Vorderschnitt
Permanent Match lighter, silver-plated, removable wick, friction surface on the fore edge
Um / *Around* 1900
5,5 x 2,6 x 0,8 cm

3.040
Aufklappbare Beindose mit aufgeklebtem Bild, Reibfläche am Vorderschnitt
Hinged box made of bone with a sticker, friction surface on the fore edge
Um / *Around* 1900
5 x 3 x 1,2 cm

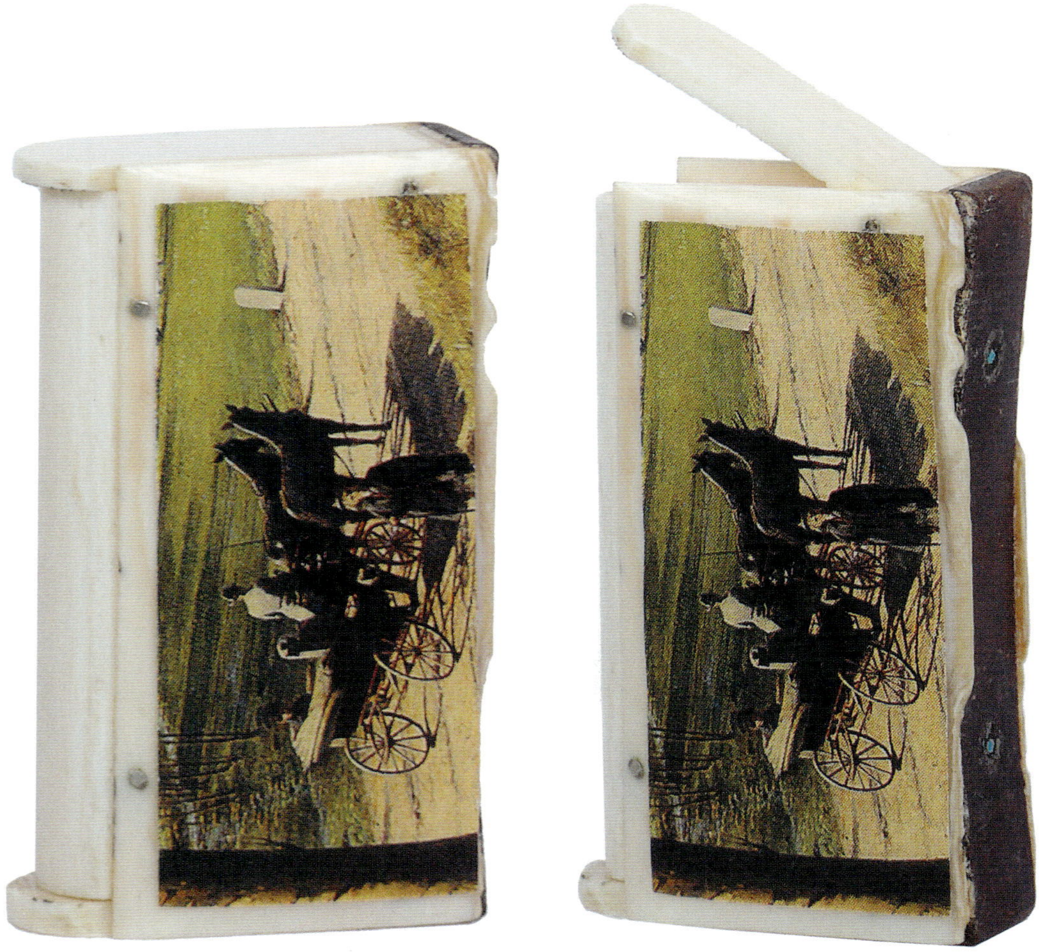

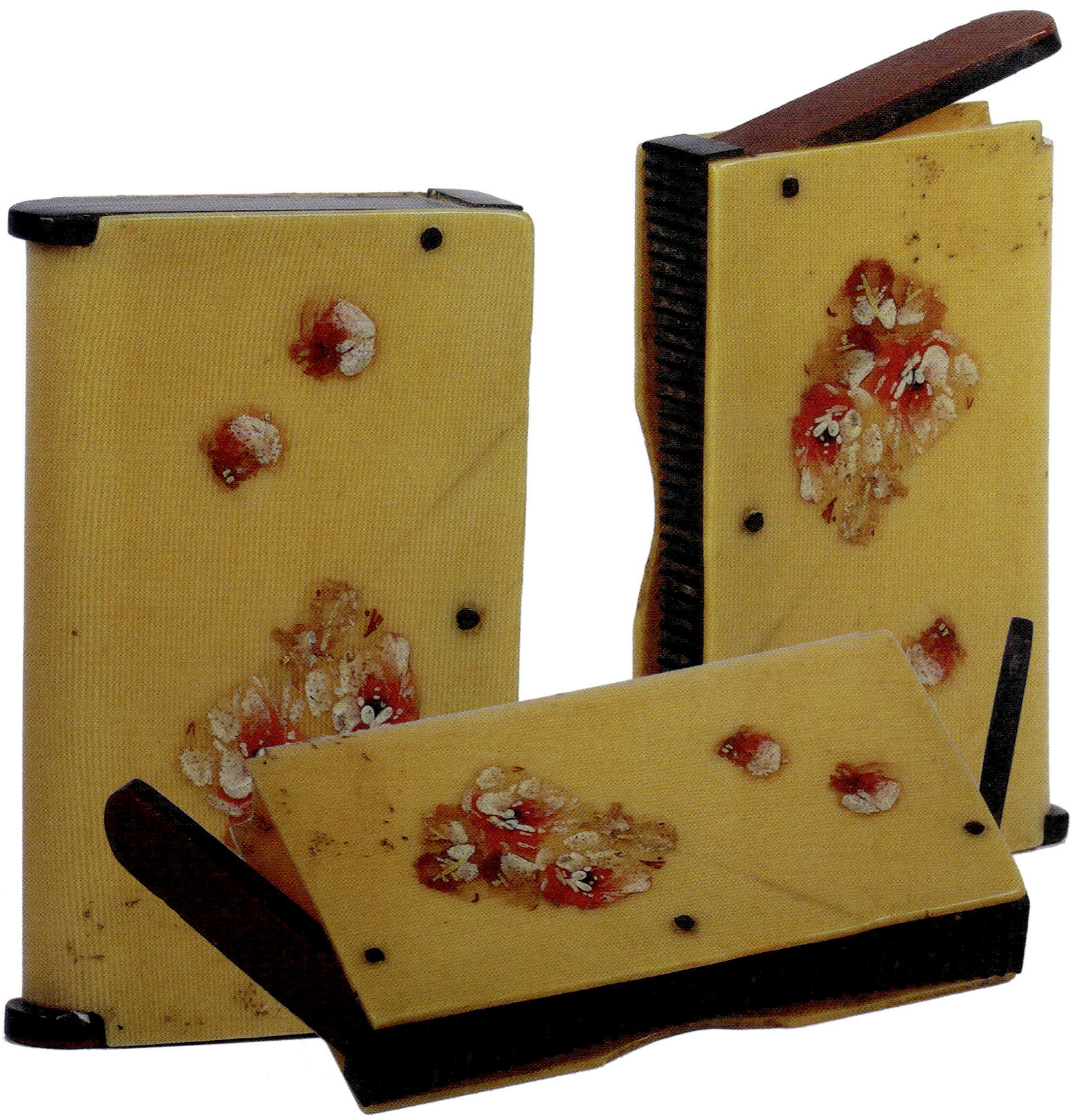

3.041
Aufklappbare Kunststoffdose, Reibfläche am Vorderschnitt
Hinged plastic box, friction surface on the fore edge
Anfang 20. Jh. / *Beginnig of the 20th century*
6,4 x 4,1 x 1,1 cm

3.042
Beindose mit auf-
klappbarem Kopf-
schnitt, Reibfläche
am Vorderschnitt
*Box made of bone
with hinged head,
friction surface on
the fore edge*
Um / *Around* 1900
6,8 x 4,5 x 1,2 cm

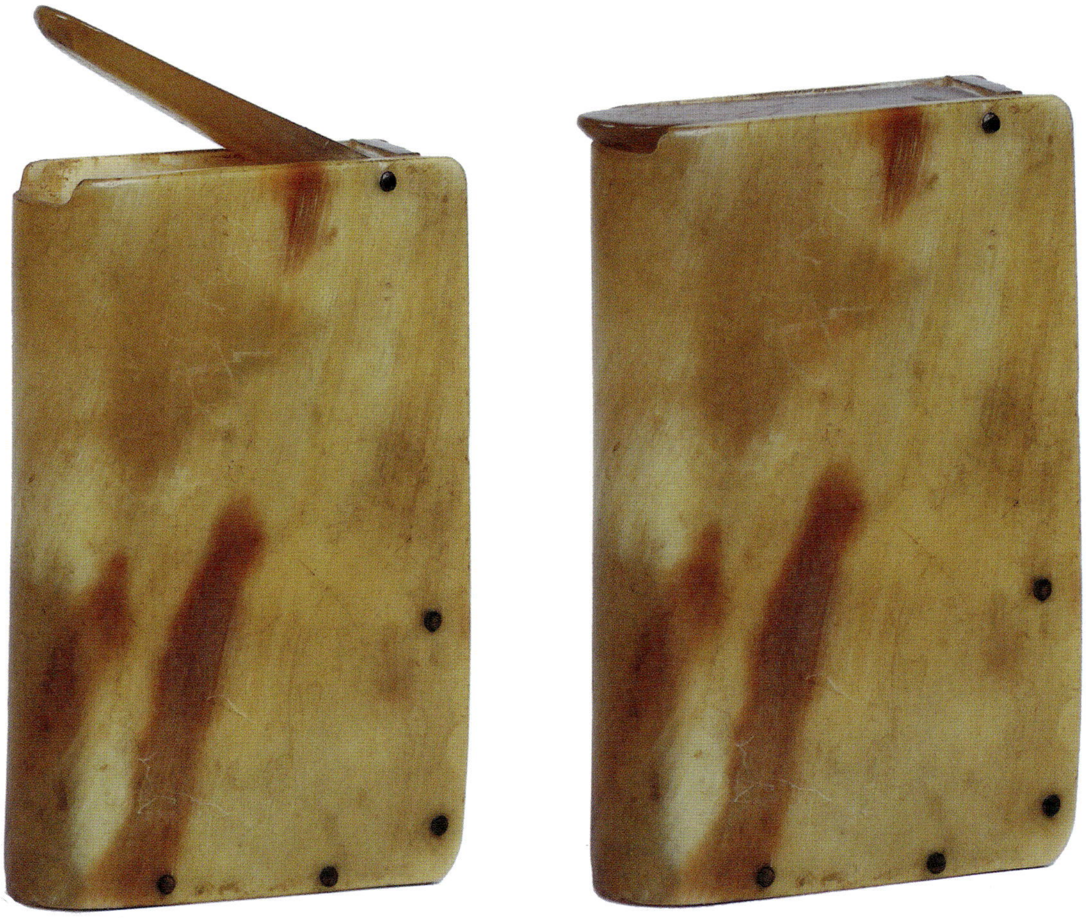

3.043
Beindose mit auf-
klappbarem Kopf-
schnitt, Reibfläche
am Vorderschnitt
*Box made of bone
with hinged head,
friction surface on
the fore edge*
Um / *Around* 1900
6,9 x 5,4 x 2,3 cm

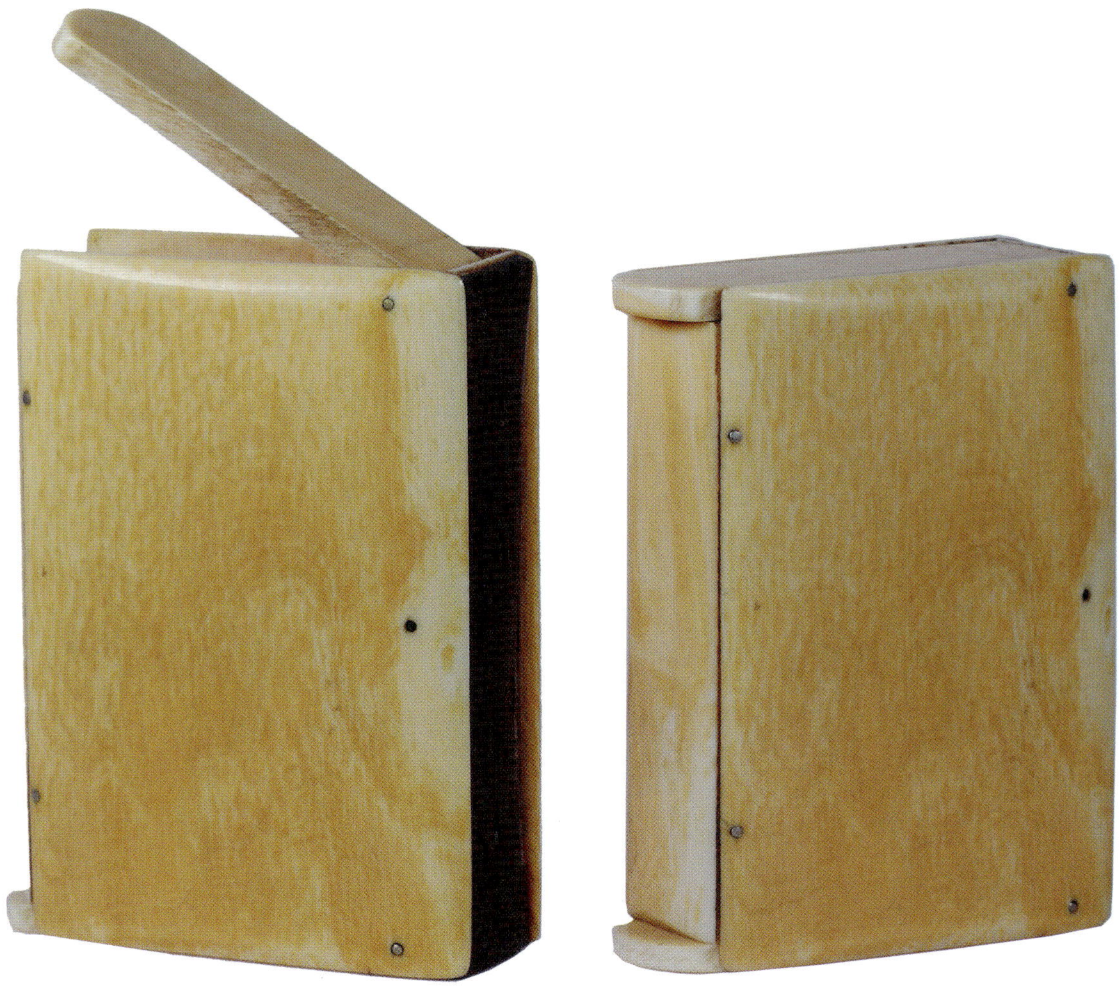

3.044
Feu Souvenir
Messingdose mit Lederrücken, ziselierte Deckel, Rückenvergoldung, dreiseitige Reibflächen
Brass box with leather spine strip, chased covers, gilt spine, friction surfaces on three sides
19. Jh. / *19th century* | 1,3 x 6,4 x 5,1 cm

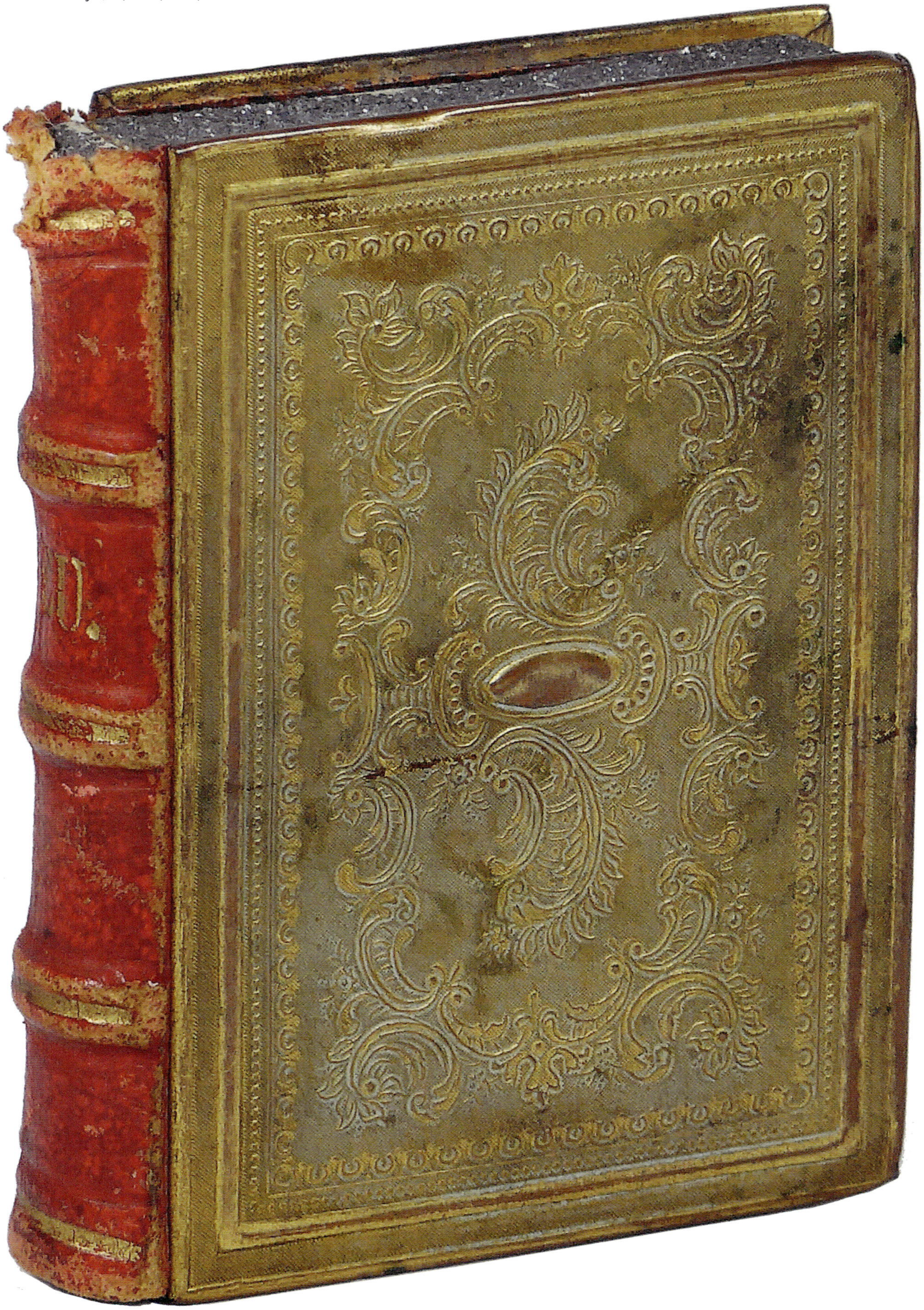

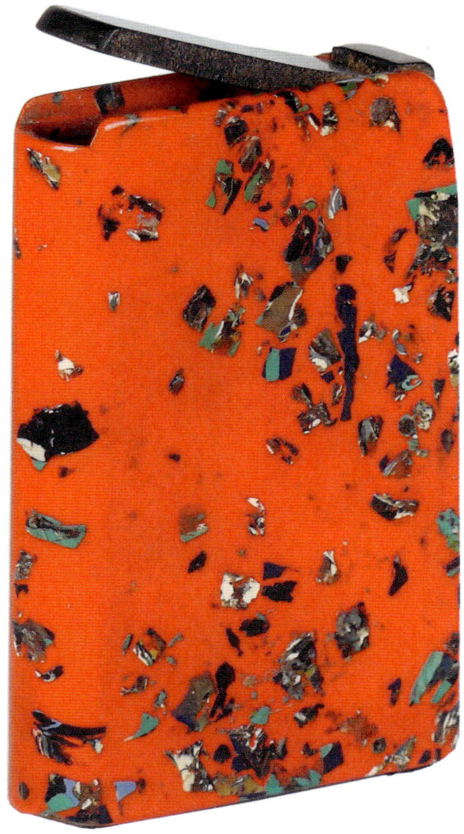

3.045
Kunststoffdose mit aufklappbarem Kopfschnitt, Feuerwehrmotive auf beiden Deckeln, Reibfläche am Vorderschnitt
Plastic box with hinged head, fire brigade motifs on both covers, friction surface on the fore edge
Ende 19. Jh. / *19th century*
7 x 4,5 x 1,3 cm

3.046
Kunststoffdose mit aufklappbarem Kopfschnitt, Reibfläche am Vorderschnitt
Plastic box with hinged head, friction surface on the fore edge
Um / *Around* 1900
6,1 x 4 x 1,1 cm

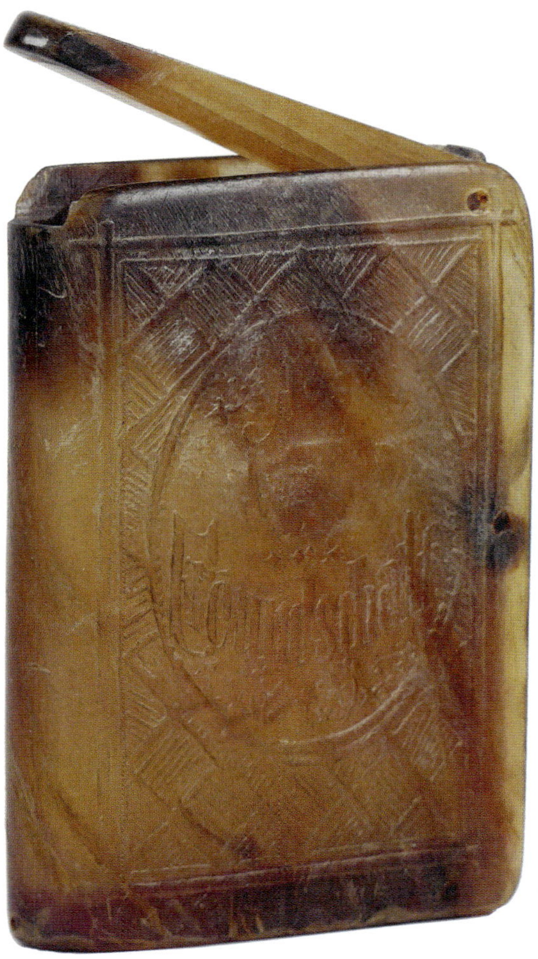

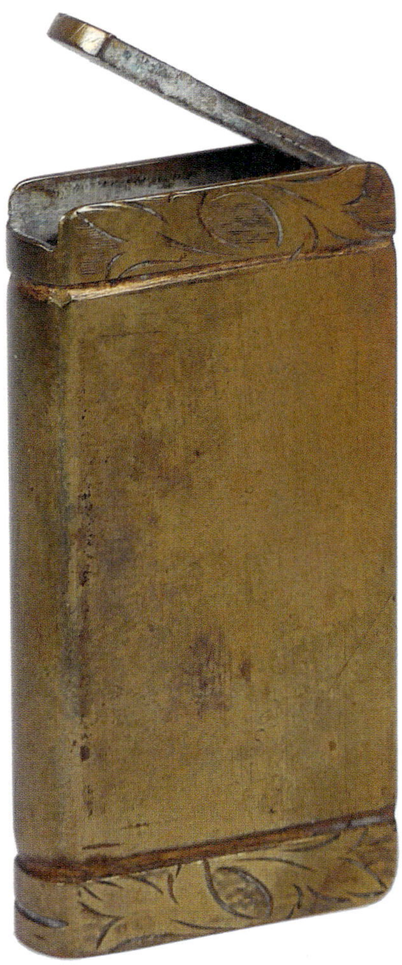

3.047
Freundschaft Glück auf
Friendship Good Luck
Kunststoffdose mit aufklappbarem Kopfschnitt, Reliefszene mit Mutter und Kind, Reibfläche am Vorderschnitt
Plastic box with hinged head, reliefed image of a mother and child, friction surface on the fore edge
Ende 19. Jh. / *End of 19th century*
6,7 x 5 x 1,4 cm

3.048
Messingdose mit aufklappbarem Kopfschnitt, Gravur auf Vorder- und Hinterdeckel, Reibfläche am Innenkopfschnittdeckel
Brass box with hinged head, engraving on the front and rear board, friction surface on the head
Um / *Around* 1900
5,8 x 2,9 x 0,9 cm

3.049
Holzdose mit aufklappbarem Kopfschnitt, Deckelgravur, Reibfläche am Fußschnitt
Wooden box with hinged head, engraving on the covers, friction surface on the foot edge
Um / *Around* 1900 | 7 x 4,5 x 2,2 cm

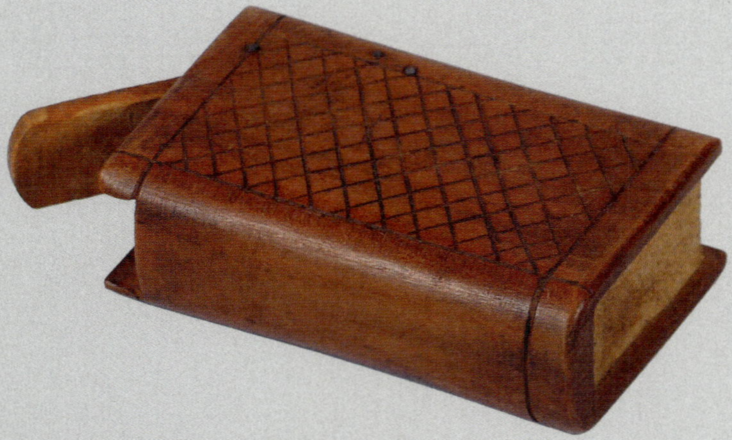

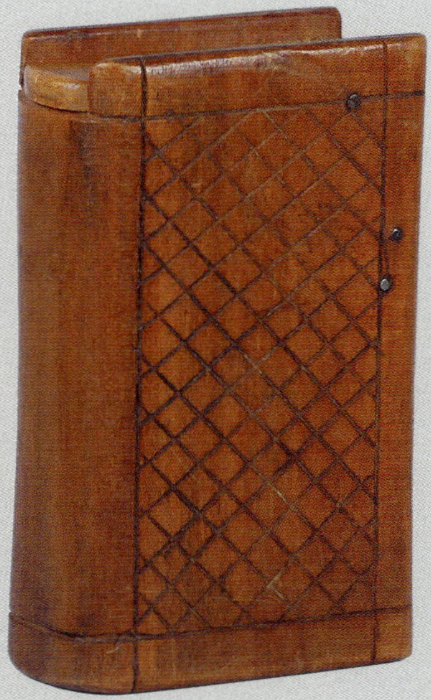

3.050
Holzdose mit aufklappbarem Kopf- und Fußschnitt, Blumen- und Schwalbenmotiv, Reibfläche am Vorderschnitt
Wooden box with hinged head and foot edges, painted flowers and swallows, friction surface on the fore edge
Um / *Around* 1900
6 x 4,3 x 1,3 cm

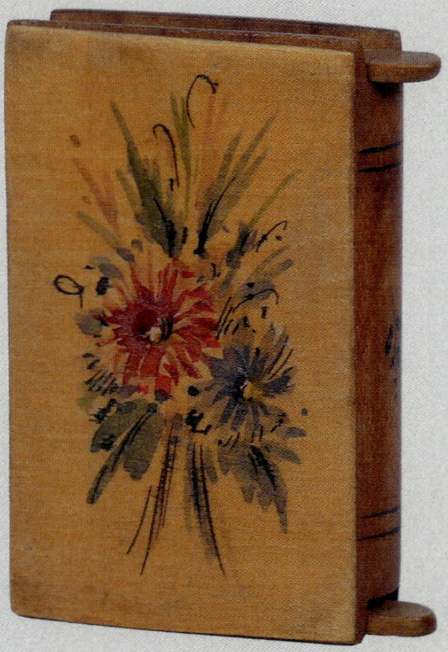

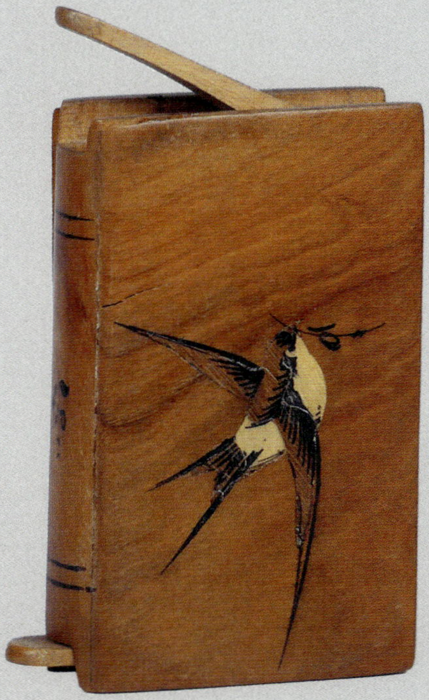

3.051
Holzdose mit aufklappbarem Kopf- und Fußschnitt, gemaltes Schwalbenmotiv, Reibfläche am Vorderschnitt
Wooden box with hinged head and foot edge, painting of a swallow, friction surface on the fore edge
Um / *Around* 1900
4,9 x 3,9 x 1,1 cm

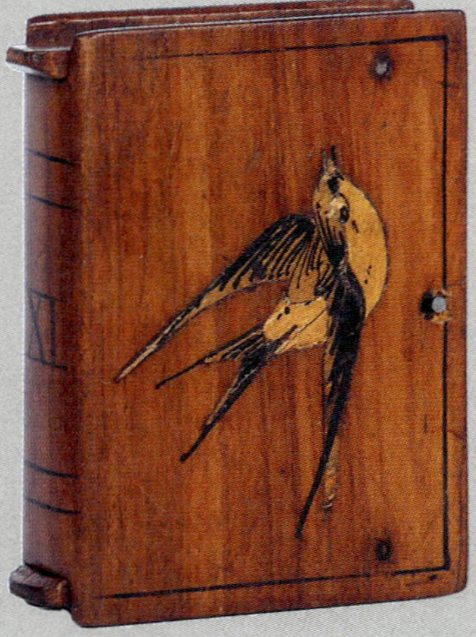

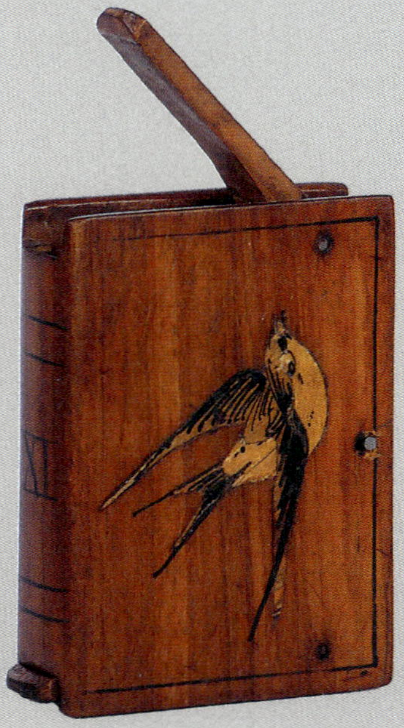

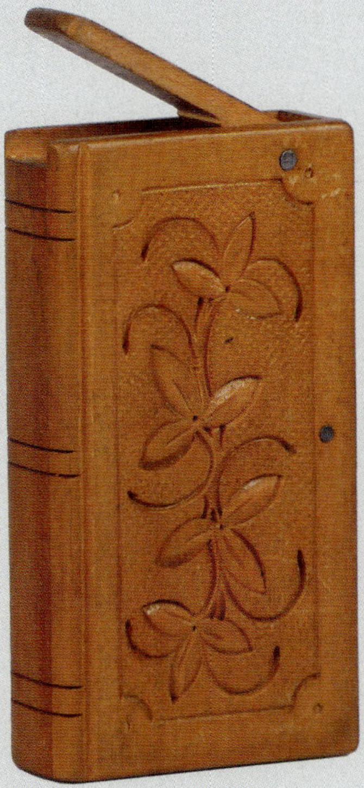

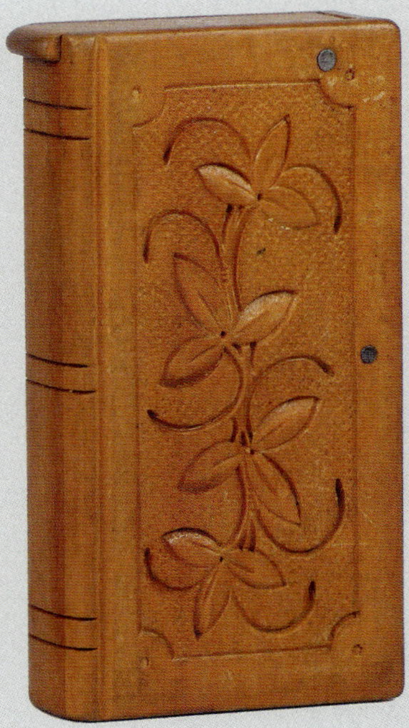

3.052
Holzdose mit aufklappbarem Kopfschnitt, geschnitztes Blumenmotiv, Reibfläche am Fußschnitt
Wooden box with hinged head, carved flower pattern, friction surface on the foot edge
Anfang 20. Jh. / *Beginning of the 20th century*
6,8 x 3,8 x 1,4 cm

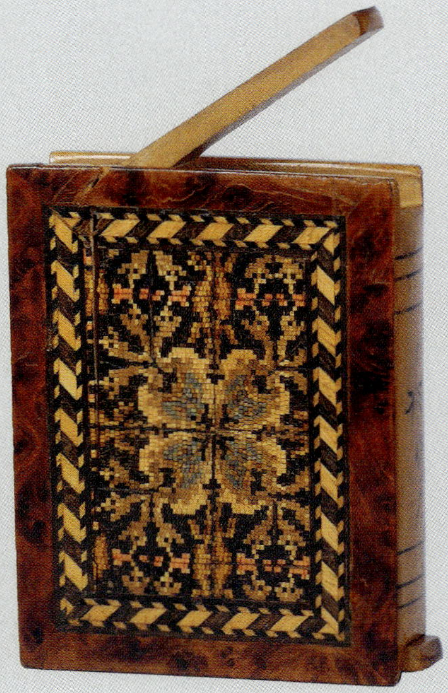

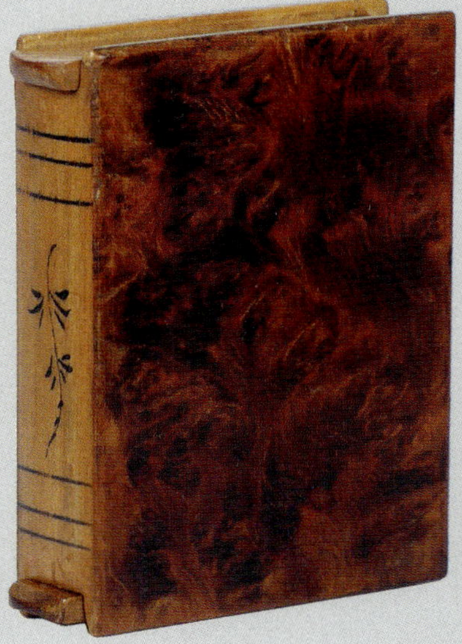

3.053
Wurzelholzdose mit aufklappbarem Kopf- und Fußschnitt, Holzeinlegearbeit am Vorderdeckel
Root wood box with hinged head and foot edge, wooden marquetry on the front board
Um / *Around* 1900
6 x 5 x 1,3 cm

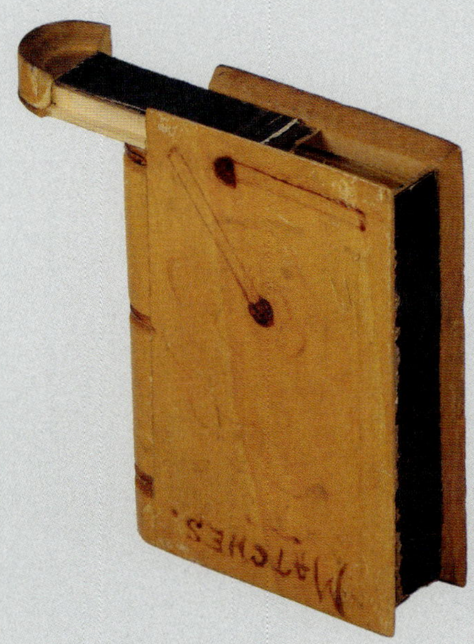

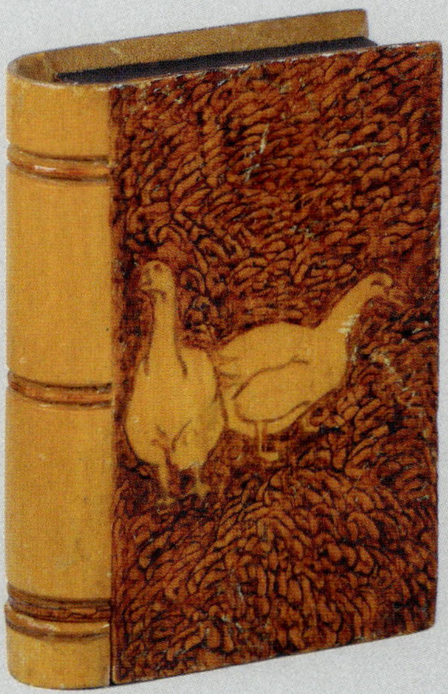

3.054
Matches
Holzdose mit Schieber am Fußschnitt, geschnitztes Gänsemotiv und Streichholzmotiv, dreiseitige Reibflächen
Wooden box with slider at the foot edge, carved gooses and matches, friction surfaces on three sides
Anfang 20. Jh. / *Beginning of the 20th century*
7 x 5,2 x 1,7 cm

3.055
Feu
Lederdose mit Einschub, Futter Marmorpapier, Seidenstickerei, Titelvergoldung
Leather box with drawer, marbled paper lining, silk embroidery, gilt title
19. Jh. / *19th century*
1,3 x 7,5 x 5,7 cm

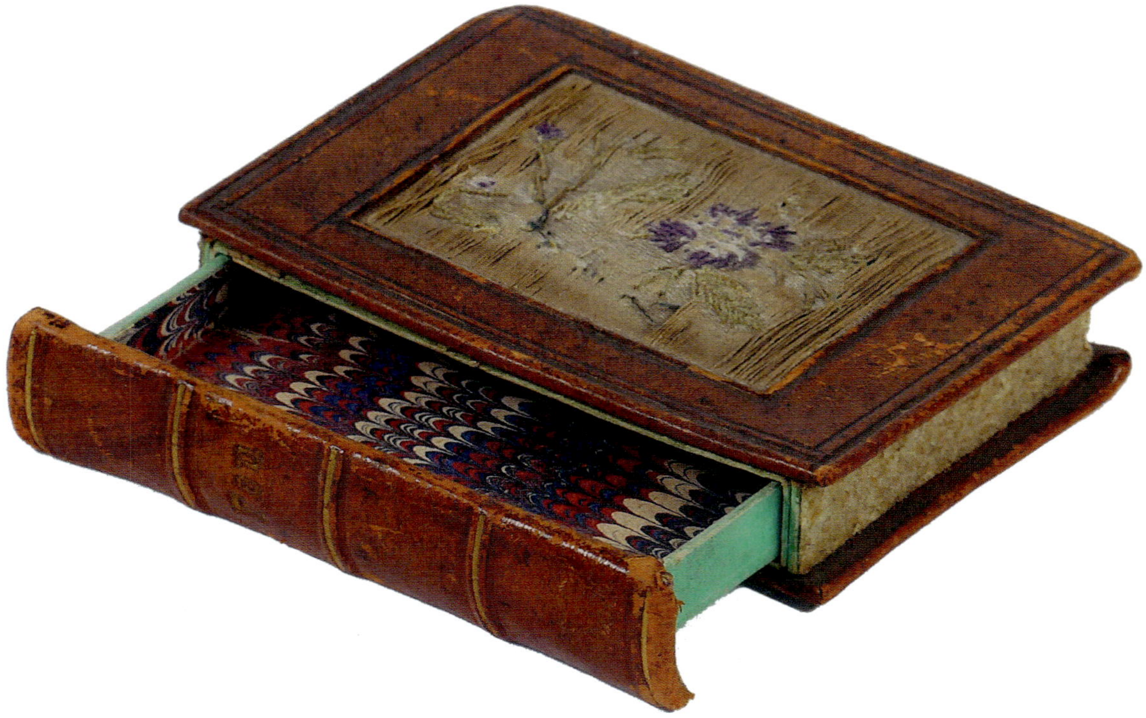

3.056
IH
Zwillingslederdose mit Hals, Vergoldungen, Reibflächen am Kopf- und Fußschnitt
Twin leather box with neck, gildings, friction surfaces on the head and foot edges
Um / *Around* 1900
2 x 5 x 4,6 cm

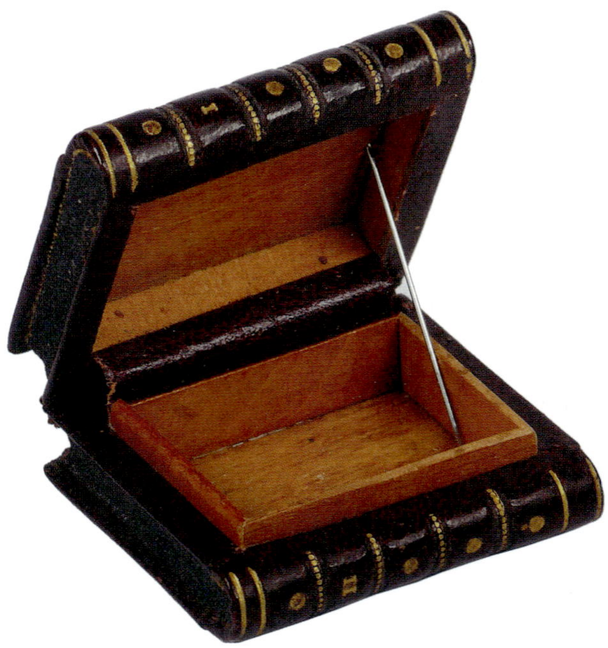

3.057
Lederdose mit eingelegter ovaler Gobelinstickerei, Vergoldungen, dreiseitige Reibflächen
Leather box with inserted oval Gobelin embroidery, gildings, friction surfaces on three sides
19. Jh. / *19th century*
1,1 x 5,8 x 4 cm

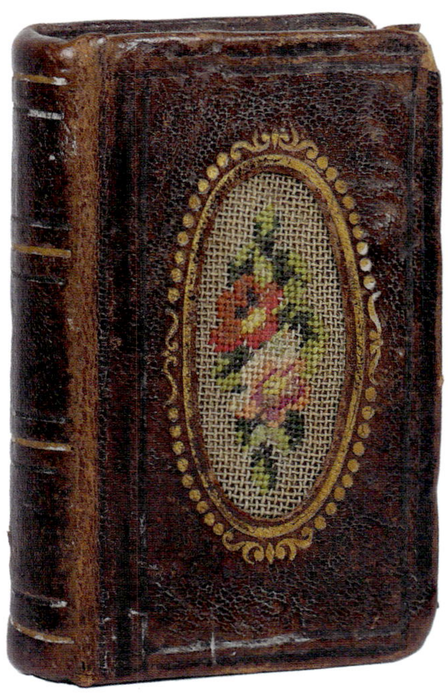

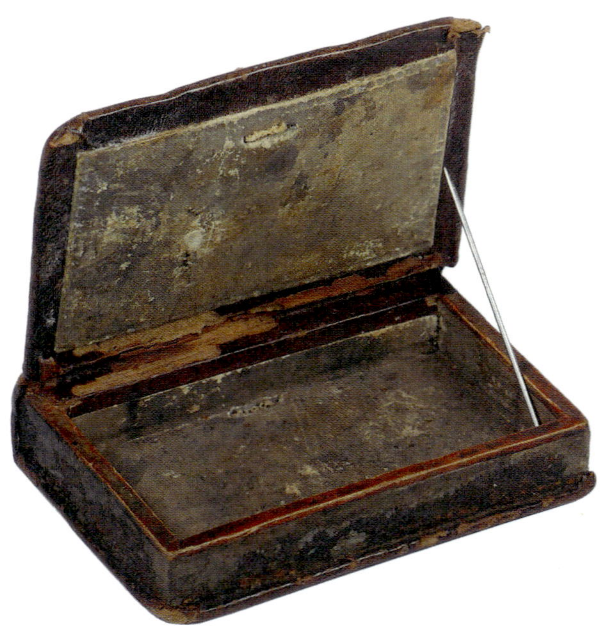

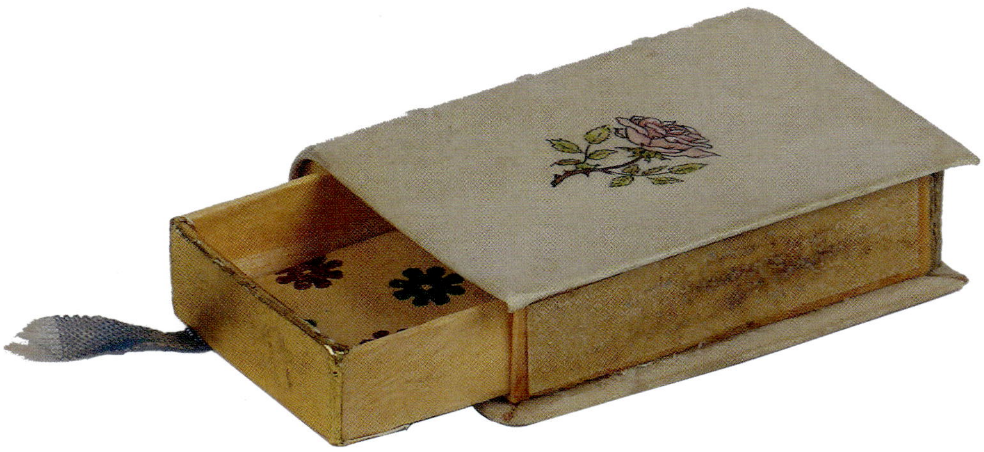

3.058
Pergamentschachtel, Deckel mit Blumenmotiv, Goldschnitt, Zugbänder, Reibfläche am Vorderschnitt
Parchment box, flowers on the front board, gilt edges, drawstring, friction surface on the fore edge
Mitte 20. Jh. / *Mid of the 20th century*
1,5 x 5,9 x 4,5 cm

3.059
Blechdose mit aufklappbarem Vorderschnitt, Reibfläche am Vorder- und Fußschnitt
Tin box with hinged fore edge, friction surface at the fore and foot edges
Um / *Around* 1900 | 5,8 x 5,7 x 1,9 cm

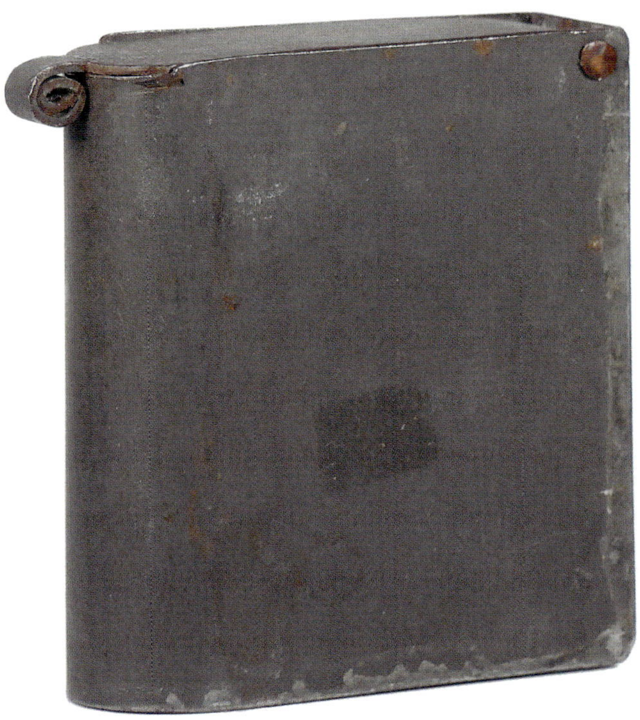

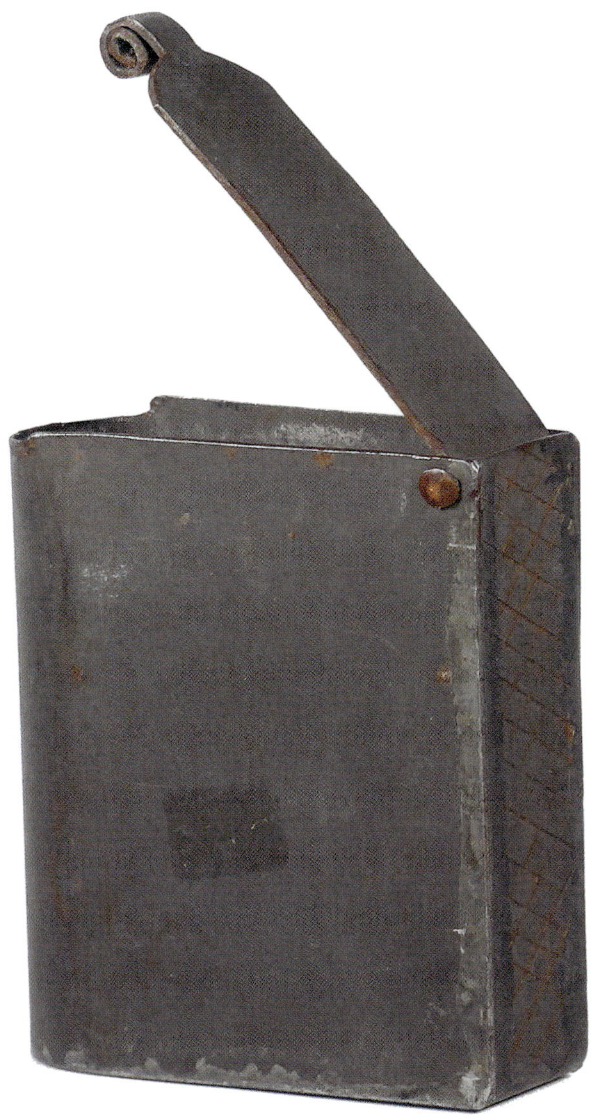

3.060
Bakelitdose mit aufklappbarem Kopfschnitt, Rücken- und Deckelverzierung, Reibfläche am Vorderschnitt
Bakelite box with hinged head, spine and cover with ornaments, friction surface on the fore edge
Um / *Around* 1900
6,8 x 4,3 x 1,2 cm

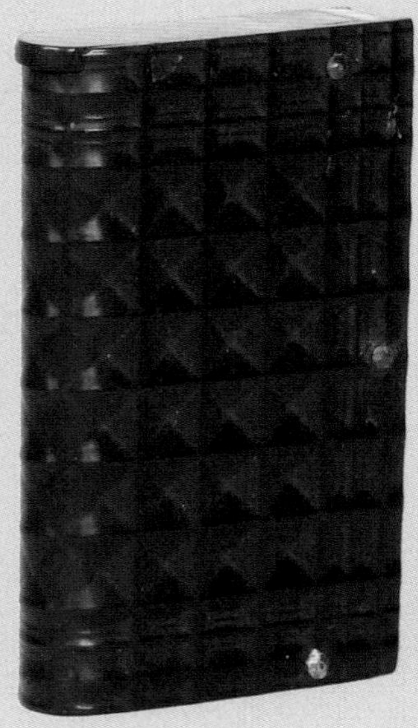

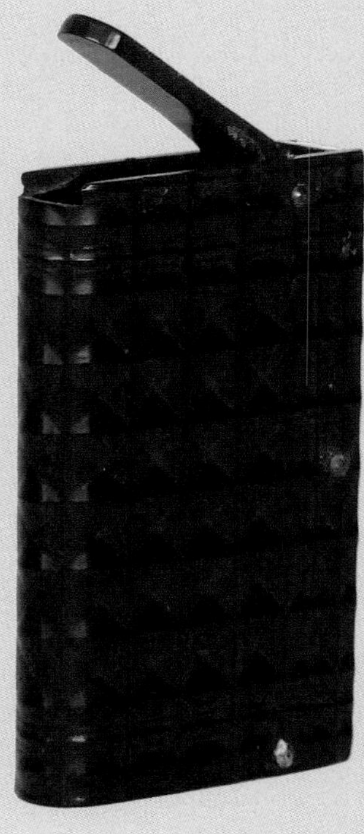

3.061
Bakelitdose mit aufklappbarem Kopfschnitt, Beschriftung, Rücken- und Deckelverzierungen, Reibfläche am Vorderdeckel
Bakelite box with hinged head, spine and cover with ornaments, friction surface on the fore edge
Um / *Around* 1900
6,5 x 4 x 1,3 cm

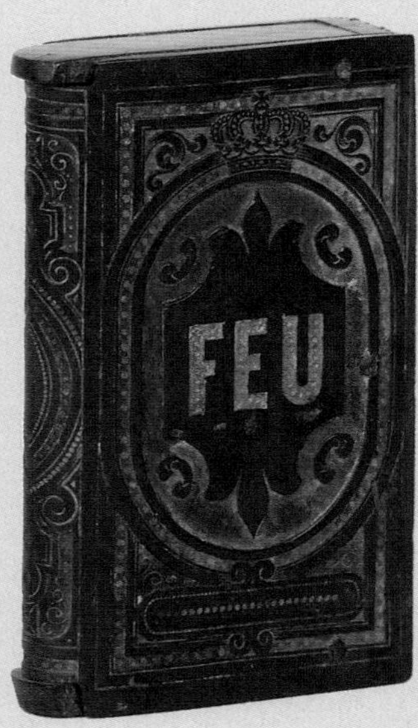

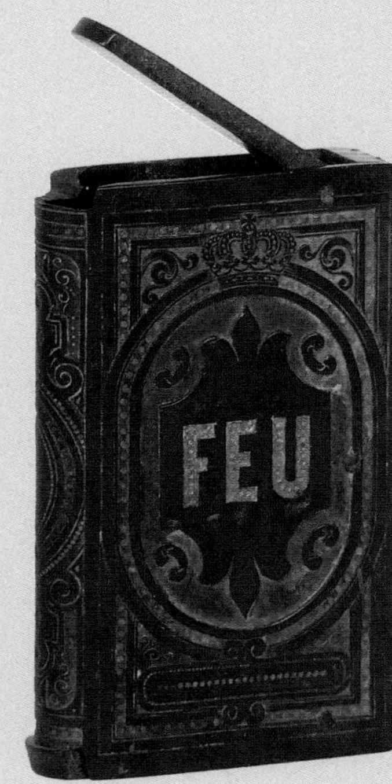

3.062
Feu, New York, Hamburg, G.W. Co.
Bakelitdose mit aufklappbarem Kopfschnitt, Rücken- und Deckelbeschriftung, Reibfläche am Vorderschnitt
Bakelite box with hinged head, lettering on the spine and cover, friction surface on the fore edge
Um / *Around* 1900
5 x 3,8 x 1,2 cm

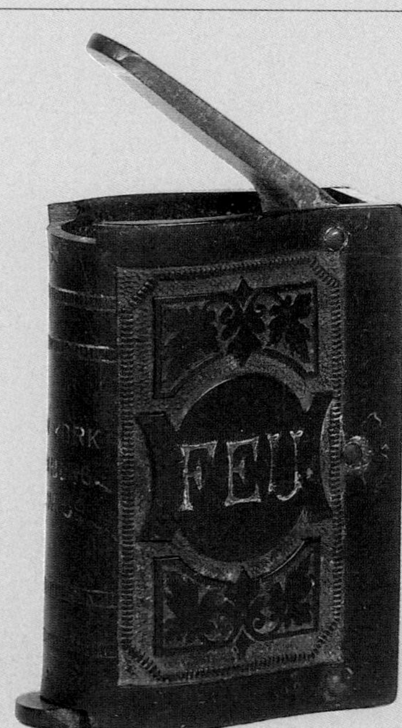

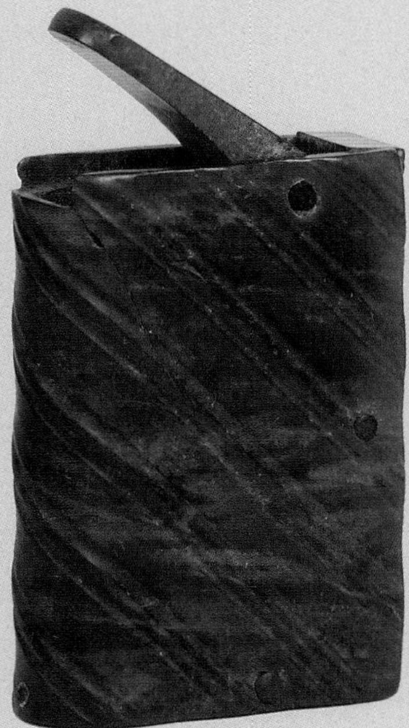
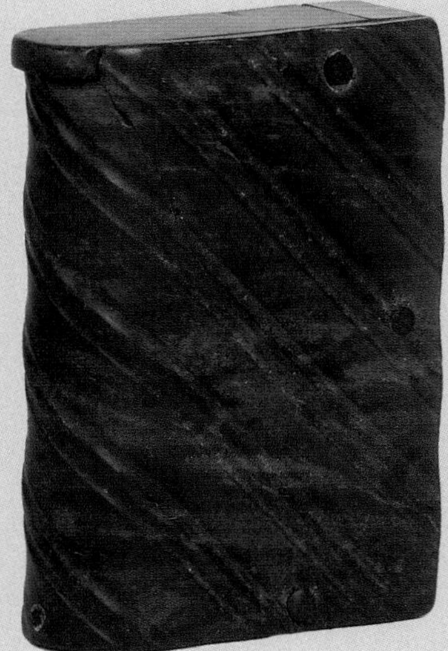

3.063
Bakelitdose mit aufklappbarem Kopfschnitt, Rücken- und Deckelverzierung, Reibfläche am Vorderschnitt
Bakelite box with hinged head, spine and cover ornaments, friction surface on the fore edge
Um / *Around* 1900
4,5 x 3,3 x 1,2 cm

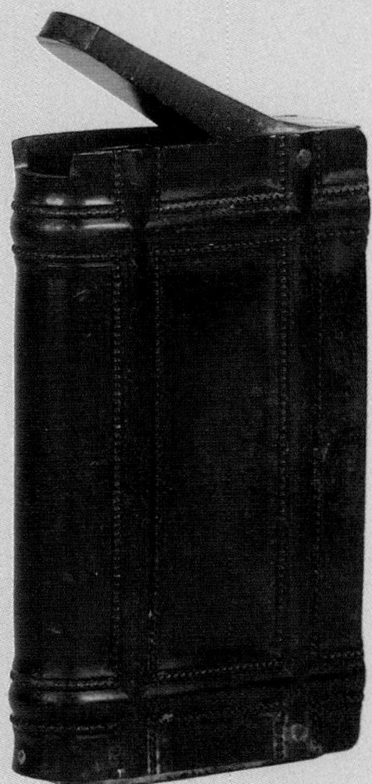
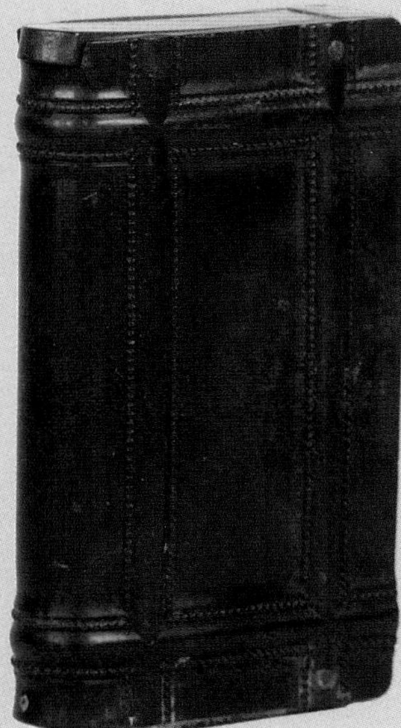

3.064
Bakelitdose mit aufklappbarem Kopfschnitt, Rücken- und Deckelbeschriftung, Reibfläche am Vorderschnitt
Bakelite box with hinged head, lettering on the spine and cover, friction surface on the fore edge
Um / *Around*1900
6,9 x 4 x 1,3 cm

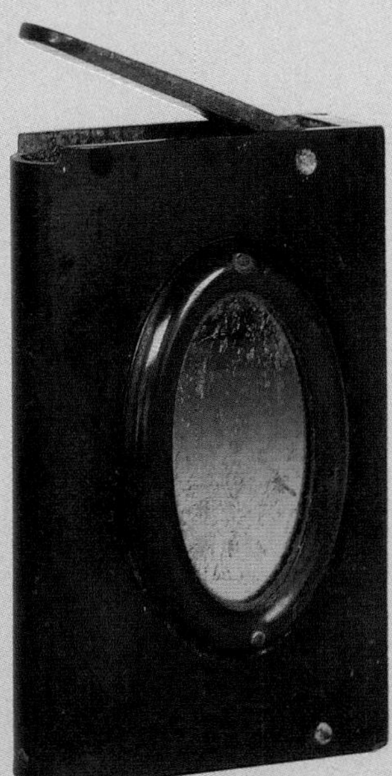
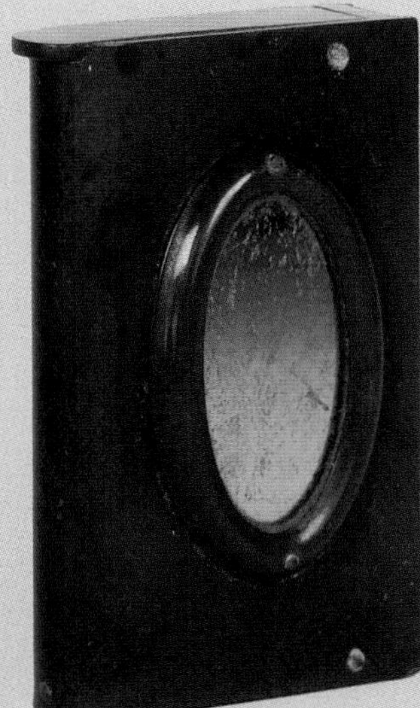

3.065
Bakelitdose mit ovalem Spiegel, aufklappbarer Kopfschnitt, Reibfläche am Vorderschnitt
Bakelite box with oval mirror, hinged head, friction surface on the fore edge
Um / *Around* 1900
6,4 x 4 x 1,2 cm

3.066
Feu
Bakelitdose mit aufklappbarem Kopfschnitt, Rücken- und Deckelverzierung, Reibfläche am Vorderschnitt
Bakelite box with hinged head, ornaments on the spine and cover, friction surface on the fore edge
Um / *Around* 1900
6,6 x 4,2 x 1,3 cm

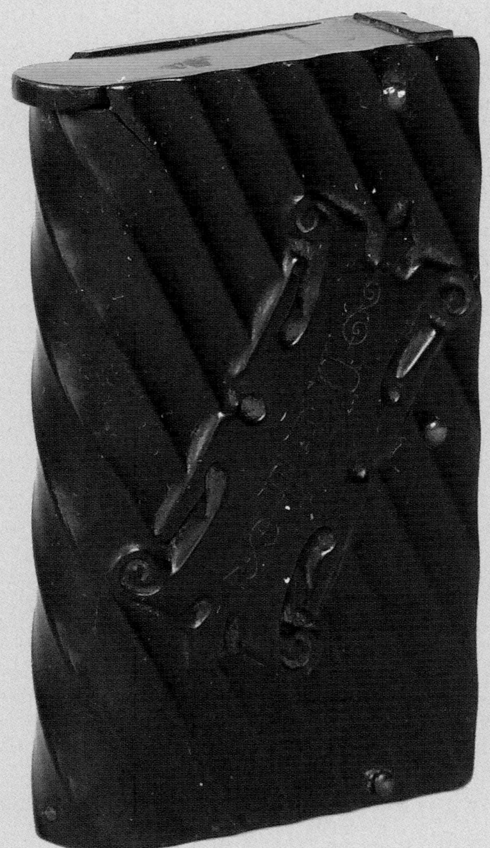

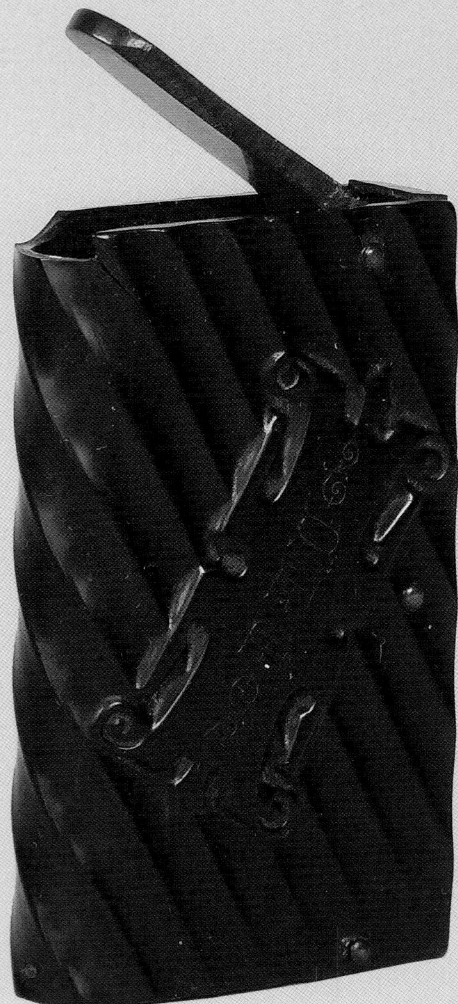

3.067
E. VII. Honi soit qui mal y pense, englischer Hosenbandorden / *Motto oft the nobel Order of the Garter*
Bakelitdose, Kopf- und Fußschnitt aufklappbar, Porträt König Eduard VII, Schriftzug auf dem Hinterdeckel
Bakelite box with hinged head and foot edge, portrait of king Edward VII, lettering on the back cover
Um / *Around* 1900
5 x 3,7 x 1,2 cm

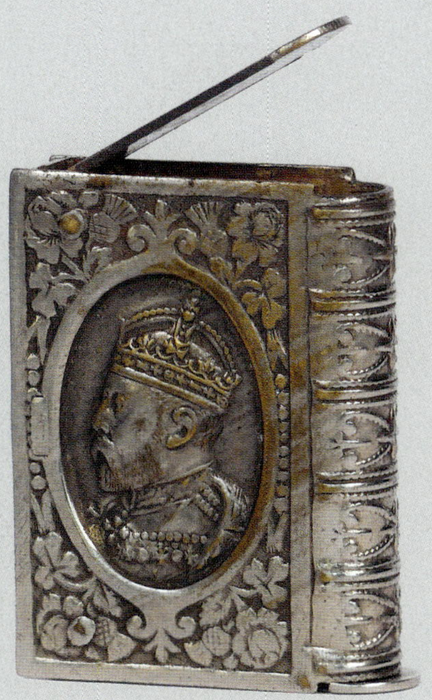

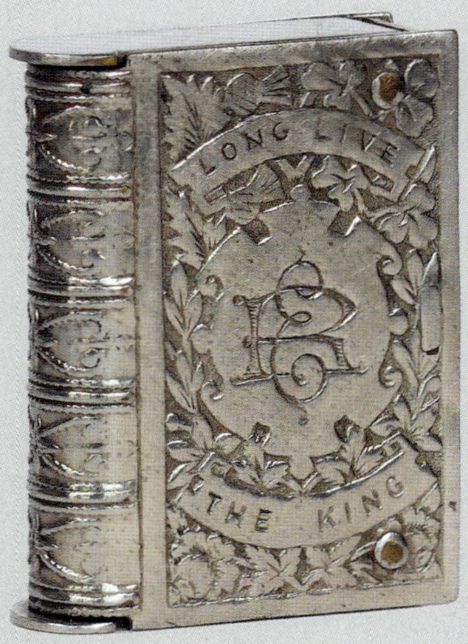

3.068
Long live the King
Metalldose mit aufklappbarem Kopf- und Fußschnitt, graviertes Monogramm, Porträt König Eduard VII auf dem Hinterdeckel, Reibfläche am Vorderschnitt
Metal box with hinged head and foot edge, engraving with monogram, portrait of King Edward VII on the rear cover, friction surface on the fore edge
Um / *Around* 1900
4,5 x 3,5 x 1,1 cm

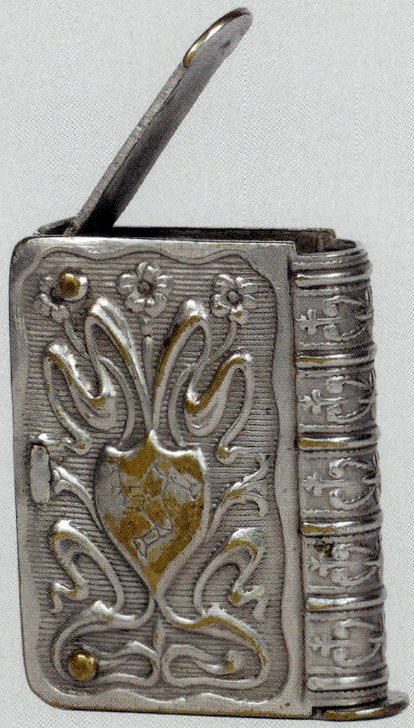

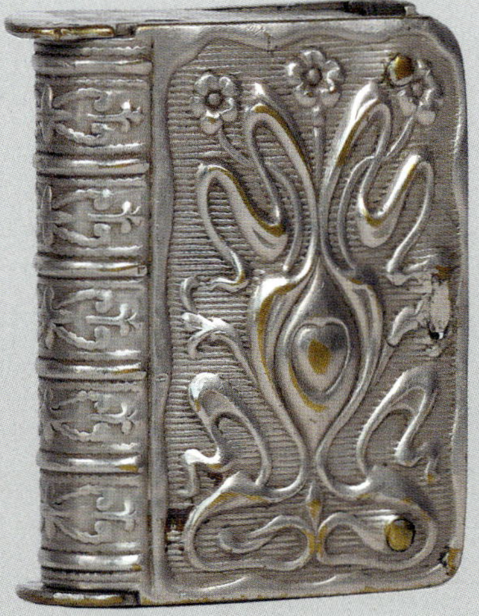

3.069
Metalldose mit aufklappbarem Kopf- und Fußschnitt, Deckel mit Relief, Reibfläche am Vorderschnitt
Metal box with hinged head and foot edge, relieved covers, friction surface on the fore edge
Jugenstil / *Art Nouveau*
4,4 x 3,6 x 1,1 cm

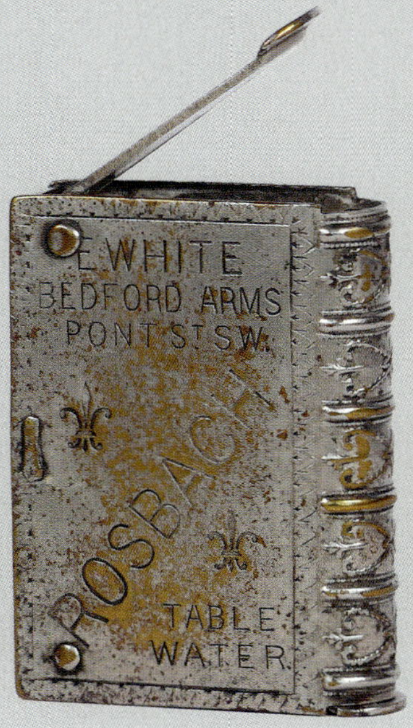

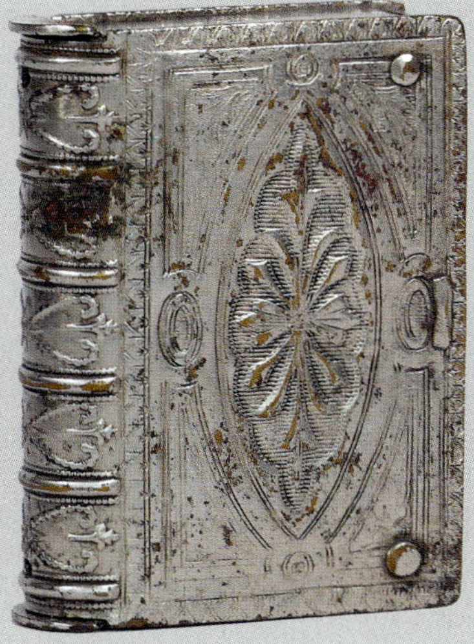

3.070
Rosbach, Table Water
Metalldose mit aufklappbarem Kopf- und Fußschnitt, Gravur auf Deckel, Reibfläche am Vorderschnitt
Metal box with hinged head and foot edge, cover engravings, friction surface on the fore edge
Anfang 20. Jh. / *Beginning of the 20th century*
4,5 x 3,3 x 1,1 cm

3.071
Matches
Streichholzschachtelhalter aus Holz, geschnitzter Rücken und Deckel, Titelaufdruck
Wooden matchbox holder, carved spine and boards, printed titel
2,9 x 7,9 x 6 cm

3.072
Streichholzschachtelhalter aus Metall mit vergoldeten Saffian-Lederüberzug
Matchbox metal holder with gilt Saffian leather cover
3 x 14,8 x 11,1 cm

3.073
Streichholzschachtelhalter aus Karton, Hinterglasmalerei auf dem Vorderdeckel, Deckeldekor mit geprägtem Goldpapier, Veloursrücken, geprägter Goldschnitt, ausgefüttert mit Glanzpapier, Reibfläche auf dem Hinterdeckel
Cardboard matchbox holder, illustration protected by glass on the front cover, gold-tooling on the cover, velvet spine strip, gold-tooled edges, lined with glossy paper, friction surface on the back lid
Ende 19. Jh. / *End of the 19th century*
1,9 x 6,8 x 5,4 cm

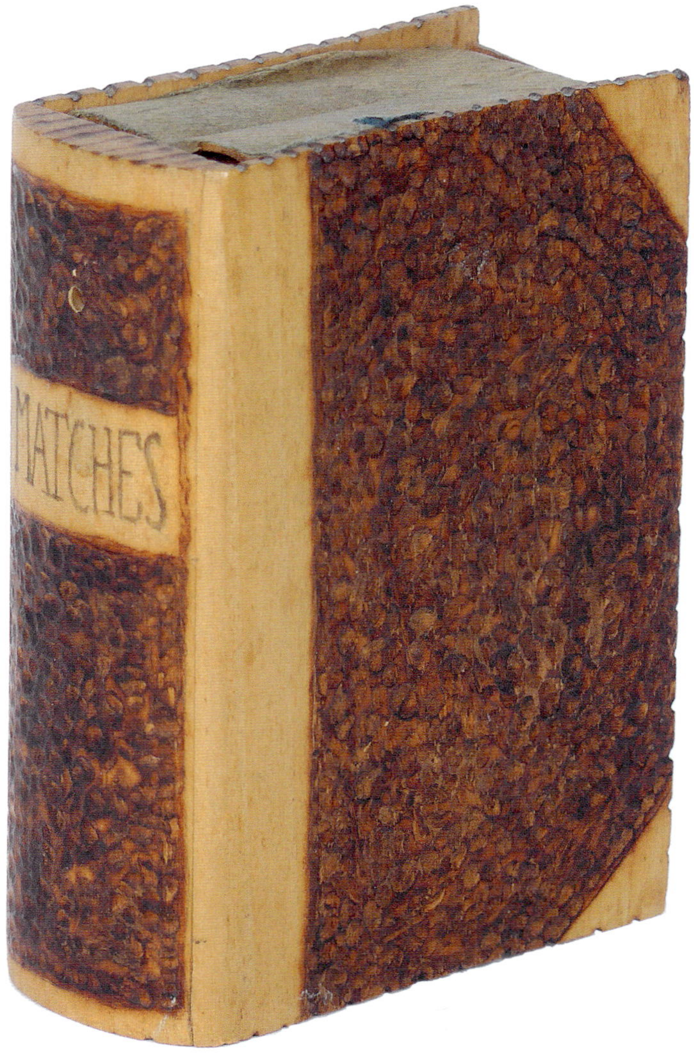

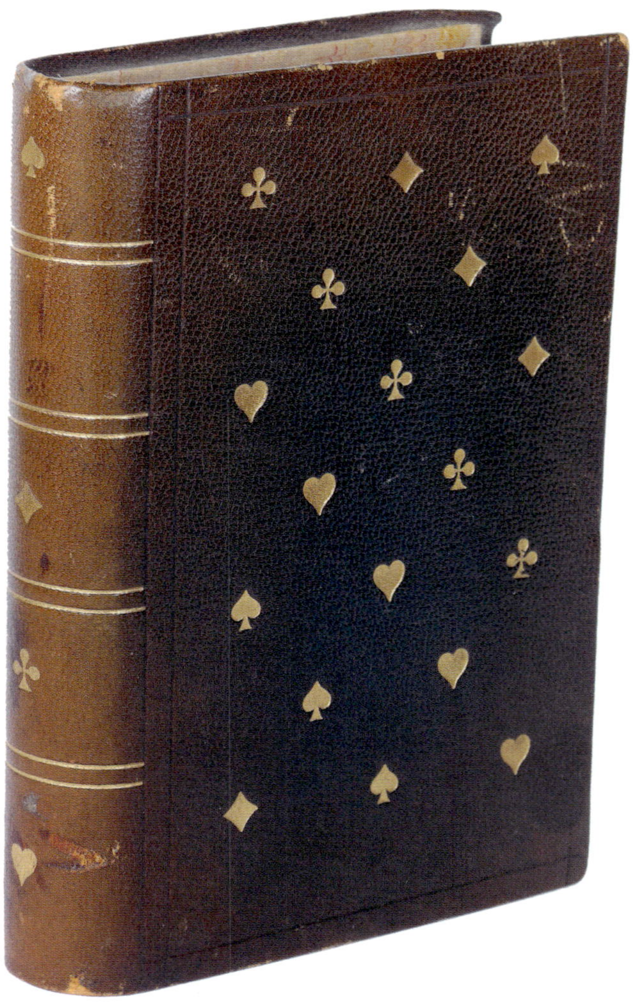

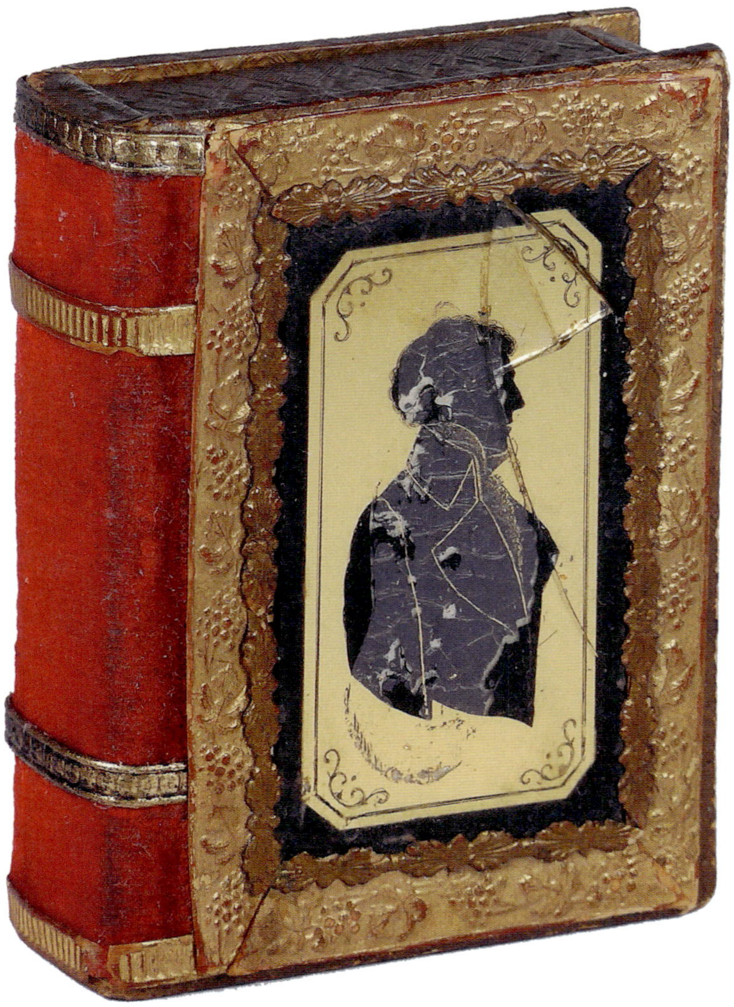

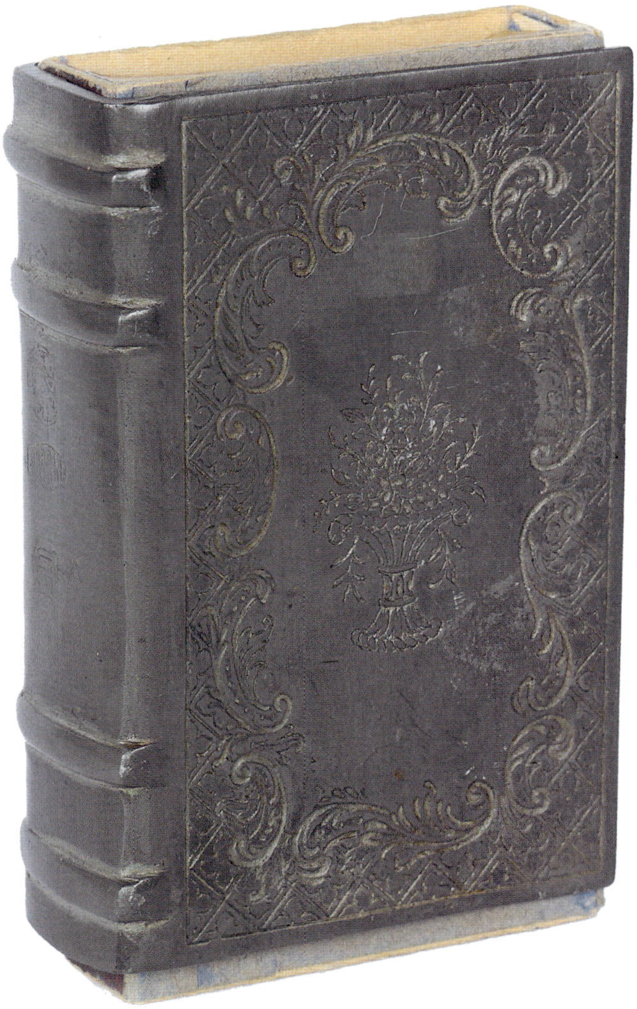

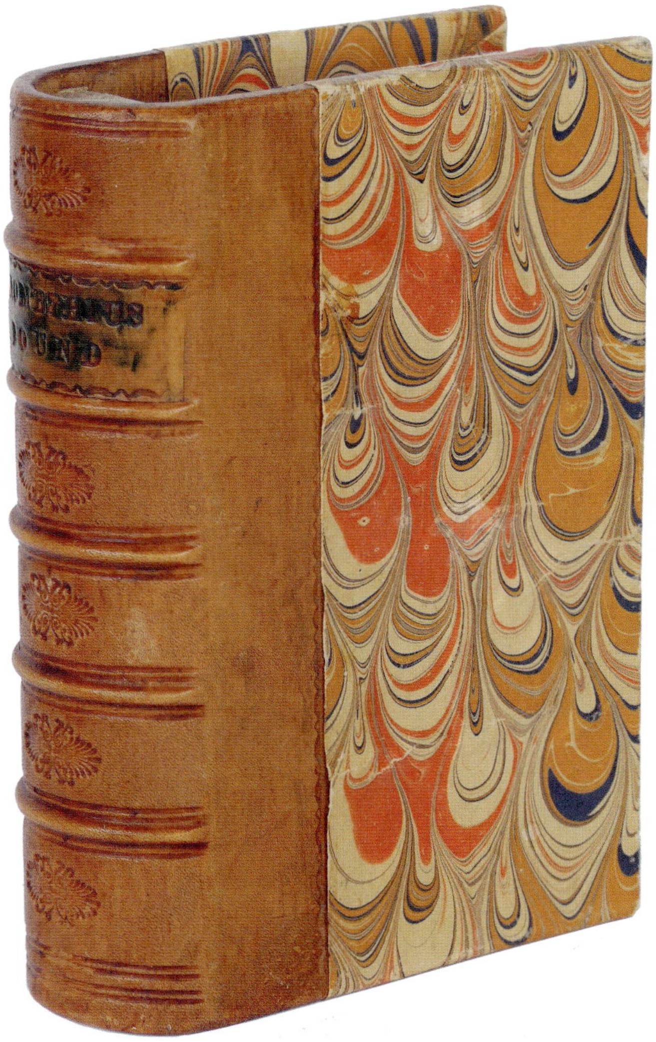

3.074
Streichholzschachtelhalter aus Zinn, punziertes Rankenwerk auf beiden Deckeln
Pewter matchbox holder, decorated with punched tendrils on both covers
3 x 11 x 7,7 cm

3.075
Promethius Bound
Streichholzschachtelhalter aus Holz, Halblederband, Pfauenmarmorpapierüberzug, Titel- und Blindprägung
Wooden matchbox holder, half leather binding and peacock marbled paper, title and blind tooling
3,7 x 12,8 x 9,5 cm

3.076
St. Dunstan's Hostel, Regent's Park, London
Blech- Streichholzschachtelhalter farbig bedruckt, Rückenbeschriftung, Männerporträts auf beiden Deckeln
Sheet metal matchbox holder printed in color, label on the spine, portraits of men on both covers
Um / *Around* 1900 | 2,3 x 6,2 x 4,2 cm

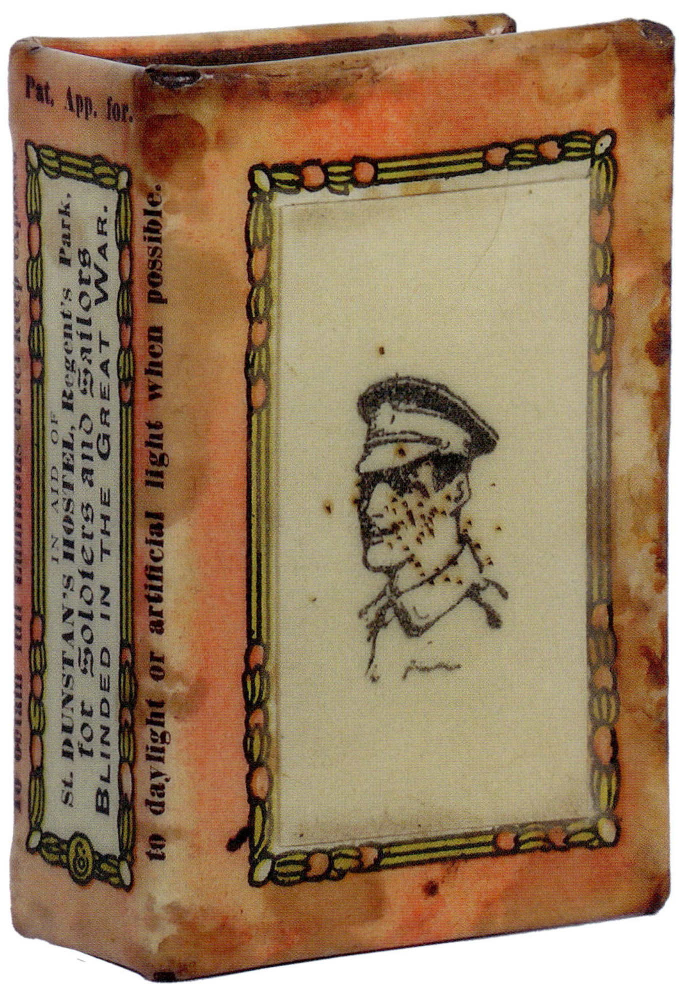

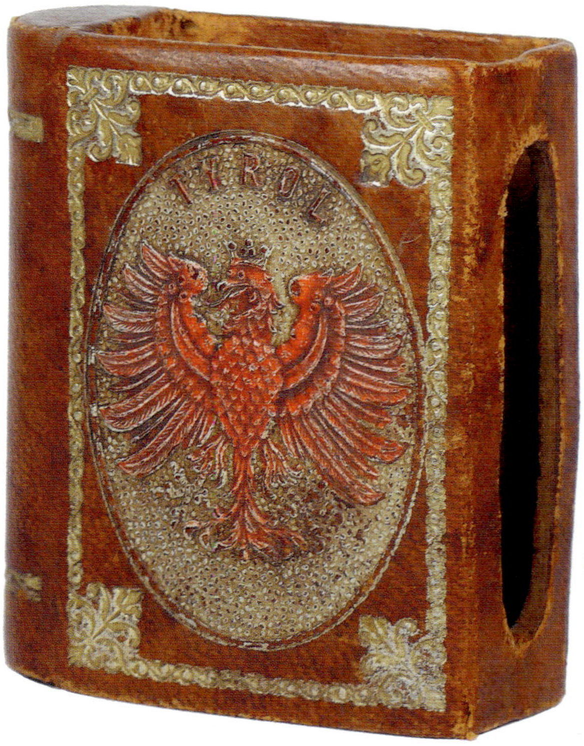

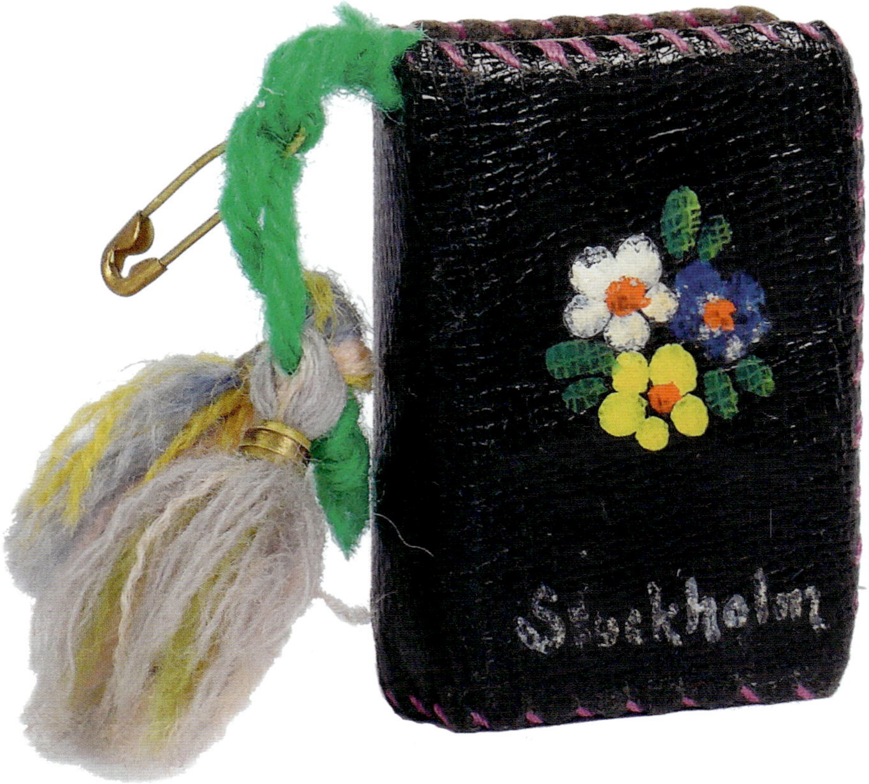

3.077
Tyrol
Ganzleder-Streichholzschachtelhalter, geprägtes farbiges Tiroler- Adlerwappen auf dem Vorderdeckel
Full leather matchbox holder, embossed colored Tyrolean emblem with eagl on the front cover
2,2 x 5,8 x 5 cm

3.078
Stockholm
Ganzleder-Streichholzschachtelhalter, bemalter Vorderdeckel, genähte Kanten, Wollschnur mit Sicherheitsnadel am Kopfschnitt
Full leather matchbox holder, painted front cover, sewn edges, woolen cord with a security pin at the head
Souvenir | 1,2 x 4,5 x 3,1 cm

3.079
Relie Cuir, Bélier 21. Mars – 20. Avril
Lederdose für Streichhölzer mit Einschub, Blindprägung auf dem Rücken und beiden Deckeln, Widder Tierkreiszeichen, Reibfläche am Vorderschnitt
Leather box for matches with drawer, blind tooling on the spine and both covers, Aries sign of the zodiac, friction surface on the fore edge
Made in France | Um / *Around* 1900
1,5 x 5,x 4 cm

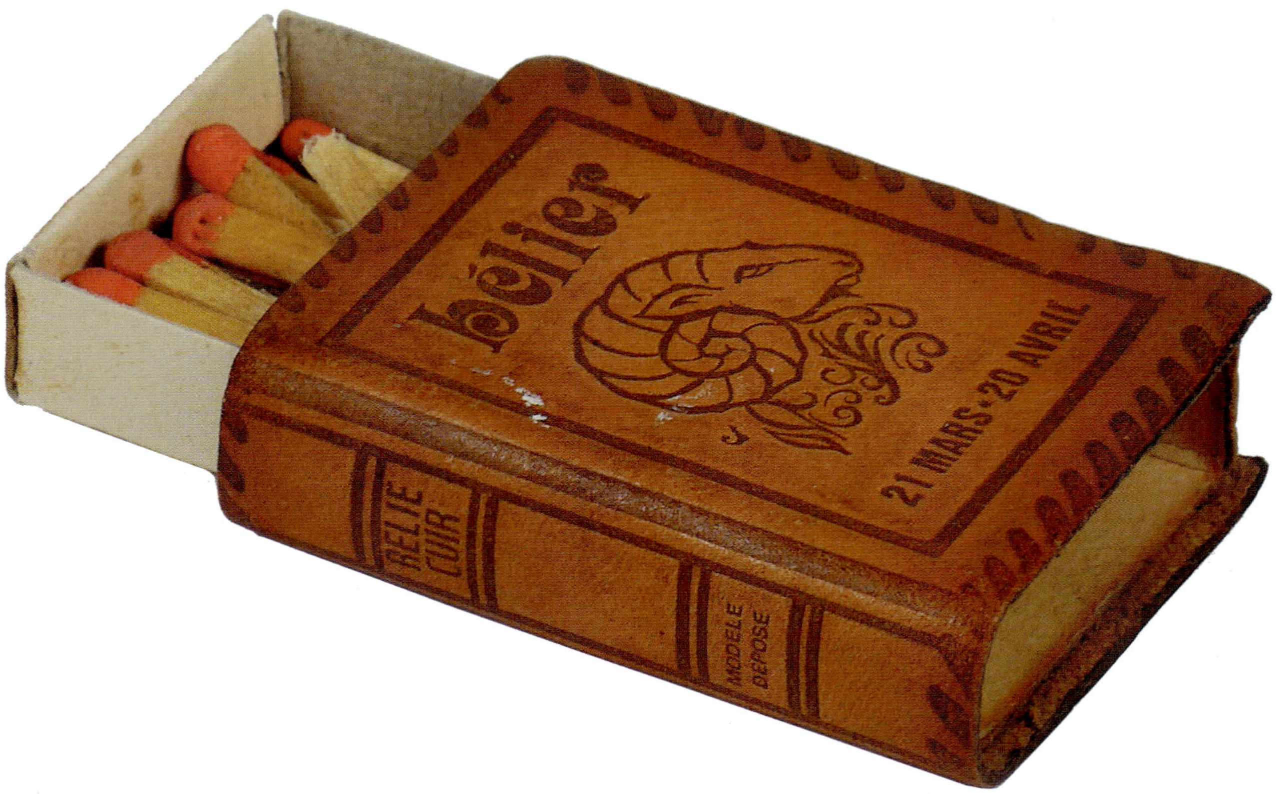

3.080
G. de Nerval, Les filles du feu
Ganzleder-Streichholzschachtelhalter, Rücken- und Deckelvergoldung
Full leather matchbox holder, gilt spine and lid
2,2 x 6,2 x 5 cm

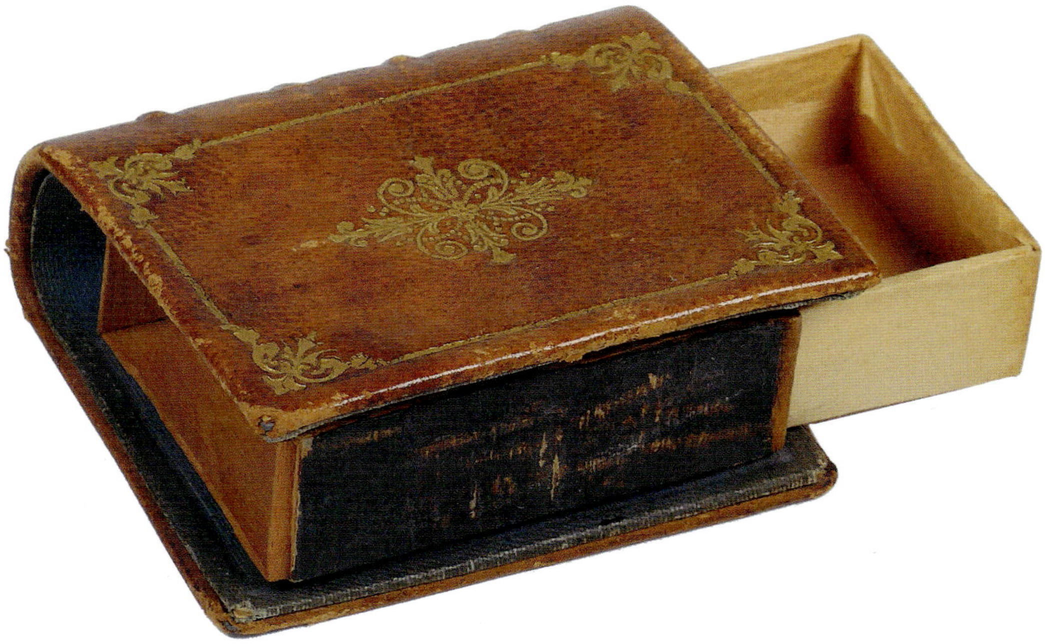

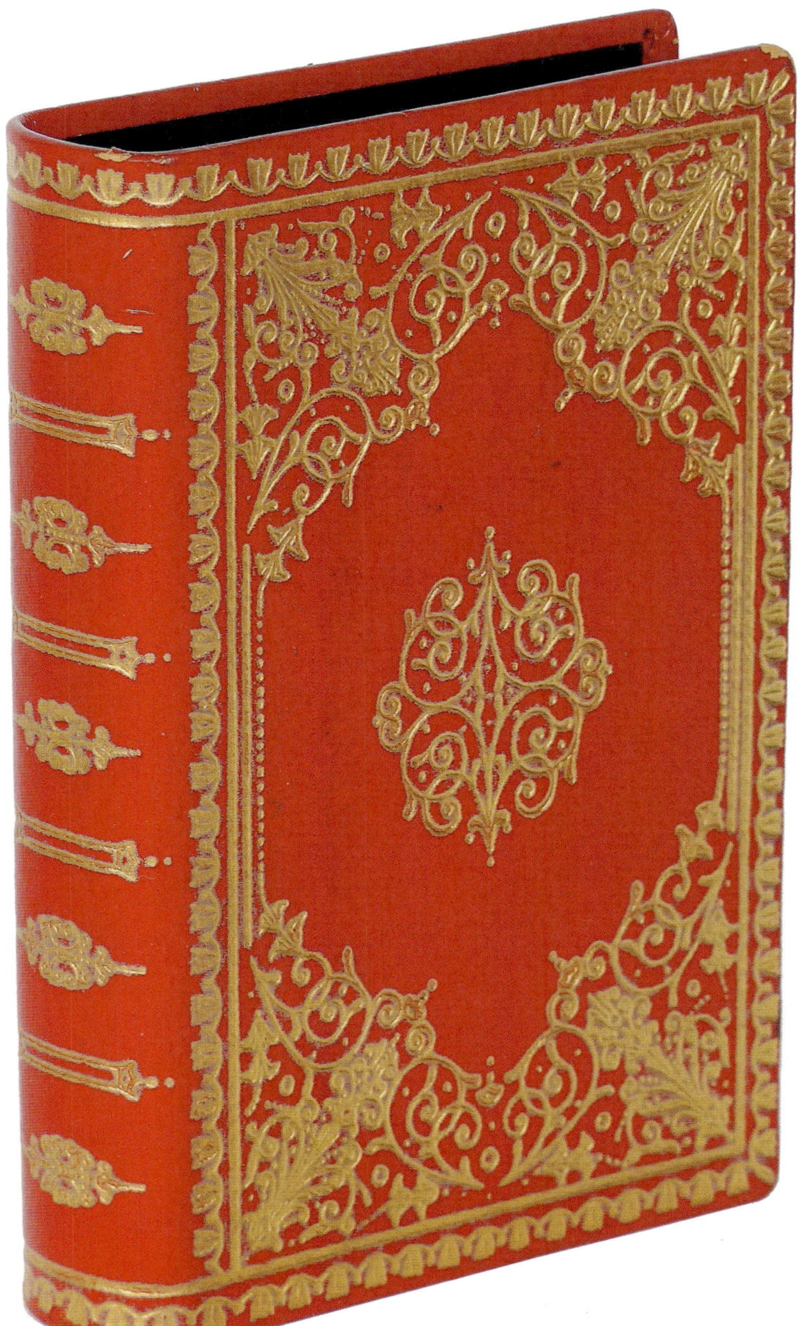

3.081
Streichholzschachtelhalter aus Metall mit vergoldetem Rindslederüberzug
Metal matchbox holder with gilt cowhide leather binding
1,8 x 9,3 x 6,4 cm

3.082
Blech-Streichholzschachtelhalter, englische Jagdszene auf dem Vorderdeckel
Sheet metal matchbox holder, English hunting theme on the front cover
2 x 6,2 x 5 cm

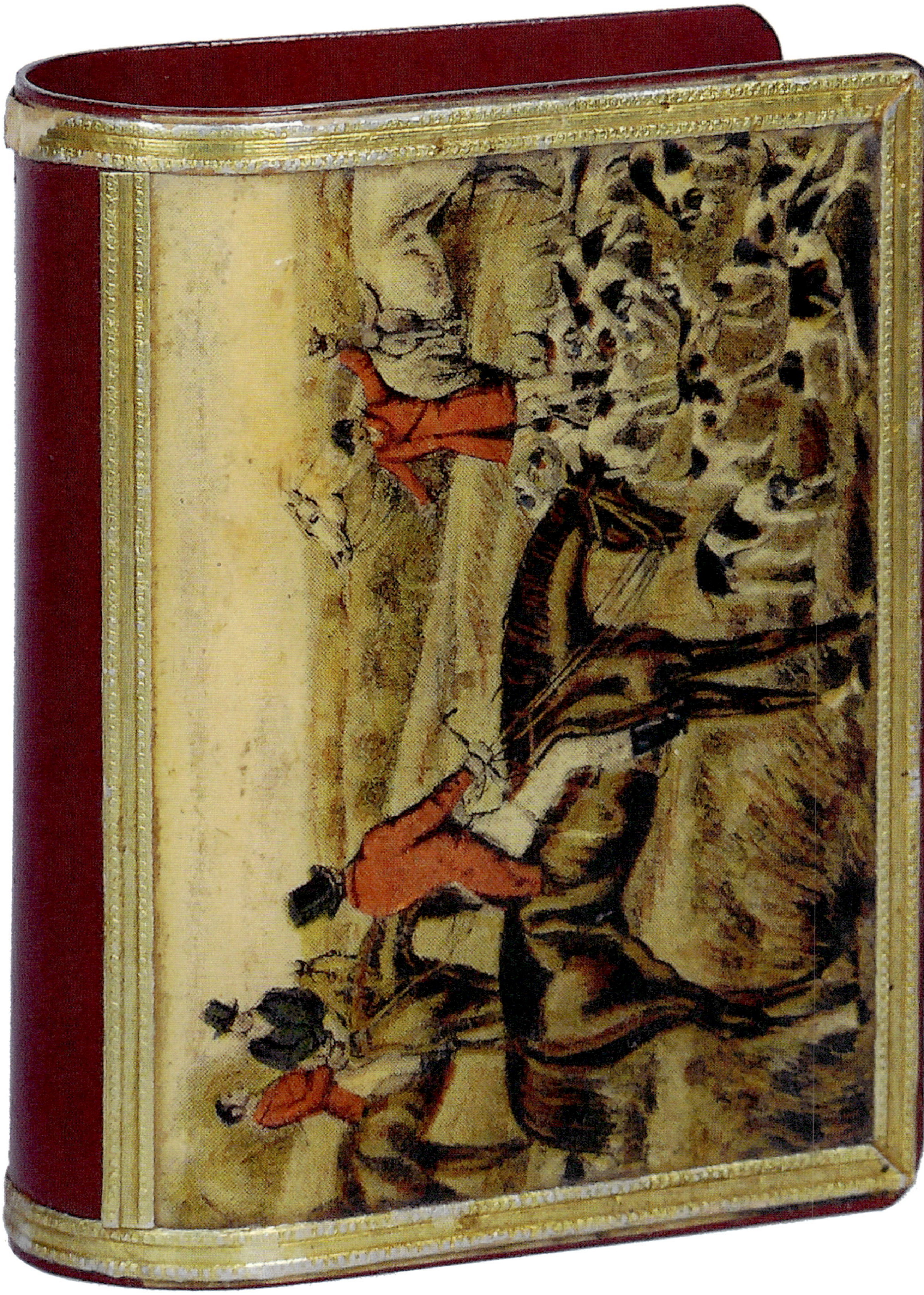

3.083
Feu
Streichholzschachtelhalter aus Metall mit vergoldeten Ziegenlederüberzug, Titelprägung
Metal matchbox holder with gilt goatskin binding, stamped title
4,2 x 12,3 x 8,1 cm

3.084
Ganzleder-Streichholzschachtelhalter, Goldprägung auf dem Rücken und beiden Deckeln
Full leather matchbox holder, gold tooling on the spine and both covers
2,1 x 5,7 x 4,8 cm

3.085
Siegfried MCMXXX
Streichholzschachtelhalter aus Metall mit Rindslederüberzug, Titel- und Deckelblindprägung, Apotheker mit Mörser
Metal matchbox holder with cow-hide leather binding,stamped title and blind tooling on the cover, pharmacist with mortar
4,3 x 12,2 x 8,5 cm

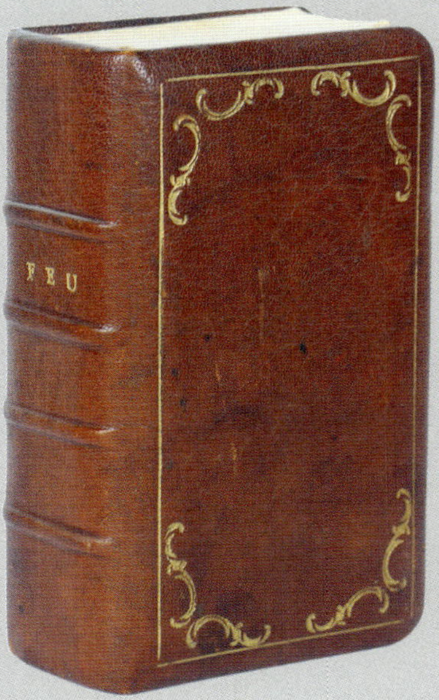

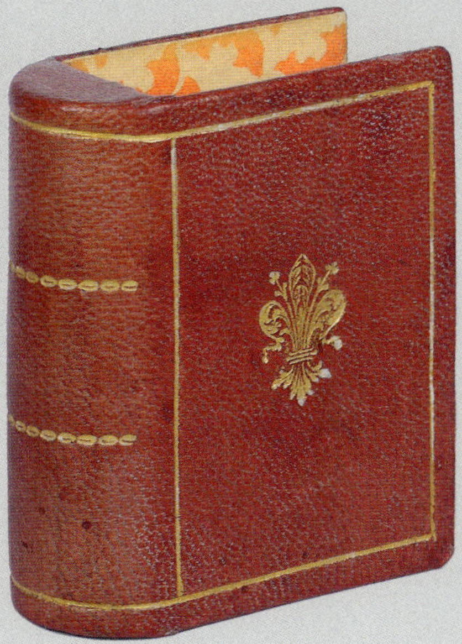

3.086
Zundhölzli BuBu Matches
Ganzleder-Streichholzschachtelhalter, Rücken- und Deckelprägung
Full leather matchbox holder, embossed spine and cover
2,5 x 6,2 x 4,5 cm

3.087
Stromeyer
Streichholzschachtelhalter aus Metall mit vergoldetem Rindslederüberzug, Titelprägung
Metal matchbox holder with gilt cow leather binding, stamped title
4,4 x 12,5 x 8,4 cm

3.088
Streichholzschachtelhalter aus Metall mit wattiertem Ziegenlederüberzug, Titel- und Deckelblindprägung, Blindprägung am Rücken
Metal matchbox holder with padded goatskin cover, stamped title and blind tooling on the cover, blind tooling on the spine
4,4 x 12,6 x 8,8 cm

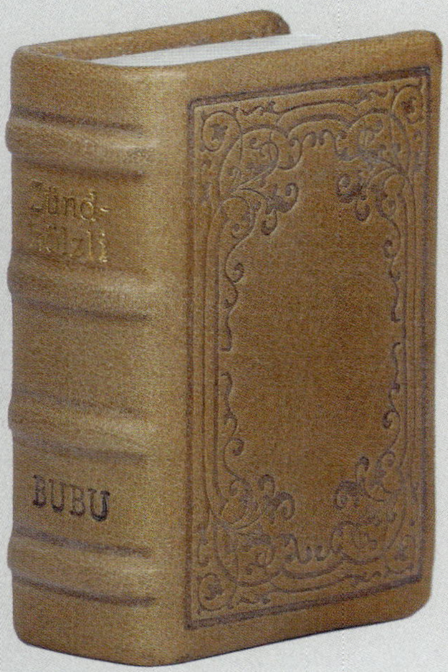

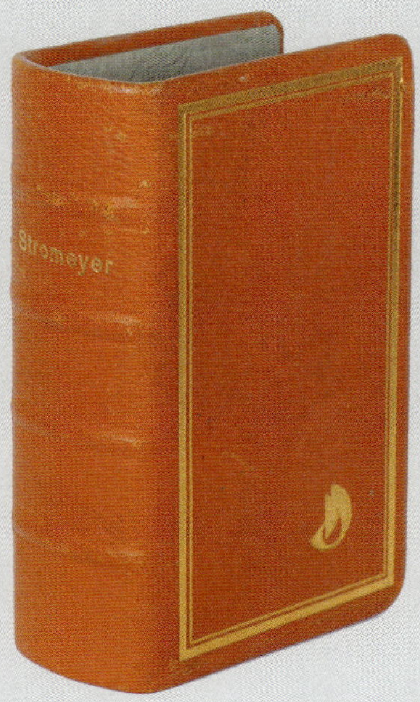

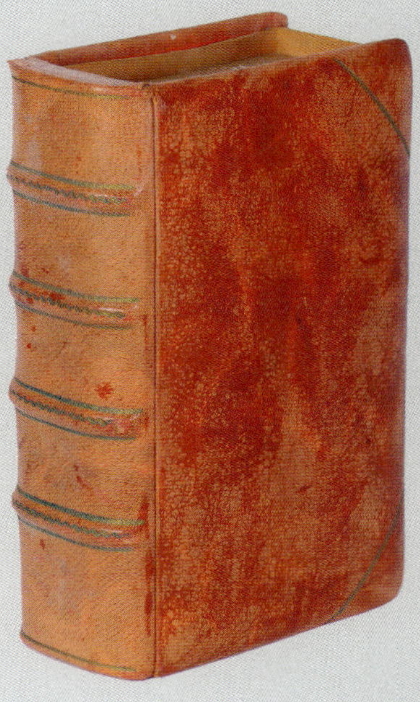

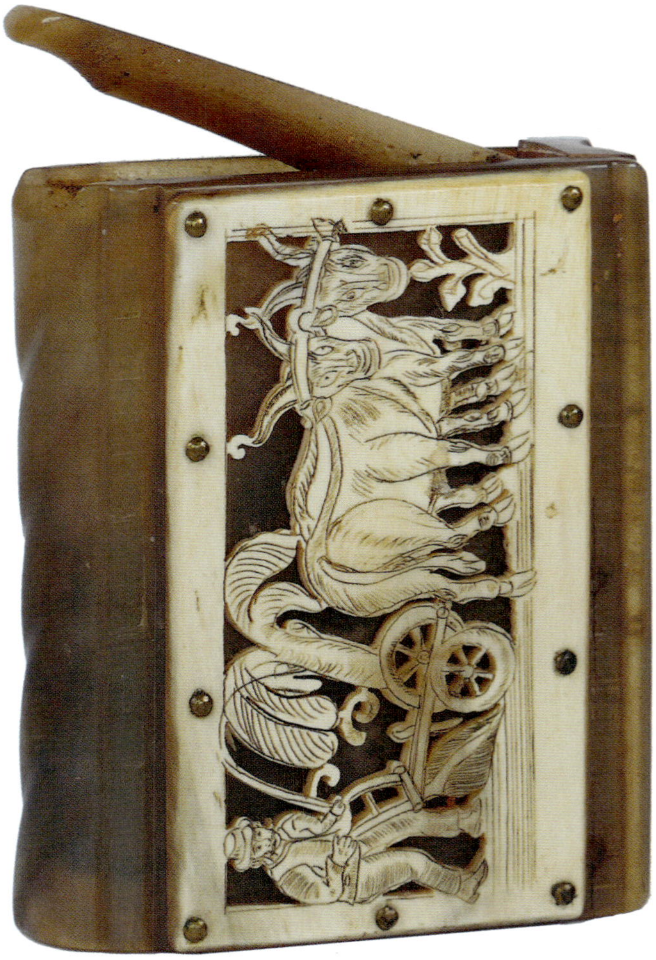

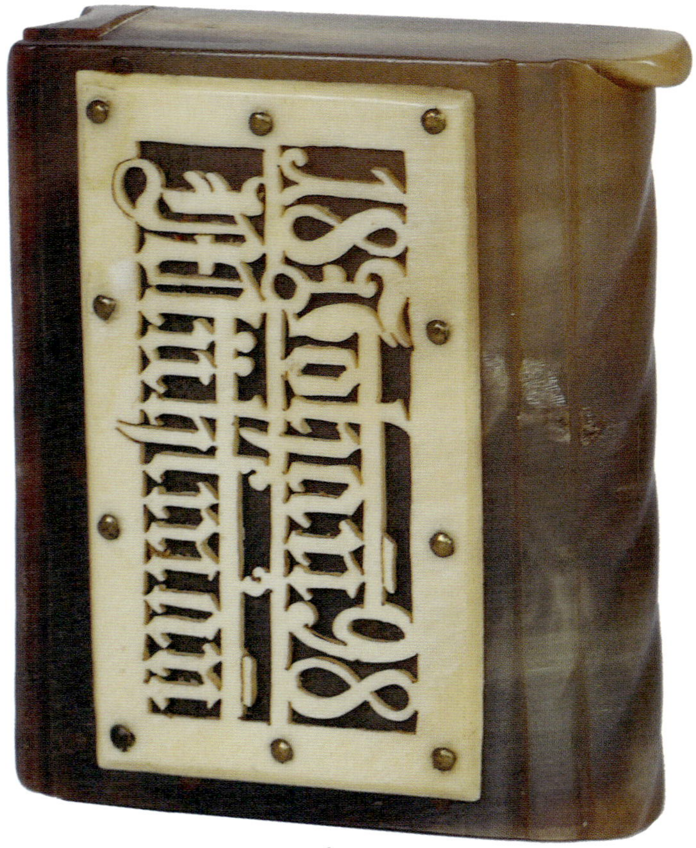

3.089
Schnupftabakdose oder Tabatiere aus Bein mit Öffnung am Kopfschnitt, ausgesägte landwirtschaftliche Szene am Vorderdeckel sowie Namenszug und Datum am Hinterdeckel
Snuffbox or tobacco box made of bone to be opened at the head, sawed out agricultural theme on the front cover, name and date on the back cover
„1898, Johann Mühlmann" | 2,2 x 6,9 x 6 cm

3.090
Schnupftabakdose oder Tabatiere aus Bein, Vorder- und Hinterdeckel graviert: „Badel H.", Messingschnitt
Snuffbox made of bone, front and back cover engraved: "Badel H.", brass edges
Mitte 19. Jh. / *Mid of the 19th century* | 2 x 8,8 x 4,8 cm

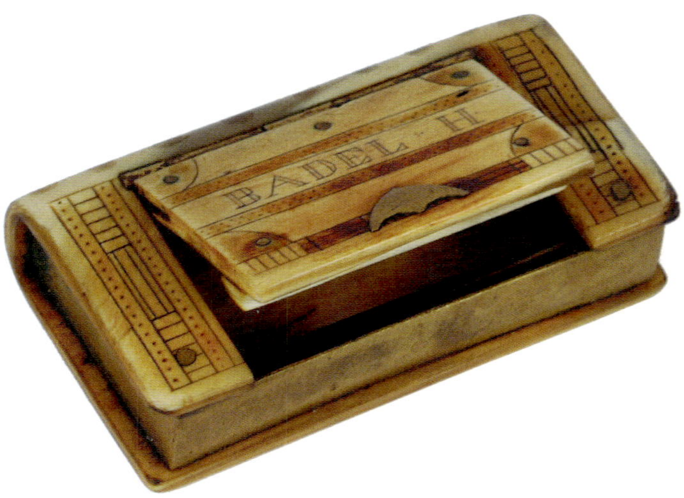

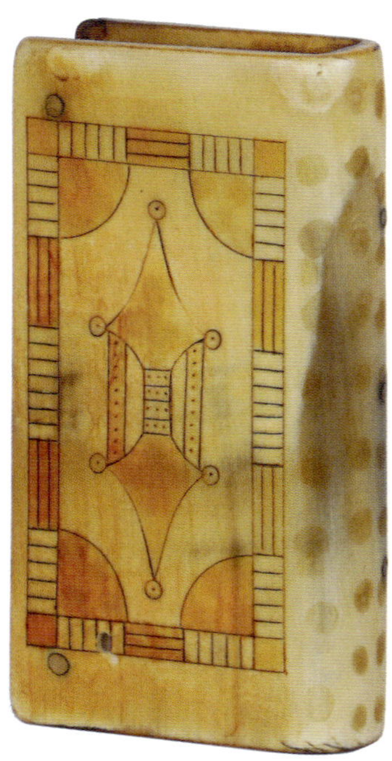

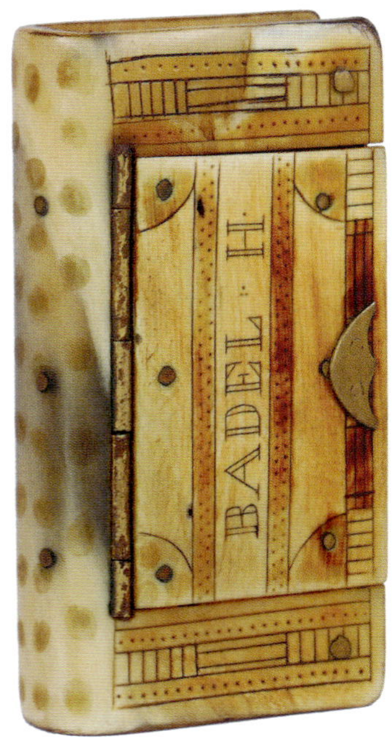

3.091
Schnupftabakdose oder Tabatiere aus Bein, allseitig graviert mit Monogramm „LC“ und mit Stadtansicht
Snuffbox or tobacco box made of bone, all over engravings with monogram “LC” and with city view
1841 | 2,1 x 9,5 x 5,5 cm

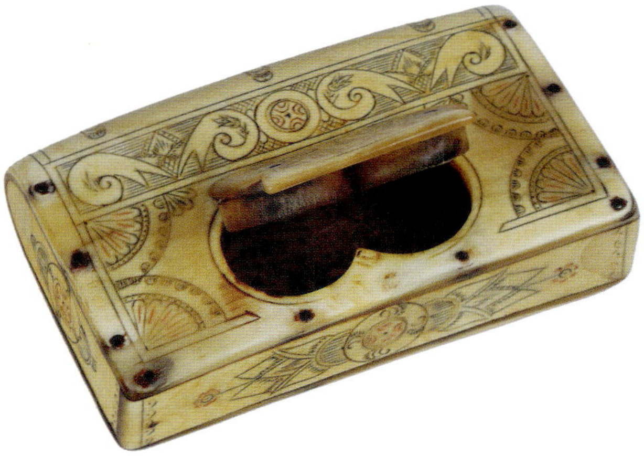

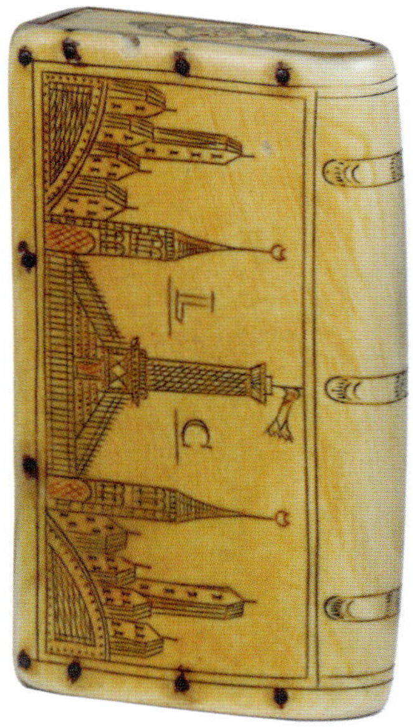

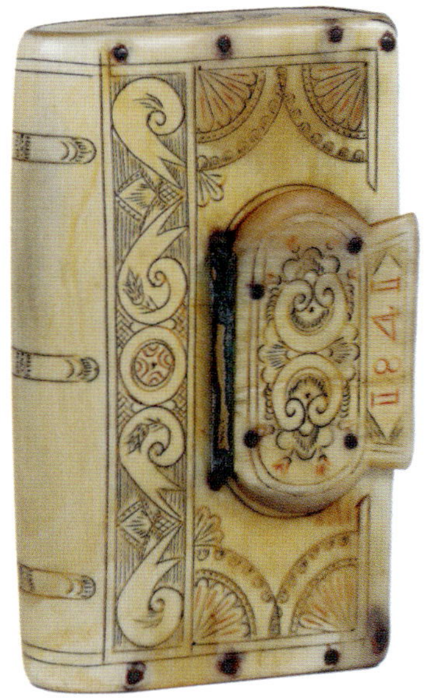

3.092
Schnupftabakdose oder Tabatiere aus Bein, Vorder- und Hinterdeckel graviert, Messingschnitt
Snuffbox or tobacco tin made of bone, engraving on the front and rear board, brass edges
Mitte 19. Jh. / *Mid of the 19th century*
2,1 x 8,1 x 5 cm

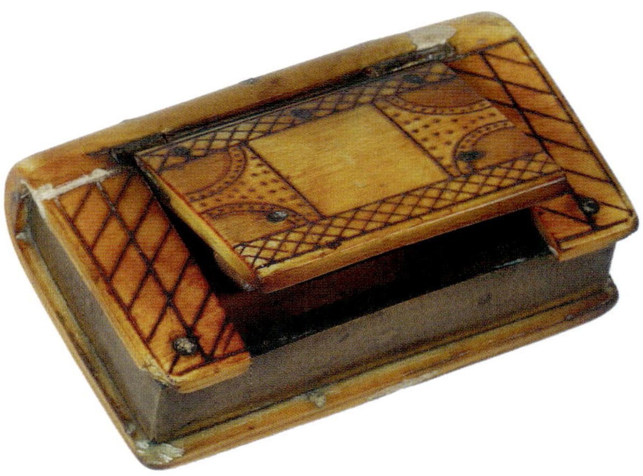

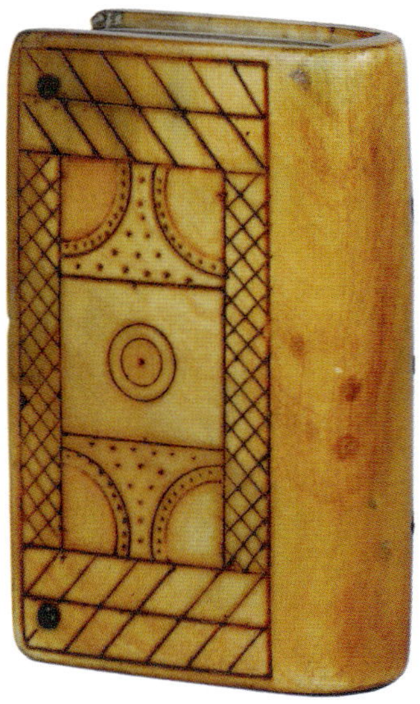

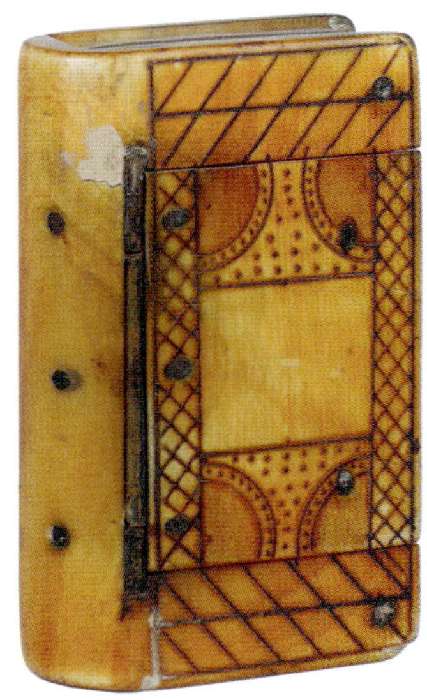

3.093
Schnupftabakdose oder Tabatiere aus Wurzelholz
Snuffbox or tobacco tin made of burl wood
Um / *Around* 1900 | 2 x 8,4 x 4,7 cm

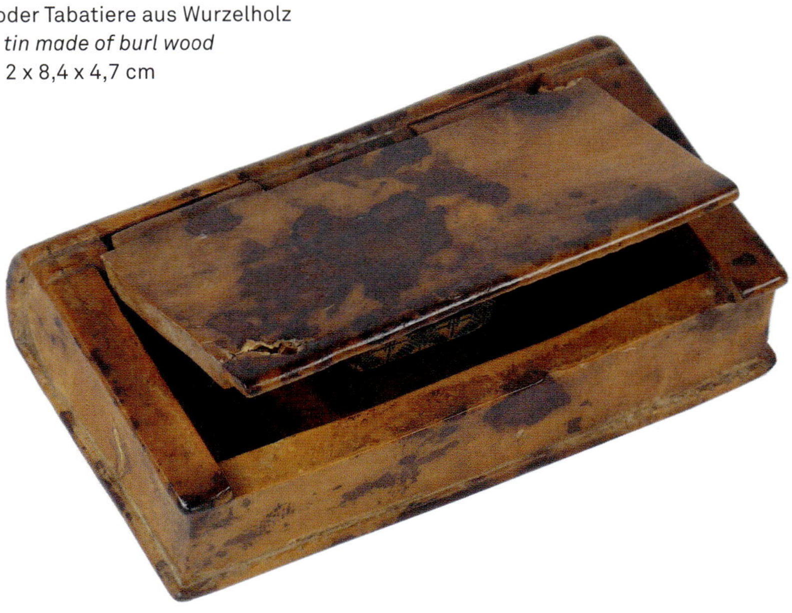

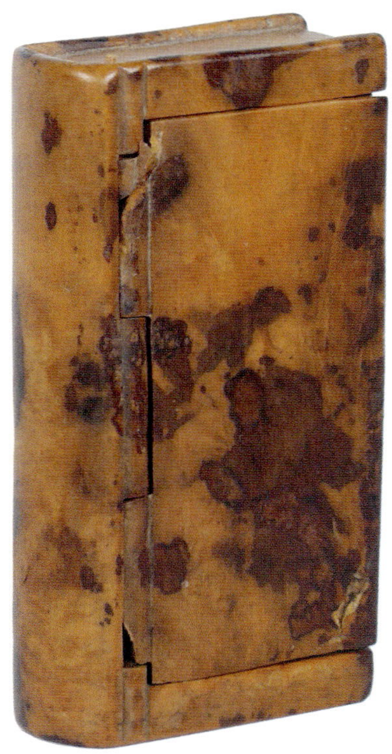

3.094
Schnupftabakdose oder Tabatiere
aus Bein, Messingschnitt
Snuffbox or tobacco box made of bone, brass edges
Um / *Around* 1900 | 1,7 x 5,8 x 4 cm

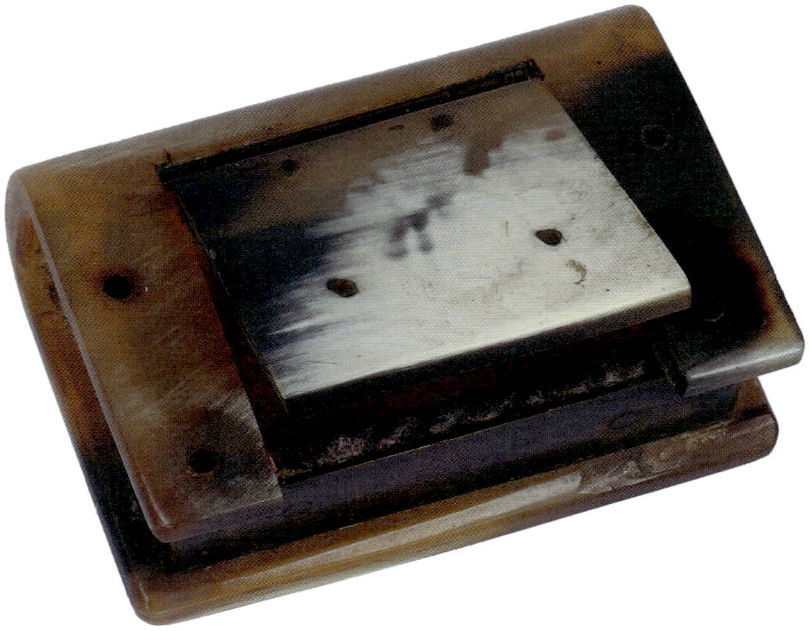

3.095
Schnupftabakdose oder Tabatiere
aus Holz, geschnitzt und farbig gefasst,
Herkunft unklar
Wooden snuffbox or tobacco box, carved and colored, origin unclear
Zeitgenössisch / *Contemporary*
2,5 x 9,7 x 6,1 cm

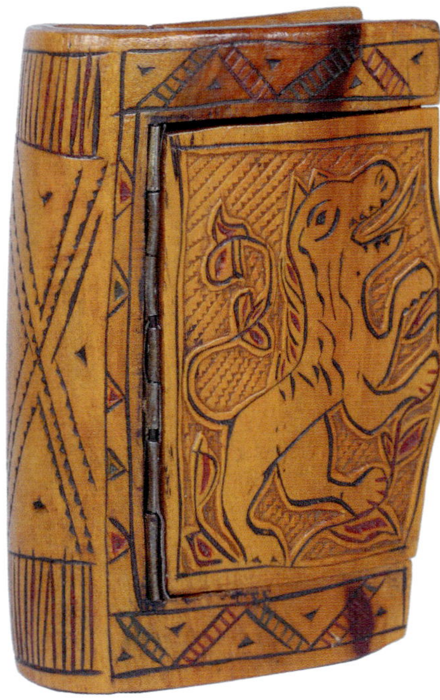

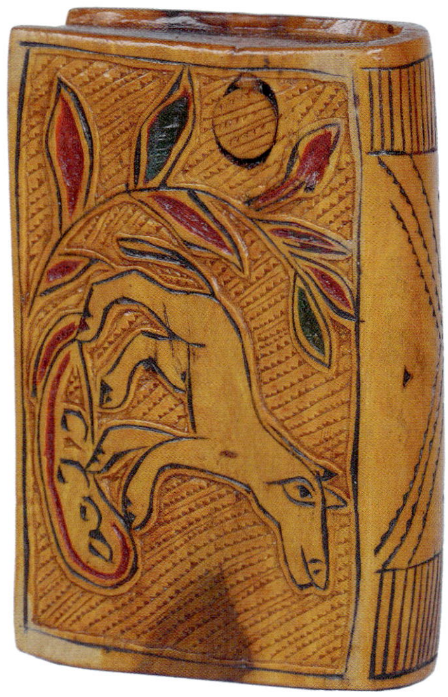

3.096
Schnupftabakdose oder Tabatiere
aus Holz mit Öffnung am Kopfschnitt
Wooden snuffbox or tobacco box to be opened at the head
Mitte 19. Jh. / *Mid of the 19th century*
2,5 x 7 x 6 cm

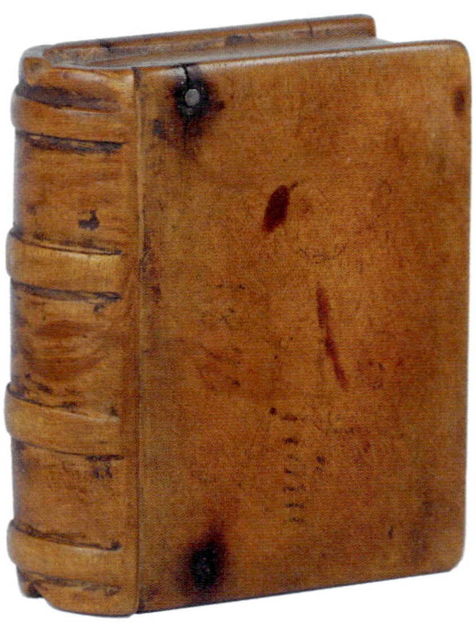

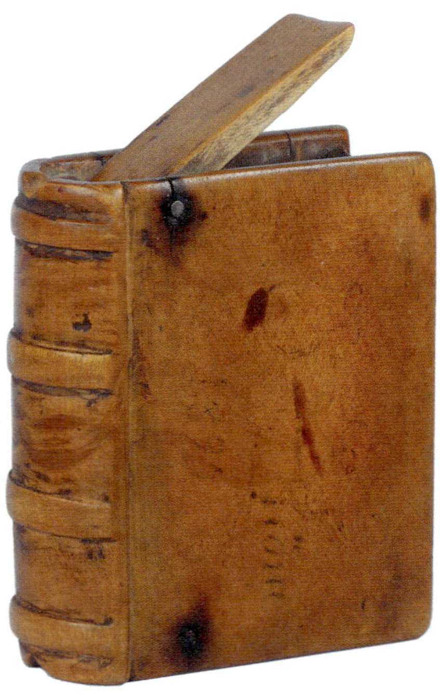

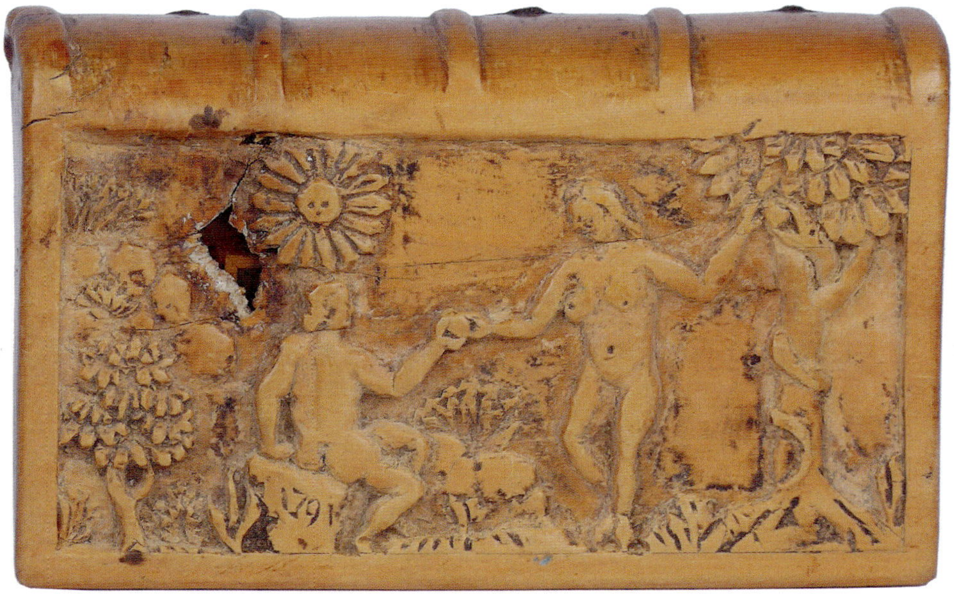

3.097
Schnupftabakdose oder Tabatiere aus Holz, geschnitzte biblische Sündenfallszene, Fragment
Wooden snuffbox or tobacco box, carved biblical scene of the Fall of Man, fragment
1791 | 2,8 x 9,8 x 6 cm

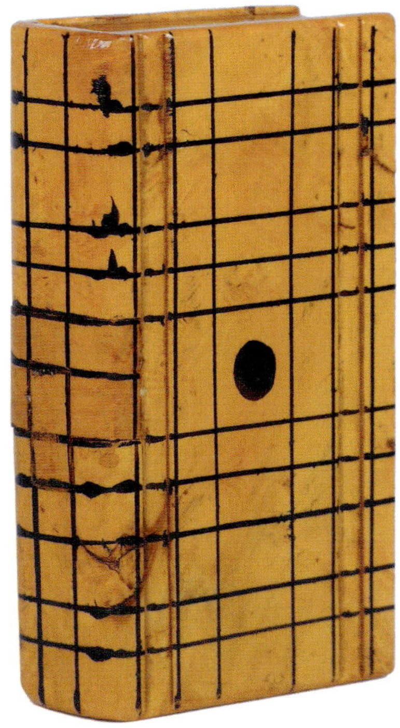

3.098
Schnupftabakdose oder Tabatiere aus Holz mit raffiniertem Geheimverschluss, geometrisches Muster auf dem Rücken und auf beiden Deckeln
Wooden snuffbox with a sophisticated secret closure, geometric pattern on the spine and on both boards
19. Jh. / *19th century* | 2 x 8,2 x 4,7 cm

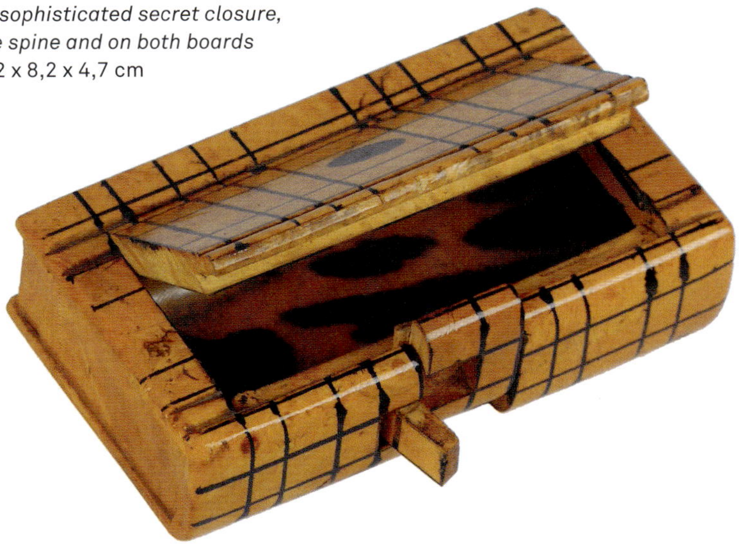

3.099
Holzdose mit verschiebbarem Vorderdeckel, feine Gravur auf beiden Deckeln
Wooden box with a sliding lid, fine engraving on both boards
Ende 19. Jh / *Late 19th century* | 1,3 x 7,8 x 4,7 cm

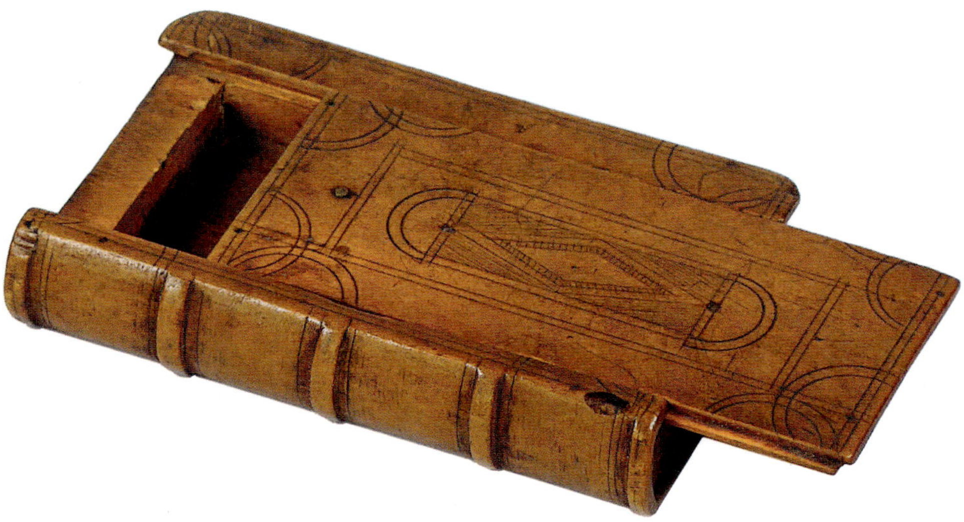

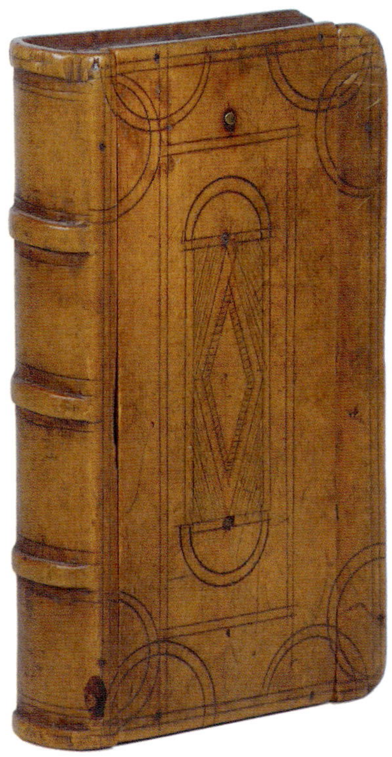

3.100
Codex Fumandi
Doppelaschenbecher aus Bronze, aufklappbar, Titel und Wappen auf dem Vorderdeckel
Double bronze ashtray, hinged, title and emblem on the front lid
4 x 14 x 10,1 cm

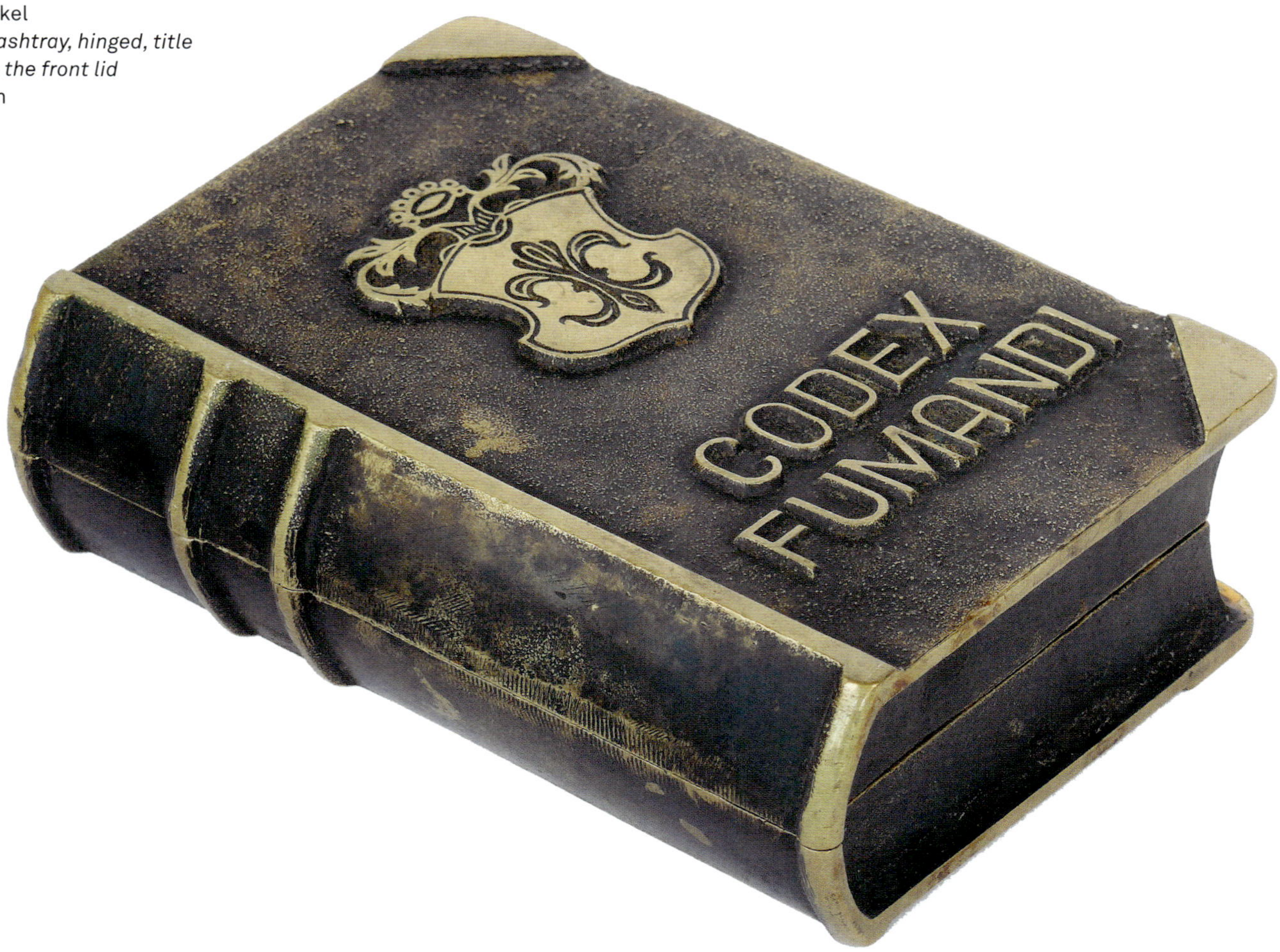

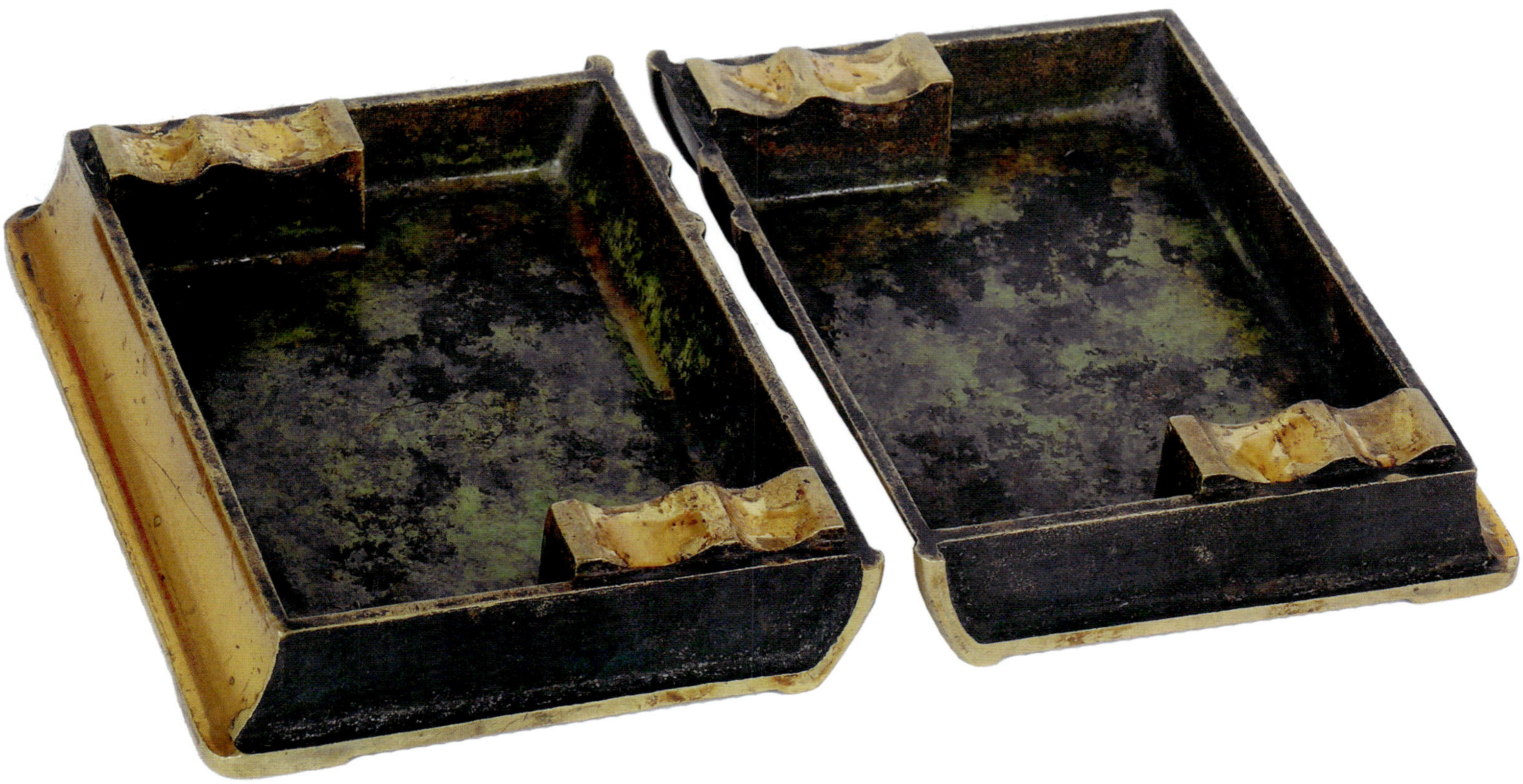

3.101
Messing-Taschenaschenbecher, aufklappbar mit integrierter Zigarettenablage, farbig bemalt, dreiseitiger Goldschnitt
Brass ashtray, hinged, with integrated cigarette holder, colored paintwork, all edges gilt
Anfang 20. Jh. / *Early 20th century*
2,4 x 4,9 x 5,3 cm

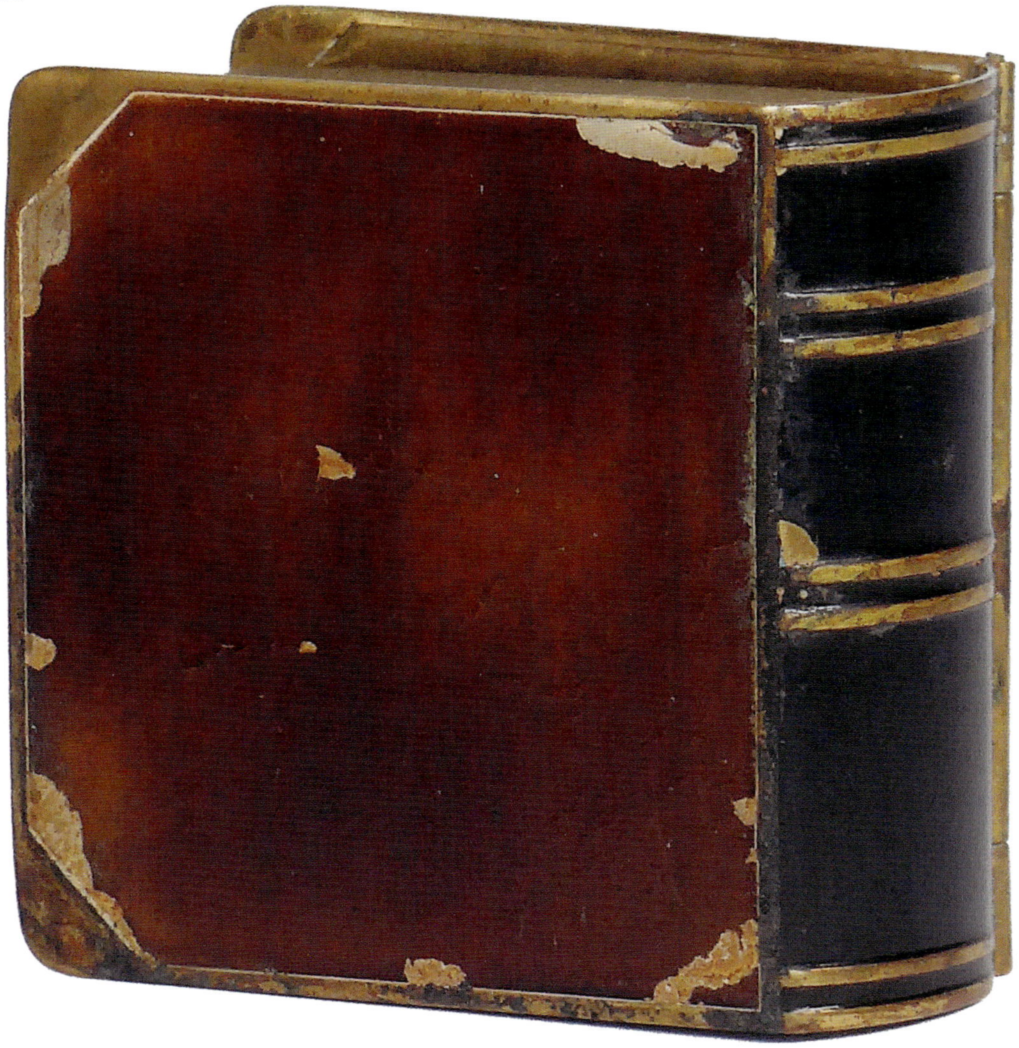

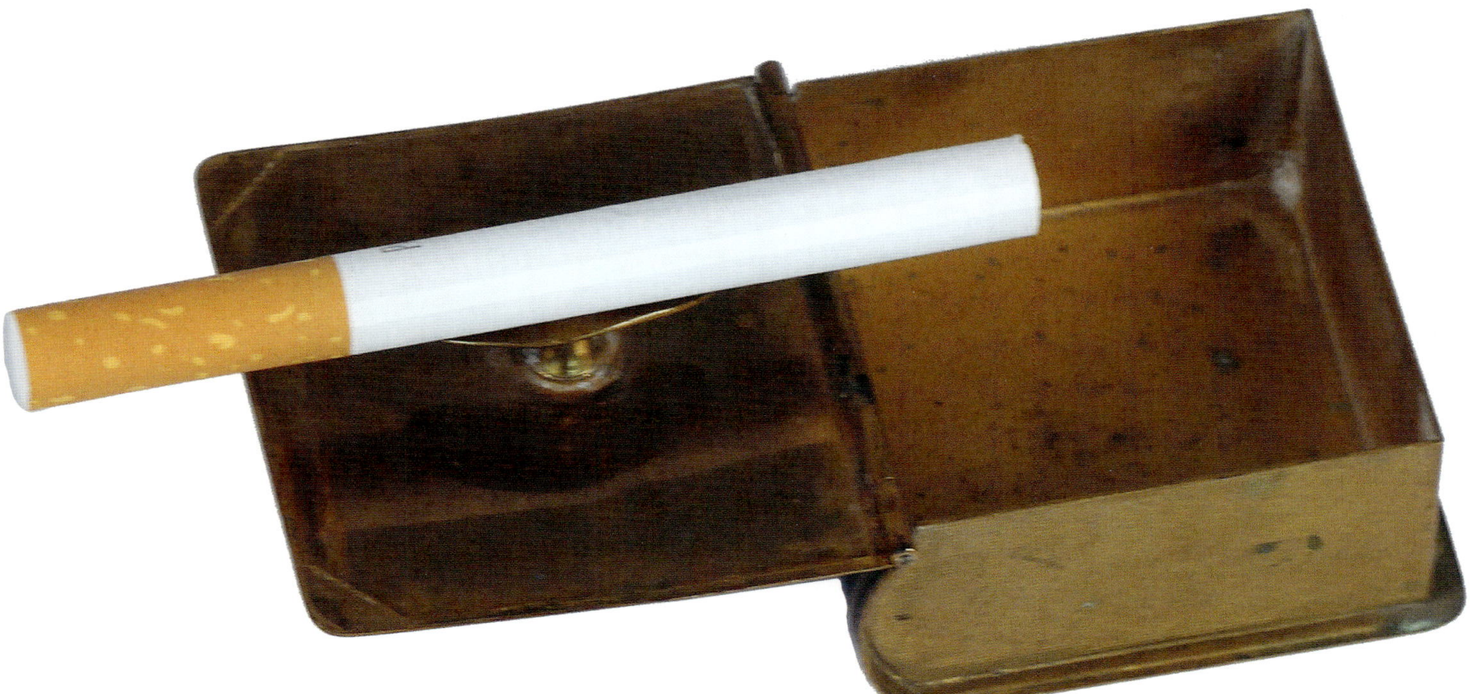

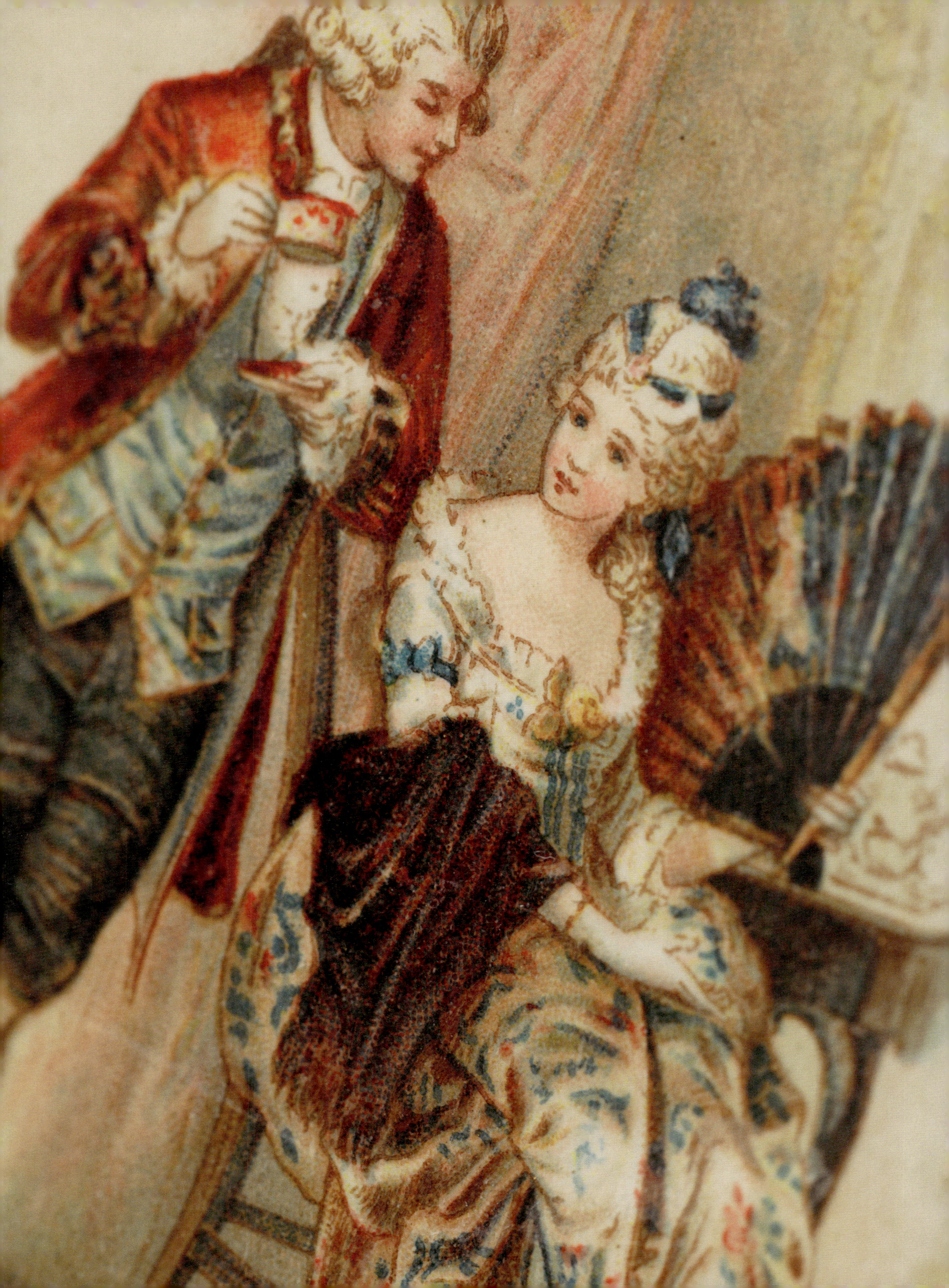

Gaumenfreudenn
Culinary Delights

Die Künstlerin, Galeristin und Antiquitätenhändlerin Hanne Bee führte in der Froschaugasse in der Zürcher Altstadt eine Galerie. Da meine Partnerin sie kannte, war es mir vergönnt, diese in ihrem zauberhaften Einfamilienhäuschen in bester Lage zu besuchen. Beim ersten Besuch entdeckte ich auf einer alten Kommode ihres Wohnzimmers eine lithografierte Blechdose mit der Bezeichnung „Bookstand" der Firma Huntley & Palmers Biscuits, die ich schon lange suchte. Reading & London fertigte die Keksdose 1905 an. Die Blechdose mit vier Metallfüßen imitiert ein Büchergestell mit erhabenem Buchrücken auf allen vier Seiten. Der Deckel in Holzimitat ist mit Scharnieren befestigt.

Trotz meiner strategisch geschickten Kaufkünste – ein Sammler darf nie in große Begeisterungsstürme ausbrechen, da es sich sonst sofort im Preis bemerkbar macht – wollte die Galeristin mir die Dose partout nicht verkaufen, was sie fadenscheinig damit begründete, sie bewahre ihren Kram darin auf. Sie versprach mir aber, die 23 Jahre älter als ich war, dass ich die Dose nach ihrem Ableben bekommen könne.

Nach vielen Jahren bemerkte ich in der NZZ ihre Todesanzeige mit der Traueradresse in Norddeutschland. Gleichentags nahm ich mit den Angehörigen Kontakt auf und schilderte ihnen mein Anliegen. Weil das Häuschen vom Hinterberg verkauft werden sollte und das Inventar ebenfalls neue Besitzer suchte, stand ich nach ca. 30 Jahren wieder vor meinem gewünschten Objekt.

Die Geschichte hat den Verwandten so gut gefallen, dass ich endlich die Huntley & Palmers Biskuitdose erwerben konnte und das zu einem Freundschaftspreis.

The artist, gallery owner and antique dealer Hanne Bee ran a gallery in Froschaugasse in Zurich's old town. Since my partner knew her, I was privileged enough to visit her enchanting single-family home in a prime location. During my first visit, I discovered a tin box on an old sideboard in her living room with a lithography entitled "Bookstand" by Huntley & Palmers Biscuits, which I had been seeking for a long time. Reading & London produced the cookie tin in 1905. The box with four metal feet imitates a bookstand with a raised book spine on all four sides. The lid in imitation wood is hinged.

Despite my strategically clever buying skills - a collector must never immediately show his enthusiasm; otherwise it affects the price ¬ the gallery owner declined to sell me the tin on the flimsy grounds that she kept her stuff in it. But she promised me that, since she was 23 years older than me, I could have the tin after her death.

After many years I noticed her obituary in the NZZ with a mourning address in Northern Germany. On the same day I contacted the relatives and told them about my request. Because the house was to be sold and the inventory was also looking for new owners, I found my desired object again after about 30 years.

The relatives liked the story so much, they finally allowed me to buy the Huntley & Palmers cookie tin at a discount price.

4.001
„Waverley“
Lithografierte Blechdose
Lithographed tin box
Huntley & Palmers Biscuits,
Reading & London
1903 | 16 x 16 x 12 cm

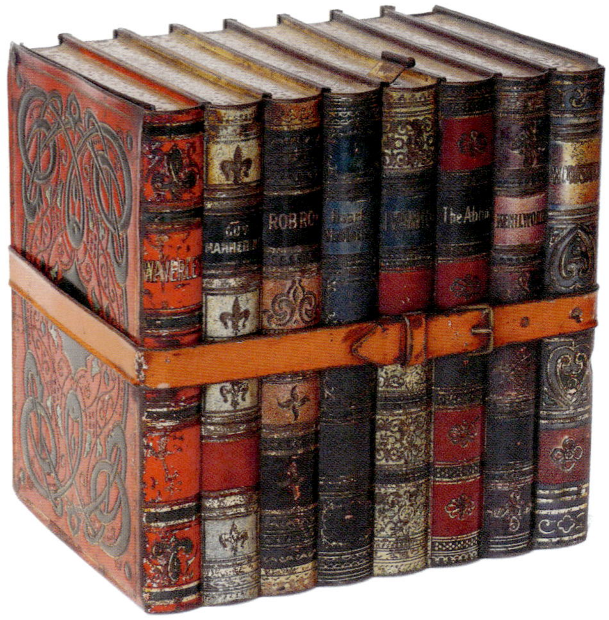

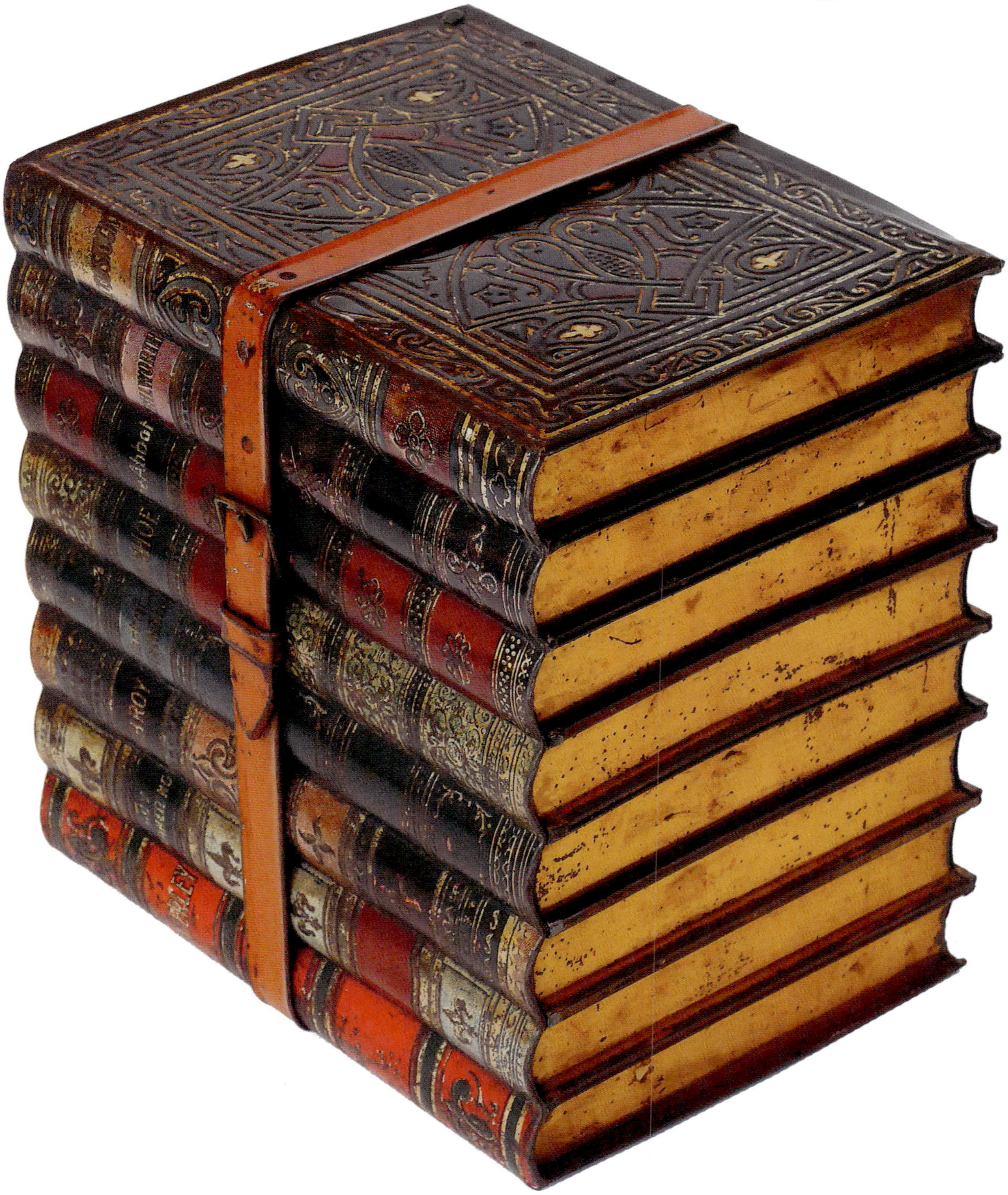

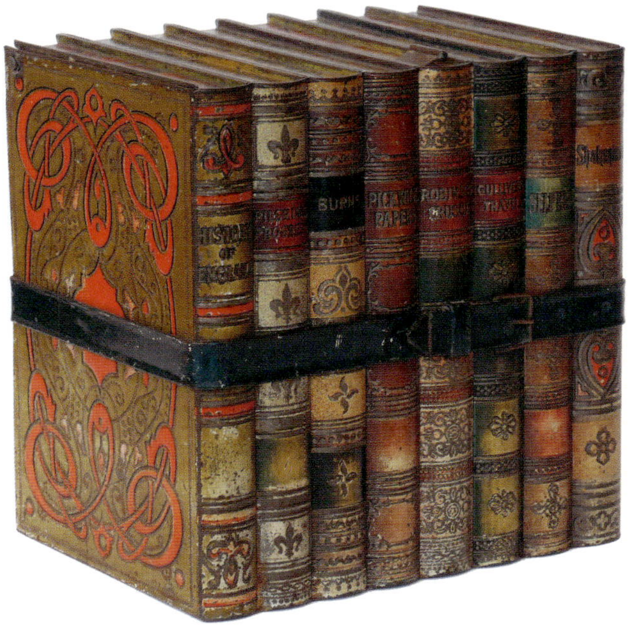

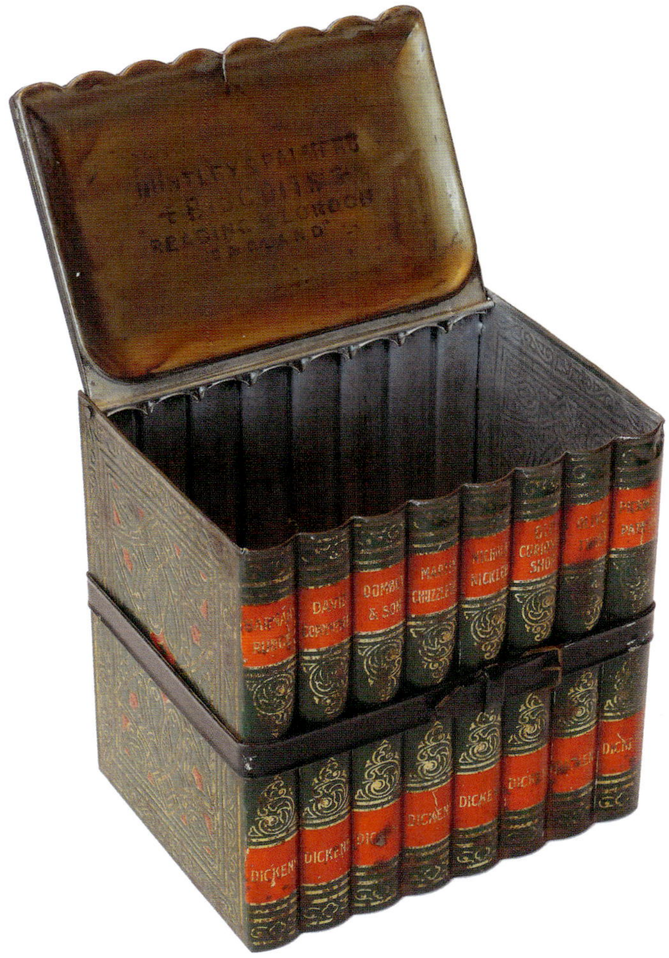

4.002
„Literature“
Lithografierte Blechdose
Lithographed tin box
Huntley & Palmers Biscuits,
Reading & London
1901 | 16 x 16 x 12 cm

4.003
„Dickens“
Lithografierte Blechdose
Lithographed tin box
Huntley & Palmers Biscuits,
Reading & London
1911 | 16 x 16 x 12 cm

4.004
„Bookstand“
Lithografierte Blechdose
Lithographed tin box
Huntley & Palmers Biscuits,
Reading & London
1905 | 16 x 12,8 x 10,9 cm

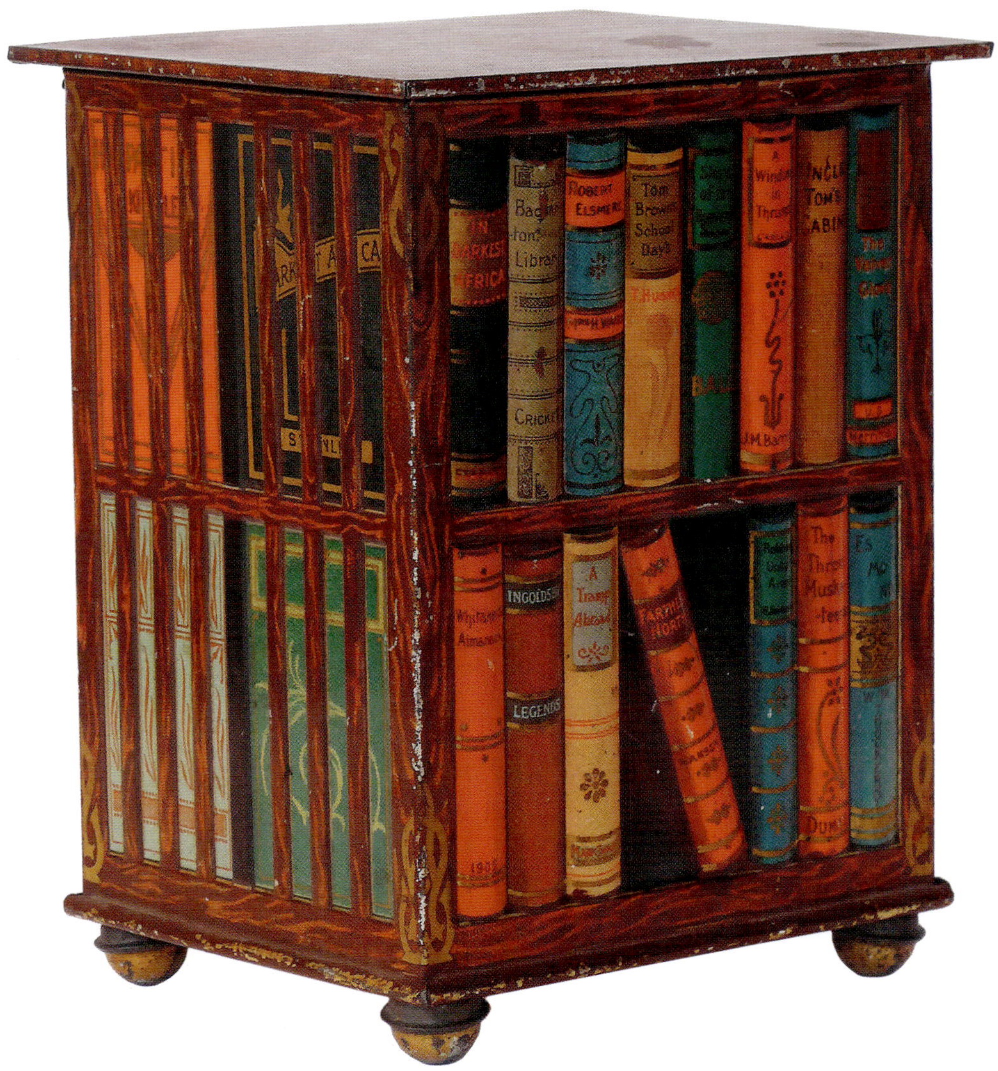

4.005
„Stories“
Lithografierte Blechdose
Lithographed tin box
Huntley & Palmers Biscuits,
Reading & London
1910 | 9,8 x 6,1 x 9,5 cm

4.006
„Book“
Lithografierte Blechdose
Lithographed tin box
Huntley & Palmers Biscuits,
Reading & London
1930 | 3,4 x 24,9 x 18 cm

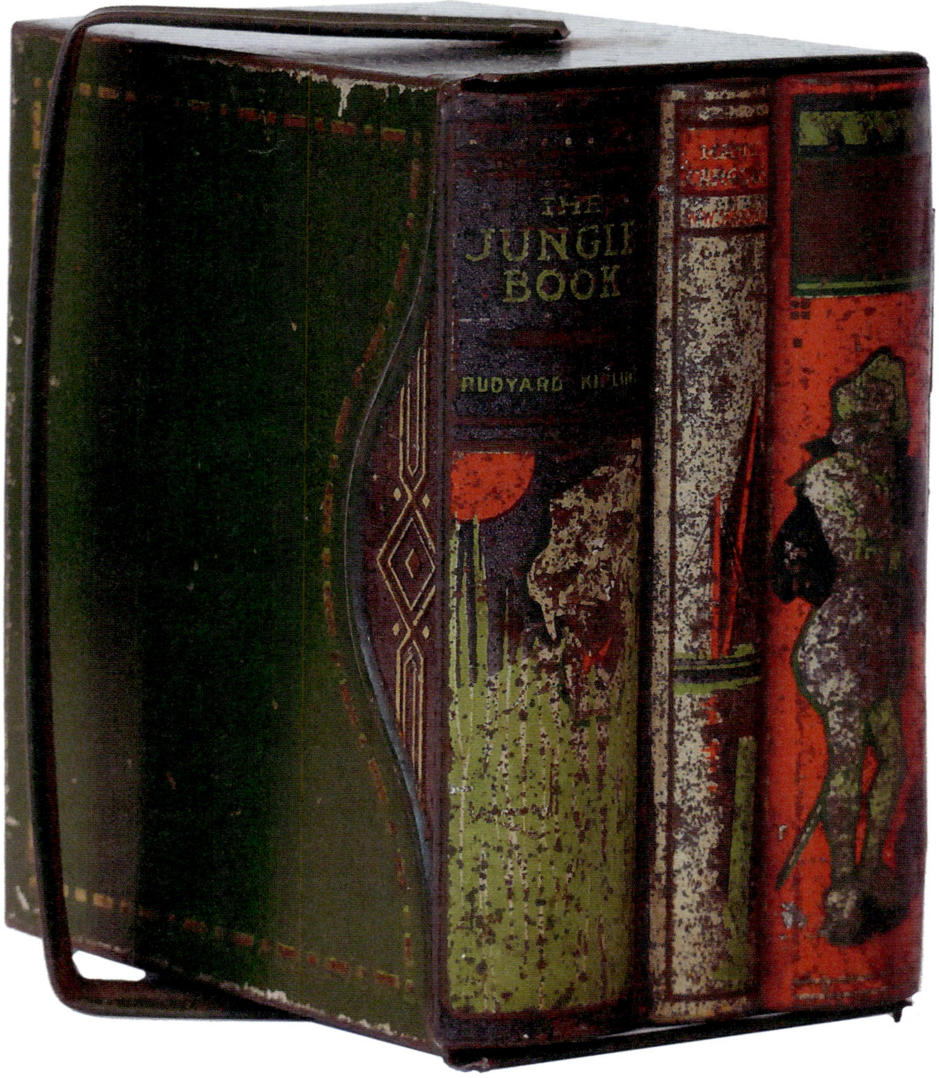

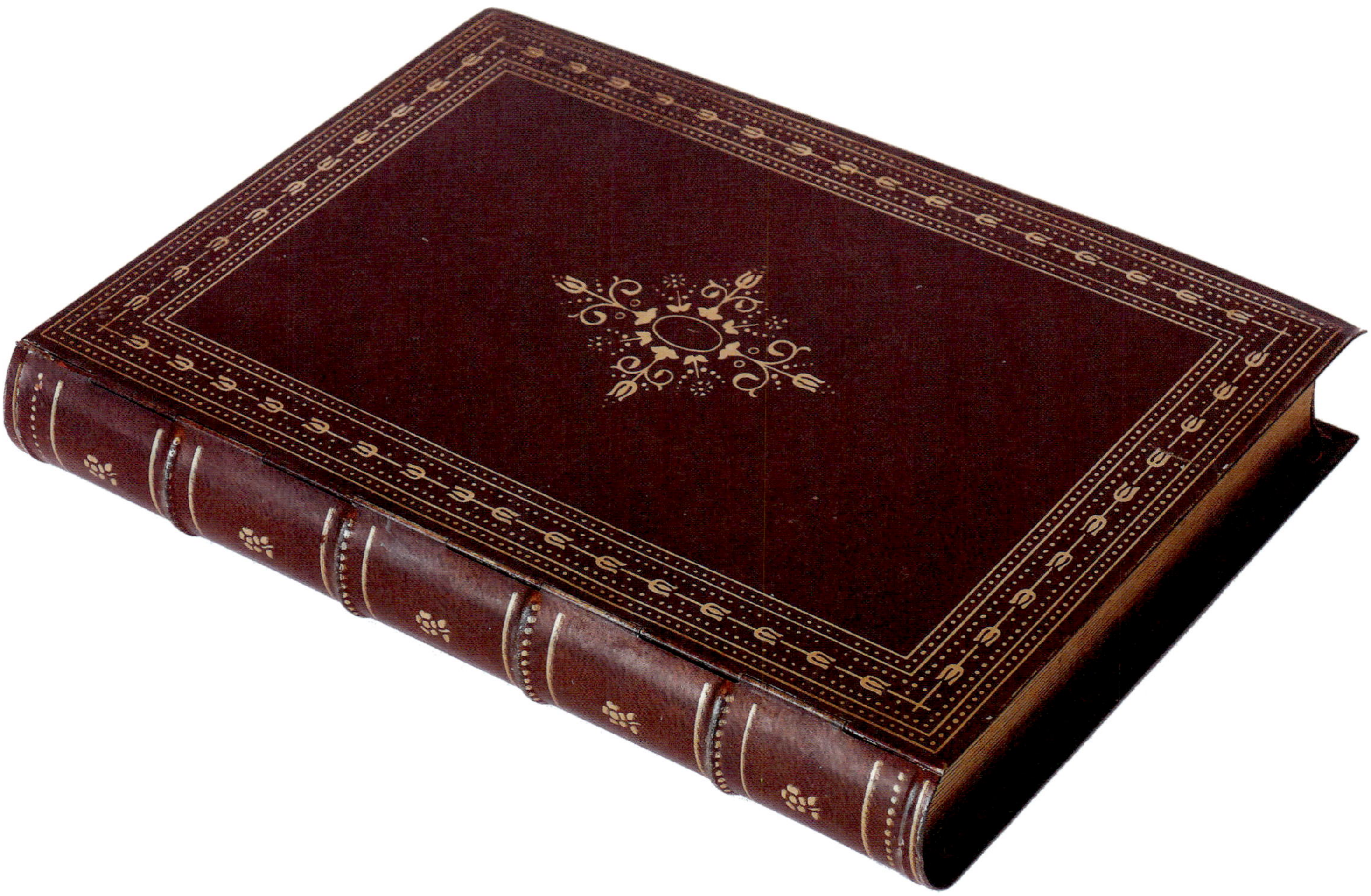

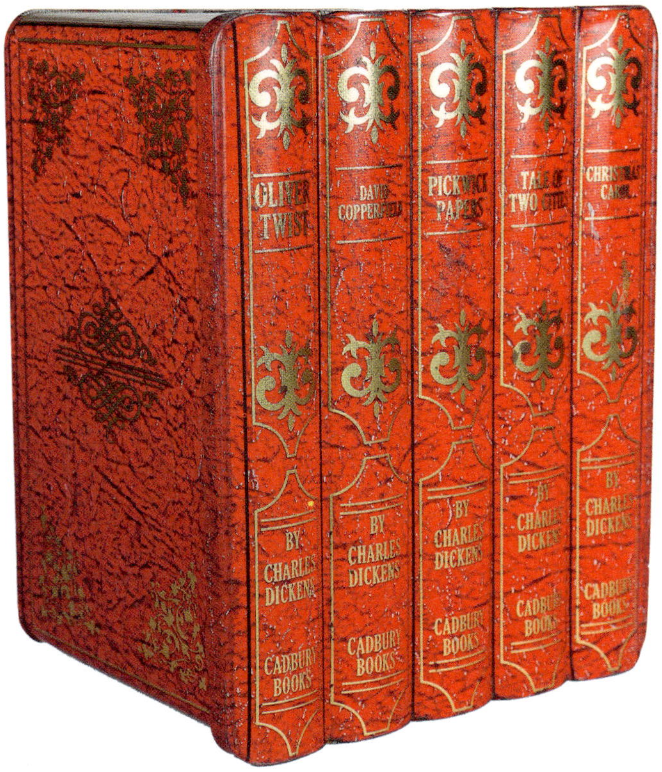

4.007
Christmas Carol, by Charles Dickens
Blechdose für Schokolade
Tin box for chocolate
Cadbury England
9,4 x 11,6 x 14,9 cm

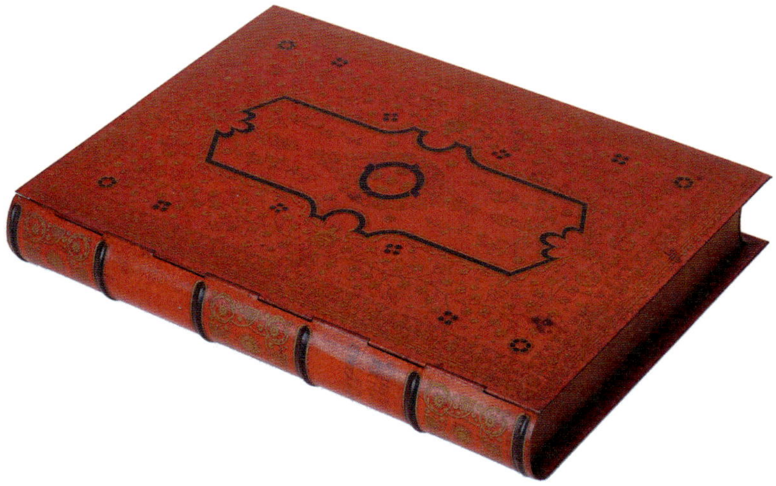

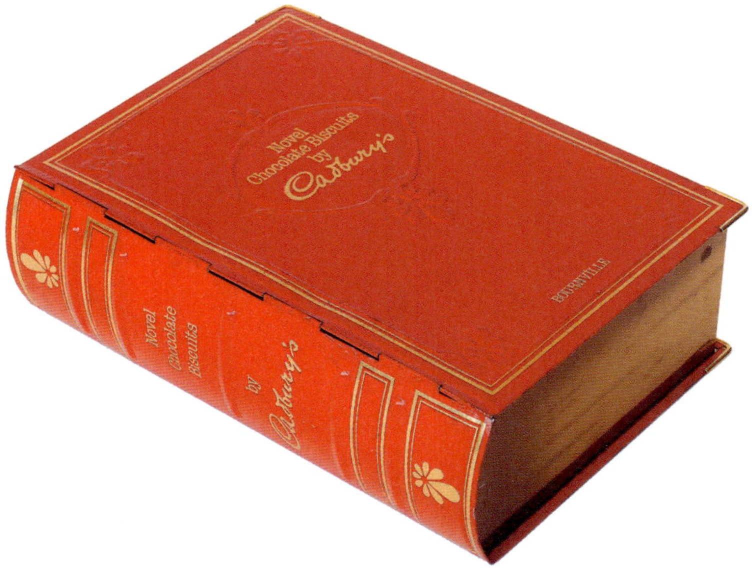

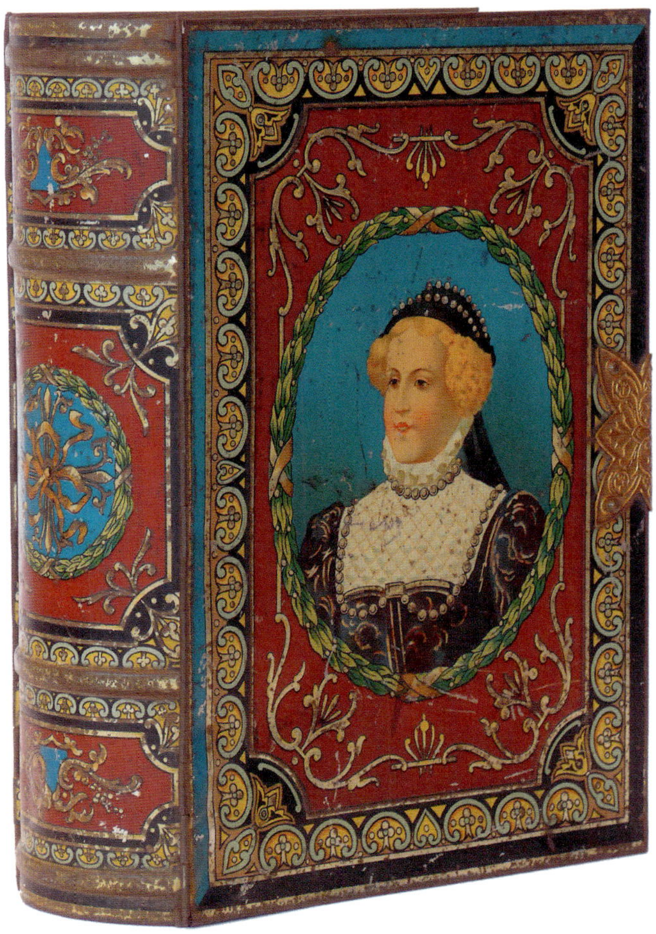

4.008
„Book“
Lithografierte Blechdose
Lithographed tin box
Huntley & Palmers Biscuits, Reading & London
1930 | 3,5 cm x 24,9 x 18 cm

4.009
Blechdose mit Reliefprägung
Tin box with relief embossing
Novel Chocolate Biscuits, Cadbury's, Bournville England
1920 | 7 x 23,5 x 17,1 cm

4.010
„Book“
Lithografierte Blechdose
Lithographed tin box
Die erste als Buch gestaltete Blechdose, der weitere von verschiedenen Herstellern folgten
The first tin box in the design of a book, followed by others from various manufacturers
Peak Frean, Biscuit Manufacturers, London | 1895 | 6,8 x 20,5 x 16 cm

4.011
Bonbons de Chocolat
Blechdose mit Reliefprägung (Segelschiff)
Tin box with relief embossing (sailing boat)
Confiserie Seila, Saint- Étienne Frankreich
Um / *Around* 1960 | 5,7 x 17,6 x 13,1 cm

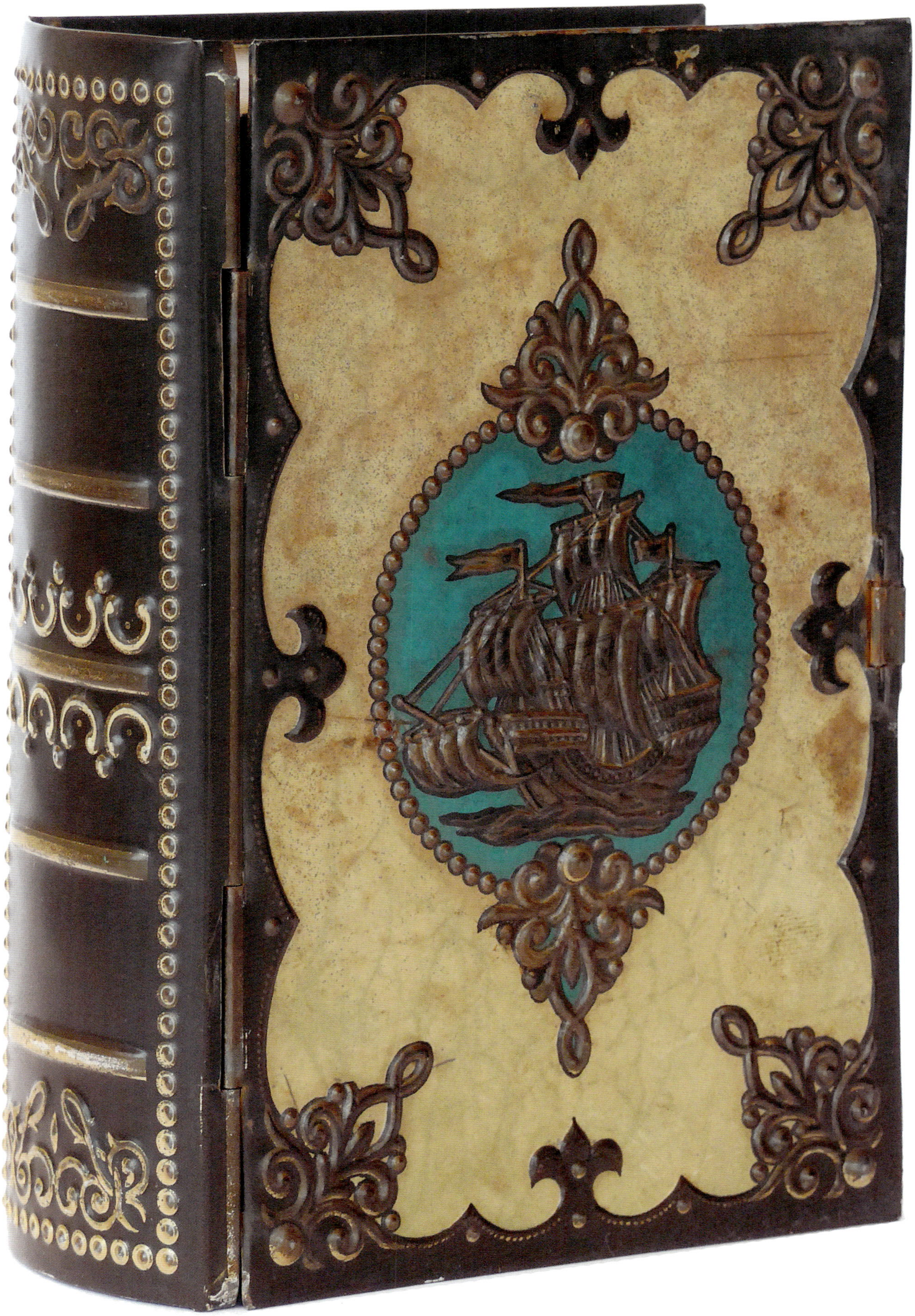

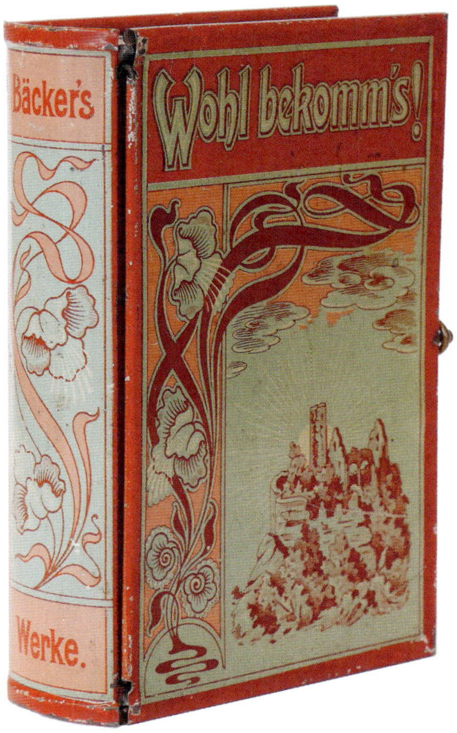

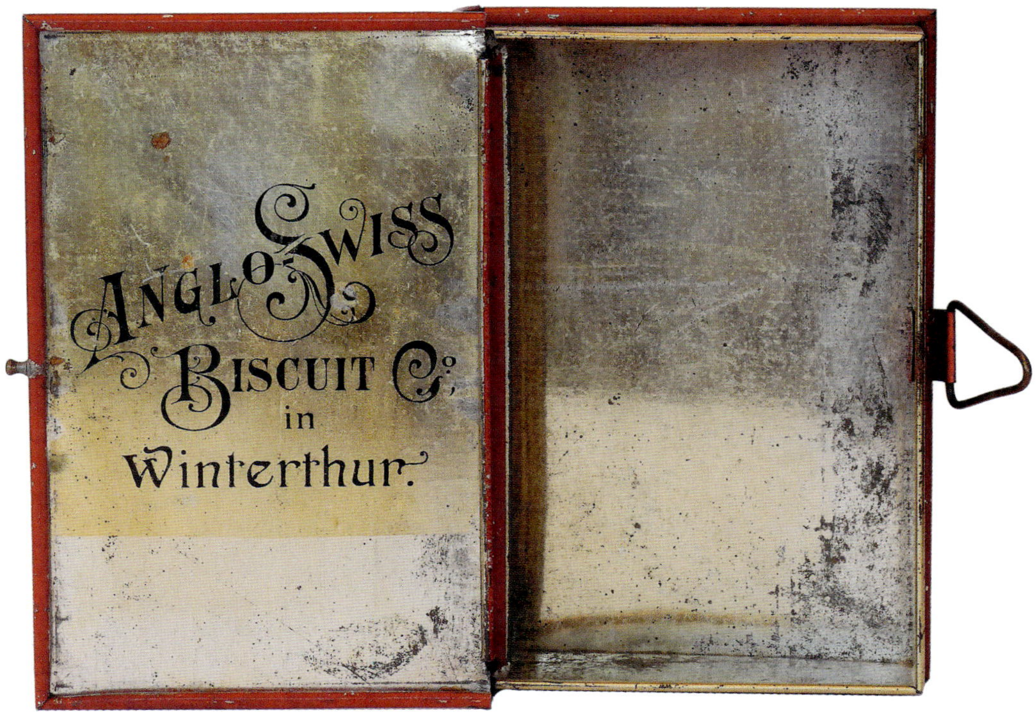

4.012
Bäcker's Werke, Wohl bekomm's!
To Baker's Works, Cheers!
Lithografierte Jugendstil-Blechdose für Biscuits
Lithographed Art Nouveau tin box for cookies
Anglo Swiss Biscuits Winterthur, Switzerland
Um / *Around* 1900 | 15,8 x 11,2 x 3,9 cm

4.013
Bonbons de Chocolat
Blechdose mit Reliefprägung (römischer Kopf)
Tin box with relief embossing (roman head)
Confiserie Seila, Saint-Étienne France
Um / *Around* 1960 | 5,7 x 17,6 x 13,1 cm

4.014
Morceaux Choisis
Lithografierte Biskuit-Blechdose, sieben erhabene Bünde, dreiseitiger Goldschnitt
Lithographed biscuit box, seven raised bands, all edges gilt
Frankreich / *France* | 5,7 x 29,4 x 19,7 cm

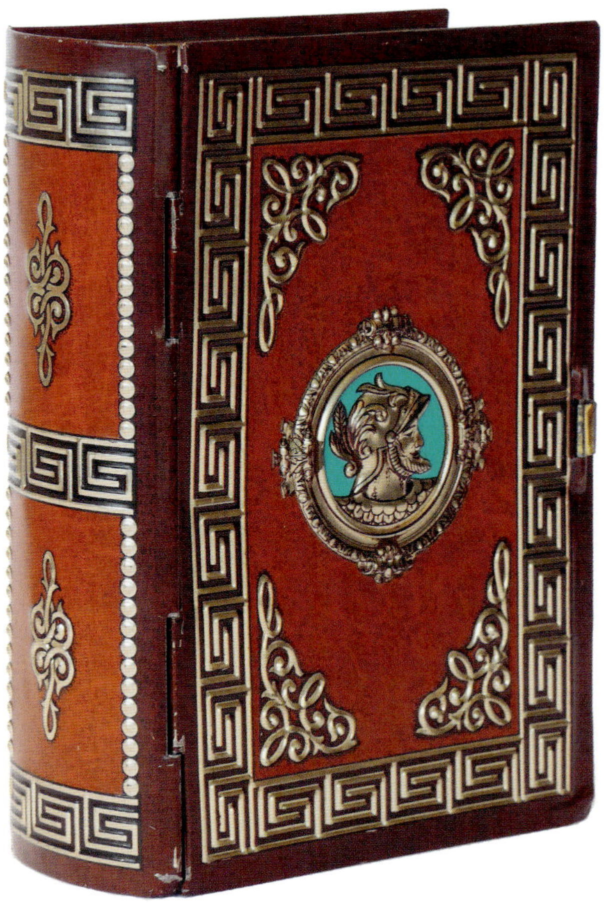

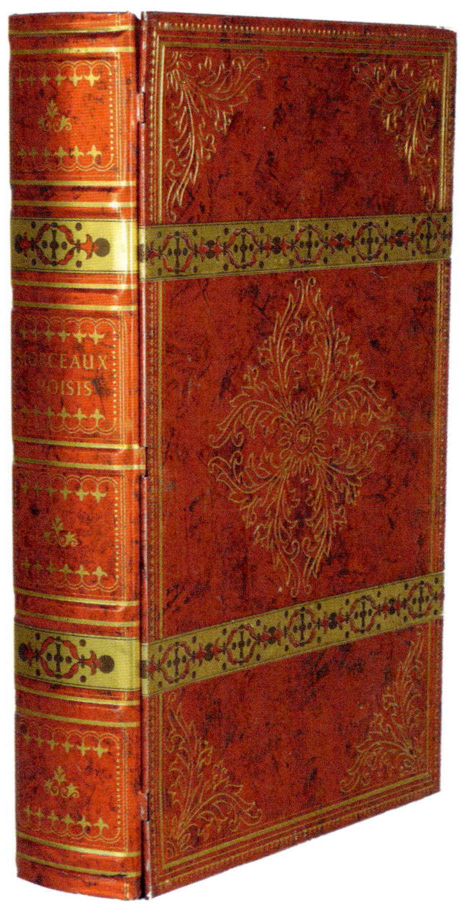

4.015
Kartondose mit Chromolithografie eines Liebespaares auf dem Vorderdeckel, dreiseitig geprägter Goldschnitt
Box with chromolithography of a lovers' couple on the cover, gold-tooled edges
Chocolat Maestrani
Um / *Around* 1930 | 2 x 8 x 6,2 cm

4.016
Kartondose mit Chromolithografie eines Liebespaares auf dem Vorderdeckel, dreiseitig geprägter Goldschnitt
Box with chromolithography of a lovers' couple on the cover, gold-tooled edges
Fabrique de Chocolat J. Klaus, Le Locle Suisse
Um / *Around* 1930 | 2 x 8 x 6,2 cm

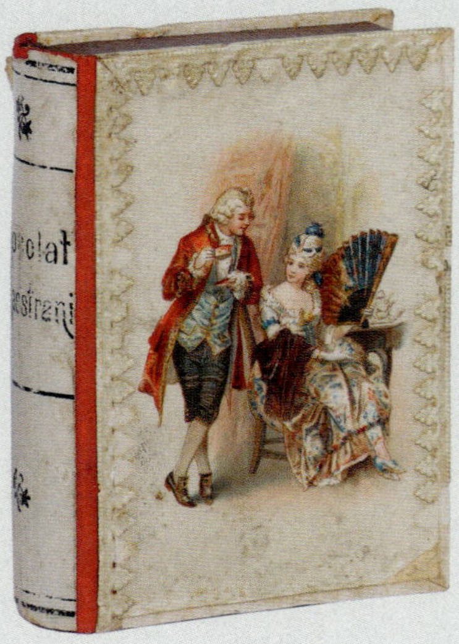

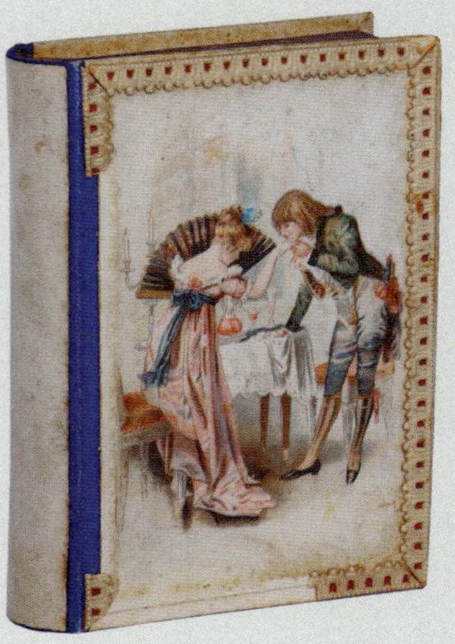

4.017
Kartondose mit Chromolithografie eines Mädchens auf dem Vorderdeckel, dreiseitig geprägter Goldschnitt
Box with chromolithography of a girl on the cover, gold-tooled edges
Chocolat Maestrani, St. Gallen Suisse
Um / *Around* 1930 | 2 x 8 x 6,2 cm

4.018
Kartondose mit Chromolithografie zweier Kinder auf dem Vorderdeckel, dreiseitig geprägter Goldschnitt
Box with chromolithography of two children on the cover, gold-tooled edges
Chocolat Maestrani
Um / *Around* 1930 | 2 x 8 x 6,2 cm

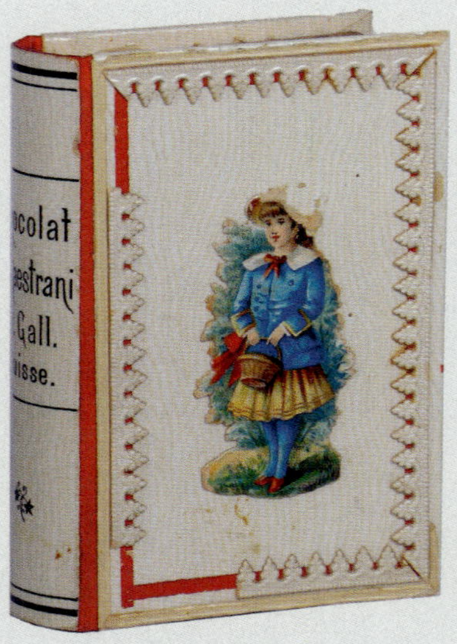

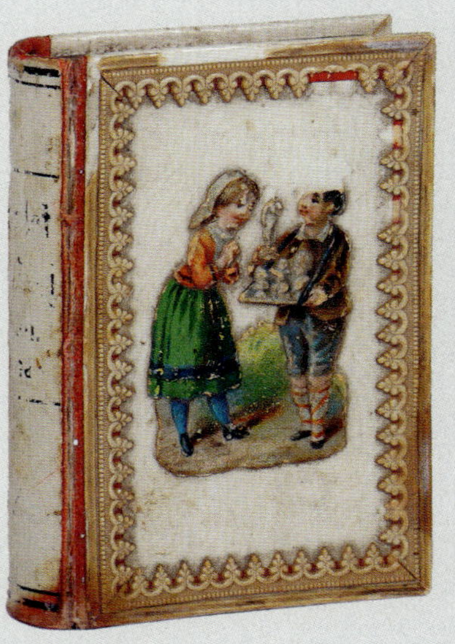

4.019
Vallotton Lausanne
Kartondose mit Chromolithografie eines Liebespaares auf dem Vorderdeckel, dreiseitig geprägter Goldschnitt
Box with chromolithography of a lovers' couple on the cover, gold-tooled edges
Um / *Around* 1930 | 2,1 x 8 x 6,4 cm

4.020
Chocolat Maestrani
Kartondose für Schokolade, Chromolithografie mit Rosensujet auf dem Vorderdeckel, dreiseitig geprägter Goldschnitt
Box for chocolate, chromolithography with a rose design on the cover, gold-tooled edges
Um / *Around* 1930 | 2 x 8 x 6,2 cm

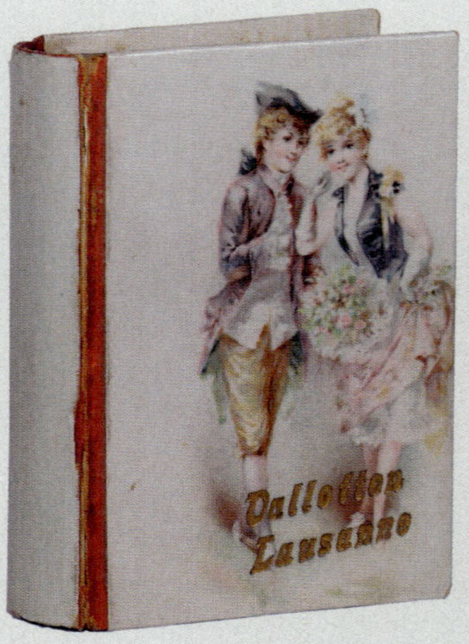

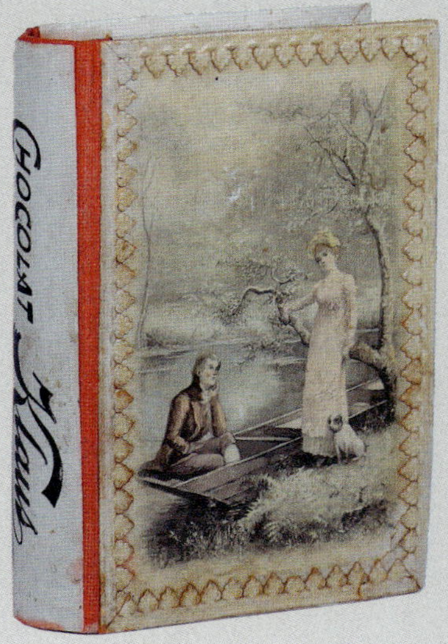

4.021
Kartondose mit Chromolithografie eines Rosensujets auf dem Vorderdeckel, dreiseitig geprägter Goldschnitt
Box with chromolithography of a rose otheme on the cover, gold-tooled edges
Chocolat Maestrani
Um / *Around* 1930 | 2 x 8 x 6,2 cm

4.022
Kartondose mit Chromolithografie eines Paares und Schiffs auf dem Vorderdeckel, dreiseitig geprägter Goldschnitt,
Box with chromolithography of a couple and a ship on the cover, gold-tooled edges
Chocolat Klaus, No. 32
Um / *Around* 1930 | 2 x 8,5 x 6,5 cm

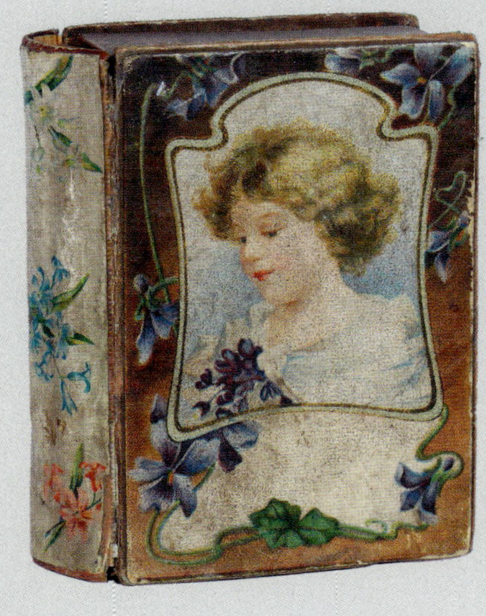

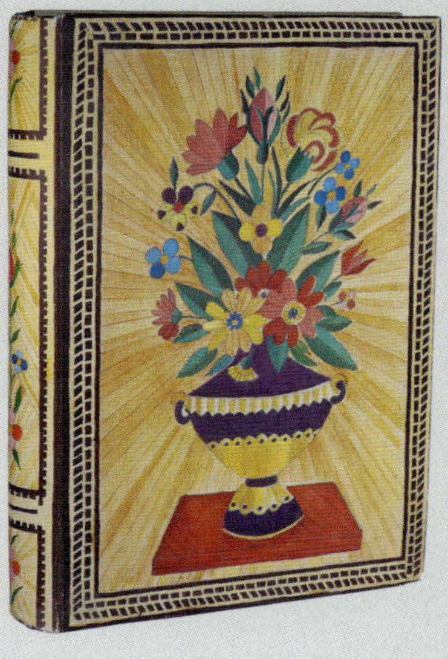

4.023
Kartondose mit Chromolithografie eines Mädchens auf dem Vorderdeckel, dreiseitig geprägter Papierschnitt
Box with chromolithography of a girl on the cover, embossed paper edges
Herkunft unbekannt/ *Origin unknown*
Jugendstil / *Art Nouveau* | 2,9 x 10,1 x 8,5 cm

4.024
Marquise de Sevigné, C. Rouzaud, Chocolats Paris
Kartonschachtel für Schokolade, geprägte farbige Vase mit Blumenbouquet auf Vorderdeckel, dreiseitiger Goldschnitt
Cardboard box for chocolate, vase with an embossed flower bouquet on the cover, all edges gilt
Um / *Around* 1900 | 4,2 x 29 x 21,8 cm

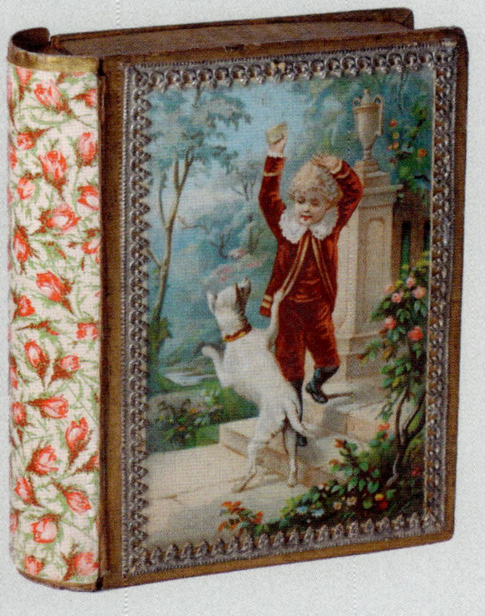

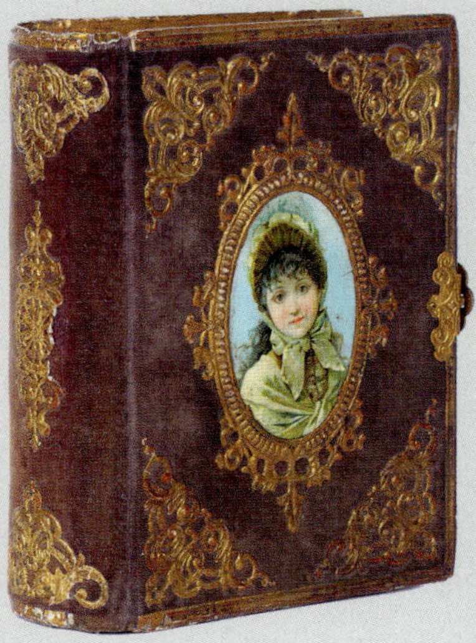

4.025
Chromolithografie eines Kindes mit Hund auf dem Vorderdeckel, eingerahmt mit Goldlitzen, Hinterdeckel mit Blumen-Buntpapier, Goldschnitt
Chromolithography of a child with a dog on the cover, framed with gold dentelle, rear board with floral paper-over-board, gilt edges
Chocolat Maestrani
19. Jh. / *19th century* | 10,5 x 9,2 x 2,5 cm

4.026
Plüschschatulle mit lithografiertem ovalen Mädchenporträt, applizierte goldgeprägte Papierverzierungen, dreiseitig geprägter Goldschnitt, Messingschließe
Box with plush-over-board, oval lithography of a girl, gilt paper ornaments, gold-tooled edges, brass buckle
Um / *Around* 1930 | 4,4 x 14 x 11,5 cm

4.027
Schokoladenverpackung mit acht Buchrücken, vier Standfüße, rückseitige Schublade, Vitrinenaufsatz mit Logo, Bändel zum Tragen
Chocolate box with eight book spines, four feet, drawer on the back, display with logo, ribbon to carry
Chocolat Kohler, Lausanne
1790–1874 | 8 x 13,5 x 4 cm

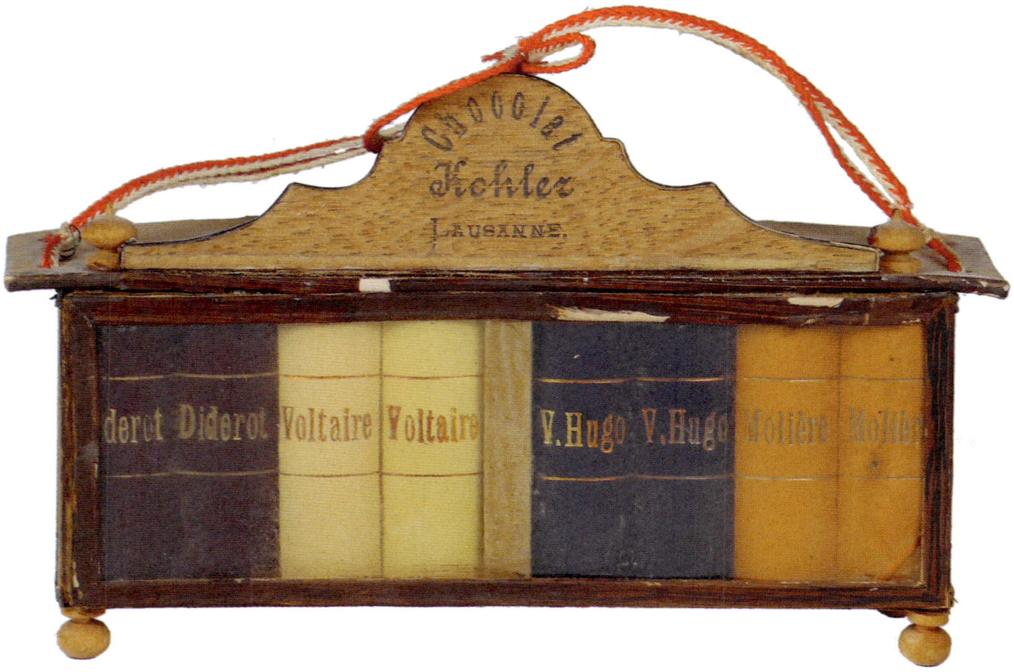

4.028
„Göthe"
Kartonkästchen mit Buchrücken aus Seide, rückseitige Schublade, Deckel mit Holzimitationspapier, vier Standfüße, Bändel zum Aufhängen, Christbaumschmuck?
Box with silk spine strips, drawer on the back, lid with faux wood paper, four feet, ribbon to be hang, Christmas tree decoration?
G.L. Männer, Hoflieferant Stuttgart
4,2 x 6 x 3 cm

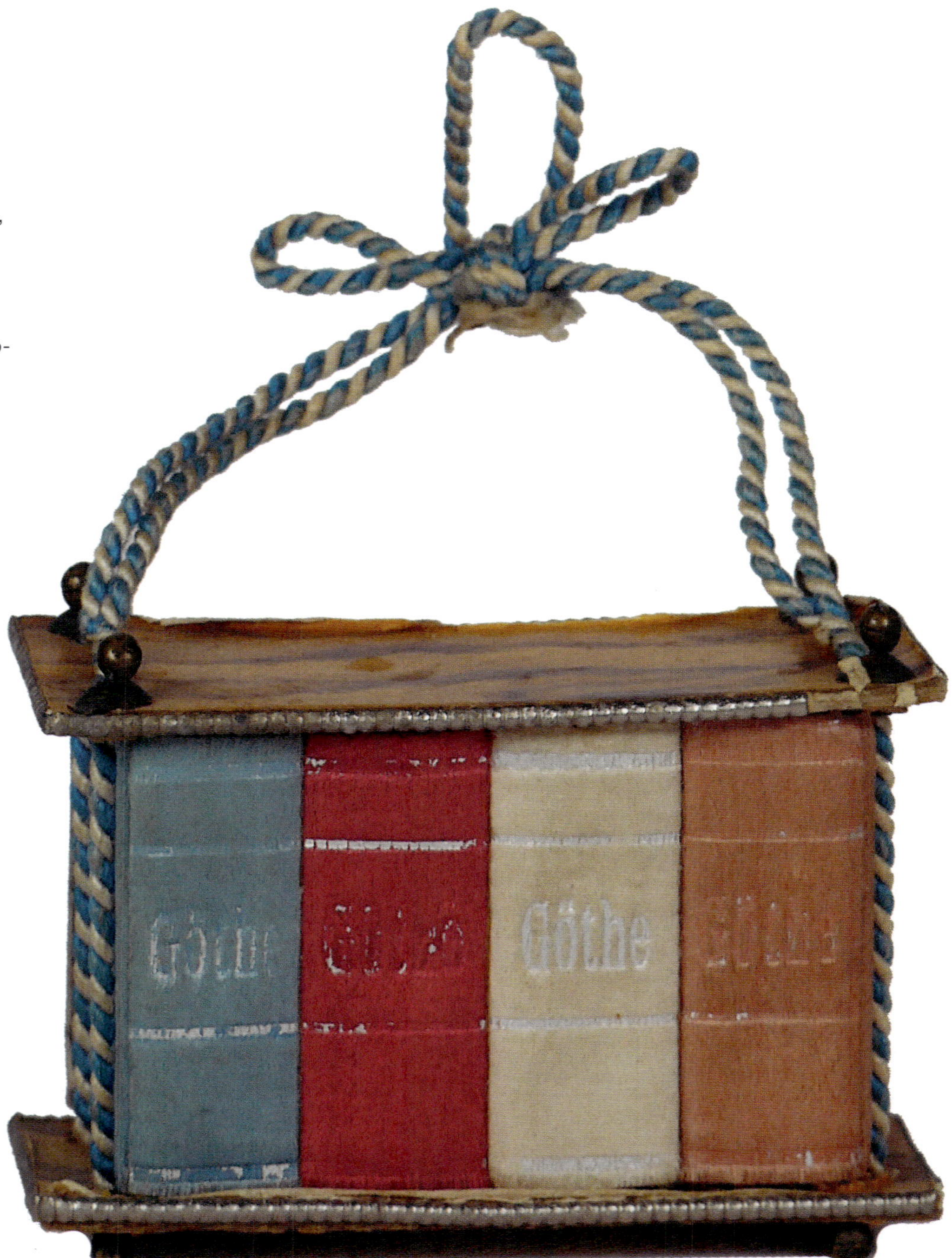

4.029
Aufgeschlagene Halbkartonschachtel, Stulpdecken mit zwei aufgeklebten Bildern von Albert Anker, dreiseitiger Goldschnitt, Gewebeboden
Open semi-cardboard box, pictures by Albert Anker glued on the slip lid, all edges gilt, fabric lining
3,9 x 24,8 x 16 cm

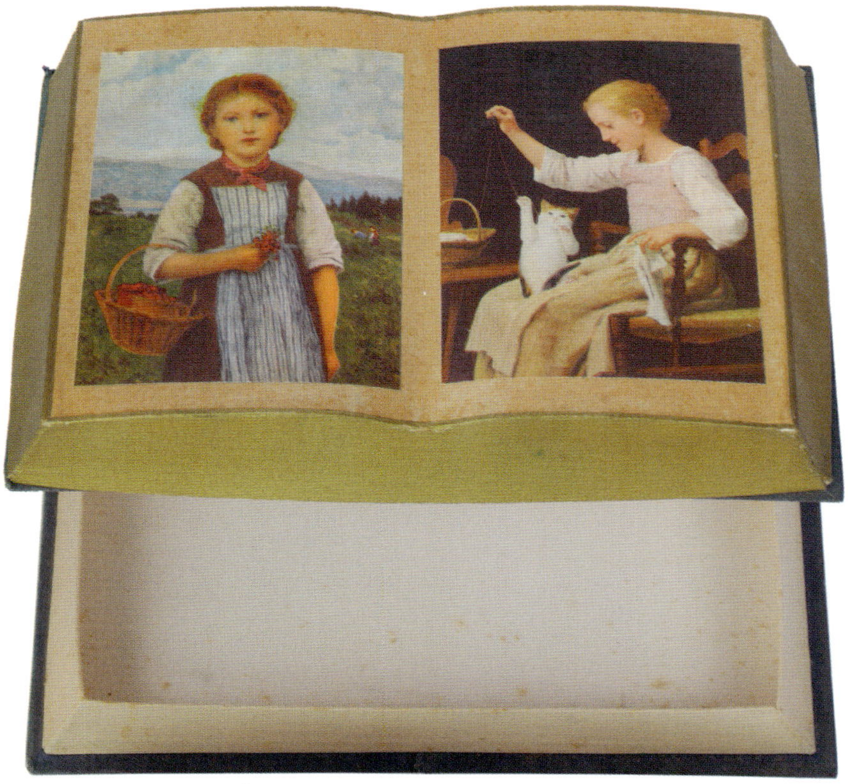

4.030
Halbgewebebuchschachtel goldfarben und farbig bedruckt, Behältnis für Schokolade, große Ecken, vier Halbkartonklappen, Moirépapiervorsatz, dreiseitiger Goldschnitt, Schuber
Half fabric box for chocolate with gold and color printing, large edges, four semi-cardboard flaps, moiré paper endpaper, all edges gilt, slipcase
Chocolat Meurice, Belgium
25,8 x 18,5 x 3,7 cm

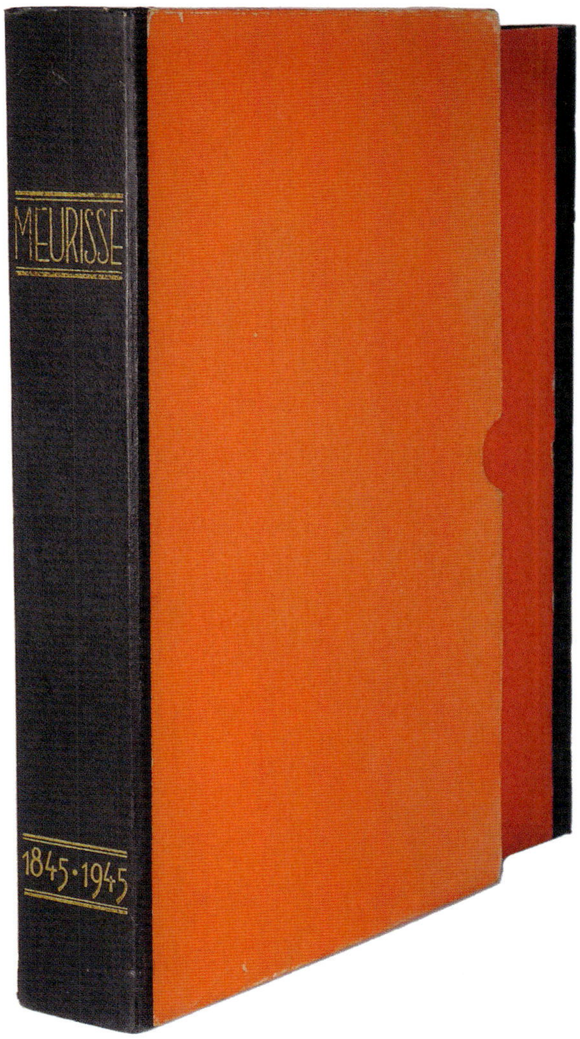

4.031
Tobler, Süsse Geschichten;
Tobler Rêves d'Or
Tobler, Sweet Stories
Wattierte Kartonschachtel mit Papierüberzug für Pralinés, Titelprägung, dreiseitiger Goldschnitt
Padded paperboard box with paper-over-board for pralines, stamped title, all edges gilt
3,3 x 20,8 x 13,5 cm

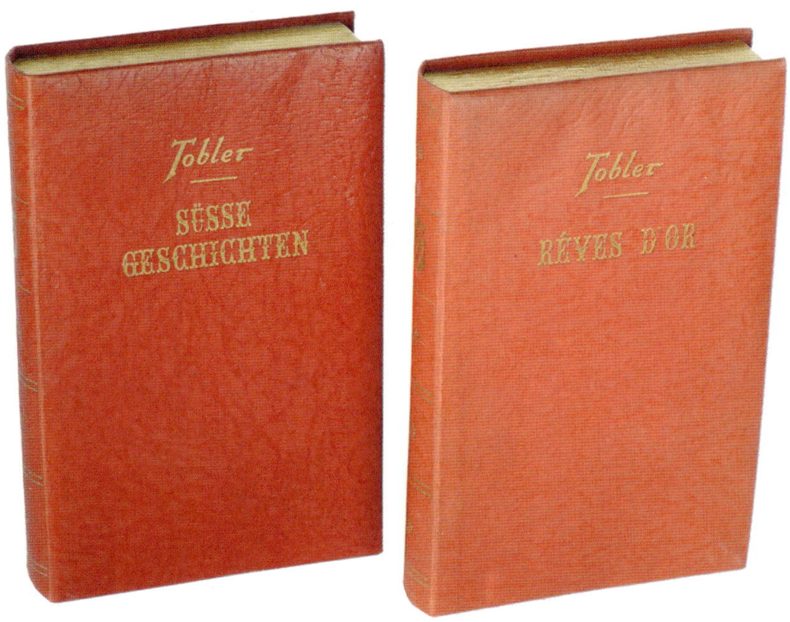

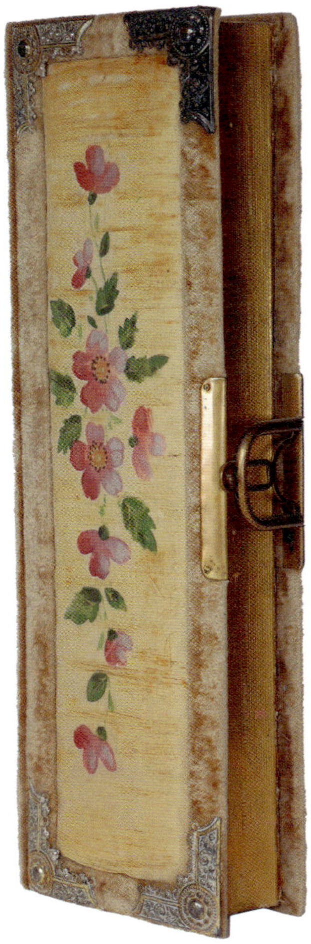

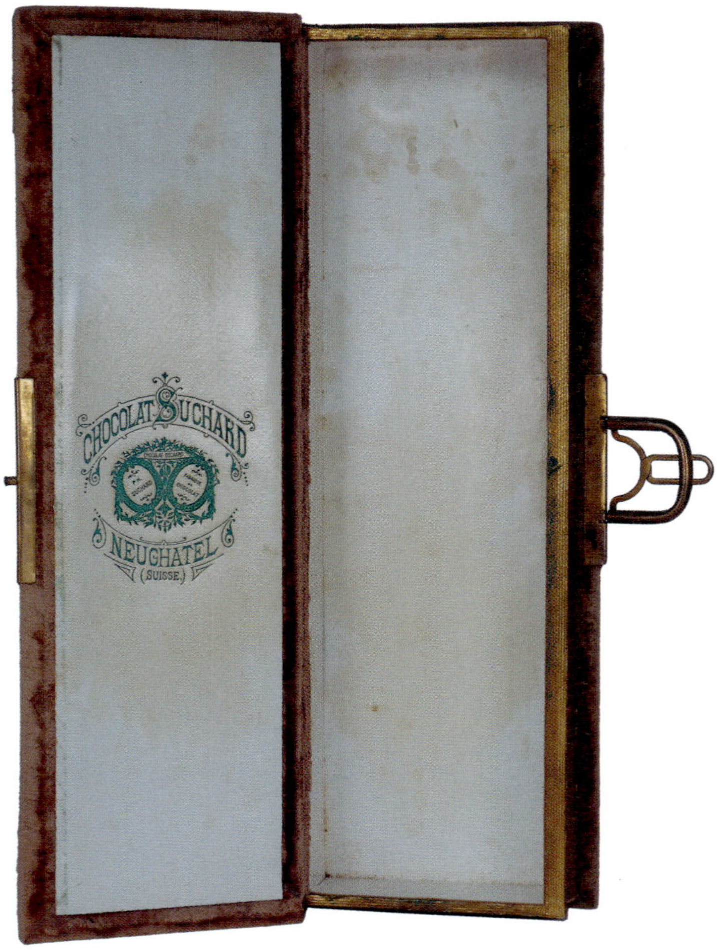

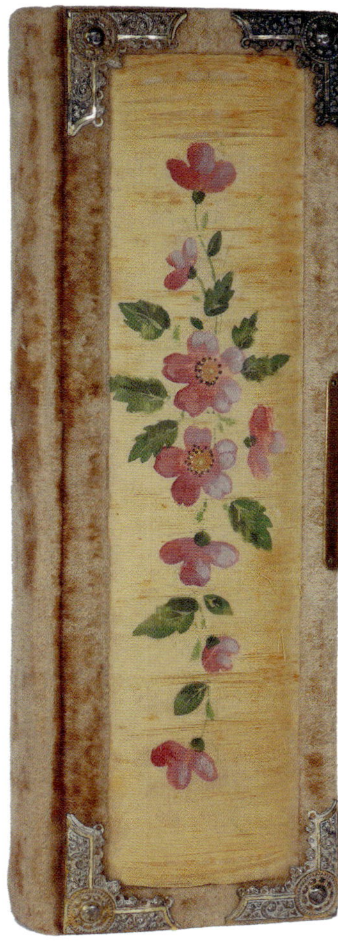

4.032
Aufwändige Schatulle aus Plüsch, Seidenmalerei auf dem Vorderdeckel, Metalleckenbeschläge, Messingschließe, geprägter Goldschnitt, ausgefüttert mit Glanzpapier, vier Messingstandfüße, Firmenstempel im Innendeckel
Extravagant box in plush, with silk painting on the front lid, metal corner fittings, brass buckle, gold-tooled edges , lined with glossy paper, four brass feet, logo on the interior of the lid
Chocolat P.H. Suchard, Neuchâtel Suisse
19. Jh. / *19th century* | 5,5 x 36 x 12,8 cm

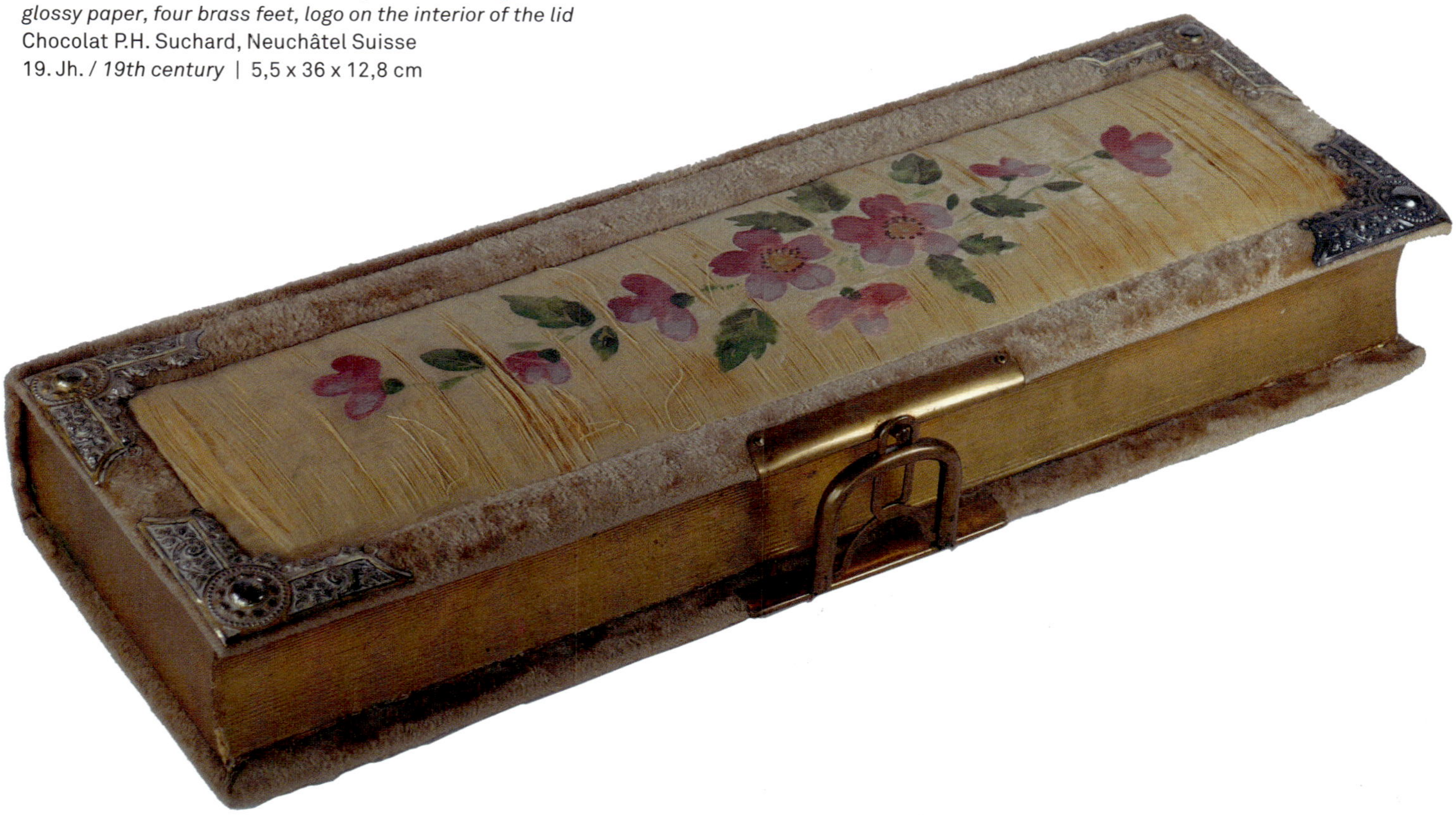

4.033
Kartonschachtel mit reliefgeprägtem Vorderdeckel, idyllische Häuserszene und Blumenmotiv, dreiseitig geprägter Goldschnitt
Box with relief embossing on the lid, illustraion of an idyllic house and flowers, embossed gold-tooled edges
Fabrique de Chocolat, J. Klaus, Locle Suisse
Spätes 19. Jh. / *Late 19th century*
2,5 x 14,2 x 10 cm

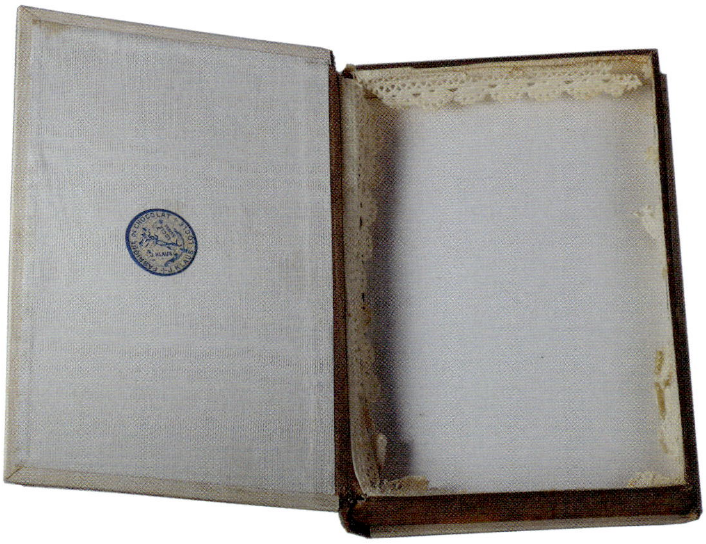

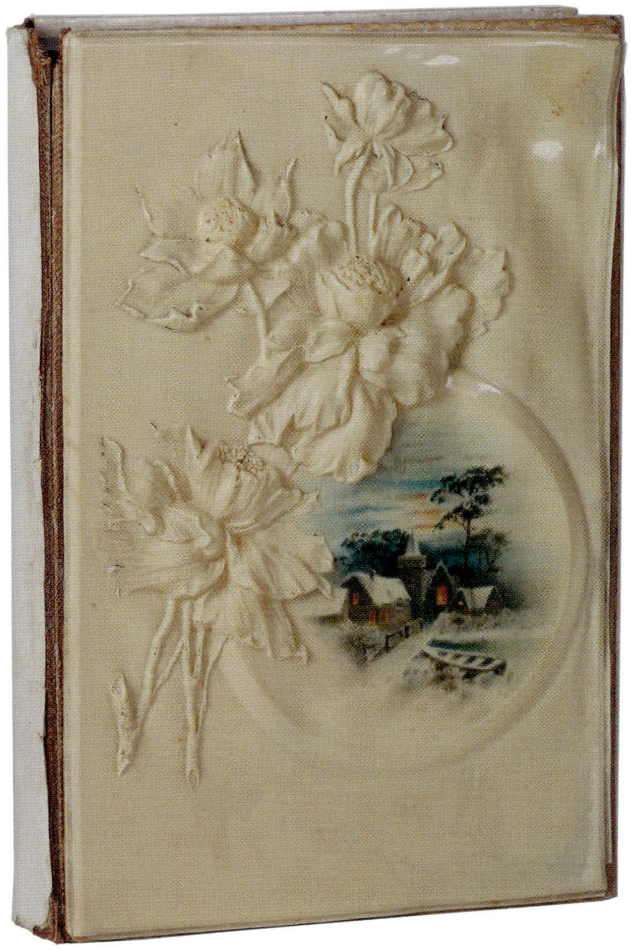

4.034
Plüschschatulle mit reliefartigem Kunststoffdeckel, romantische Häuserszene mit See auf dem Vorderdeckel, dreiseitig geprägter Goldschnitt, zwei Verschlussbändern, Spiegel mit geprägtem Krokodilleder-Imitationspapier
Box with plush cover, relief front board in plastic, romantic house with lake, gold-tooled edges , two straps, pastedown embossed crocodile skin limitation paper
3,5 x 17,1 x 13,2 cm

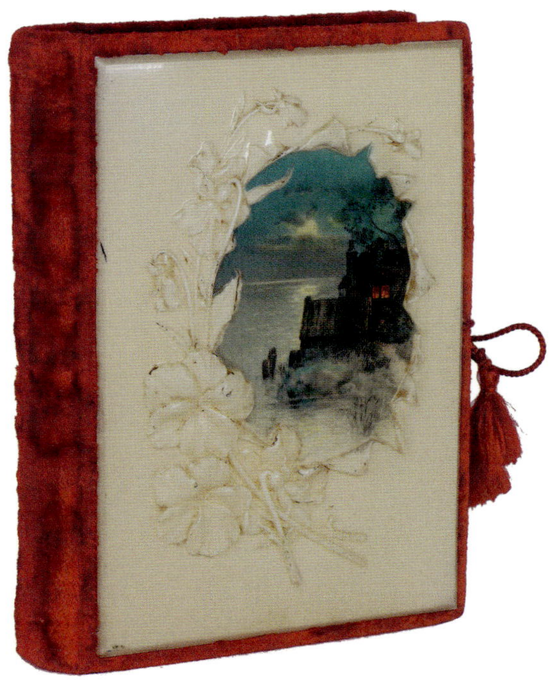

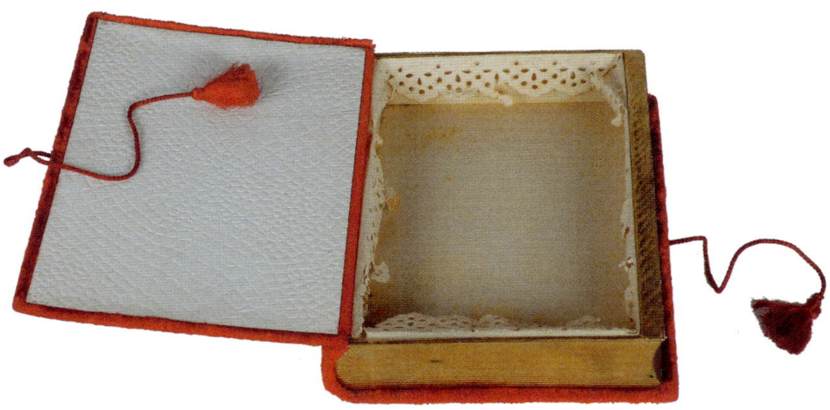

4.035
Plüschdose mit aufgesetztem Metallblumenrelief auf dem Vorderdeckel, Messingschließe, Firmenbezeichnung auf dem Vorderspiegel, dreiseitiger Goldschnitt
Box with plush cover, metal flower relief on the front cover, brass buckle, company name on the front mirror, all edges gilt
Chocolat Suchard, P.H. Suchard, Fabrique de Chocolat
19. Jh. / *19th century* | 2,2 x 10,1 x 8 cm

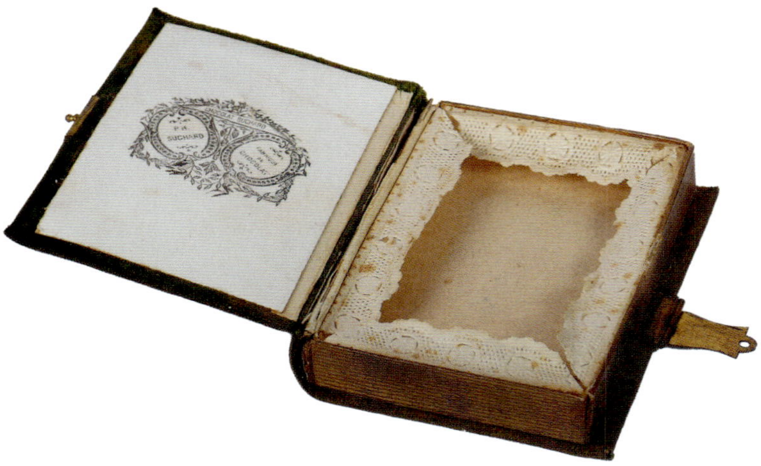

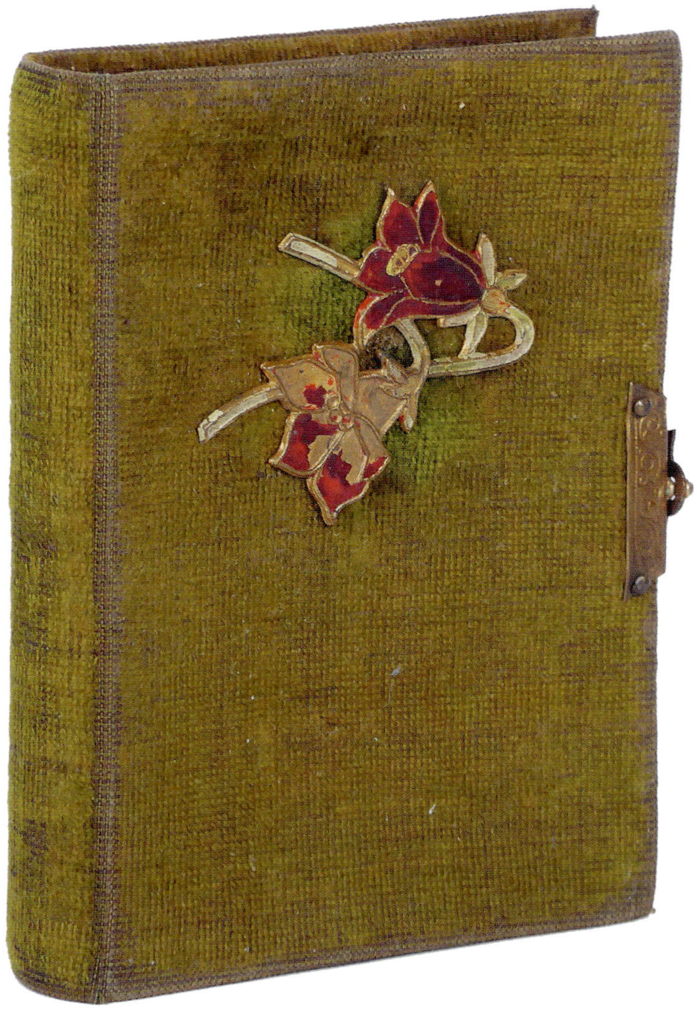

4.036
Album
Kartondose mit Papierüberzug, Vorder- und Hinterdeckel mit Prägung, ausgefüttert mit weißem Moirépapier, dreiseitiger Goldschnitt
Box with paper cover, embossed front and back cover, lined with white moiré paper, all edges gilt
Um / *Around* 1900 | 2 x 8,5 x 4,7 cm

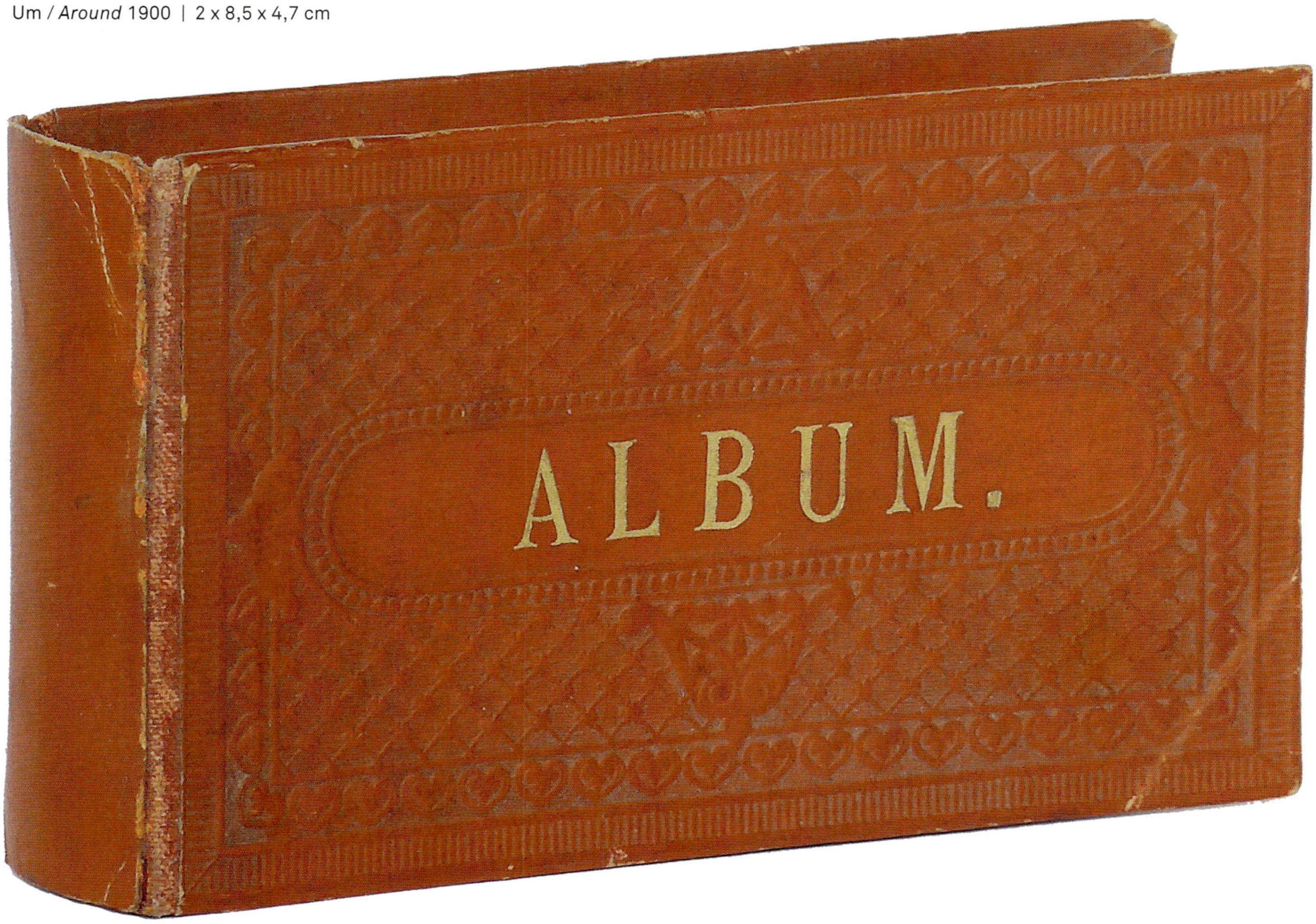

4.037
Fruits Glaces
Bombierte Kartondose mit Rücken- und Deckelgoldprägung, Messingschließe, dreiseitiger Goldschnitt, ausgefüttert mit weißem Glanzpapier
Cambered box with gilt tooling on the spine and covers, a brass buckle, all edges gilt, lined with white glossy paper
Um / *Around* 1900 | 3,5 x 14,2 x 12 cm

4.038
Kartonschachtel mit Papierüberzug, Stadtwappenaufdruck, dreiseitiger Goldschnitt
Box with paper-over-board, imprint of a city's emblem, all edges gilt
Duceau Angoulême, Chocolaterie, 18 Hotel de Ville, France
3,5 x 18,5 x 15,2 cm

4.039
Kartondose mit Messingverschluss für Dragées, goldbedruckter Vorderdeckel, dreiseitiger Goldschnitt
Cardboard box with brass closure for drops, gilt front cover, all edges gilt
Leon Braquier, Confiseur Chocolatier Verdun, Maison fondée en 1783 | 2,6 x 10,9 x 8,8 cm

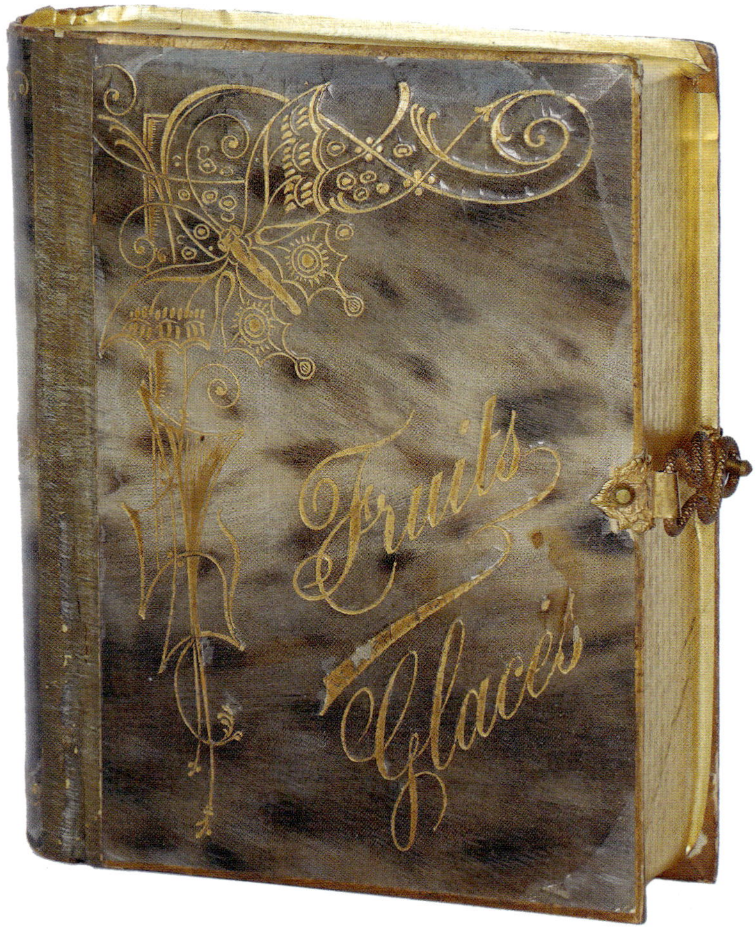

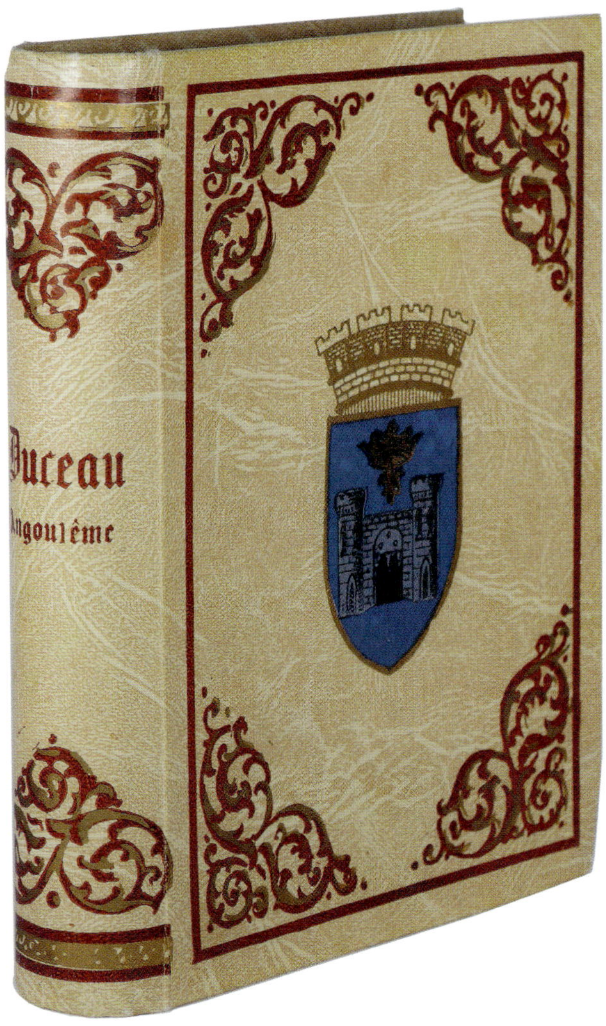

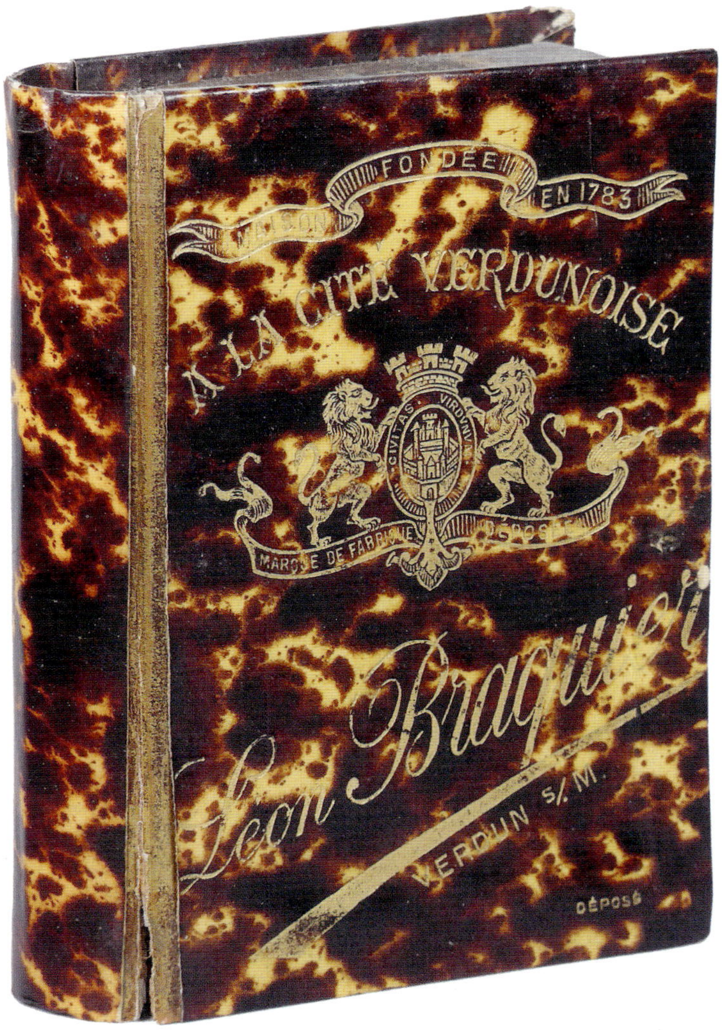

4.040
Compagnie Francaise, With the season's, Hearty greetings
Kartondose für Schokolade, Lithografierte Häuserszene mit Garten auf dem Vorderdeckel, Titelprägung auf dem Rücken- und Hinterdeckel, dreiseitiger Goldschnitt, Verschlussbänder
Cardboard box for chocolate, lithographed house with garden on the front lid, title embossing on the spine and back cover, gilt edges, straps
France
2,5 cx 9,9 x 8,2 cm

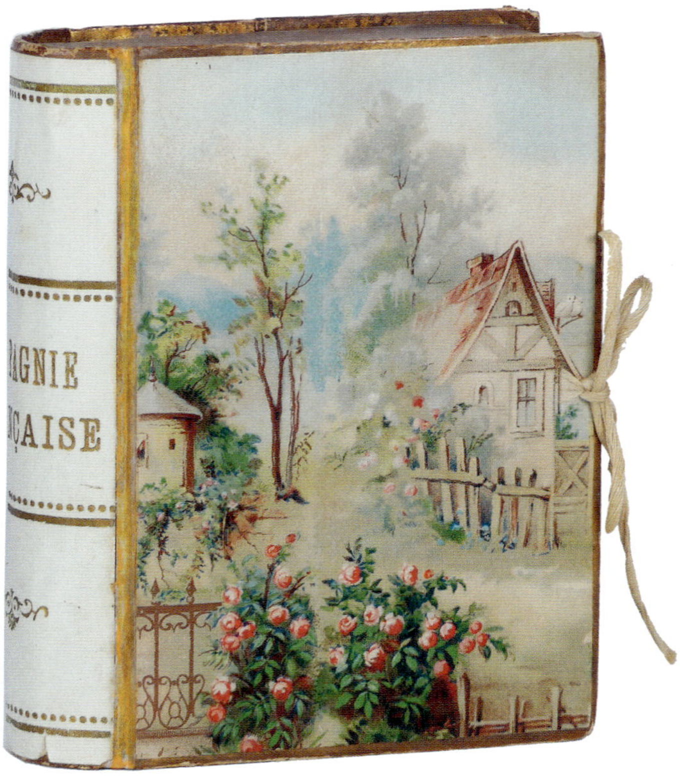

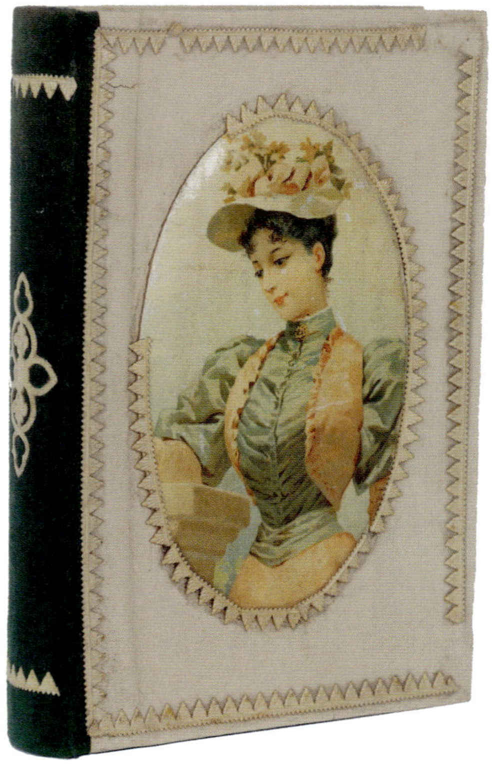

4.041
Plüschschatulle mit lithografiertem ovalen erhabenen Mädchenporträt auf dem Vorderdeckel, beiger Papierüberzug, Papierornamente, dreiseitig geprägter Goldschnitt
Box with plush cover and lithographed oval raised portrait of a girl on the front cover, beige paper-over-board, paper ornaments, gold-tooled edges
Um / *Around* 1900 | 2,6 x 15,7 x 11,5 cm

4.042
Kartonschachtel mit Papierüberzug für persisches Nougat (Gaz), Rückenbeschriftung, Persische Miniatur auf dem Vorderdeckel
Box with paper-over-board for Persian nougat (Gaz), label on the spine, Persian miniature on the front cover
Persian Nougat, Edition IV
Zeitgenössisch / *Contemporary* | 2,8 x 16 x 11 cm

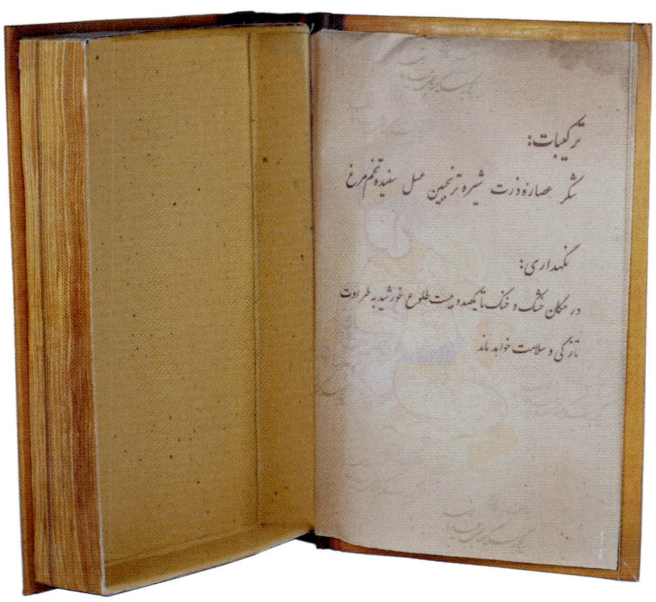

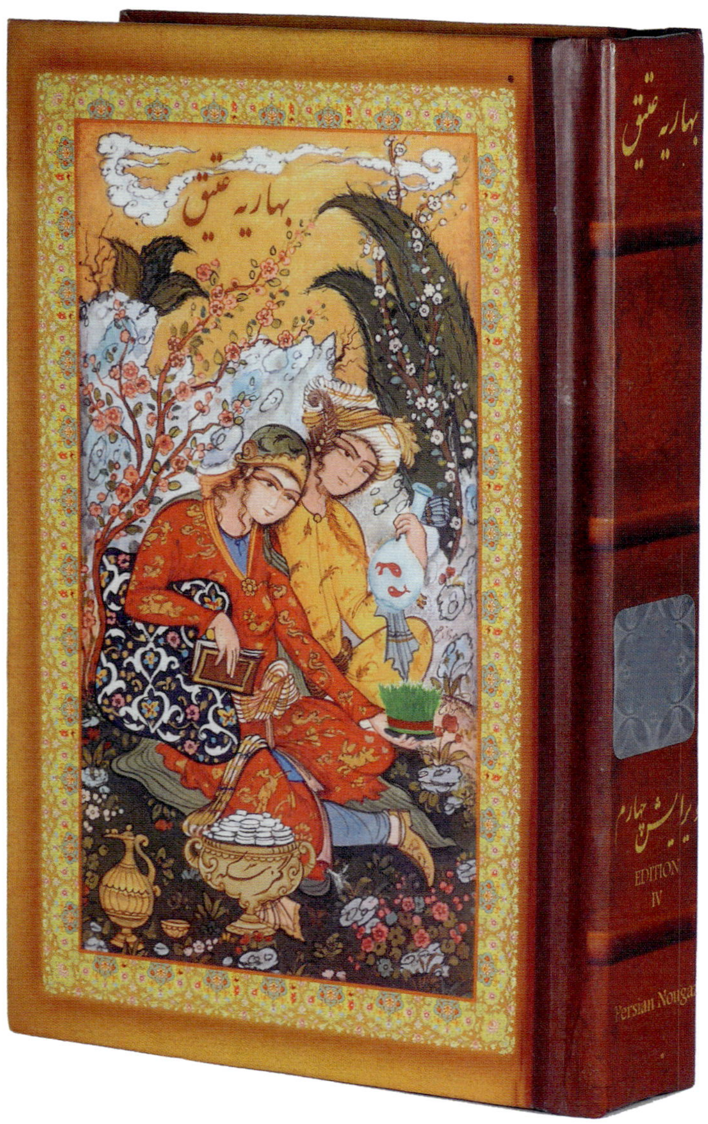

4.043
Kartondose mit Lithografie einer Häuserszene an einem Fluss, Vater und Kind mit Schafherde, Goldpapiereinfassung, Deckelvergoldung, Rücken- und Rückdeckel mit Buntpapierüberzug, dreiseitig geprägter Goldschnitt
Box with lithography of a riverside house, father and child with sheeps, gold paper lining, gilt edging, spine and rear cover with colored paper-over-board, gold-tooled edges
Lindt & Sprüngli, Berne, Zürich
Um / *Around* 1900 | 2,4 x 14,4 x 10,5 cm

4.044
Kartonschachtel gerillt, Chromolithografie eines Liebespaares auf dem Vorderdeckel, Verschlusslasche, dreiseitiger Goldschnitt
Grooved box, chromolithography of a couple of lovers on the front cover, closure strap, all edges gilt
Spätes 19. Jh. / *Late 19th century* | 2 x 9 x 6,5 cm

4.045
Kartondose mit Lithografie einer romantischen Waldszene mit Fluss, elegante Dame mit Strohhut, Goldpapiereinfassung, geprägte Goldpapierbordüre auf dem Vorderdeckel, Rücken und Rückdeckel mit Papier- Blumenmusterüberzug, dreiseitig geprägter Goldschnitt
Box with lithography of a romantic forest and a river, elegant lady with straw hat, gold paper binding, gilt embossed paper dentelle on the front lid, spine and rear lid with floral pattern paper cover, gold-tooled edges
Chocolat Lindt & Sprüngli, Berne, Zürich
Um / *Around* 1900 | 2,4 x 10,2 x 8,5 cm

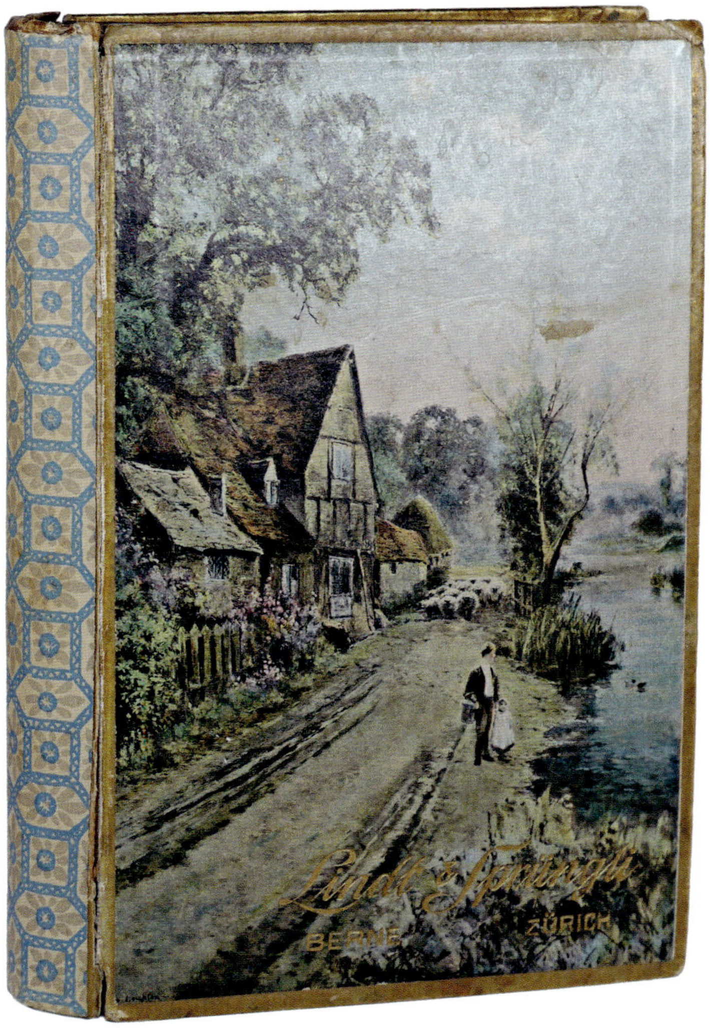

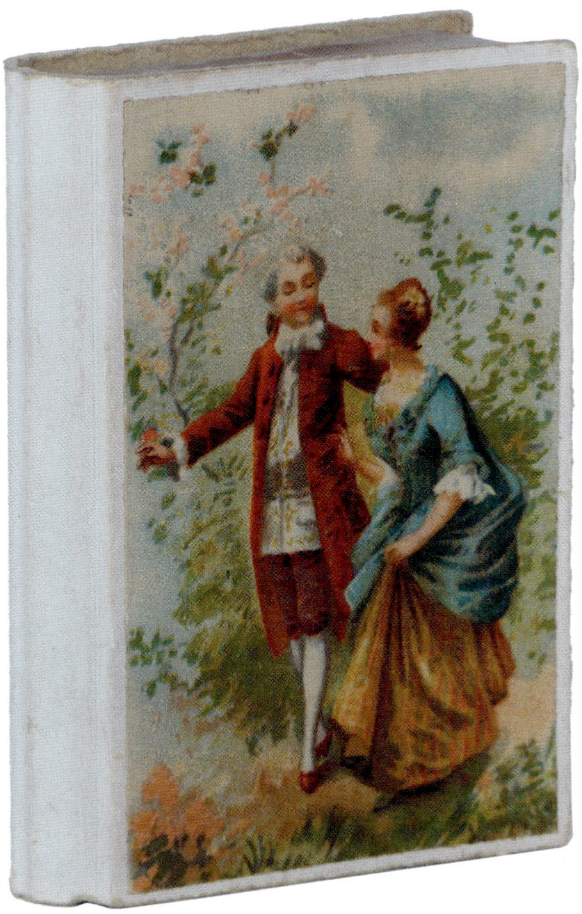

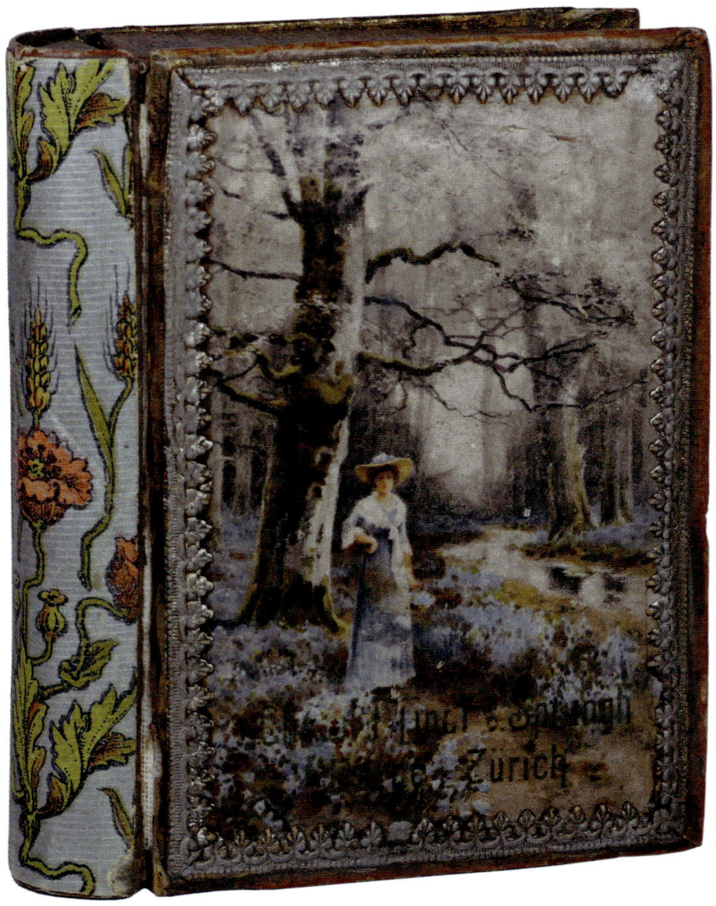

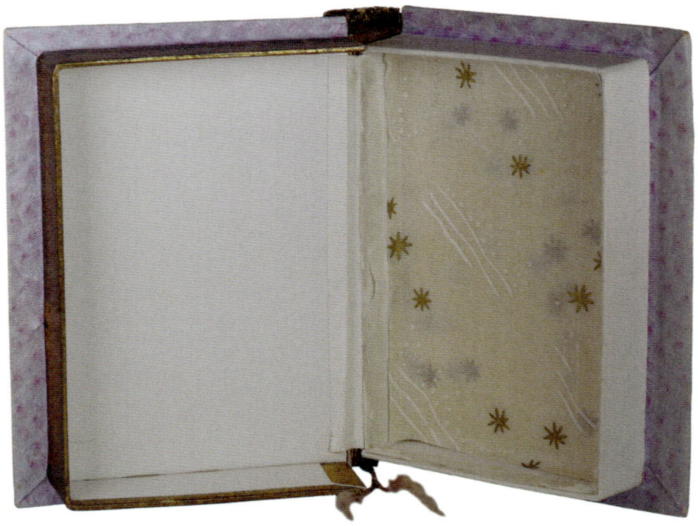

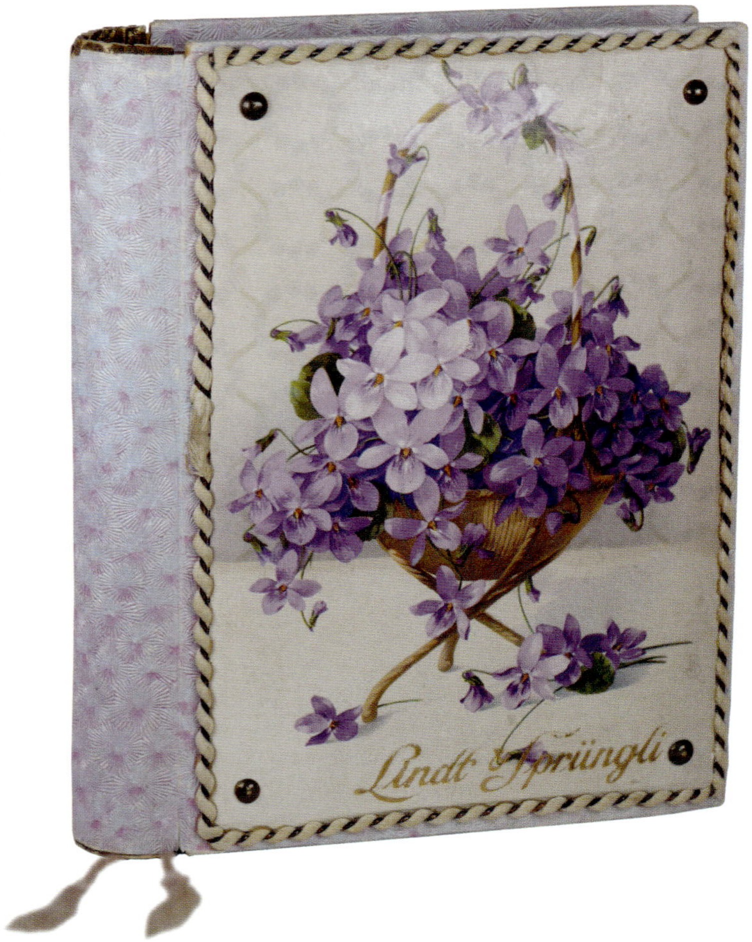

4.046
Kartondose mit Lithografie eines Blumenkorbs, geflochtene Schnurkantenbordüre, Rücken und Rückdeckel mit geprägtem Buntpapierüberzug, dreiseitig geprägter Goldschnitt, zwei Lesezeichenschnurbänder mit Quasten am Fußschnitt
Box with a lithography of a flower basket, a braided cord edge, spine and rear cover with embossed color paper-over-board, gold-tooled edges, two bookmark ribbons with tassels on the foot
Chocolat Lindt & Sprüngli, Switzerland
Um / *Around* 1900 | 3 x 13,8 x 11,6 cm

4.047
Kartondose für Schokolade, lithografierter Blumenkorb, Rückentitel, Firmenkleber am Rückdeckel, dreiseitig geprägter Goldschnitt
Box with lithography of a flower basket, title on the back, company sticker on the back cover, gold-tooled edges
Chocolats Lindt & Sprüngli, Berne & Zürich, Switzerland
Um / *Around* 1900 | 1,8 x 7 x 12,5 cm

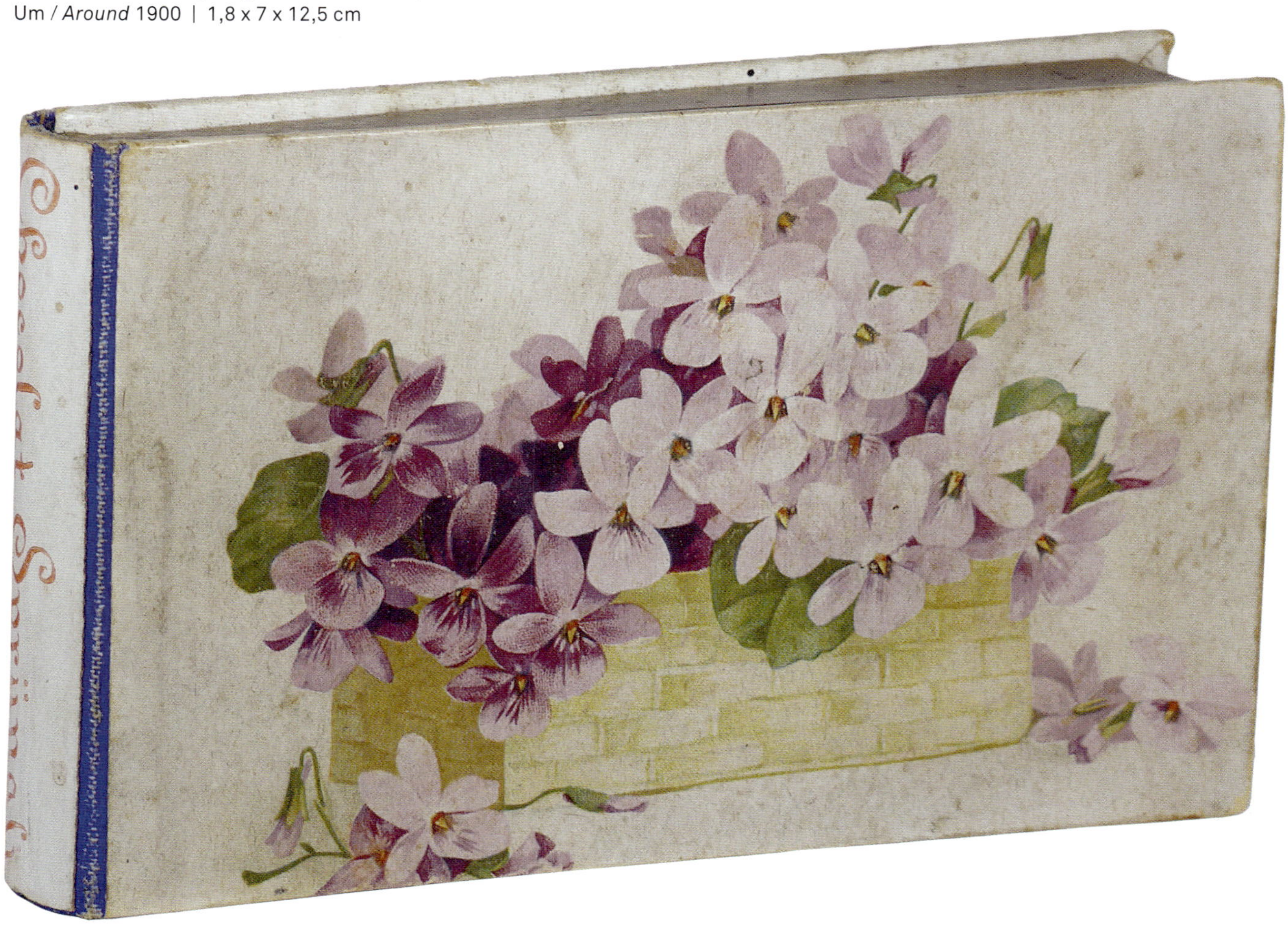

4.048
Kartondose mit bombiertem Deckel, Überzug mit Krokodil-Imitationspapier, Deckel- und Rückenvergoldung, dreiseitig geprägter Goldschnitt
Box with cambered cover, crocodile skin imitation paper, gilt cover and spine, gold-tooled edges
Chocolat Lindt & Sprüngli, Berne, Zürich, Switzerland
Um / *Around* 1900 | 2,2 x 8,7 x 10,8 cm

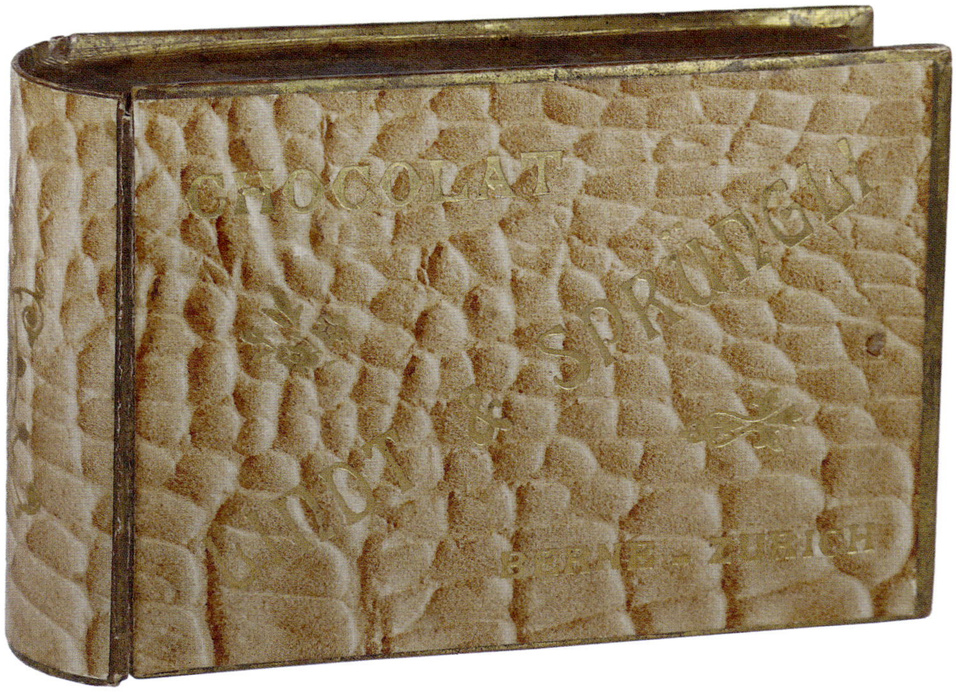

4.049
Kartondose mit Lithografie mit romantischer Bauernhausszene mit arbeitendem Bauernpaar, geprägte Goldpapierbordüre auf dem Vorderdeckel, vergoldeter Kaliko- Buchrücken, dreiseitig geprägter Goldschnitt
Box with lithography of a romantic farmhouse with a working farmer couple, gilt embossed dentelle on the front cover, gilt calico spine, gold-tooled edges
Chocolat Lindt & Sprüngli, Zürich, Switzerland
Um / *Around* 1920 | 2,2, x 8 x 13,8

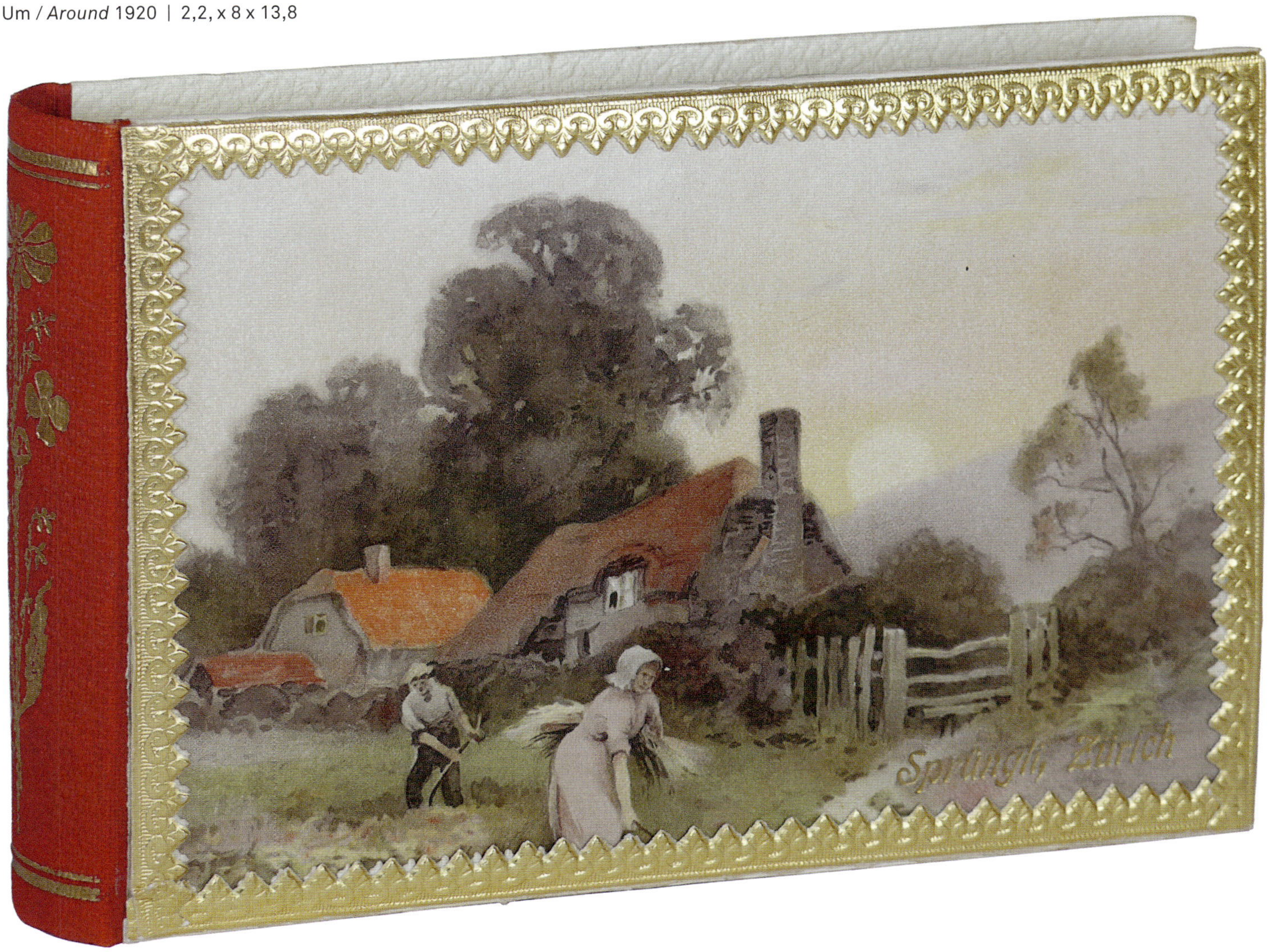

4.050
S, Sugar, P
Bakelitdose für Salz, Zucker und Pfeffer auf Messingstand
Bakelite box for salt, sugar and pepper with brass base
Davis Producte, Brooklyn N.Y., *Made in U.S.A.*
Art Déco | 7 x 15 x 6,5 cm

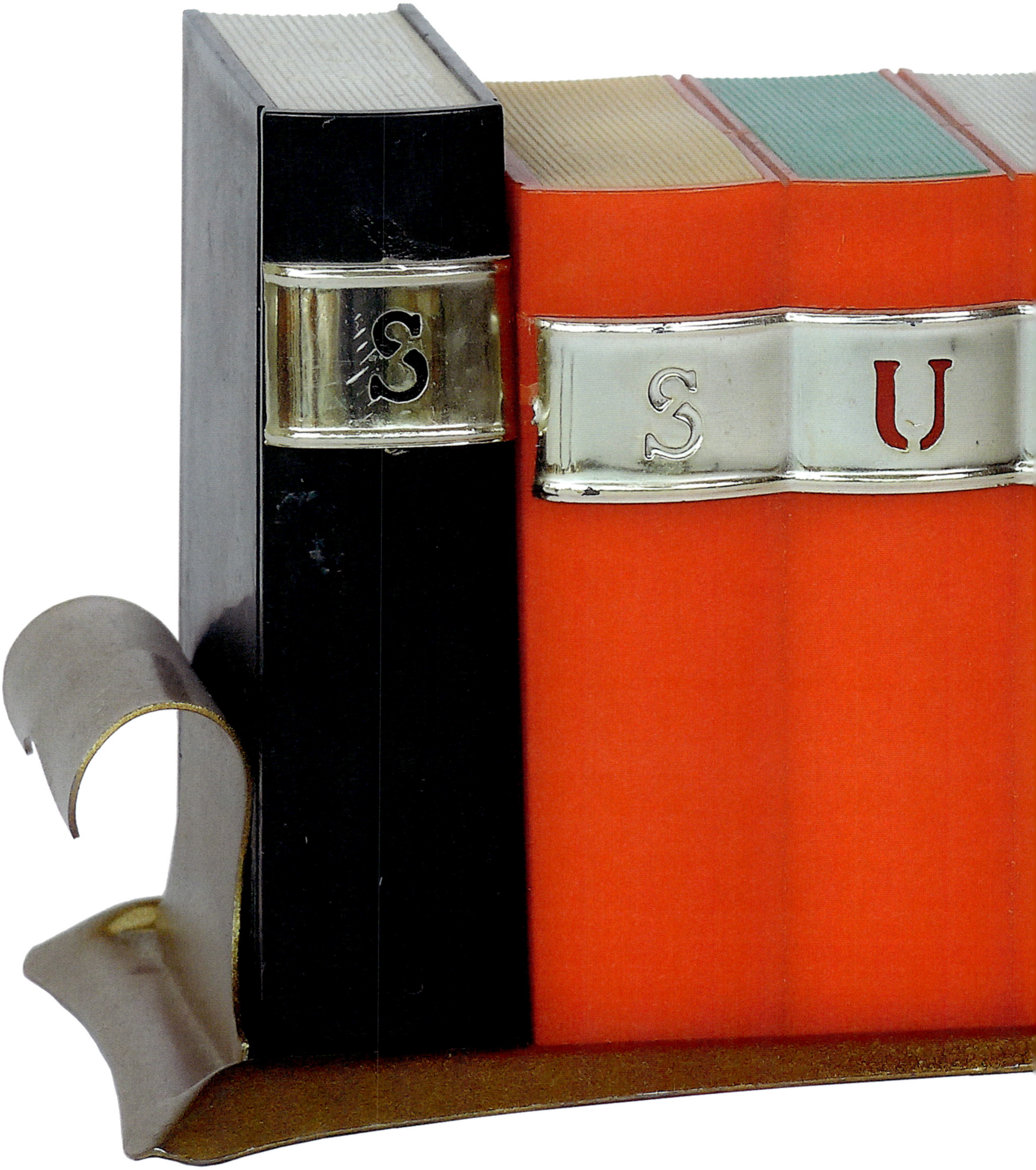

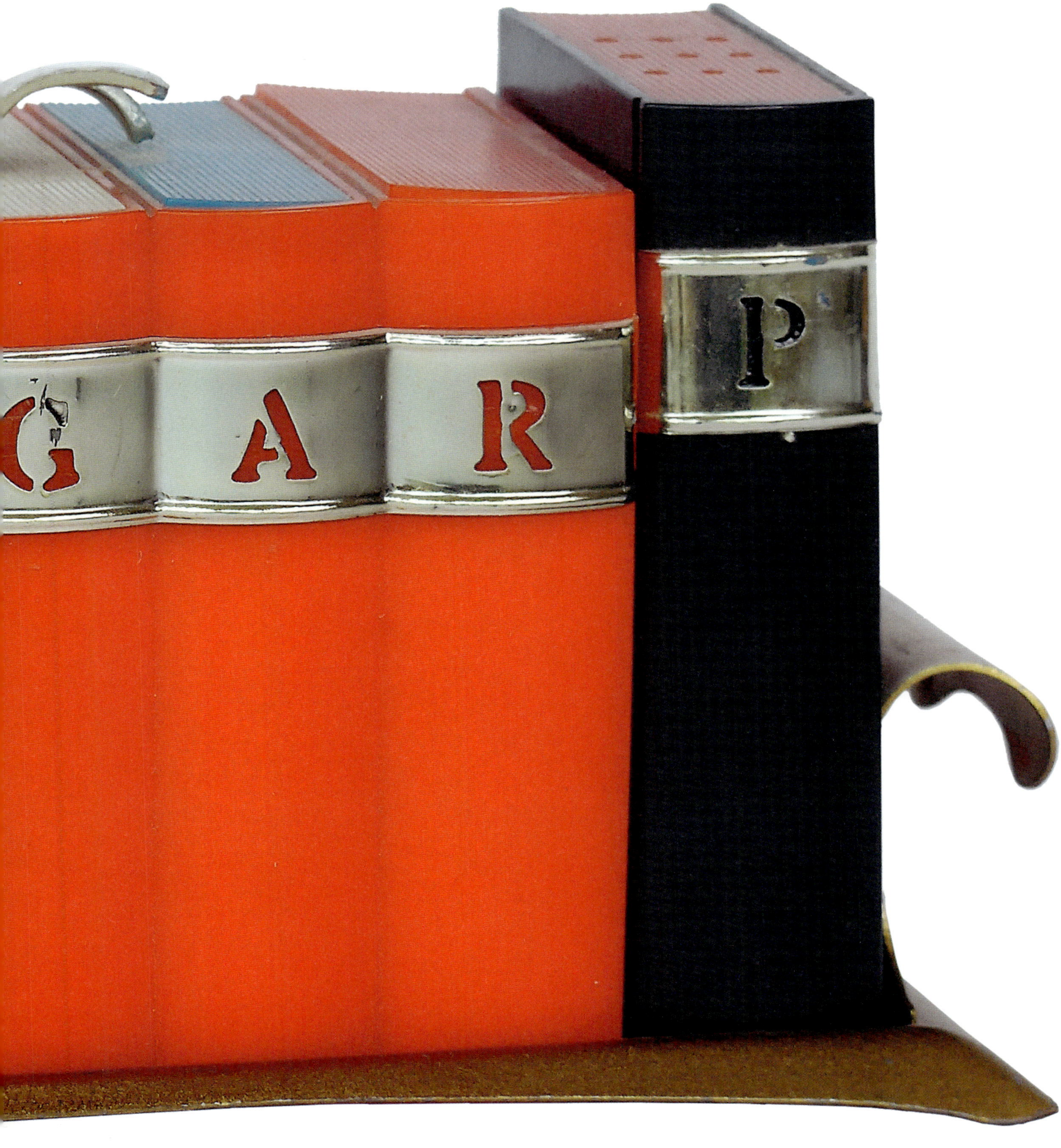
G A R
P

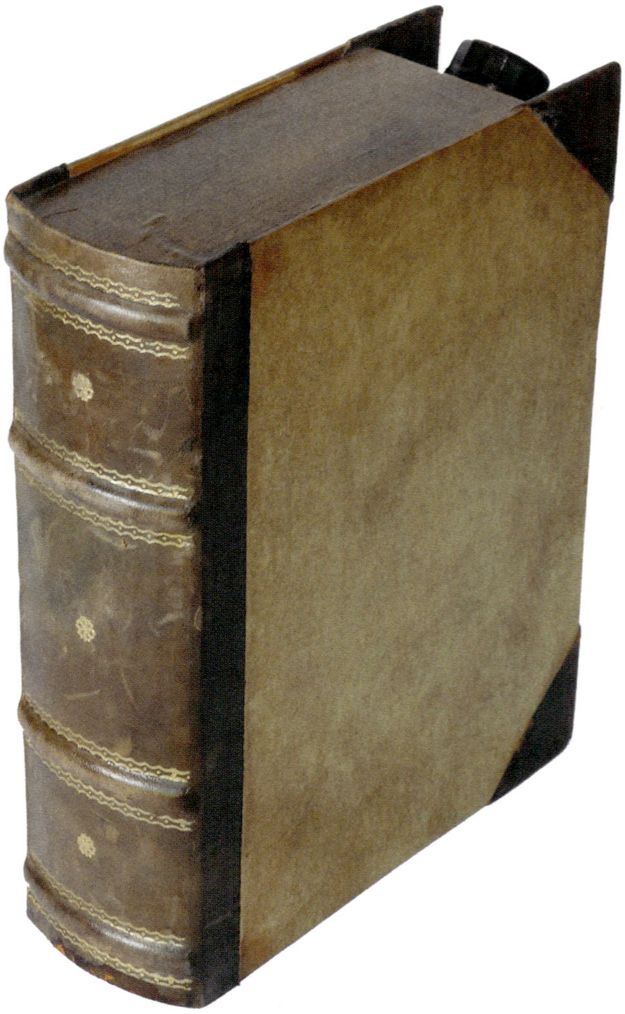

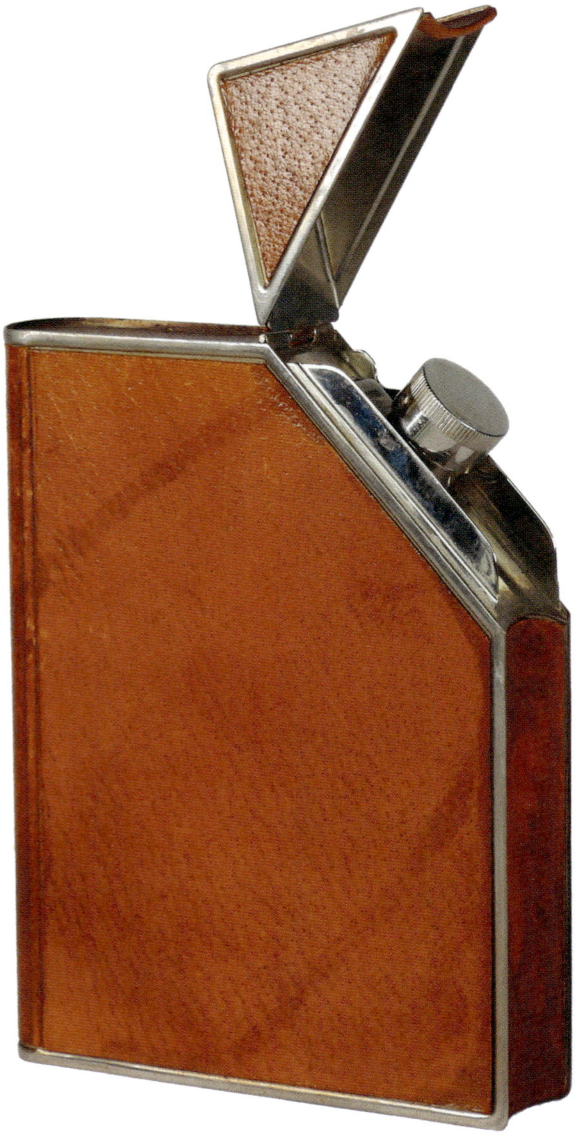

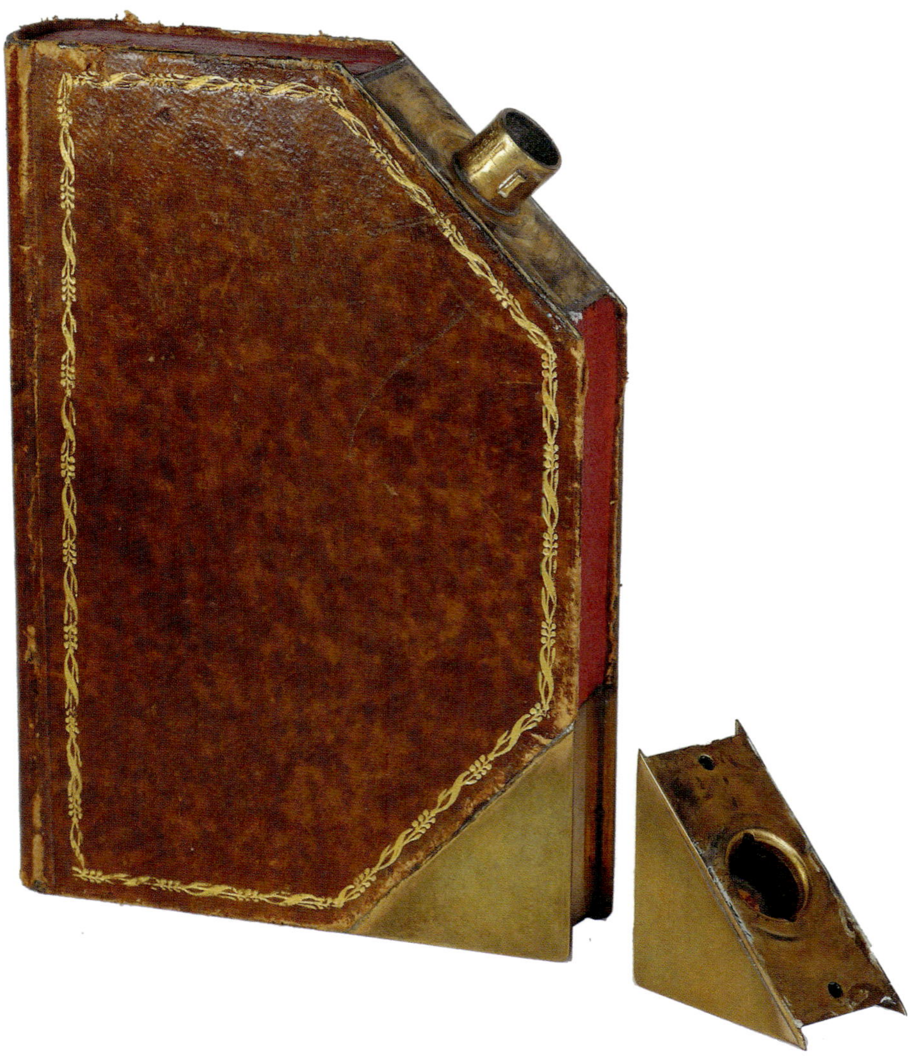

4.051
Glas-Trinkflache getarnt in einem Halbledereinband, Rückenvergoldung, vier erhabene Bünde, Schraubverschluss
Bottle made of glass camouflaged in a half leather binding, gilt spine, four raised bands, screw cap
22,8 x 18,5 x 6,5 cm

4.052
Taschen-Trinkflasche mit Schweinslederüberzug, Metallkantenverstärkung, aufklappbare obere Ecke
Pocket bottle with a pigskin cover, reinforced with metal edges, upper corner hinged
Made in Germany | 14,2 x 11,2 x 2,6 cm

4.053
Taschen-Trinkflasche, Messingbehältnis in Buchform mit Lederüberzug, Handvergoldung auf Vorder- und Hinterdeckel, dreiseitiger roter Lederschnitt, obere Messingecke abschraubbar
Pocket drinking bottle, brass container with leather cover, hand gilding on front and back cover, red leather edges, removable upper brass edge
Made in Germany | 15,9 x 11,3 x 2,6 cm

4.054
The Last Swallow from Canada
Kaliko-Dose mit einem Minifläschchen, Titelprägung auf dem Vorderdeckel, dreiseitig geprägter Goldschnitt
Box made of calico with a mini-bottle, stamped title on the front cover, gold-tooled edges
"Canadian Rye" Whisky
2 x 5,4 x 3,1 cm

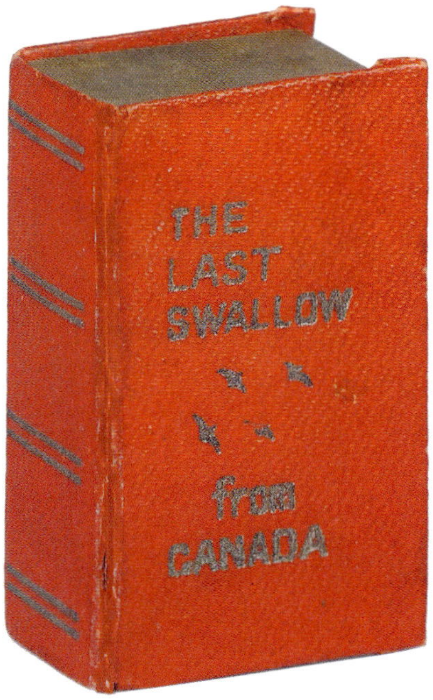

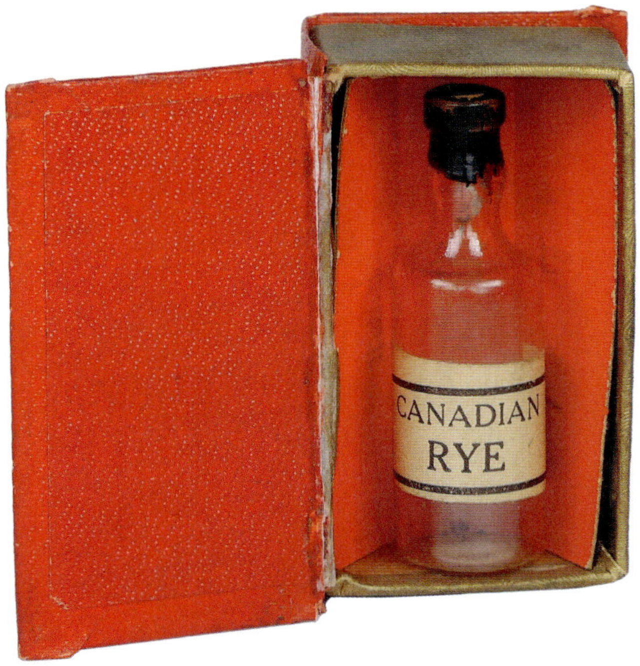

4.055
Geheimversteck für eine Schnaps-Bar in vier ausgehöhlten echten Lederbänden, Inhalt mit zwei Flaschen und vier Gläsern
Secret hiding place for a liquor bar in four hollowed out books with genuine leather binding, two bottles and four glasses.
14,5 x 20 x 14 cm

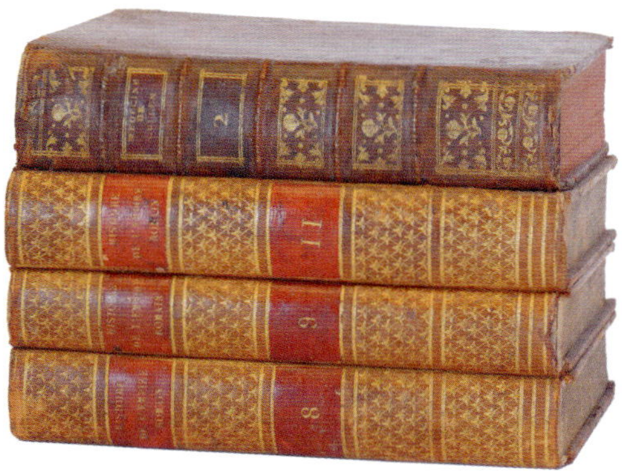

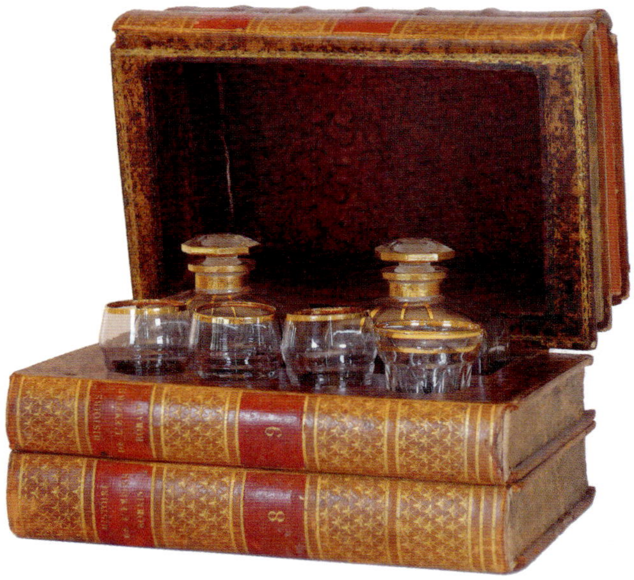

4.056
8 Whisky-Sorten in einer Schachtel
8 types of whisky in a box
Scotland's Whiskies Volume 2 Gordon & Mac Phail
Zeitgenössisch / *Contemporary*
25,5 x 17,3 x 4,5 cm

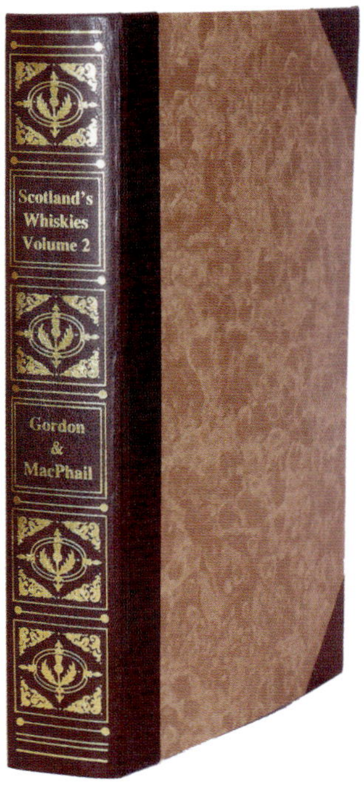

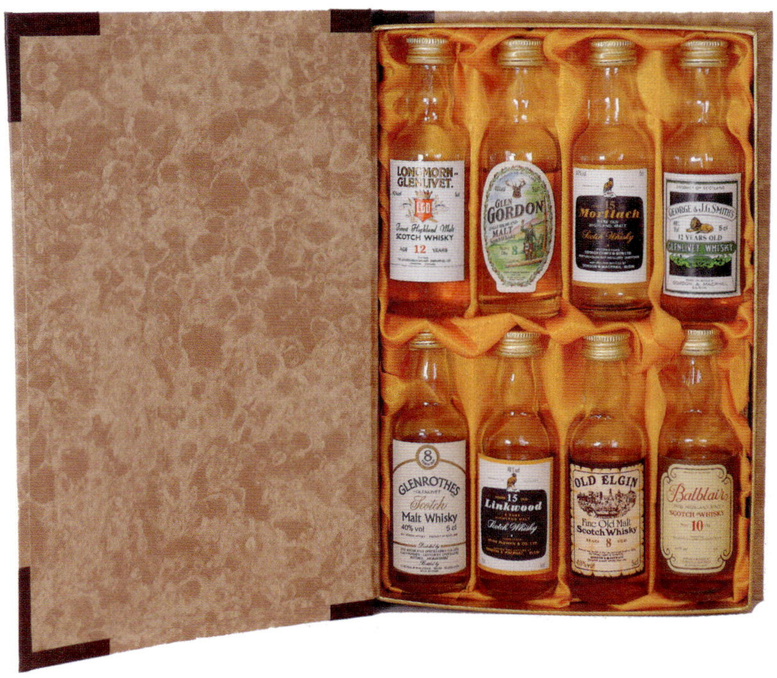

4.057
The Story of the Four Swallows from Montreal
Kaliko Schächtelchen mit vier Glasfläschchen: Port, Brandy, Irish Scotch. Goldbedruckter Rücken und Vorderdeckel, dreiseitiger Goldschnitt
Calico box with four glass bottles: Port, Brandy, Irish, Scotch. Gold printed spine and cover, all edges gilt
1,8 x 9 x 6 cm

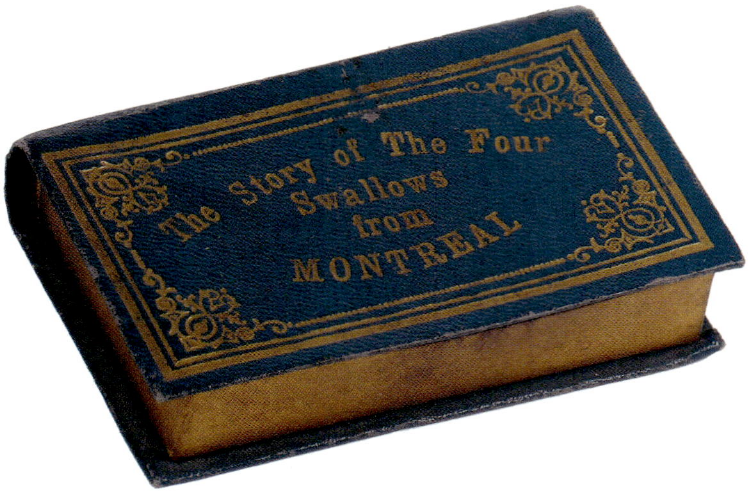

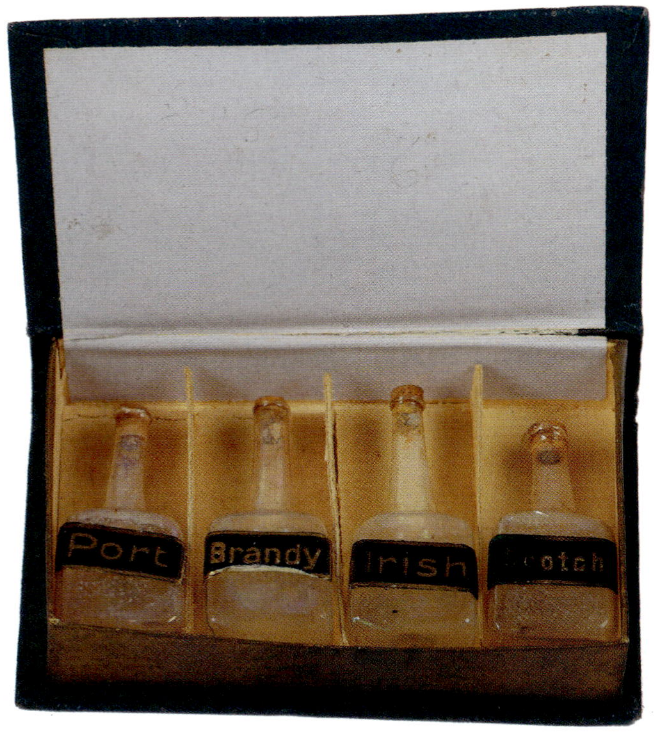

4.058
Alcohol. The Story of the Four Swallows from Montreal
Kaliko Schächtelchen mit Einschub, vier Glasfläschchen: Port, Brandy, Irish, Scotch. Rückenschild, goldbedruckter Vorderdeckel, dreiseitiger Goldschnitt
Calico box with drawer, four glass bottles: Port, Brandy, Irish, Scotch. Spine label, cover priented in gold, all edges gilt
2 x 9 x 6,5 cm

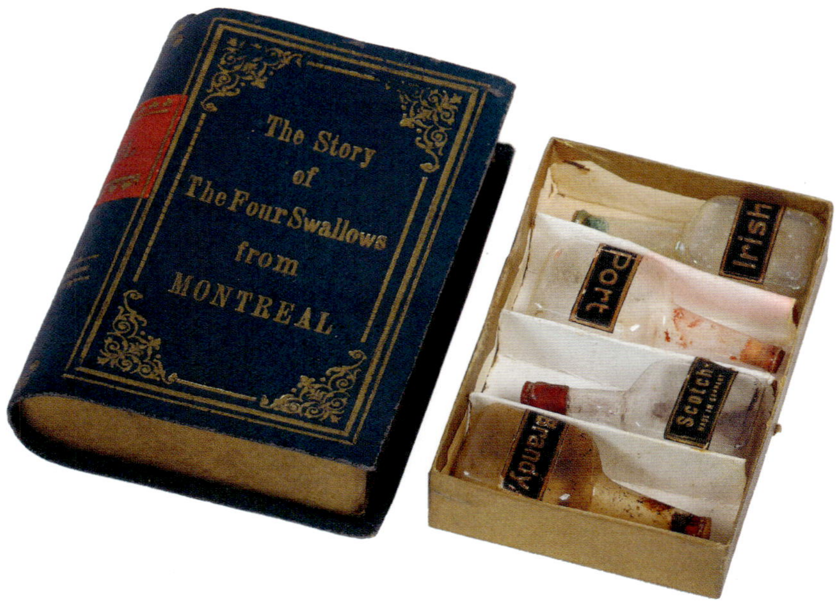

4.059
Zwei Schnapsflaschen aus Glas getarnt in zwei Buchdecken. Monogrammiert „M.D.S.“, mit einem Lederriemen zusammenhaltend
Two glass bottles for liquor disguised by two book covers, with the monogram "M.D.S.", held together with a leather strap
11,5 x 7,3 x 5,6 cm

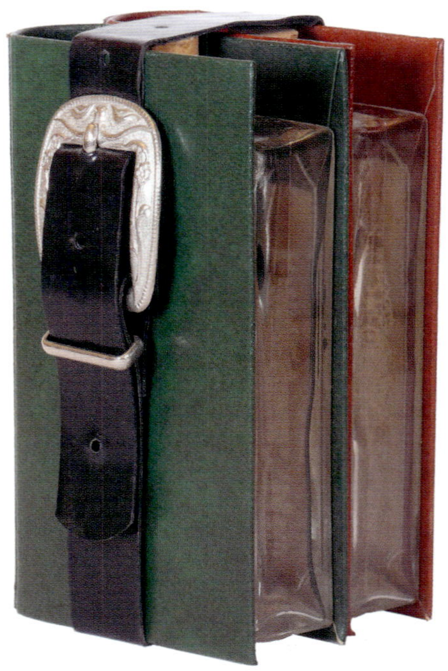

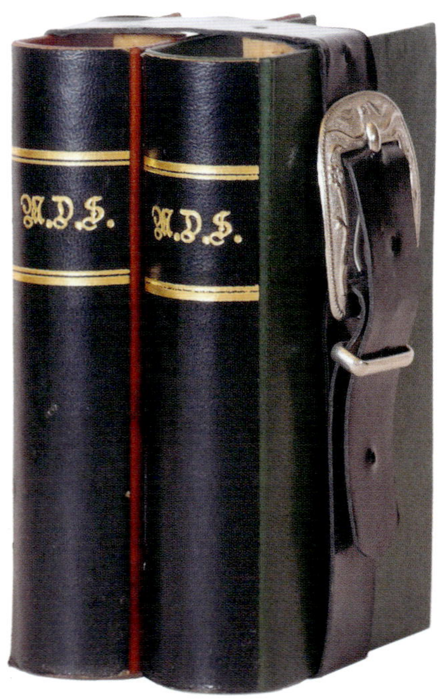

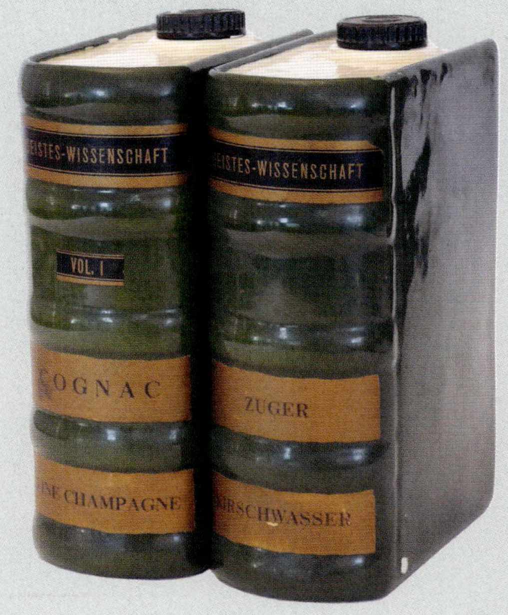

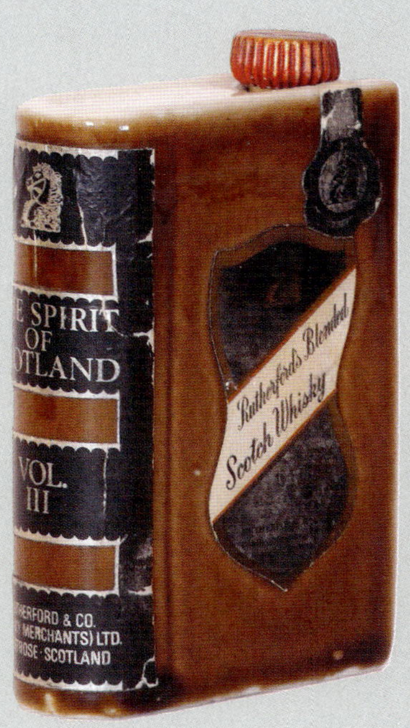

4.060
Geistes-Wissen-schaft, Humanities, Vol. I, Cognac, Fine Champagne
Keramiktrinkflasche
Ceramic bottle
17,2 x 12,5 x 6,2 cm

4.061
The Spirit of Irland, Vol. III., Rutherfords Blended, Scotch Whisky
Porzellantrinkflasche
Porcelain bottle
Montrose Scotland
9 x 6,3 x 2,7 cm

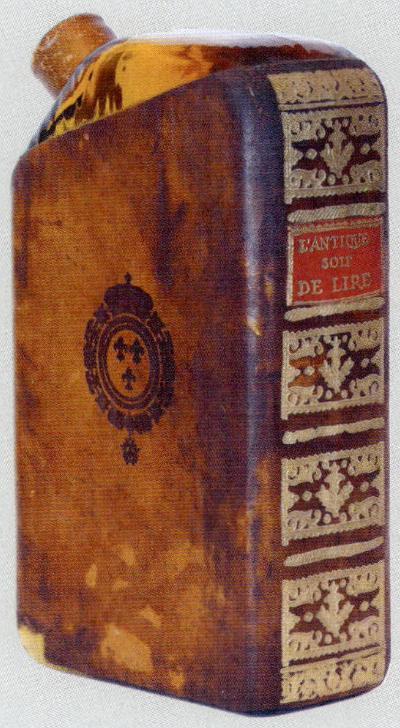

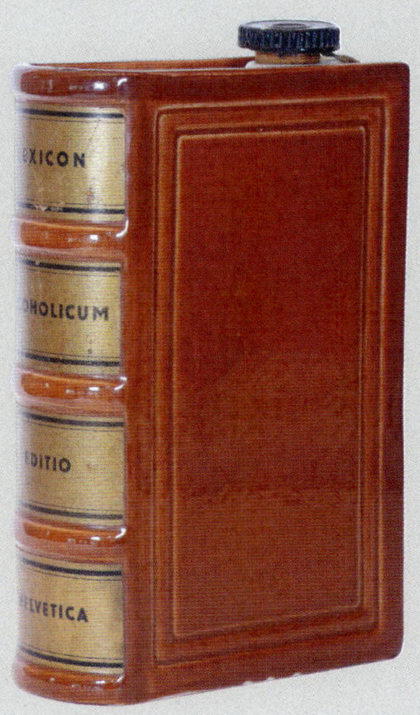

4.062
L'antique soif de lire
Schnapsflasche aus Glas, Schnapsbibel genannt, Lederüberzug, Rücken reich vergoldet
Glass bottle for liquor, also called "booze bible" in German, leather binding, elaborated gilt spine
20 x 11,5 x 6 cm

4.063
Lexicon Alcoholicum Editio Helvetica
Keramiktrinkflasche
Ceramic bottle
18,5 x 12,5 x 5,1 cm

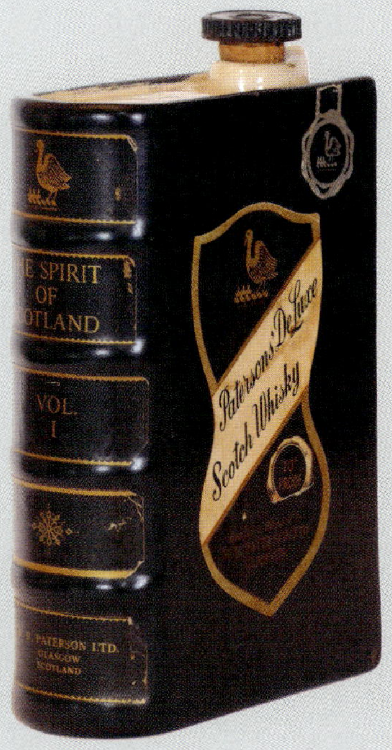

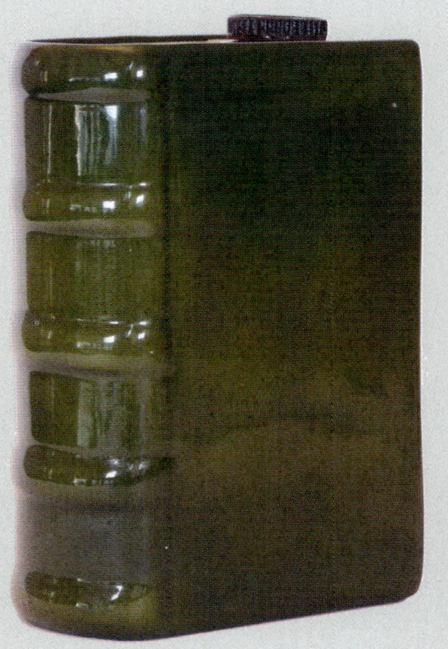

4.064
The Sprit of Scotland, Vol. I. W.R. Paterson LTD. De Luxe Scotch Whisky, Glasgow
Keramiktrinkflasche
Ceramic bottle
18 x 12,8 x 5,5 cm

4.065
Keramiktrinkflasche
Ceramic bottle
17,2 x 12,5 x 6,4 cm

4.066
Keramiktrinkflasche
Ceramic bottle
17,2 x 13,8 x 6,4 cm

4.067
Band 2, Alpen-kräuter Geist von A.L.Kohol, / *Vol. 2, Alpine Herbal Spirit by A.L.Kohol*
Keramiktrinkflasche
Ceramic bottle
14,1 x 10,5 x 4,3 cm

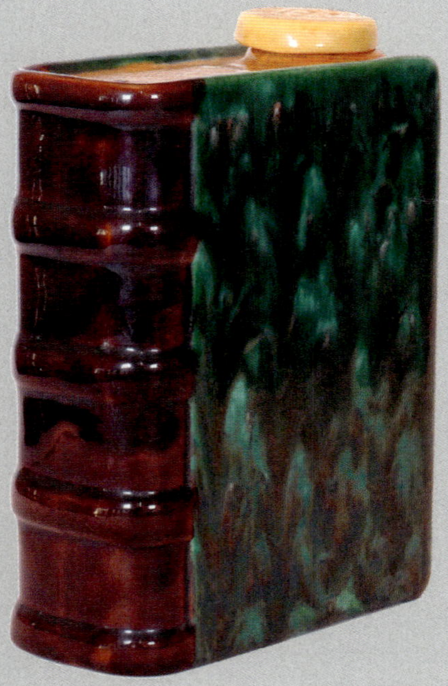

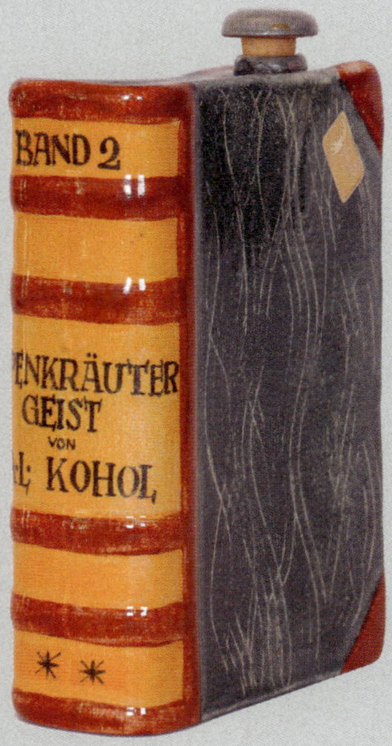

4.068
Pellisson Cognac
Keramiktrinkflasche
Ceramic bottle
13,9 x 10 x 5,2 cm

4.069
Jihoceska fruta
Keramiktrinkflasche, angedeutete erhabene Beschläge auf dem Vorderdeckel
Ceramic bottle with hinted raised fittings on the front cover
Tschechien / *Czech Republic*
14 x 11 x 4 cm

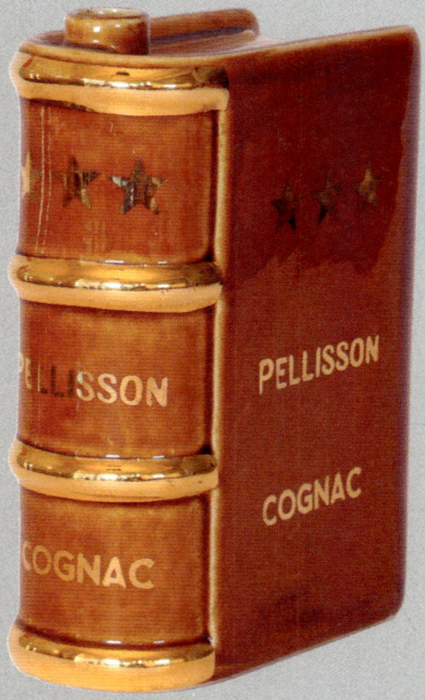

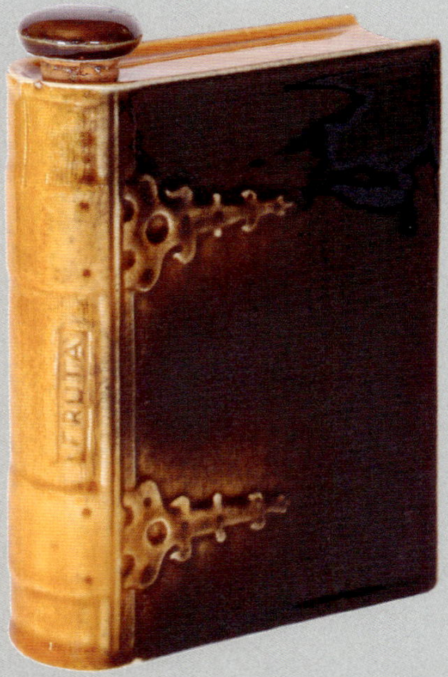

4.070
The Spirit of Burns,
Rutherford Whisky
Porzellantrinkflasche
Porcelain bottle
Montrose, Scotland
9 x 6 x 2,7 cm

4.71
The Spirit of Ireland, Vol. III., W. R. Peterson, De Luxe Irish Whiskey
Porzellantrinkflasche
Porcelain bottle
Glasgow, Scotland
9,2 x 6,3 x 2,7 cm

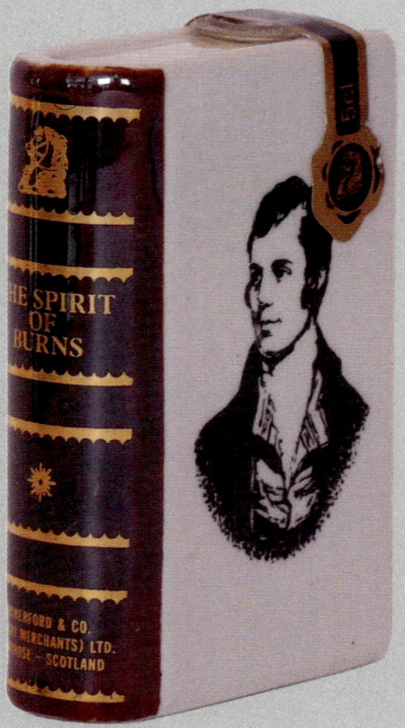

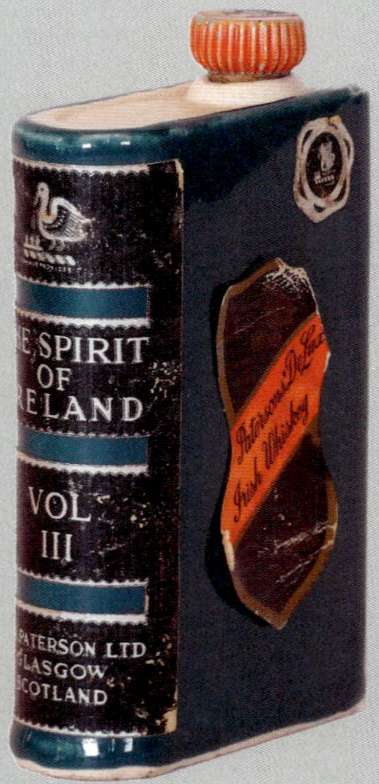

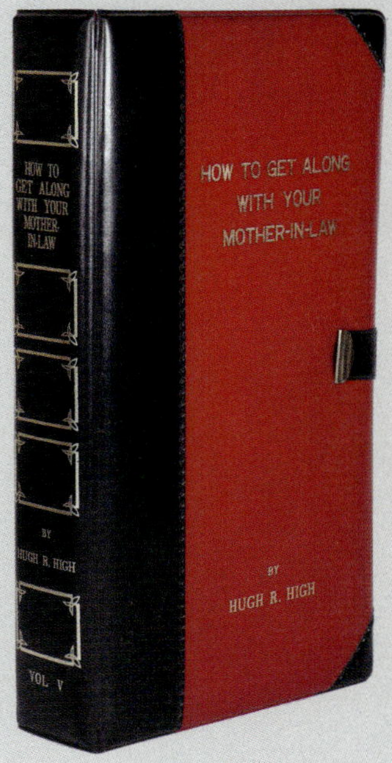

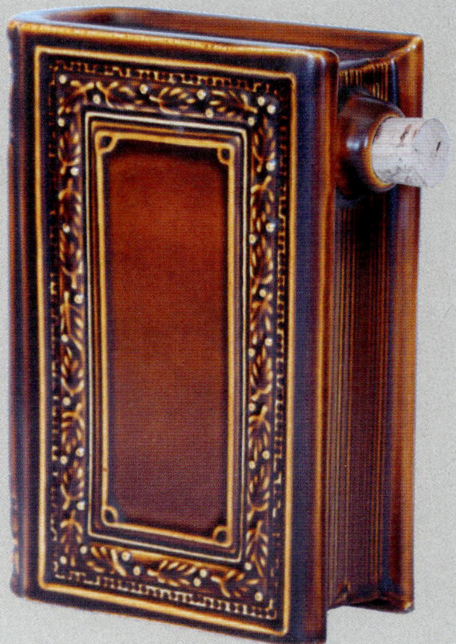

4.072
How to get along with your mother-in-law, by Hugh R. High, Vol. V
Kunstlederbehältnis, Trinkflasche und zwei Becher, Titelprägung
Synthetic leather box with bottle and two cups, stamped title
24,9 x 14,3 x 5,4 cm

4.073
J.R. Whisky, Der Tag geht / *The Day Goes By*
Keramiktrinkflasche
Ceramic bottle
17,5 x 12 x 6 cm

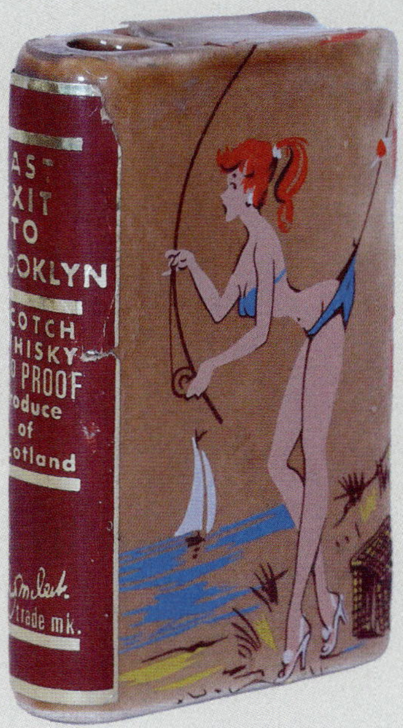

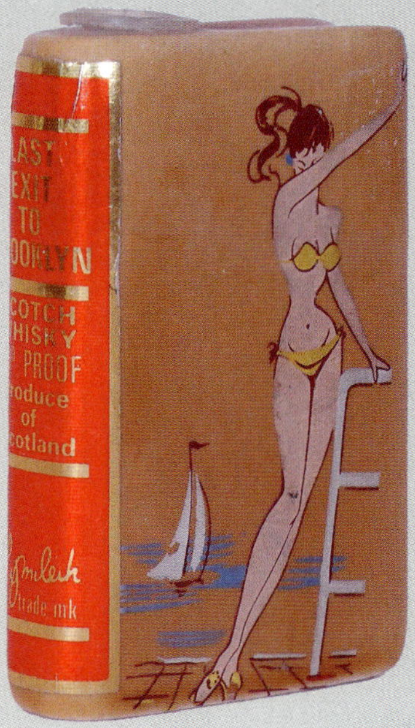

4.074
Last Exit to Brooklyn, Scotch Whisky 70° Proof
Trinkflasche aus Steinzeug
Stoneware bottle
Produce of Scotland
7,8 x 5,5 x 1,8 cm

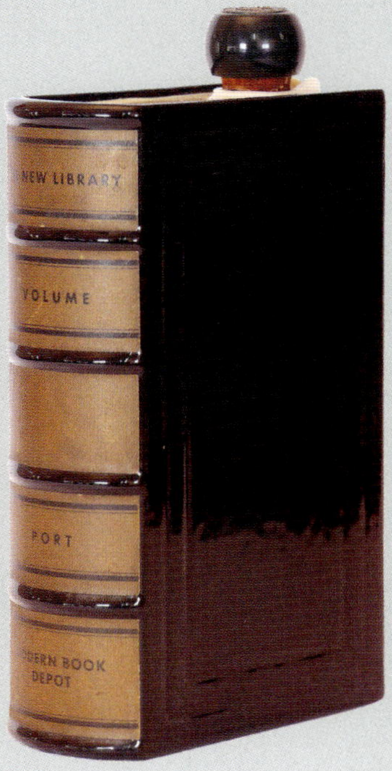

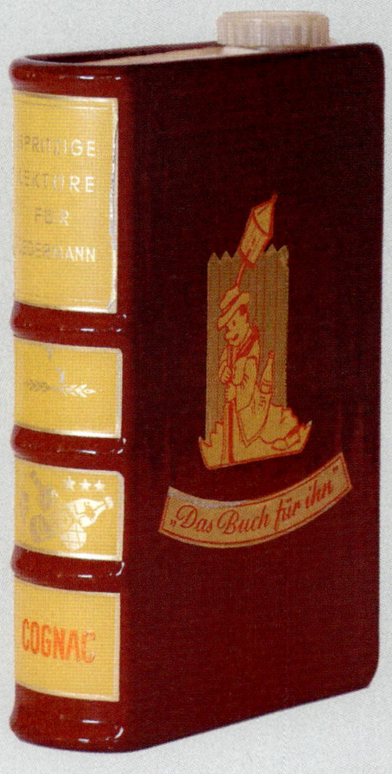

4.075
The New Library, Volume, Port, Modern Book Depot
Keramiktrinkflasche
Ceramic bottle
Made in Germany
18 x 12 x 5,2 cm

4.076
Spritzige Lektüre für Jedermann, Cognac. Das Buch für ihn. / *Great reading for everyone, cognac. The book for him.*
Keramiktrinkflasche
Ceramic bottle
West Germany
16,1 x 11,5 x 3,7 cm

4.077
De Luxe Edition, Bar Set
Barbesteck in einer Buchschachtel. 40 Rezepte für Cocktails
Bartender tools in a bookcase, 40 recipes for cocktails
26,8 x 20,2 x 5 cm

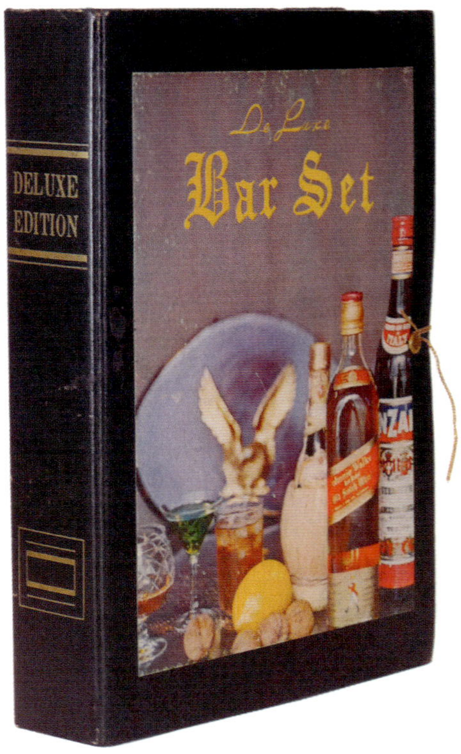

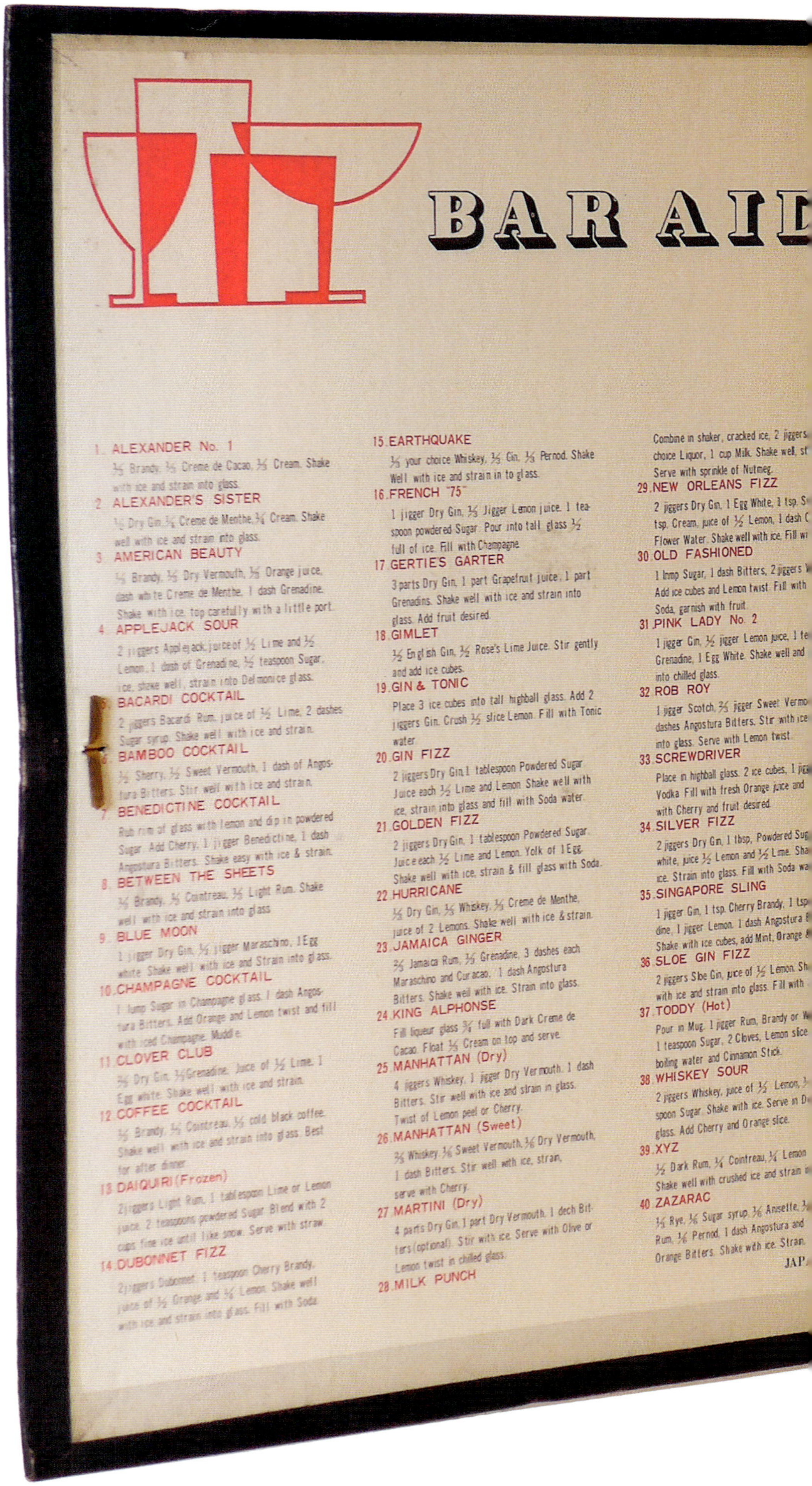

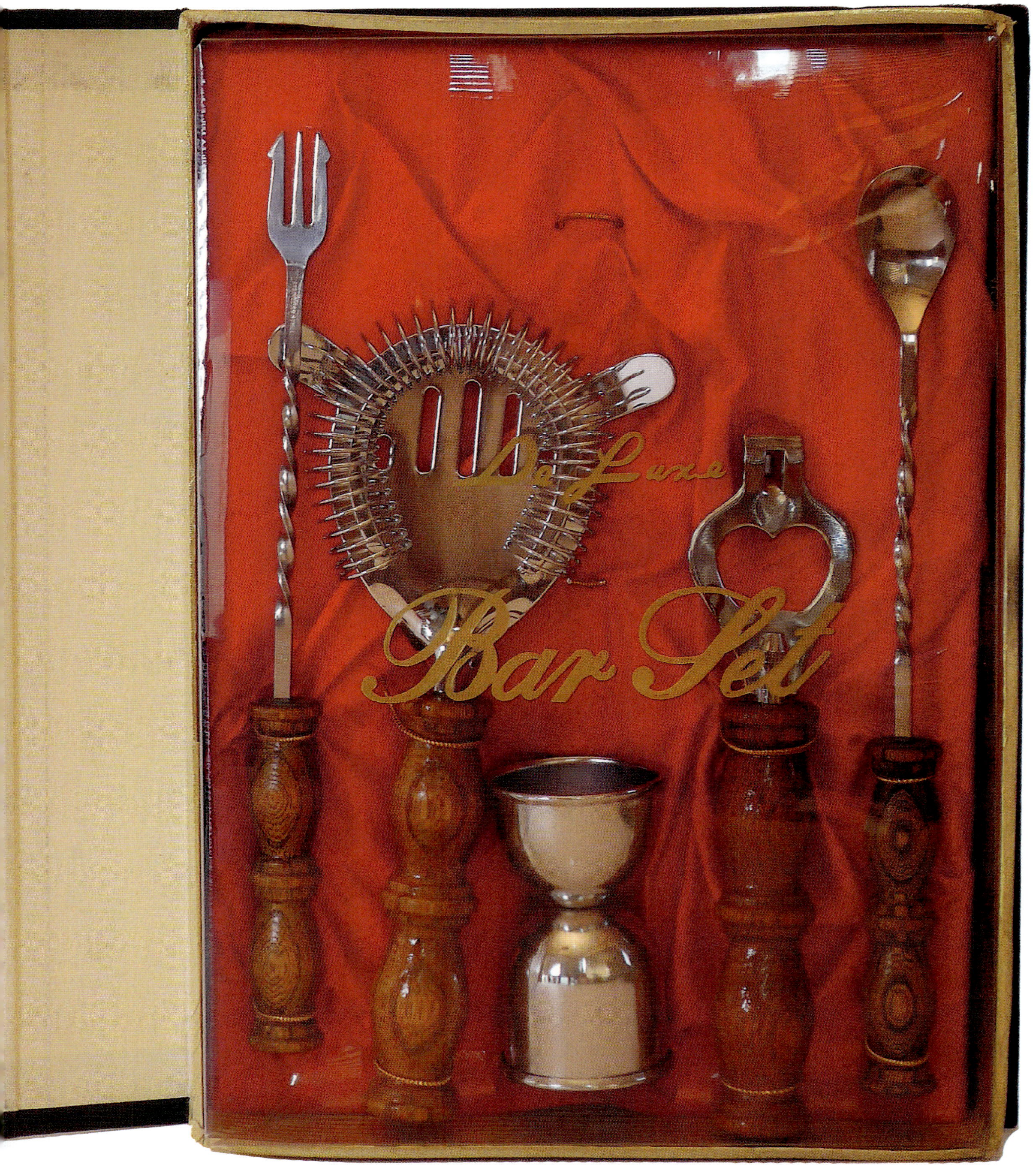
De Luxe
Bar Set

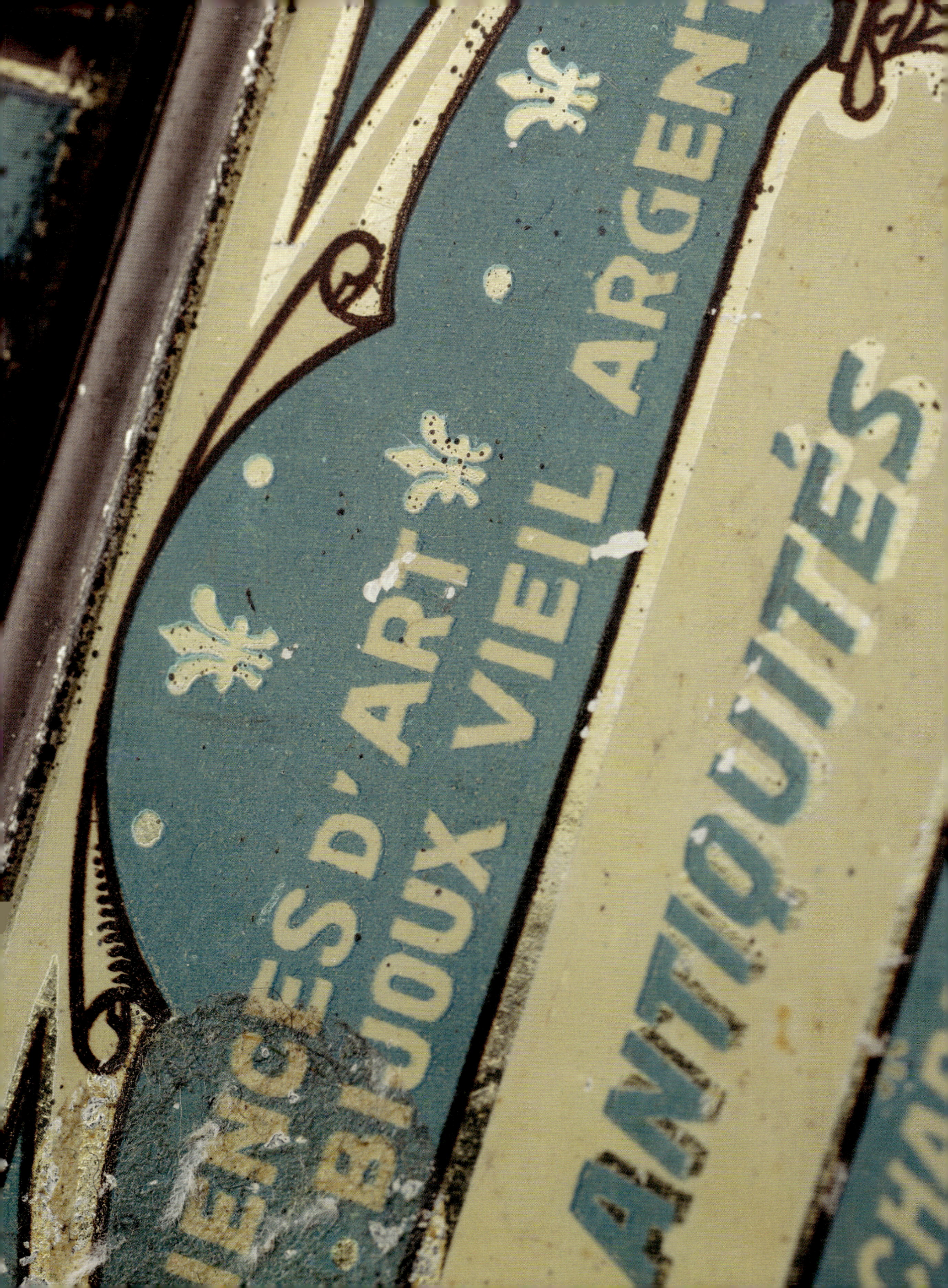
ES D'ART
BIJOUX VIEIL ARGEN
ANTIQUITÉS

Dosen
Boxes

Mein ehemaliger Lehrer an der Gewerbeschule sammelte passioniert Buntpapiere. Der Buchbindermeister veröffentlichte das berühmte Werk „Buntpapiere". Darin sind Seiten mit Original Papiermustern enthalten. Er hatte die Fähigkeit, seine Schüler für den Beruf des Buchbinders zu begeistern. An meiner Sammelleidenschaft ist er sicher nicht ganz unschuldig. Ich glaube sogar, dass ich sein Lieblingsschüler war.

Als Buchbindermeister hatte er auch eine tolle Sammlung schöner Einbände zusammengetragen. Lange Zeit wusste ich nichts von seiner Buchattrappen-Sammlung. Während seiner Ferien in Poschiavo beschäftigte er sich auch mit dem Bearbeiten von Sassalbo Kalkstein. Es entstanden wunderbare Bücher aus Stein.

Nach seinem Tod fragte mich sein Sohn, ob ich Interesse hätte, die Kollektion seines Vaters zu übernehmen. Mit Freude empfing ich die ca. 50 Objekte. Ihr Highlight ist der aufklappbare Holzschemel in Buchform mit einem eingelassenen Messing-Monogram: „AM".

My former teacher at the vocational school passionately collected colored papers. The master bookbinder published the famous work "Buntpapiere" ("Colored Papers"). It contains pages with original paper samples. He was able to inspire enthusiasm for the bookbinding profession among his students. He certainly played a part in my passion for collecting and I even believe I was his favorite student.

As a master bookbinder, he also had a great collection of beautiful bindings. For a long time I knew nothing about his collection of fake books. During his holidays in Poschiavo, he also worked on Sassalbo limestone, producing wonderful books made of stone.

After his death, his son asked me if I was interested in adopting his father's collection. I gladly received around 50 objects. Their highlight is a fold-out wooden stool in a book design with an embedded brass monogram: "AM".

5.001
Gourmets Delight
Lithografierte Blechdose
Lithographed tin box
Victoria Biscuit, Brüssel
Belgien / *Belgium*
Um / *Around* 1960
5,5 x 24 x 17,2 cm

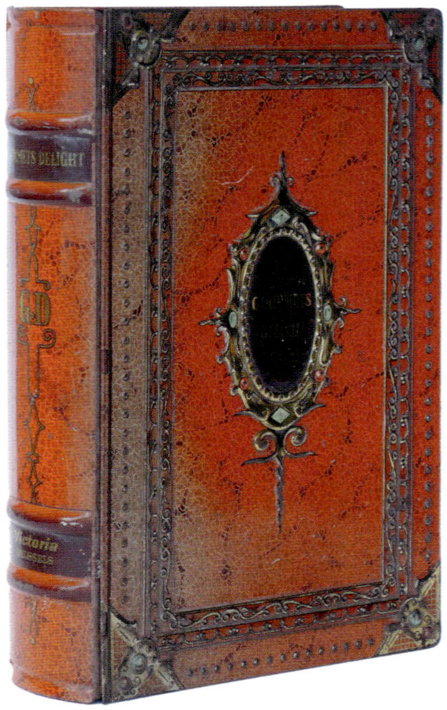

5.002
Gourmets Delight
Lithografierte Blechdose
Victoria Biscuit, Dortrecht,
Niederlande / *The Netherlands*
Um / *Around* 1960
5,5, x 24 x 17,2 cm

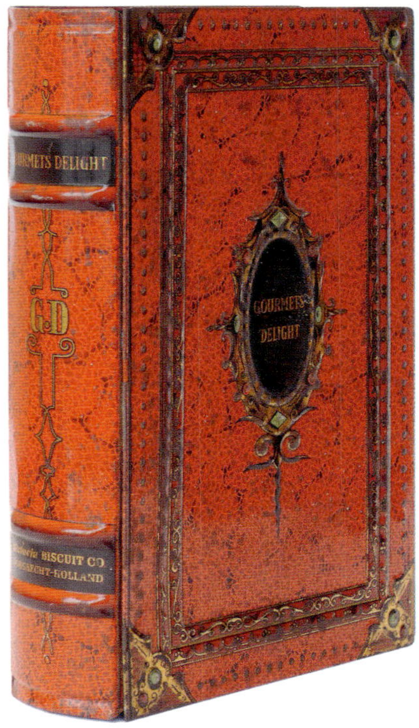

5.003
Café, Poivre, Amidon, Thé
Lithografierte Blechdosen
zur Aufbewahrung von Lebensmitteln.
Lithographed tin box for storing food
Frankreich / *France*
Um / *Around* 1900
15,5 x 11,5 x 6,5 cm

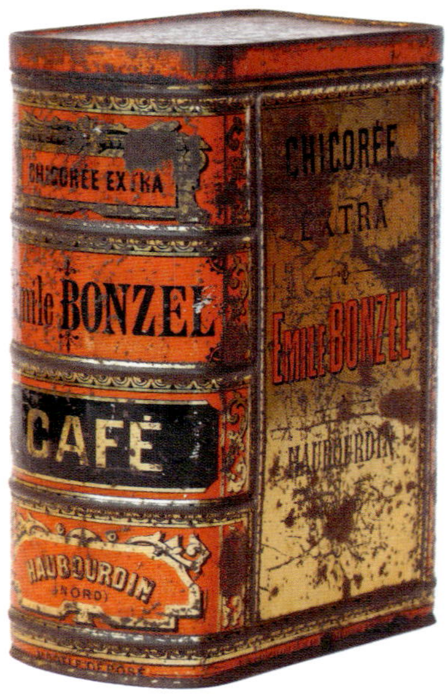

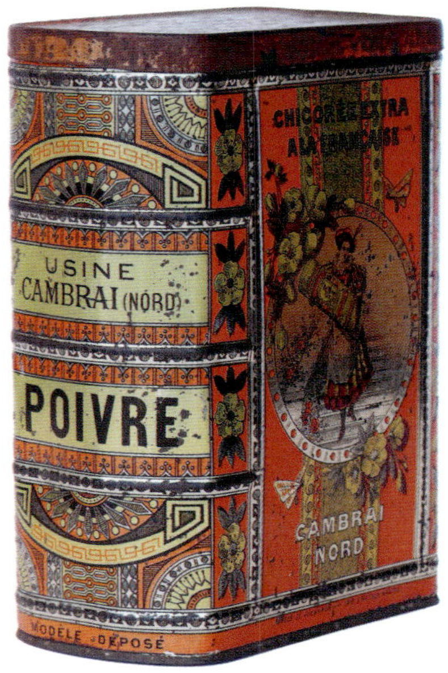

5.004
Café, Poivre, Amidon, Thé
Lithografierte Blechdosen zur Aufbe-
wahrung von Lebensmitteln
Lithographed tin cans for storing food
Frankreich / *France*
Um / *Around* 1900
15,5 x 11,5 x 6,5 cm

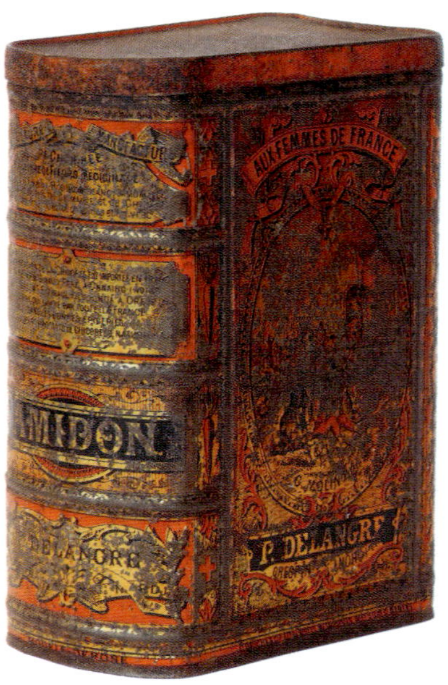

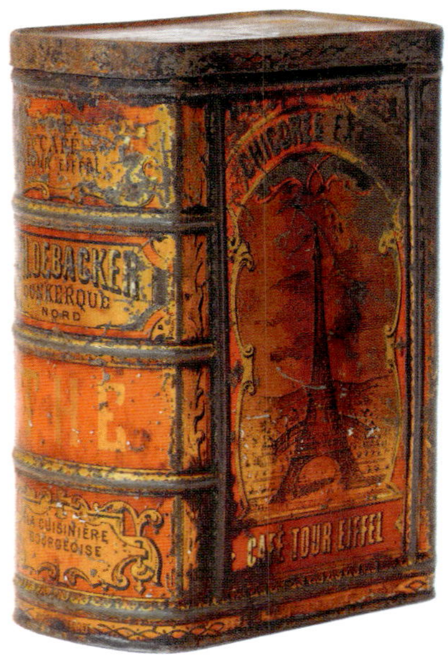

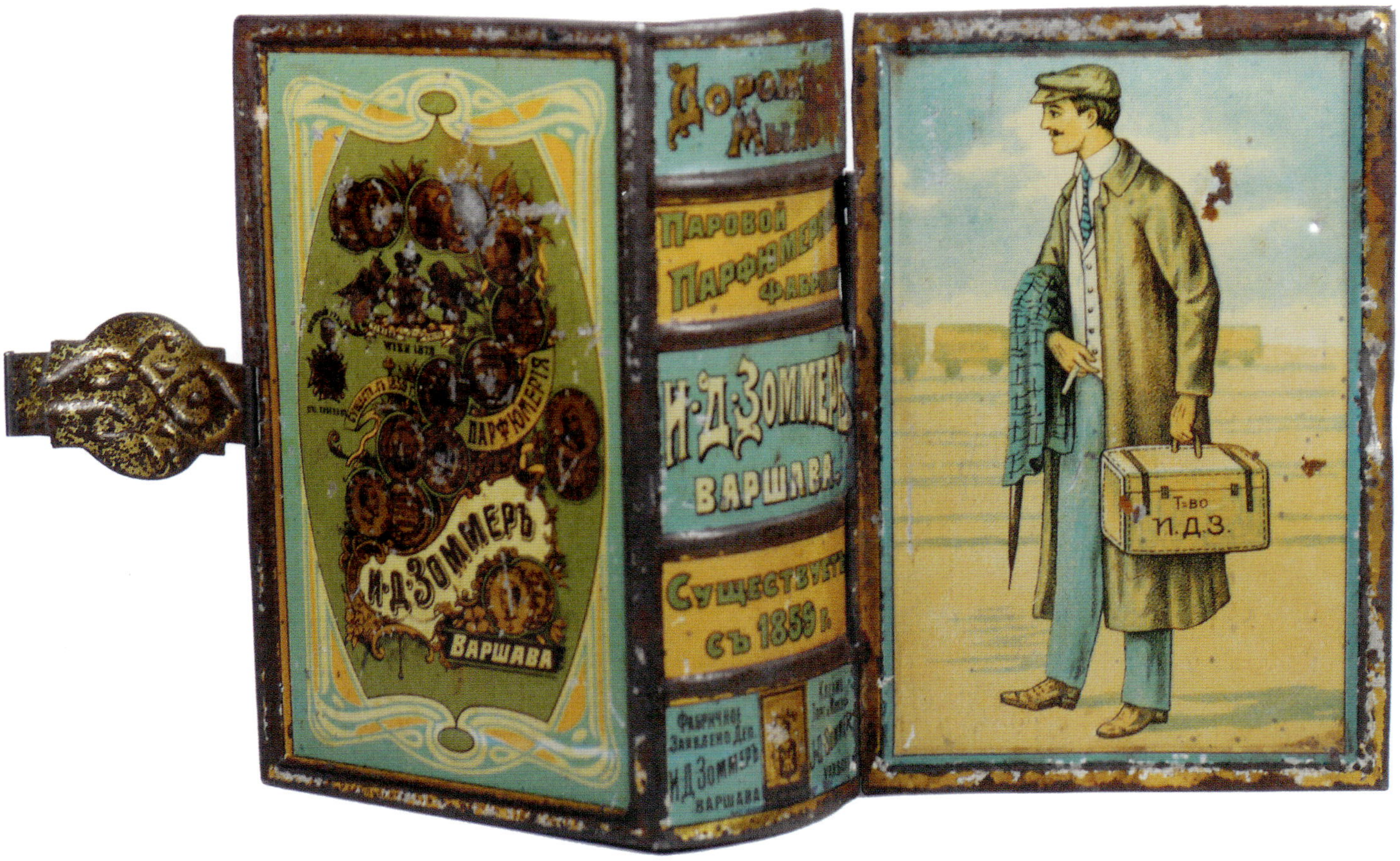

5.005
Lithografierte Blechdosen für Reiseseifen, Warschau und Moskau, die dampfbetriebene Parfümeriefabrik Sommer J.D. in Warschau existiert seit 1859
Tin soap boxes for travelers with lithographs, Warsaw and Moscow, the steam-powered perfumery factory Sommer J.D. in Warsaw exists since 1859
Um / *Around* 1900 | 3,3 x 9 x 6,7 cm

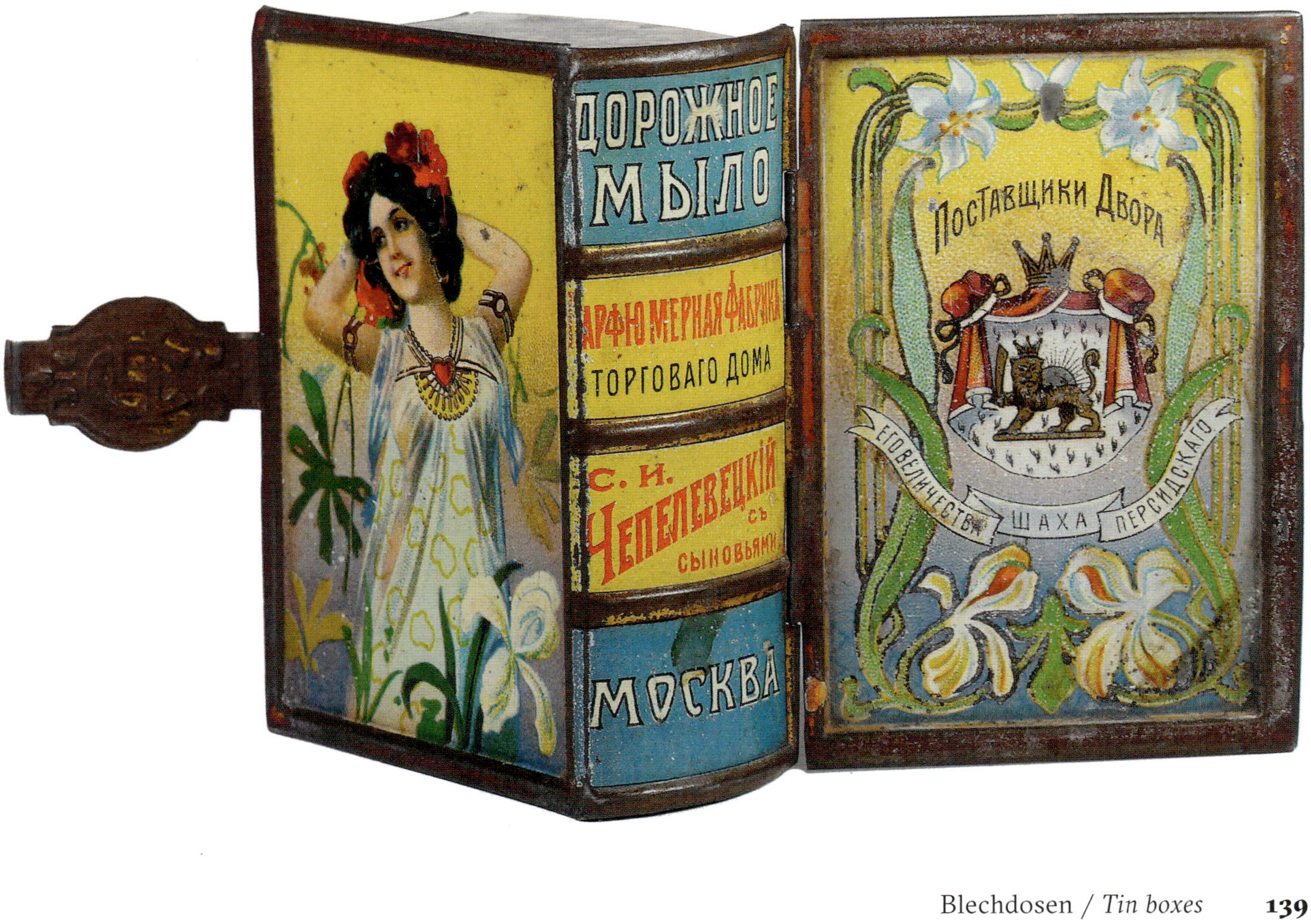

5.006
Passementerie Parfumerie Merceri Rubans.
Blechdöschen für Pastillen
Tin box for drops
Grand Magasins des Cordeliers Nouveautés, Lyon, Frankreich / *France*
1,4 x 5 x 3,8 cm

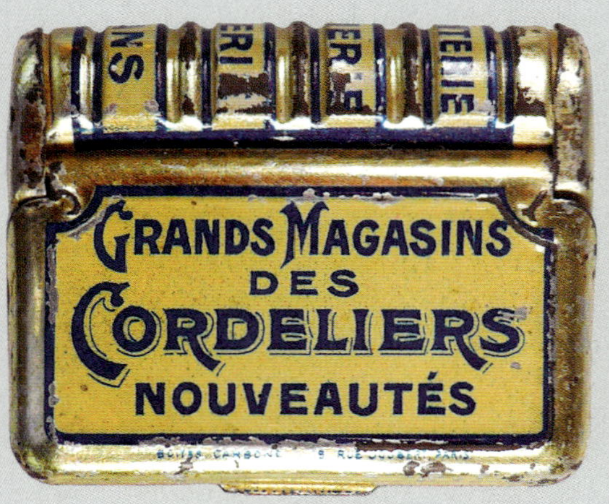

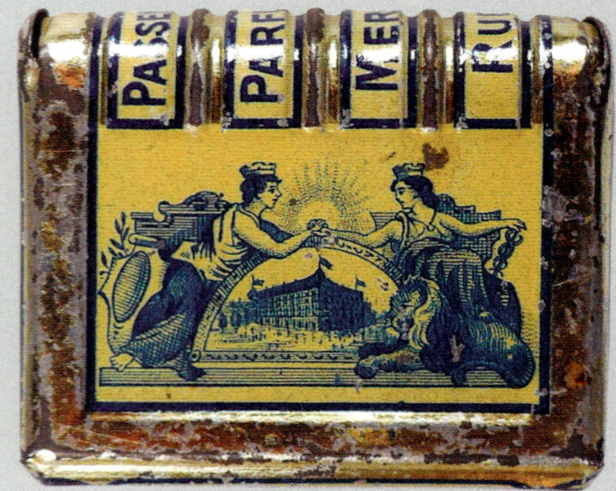

5.007
Suc Bechique Pectoral Parrayoe.
Tin box for drops
Pharmacie Parrayon-Bouchet, Lyon
Frankreich / *France*
1,4 x 5 x 3,8 cm

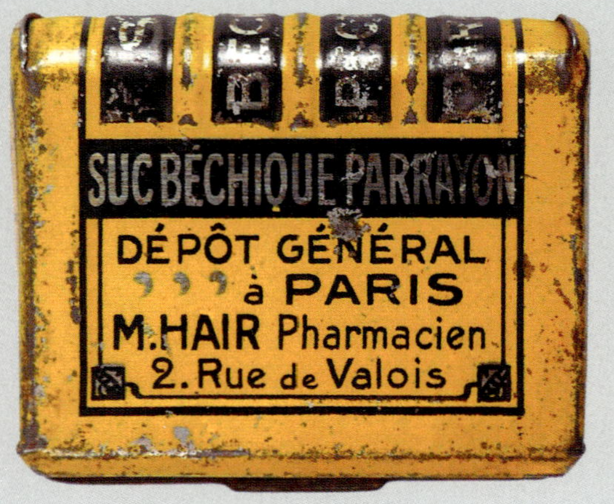

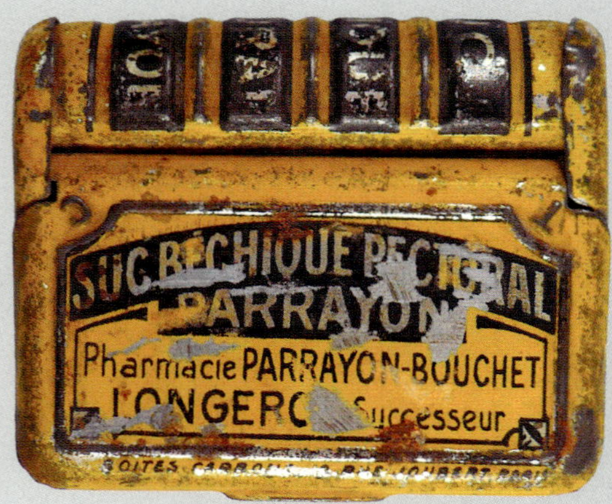

5.008
Mannine Valbay Burgaties Agréable.
Blechdöschen für Zündhölzer
Tin box for matches
Pharmacies Balvay Paris, Frankreich / *France*
1,4 x 5 x 3,8 cm

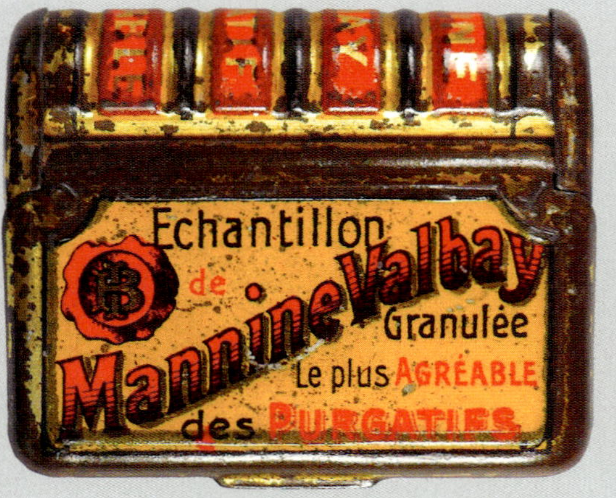

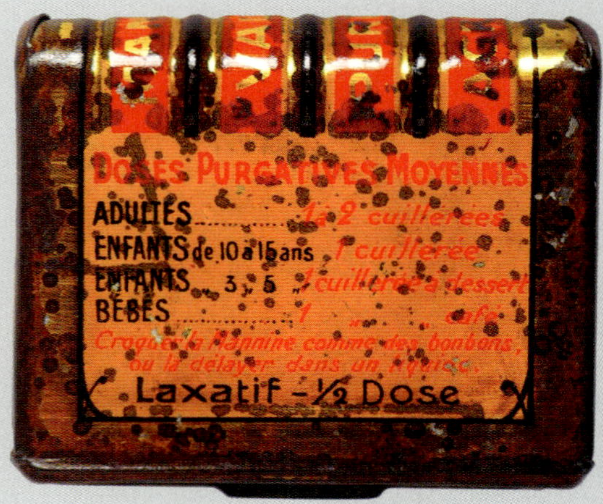

5.009
Téléphone 212–43 Prix Tres Réduits
Blechdöschen für Zündhölzer
Tin box for matches
Pharmacie des deux Mondes, Paris, Frankreich / *France*
1,4 x 5 x 3,8 cm

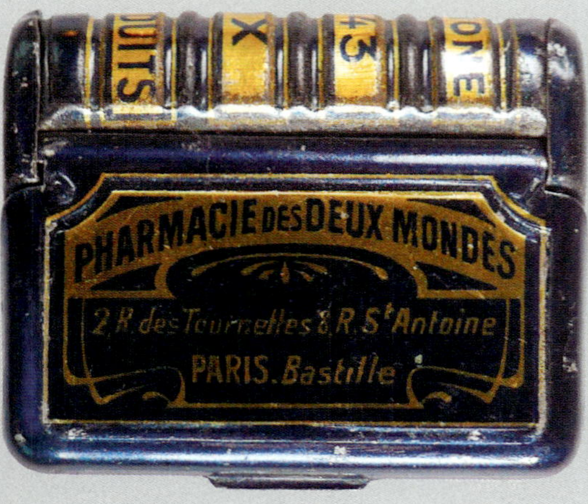

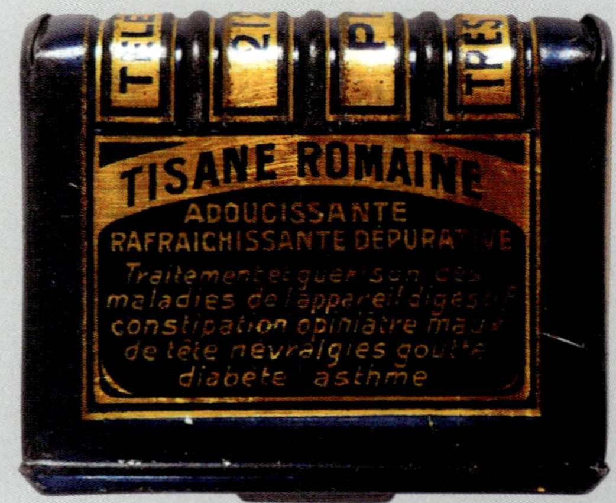

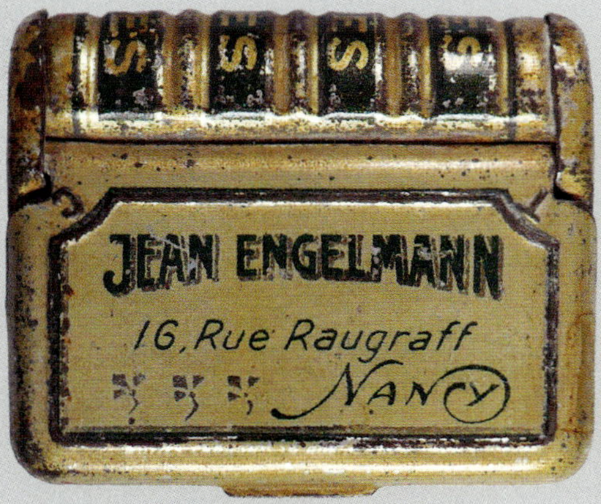

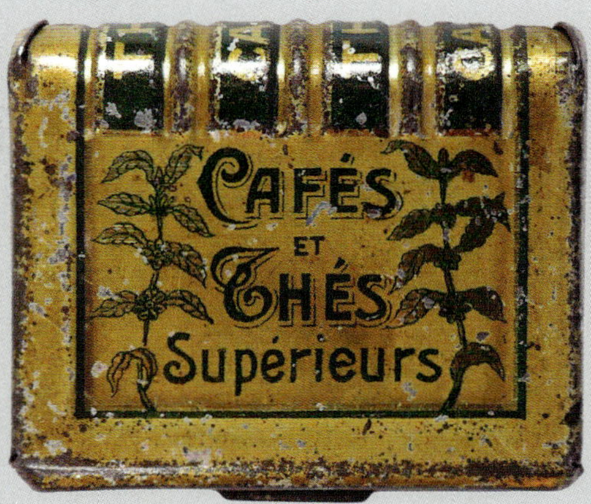

5.010
Thes Cafés, Thes Cafés. Cafés et Thes Supérieurs,
Blechdöschen für Zündhölzer
Tin box for matches
Jean Engelmann, Nancy, Frankreich / *France*
1,4 x 5 x 3,8 cm

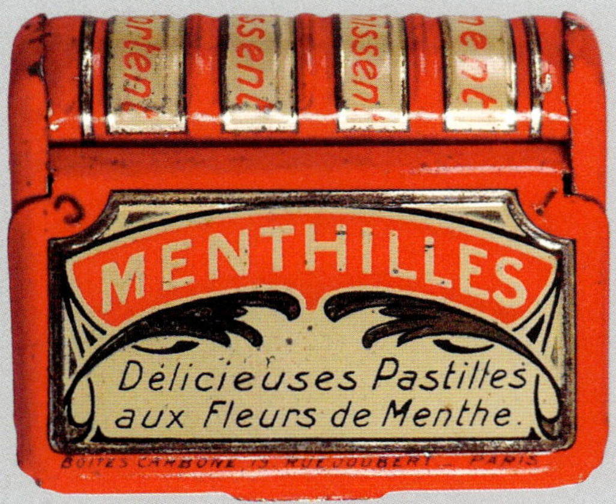

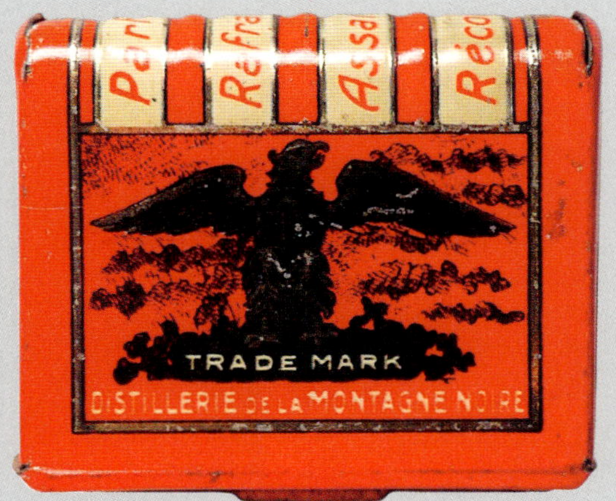

5.011
Parfument Rafraichissen Assainissen Réconforten Menthilles,
Blechdöschen für Zündhölzer
Tin box for matches
Raissac & Cie.
Frankreich / *France*
1,4 x 5 x 3,8 cm

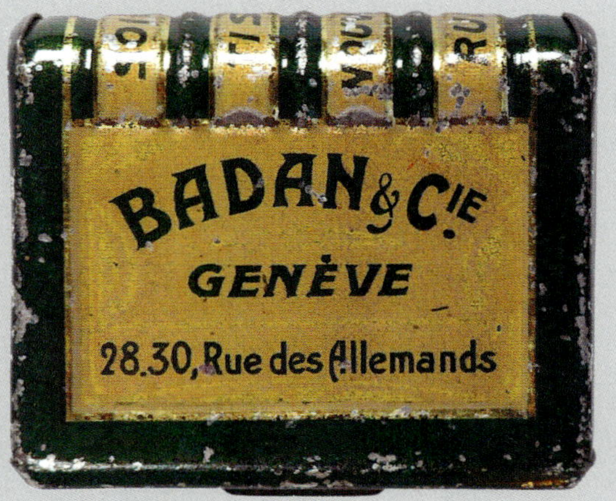

5.012
Soieries Tissue Nouveautés Rubans
Blechdöschen für Pastillen
Tin box for drops
Badan & Cie, Genéve, Schweiz / *Switzerland*
1,4 x 5 x 3,8 cm

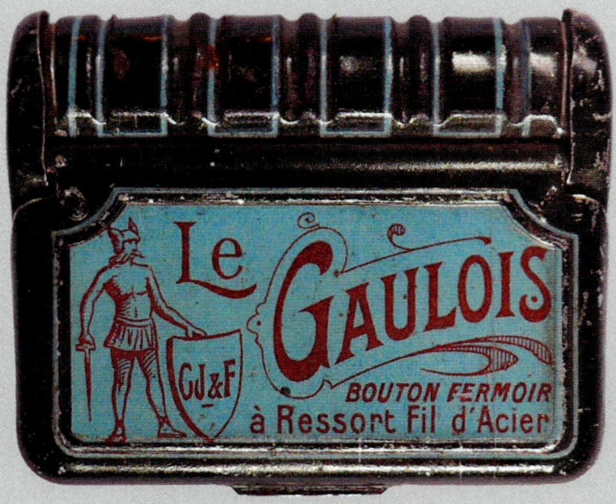

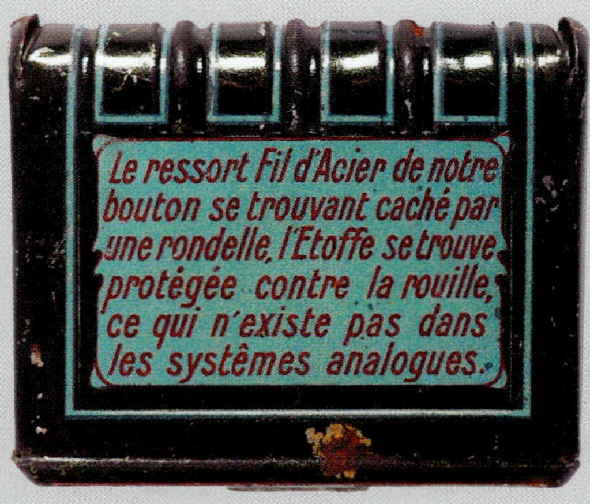

5.013
Le Gaulois Bouton Fermoir à Ressort Fil d'Acier
Blechdöschen für Pastillen
Tin box for drops
Frankreich / *France*
1,4 x 5 x 3,8 cm

5.014
Tablettes Oxyment-hal Perraudin,
Blechdöschen für Zündhölzer
Tin box for matches
Pharmacie Perraudin, Paris
Frankreich / *France*
1,4 x 3,5 x 3,8 cm

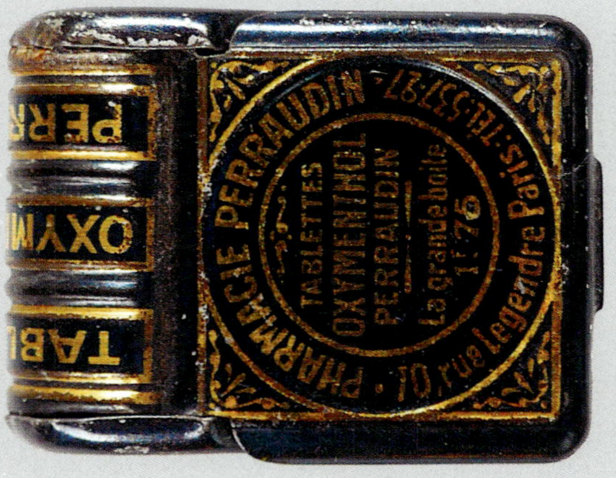

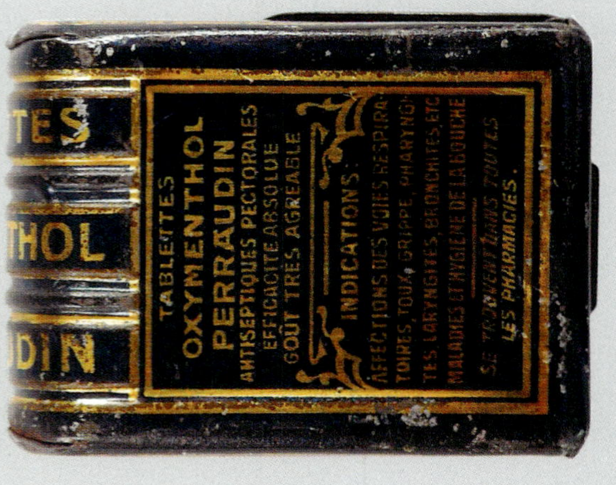

5.015
Deutsche Zündholzfabrik AG Diamant, Rheiman Baden
Blechdöschen für Zündhölzer
Tin box for matches
Deutschland / *Germany*
1,4 x 3,5 x 4,4 cm

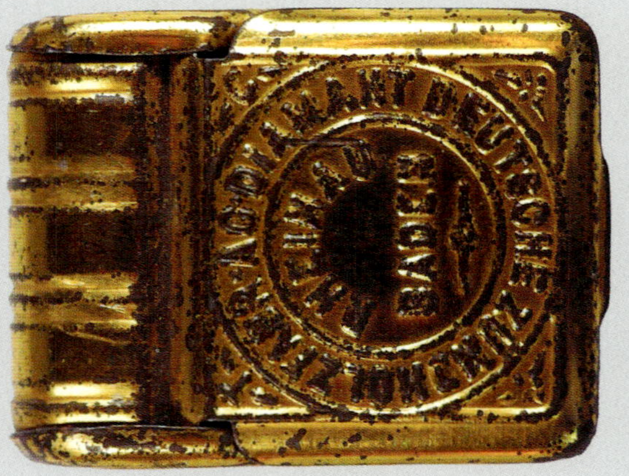

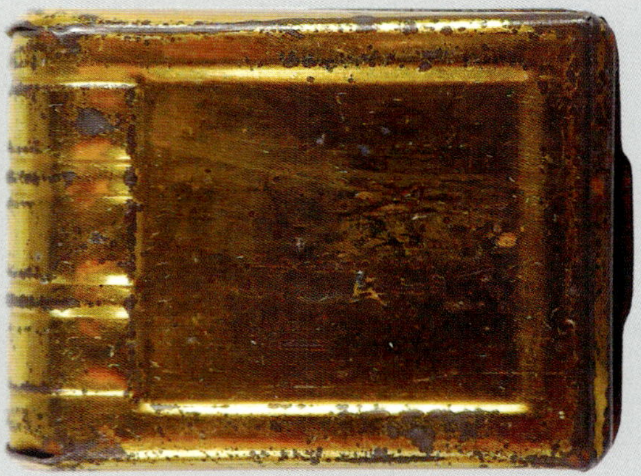

5.016
Blechdöschen für Pastillen
Tin box for drops
Herkunft unbekannt / *Origin unknown*
1,4 x 3,5 x 4,4 cm

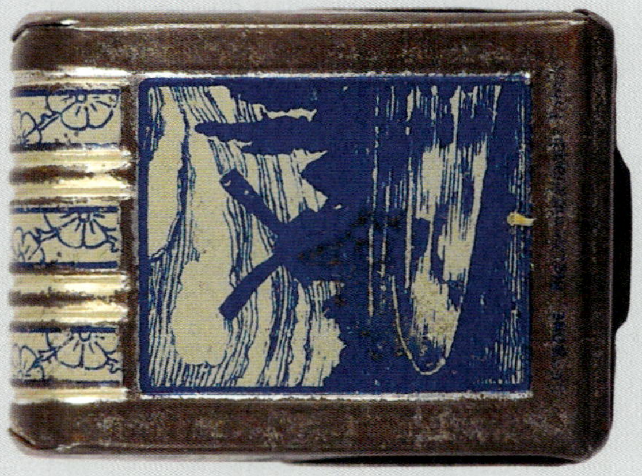

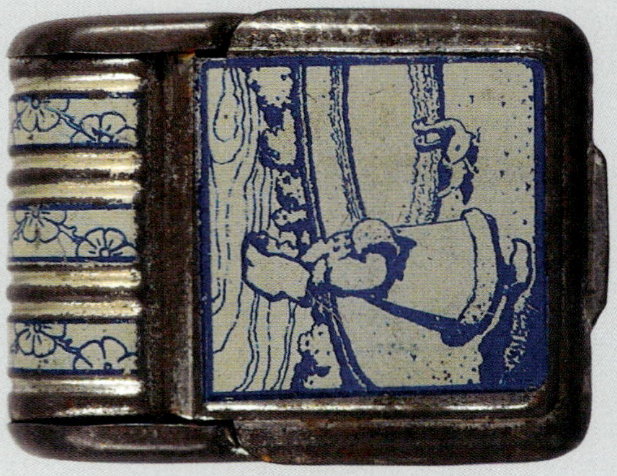

5.017
Guerison de la constipation Laxiline, Cooperation Pharmaceutique Francaise
Blechdöschen für Zündhözer
Tin box for matches
Frankreich / *France*
21,4 x 3,5 x 4,5 cm

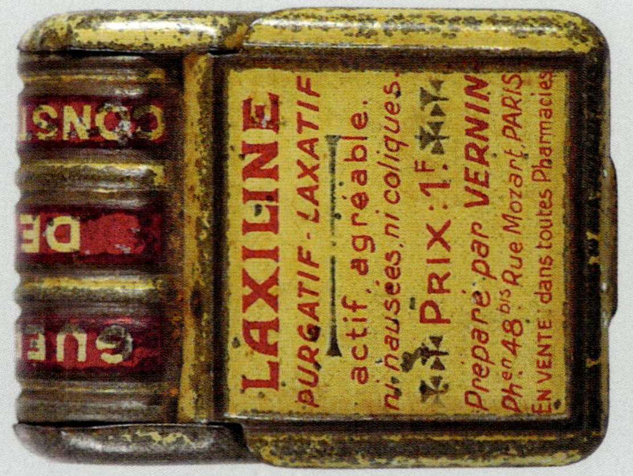

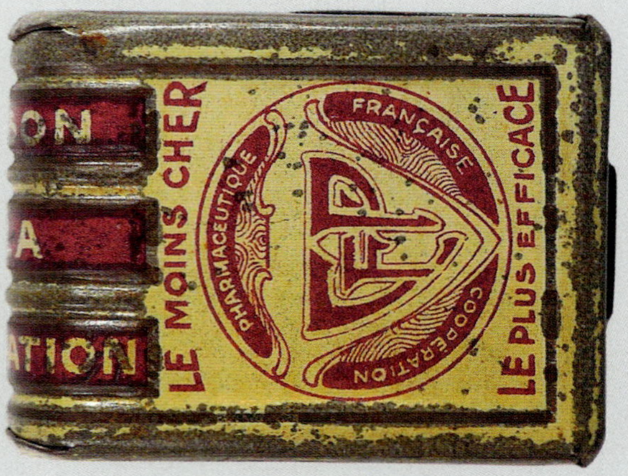

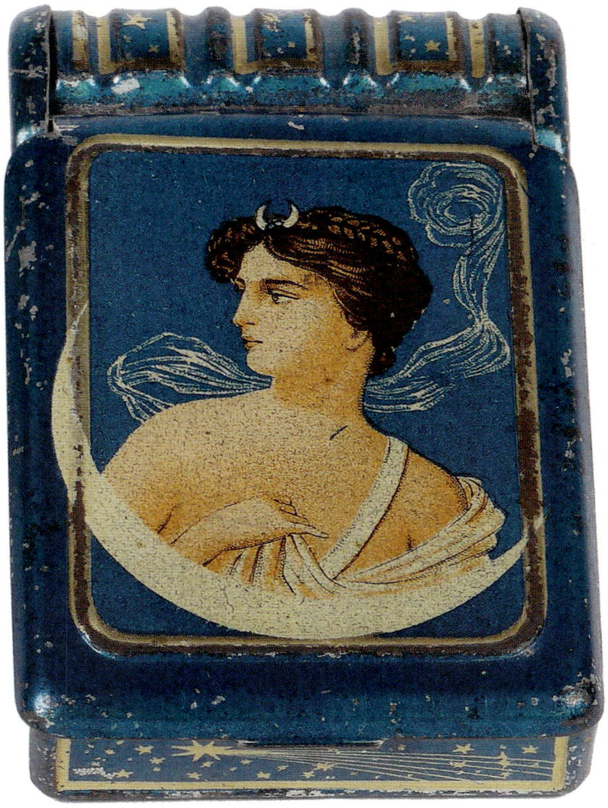

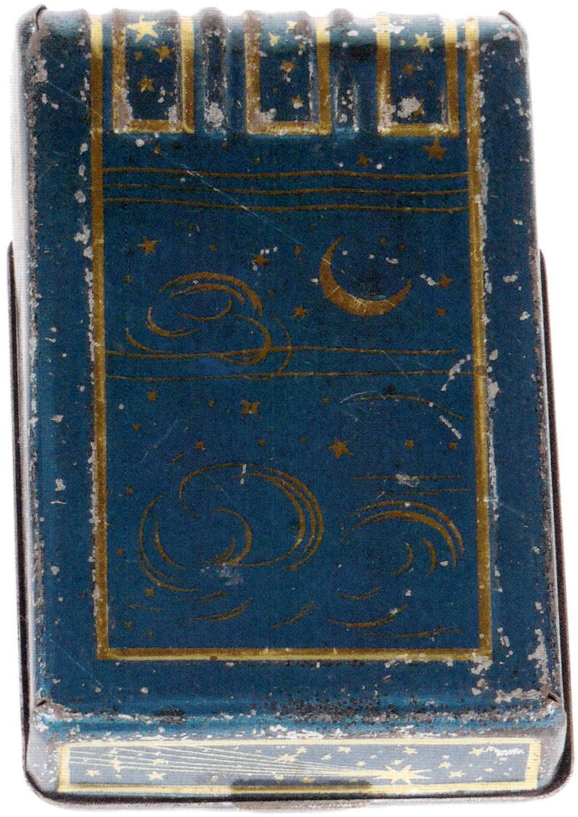

5.018
Lithografierte Blechdose mit Damenporträt auf dem Vorderdeckel, vermutlich für Bonbons
Lithographed tin box with portrait of a lady on the lid, probably for sweets
Um / *Around* 1900 | 1,5 x 5,2 x 8 cm

5.019
Lithografierte Blechdose mit harfenspielender Dame auf dem Vorderdeckel und Schlittschuh laufender Dame auf dem Rückdeckel, vermutlich für Bonbons
Lithographed tin box with harp playing lady on the lid and skating lady on the back, probably for sweets
Jugendstil / *Art Nouveau* | 1,6 x 5,1 x 8 cm

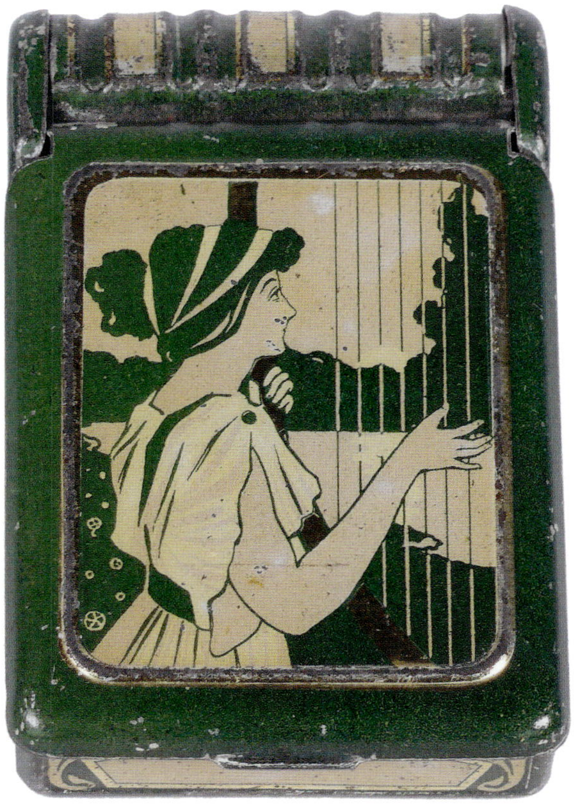

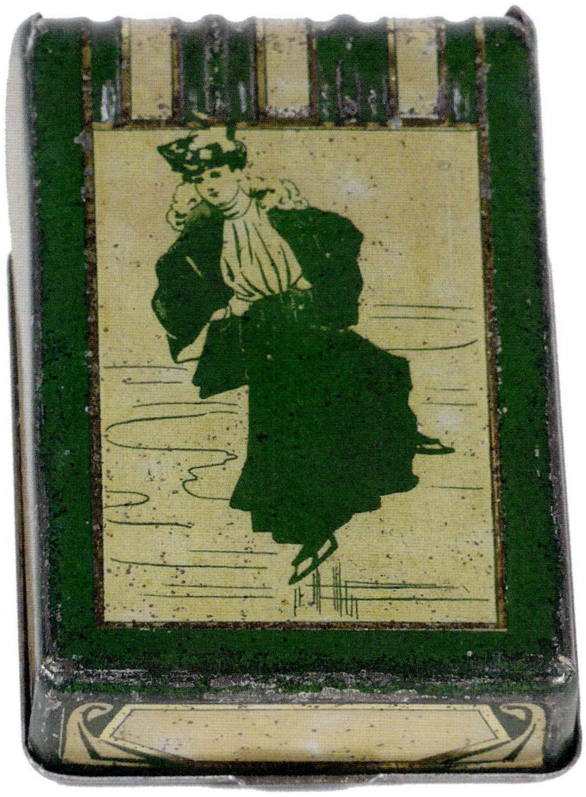

5.020
Specialite Bonbons
Lithografierte Blechdose mit Blumenkorb auf beiden Deckeln
Lithographed tin box with the image of a flower basket on both covers
Frankreich / *France*
Um / *Around* 1900
2,5 x 7,5 x 5,2 cm

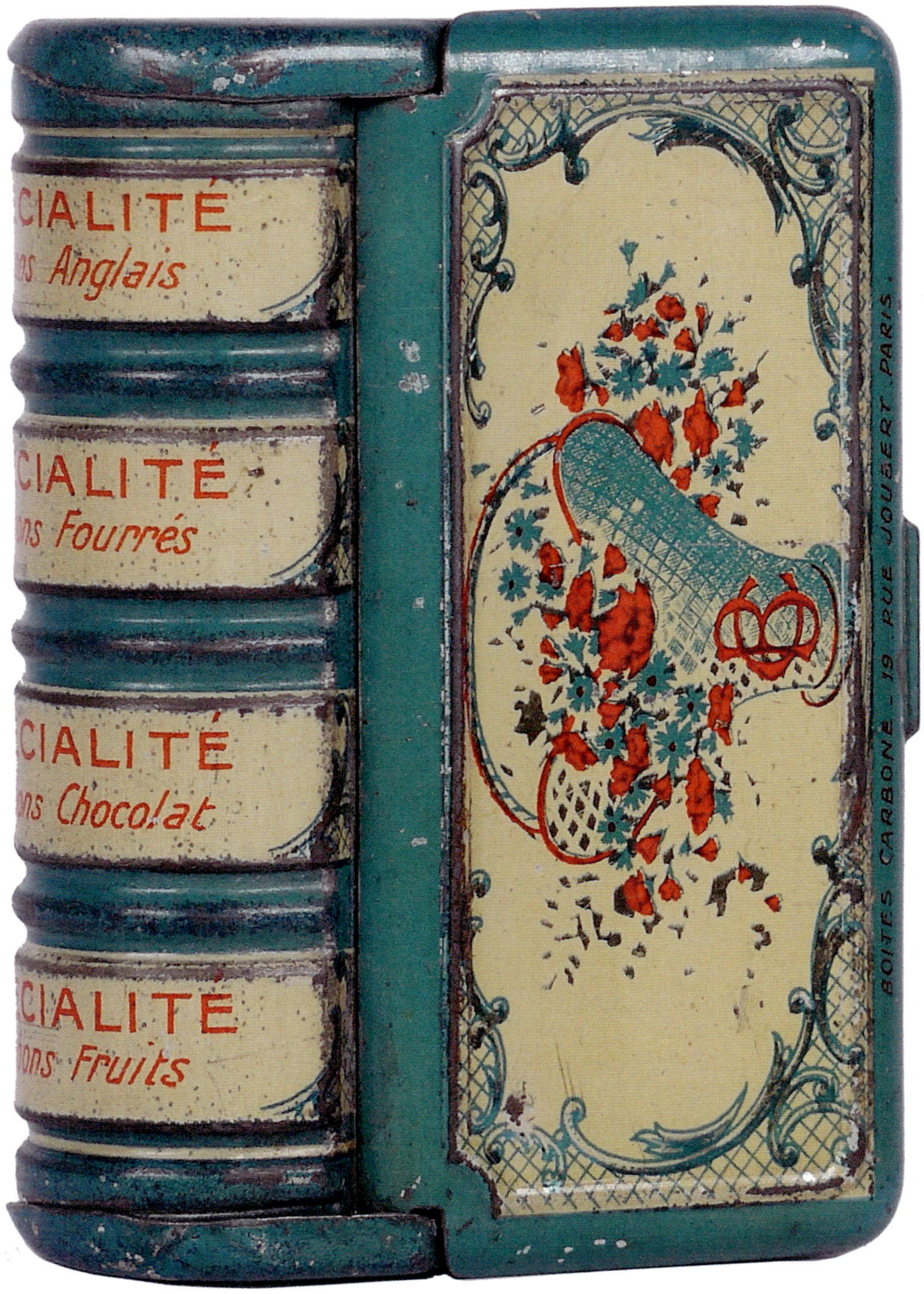

5.021
Pastilles Brachat, Paris.
Guérit toux Rhumes Bronchites toutes Pharmacies
Blechdöschen für Zündhölzer
Tin box for matches
Frankreich / *France*
1,4 x 3,5 x 4,4 cm

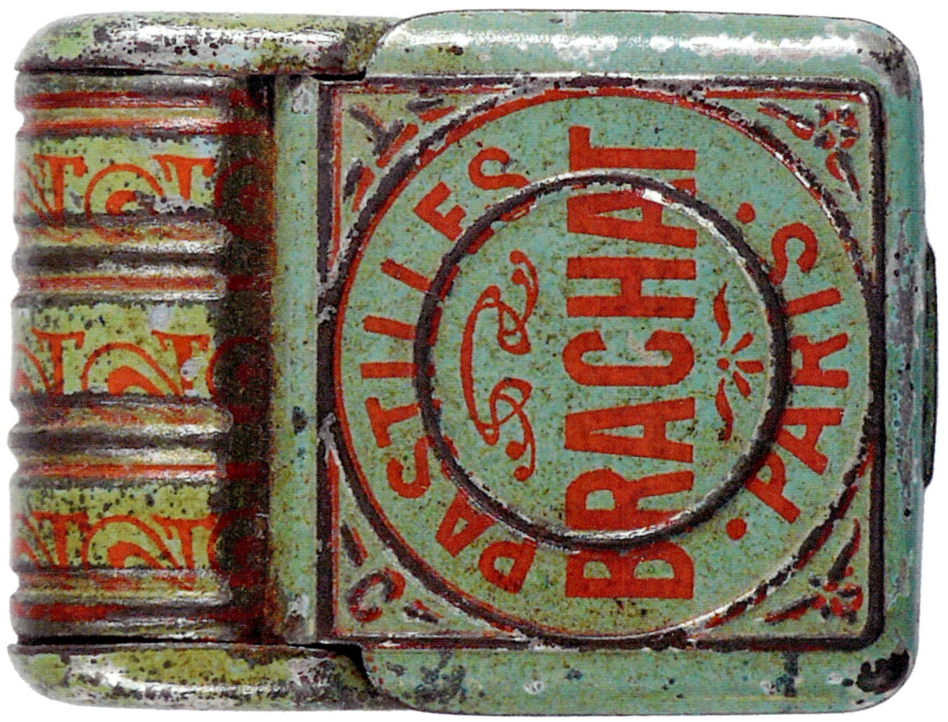

5.022
Veritables Pastilles du Docteur Coudert, Paris
Lithografierte Blechdose
für Pastillen
Lithographed tin box for drops
Frankreich / *France*
Um / *Around* 1900
1,3 x 8,9 x 7,7 cm

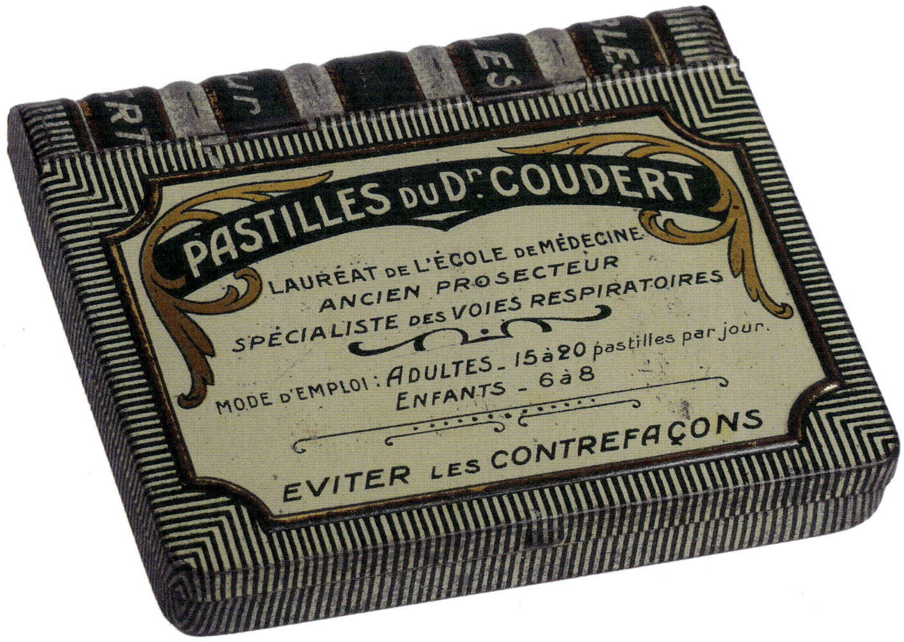

5.023
Souvenir de Chambord
Lithografierte Blechdose
Lithopgraphed tin box
Frankreich / *France*
Um / *Around* 1900
2 x 9 x 8,2 cm

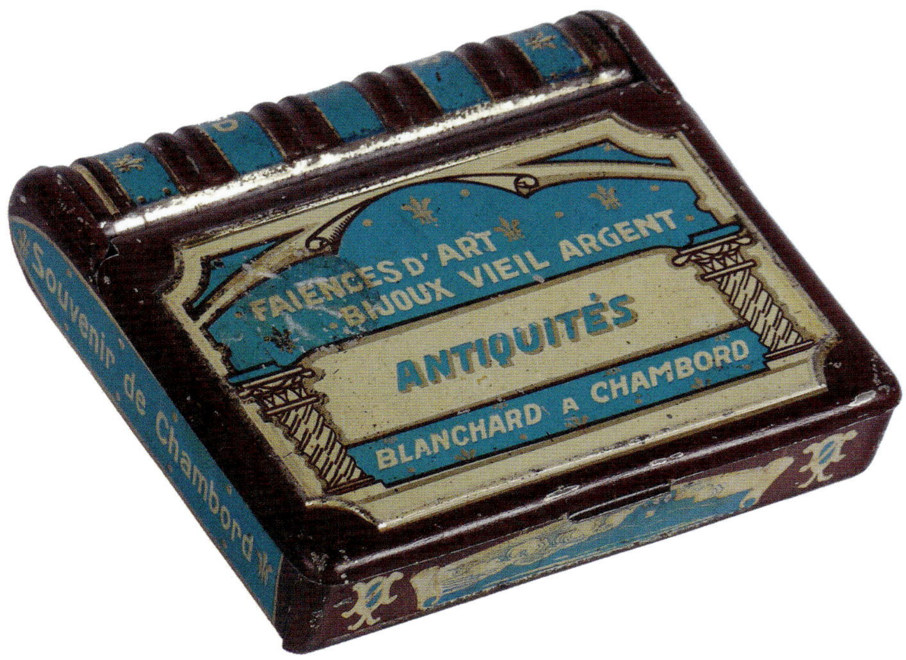

5.024
Epingles en Acier Première Qualité
Lithografierte Blechdose für Sicherheitsnadeln
Lithopgraphed tin box for safety pins
Frankreich / *France*
Um / *Around* 1900
2,1 x 9 x 8,1 cm

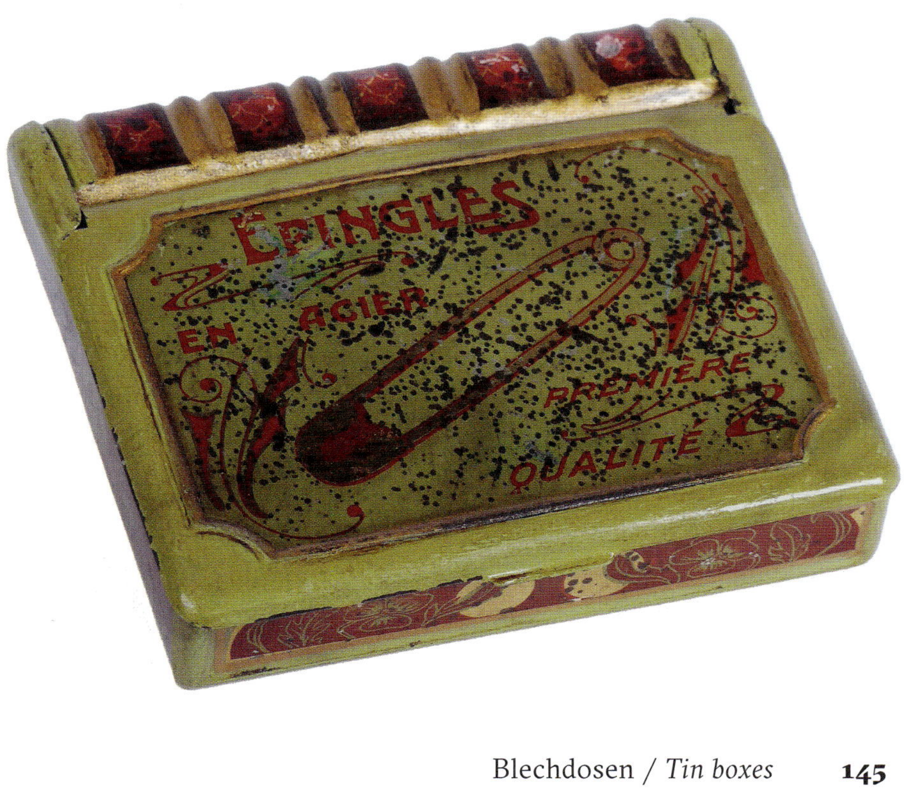

5.025
La Poule au Pot du Bouillon Kub
Lithografierte Blechdose für Bouillon
Lithographed tin box for bouillon
Frankreich / *France*
Um / *Around* 1900
1,9 x 9,7 x 7,7 cm

5.026
Emulsion Elixir Granulé Comprimés Ampoules
Lithografierte Blechdose für Histogenol Nalin
Lithographed tin box for Histogenol Nalin
Frankreich / *France*
Um / *Around* 1900
2 x 9 x 8,2 cm

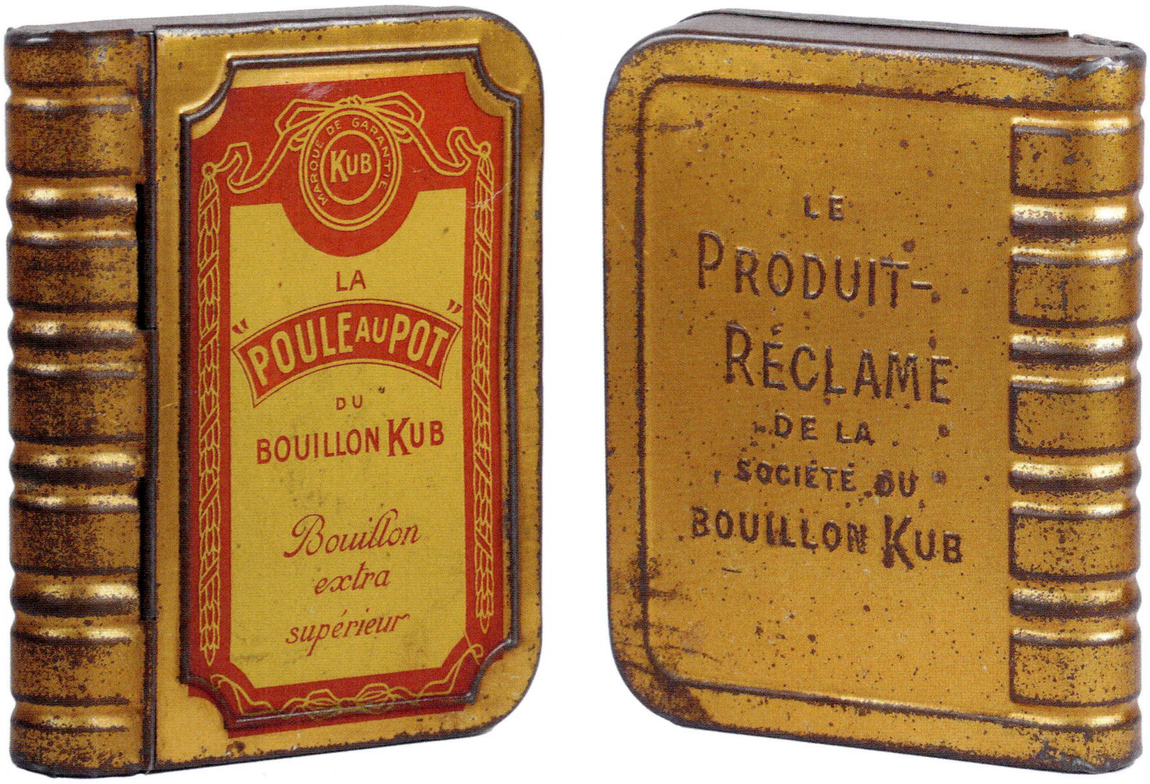

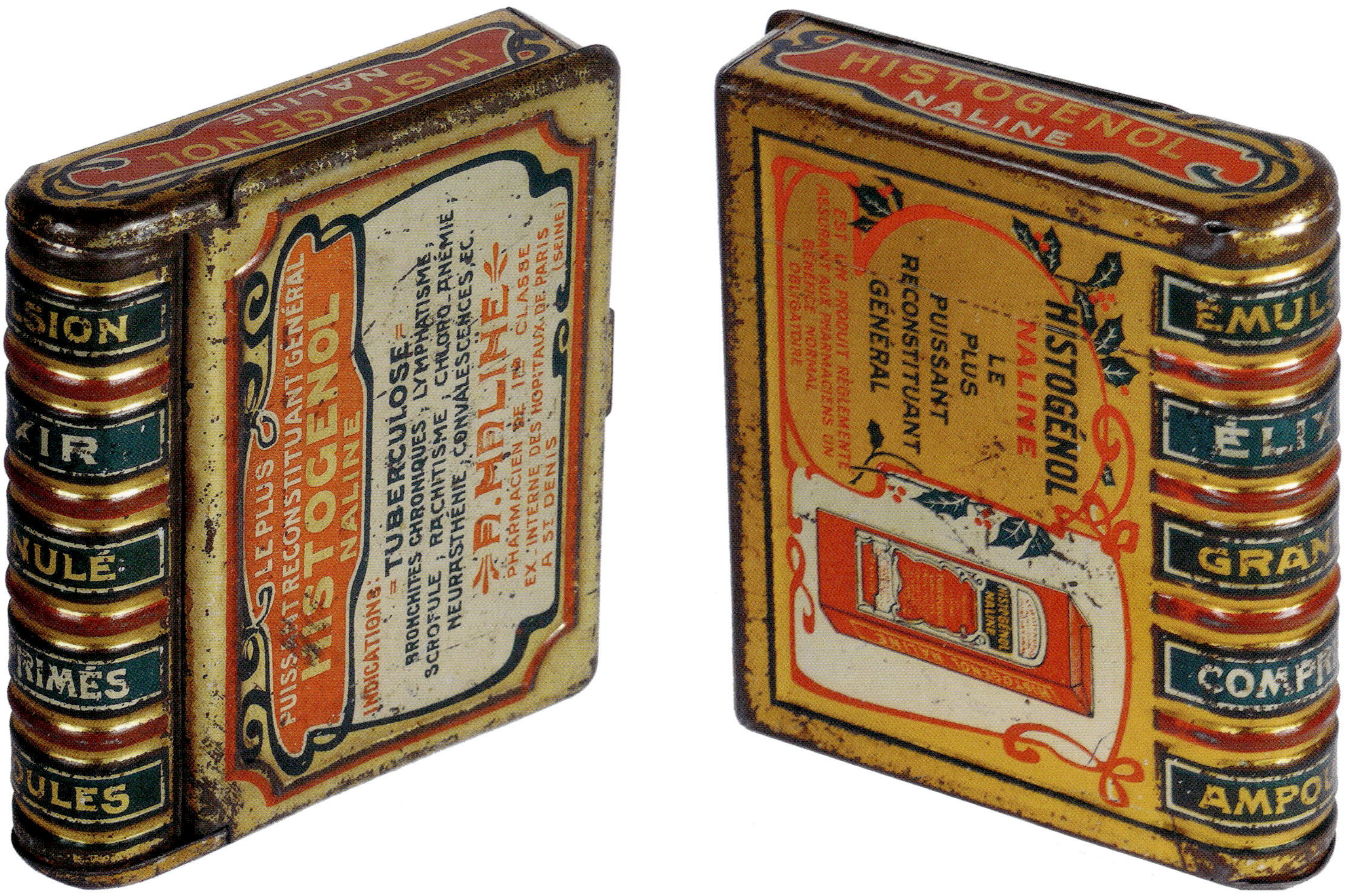

5.027
„Le Zéphyr“ Drortes Ondulées Fines Demi-Fines
Lithografierte Blechdose für Haarnadeln
Lithographed tin box for hairpins
Frankreich / *France*
Um / *Around* 1900
1,4 x 7,5 x 5,5 cm

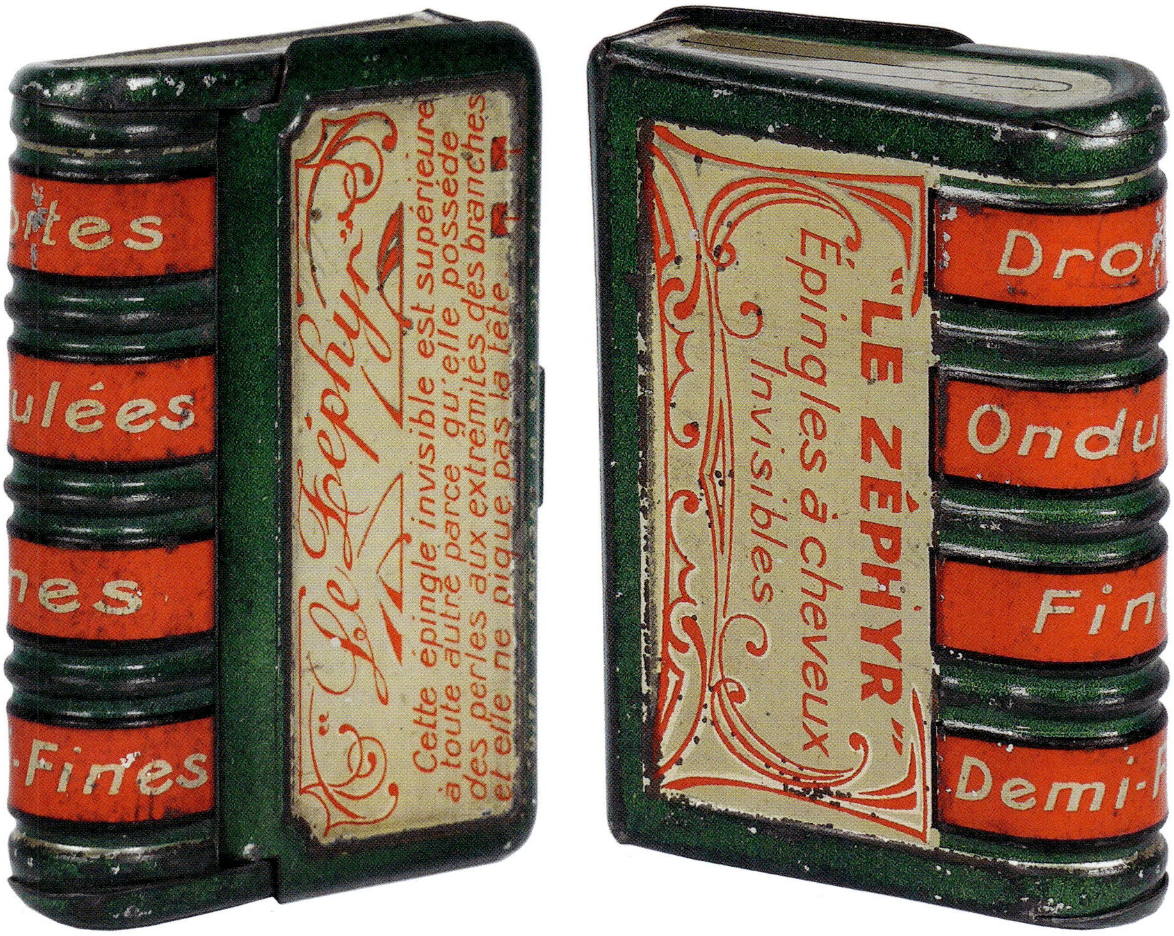

5.028
Elixir Femina, T. A. Games, Pharmacien de l'École Supérieure de Paris
Lithografierte Blechdose für Pastillen
Lithographed tin box for drops
Frankreich / *France*
Um / *Around* 1900
2,5 x 7,5 x 5,1 cm

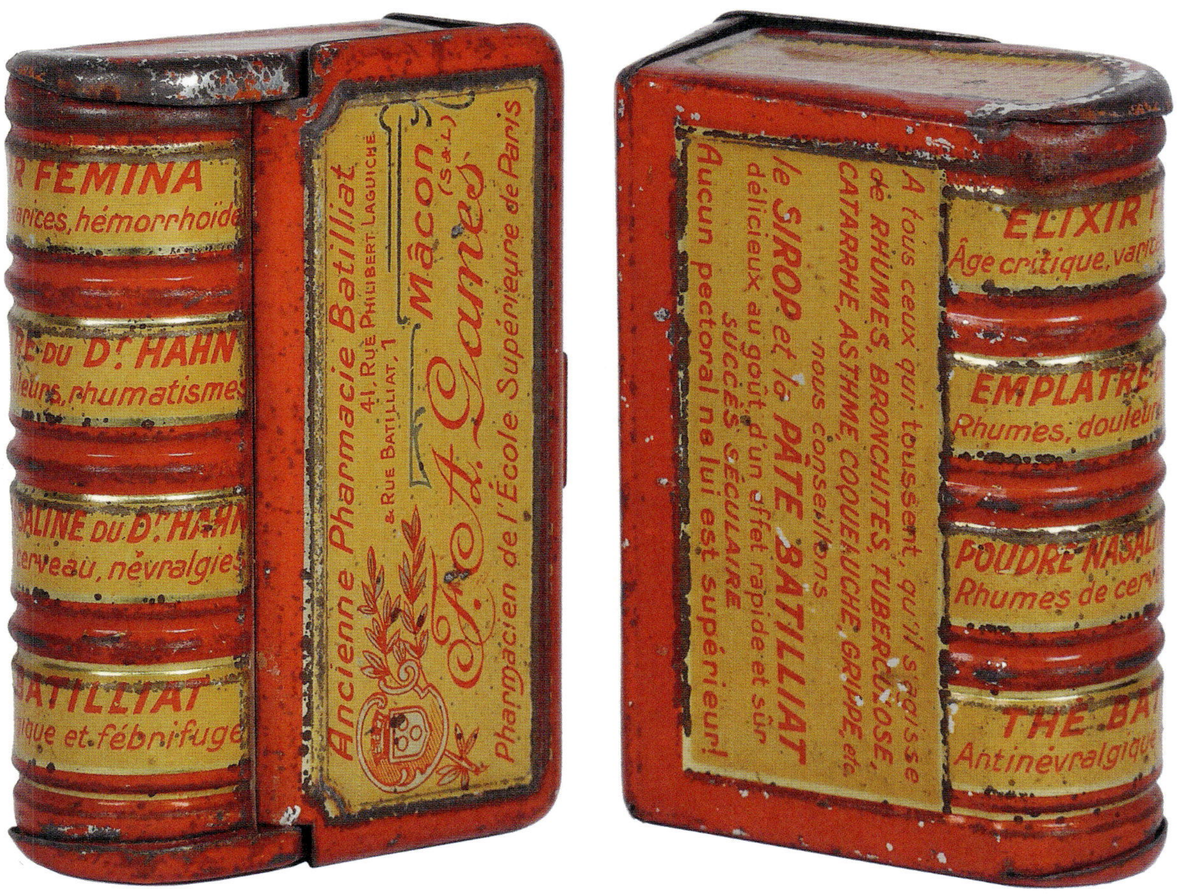

5.029
Aventures Merveilleuses du Chevalier Bayard
Lithografierte Blechdose mit Verschluss
Lithographed tin box with closure
Frankreich / *France*
4,5 x 19,2 x 5,2 cm

5.030
Histoire de la Musique
Lithografierte Blechdose mit Verschluss
Lithographed tin box with closure
Frankreich / *France*
24,x 19,2 x 5,2 cm

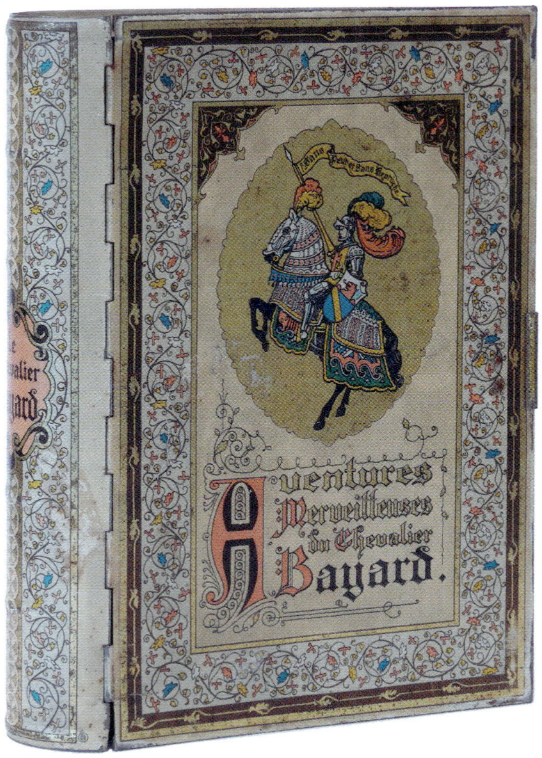

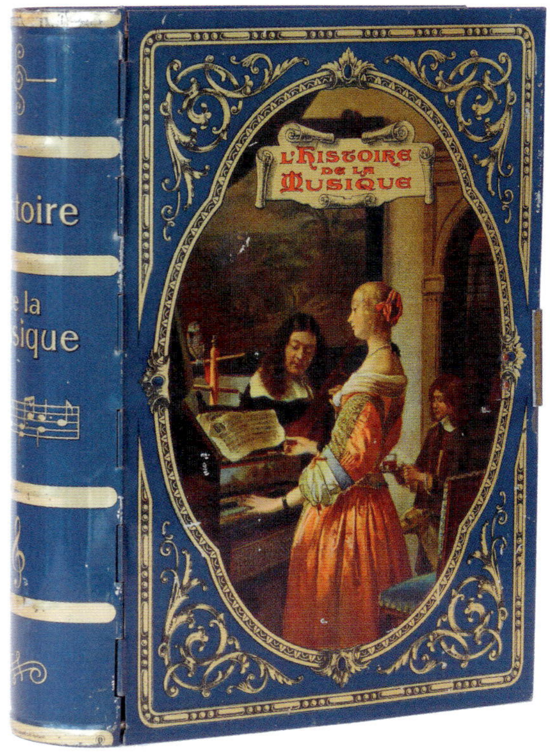

5.031
Machiavelli il Principe
Lithografierte Blechdose einem Jean-Grolier-Einband aus dem 16. Jahrhundert nahekommend
Lithographed tin box similar to a Jean-Grolier binding from the 16th century
26,4 x 19,5 x 5,7 cm

5.032
Chroniques d'Enguerrand de Monstrelet
Lithografierte Blechdose mit Ritterszene aus dem 15. Jahrhundert
Lithographed tin box with a knight theme from the 15th century
26,4 x 19 x 5,7 cm

5.033
Contes de Fées
Lithografierte Blechdose mit Schließe, abschließbar
Lithographed tin box with clasp, lockable
Frankreich / *France*
24,5 x 19,2 x 5,2 cm

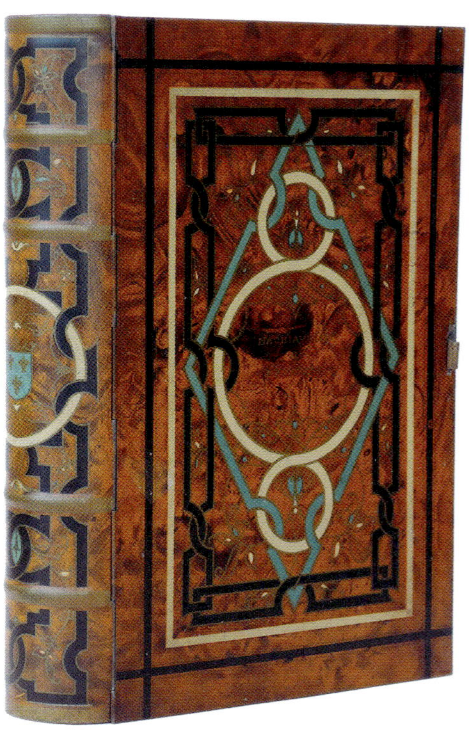

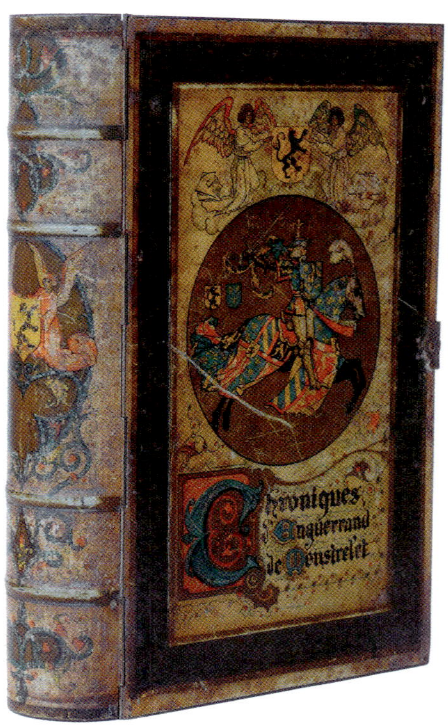

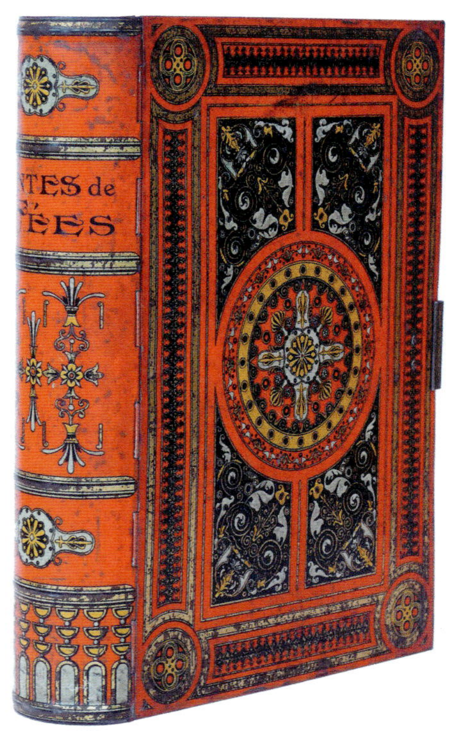

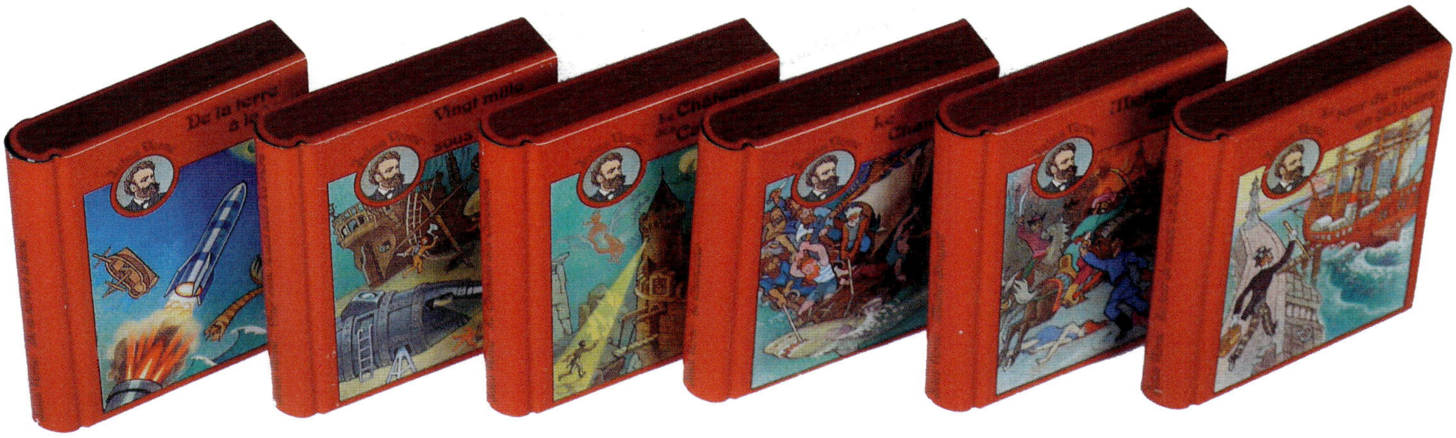

5.034
Sechs Blechdöschen für Apfeltraubenzucker, rot lackiert, die Sujets im Offsetdruck zeigen die abenteuerlichen Geschichten von Jules Verne, Kartonschuber
Six tin boxes for apple-grape sugar, painted in red, image of the adventurous stories of Jules Verne in offset printing, cardboard slip case
Läckerli-Huus, Basel, Switzerland
Um / *Around* 1900 | 6,2 x 7,9 x 5,6 cm

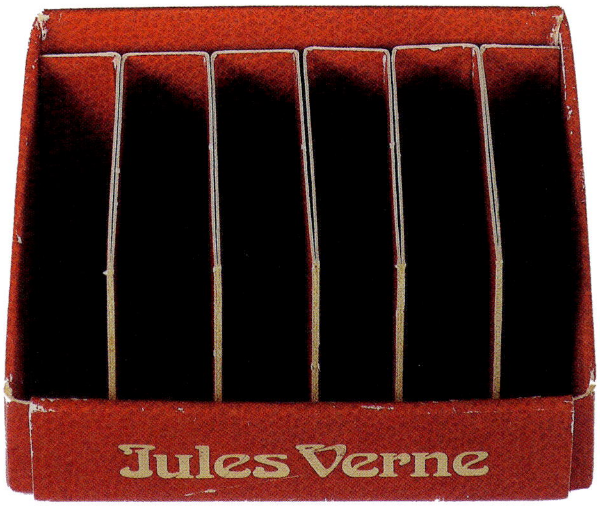

5.035
World's Fair 1939
Kunststoffdose mit Metalldeckel von der Weltausstellung 1939–1940 in New York, vermutlich für ein Leporello, geprägter Obelisk, eine weiße Kugel auf dem Vorderdeckel
Plastic box with metal lid from the world exhibition 1939-1940 in New York, probably for a leporello, embossed obelisk, a white ball on the front lid
0,6 x 3,5 x 2,8 cm

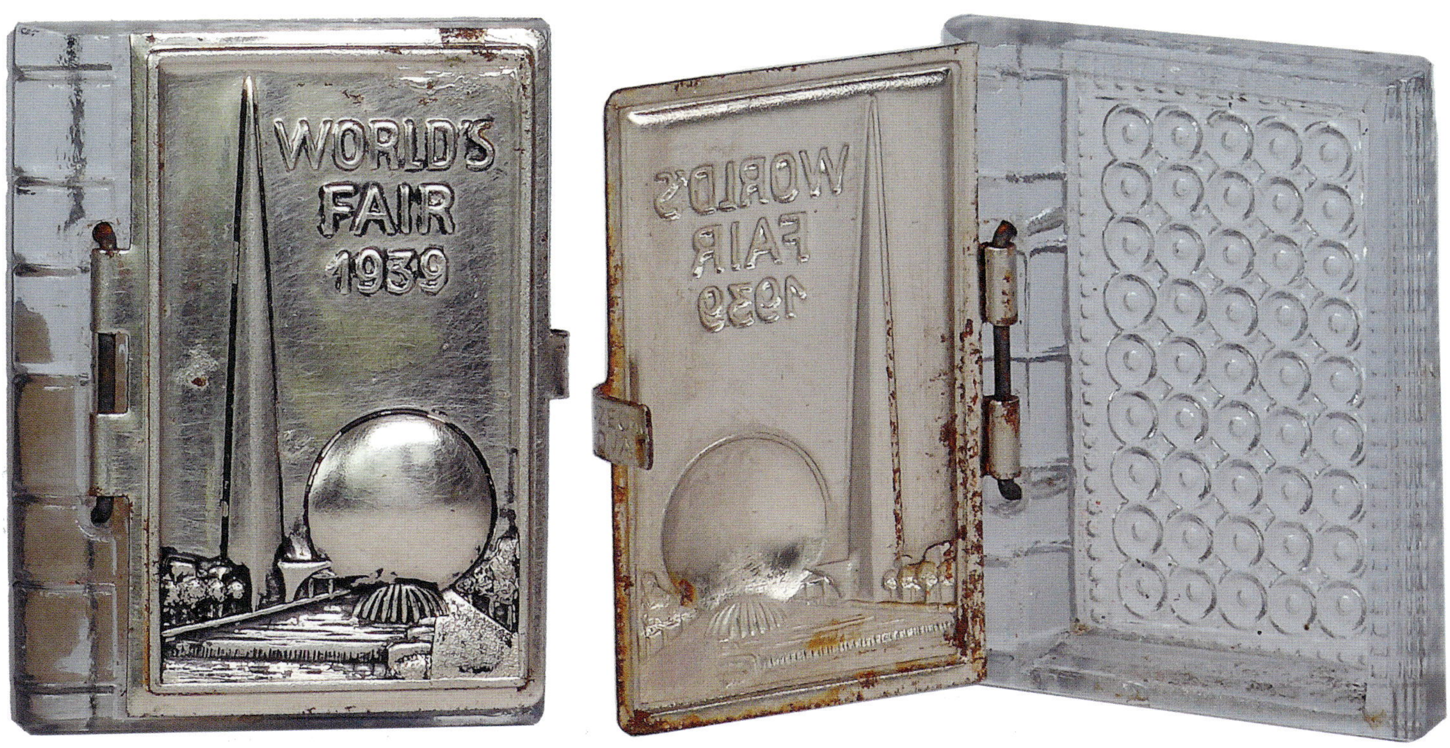

5.036
Blechdose als Laterne, schwarz lackiert, zwei romantische Ansichten in Goldton auf beiden Deckeln, Haltegriff, Vorrichtung zum Aufhängen, aufklappbar, Frontansicht verglast, Kerzenhalterung
Tin box used as lantern, varnished in black, two romantic themes in gold on both covers, handle, device for hanging up, hinged, glazed front cover, candle holder
13 x 8,5 x 2,2 cm

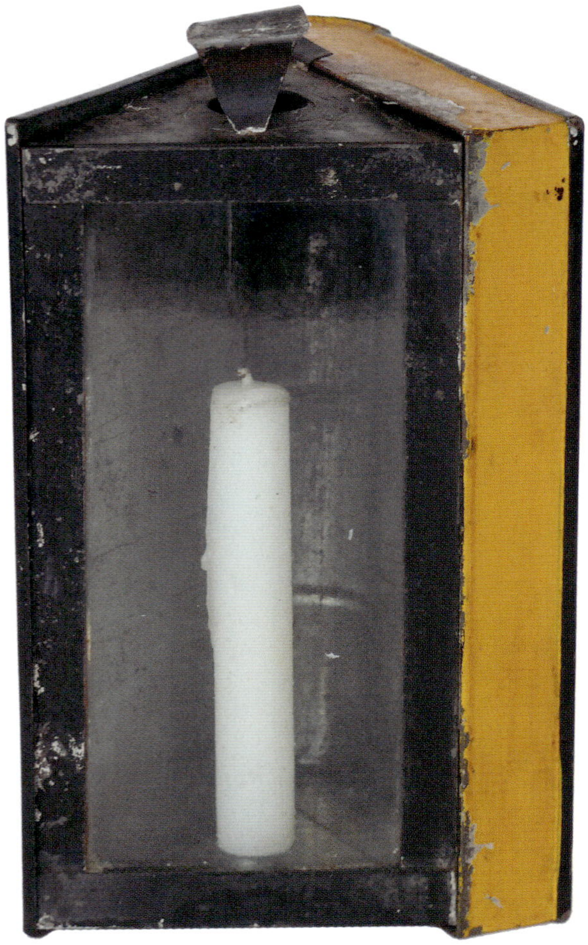

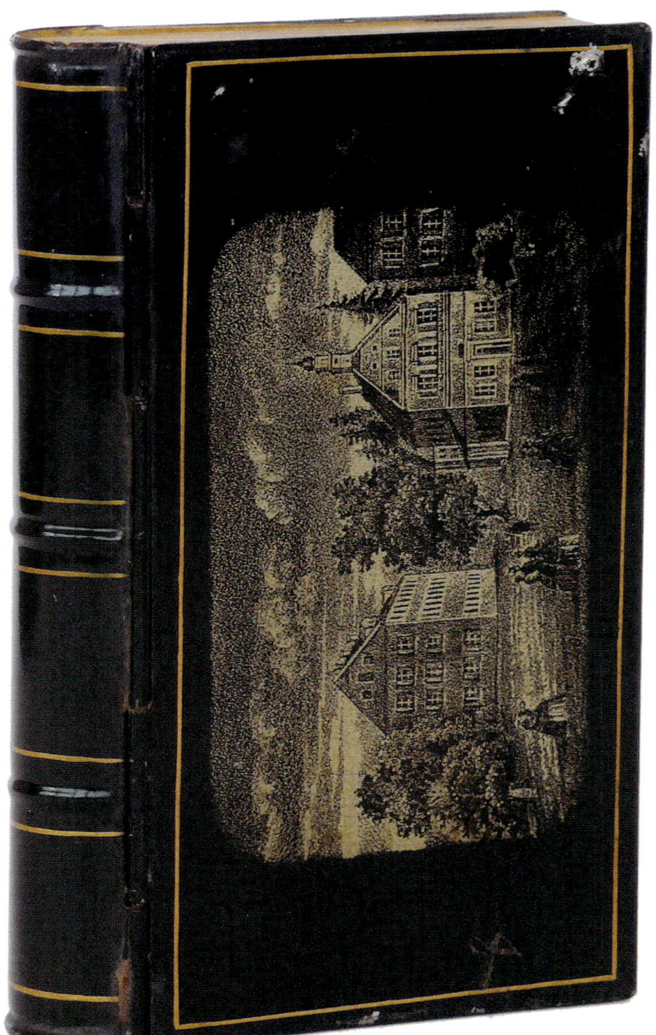

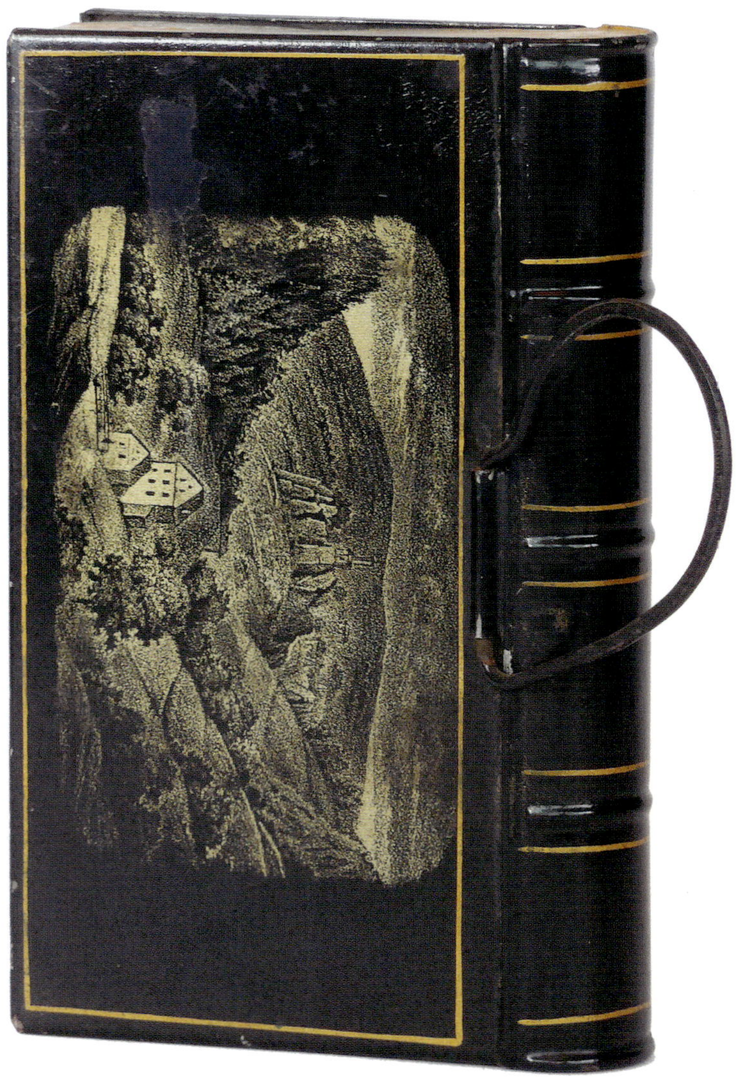

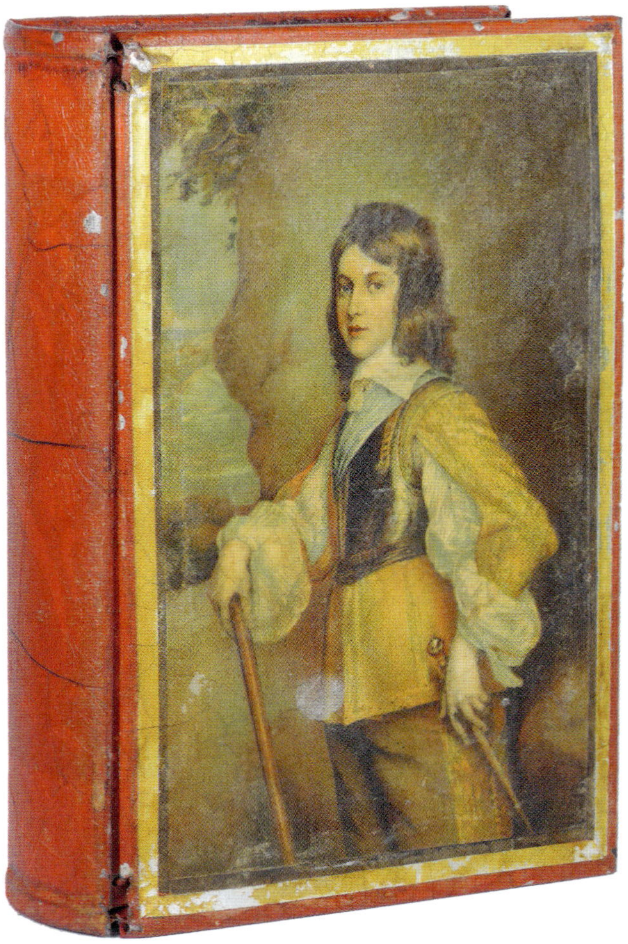

5.037
Lithografierte Blechdose mit adligen Jünglingsszene auf dem Vorderdeckel, ausgefüttert mit Buntpapier, dreiseitiger Goldschnitt
Lithographed tin box with the image of young man on the front cover, lined with colored paper, all edges gilt
3,9 x 15,8 x 11,3 cm

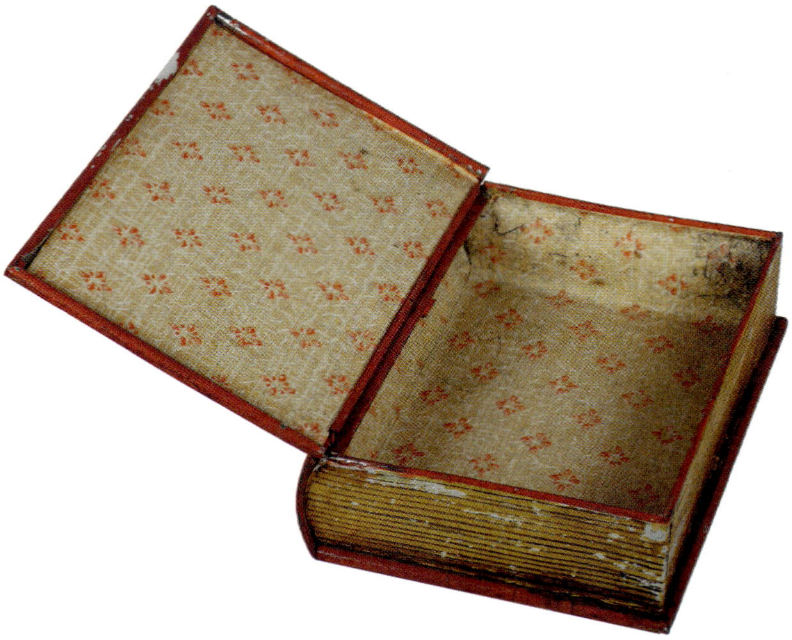

5.038–5.040
Blechbehältnisse in Buchform mit Fingergriff für die Krümel-Tischreinigung
Sheet metal boxes in the design of a book with a grip for cleaning the table of crumbs
3,2 x 23 x 15 cm

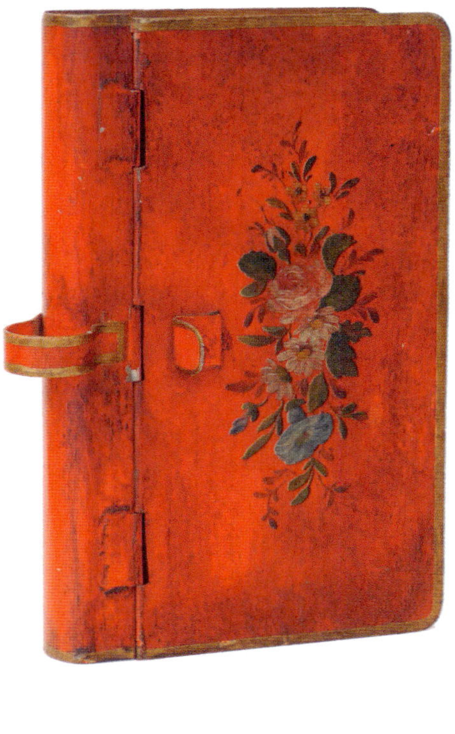

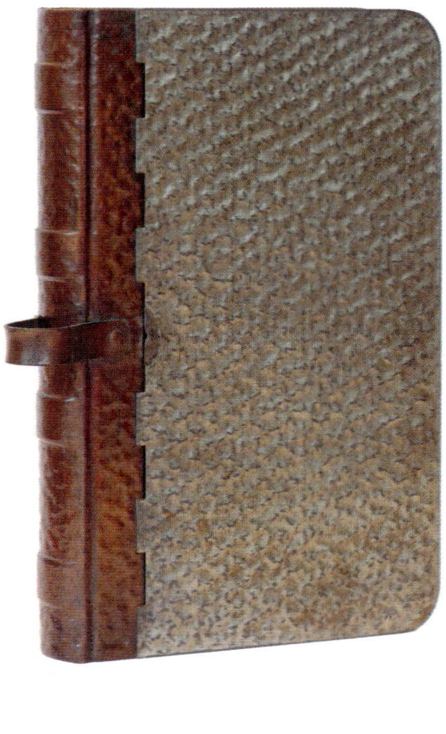

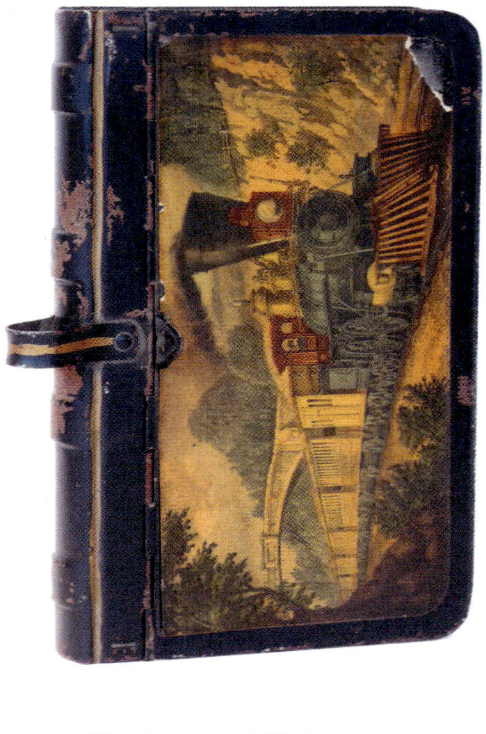

5.041
Metalldose, reliefierter Vorderdeckel, drei Putten mit Rankenwerk, ziselierter Rückdeckel, Blumendekor, Holzeinlage
Metal box, front cover in relief, three putti with tendrils, chased back cover, floral ornaments, wooden inlay
2,6 x 10,5 x 9,2 cm

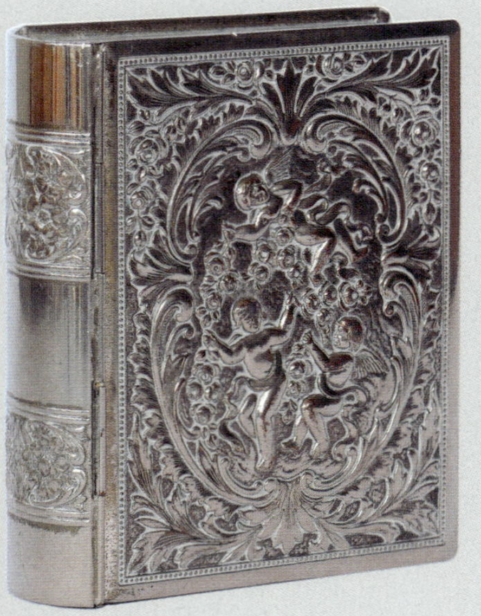

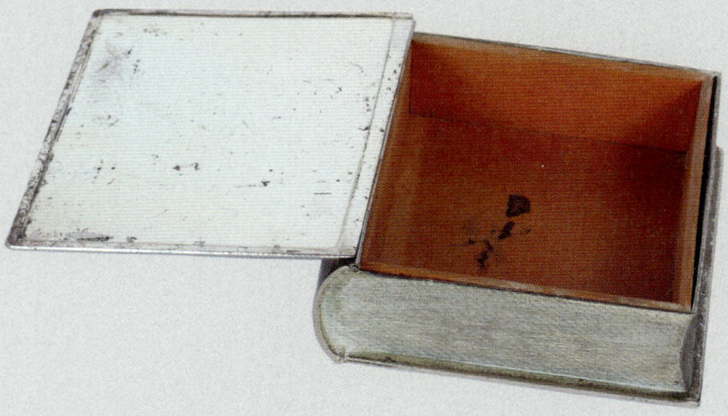

5.042
Metalldose mit zwei aufgesetzten Porträts und zwei Monogramme, „E.R.,V.R." König Eduard VII und Königin Victoria des Vereinigten Königreiches von Großbritannien und Irland
Metal box with two portraits and two monograms, "E.R.,V.R." King Edward VII and Queen Victoria, of the United Kingdom of Great Britain and Ireland
1,7 x 6,9 x 5,5 cm

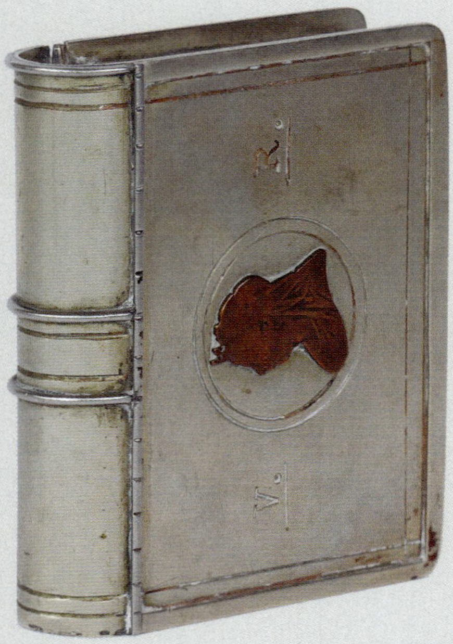

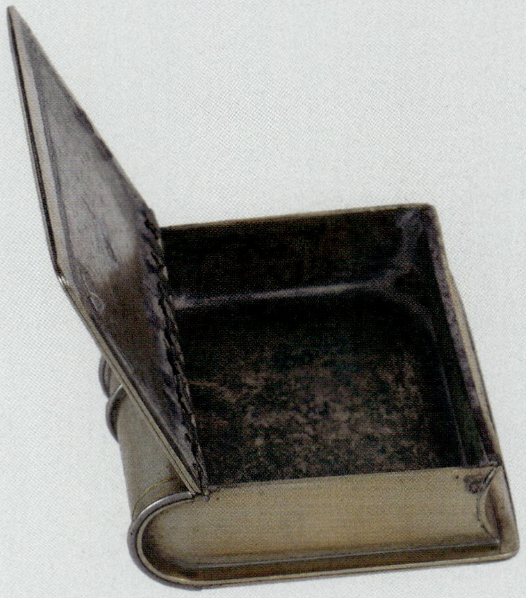

5.043
Metalldose getrieben und ziseliert
Embossed and chased metal box
2,6 x 10,8 x 7,1 cm

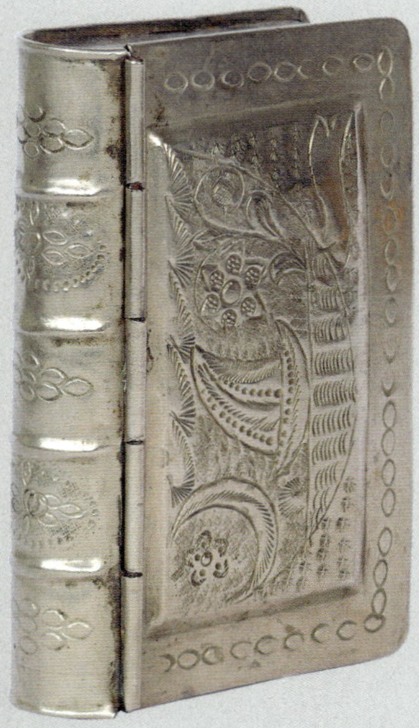

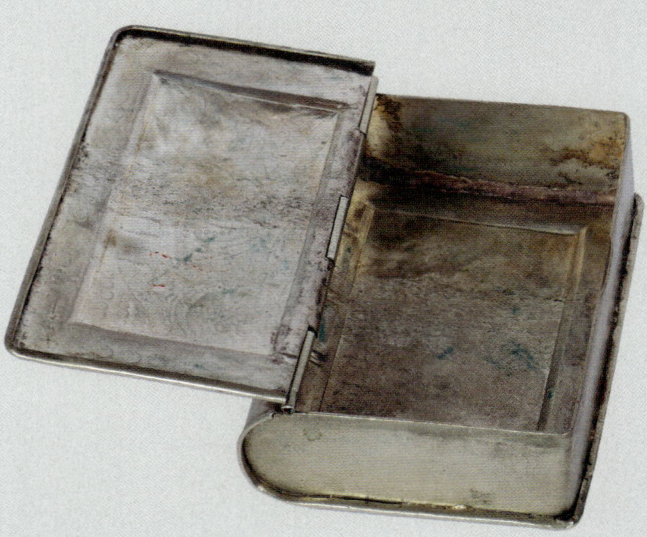

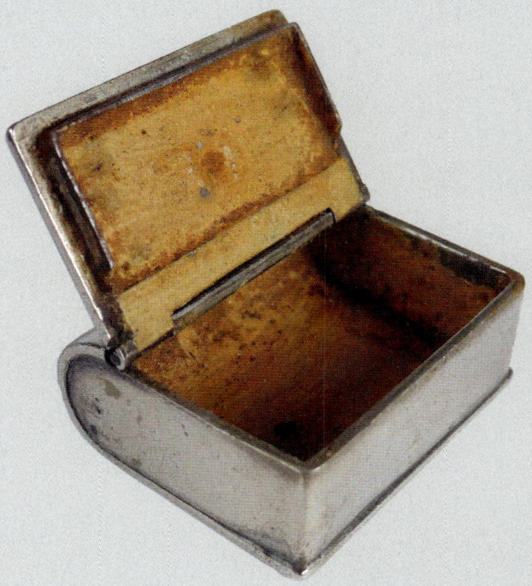

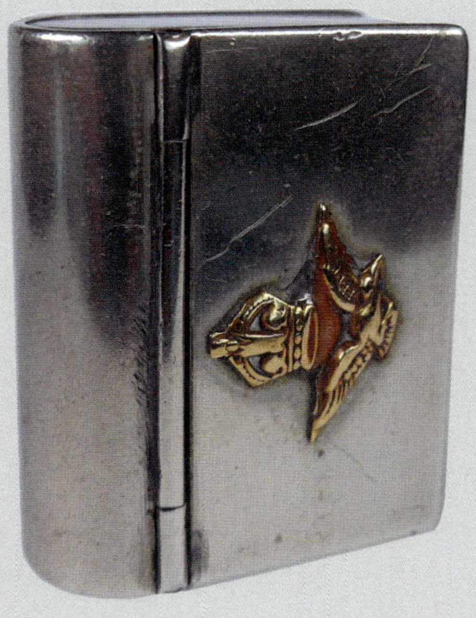

5.044
Metalldose mit aufgesetztem Adler und Krone aus Messing auf dem Vorderdeckel, Innenbemalung, Pillendose (?)
Metal box with an eagle and brass crown on the lid, painted interior, pillbox (?)
1,1 x 3,1 x 2,5 cm

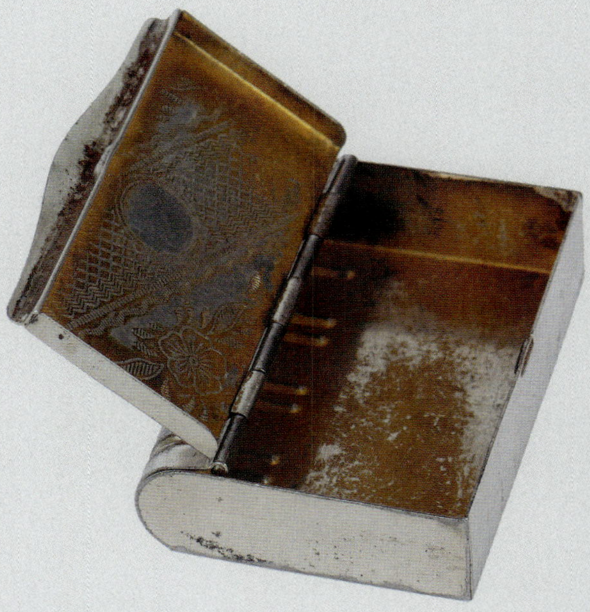

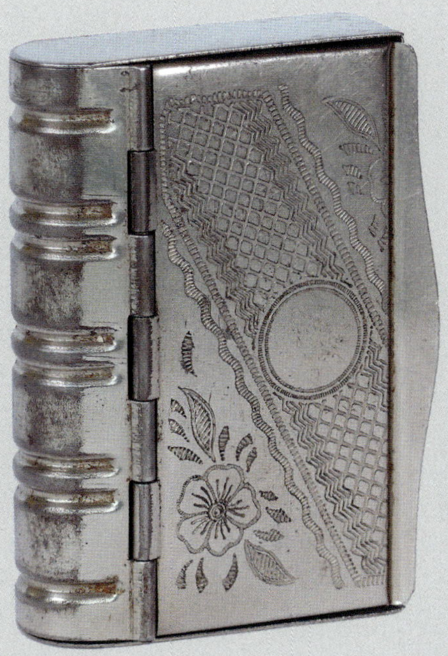

5.045
Metalldose mit graviertem Vorderdeckel
Metal box with engraving on the lid
1,9 x 8,3 x 5,4 cm

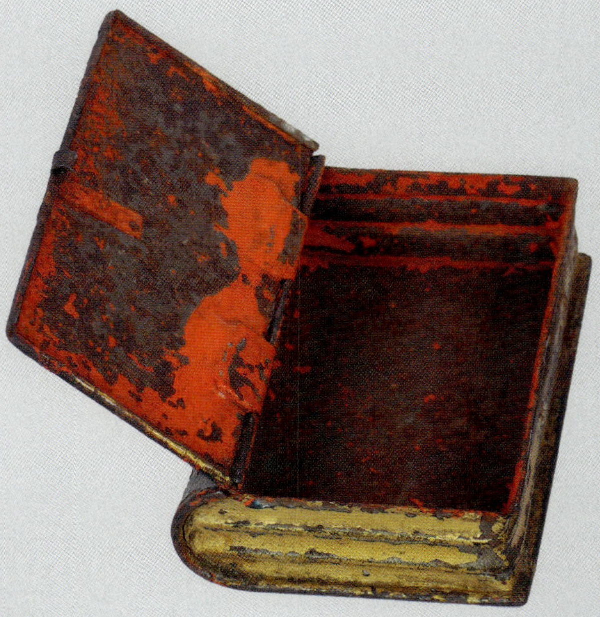

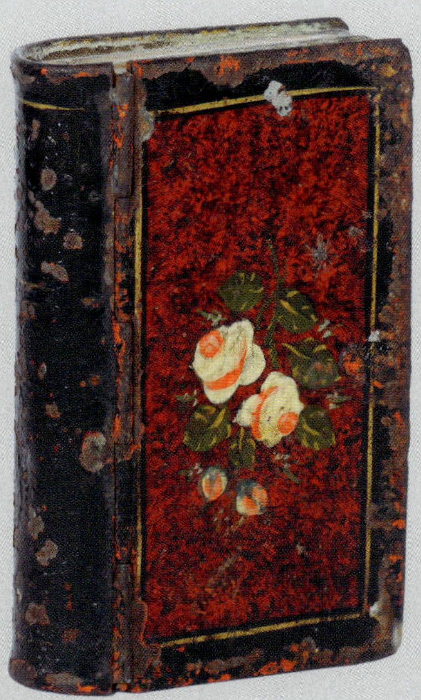

5.046
Blechdose bemalt mit Blumenmotiv auf dem Vorder- und Rückdeckel, dreiseitiger Goldschnitt
Tin box with painted flowers on lid and bottom, all edges gilt
2,3 x 9,6 x 6,2 cm

5.047
Metalldose mit asiatischer Gravur auf dem Vorder- und Rückdeckel
Metal box with Asian engraving on both covers
Um / *Around* 1930
0,8 x 4,9 x 3,5 cm

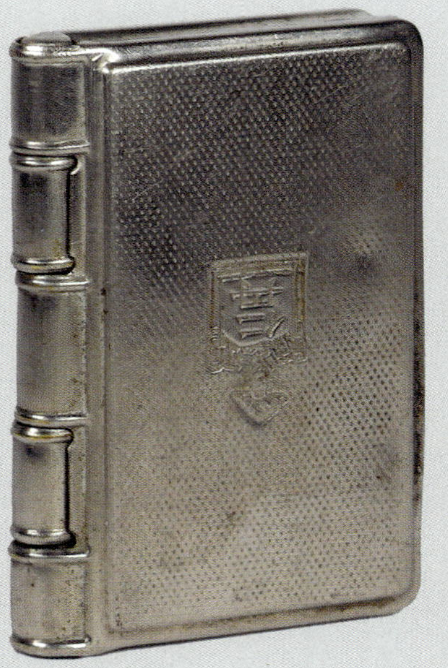

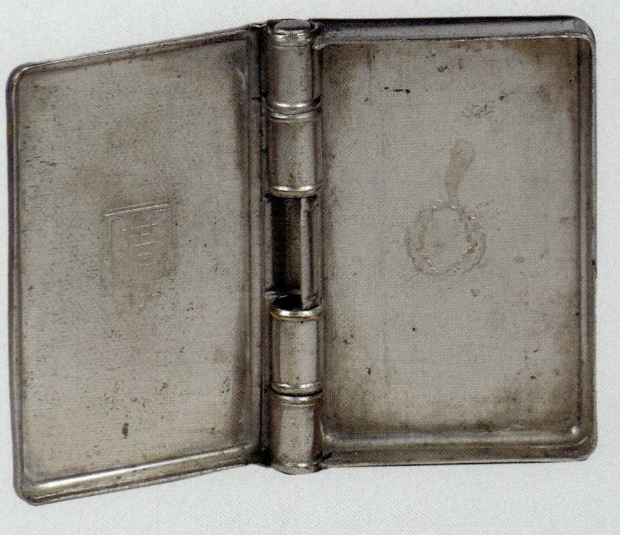

5.048
Metalldose mit geprägter Rücken- und Deckelverzierung
Metal box with embossed spine and covers with ornaments
Jugendstil / *Art Nouveau*
1,1 x 6,5 x 3,6 cm

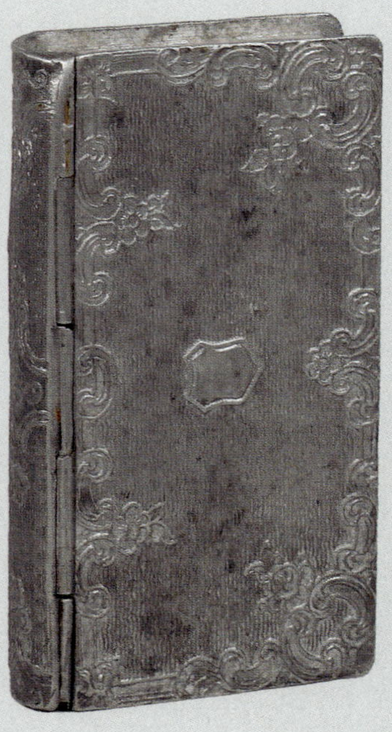

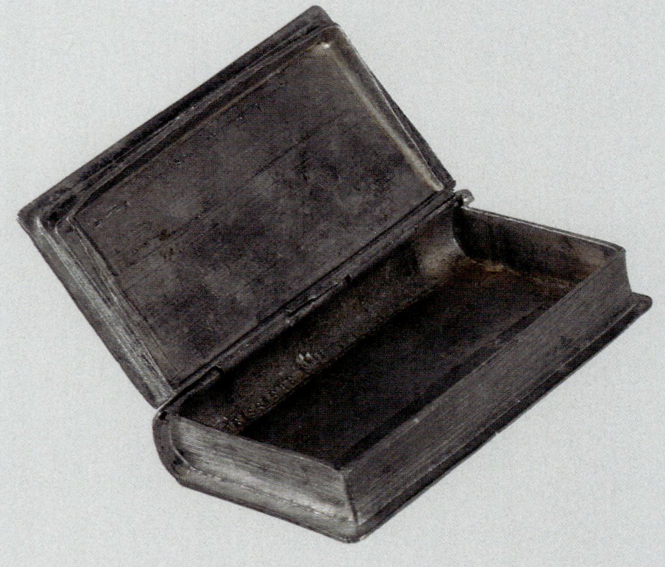

5.049
Metalldose mit Schiebeverschluss auf dem Vorderdeckel, drei Innenfächer, Verwendungszweck unklar
Metal box with a sliding closure on the front cover, three inner compartments, use unclear
2,2 x 9,7 x 6,5 cm

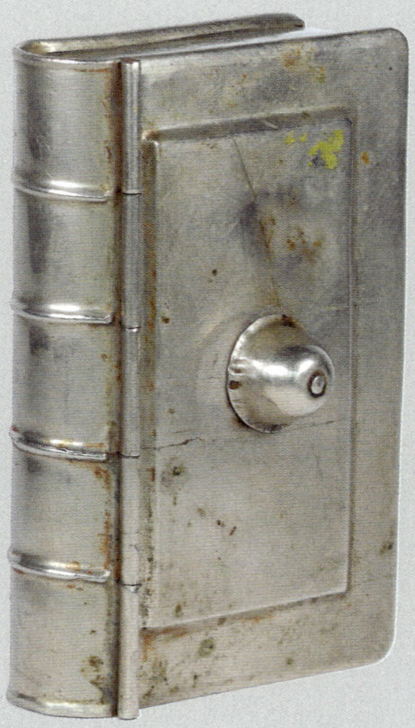

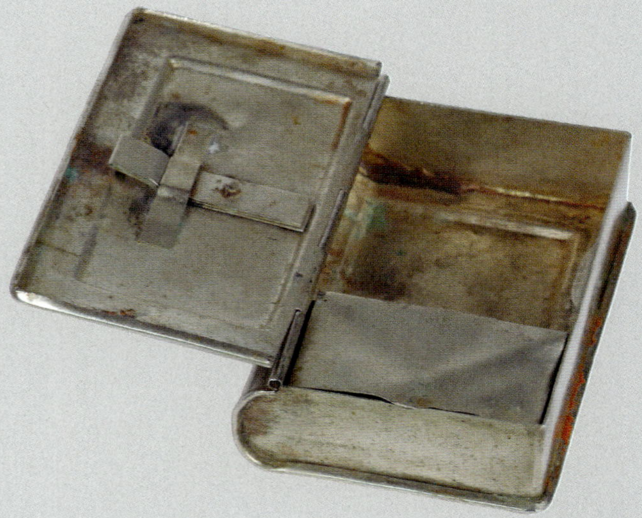

5.050
Gott mit uns / ***God with us*** **1914/15**
Metalldose mit Relief des Marktplatzes mit Rathaus von Neubreisach auf dem Vorderdeckel, Rückenbeschriftung mit Eisernem Kreuz, ausgefüttert mit blauem Stoff
Metal box with a relief showing the marketplace of the city hall of Neubreisach on the lid, labelled with an iron cross on the spine, lined with blue fabric
3,5 x 10 x 7,9 cm

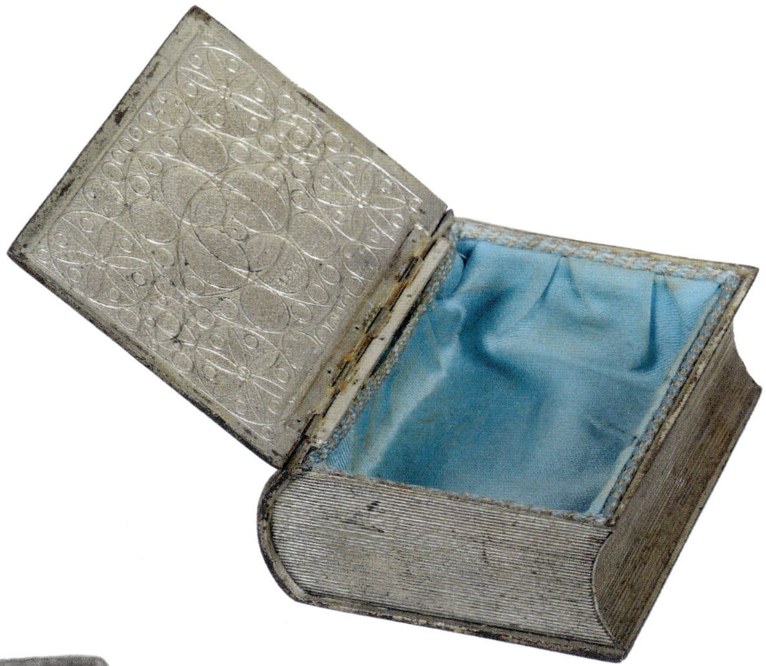

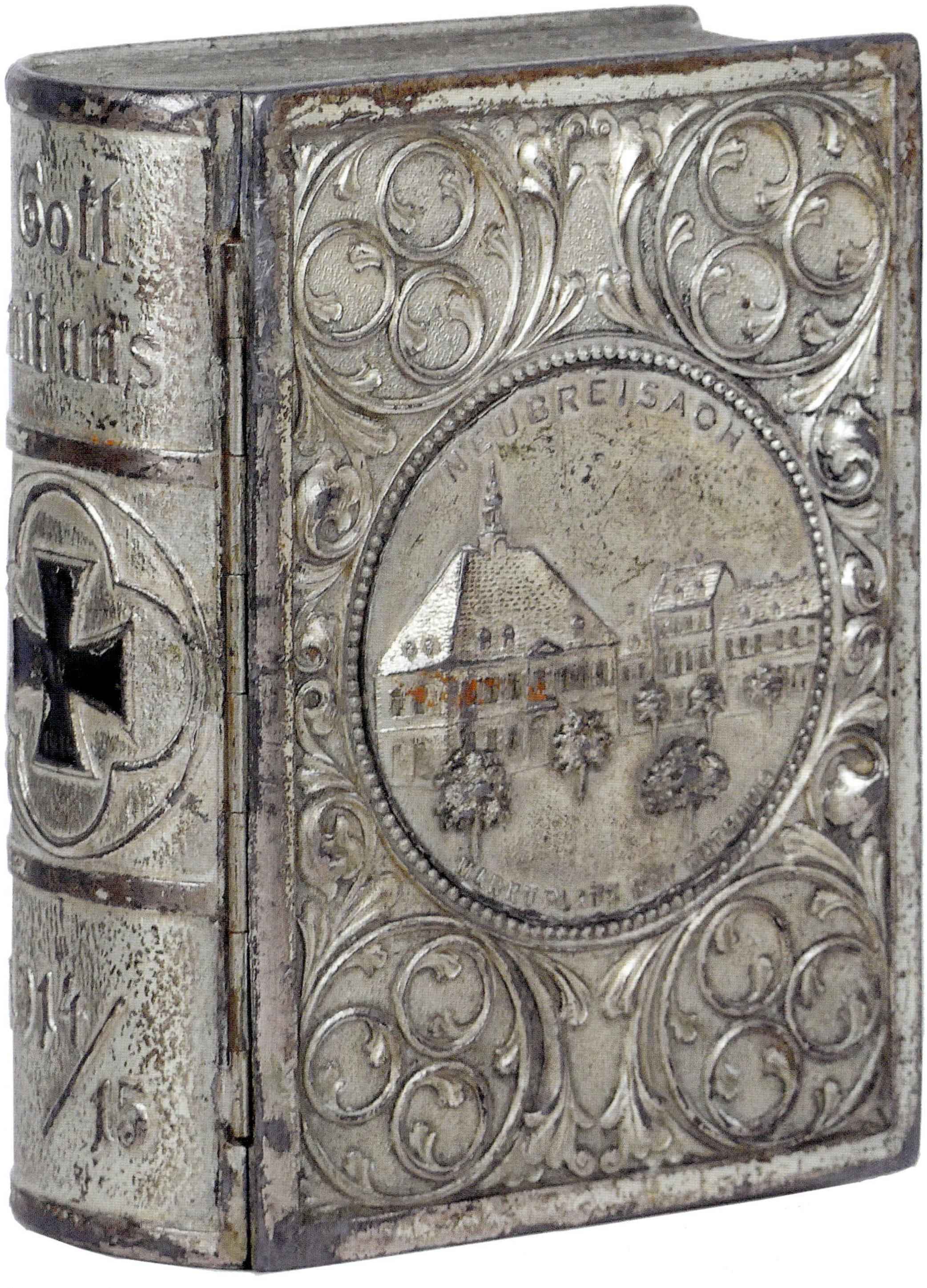

5.051
Adela 1862,
From in Cordingley
to Henry Stevenson
Messingdose
mit Gravur auf dem
Vorderdeckel
Brass box with
engraving on the lid
2,3 x 7,5 x 5,4 cm

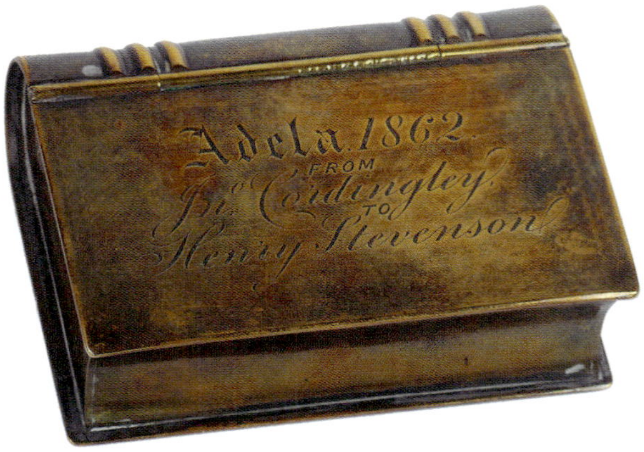

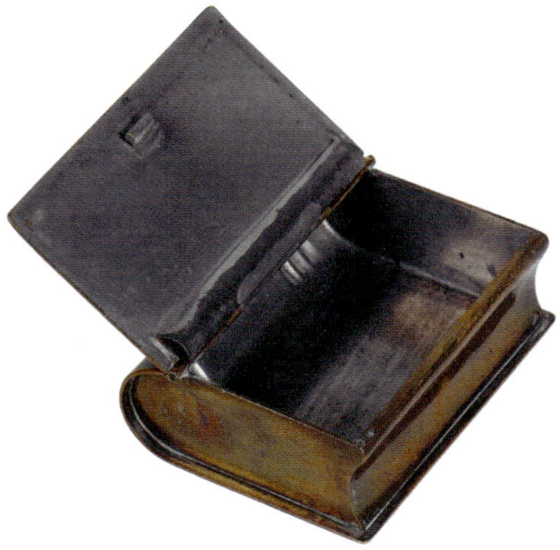

5.052
Kupferdose mit
erhabenen heral-
dischen Lilien, um-
laufende Zierkanten
mit Drachen, hohl,
nicht zu öffnen, Ver-
wendungszweck und
Herkunft unklar
Copper box with
raised heraldic lilies,
edges with dragons,
hollowed, can not be
opened, purpose
and origin unknown
14 x 10,3 x 4,3 cm

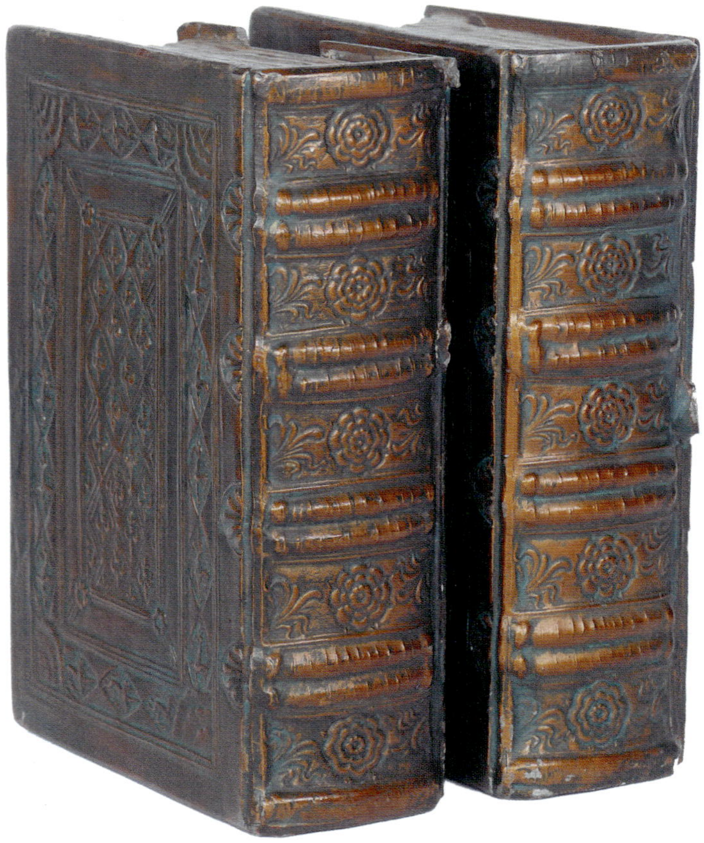

5.053
Metalldose mit ge-
prägter Blumenranke
auf beiden Deckeln,
Pillendose (?)
Metal box with em-
bossed flower tendril
on both covers, pill
box (?)
Jugendstil / *Art*
Nouveau
1,1 x 4,5 x 2,9 cm

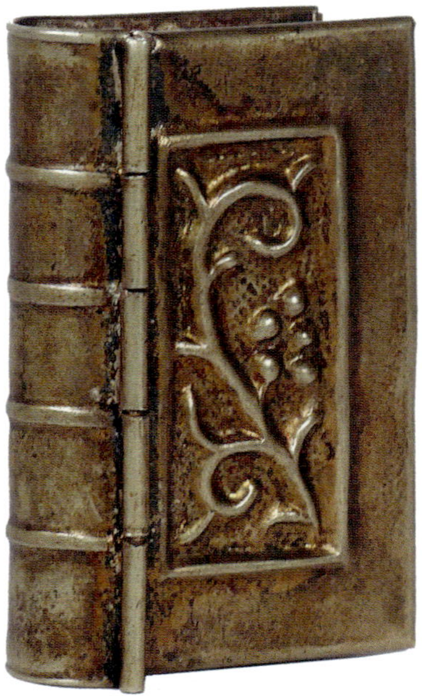

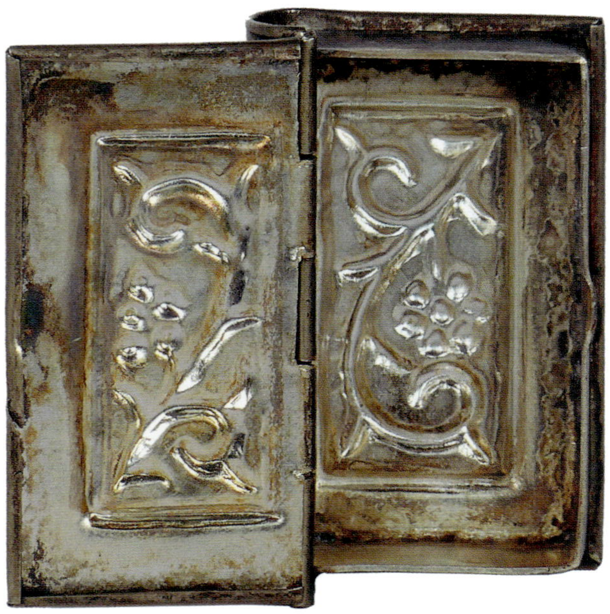

5.054
Messingdose mit kunstvoll ziselierten Ornamenten, farbig gefasst, dreiseitig gravierte Buchschnitte
Brass box with elaborated engraved ornaments, colored frames, engraved edges
Wohl persisch / *Probably Persian*
3,8 x 11,3 x 8 cm

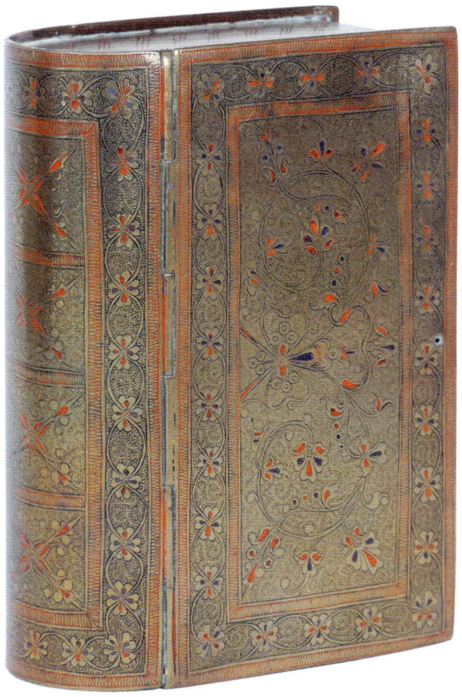

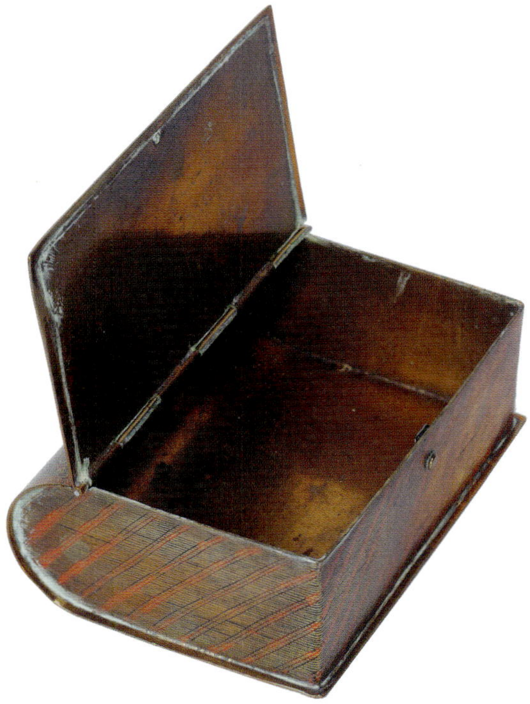

5.055
Messingdose mit Deckelgravur
Brass box with engraving on the lid
2,3 x 8,7 x 6,6 cm

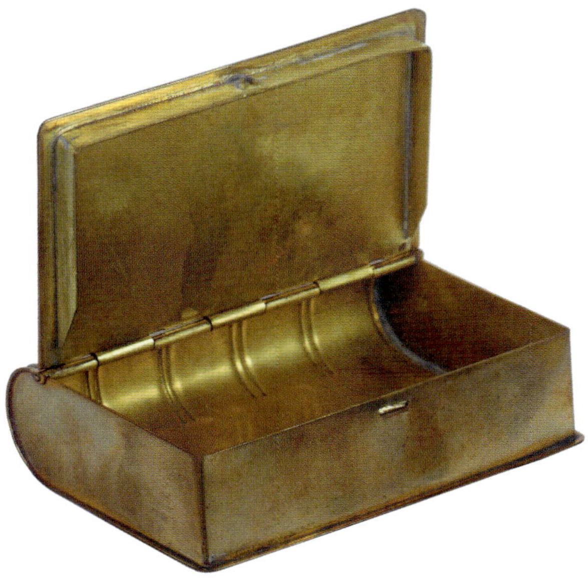

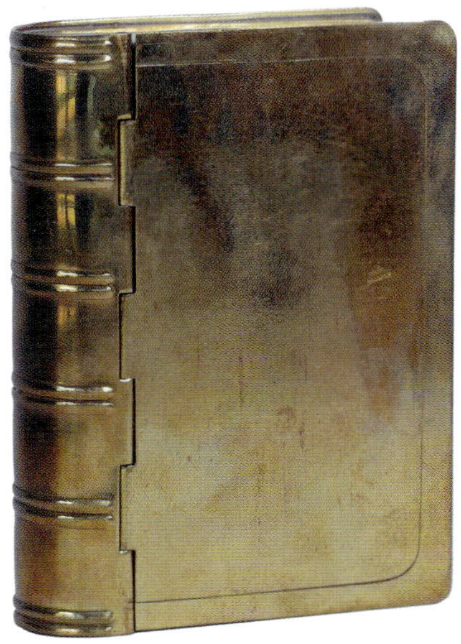

5.056
Messingdose mit aufgesetzter Deckeldekoration
Brass box applied decoration on the lid
2,3 x 6,8 x 5,4 cm

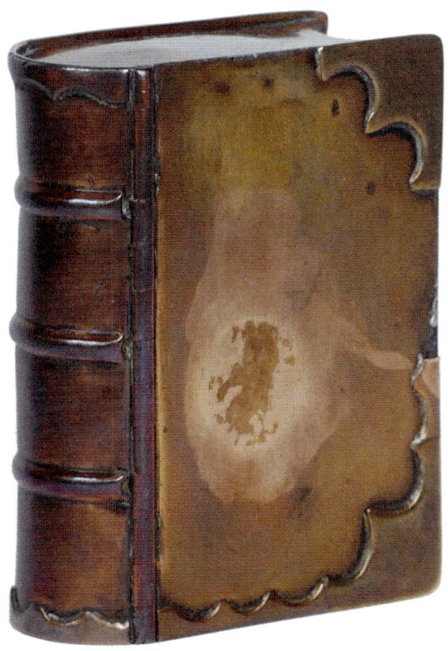

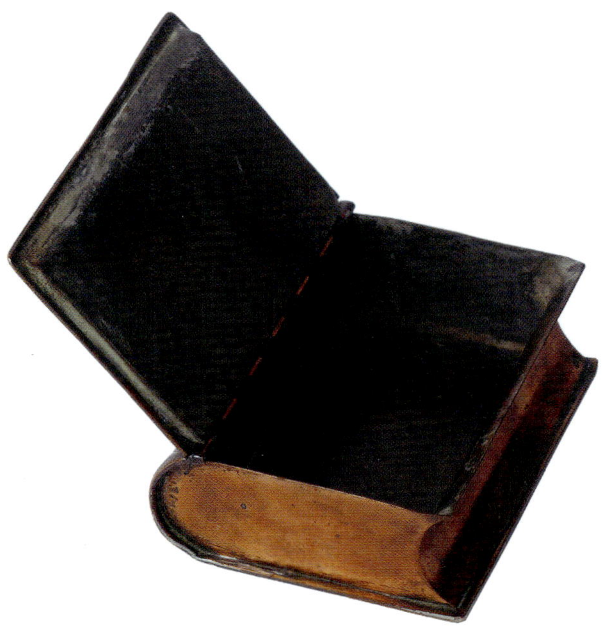

5.057
Holzdose mit raffiniertem Verschlussmechanismus, Kopfschnitt und Rücken verschiebbar, geschnitztes Männerporträt auf dem Rückdeckel
Wooden box with ingenious closing mechanism, sliding head and spine, carved portrait of a man on the back cover
11,3 x 6,7 x 2,2 cm

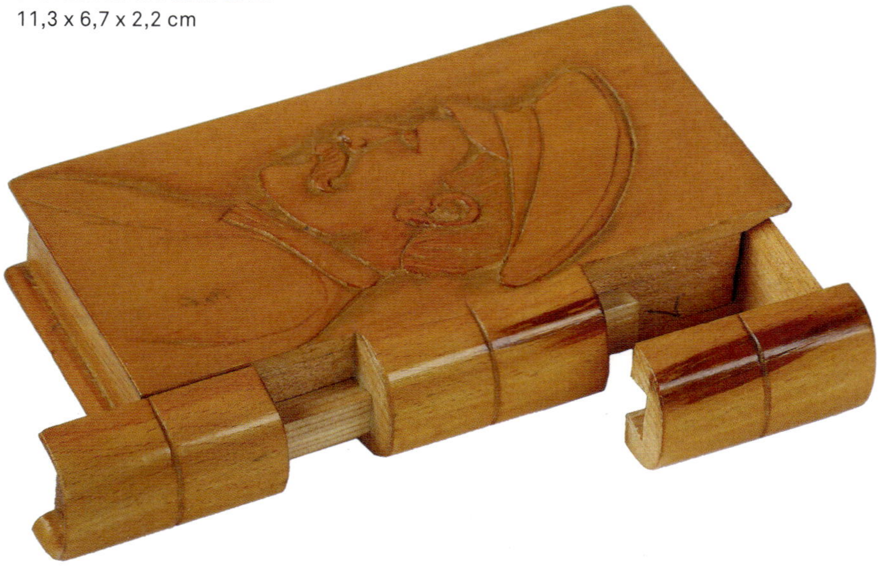

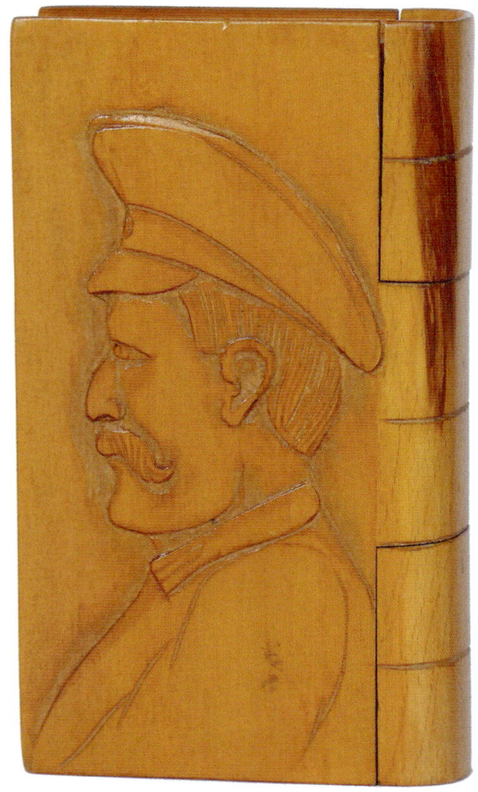

5.058
Holzschemel in Buchform. Die Seitenteile und die Zwischenverstrebung sind zusammenklappbar. Messingmonogramm „AM" auf dem Vorderdeckel
Wooden stool in the design of a book, the lateral parts and the intermediate bracing are foldable, brass monogram "AM" on the top
13,2 x 26,7 x 13 cm

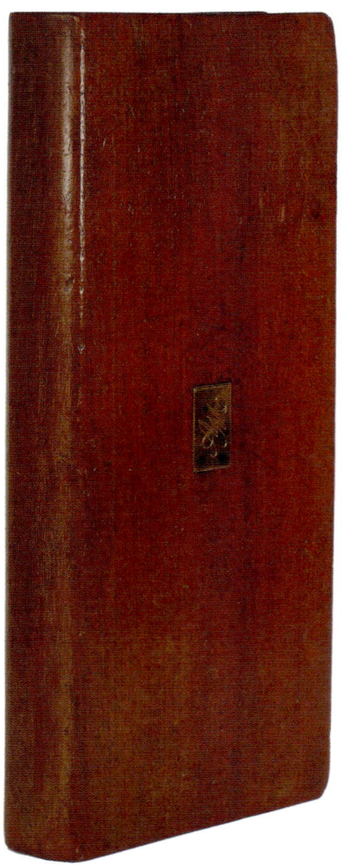

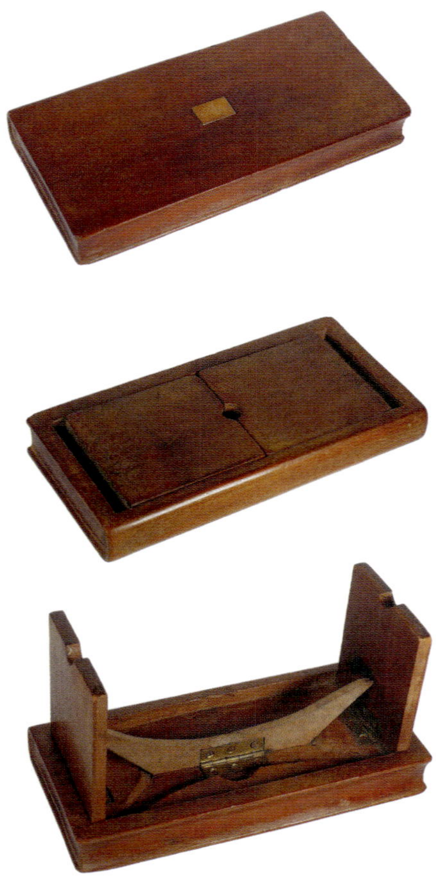

5.059
Holzschatulle aus dem Souvenir-Mekka der Ukrainischen Karpaten, bemalte Kerbschnitzerei auf dem Rücken und Deckel
Wooden box from the souvenir mecca of the Ukrainian Carpathians, decorated with a painted carving on the spine and lid
Zeitgenössisch / *Contemporary*
4,8 x 23,5 x 15,1 cm

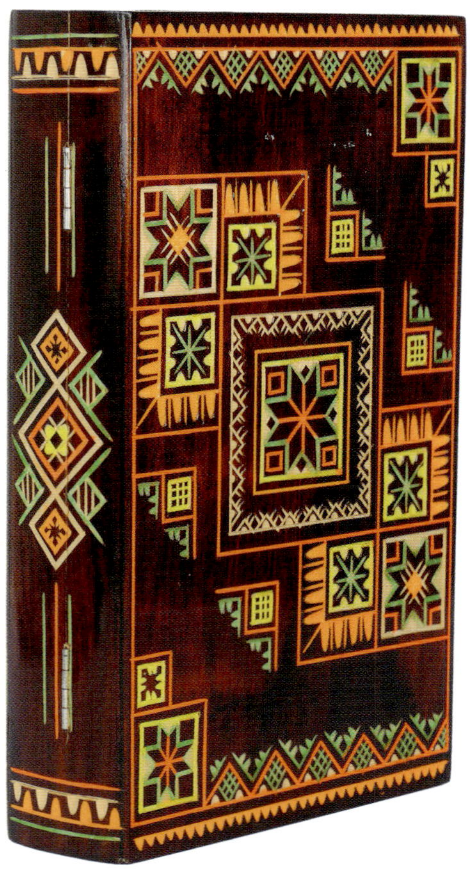

5.060

Holz-Schatulle. Aufwändig schwarz lackiertes Behältnis im Stil des Historismus. Porträt Maria von Burgund (1457–1482) auf dem Vorderdeckel, verheiratet mit Maximilian, Herzog von Burgund und ab 1493 Kaiser Maximilian I.

Elaborated black lacquered wooden box in the style of Historicism, on the front cover a portrait of Mary of Burgundy (1457–1482), married to Maximilian, Duke of Burgundy and from 1493 Emperor Maximilian I
18,5 x 15,5 x 4 cm

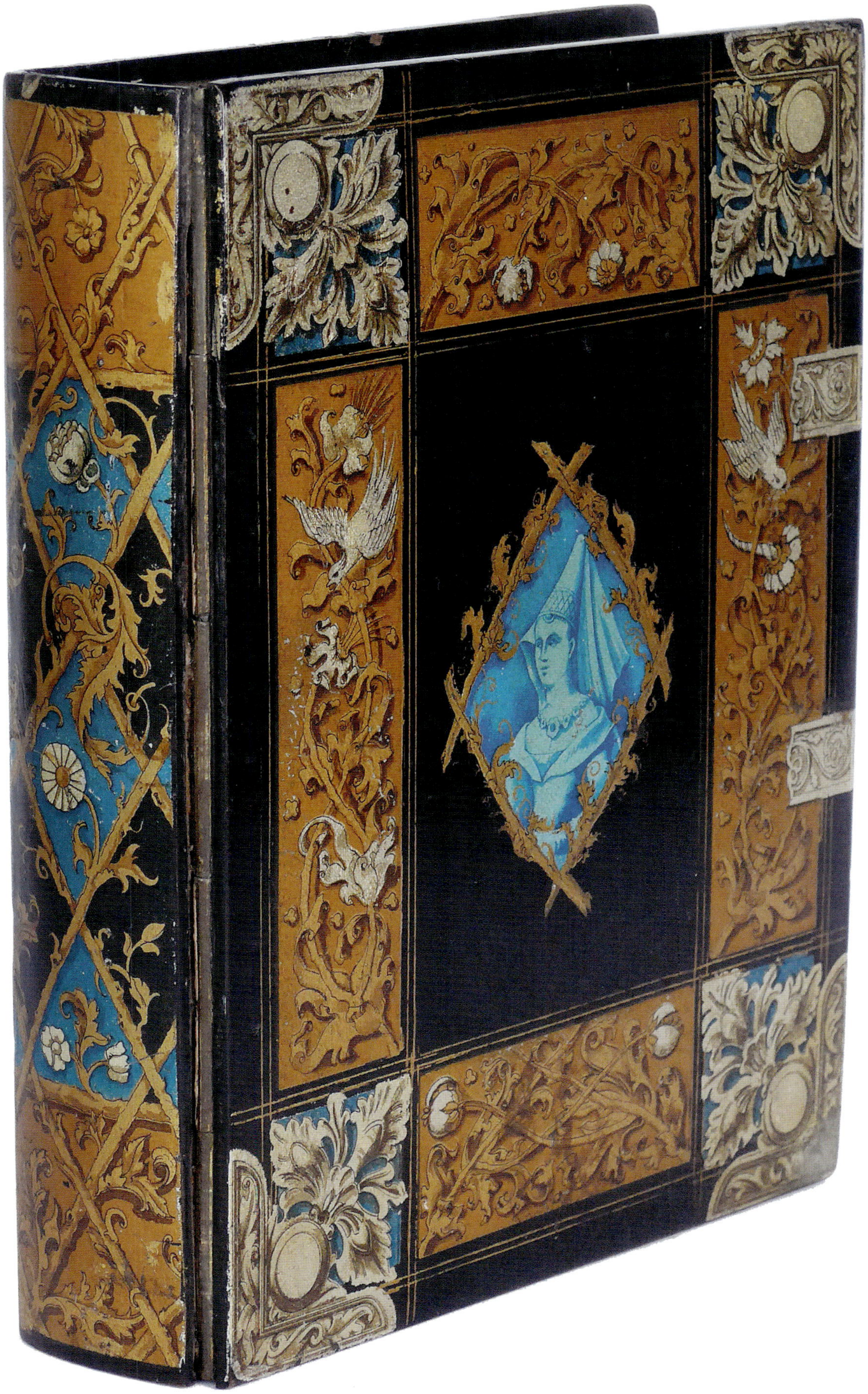

5.061
Holzdose mit Hals, Scharnier, geschnitzter Vorderdeckel mit Blumenmotiv und Verschluss-Lederriemen
Wooden box with neck, hinges, carved flowers on the lid, leather strap closure
4,6 x 10,6 x 6,5 cm

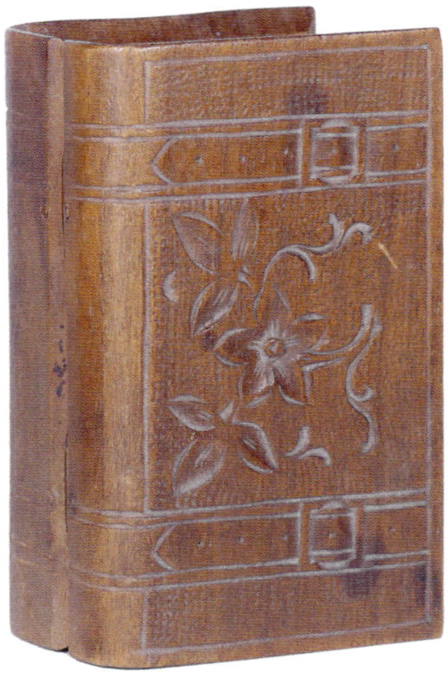

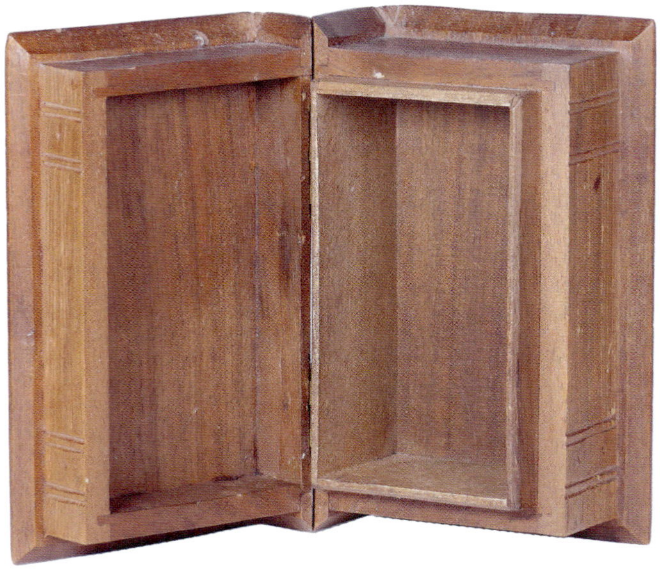

5.062
Eidg. Schützenfest Lausanne 1954. Stadtschützen Bern, Stiftung-Fritz Vonäsch
Swiss Federal Shooting Festival Lausanne 1954, wooden box by the Fritz Vonäsch Foundation
Holzkasten mit Türe, Blindprägung auf Rücken und Deckel, geschnitztes Holzrelief eines Schützen auf der Front, Holzstand, fünf Stoff bezogene Einlagen für die Abzeichen
Box with door, blind tooling on the spine and lid, carved wooden relief of a shooter on the lid, wooden stand, five inserts covered with fabric for storing badges
33,5 x 32,5 x 8 cm

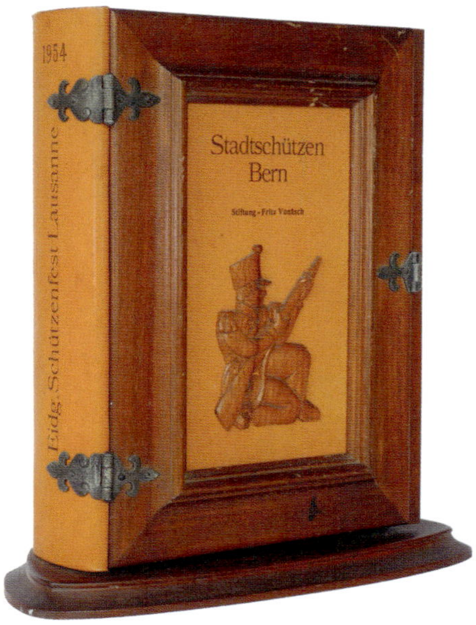

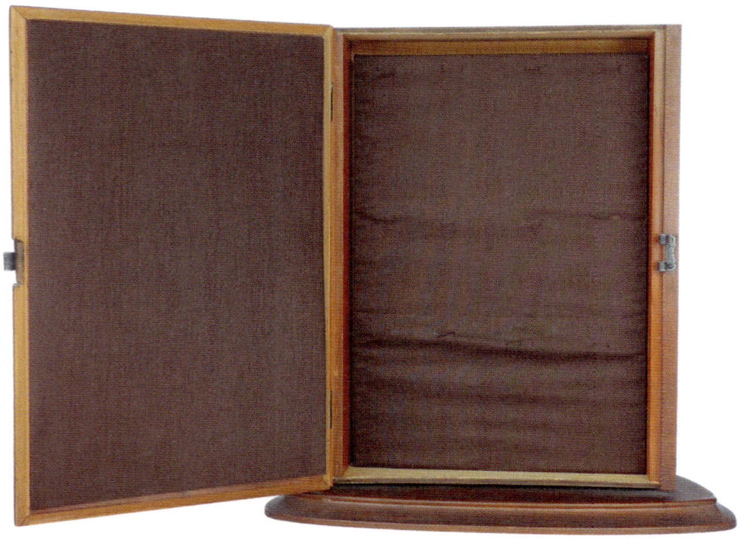

5.063
Holzschatulle mit Schublade am Buchrücken, Holzeinlegearbeit auf dem Vorderdeckel, dreiseitiger Goldschnitt
Wooden box with drawer at the spine, wooden marquetry on the lid, all edges gilt
3,1 x 14,8 x 11,3 cm

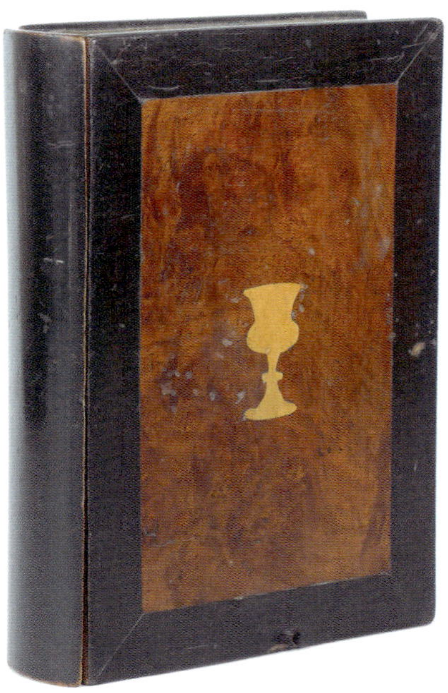

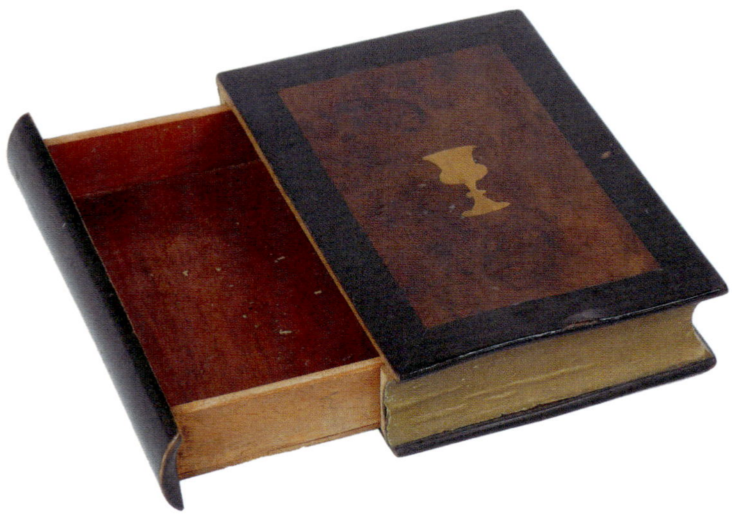

5.064
Nussbaumholzschatulle mit verschiebbarem Rücken zum Öffnen und Schließen, verschiebbarer Fußschnitt, Rosenintarsien auf dem Vorderdeckel, Filzboden
Walnut wood box with a sliding closure at the spine, sliding foot edge, drawer, marquetry of roses on the front cover, felt on the bottom
4,5 x 26,3 x 19,7 cm

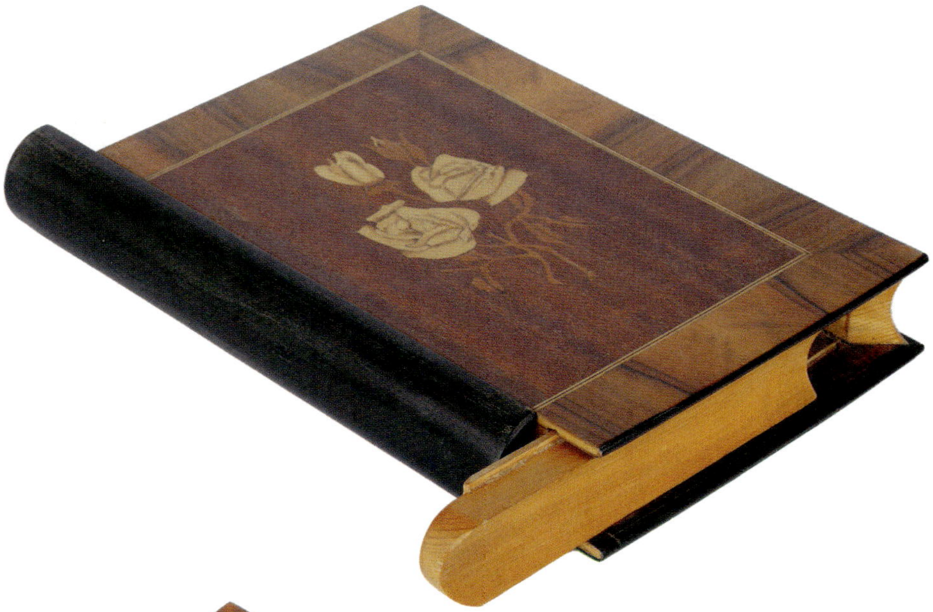

5.065
Nussbaumholzschatulle mit verschiebbarem Rücken zum Öffnen und Schließen, verschiebbarer Fußschnitt, Schublade, Rosenintarsien auf dem Vorderdeckel
Walnut wood box with a sliding closure at the spine, sliding foot edge, drawer, marquetry of roses on the cover
4,4 x 24,2 x 17 cm

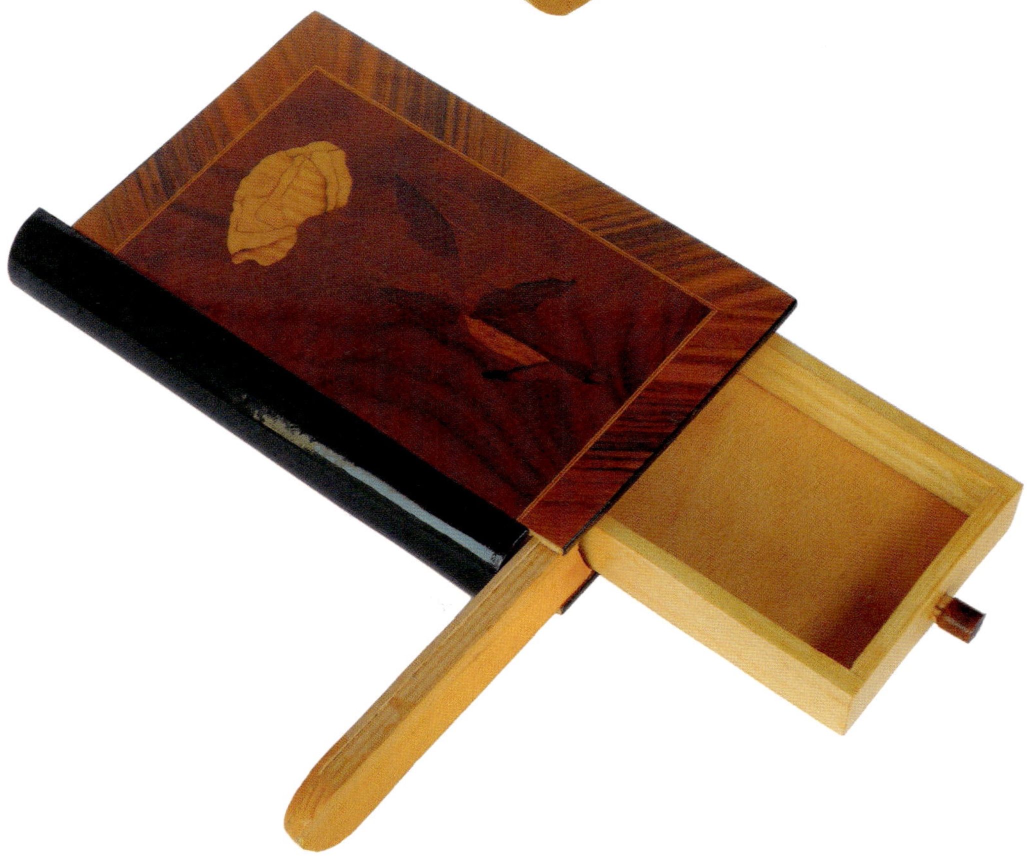

5.066
Wurzelholzschatulle mit Geheimverschluss, am Rücken ein Bund um Schublade zu öffnen, Holzeinlegearbeiten auf beiden Deckeln
Burl wood box with secret lock, a band on the spine is used to open the drawer, wooden marquetry on both boards
4,7 x 26,3 x 16,5 cm

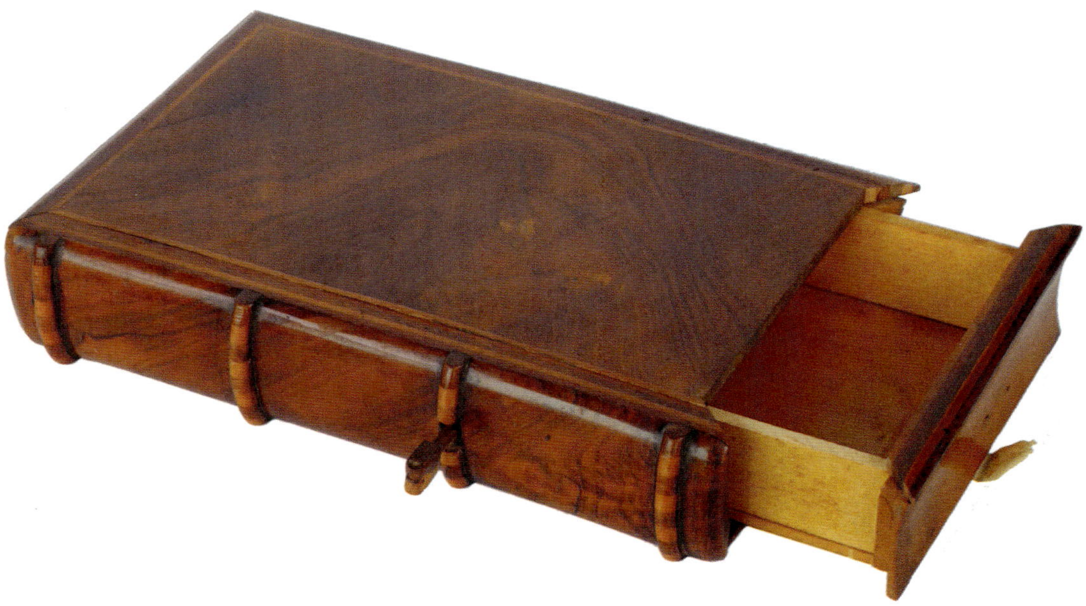

5.067
Holzschatulle mit Schublade am Buchrücken, Holz- und Beineinlegearbeiten
Wooden box with a drawer on the spine of the book, marquetry of wood and bone
3,7 x 17,6 x 11,3 cm

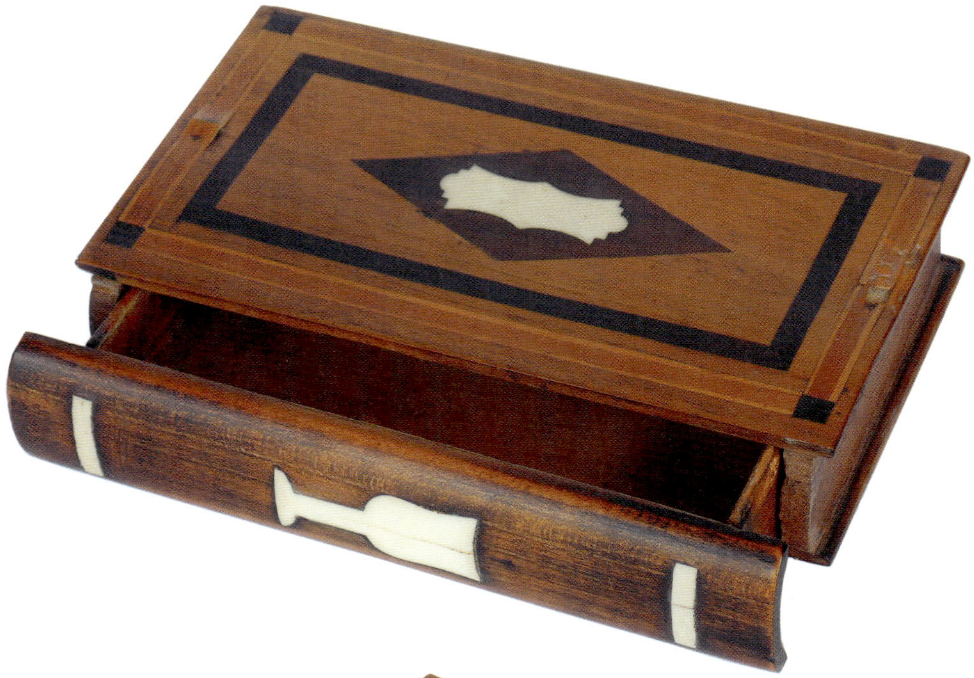

5.068
Holzschatulle mit Schublade am Rücken, Einlegearbeiten am Rücken und Vorderdeckel aus Holz und Metall
Wooden box with a drawer at the spine, marquetry on the spine and front cover made of wood and metal
4,2 x 19,8 x 14,3 cm

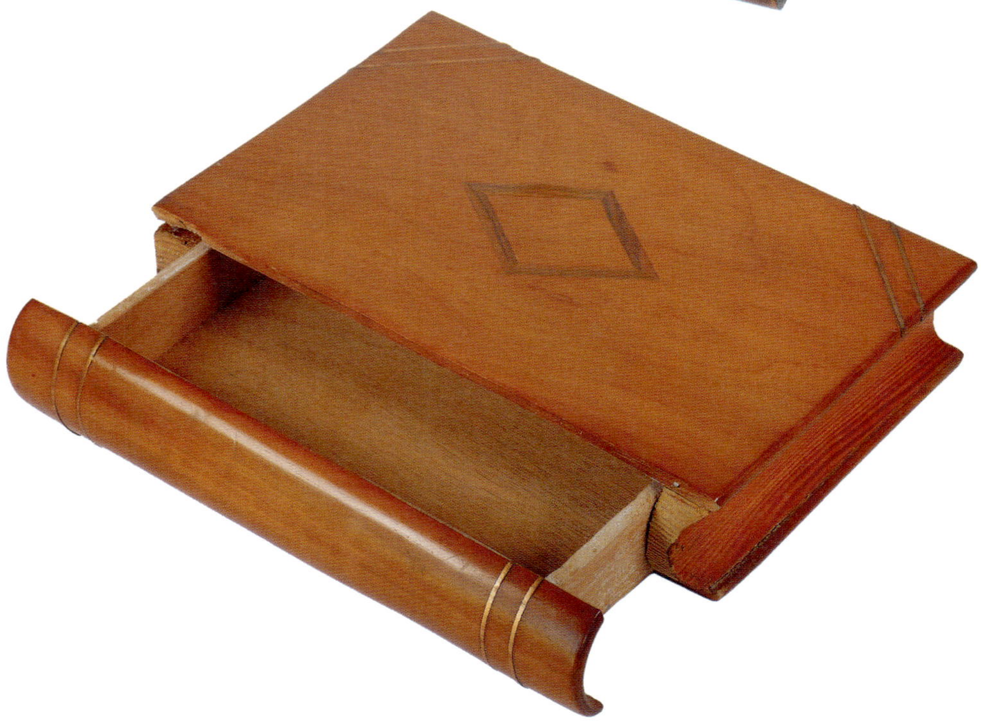

5.069
Holzschatulle mit Schublade am Buchrücken, Holz- und Perlmutteinlegearbeiten, Monogramm „MAH“
Wooden box with a drawer at the spine, wood and mother of pearl marquetry, monogram “MAH”
3,7 x 15,7 x 10,3 cm

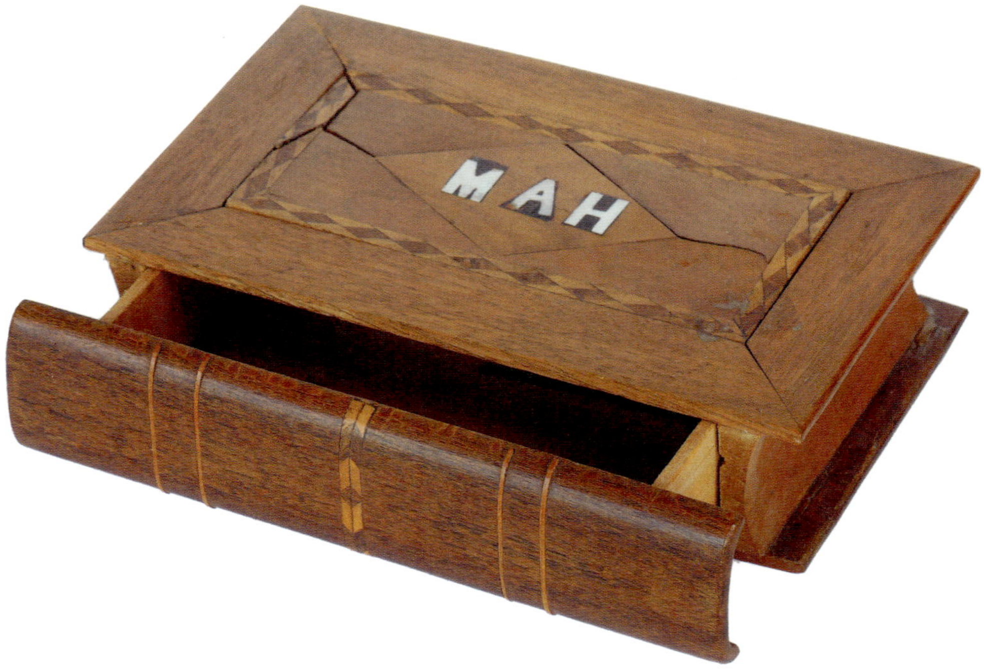

5.070
A. Farewell to Arms
Handbemaltes Früchtestilleben auf der Lederdose, Rückentitel, Messingverschluss, dreiseitiger Goldschnitt, ausgefüttert mit Plüschpapier
Leather box with a hand-painted fruit still life, title on the spine, brass closure, all edges gilt, lined with plush paper
4 x 15,5 x 11 cm

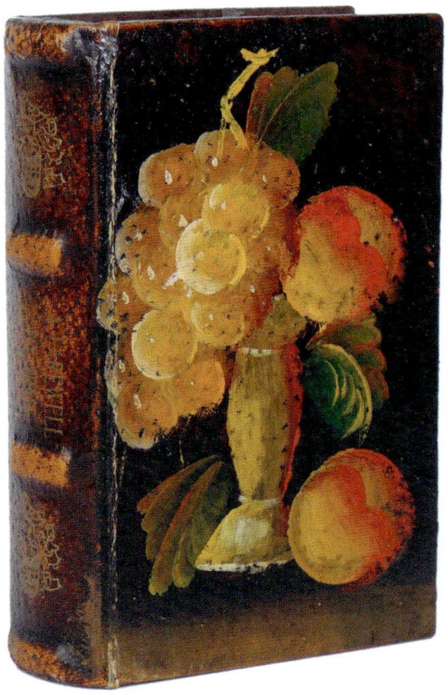

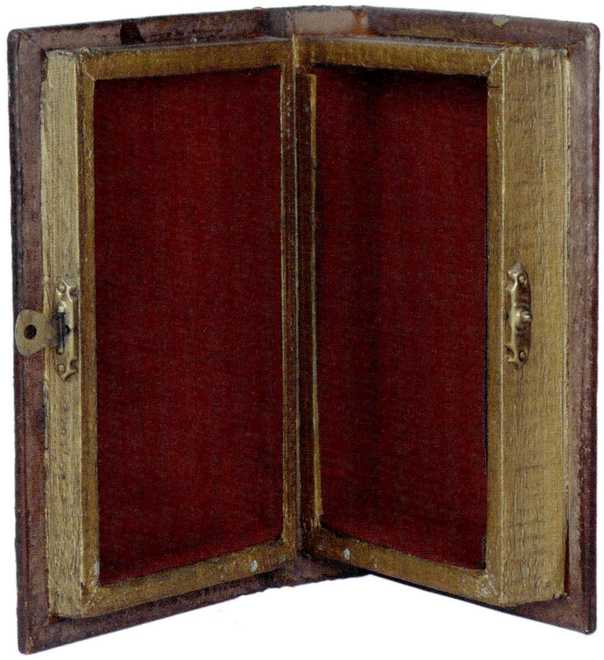

5.071
Holzdose mit Schublade am Vorderschnitt, Einlegarbeiten auf beiden Deckeln
Wooden box with drawer at the front edge, marquetry on both boards
3,6 x 17,7 x 11,6 cm

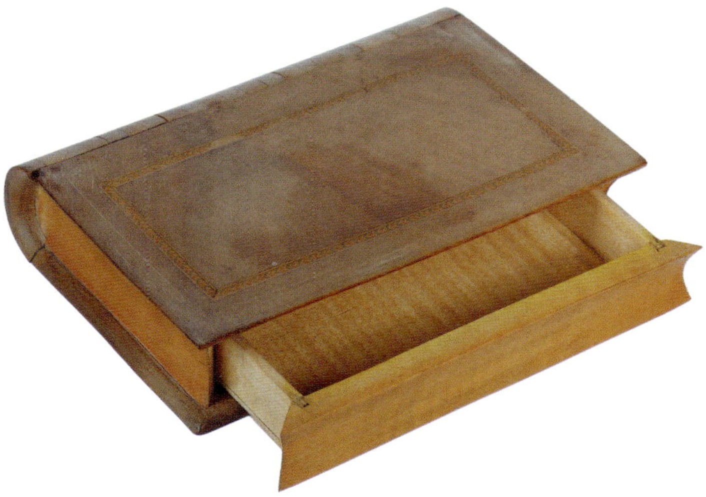

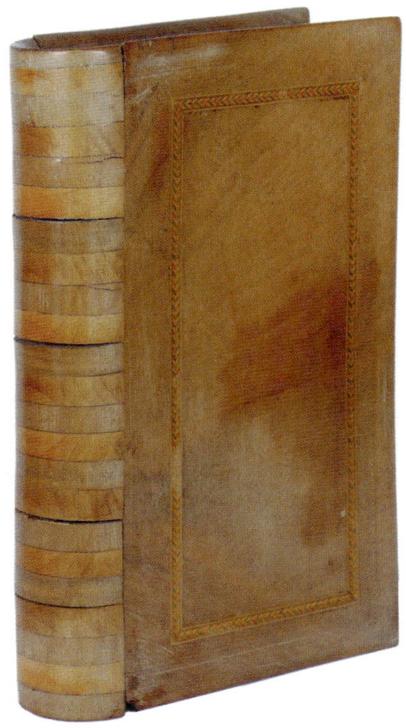

5.072
Nussbaum-Holzdose mit Einlegearbeiten, Blumenmalerei auf dem Vorderdeckel, Innenboden mit Plüsch und Bordüre ausgelegt
Walnut wood box with marquetry, painted flowers on the front board, inner bottom and border of plush
4,5 x 14,2 x 12,4 cm

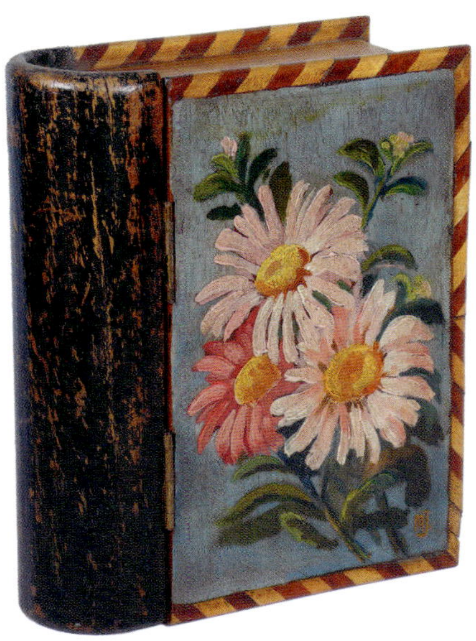

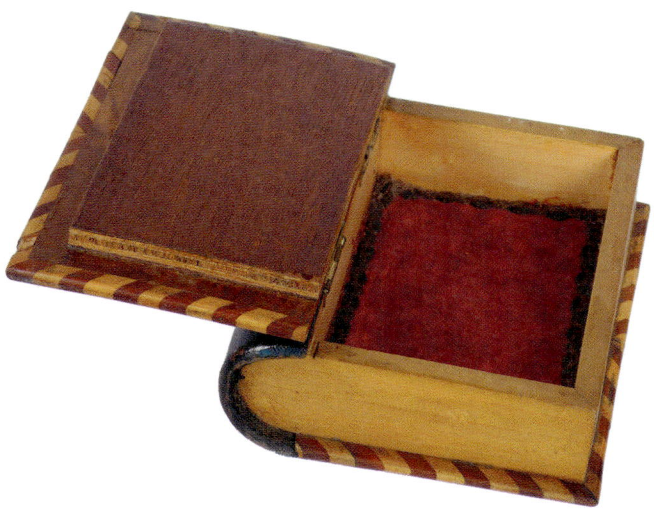

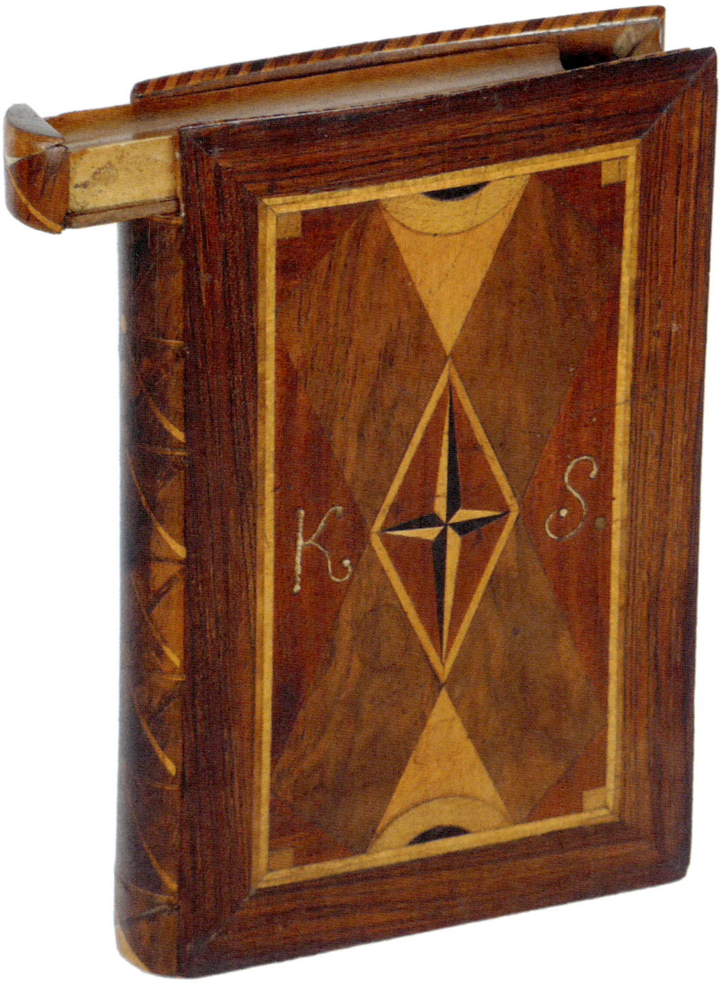

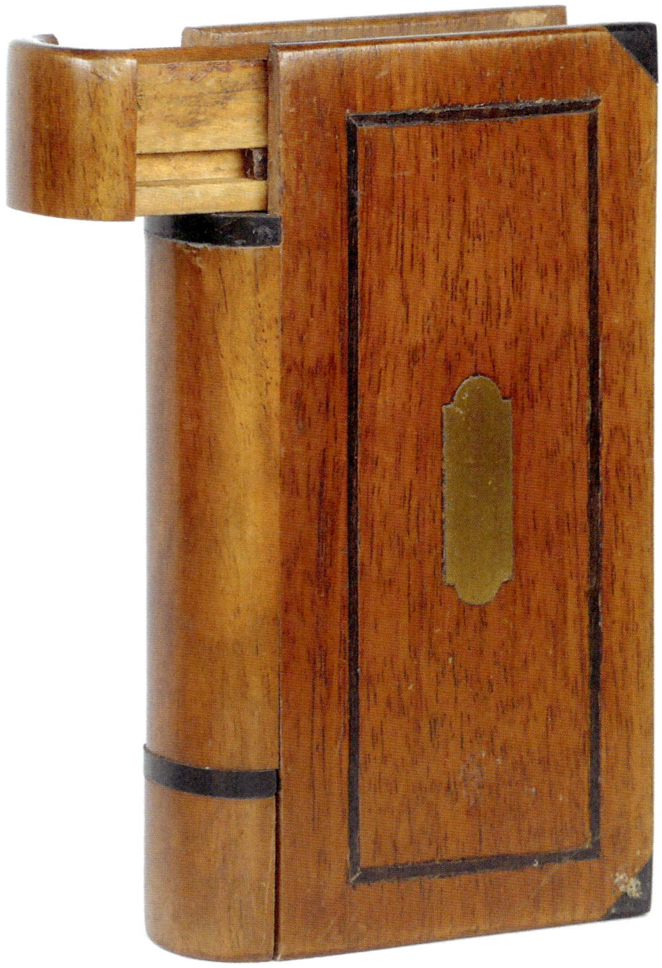

5.073
Holzdose mit Schieber am Kopfschnitt, Holzeinlegearbeiten auf Rücken und beiden Deckeln, Monogramm „KS“, zwei Fächer, vermutlich für Zigarren
Wooden box with a slider at the head, wood marquetry on the spine and both covers, monogram “KS”, two compartments, probably for cigars
13,8 x 9,2 x 2 cm

5.074
Holzdose mit Schieber am Kopfschnitt, Holzeinlegearbeit am Rücken und beiden Deckeln, zwei eingelegte Messingschilder
Wooden box with slider at the head part, wood marquetry on the spine and on both covers, two inserted brass plates
Um / *Around* 1900 | 12 x 6,8 x 2,7 cm

5.075
Holzschatulle mit Kerbschnitzerei auf dem Vorderdeckel, Scharnier, verschiedene Innenfächer, Verwendungszweck unklar
Wooden box with carving on the lid, hinges, various inner compartments, purpose unclear
4,5 x 20,5 x 15,7 cm

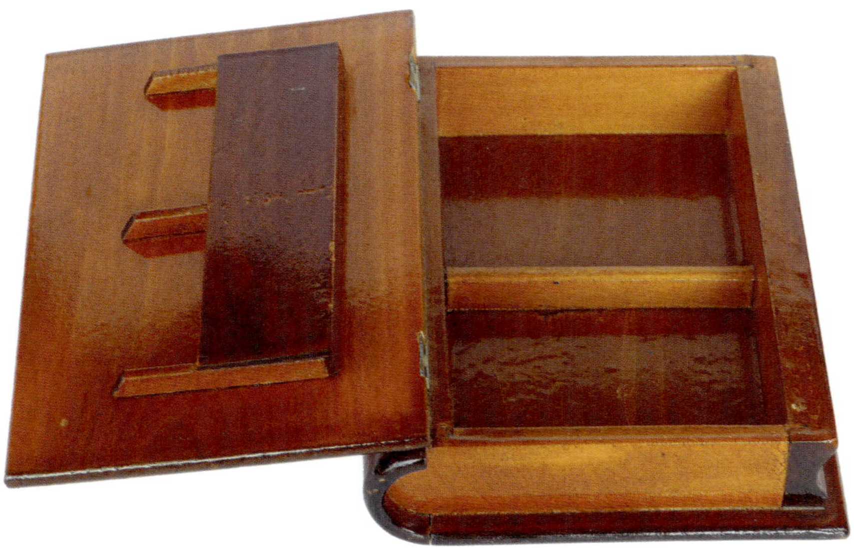

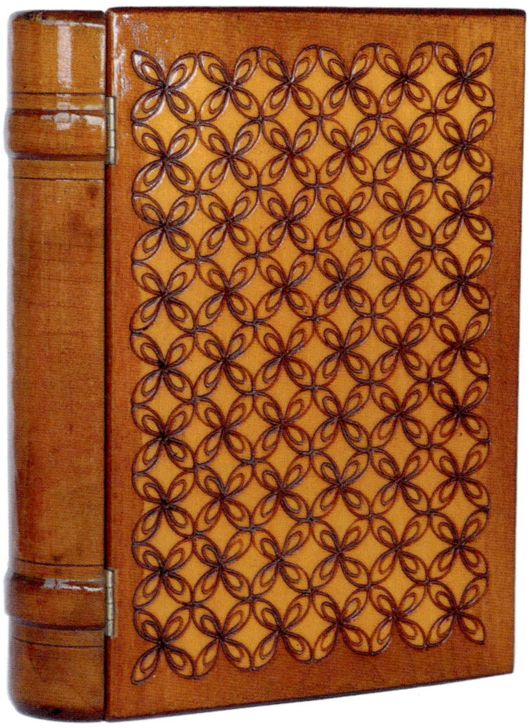

5.076
Holzdose mit Schublade am Kopfschnitt, Holzeinlegearbeten am Rücken und beiden Deckeln, läßt sich öffnen beim Verschieben des mittleren Bundes
Wooden box with drawer at the head, wood marquetry on the spine and both-boards, to be opened by using the band in the middle
2,8 x 10,3 x 7,8 cm

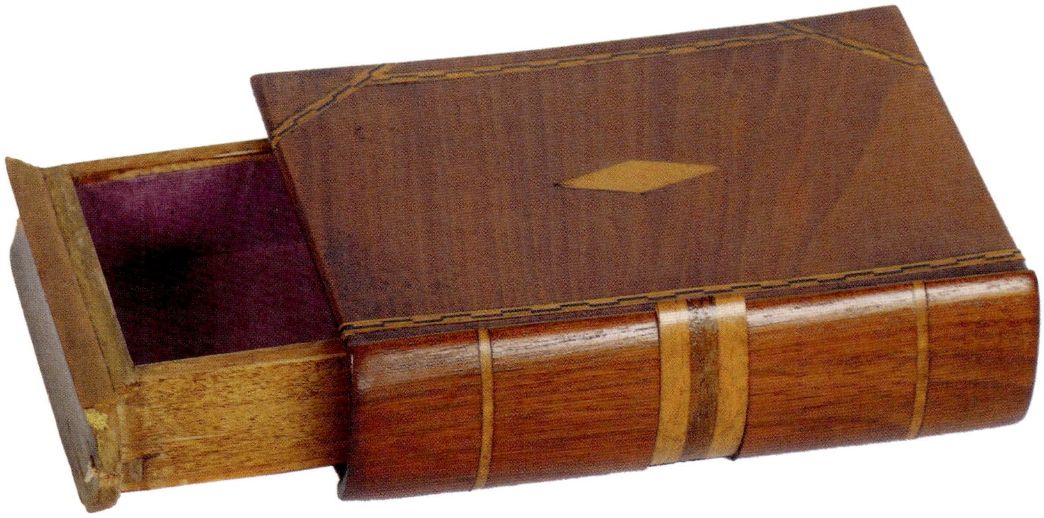

5.077
Holzdose mit drei Schubladen am Vorderschnitt, bemalte Schnitzereien auf dem Vorder- und Rückdeckel
Wooden box with three drawers at the fore edge, painted carvings on the front and back cover
12 x 8,3 x 5,9 cm

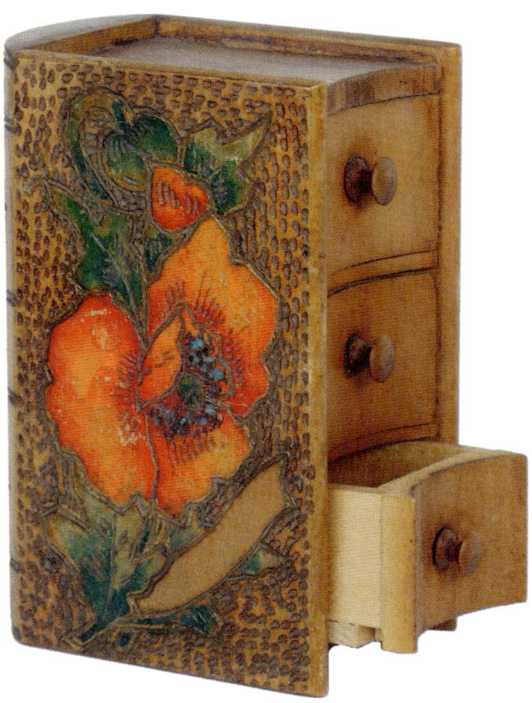

5.078
Holzdose mit geschnitzten Pflanzen- und Ledergurtmotiv auf dem Vorderdeckel
Wooden box with a carved image of a plant and a leather belt on the lid
3 x 7,6 x 5,2 cm

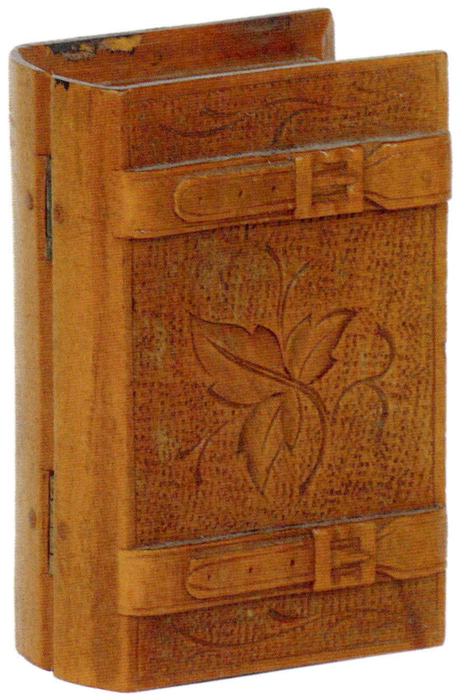

5.079
Holzdose mit geschnitztem Blumenmotiv auf dem Vorderdeckel, eingebauter Thermometer
Wooden box with carved flowers on the lid, thermometer inside
9,3 x 3,6 x 1,8 cm

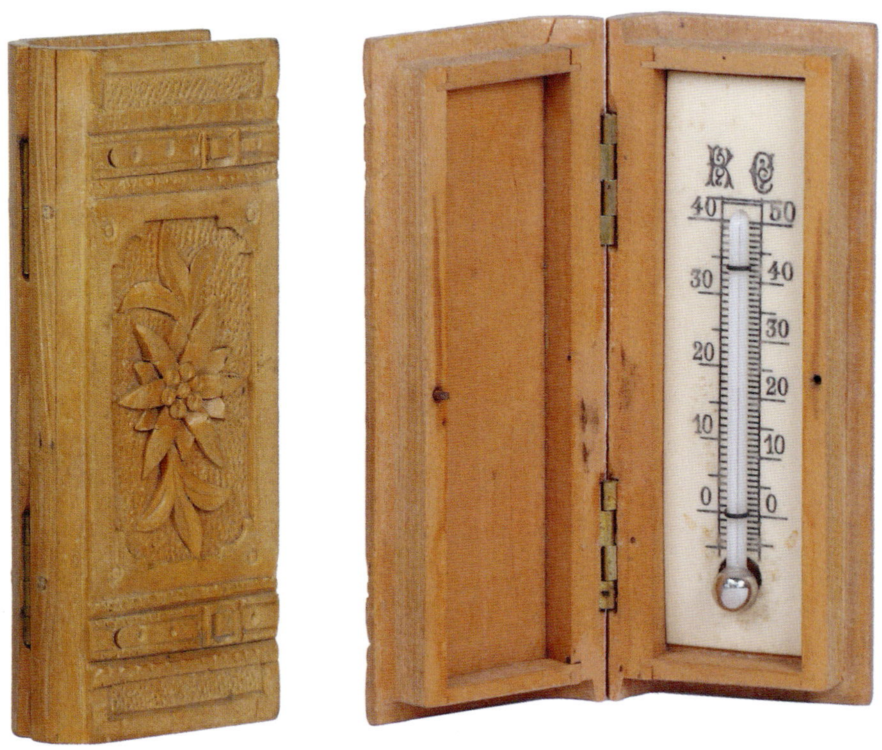

5.080
Holzdose mit ausschwenkbarem Vorderschnitt, Holzeinlegearbeit mit Monogramm „HAK“, dreiseitiger gelber Farbschnitt
Wooden box with hinged fore edge, wooden marquetry with monogram "HAK", all edges in in yellow
Ende 19. Jh. / *End of the 19th century*
3,2 x 8,7 x 7,6 cm

5.081
Wurzelholzdose mit schwenkbarem „Buchblock“, vier Intarsien-Bünde, hebräisch
Burl wood box with pivotable „book block", four bands made of marquetry, Hebrew
3 x 11,9 x 9 cm

5.082
Wurzelholzdose mit schwenkbarem „Buchblock“, drei Intarsien-Bünde, hebräisch
Burl wood box with pivotable "book block", three bands made of marquetry, Hebrew
3,3 x 10,2 x 8 cm

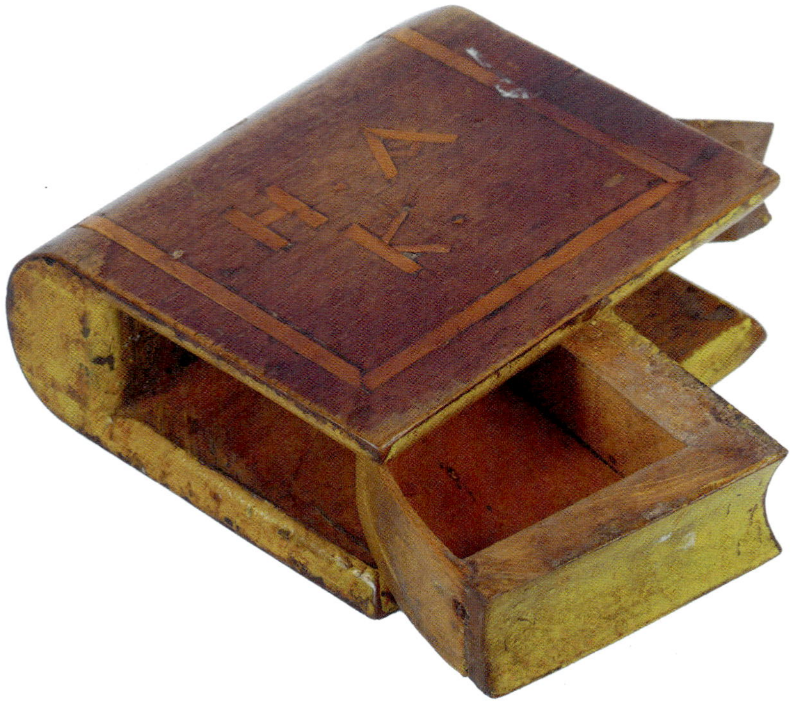

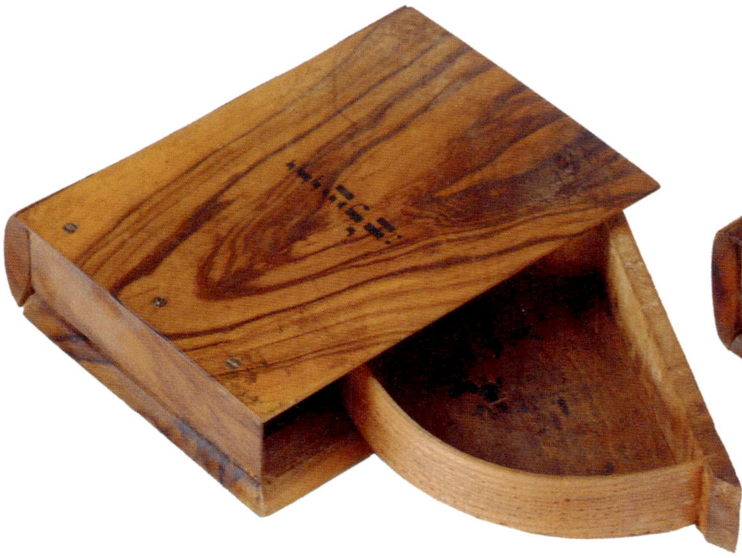

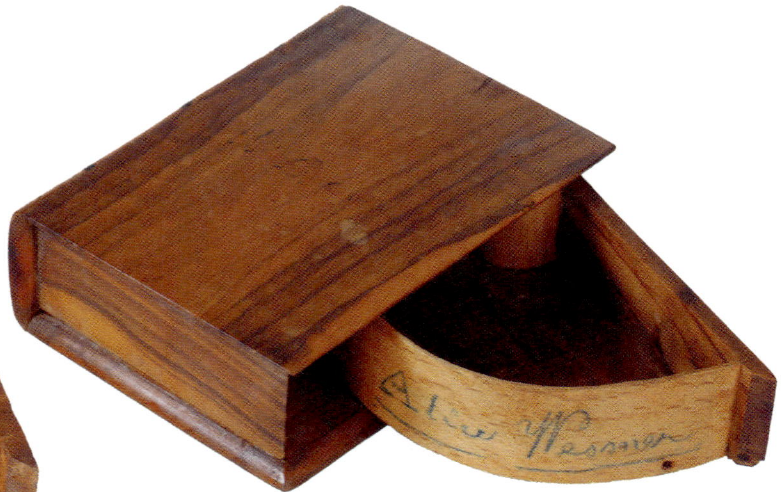

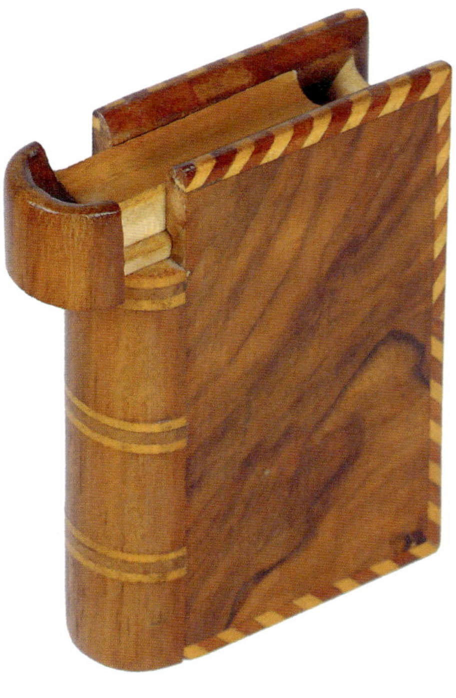

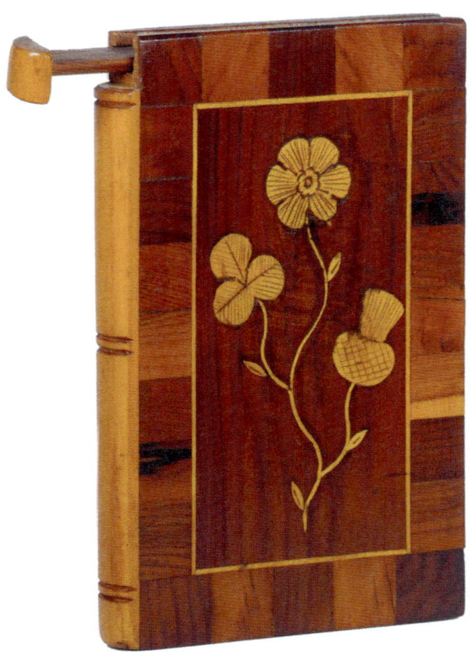

5.083
Holzdose mit Schieber am Kopfschnitt, Kanten-Holzeinlegearbeit, zwei Fächer für Nähnadeln (?)
Wooden box with slider at the head, wood marquetry on the edges, two compartments for needles (?)
Ende 19. Jh. / *End of the 19th century*
7,8 x 5,5 x 5,5 cm

5.084
Killarney Lakes
Souvenir-Holzdose aus dem Südwesten Irlands, Schieber am Kopfschnitt, Intarsien am Vorder- und Rückdeckel
Wooden souvenir box from the southwest of Ireland, slider at the head edge, marquetry on the front and back cover
Um / *Around* 1900 | 11,2 x 7,3 x 1 cm

5.085
Holzdose mit Schieber am Kopfschnitt
Wooden box with slider at the head
Um / *Around* 1900
10 x 7,9 x 2,5 cm

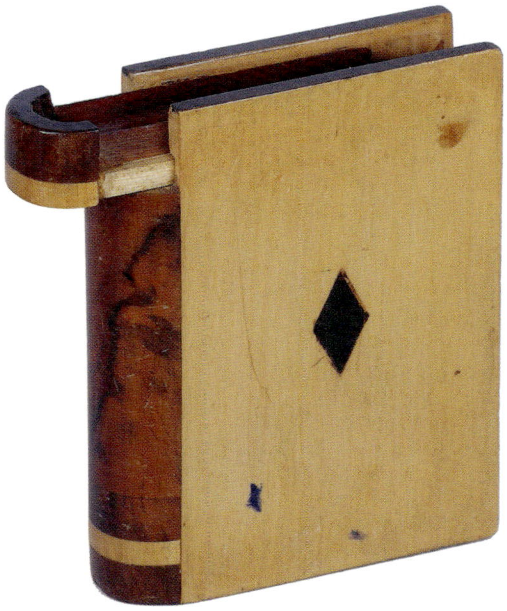

5.086
Wurzelholzschatulle, ausziehbarer Rücken mit Schublade, Holzeinlegearbeiten auf beiden Deckeln
Burl wood box, pull out spine containing a drawer, wood marquetry on both boards
4,7 x 23,2 x 16,2 cm

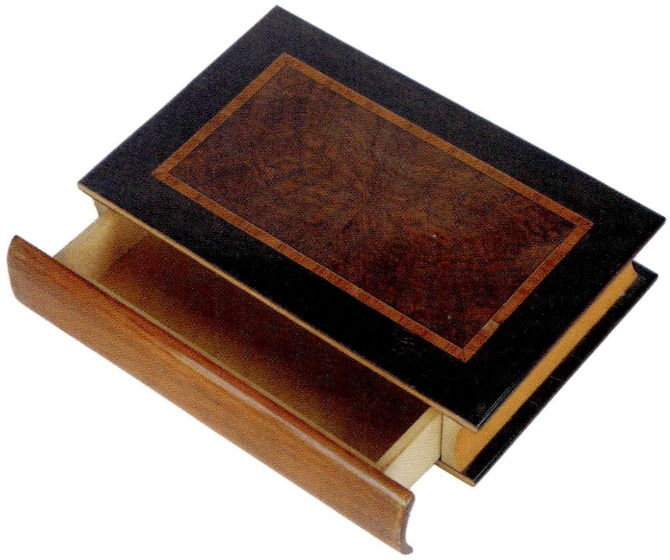

5.087
Holzdose mit Schublade am Kopfschnitt, verschiebbarer mittlerer Bund zum Öffnen, Holzeinlegearbeiten, dreiseitiger Goldschnitt
Wooden box with drawer at the head part, to be opened with a movable band in the middle, wood marquetry, all edges gilt
3,5 x 14,4 x 11 cm

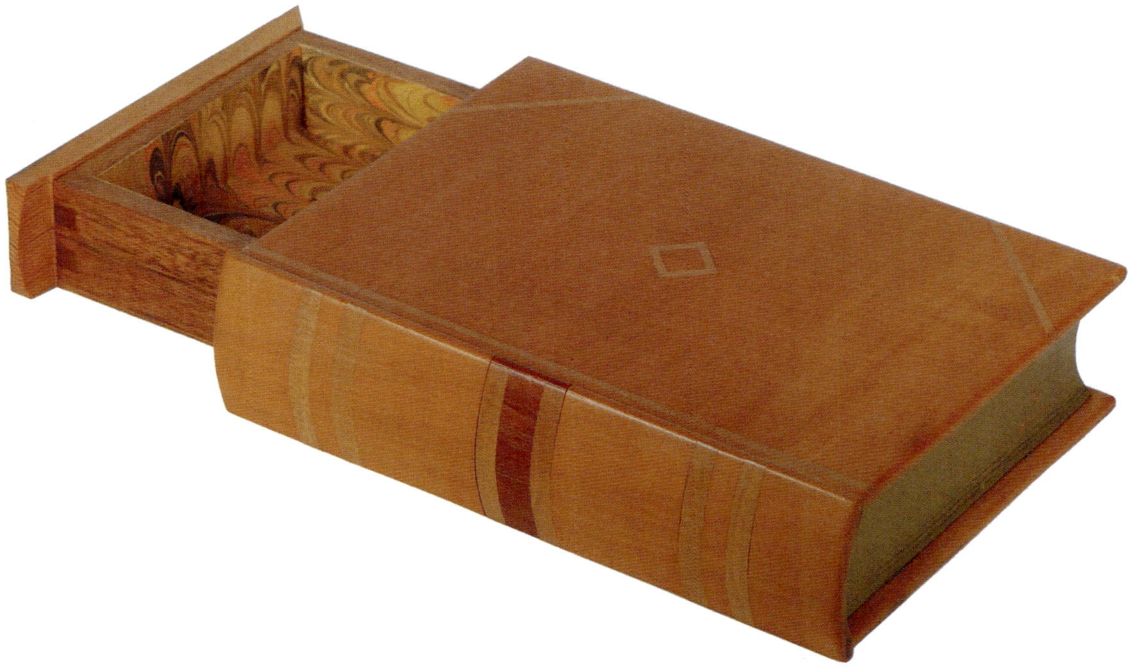

5.088
Holzdose mit aufklappbarem Kopfschnitt, Holzeinlegearbeiten auf beiden Deckeln: Herz mit Kreuz und Anker, Kelch
Wooden box with hinged head, wood marquetry on both boards: heart with cross and anchor, chalice
9,2 x 7 x 1,5 cm

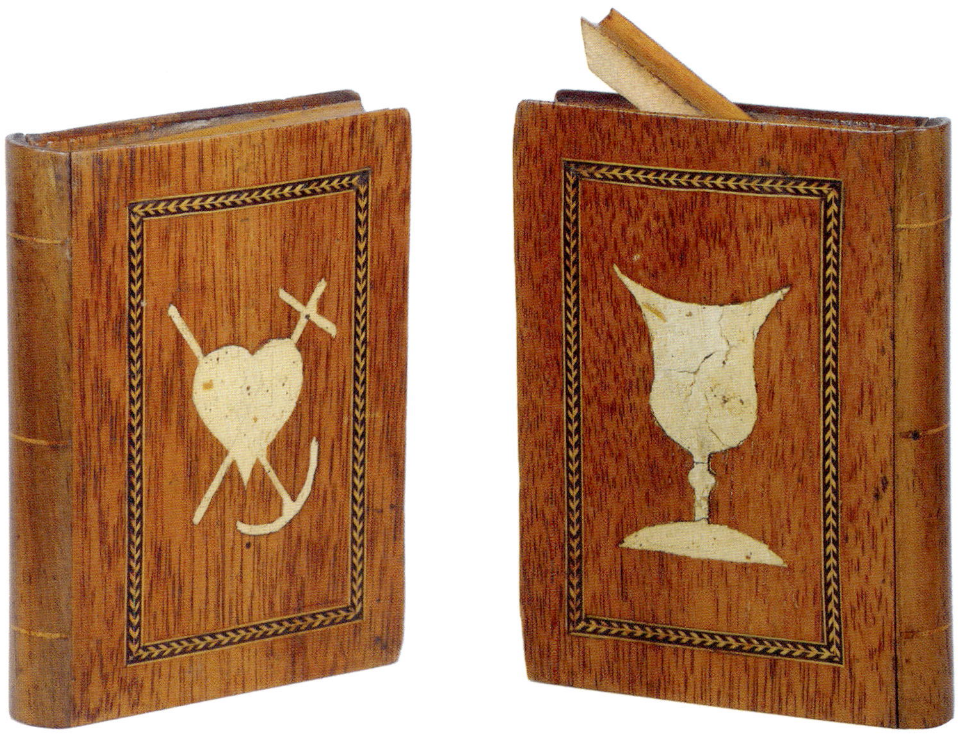

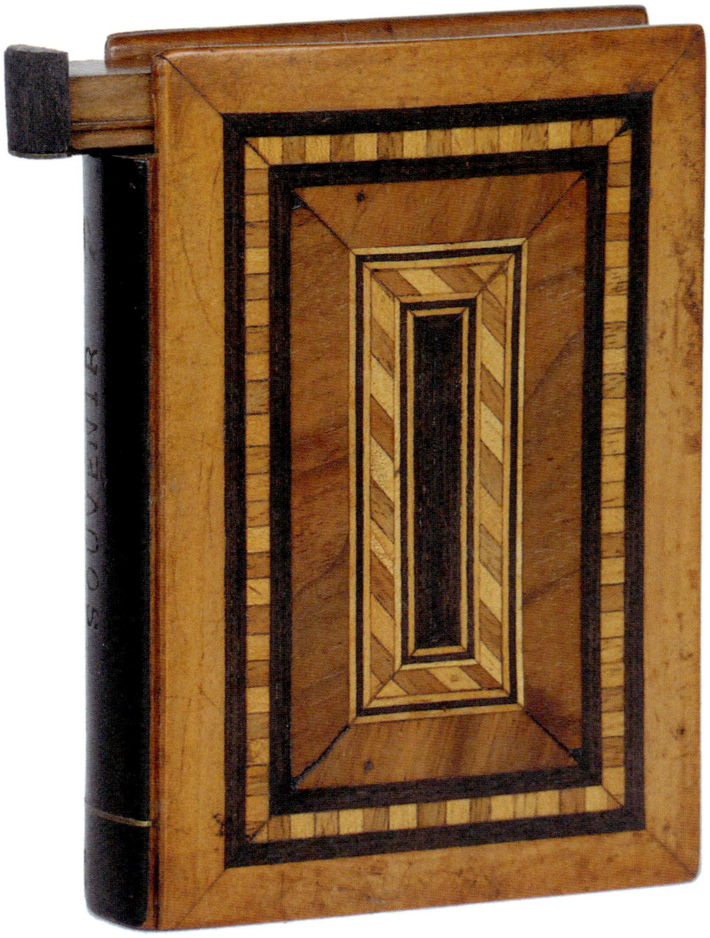

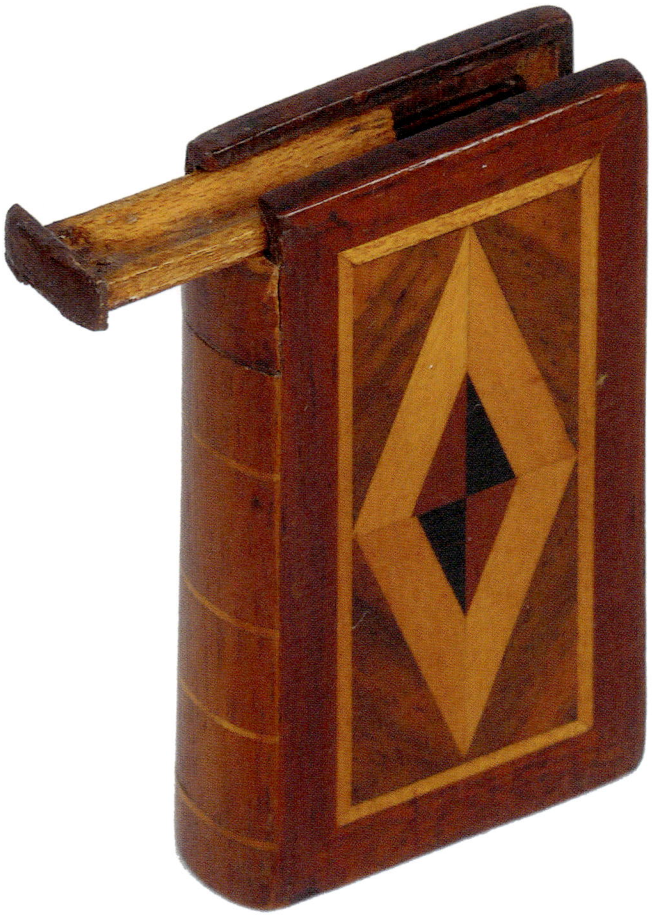

5.089
Souvenir
Holzdose mit Schieber am Kopfschnitt, Intarsien auf Vorder- und Rückdeckel
Wooden box with slider at the head part, marquetry on both boards
Spätes 19. Jh. / *Late 19th century*
11,8 x 8,5 x 2 cm

5.090
Holzdose mit Schieber am Kopfschnitt, Intarsien auf beiden Deckeln
Wooden box with slider at the head, marquetry on both boards
Um / *Around* 1900 | 6,4 x 3,5 x 1,3 cm

5.091
Holzschatulle mit Messingscharnier, vier schwarze eingelegte Holzstreifen auf dem Vorderdeckel, dreiseitiger Imitationsbuchschnitt
Wooden box with brass hinge, black wood marquetry on the front board, all edges imitating a book
Art Déco | 3,7 x 23 x 15,2 cm

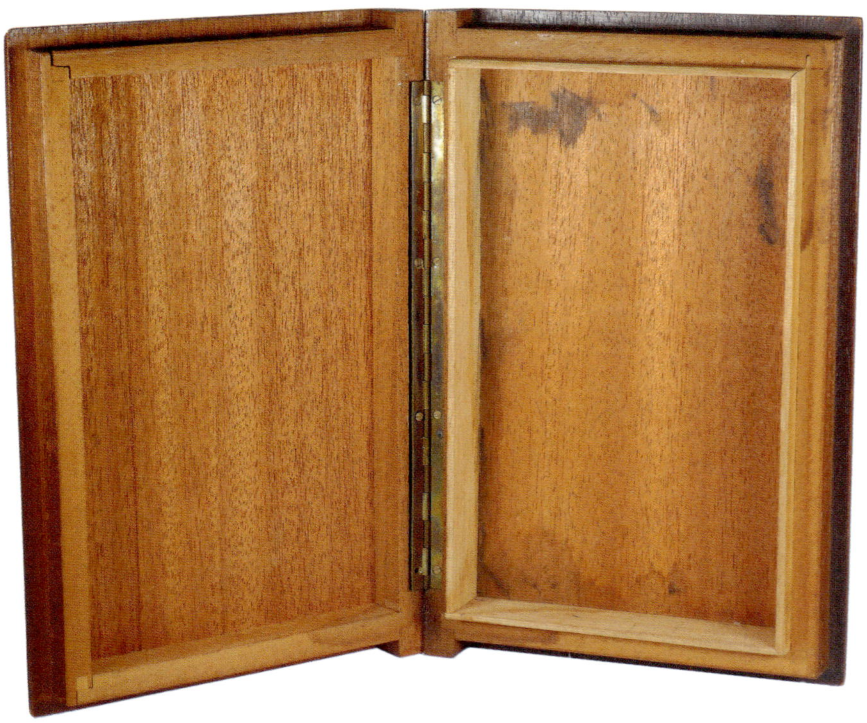

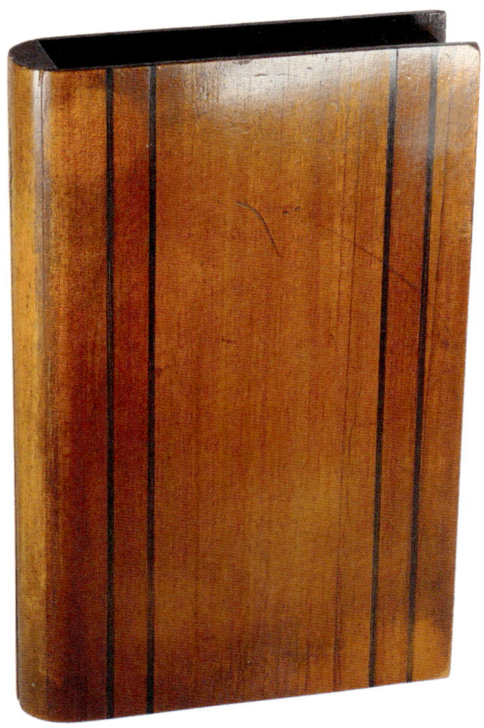

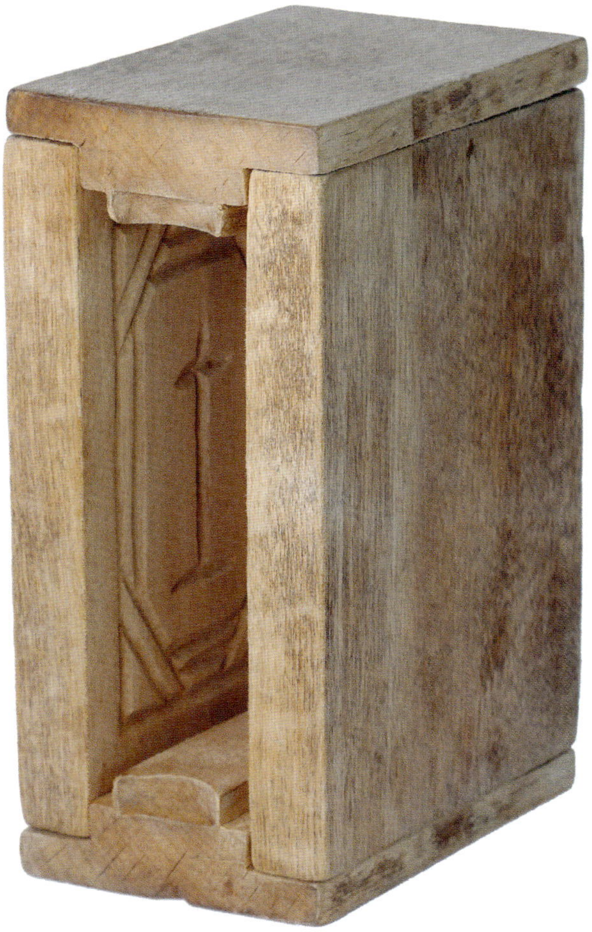

5.092
Buttermodel aus Holz, vierteiliges Klapp- oder Passmodel mit einem Gebetsbuch als Motiv
Wooden butter mould, four-piece folding mould with a carved prayer book
Um / *Around* 1900 | 5,7 x 12,3 x 8 cm

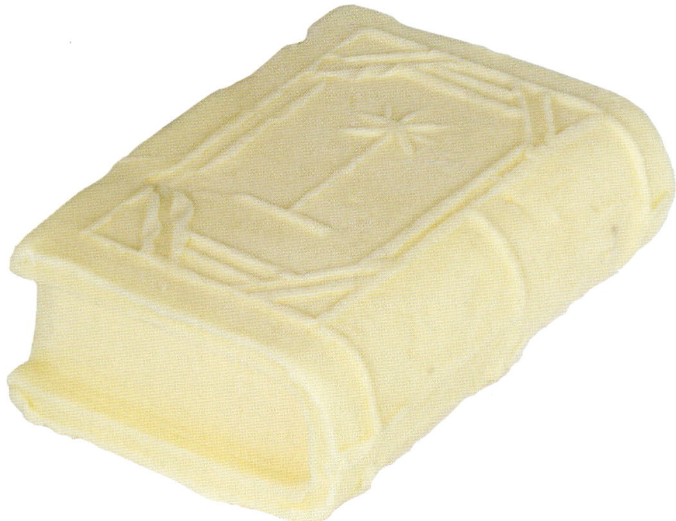

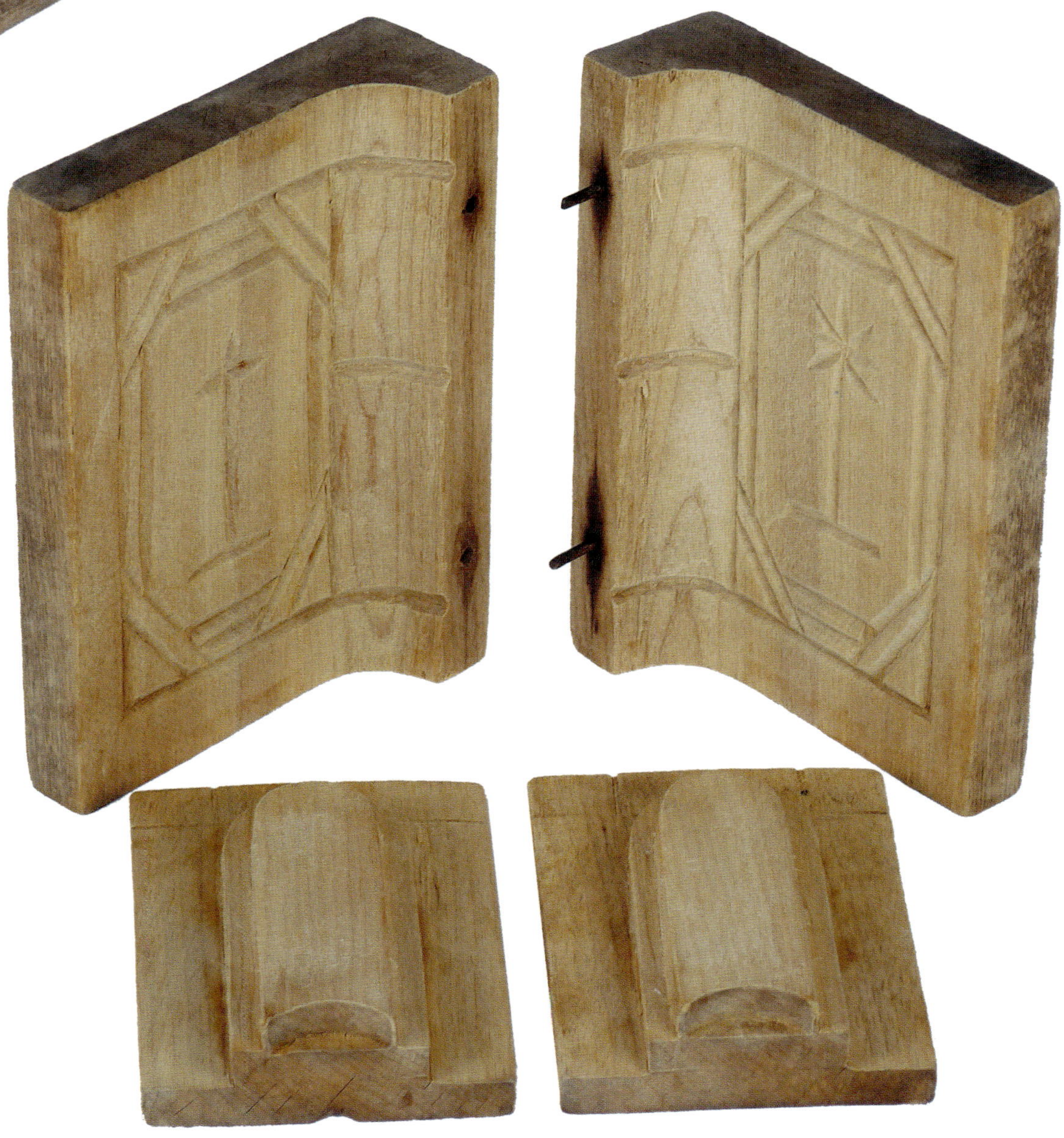

5.093–5.101
Lithografierte englische Blechspardosen
English tin money boxes with lithography
Um / *Around* 1920

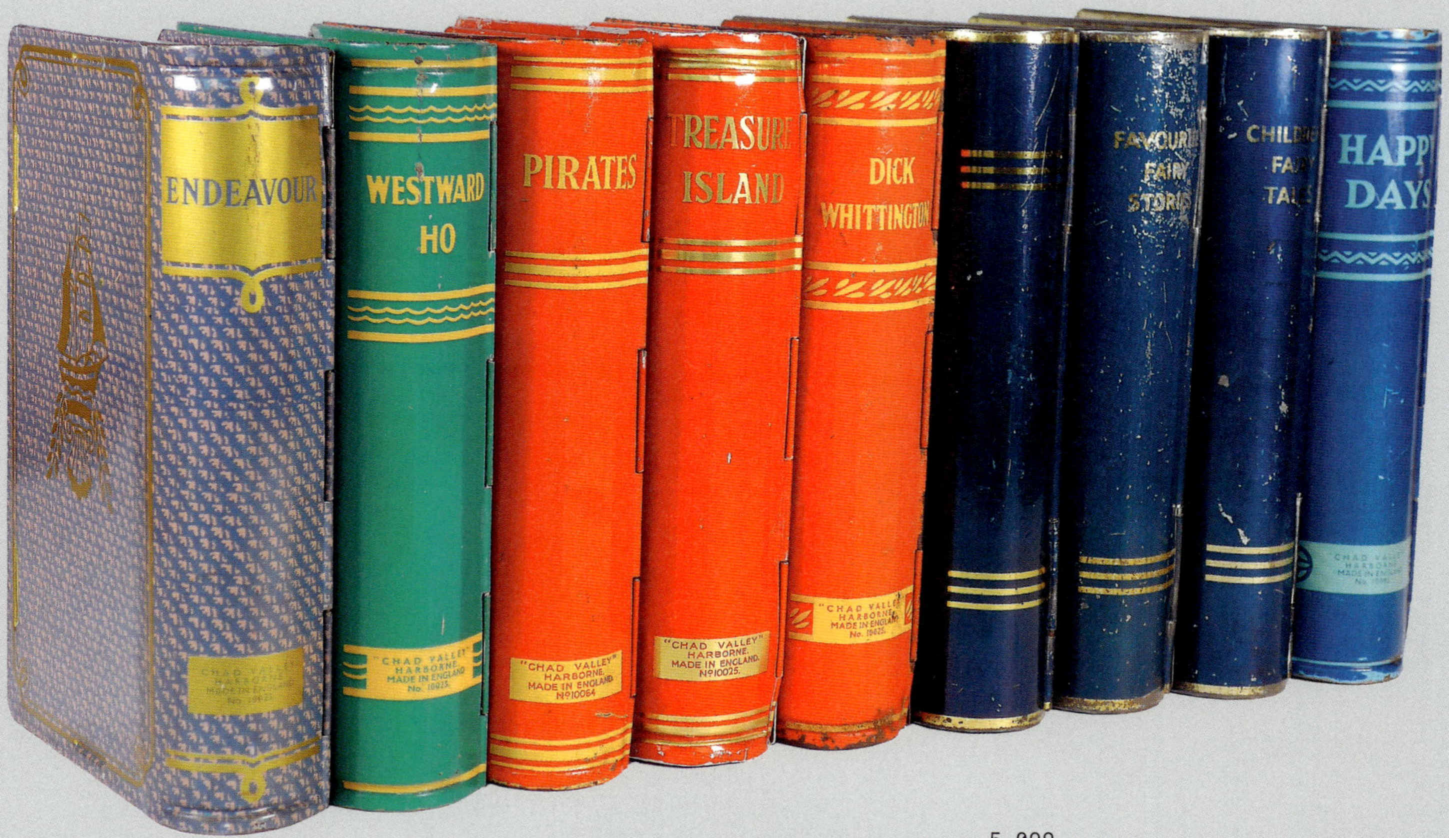

5.093
Endeavour
Ein Segelschiff kommandiert von James Cook. Lithografierte Blechspardose abschließbar
A sailing ship commanded by James Cook.. Lockable lithographed tin money box
"Chad Valley" Harborne, No.10025
Made in England
Um / *Around* 1920 | 14,4 x 10,3 x 3,3 cm

5.094
Treasure Island
Romantisches Seefahrer-Abenteuer mit dem flüchtenden Jim Hawkins. Llithografierte Blechspardose, abschließbar
A romantic sailor's adventure with the fleeing Jim Hawkins. Lithographed tin money box, lockable
"Chad Valley" Harborne, No.10025
Made in England
Um / *Around* 1920 | 14, 4 x 10,3 x 3,3 cm

5.095
Cinderella, Favorite Fairy Stories
Die junge Ella wird von der Stiefmutter und deren Töchtern hämisch "Cinderella" genannt. Am Ende heiratet sie den Prinzen. Lithografierte Blechspardose, abschließbar
Young Ella is maliciously called "Cinderella" by her stepmother and the other daughters. In the end she marries the prince. Lithographed tin money box, lockable
Made in England
Um / *Around* 1900 | 14,4 x 10,3 x 3,3 cm

5.096
Westward Ho
James Cook mit seinem Segelschiff. Lithografierte Blechspardose abschließbar
James Cook with his sailing ship. Lithographed tin money box, lockable
"Chad Valley" Harborne, No.10025
Made in England
Um / *Around* 1920 | 14,4 x 10,3 x 3,3 cm

5.097
Childrens Fairy Tales
„Aladin und die Wunderlampe" aus 1001 Nacht. Mit Unterstützung des hilfreichen Geistes wird Aladin reich und mächtig und heiratet die schöne Tochter des Sultans. Lithografierte Blechspardose, abschließbar
"Aladdin and the Magic Lamp" from The Arabian Nights. With the help of the spirit Aladdin becomes rich and powerful and marries the beautiful daughter of the Sultan. Lithographed tin money box, lockable
Made in England
Um / *Around* 1900 | 14,4 x 10,3 x 3,3 cm

5.098
Happy Days
Kindergeburtstag, Sankt Nikolaus mit Schlitten, spielende Kinder am Strand. Lithografierte Blechspardose, abschließbar
Children's birthday party, St. Nicholas with sleigh, children playing on the beach. Lithographed tin money box, lockable
"Chad Valley" Harborne, No.10095
Made in England
Um / *Around* 1920 | 14,4 x 10,3 x 3,3 cm

5.099
Pirates
Zwei fechtende Seefahrer, lithografierte Blechspardose, abschließbar
Two fencing sailors. Lithographed tin money box, lockable
"Chad Valley" Harborne, No.10064
Made in England
Um / *Around* 1920 | 14,4 x 10,3 x 3,3 cm

5.100
Dick Whittington & His Cat. Der wandernde Waisenknabe
Dick Whittington, Waise und später Stadtrat, Oberbürgermeister und in den Ritterstand erhoben, mit seiner ratten- und mäusefangender Katze. Lithografierte Blechspardose, abschließbar
Dick Whittington, orphan and later councilman, Lord Mayor and a noble knight, with his rat and mouse catching cat. Lithographed tin money box, lockable
"Chad Valley" Harborne, No.10025
Made in England | Um / *Around* 1920
14,4 x 10,3 x 3,3 cm

5.101
Favourite Faire Stories Jack and the Beanstalk.
Englisches Märchen. Die erste Version stammt von Benjamin Tabarl (1807). Lithografierte Blechspardose, abschließbar
The first version of the fairy tale was written by Benjamin Tabarl (1807). Lithographed tin money box, lockable
Made in England
Um / *Around* 1920 | 14,4 x 10,3 x 3,3 cm

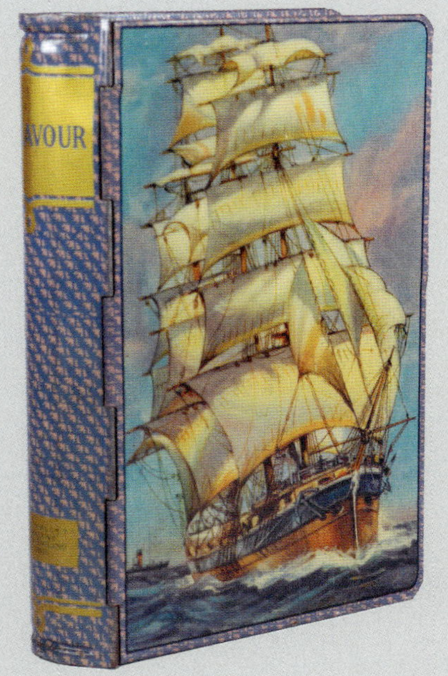
VOUR

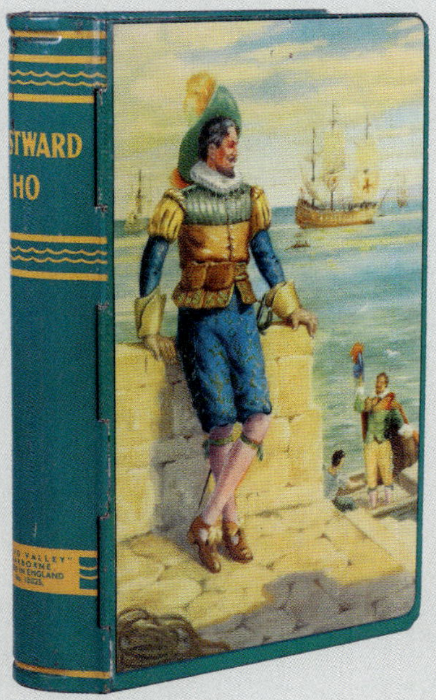
STWARD
HO

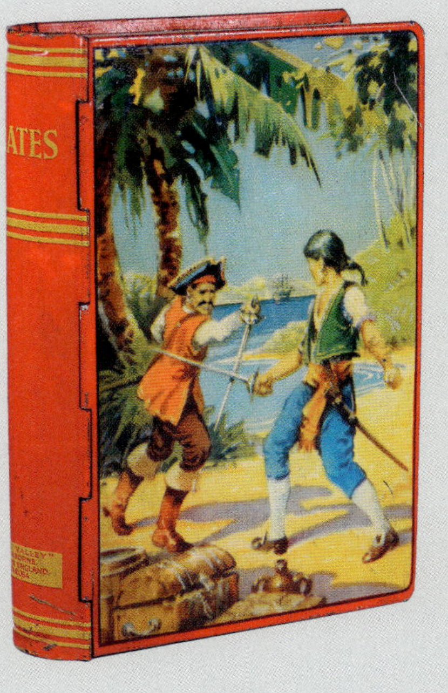
ATES

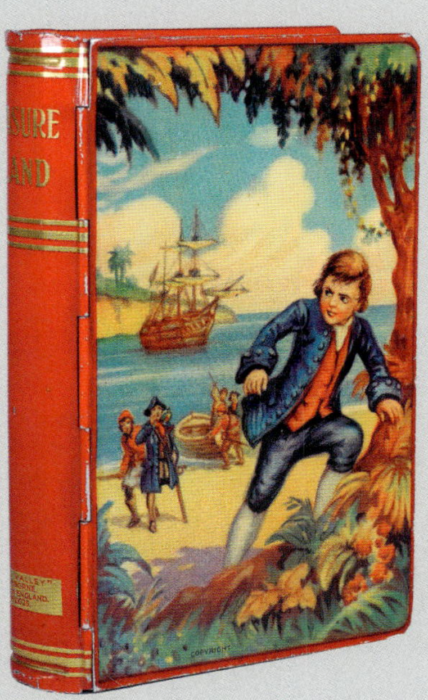
SURE
AND

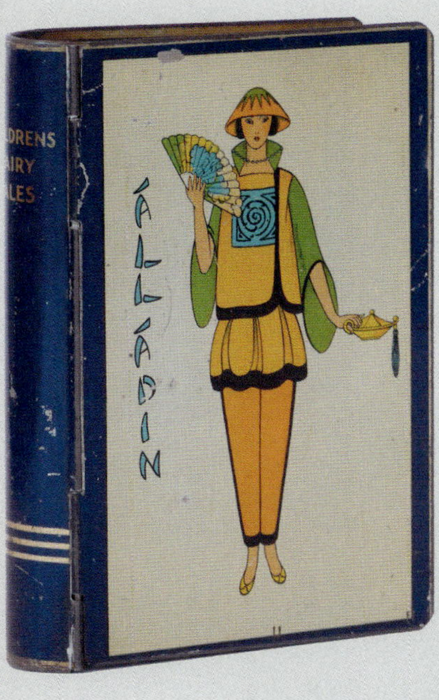
DRENS
AIRY
LES
ALLADIN

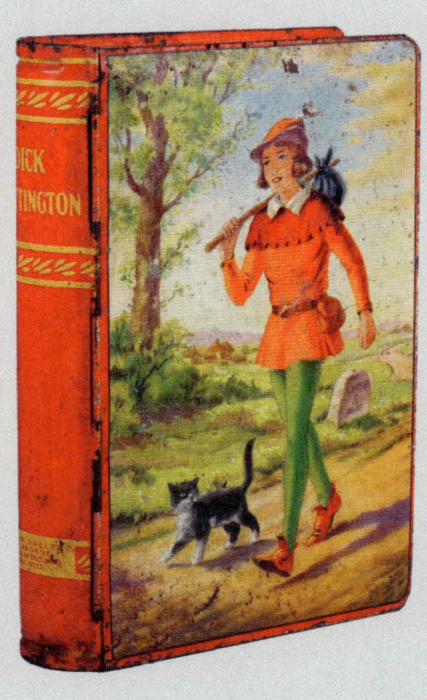
DICK
TINGTON

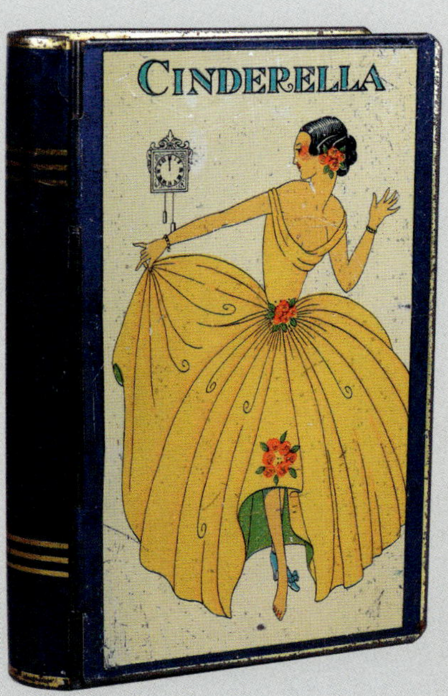
CINDERELLA

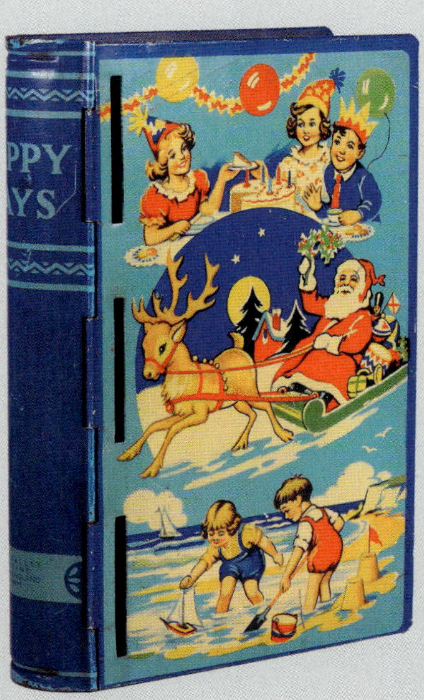
PPY
AYS

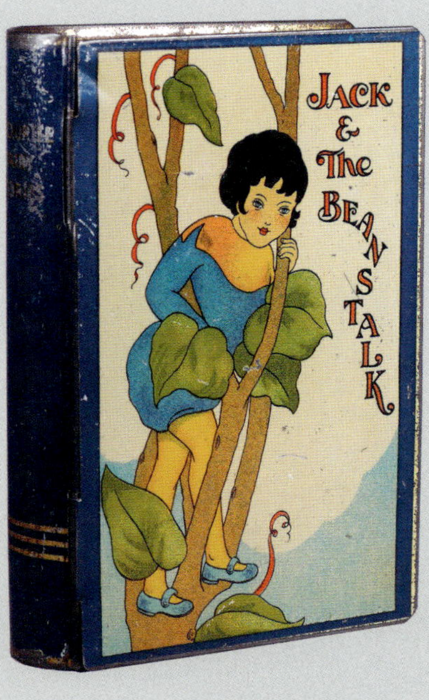
JACK
&
The
BEAN
STALK

5.102
Hotpoint, USA Bank
Spardose mit geprägtem weinrotem Kunstledereinband mit Zählwerk, abschließbar
Money box with embossed wine-red imitation leather cover with a counter, lockable
Um / *Around* 1900 | 10,9 x 8 x 2,5 cm

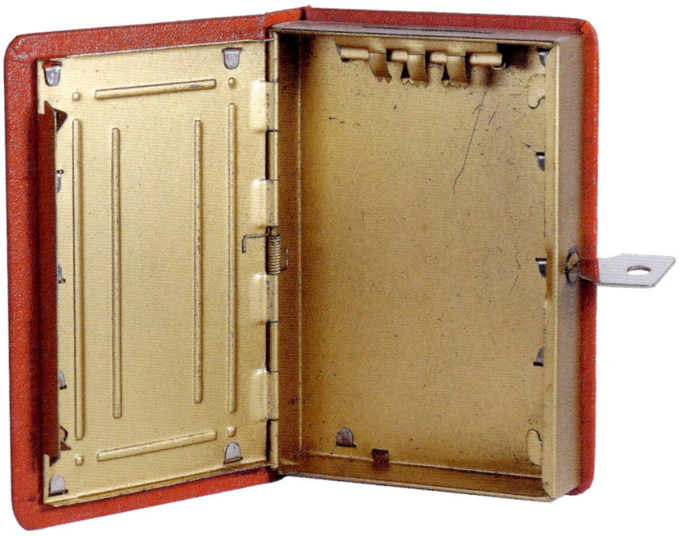

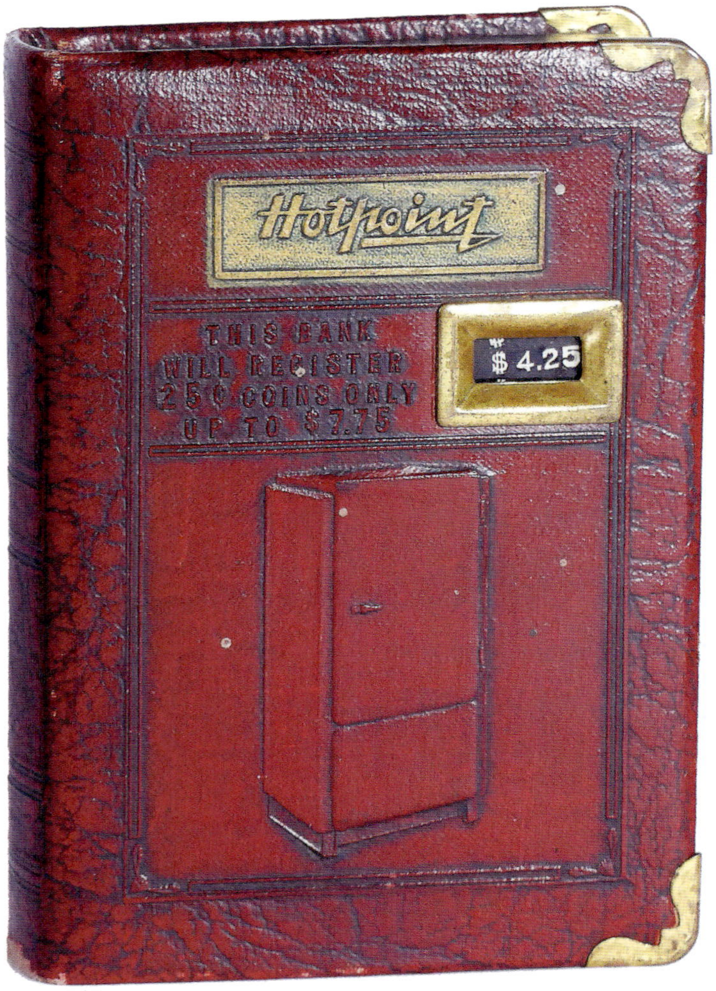

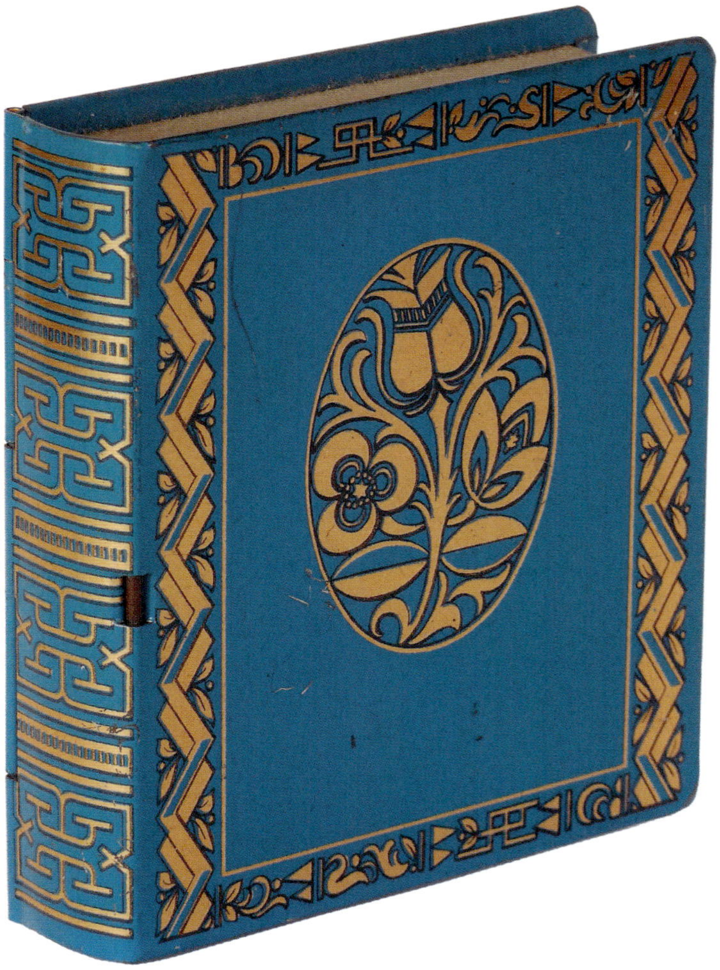

5.103
Sparbuch
Blechspardose mit Zählanzeige, aufklappbarer Vorderdeckel, abschließbar
Sheet metal money box with counter display, hinged front cover, lockable
Made in Germany | 10 x 9,2 x 2,3 cm

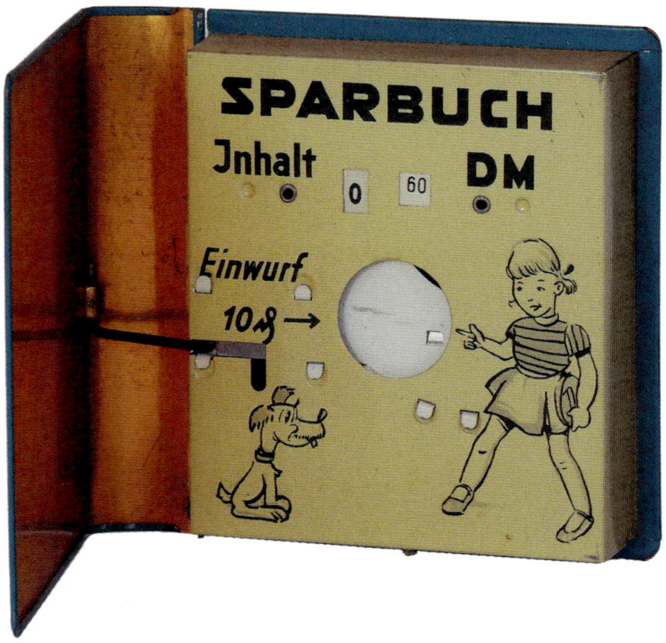

5.104

British and Foreign Bible Society. Thank Offerings

Christliche karitative Organisation mit dem Ziel, die Bibel weltweit verfügbar zu machen (gegründet 4. März 1804). Spardose aus Holz mit Schieber am Fußschnitt zum Öffnen

Christian charity organization with the aim of making the Bible available all over the world (founded March 4, 1804). Wooden money box with an opening slider at the foot edge

16,4 x 11,2 x 4,3 cm

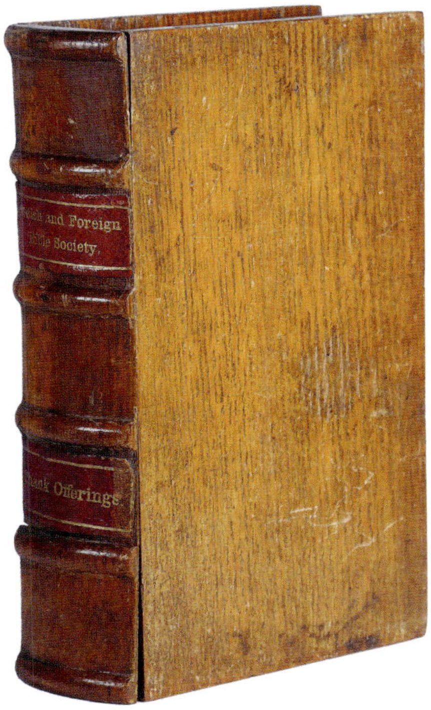

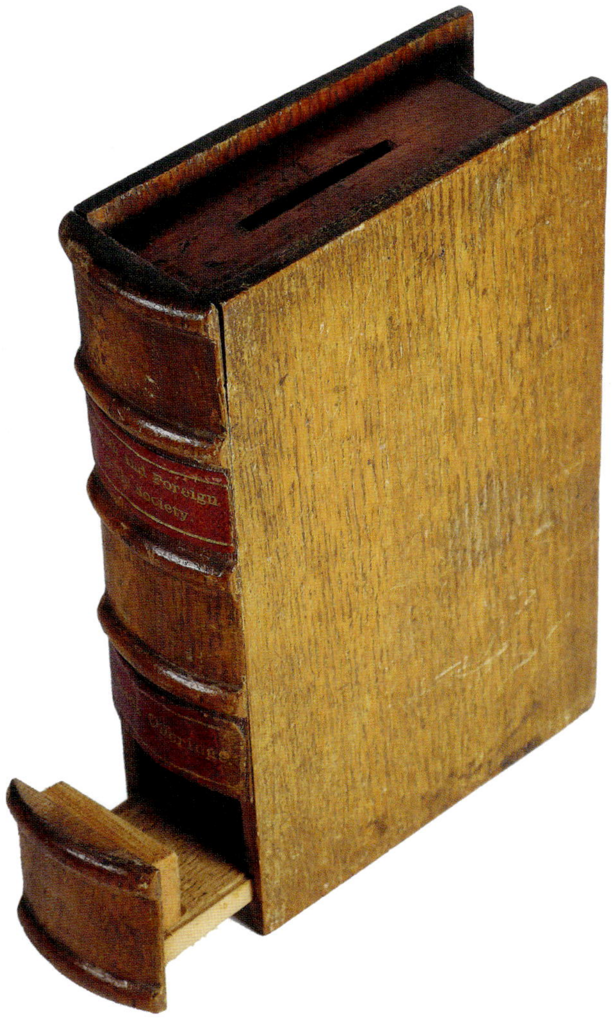

5.105

Spardose aus Nussbaumholz, mit raffiniertem verschiebbarem Mechanismus zum Öffnen und Schließen, Kammmarmorschnitt

Walnut wood money box, with a elaborated closure system with a sliding mechanism, comb marbled edges.

19. Jh. / *19th century* | 13 x 8,8 x 3,2 cm

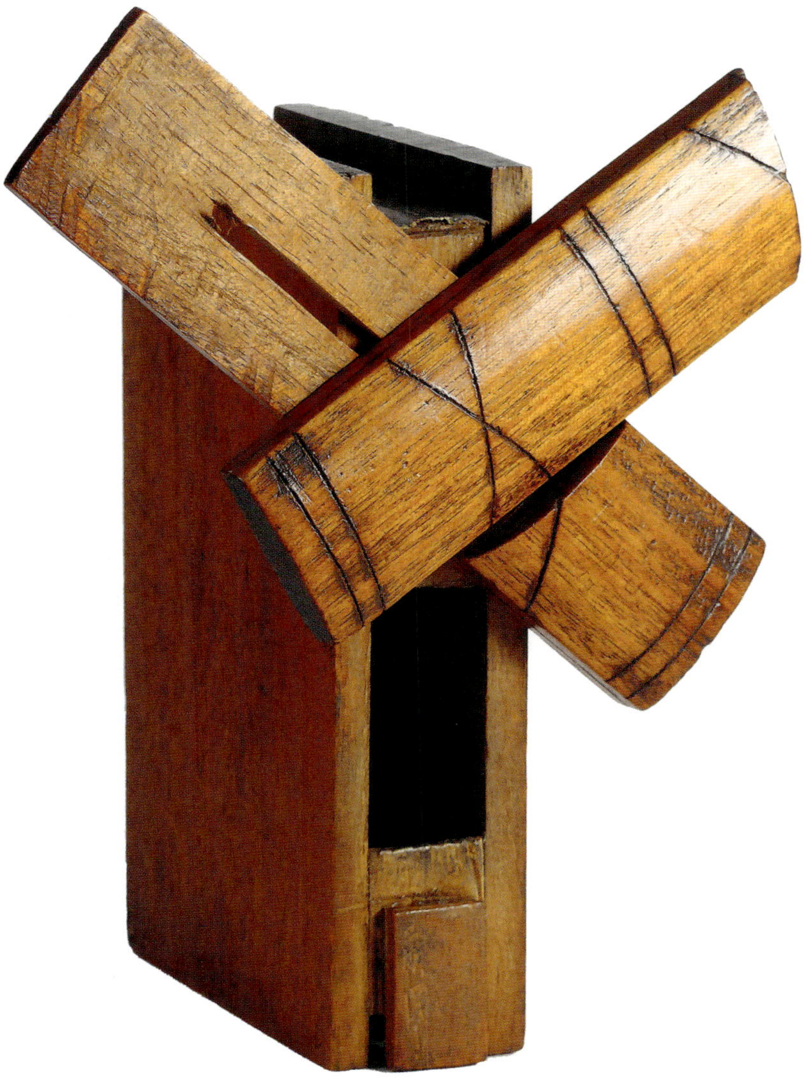

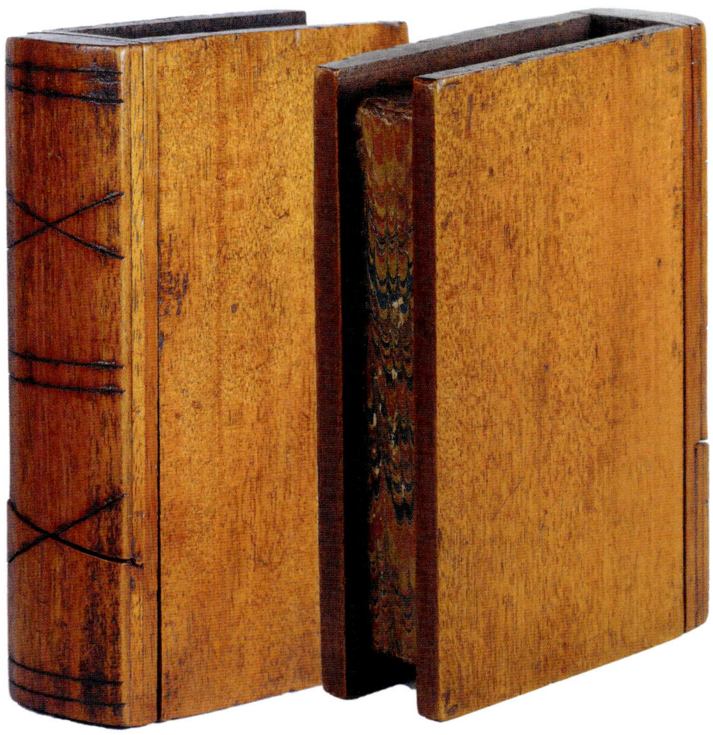

5.106
Golden Gate International Exposition 1930, Treasure Island
Spardose mit geprägtem braunem Lederimitationseinband, abschließbar
Money box with embossed brown imitation leather binding, lockable
Made in USA | 1939 | 8,8 x 8 x 2,5 cm

5.107
Post Office Savings Bank, Nr. 511461
Spardose mit geprägtem grünem Lederimitationseinband
Money box with embossed green imitation leather binding
11,9 x 7,6 x 2,2 cm

5.108
Chicago USA
Spardose mit dunkelblauem Lederimitationseinband, abschließbar
Money box with a navy blue imitation leather binding, lockable
9,5 x 6 x 0,8 cm

5.109
Caja Nacional de Ahorros, Chile Nr. 355
Spardose mit geprägtem rotem Lederimitationseinband, abschließbar
Money box with red imitation leather binding, lockable
9,8 x 6,5 cx 1,5 cm

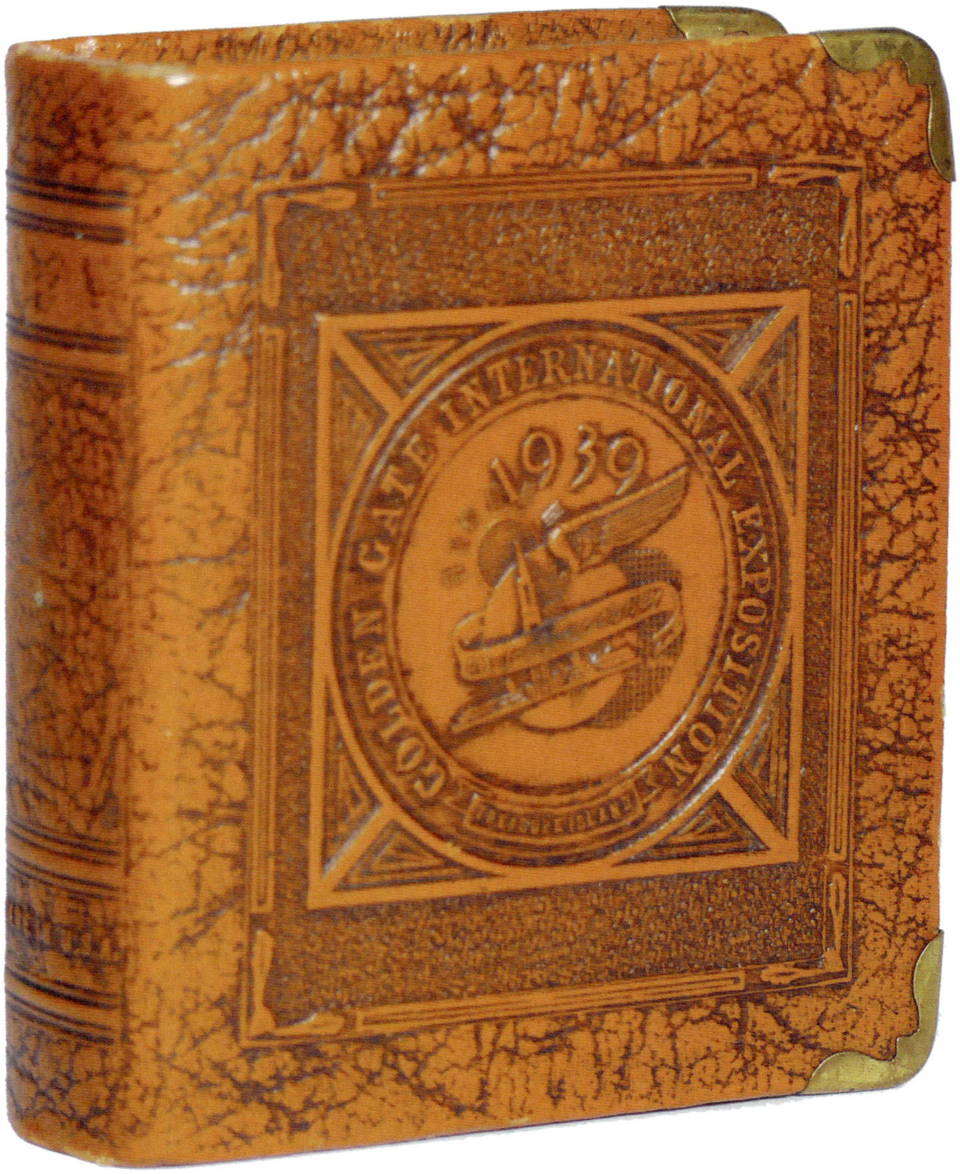

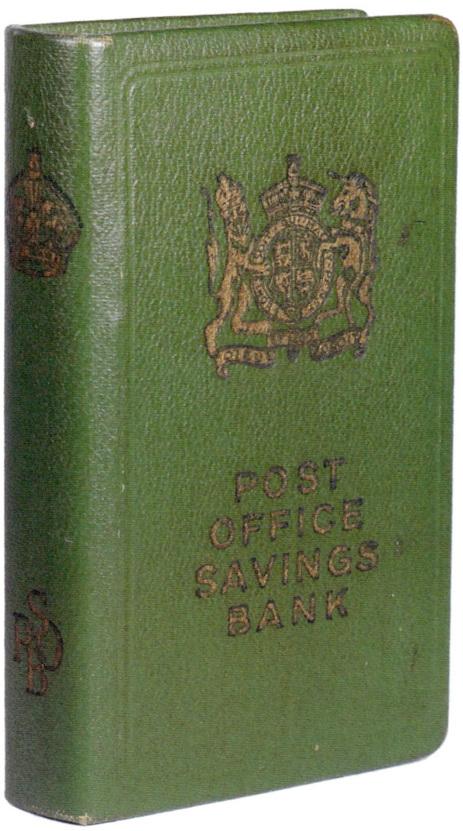

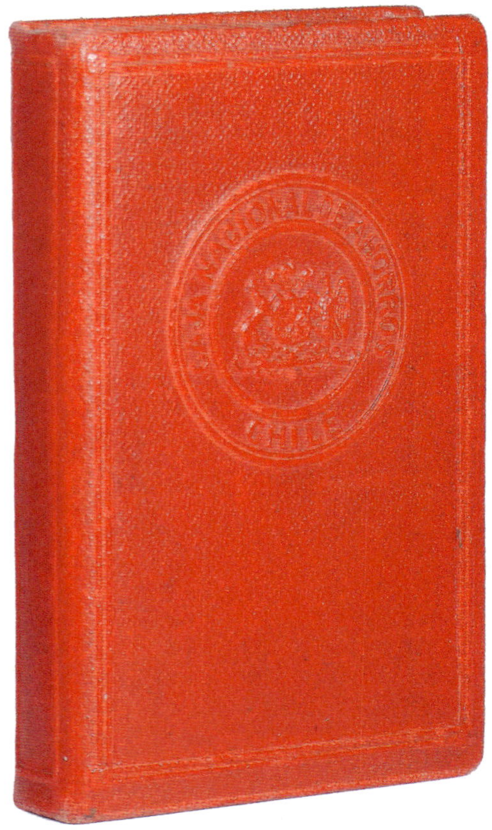

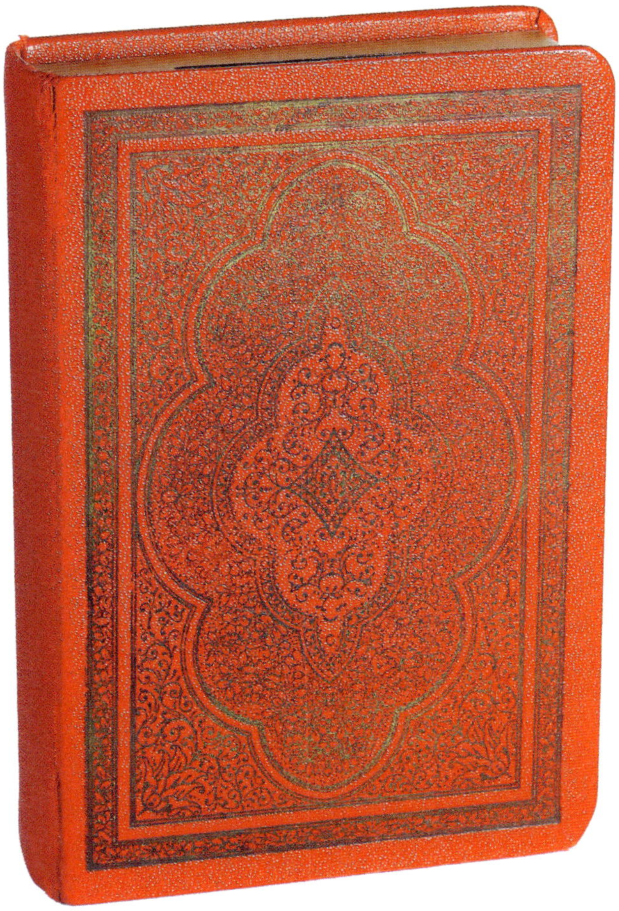

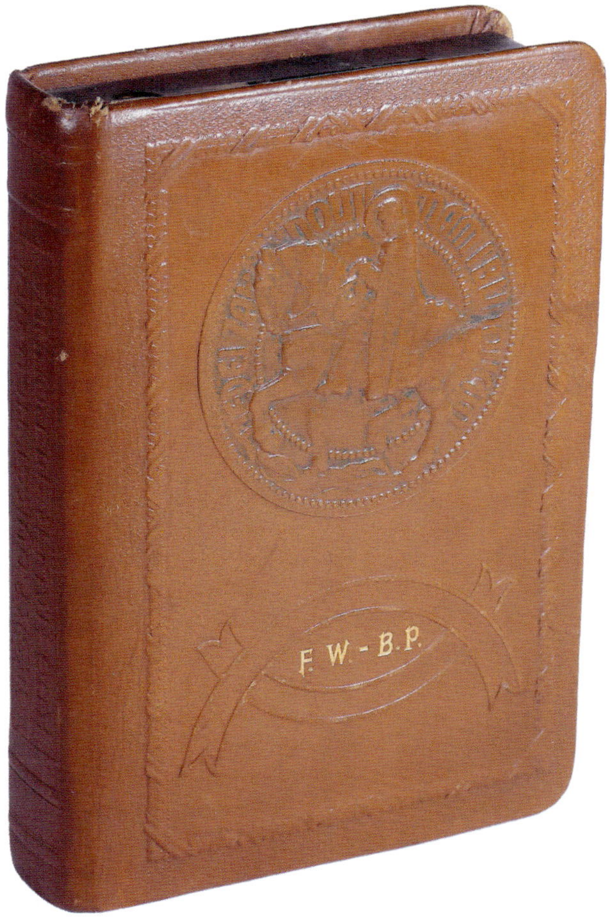

5.110
Spardose mit rotem Lederimitationseinband, schwarze Prägung auf Vorderdeckel, abschließbar
Money box with red leather imitation cover, black embossing on the cover, lockable
Herkunft unbekannt / *Origin unknown*
13,2 x 9,4 x 2,7 cm

5.111
Cesky dukat neuvidi kdo halerem pohrda. Tresoria Praha
Spardose mit geprägtem hellbraunem Ledereinband, Illustration eines Pferdes mit Reiter, abschließbar
Money box with embossed light brown leather binding, illustration of a horse and a rider, lockable
13,2 x 9,4 x 2,7 cm

5.112
Post Office, Savings Bank, Nr. 513789
Spardose mit rotem Lederimitations-einband, ovales Messingschild, abschließbar
Money box with red imitation leather binding, an oval brass plate, lockable
12,7 x 8,9 x 2,1 cm

5.113
Post Office, Savings Bank, Nr.437779
Spardose mit grünem Lederimitationseinband, ovales Messingschild, abschließbar
Money box with green imitation leather binding, an oval brass plate, lockable
12,7 x 8,9 x 2,1 cm

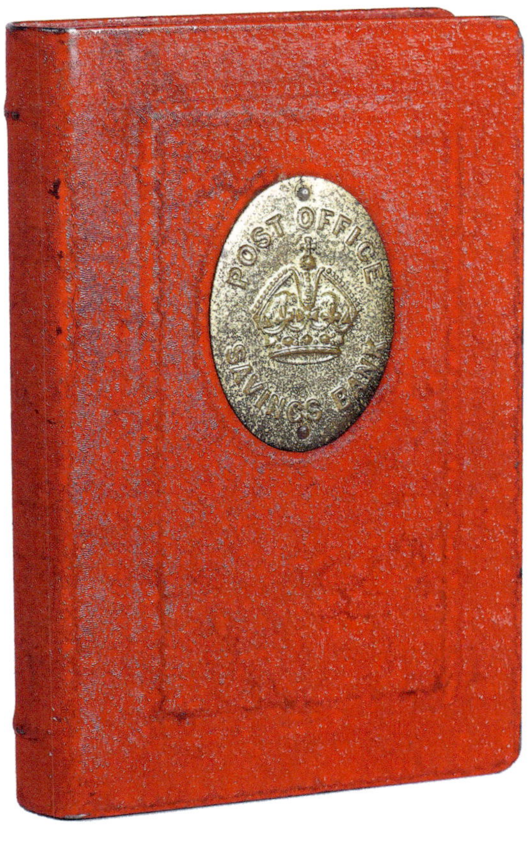

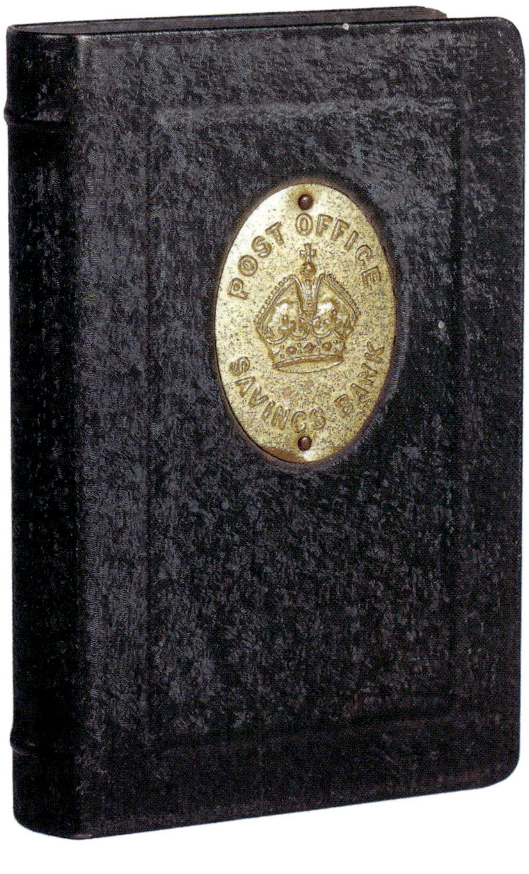

5.114
Somogjmegyei Takarekpénztar Kaposvarott
Spardose mit geprägtem dunkelblauem Lederimitationseinband, Nr.191, abschließbar
Money box with embossed dark blue imitation leather binding, No.191, lockable
Ungarn / *Hungary*
11,6 x 7,5 x 2,2 cm

5.115
How To Win, Grant, A Mutual Savings Bank
Spardose mit geprägtem beigen Lederimitationseinband, abschließbar
Money box with embossed brown imitation leather binding, lockable
7,5 x 5,5 x 1 cm

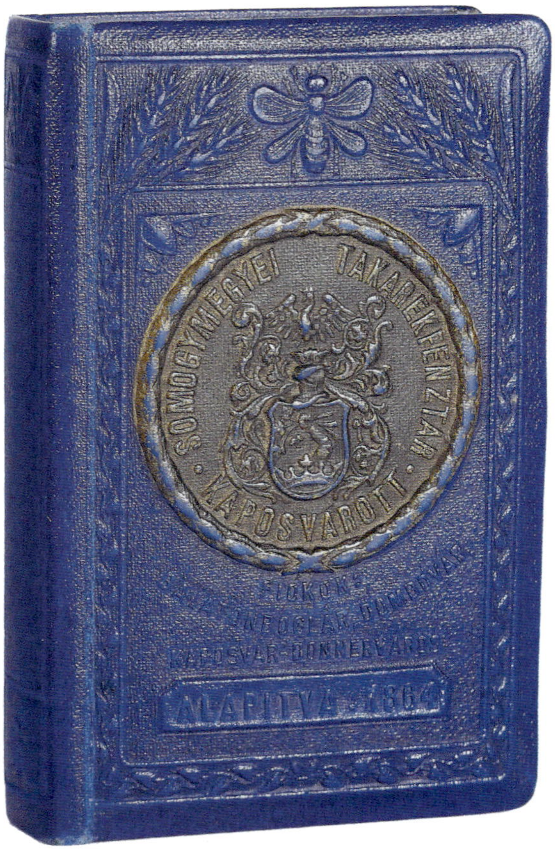

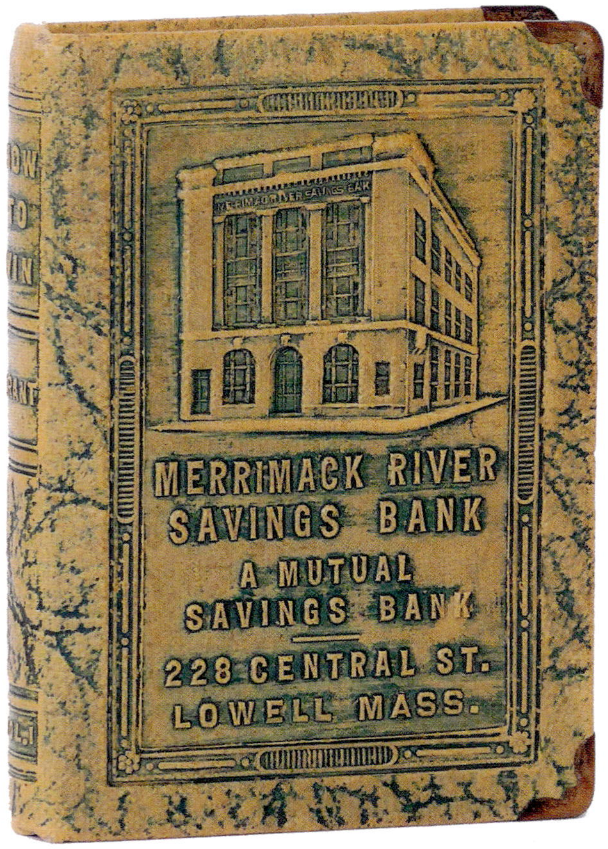

5.116
Baby's Bank
Spardose mit geprägtem Lederimitationseinband, abschließbar
Money box with embossed imitation leather binding, lockable
9,4 x 5,8 x 1,1 cm

5.117
Economia e Riquesa, Benjamin Franklin, Vol. l, Nr. 5297. A.
Spardose mit braunem Lederimitationseinband, abschließbar
Money box with brown imitation leather binding, lockable
Piano J&C. Casa Bancaria Lissabon / *Lisbon*
11,6 x 8,9 x 2,5 cm

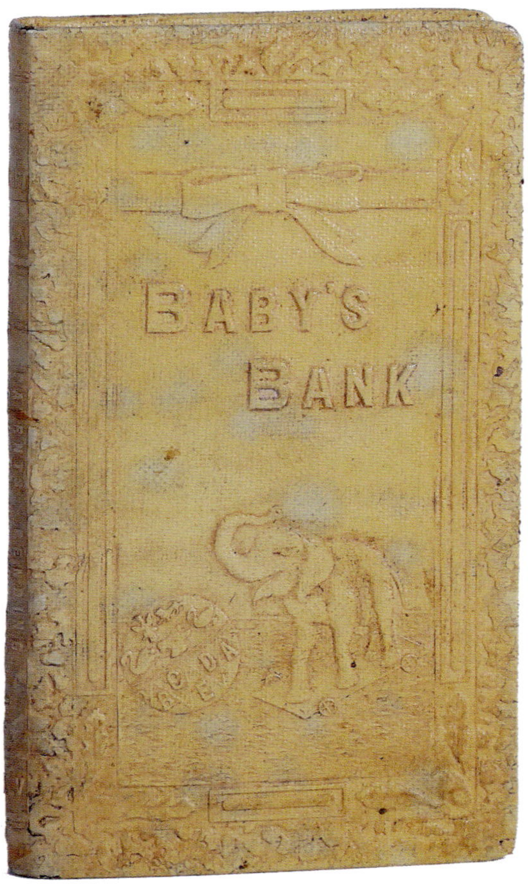

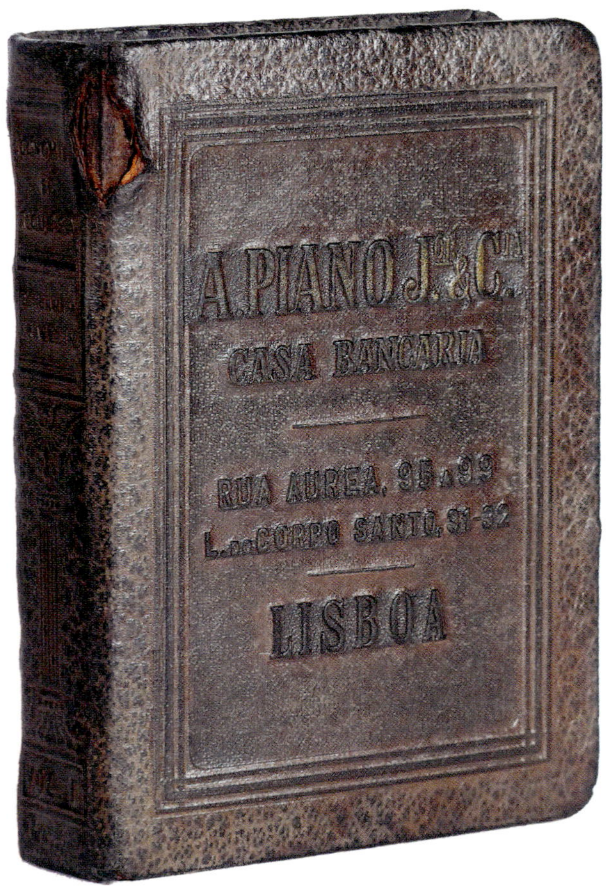

5.118
Cassabuch
Blechspardose dunkelgrün lackiert, abschließbar
Tin money box varnished in dark green, lockable
10 x 7,2 x 3,4 cm

5.119
Lithografierte Blechspardose, abschließbar, Neujahrszenen: Kaminfeger, Schwein, Glücksklee und Hufeisen
Lithographed tin money box, lockable, illustration of New Year themes: Chimney sweeper, pig, lucky clover and horseshoe
Made in Germany, US Zone, Nr. 683
12,3 x 8,1 x 2,8 cm

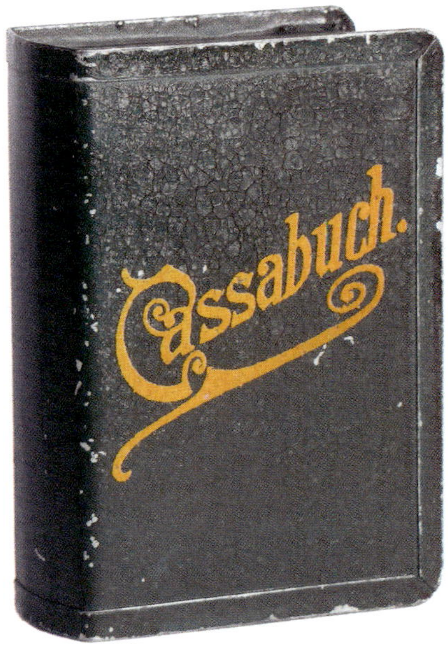

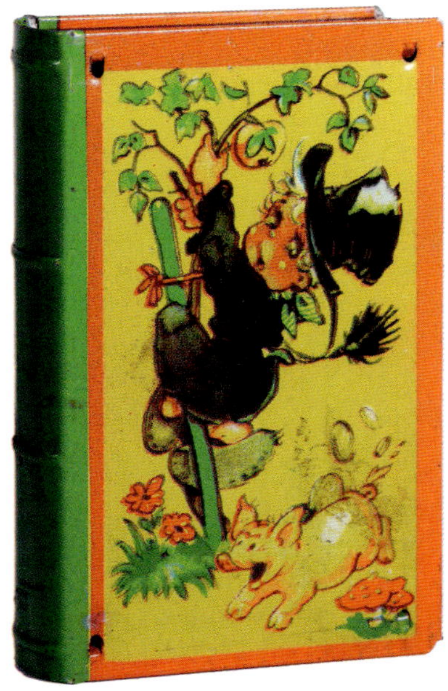

5.120
Cassa di Risparmio delle Provincie Lombarde, Mailand, 717940 L
Metallspardose weinrot lackiert, abschließbar,
Metal money box painted in wine red, lockable
Made in Italy, Italora S. A. | 13 x 9,8 x 4,3 cm

5.121
Die grosse Bertelsmann Lexikothek, über 150 Jahre Bertelsmann lesen, hören, sehen
The great Bertelsmann encyclopedia, over 150 years of reading, listening and seeing Bertelsmann
Spardose aus blau/weißem Kunststoff
Money box made of blue and white plastic
7,9 x 6,6 x 3,5 cm

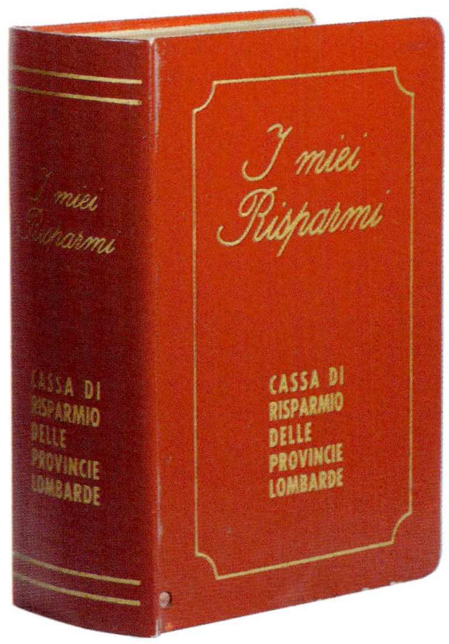

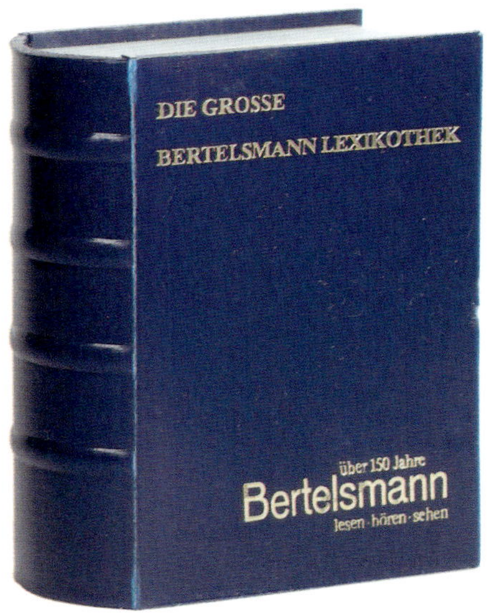

5.122
Master Simpson
Gemälde von Arthur Williams Devis (1762–1822), lithografierte Blechspardose, abschließbar
Painting by Arthur Williams Devis (1762–1822), lithographed tin money box, lockable
London, England | 17,6 x 13,3 x 4,2 cm

5.123
Dignity & Impudence
Gemälde von Sir Edwin Henry Landseer, 1802–1873, gemalt 1839, lithografierte Blechspardose, abschließbar
Painting by Sir Edwin Henry Landseer, 1802–1873, painted 1839, lithographed tin money box, lockable
London, England | 17,6 x 13,4 x 4,2 cm

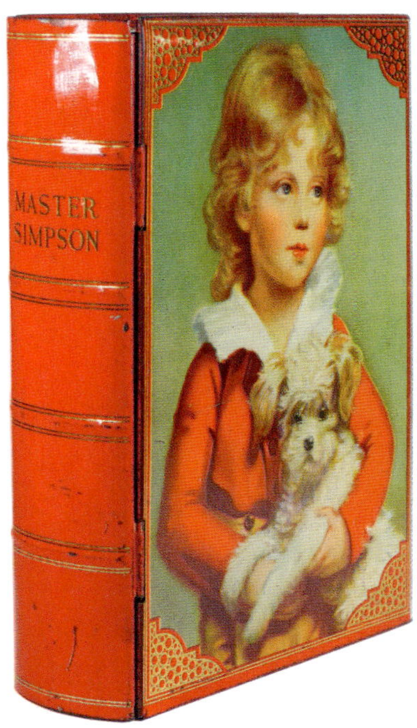

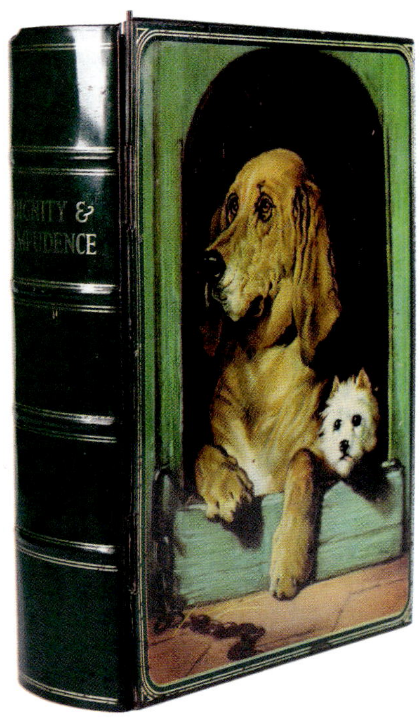

5.124
Les Finances
Spardose aus Blech mit dunkelblauem Überzug, abschließbar
Sheet metal money box with navy blue cover, lockable
Wohl Frankreich / *Probably made in France*
9 x 6,1 x 3,5 cm

5.125
The World Book Encyclopedia, Chicago
Spardose aus beigem Kunststoff mit Schieber zum Öffnen
Money box made of beige plastic with an opening slide
USA

5.126
Book, Spardosen, Holzbehältnisse farbig bemalt, drei- und vierbändig, aufschiebbare Seitenwände
Book, money boxes, wooden containers painted in different colors, three and four volumes, sliding side partitions
11,5 x 9 x 8 cm

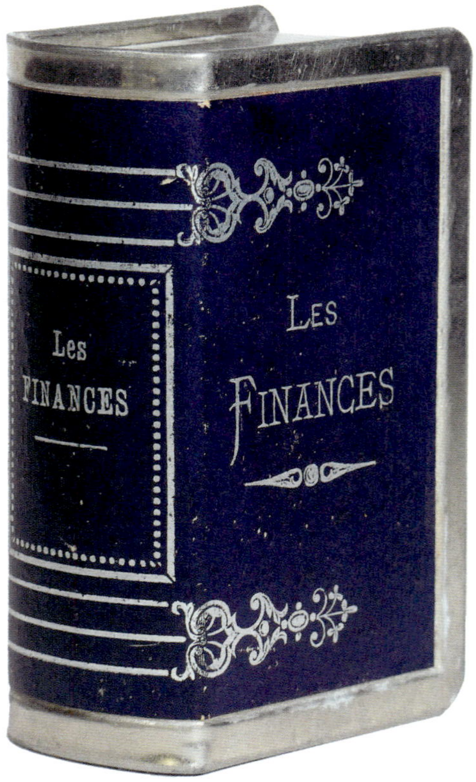

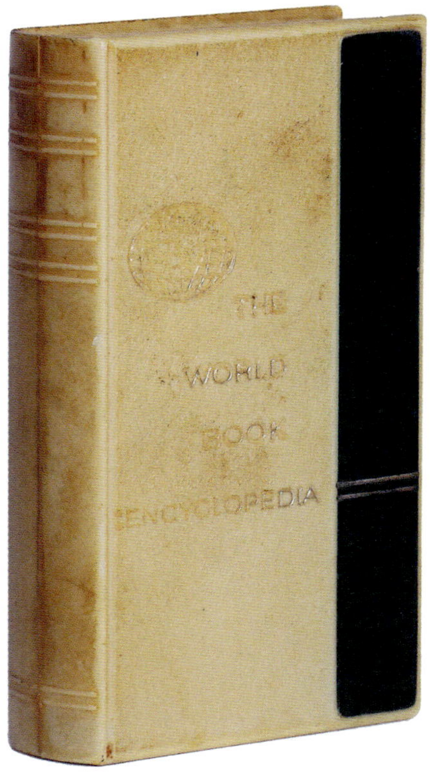

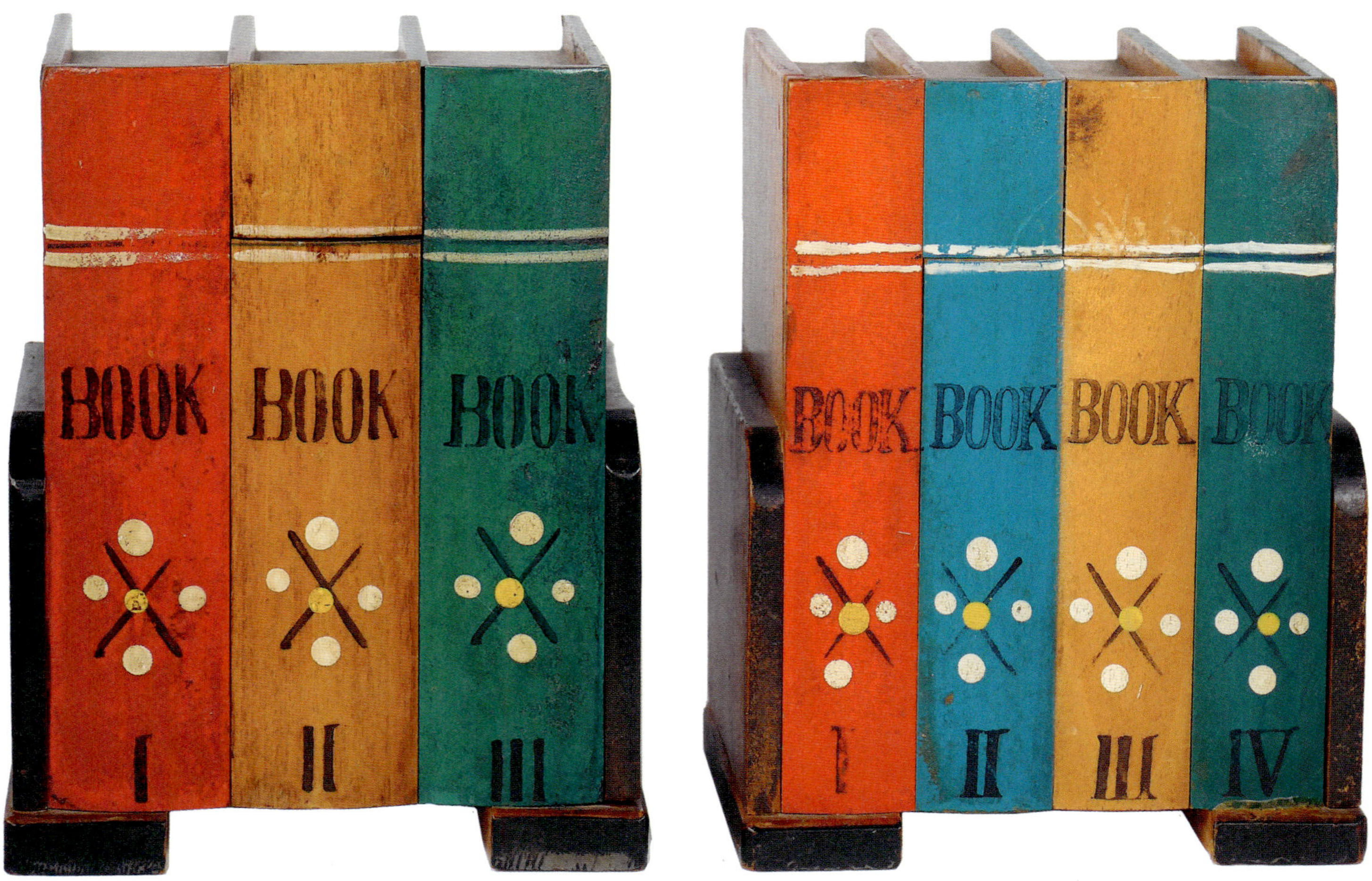

5.127
Massiver Blechtresor in Buchform, farbig bemalt, am Vorderdeckel abschließbar, Tragegriff, dreiseitiger Farbschnitt
Massive sheet metal safe, painted in different colors, lockable at the lid, handle, colored edges
Um / *Around* 1900
13,3 x 38 x 24,7 cm

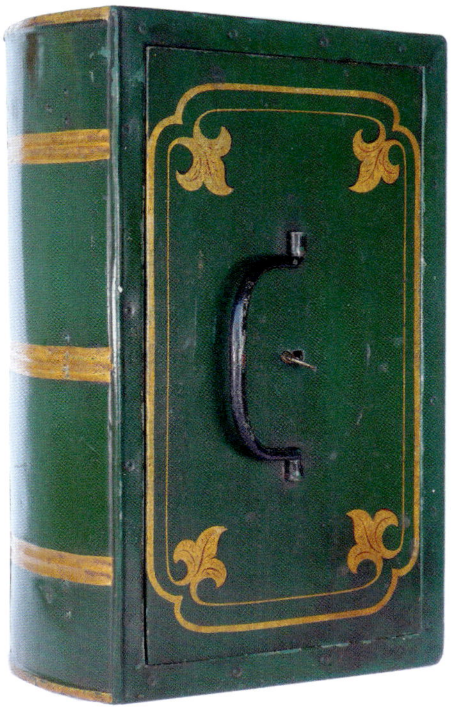

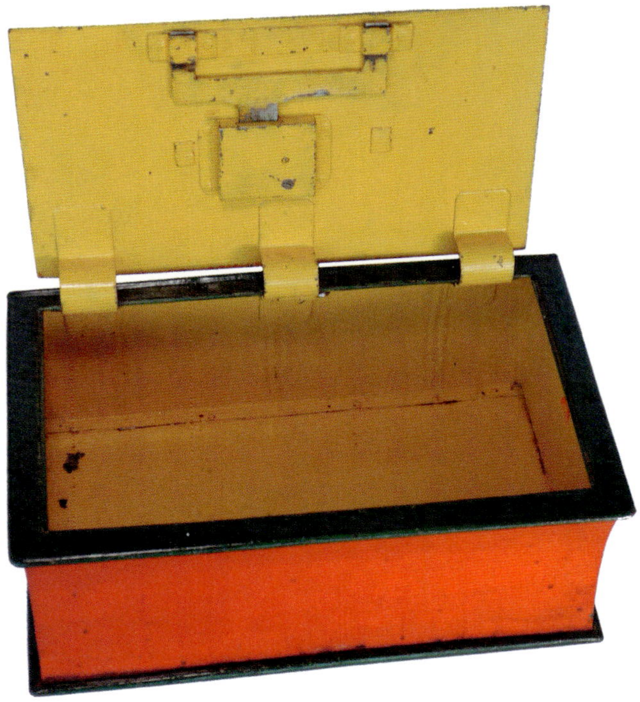

5.128
Bonbons de Chocolat Confiserie Seila, Saint Étienne
Blechdose mit Reliefprägung (Segelschiff)
Tin box with relief embossing (sailing ship)
Frankreich / *France*
Um / *Around* 1960
5,7 x 17,6 x13,1 cm

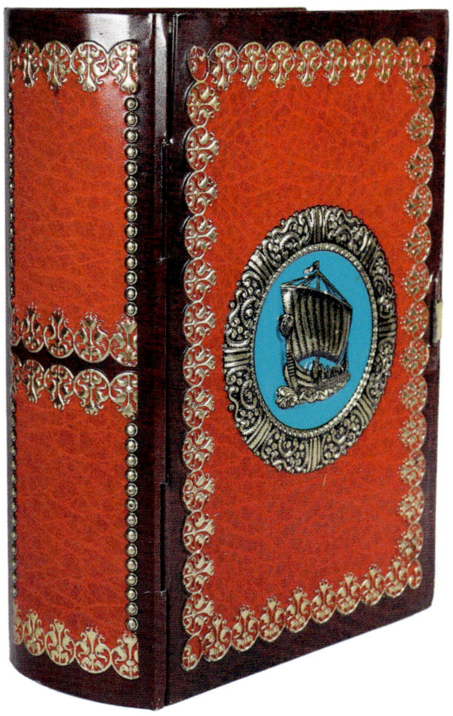

5.129
Uegy Szorgalmas es Takarckos
Spardose aus Metall mit Prägung
Metal money box with embossing
Ungarn / *Hungary*
8,7 x 6,7 x 2,6 cm

5.130
Old King Cole, Humpty Dumpty, Hey Diddle, Little Boy Blue
Szenen aus einem englischen Märchen, Spardose mit blauem Kunstledereinband mit farbigem Aufdruck, abschließbar
Scenery from an English fairy tale. Money box with blue imitation leather binding with color printing, lockable
11,9 x 7,7 x 2,3 cm

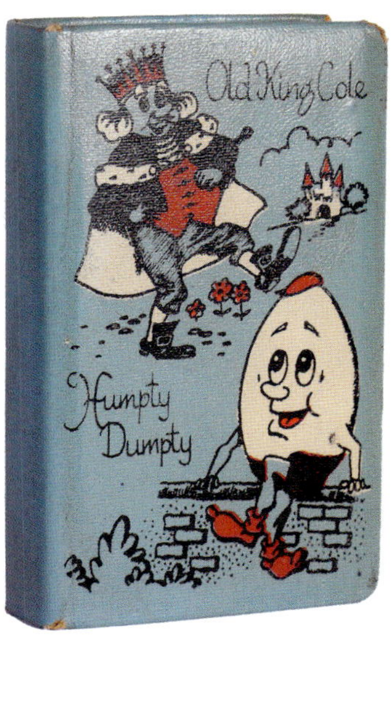

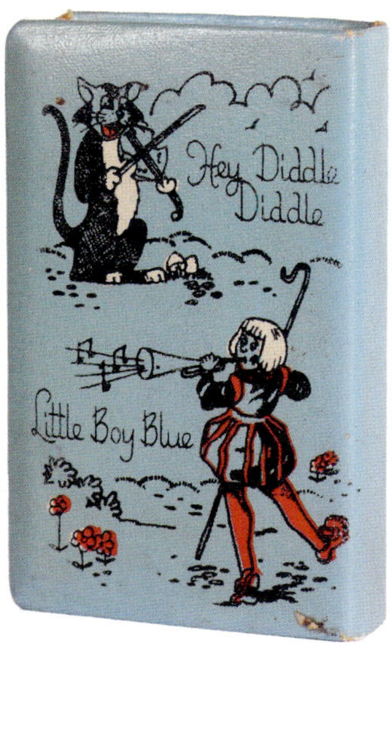

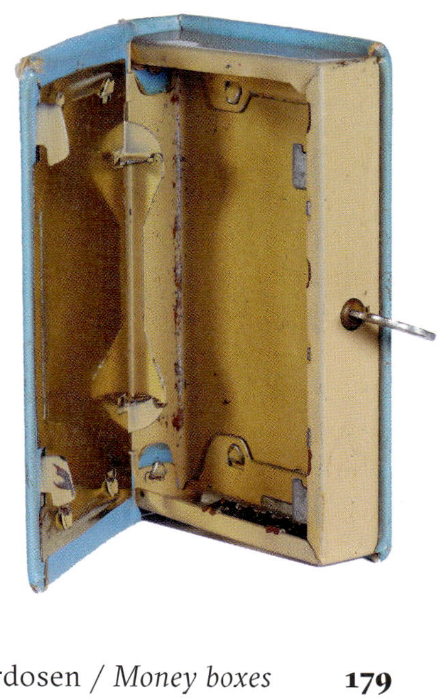

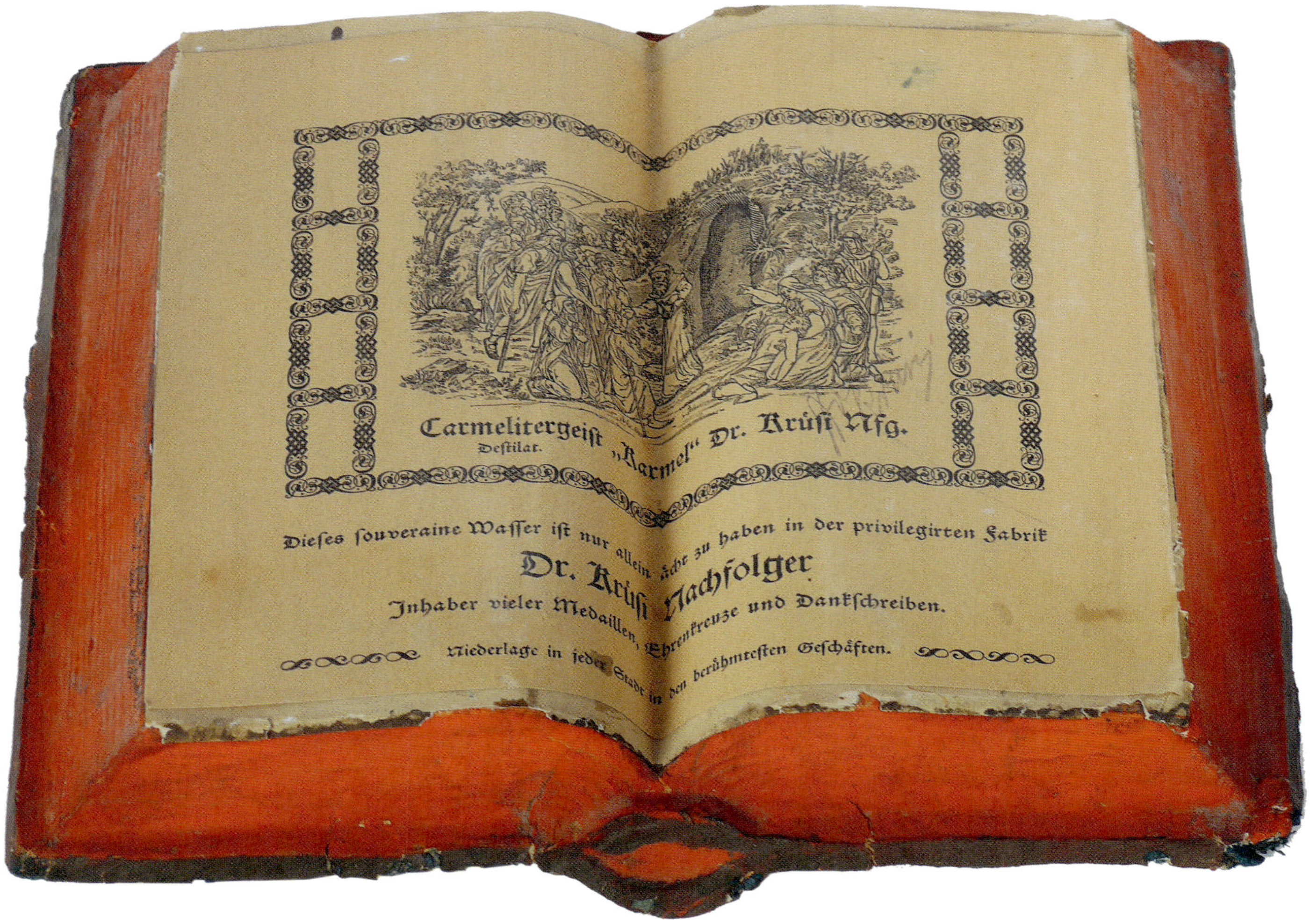

5.131
Carmelitergeist „Karmel“, Dr. Krüsi Nfg
Carmelite Spirit „Carmel“, Dr. Krüsi Nfg
Aufgeschlagenes Buch aus Fasern und Gips für Werbezwecke, beklebt und bemalt
Open book made of fabric and plaster for advertising purposes, laminated and painted
3,8 x 25,5 x 22,2 cm

5.132
Halbkalikodose mit großen Ecken, Steinmarmorpapierüberzug, dreiseitiger Goldschnitt, ausgefüttert mit farbigen Walzendruckpapier
Semi calico box with large corners, stone marbeled paper-overboard, all edges gilt, lined with roller printed color paper
Um / *Around* 1900 | 2,1 x 8 x 6 cm

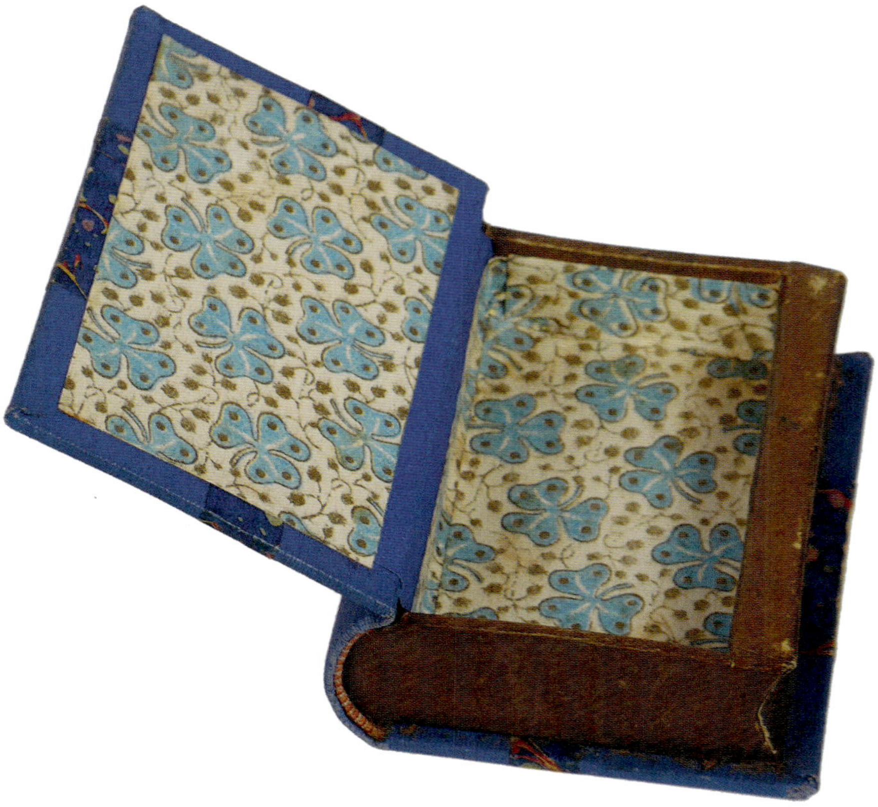

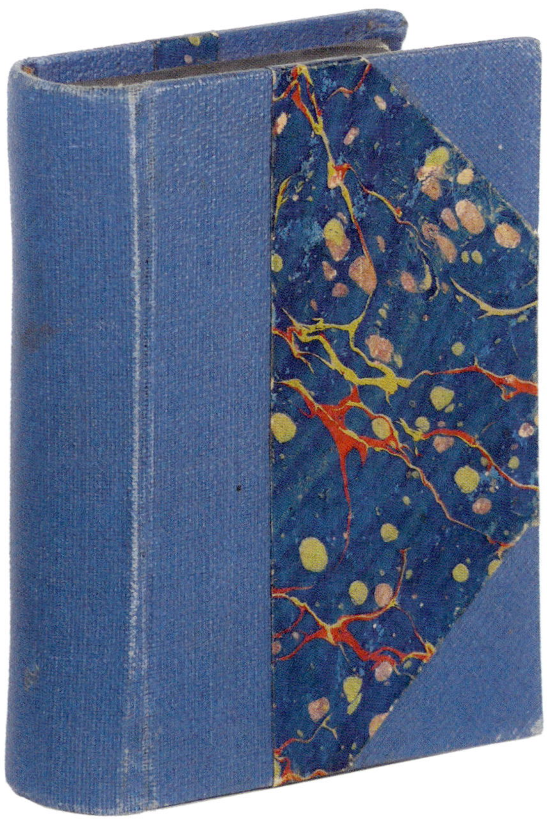

5.133

Buchschachtel mit Stulpdeckel, lithografiertes Damenbildnis auf dem Vorderdeckel, Rücken aus geprägtem Goldpapier, eingefasst mit Goldlitzen, dreiseitiger Goldschnitt

Box with slip lid, lithographed portrait of a lady on the front cover, spine strip of embossed gold paper, edged with gold braids, all edges gilt
2 x 11,8 x 8,1 cm

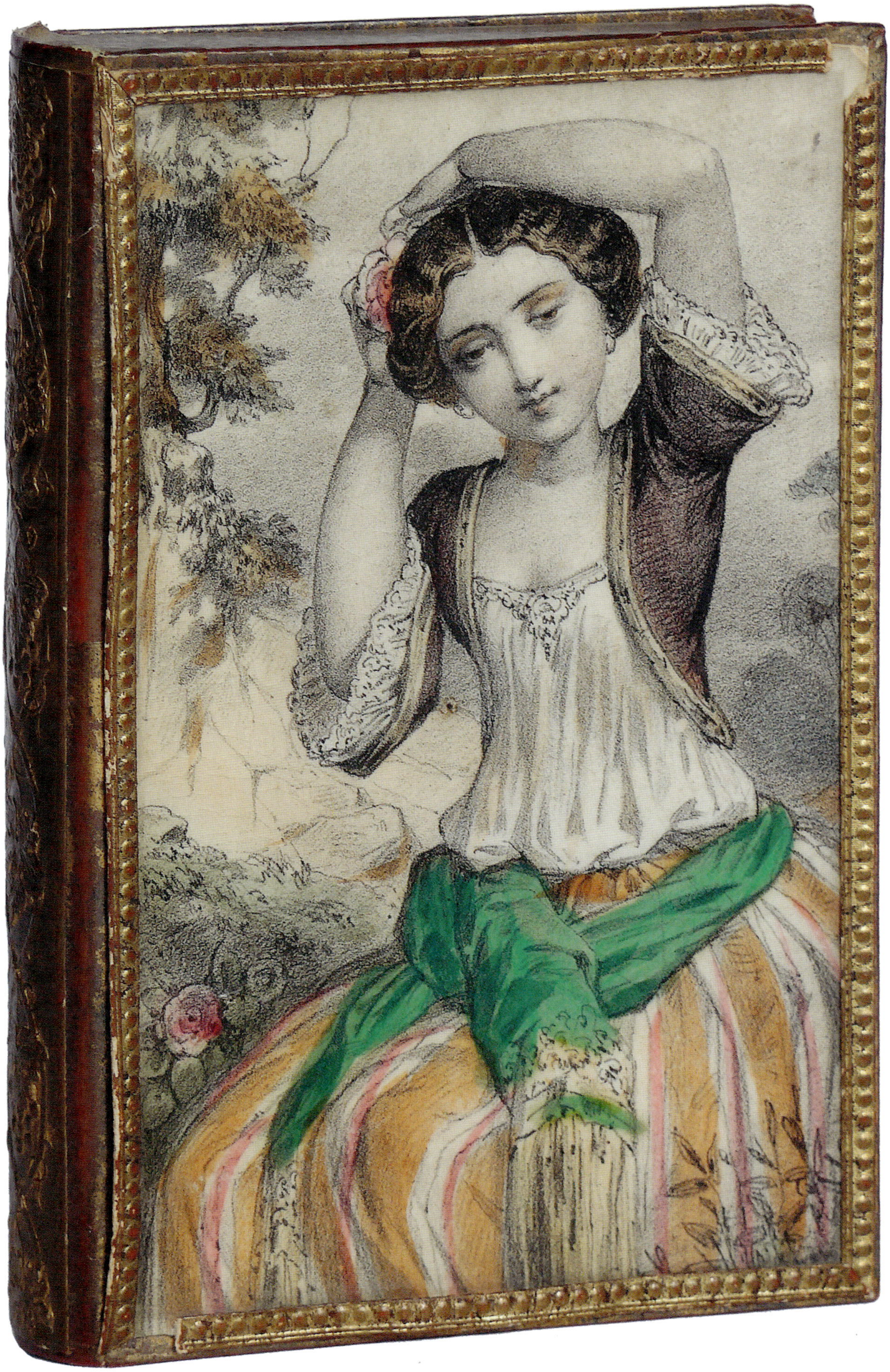

5.134
Holzdose mit Lederüberzug und reich ornamentierten vergoldetem Vorderdeckel, dreiseitiger Goldschnitt
Wooden box with leather cover and richly ornamented gilt lid, all edges gilt
3 x 10,4 x 9,7 cm

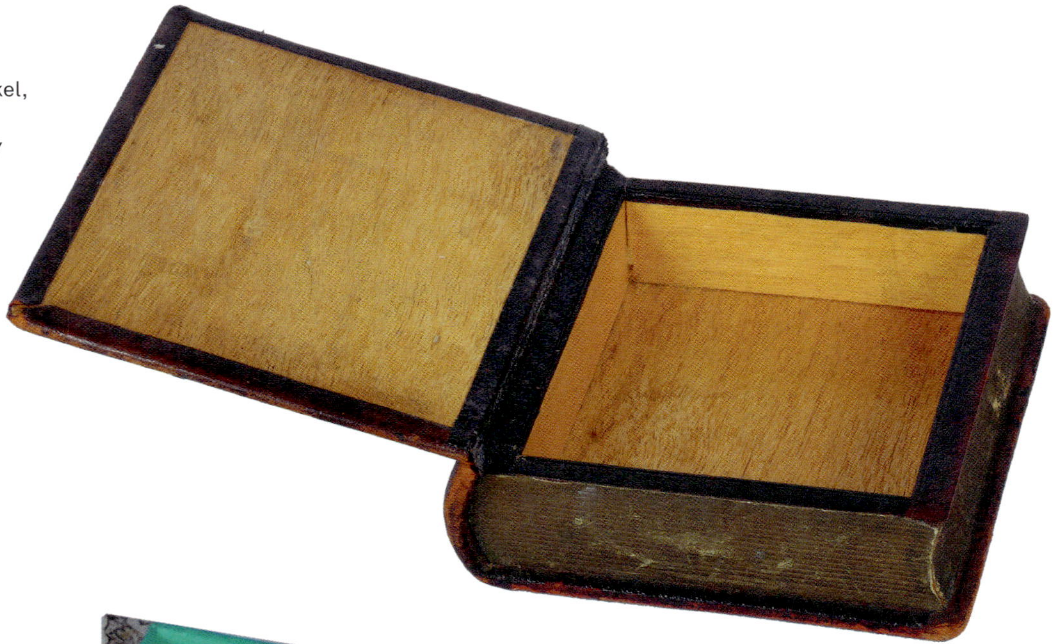

5.135
Kartondöschen mit farbiger und goldener Prägung, Blumenmotiv, dreiseitig geprägter Goldschnitt, ausgefüttert mit gelbem Glanzpapier
Cardboard box with embossing in color and gold and flowers, gold tooling, lined with glossy yellow paper
19. Jh / *19th century* | 7,3 x 5,6 x 1,4 cm

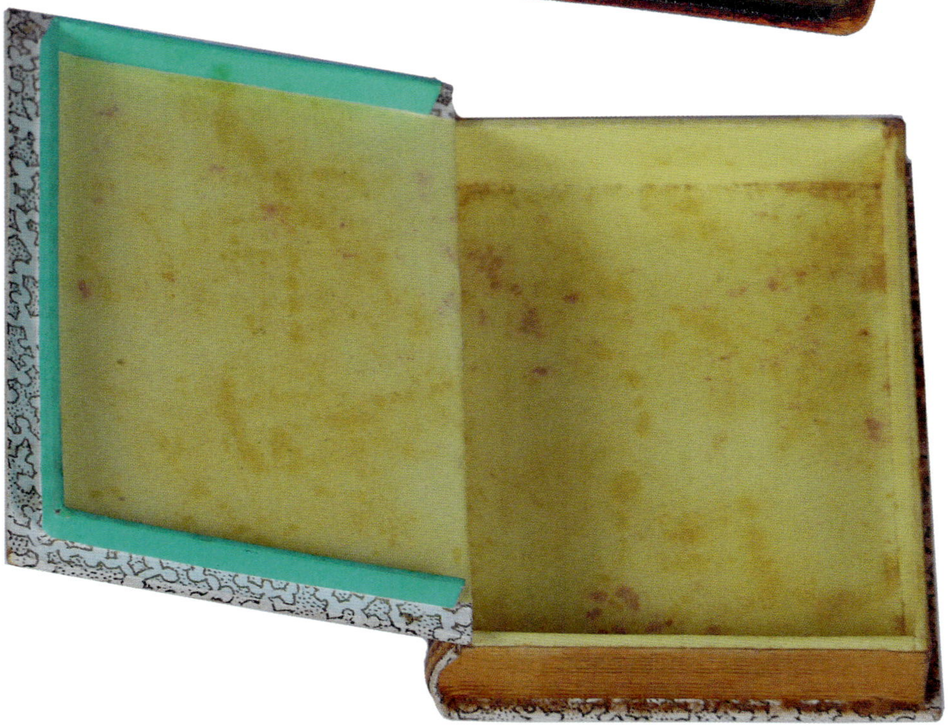

5.136
Halbkaliko-Buchkassette mit Wolkenmarmorpapierüberzug, große Ecken, dreiseitiger Kammmarmorschnitt, ausgefüttert mit lithografiertem Buntpapier
Semi-calico box with cloudy marbled paper-over-board, large corners, comb marbled edges, lined with lithographed colored paper
23,3 x 15,5 x 3,5 cm

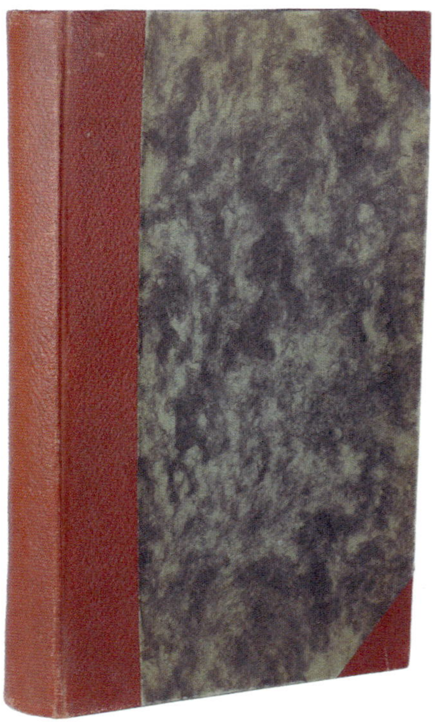

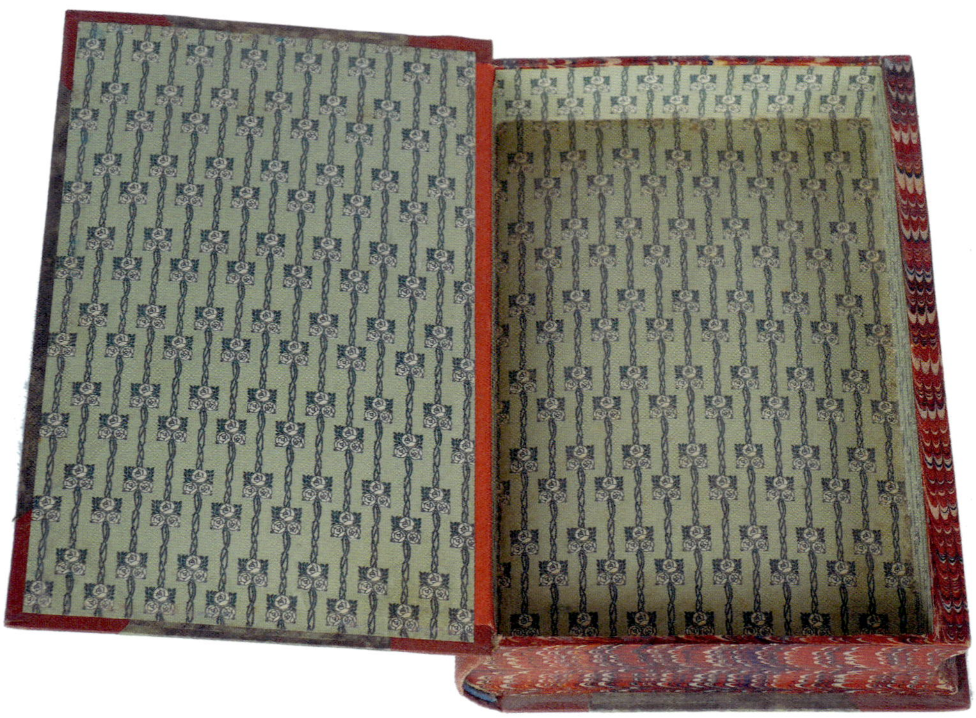

5.137
Saint-Simon, Memoires, Tome 9
Lederschatulle mit reicher Vergoldung auf dem Rücken und beiden Deckeln, Schnitt und ausgefüttert mit Wellenmarmorpapier
Leather box with rich gilding on the spine and both covers, marbel paper edges and lining
4,5 x 21 x 14,9 cm

5.138
Jahrbuch des S.A.C. XXIII / *1887 Yearbook*
Kaliko-Buchschachtel mit Gold- und Blindprägung, dreiseitiger Steinmarmorpapierschnitt, ausgefüttert mit farbigem lithografiertem Buntpapier
Calico box with gold and blind embossing, stone marble paper edges, lined with lithographed colored paper
3,2 x 18,6 x 13,2 cm

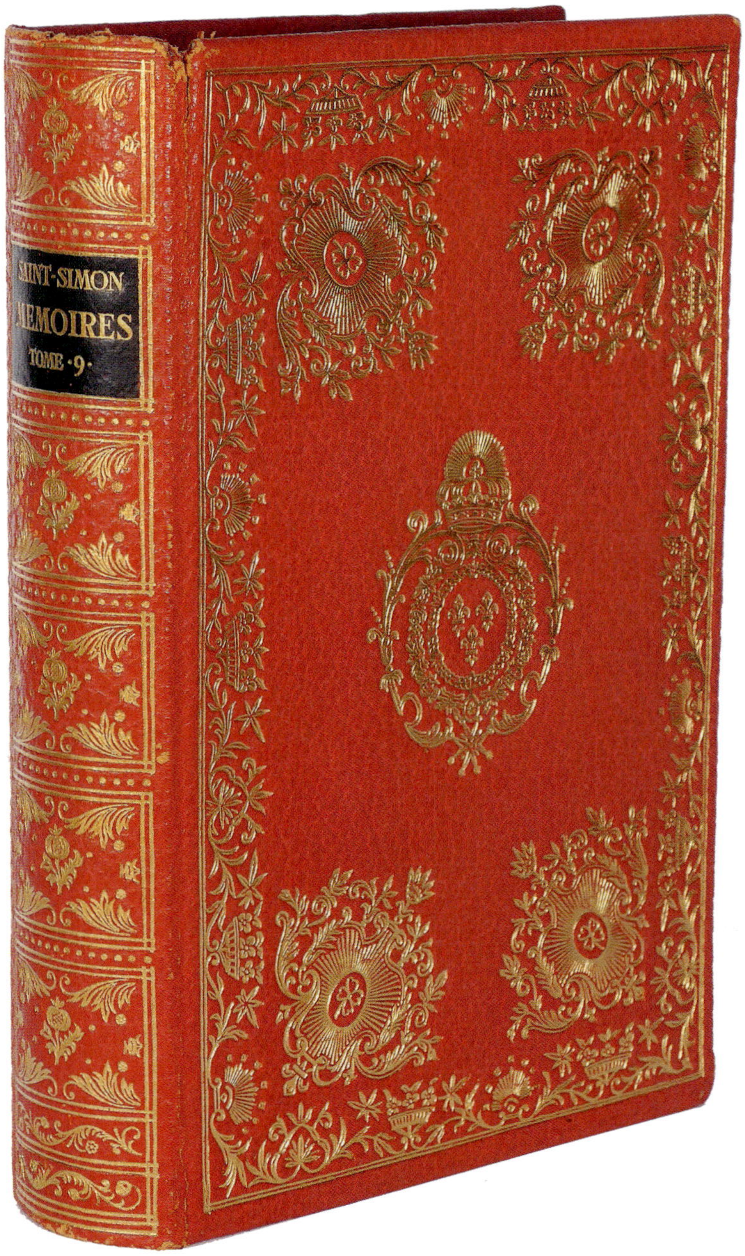

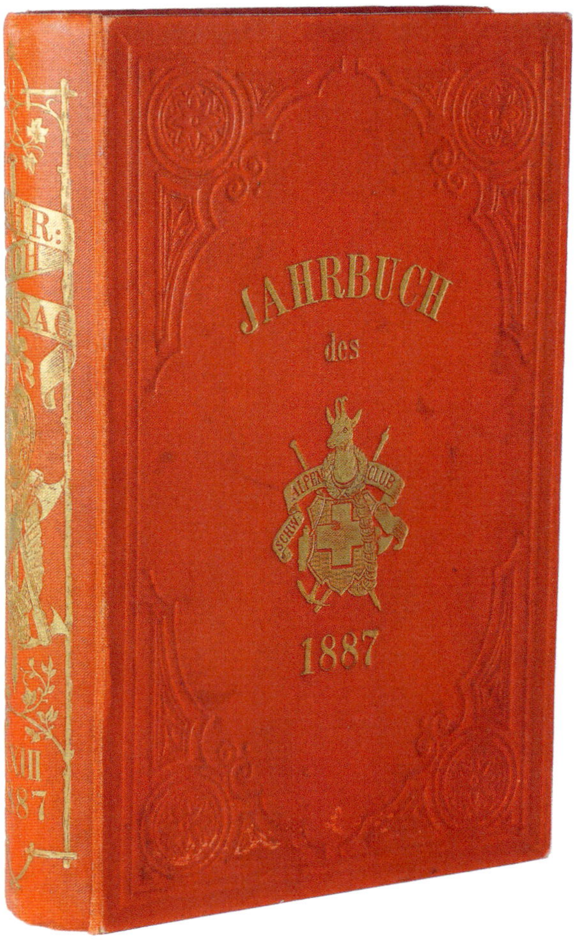

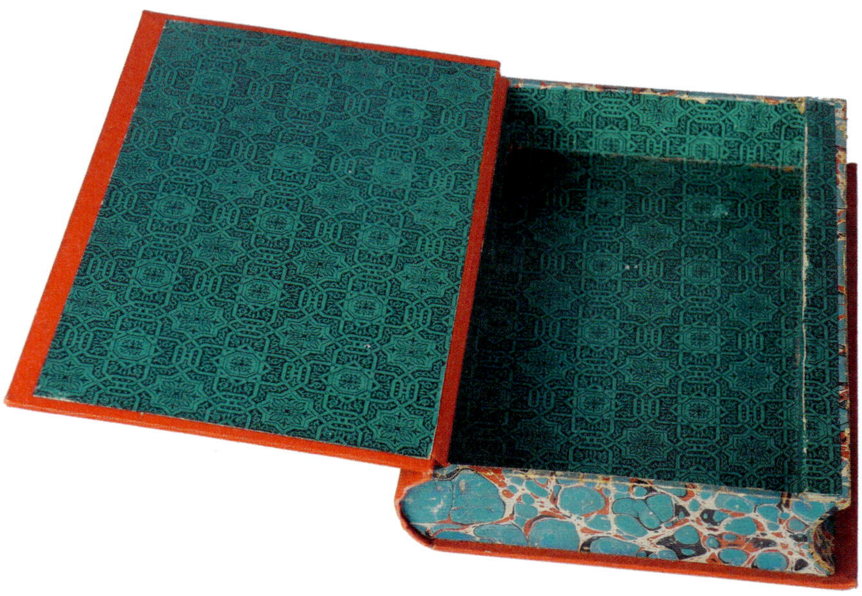

5.139
Memoires des vide-goussets
Ganzledereinbanddecke mit Holzschachtel, Rücken- und Deckelvergoldung, Spiegel und Buchschnitt mit Schneckenmarmorpapier
Full leather cover with wooden box, gilt spine and cover, marbled paper pastedown and edges with marbled paper
5 x 19,5 x 12,2 cm

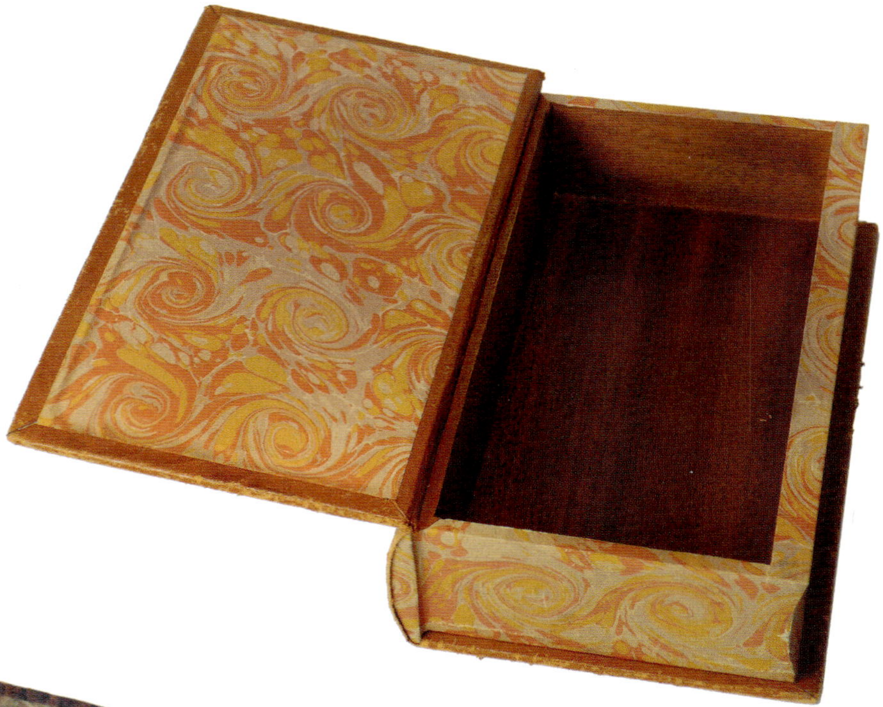

5.140
E. Lancosme: Lgocratine
Halblederdose mit Papierüberzug, vier erhabene Bünde, Titelprägung, ausgefüttert mit Fantasiemarmorpapier
Semi-leather box with paper-overboard, stamped title, marbled paper lining
3 x 12,1 x 9,1 cm

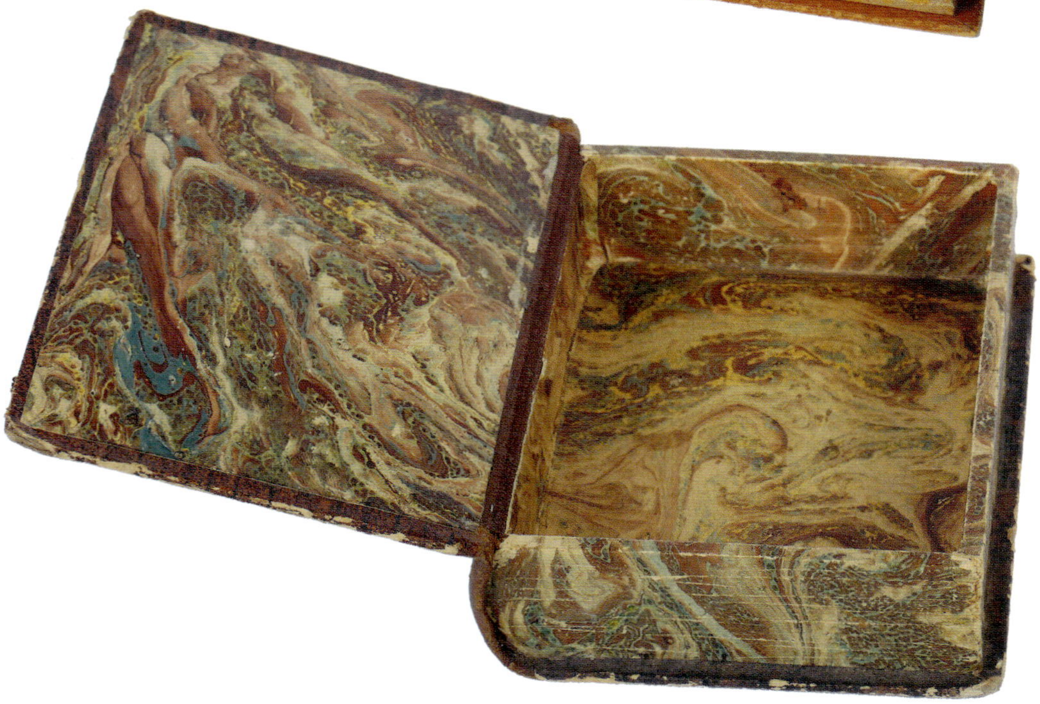

5.141
Das erste Jahr im neuen Haushalt
The first year of the new household
Kaliko-Buchschachtel mit Gold- und Farbprägung, dreiseitiger Kammmarmorpapierschnitt, ausgefüttert mit Walzendruckpapier
Calico box with gold and color embossing, comb marbled paper edges, lined with roller printed paper
Jugendstil / *Art Nouveau*
3,2 x 17,1 x 11,7 cm

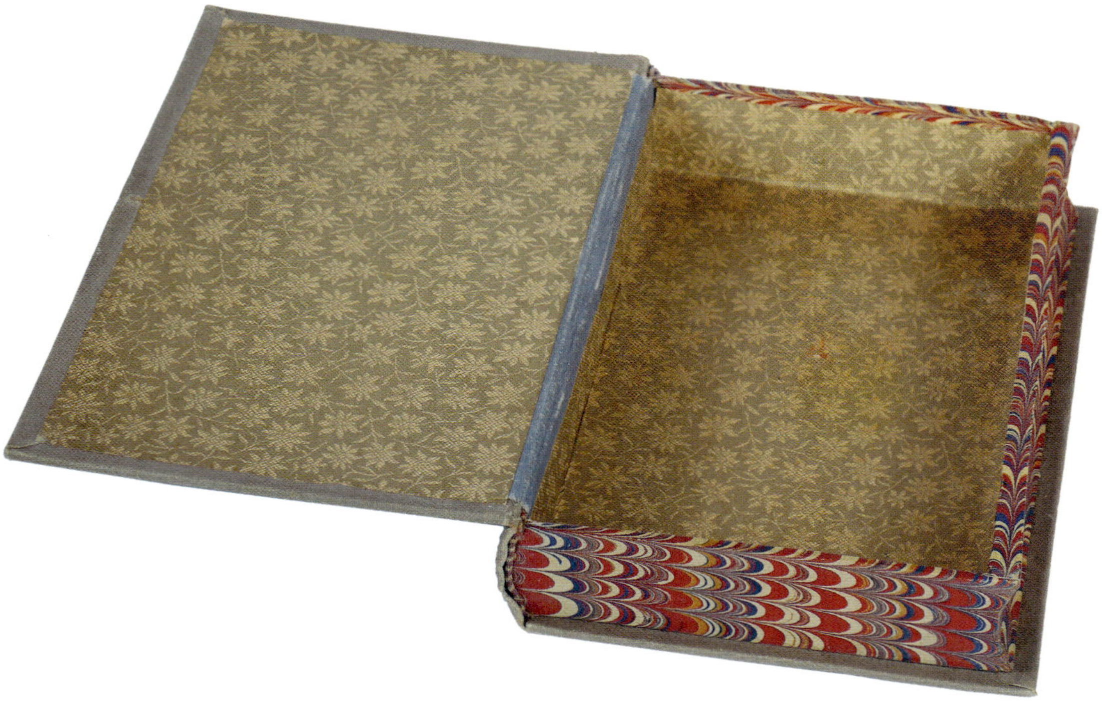

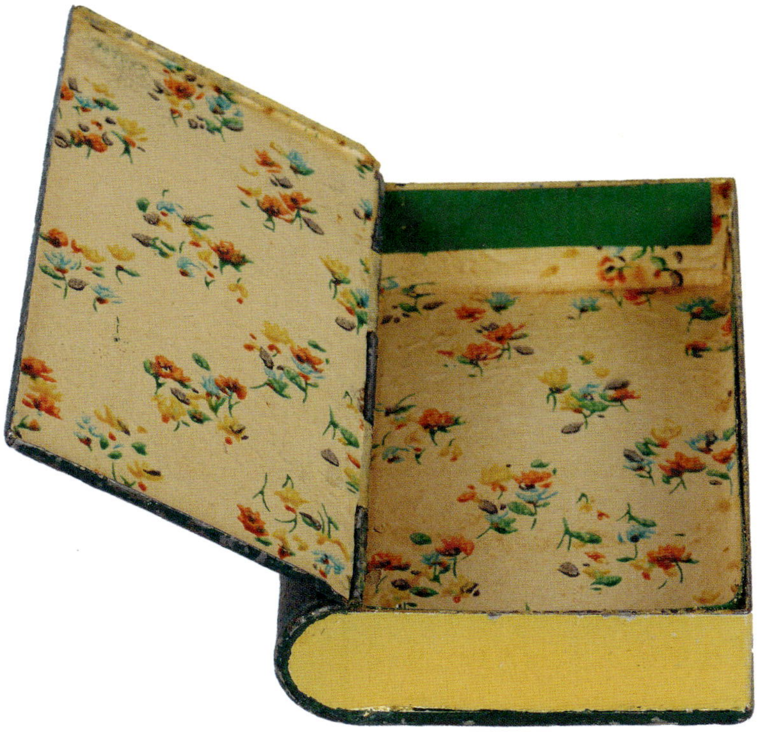

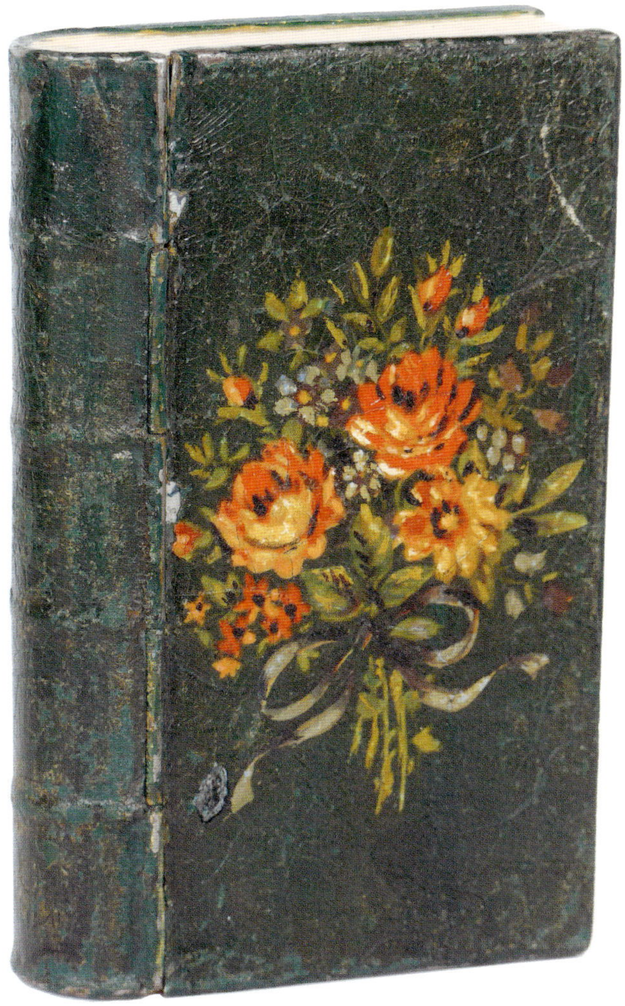

5.142
Metalldose mit Blumendekor farbig bemalt, ausgefüttert mit Buntpapier, dreiseitiger Goldschnitt
Metal box with painted flowers in color, lined with colored paper, all edges gilt
2,5 x 12,8 x 8,3 cm

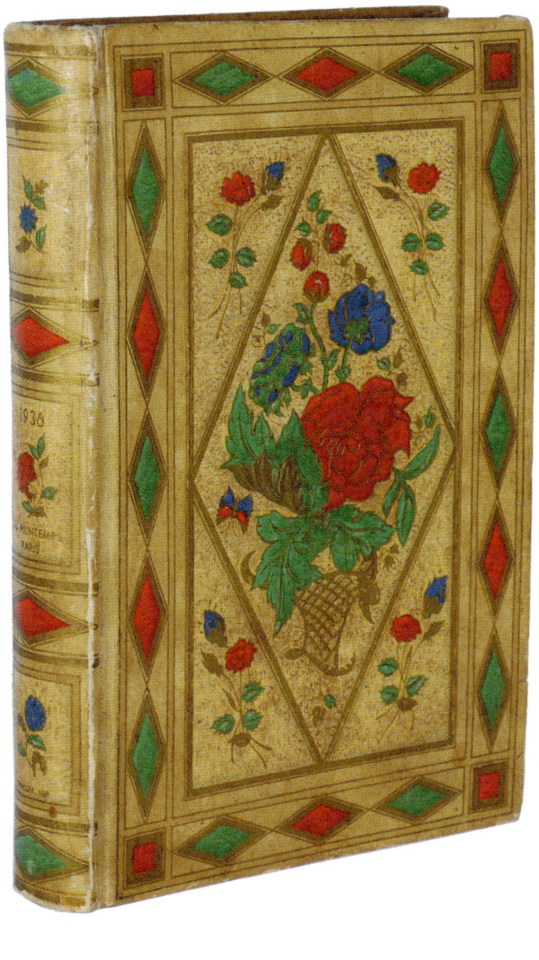

5.143
Au Printemps Paris, 1936, Draeger IMP
Farbig geprägter Pappband mit Blumendekor, Buchschnitt und ausgefüttert mit lithografiertem Buntpapier
Color embossed cardboard volume with floral decor, edging and lining made of lithographed colored paper
2,8 x 21 x 14,9 cm

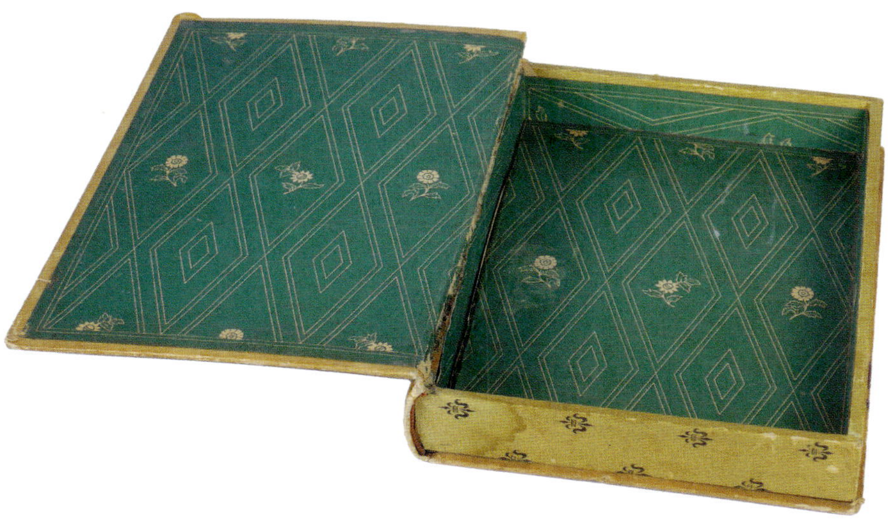

5.144
Klassisches Vergissmeinnicht
Traditional forget-me-not
Kaliko-Einband farbig geprägt, Schließe, geprägter Goldschnitt
Color embossed calico binding, buckle, gold-tooled edges
Jugendstil / *Art Nouveau*
9,3 x 7 x 1,7 cm

5.145
Damenkalender / *Ladies Calendar*
Gewebeschachtel mit Gold- und Farbprägung, dreiseitiger Buntpapierschnitt
Woven box with gold tooling and color embossing, all edges of colored paper
12,5 x 9 x 2,4 cm

5.146
Album
Kaliko-Buchschachtel mit Reliefprägung für Fotografien, ausgefüttert mit Moirépapier, dreiseitig geprägter Goldschnitt, Messingschließe
Calico box with relief embossing for photos, lined with moiré paper, gold-tooled edges, brass clasp
S.P. Christmann, Kunstverlag / *Art Publishing House,* Berlin, Deutschland / *Germany*
Um / *Around* 1900 | 2,4 x 12,4 x 9,3 cm

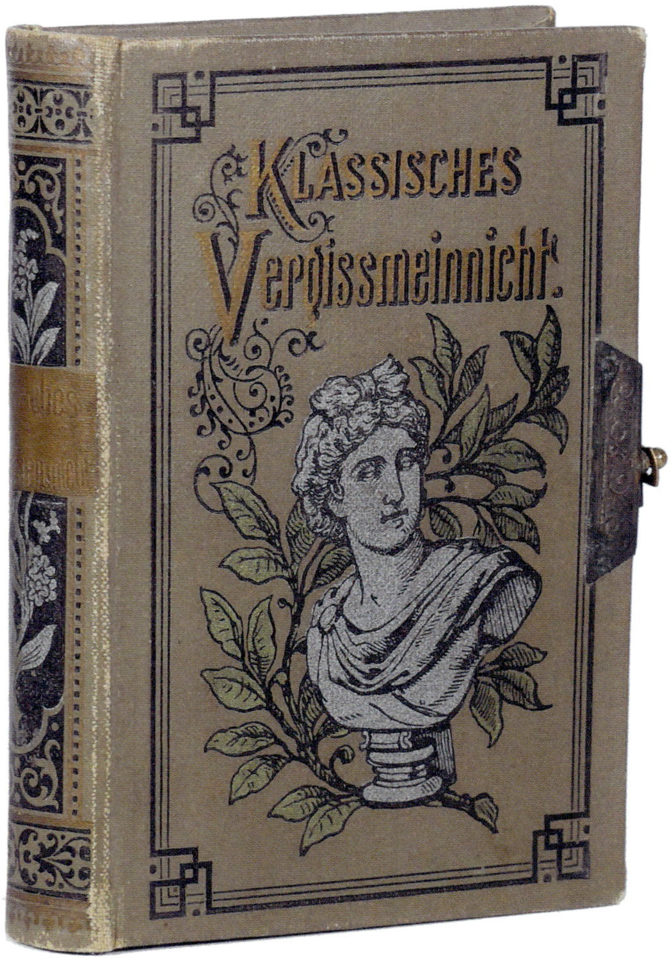

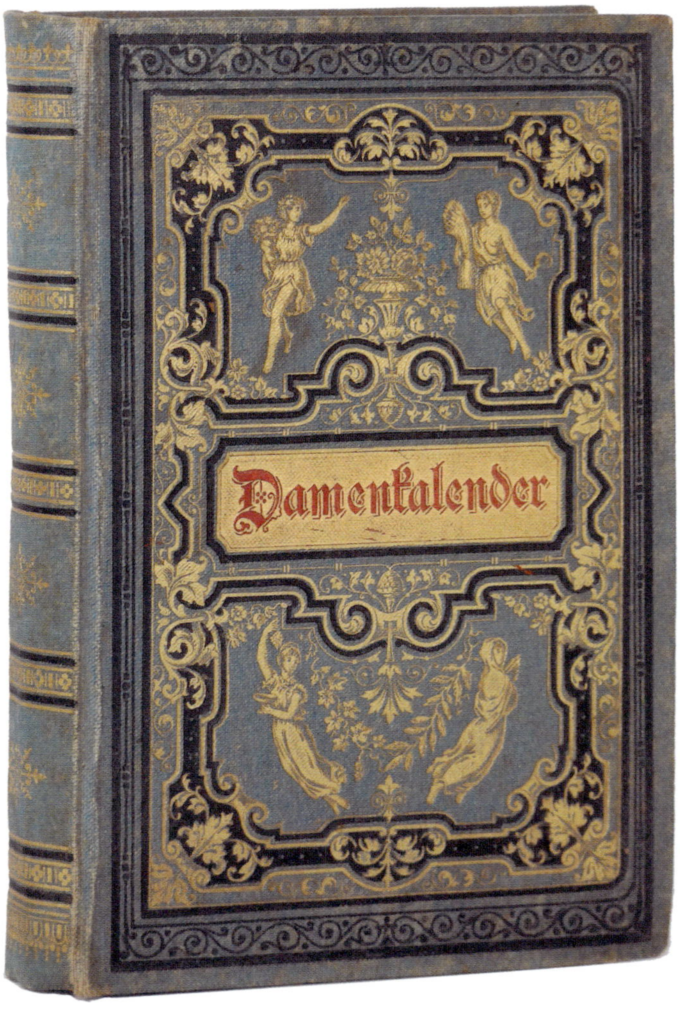

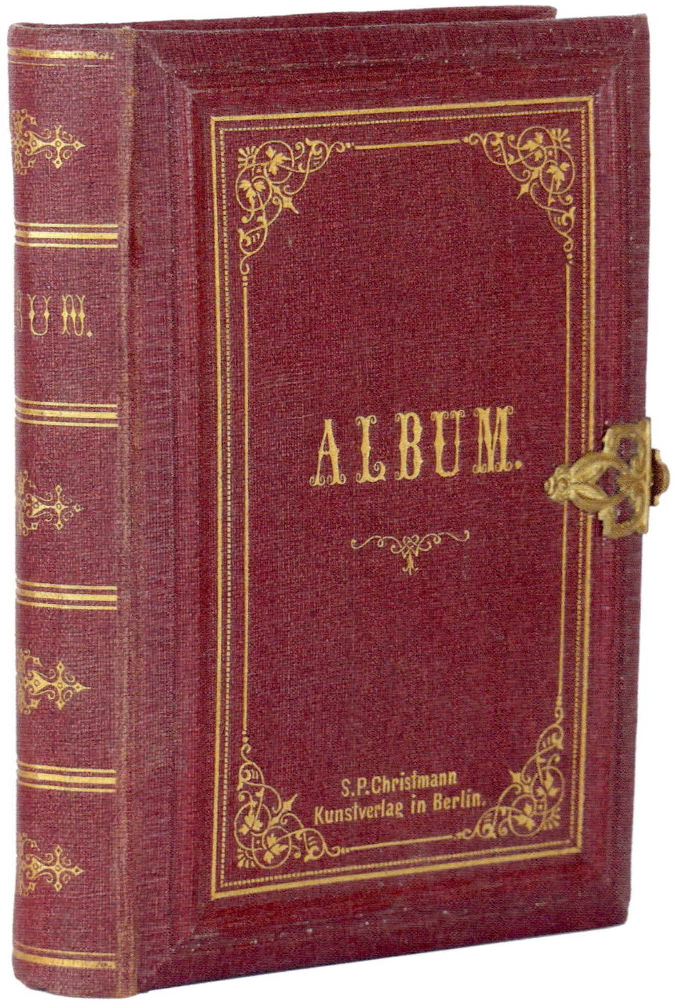

5.147
Kartondöschen mit farbiger und goldener Prägung, Blumenmotiv, dreiseitig geprägter Goldschnitt, ausgefüttert mit gelbem Glanzpapier
Cardboard box with color and gold tooling, flower illustration, gold-tooled edges, lined with yellow glossy paper
19. Jh. / *19th century* | 7,3 x 5,6 x 1,4 cm

5.148
Das Geld aller Völker, Herausgegeben von Commissionsrath Adolf Henze
The Money of All Nations, published by Commissioner Adolf Henze
Goldgeprägter Kaliko-Einband mit Schließe, dreiseitiger Pfauenmarmorpapierschnitt, ausgefüttert mit lithografiertem Buntpapier
Gold embossed calico binding with buckle, peacock marbled paper edges, lined with lithographed color paper
Leipzig, Deutschland / *Germany*
Um / *Around* 1900 | 28,5 x 20,4 x 3 cm

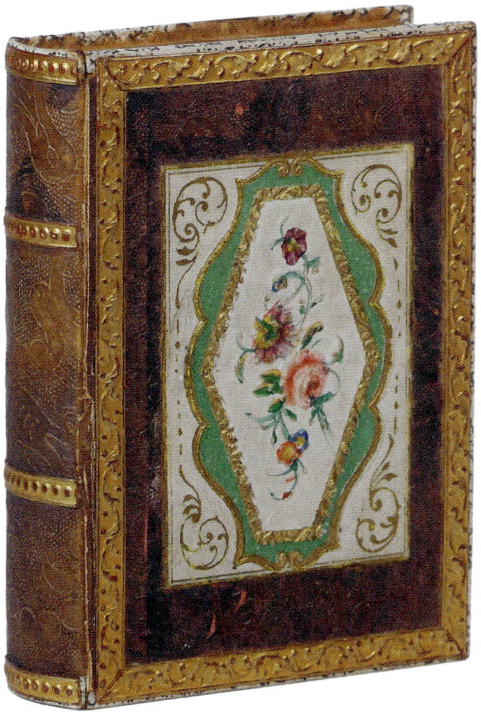

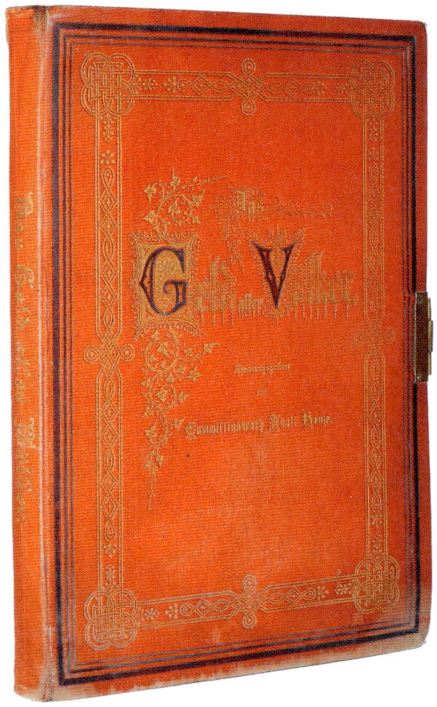

5.149
Odds & Ends, Germany
Lederschatulle mit goldgeprägtem Rücken- und Vorderdeckel, ovales Sichtfenster mit Gobelinstickerei, dreiseitiger Goldschnitt
Leather box with gold-tooling on the rear and front covers, oval display with Gobelin embroidery, all edges gilt
9,7 x 9,7 x 3,5 cm

5.150
En Souvenir du Baptème de Jean-Pierre, 19. Oktober 1929. Le Manoir de Brüssous Forges
Lackschachtel mit Schublade am Rücken, Häuserszene auf Vorder- und Rückdeckel, zwei Fächer, ausgefüttert mit Moirépapier, dreiseitiger Marmorschnitt
Varnished box with drawer at the spine, illustration of a house on the front and back covesr, two compartments, lined with moiré paper, marbled edges
3,6 x 17,9 x 16,5 cm

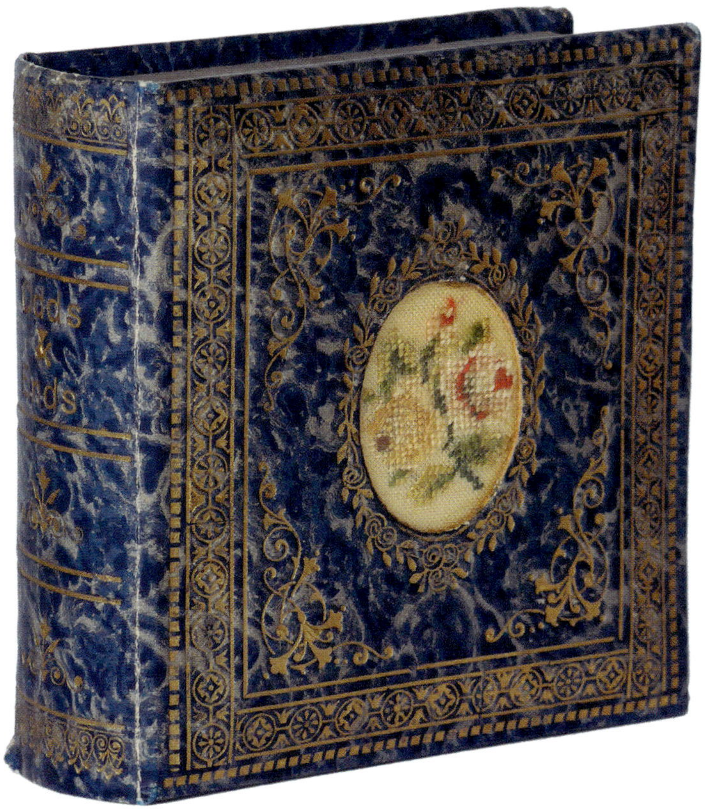

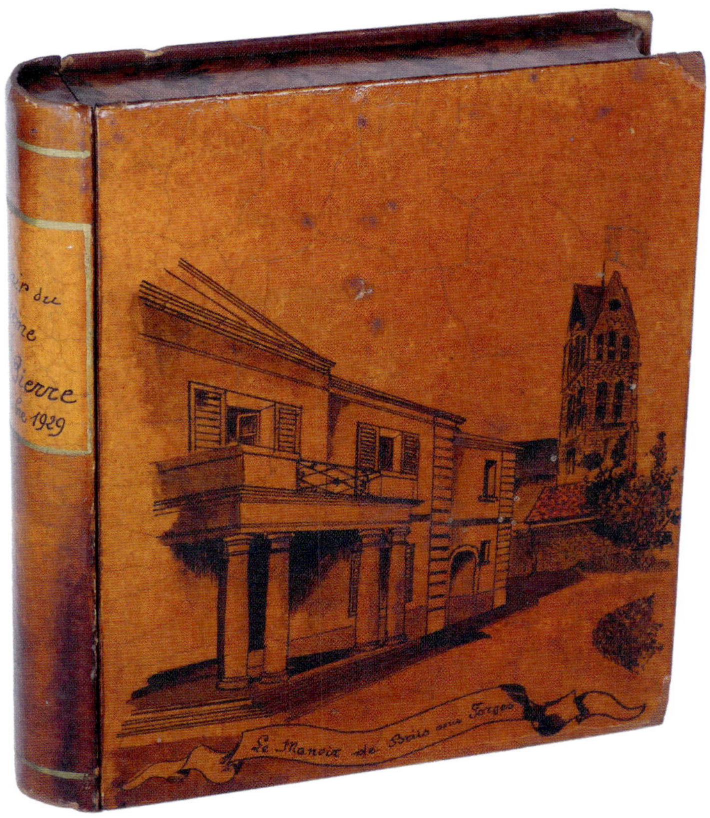

5.151
Europäische Wanderbilder 1
European migratory images 1
Saffian-Lederschatulle für Fotos im Stil eines Lyonesereinbandes, Lederauflagen, Rücken- und Deckelschilder, Handvergoldung, Futter weißes Moirépapier, Buchschnitt mit silbernen Walzendruckpapier
Box in Saffian leather for photos in the style of a Lyonese book cover, leather overlays, labels on the spine and cover, manual gilding, white moiré paper lining, edges in silver roller printed paper
4,3 x 20,7 x 15,4 cm

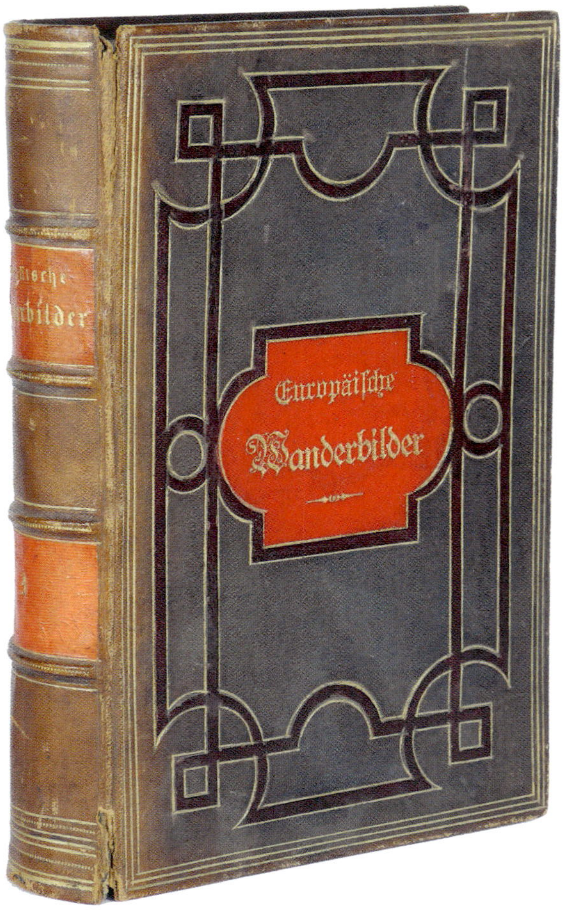

5.152
Traité de droit civil, Des obligations I
Saffian-Einbanddecke in Halbleder mit Holzkern, Titelprägung, Gustavmarmorpapierüberzug, Futter Steinmarmorpapier
Half leather Saffian binding with wooden core, stamped titel, "Gustav" marbled over-paperboard, stone marbeled paper lining
4,5 x 22,1 x 15 cm

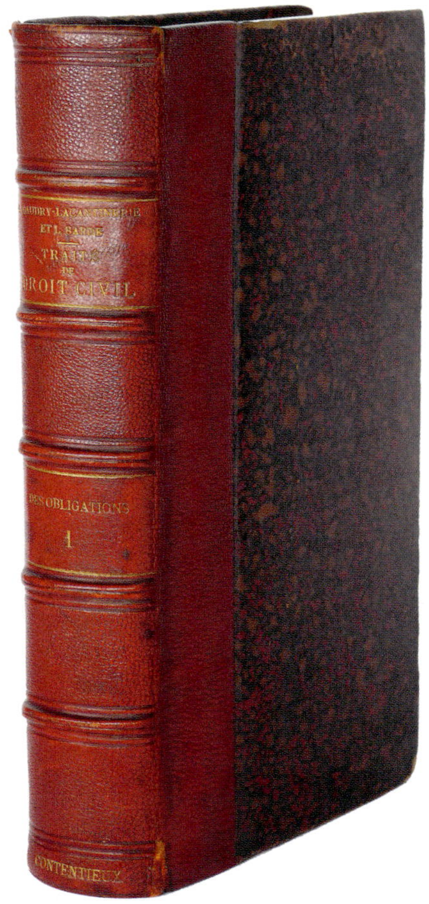

5.153
Kartondose mit französischem Fantasie- Marmorpapierüberzug, dreiseitiger Goldschnitt, ausgefüttert mit Holzmodeldruckpapier
Cardboard box with French marbled paper cover, all edges gilt, lined with printed faux wood paper
Ende 19. Jh. / *End of the 19th century*
2,3 x 10,3 x 7,7 cm

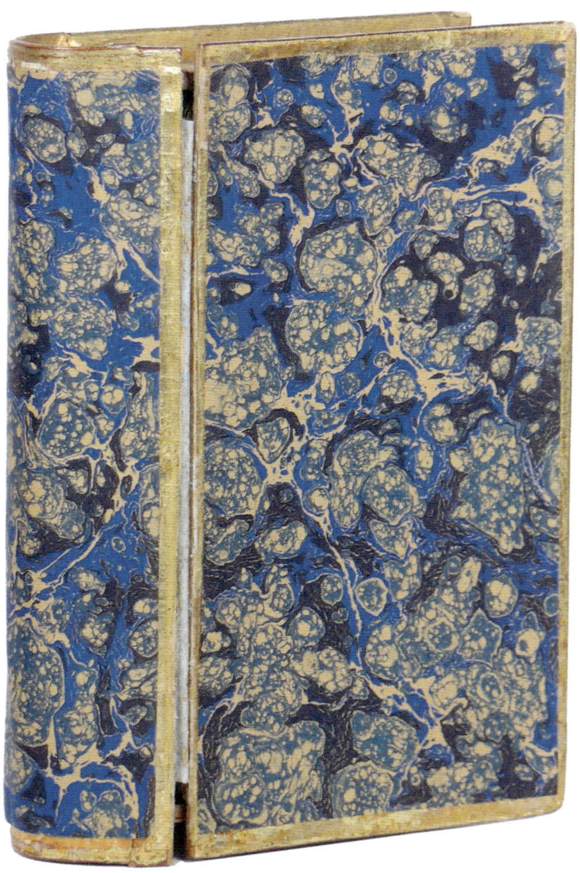

5.154
Memoires des videgoussets
Ganzledereinbanddecke mit Holzschachtel, Rücken- und Deckelvergoldung, Spiegel und Buchschnitt mit Schneckenmarmorpapier
Full leather binding with wooden box, gilding on the spine and lid, scroll marbled pastedown and edges
5 x 19,5 x 12,2 cm

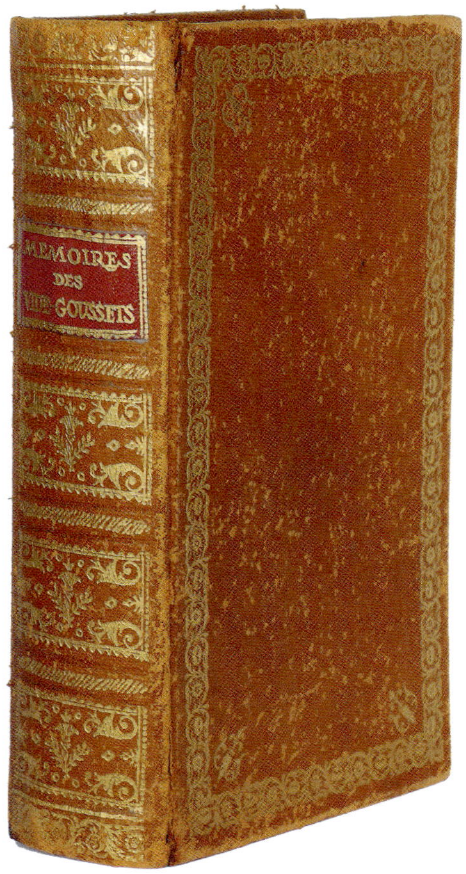

5.155
Memoires des Vide-Goussets
Kalbslederschatulle mit Rücken- und Deckelvergoldung, Titelschild, dreiseitiger Lederschnitt, Lederspiegel
Calf leather box with gilt spine and cover, label, leather edges, leather pastedown
5 x 19,7 x 12,3 cm

5.156
My Books, Rodrigues 42 Piccadilly, London Where is it, Engagements, Journal, Cash Book
Lederkästchen mit Vergoldung, abschließbar, vier Lederbände mit dreiseitigem Goldschnitt und Rahmenvergoldung
Small leather box with gilding, lockable, four volumes in leather with all edges gilt
11,3 x 8,1 x 4,3 cm

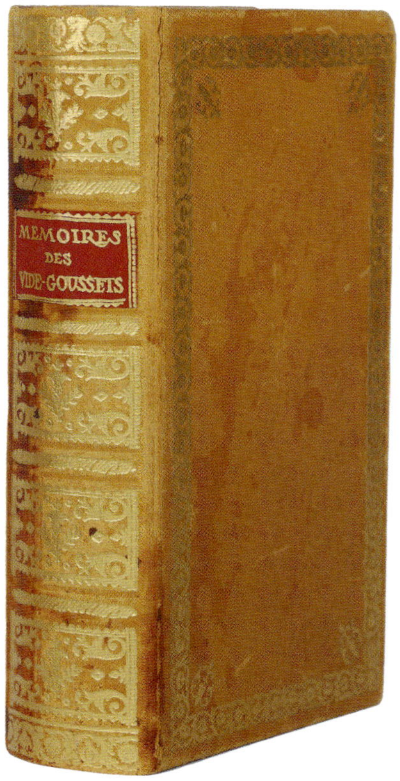

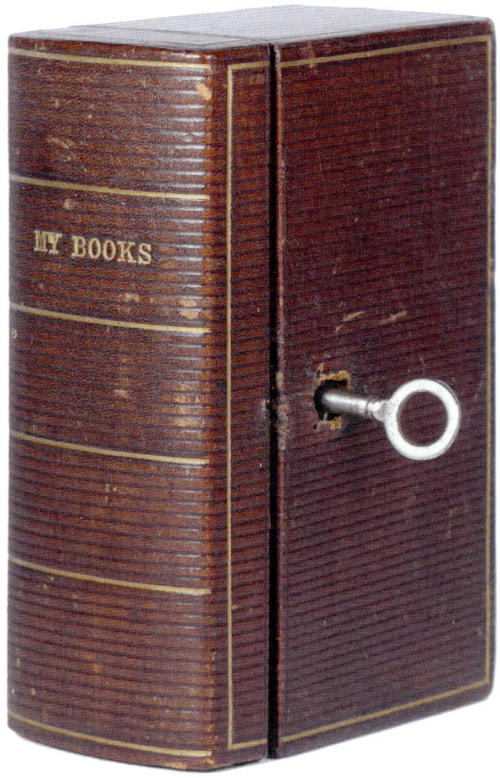

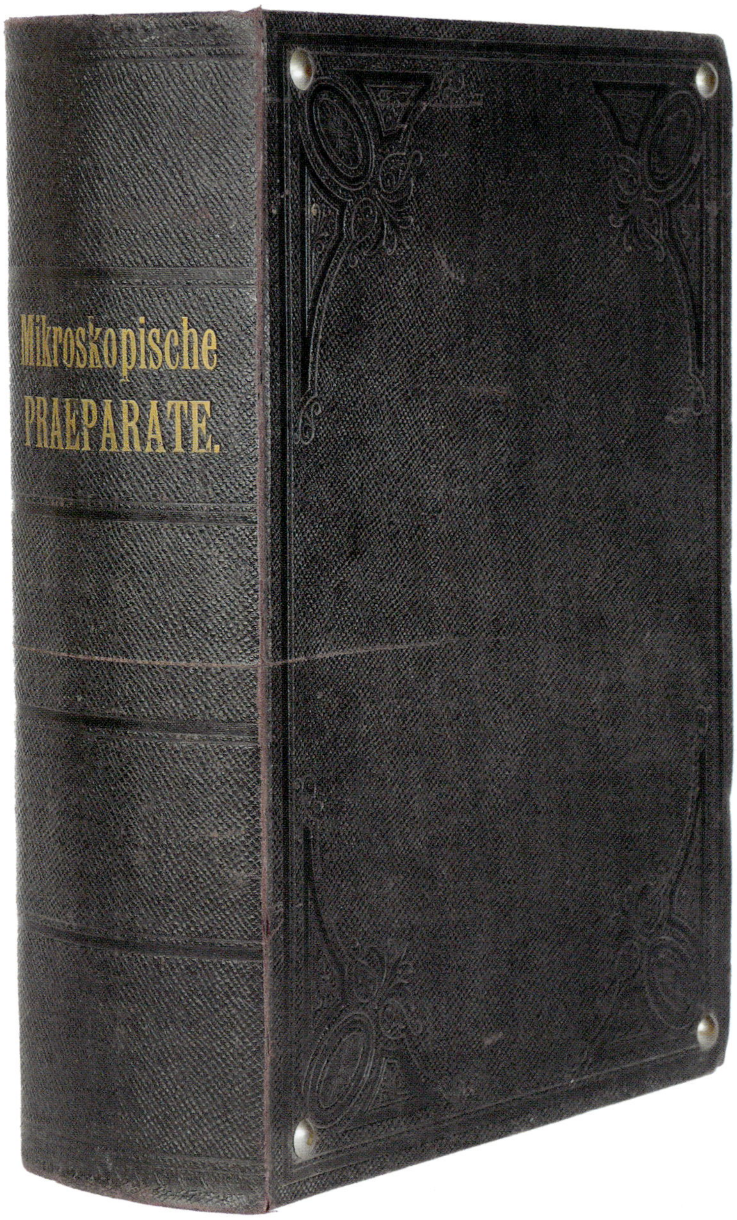

5.157
Mikroskopische Praeparate
Microscopic Preparations
Kaliko-Buchschachtel mit zwei Abteilungen, nummerierte Zahnleisten, Gold- und Blindprägung, Kammmarmorschnitt, Futter schwarzes Spitzkaro geprägtes Papier
Calico book box with two compartments, numbered dental ridges, gold and blind tooling, comb marbled edges, lining black checkered paper
E. Leitz, Berlin N.W., Deutschland / *Germany* | Jugendstil / *Art Nouveau*
7,6 x 27,9 x 21, 2 cm

5.158
Wattierter Kalbsledereinband mit Rücken- und Deckelvergoldung, oberes Buch mit Scharnieröffnung, Holzschachtel mit Hals, dreiseitiger Farbschnitt, Stoffboden
Padded calfskin binding with gilt spine and cover, upper book with hinged opening, wooden box with neck, all edges in color, bottom in fabric
4,6 x 10,5 x 10,1 cm

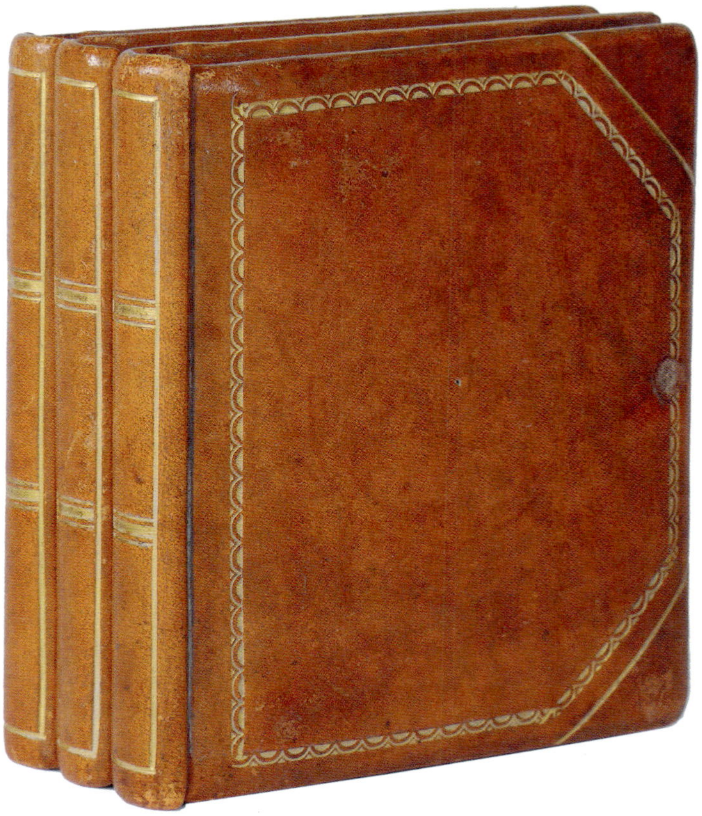

5.159
Lose Blätter / ***Loose sheets***
Saffian-Lederschatulle für lose Blätter im Stil eines Lyoneser Einbandes, geprägtes verschlungenes Bandwerk, Rücken- und Deckelvergoldung, dreiseitiger Buchschnitt mit lithografiertem Buntpapier, Zugbänder
Box in Saffian leather for photos in the style of a Lyonese book cover, gilding on the spine and cover, all edges made of lithogaphed paper, drawstrings
3 x 22,3 x 16,2 cm

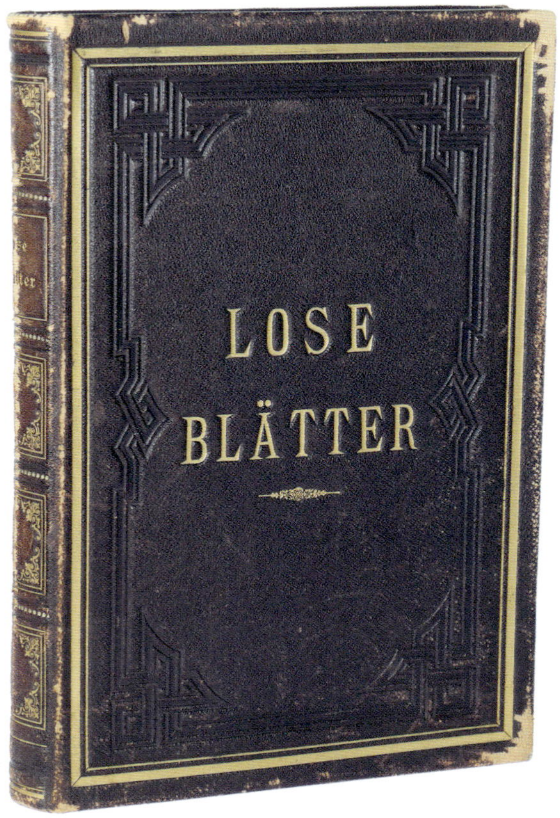

5.160
Lourdes
Schweinslederdose für Raucherwaren, Gold- und Blindprägung, genähte Deckelkante, ausgefüttert mit Spaltleder, dreiseitiger Messingschnitt
Pigskin leather box for smoking goods, gold and blind embossing, sewn cover, lined with split leather, brass edges
3,2 x 10,8 x 9,1 cm

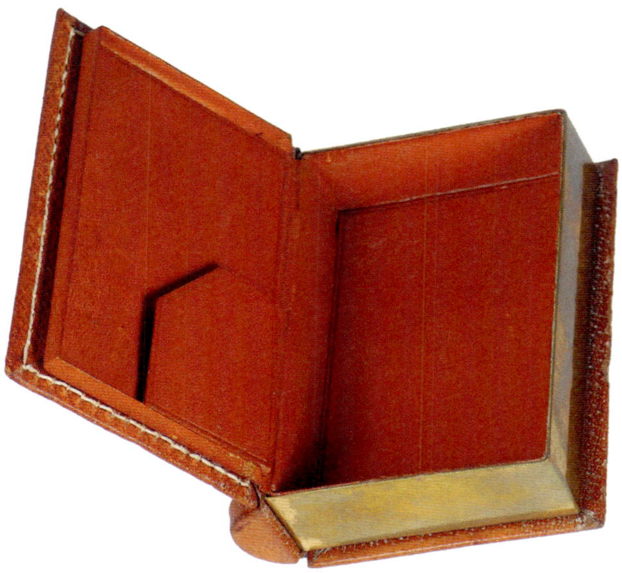

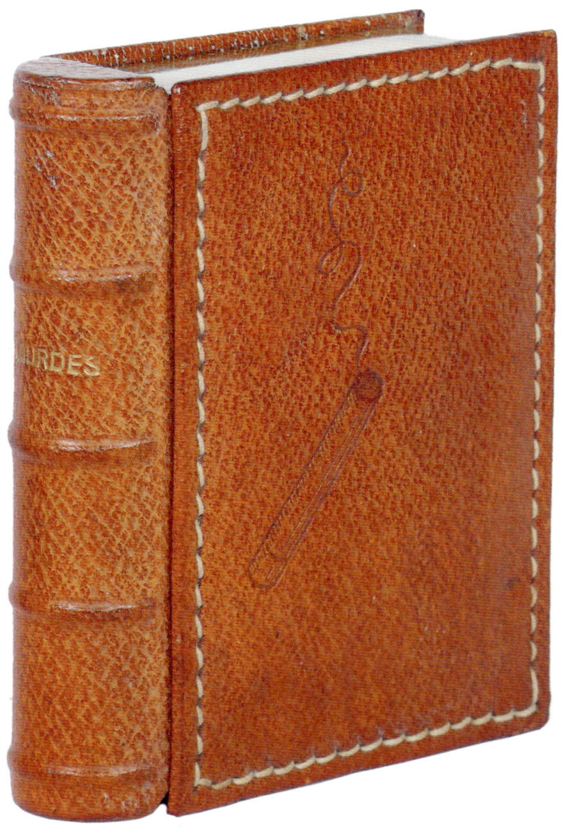

5.161
Reliefgeprägte Lederschatulle mit Amoretten-Szene, Kanten mit Lederriemchen umflochten, ausgefüttert mit Moiréseide, dreiseitiger Goldschnitt
Embossed leather box with cupid theme, edges braided with leather straps, lined with moiré silk, all edges gilt
3,3 x 13,9 x 10,5 cm

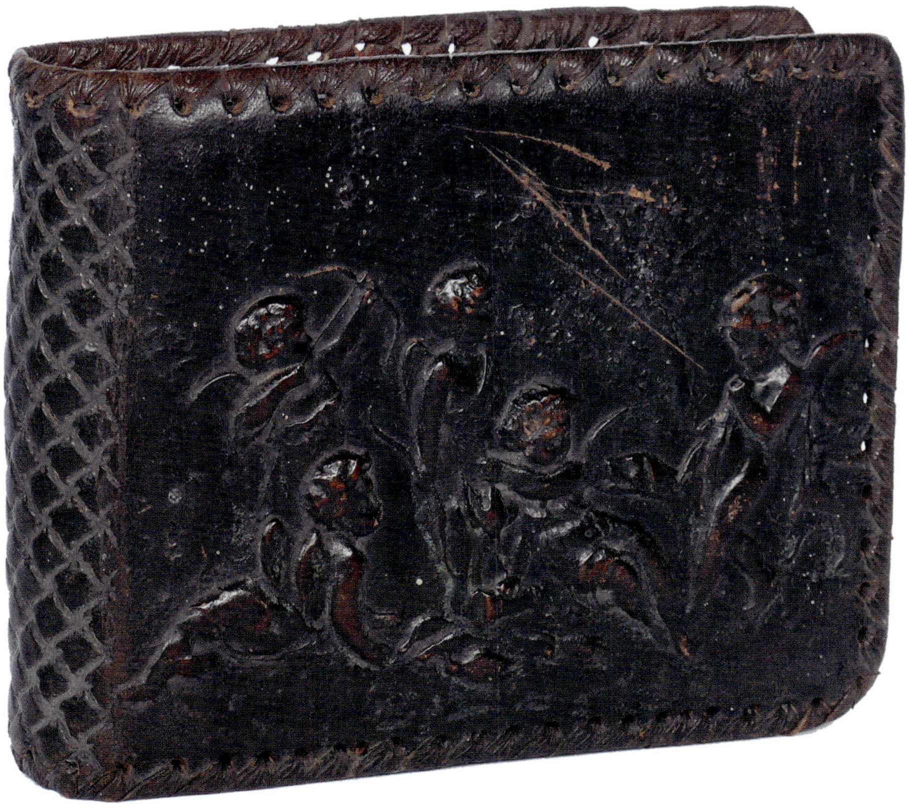

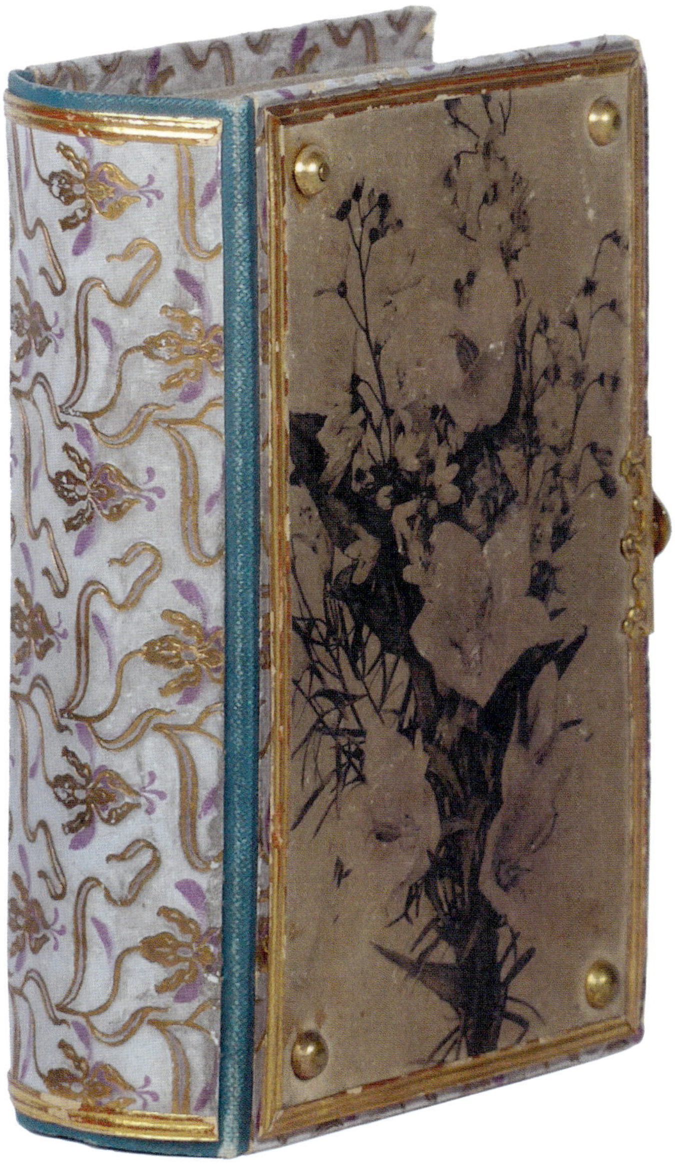

5.162
Kartondose mit Pflanzenmotiv auf dem Vorderdeckel, goldgeprägter Rücken und Rückdeckel, Messingschließe, dreiseitiger Goldschnitt, Futter weißes Moiré- und Glanzpapier
Cardboard box with vegetal ornament on the lid, gold-tooled spine and back cover, brass buckle, all edges gilt, white moiré and glossy paper lining
Ende 19. Jh. / *End oft he 19th century*
3,2 x 10,5 x 7,5 cm

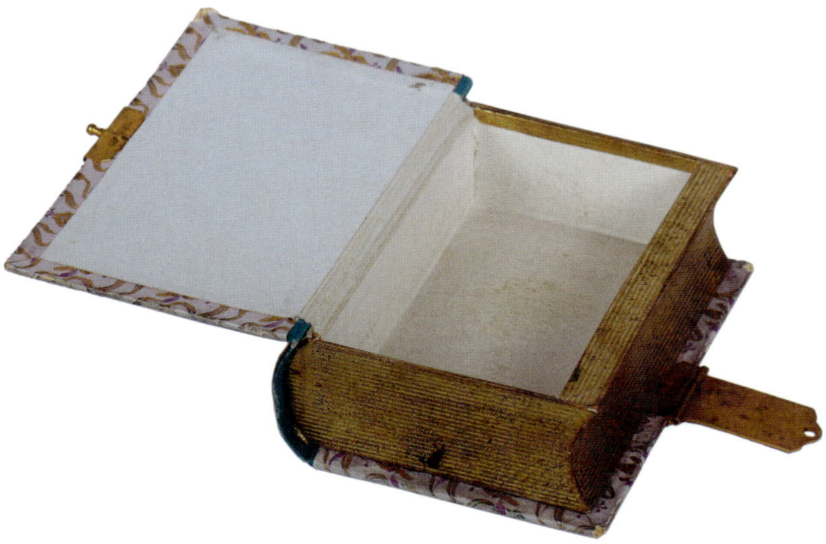

5.163
Plüsch-Schatulle. Prunk-Behältnis mit Beschlägen und Schließe, wattierte Deckel, dreiseitiger Goldschnitt, ausgefüttert mit grünem Steinmarmorpapier
Casket with plush cover. Splendid box with fittings and clasp, padded lid, all edges gilt, lined with green stone marbled paper
Um / *Around* 1900 | 28 x 21,5 x 7 cm

5.164
Tom XVII
Lederdose mit Handvergoldung, zwei erhabene Bünde, ausgefüttert mit Schneckenmarmorpapier, drei Fächer, Aufbewahrungsbehältnis für Siegelringabdrucke
Leather box with manual gilding,two raised bands, lined with marbled paper, three compartments, storage for signet ring imprints
1941–1976, Hans Trautweiler Goldsmith
Basel, Switzerland
3,3 x 4,6 x 10,5 cm

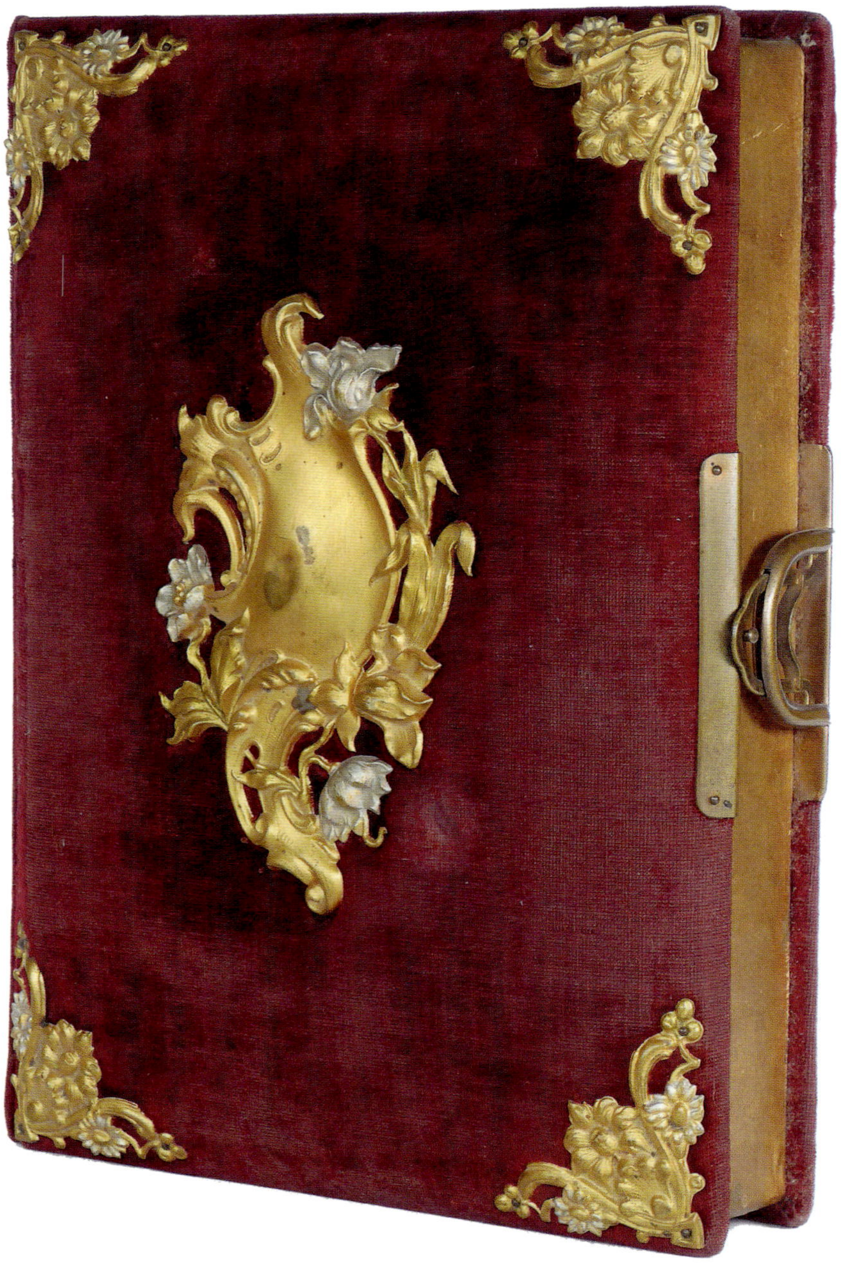

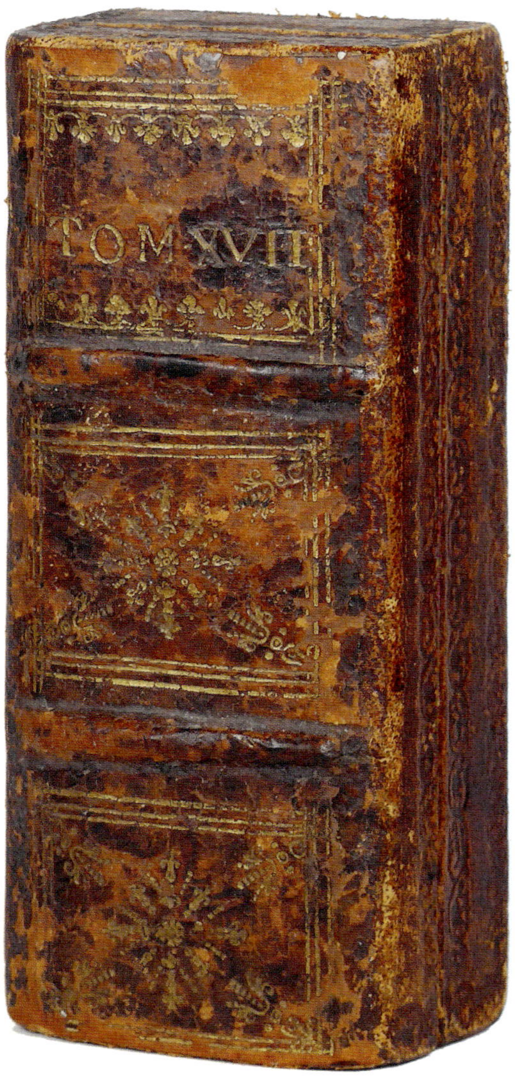

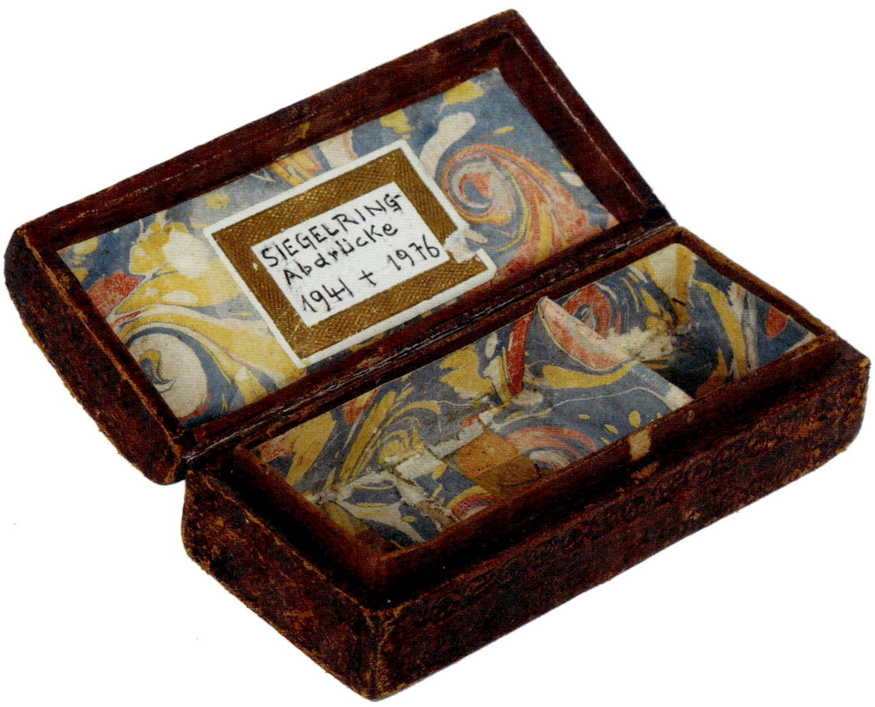

5.165

Souvenir

Gold- und farbgeprägtes Lederbändchen mit zwei Fächern und zwei Lederlaschen, dreiseitig geprägter Goldschnitt, Messingschließe, Verwendungszweck unklar

Gold-tooled and color embossed leather volume with two compartments and two leather straps, gold-tooled edges, brass buckle, use unclear

19. Jh. / *19th century* | 8 x 5 x 3,5 cm

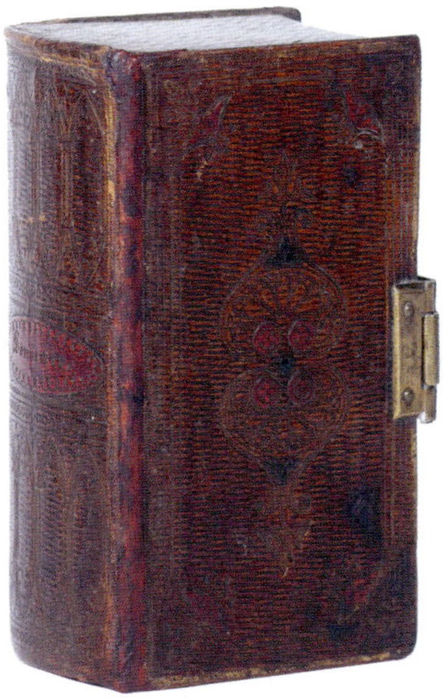

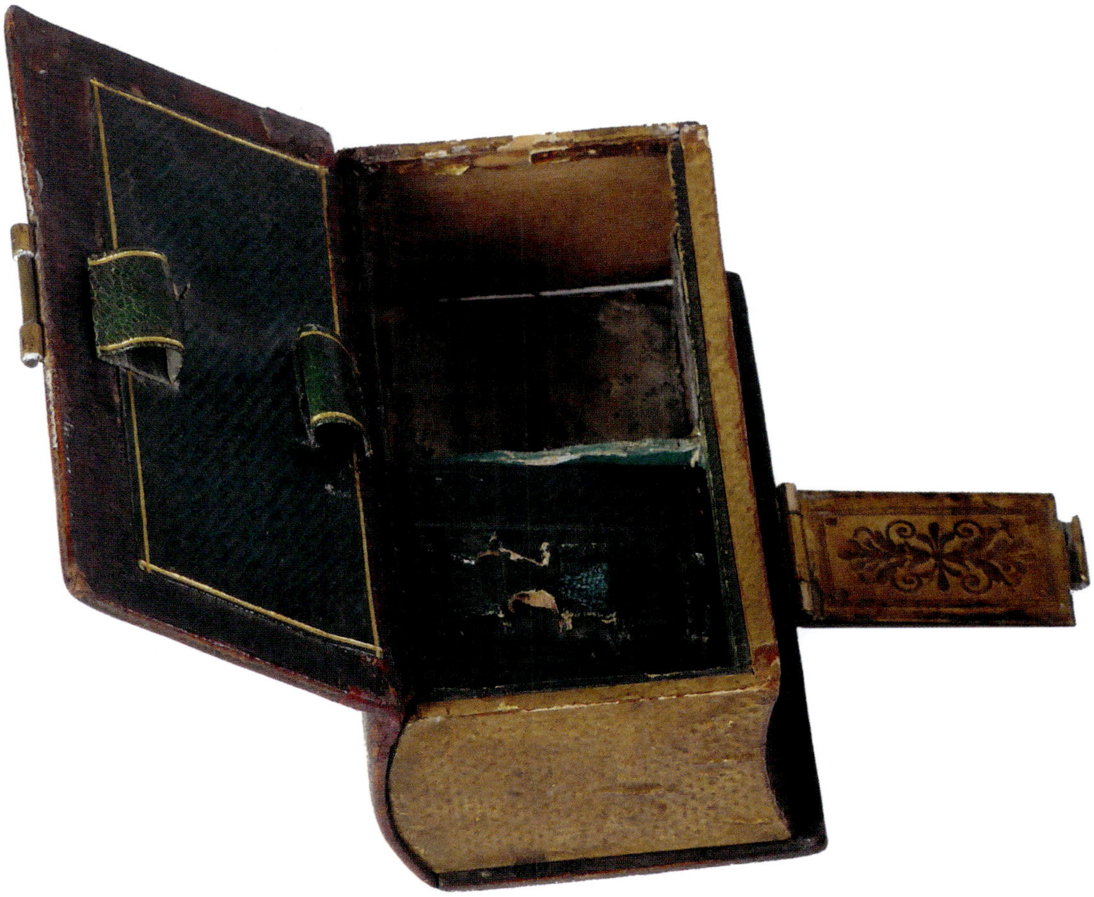

5.166

Plüschschatulle mit montierter Fotografie unter Plexiglas auf dem Vorderdeckel, ausgefüttert mit Kunstleder, zwei Messingecken, dreiseitiger Goldschnitt

Box coverd with plush and with a photography behind plexiglass on the lid, lined with imitation leather, two brass corners, all edges gilt

3,5 x 16 x 12,1 cm

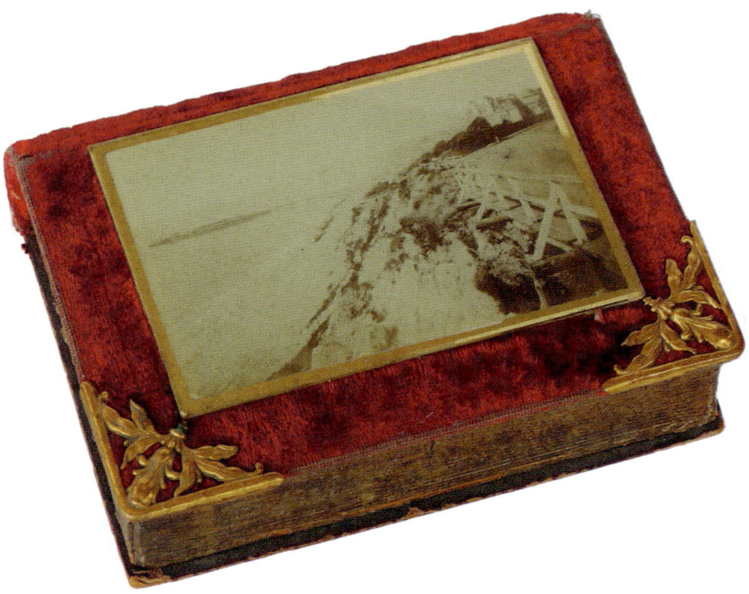

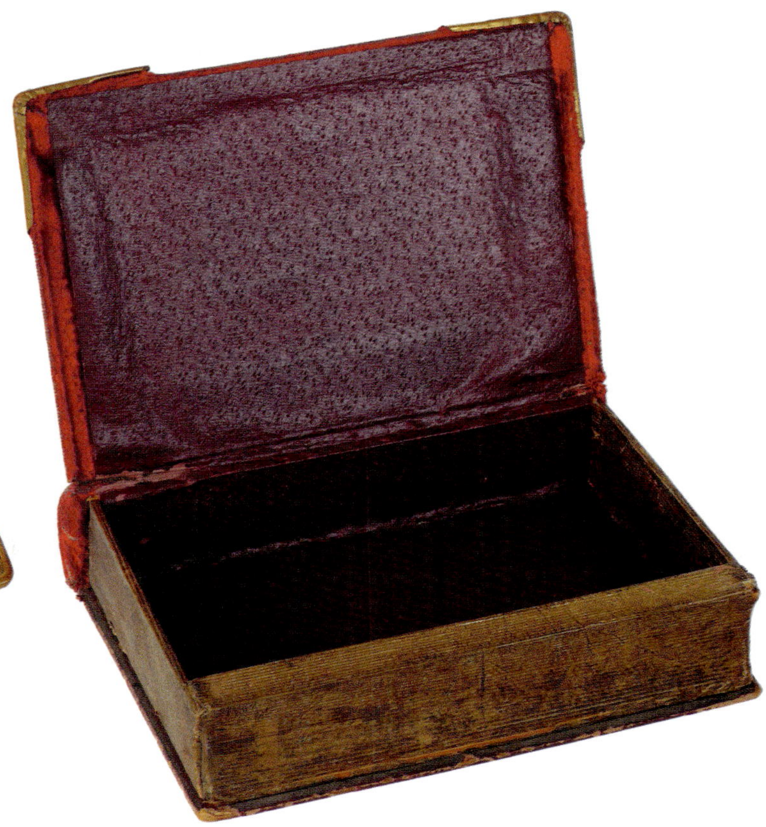

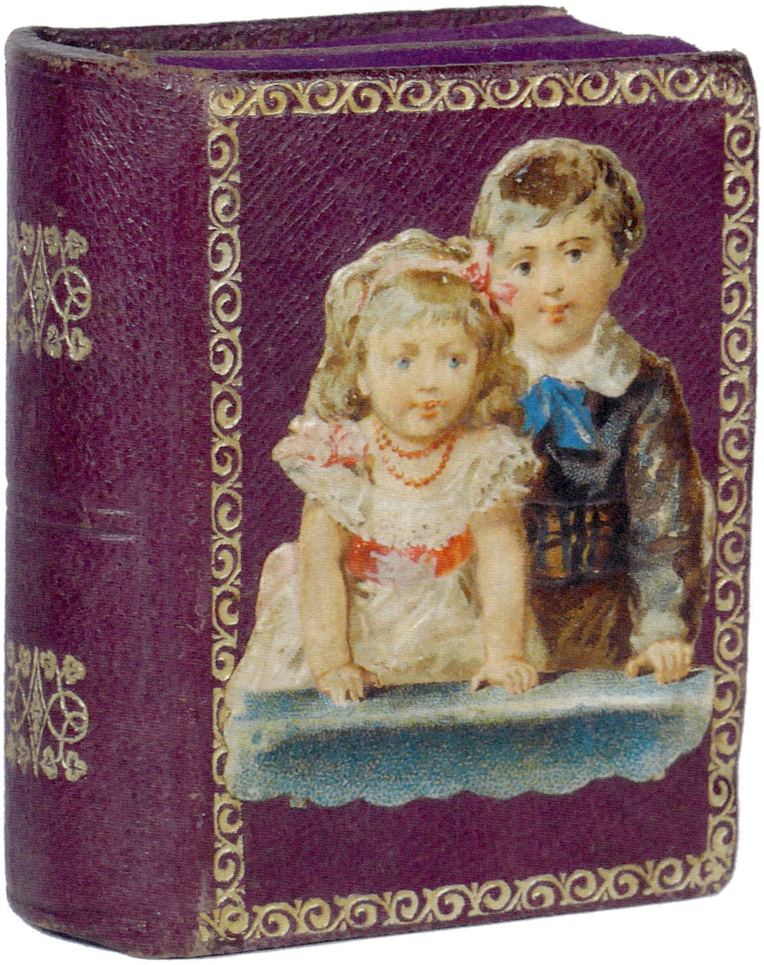

5.167
Ganzlederdöschen handvergoldet, aufgeklebtes geprägtes Kinderporträt, ausgefüttert mit Goldpapier und farbigem Buntpapier
Full leather box, manual gilding, embossed portrait of a child, lined with gold and colored paper
Registered May.12.1879
7,3 x 6,1 x 3 cm

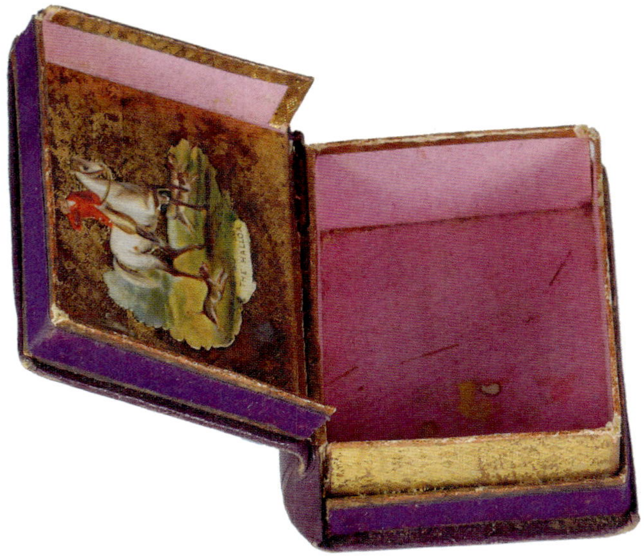

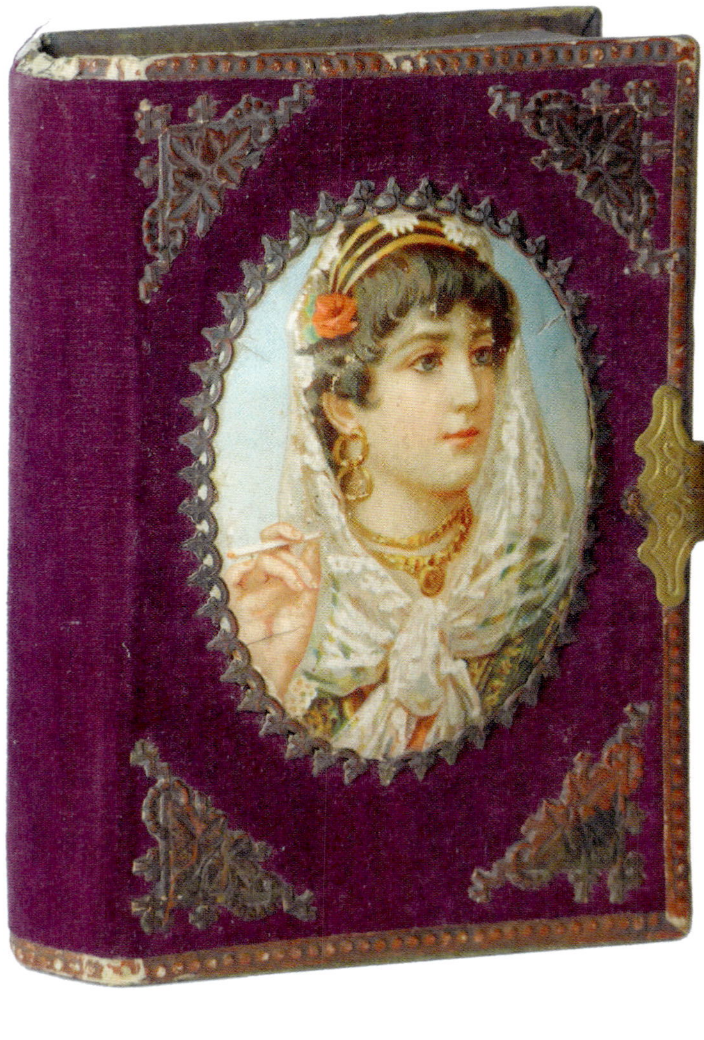

5.168
Samtschatulle mit ovalem erhabenem Damenporträt, Ecken- und Kantenverzierungen aus geprägtem Goldpapier, dreiseitig geprägter Goldschnitt, Messingschließe
Casket with velvet cover with an raised oval portrait of a lady, corners and edges decorated with embossed gold paper, gold-tooled edges, brass buckle
Spätes 19. Jh. / *Late 19th century*
11,3 x 8,7 x 3 cm

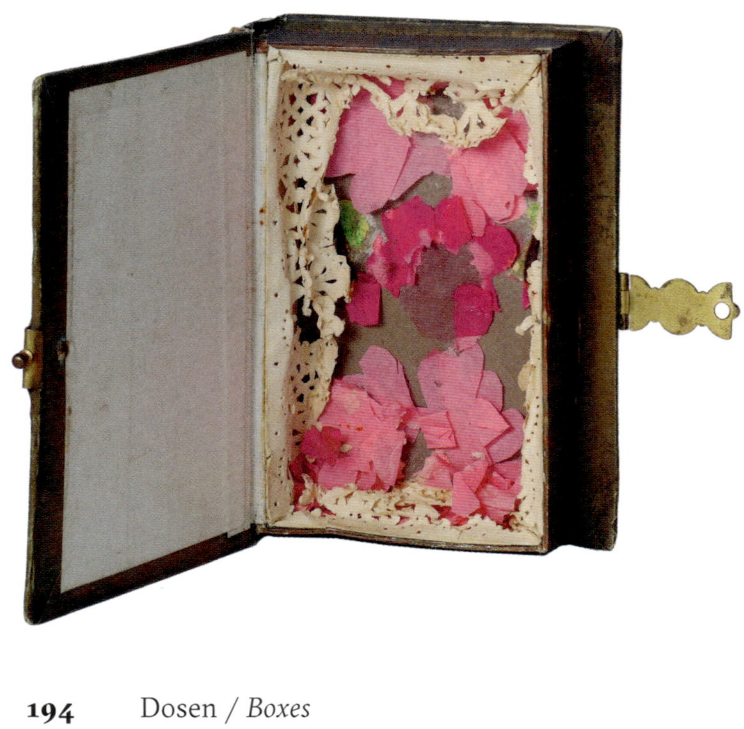

5.169
Herzlichen Glückwunsch zur Verlobung
Congratulations on the engagement
Plüschkassette mit Metallschließe, aufgeklebte Glückwunschkarte auf Vorderdeckel, dreiseitiger Farbschnitt, vier Messingstandfüße, ausgefüttert mit Silberpapier
Box covered with plush and with metal clasp, greeting card glued on the lid, colored edges, four brass feet, lined with silver paper
4,7 x 19,9 x 15 cm

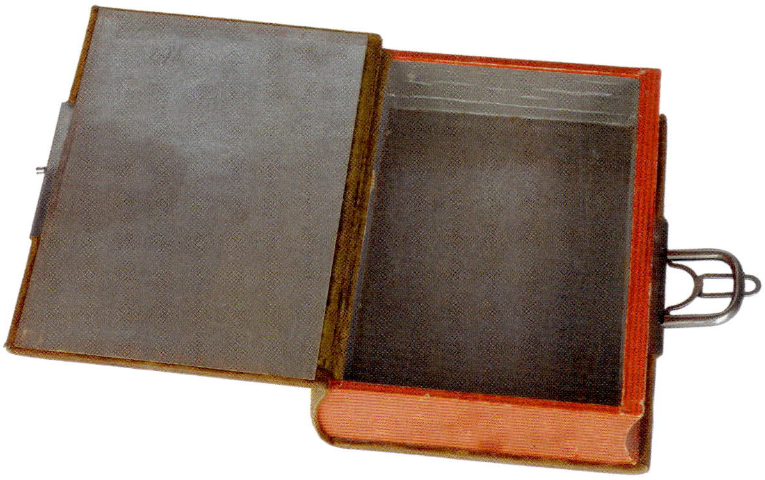

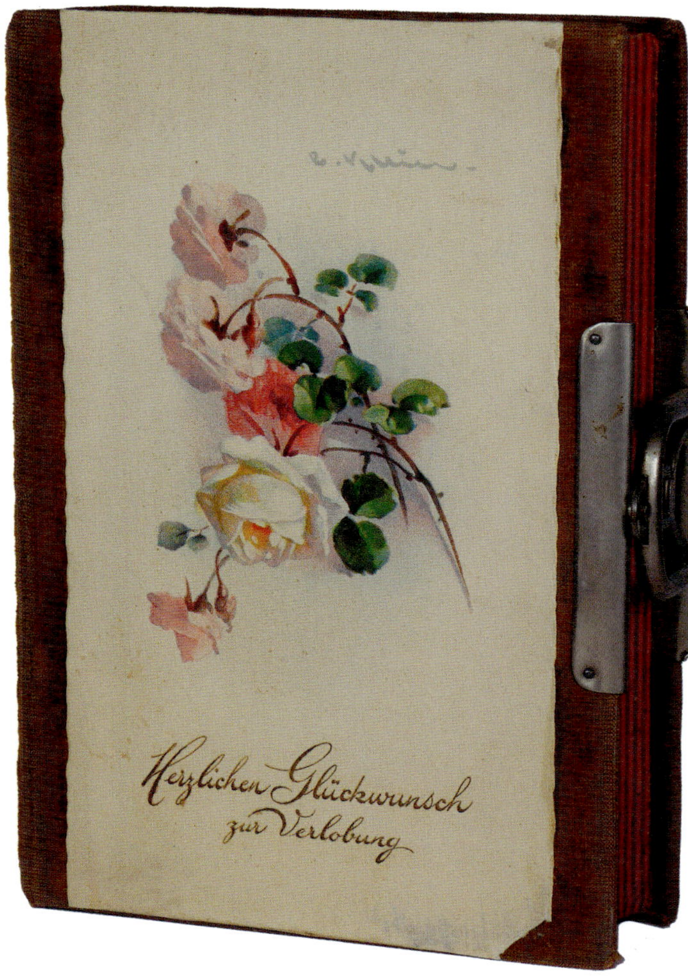

5.170
Kartondose mit geprägtem Papierüberzug, eingefasst mit Goldlitzen, eingeklebte Papierblume auf dem Innendeckel, dreiseitig geprägter Papierschnitt, Schmuckdöschen (?)
Cardboard box with embossed paper-overboard, edged with gold braids, a paper flower pasted on the inner lid, embossed paper edges, box for jewels (?)
Um / *Around* 1900 | 0,9 x 4 x 3,3 cm

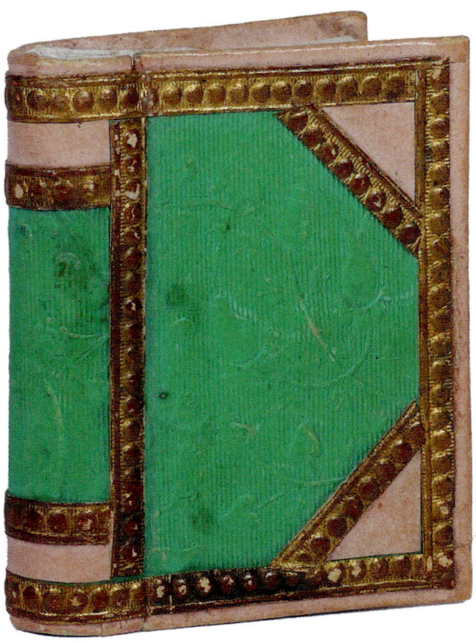

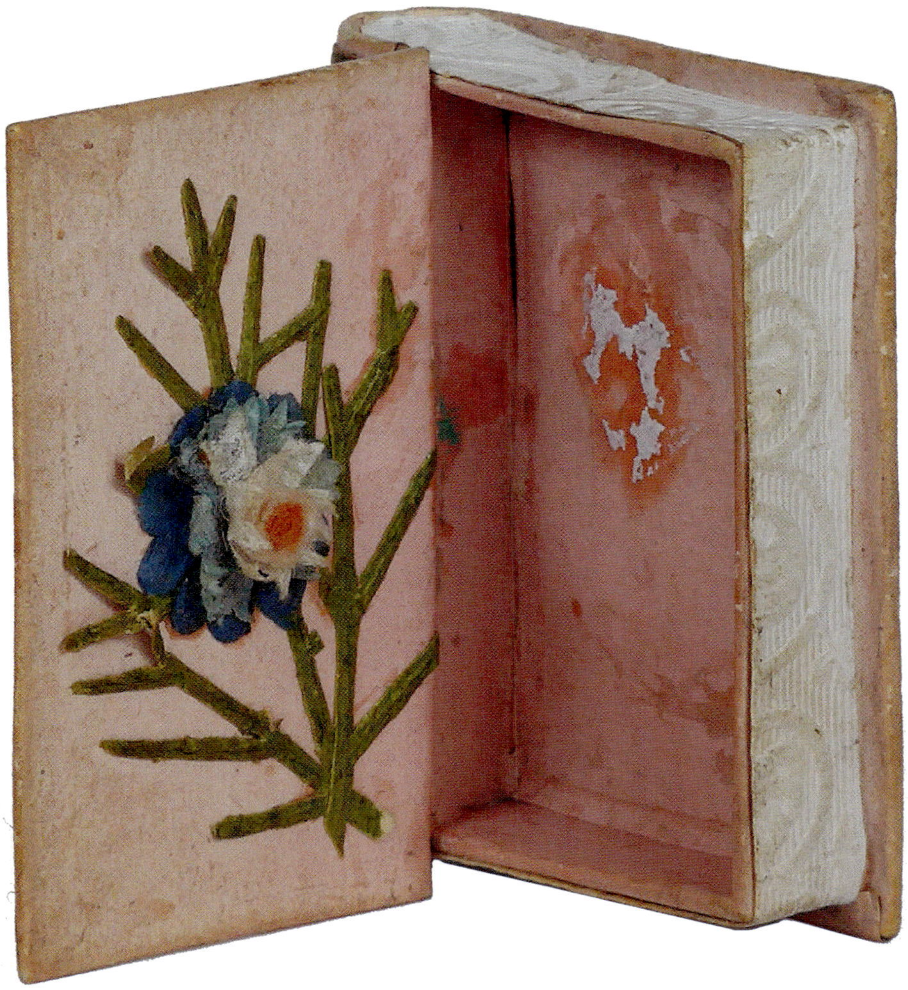

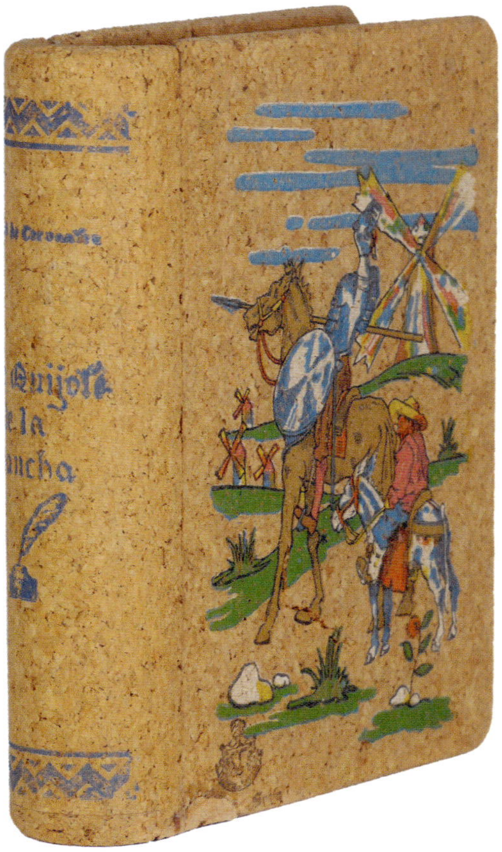

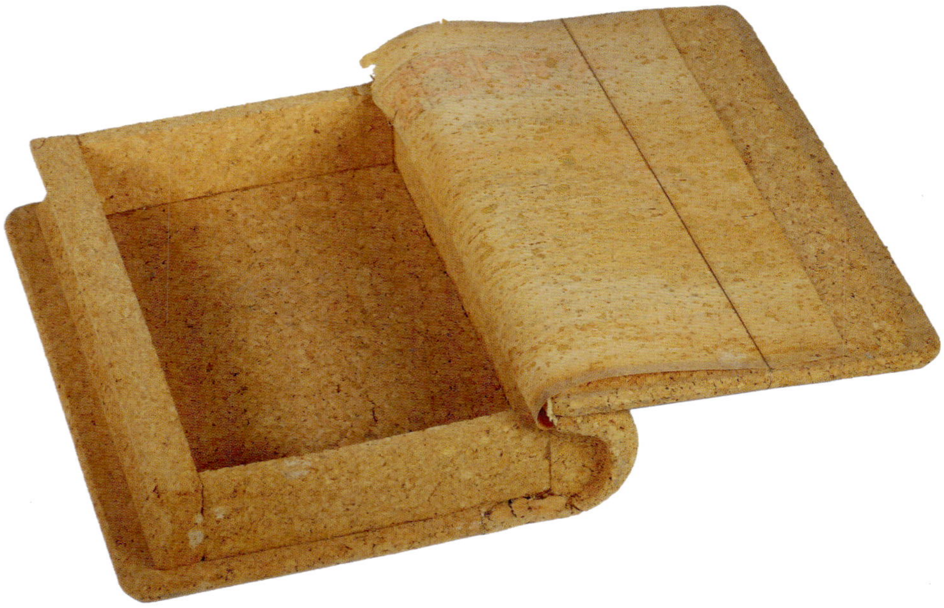

5.171
Miguel de Cervantes: Don Quijote de la Mancha
Korkbuch mit farbigem Aufdruck auf beiden Deckeln, ein Deckblatt aus Kork
Cork book with colored imprint on both covers, flyleaf made of cork
3,7 x 15,5 x 13,3 cm

5.172
Classic Winnie the Pooh, Gund
Verpackungsbuchschachtel für einen Teddybären der amerikanischen Firma Gund
Packaging box for a teddy bear by the American company Gund
21,3 x 15, 3 x 6,7 cm

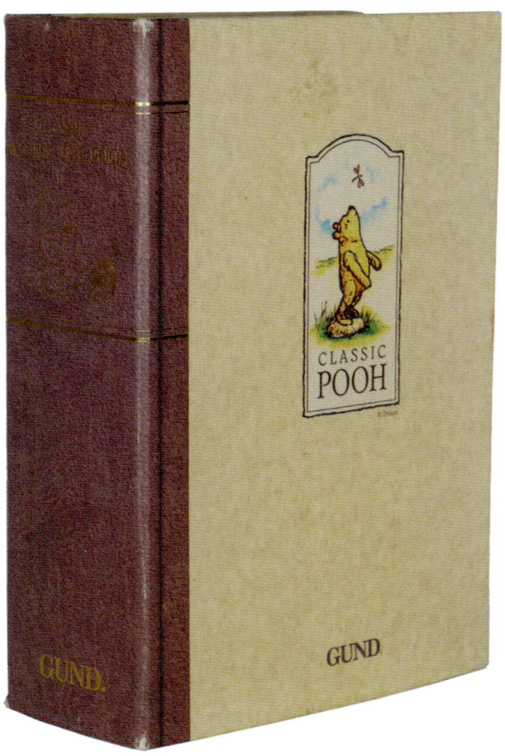

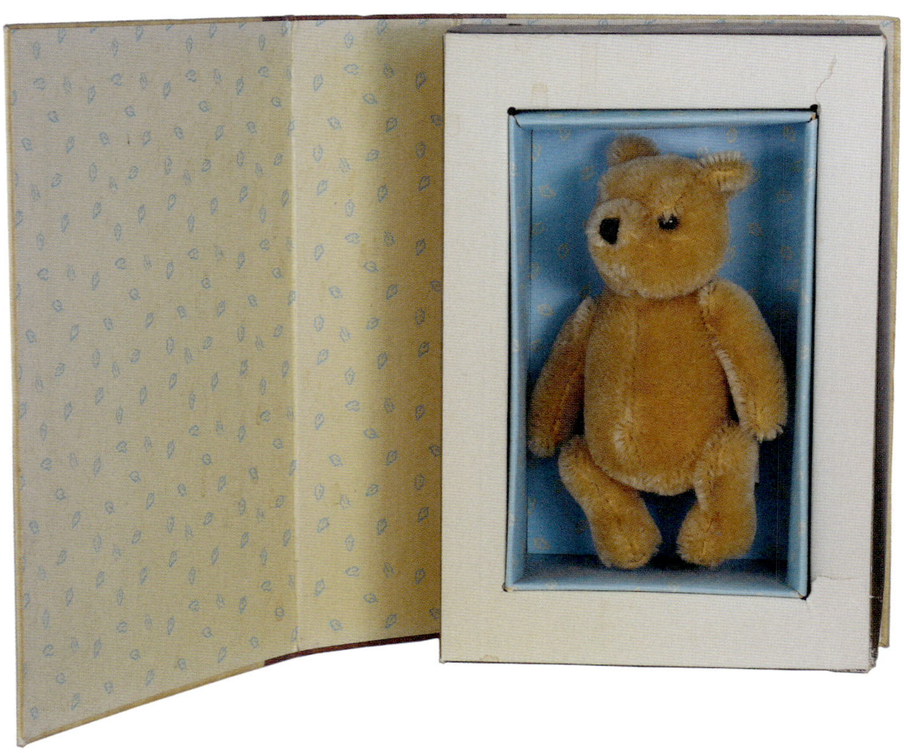

5.173
Schuber mit Stulpdeckel auf dem Kopfschnitt, Buntpapierüberzug, Eingriffkerbe
Slipcase with slip lid at the head, colored paper-over-board
19. Jh. / *19th century*
18,2 x 13 x 5,3 cm

5.174
Schuber mit Stulpdeckel auf der Vorderschnittseite, Buntpapierüberzug, eingefasst mit Ornament-Papierstreifen, Eingriffkerbe
Slipcase with slip lid at the fore edge, colored paper-over-board, edged with ornamental paper strips
19. Jh. / *19th century*
19,9 x 13,2 x 5,5 cm

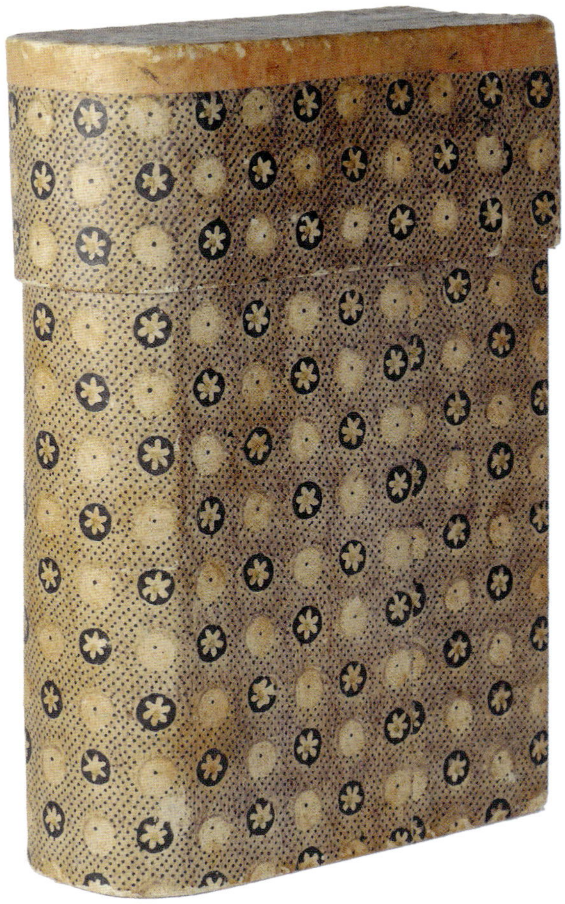

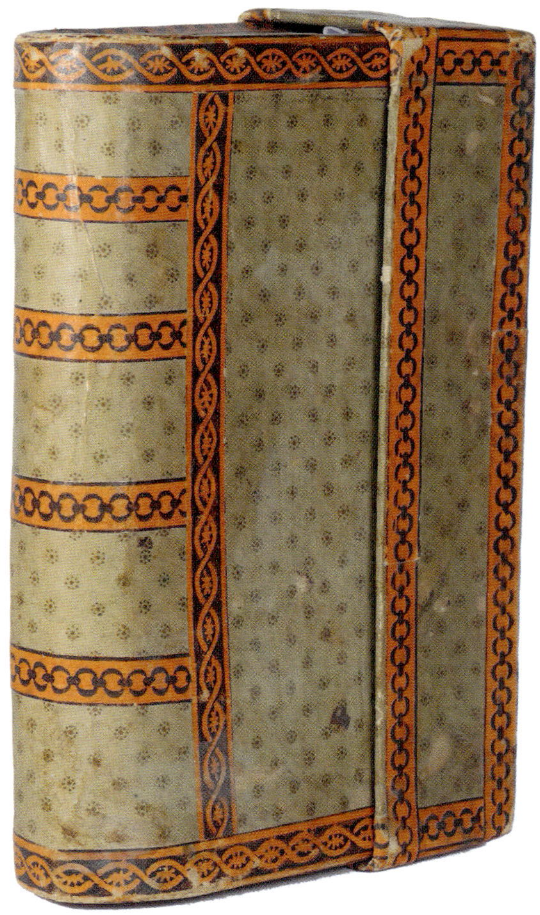

5.175
Lederschuber mit Hals, blindgeprägter Einband, ausgefüttert mit Kattunpapier
Leather slipcase with neck, blind tooling, calico paper lining
18. Jh. / *18th century*
20,5 x 3,7 x 14,7 cm

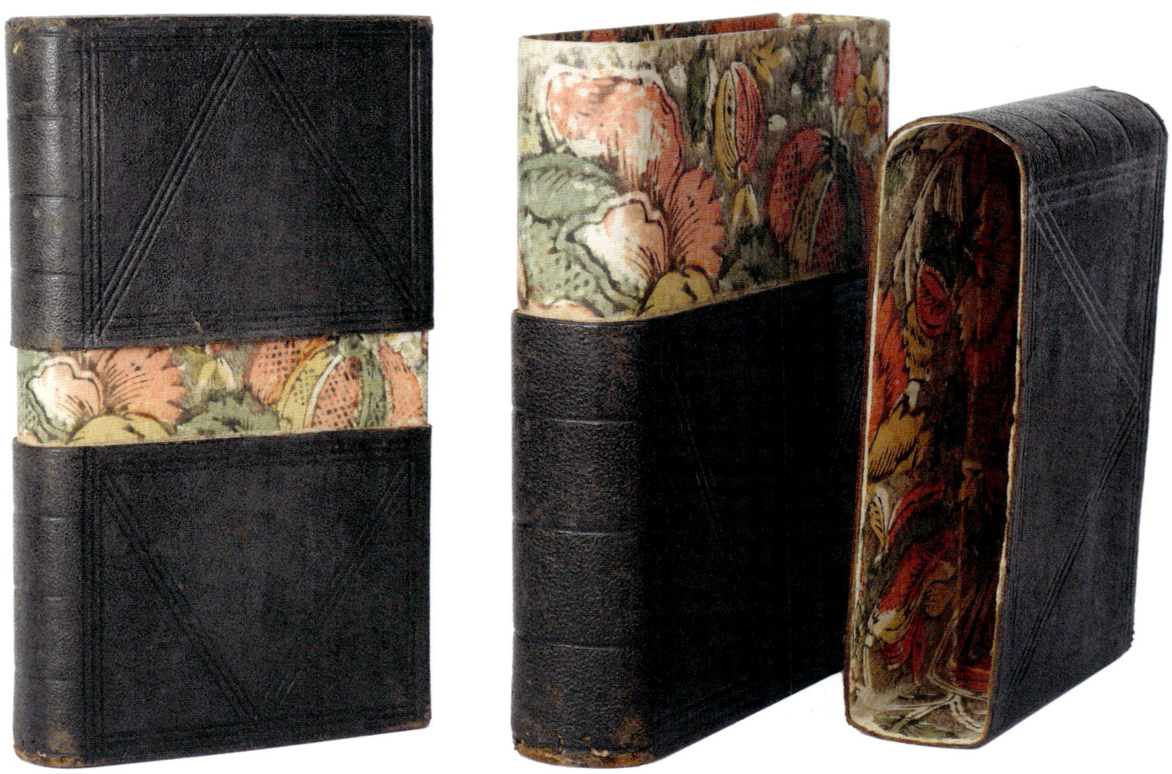

5.176
Lederdose mit Hals, Handvergoldung, ausgefüttert mit Kleisterpapier
Leather box with neck, manual gilding, lined with paste paper
Ende 19. Jh. / End of the *19th century*
10 x 6,8 x 1,8 cm

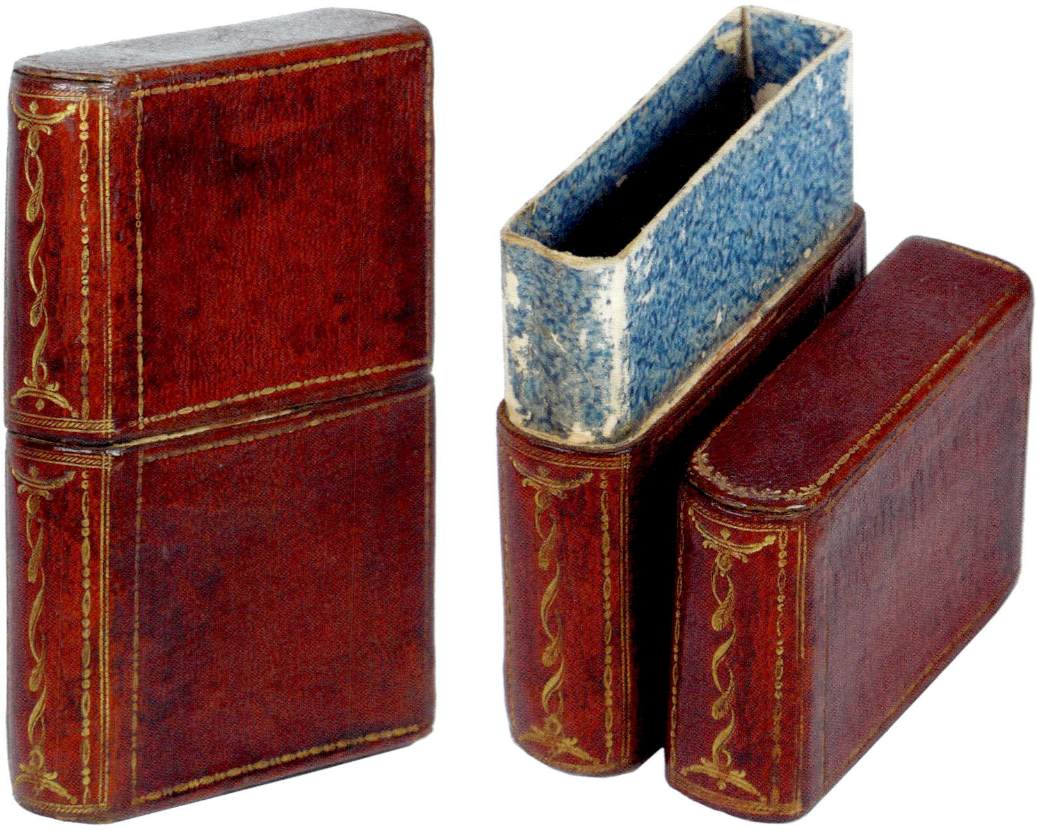

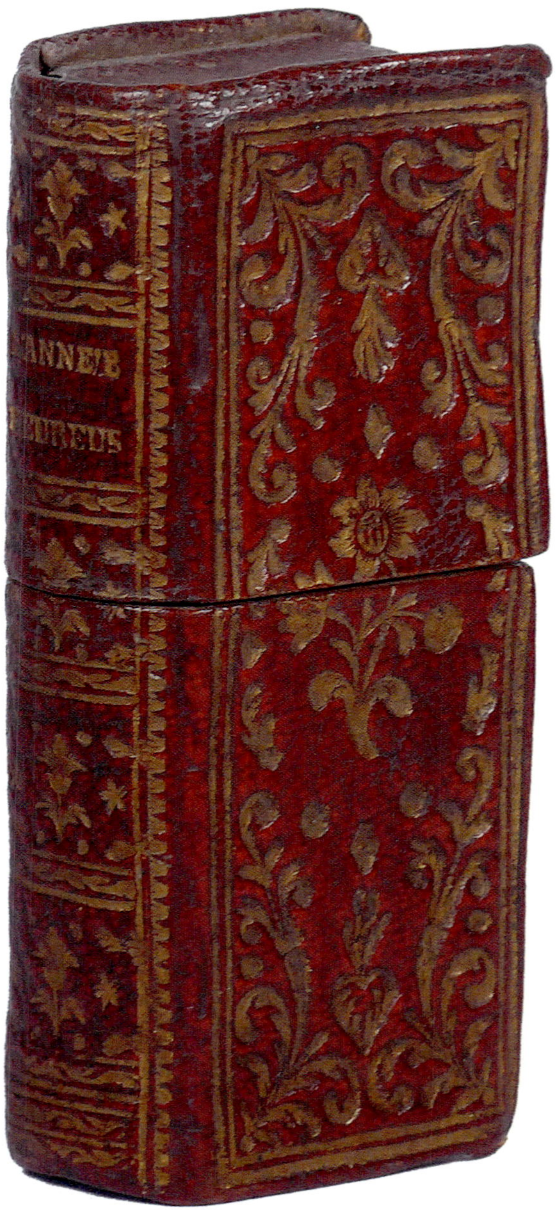

5.177
Lederdose mit Hals, Rücken- und Deckelvergoldung, dreiseitige Schnittvergoldung, *Verwendungszweck unklar*
Leather box with neck, gilt spine and covers, all edges gilt, use unclear
19. Jh. / *19th century* | 7,8 x 3,7 x 2,2 cm

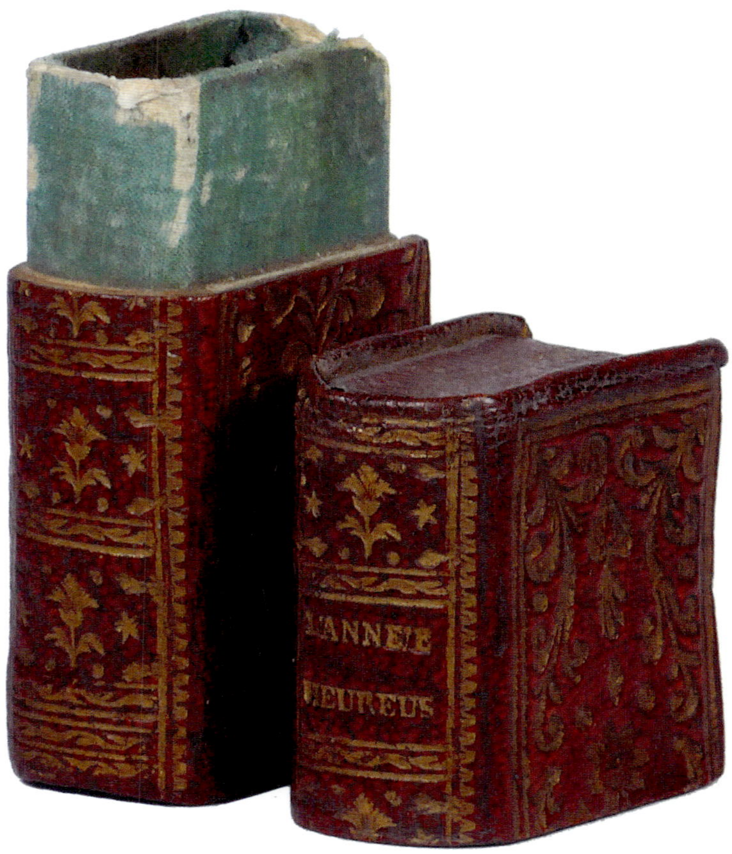

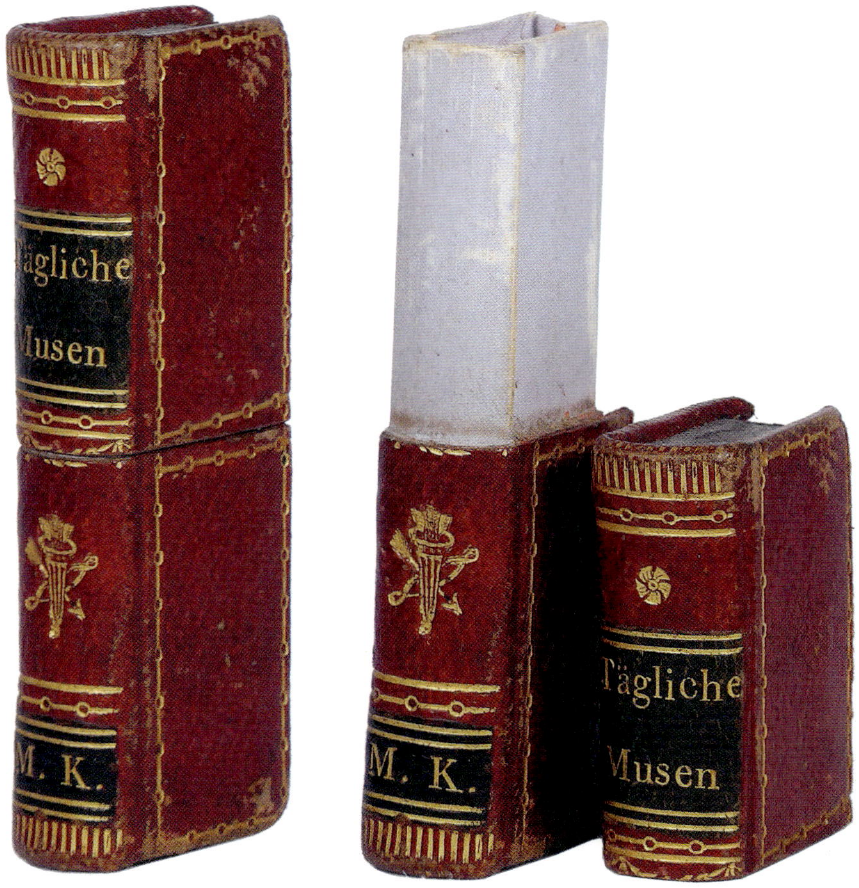

5.178

Tägliche Musen, M.K / ***Daily Muses, M.K***

Lederdose mit Hals, Titelschild und Monogramm, Rücken- und Deckelvergoldung, Kantenvergoldung, Verwendungszweck unklar

Leather box with neck, title label and monogram, gilt spine, covers and edges, use unclear

19. Jh. / *19th century* | 7 x 2,7 x 1,2 cm

5.179

Sainte Bible, 1–12

Marmorierte Kalbsleder-Buchschachteln mit Hals, Titelschilder und Bandzahlen aus rotem Leder, handvergoldet, ausgefüttert mit Steinmarmorpapier

Marbled calfskin boxes with neck, label and numbers of all volumes in red leather, manual gilding, lined with stone marble paper

24,2 x 16,8 x 5,4cm / 3,6 cm

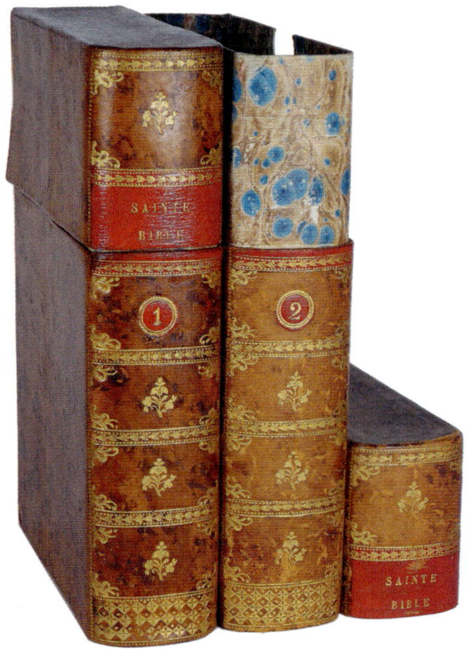

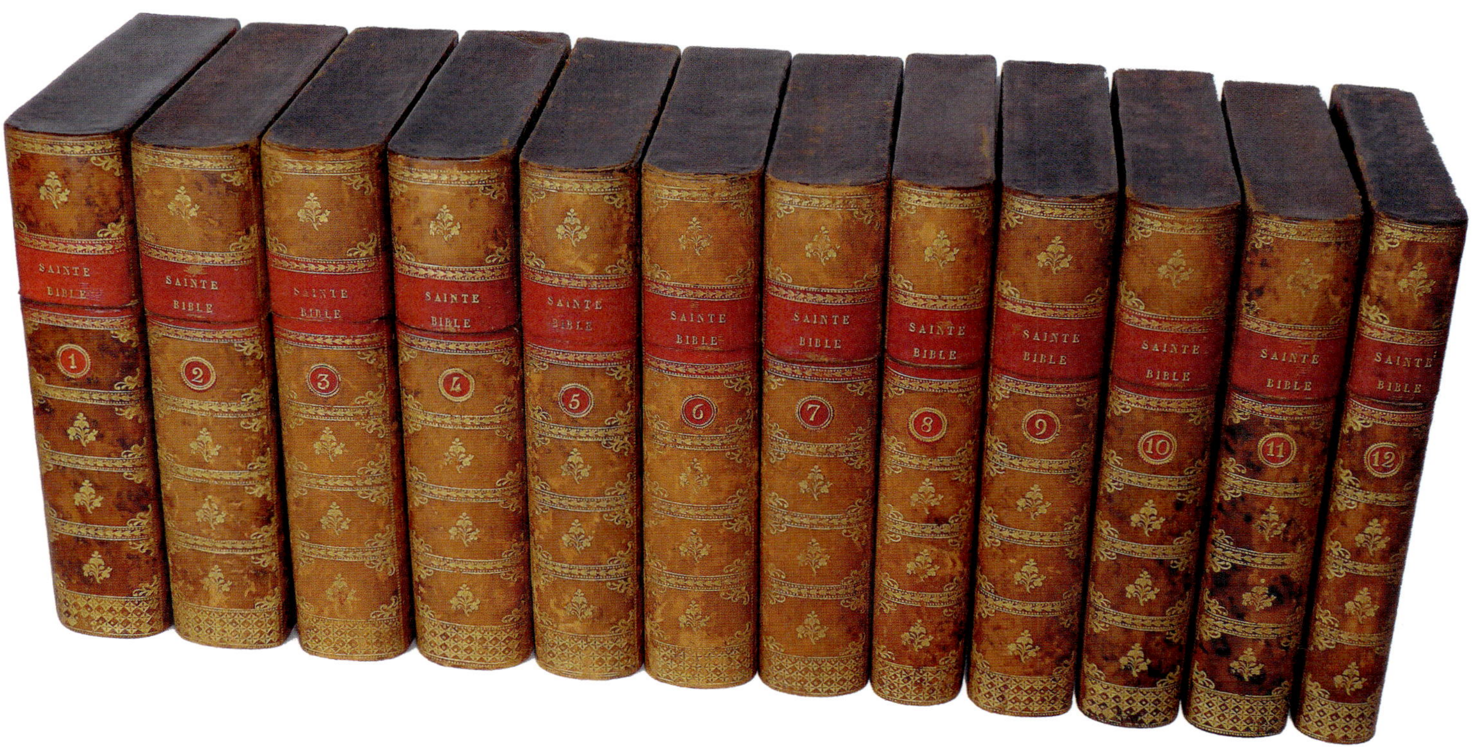

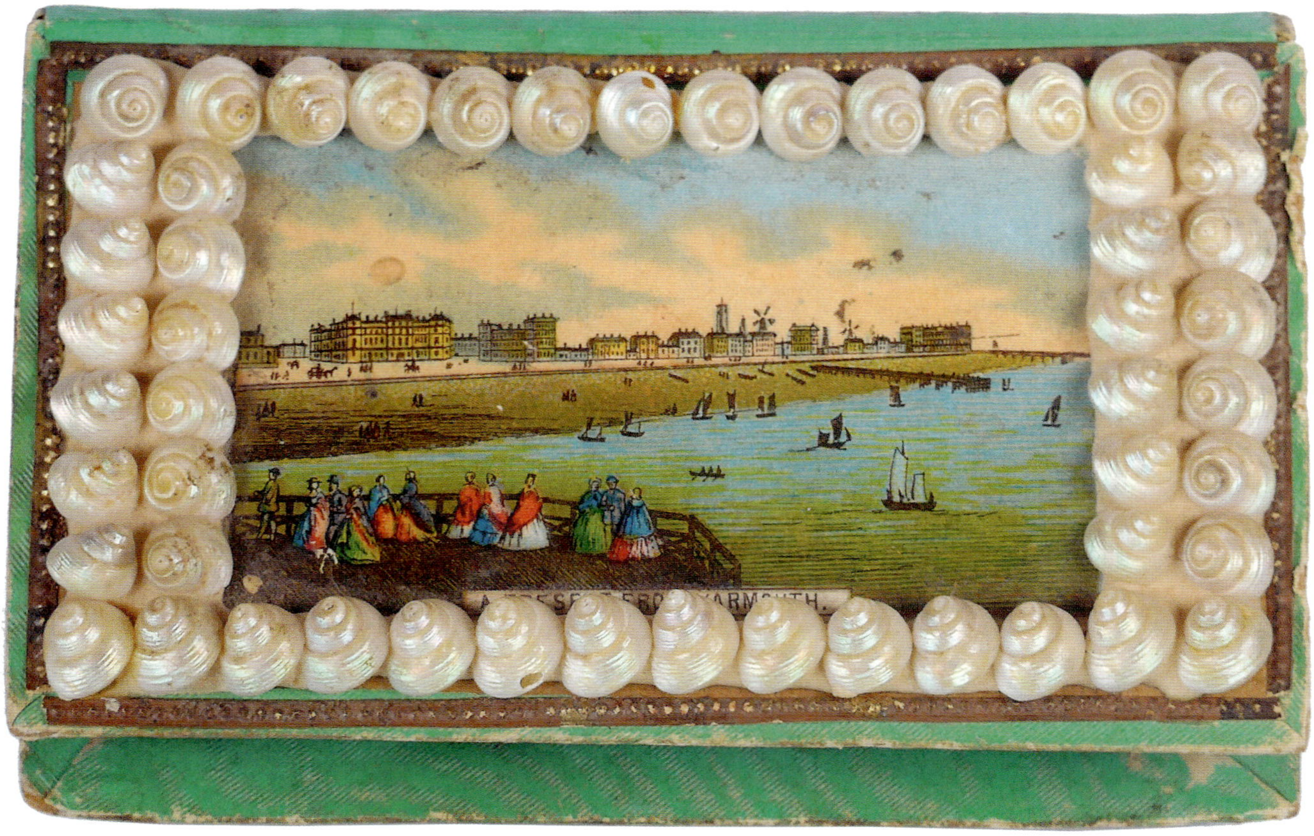

5.180
A. Present from Yarmout
Bombierte Plüschsouvenirdose, beidseitiges Dekor mit Schneckenhäuschen, Prägedruck auf dem Vorderdeckel, Chromolithografie einer Stadtansicht auf dem Rückdeckel, ausgefüttert mit weißem Moirépapier, dreiseitig geprägter Goldschnitt
Cambered souvenir box with plush cover, decoration on both sides with snail shells, embossing on the lid, chromolithography of a city view on the bottom, lined with white moiré paper, gold-tooled edges
Yarmout, England | 4 x 11,6 x 7,6 cm

5.181
Kartondose mit Samtrücken, Glasperlendeckel umrandet mit Goldlitzen, dreiseitiger Goldschnitt, ausgefüttert mit Moirépapier
Cardboard box with a spine strip made of velvet, both covers decorated with snail shells, all edges gilt, lined with white moiré paper
Ende 19. Jh. / *Late 19th century* | 2,2 x 7,8 x 5,8 cm

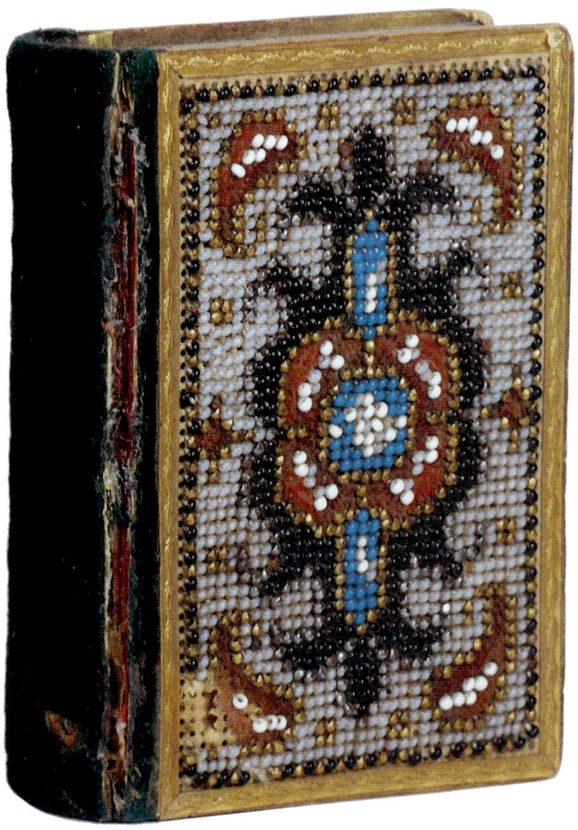

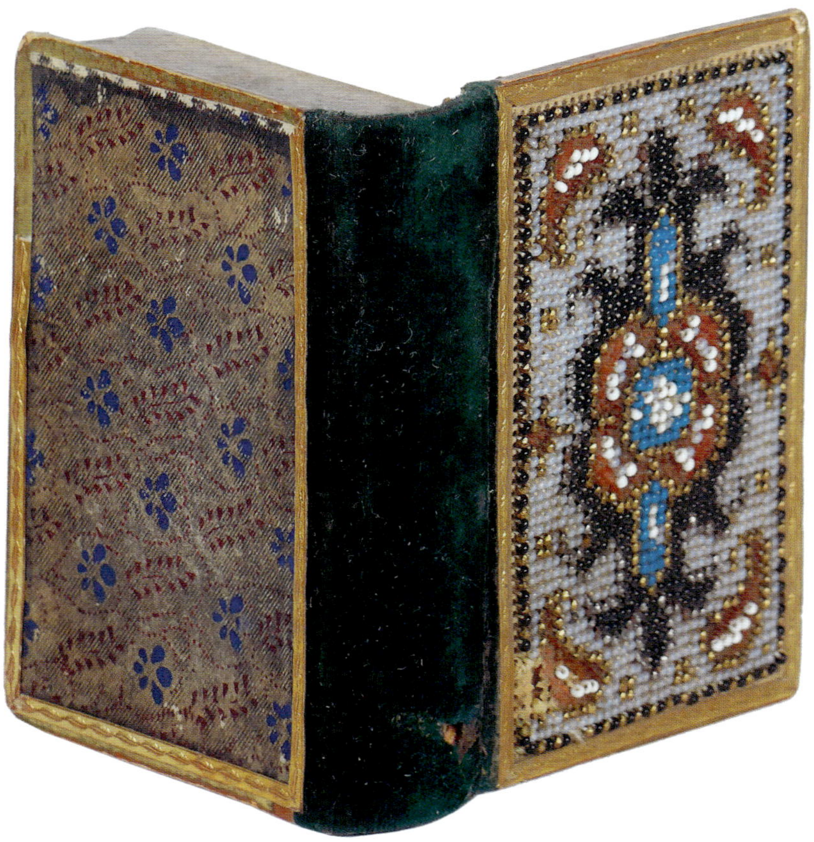

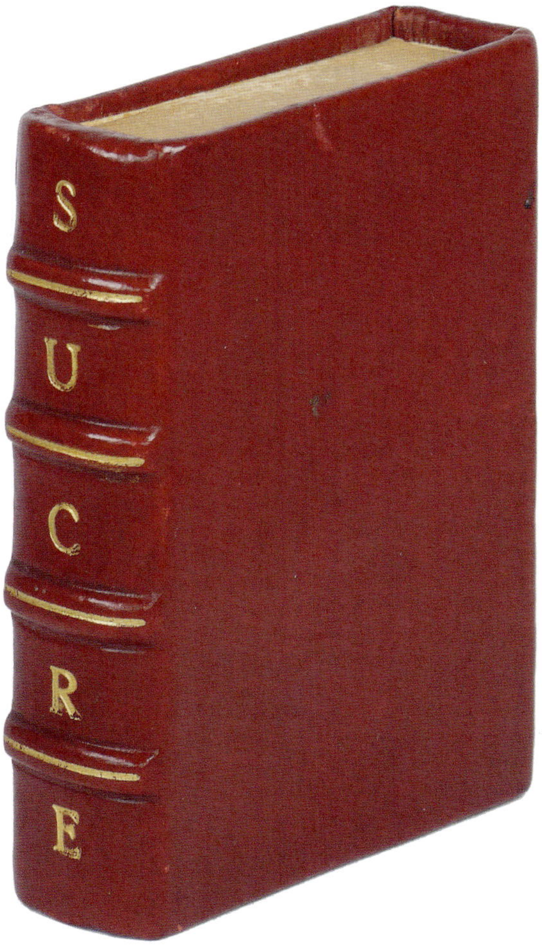

5.182
Sucre, J. H. Waser Zürich
Ganzlederschuber mit Kartonschachtel-einzug zur Aufbewahrung von Zucker (?), Handvergoldung
Full leather slipcase with cardboard box for the storage of sugar (?), manual gilding
1,8 x 7,1 x 5,6 cm

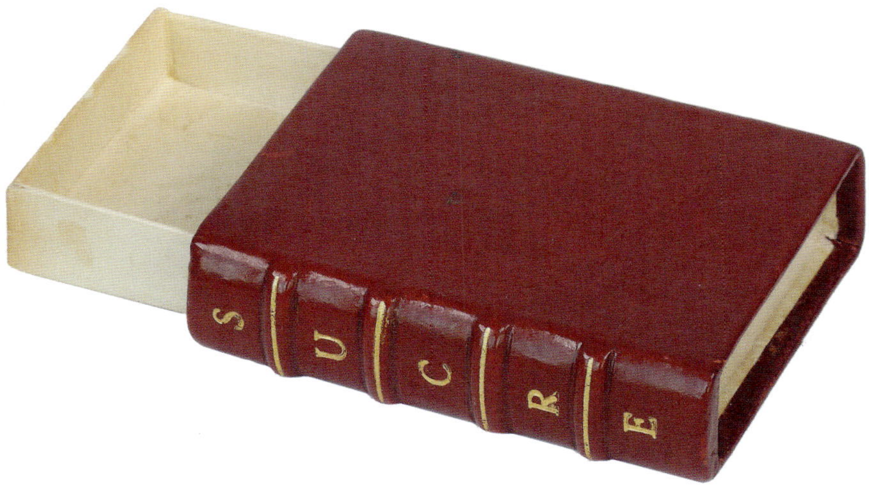

5.183
Dose mit Metallrücken und Kunststoffdeckel, zwei Scharniere auf Deckel übergreifend, vier Standfüße, dreiseitiger Goldschnitt
Box with metal spine and plastic lid, two hinges overlapping the lid, four feet, all edges gilt
5 x 15,3 x 10,6 cm

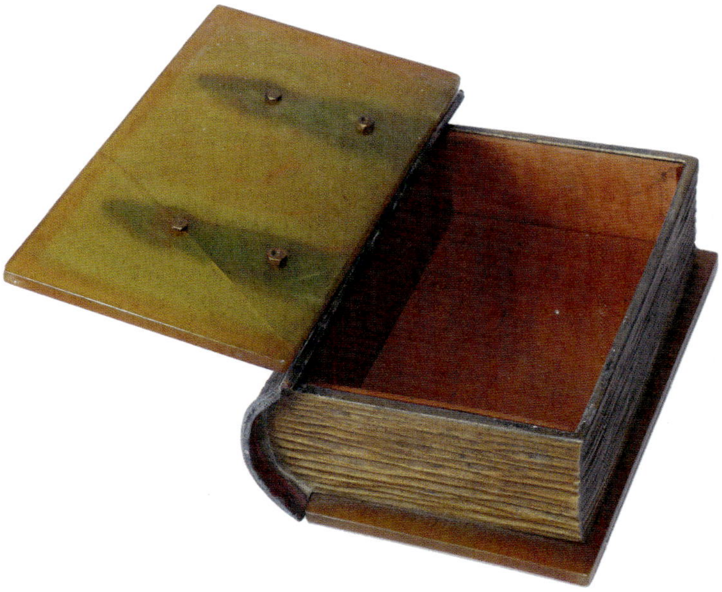

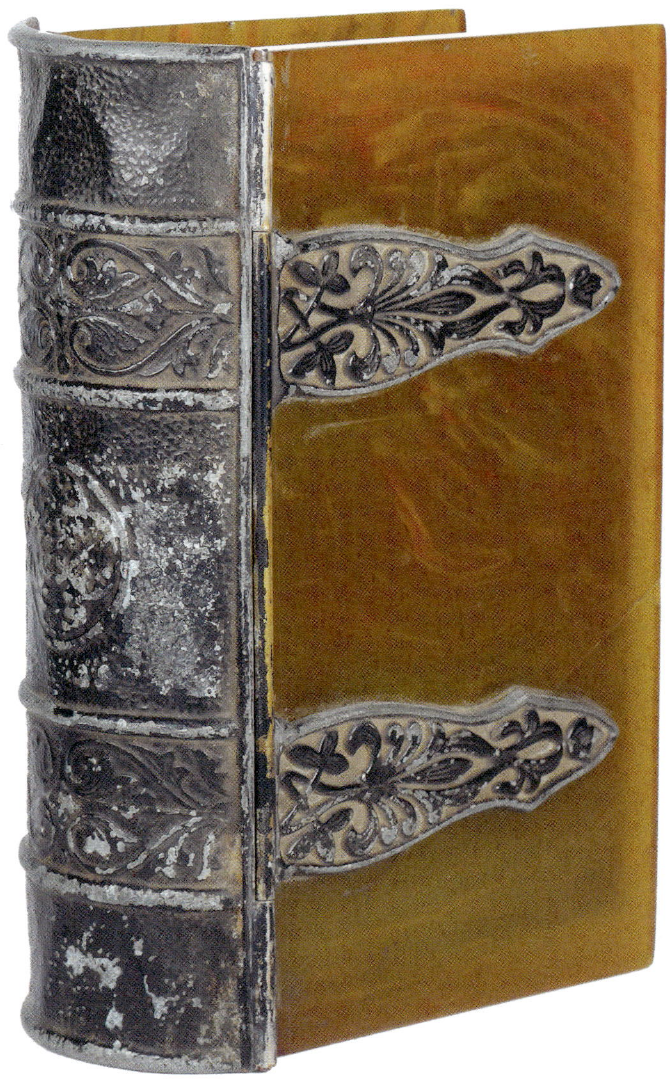

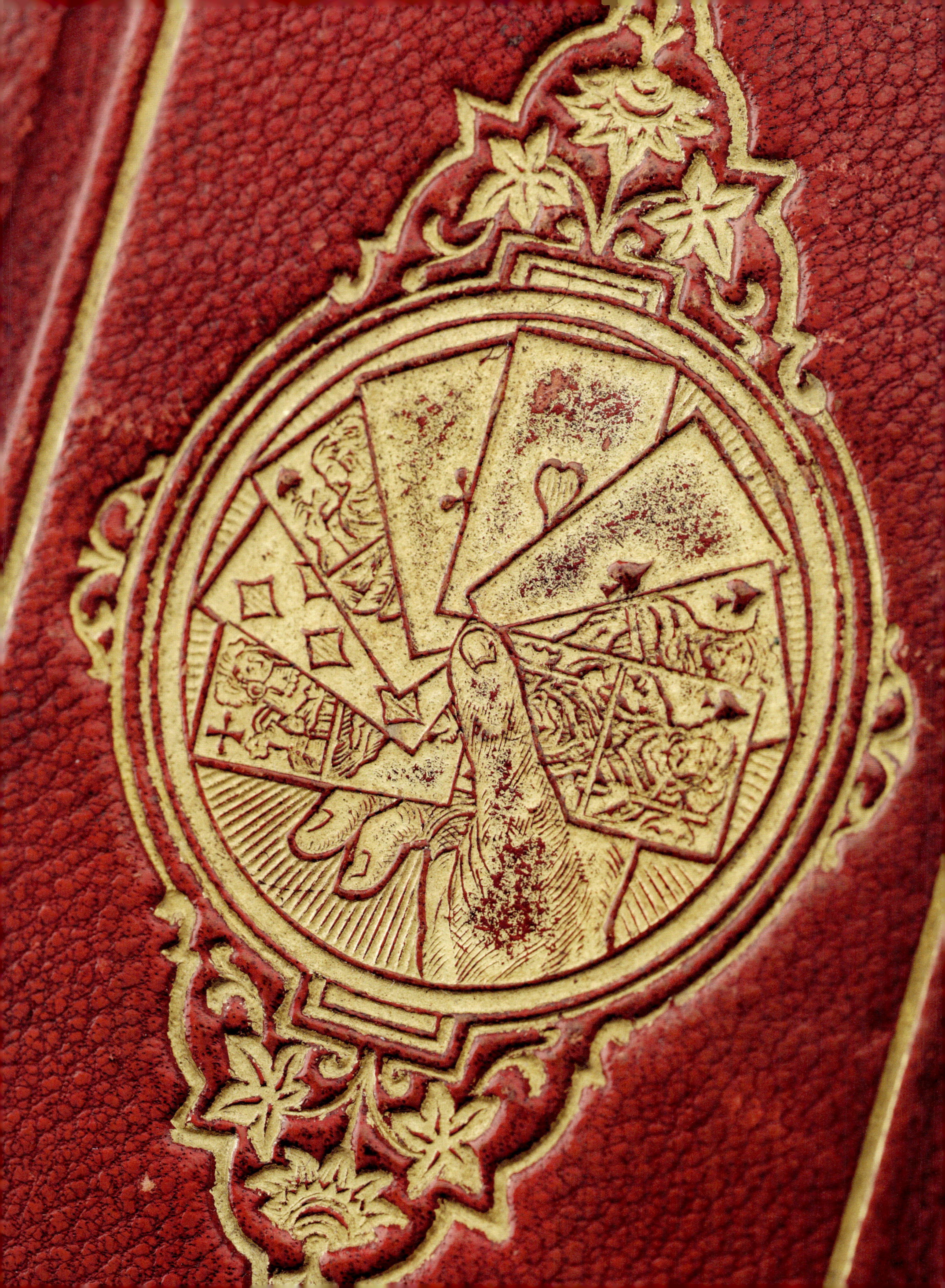

Spiel
Playful Things

Auktionen sind immer nervenaufreibend und stressig. Der Zeitaufwand für das Katalogstudium, die Vorbesichtigung, die Auktionssitzung und das Abholen ist beträchtlich. Zudem sind je nach Publikum die Gebote unberechenbar.

Zusatzkosten wie das Aufgeld und die Mehrwertsteuer sollten immer im Auge behalten werden. Auch wenn man sich ein Limit setzt, lässt man sich immer wieder im Auktionsfieber dazu verleiten, einen potentiellen Käufer zu überbieten.

Ein bekanntes Berner Auktionshaus versteigerte eine äußerst rare Vogelspieldose in Gestalt eines reich verzierten Folianten im Stil des Historismus des späten 19. Jahrhunderts. Ein kleiner bunter Vogel, verborgen unter dem aufklappbaren Medaillon des vorderen Buchdeckels, erscheint, bewegt sich und „singt", auslösbar durch einen seitlichen Hebel am Vorderschnitt. Der Buchrücken beinhaltet ein Innenfach für den Schlüssel. Das in Deutschland hergestellte Objekt mit mechanischem Laufwerk und aus Silber mit 800er- Stempel zieren vier Cabochons aus Rosenquarz, ein Halbmond und eine Krone, ein Firmenwappen sowie zwei reliefartige Medaillons mit den Namen „Christof Fuger Ab Haimendorf" und „Maria Georg Pfintzigen". Es ist wahrscheinlich, dass das Uhrwerk aus der Schweiz stammt.

Anwesende im Saal, telefonische Mitbieter und Interessenten, die schriftliche Angebote einreichten – allesamt keine Buchattrappen Sammler, sondern Silberwaren- und Spieldosenliebhaber waren –, kämpften mit mir um das begehrte Sammlerstück. Ich habe schließlich den Zuschlag bekommen und die begehrte Zimelie in meine Sammlung aufgenommen.

Auctions are always exhausting and stressful. The time required to study the catalogue, preview the items, carry out the actual auction and pick up the purchases is considerable. Moreover, depending on the participants, the bids are unpredictable. Additional costs such as the mark-up and VAT should always be taken into account. Even if you set yourself a limit, the thrill of the auction often seduces you into outbidding a potential buyer.

A well-known auction house in Bern auctioned off an extremely rare birdsong music-box in the design of a book that was richly decorated in a late 19th-century historicist style. A small colorful bird, hidden under the hinged medallion of the front cover of the book, appears, moves and "sings", triggered by a side lever near the front. The book's spine contains an inner pocket for the key. The object, made in Germany, with a mechanical drive and a silver 800 stamp, is decorated with four rose quartz cabochons, a crescent moon and a crown, as well as a company coat of arms and two relief-like medallions with the names "Christof Fuger Ab Haimendorf" and "Maria Georg Pfintzigen". The clockwork probably comes from Switzerland.

Those present in the auction room, telephone bidders and interested parties who had submitted written offers, none of whom were fake-book collectors but silverware and music boxes enthusiasts, competed with me for the highly coveted collector's item. I finally won the bid and added the coveted cimelia to my collection.

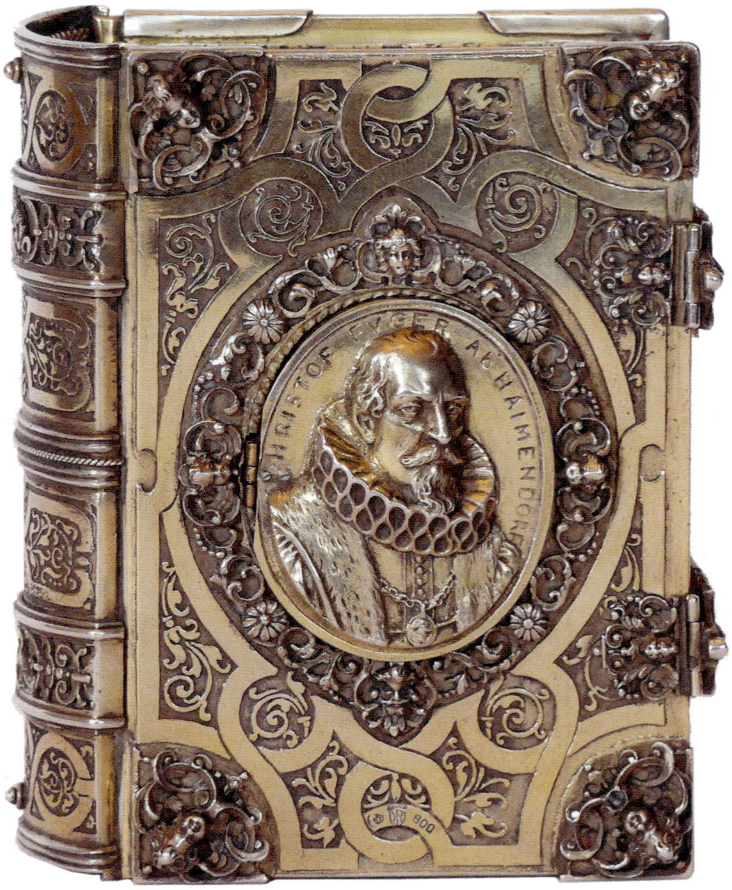

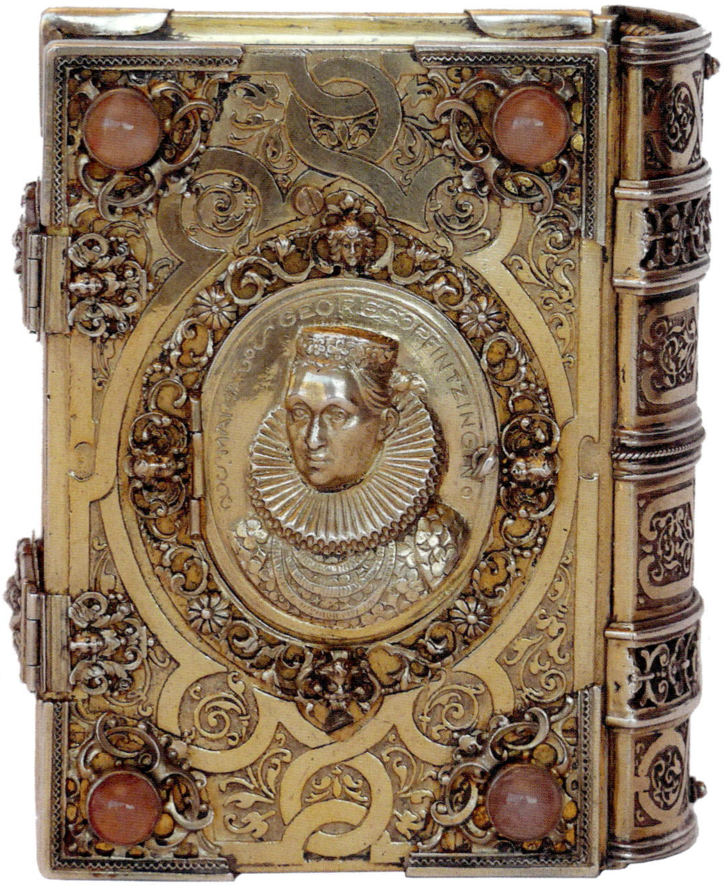

6.001

Singvogel-Spieldose

Korpus in Gestalt eines reich verzierten Folianten im Stil des Historismus. Mechanisches Laufwerk mit „Singstimme“. Ein kleiner bunter Vogel, verborgen unter dem aufklappbaren Medaillon des vorderen Buchdeckels, erscheint, bewegt sich und „singt“, auslösbar durch einen seitlichen Hebel am Vorderschnitt. Schlüsselaufzug unter dem aufklapp- baren Medaillon des hinteren Buchdeckels.
Die beiden reliefierten Bildnismedaillons sind bezeichnet mit „Christof Fuger Ab Haimendorf“ und „Maria Georg Pfintzingen“. Aufschiebbarer Buchrücken mit Innenfach für Schlüssel. Vier Cabochons aus Rosenquarz. Silber, 800er-Stempel, Halbmond und Krone, Firmenwappen.
Es ist wahrscheinlich, dass das Uhrwerk aus der Schweiz stammt und von einem Gold- bzw. Silberschmied in die Buchdose eingearbeitet wurde.

Songbird music box

Body in the shape of a richly decorated folio in the Historicist style. Mechanical drive with „singing voice“. A small colorful bird, hidden under the hinged medallion on the front cover of the book, appears, moves and „sings“, triggered by a lateral lever on the front cover. A small winding key under the hinged medallion of the rear cover. Inscriptions on the two portrait medallions in relief: „Christof Fuger Ab Haimendorf“ and „Maria Georg Pfintzingen“. Slide-on spine with interior pocket for keys. Four cabochons of rose quartz. Silver, stamp 800, half moon and crown, company emblem.
It is likely that the mechanism originates from Switzerland and was inserted by a goldsmith or silversmith.

Deutschland / *Germany* | 5,7 x 10,4 x 8,7 cm

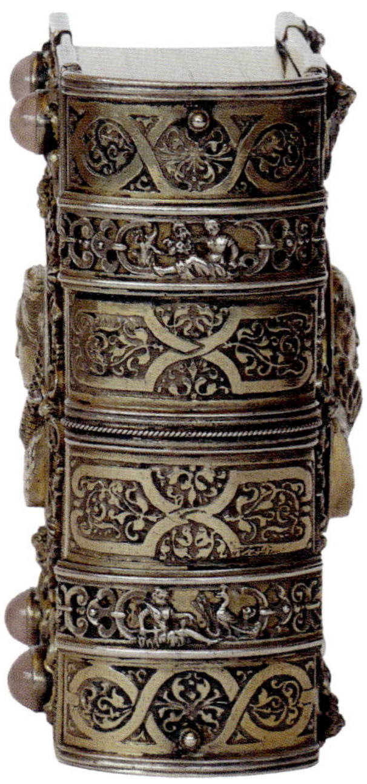

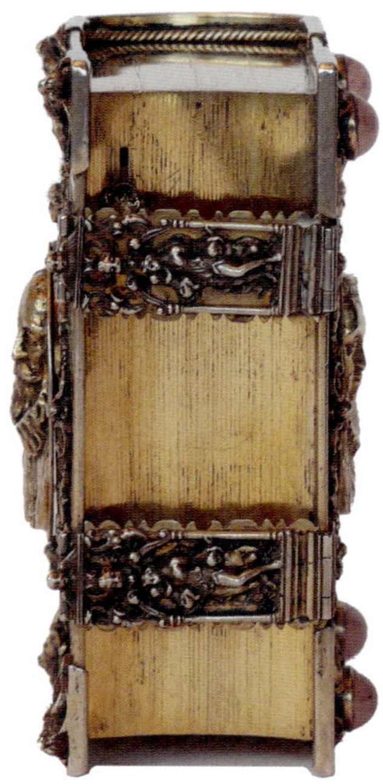

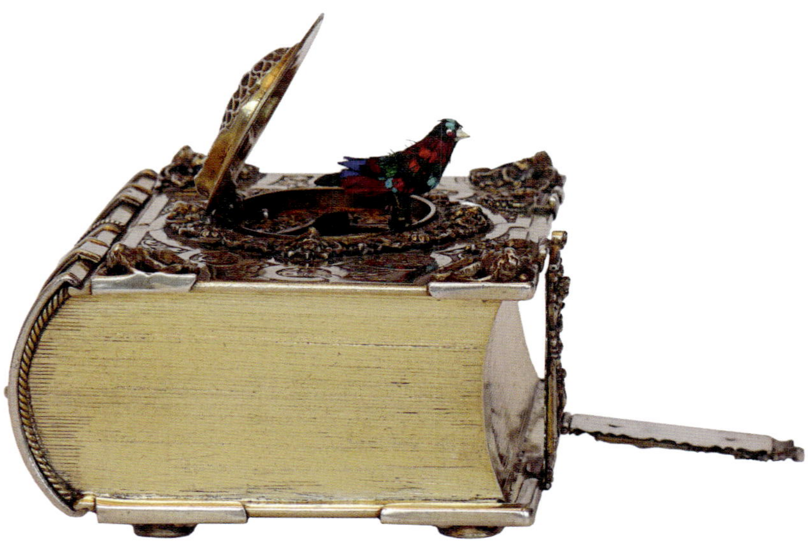

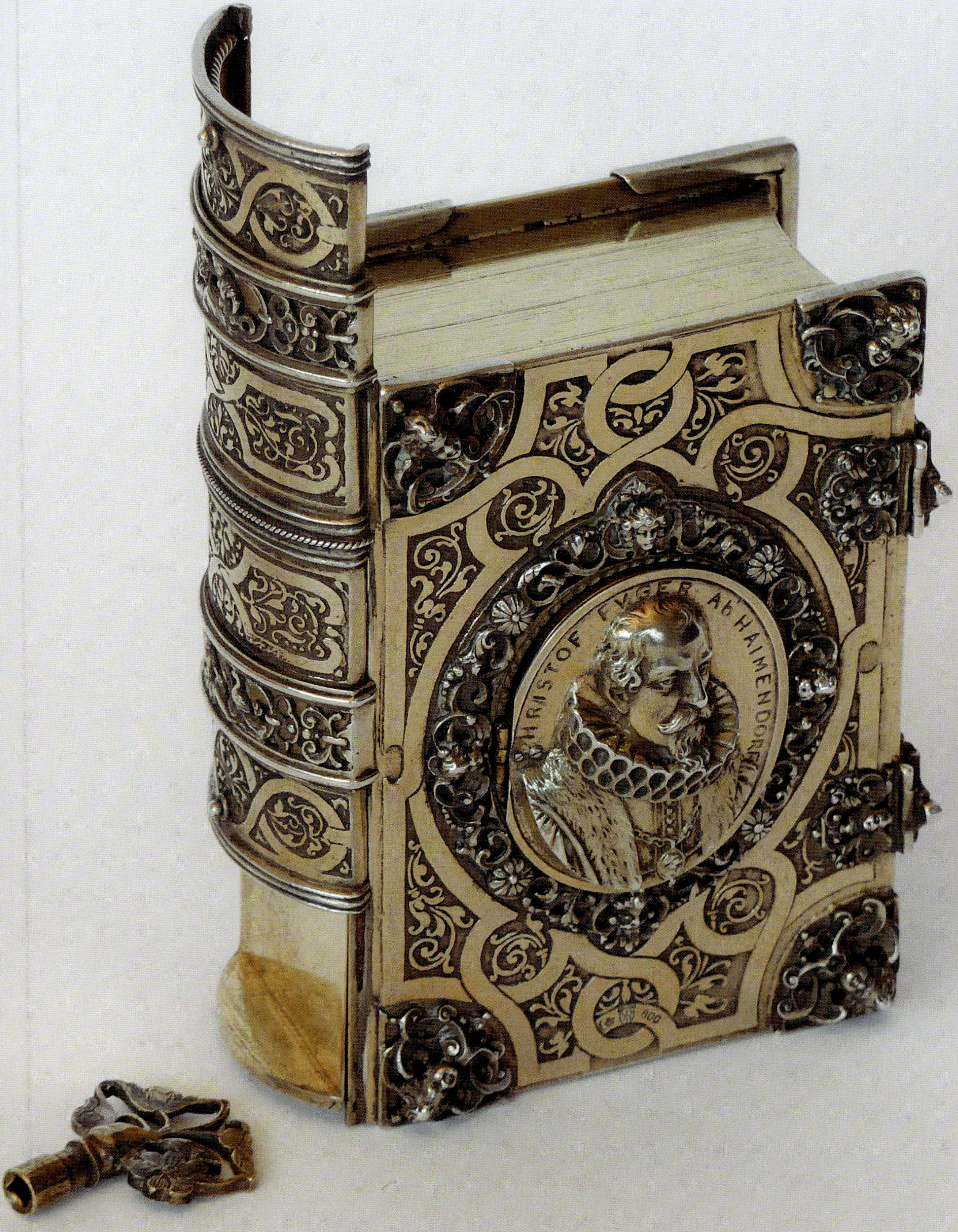

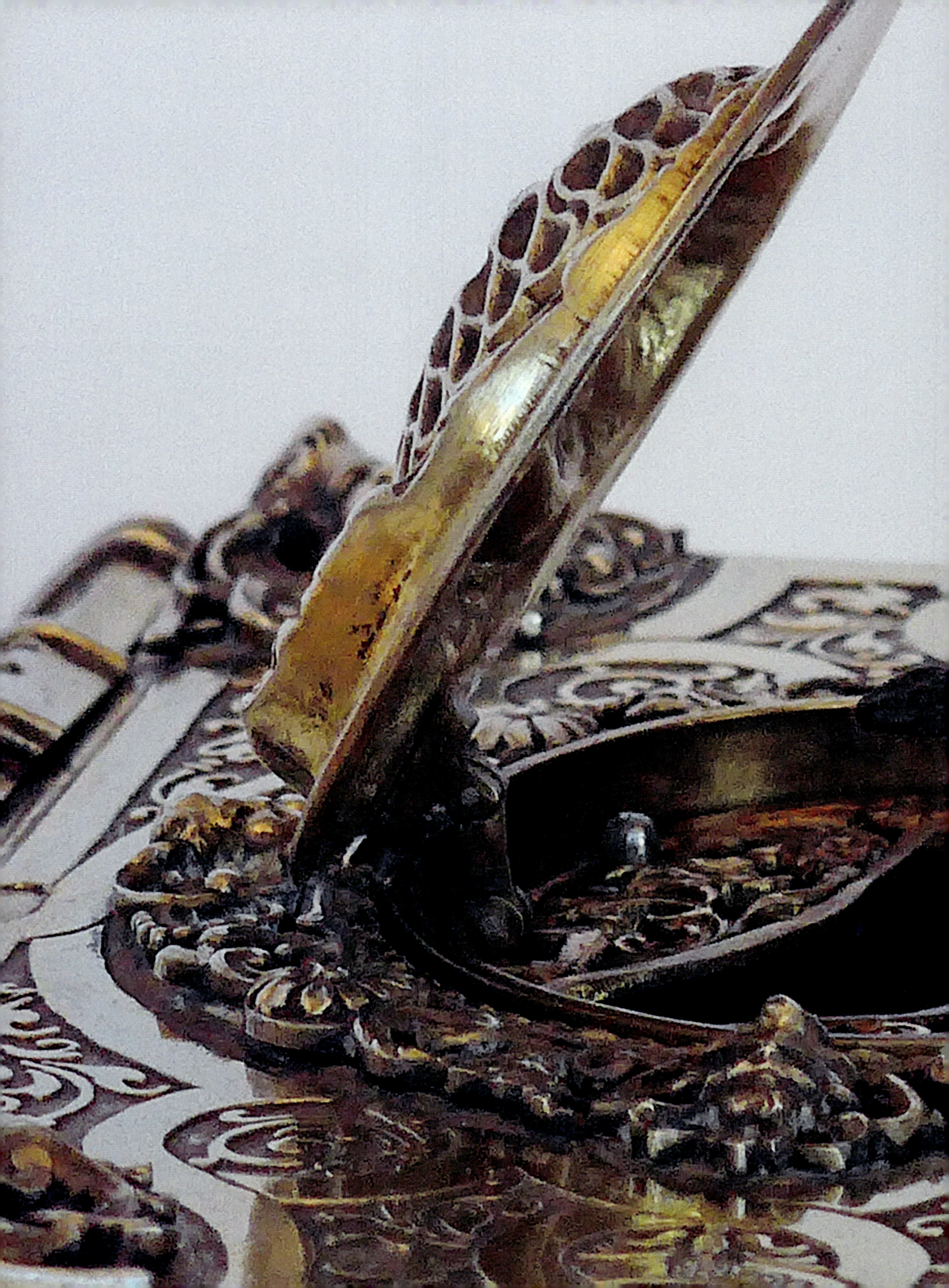

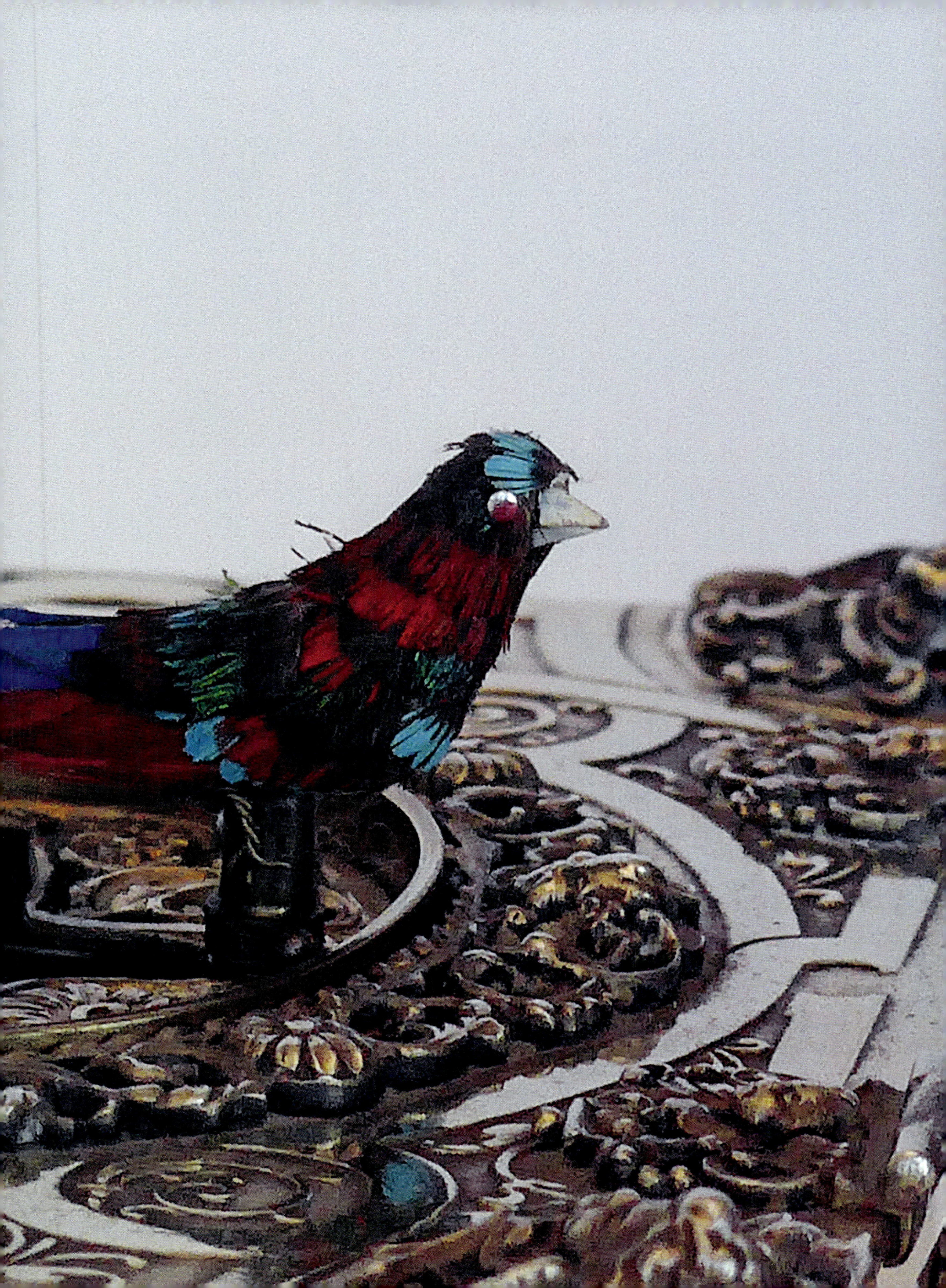

6.002
Laura
Lederdose mit Walzenspieldose und Geheimfach, Reliefprägung auf beiden Deckeln, Messingschließe, dreiseitiger Goldschnitt, ausgefüttert mit Moiréseide
Leather box with cylindrical music box and secret compartment, relief embossing on both covers, brass buckle, all edges gilt, moiré silk lining
6,5 x 15 x 12,6 cm

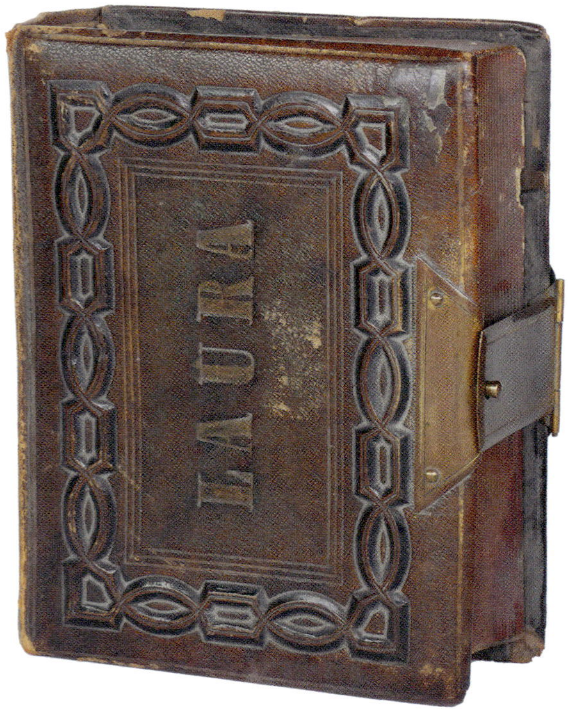

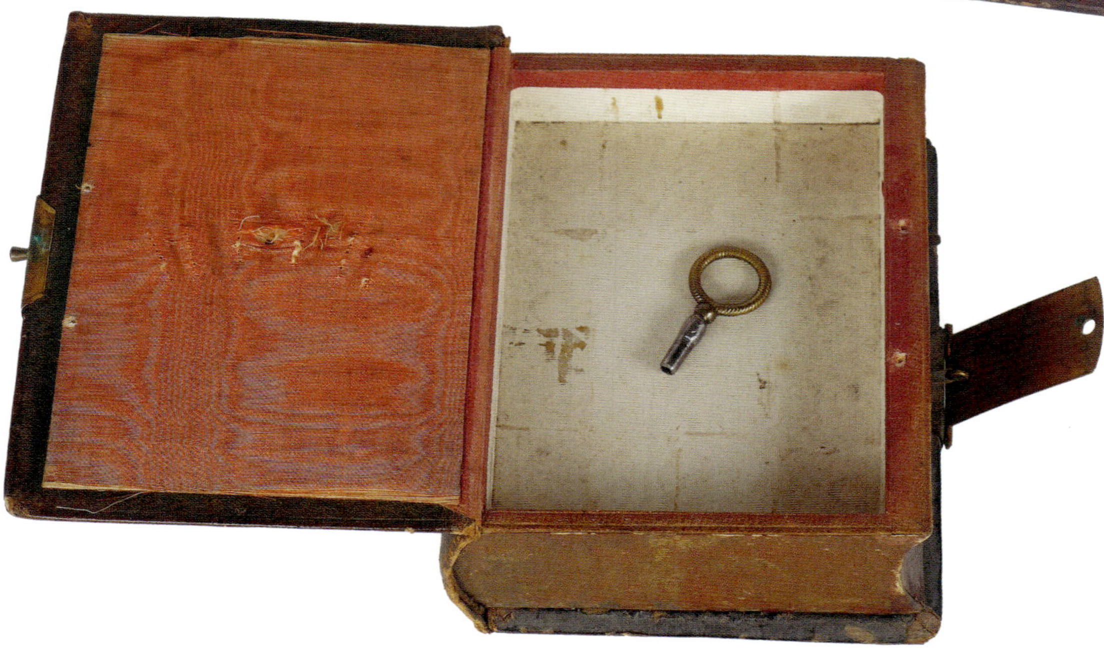

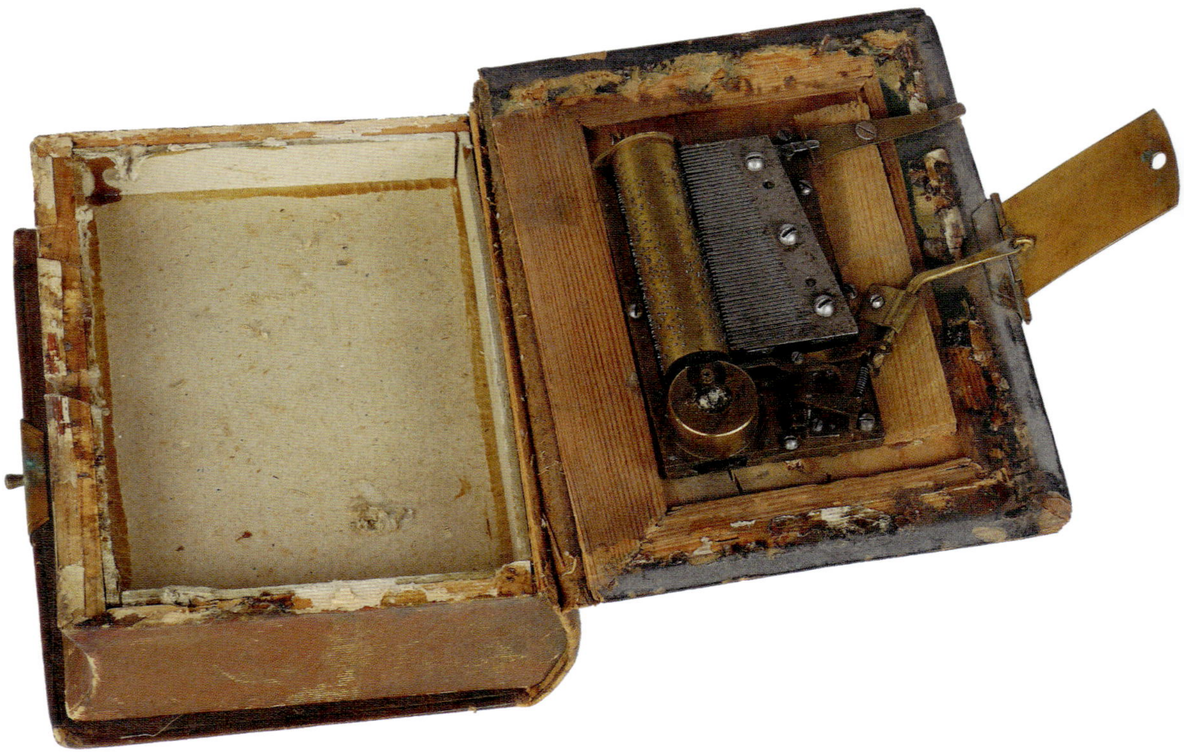

6.003
Bubuphon
Ziegenlederschatulle mit eingebauter Walzenpieldose, dreiseitiger Goldschnitt
Goatskin box with integrated cylindrical music box, all edges gilt
Bubu AG Mönchaltof
Neujahrsgabe / *a New Year's edition*, 1985
4,3 x 9,5 x 7,7 cm

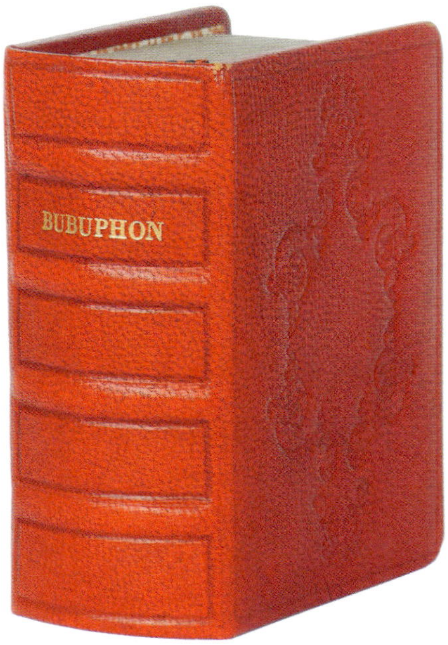

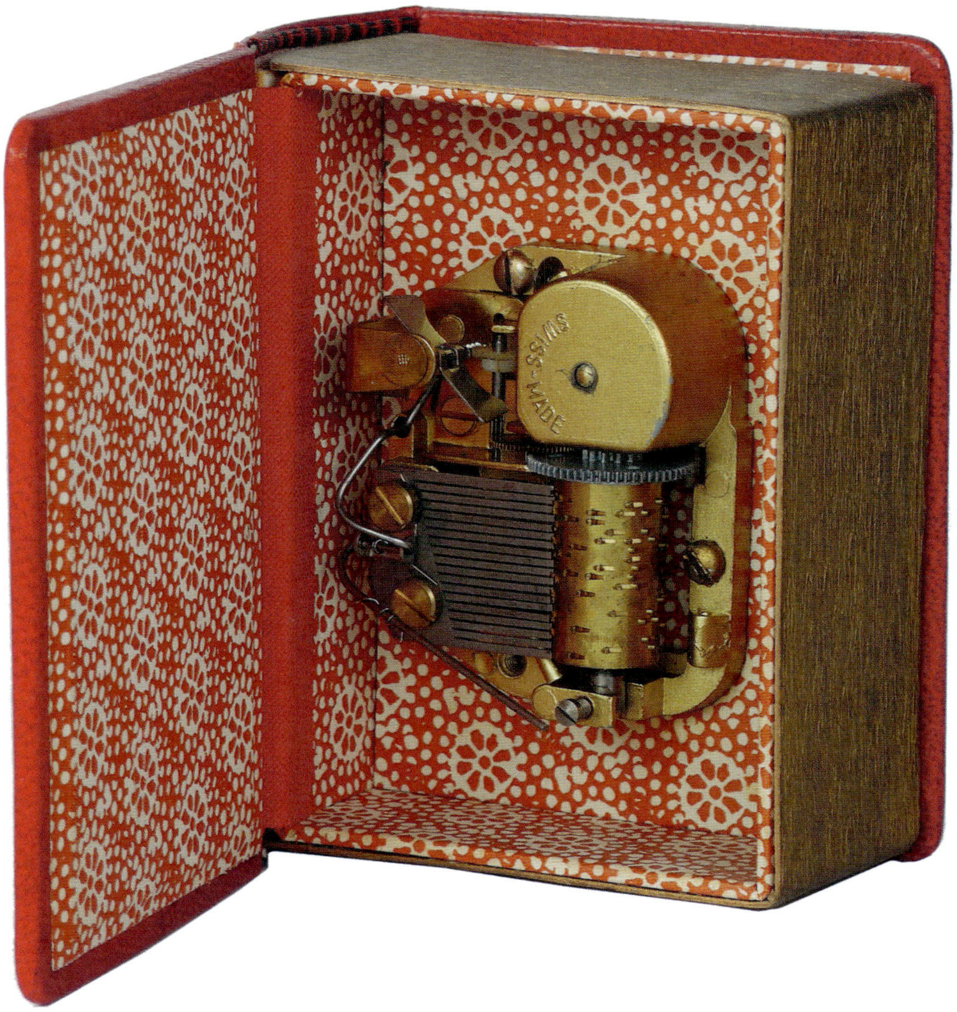

6.004
Fotoalbum mit Spieldose
Photoalbum with Music Box
Ausgehöhltes Album für eine Walzenspieldose, Lederband mit blindgeprägtem Jugendstil-Dekor, mittels der Messingschließe wird die Spielfunktion ausgelöst
Hollowed album with a cylindrical music box, leather strap with blind embossed Art Nouveau decoration, the brass buckle is used to trigger the play function
28,8 x 21,8 x 7 cm

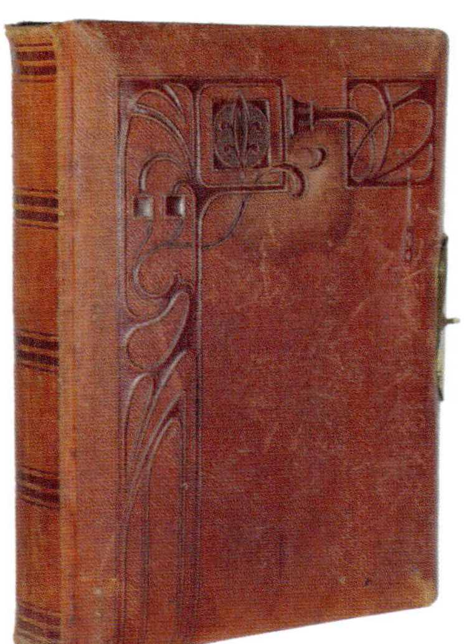

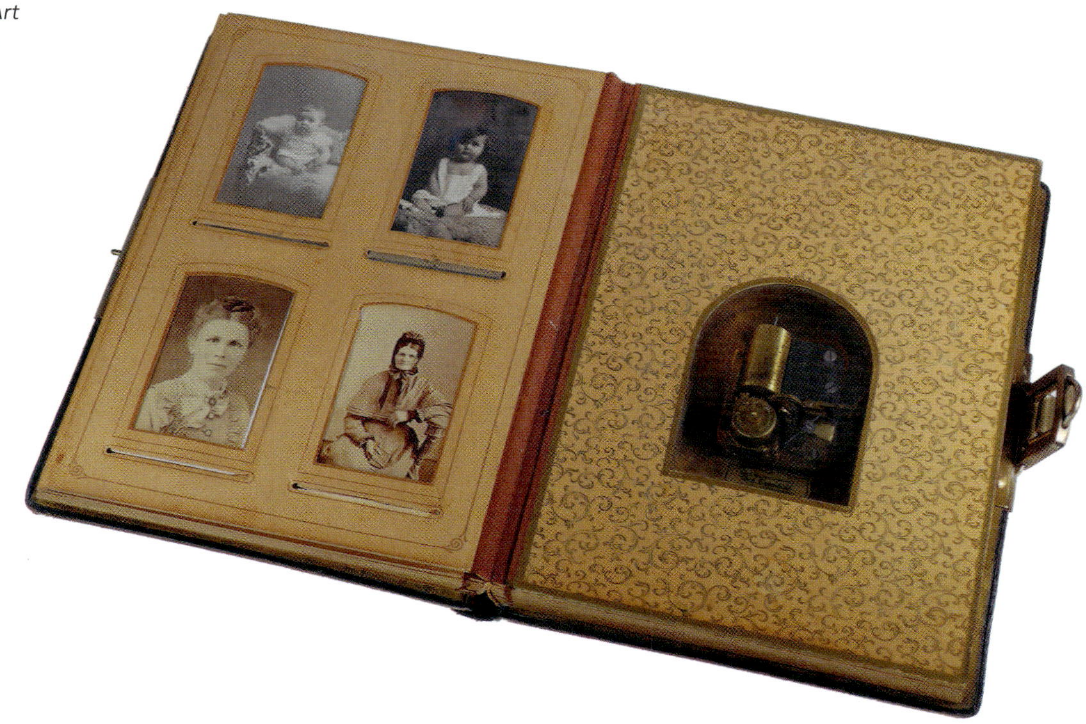

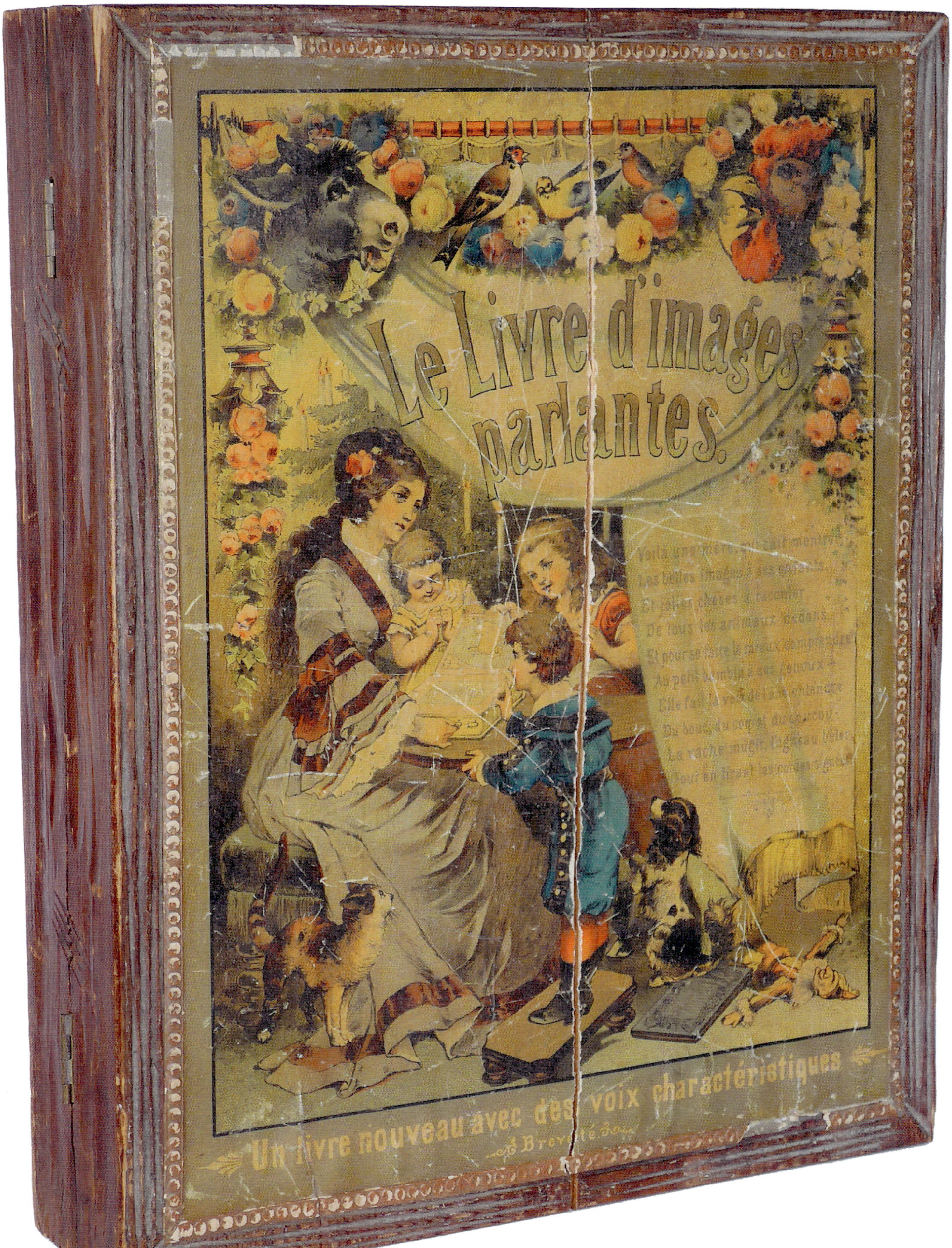
Le Livre d'images parlantes.
Un livre nouveau avec des voix charactéristiques

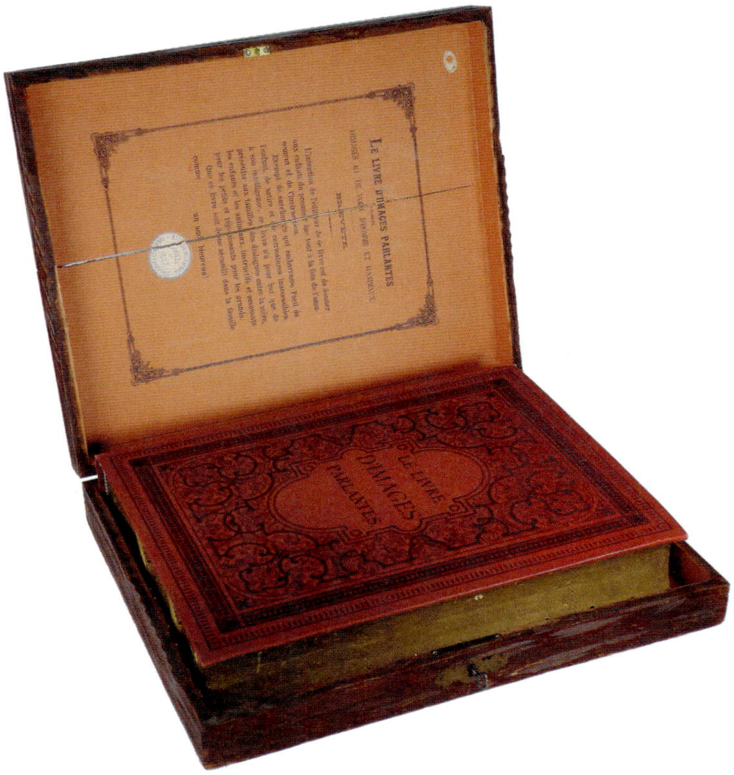

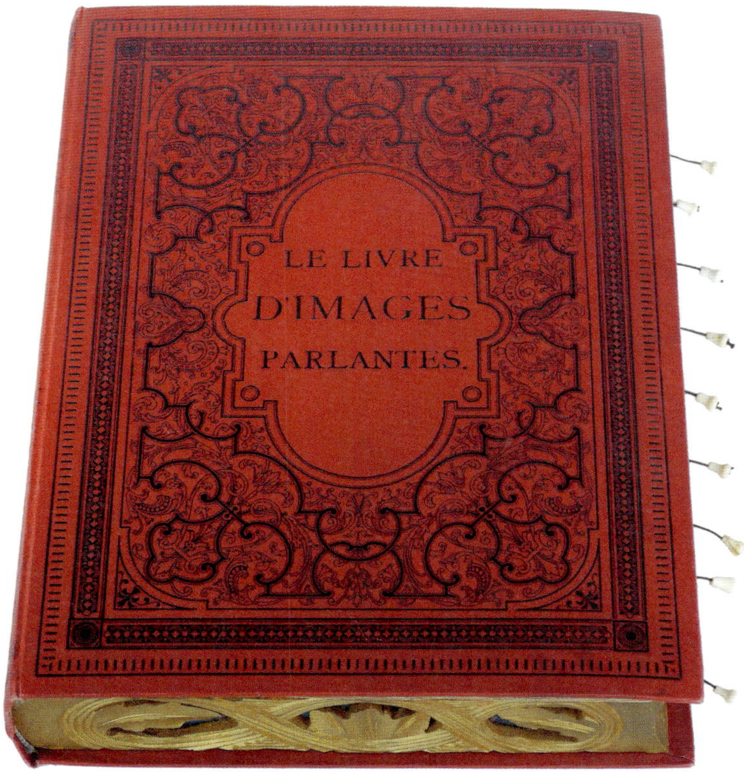

6.005

Le livre d'images parlantes pour les chers petits. Un livre nouveau avec des voix charactéristiques: Le Coq, L'Ane, L'Agneau, Le Nid, La Vache, Le Coucou, Le Bouc, Les Enfants

„Sprechendes Buch", Kalikoeinband mit Prägung in Originalhollzkiste mit Schloss,, Chromolithografien mit Text. Mit den Zugschnüren am Vorderschnitt können die Tierstimmen mit Blasbälgen ausgelöst werden. „Lautsprecher" am Kopf- und Fußschnitt

"Talking Book", calico binding with embossing in a wooden box with lock, chromolithographs with text. With the drawstrings on the front cover the animal voices can be triggered by bellows. "Speakers" at the head and foot edges.

Theodor Brand, Paris | Um / *Around* 1880 | 32 x 24,8 x 5,5 cm

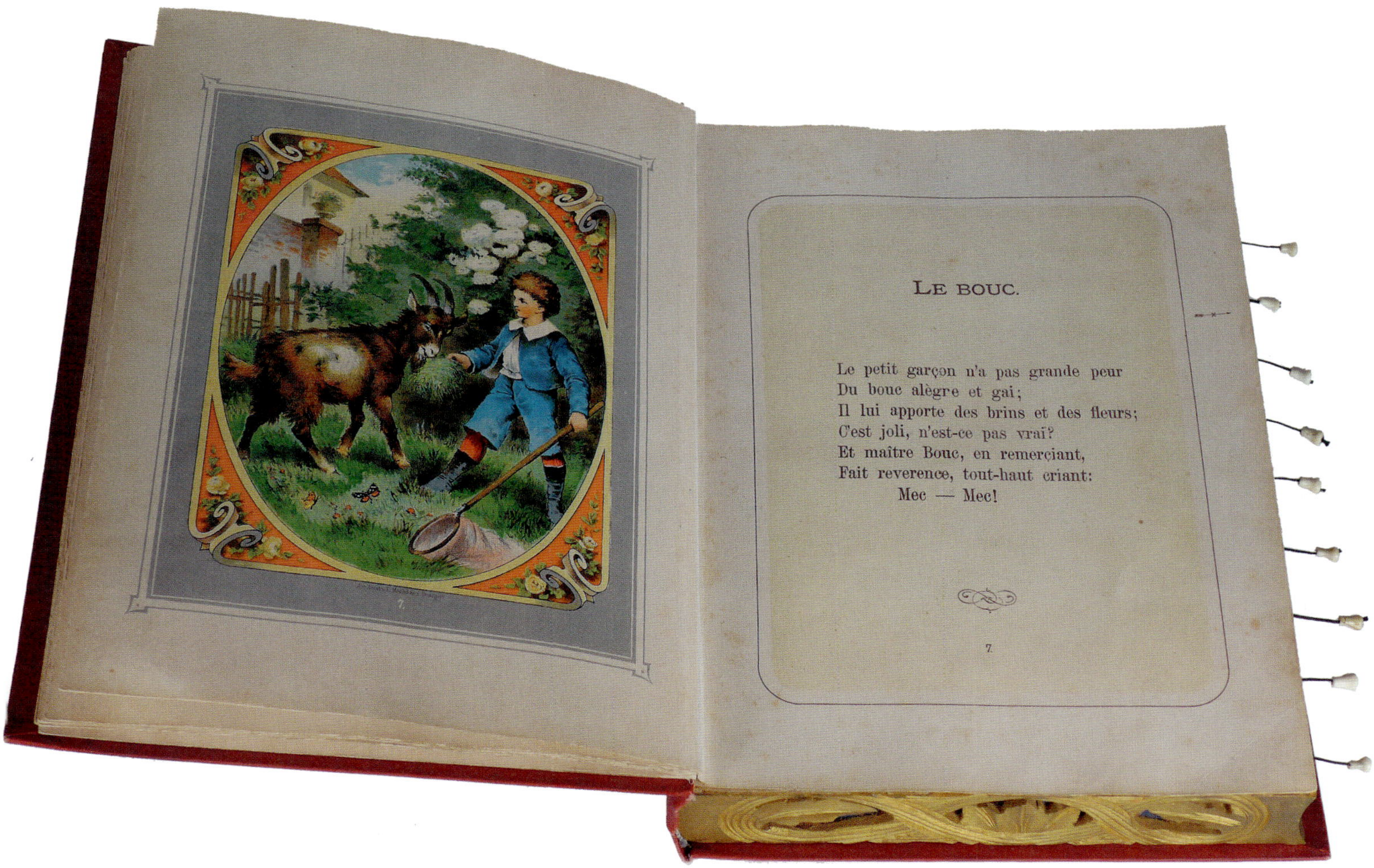

6.006
Ganzlederdose für ein Domino-Legespiel mit Verschluss-lasche, Goldprägung auf dem Vorderdeckel, dreiseitiger Goldschnitt, Kunststoffspielsteine
Full leather box for a Domino Legend game with closing flap, gold tooling on the lid, all edges gilt, plastic tokens
9 x 7,8 x 1,7 cm

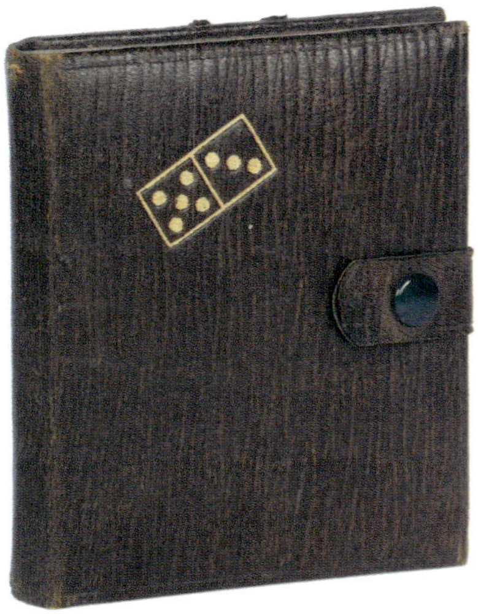

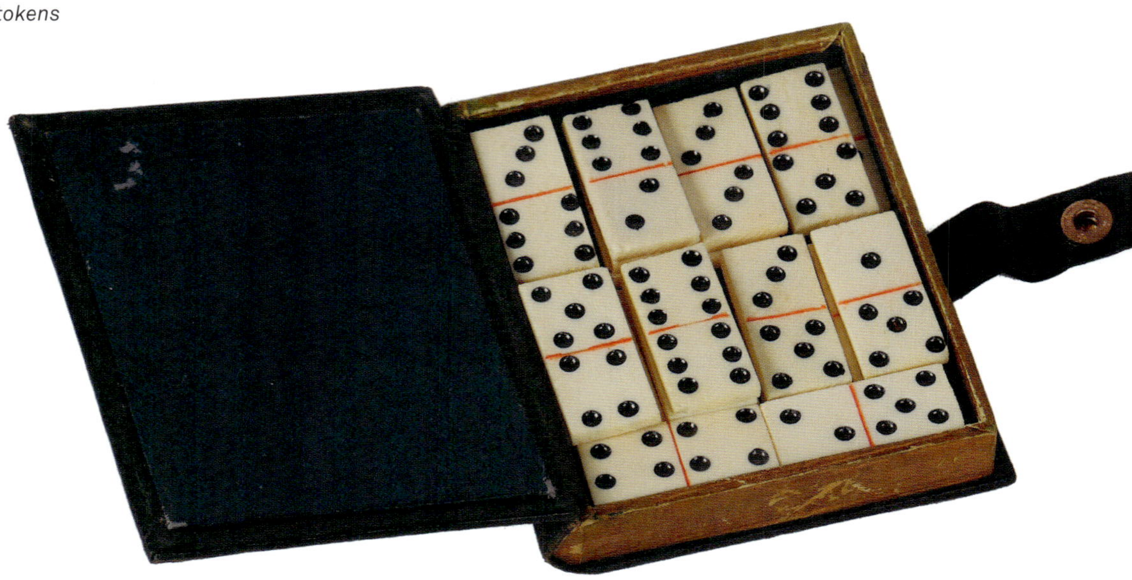

6.007
English Games, Vol. 1 + 2, Backgammon
Marmorierter Ganzlederband mit Vergoldung, zwei Bände aufklappbar, dreiseitiger Marmorschnitt, auf Vorder- und Hinterdeckel, Lederintarsien-Schachbrett
Marbled full leather volumes with gilding, hinged, all edges marbeled, leather inlays, chessboard on the front and back covers.
7,2 x 42,2 x 21,2 cm

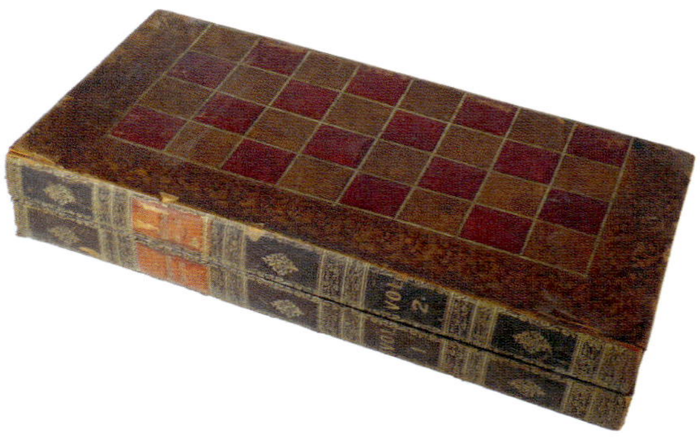

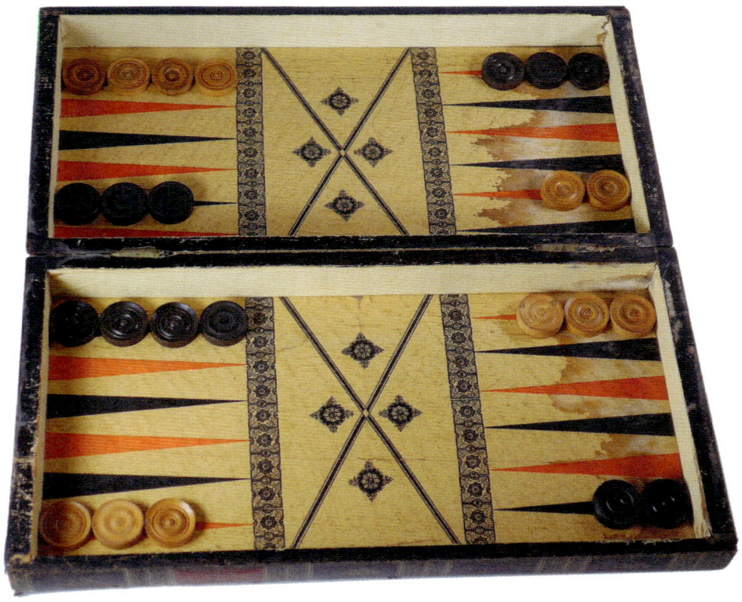

6.008
Chess, Vol. 524, E.S. Lowe
Reliefgeprägte Ledereinbanddecke, aufklappbar mit Verschluss-druckknopf, Holz-Spielbrett mit Schublade für die Spielsteine
Relief embossed leather cover, hinged with snap fastener, wooden game board with drawer to storage tokens
2,4 x 11,7 x 12,2 cm

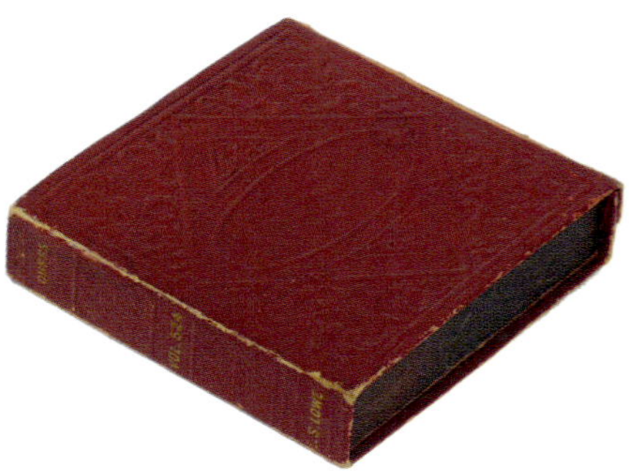

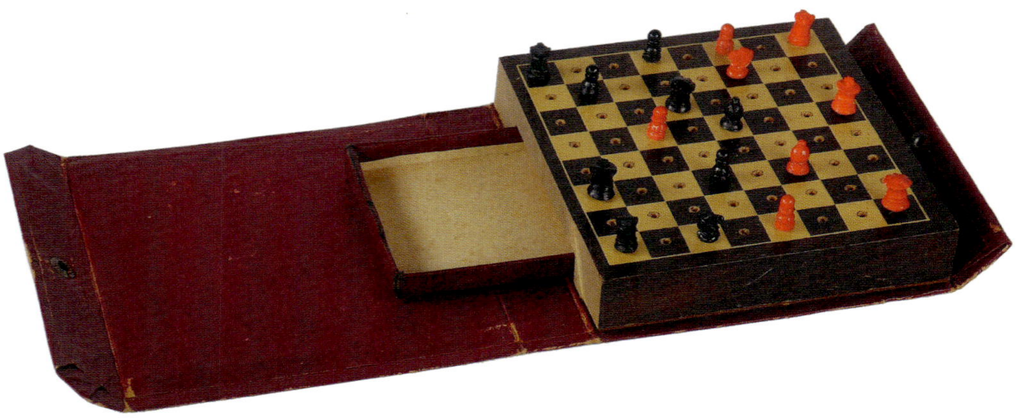

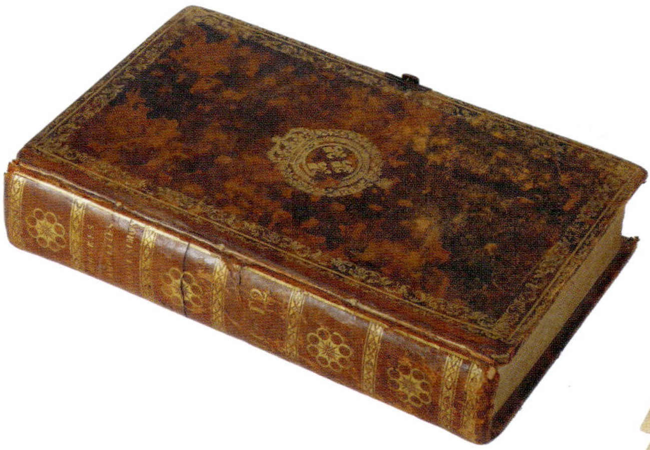

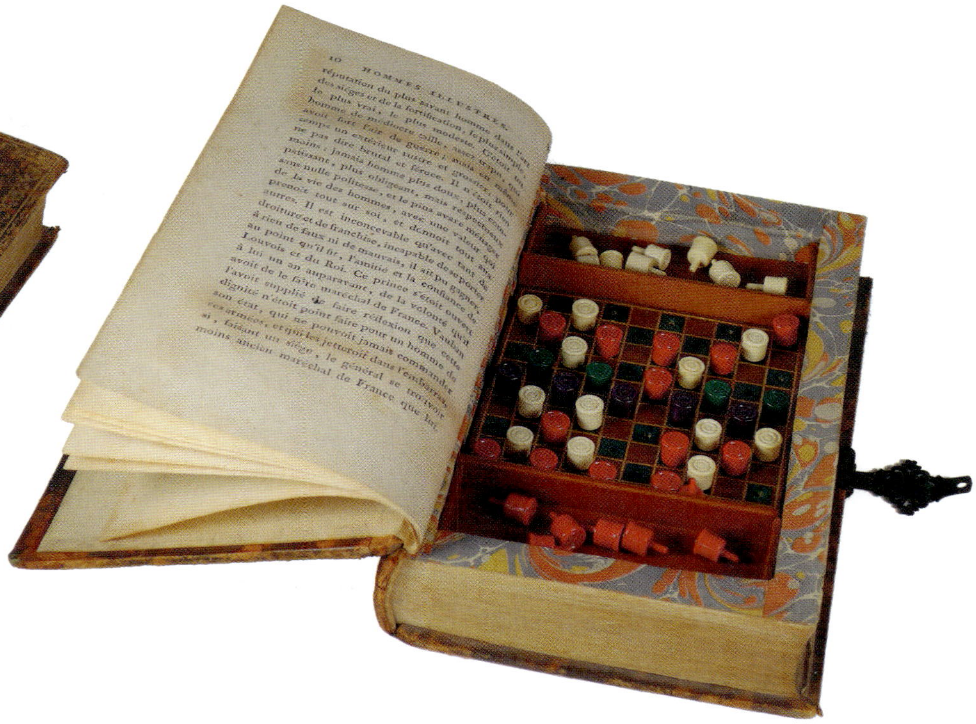

6.009
Oeuvres Complettes de Saint-Simon
Marmorierter Kalbsledereinband mit Vergoldung und Supralibros, Schließe, ausgehöhlter Buchblock für ein Brettspiel
Marbled calfskin binding with gilding and Supralibros, buckle, hollowed book block with a board game
3,8 x 20,8 x 13,3 cm

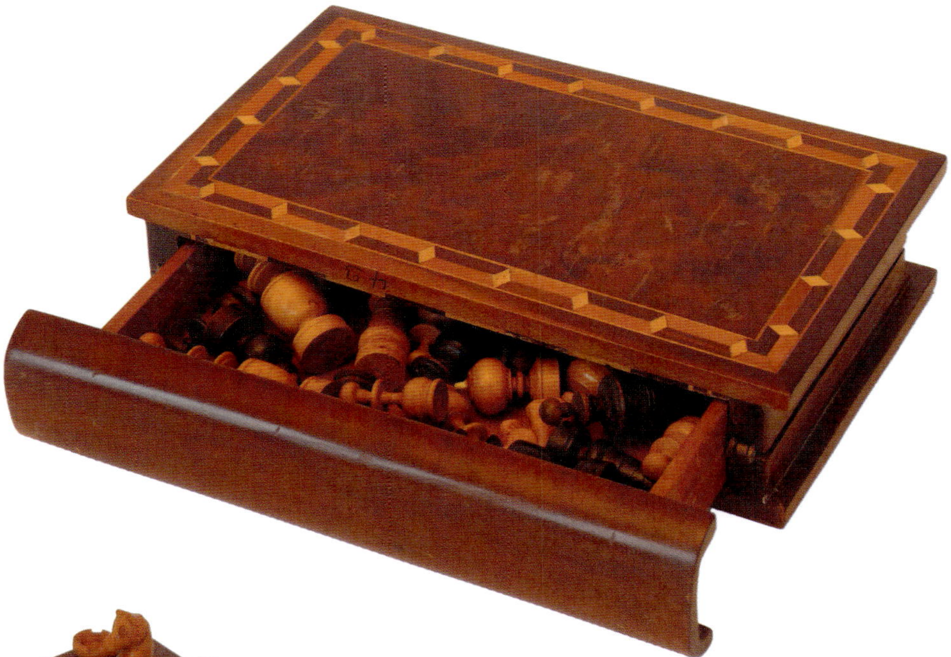

6.010
Schachspiel in Holzbuchkassette mit Einlegearbeiten auf Vorder- und Hinterdeckel, aufklappbar, Intarsien-Schachbrett mit Zierader, Schublade zum Versorgen der Figuren, Biedermeier
Chess game in a wooden box with marquetry on the front and back cover, hinged, chessboard with marquetry and décor like a vein, drawer for the pieces, Biedermeier style
22 x 14,8 x 5,2 cm

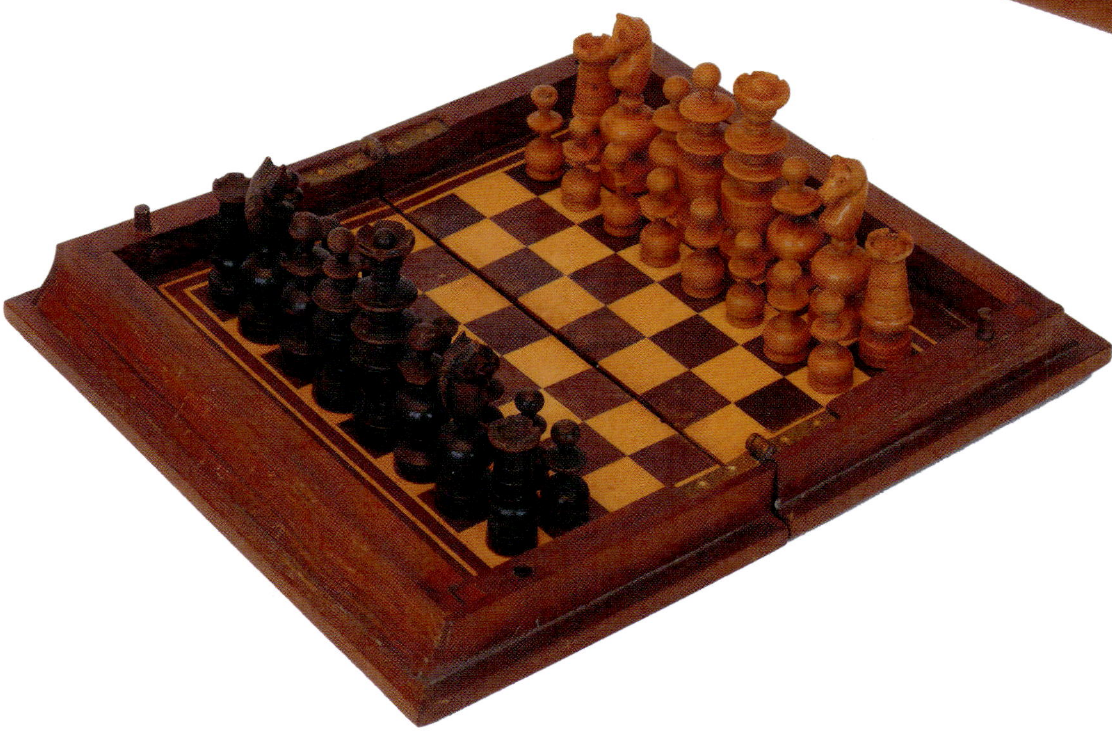

6.011
Blechdose für Spielkarten, schwarz lackiert mit farbigem Aufdruck, beidseitig zu öffnen
Tin box for playing cards, varnished in black with a colored imprint, opening on both sides
10,2 x 8,9 x 3,9 cm

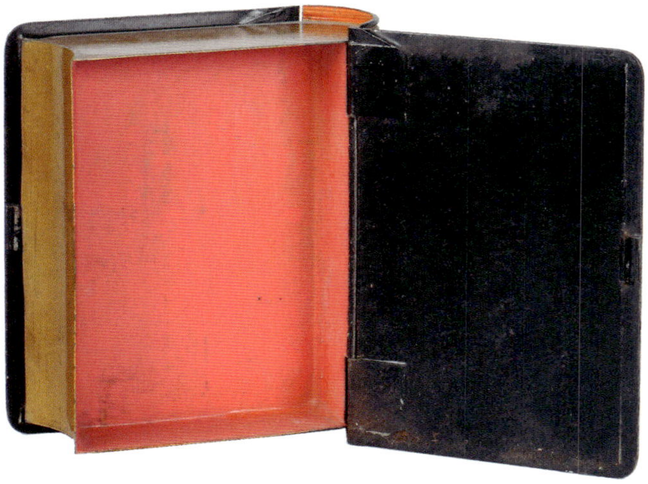

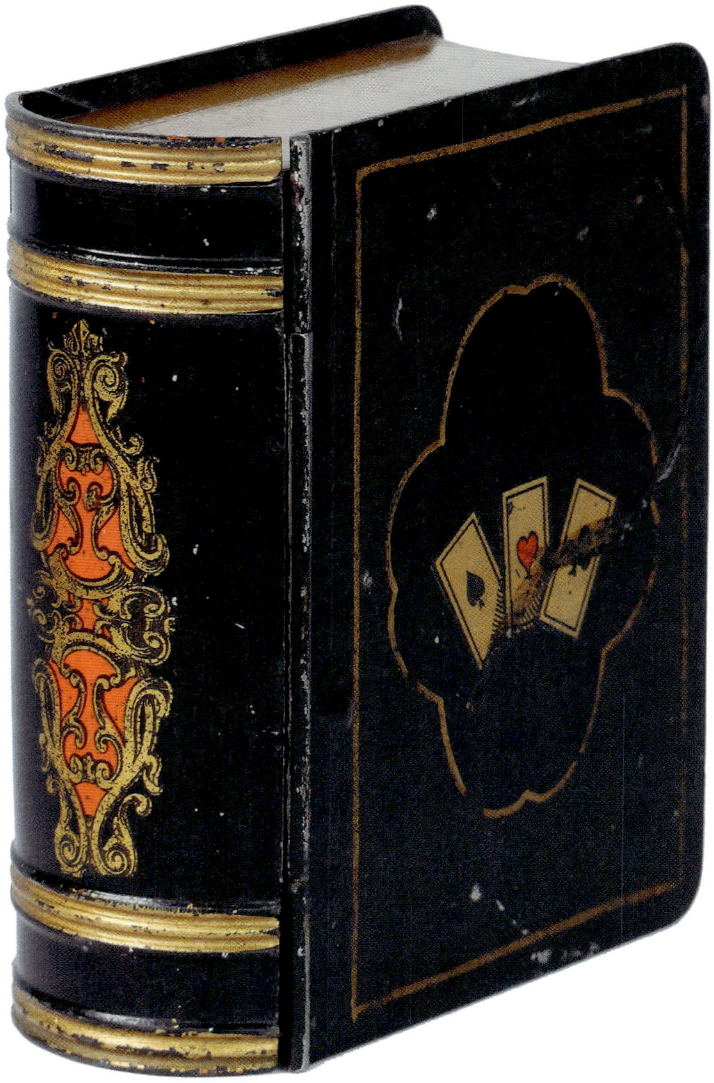

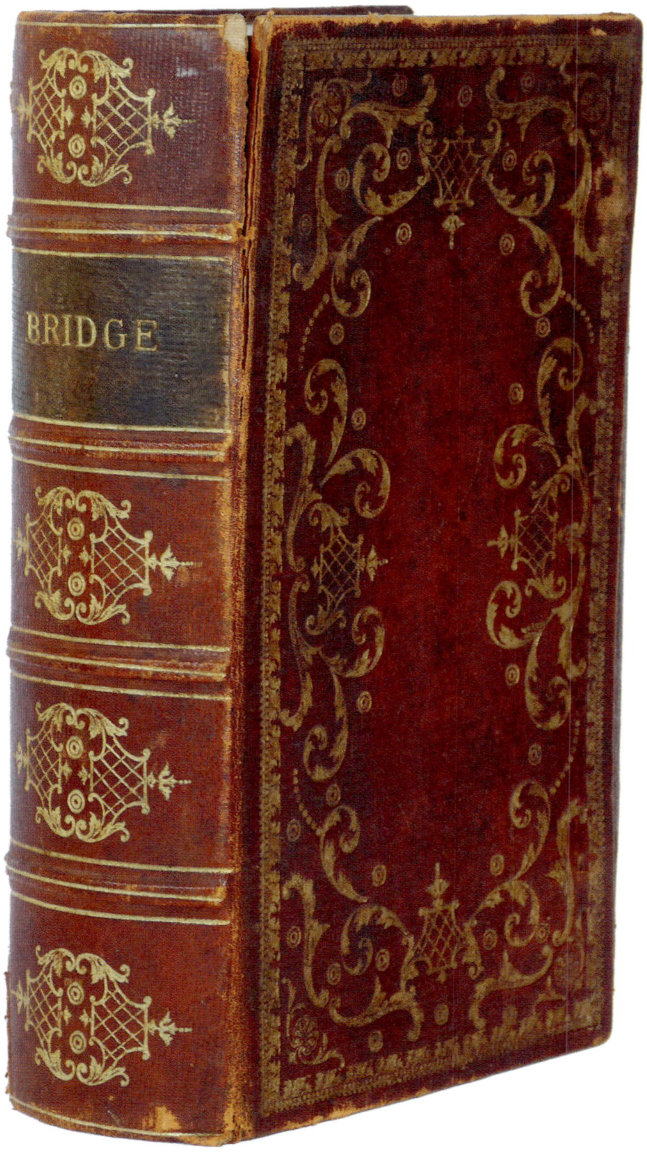

6.012
Bridge
Ganzleder-Buchkassette für Kartenspiele, Handvergoldung auf Rücken und Vorderdeckel, Titelschild, Innenfächer und Ledertasche, aufklappbarer Vorderschnitt, dreiseitiger Schneckenmarmorschnitt, zwei Druckknopfverschlüsse
Full leather book box for playing cards, manual gilding on the spine and cover, label, interior compartments and a leather pocket, hinged fore edge, scroll marble edges, two snap fasteners
5,8 x 20,5 x 12,9 cm

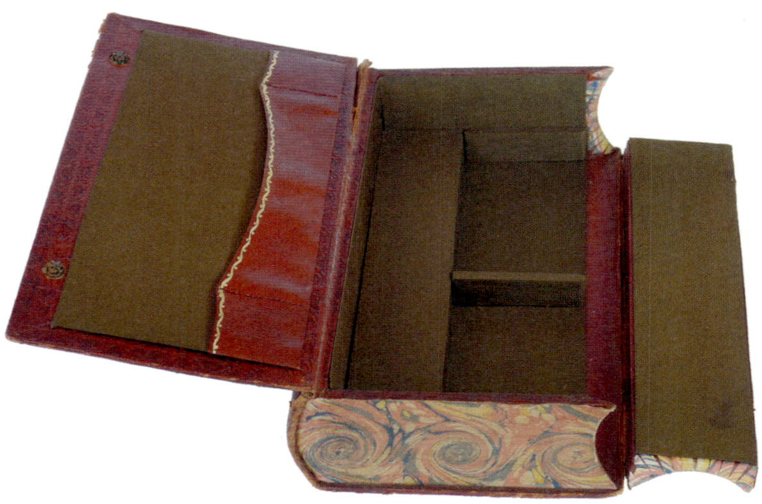

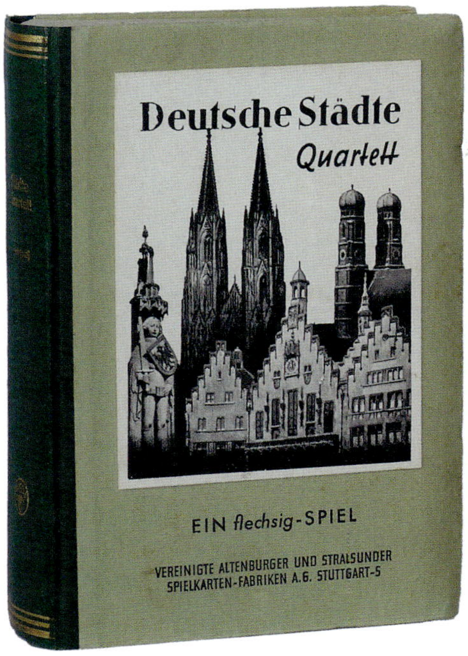

6.013
Städte-Quartett / ***City Quartet***
Ein flechsig Spiel, Halbgewebebuchschachtel mit 36 Spielkarten
A tough game, semi-woven fabric book box with 36 playing cards
Vereinigte Altenburger und Stralsunder Spielkartenfabriken AG Stuttgart-5, Germany
Um / *Around* 1950 | 13,6 x 9,9 x 2,5 cm

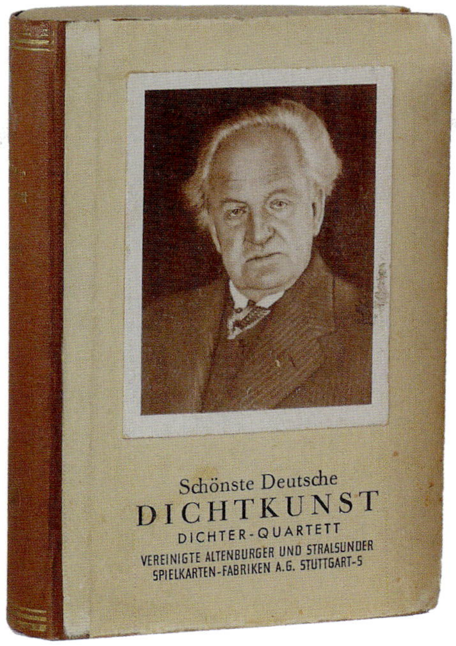

6.014
Dichter-Quartett / ***The Poet's Quartet***
Schönste Deutsche Dichtkunst
Halbgewebe-Buchschachtel mit 36 Spielkarten
The Most Beautiful German Poetry
Semi-woven fabric book box with 36 playing cards
Vereinigte Altenburger und Stralsunder Spielkarten-Fabriken AG Stuttgart-5, Germany
Um / *Around* 1950 | 13,5 x 10 x 2,5 cm

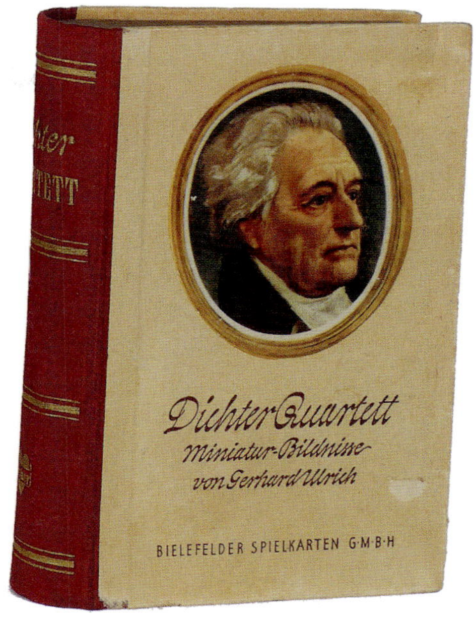

6.015
Dichter-Quartett / ***The Poet's Quartet***
Miniatur-Bildnisse von Gerhard Ulrich,
Halbgewebe-Buchschachtel mit 36 Spielkarten
Miniature portraits of Gerhard Ulrich,
Book box in half cloth binding with 36 playing cards
Bielefelder Spielkarten GmbH.
Um / *Around* 1950 | 12,7 x 9,4 x 3,3 cm

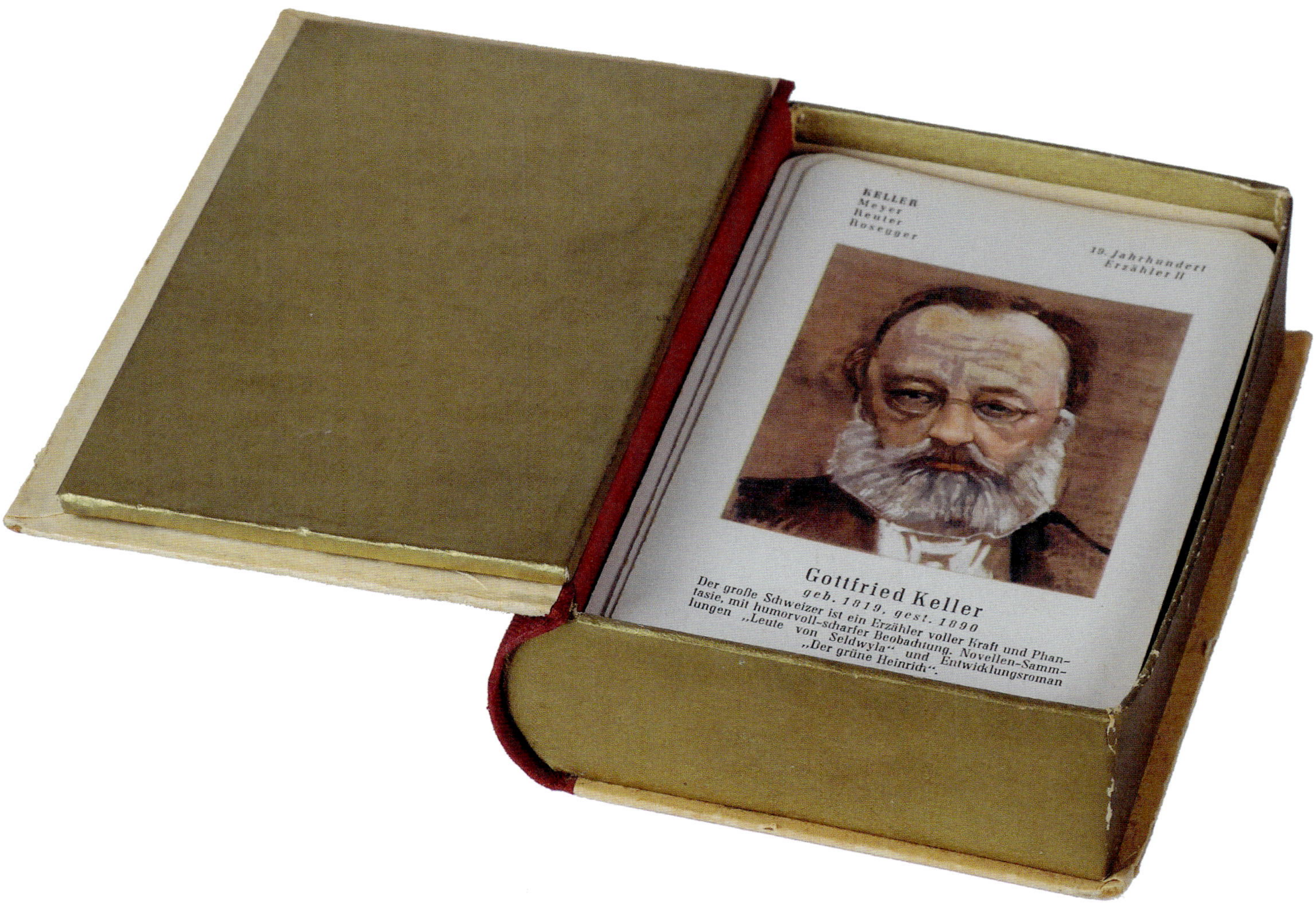

6.016
Lexicon, By Atozed,
Waddington's, Card Game
Kaliko-Schuber für Spielkarten
Calico slipcase for playing cards
England | Um / *Around* 1930
9,9 x 7,2 x 2.7 cm

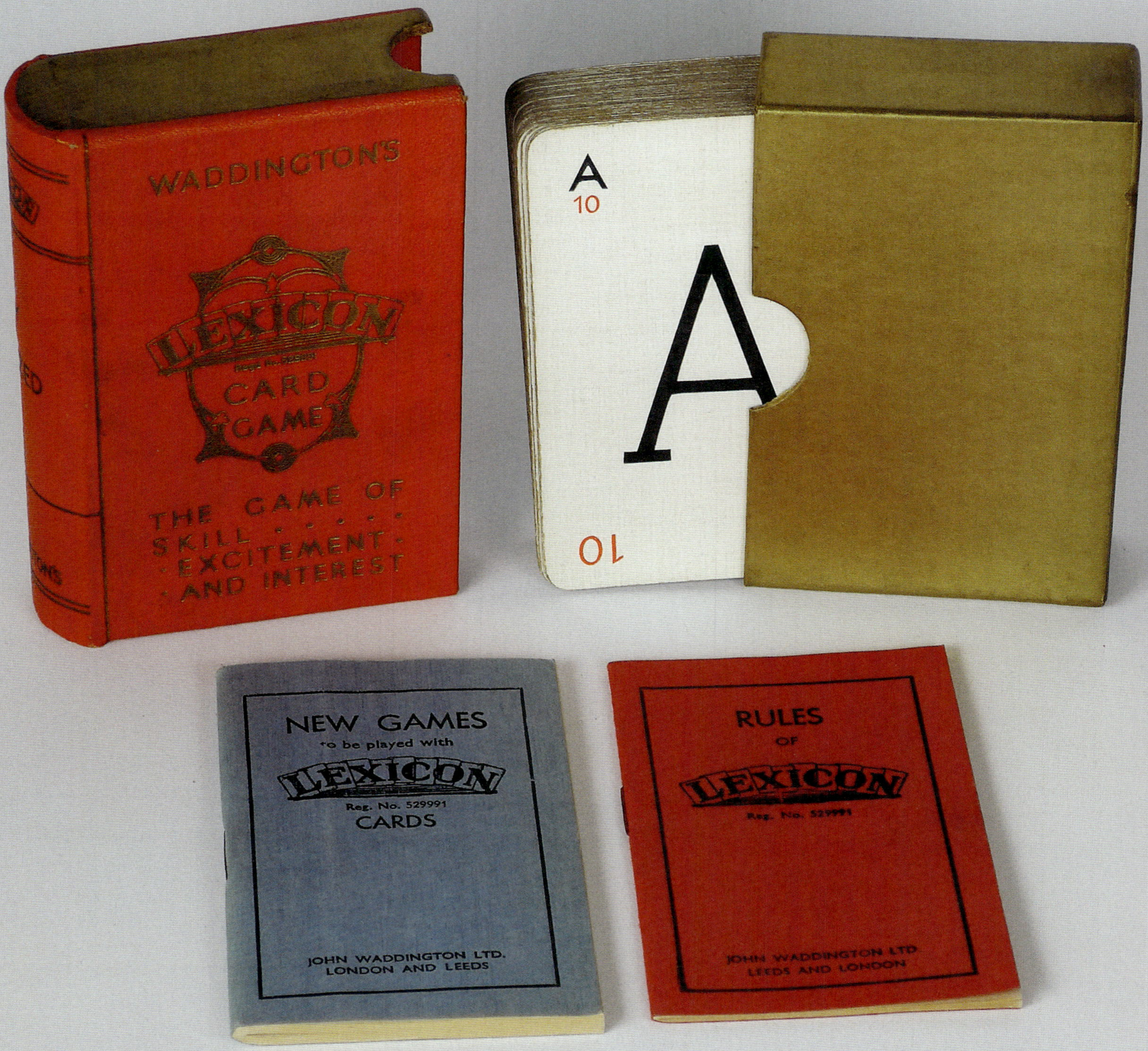

6.017
Lexicon, By Atozed, Waddington's, Card Game
Kaliko-Schuber für Spielkarten
Calico slipcase for playing cards
England
Um / *Around* 1930
13,1 x 9,9 x 2,7 cm

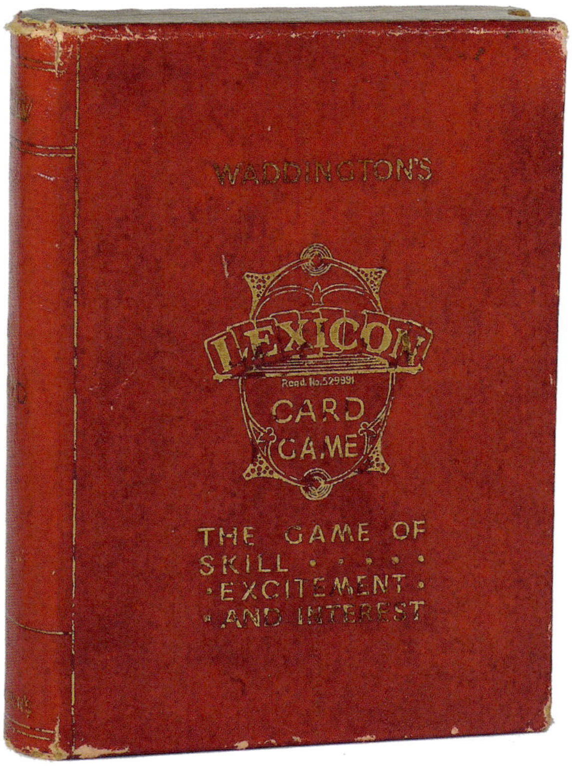

6.018
Bridge Markers
Kunstlederschuber mit Spielberichtsbogen und Bleistifte
Synthetic leather slipcase with play report sheet and pencils
Um / *Around* 1930 | 13 x 10,2 x 2,3 cm

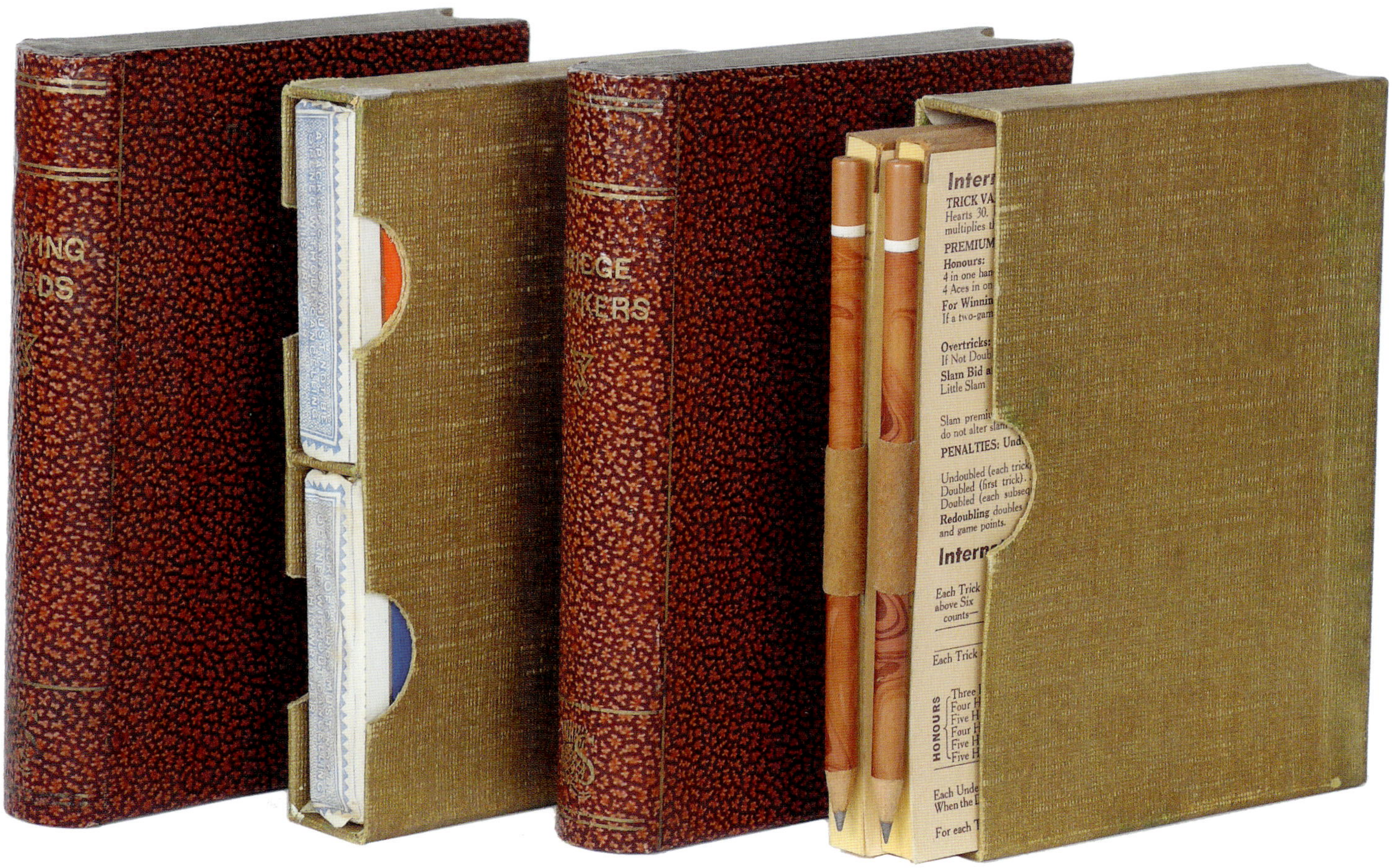

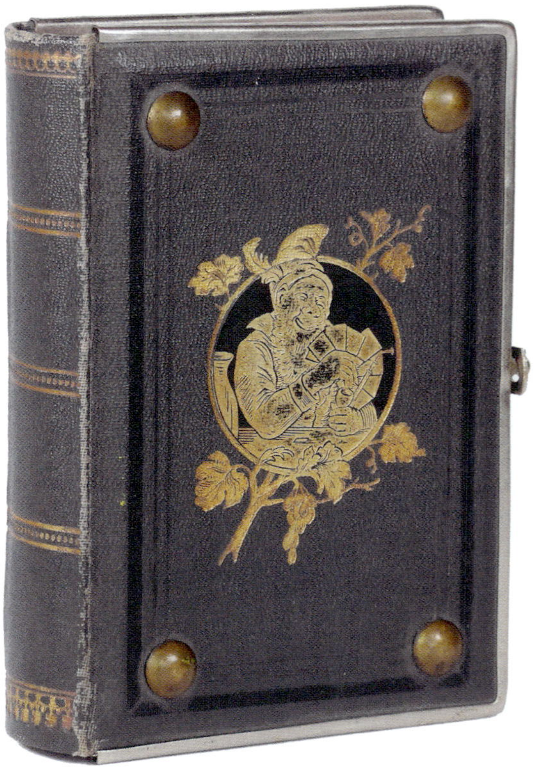

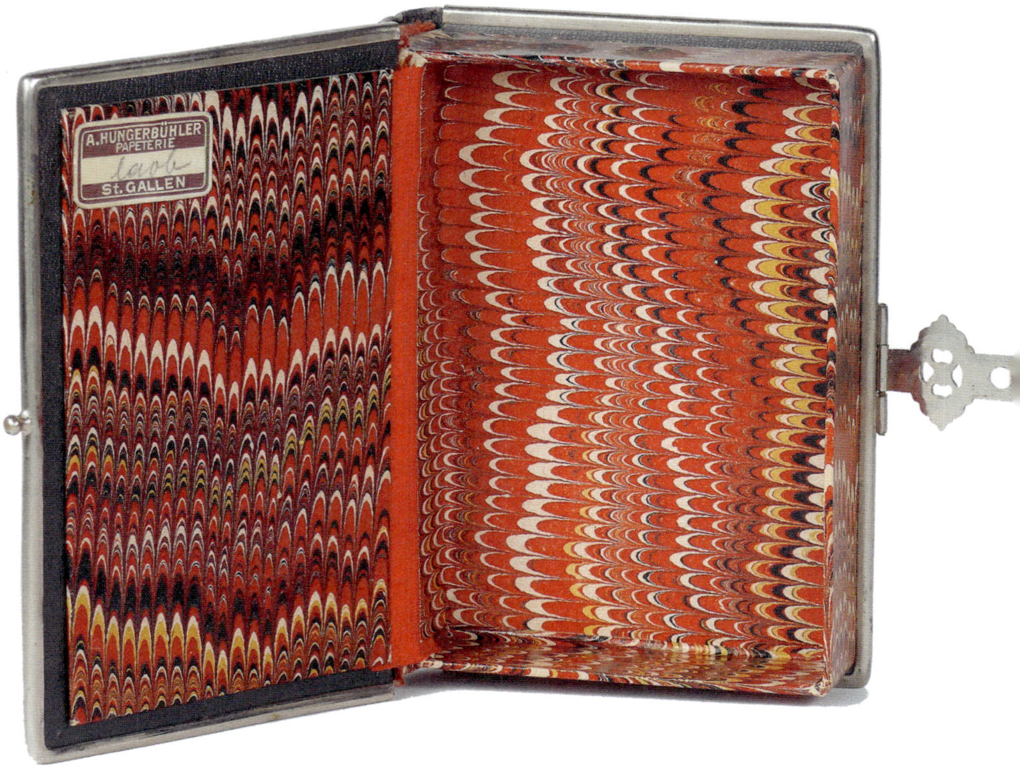

6.019
Kaliko-Dose für Spielkarten, Goldprägung mit jassendem Zwerg, Schnitt und ausgefüttert mit Kammmarmorpapier, Kantenschoner, Schließe und je vier Buckel
Calico box for playing cards, gold embossing showing a jass dwarf, edges and lining comb marbled paper, edge protectors, buckle and four humps each
Hungerbühler, Papeterie | St. Gallen, Schwitzerland | 10,5 x 7,6 x 2,3 cm

6.020
Drei Minilederschuber für Spielkarten mit Verschlussriemen, Metallrückenverzierung
Three mini leather slipcases for playing cards with closure straps, metallic ornaments on the spine
4,5 x 6,4 x 4 cm

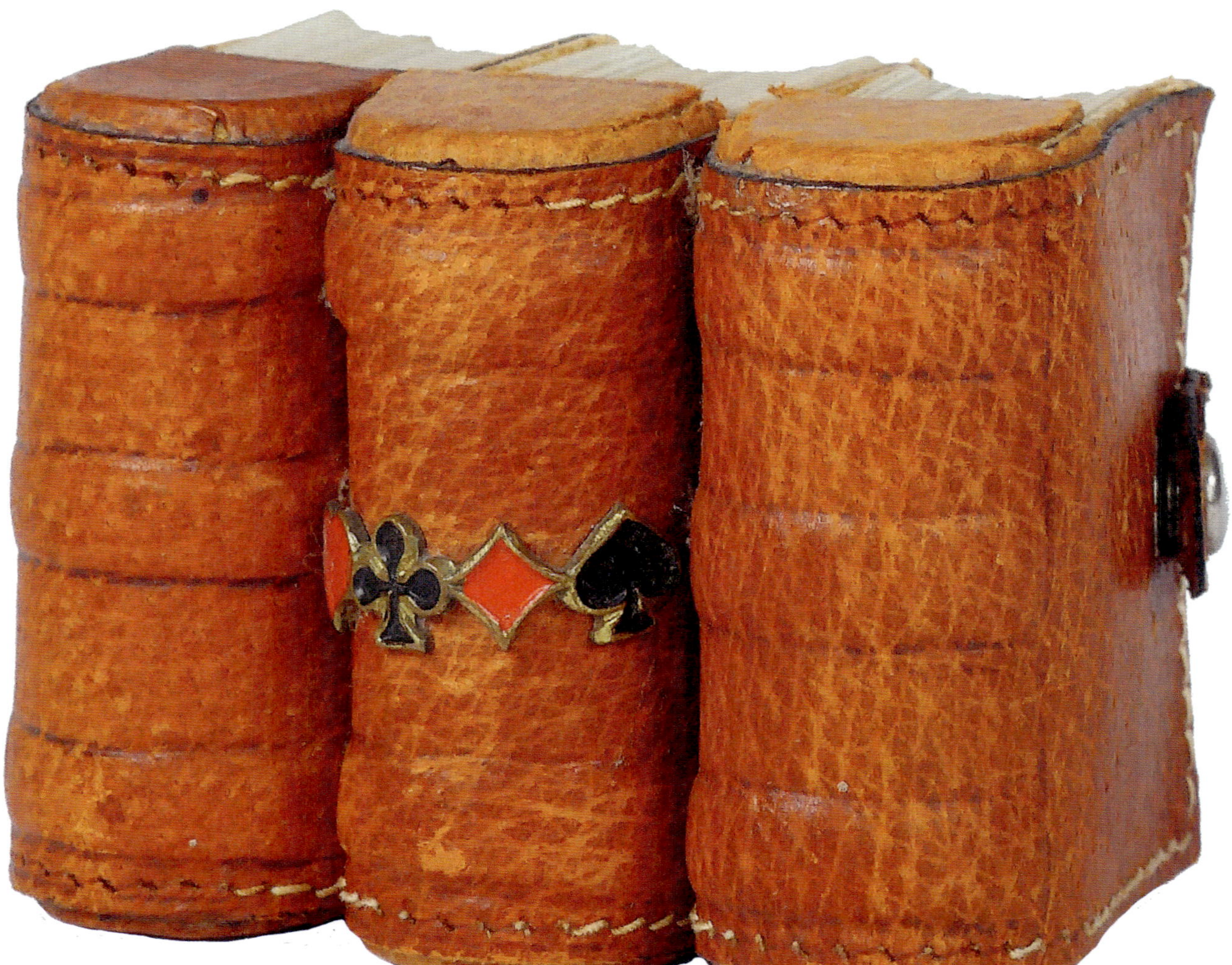

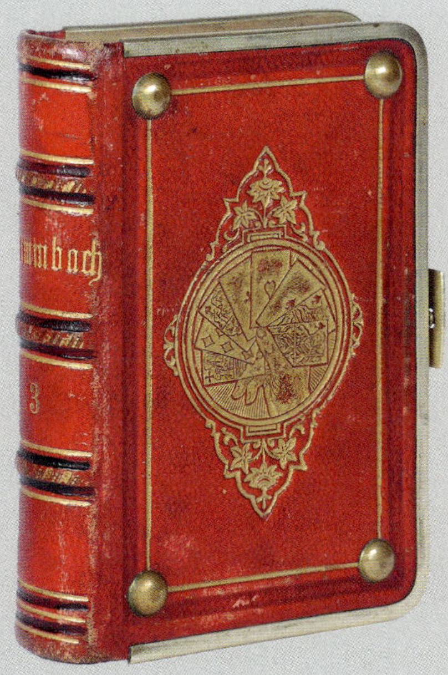

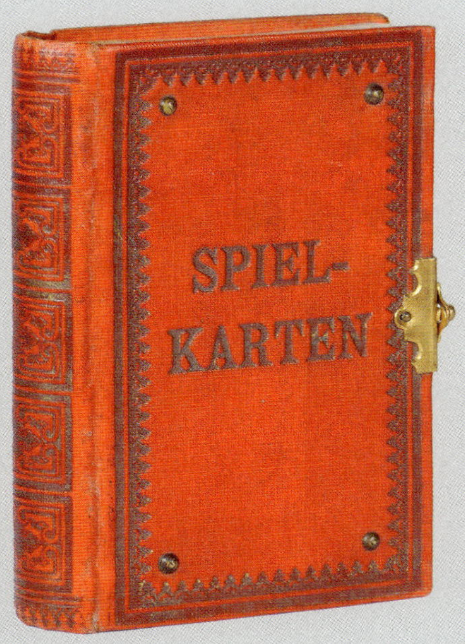

6.021
Stammbuch 3 *Family album 3*
Ganzlederdose für Spielkarten, Prägung auf dem Vorder- und Hinterdeckel, zweiseitiger Marmorschnitt, Kantenschoner, Schließen und je vier Buckel
full leather box for playing cards, embossing on the covers, double-sided marble edges, edge protectors, clasps and four humps each
Buchbinderei Schubert Zürich, Switzerland
10,1 x 7,3 x 2,2 cm

6.022
Spielkarten, Kaliko-Dose für Spielkarten, Prägung auf dem Vorderdeckel, zweiseitiger Buntpapierschnitt, Schließe und je vier Buckel
Playing cards, calico box for playing cards, embossing on the front cover, two-sided color paper edges, clasp and four humps each
10 x 7,4 x 2,2 cm

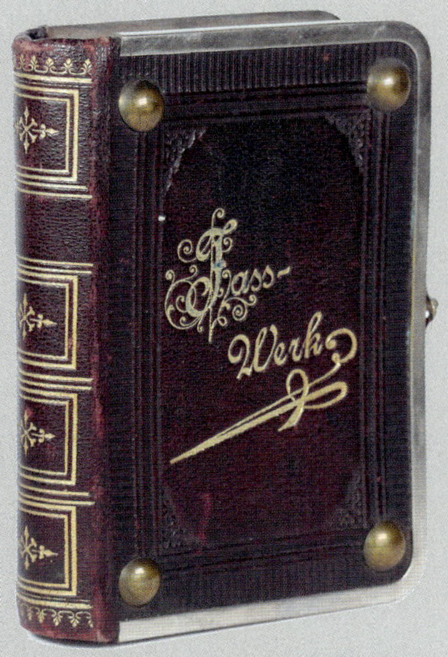

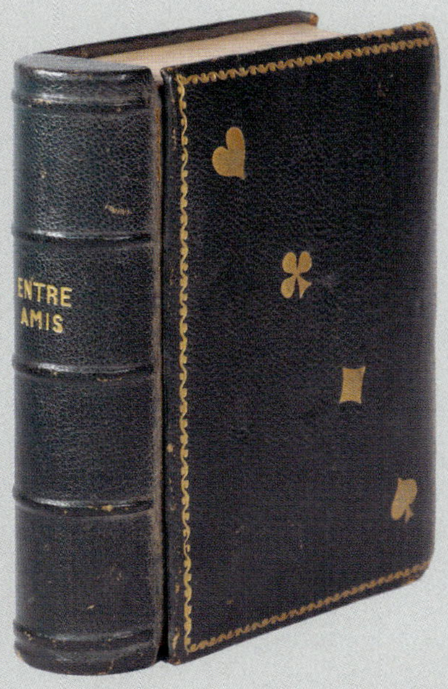

6.023
Jass-Werk
Ganzlederdose für Spielkarten, Goldprägung, zweiseitiger Kammmarmorschnitt, Kantenschoner, Schließe und je vier Buckel
Full leather box for playing cards, gold tooling, double-sided combed marble edges, edge protectors, buckle and four humps
10,6 x 8,1 x 2,5 cm

6.024
Entre Amis
Wattierter Ganzledereinband mit Vergoldung, Box für Spielkarten, Tasche für ein Notizbüchlein, Zuglasche
Padded full leather binding with gilding, box for playing cards, pocket for a notebook, pull tab
11,3 x 10,4 x 3,4 cm

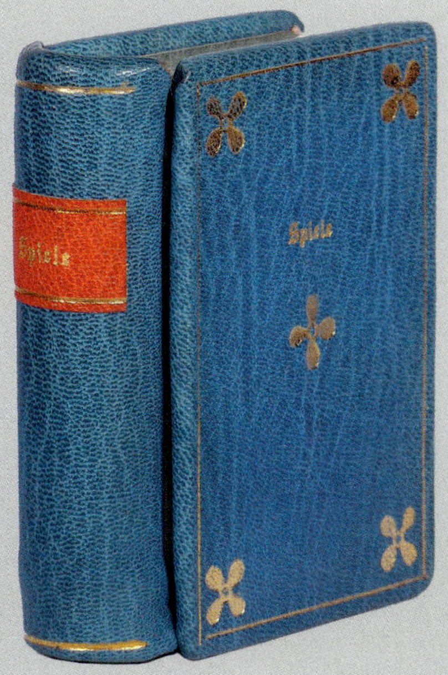

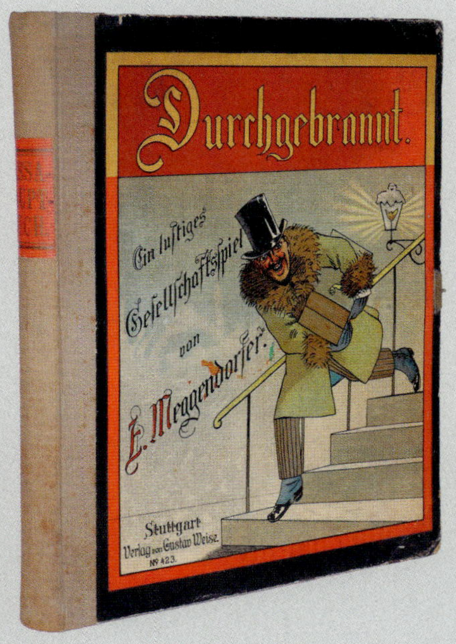

6.025
Spiele / *Games*
Lederbox mit Schublade, zwei Kartenspiele, fünf Würfel, Rückenschild, Rücken- und Deckelvergoldung, dreiseitiger Goldschnitt.
Leather box with drawer, two card games, five dices, spine label, gilt spine, cover and edges
Sybille und August Wirz Winterthur, Switzerland
8,9 x 7,6 x 2,9 cm

6.026
Cassa-Haupt-Buch, Durchgebrannt
Cassa-book, Burnt out
Gesellschaftsspiel mit 14 Spielkarten, ca. 100 Zahlenchips und drei Würfel
A parlor game with 14 playing cards, about 100 chips and three dices
E. Meggendorfer, Stuttgart, Gustav Weise, No.423
1895–1914 | 3,2 x 31,1 x 27,5 cm

6.027
Zwillingsbuch aus Holz für Spielkarten, rot/schwarz lackiert mit Jasskarten- und Würfelmotiv, beide Rücken ausschwenkbar zum Versorgen der Karten, Schublade im Buchstand
Wooden twin book for playing cards, varnished in red/black with illustrations of Jass cards and dices, both spines swing out to supply the cards, a drawer in the bookstand
15,5 x 11,2 x 8,5 cm

6.028
Byrrh. Une partie qui finit bien finit toujours par un Byrrh
Blechdose für Spielkarten, rot lackiert mit farbigem Aufdruck
Tin box for playing cards, varnished in red with a colored imprint
Frankreich / *France*
Um / *Around* 1940
10,5 x 6,9 x 2,3 cm

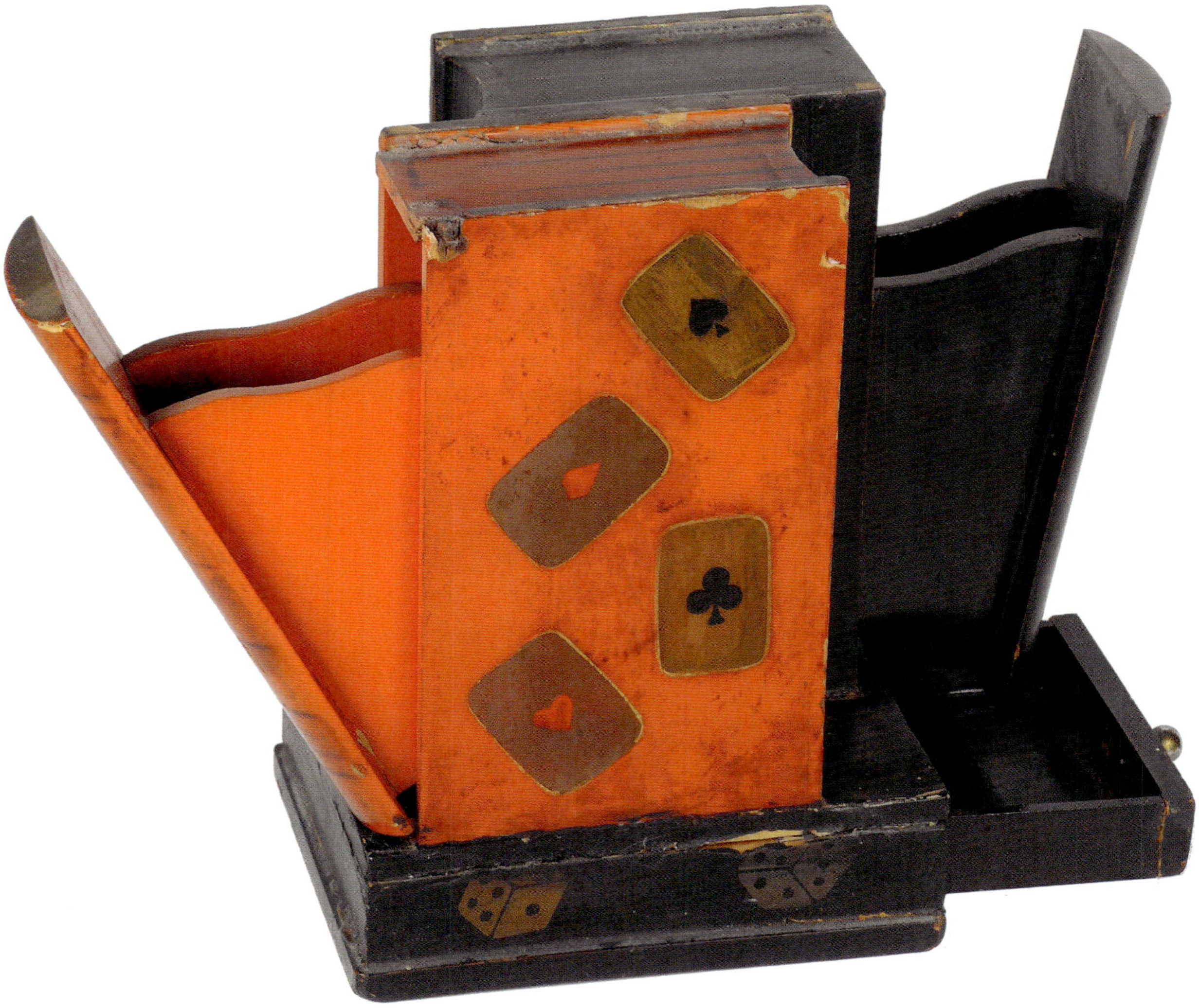

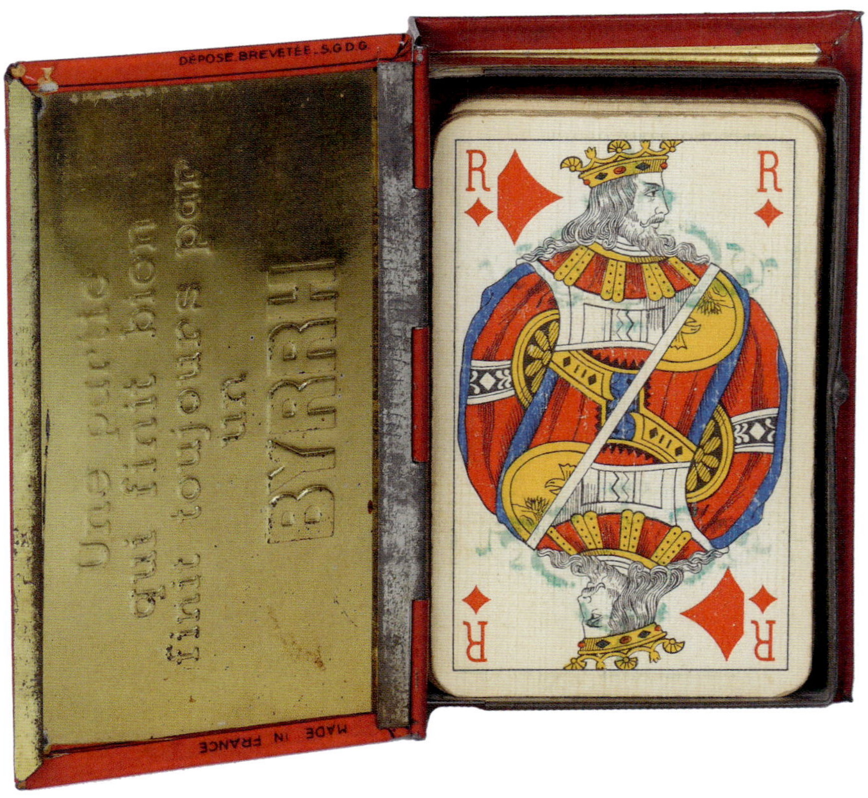

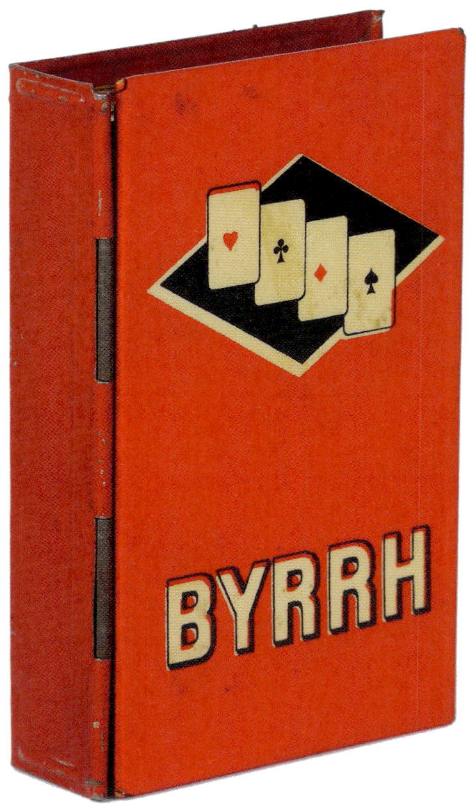

6.029
Lederdose mit vier Fächern für Spielkarten, zwei eingelegte Spielkarten auf dem Vorderdeckel, Handvergoldung, ausgefüttert mit Spaltleder
Leather box with four compartments for playing cards, two inserted playing cards on the lid, manual gilding, lined with split leather
Spulcioni Firenze, Italy
7,3 x 11 x 11,6 cm

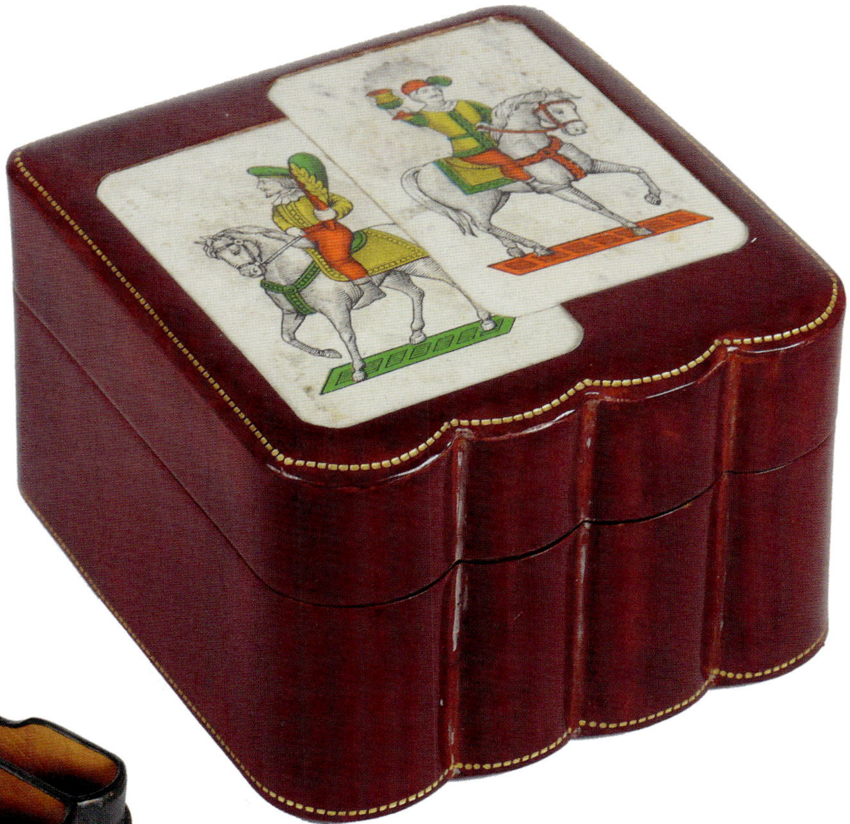

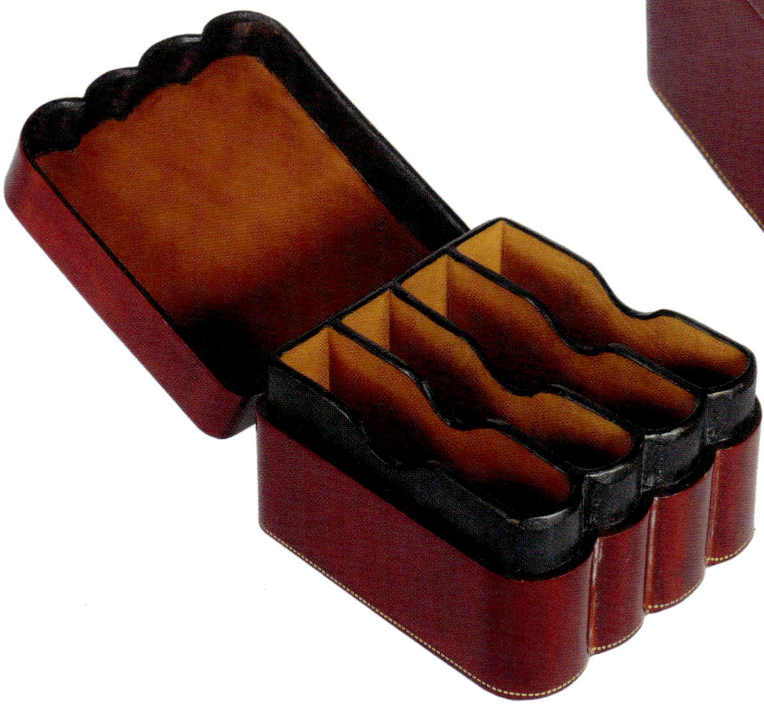

6.030
Otto Benz, Fabrik elektrischer Maschinen Dübendorf
Factory of electrical machines
Gewebekassette für Spielkarten, Titelschild, vier Fächer für Spielkarten, Kreide und Schwamm, einschiebbare Schiefertafel
Box made of fabric for playing cards, label plate, four compartments for playing cards, chalk and sponge, insertable slate
3,5 x 21,9 x 15,8 cm

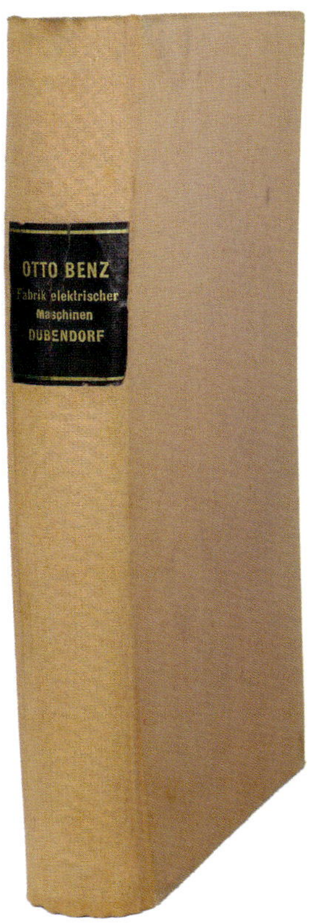

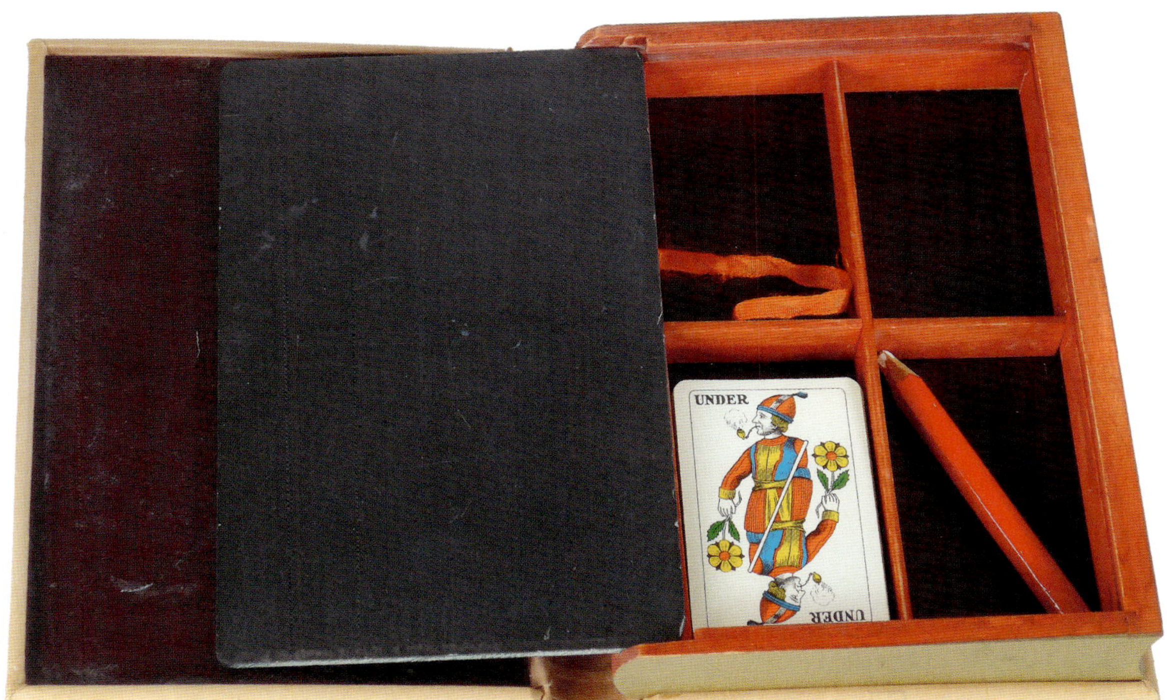

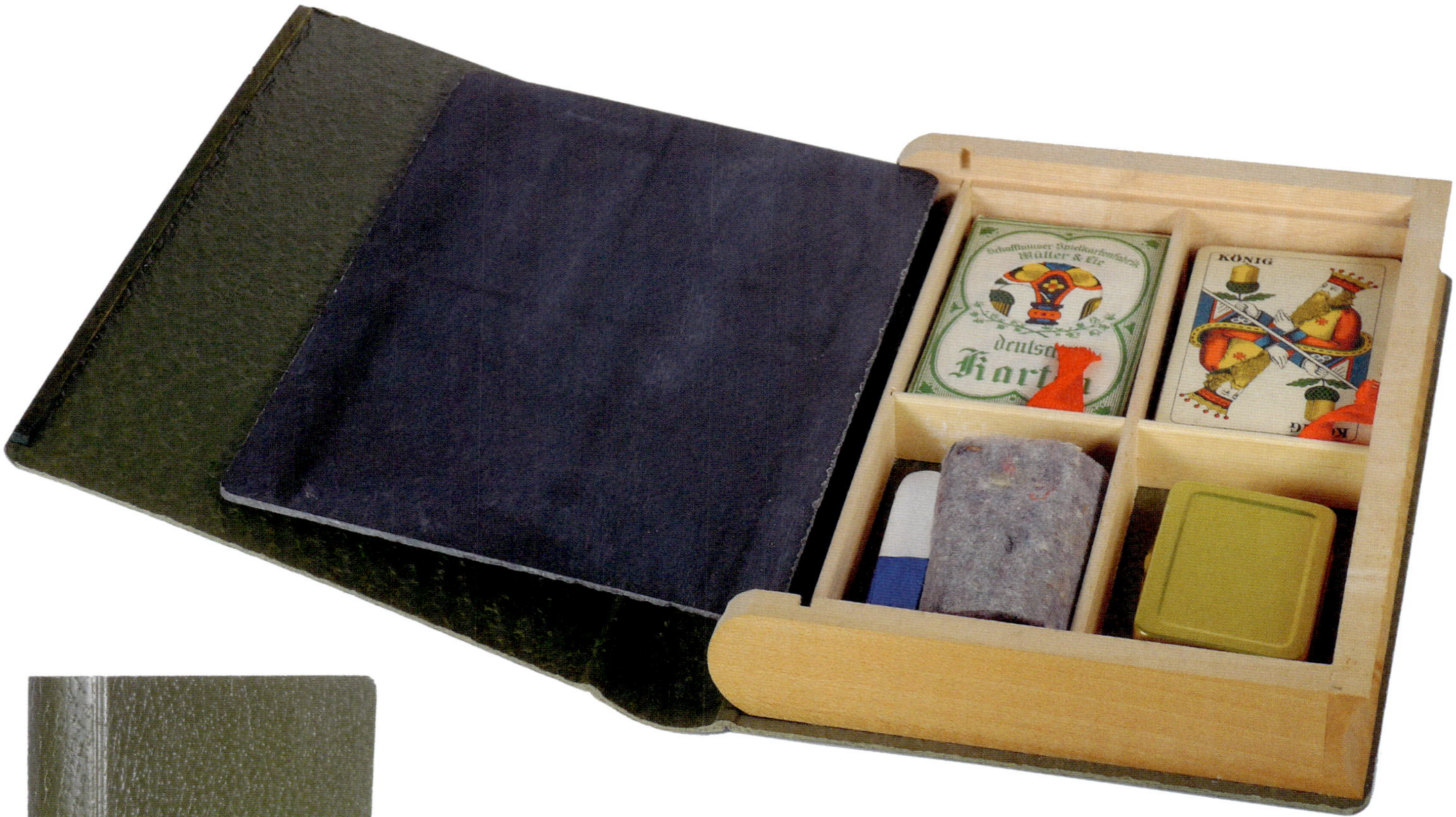

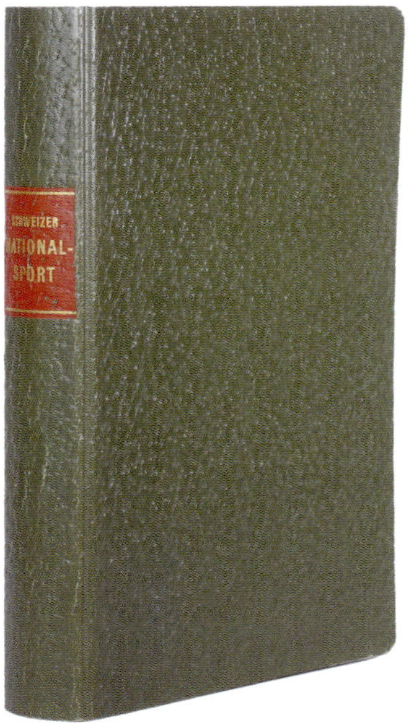

6.031
Schweizer Nationalsport / ***Swiss National Sport***
Kartonkassette für Spielkarten, Titelschild, vier Fächer für Karten, Kreide, Schwamm, einschiebbare Schiefertafel
Cardboard box for playing cards, title plate, four compartments for cards, chalk, sponge, insertable slate
3,5 x 21,9 x 15,8 cm

6.032
Maroquin-Box für Spielkarten, Rücken- und Deckelvergoldung, Druckknopfverschluss, Zugbänder
Maroquin box for playing cards, gilding on the spine and lid, snap fastener, drawstring
13 x 9,5 x 2,9 cm

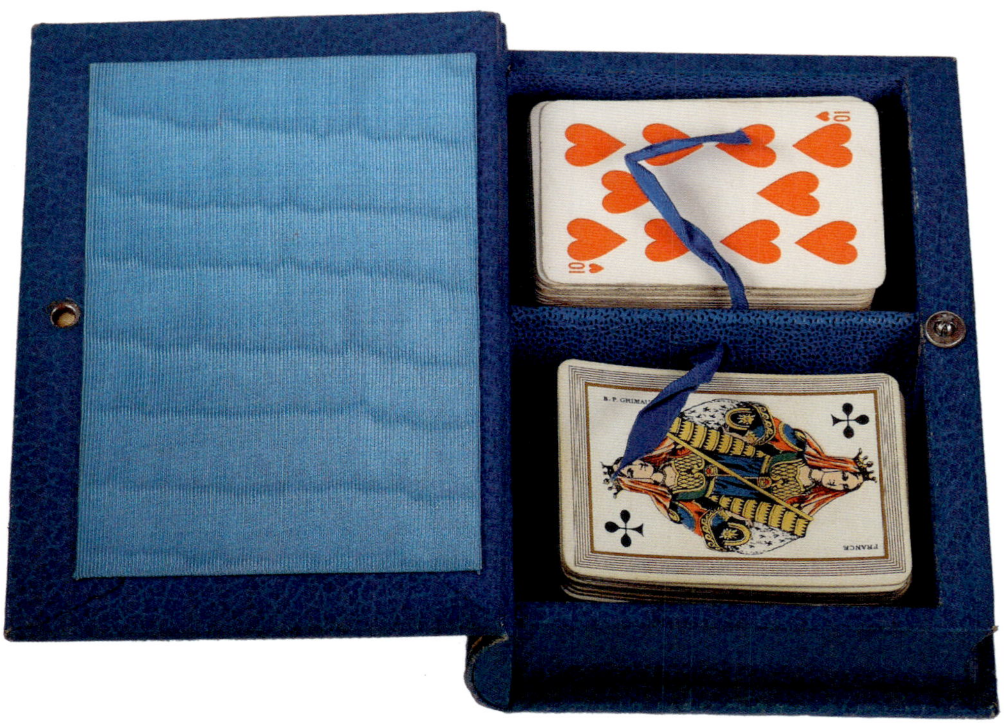

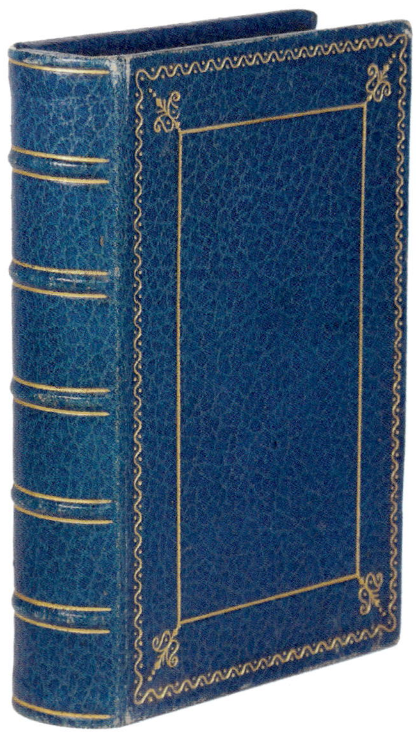

6.033
Boite à Cartes, Suze Apéritif
Holzdose für Spielkarten, schwarz/rot lackiert mit Schieber am Vorderschnitt zum Öffnen
Wooden box for playing cards, varnished in black/red with a sliding opening on the fore edge
Frankreich / *France* | 12,5 x 7,5 x 3 cm

6.034
Wort-Spiel Jeux de mots Pun
Wer beginnt, hat aus seinen Buchstaben ein Wort zu bilden. Gerillte Buchschachtel mit 50 Buchstabentäfelchen
The one who begins has to form a word from his letters. Grooved book box with 50 letter plates
1,3 x 8,9 x 1,7 cm

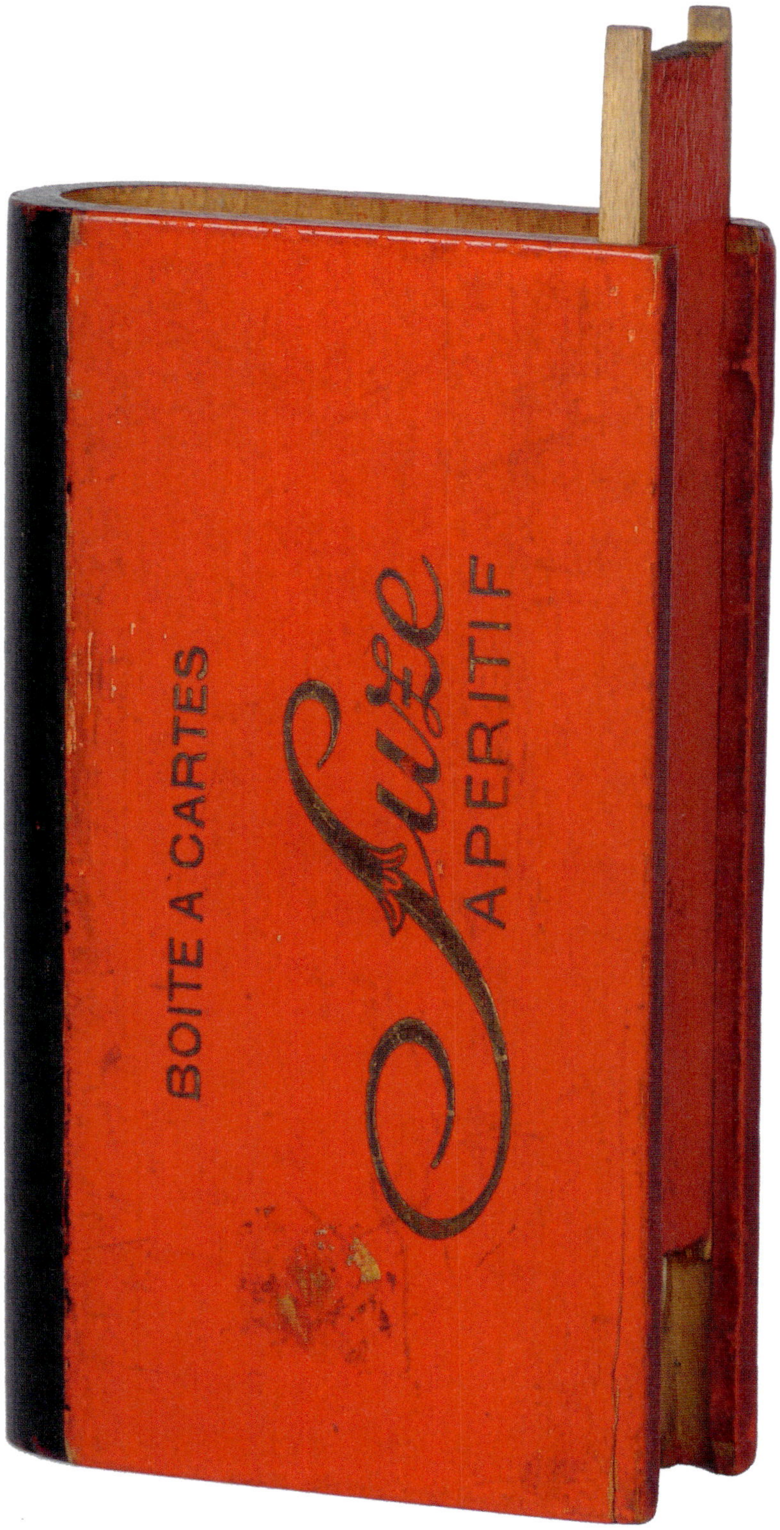

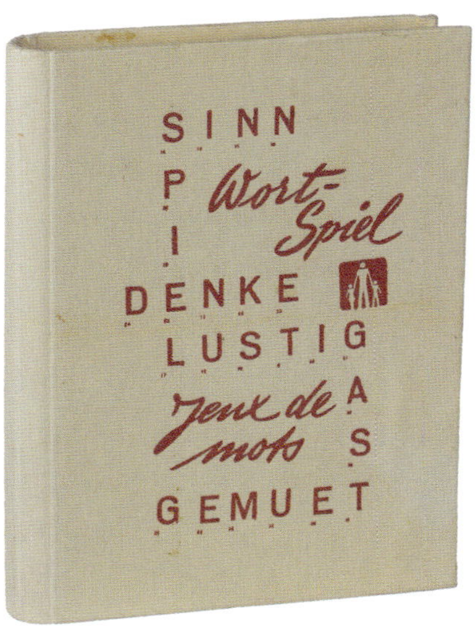

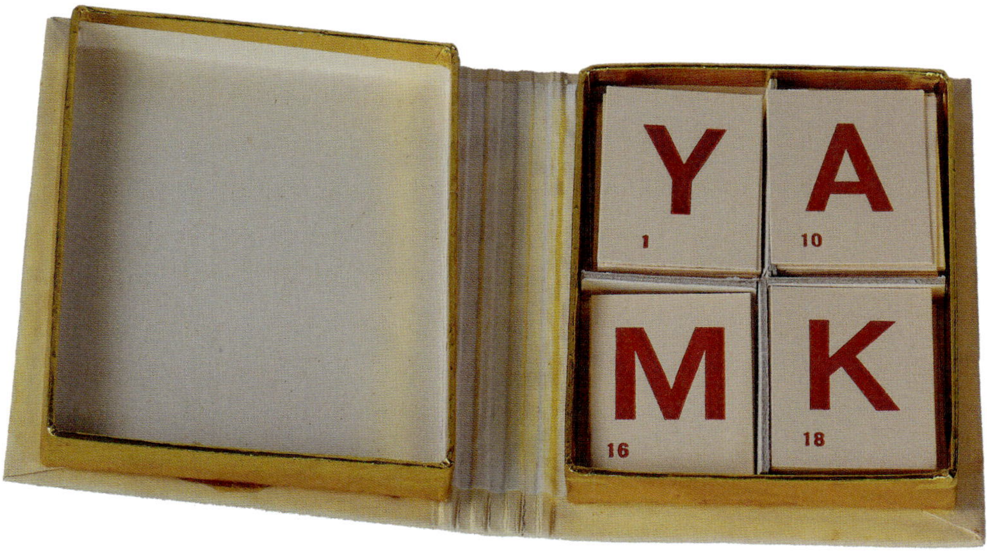

Schöner Bücher Schein

Bruno Weber

Wer wissen will, muss fühlen. Scheinbücher bieten dazu gute Gelegenheit, sie sind aparte Vorspiegelungen, unbrauchbar und nützlich zugleich, man verwendet sie als listige Fühler des Wissens. Schöne Bücher, die vielversprechend scheinen, aber nicht enthalten, was zur Erscheinung kommen soll, werden als ein schöner Bücherschein wahrgenommen: Buchattrappen, imaginierte Bücher, Livres feints, Faux books, „Objekte und Gestaltungen, die Bücher vortäuschen, ohne es zu sein". Diese im Lexikon des gesamten Buchwesens 1987 formulierte Definition stammt vom Pilgerzeichenforscher Kurt Köster (1912–1986), seit 1954 Direktor und von 1969 bis 1975 Generaldirektor der Deutschen Bibliothek in Frankfurt am Main, der Scheinbücher als „Buchverfremdung" begriff und erkundete. Die Buchverfremdungen sind Codices, herzuleiten von lateinisch caudex für Holz vom Baumstamm, welche beliebig viele Einzelbogen in Lagen zu je vier Seiten von Blättern aus Papyrus, Pergament oder Papier, von Hand beschrieben oder bedruckt, als lesbare Informationsträger enthalten sollen, oben und unten von Holzbrettern umfasst und seitlich gebunden. Solche Bände, angeblich Manuskript oder Druckschrift in geschlossenem Zustand, sind kostbare Bücher, mit Charme und besonderen haptischen Qualitäten ausgestattet, die scheinen wie sie sind, aber mehr sind, wie sie scheinen: Zimelien, weil sie die Illusion des richtigen Sachverhalts verkörpern. Denn sie sind anders, und dieses Andere ist ein Mehr. Wie sie als Buch ins Auge fallen, also wahrscheinlich sind und als glaubwürdig wahrgenommen werden, sind sie bloß anscheinend, mithin scheinbar: Faux books und Livres feints, imaginierte Bücher, Buchattrappen.

Als einleuchtende Fiktion sind Scheinbücher zweifellos trügerisch, doch nicht wesenlos, nicht ohne Bedeutung: Seien sie dicht und fest, gediegen hart und homogen, kompakt, massiv, schwer und undurchdringlich wie ein Block, Klotz oder Stein, ein Gebilde zu Verborgenem und Geheimplatz, oder seien sie hohl und leer als Gefäß für Flüssiges aller Art, Flakon oder Phiole, zumal Gehäuse und Behälter für Festes aller Art, Büchse, Dose und Etui, Futteral, Kapsel, Kassette, Schachtel, Schatulle oder Tresor, als Reliquiar, Klappsonnenuhr und Musikinstrument. Was fest ist, befestigt (ein Briefbeschwerer), auch was hohl ist, bildet (ein Vanity case). Den Unterschied zwischen beiden Aggregatzuständen beleuchtet folgende Anekdote. Zwei Scheinbücher treffen sich in der Sauna. Fragt einer den andern: „Warum bist du so dicht?" Der beteuert: „Ich bin vom Dichter, ungelesen, so bleib ich was ich bin. Warum bist du so hohl?" Meint jener: „Bin doch ein Bestseller, innerlich umschmeichelt vom Altneuen, so bleib ich was ich bin." Also sind Scheinbücher im Strom des Ewigwechselnden das Bleibende. Dies hat kein Geringerer als Friedrich Schiller begriffen, in dessen Schauspiel Wilhelm Tell (1804) die Nachbildung des Steinernen Buchs in der Hohlen Gasse bei Küssnacht zur Darstellung kommt (4. Aufzug 3. Szene): „Auf dieses Buch von Stein will ich mich setzen / Dem Wanderer zur kurzen Ruh bereitet."

Wer sich von Buchattrappen täuschen lässt, wird belohnt. Wir lassen uns gern von derlei befremdlichen Gegenständen täuschen, deren Form erkennbar, Funktion einsichtig, Rarität eindeutig erscheint. Nur können sie nicht rundheraus gelesen werden, denn sie sind in ihrer geschlossenen Gesellschaft erlesen. So repräsentieren Scheinbücher in erfreulicher Weise die Wissenschaft des mehrdeutigen Seins. Die Nichtübereinstimmung von Schein und Sein, Form und Funktion ist ihr wesentliches Merkmal. Wir durchschauen dies und freuen uns über dieses Wissen. So empfand es auch der Landesfürst und erfahrene Diplomat Jean de France, Ier duc de Berry (1360–1416), ein leidenschaftlicher Sammler von Juwelen, Goldschmiedearbeiten und Medaillen, Mäzen der Christine de Pisan und extravaganter Bibliophile, der über eine gelehrte Bibliothek von 300 Handschriften verfügte, wie er am Neujahrstag anno 1411 in seinem Palast in Bourges ein besonderes Kleinod als Codex in Empfang nahm: „Un livre contrefait d'une pièce de bois paincte en semblance d'un livre, où il n'a nuls fueillets ne rien escript; couvert de veluiau blanc, à deux fermouers d'argent dorez, esmaillez aux armes de Monseigneur; lequel livre Pol de Limbourc et ses deux freres donnerent à mondit Seigneur ausdictes estrainnes mil CCCC et X." Nach dieser Inventarnotiz von 1416 war die Gabe, das erste bezeugte und berühmteste Scheinbuch der Buchgeschichte, ein bemalter Holzklotz als Buch ohne Blätter und Schrift, in weißen Samteinband mit vergoldeten und heraldisch emaillierten Silberschließen gelegt. Dies, nachdem seine Hersteller, der Maler Paul de Limbourg und seine Brüder, die Goldschmiede Jean und Herman de Limbourg (um 1385/1388–1416), von 1405 bis 1409 das kostbare Stundenbuch Les Belles Heures du duc de Berry geschrieben und illuminiert hatten, nun auch die noch prächtigeren, 1416 unvollendet gebliebenen Très Riches Heures du duc de Berry in Arbeit hatten. Der Mäzen bedankte sich beim einfallsreichen Maler, seinem Lieblingskünstler, für die Vorspiegelung des neuen Wunderwerks, indem er ihm in der Hauptstadt Bourges den Palast des vormaligen Schatzmeisters Christoph de la Mer an der Rue Porte-Jaune (Nr. 5, Neubau des 18. Jahrhunderts) zur Verfügung stellte, eine Liegenschaft von fürstlichem Anschein, „une des plus grans et plus spacieuse et notable", wie es in einer Urkunde von 1434 heißt, in der König Charles VII deren Rückgabe an die Krone besiegelte. Wenn er sich nicht in Paris befand, wohnte Paul hier mit seiner Frau Gillette bis zu seinem frühen Tod 1416.

Auch die Erzherzogin Margarete von Österreich (1480–1530), seit 1507 Statthalterin der habsburgischen Niederlande, Mäzenin der Künste und Porträtsammlerin, besaß in ihrem Palast in Mechelen, Hauptresidenz der großen Regentin, neben der Bibliothek von nahezu vierhundert Büchern (größtenteils Handschriften) einen solchen „fainct livre" als Kästchen in violettem Samteinband, ebenfalls mit silbevergoldeten und wappengeschmückten Schließen. Es diente für ihre Malutensilien, wenn sie bei Gelegenheit als Porträt malerin zum Pinsel griff. Zudem war auch „ung cadrant fait en manière d'ung petit livret", eine Klappsonnenuhr in Form eines Codex in Silber, ihr Eigentum. Die frühesten bekannten Scheinbücher hatten sakralen Charakter, sie wurden im 6. und 7. Jahrhundert als Amulettkapsel, silbervergoldet oder aus Goldblech und juwelengeschmückt, am Gürtel oder an einer Halskette getragen. Alle diese und tausend andere Scheinbücher wurden, ob fest oder hohl, nach dem Wunsch der meist adeligen Auftraggeber bis in das 19. Jahrhundert in Einzelanfertigung hergestellt, waren Unikate, Luxusobjekte von festgelegter Bedeutung für einen bestimmten Verwendungszweck. Erst die industriell produzierten buchförmigen Dosen und Flakons bedienten zu sinnvoller Anwendung eine breitere Kundschaft von Kennern und belesenen Liebhabern. Der Buchbesitz von Verpackungsmaterial für nicht lesbaren, leicht zu fassenden Inhalt, ein Feuerzeug, ein geistiges Getränk oder Pralinés, Salz und Pfeffer, auch ohne Deckel wie etwa ein Bleistiftspitzer, kennzeichnet uns als Angehörige der gebildeten Schicht. Das wirklich nützliche Scheinbuch ist im bürgerlichen Haushalt (neben dem Gesangbuch, das dem seelischen Heil dient) sozusagen das Zweitbuch für die praktische Seite des Daseins.

Bei den hohlen Vexierbüchern sind zwei besonders unsympathische Vertreter der Erwähnung wert. Einerseits inkommodieren die als Officium Beatae Mariae Virginis getarnten Codices mit eingebauten Steinschlosspistolen, deren Abzug am Unterschnitt funktioniert, ein Austritt der abgefeuerten Kugel am Oberschnitt festgestellt werden könnte; italienische Exemplare mit Impressum 1625 und 1627 sowie ein späteres, kurpfälzisches mit zwei Terzerolen sind überliefert. Anderseits imponieren die gepolsterten aufklappbaren Bücher-Nachtstühle, als voluminöser Stapel von l iegenden Folianten konstruiert und assoziativ Voyage des Pays-Bas Tom. I–IV oder Spectacle de la Nature betitelt; mehrere dieser „Chaises percées", meist französische Gebrauchsmöbel aus dem 17. und 18. Jahrhundert, sind bekannt.

Neben solchen materiellen Zeugen der Scheinbuch-Bibliophilie aus zwölf Jahrhunderten ist auch der immateriellen fingierten Büchersammlungen, mit bedeutungsvollen Codices ohne unmittelbaren Zugriff, zu gedenken. Im Porträt „mit dem Renaissancepilaster" des Desiderius Erasmus von Rotterdam (1469–1536) aus Longford Castle (National Gallery London) malte Hans Holbein d. J. in Basel 1523 zwei Scheinbücher. Auf dem liegenden mit offenen Bändern ruhen die ausdrucksvollen Hände des in Halbfigur abgebildeten, stets fröstelnden Humanisten, als ob er sich daran wärmen wollte. Der goldgeprägte rote Folioband ist am Oberschnitt in griechischen Majuskeln ERAKLEIOI PONOI (Herkulische Mühen), am Vorderschnitt lateinisch ERASMI ROTERO (des Erasmus Roterodamus) bezeichnet. Er symbolisiert die berühmten Adagiorum Chiliades des Erasmus, eine umfangreiche Sammlung von Sprichwörtern antiker Autoren (Erstdruck 1508), wo der forschende, äußerst produktive Gelehrte im Essay „Herculei labores" von seinen selbstlosen und erdrückenden, ja herkulischen Plagen spricht. Das prachtvolle Scheinbuch vergegenwärtigt somit Erasmus als wahren Renaissance-Herkules, der die verborgenen Schriftdenkmäler der Alten unter Neid und Missgunst der Zeitgenossen zutage fördert. Das aufgestellte andere Scheinbuch, ein brauner Lederband mit geschlossenen Schließen, ist römisch 1523 datiert und trägt am Vorderschnitt die von Erasmus verfasste Künstlersignatur: ILLE EGO IOANNES HOLBEIN, NON FACILE VLLVS TAM MICHI MIMVS ERIT, QVAM MICHI MOMVS ERIT (Ich bin jener Johannes Holbein, schwerlich wird irgendjemand mich ebenso nachahmen wie er mich tadeln wird). Das Distichon rühmt Holbein als einen unnachahmlichen, den antiken Meistern Apollodoros, Zeuxis und Parrhasios vergleichbaren Künstler, der quasi durch Impressum ausgewiesene Foliant legitimiert ihn als dem Gelehrten ebenbürtigen Autor.

Das geistvollste Experiment einer fiktionalen Scheinbuchsammlung dürfte die Porte de Turgot von 1774 darstellen, die in Limoges archivierte Geheimtür aus dem Arbeitskabinett von Anne Robert Jacques Turgot (1727–1781), von 1761 bis 1774 Intendant des Limousin, danach Finanzminister in Paris bis 1776. Diese Bibliotheca ficta des streitbaren Reformpolitikers enthält auf den stempelvergoldeten Kalblederrücken von 76 aufgestellten Bänden in Quart- bis Großfolioformat 58 erfundene Werktitel mit giftigen Anspielungen, die von Ironie und Sarkasmus triefen. Schon wenige Schritte weiter gelangt man mit Mon Faust von Paul Valéry (1871–1945), einer 1940 geschriebenen Szenenfolge, in das Niemandsland des Fiktionalen (Erstdruck 1941). In der fünften Szene des dritten Akts tritt Fausts phantastische „bibliothèque illuminée et gorgée de livres" in Erscheinung, eine Versammlung von Scheinbüchern mit sämtlichen „excréments de l'esprit", die sich als ein gigantischer Misthaufen der Jahrhunderte erweist, „l'édifice monumental de l'ILLISIBLE" aus toter Vergangenheit. Einer der berühmtesten Sätze in Pascals Pensées wird parodiert, wo anstelle der „espaces infinis“ des gestirnten Himmels die unzähligen Bände stehen: „Le silence éternel de ces volumes innombrables m'effraie.“ Da manifestiert sich mit Heraklits Œuvres complètes in zehn Foliobänden und einer absurden Abhandlung von Descartes, betitelt Traité de l'Oraison de la Raison, der Triumph von Irrationalität und Irrsinn.

Noch einen Schritt weiter kommt man zum faszinierenden Erlebnisbericht, den sich Jorge Luis Borges (1899–1986) erdacht hat: Die Bibliothek von Babel (Erstdruck 1941). Dieses utopische Universum, „das andere die Bibliothek nennen“, besteht seit ewig aus einer wahrscheinlich unendlichen Zahl von künstlich beleuchteten Waben, dem Zellenwerk des Bienenstocks nachgebildet, als ein horizontal und vertikal grenzenloses, „überall vorhandenes und fortdauerndes System sechseckiger Galerien“. Diese bergen jede für sich 20 Regale zu je 32 Büchern mit unabänderlich 410 Seiten, welche immer 40 Zeilen von generell 80 Buchstaben enthalten, das heißt insgesamt 839680000 orthographische Zeichen pro Galerie, nicht ganz eine Milliarde. Alles ist in sämtlichen möglichen Sprachen schon geschrieben worden, wie „Geschichte der Zukunft“, wie „Autobiographie der Erzengel“. Die Bücher sind alles geschlossene Scheinbücher, gewiss nicht unsinnig, total unverständlich. So liest man auf Rückenschildern Gekämmter Donner und Gipskrampf oder Axaxas Mlö, was keinen Rückschluss auf den Inhalt zulässt, der fast ausnahmslos, bis auf ein zufälliges Zeilenfragment „O Zeit, deine Pyramiden“, unintelligibel bleibt. Die Bibliothek wird von verzweifelten Bibliothekaren und unschlüssigen Inquisitoren betreut. Ihre Unabsehbarkeit erinnert an die architektonischen Raumvisionen von Piranesis Carceri (1749/50 und 1761), ihre Undurchschaubarkeit an Kafkas Romanfragment Das Schloss (1926). Die totalitäre Struktur, zweifellos höllisch, ist ein gottähnliches Wesen, „erleuchtet, einsam, unendlich, vollkommen, unbeweglich, gewappnet mit kostbaren Büchern, überflüssig, unverweslich, geheim“.

Auch die Scheinbücher-Sammlung Armin Müller ist gewissermaßen erleuchtet und einsam, in tausendfünfhundert Objekten von besonderer Eigenart kostbar, überflüssig und geheim. Sie umfasst im großen Ganzen die Zeitspanne zwischen Neunzehnhundert und Art déco, offenbart in räumlicher Hinsicht einen ungeahnten Reichtum von Formen und Funktionen. Die meisten Scheinbücher sind Behälter, hohl, zu irgendeiner Füllung vorgesehen. Alle zeugen von der unglaublichen Belesenheit ihres umsichtigen Sammlers, der nur die aussagekräftigsten Stücke ins Auge fasst. Das älteste ist ein Blindprägeband des 16. Jahrhunderts, der im 18. mit Pfauenmarmor ausgekleidet wurde. Als wertvollster Gegenstand stellt sich eine niedliche Vogelspieldose des späten 19. Jahrhunderts mit flötendem Wohllaut zur Schau. Kleiner als ein Quadratzentimeter gibt sich ein Anhänger in Gold als offene Holy Bible. Das größte Gebilde überrascht als Eigenbau einer Holzbibliothek, vom Sammler selbst mit 120 Scheinbüchern in angenehm hölzerner Wesensart angefertigt. Man wird bei der Betrachtung und in Gegenwart so vieler brillanter Zeugnisse von werthaltigem Nonsens, von subtiler Ironie und allfällig tieferer Bedeutung, nicht müde, zu schauen, zu staunen und zu bewundern. Eine solche Anhäufung von Kunst und Illusion in überschaubaren Großfamilien und akribisch geordneten Kleinsiedlungen ist sehr selten. Es ist zu hoffen, dass dereinst eine interessierte und geeignete Institution, Bibliothek oder Museum, sich bereit erklären wird, die einzigartige Sammlung in ihre auch sonst ungemein bibliophilen Bestände aufzunehmen, zu pflegen, zu ergänzen und der Nachwelt zu erhalten. Sind Scheinbücher etwas Originelles? Je nachdem wie, im Kunstwerk und bei aller Verfremdung, der Geist fluktuiert. Sie sind tatsächlich originär, Ausguss einer seltsamen Erfindung, die sich Täuschung als interesseloses Wohlgefallen zum Ziel setzt. Kunst und Illusion amalgamieren im singulären Outfit zum schlichten Output von Dichtung und Wahrheit: Fake as alternative reality. Das wirklich gute Scheinbuch enthüllt durch seine entwaffnende Inhaltslosigkeit und völlige Präsenz, ein augenzwinkerndes Als-ob von Status und übersättigtem Luxus, das nur subjektive Geltung, kein objektives Urteil zulässt, seine Symbolträchtigkeit, wir erkennen in ihm das Zwecklose der Daseinsberechtigung. Das wirklich erhellende Scheinbuch ermöglicht einen Transfer von Bedeutung, ursprünglich, fremdbestimmt und eigenbedeutsam zugleich. So sind Scheinbücher, was auch immer sie waren, historische Realität. Seit es lesbare Bücher in der Gestalt von Codices gab, waren dergleichen Scheinbücher zum Blickfang als verwirrende Gabe zuhanden. Im Zeitalter des Online gehören sie zur Steinzeit des Buchs. Sie repräsentieren in ihrem Design avant la lettre ein europäisches Kulturgut, jedes unwiederbringliche Sammlerstück ist museal zu würdigen. Dem Begleitphänomen der Schriftlichkeit gebührt Wohlwollen und Respekt, hat es doch zur Hochschätzung des Buchs als Medium von Wissen und Erleben unschätzbar beigetragen. Wo immer Bücher waren, gab es auch Scheinbücher, die ungelesenen, daher in allen Bibliotheken zum herausragenden Lehr- oder Lesebuch das unscheinbare immergrüne Scheinbuch, wie zum Stern die Dunkle Materie, cum grano salis wie zum Geist, der das Nichts umfängt, das geisthaltige Nichts. Ohne Scheinbuch kein real existierendes Buch, wie dieses darlegt: Schöner Bücherschein. Wer augenscheinlich fühlen will, muss auch wissen. Quod erat demonstrandum.

Beautiful bogus books

Bruno Weber

Who wants to know what's inside, must feel the inside. Fake books offer a good opportunity, they are distinctive pretences, useless and useful at the same time, they are used as cunning sensors of knowledge. Beautiful books that seem promising, but do not contain what you would normally see from a beautiful bookshelf: book dummies, imagined books, livres feints, faux books, 'objects and designs that pretend being books without being it'. This definition formulated in 'Lexikon des gesamten Buchwesens' in 1987 is from the researcher for pilgrim signs Kurt Köster (1912–1986), since 1954 director and from 1969 to 1975 general director of the German library in Frankfurt am Main, who understood and explored fake books as 'book alienation'. The book alienations are codices derived from the Latin phrase 'caudex' for wood from the tree trunk, which should contain any number of single sheets in layers of four pages of papyrus, parchment or paper, hand-written or printed, as readable information carriers, covered at the top and bottom by wooden boards and tied laterally. Such volumes are selected as they belong together as a unique group as in manuscripts or pamphlets, they are precious books, equipped with charm and special haptic qualities that seem to be what they pretend to be, but are more so: cimelia, because they are impersonating the correct factual circumstance. As they are different, and this difference is significant. As they are visible as books and probably are and perceived as credible, they are apparently there and therefore seemingly: faux books and 'Livres feints'.

As a plausible fiction, bogus books are undoubtedly illusive, but not unsubstantial, not without significance: Be they tight and firm, solid hard and homogeneous, compact, massive, heavy and impenetrable like a block, pad or stone, a structure to the hidden and secret place; or they are hollow and empty as a container for liquids of all kinds, flagons or phials, particularly enclosures and containers for solids of all kinds, tin can and case, sheath, capsule, cartridge, carton, casket or safe, as a reliquary, clap sundial and musical instrument. What is stable secures (a paperweight); even what is hollow educates (a vanity case). The difference between the two aggregate states is illuminated by the following anecdote. Two fake books meet in the sauna. One asks the other: "Why are you so dense?" He asserts: "I am from the poet, unread, so I remain what I am. Why are you so hollow?" The other one replies: "I'm a bestseller, internally flattered by the new that looks old, so I stay what I am." So fiction books in the stream of the ever-changing are the enduring. This has been understood by none other than Friedrich Schiller, in whose play 'Wilhelm Tell' (1804) the replica of the stone book in the 'Hohle Gasse' near Küssnacht (Act 4, scene 3), depicts: "I want to sit down on this book of stone, which provides the wanderer for a short rest."

Those who allow to be fooled by book dummies will be rewarded. We like to be fooled by such strange objects whose shape is recognisable, function evident and rarity clear. Only they cannot be read straight out because they are selected in their closed cluster. Thus, fake books happily represent the science of ambiguous being. The evident nonconformity of appearance and reality, form and function is its essential feature. We see through this and are happy about this knowledge. This was also the feeling of the sovereign and experienced diplomat Jean de France, Ier duc de Berry (1360–1416), a passionate collector of jewellery, goldsmiths work and medals, patron of Christine de Pisan and extravagant bibliophile, who possessed an informative library of three hundred manuscripts as he received a special jewel as a codex on New Year's Day, in 1411, at his palace in Bourges: "Un livre contrefait d'une pièce de bois paincte en semblance d'un livre, où il n'a nuls fueillets ne rien escript; couvert de veluiau blanc, à deux fermouers d'argent dorez, esmaillez aux armes de Monseigneur; lequel livre Pol de Limbourc et ses deux freres donnerent à mondit Seigneur ausdictes estrainnes mil CCCC et X." According to this inventory note from 1416, this gift was the first witnessed and most famous illusory book in book history, a painted block of wood as a book without sheets and writing covered in white velvet closed with gold-plated and heraldic enamelled silver clasp. This first illusory book has been made, after his manufacturers, the painter Paul de Limbourg and his brothers, the goldsmiths Jean and Herman de Limbourg (around 1385/1388–1416), wrote and illuminated the precious book of hours 'Les Belles Heures du duc de Berry' from 1405 to 1409. And now they worked on the even more magnificant, 1416 unfinished, 'Très Riches Heures du duc de Berry'. The patron thanked the imaginative painter, his favourite artist, for the illusion of the new miracle by providing him the palace of the former treasurer Christoph de la Mer on Rue Porte-Jaune (No. 5, new building of the 18th century) in the capital Bourges, a property of princely appearance, "une des plus grans et plus spacieuse et notable", as stated in a document of 1434, in which King Charles VII sealed their return to the crown. When he was not in Paris, Paul lived here with his wife Gillette until his early death in 1416.

The Archduchess Margaret of Austria (1480–1530), since 1507 governor of the Habsburg Netherlands, patron of the arts and portrait collector, owned besides a library of nearly four hundred books (mostly manuscripts) in her palace in Mechelen, the main residence of the great regent, such a 'fainct livre' as a box with a violet velvet cover, which also had silver-gilt and heraldic embossed clasps. It served her well as a container for her painting utensils, when she occasionally grabbed the brush as a portrait painter. In addition, "ung cadrant fait en manière d'ung petit livret", a clap sundial in the form of a silver codex, was her property. The earliest known fake books had sacral character, in the 6th and 7th century they were worn as an amulet capsule, silver gilt or gold plating and jewelled, worn on the belt or as a necklace. All these and a thousand other bogus books, whether solid or hollow, were custom made according to the wishes of the mostly aristocratic patrons as unique luxury objects of fixed meaning for a particular purpose until the 19th century. Only the industrially produced book-shaped cans and bottles had meaningful applications to a wider clientele of connoisseurs and well-read lovers. The book possession of packaging material for unreadable, but easy-to-handle content, a lighter, liquor or pralines, salt and pepper, even without a lid such as a pencil sharpener, characterises us as members of the ill-educated section of society. The really useful fake book is in the bourgeois middle-class household (next to the hymnbook, which serves as the spiritual salvation), so to speak, the second book for the practical side of existence.

Two particularly unsympathetic representatives are especially noteworthy among the puzzle books. On the one hand, as in 'Officium Beatae Mariae Virginis' camouflaged codices, with built-in flintlock pistols whose triggering works on the foot cut, could incur an exit of the fired bullet at the upper section. Italian copies with imprint 1625 and 1627 are handed down, as well as a later copy, from the Electoral Palatinate with two terzeroles. On the other hand, impress the cushioned hinged book-night commodes, constructed as a voluminous stack of recumbent folios and associatively titled by 'Voyage des Pays-Bas' vol. I–IV or 'Spectacle de la Nature' titled; several of these „Chaises percées", mostly French utility furniture from the 17th and 18th centuries, are known.

In addition to such material witnesses of the fictitious bibliophilia of twelve centuries, the immaterial fictitious collection of books, with meaningful codices without direct access, must be commemorated. In the portrait "with the Renaissance pilaster" by Desiderius Erasmus of Rotterdam (1469–1536) from Longford Castle (National Gallery London), Hans Holbein d. J. in Basel 1523 painted two fake books. On the recumbent, with a loose band, rest the expressive hands of the half-figure, the always shivering humanist, as if he wanted to warm himself on it. The gold embossed red folio band is designated on the upper section in Greek capital letters ERAKLEIOI PONOI (Herculean troubles), at the front section in Latin ERASMI ROTERO (Erasmus Roterodamus). It symbolises the famous 'Adagiorum Chiliades' of Erasmus, an extensive collection of proverbs of ancient authors (first print 1508), where the researching, extremely productive scholar in the essay "Herculei labores" speaks of his selfless and crushing, even Herculean plagues. The magnificent mock book thus visualises Erasmus as a true Renaissance Hercules, who brings to light the hidden monuments of the ancients under the envy and resentment of their contemporaries. The arrayed other fake book, a brown leather strap with closed closures, is dated Roman in 1523 and bears at the front cut the artist's signature written by Erasmus: ILLE EGO IOANNES HOLBEIN, NON FACILE VLLVS TAM MICHI MIMVS ERIT, QVAM MICHI MOMVS ERIT (I am that Johannes Holbein, hardly anyone will imitate me as he will censure me). The distichon praises Holbein as an inimitable artist, comparable to the ancient masters of Apollodoros, Zeuxis and Parrhasios, and the folio, which is more or less indicated by the imprint, legitimises him as an author of equal rank.

The most brilliant experiment of a fictional faux book collection is the 'Porte de Turgot' of 1774, the secret door archived in Limoges from the cabinet of Anne Robert Jacques Turgot (1727–1781), from 1761 to 1774 director of the Limousin, finance minister in Paris until 1776. This 'Bibliotheca ficta' of the controversial reform politician contains on the stamp gilded calf leather backs of 76 arrayed volumes in quarto-to large-folio format, 58 invented working titles with poisonous allusions that drip with irony and sarcasm. Just a few steps further with 'Mon Faust' by Paul Valéry (1871–1945), a scene sequence written in 1940, one arrives in the no man's land of the fictional (first print 1941). In the fifth scene of the third act, Faust's fantastic "bibliothèque illuminée et gorgée de livres" appears, with a collection of fake books with all the "excréments de l'esprit" that resulted in a gigantic dunghill of the centuries,"l'édifice monumental de l'ILLISIBLE" from the past. One of the most famous sentences in Pascal's 'Pensées' is parodied, where instead of the "espaces infinis" of the starry heavens the innumerable volumes are: "Le silence éternel de ces volumes innombrables m'effraie." Heraklit's 'Œuvres complètes' manifest themselves in ten folio volumes and one absurd essay by Descartes, entitled 'Traité de l'Oraison de la Raison', the triumph of irrationality and madness.

One step further is the fascinating adventure report that Jorge Luis Borges (1899–1986) devised: 'The Library of Babel' (first edition 1941). This utopian universe, "that others name the library", existed for a long period of time and of a probably infinite number of artificially illuminated honeycombs, imitating the cells of the beehive, as a horizontally and vertically boundless, "universally existing and enduring system of hexagonal galleries". Each of them holds 20 shelves of 32 books with an immutable 410 pages, which always contains 40 lines with generally 80 letters, i.e. a total of 839'680000 orthographic signs per gallery, not quite a billion. Everything has already been written in all possible languages, such as "history of the future" and "autobiography of the archangels". The books are all closed fake books; certainly not nonsensical, or totally incomprehensible. Thus, one can read on spine signs 'Gekämmter Donner' and 'Gipskrampf' or 'Axaxas Mlö', which allows no conclusion as to the content which remains almost invariably unintelligible except for a random line fragment "O time, your pyramids". The library is looked after by desperate librarians and undecided inquisitors. Their unforeseeability is reminiscent of the architectural visions of Piranesis 'Carceri' (1749/50 and 1761), their impenetrability of Kafka's novel Fragment 'Das Schloss' (1926). The totalitarian structure, doubtlessly hellish, is a godlike being, "enlightened, lonely, infinite, perfect, immovable, armed with precious books, superfluous, imperishable, secret".

The fictitious book collection of Armin Müller is also enlightened and lonely, precious in a thousand and five hundred objects of a special nature, superfluous and secret. On the whole, it covers the period between the nineteen hundred and art deco, revealing in spatial terms an unimagined wealth of forms and functions. Most fake books are containers, hollow, intended for any filling. All testify to the incredible literacy of their prudent collector, who only contemplates the most meaningful pieces. The oldest is a 16th century blind embossed volume, which was lined with peacock marble in the 18th century. The most valuable item on display, a cute bird's music box from the late 19th century, has a noble sound. Less than a square centimetre in size is a pendant in gold as an open 'Holy Bible'. The largest object surprises as a self-made wooden library, made by the collector himself consisting of 120 dummy books in a variety of wonderful woods. One never gets tired of looking at, wondering and admiring, in the presence of so many brilliant testimonies of valuable nonsense, subtle irony and possibly deeper meaning. Such an accumulation of art and illusion in manageable large families and meticulously organised small settlements is very rare. It is to be hoped that one day an interested and suitable institution, library or museum will agree to include, nurture, supplement and preserve this unique collection for posterity in its otherwise prodigious bibliophilic collections.

Are fake books extraordinary? Depending on how, in the work of art and alienation, the mind fluctuates. They are, in fact, original, the spout of a strange invention that seeks delusion as an apathetic pleasure. Art and illusion amalgamate in a singular outfit to the simple output of poetry and truth: fake as alternative reality. The really good pseudo-book reveals its symbolic character through its disarming lack of reading and complete presence, a winking as if of status and oversaturated luxury, which allows only subjective validity, no objective judgment, we recognise in it the uselessness of the raison d'être. The really enlightening illusory books simultaneously enable a transfer of meaning, original, foreign-determined and significant. So are fake books, whatever they were, historical reality. Since there were readable books in the guise of codices, such fake books were eye-catching as a confusing gift. In the age of online, they belong to the Stone Age of books. In their design 'avant la lettre' they represent a European cultural asset, every irretrievable collector's item is to be worthy of a museum. Benevolence and respect are necessary for the accompanying phenomenon of the written form, since it has contributed inestimably to the esteem of the book as a medium of knowledge and experience. Wherever there were books, there were also bogus books, the unread ones, hence in all libraries the outstanding textbook or reading book, the inconspicuous evergreen illusory book, as to the star the dark matter, 'cum grano salis' as to the spirit, which embraces the nothingness, the spiritually of nothing. Without a bogus book, there is no real existing book, as 'beautiful bogus books' expounds. Who wants to have feelings, must have knowledge. Quod erat demonstrandum.

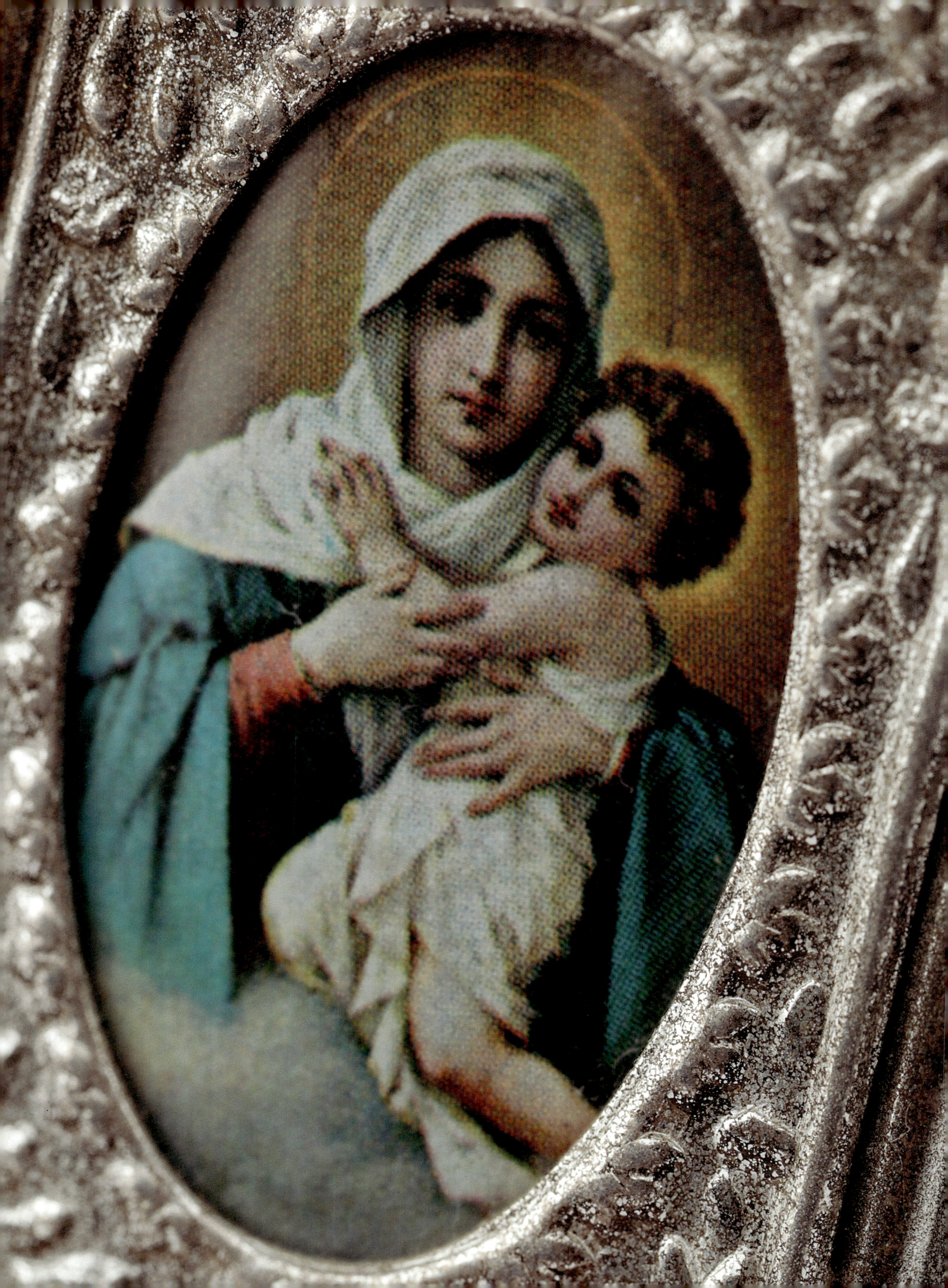

Geist & Seele
Spirit & Soul

Eine sehr interessante und gesprächige Trödlerhändlerin in der Winterthurer Altstadt habe ich immer wieder gern besucht. Ganz selten hat sie mir etwas Passendes für meine Sammlung anbieten können. Dafür war ich aber immer über den neuesten Klatsch in der Stadt informiert.

Zu meiner Entlastung brachte ich ihr gelegentlich ein paar nicht sammlungswürdige „Antiquitäten". In meiner Buchattrappen Sammlung befanden sich einige kitschige Objekte die ich jeweils als Anfangssünden der Sammlung bezeichnete. Es handelte sich um Trinkflaschen aus Keramik, auch Schnapsbibeln genannt, oder kitschige neue Spardosen, aufgeschlagene Bücher mit eingraviertem Text, die für Grabstätten verwendet werden. Zu meiner Freude nahm die Händlerin sie zum Wiederverkauf gerne an. Eines Tages entdeckte ein befreundetes Ehepaar, das den Laden ebenfalls häufig aufsuchte, die „Schätze" und wollte die Objekte für mich erwerben, war aber dann doch etwas unsicher, und hat mich vor dem Kauf zum Glück noch informiert. Irgend jemand hat nun doch Freude daran …

I often enjoyed visiting a very interesting and talkative second-hand dealer in Winterthur's old town. She only rarely offered me something that was suitable for my collection. But I was always up to date with the latest gossip from the city.

I occasionally brought her some "antiques" that I wanted to pass on since they were not worth collecting. In my collection of fake books there were some kitschy objects that I regarded as beginner's mistakes. They were ceramic drinking bottles, also known as liquor bibles, cheesy new money boxes, or opened books with an engraved text, which are used for graves. To my delight, the dealer gladly accepted them for resale. One day a couple of friends, who also visited the shop frequently, discovered the "treasures" and wanted to buy the objects for me. But they were a little insecure and fortunately informed me before buying. So now, someone else can enjoy them after all …

7.001

Arbeit ist des Bürgers Zierde, Segen ist der Mühe Preis

Work adorns the burgher greatly, Blessing is our labour's prize

Aufgeschlagenes Buch aus Metall mit Spruch und Porträt von Friedrich Schiller

Open book made of metal with a saying and portrait of Friedrich Schiller

1,3 x 13,5 x 10 cm

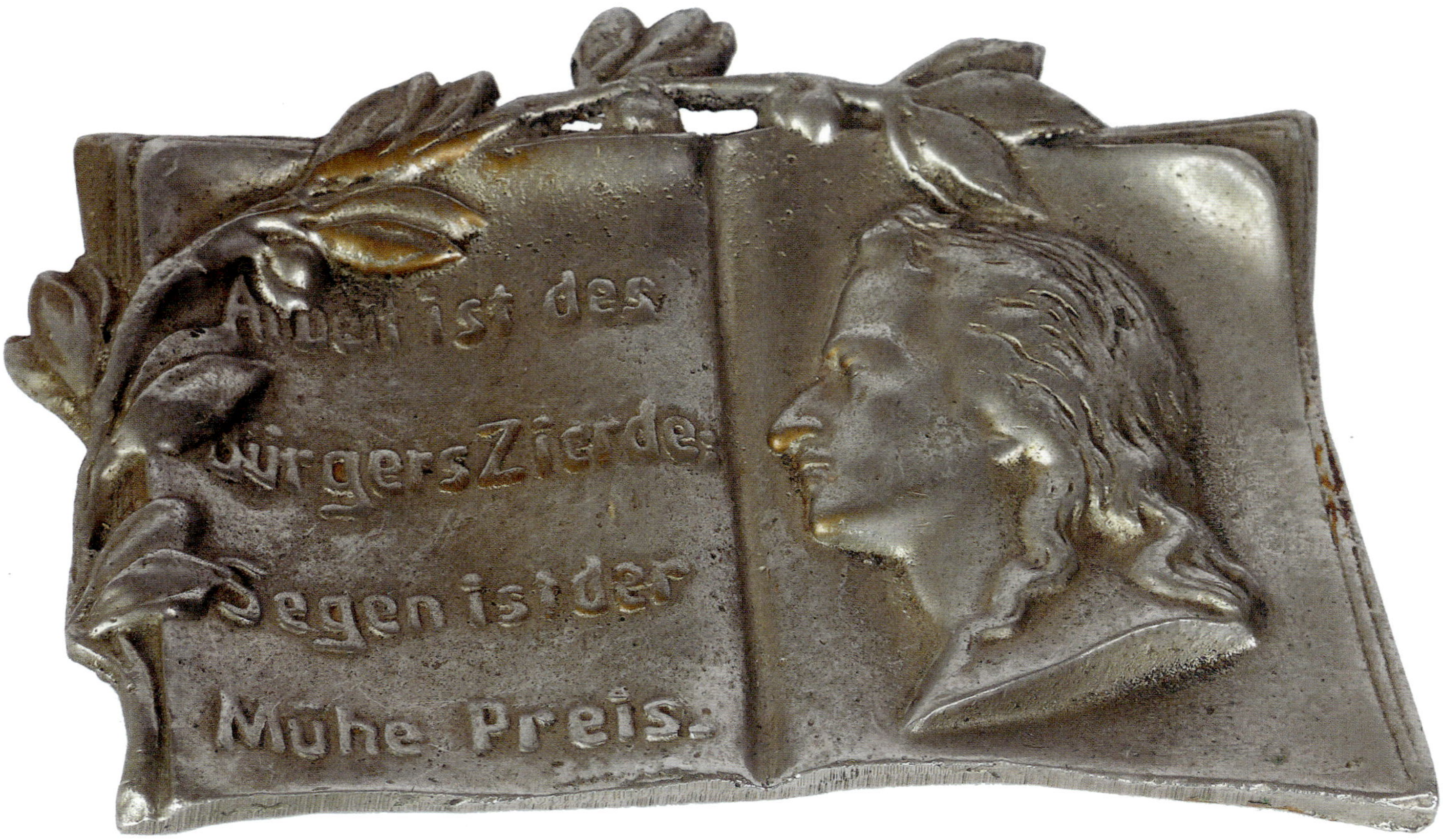

7.002

Le livre de la vie

Aufgeschlagenes Buch aus Kupferblech, erhabenes Blumensujet und Spruch von Alphonse Lamartine

Open book made of copper sheet, raised floral ornament and saying by Alphonse Lamartine

0,8 x 11 x 8 cm

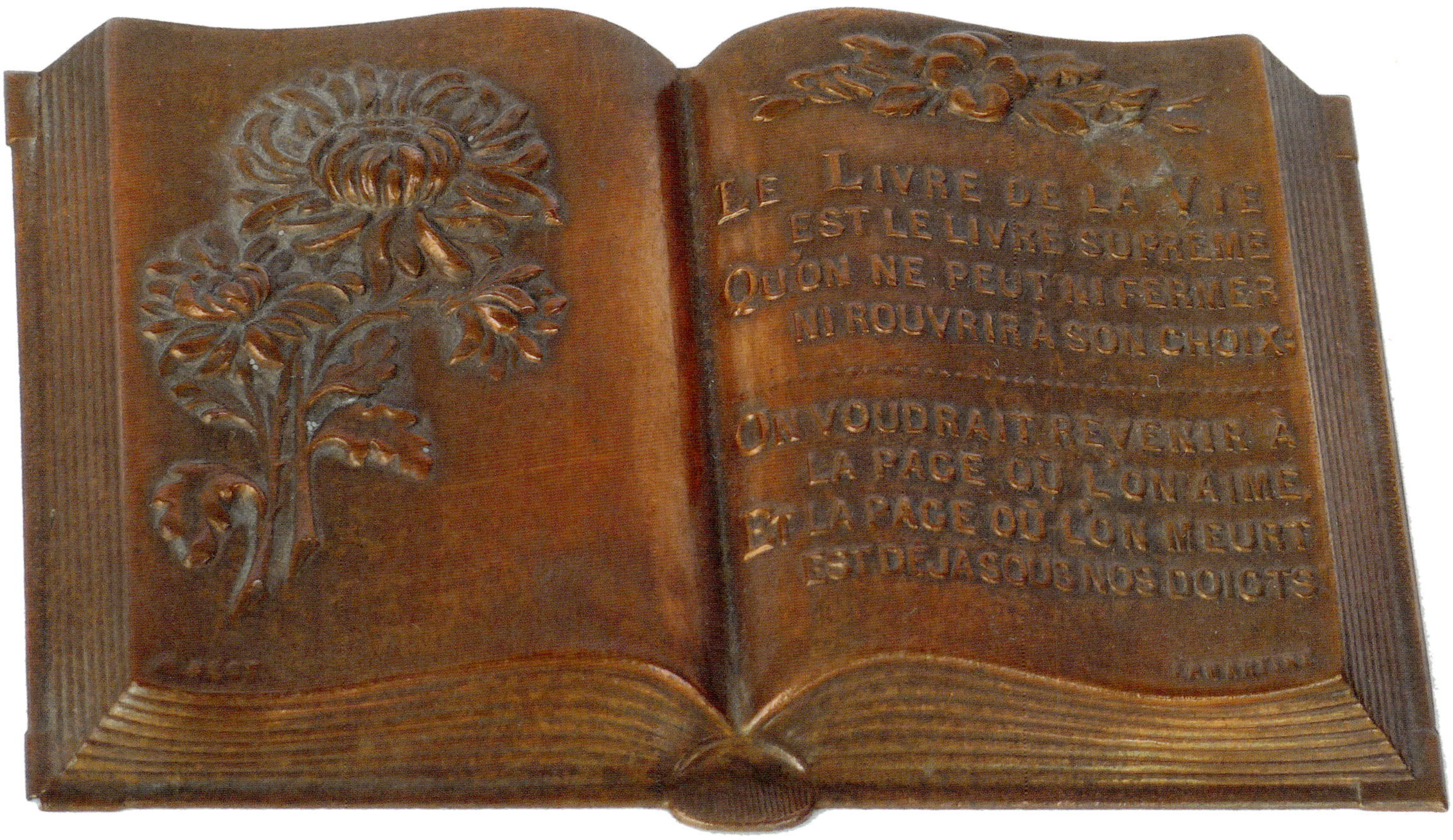

7.003
Metall-Rosenkranz-dose mit farbigem Abbild von Maria mit dem Kind auf dem Vorderdeckel, verzierter Rückdeckel
Rosary metal box with colored image of Mary with Child on the cover, back cover with ornaments
Um / *Around* 1900
1,3 x 4 x 3,2 cm

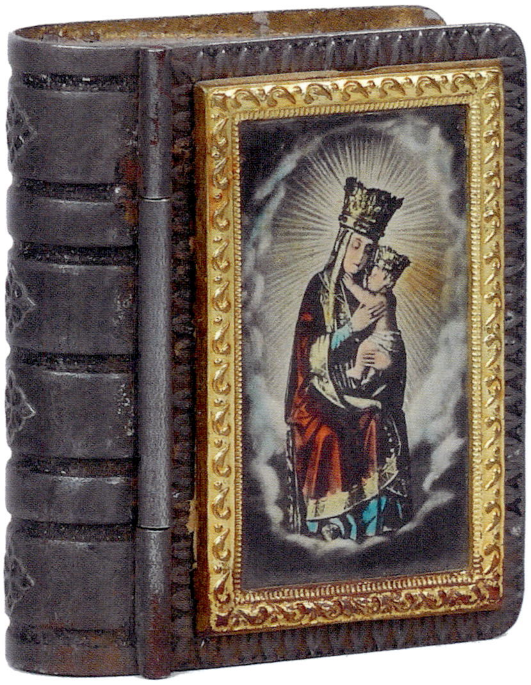

7.004
JHS
Metall-Rosenkranz-dose mit Kreuz und Monogramm „JHS“ auf dem Vorderdeckel, geprägte Verzierungen auf beiden Deckeln
Rosary metal box with cross and monogram „JHS" on the front cover, embossed ornaments on both covers
Um / *Around* 1900
1,2 x 6,2 x 4,8 cm

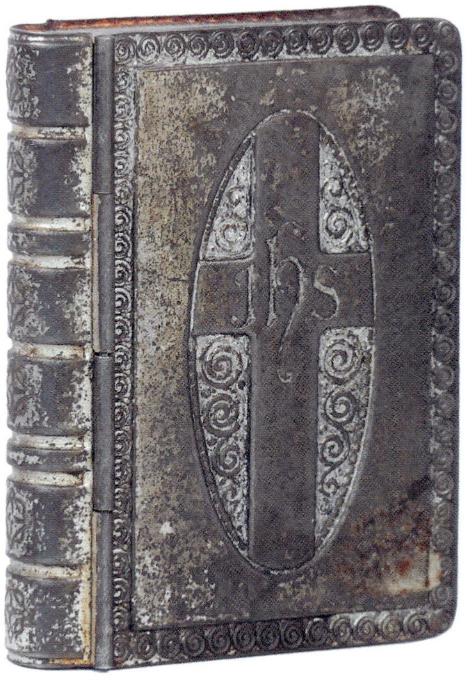

7.005
Metall-Rosenkranz-dose mit getriebener Abbildung von Maria mit Kind auf dem Vorderdeckel, geprägte Verzierungen auf dem Hinterdeckel, mit Rosenkranz
Rosary metal box with embossed portrait of Mary with Child on the front ocver, embossed ornaments on the back cover, with rosary
Um / *Around* 1900
1 x 4,8 x 3,5 cm

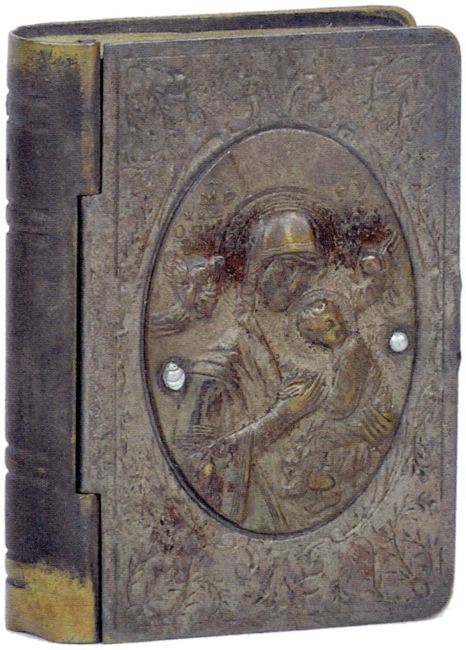

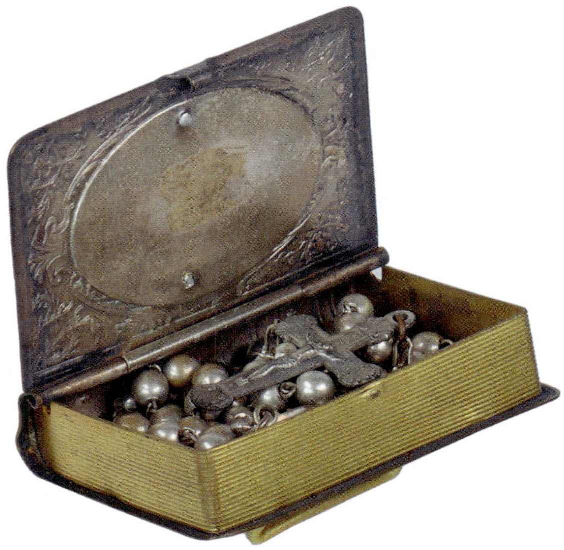

7.006
Metall-Rosenkranz-dose mit farbigem, ovalem Abbild von Maria mit dem Kind auf dem Vorderdeckel, geprägtes Monogramm „JHS“ auf dem Hinterdeckel, mit Rosenkranz
Rosary metal box with a colored, oval image of Mary with Child on the front cover, embossed monogram "JHS" on the back, with rosary
Nach / *After* 1900
1,3 x 5,1 x 4,1 cm

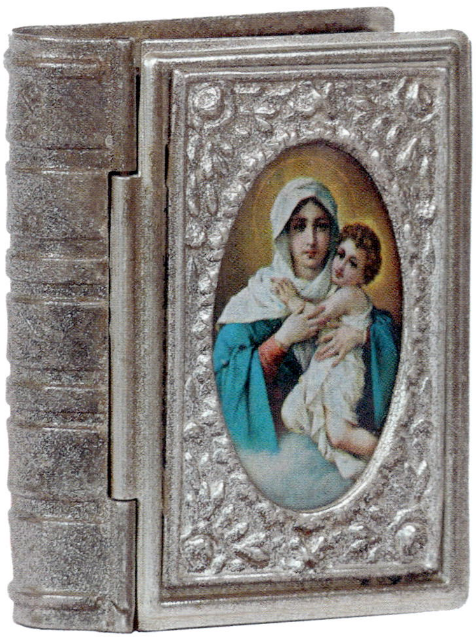

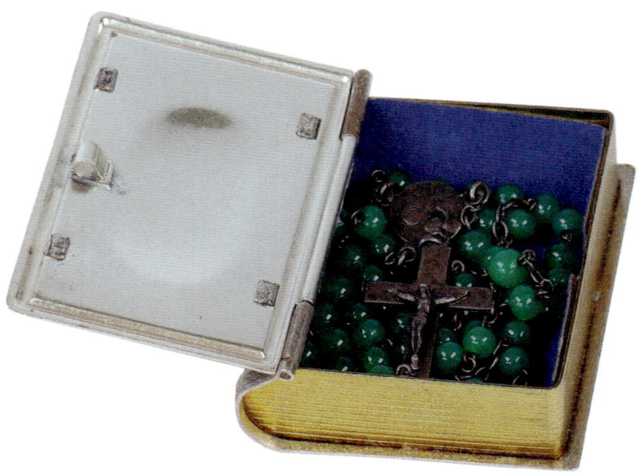

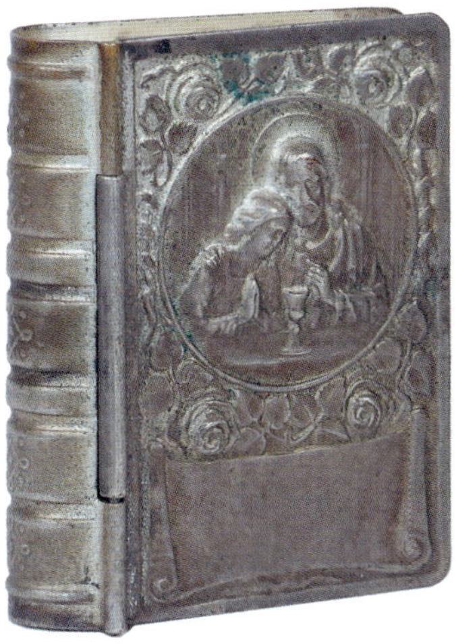

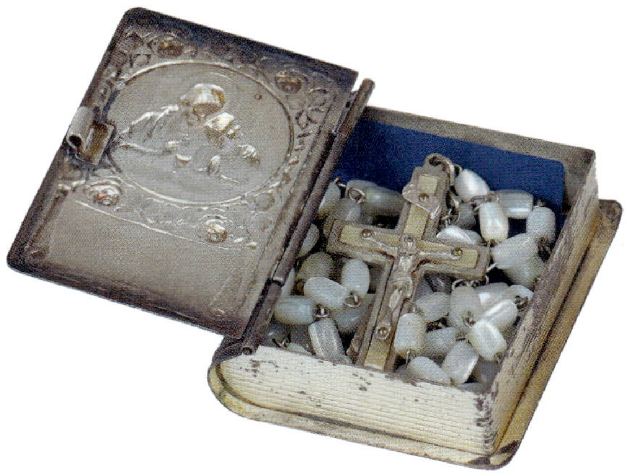

7.007
Metall-Rosenkranzdose mit getriebener Abbildung von Jesus mit Kind und Kelch auf dem Vorderdeckel, geprägtes Kreuz mit Monogramm „JHS“ auf dem Hinterdeckel, mit Rosenkranz
Rosary metal box with an embossed image of Jesus with Child and chalice on the front cover, embossed cross with monogram "JHS" on the back, with rosary
Um / *Around* 1900 | 1,4 x 5,1 x 4,3 cm

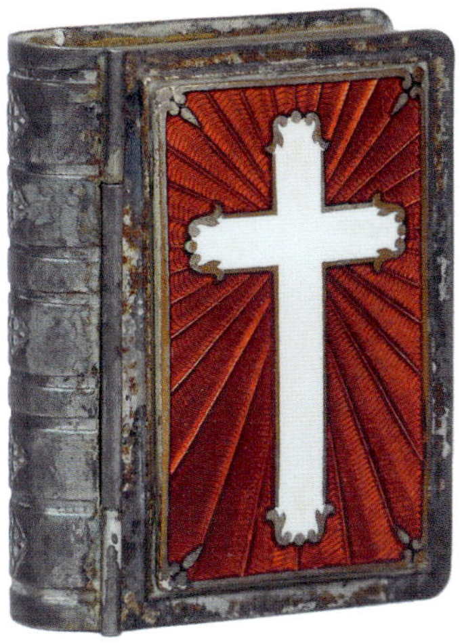

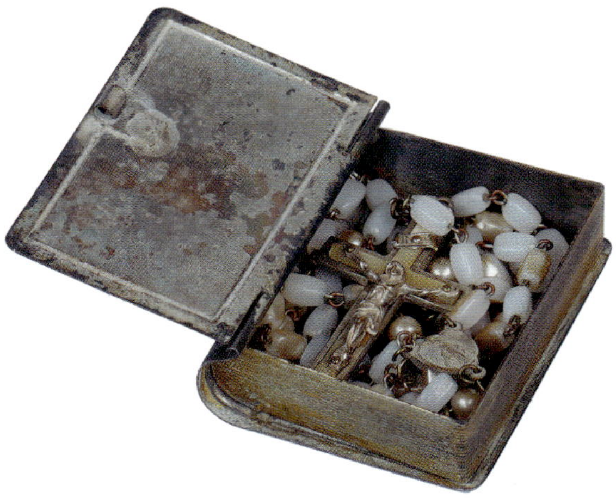

7.008
Metall-Rosenkranzdose mit farbigem Emailkreuz auf dem Vorderdeckel, mit Rosenkranz
Rosary metal box with a colored enamel cross on the front cover, with rosary
Um / *Around* 1900 | 1,4 x 5,1 x 4 cm

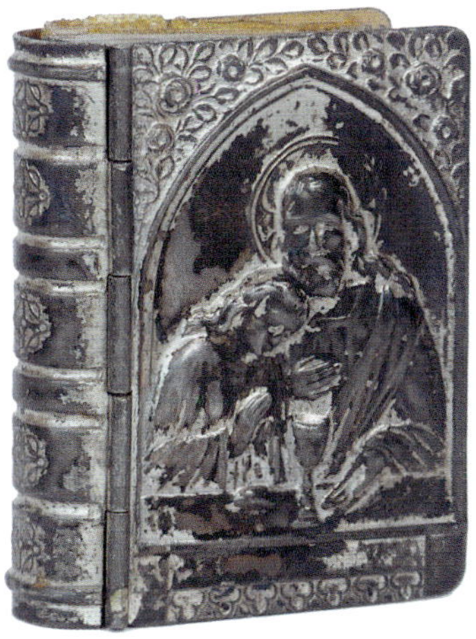

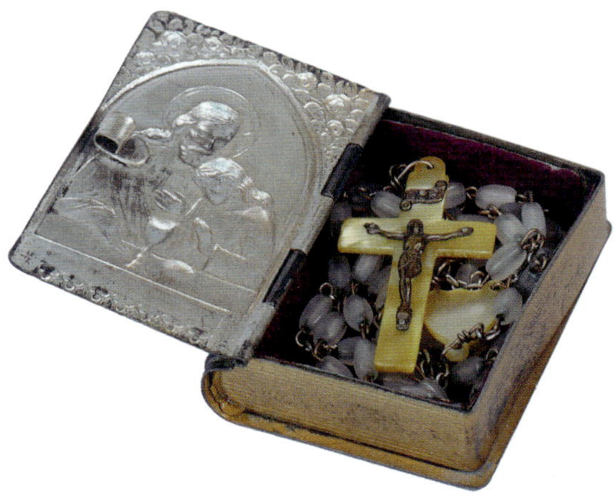

7.009
Metall-Rosenkranzdose mit getriebener Abbildung von Jesus mit Kind und Kelch auf dem Vorderdeckel, Gravur auf dem Hinterdeckel: „Andenken an meine erste heilige Communion“, mit Rosenkranz
Rosary metal rosary box with embossed image of Jesus with Child and chalice on the front cover, engraving on the back: "Souvenir of my first holy communion", with rosary
Um / *Around* 1900 | 1,4 x 5,1 x 4 cm

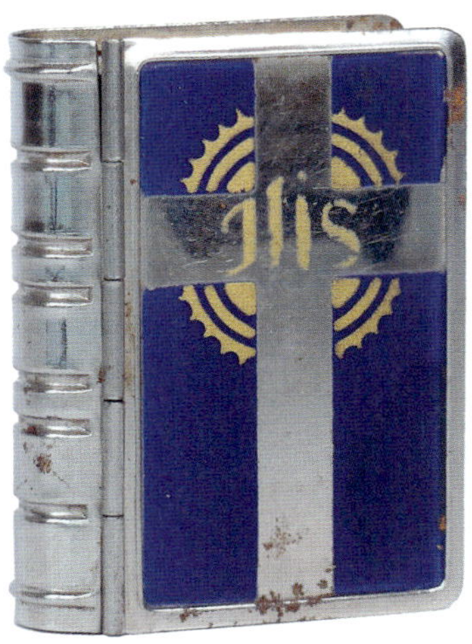

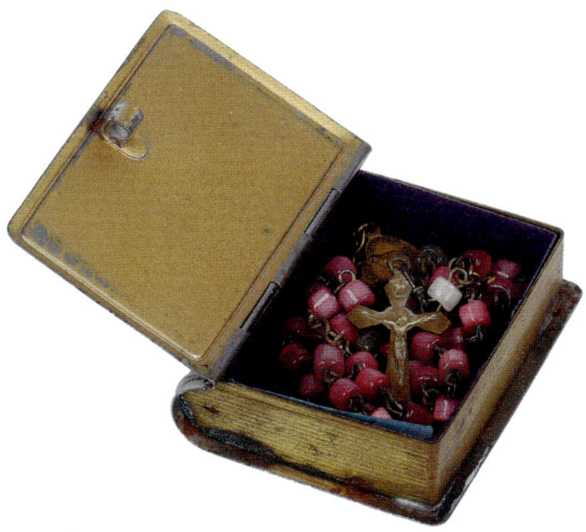

7.010
JHS
Metall-Rosenkranzdose mit Kreuz und Monogramm „JHS“ auf dem Vorderdeckel, mit Rosenkranz
Rosary metal box with cross and monogram "JHS" on the front cover, embossed decorations on both covers
Nach / *After* 1900 | 1,2 x 5,2 x 4,1 cm

7.011
Andenken an Muttergottesberg bei Grulich, Tchechien
Souvenir of the Mountain of the Mother of God, near Králíky, Czech Republic
Bakelit-Rosenkranzdose mit abgebildeter Maria mit Kind auf dem Vorderdeckel, ausgefüttert mit Buntpapier, Messingschließe, dreiseitiger Goldschnitt
Rosary box made of bakelite with depiction of Mary with Child on the front cover, lined with multicolored paper, brass buckle, all edges gilt
Um / *Around* 1900 | 1,8 x 5,2 x 4 cm

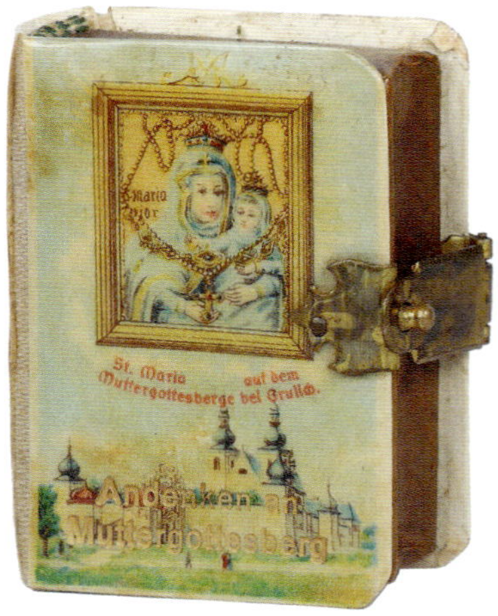

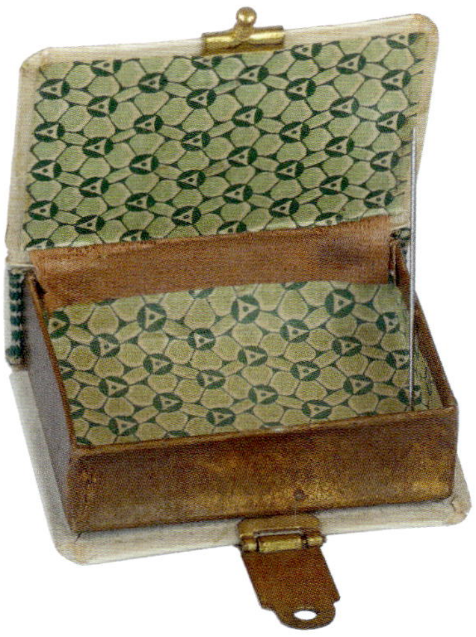

7.012
Metall-Rosenkranzdose mit getriebenem Porträt von Maria mit dem Kind auf dem Vorderdeckel, geprägtes Kreuz mit Monogramm „JHS“ auf dem Hinterdeckel
Rosary metal box with embossed portrait of Mary with Child on the front cover, embossed cross with monogram „JHS” on the back
Um / *Around* 1900 | 1,3 x 5,2 x 4,3 cm

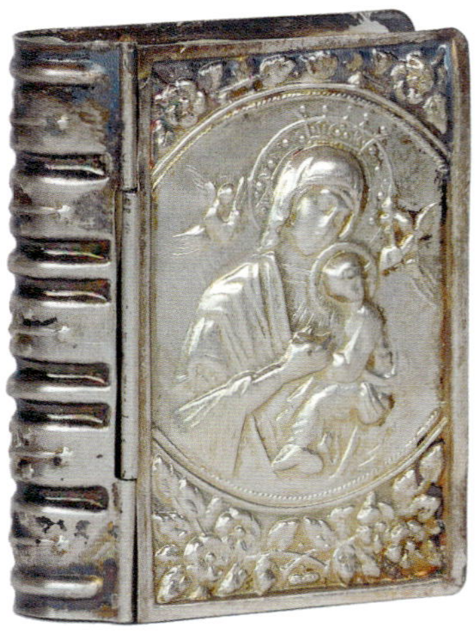

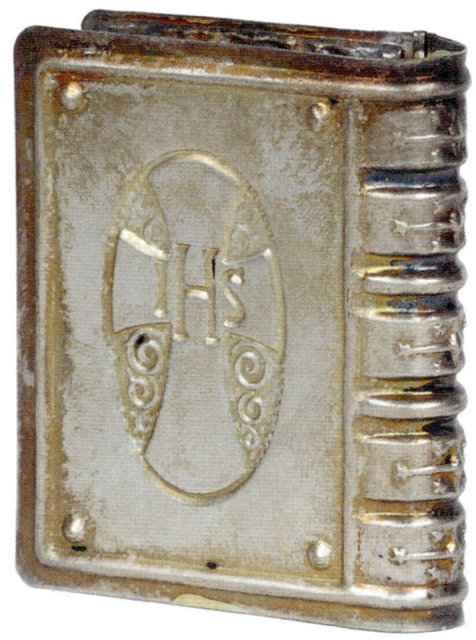

7.013
Pius XII Pont Max
Metall-Rosenkranzdose mit getriebenem Porträt von Papst Pius XII auf dem Vorderdeckel, geprägter Strahlenkranz mit Monogramm „JHS“ auf dem Hinterdeckel
Rosary metal box with engraved portrait of Pope Pius XII on the front cover, embossed rosary with monogram „JHS” on the back
Um / *Around* 1900 | 1,3 x 6 x 5,1 cm

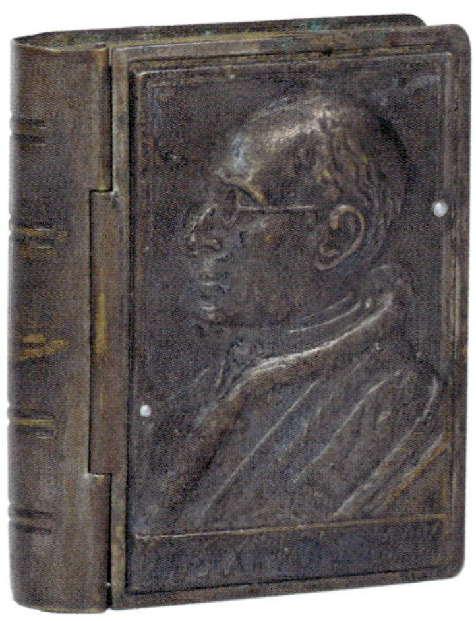

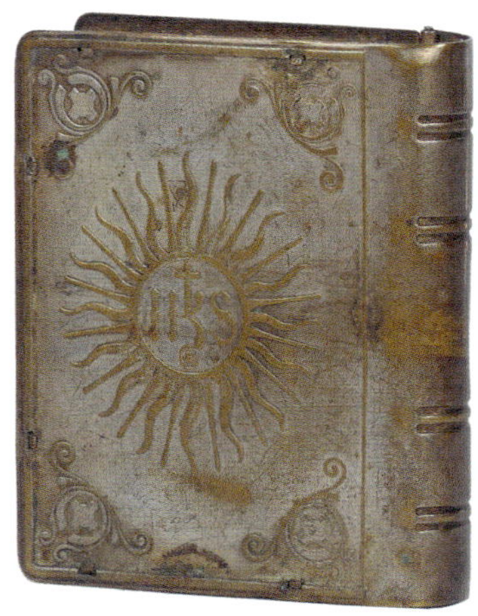

7.014
Kunststoff-Rosenkranzdose mit aufgesetztem Kreuz auf dem Vorderdeckel, abnehmbarer Deckel, mit Rosenkranz
Rosary box with cross on the front cover, removable cover, with rosary
1,1 x 4,8 x 3,3 cm

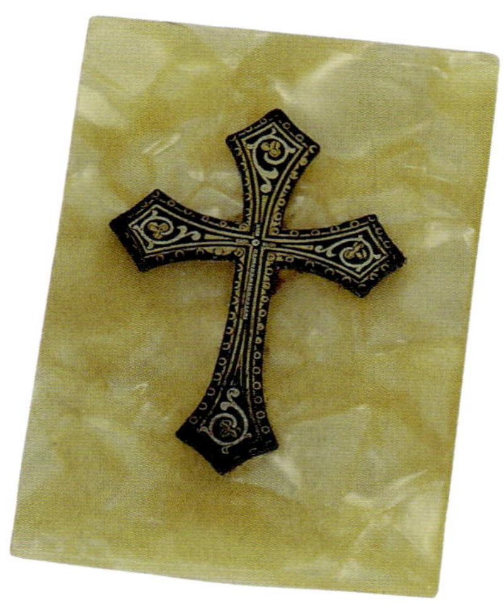

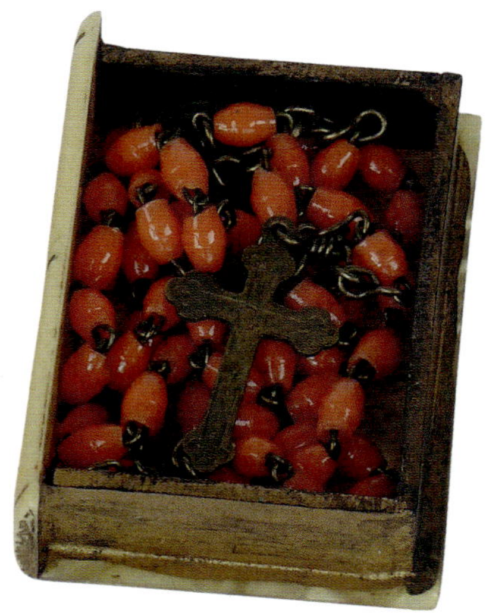

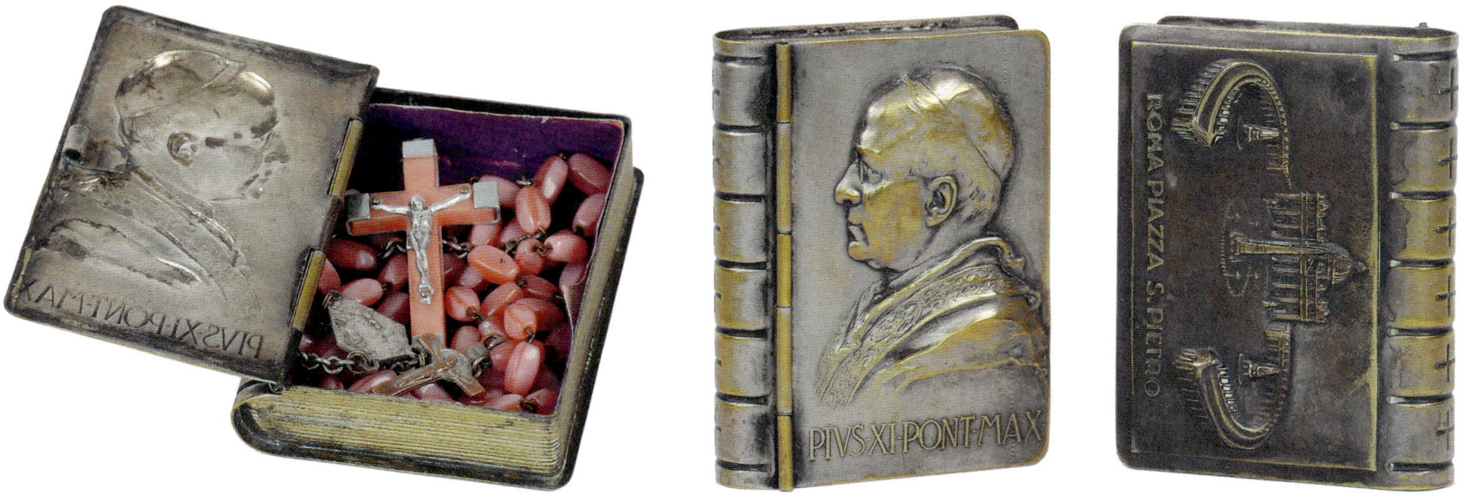

7.015

Pius XI Pont Max

Metall-Rosenkranzdose mit getriebenem Porträt von Papst Pius XI. auf dem Vorderdeckel, geprägte Roma Piazza S. Pietro auf dem Hinterdeckel, mit Rosenkranz

Rosary metal box with embossed portrait of Pope Pius XI on the front cover, embossed Roma Piazza S. Pietro on the back, with rosary

Um / *Around* 1900 | 1,3 x 6,2 x 4,6 cm

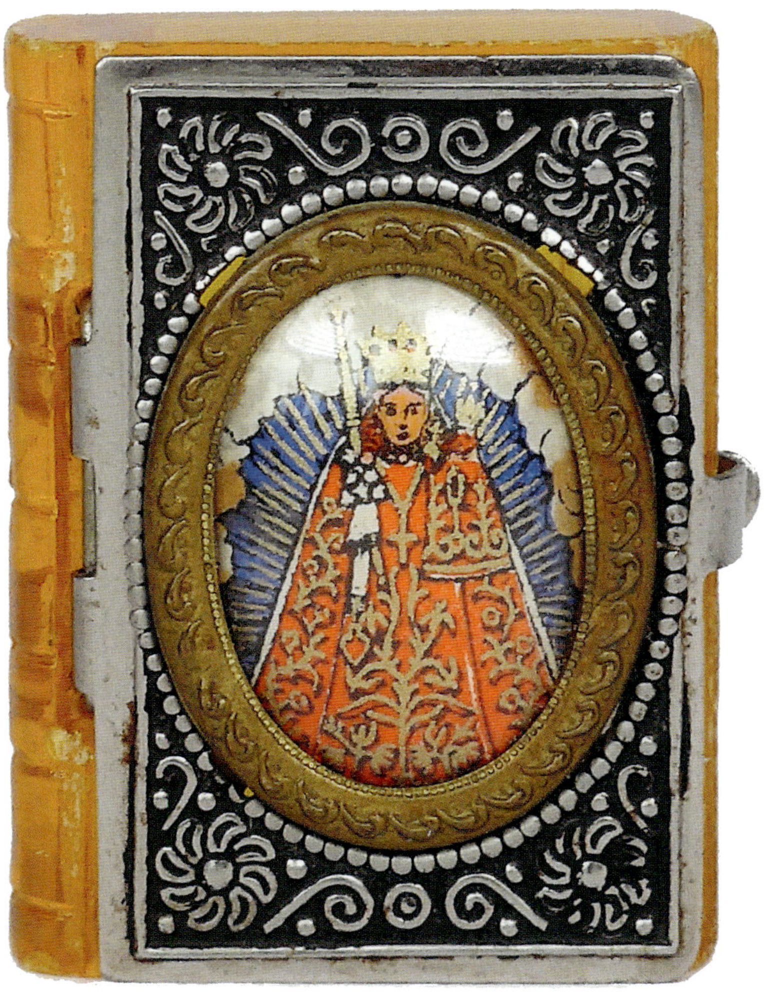

7.016

Kunststoff-Rosenkranzdose mit Metalldeckel, ovales Medaillon mit gekrönter Maria auf dem Vorderdeckel, mit Rosenkranz

Rosary box made of plastic with metal lid, oval medallion with crowned Maria on the front cover, with rosary

0,8 x 3,5 x 2,5 cm

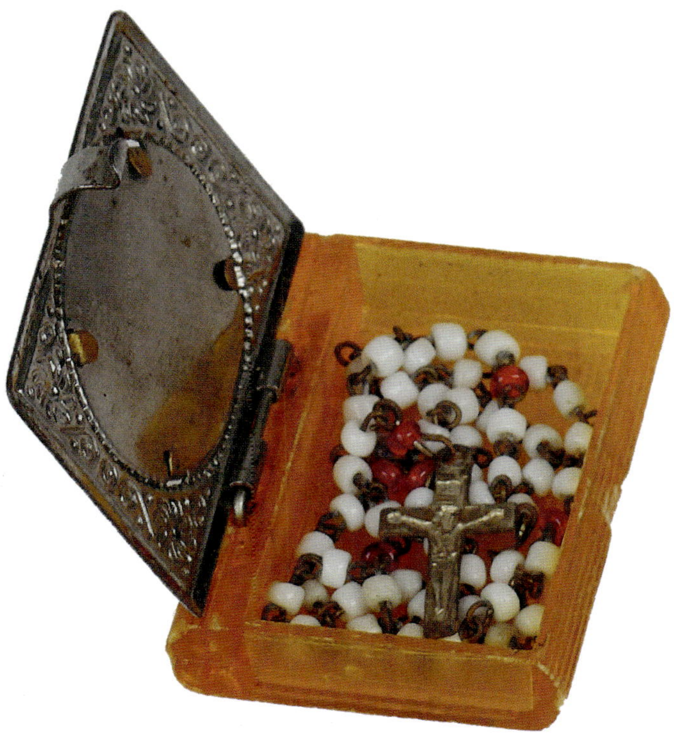

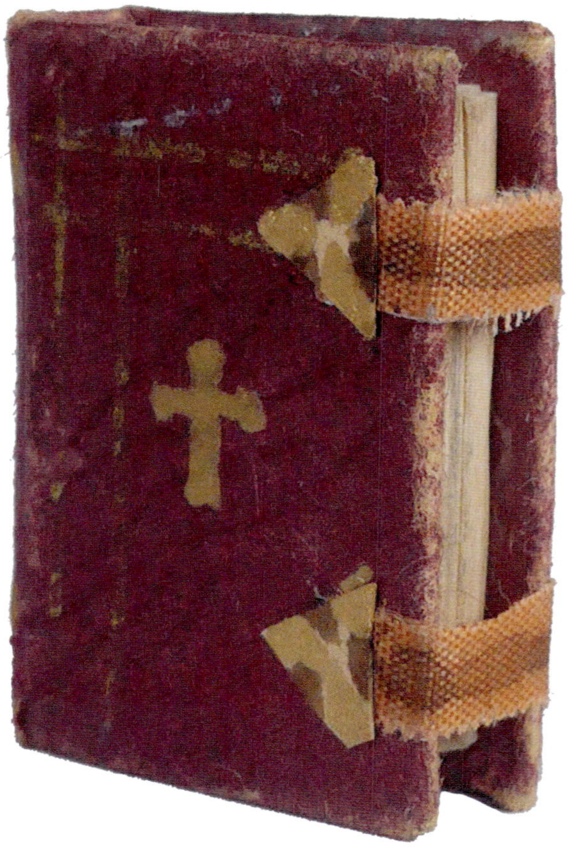

7.017
Kartoneinbanddecke mit Papierüberzug, zugeklebter Buchblock, Goldbemalung mit Kreuz auf dem Vorderdeckel, zwei Scheinstoffschließen
Paperback cover with paper-over-board, sealed book block, cross painted in gold on the front cover, two fake cloth clasps
3,5 x 2,6 x 0,9 cm

7.018
Martha
Holzschatulle, Vorderschnitt abnehmbar, Metalleinlegearbeit mit Kreuz, bemalter Rückentitel und Vorderdeckel
Wooden casket, removable fore edge, metal marquetry with cross, title painted on the spine and paintings on the front cover
4 x 17 x 11,3 cm

7.019
Gewebedose mit geprägtem Kreuz auf dem Vorderdeckel, ausgefüttert mit Moirépapier, dreiseitiger Goldschnitt, für Bibelsprüche, Zugbänder
Textile box with embossed cross on the front cover, lined with moiré paper, all edges gilt, used for bible verses, drawstring
2,3 x 11,5 x 8,9 cm

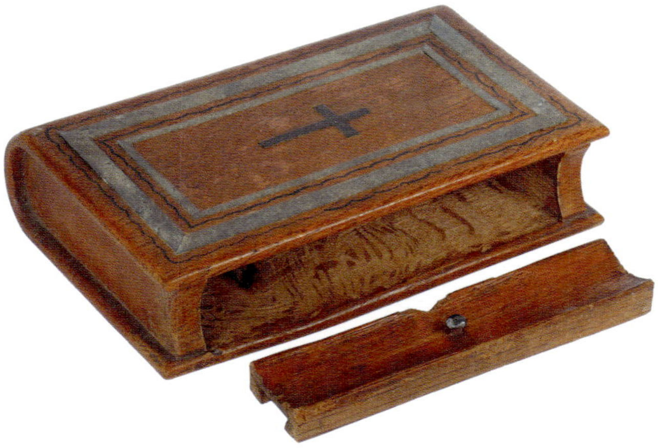

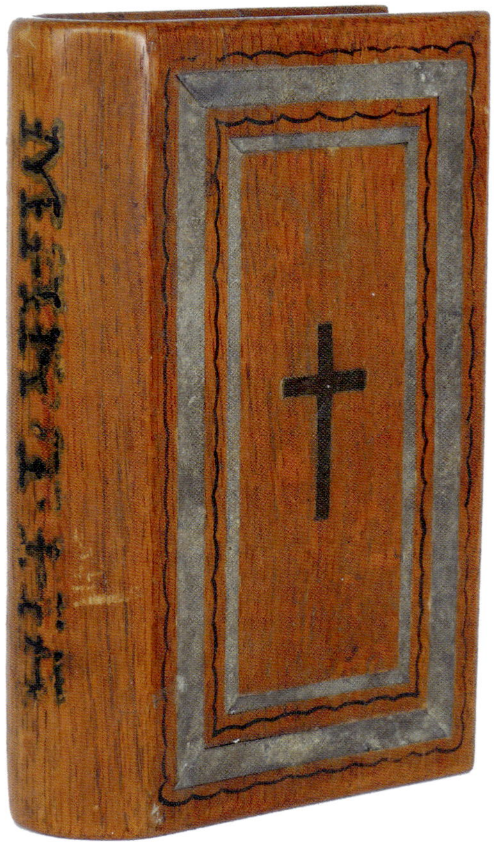

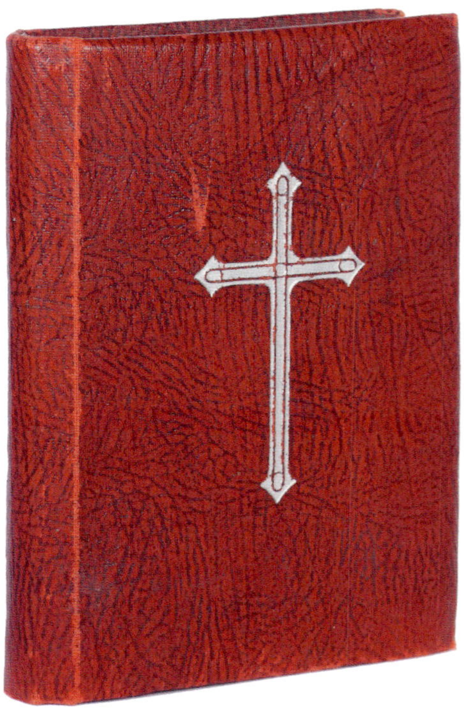

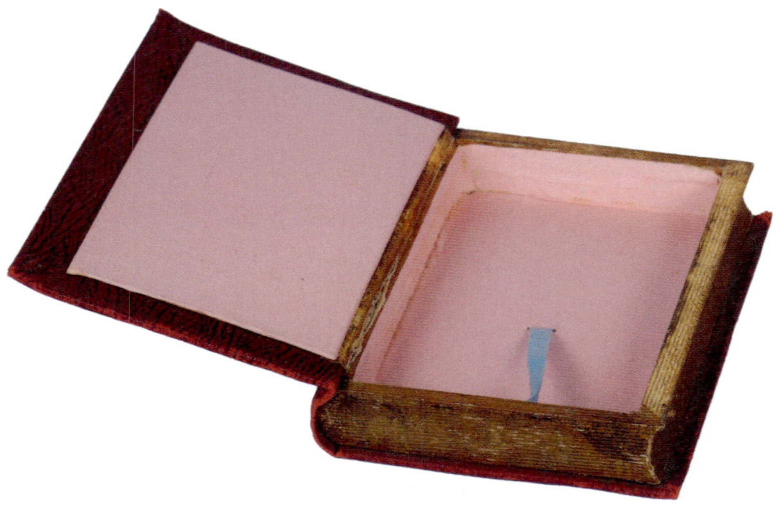

7.020
Holzdose mit Schublade am Rücken, Holzeinlegearbeit mit Kreuz auf beiden Deckeln, zwei eingelegte Scheinbünde am Rücken
Wooden box with drawer on the spine, wooden marquetry with cross on both covers, two inlaid fake bands on the spine
2,7 x 10 x 7 cm

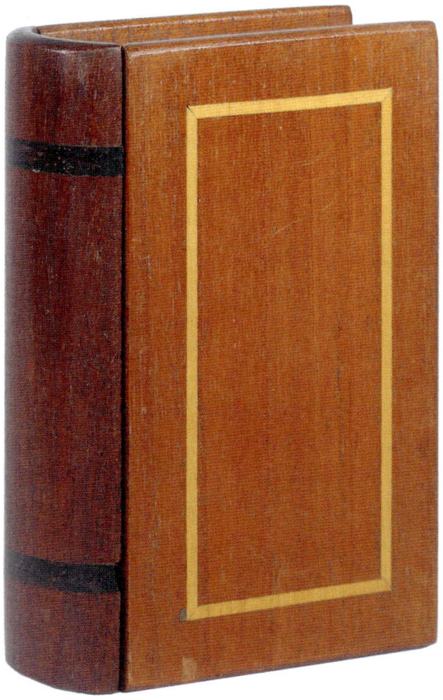

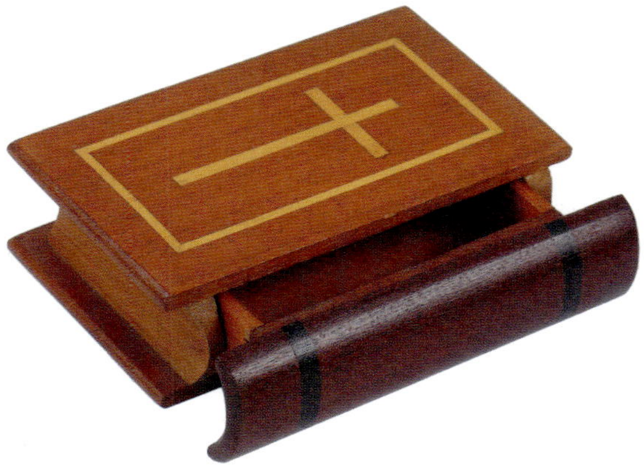

7.021
Tautropfen
Dewdrops
Kaliko-Klapschachtel mit Bibelsprüchen, Rücken- und Deckelprägung, dreiseitiger Goldschnitt, Zugbänder
Calico box with bible verses, embossed spine and cover, all edges gilt, drawstrings
2,1 x 10,8 x 8,5 cm

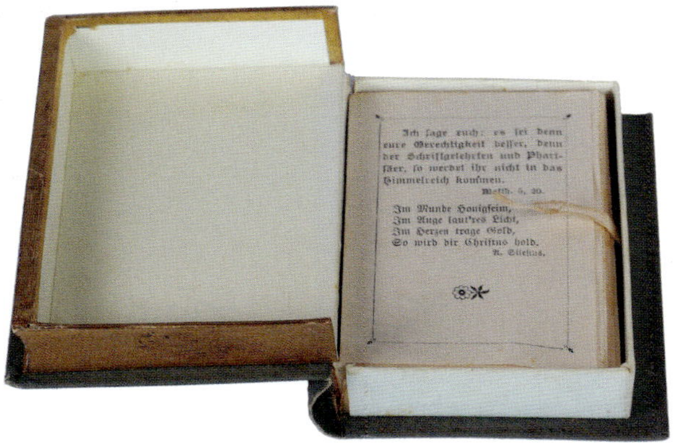

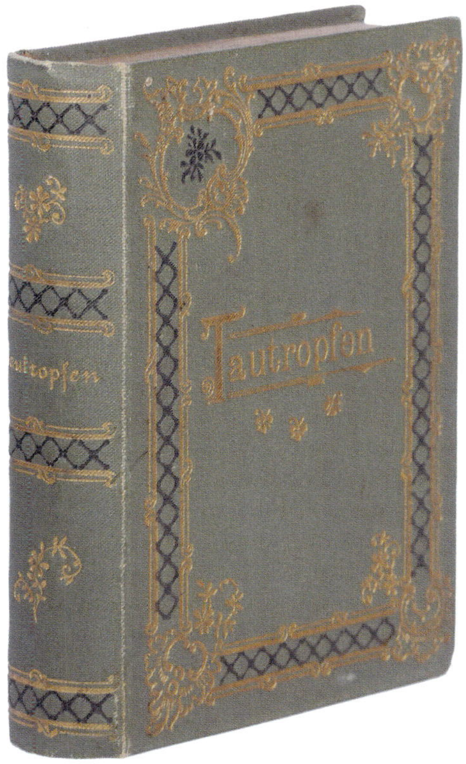

7.022
Lichtstrahlen / ***Rays of Light***
Kartondose mit Schuber, Bibelsprüche enthaltend, Rücken- und Deckelprägung, dreiseitiger Goldschnitt
Box with a slipcase containing bible verses, embossed spine and cover, all edges gilt
2,2 x 8,6 x 7 cm

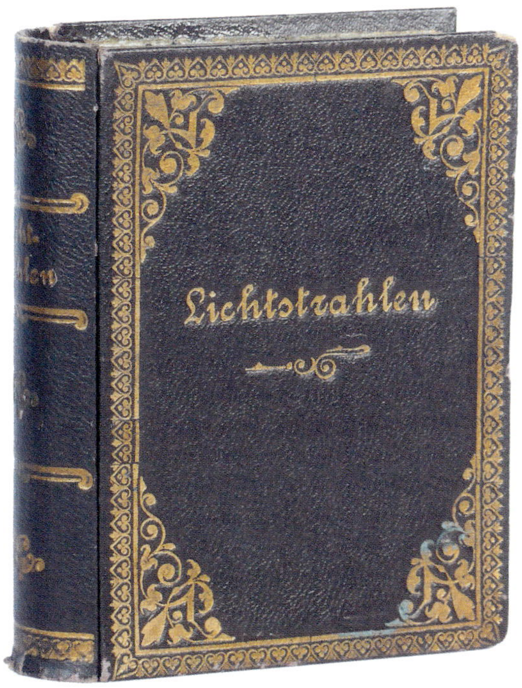

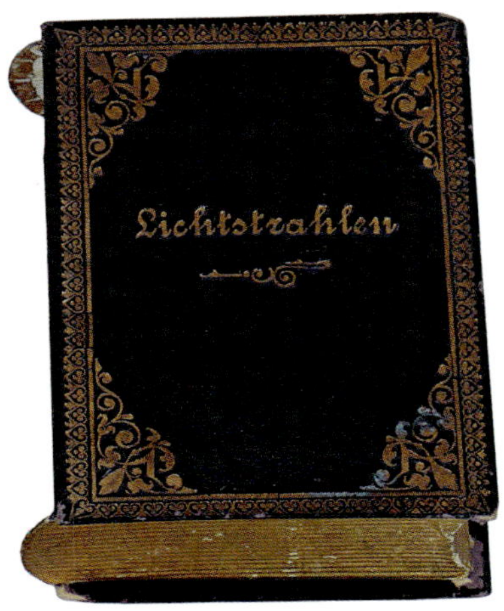

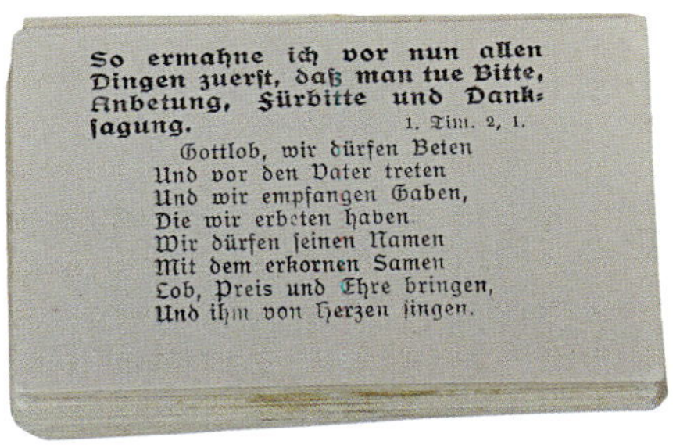

7.023
Lichtstrahlen
Rays of Light
Kartondose mit Schuber, Bibelsprüche enthaltend, Rücken- und Deckelprägung, dreiseitiger Goldschnitt
Box with a slipcase containing bible verses, embossed spine and cover, all edges gilt
2,2 x 8,6 x 7 cm

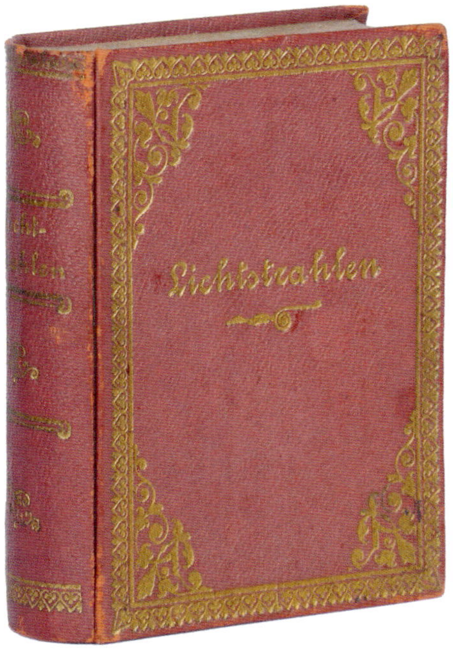

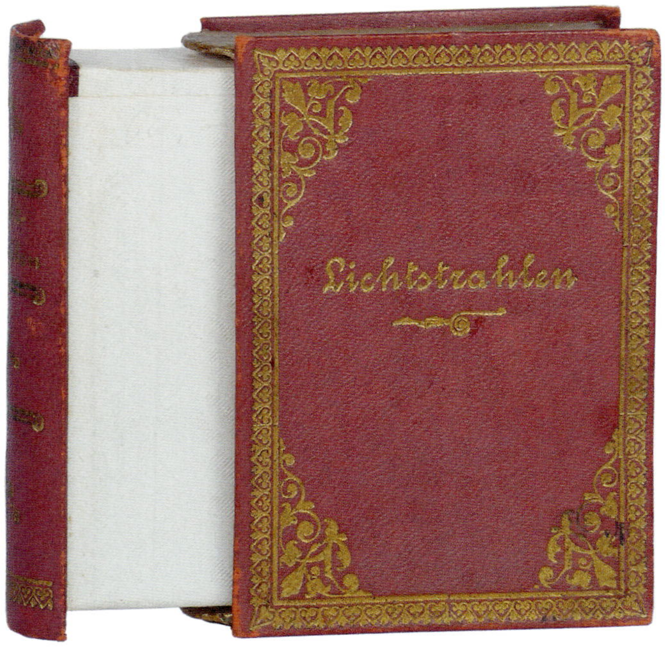

7.024
Firmungs-Andenken, Zur Erinnerung von deiner Pathin Yoaela Gebhart, für Maria Gebhart, 1914
Souvenirs of the Confirmation, In memory of your godmother Yoaela Gebhart, for Maria Gebhart, 1914
Kartondose mit Papierüberzug, Prägung auf Rücken- und Vorderdeckel, dreiseitiger Goldschnitt
Box with paper-overboard, embossing on the spine and cover, all edges gilt
Albert Ade, Uhren & Goldwaren, Kempten, Fischerstraße
2,3 x 8,9 x 7,6 cm

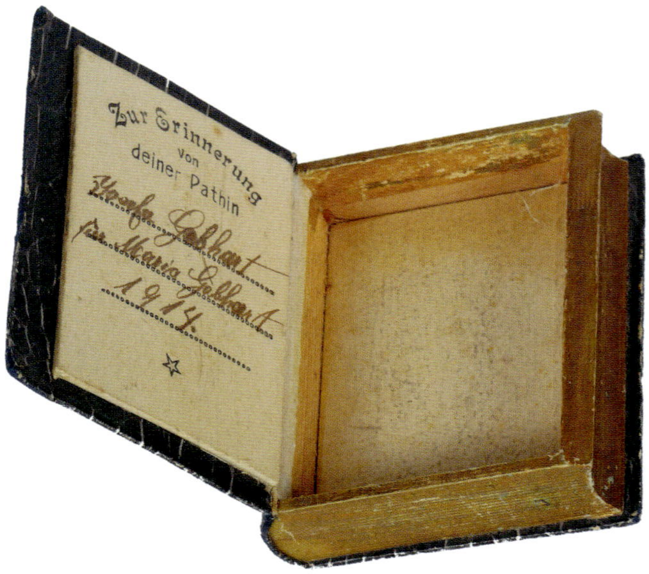

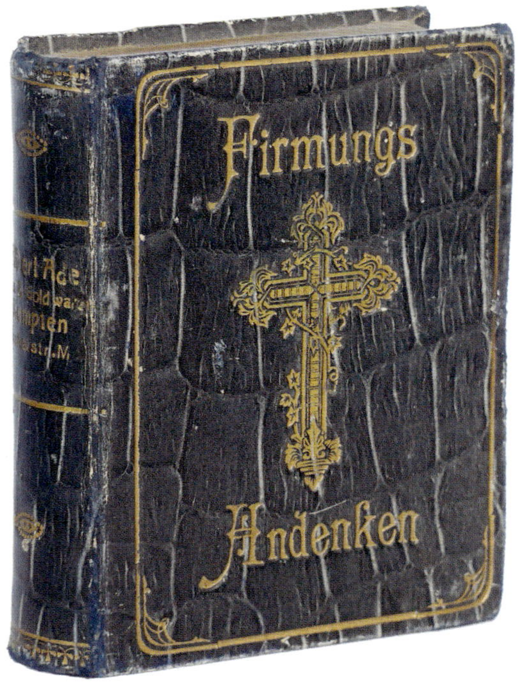

7.025
Carl Grünbaum
Geschenk-Ganzlederdose anlässlich der Firmung von 1830, Rücken- und Deckelvergoldung, dreiseitiger Goldschnitt, ausgefüttert mit Glanzpapier, Zugbänder, Denkzettel
Full leather gift box on the occasion of the confirmation in 1830, cover gilding, all edges gilt, lined with glossy paper, drawstring, containing a lesson
1,7 x 8,5 x 11,5

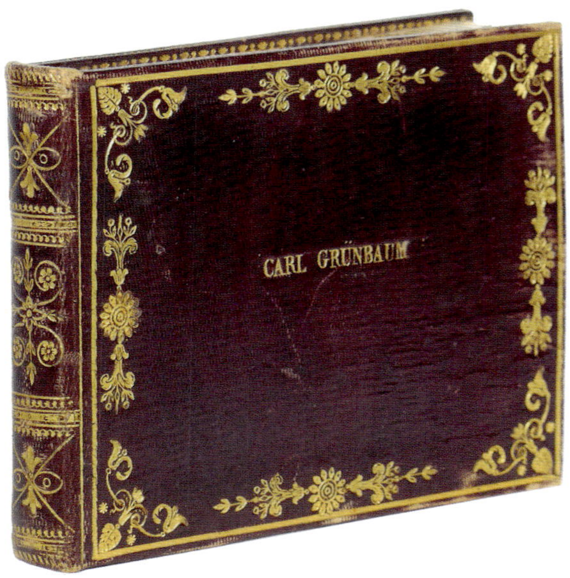

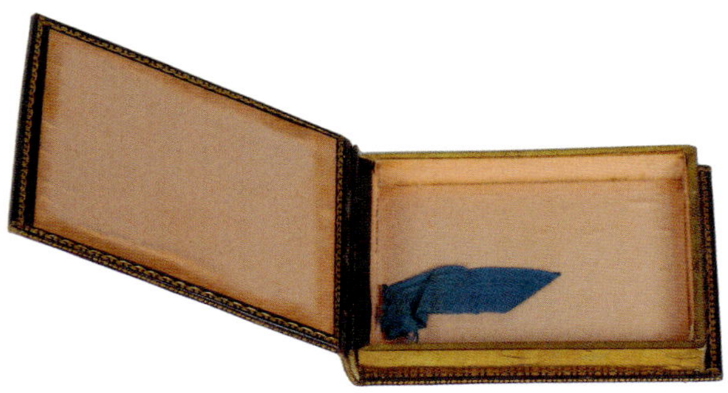

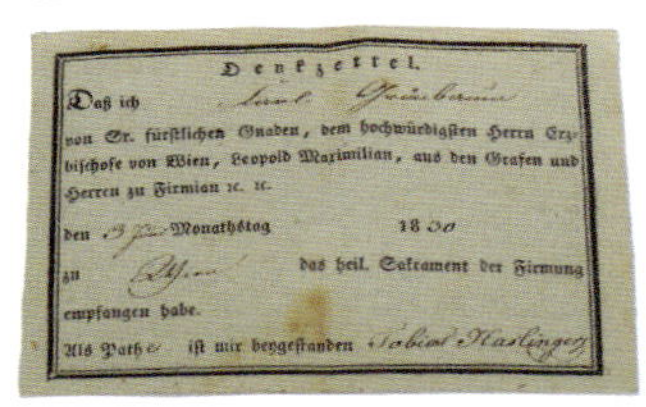
Denkzettel.
Daß ich
von Sr. fürstlichen Gnaden, dem hochwürdigsten Herrn Erzbischofe von Wien, Leopold Maximilian, aus den Grafen und Herren zu Firmian ꝛc. ꝛc.
den Monathstag 1830
zu das heil. Sakrament der Firmung empfangen habe.
Als Pathe ist mir beygestanden Tobias Haslinger

7.026
Catacombe S. Calisto Roma
Andenken-Holzdose mit vierzehn runden-eingelegten, metallenen Kreuzigungsszenen, aufklappbar, Kruzifix auf Vorderdeckel
Hinged wooden souvenir box with 14 illustrations of the crucifixion made of metal, crucifix on the lid
10,8 x 7,5 x 1,8 cm

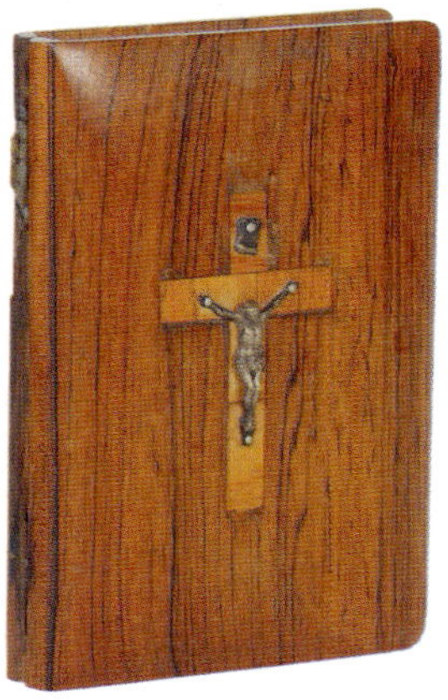

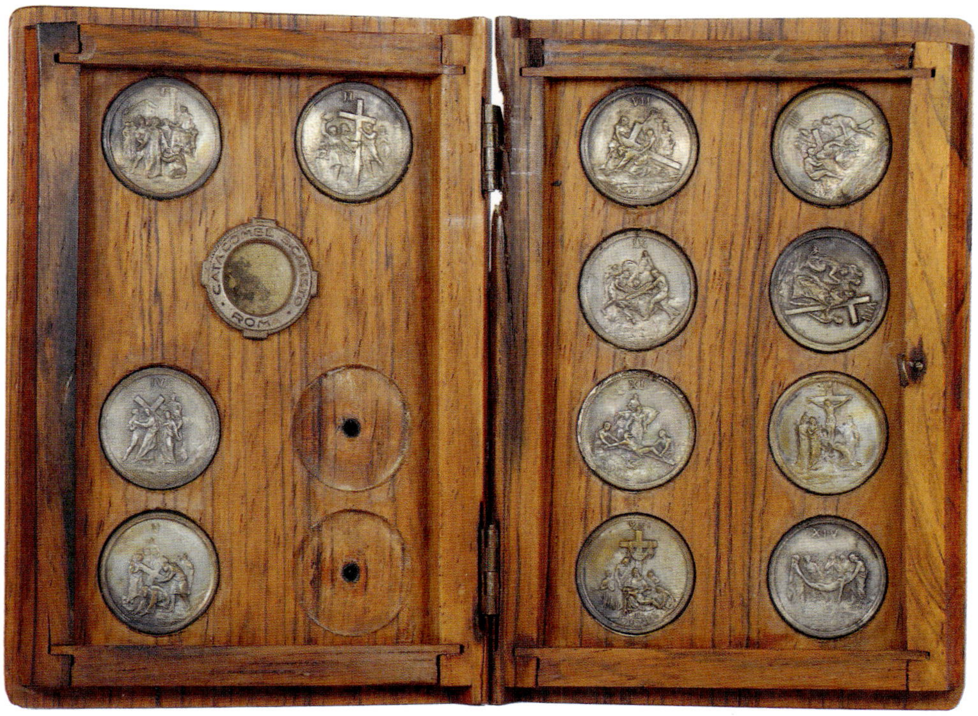

7.027
Roma
Kunststoffdose mit vierzehn runden, metallenen Kreuzigungsszenen, Kruzifix im Innendeckel, Andenken
Plastic box with 14 round illustrations of the crucifixion made of metal, crucifix on the interior of the lid, souvenir
11,1 x 7 x 1,5 cm

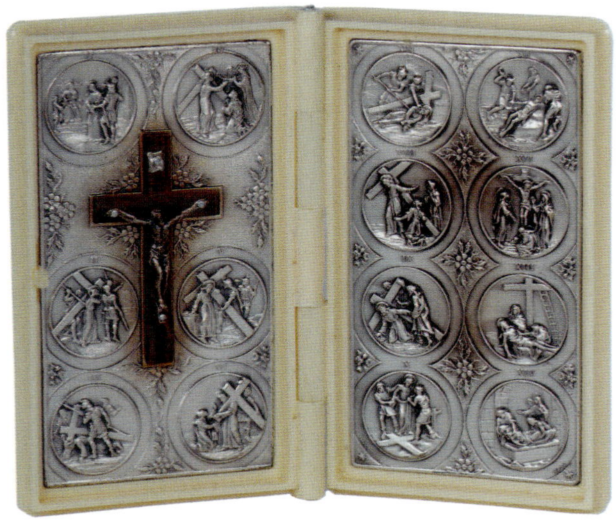

7.028
Biblia
Kalikodose mit einschiebbarem Schuber, 80 Bibelsprüche, 4. Aufl., Rücken- und Deckelvergoldung, dreiseitiger Goldschnitt
Calico box with slipcase, 80 bible verses, 4th ed, gilt spine and covers, all edges gilt
Verlag der Buchhandlung der Ev. Gesellschaft
Stuttgart, Germany
1896 | 6,4 x 5,2 x 2,2 cm

7.029
Biblia
Kalikodose im Schuber, Rücken- und Deckelvergoldung, dreiseitiger Goldschnitt, 80 Bibelsprüche
Calico box in a slipcase, gilt spine and cover, all edges gilt, 80 bible verses
Verlag der Buchhandlung Ev. Gesellschaft
Stuttgart, Germany
1900 | 6,6 x 5,3 x 2,1 cm

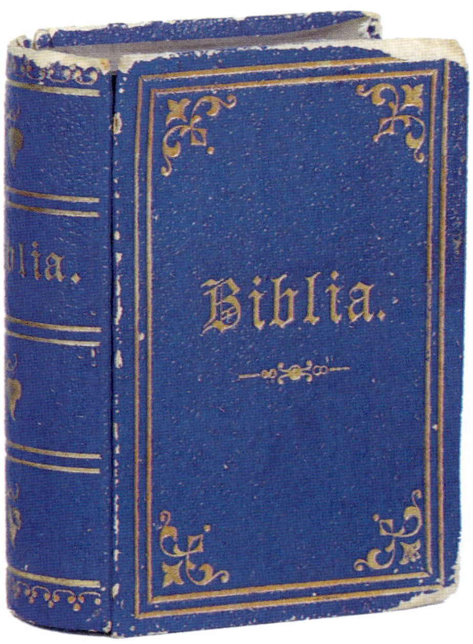

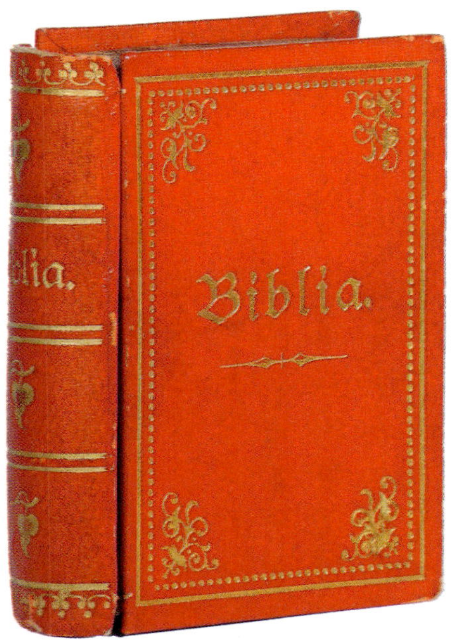

7.030
Worte des Lebens / *Words of Life*
Kalikodose mit Kaetonschuber, 120 Bibelsprüche mit Versen von Gerhard Tersteegen, Rücken- und Deckelvergoldung, dreiseitiger Goldschnitt
Calicos box with a cardboard slipcase, 120 bible verses by Gerhard Tersteegen, gilt spine and cover, all edges gilt
Um / *Around* 1900 | 9,6 x 7,7 x 2,2 cm

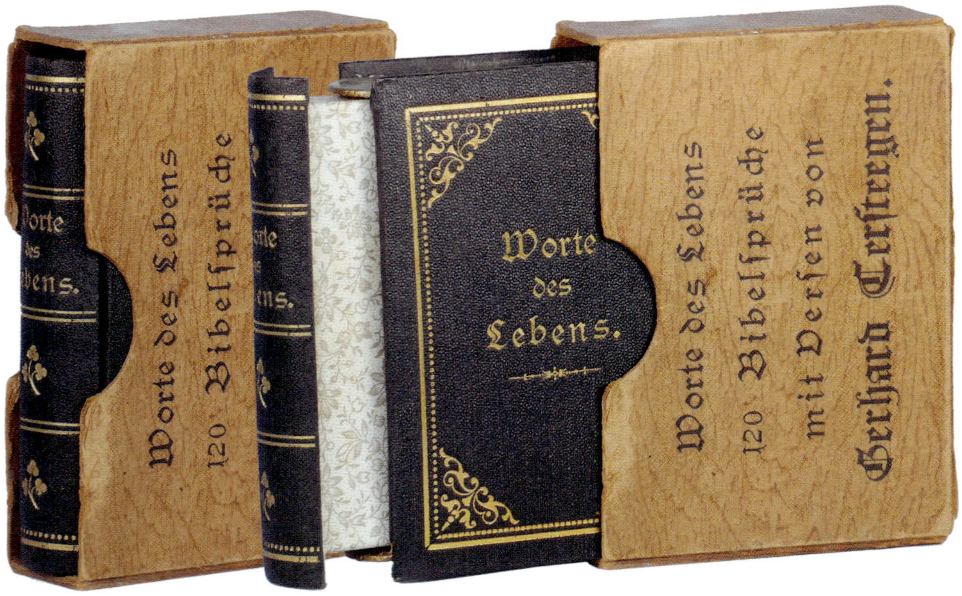

7.031
Kalikodose in Kartonschuber, 80 Bibelsprüch, Rücken- und Deckelvergoldung, dreiseitiger Goldschnitt
Calico box in a slipcase, gilt spine and cover, all edges gilt, 80 bible verses from the bible
Verlag der Buchhandlung Ev. Gesellschaft Stuttgart, Germany 1900 | 6,4 x 5,3 x 2,1 cm

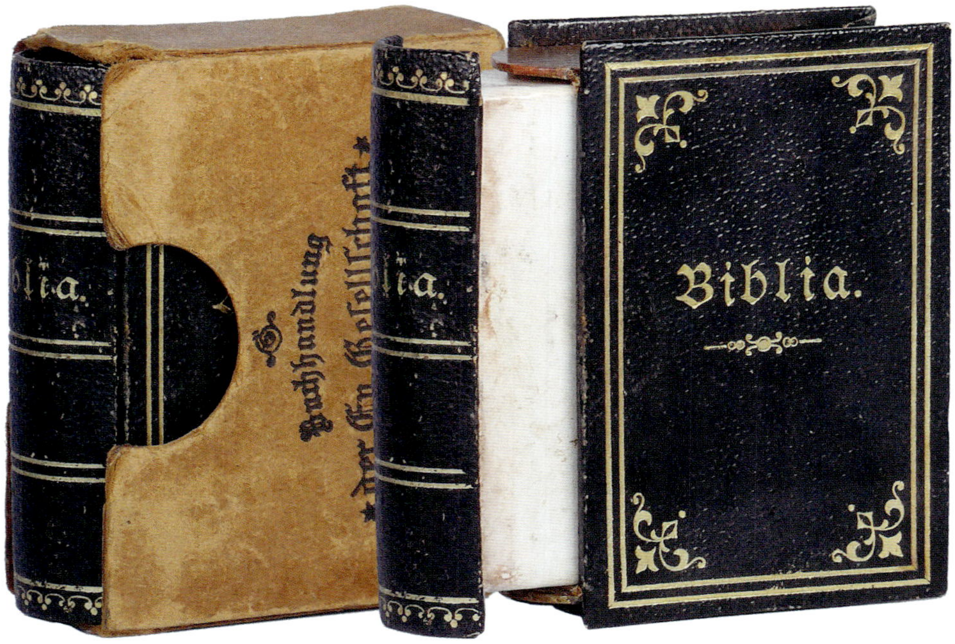

7.032
Kunststoffdose mit erhabenem Blumenmotiv auf dem Vorderdeckel
Plastic box with raised flowers on the front cover
2,3 x 12,7 x 7,5 cm

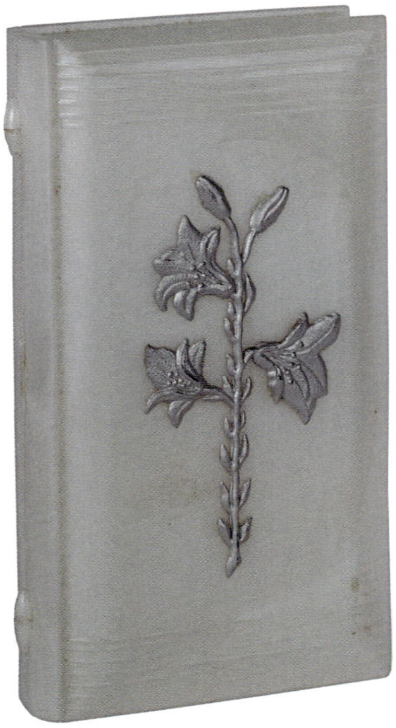

7.033
Holy Bible, FLT
Aufgeschlagene Bibel aus Metall mit zwei Händen
Open Bible made of metal with two hands
1,3 x 7,5 x 7,6 cm

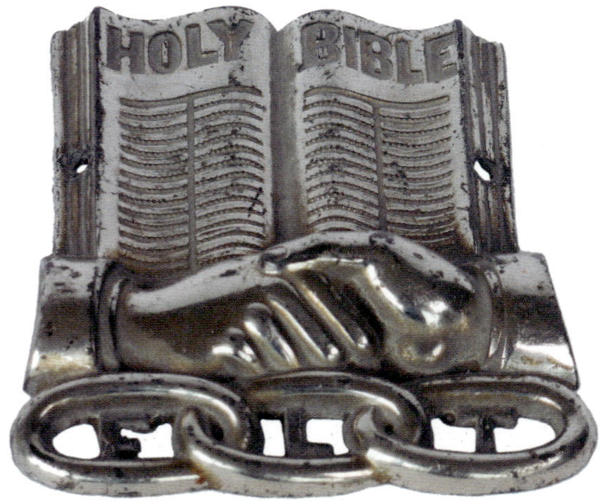

7.034

Christliches Vergissmeinnicht / ***Christian Forget-Me-Not***

Kaliko-Buchschachtel mit Farb- und Goldprägung, dreiseitiger Goldschnitt mit geprägtem Papier, ausgefüttert mit lithografiertem Buntpapier

Calico book box with color and gold tooling, all edges gilt with embossed paper, lined with lithographed colored paper

Um / *Around1900* | 2,6 x 12,3 x 9,6 cm

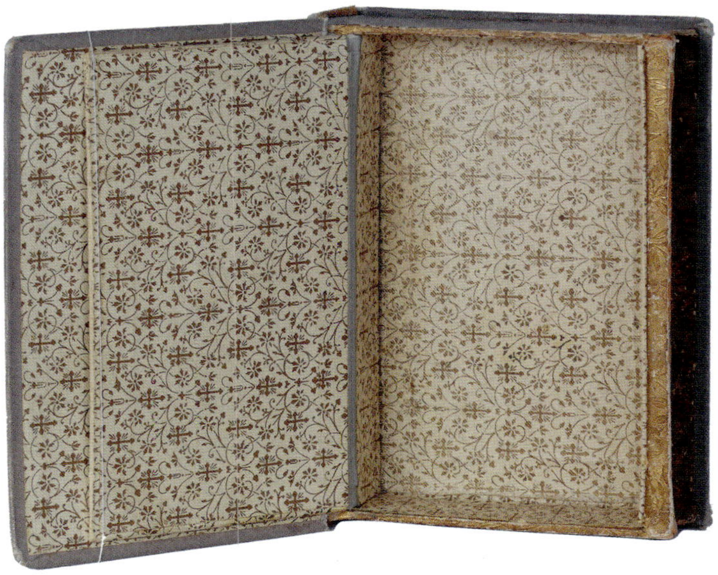

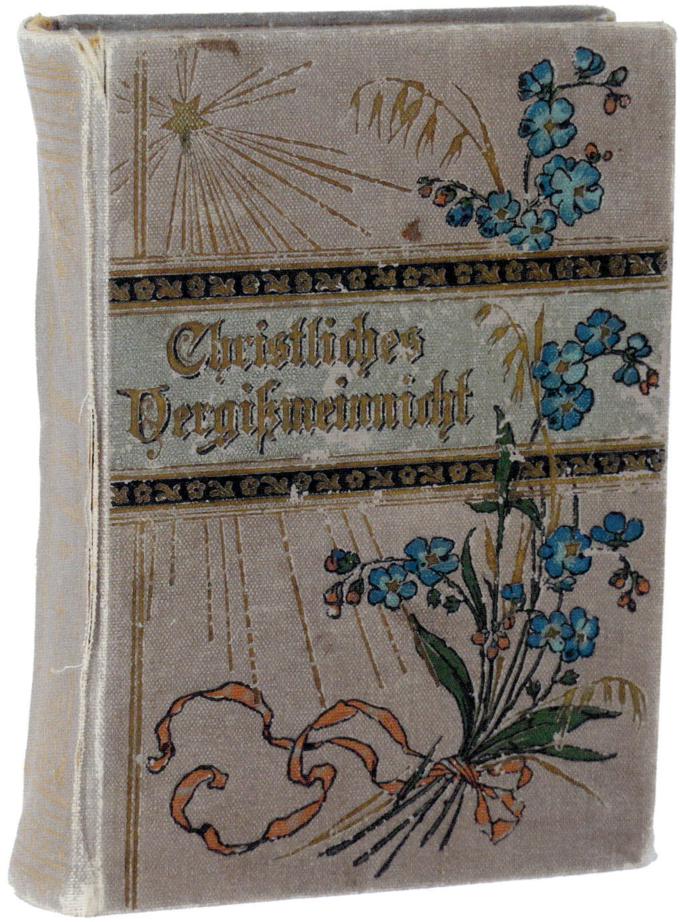

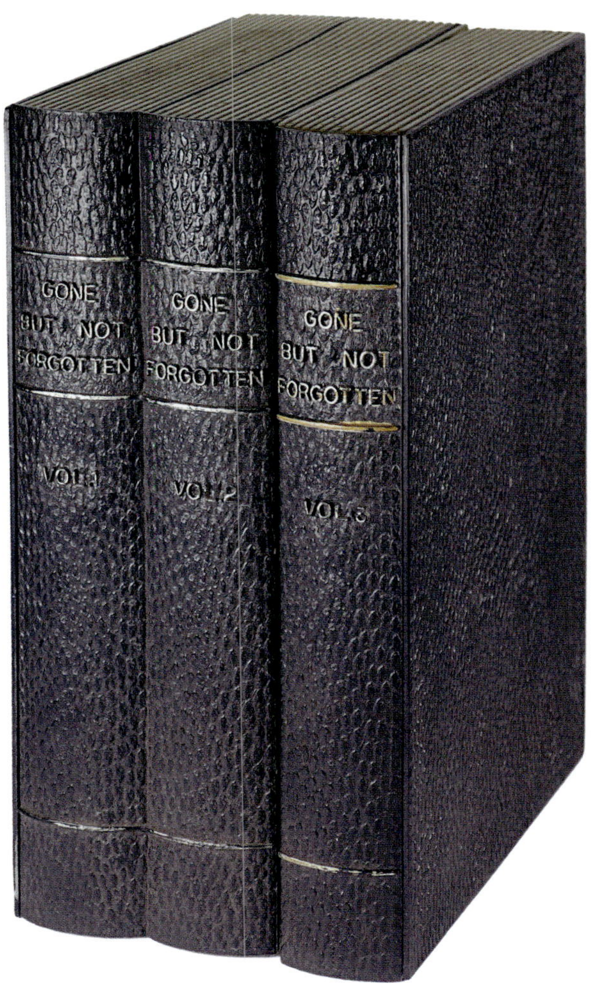

7.035

Gone But Not Forgotten, Vol. 1–3

Kunststoffdose zweiteilig mit abnehmbarem Deckel, zur Aufbewahrung von Trauer- und Beileidsschreiben, drei erhabene Titel

Plastic box in two parts with removable covers, for storing letters of mourning and condolence, three raised titles

18,3 x 8,8 x 13,8 cm

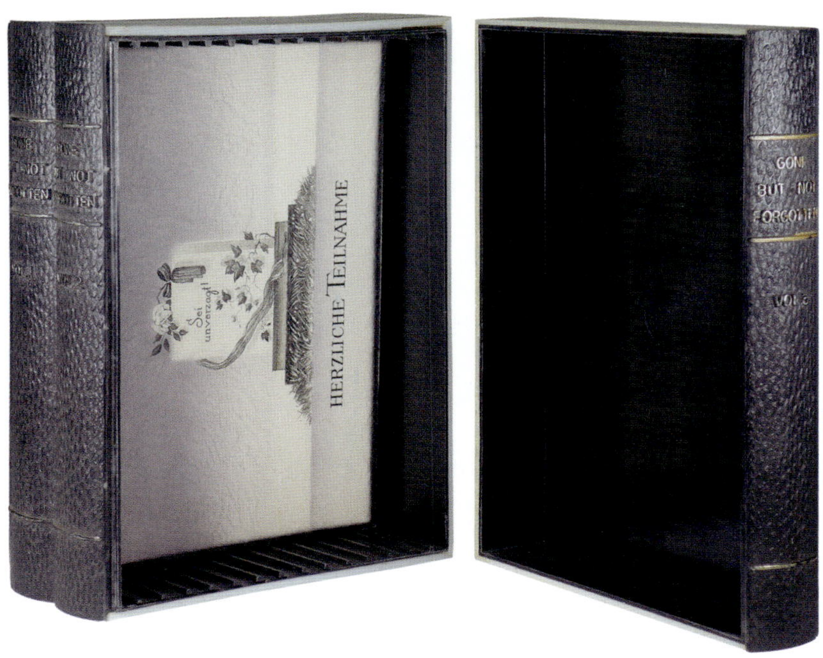

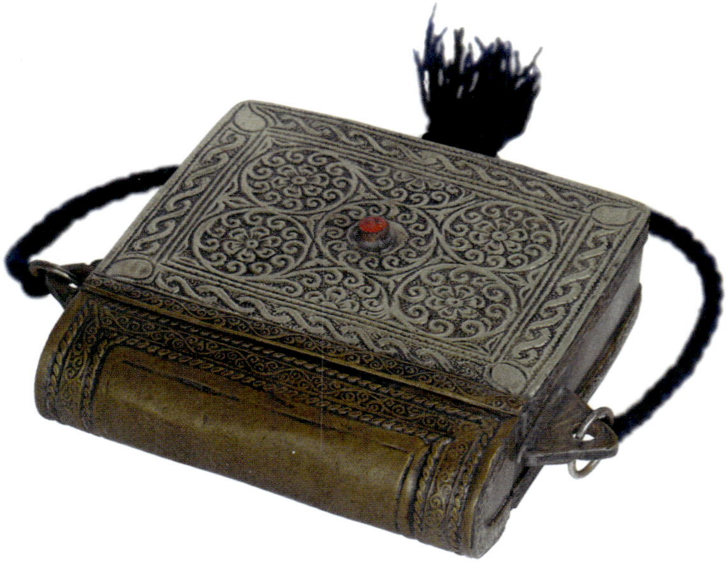

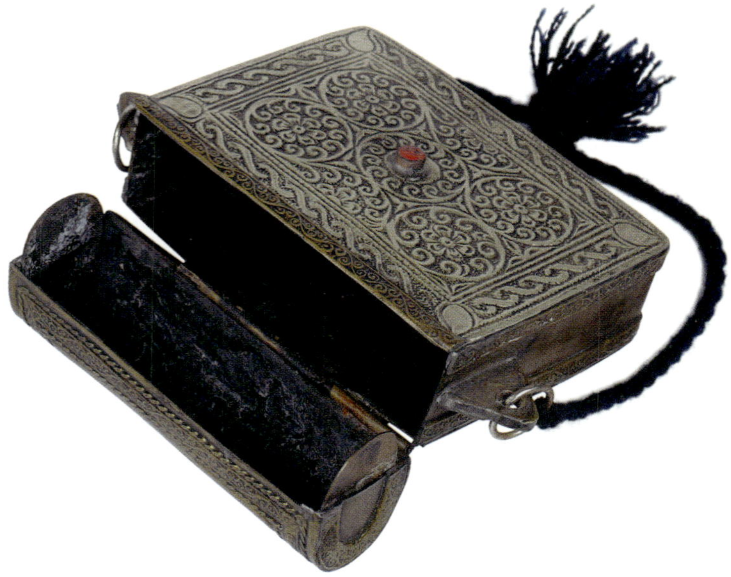

7.036
Wohl arabischer Koranbehälter aus Metall, ziseliert und verziert mit farbigen Halbedelsteinen, zwei Ösen für Tragkette
Arabic Koran container made of metal, chased and decorated with colored semi-precious stones, two eyelets for a chain
15,7 x 11,8 x 3,5 cm

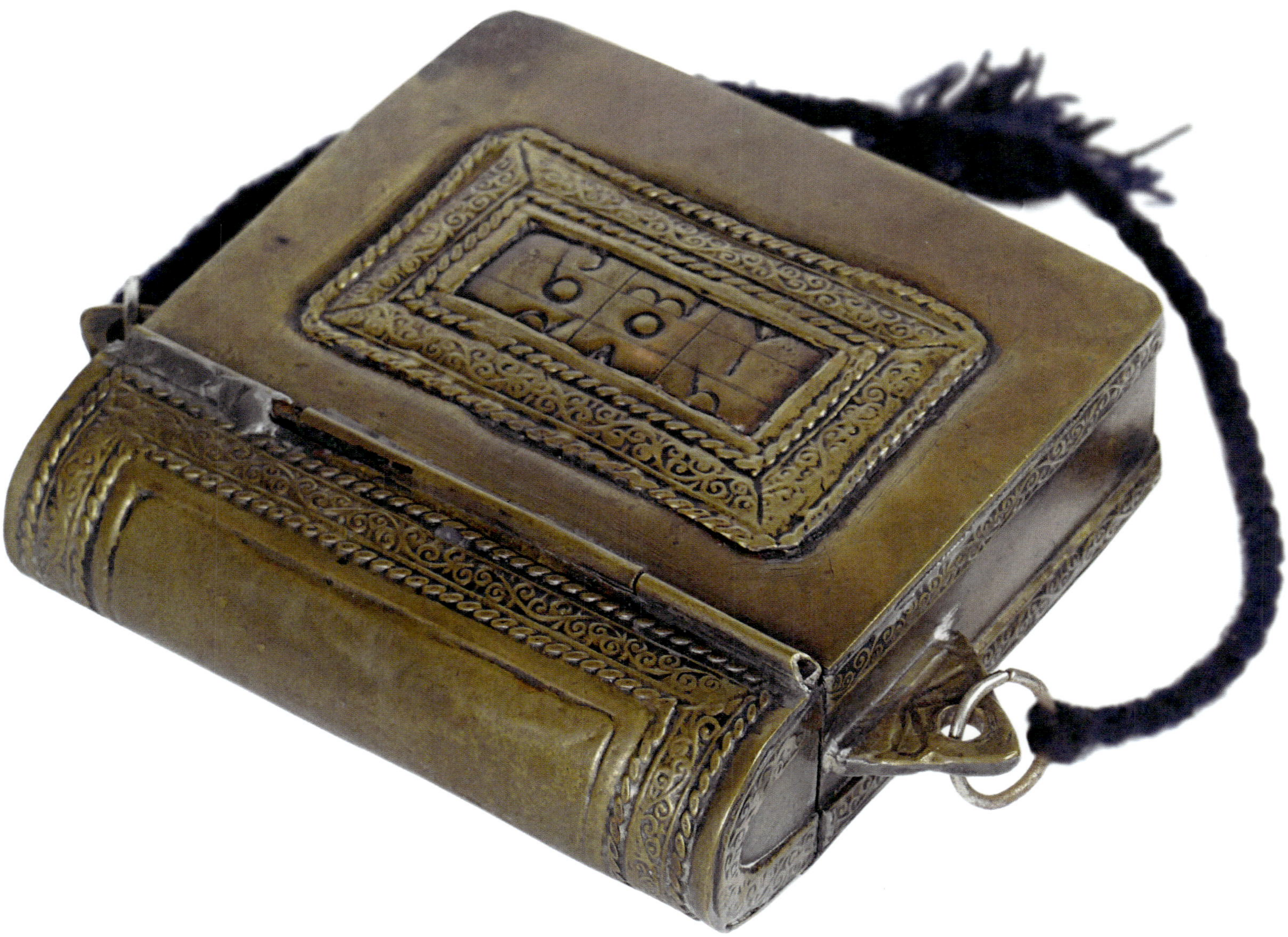

7.037
Wohl arabischer Koranbehälter aus Metall, ziseliert und verziert mit farbigen Halbedelsteinen, zwei Ösen für Tragkette
Arabic Koran container made of metal, chased and decorated with colored semi-precious stones, two eyelets for a chain
16,2 x 12 x 4 cm

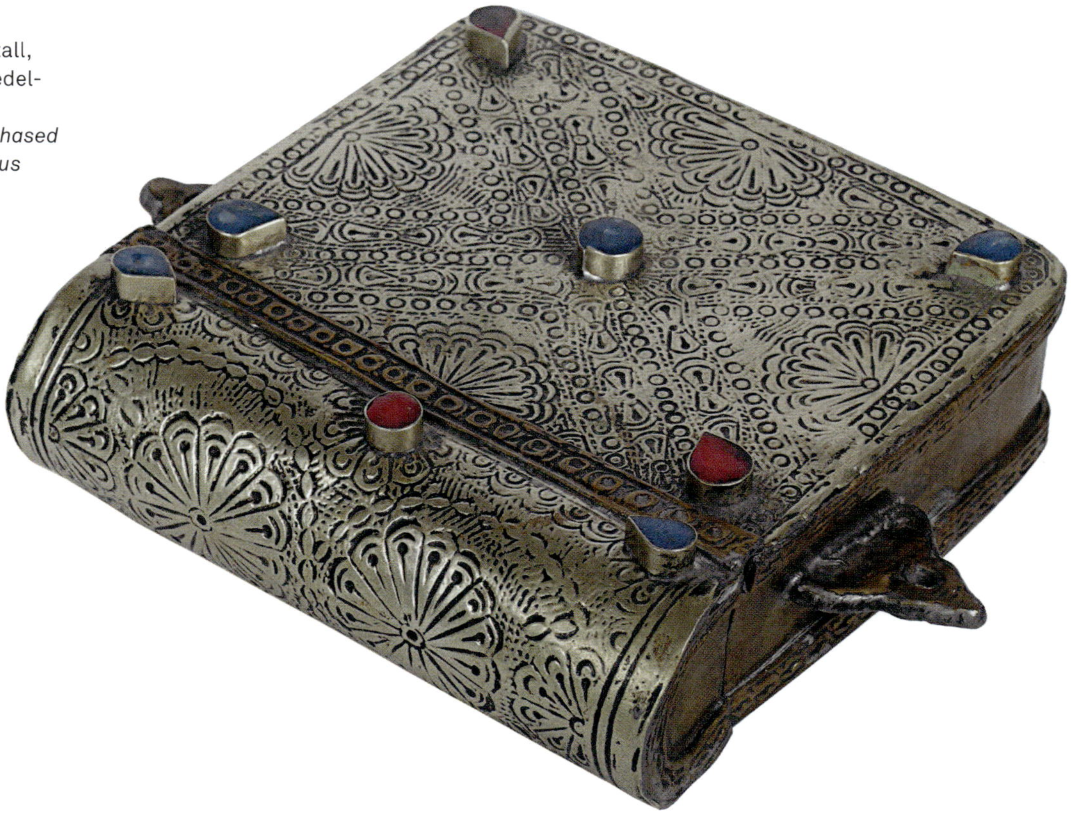

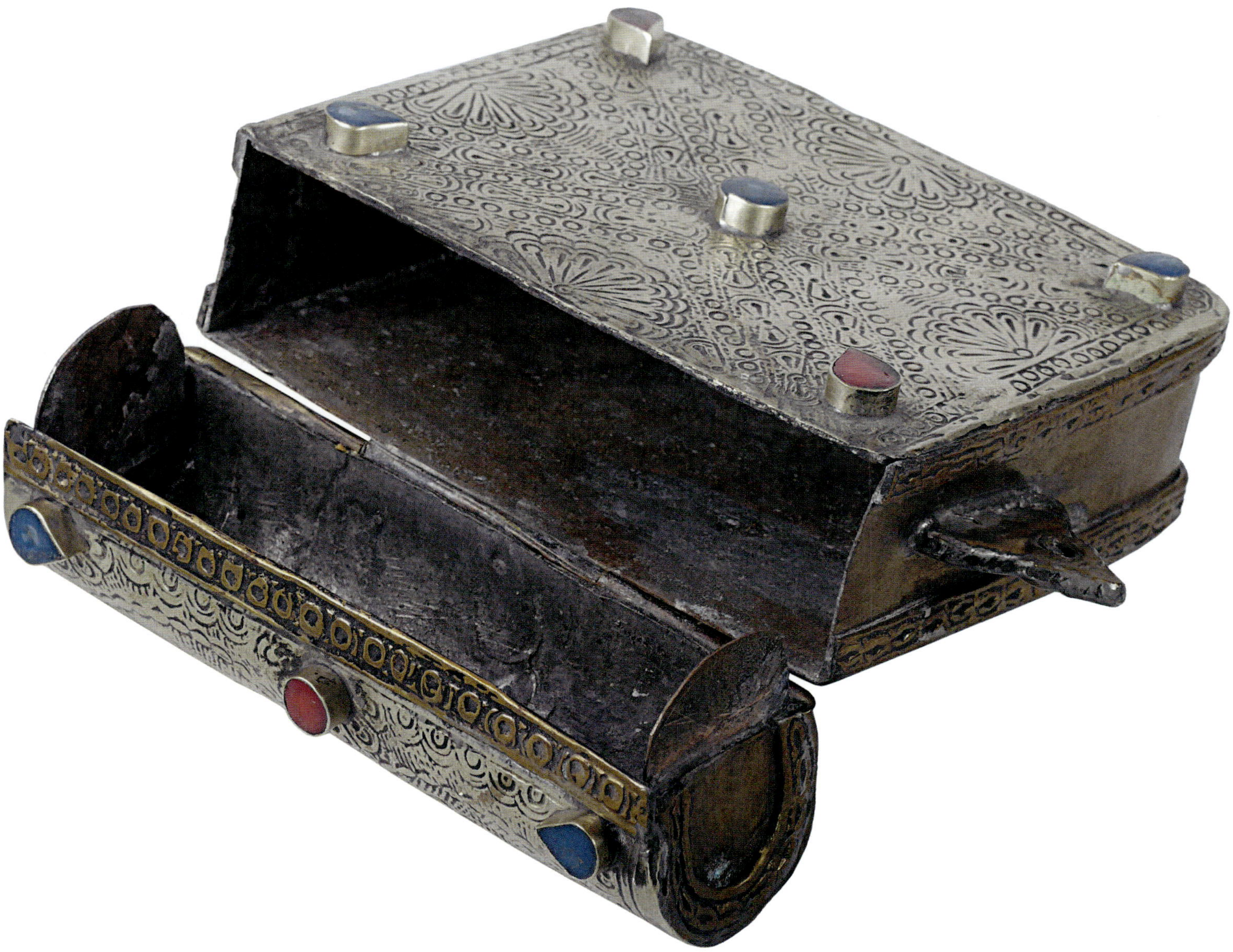

7.038–7.054
Wachsstöcke oder Wachsbücher sind Nachbildungen von Gebetsbüchern, umgeben von Rankenwerk und floralem Dekor in farbiger Wachsbossierung
Wax tapers or wax books are replicas of prayer books with wax embossed floral ornaments and tendrils
Um / *Around* 1900

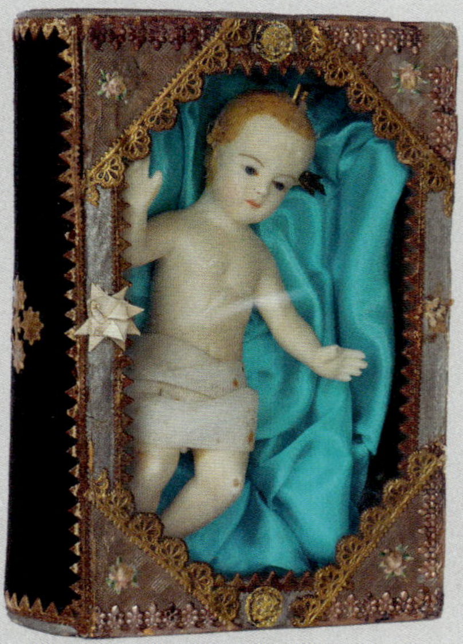

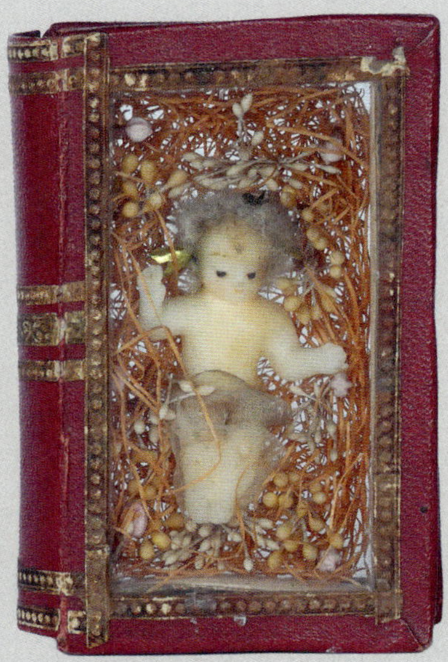

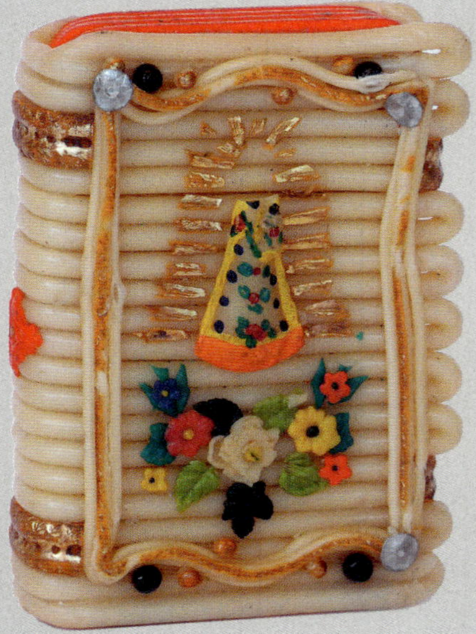

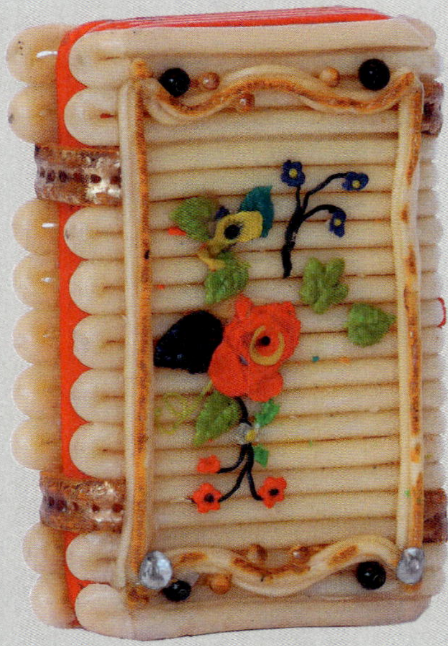

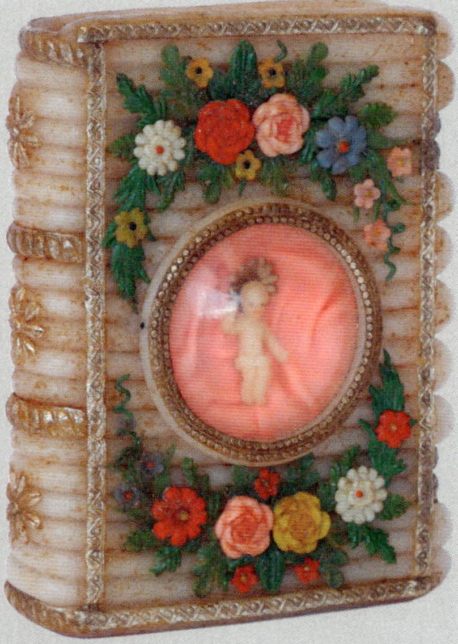

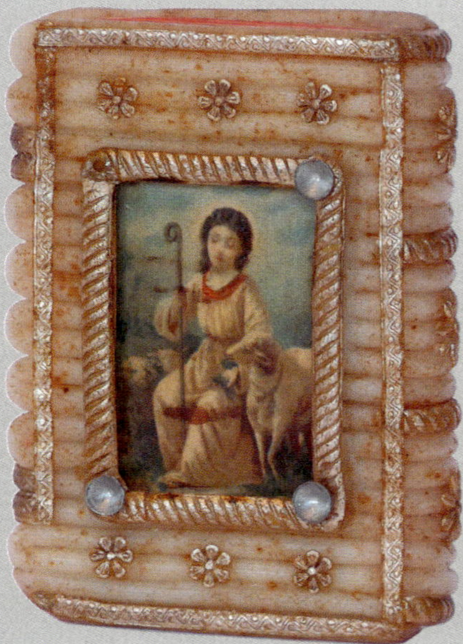

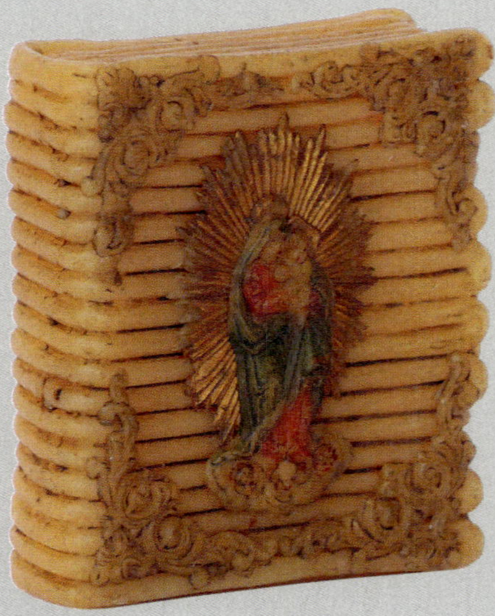

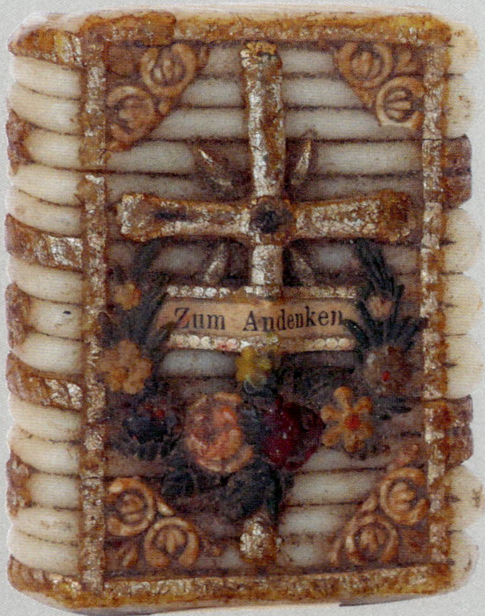

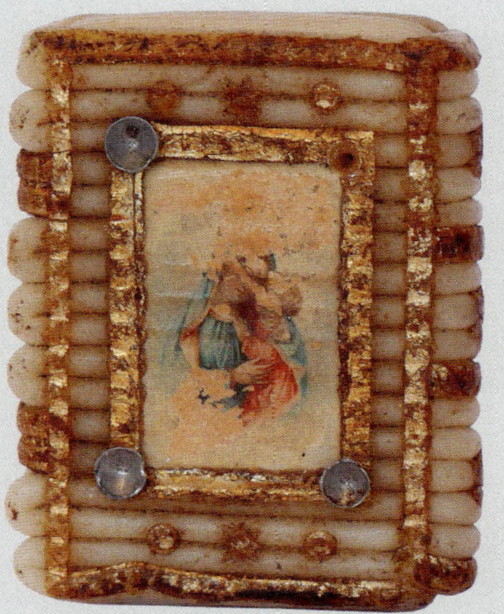

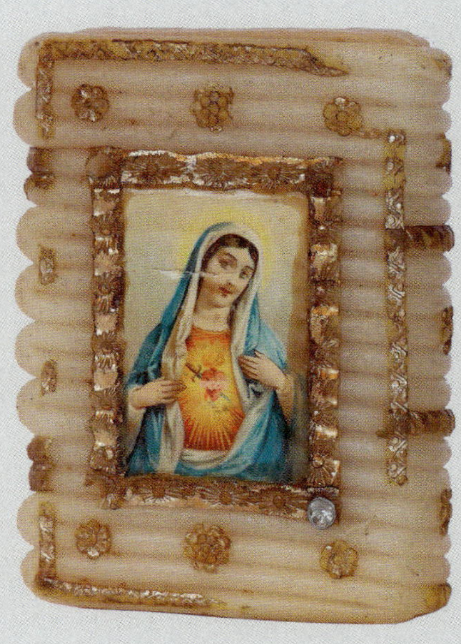
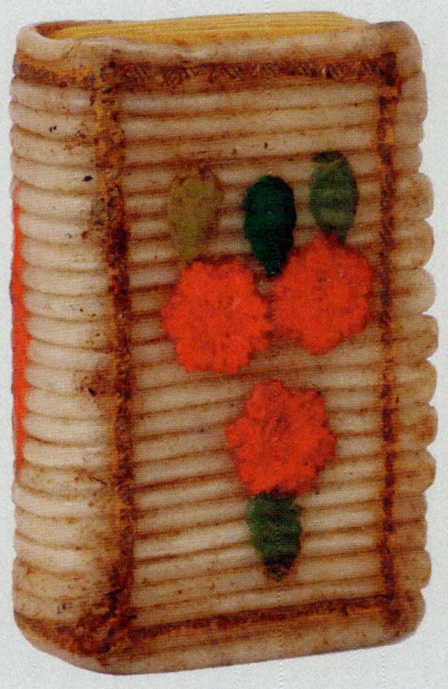
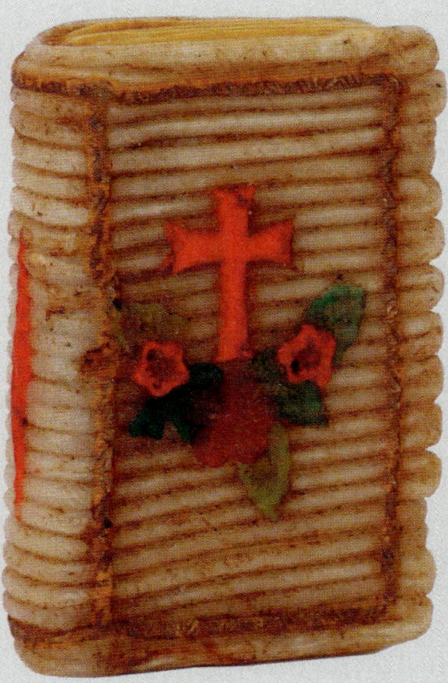
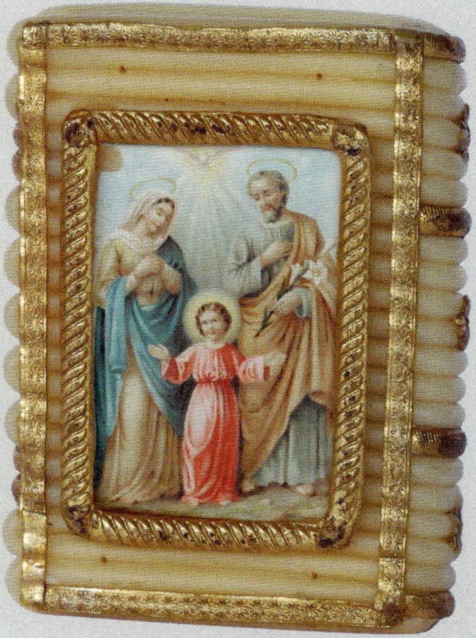
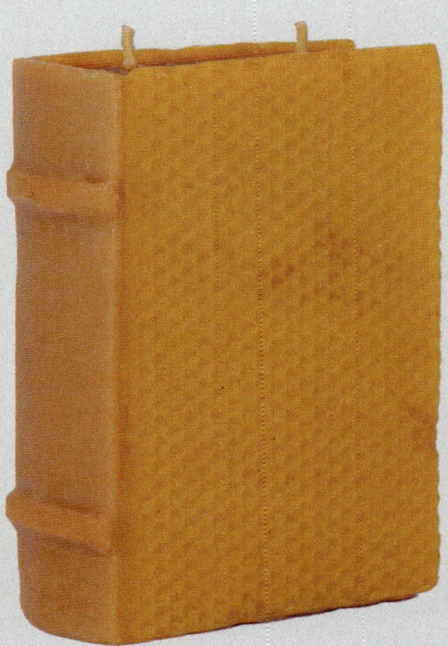
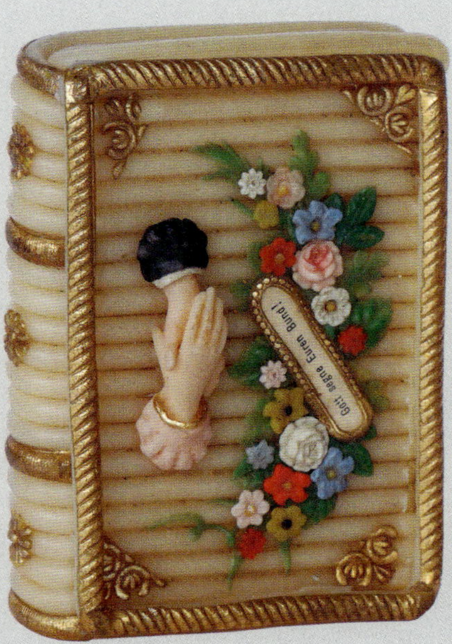
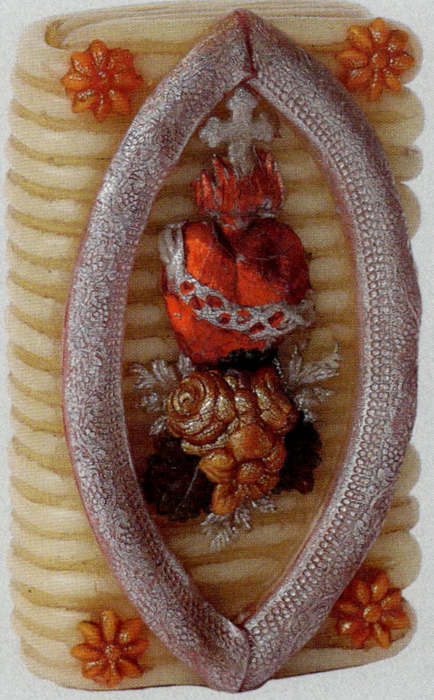

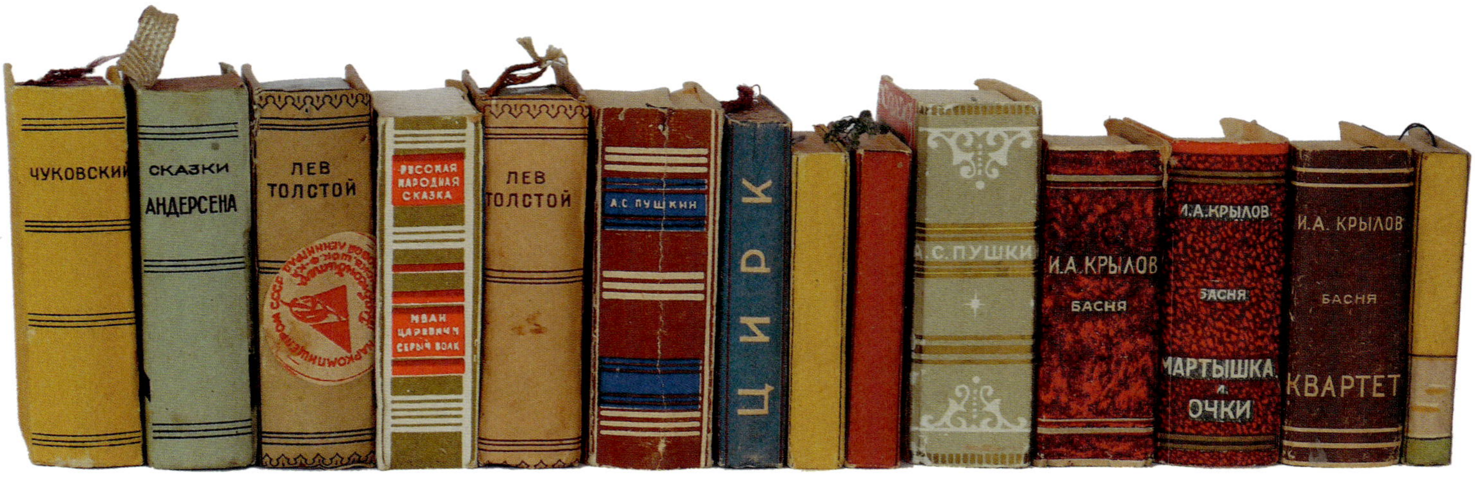

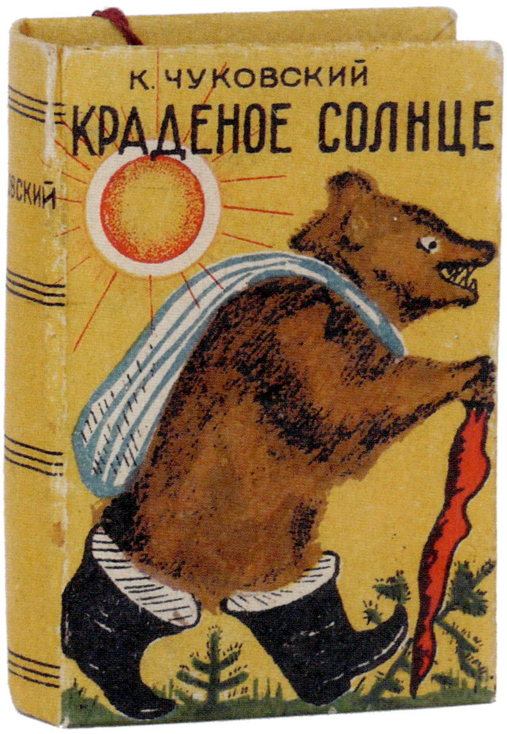

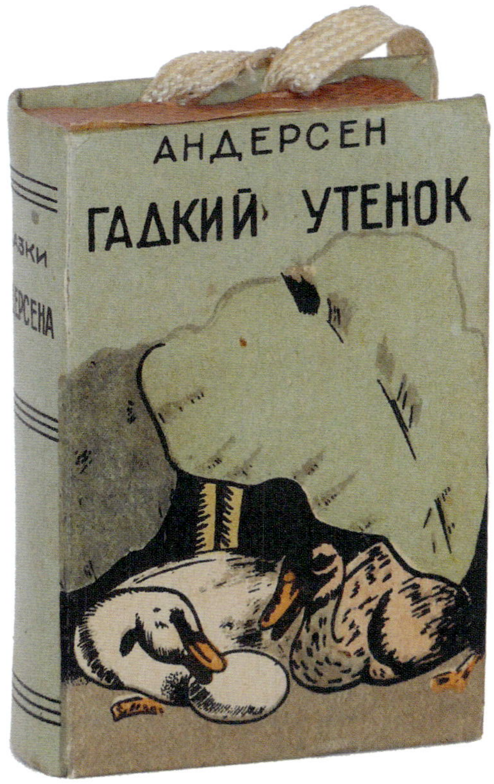

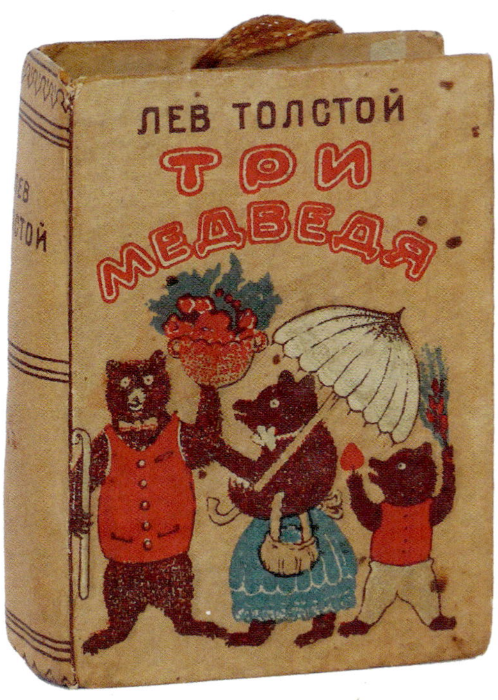

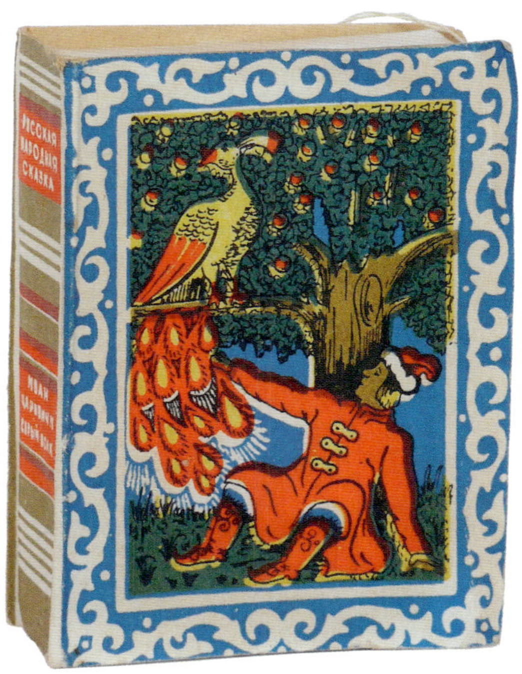

Die gestohlene Sonne
The Stolen Sun
8,1 x 5,8 x 2,4 cm

Das hässliche Entlein
The Ugly Duckling
8,1 x 5,8 x 2,4 cm

Die drei Bären
The Three Bears
8,1 x 5,8 x 2,4 cm

Iwan der Zarensohn „Grauer Wolf“
Ivan and The Grey Wolf
7,7 x 5,9 x 2,1 cm

Kater Bajun
The Bajun Cat
7,8 x 6 x 2,7 cm

Zirkus
The Circus
7,5 x 6 x 1 cm

Martyschka (Affe) und die Brillen
The Monkey and The Spectacles
6,9 x 5,5 x 1,2 cm

Die Kinderchen im Käfig
Kids in a Cage
7 x 5,6 x 1,1 cm

Teurer als ein farbiges Korn (Hühnerbeinige Hütte der Hexe Jaga)
The Hat on Hen's Legs of Baba Yaga
8 x 6 x 2,7 cm

Der Hahn und die Perle
The Cock And The Pearl
7,1 x 5,2 x 2,5 cm

Das Quartett (Esel, Bär, Ziegenbock, Affe)
The Quartet (Donkey, Bear, Goat, Monkey)
7,2 x 5,5 x 2,7 cm

Der kleine goldene Fisch
The Golden Fish
7 x 5,5 x 1,1 cm

7.055–7.067

Russischer Christbaumschmuck / ***Russian Chrsitmas tree decoration***

Behältnisse aus Pappe in Buchform für Süßigkeiten, der Vorderdeckel kann geöffnet öffnen, lithografierte Märchenszenen, Laschen zum Aufhängen

Cardboard boxes in the style of a book for sweets, the front cover can be opened. Lithographed fairytale scenes. Tabs to hang up

Um / *Around* 1930.

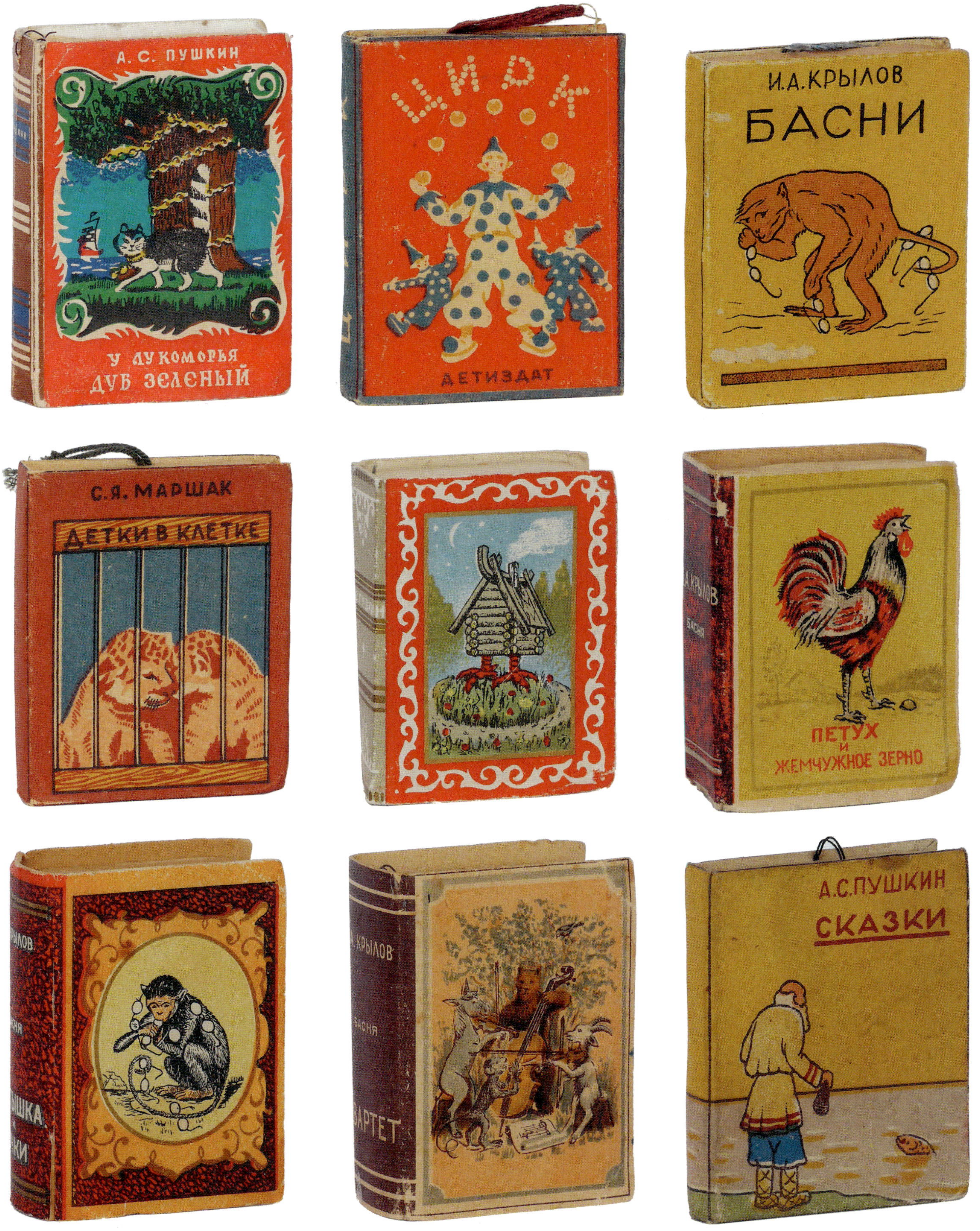

7.068–7.078
Zeitgenössischer Christbaumschmuck, Büchergestell, Eulen mit Büchern
Contemporary Christmas tree decorations, bookcase, owls holding books

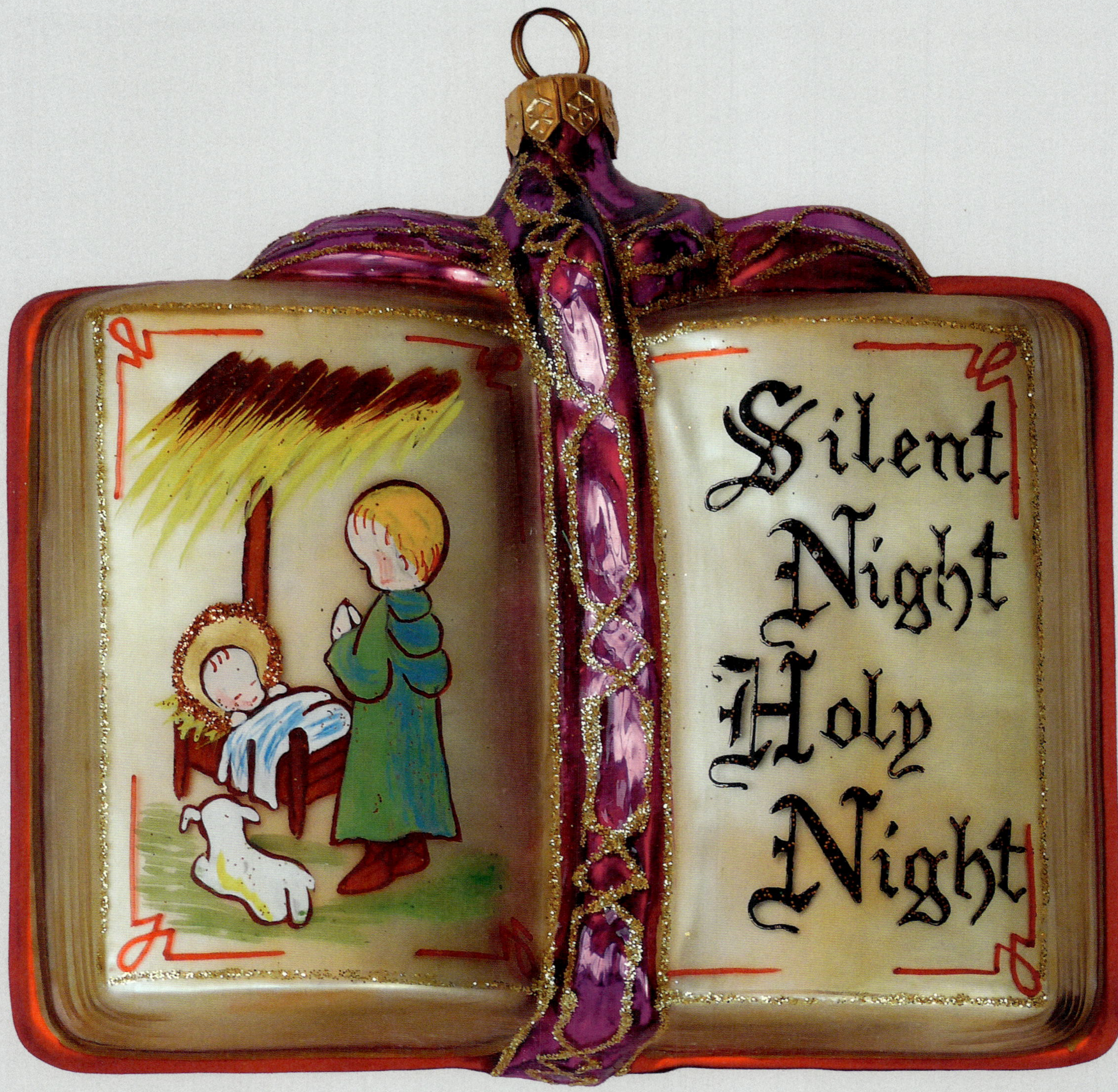

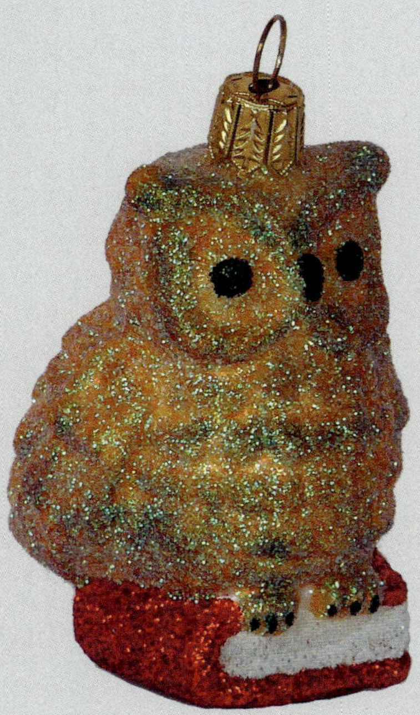

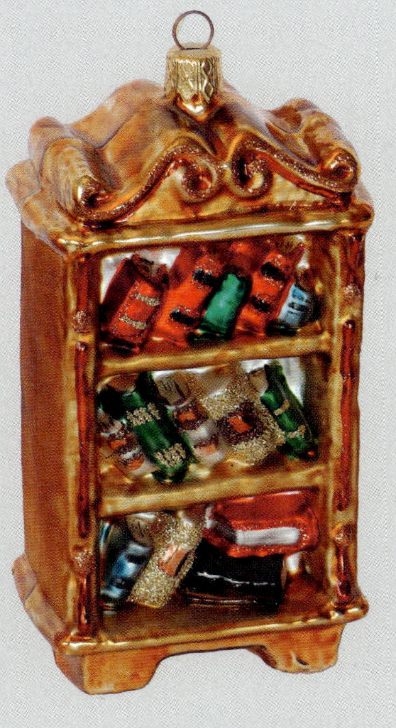

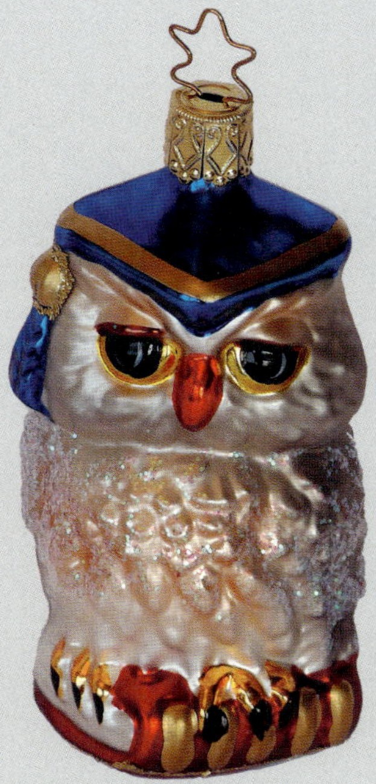

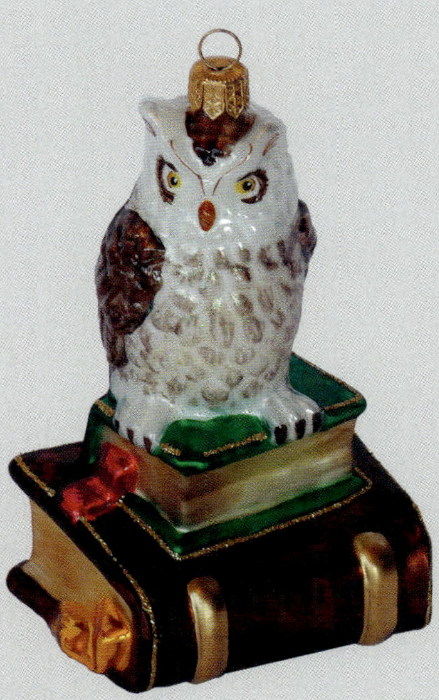

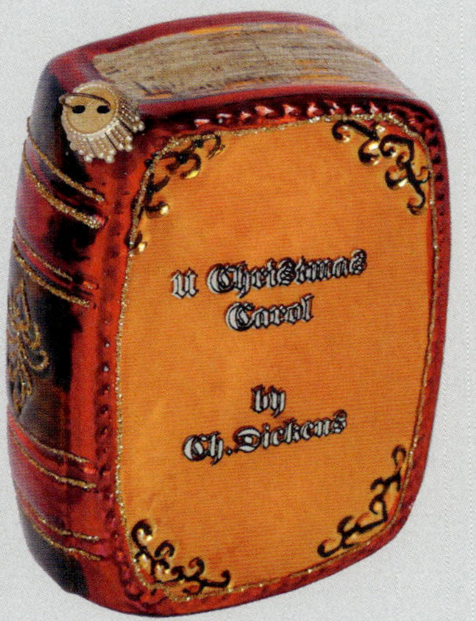
Christmas
Carol
by
Ch.Dickens

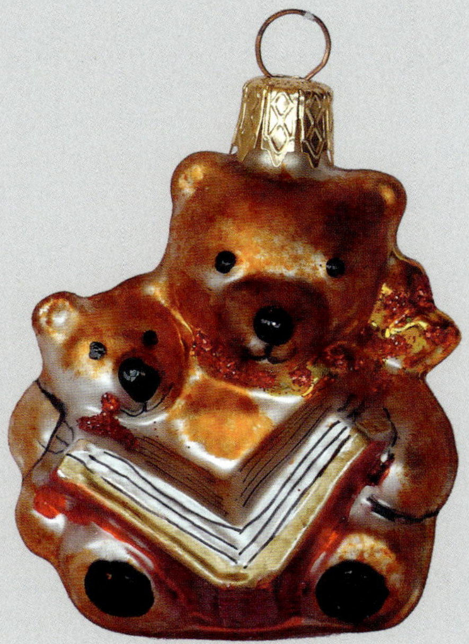

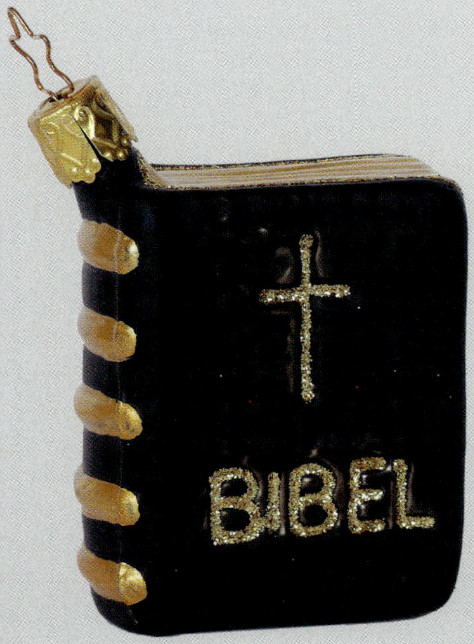
BIBEL

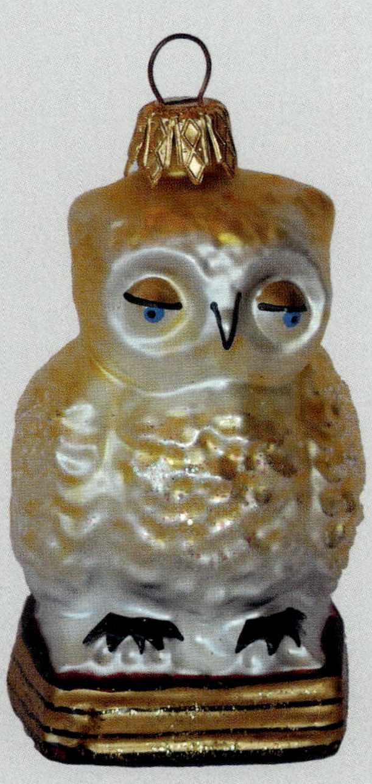

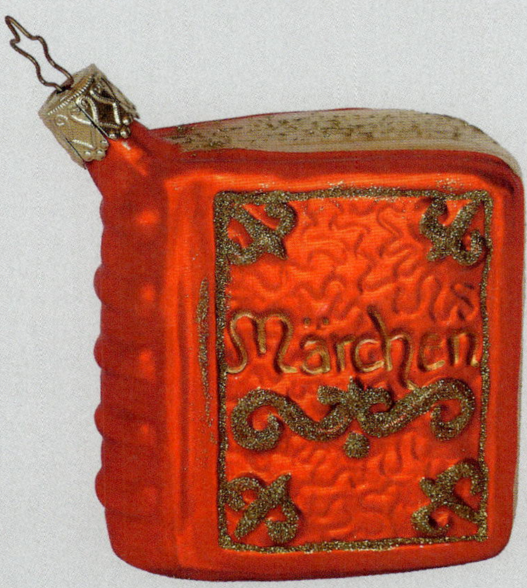
Märchen

7.079
Dresdner Pappe, Candy Container
Christbaumschmuck-Anhänger mit Winterszene, dreiseitiger Goldschnitt aus geprägtem Papier, Vorderdeckel kann geöffnet werden, Lasche zum Aufhängen
Christmas tree decoration pendant with a winter lanscape, gold-tooled paper, front cover can be opened, flap to hang up
Um / *Around* 1890 | 8,2 x 6,9 x 2,3 cm

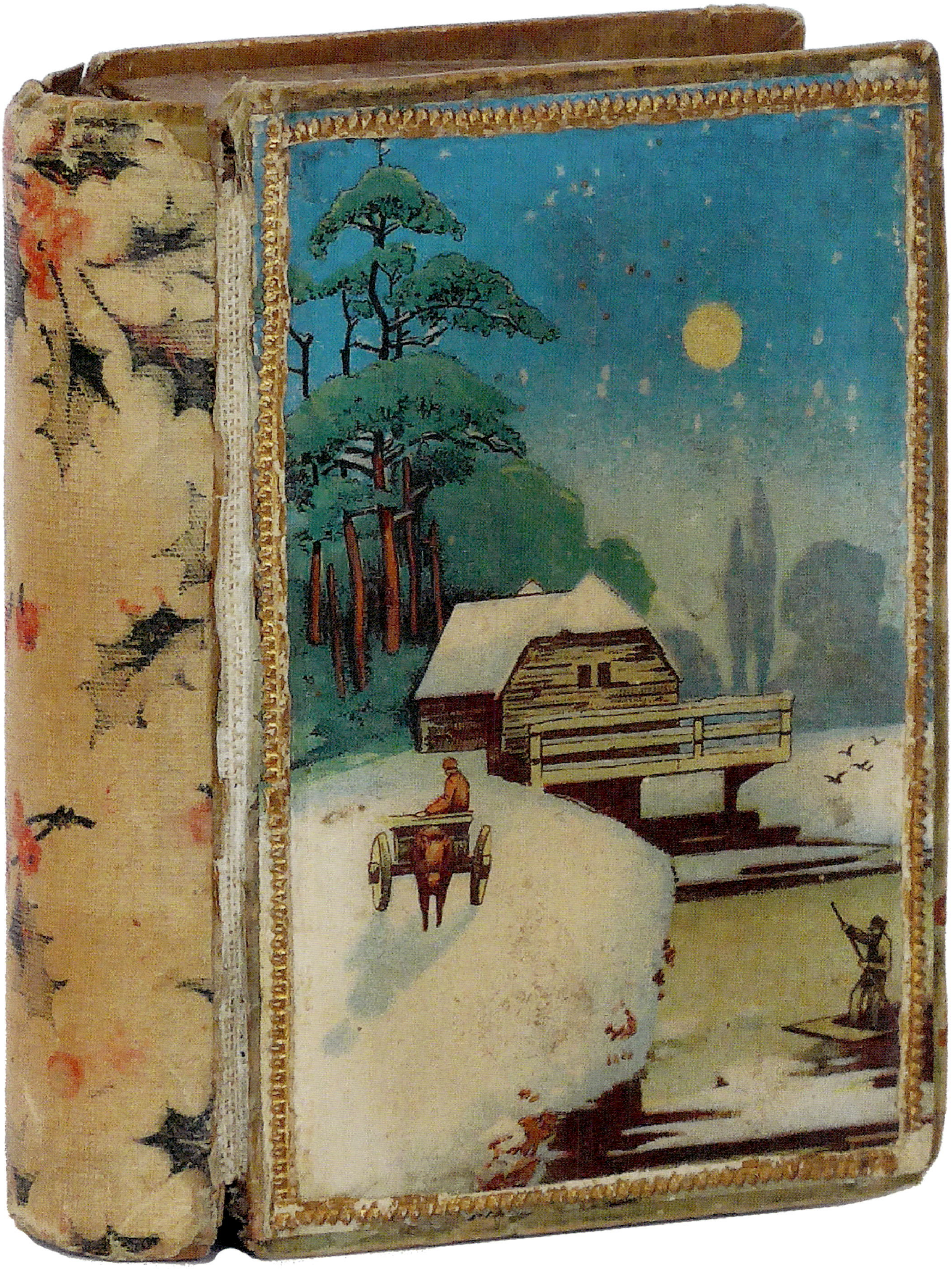

7.080
Christbaumschmuck- Anhänger mit Achatmarmor-Überzug, dreiseitiger gelber Farbschnitt, der Vorderdeckel kann geöffnet werden.
Christmas tree ornament pendant with agate marbled cover, yellow colored edges, the front cover can tbe opened
Herkunft unbekannt / *Origin unknown*
7 x 5,5 x 1,3 cm

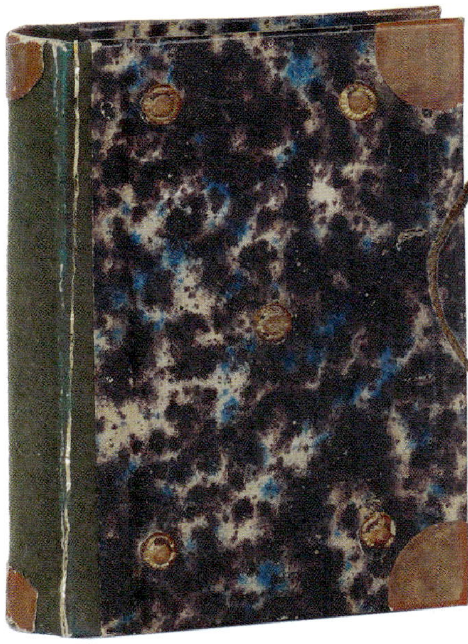

7.081
Christbaumschmuck-Anhänger aus Leder, dreiseitiger Goldschnitt
Christmas tree pendant made of leather, all edges gilt
Herkunft unbekannt / *Origin unknown*
5,7 x 4 x 1,6 cm

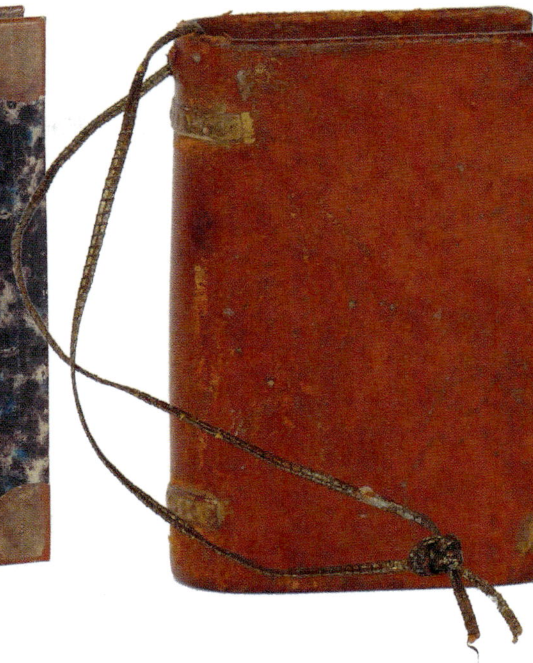

7.082
Salomé Comédie en 6 actes
Christbaumschmuckanhänger, Vorderdeckel mit Abbildung von Salomé, kann geöffnet werden
Christmas tree pendant, front cover with an illustration of Salomé, can be opened
Frankreich / *France* | Um / *Around* 1910
7,6 x 5,5 x 2 cm

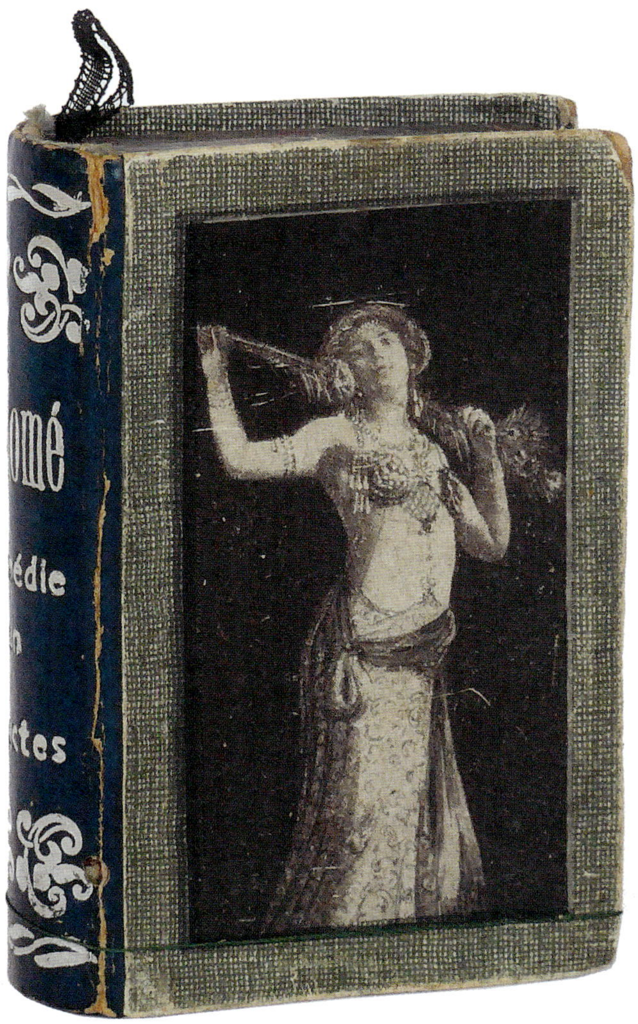

7.083
Christbaumschmuck-Anhänger aus Samt, eingefasst mit Goldlitze, dreiseitiger Goldschnitt
Christmas tree decoration made of velvet, edged with gold braid, all edges gilt
Zeitgenössisch / *Contemporary*
4,4 x 3,4 x 0,7 cm

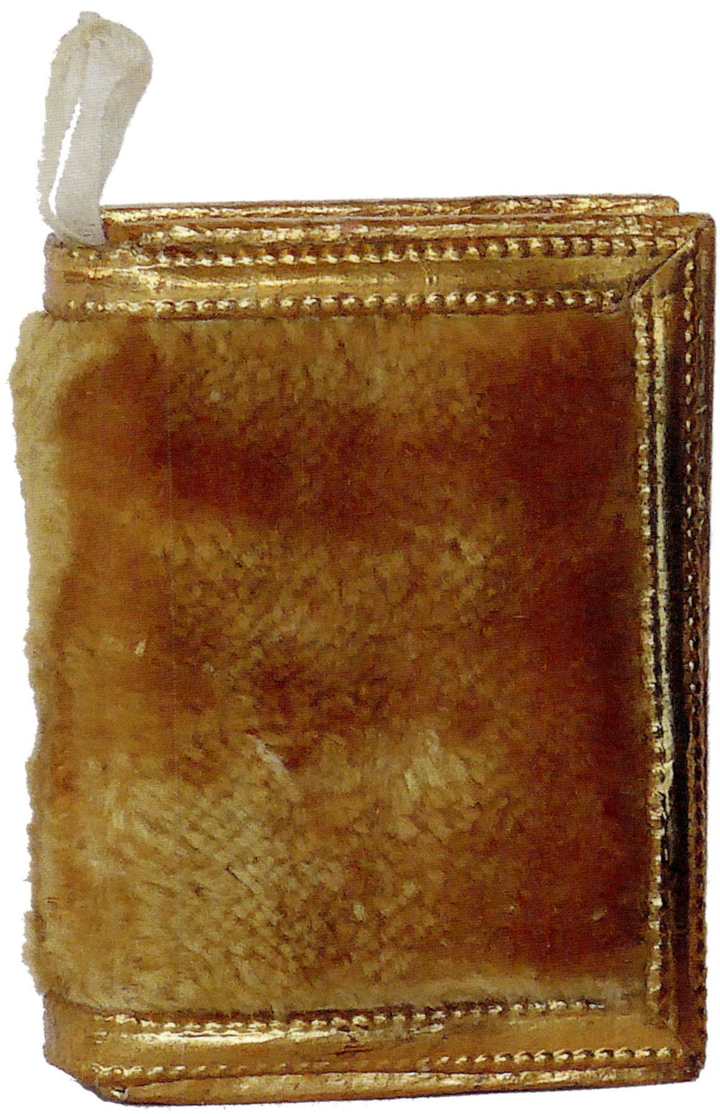

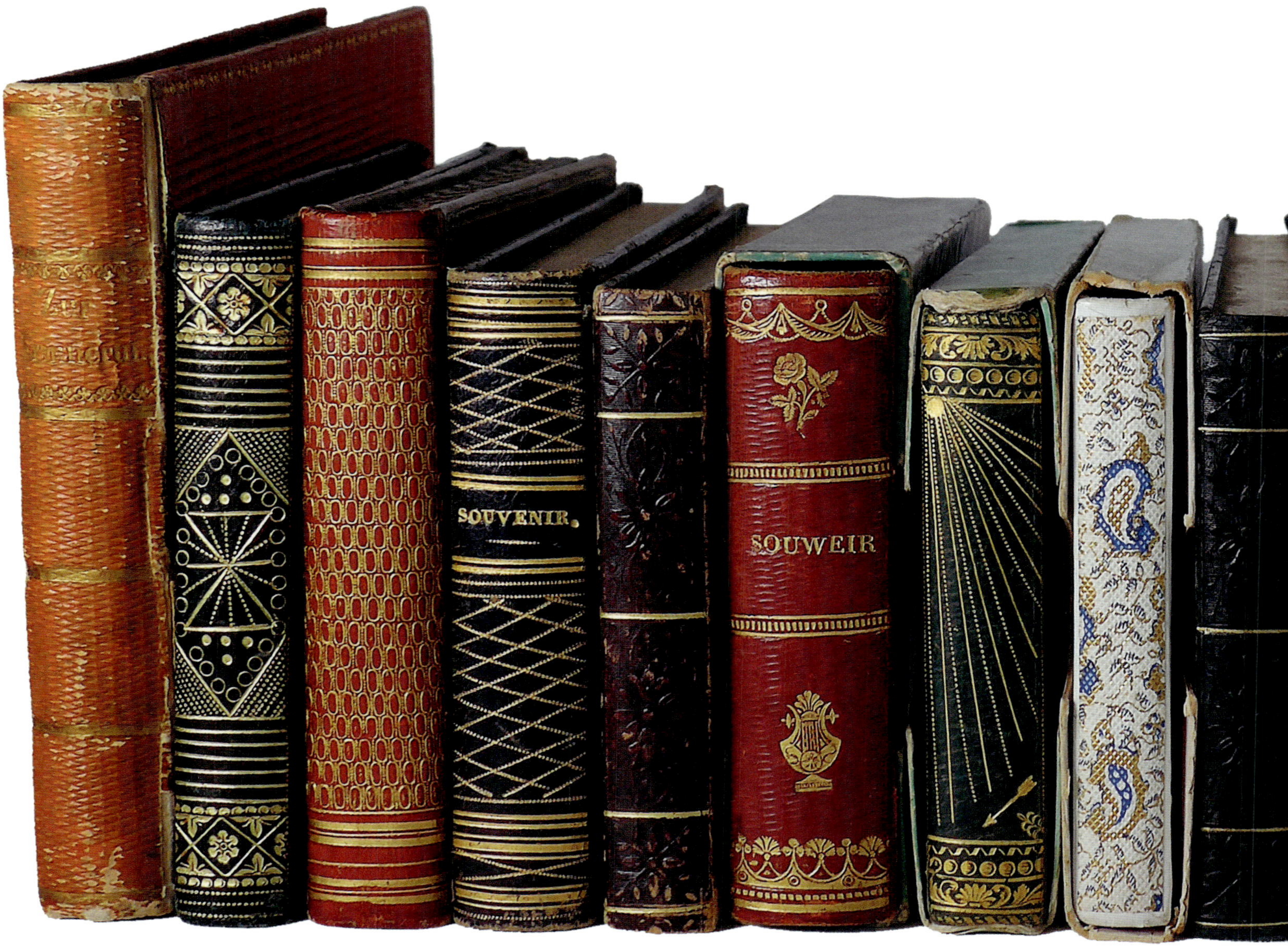

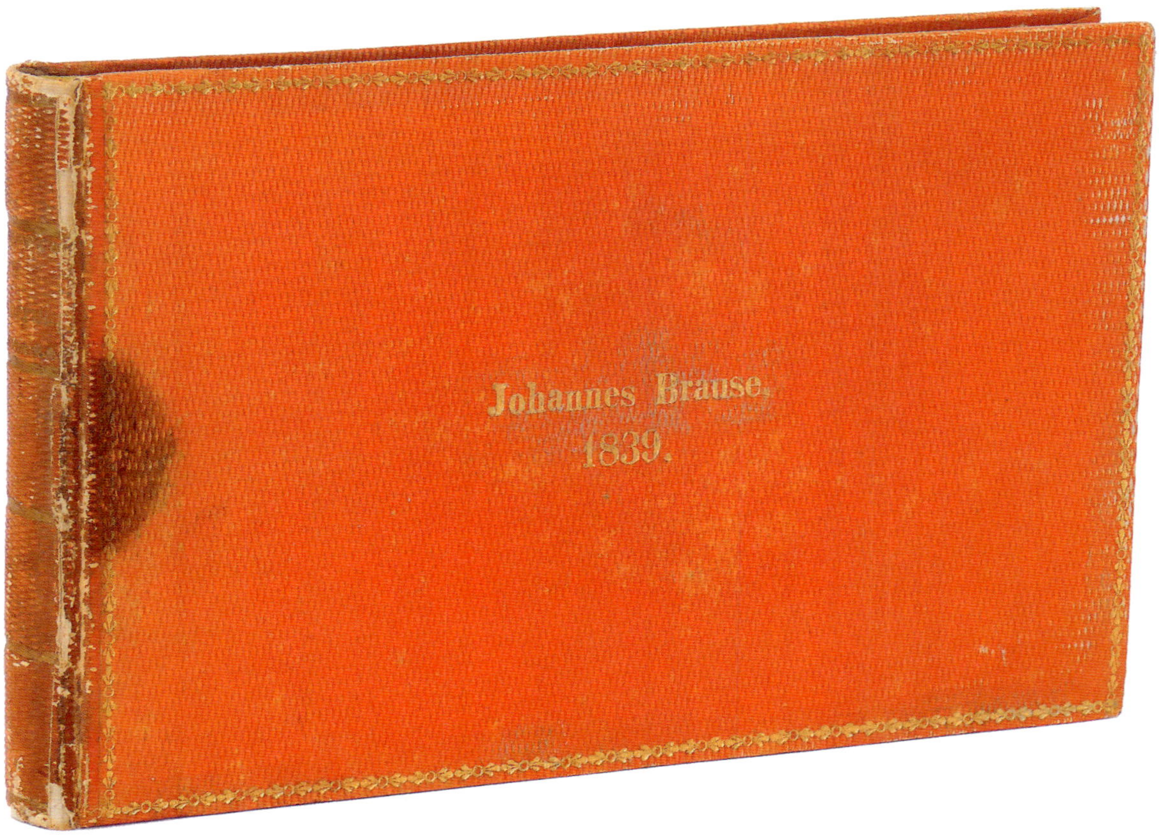

7.104
Zur Erinnerung, Johannes Brause 1839 Buchkassette mit geprägtem Papierüberzug, Titel- und Deckelvergoldung, 37 Blätter mit Goldschnitt, 15 Blätter beschriftet von 1840–1846, Zugbänder
As a reminder, Johannes Brause 1839 book box with embossed paper-over-board, gilt title and lid, 37 leaves with gilt edges, 15 leaves with lettering from 1840-1846, drawstring
1,9 x 20,2 x 12 cm

7.084–7.103
20 Freundschafts- und Stammbücher, Souvenir und Poesiealben
20 friendship and family books, souvenirs and poetry albums

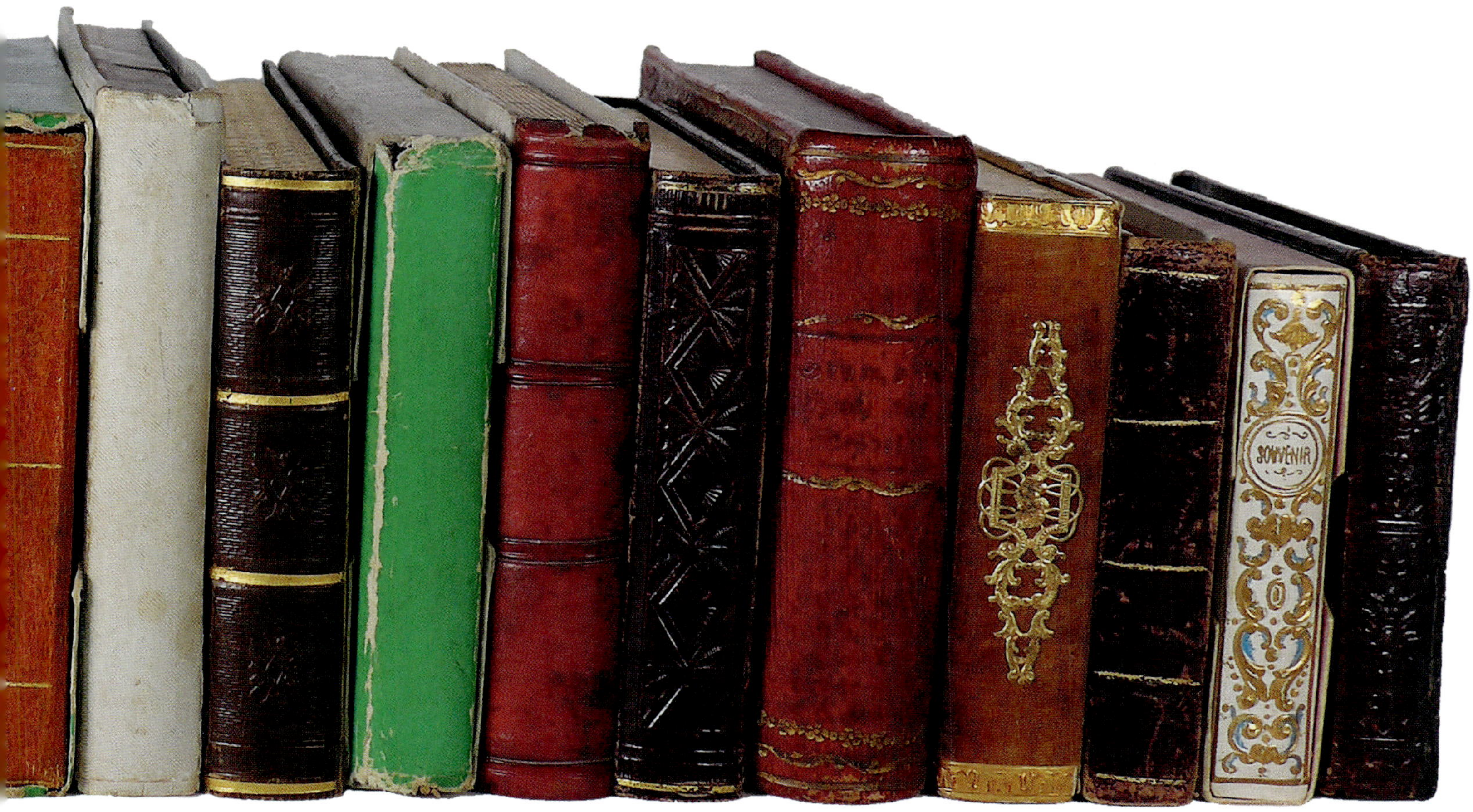

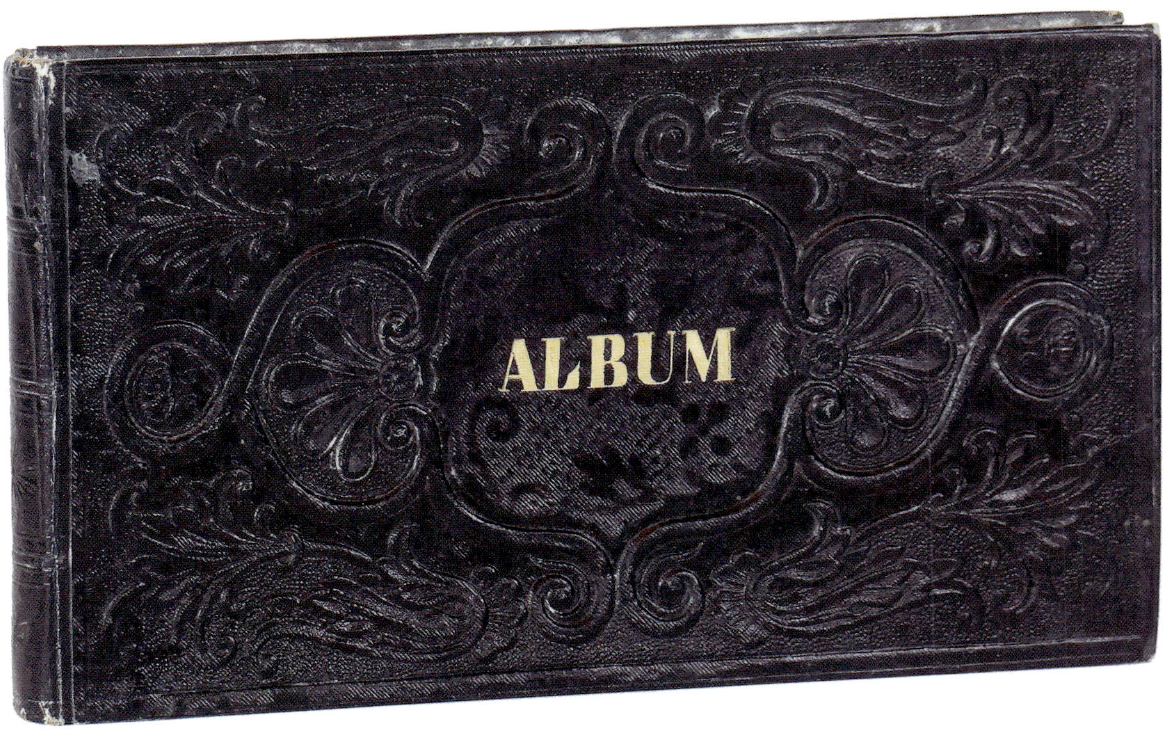

7.105
Poesiealbum, auch Souvenir
Autograph Book
Ganzleder-Buchkassette mit Prägung, Deckelvergoldung, dreiseitiger Goldschnitt, kolorierter Frontispiz, 19 handbeschriftete Blätter von 1847–1840, Zugbänder, Papierchemise und Schuber
Full leather book case with embossing, gilt cover and edges, colored frontispiece, 19 handwritten sheets from 1847 to 1840, drawstrings, paper chemise and slipcase
1,1 x 15,3 x 8,4 cm

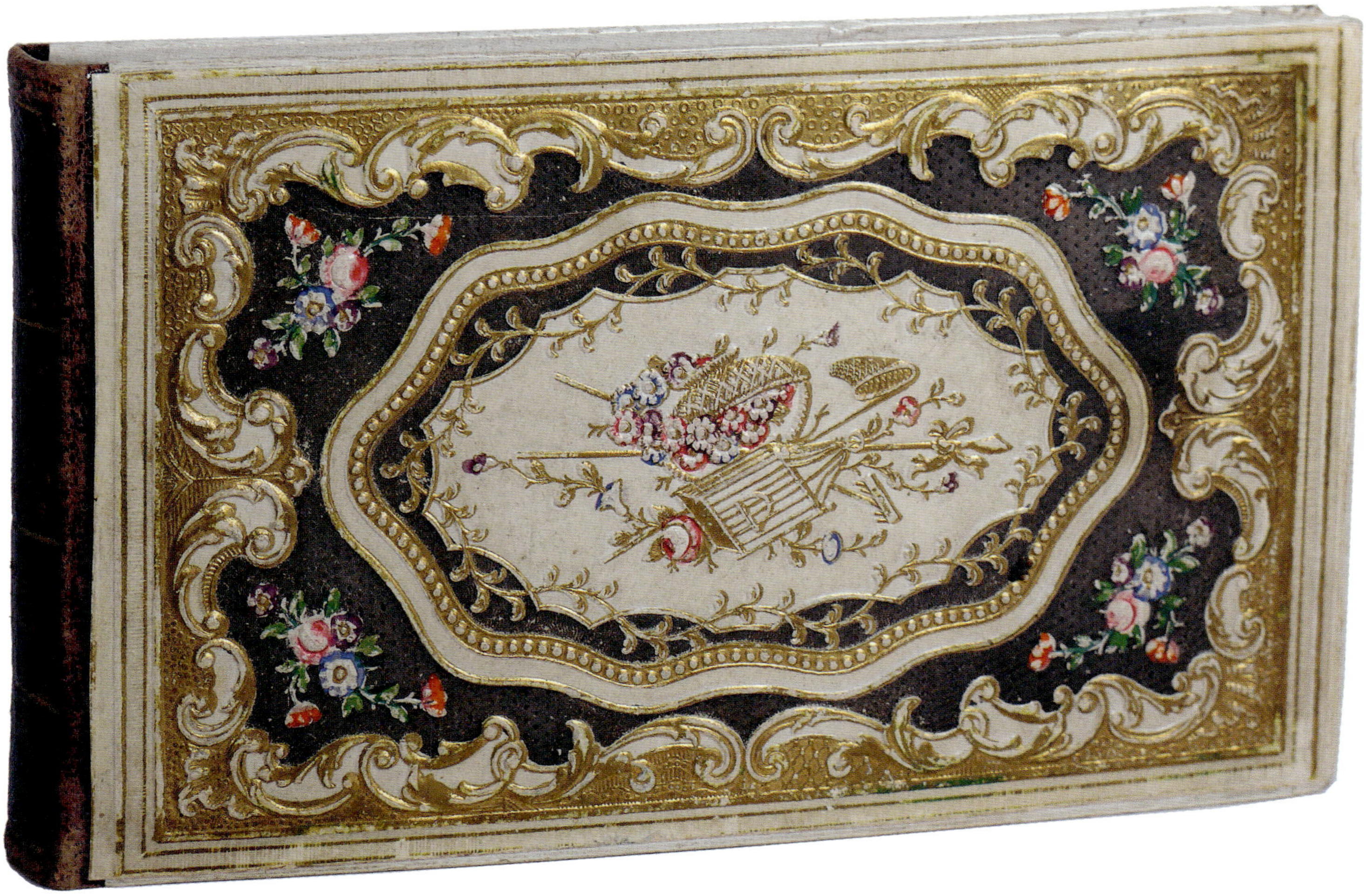

7.106
Halblederkassette mit farb- und goldgeprägtem Papierüberzug, dreiseitiger Goldschnitt, Stahlstich-Frontispiz, Zuglasche, geprägte Karte von 1860
Half leather case with color embossed and gold-tooled paper-over-board, all edges gilt, steel engraved frontispiece, pull tab, embossed map from 1860
1,2 x 13,3 x 7,6 cm

7.107
Ganzleder-Buchkassette mit Prägung, Rücken- und Deckelvergoldung, dreiseitiger Goldschnitt, koloriertes Frontispiz, Stickereien, Haarandenken von 1858, Zugbänder
Full leather box with embossing, gilt spine and cover all edges gilt, colored frontispiece, embroideries, hair souvenirs from 1858, drawstring
1,1 x 17,1 x 9,4 cm

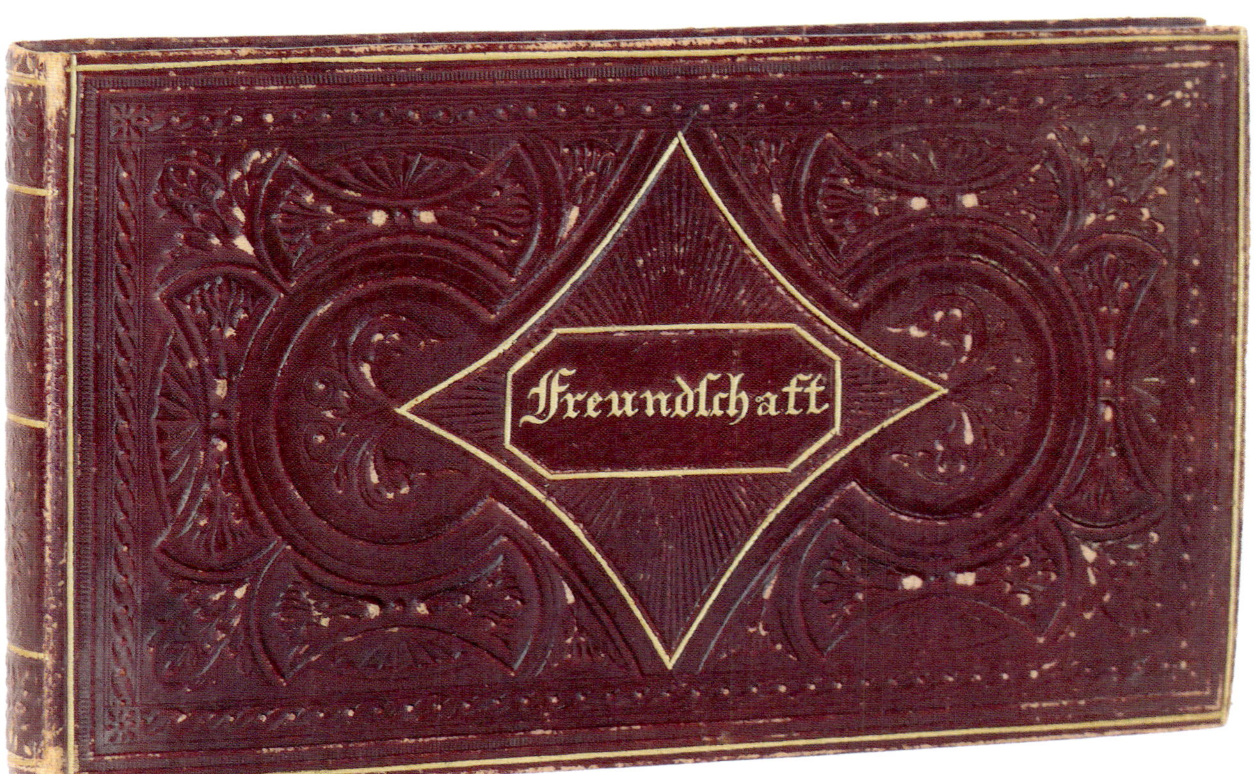

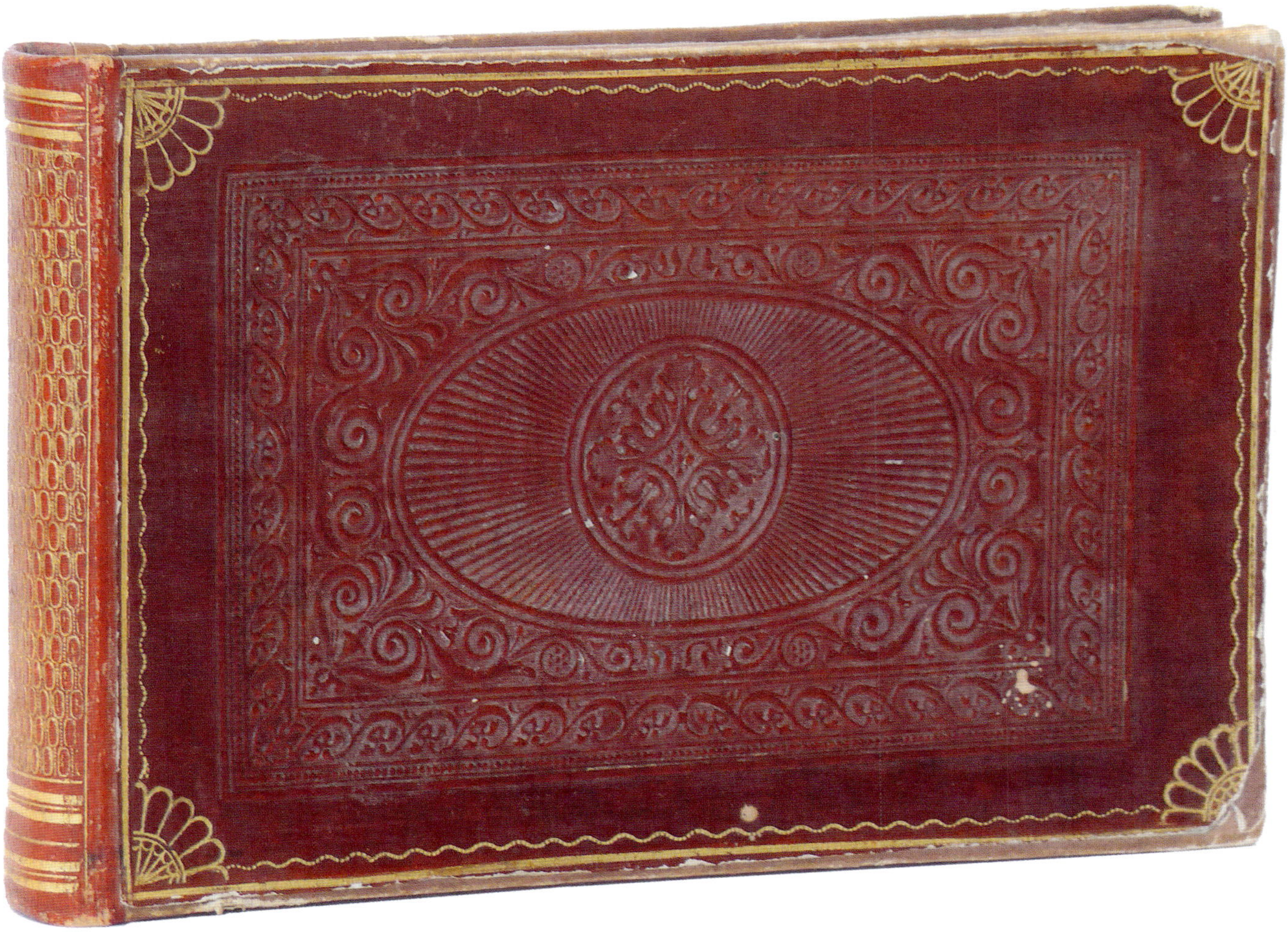

7.108
Halbleder-Buchkassette mit geprägtem Überzug, Rücken- und Deckelvergoldung, dreiseitig geprägter Goldschnitt, Zugbänder
Semi-leather box with embossed cover, gilt spine and cover, gold-tooled edges, drawstring
1,9 x 16,7 x 10,2 cm

7.109
Souvenir
Leder-Buchkassette mit Prägung, Rücken- und Deckelvergoldung, Innenkantenvergoldung, dreiseitiger Goldschnitt, Zugbänder
Leather box with embossing, gilt spine and cover, interior gilt edging, all edges gilt, drawstring
2 x 17,2 x 9,6 cm

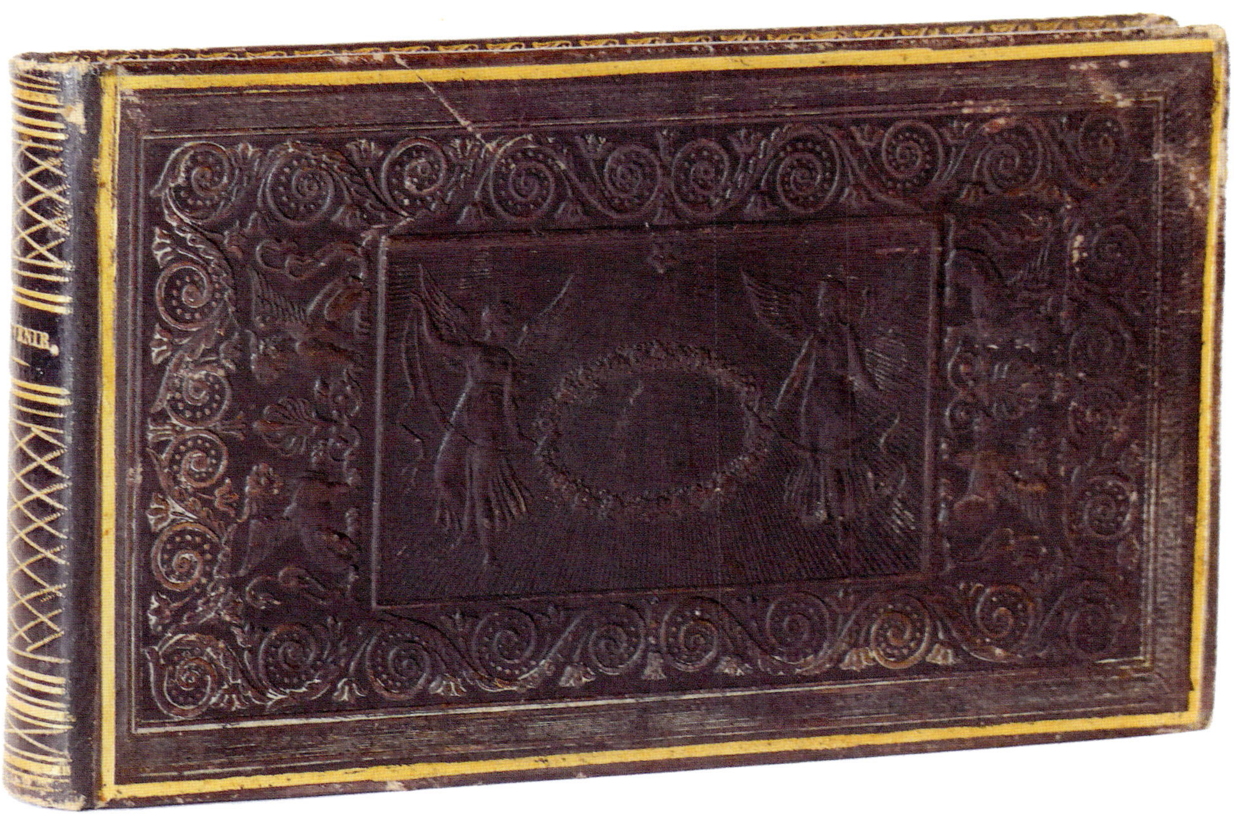

7.110
Souvenir
Ganzleder-Buchkassette mit Prägung, Rücken- und Deckelvergoldung im Kathedralstil, Innenkantenvergoldung, dreiseitiger Goldschnitt, geprägter Spiegel und Frontispiz, 14 handbeschriebene Blätter mit Goldschnitt von 1841–1870, Zugbänder, Papierchemise mit Schuber
Full leather box with embossing, spine and cover gilding in cathedral style, interiror dentelle in gold, all edges gilt, embossed pastedown and frontispiece, 14 hand-written leaves with gilt edges from 1841–1870, drawstring, paper chemise with slipcase
1,1 x 15,6 x 9 cm

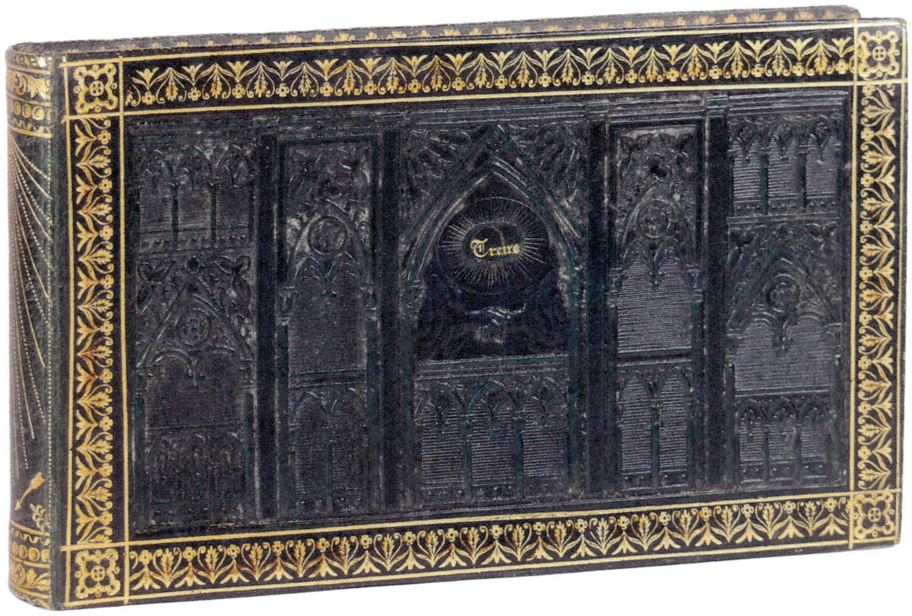

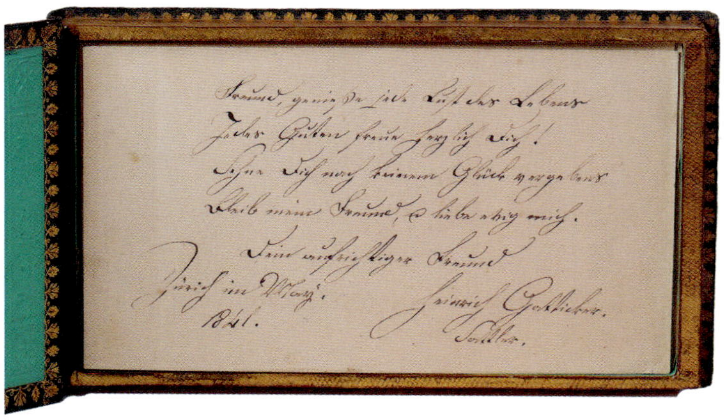

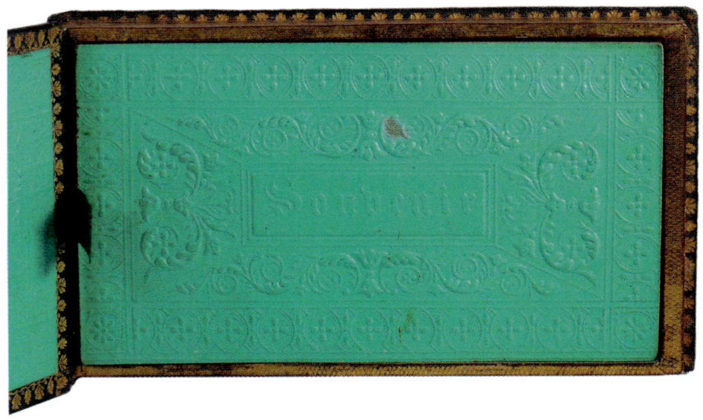

7.111
Ganzleder-Buchkassette mit Goldprägung, Verschlusslasche, dreiseitiger Goldschnitt, geprägter Vorderspiegel, Zuglasche
Full leather book case with gold tooling, embossed pastedown, all edges gilt, closure strap
1,1 x 13 x 8,3 cm

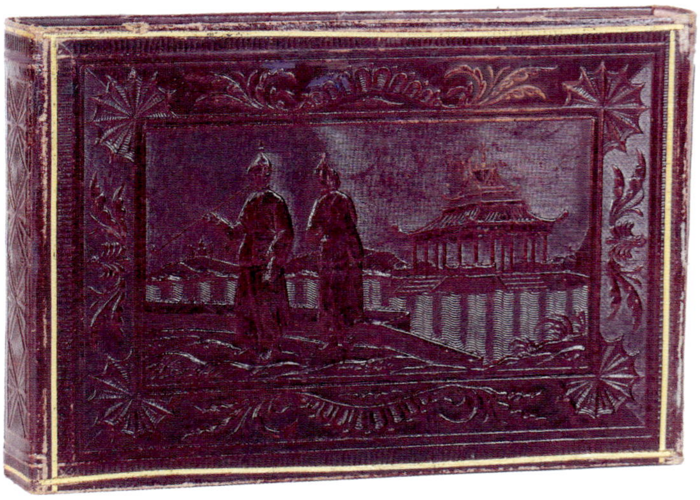

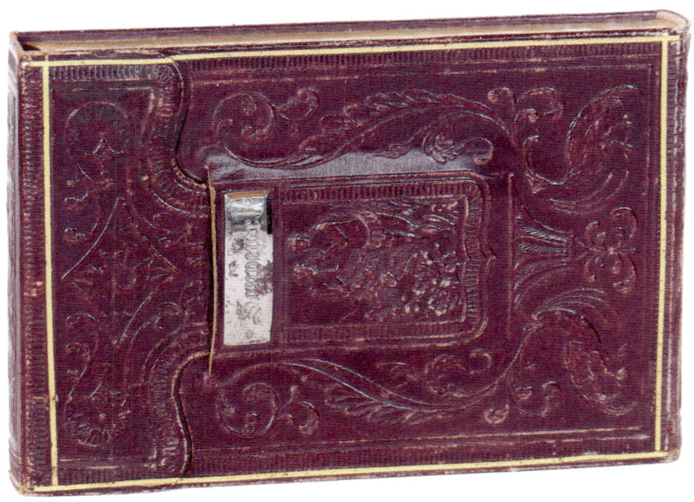

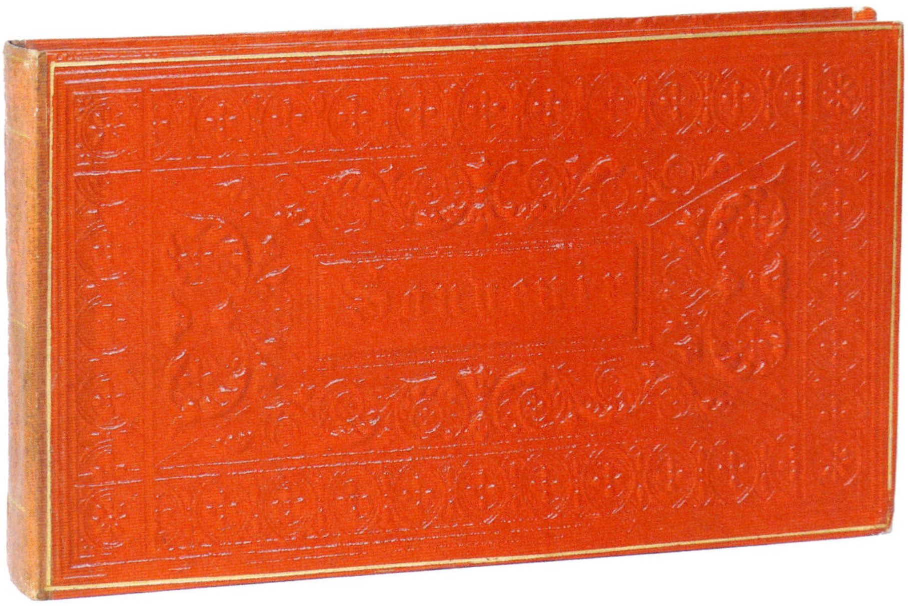

7.112

Poesielabum Souvenir / *Autograph Book*
Ganzleder-Buchkassette mit Prägung, Rücken- und Deckelvergoldung, dreiseitiger Goldschnitt, kolorierte Umrissradierung, 38 handbeschriebene Blätter mit Goldschnitt von 1840–1842, Zugbänder, Schuber
Full leather book box with embossing, gilt cover and spine, gilt edges, colored frontispiece, 19 handwritten leaves from 1840 to 1842, drawstring, paper chemise and slipcase
1,5 x 15,5 x 8,5 cm

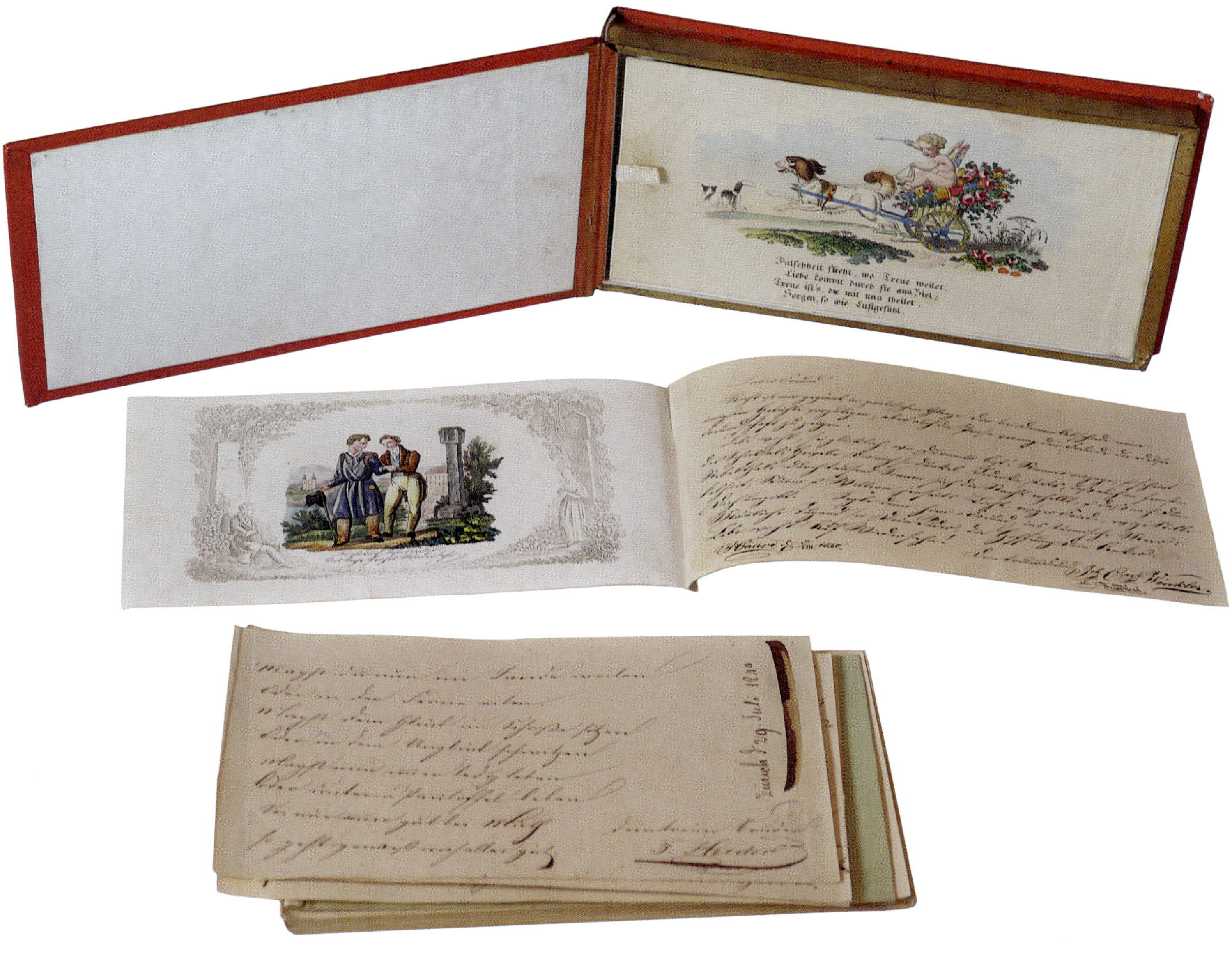

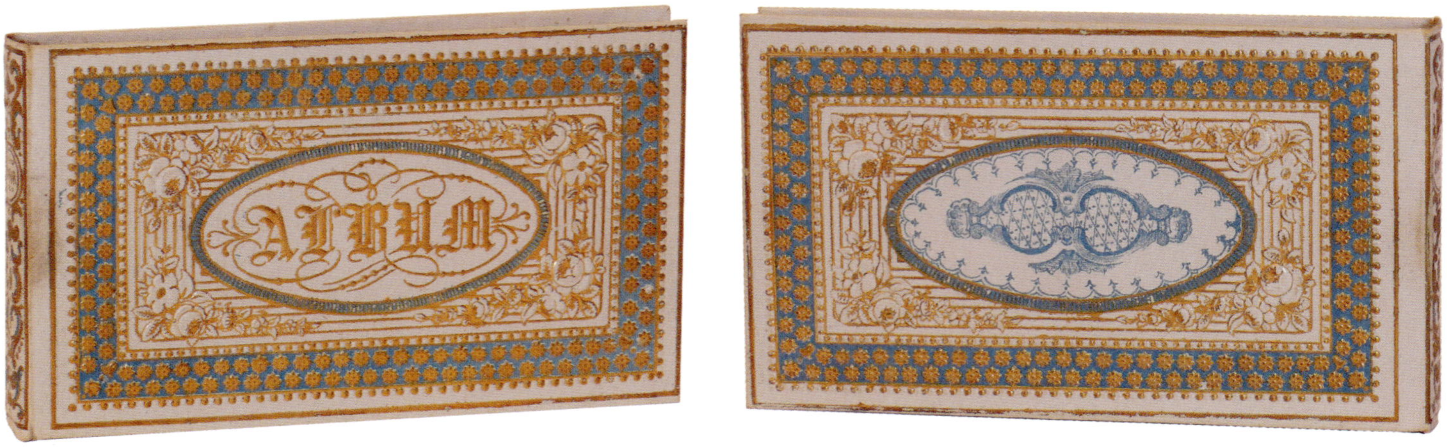

7.113
Poesiealbum, auch Album / ***Autograph Book***
Buchkassette mit farb- und goldgeprägtem Papierüberzug, dreiseitiger Goldschnitt, 35 Blätter mit Goldschnitt, Zuglasche, Schuber
Book box with gold-tooled and color embossed paper-over-board, all edges gilt, 35 leaves with gilt edges, pull tab, slipcase
1,3 x 12,4 x 7 cm

7.114
Poesiealbum, auch Album / ***Autograph Book***
Ganzleder-Buchkassette mit Blind-, Gold- und Farbprägung, Innenkantenvergoldung, vier Klappen und Spiegel aus Moireseide, 32 Blätter mit Goldschnitt, Stammbucheintragungen von 1842–1847, dreiseitiger Goldschnitt, Zugbänder, Schuber
Full leather box with blin and gold tooling as well as color embossing, gilt interior edges, four flaps and pastedown of moiré silk, 32 leaves with gilt edges, family book records from 1842–1847, all edges gilt, drawstring, slipcase
18 x 27,6 x 2,7 cm

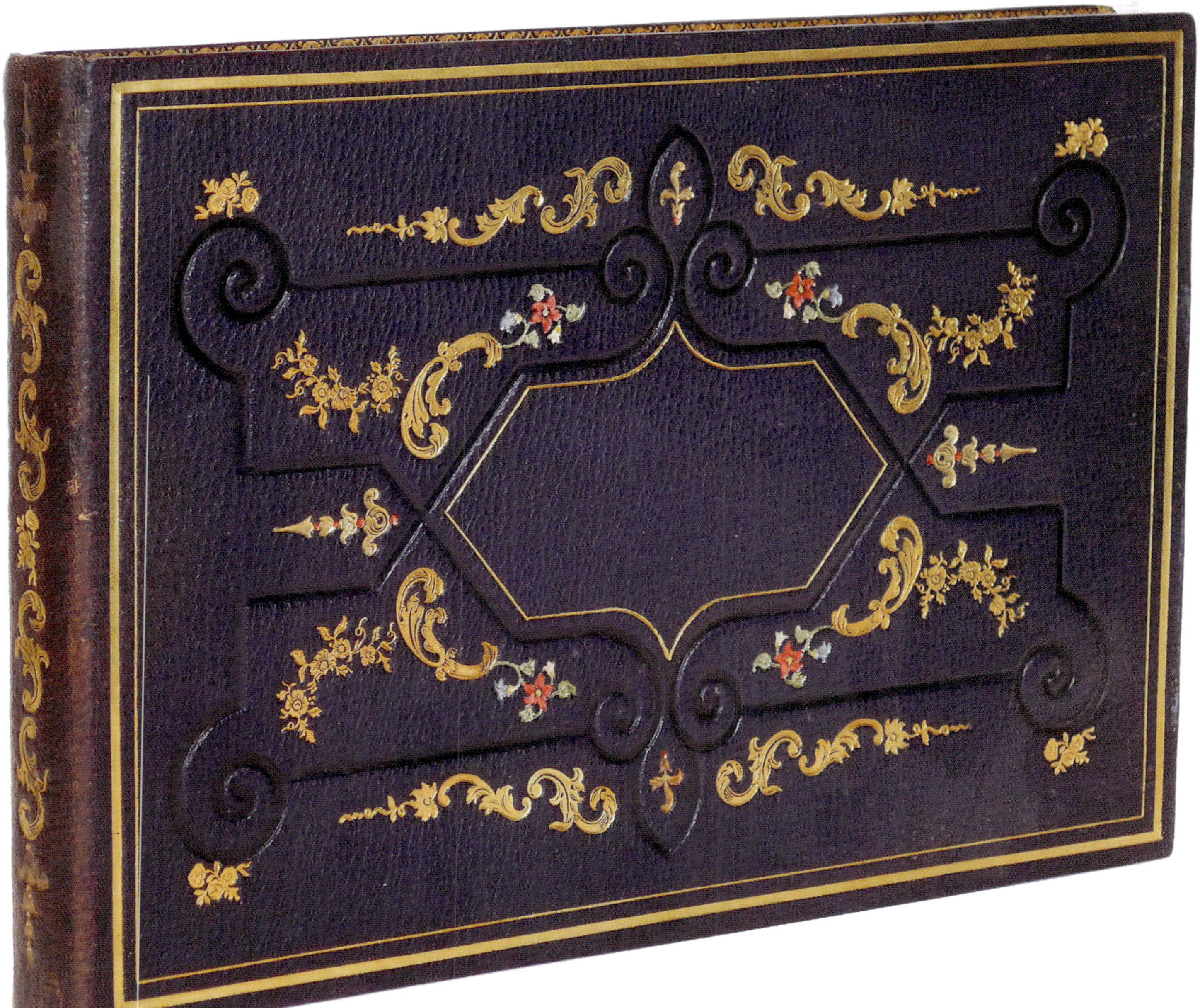

7.115
Souvenir
Samt-Buchkassette mit aufgeklebten Goldpapierbordüren- und Verzierungen, Spiegel und Frontispiz mit farbiger Lithografie, 22 Blätter mit Goldschnitt, 16 Blätter handbeschriftet, drei Originalzeichnungen, Zuglasche
Book case covered with velvet, dentelle and ornaments of gold paper, pastedown and frontispiece with color lithography, 22 leaves with gilt edges, 16 handwritten leaves, three original drawings, pull tab
1,8 x 12,8 x 8,1 cm

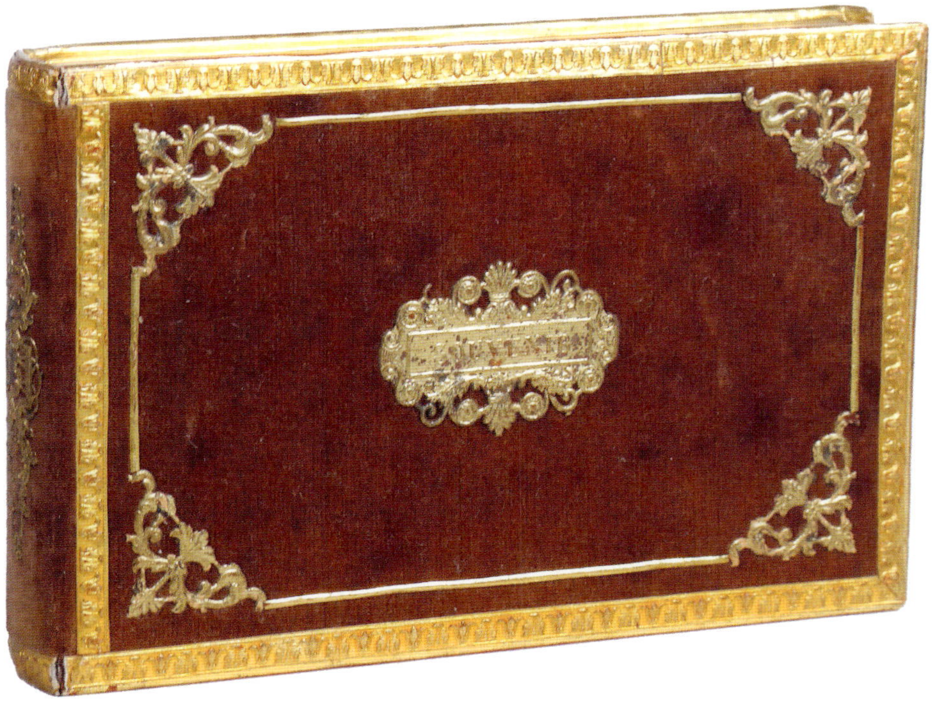

7.116
Souvenir
Halbleder-Buchkassette mit geprägtem Papierüberzug, Titel- und Deckelvergoldung, dreiseitiger grüner Farbschnitt, Umrissradierung von 1826, Heiligenbilder, Zugbänder, Schuber
Half leather binding box with embossed paper-over-board, gilt front cover, green edges, outline etching from 1826, holy pictures, slip case
2,3 x 16,4 x 9,5

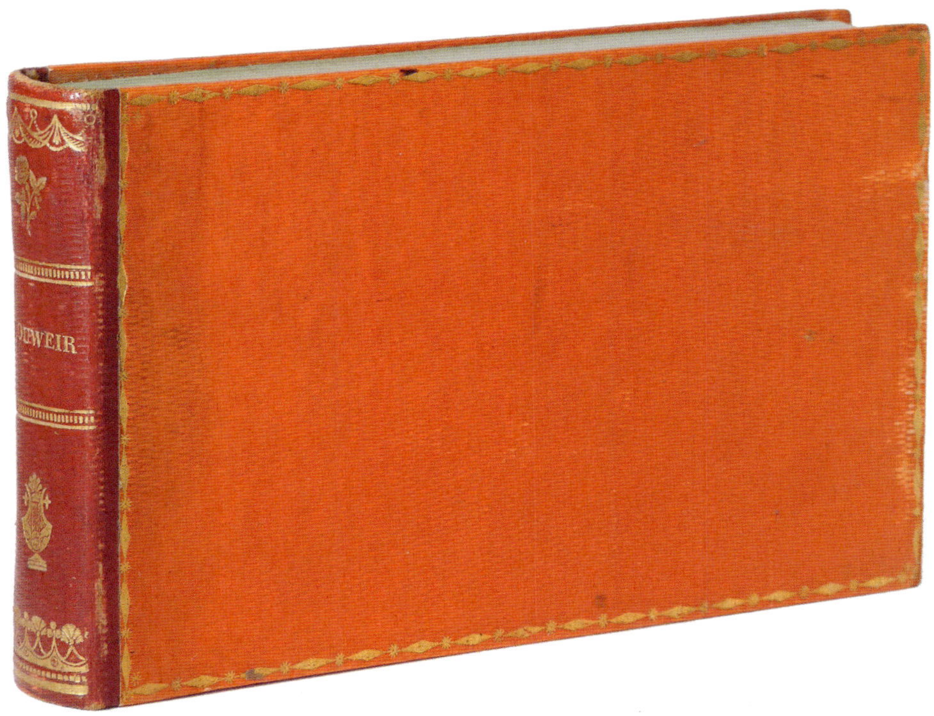

7.117
Ganzleder-Buchkassette mit Rücken- und Deckelvergoldung, dreiseitiger Goldschnitt, 25 handbeschriftete Blätter mit Goldschnitt Frontispiz-Originalzeichnung, 1829–1830, Zuglasche
Full leather book box with gilt spine and cover, gilt edges, 25 hand-labeled leaves with gilt edges, frontispiece original drawing, 1829–1830, pull tab
2,2 x 15,3 x 8,8 cm

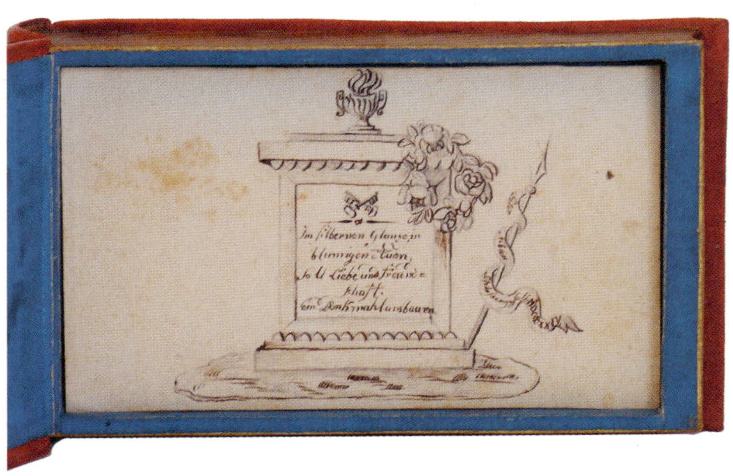

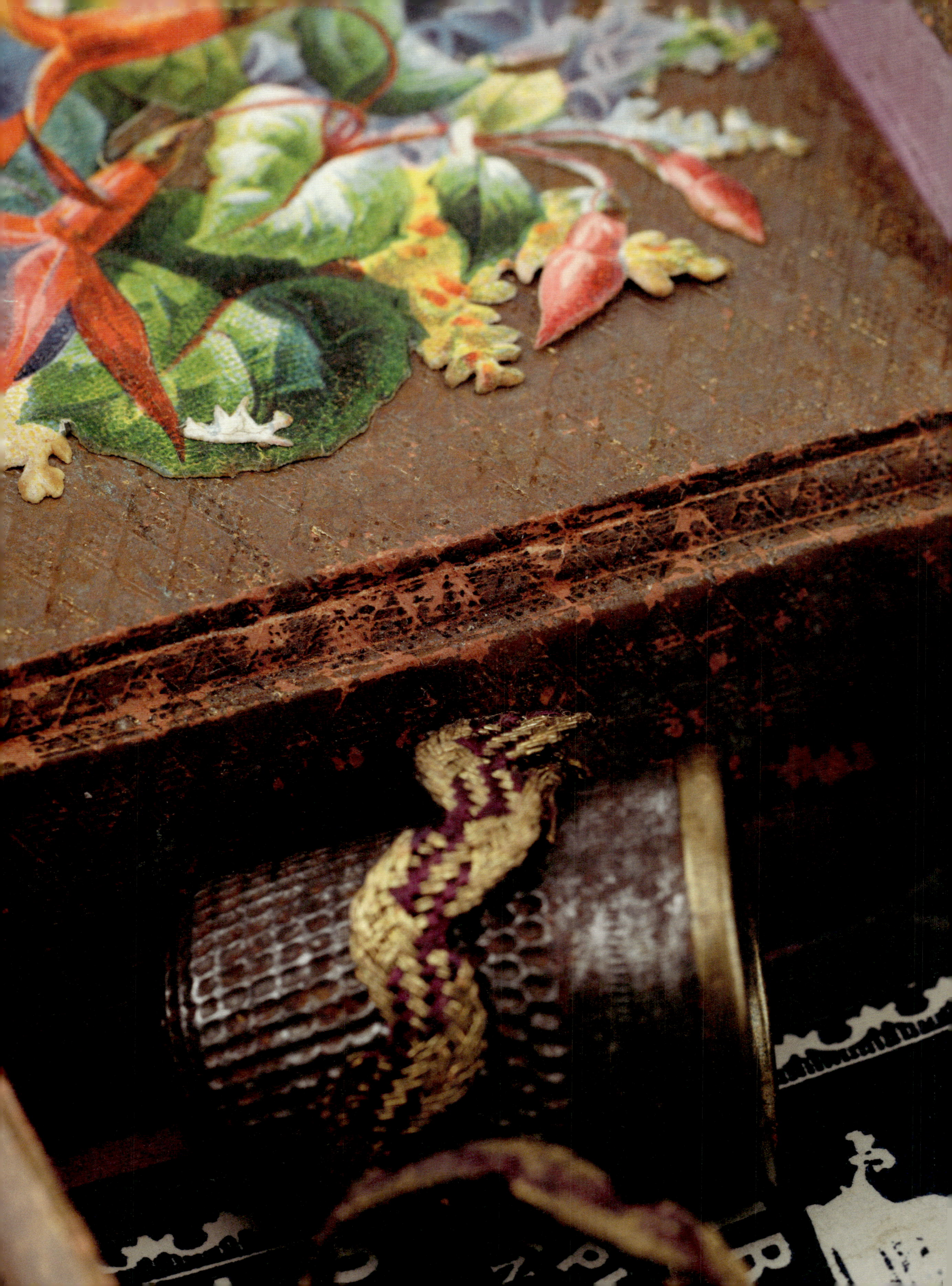

Kleidung
Clothing

Wer nach Antiquitäten sucht, findet im bayerischen Lindau am Bodensee neben einem Auktionshaus zahlreiche kleine Läden mit antikem Angebot. Sehenswert ist die ehemalige Reichsstädtische Bibliothek mit ca. 15.000 Bänden und mehr als 140 Wiegendrucken. Die Buchbestände basieren vermutlich auf ein aufgelöstes Franziskanerkloster von 1528. Das wohl bekannteste Wahrzeichen der denkmalgeschützten Stadt ist die Hafeneinfahrt mit der sechs Meter hohen Löwenstatue sowie dem neuen Leuchtturm. Das historische Zentrum steht unter Denkmalschutz.

In der Burggasse 4 betreibt Wilfried Gottschalk ein Stein- Atelier, „Dein Stein, – creare dalla natura". Unter anderem fertigt er ausgefallene kleine Kunstwerke aus Bodensee-Steinen. In der Auslage entdeckte ich in einem Körbchen runde flache Steine mit je zwei Löchern, gedacht als Kleiderknöpfe. Da ich bei Knopfhändlerinnen äußerst selten Knöpfe in Buchform finden konnte, bat ich den Steinhändler welche anzufertigen. Spontan erklärte er sich bereit und machte sich mit Hilfe einer kleinen Skizze sofort an die Arbeit. Am gleichen Tag der Abreise durfte ich das kleine Kunstwerk bereits abholen. Ich war entzückt mit welcher Akribie er den Knopf fertigte. Obwohl nur 3 × 2,4 × 0,5 cm groß sind Feinheiten wie ein gerundeter Rücken, drei erhabene Bünde und Stehkanten deutlich erkennbar.

Ich erkundige mich gelegentlich bei Knopfhändlerinnen nach solchen Objekten – meistens sind es Frauen, die sich mit dieser Materie befassen – doch ohne Erfolg. Deshalb habe ich trotz meiner langjährigen Sammlertätigkeit nur eine Handvoll Knöpfe in Buchform gefunden.

Anyone seeking antiques will find numerous small shops with antique offers by an auction house in the Bavarian town of Lindau on Lake Constance,. The former Reichsstädtische Bibliothek with about 15,000 volumes and more than 140 incunabula is worth seeing. The book collections are presumably based on a dissolved Franciscan monastery from 1528. The most famous monument of the heritage-listed city is probably the entrance to the harbor with its six-meter high lion statue and the new lighthouse. The historical center is heritage-protected.

In Burggasse 4, Wilfried Gottschalk runs a stone studio, "Dein Stein,—creare dalla natura". Among other things, he produces unusual small works of art out of stones from Lake Constance.

In the display I discovered round, flat stones in a basket, each with two holes intended as buttons on clothes. Since I could rarely find buttons in the design of a book at button dealers, I asked the stone dealer to make some. He spontaneously agreed and immediately got to work with the help of a small sketch. The small artwork was even ready for collection on the day of my departure. I was delighted with the meticulousness with which he crafted the button. Although only 3 × 2.4 × 0.5 cm in size, delicate details such as a rounded spine, three raised cords and standing edges are clearly visible.

I occasionally inquire about such objects from button dealers—it is usually women who deal with this field—but without success. Therefore, despite my many years of collecting, I have only found a handful of fake book buttons.

8.001
Toi et moi
Tonknopf bemalt und gebrannt mit Öse, Titel auf dem Vorderdeckel, dreiseitiger Goldschnitt
Painted and fired clay button with eyelet, title on the front cover, all edges gilt
Erste Hälfte des 20. Jh / *First half of the 20th century*
2,2 x 1,7 x 0,4 cm

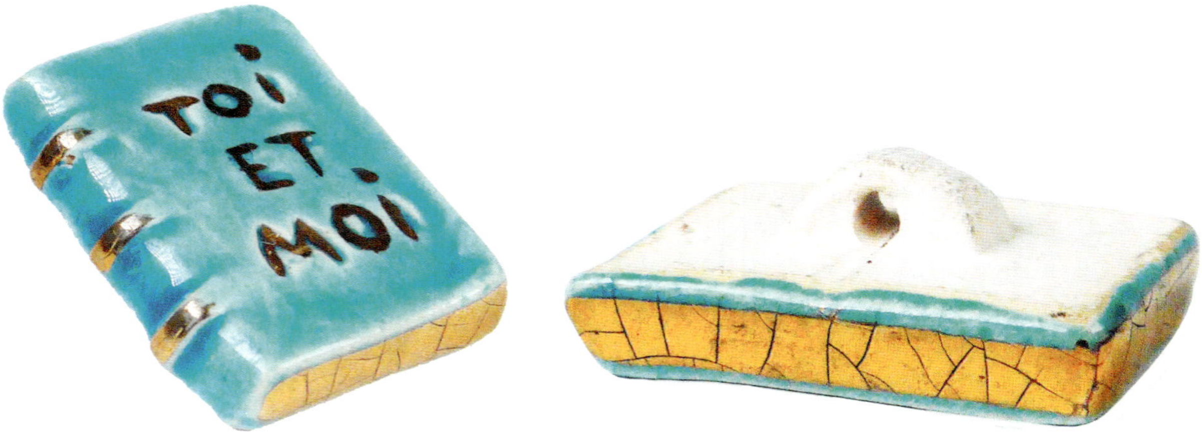

8.002
Knöpfe aus Kunststoff, zweifarbig, zwei Löcher
Lake Constance stone buttons with in two colors with two holes
Art Déco
Erste Hälfte des 20. Jh / *First half of the 20th century*
2,8 x 1,6 x 0,6 cm

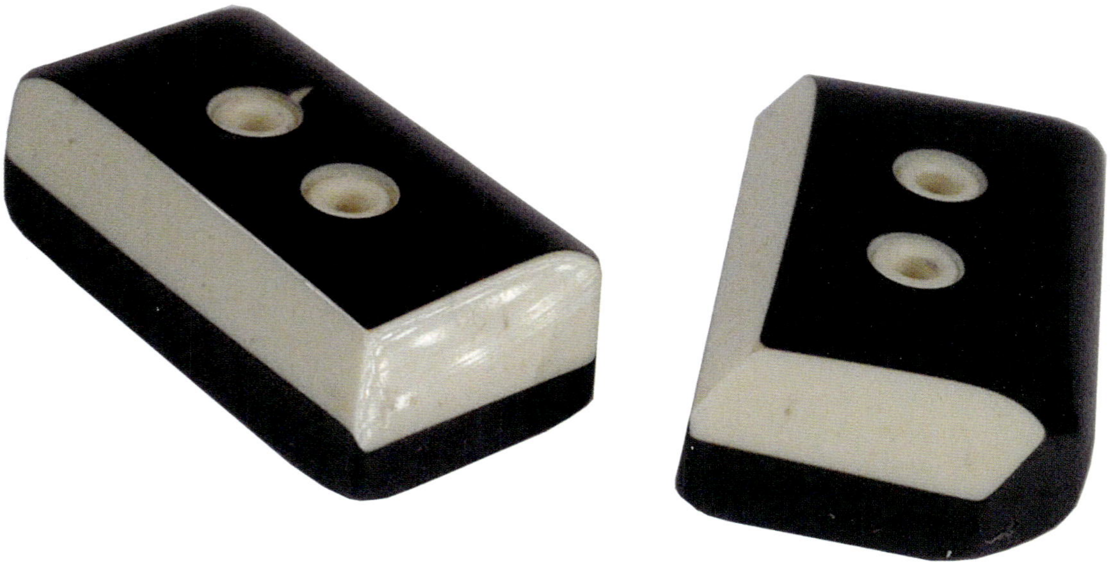

8.003
Kunststoffknopf gegossen und vergoldet in der Form eines verschlissenen Buches, zwei Metallösen
Plastic button cast and gilded in the shape of a used book, two metal eyelets
Erste Hälfte des 20. Jh / *First half of the 20th century* | 3,2 x 2,7 x 1,1 cm

8.004
Bodensee-Steinknopf mit zwei Löchern
Lake Constance stone button with two holes
Hersteller / *Manufacturer*: Wilfried Gottschalk
Lindau, Deutschland / *Germany*
2018 | 3 x 2,4 x 0,5 cm

8.005
Knöpfe aus Holz, Metallöse und zwei Löcher, zweifarbig gefärbt, vier angedeutete Bünde
wooden buttons, metal eyelet and two holes, dyed in two colors, four indicated bands
Erste Hälfte des 20. Jh. / *First half of the 20th century* | 2,8 x 2,3 x 0,6 cm

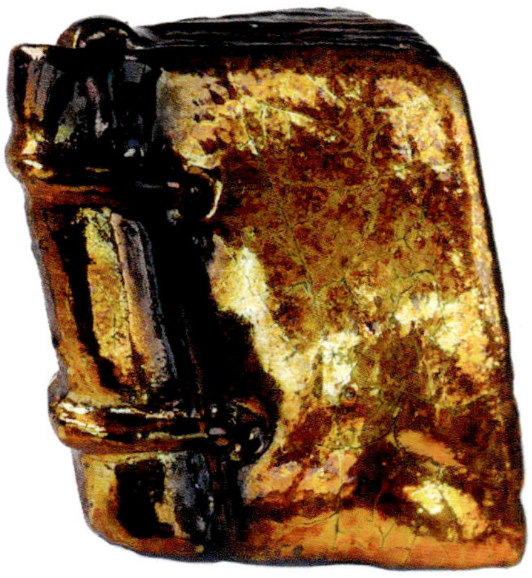

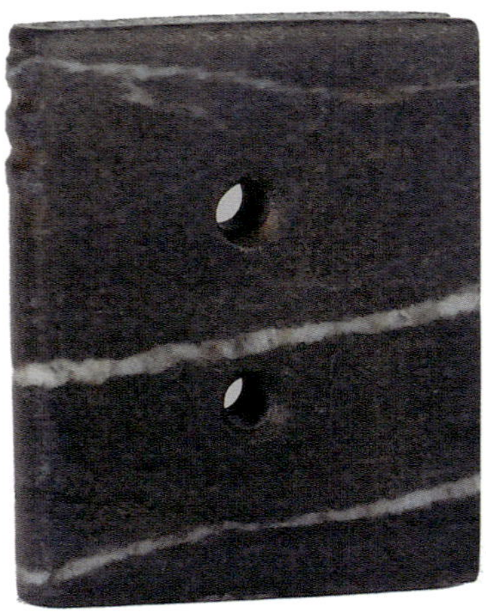

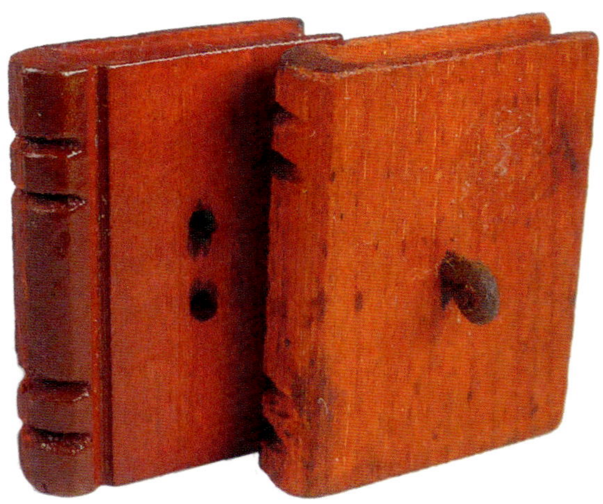

8.006
Manschettenknopf aus Perlmutt, gravierter Vorderdeckel, Scheinmessingschließe
Cufflink of mother-of-pearl, engraved front cover, fake brass buckle
Erste Hälfte des 20. Jh. / *First half of the 20th century*
2,2 x 1,5 x 0,5 cm

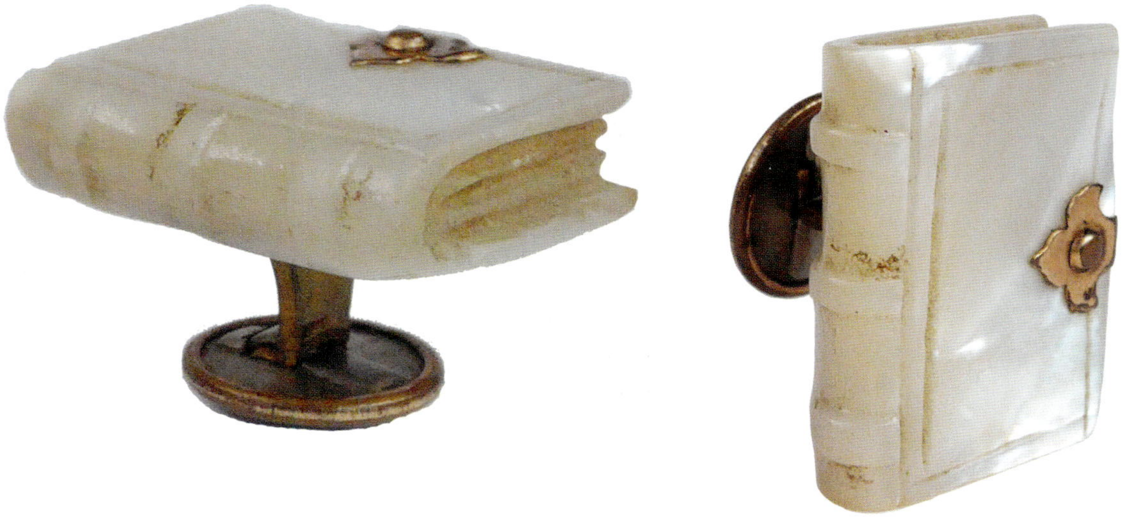

8.007
usership
Manschettenknöpfe aus Spritzguss in der Form eines aufgeschlagenen Buches, Beschriftung auf dem Buchblock
Injection moulded cufflinks in the design of an open book, inscription on the book block
Erste Hälfte des 20. Jh. / *First half of the 20th century*
0,3 x 2,5 x 1,8 cm

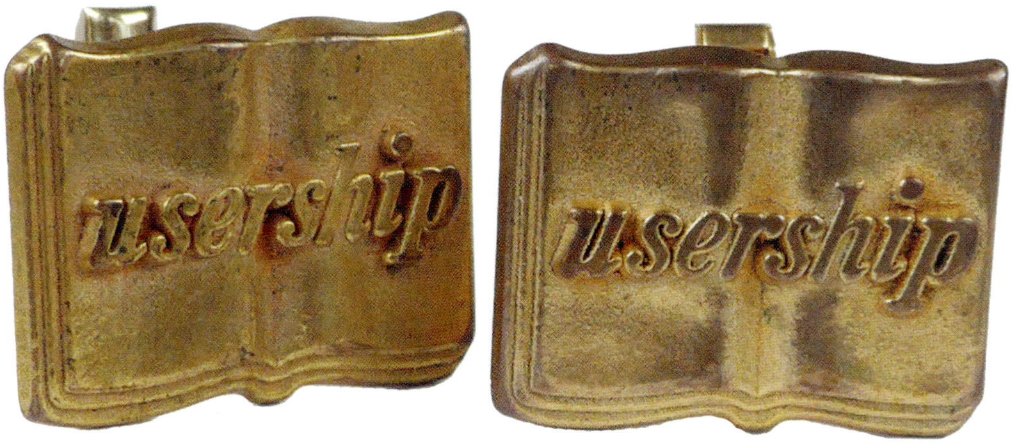

8.008
Manschettenknöpfe aus Spritzguss mit Kette
Injection moulded cufflinks with chain
Erste Hälfte des 20. Jh. / *First half of the 20th century*
0,3 x 1,2 x 0,8 cm

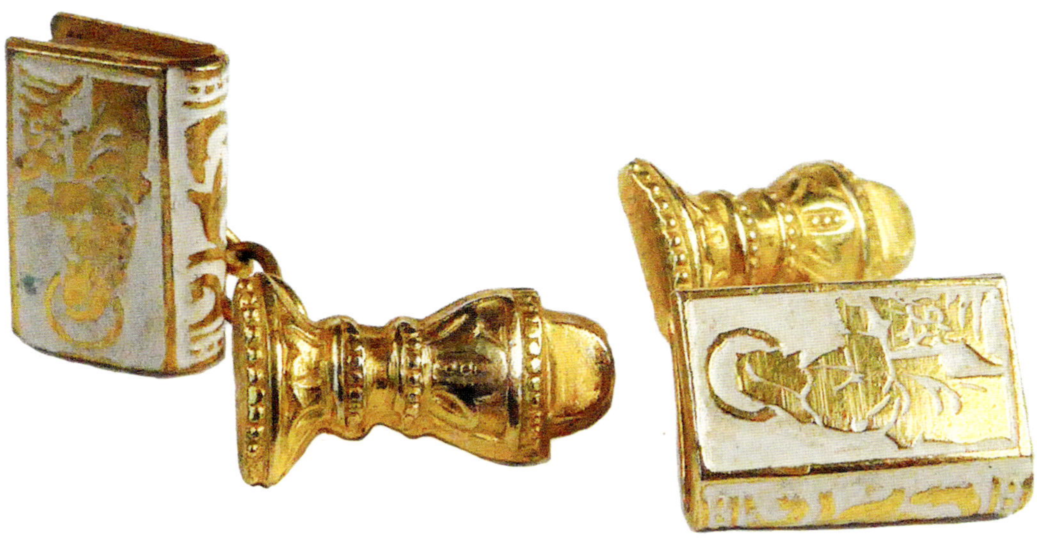

8.009
Jet Black
Manschettenknöpfe mit Kette, Kopfgoldschnitt
Cufflinks with chains, gilt head edge
Erste Hälfte des 20. Jh. / *First half of the 20th century*
0,2 x 1 x 1 cm

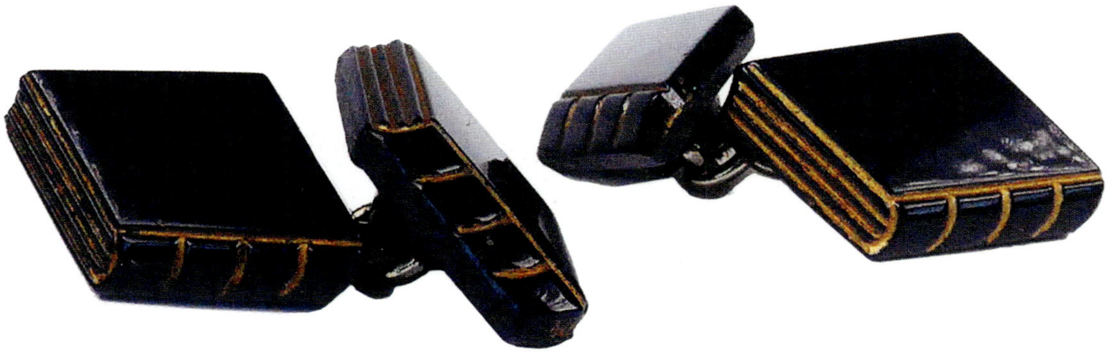

8.010
Lady's Companion
Lederdose mit Hals, Rücken und Deckel handvergoldet, Fächer für Nähzubehör
Leather box with neck, manual gilding on the spine and cover, compartments for sewing kits
Spätes 19. Jh. / *Late 19th century*

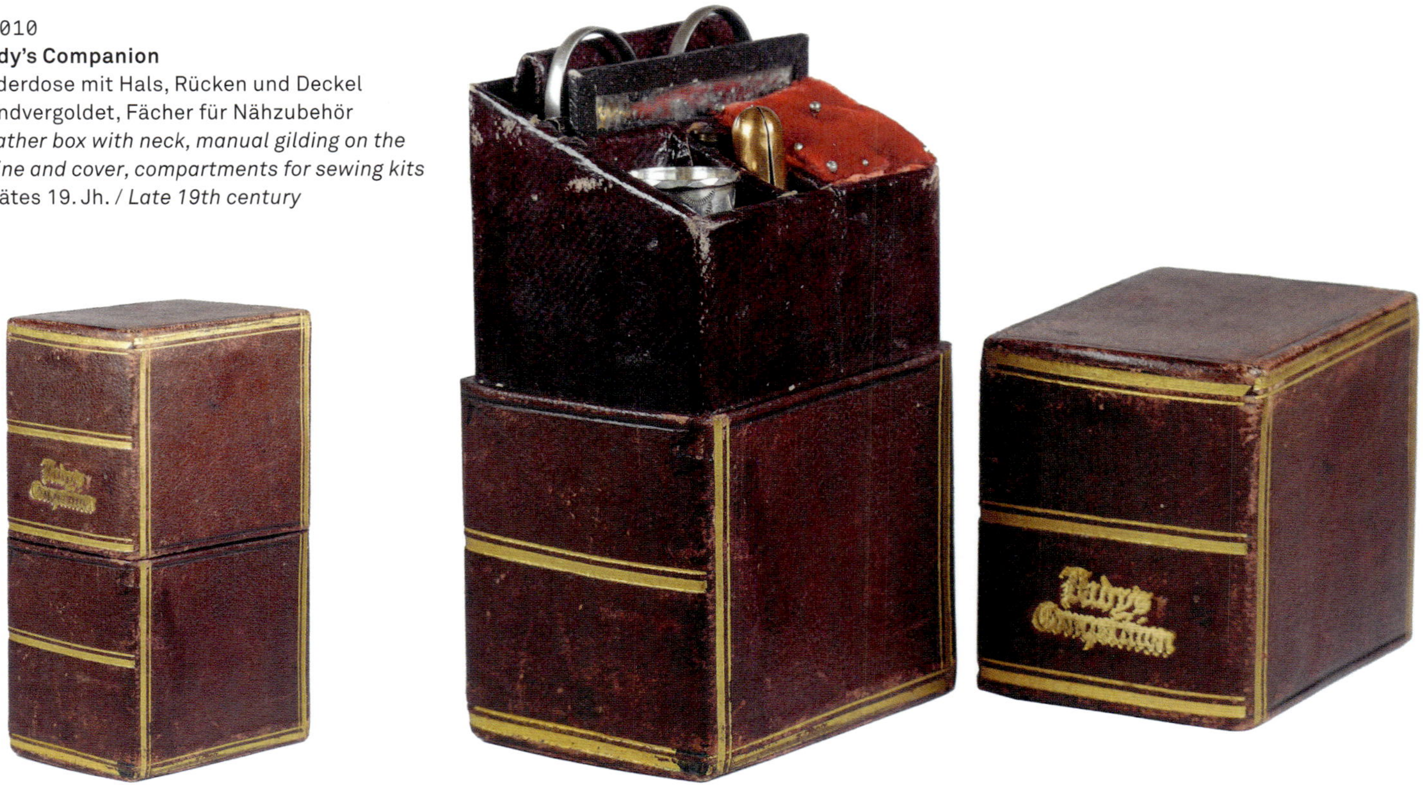

8.011
Lady's Companion
Lederdose mit Hals, Rücken und Deckel handvergoldet, Fächer für Nähzubehör
Leather box with neck, manual gilding on the spine and lid, compartments for sewing kits
Spätes 19. Jh. / *Late 19th century*

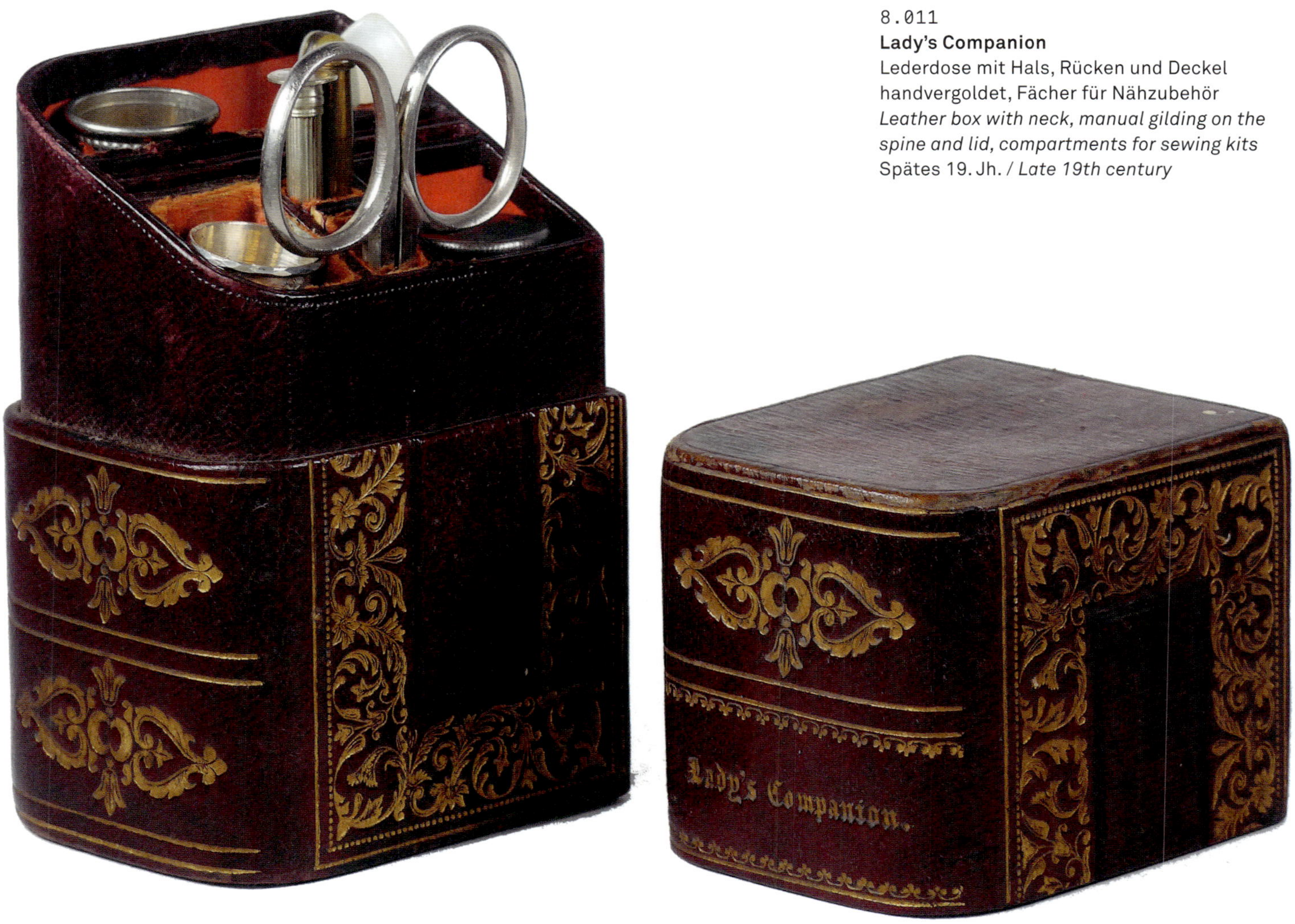

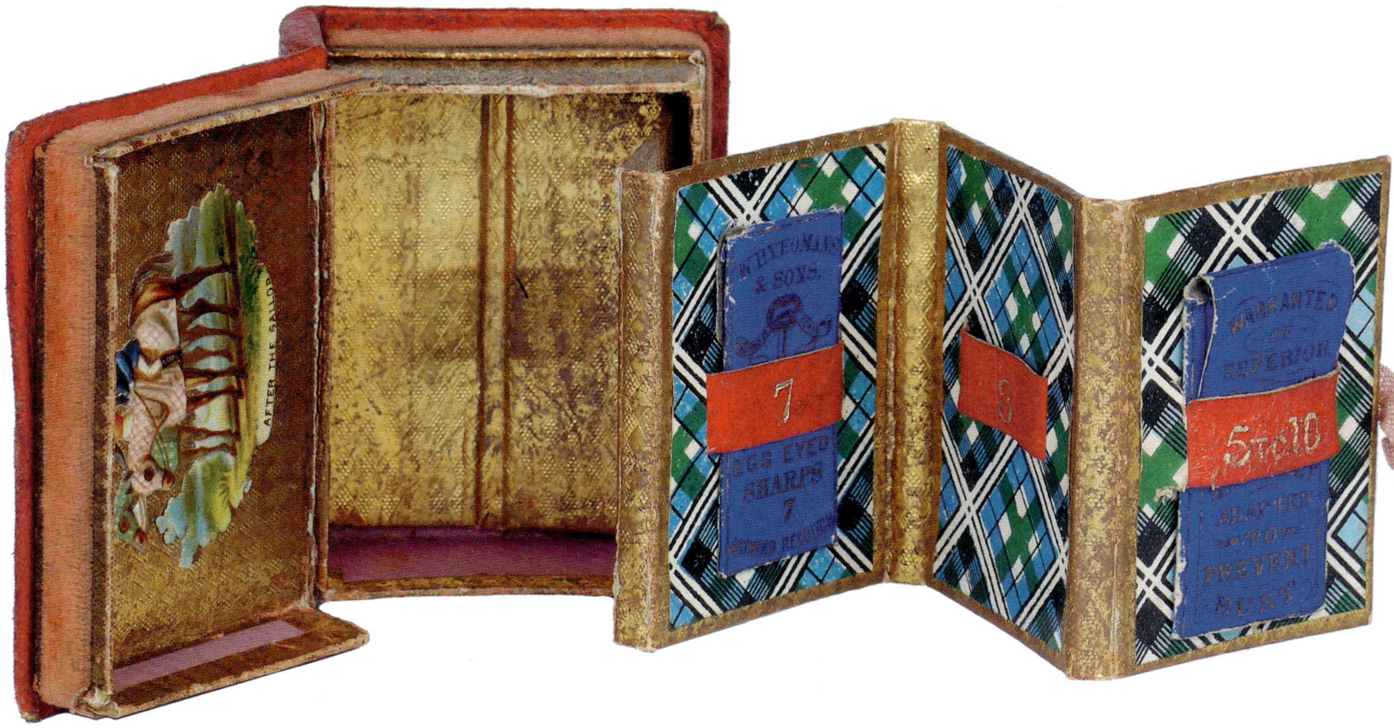

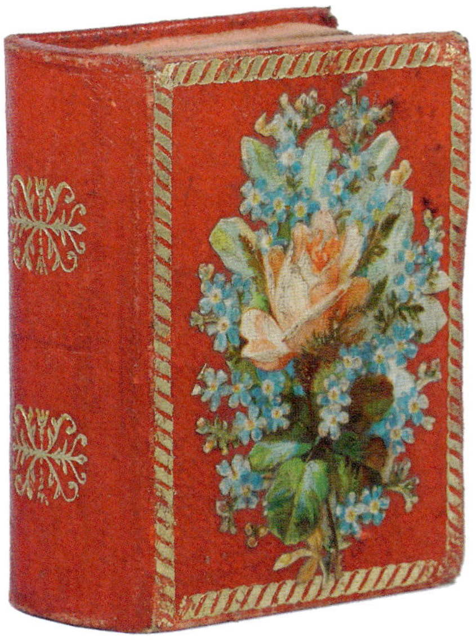

8.012
Lederdose für Nähnadeln, Registered May 12, 1879
Rücken- und Deckelvergoldung, aufgeklebtes gestanztes Blumenmotiv auf dem Vorderdeckel, Leporello mit Nadelbriefchen, ausgefüttert mit geprägtem Goldpapier
Leather box for sewing needles, gilt spine and board, decorated with stamped flowers on the front cover, leporello with pin letters, lined with embossed gold paper
6,9 x 5,5 x 2,7 cm

8.013
Lederdose für Nähnadeln,
Registered May 12. 1879
Rücken- und Deckelvergoldung, aufgeklebtes gestanztes Blumenmotiv auf dem Vorderdeckel. Leporello mit Nadelbriefchen, ausgefüttert mit geprägtem Goldpapier
Leather box for needles, gilt spine and cover, decorated with stamped flowers on the cover, leporello with pin letters, lined with embossed gold paper
6,9 x 5,5 x 2,7 cm

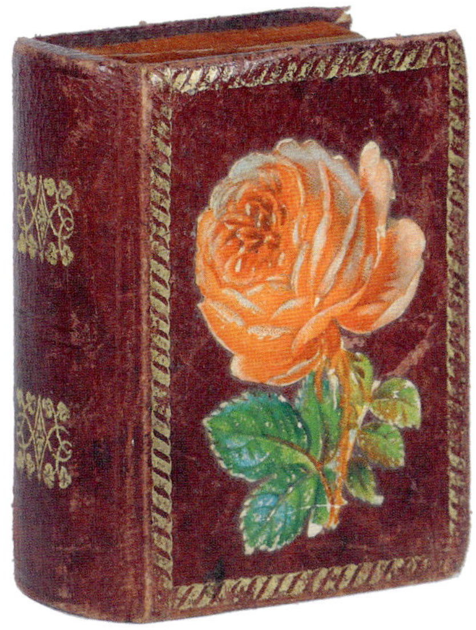

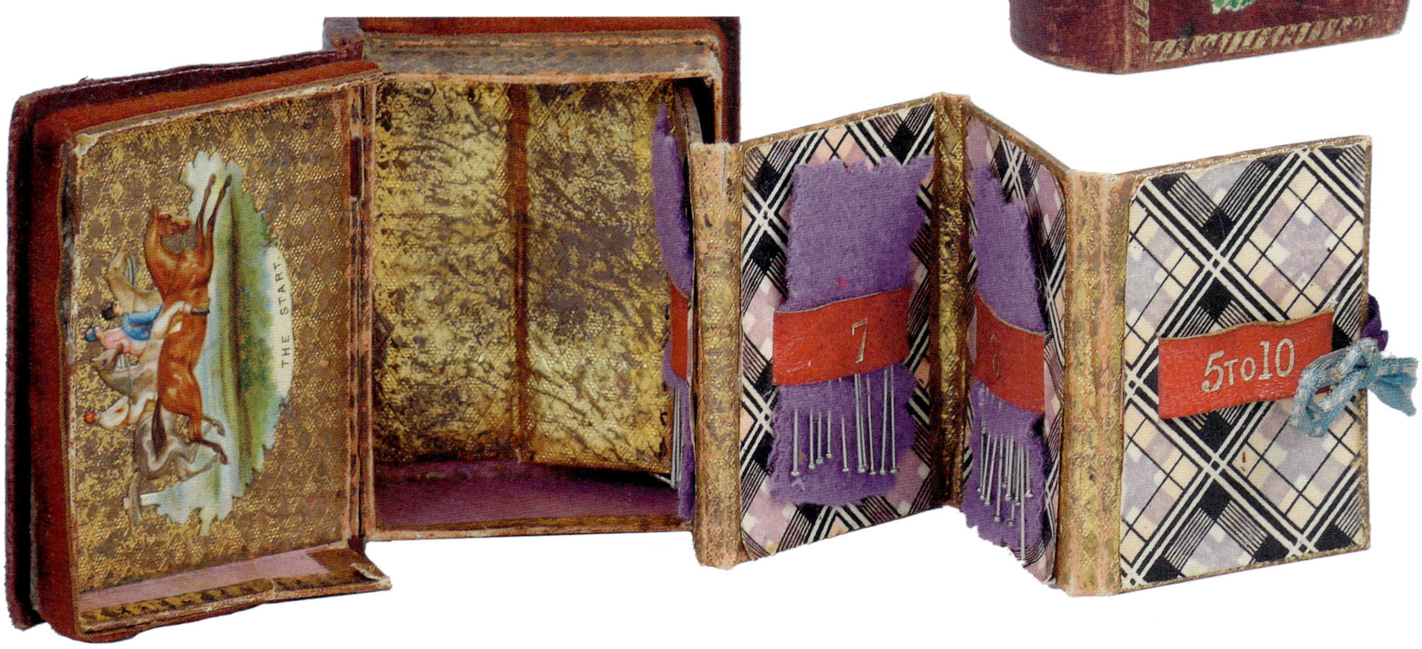

8.014
Ed. Kirchhofer, Elektr. Inst.,Tel. 783
Ed. Kirchhofer, electrician, tel. 783
Kunststoffdose mit Nähzeug,
Deckelbeschriftung, Werbegeschenk
Plastic box with sewing kit, lettering on the cover, advertising gift
1 x 7,5 x 5 cm

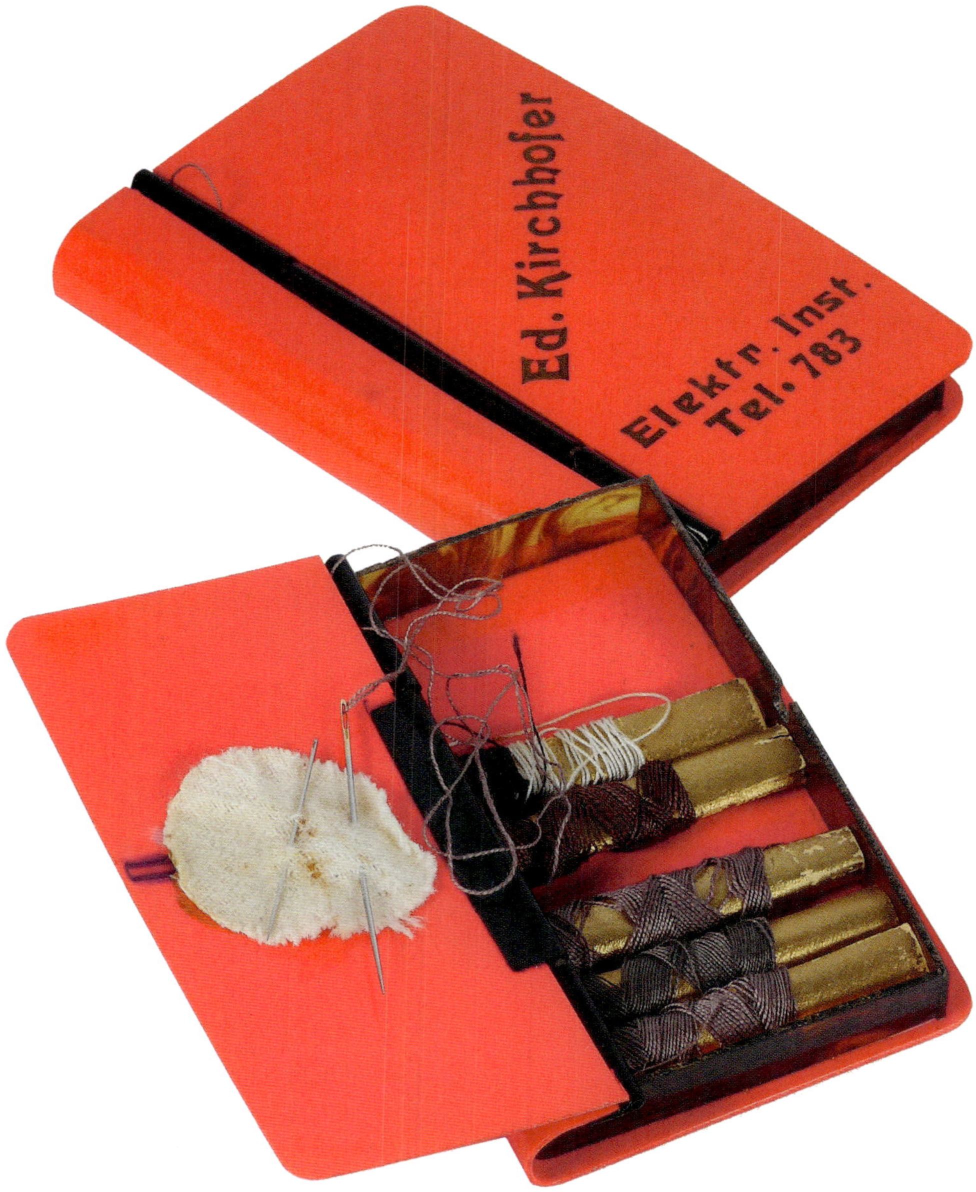

8.015
Städtische Sparkasse Nürnberg, Stopfgarn Lexikon / *Municpal bank of Nuremberg, Darning Yarn Dictionary*
Kartondose mit Nähzeug, Goldprägung auf dem Vorderdeckel, dreiseitiger Goldschnitt, Schnurschließe
Cardboard box with a sewing kit, gold tooling on the front cover, all edges gilt, cord clasp
1,3 x 6,2 x 4,7 cm

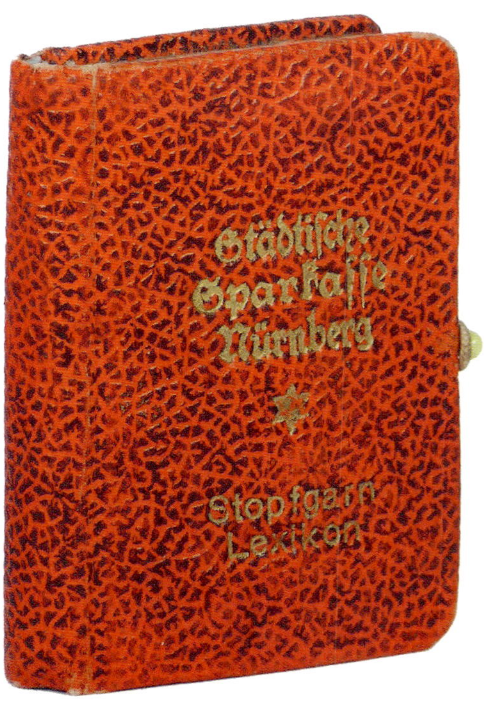

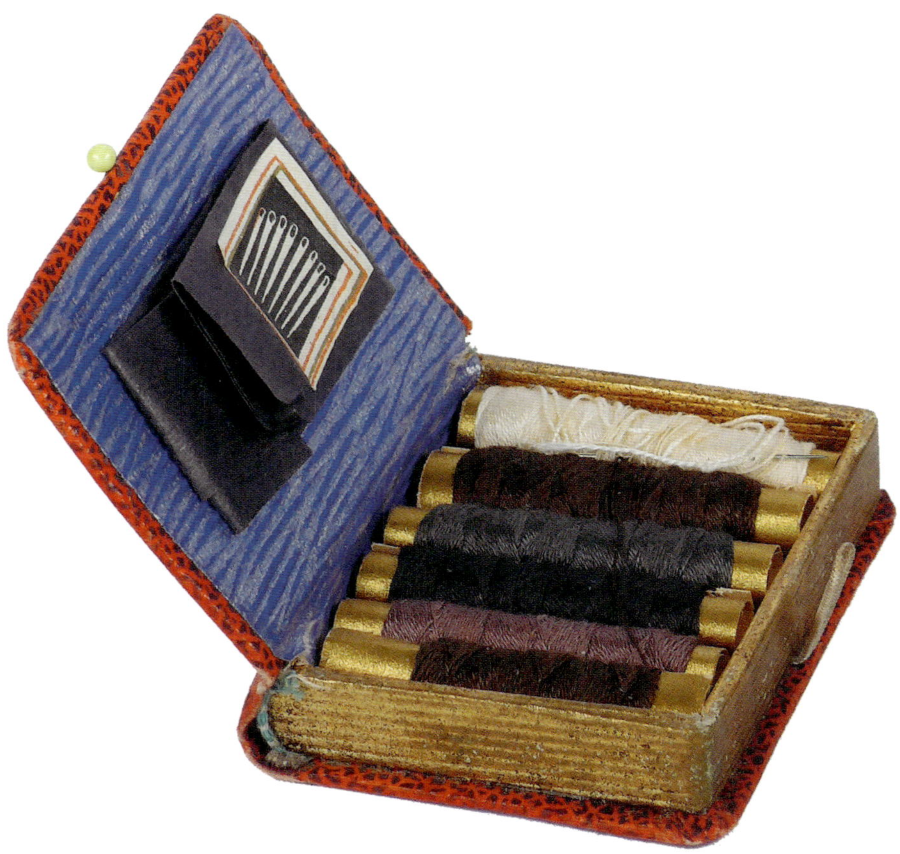

8.016
Baedeker's Reise-Begleiter
Baedeker's Travel Companion
Reisenähzeug in Baedeker-Buchattrappe, Kalikoeinband mit Prägung, dreiseitiger Kammmarmorschnitt, aufklappbar, für Faden, Nadeln, Knöpfe etc.
Travel kit in a fake book by Baedeker, calico cover with embossing, marbled edges, can be opened to store thread, needles, buttons etc.
Um / *Around* 1900 | 13,3 x 10,6 x 4 cm

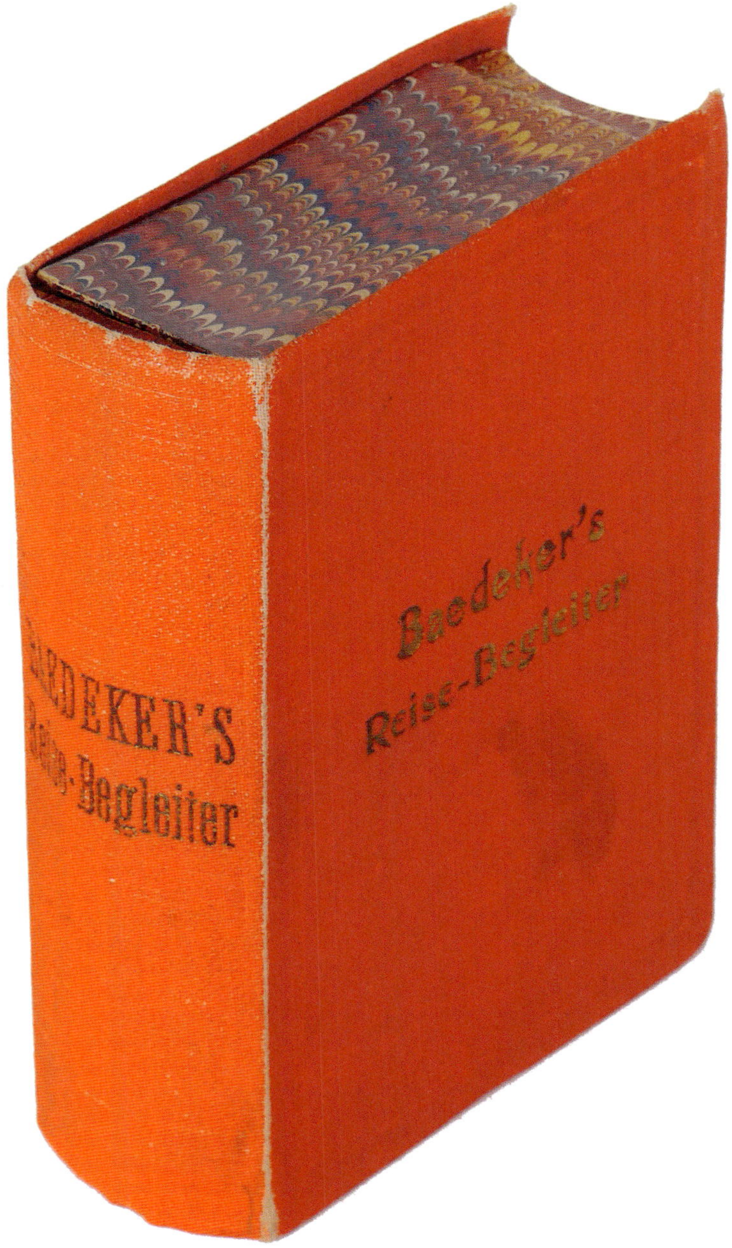

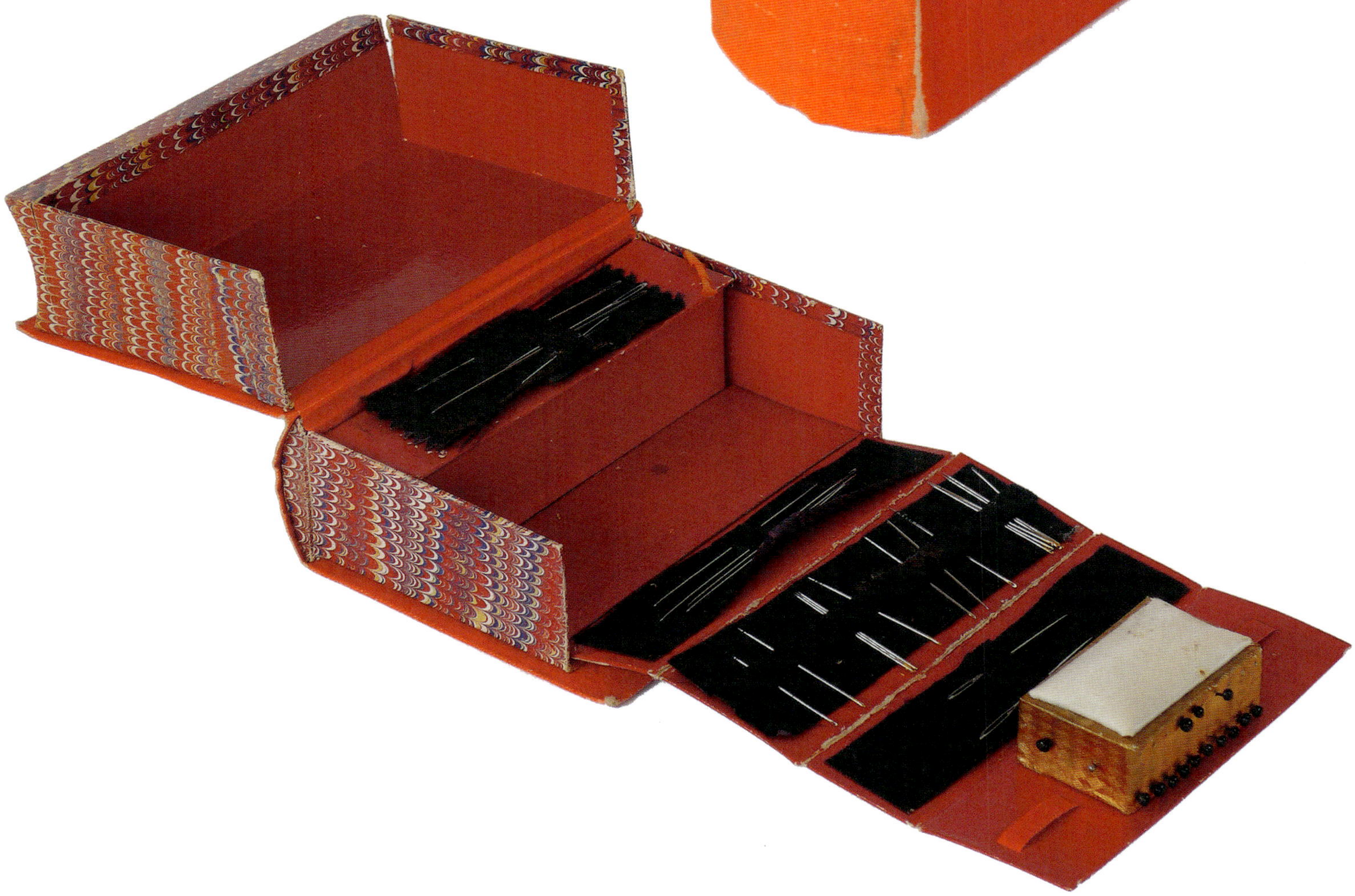

8.017
Gewebedose für Nähzeug, zwei seitlich schwenkbare Behältnisse, ovales Foto mit Stadtansicht von La Chaux-de-Fonds auf dem Vorderdeckel, vergoldete Zierlinien auf dem Vorderdeckel und Rücken, Messingschließe
Fabric box for a sewing kit, two laterally sliding containers, oval photo with a city view of La Chaux-de-Fonds on the lid, gilt ornamental lines on the lid and spine, brass buckle
Um / *Around* 1900
4,6 x 12,7 x 7,3 cm

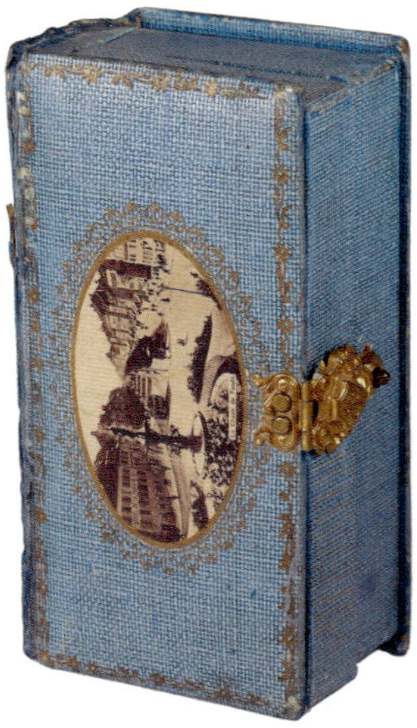

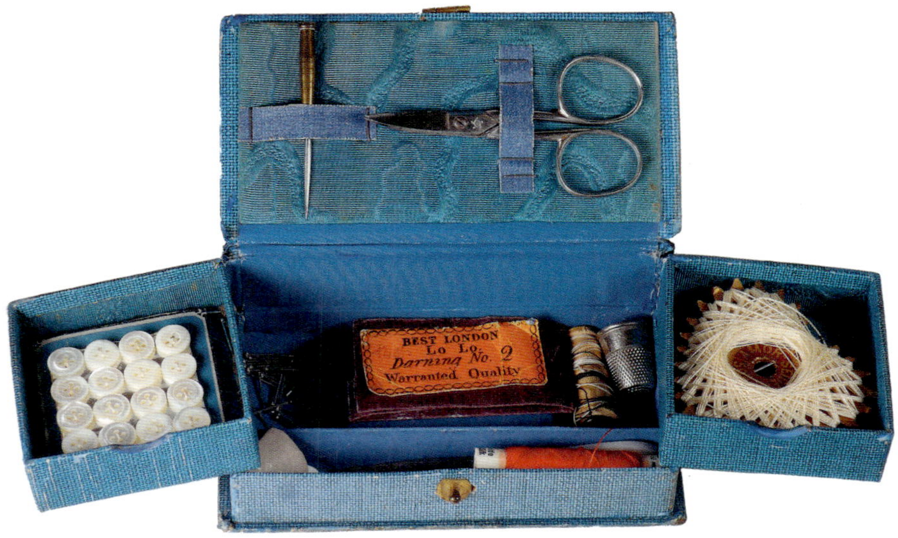

8.018
Kunststoffdose mit Nähzeug, Deckelbeschriftungen, Messingverschluss, Kartonschuber, Werbegeschenk
Plastic box with a sewing kit, lettering on the lid, brass closure, cardboard slipcase, promotional gift
Robert Gasser Lederwaren / *Leather Goods*
Sihlporte Zurich, Switzerland
0,7 x 6,6 x 5,3 cm

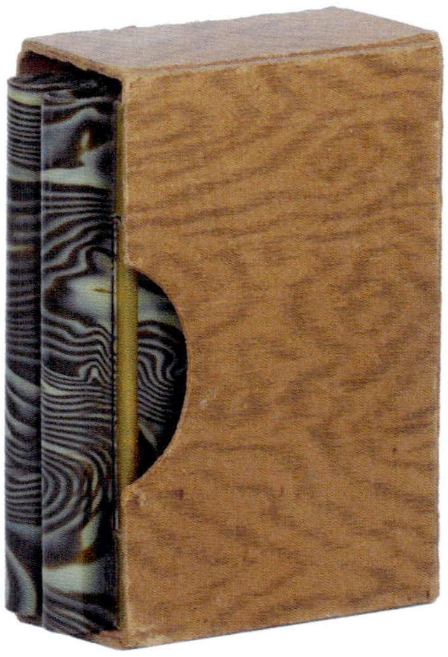

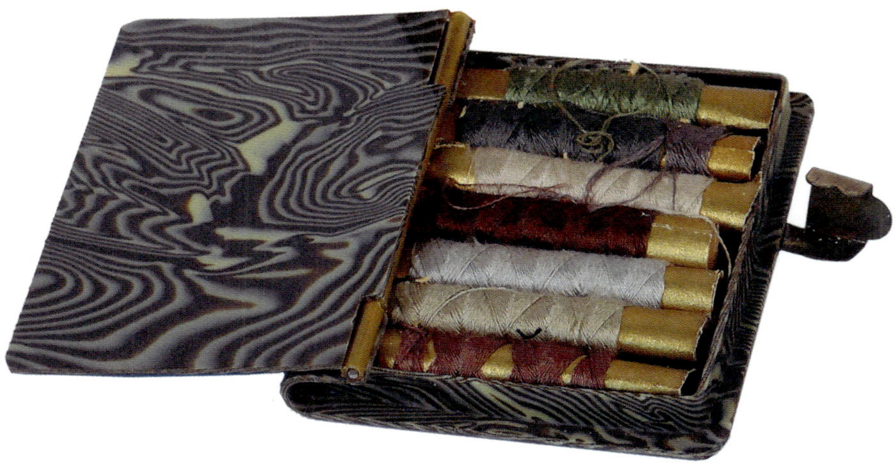

8.019
Ohne Fleiss, kein Preis, Zum Andenken
No pains, no gains, In memory
Halbgewebeschachtel für Nähzeug, Biedermeier-Kindertanzszene auf dem Vorderdeckel, Rücken- und Deckelprägung, vier Fächer für die Utensilien, Spiegel im Innendeckel, Buntpapierbuchschnitt
Semi-woven fabric box with a sewing kit, an illustration of dancing children in Biedermeier style on the lid, embossed spine and lid, four compartments for utensils, mirror on the inner side of the lid, colored paper edges
3,8 x 17,7 x 12,1 cm

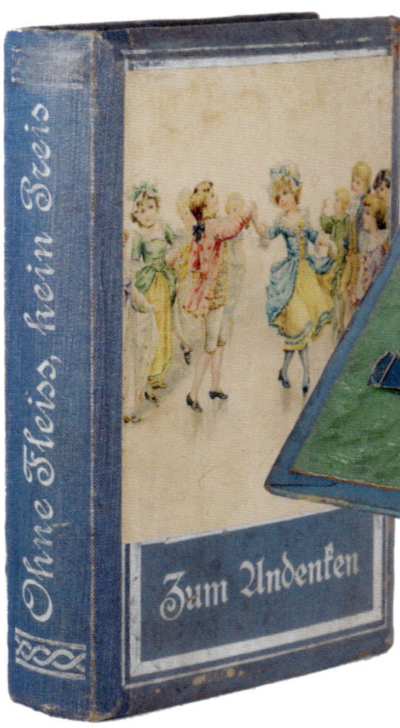

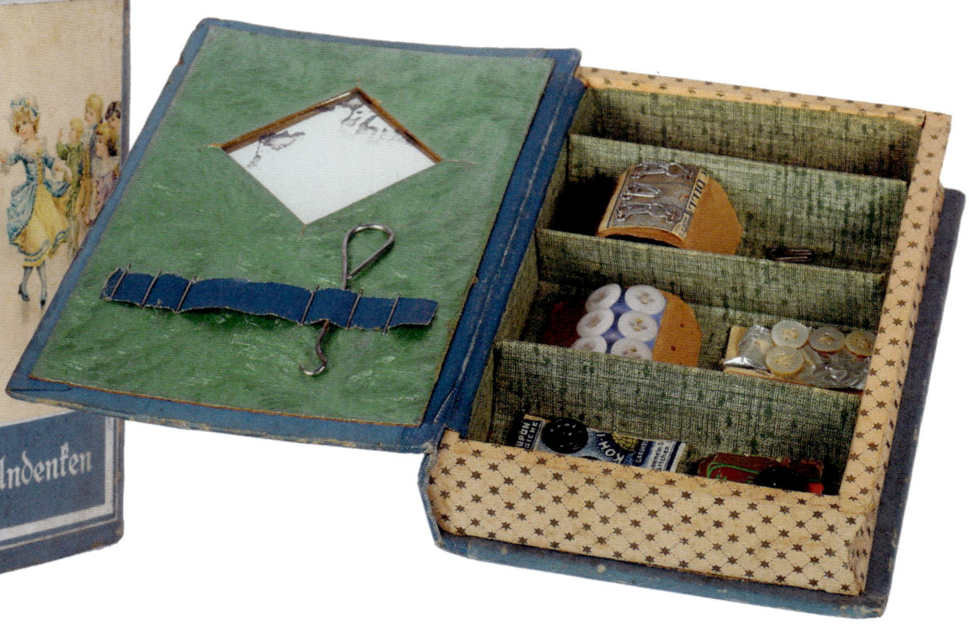

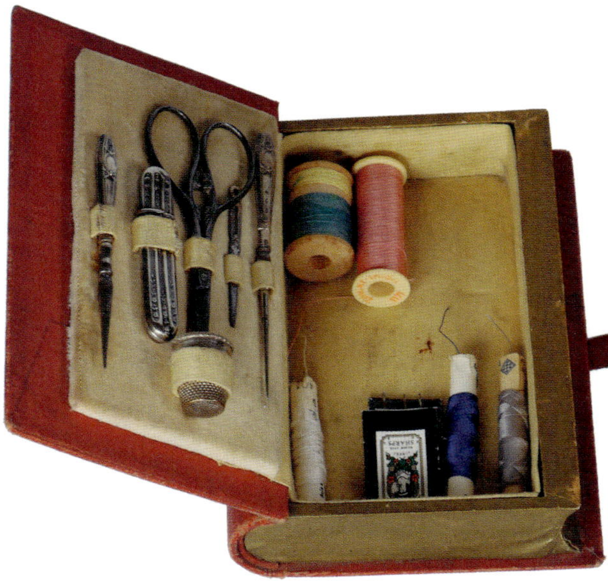

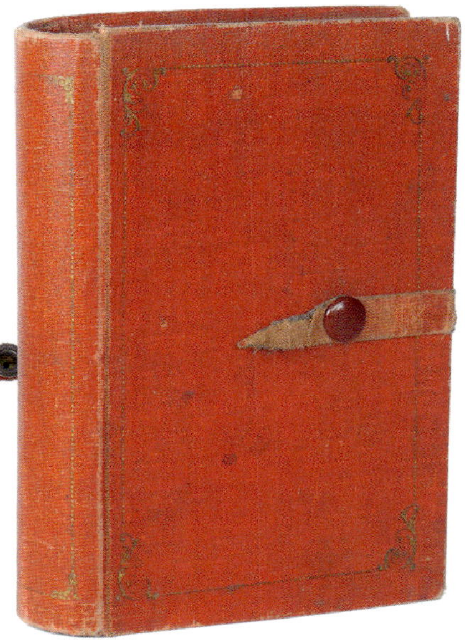

8.020
Buchschatulle für Nähzeug, Ganzgewebeeinband mit Goldprägung, Druckknopfverschluss, Nähzeugutensilien, dreiseitiger Goldschnitt
Box with a sewing kit, full cloth cover with gold embossing, snap fastener, sewing kit accessories, all edges gilt
Jugendstil / *Art Nouveau*
3,6 x 11,1 x 3,5 cm

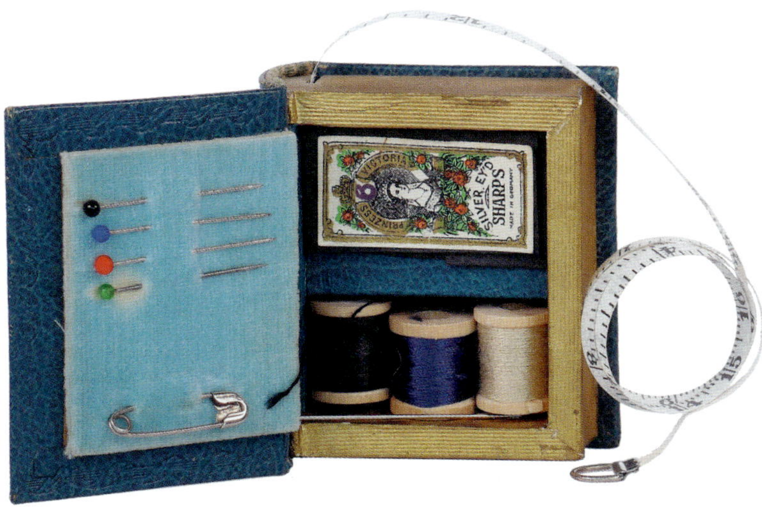

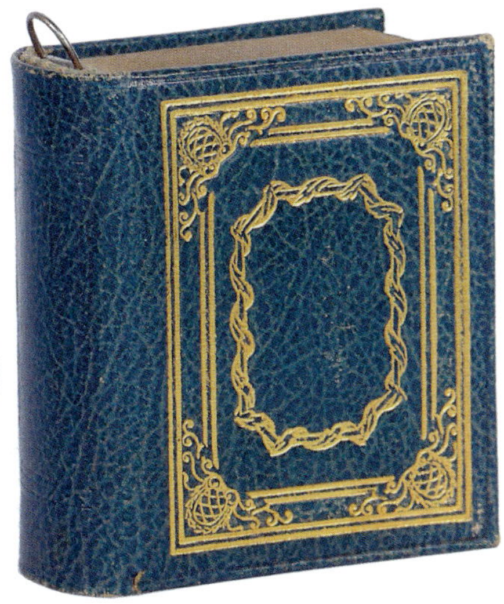

8.021
Ganzlederdose für Nähzeug, zwei Fächer für Nadeln und Faden, vergoldeter Vorderdeckel, Wattierter Vorderspiegel als Nadelkissen, Rollmaßband am Kopfschnitt, dreiseitig geprägter Goldschnitt
Leather box with sewing kit, two compartments for needles and threads, gold-plated cover, padded pastedown for needles, measuring tape at the head, gold-tooled edges
2,2 x 6 x 5,5 cm

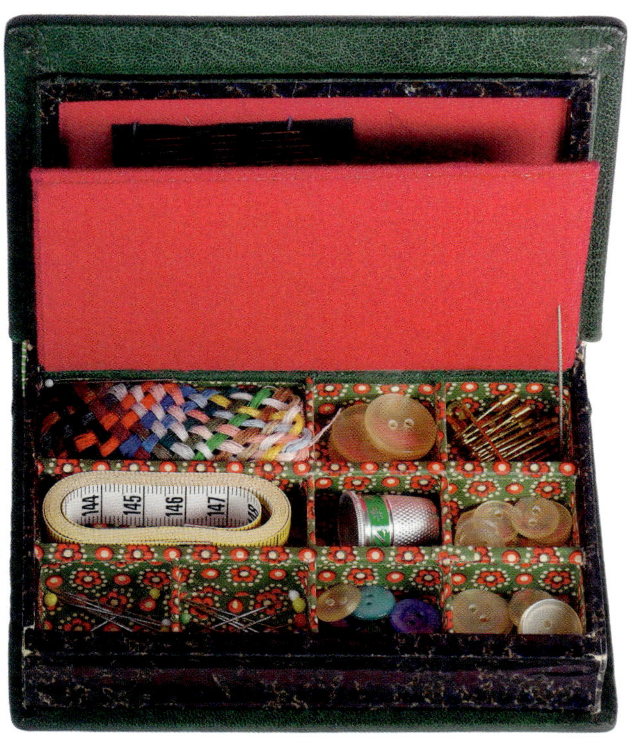

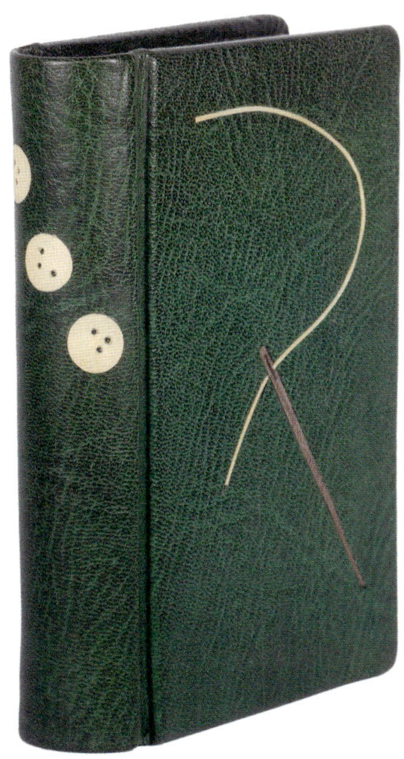

8.022
Nähzeug in einer Ganzlederkassette, zehn Fächer, Lederintarsien auf dem Rücken und beiden Deckeln, dreiseitiger Agatapierschnitt
Sewing things in a full leather box, ten compartments, leather marquetry on the spine and both covers, agate paper edges
Hersteller Sybille und August Wirz / *Manufacturer: Sybille and August Wirz* Winterthur, Switzerland
14,2 x 10,9 x 3,1 cm

8.023
Thimble Book 3
Lederdose mit Fingerhut, Messingschließe, Rückenschild, dreiseitig geprägter Goldschnitt
Leather box with thimble, brass buckle, label on the spine, gold-tooled edges
Spätes 19. Jh. / *Late 19th century*
2,3 x 4,1 x 4 cm

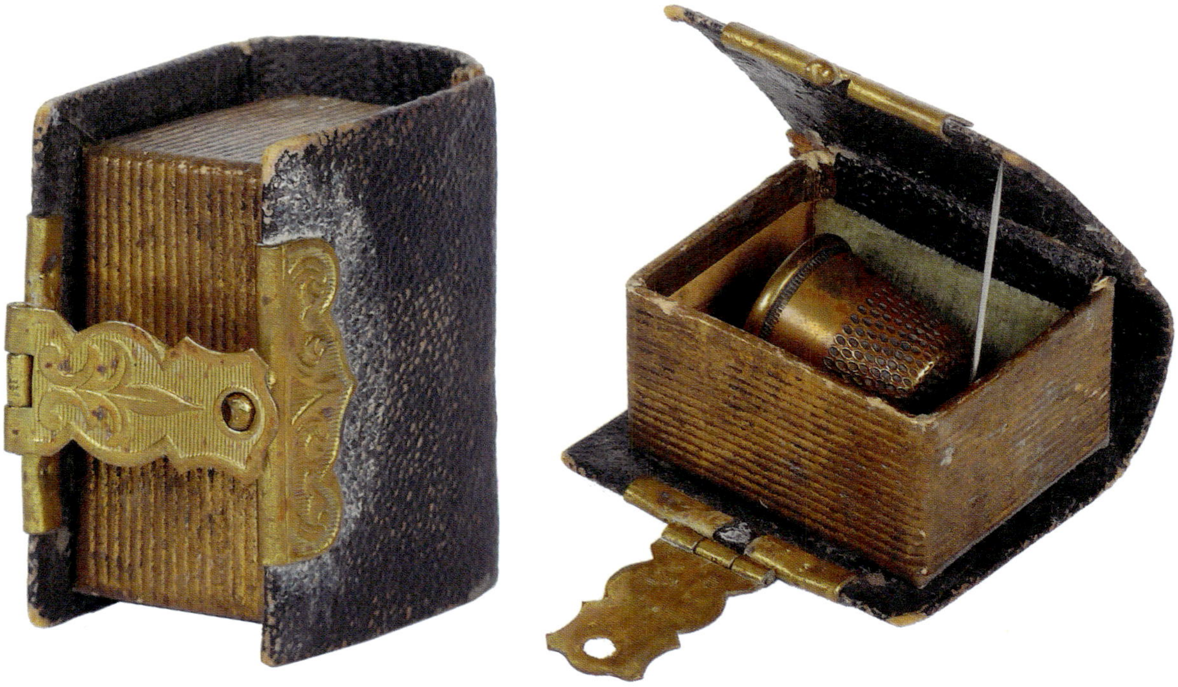

8.024
Plüschdose für Nähnadeln und Fingerhüte, Kanteneinfassungen mit Goldlitzen, aufgeklebtes gestanztes Vogelmotiv auf dem Vorderdeckel, Titelschild „Forget me not" auf dem Rücken, ausgefüttert mit geprägtem Goldpapier
Box with plush cover for sewing needles and thimbles, edging with gold braids, embossed sticker with a bird on the cover, title label "Forget me not" on the spine, lined with embossed gold paper
Um / *Around* 1880
6,7 x 6,1 x 2,7cm

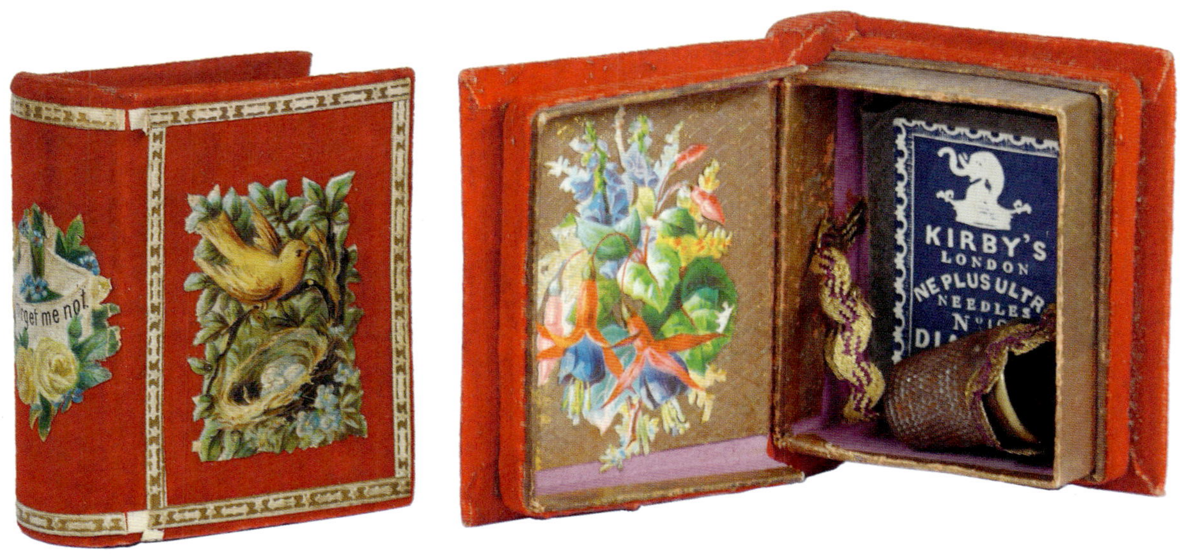

8.025
Minerva Budapest
Kartondose mit geprägtem Papierüberzug, Rollmaßband am Kopfschnitt, Rücken- und Deckelvergoldung, dreiseitiger Goldschnitt
Cardboard box with embossed paper-over-board, measuring tape at the head, gilt on the spine and cover, all edges gilt
5 x 3,8 x 1,8 cm

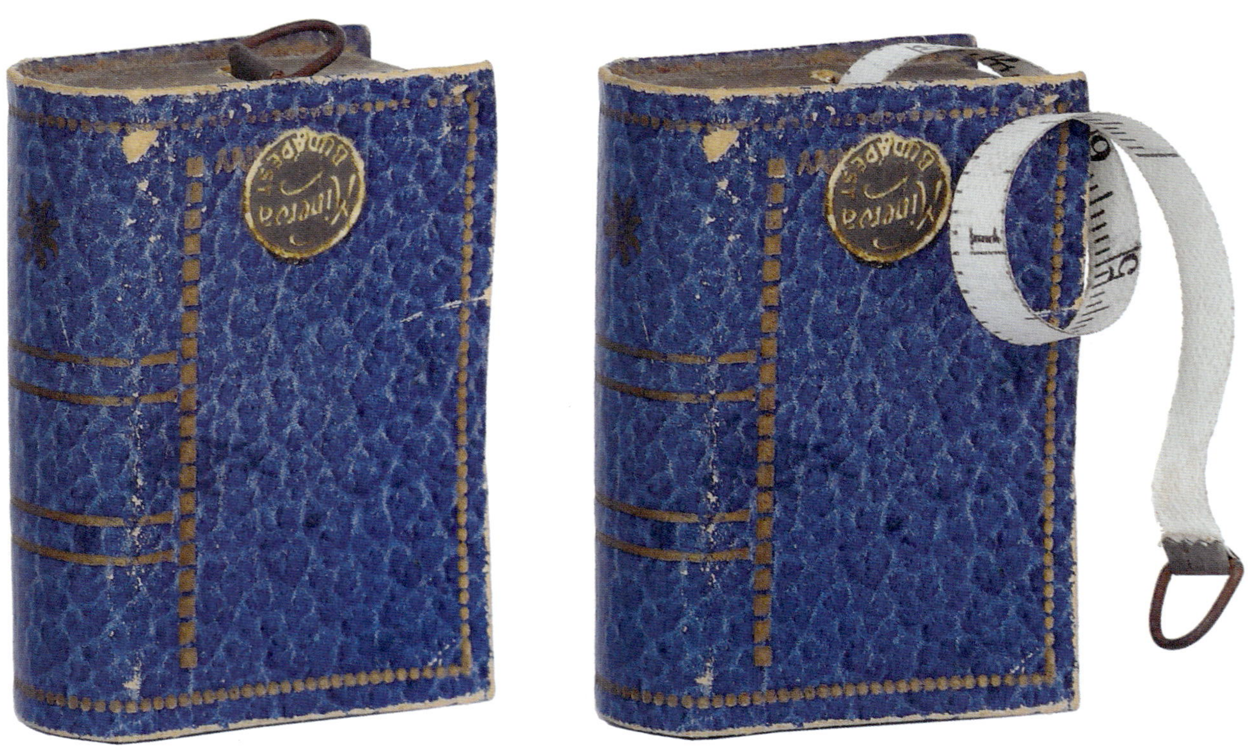

8.026
Aufgeschlagenes Kartonbuch mit einem Text von Alphonse de Lamartine (1790–1869), Aquarell mit romantischer Waldszene und Brunnen, Velourseinband mit geprägtem Goldpapierdekor, vermutlich für Stecknadeln
Open carboard book with a text by Alphonse de Lamartine (1790–1869), romantic watercolor illustration of a forest and fountain, covered with velour, gold tooling decor, probably for pins
Um / *Around1900*
0,3 x 9,2 x 6 cm

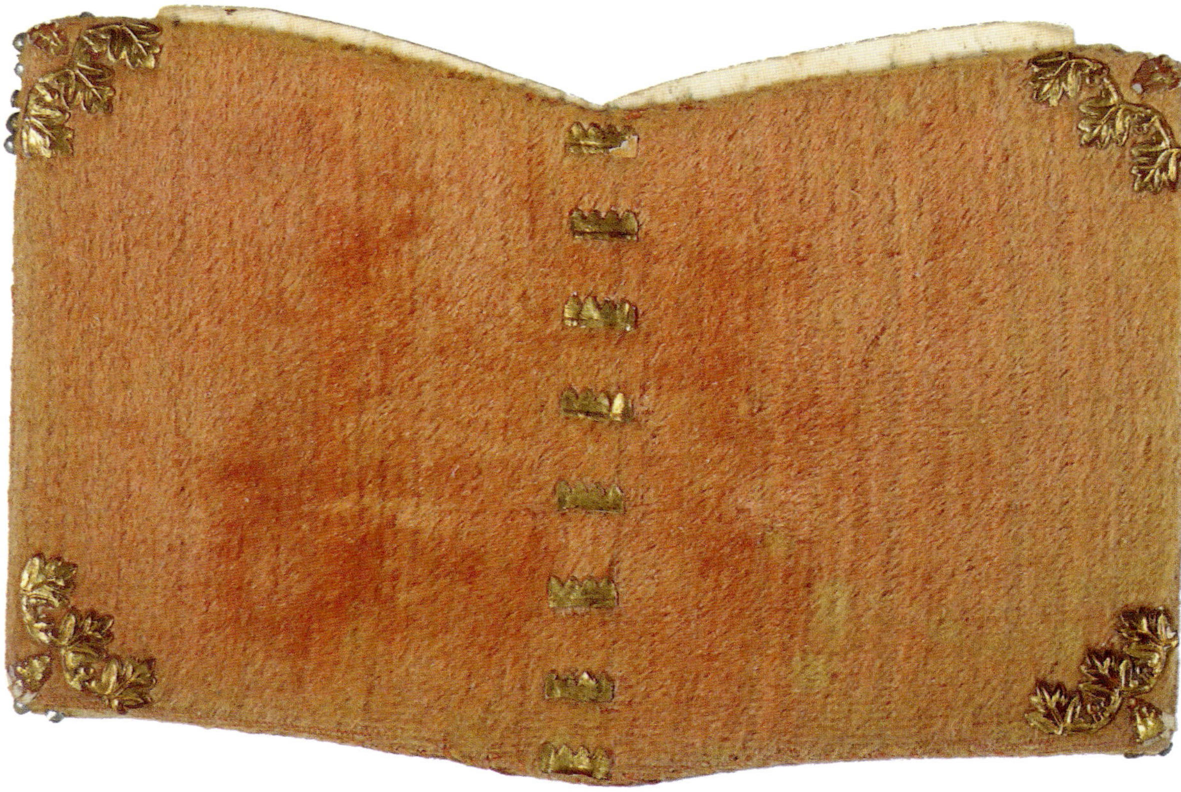

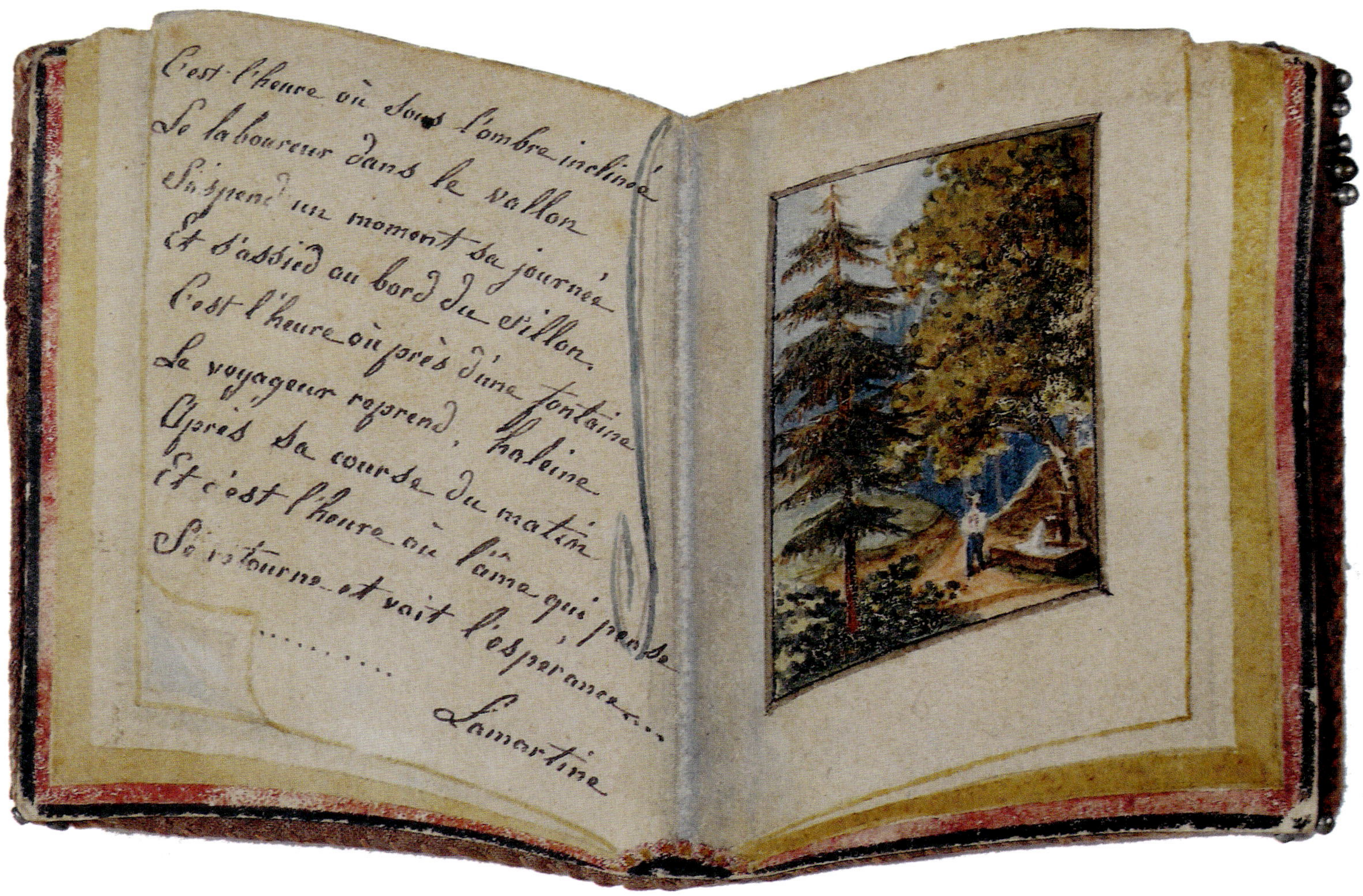

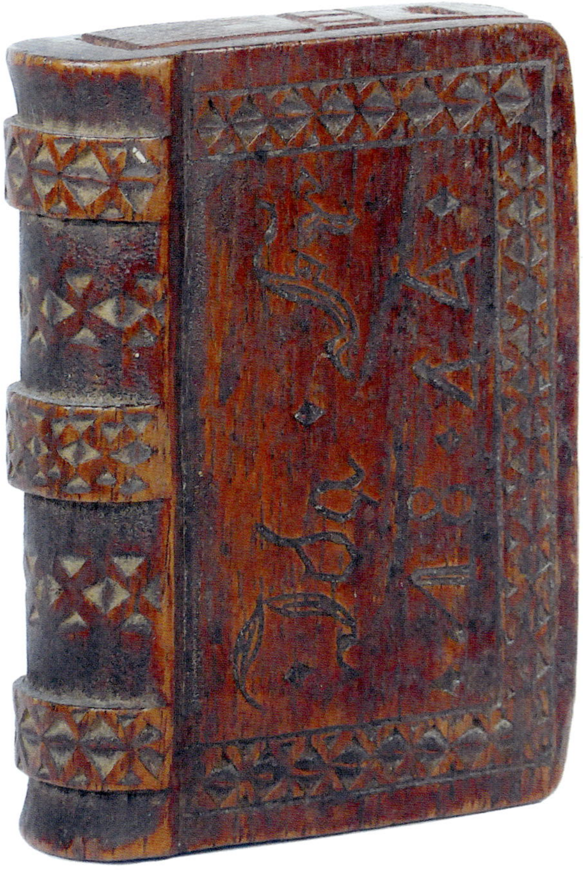

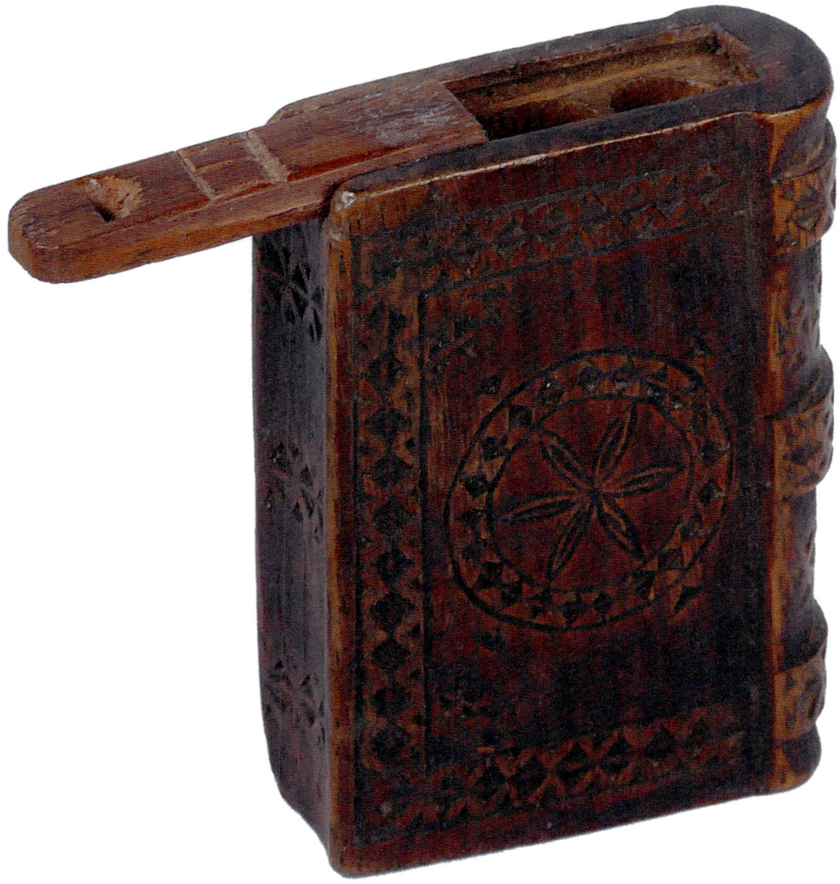

8.027
Jda Fr 1844
Holzdose mit Schieber am Kopfschnitt, Kerbschnitzerei, gravierter Namenszug und Jahreszahl, drei Löcher im Kopfschnitt für Nähnadeln
Wooden box with a slider at the head, notched carving, engraved name and year, head with-three holes for needles.
7,2 x 5,2 x 2 cm

8.028
Holzdose mit Schieber am Kopfschnitt, Holzeinlegearbeiten am Rücken und auf beiden Deckeln, zwei Löcher im Buchkern für Nadeln
Wooden box with a slider at the head, wooden marquetry on the spine and both covers, two holes for needles in the core of the book
Ende 19. Jh. / *Late 19th century*
7,2 x 5,1 x 2,3 cm

8.029
Holzdose für Nähnadeln, Schieber und Löcher am Kopfschnitt für Nadeln, Schnitzerei auf dem Vorderdeckel, geschnitztes Monogramm auf dem Rücken „SG"
Wooden box for sewing needles, head with a slider and holes for needles, carving on the front cover, carved monogram on the back "SG"
8,6 x 5,3 x 1,5 cm

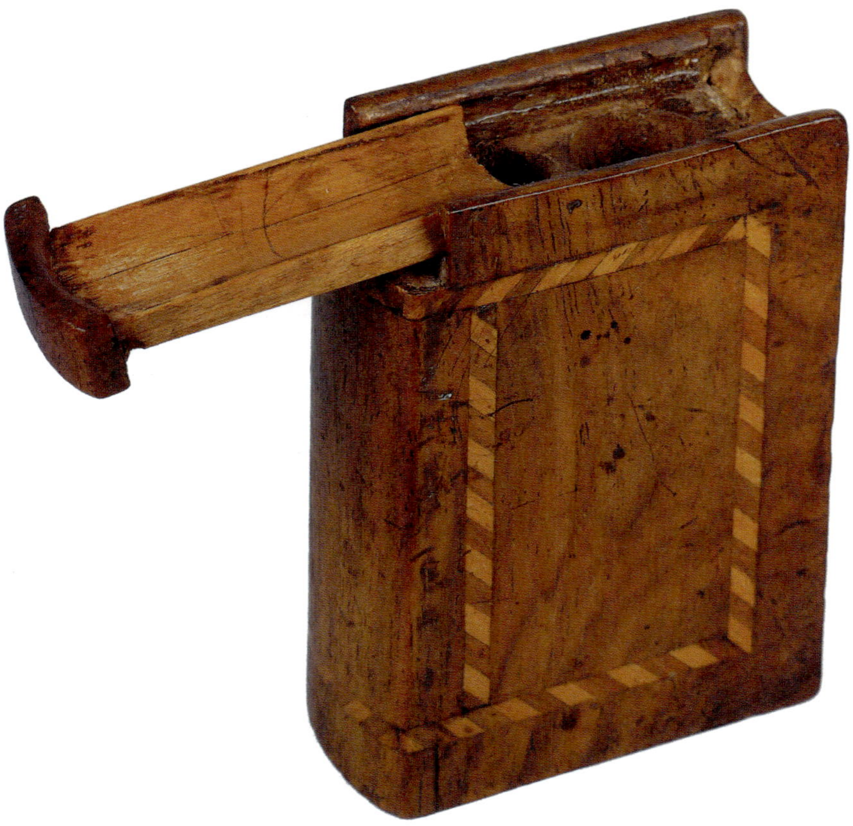

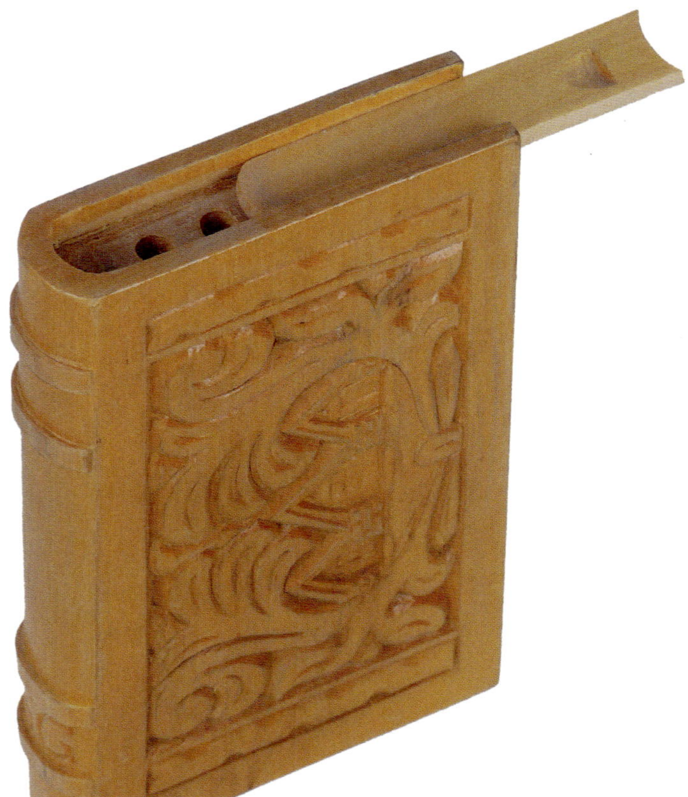

8.030
Souvenir
Nadelkissen, Rücken und Deckelkanten mit geprägtem Goldpapier verziert, Deckelbezug mit blauem Spitzkaro Papier, rotes Lederschild, mit weichem Stoff gefüllt
Pin cushion, gold tooling on the spine and cover edges, blue checked paper on the cover, label in read leather, filled with soft fabric
Spätes 19. Jh. / *Late 19th century*
7,1 x 5,1 x 1,6 cm

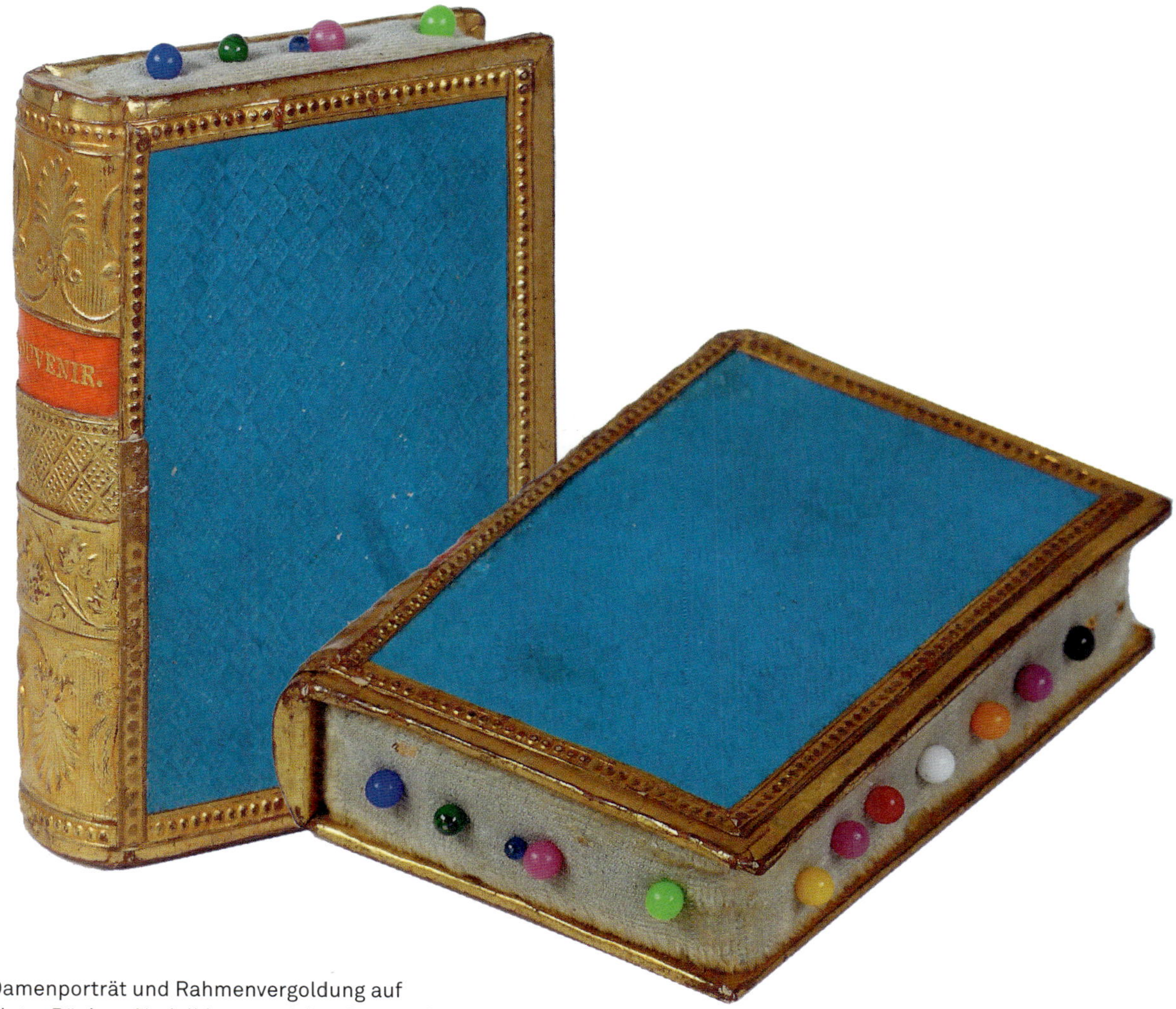

8.031
Lederdose für Nähnadeln mit Damenporträt und Rahmenvergoldung auf dem Vorderdeckel, handvergoldeter Rücken, Nadelkissen auf dem Innenspiegel, ausgefüttert mit Buntpapier, dreiseitiger Goldschnitt
Leather box for sewing needles with the portrait of a lady and a gilt frame on the lid, manual gilding on the spine, needle cushions on the inside, lined with colored paper, all edges gilt
Um / *Around* 1900 | 1,5 x 4,8 x 3 cm

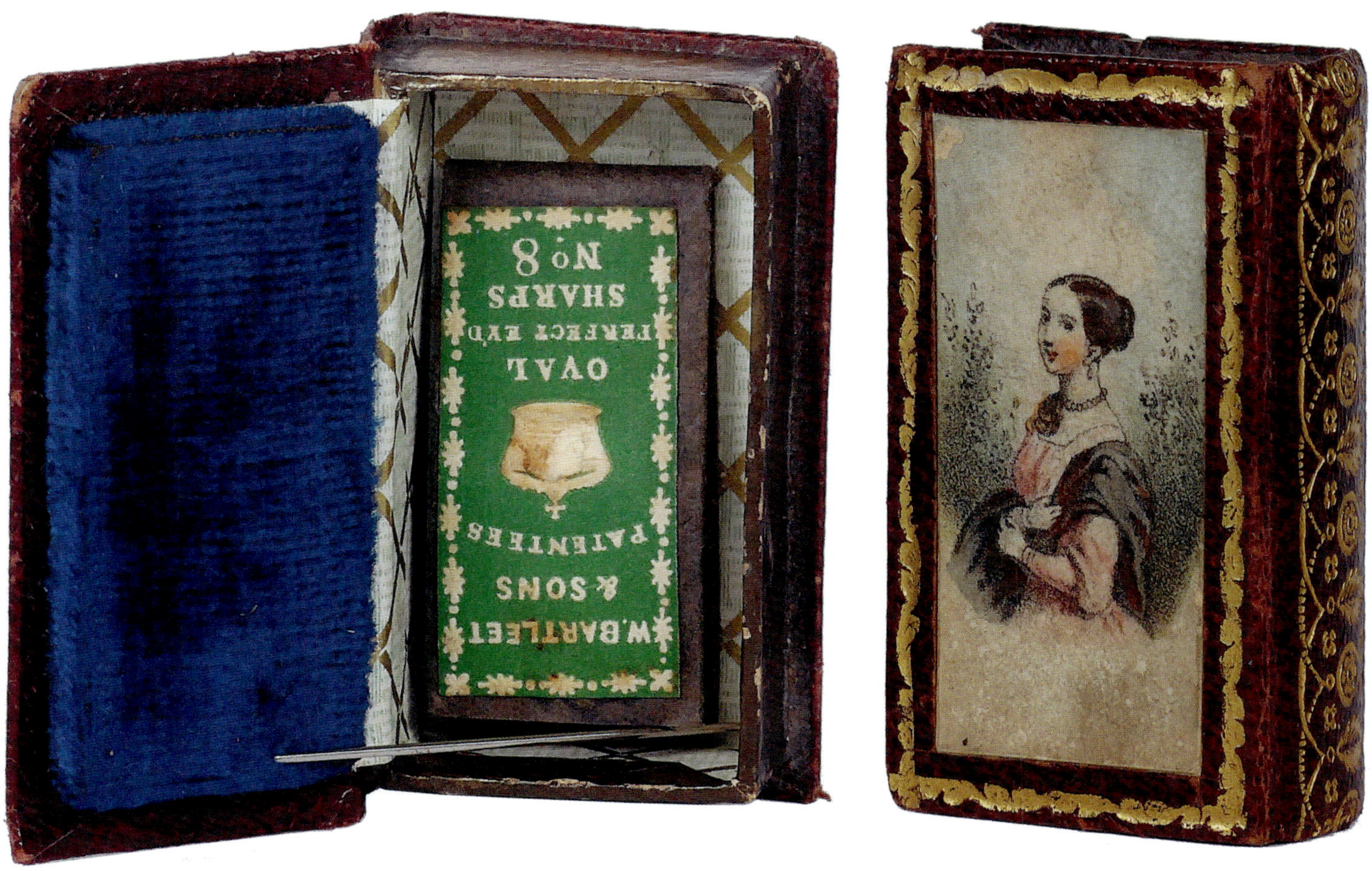

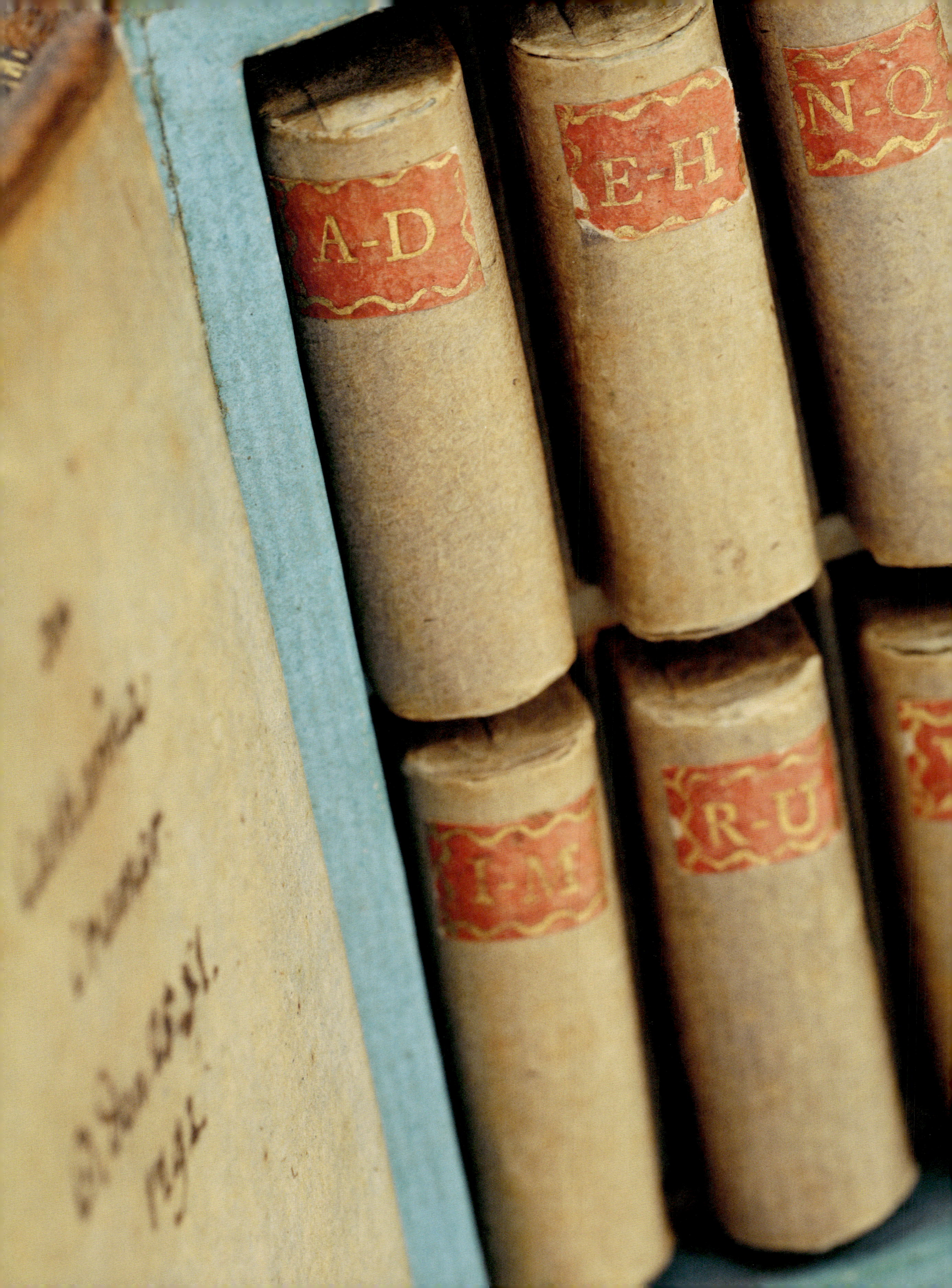
A-D
E-H
N-Q
I-M
R-U

Bibliotheken
Libraries

Ein weiteres Lieblingsstück hatte ein Zürcher Auktionshaus im Angebot. Beim begehrten Objekt handelt es sich um eine Buchschachtel aus Leder mit dem handvergoldeten Titel „Bibliothek“. Im Innern verbergen sich sechs Schuber aus Halbkarton mit 225 handgeschriebenen, grün umrandeten Kärtchen mit dem jeweiligen Thema, „Abendmahl – Zweck“. Der Autor ist der berühmte Johann Caspar Lavater, 1741–1801, Zürich. Er war ein bildbesessener Pfarrer, Philosoph, Schriftsteller sowie ein Hauptvertreter der Physiognomie. Auf dem Spiegel dieses Scheinbuchs ist die Widmung zu lesen: „An Catharina Cramer den 25. Xl 1792“. Für das museumswürdige Sammlerstück interessierten sich natürlich auch Bibliophile Sammler, Bibliotheken und Bewunderer Johann Caspar Lavaters.

Another favorite piece was on offer at a Zurich auction house. The coveted object is a leather book box decorated with the hand-gilded title "Library". Inside are six slipcases made of semi-stiff cardboard with 225 handwritten cards with green borders, denoting the respective theme, "The Last Supper – Purpose". The author is the famous Johann Caspar Lavater, 1741 - 1801, Zurich. He was a picture-obsessed pastor, philosopher, writer and leading protagonist of the study of physiognomy. There is a dedication on the mirror of this fake book: "To Catharina Cramer on the 25th Xl 1792". Naturally, bibliophile collectors, libraries and admirers of Johann Caspar Lavater were also interested in this museum-worthy collector's item.

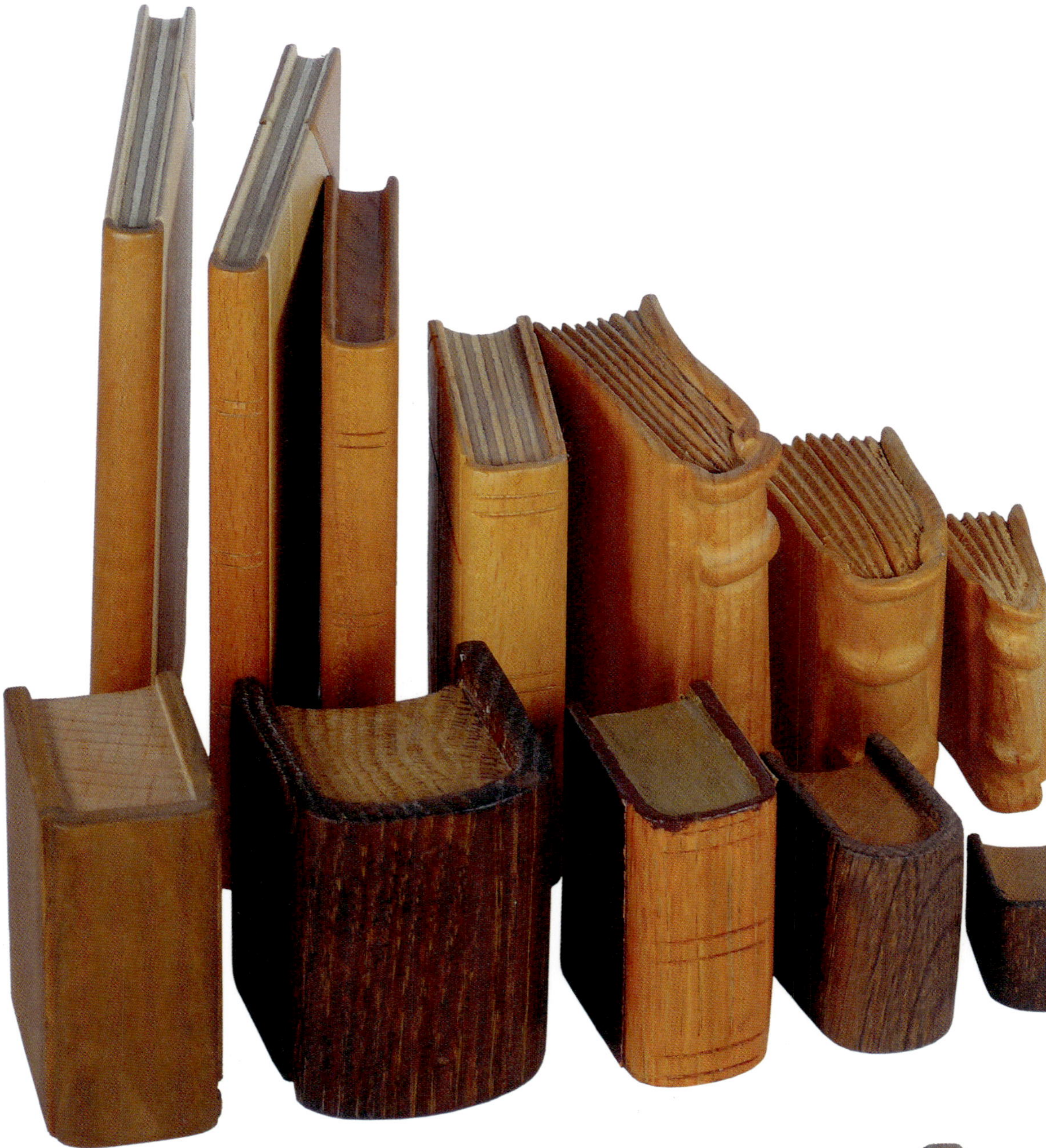

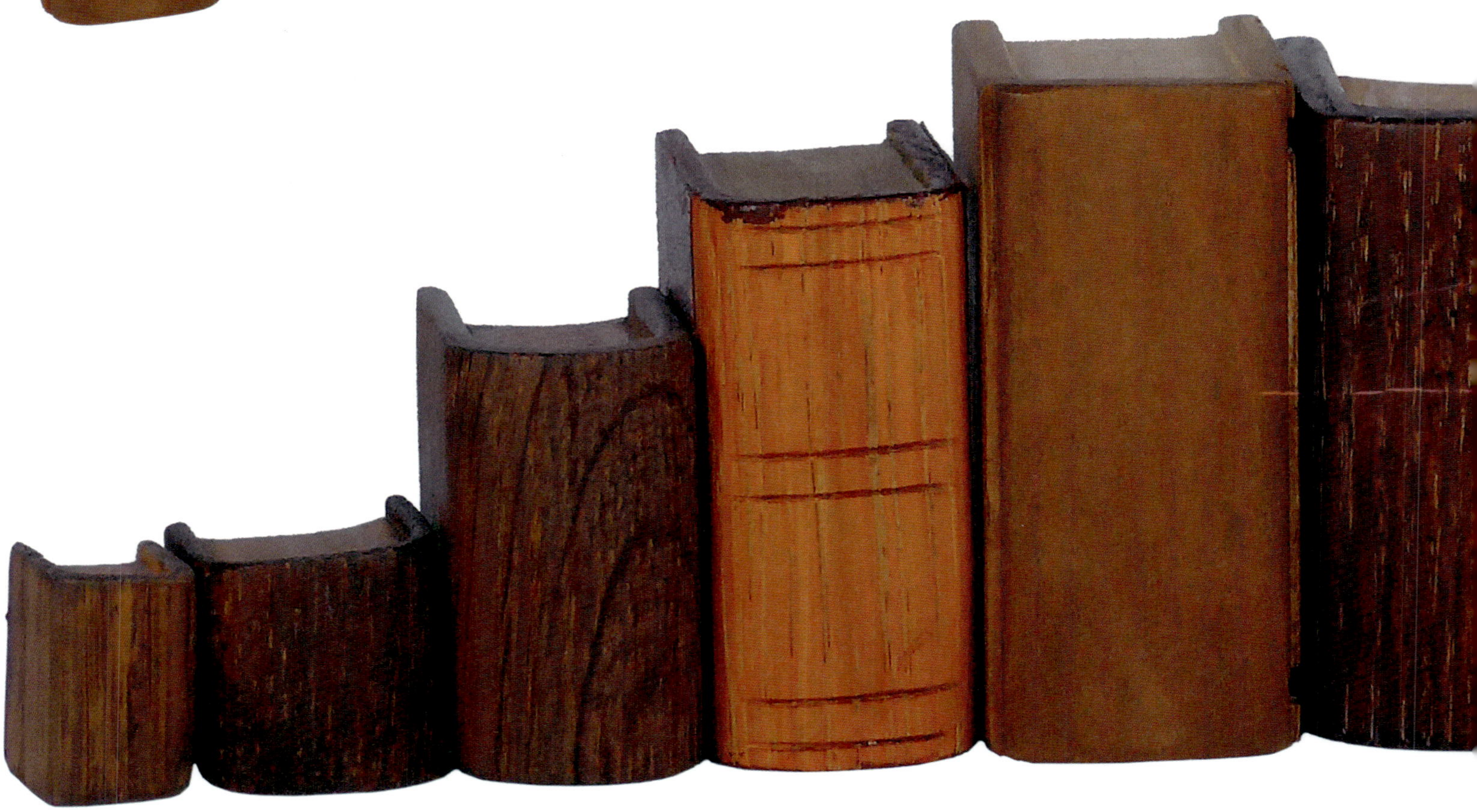

9.001–9.013
Dreizehn Holzobjekte in Buchform, verschiedene Holzarten und Formate, Zierobjekte
Thirteen wooden objects in the design of a book, different types and sizes of wood, used for decoration
Zeitgenössisch / *Contemporary*

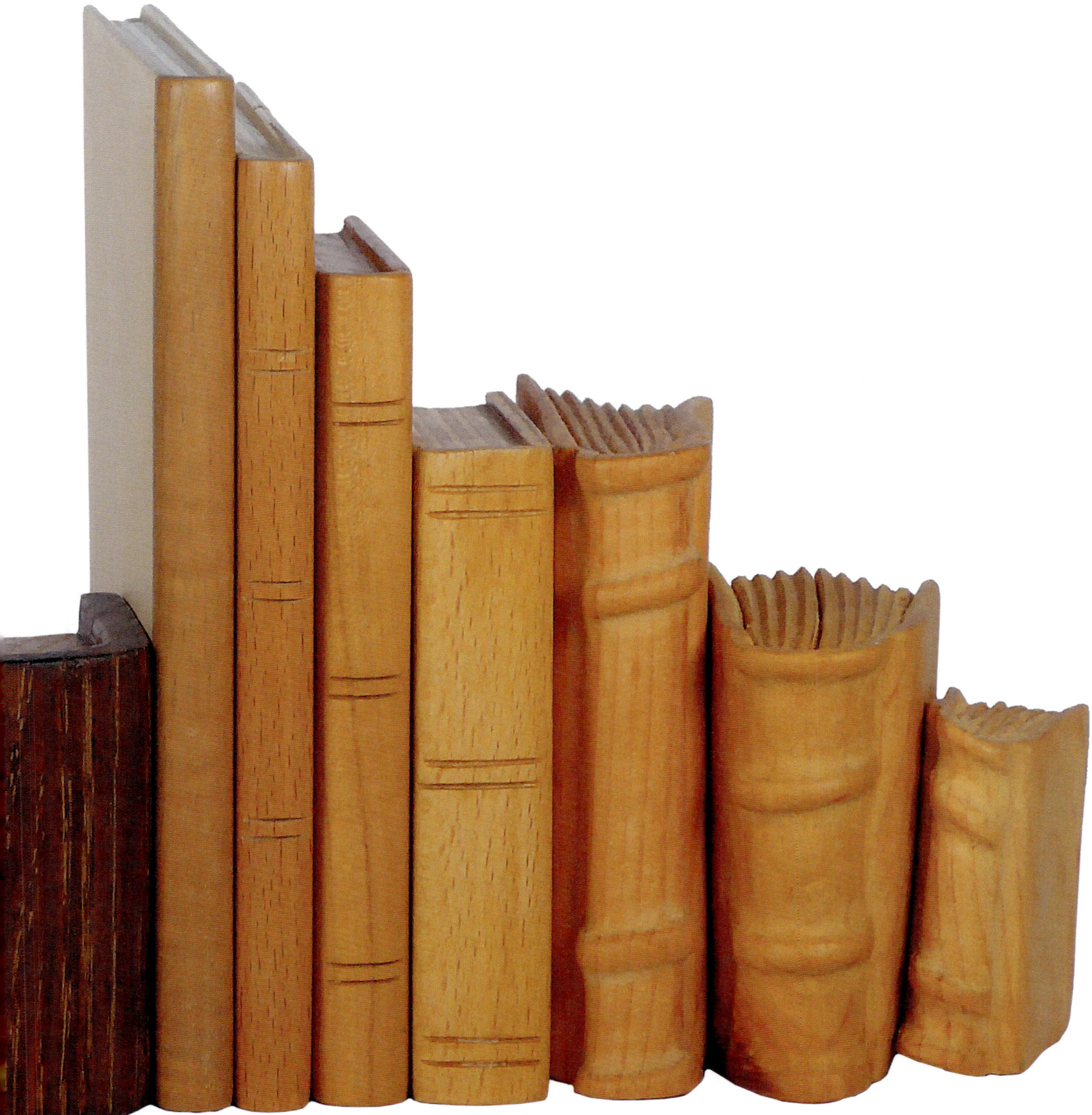

9.014
Holzbibliothek, Xylothek
Wood library, xylotheque
Zwölf Holzarten in Buchform, nummeriert, Schuber mit Holzimitationspapierüberzug
Twelve types of wood in the design of a book, each numbered, slipcase with faux wood paper-over-board
12,3 x 11,4 x 7,1 cm

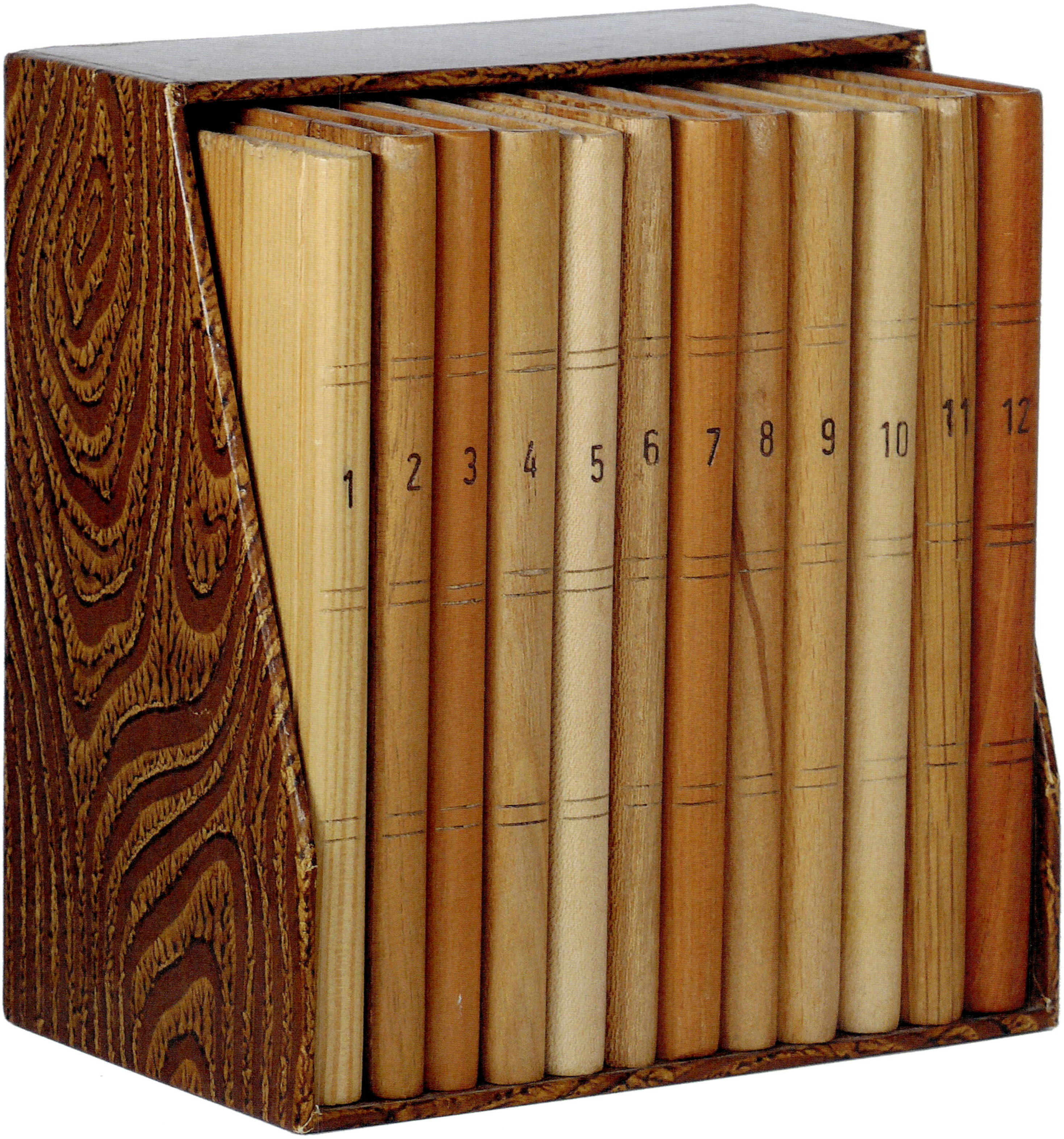

9.015

Holzmustersammlung Furniere

Sample collection of wood veneers

Nachgebaute Holzschatulle mit Schublade am Buchrücken, drei Innenfächer für hundertzehn Arten Holzfurniere, Rückenschild, für Lehrzwecke

Replica of a wooden box with drawer on the spine, three inner compartments for one hundred and eighteen kinds of wood veneers, label on the spine, for educational purposes

Runkel, Bad Oeynhausen, Deutschland / *Germany* | 7 x 38 x 26,2 cm

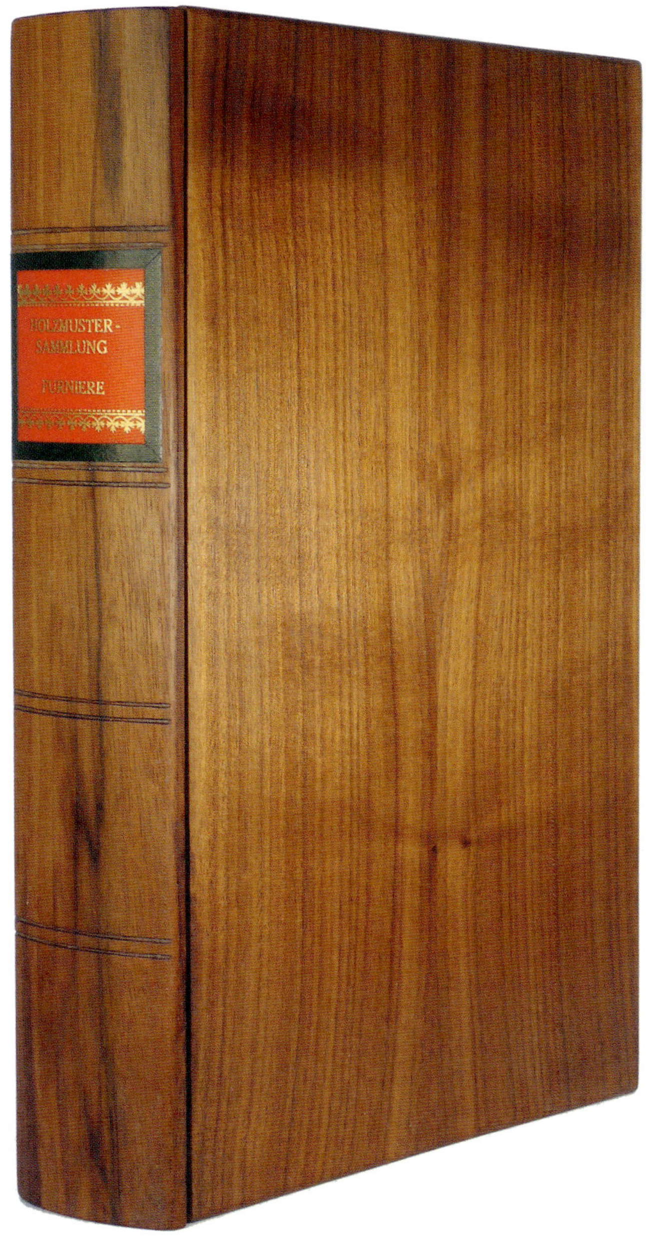

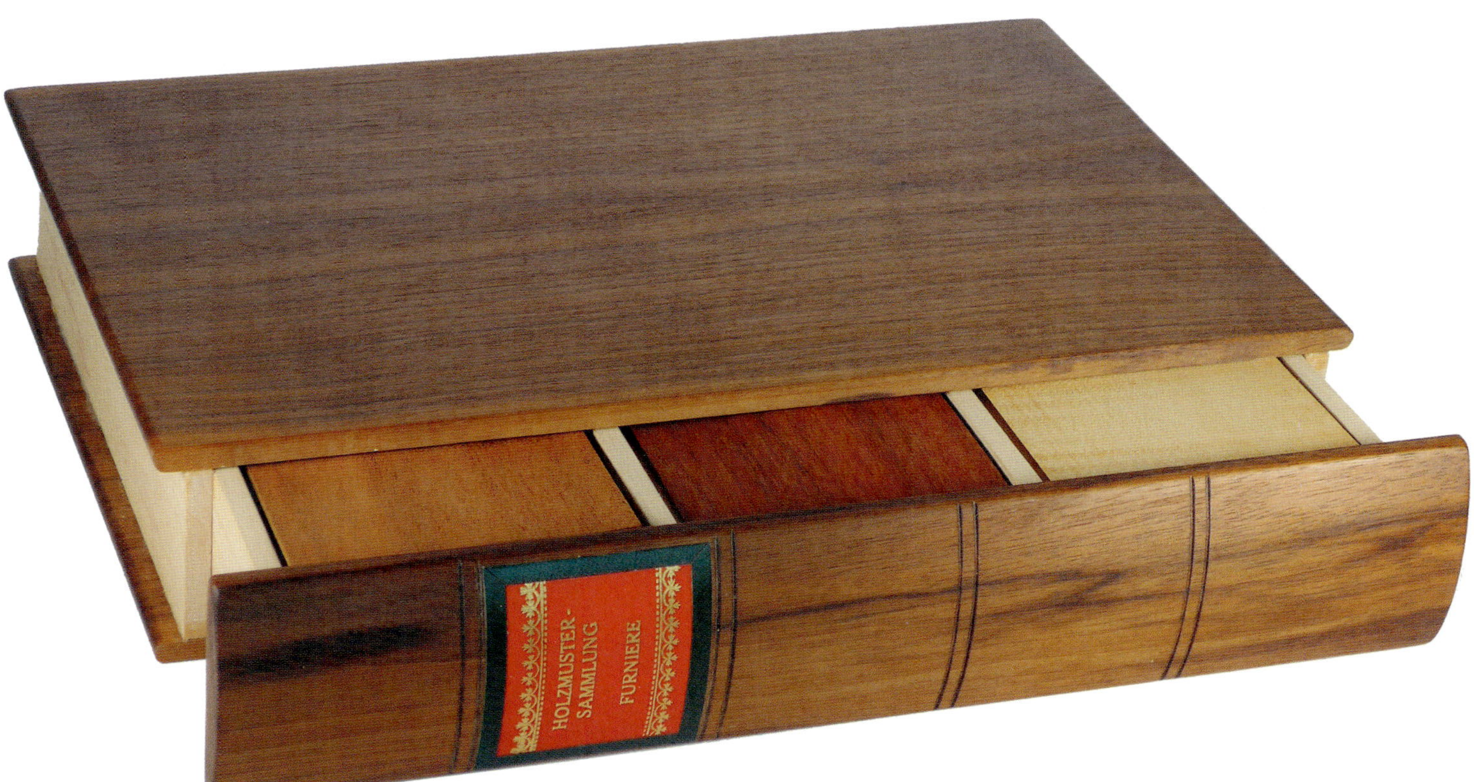

9.016
Holzbibliothek, Xylothek
Wood library, xylotheque
Bäume in Buchformat nach historischer Vorlage des 18. Jahrhunderts: Stieleiche, Weisserle, Vogelkirsche, Bergahorn und Birke, dreiteilig mit Rückenschild, Innenleben der Birke: Blätterzweig, Ast, Rinde, Stammquerschnitt, Fach für Samen
Trees in the design of a book according to historical designs of the 18th century: English oak, white alder, bird cherry, sycamore maple and birch, three parts with label on the spine, inner life of the birch: leaf branch, branch, bark, stem cross-section, compartment for seeds
20 x 10 x 4 cm

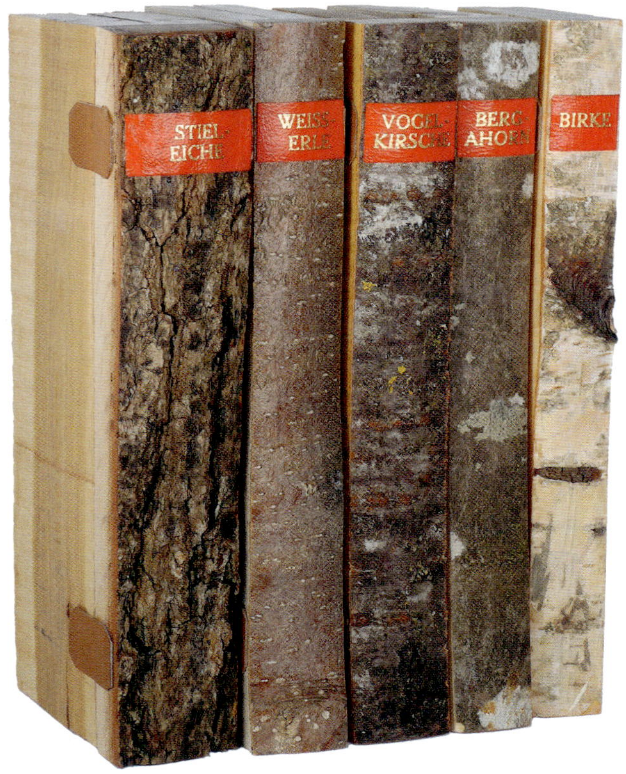

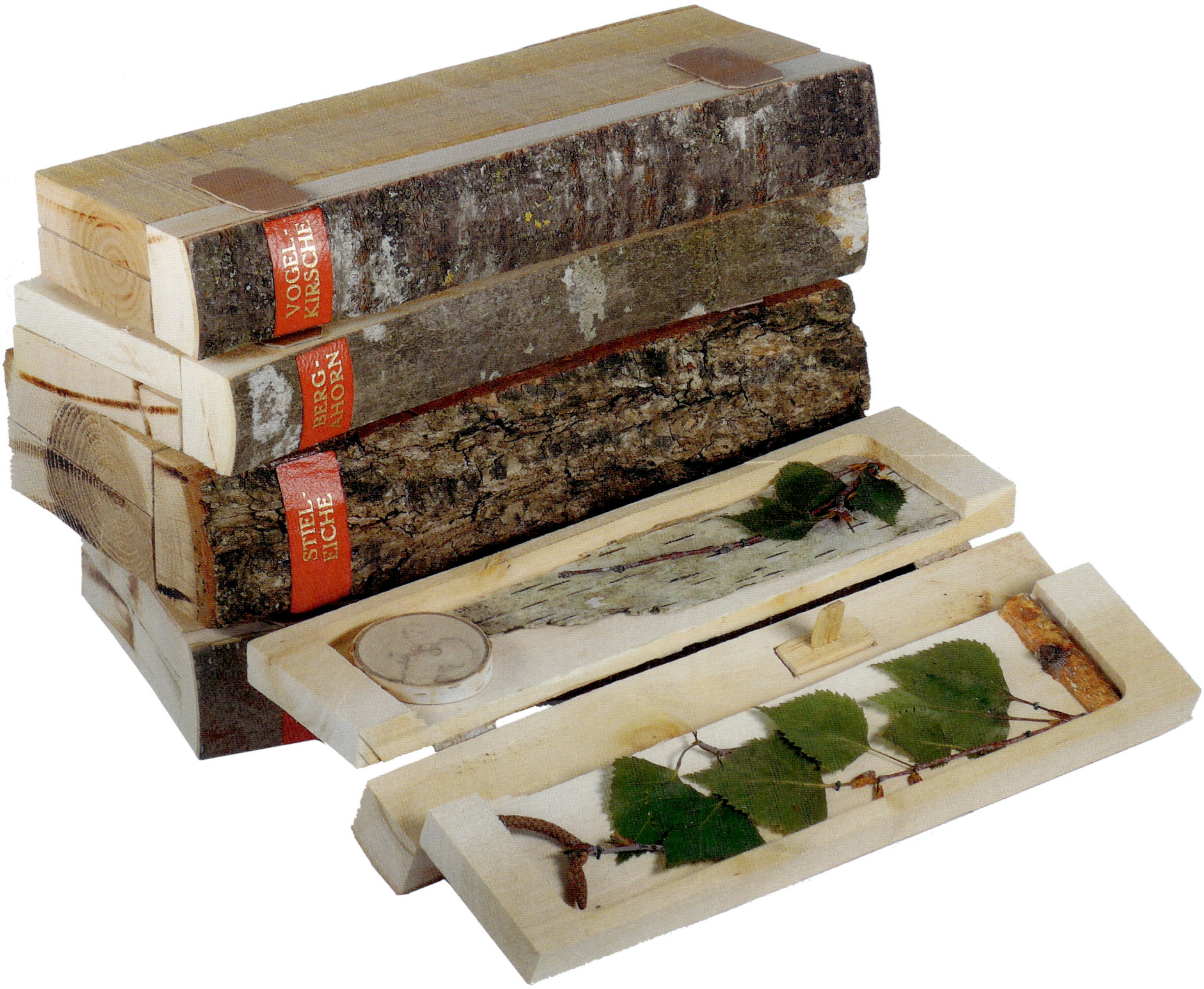

9.017

Holzbibliothek, Xylothek

Wood library, xylotheque

Nachgebaute Holzbibliothek mit 120 Büchern im Format 11,7 × 4,9 × 1,5 cm, alphabetisch geordnet, nummerierte Lederschilder, Büchergestell mit Holzimitationspapier überzogen

Replica of a wooden library with 120 books measuring 11,7 × 4,9 × 1,5 cm, arranged alphabetically, leather labels with numbers, bookcase covered with faux wood paper

53 x 47,8 x 6,2 cm

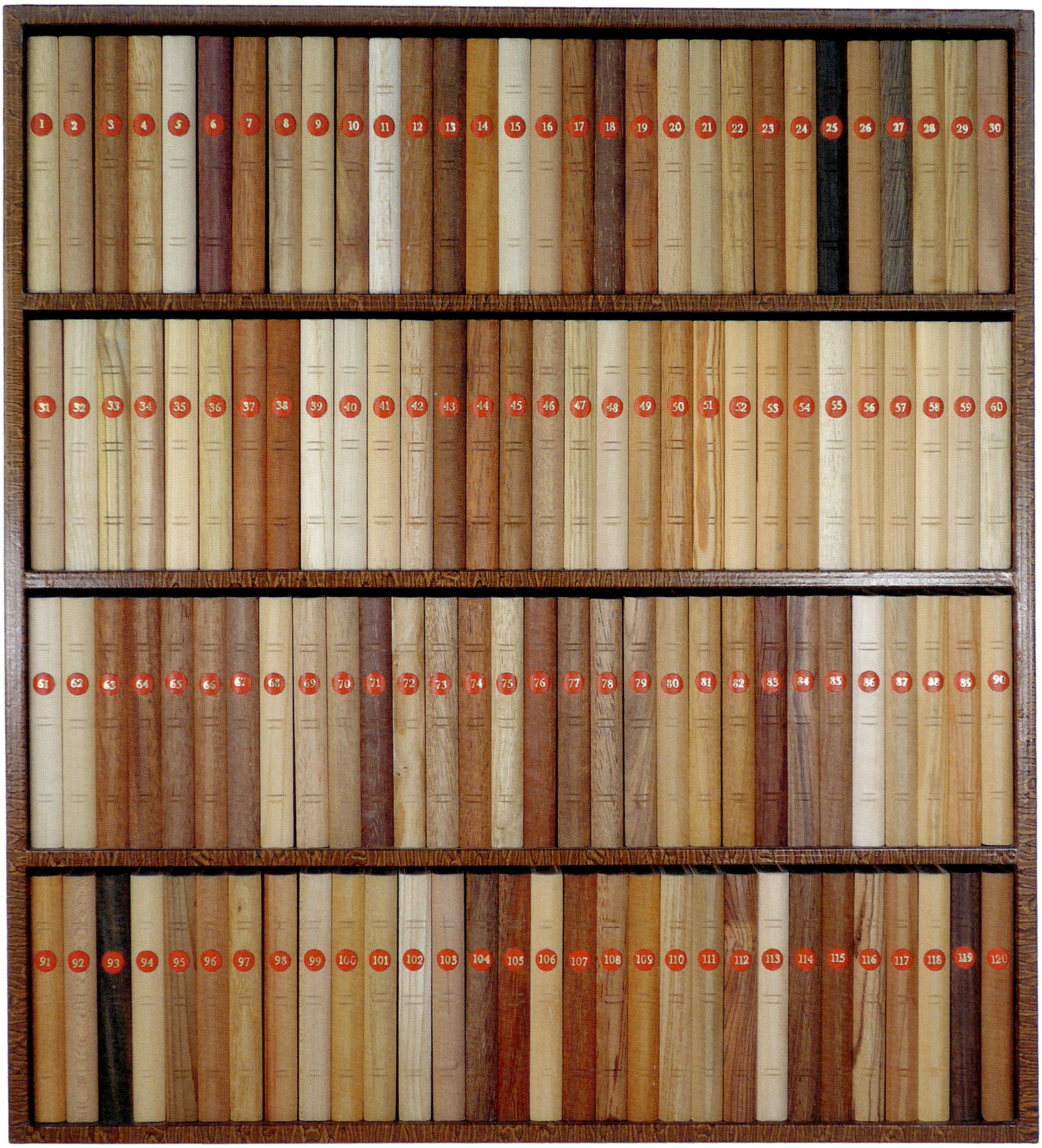

9.018
Speckstein-Buch mit fünf angedeuteten Bünden
Soapstone book with five indicated bands
9,8 x 7,5 x1,3 cm

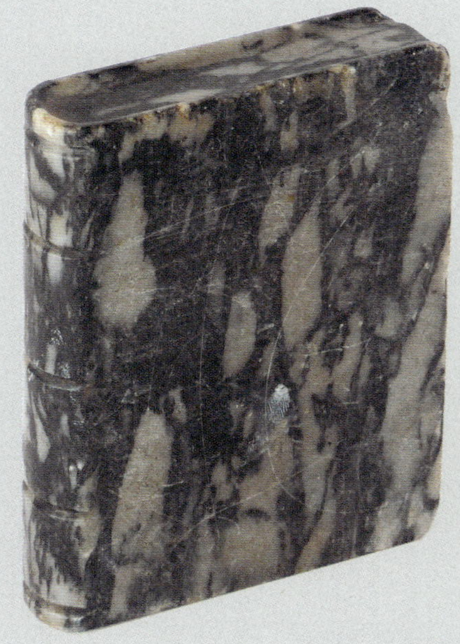

9.019
Kalksteinbruch mit drei erhabenen Bünden, Zierobjekt
Limestone book with three raised bands, for decoration
3 x 2,1 x 1,2 cm

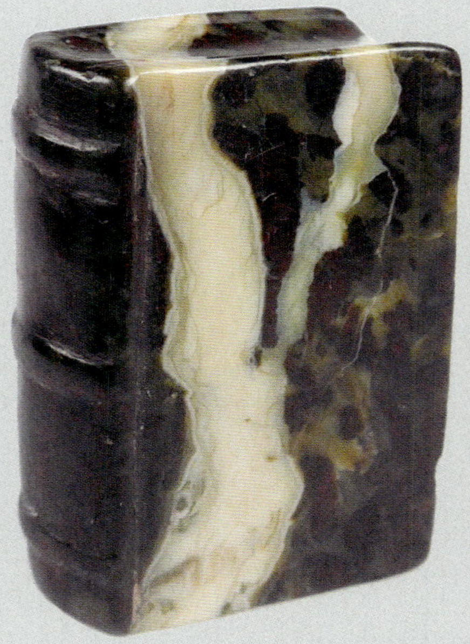

9.020
Lichtenstein Klammen
Kalksteinbruch aus dem Land Salzburg Österreich, gravierter Vorder- und Rückdeckel, Souvenirobjekt
Limestone from the province of Salzburger Land, Austria, engraved front and back cover, souvenir
5,1 x 3,8 x 1 cm

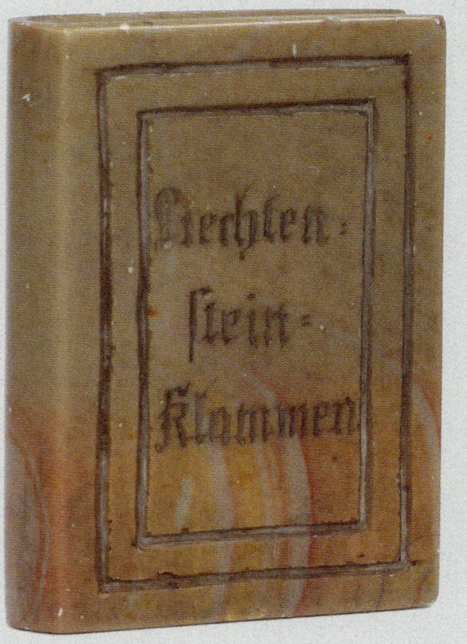

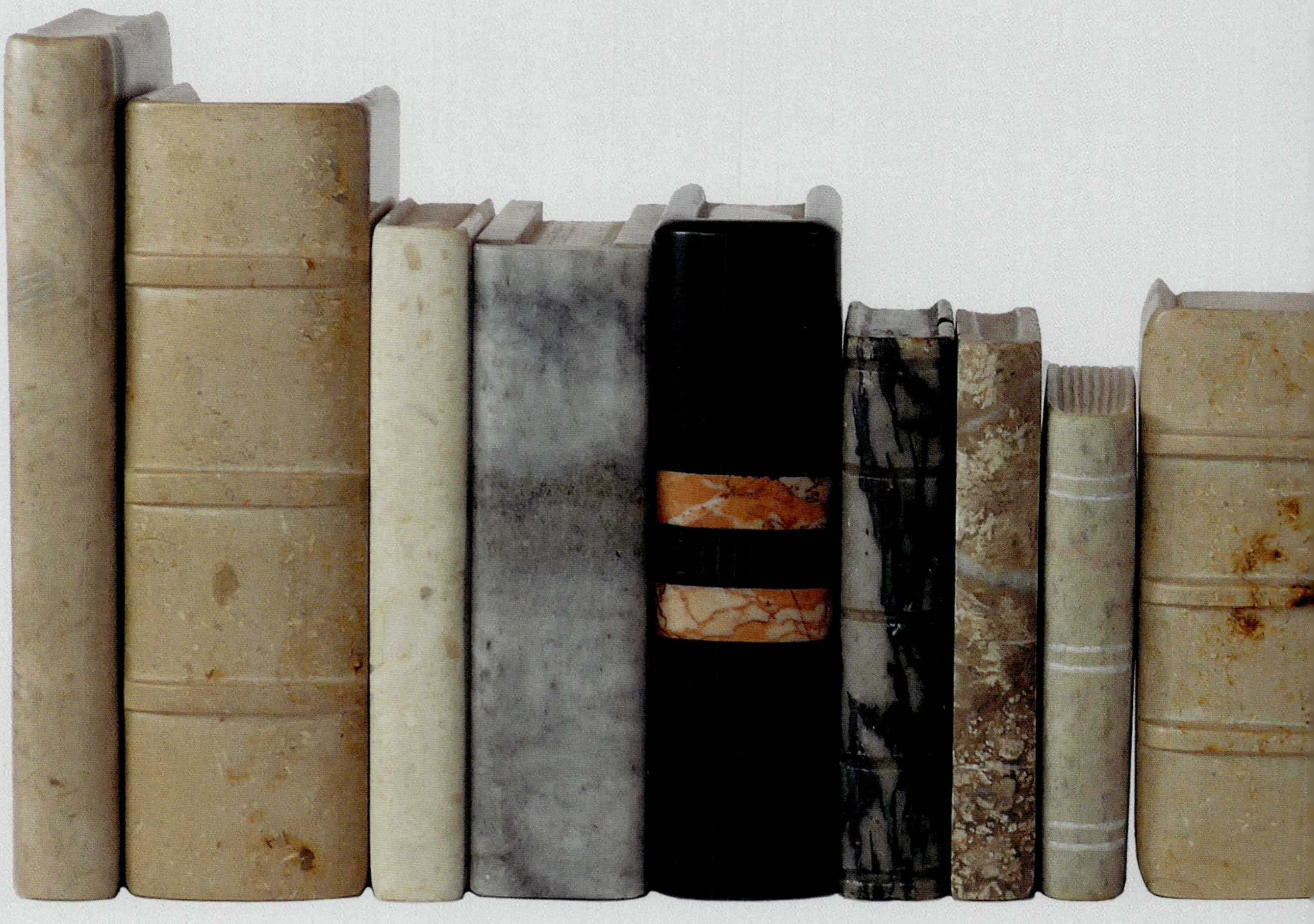

9.021
Jurakalk-Buch (auch Jura-Marmor) mit angedeutetem Falz
Jurassic marble book with suggested fold
15 x 10 x 1,9 cm

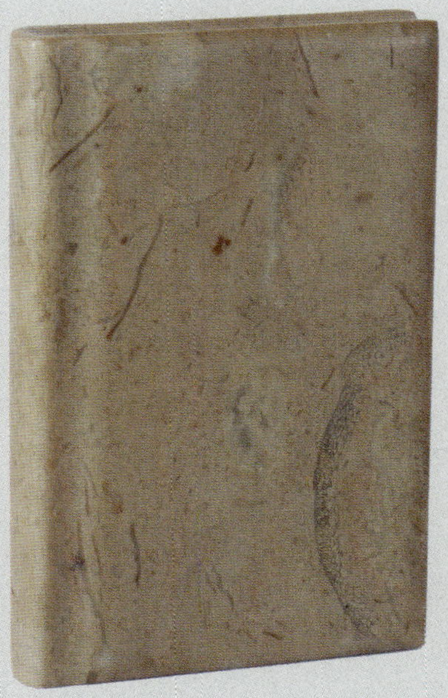

9.022
Sassalbo-Kalkstein-Buch mit drei erhabenen Bünden
Sassalbo limestone book with three raised bands
13,8 x 7,9 x 4,3 cm

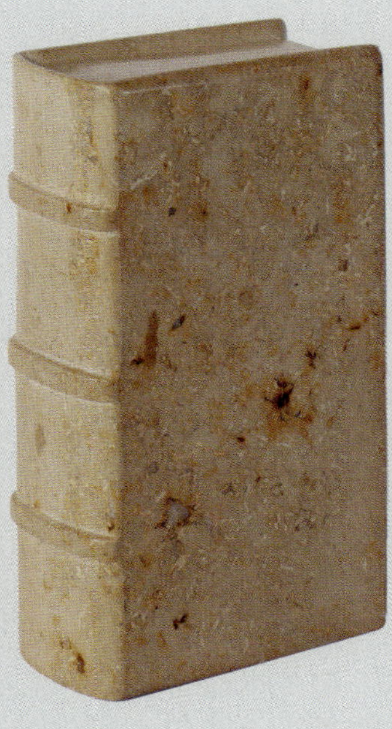

9.023
Marmor-Buch mit aufgesetzten Deckeln und Rücken
Marble book with attached covers and spine
11,4 x 9,7 x 3 cm

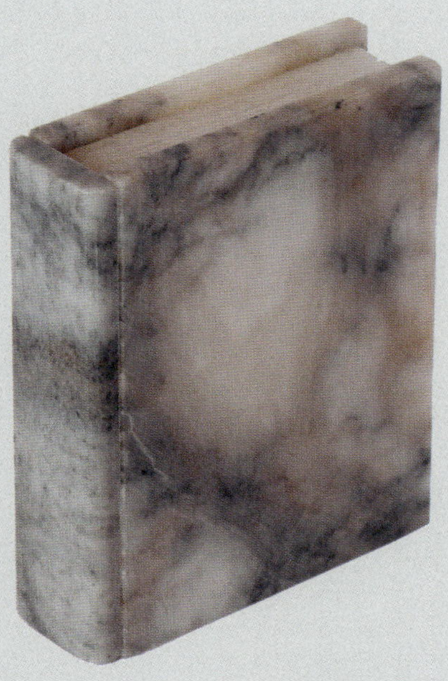

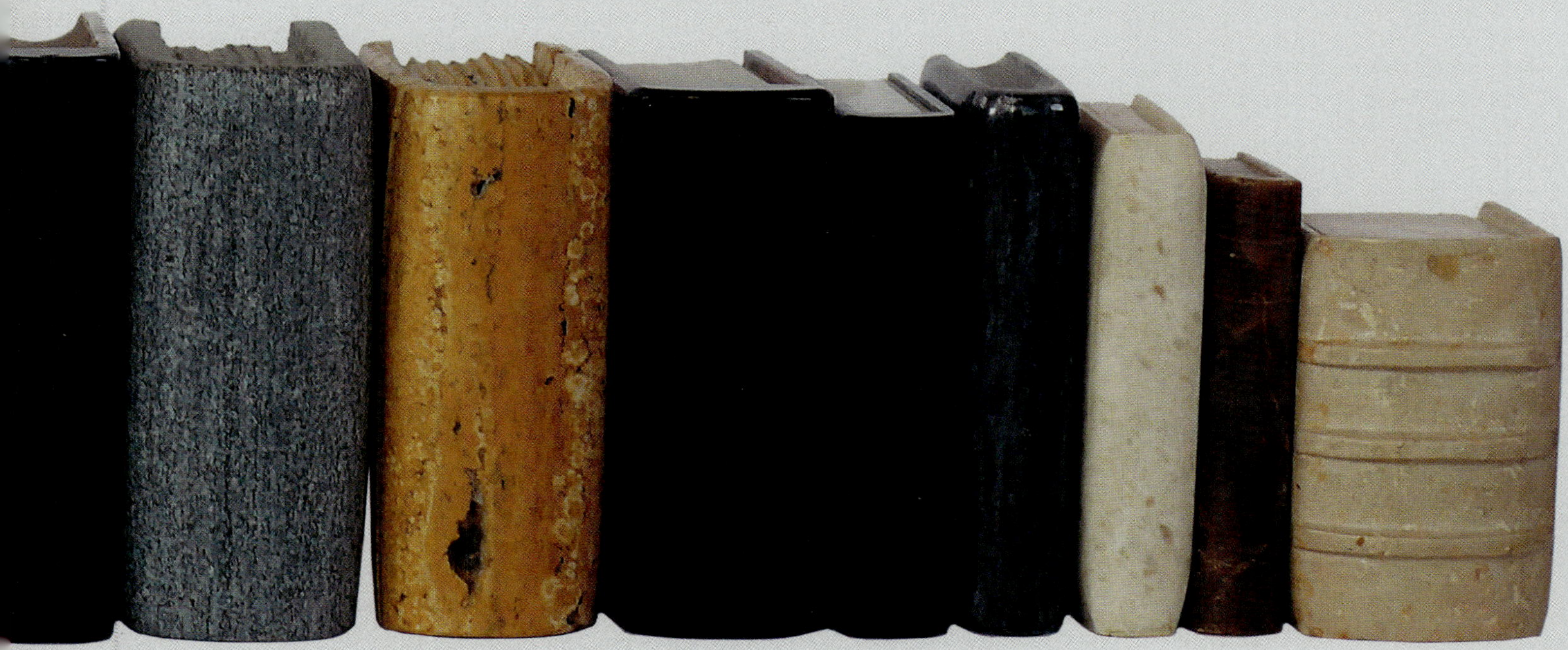

9.024
Marmor-Buch mit aufgesetztem Deckel und Rücken, angedeuteter Falz
Marble book with attached cover and spine, indicated fold
9,4 x 7,1 x 2,2 cm

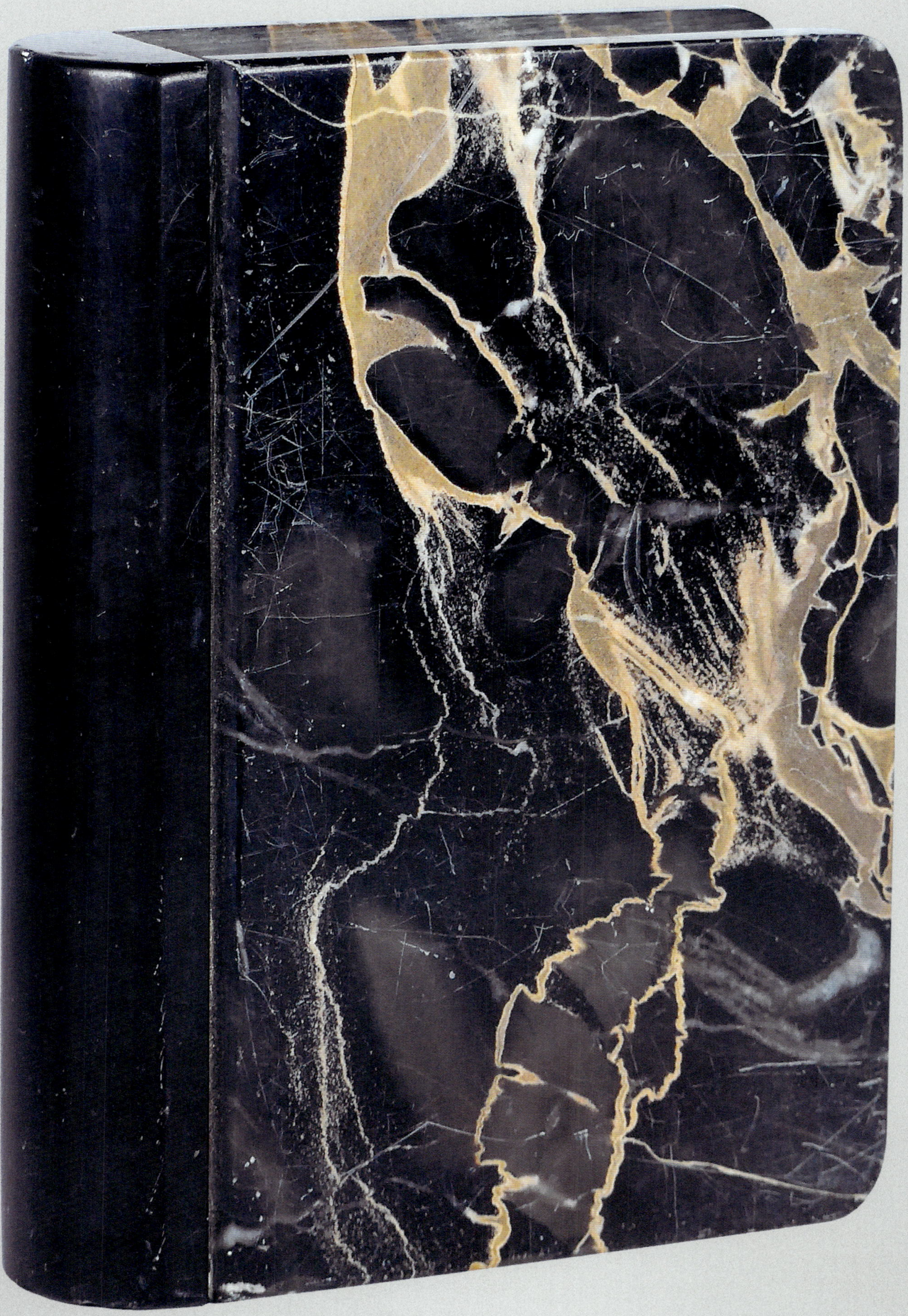

9.025
Marmor-Buch mit aufgesetzten Deckeln und Rücken, zweifarbig, eingelegte Bünde, Gravur, „Bibel, Kreuz mit Rankenwerk“, Monogramm „E.S.“
Marble book with attached covers and spine, two colors, inlaid bands, engraving, „Bible, cross with tendrils“, monogram „E.S.“.
11,8 x 8,6 x 3,3 cm

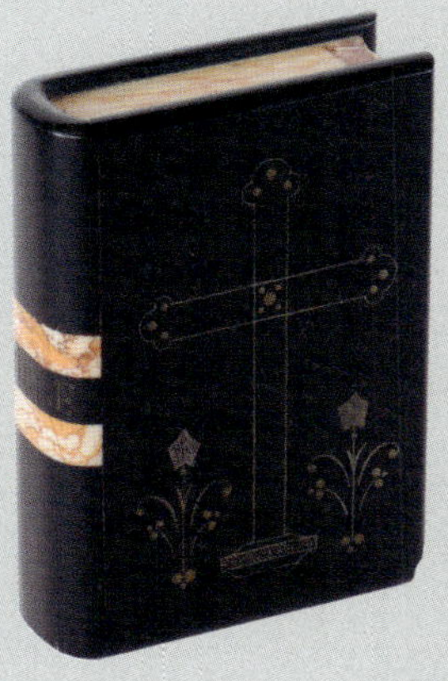

9.026
Marmor-Buch mit Gravur auf dem Rücken „Krieg 1916“
Marble book with engraving on the spine "War 1916"
11,5 x 8,7 x 3,5 cm

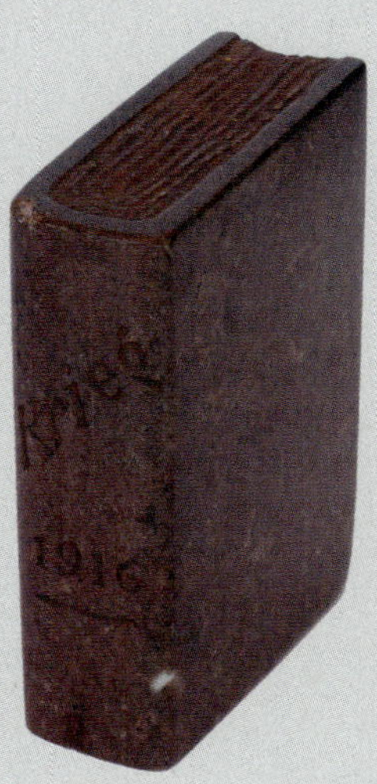

9.027
Sassalbo-Kalkstein-Buch mit drei erhabenen Bünden
Sassalbo and limestone book with three raised bands“
10,3 x 5,7 x 4 cm

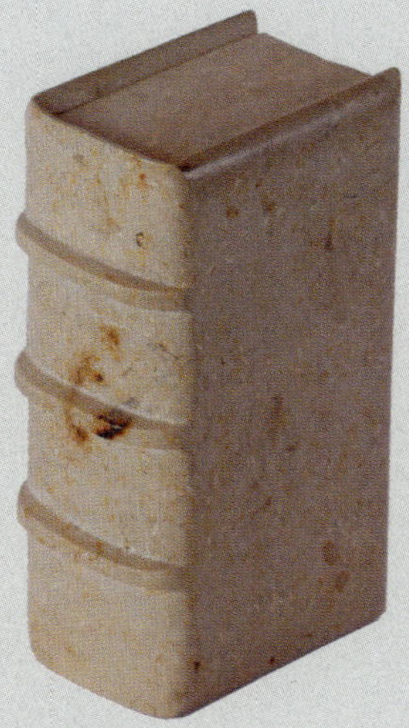

9.028
Marmor-Buch mit aufgesetztem Rücken, zweifarbig, signiert „A. Buess“
Two colors marble book with attached spine, signed "A. Buess"
8,8 x 6,2 x 2 cm

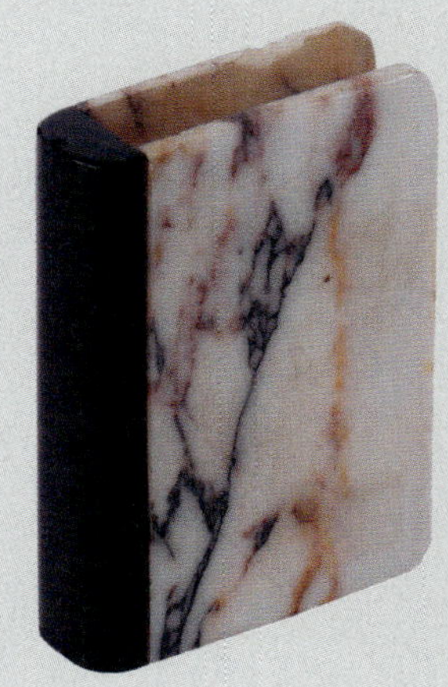

9.029
Marmorbuch mit vier erhabenen Bünden, Zierobjekt
Marble book with four raised bands, for decoration
2,6 x 2 x 0,8 cm

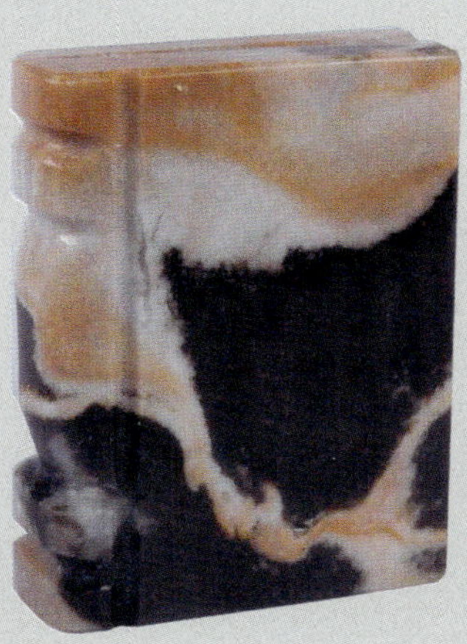

9.030
Onyx-Buch mit drei angedeuteten Bünden, Zierobjekt
Onyx book with three hinted bands, for decoration
3,3 x 2,5 x 0,8 cm

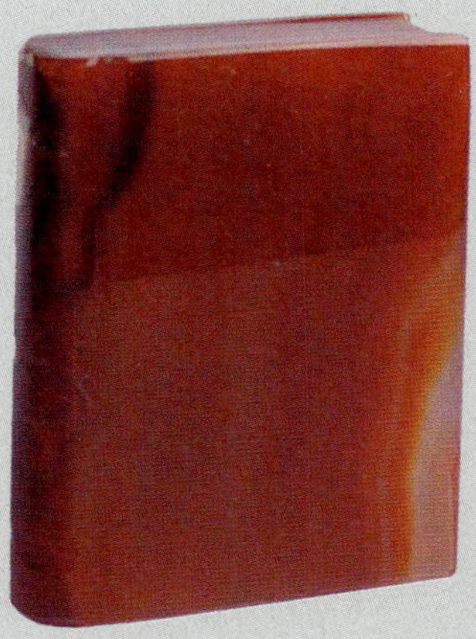

9.031
Marmorbuch mit vier angedeuteten Bünden, Zierobjekt, Handschmeichler
Marble book with four hinted bands, decorative object, a worry stone
5,3 x 4,3 x 0,7 cm

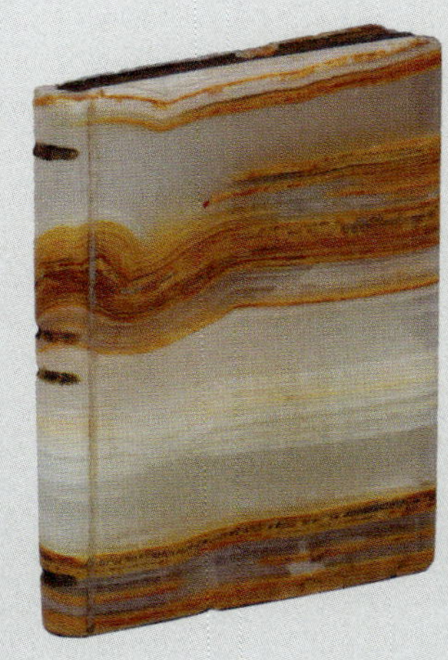

9.032
Wachauer-Marmor-Buch mit angedeutetem Falz
Book made of marble from Wachau with hinted fold
8,2 x 5,4 x 1,8 cm

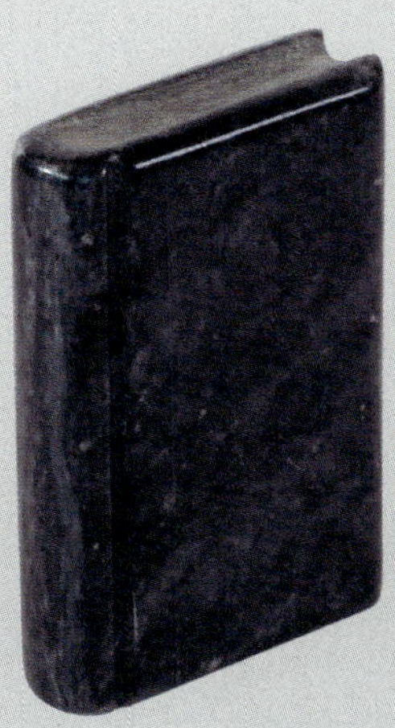

9.033
Marmor-Buch, drei erhabene Bünde, Verwendungszweck unklar
Marble book, three raised bands, use unclear
25,5 x 15,1 x 3,2 cm

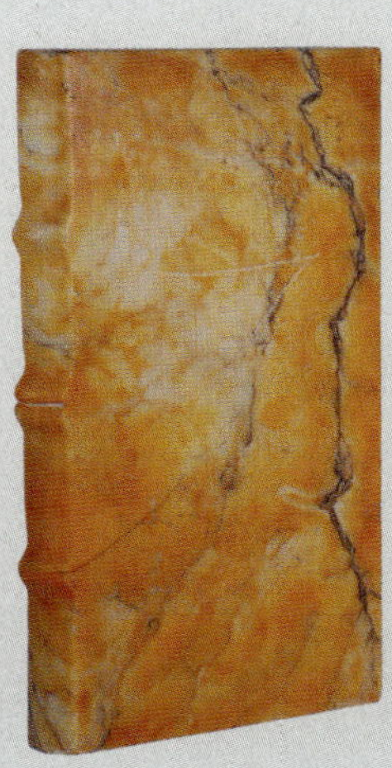

9.034
Kalkstein-Buch mit drei erhabenen Bünden
Limestone book with three raised bands
9,8 x 6,5 x 1,5 cm

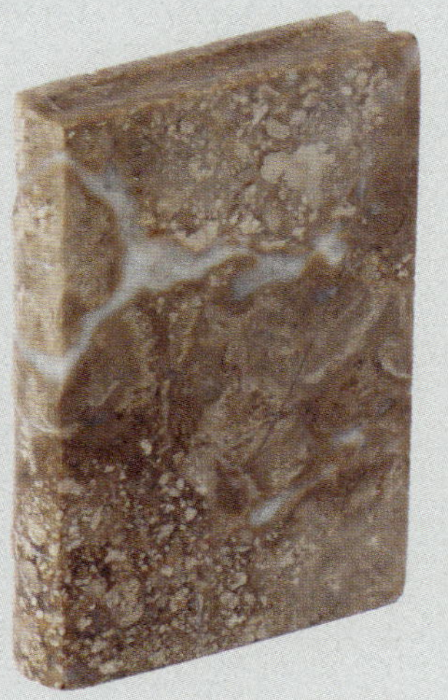

9.035
Kalkstein-Buch (Untersberger-Marmor) mit fünf angedeuteten Bünden, Gravur auf Vorderdeckel „Armin“
Limestone book with five indicated bands, engraving on the front cover "Armin"
8,7 x 6,5 x 1,6 cm

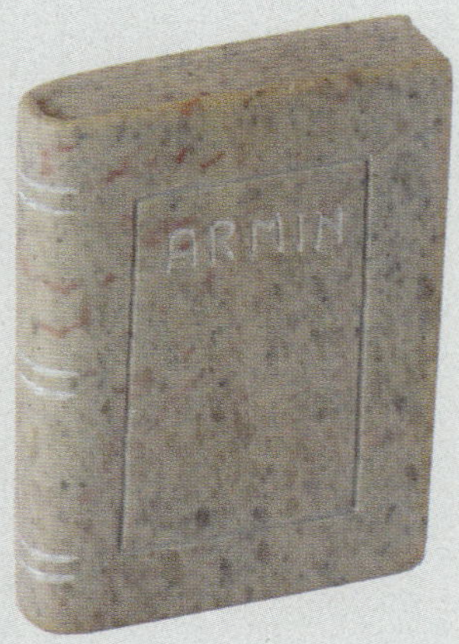

9.036
Jurakalk-Buch mit glattem Rücken
Jurassic limestone book with a smooth spine
4,5 x 3,8 x 2,2 cm

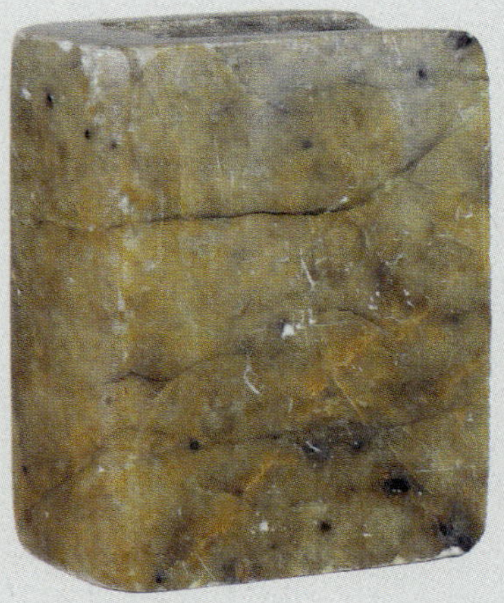

9.037
Buch mit glattem Rücken aus Tessiner Gneisgranit
Book with smooth spine made of gneiss and granite from the Canton of Ticino
8,6 x 7 x 3,6 cm

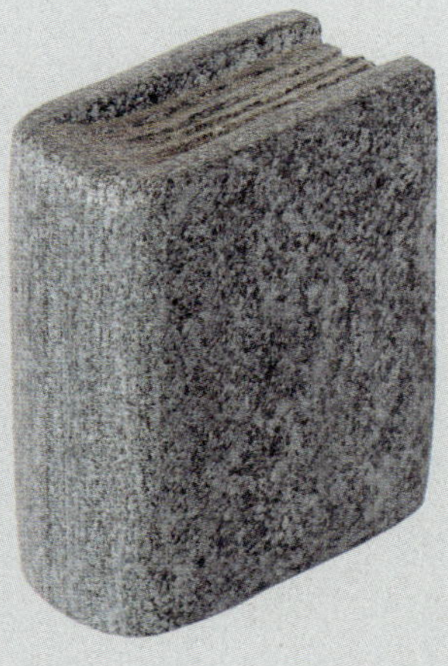

9.038
Travertin-Buch mit angedeutetem Falz
Book made of travertine with a slightly indicated fold
8,3 x 7 x 3,5 cm

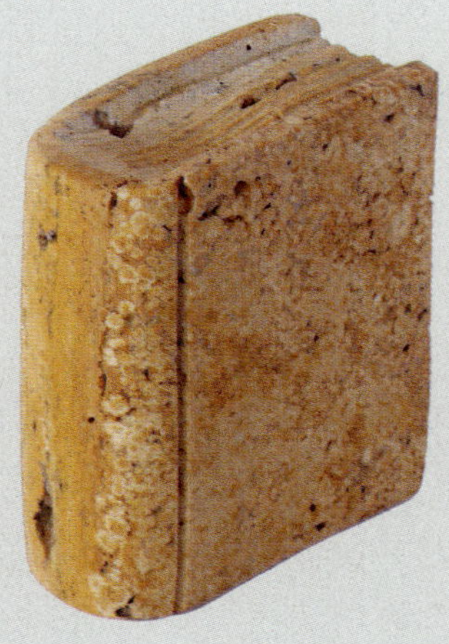

9.039
Foidgestein-Buch mit aufgesetzten Deckeln und Rücken, zweifarbig
Book made of foidite stone in two colors with attached covers and spine
7,9 x 5,6 x 1,9 cm

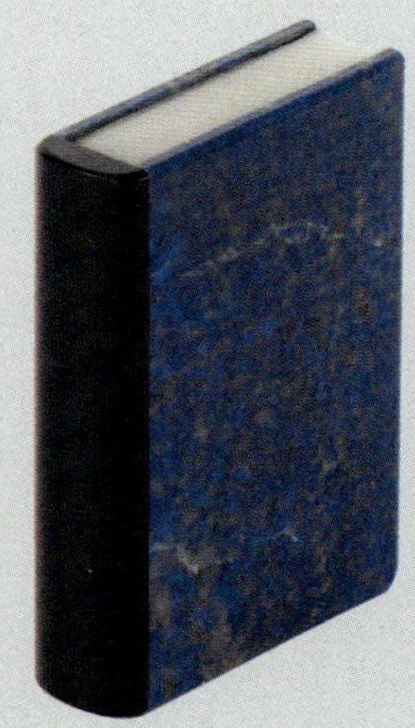

9.040
Onyx-Buch mit angedeuteten Bünden, Gravur auf Vorderdeckel „HYMNS“
Onyx book with indicated cords, engraving on the front cover "HYMNS"
6,8 x 4,3 x 1,3 cm

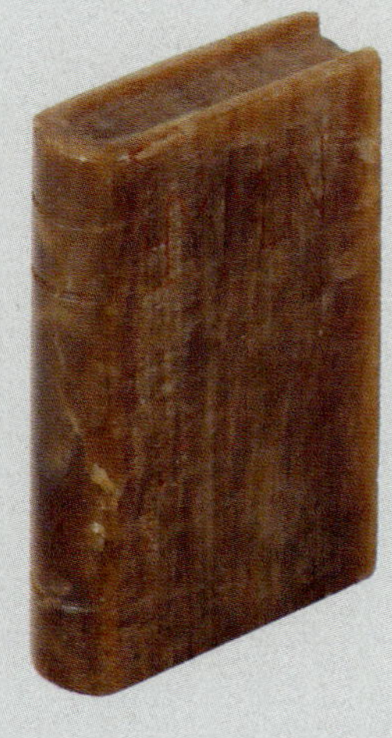

9.041
Sassalbo-Kalkstein-Buch mit drei erhabenen Bünden
Sassalbo limestone book with three raised bands
6 x 5,5 x 4 cm

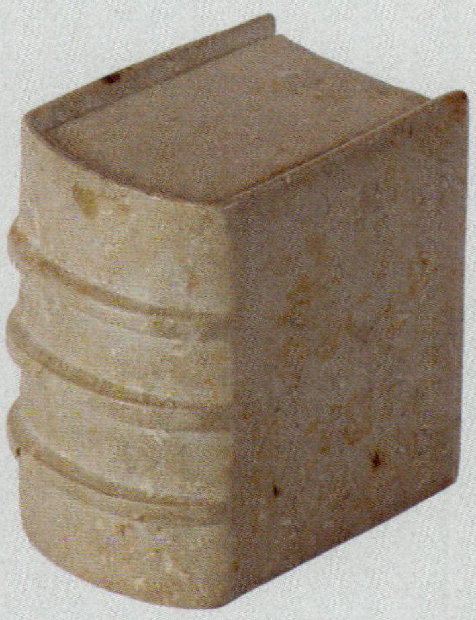

9.042
Sassalbo-Kalkstein-Buch mit glattem Rücken
Sassalbo limestone book with a smooth spine
7,7 x 4,7 x 1,5 cm

9.043
Kalkstein-Buch mit aufgesetzten Deckeln und Rücken, große Ecken, zweifarbig, Schnitt Carrara-Marmor
Book made of limestown in two colors with attached covers and spine, large corners, edges made of Carrara marble
8,1 x 6,7 x 3,2 cm

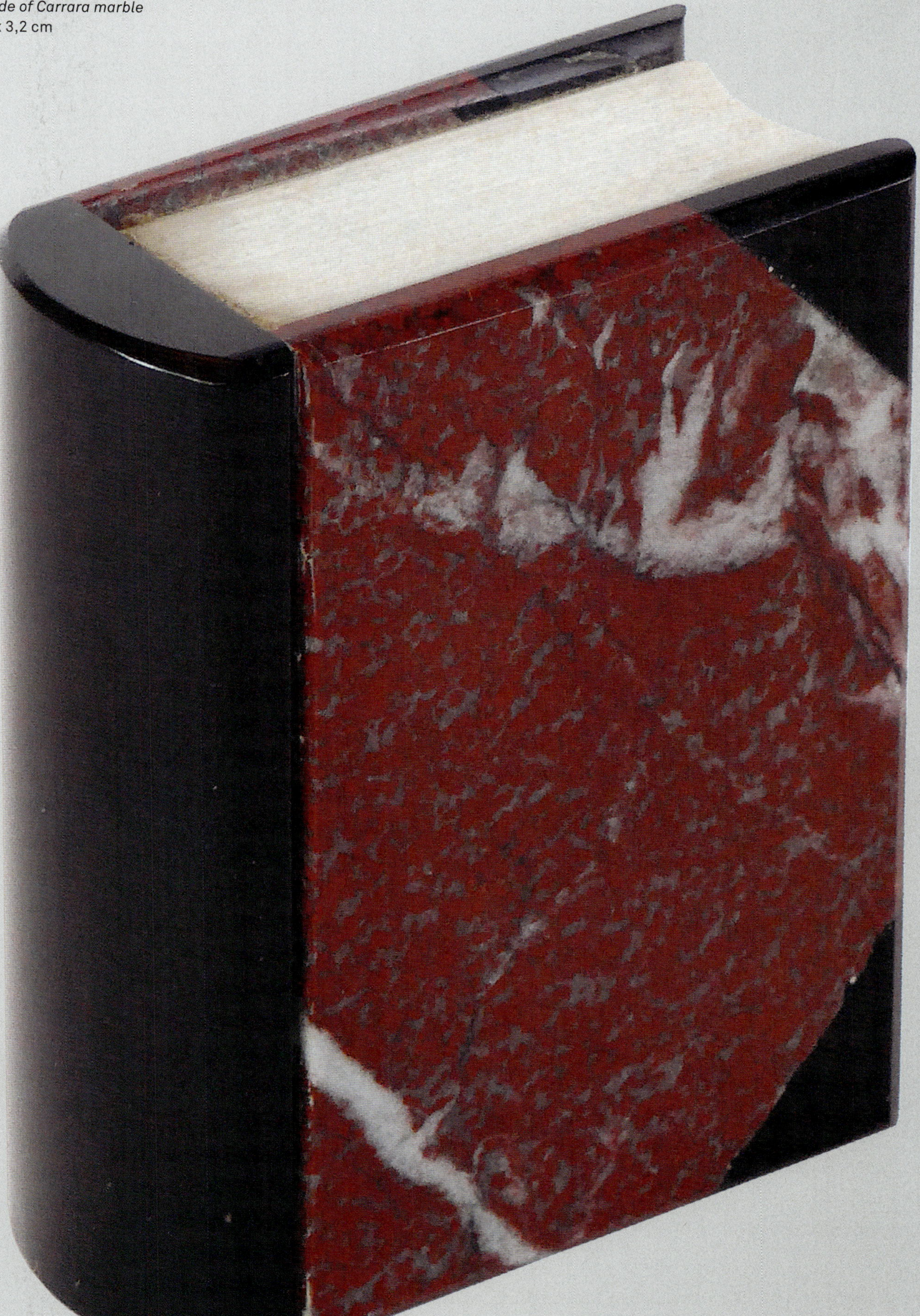

9.044

Bibliothek Johann Caspar Lavater, 1741–1801, Zürich
Buchschatulle aus Leder mit sechs als Büchlein gestalteten Behältnissen, die akribisch grün umrandeten handgeschriebenen Kärtchen zu verschiedenen Themen. 225 Kärtchen von „Abendmahl – Zweck". Einband mit Handvergoldung und Titelschild. Grüner Farbschnitt, zwei Verschlussriegel. Lavater war ein bildbesessener Pfarrer, Philosoph, Schriftsteller sowie ein Hauptvertreter der Physiognomie. Widmung auf Spiegel: „An Catharina Cramer, den 25.XI 1792"

Library Johann Caspar Lavater, 1741–1801, Zurich
A leather box with six containers designed as booklets contaning handwritten cards on different topics with meticulous applied green edges, 225 cards by "Abendmahl – Zweck", manual gilding on the covers, title label, green edges, two closure latches. Lavater was an image-obsessed priest, philosopher, writer and a main representative of physiognomy. Dedication on the pastedown: "To Catharina Cramer, the 25th of XI 1792"
9,5 x 6,4 x 3,9 cm

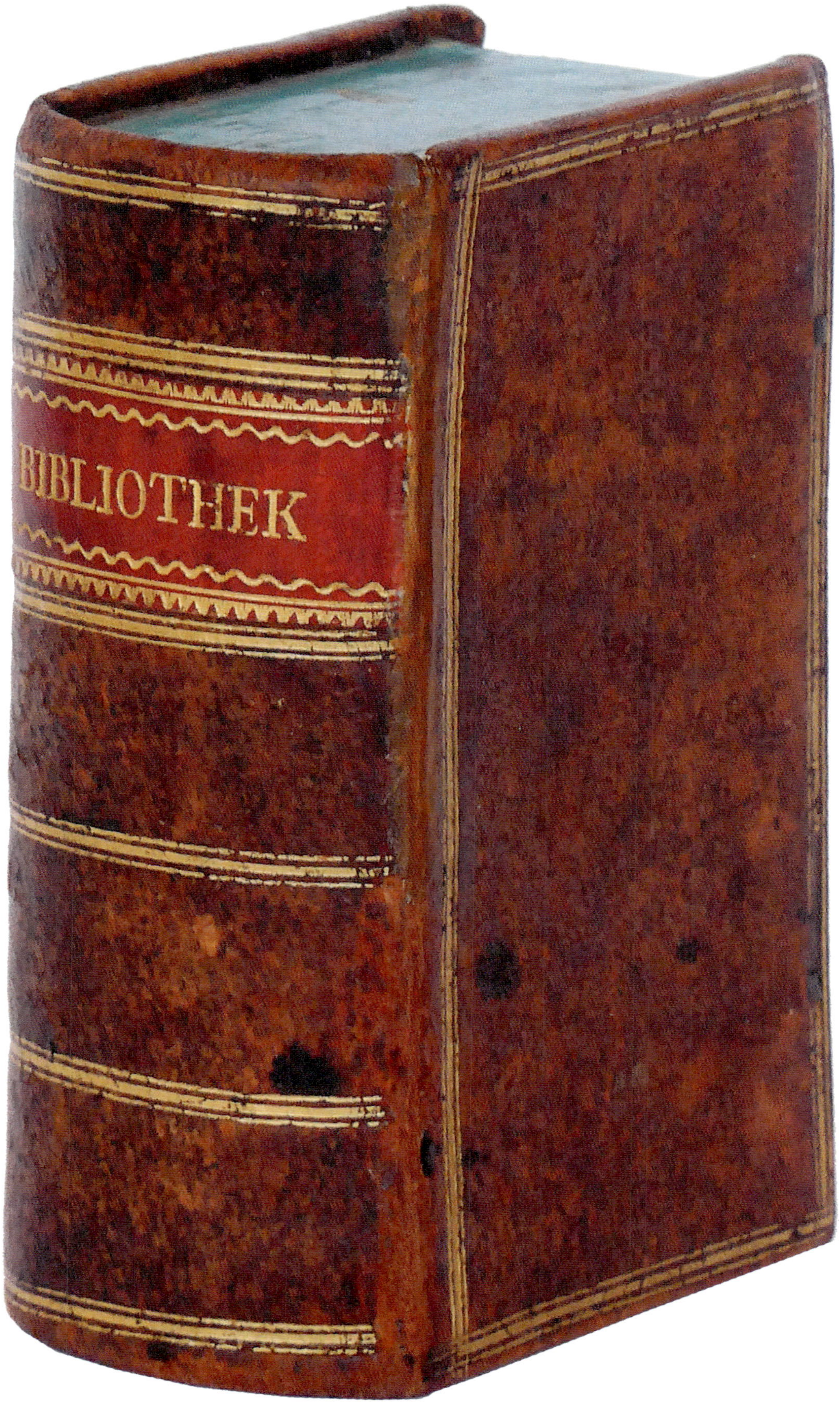

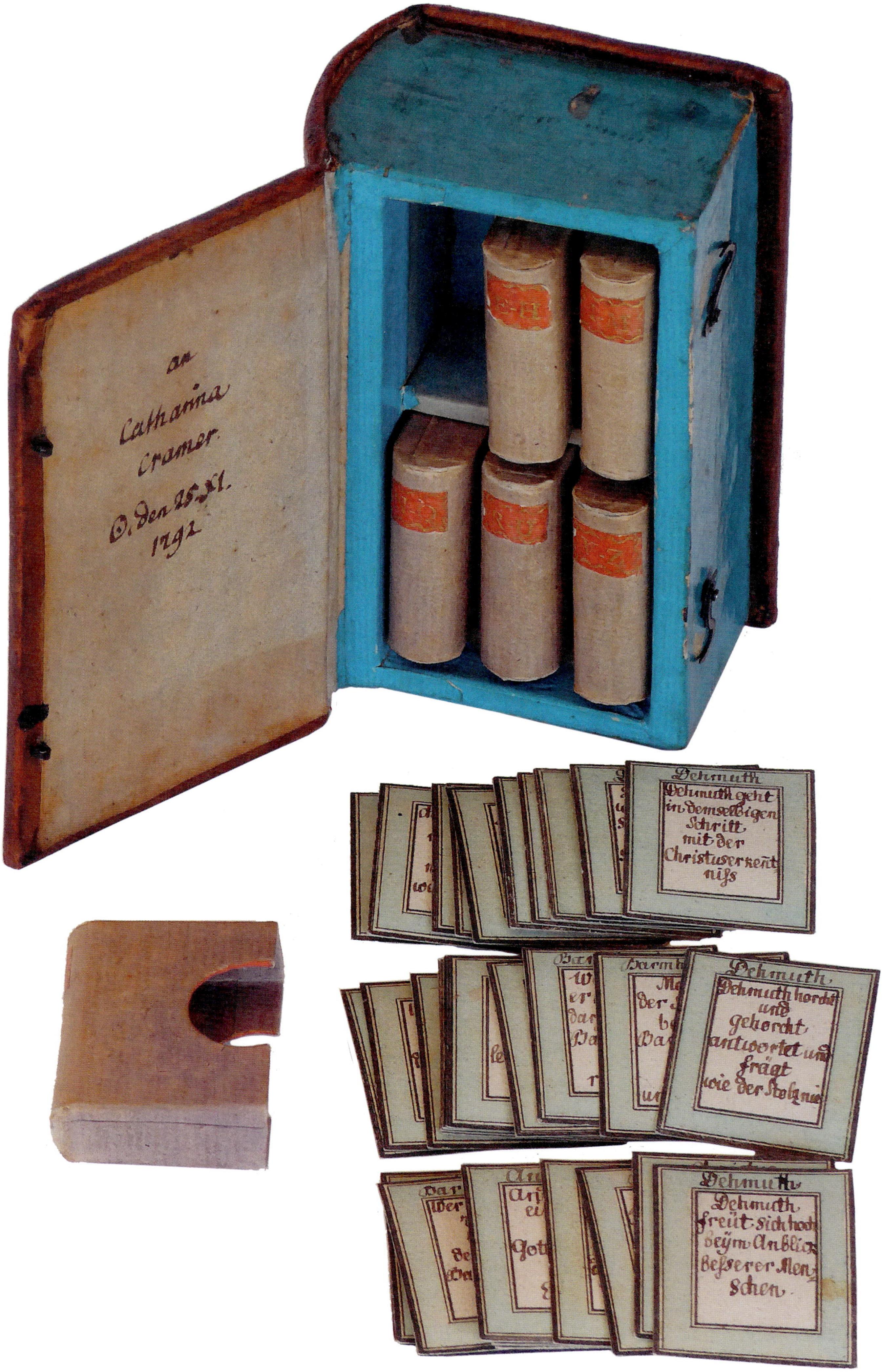
an
Catharina
Cramer
Dehmuth
Dehmuth geht in demselbigen Schritt mit der Christuserkentniß
Dehmuth
Dehmuth horcht und gehorcht antwortet und frägt wie der Stolz nie
Dehmuth
Dehmuth freüt sich hoch beÿm Anblick beßerer Menschen

9.045
Goethe, Schiller, Schwan, Lessing
Miniholzbücher mit rotem Papierrücken, schwarz lackiert, golden beschriftet und verziert, dreiseitiger Goldschnitt, Puppenstubenbibliothek
Wooden mini books with red paper spine strips black varnish, golden lettering and ornaments, all edges gilt, a dollhouse's library
3,5 x 2,7 x 0,8 cm

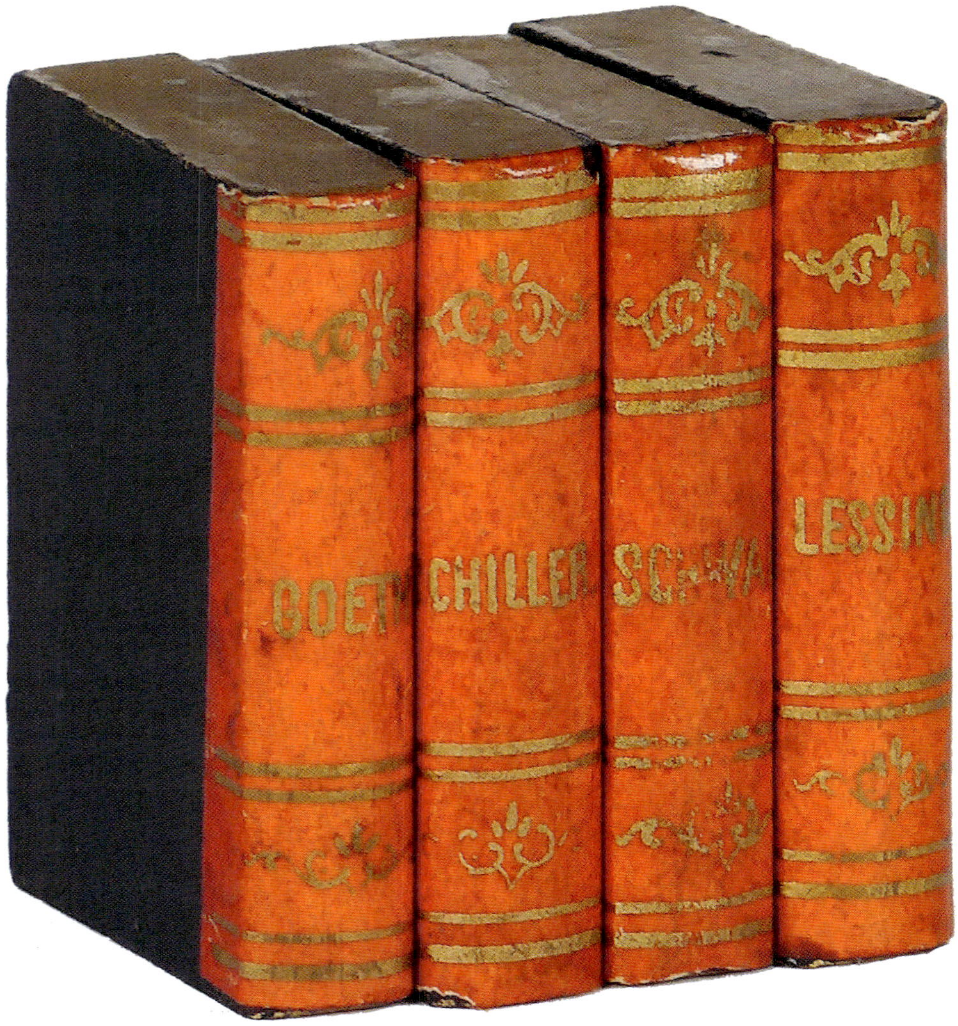

9.046
The Language
Vier Lilliput Langenscheidt Wörterbücher in einer Halblederkassette mit großen Ecken, Rückenschild, Steinmarmorüberzug, kleine Box mit Notizblock, Gummi und Bleistift, Vergrößerungsglas, dreiseitiger Kammmarmorschnitt.
Four Lilliput dictionaries by Langenscheidt in a half leather case with large corners, label on the spine, stone marbled paper cover, small box with notepad, rubber and pencil, magnifying glass, all edges comb marbled
Hersteller / *Manufacturer*: Sybille & August Wirz Winterthur, Switzerland
12,5 x 11,8 x 5,3 cm

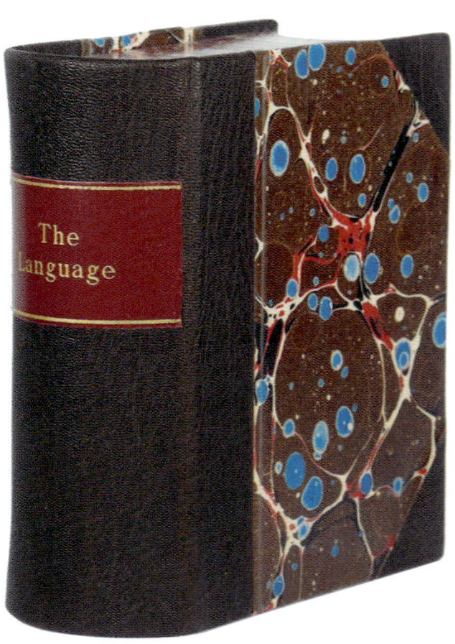

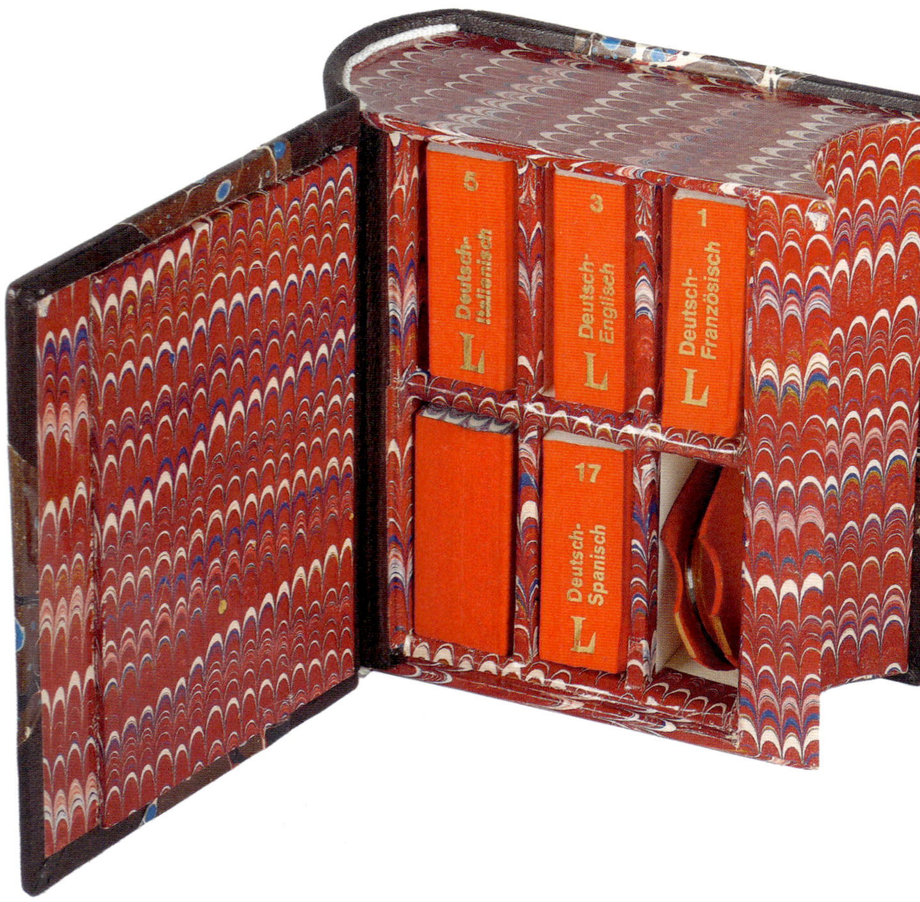

9.047
Ausgehöhlter Saffianhalbledereinband mit eingebautem Büchergestell, Miniatur Bibliothek, verschiedene Scheinbuchein-bandarten und Epochen
Saffian half leather binding with integrated book support, miniature library, various types of fake book bindings and epochs
22,1 x 15 x 4,5 cm

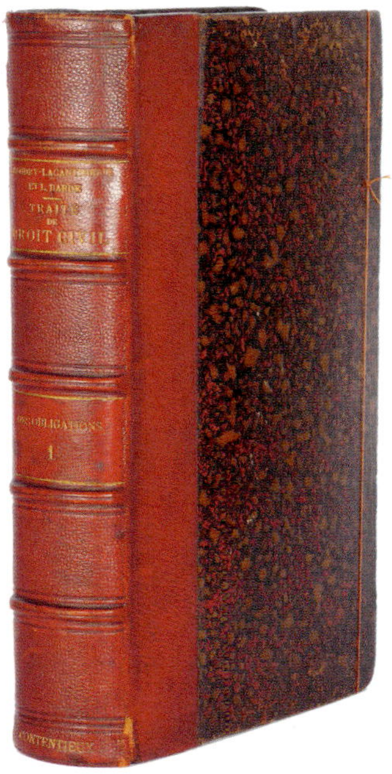

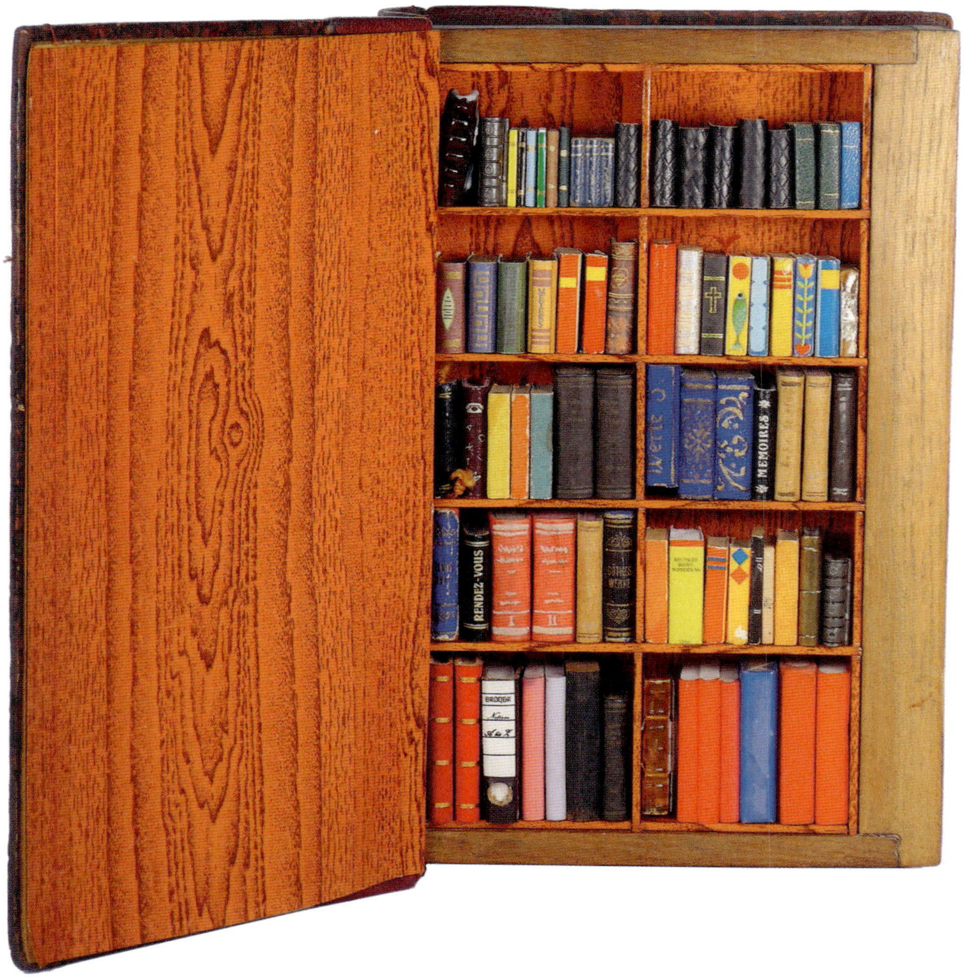

9.048
Müller's Bücherei / *Library*
Sechzehn Bucheinbandarten in einer Ganz-lederkassette, ausziehbare Tablare, Titelschild und Rückenvergoldung, Messingschließe, dreiseitiger Goldschnitt, Goldpapierspiegel
Sixteen types of book bindings in a full leather box, pull-out shelves, gilt title and spine, brass buckle, all edges gilt, golden inner lid
Hersteller / *Manufacturer*: Sybille & August Wirz Winterthur, Switzerland
18 x 13,1 x 6 cm

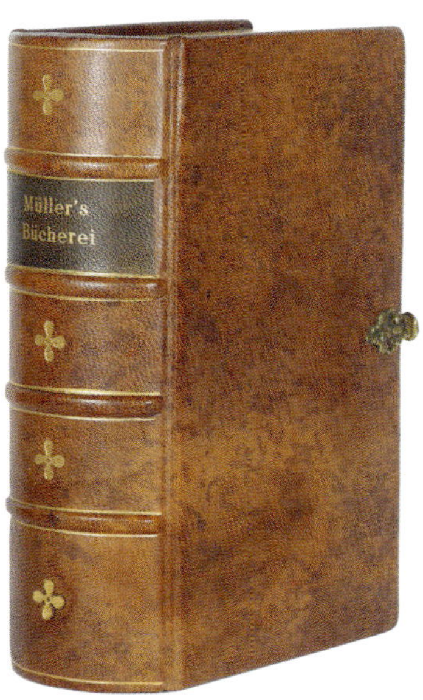

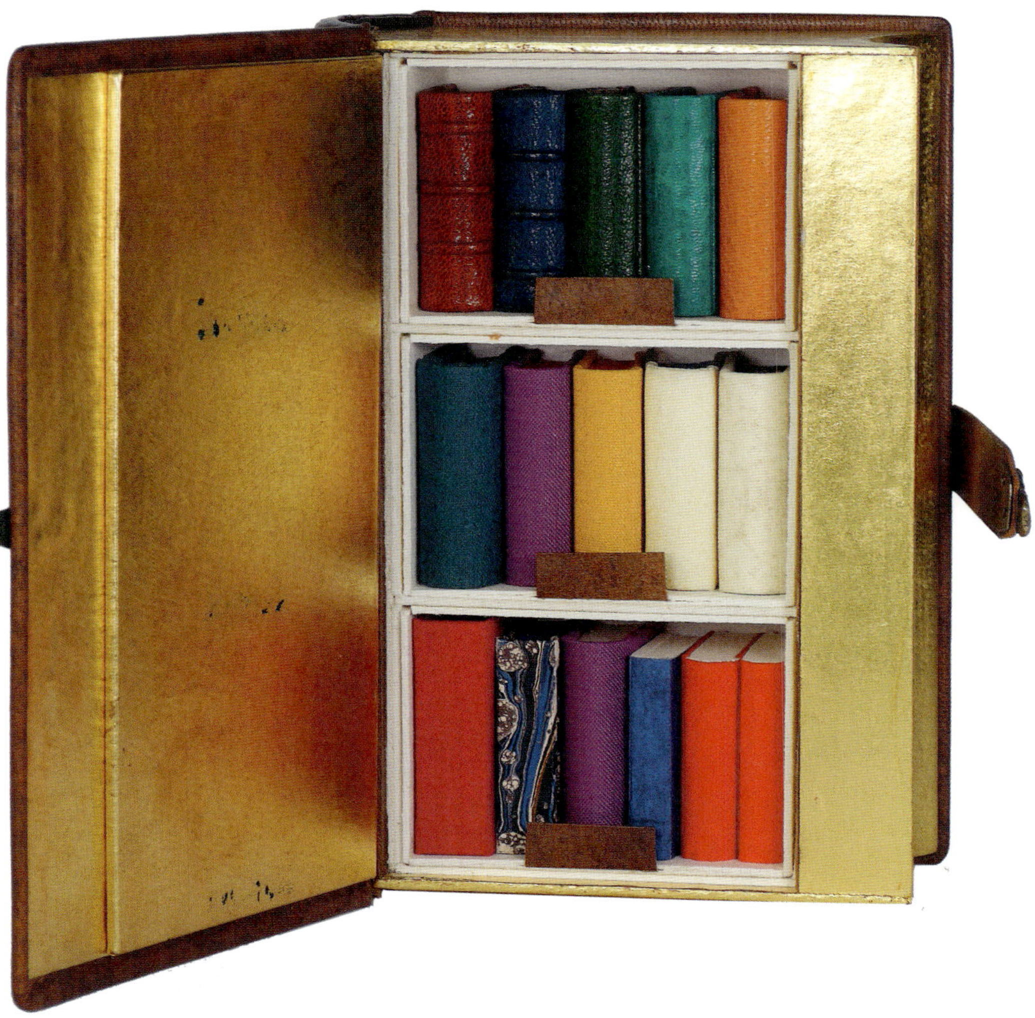

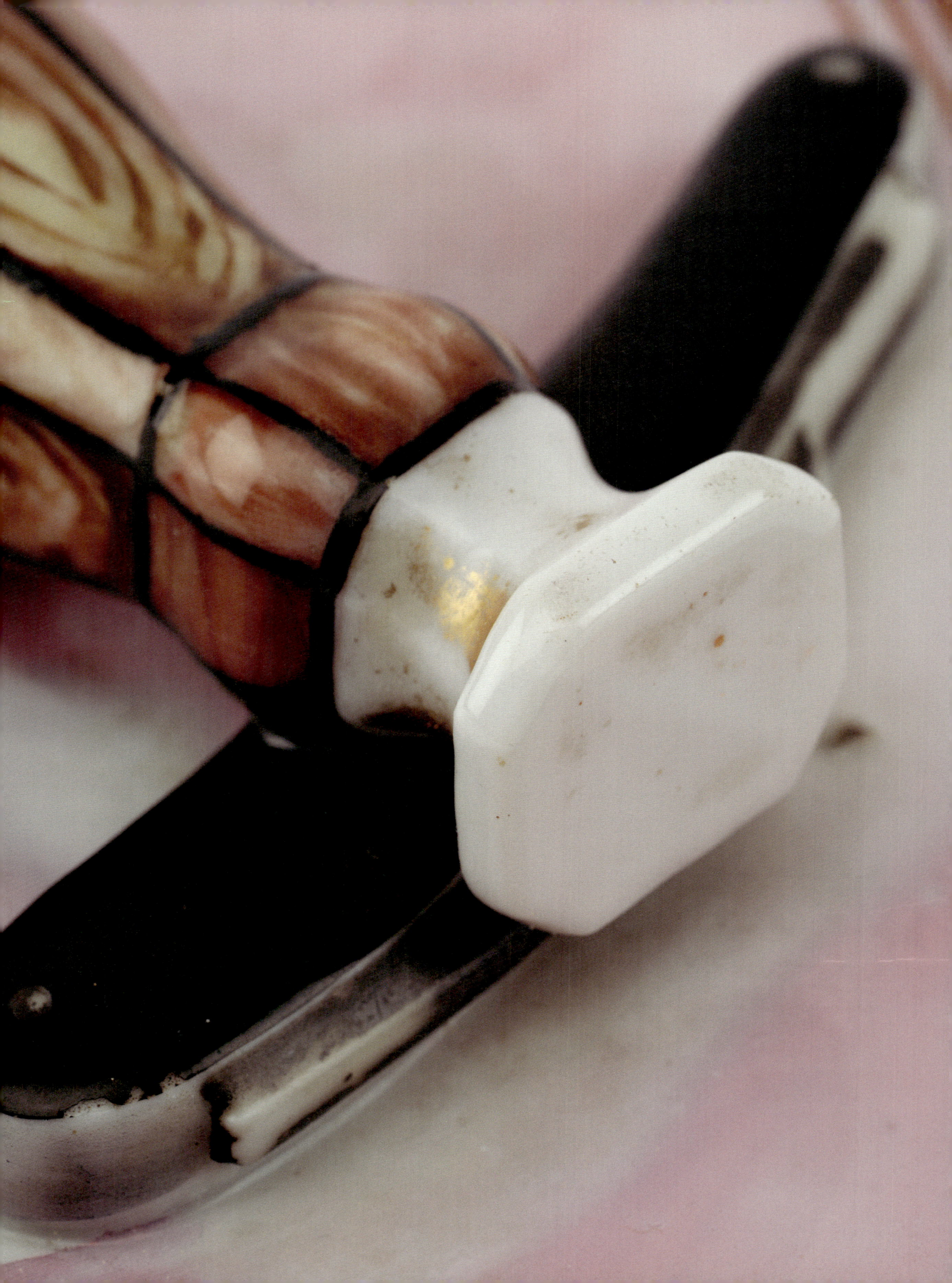

Büro
Office

Es gibt kaum Objekte, die echten Büchern so ähneln wie Büroartikelschachteln oder Stammbücher und Poesiealben mit kunstvoll handvergoldeten Lederrücken. Sie weisen die hohe Qualität eines von einem Fachmann gefertigten Buches auf. Oftmals wurden dieselben Materialien verwendet, wie sie auch in Handbuchbindereien zur Anwendung kommen: Buntpapier, Gewebe, Karton, Leder und Prägungen in Farbe oder in Gold.

Im täglichen Gebrauch leisten Bürobutler als Aufbewahrungshilfen für Briefmarken, Gummibänder, Büroklammern, Federn, Radiergummis oder Fotoecken große Dienste. Ebenso praktisch sind die Schreibzeugschatulle aus Bakelit mit zehn Klassiker-Buchrücken, die Blechdose mit eingebautem Bleistiftspitzer, das Reisetintenfässchen in einem rotem Ledereinband, verschiedene Radiergummis, die Löschwiege aus Messing mit sitzender Eule auf einem aufgeschlagenen Buch, die Signierapparate für Pharmazeuten und das Bronzepetschaft mit Totenkopf auf einem geschlossenen Buch.

Die Briefbeschwerer meiner Sammlung sind aus Keramik und Glas. Filz oder Stoff auf der Unterseite verhindert das Verrutschen. Die sogenannten „Millefiore Glass Paperweights“ sind sehr beliebte Sammlerstücke, die auf Auktionen gehandelt werden. Lange gesucht habe ich Briefbeschwerer aus Vollglas. Eine Glasmanufaktur wäre bereit gewesen, das gewünschte Objekt herzustellen, doch hätte die Fertigung mein Sammlerbudget arg strapaziert. Kurz darauf fand ich zum Glück zwei wunderbare antike Stücke aus Vollglas zu einem vernünftigen Preis im Antiquitätenhandel.

Für Ordnung und Übersicht sorgen mehrheitlich um 1900 gefertigte Schatullen und Behältnisse für Postkarten und Fotos aus den unterschiedlichsten Materialien wie Blech, Karton, Papier, Leder, Gewebe und Kunststoff.

Hardly any objects resemble real books as much as office-supply boxes, family albums, and poetry albums with artistically hand-gilded leather spines. They show the high quality of a book made by a specialist. Often the same materials have been used as those used in manual binderies: colored paper, fabric, cardboard, leather, and embossing in color or gold.

In daily use, so-called "office butlers" are very useful for storing stamps, elastic bands, paper clips, pens, erasers or photo corners. Equally useful are a bakelite pencil box with ten classic book spines, the tin box with a built-in pencil sharpener, the travel inkwell in a red leather cover, various erasers, the rocker blotter made of brass with an owl sitting on an open book, the signing apparatus for pharmacists, and the bronze skull-and-crossbones shaft on a closed book.

The paperweights in my collection are made of ceramic and glass. Felt or cloth on the bottom prevents them from slipping. The so-called "Millefiore Glass Paperweights" are very popular collector's items which are traded at auctions. For a long time, I had been looking for paperweights made of solid glass. A glass manufacturer was ready to produce the desired object, but the production would have exceeded my collector's budget. Shortly afterwards I found two wonderful antique pieces made of solid glass at a reasonable price in antique shops.

The caskets and containers for postcards and photos, mostly from around 1900, keep things organized and are manufactured from the most diverse materials, such as sheet metal, cardboard, paper, leather, fabric, and plastic.

10.001
Briefbeschwerer aus Keramik, farbig bemalt, Petschaft und Messer als Griff, Bleistift mit Lasche am Vorderschnitt, Gewebeboden, dreiseitiger Goldschnitt
Ceramic paperweight, painted in color, a seal and knife as handle, pencil with flap at the fore edge, bottom made of fabric, all edges gilt
4,4 x 15,1 x 9,4 cm

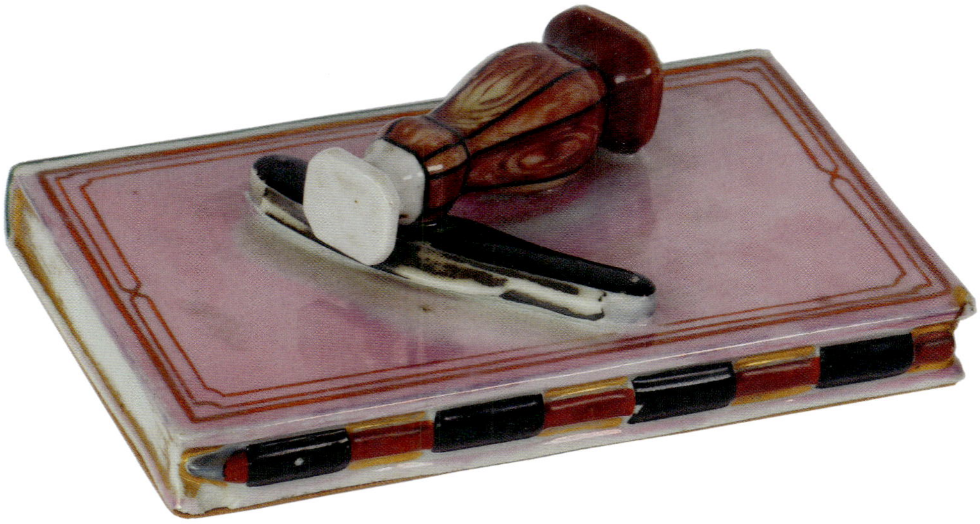

10.002
The complete ancier, Izaak Walton
Briefbeschwerer aus bemaltem Stein und Relief-Metallfisch auf dem Vorderdeckel, zwei Titelschilder, dreiseitiger Goldschnitt, Filzboden
Paperweight made of painted stone and a metallic fish in relief on the front cover, two title labels, all edges gilt, bottom made of felt
3,5 x 13,9 x 9 cm

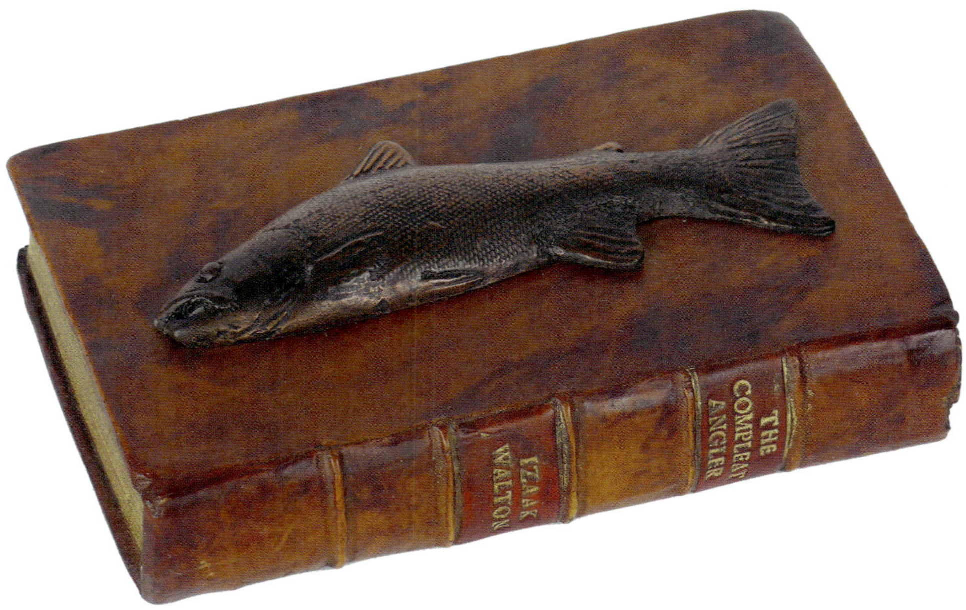

10.003
Some books are to be tasted others, To be swallowed and some few, To be chewed and digested
Briefbeschwerer aus Keramik, florales Goldmuster mit ovalem Titelschild auf der Vorderseite, dreiseitiger Goldschnitt, Filzboden
Ceramic paperweight, floral ornaments in gold with an oval title on the cover, all edges gilt, bottom made of felt
2 x 10,7 x 7,2 cm

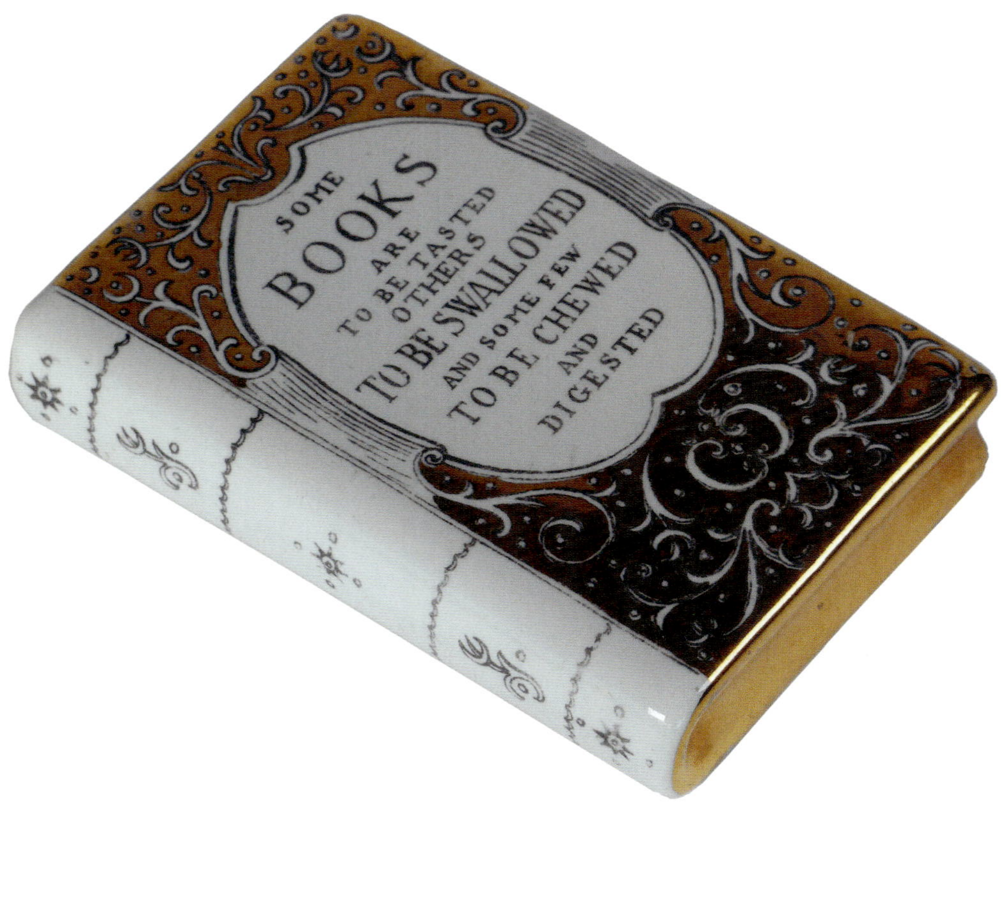

10.004
Briefbeschwerer aus Keramik, florales Goldmuster mit ovalem Damenporträt auf der Vorderseite, Filzboden
Ceramic paperweight, floral pattern in gold, oval plate with the portrait of a lady on the cover, bottom made of felt
2 x 14 x 8,1 cm

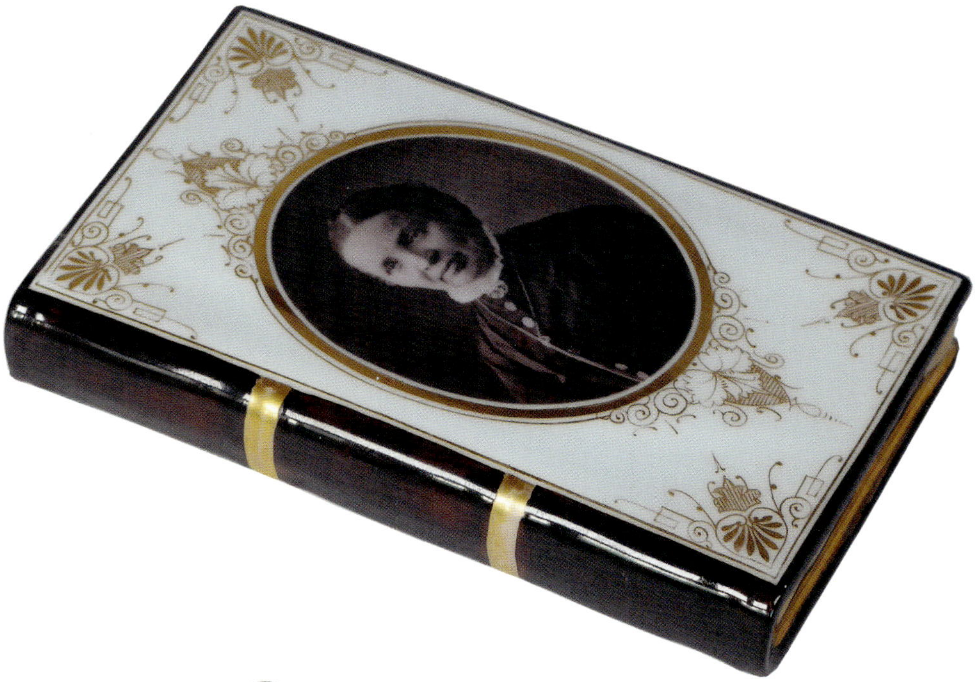

10.005
Briefbeschwerer aus Keramik, florales Goldmuster und Blumenbouquet auf der Vorderseite, dreiseitiger Goldschnitt, Filzboden
Ceramic paperweight, floral design in gold with an oval plate on the cover, all edges gilt, bottom made of felt
2 x 13,6 x 8 cm

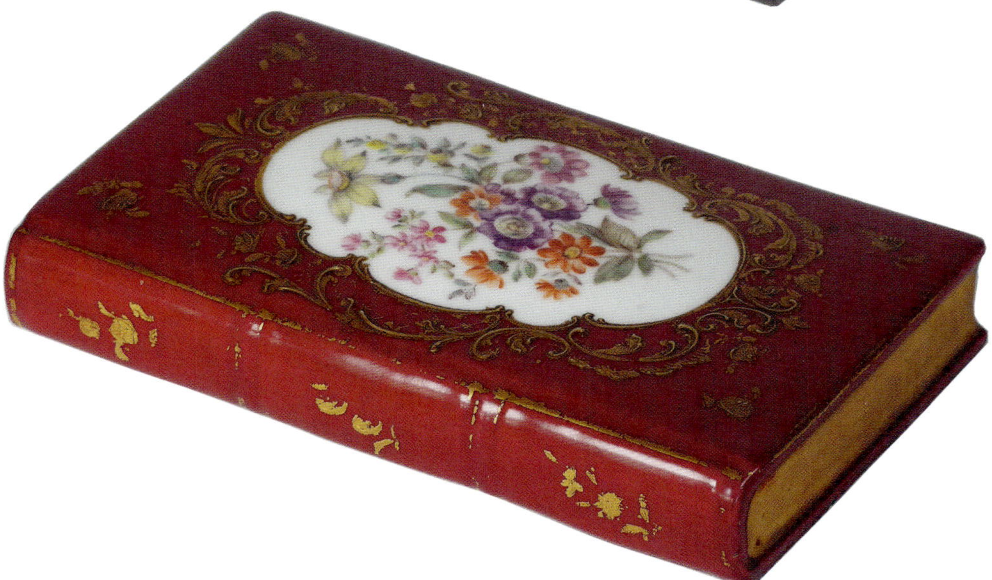

10.006
Briefbeschwerer aus Vollglas, geätzt und geschliffen, Hinterseite dunkel bemalt
Paperweight made of solid glass, etched and cut, the back is painted in dark color
Um / *Around1900* | 3 x 11 x 8,5 cm

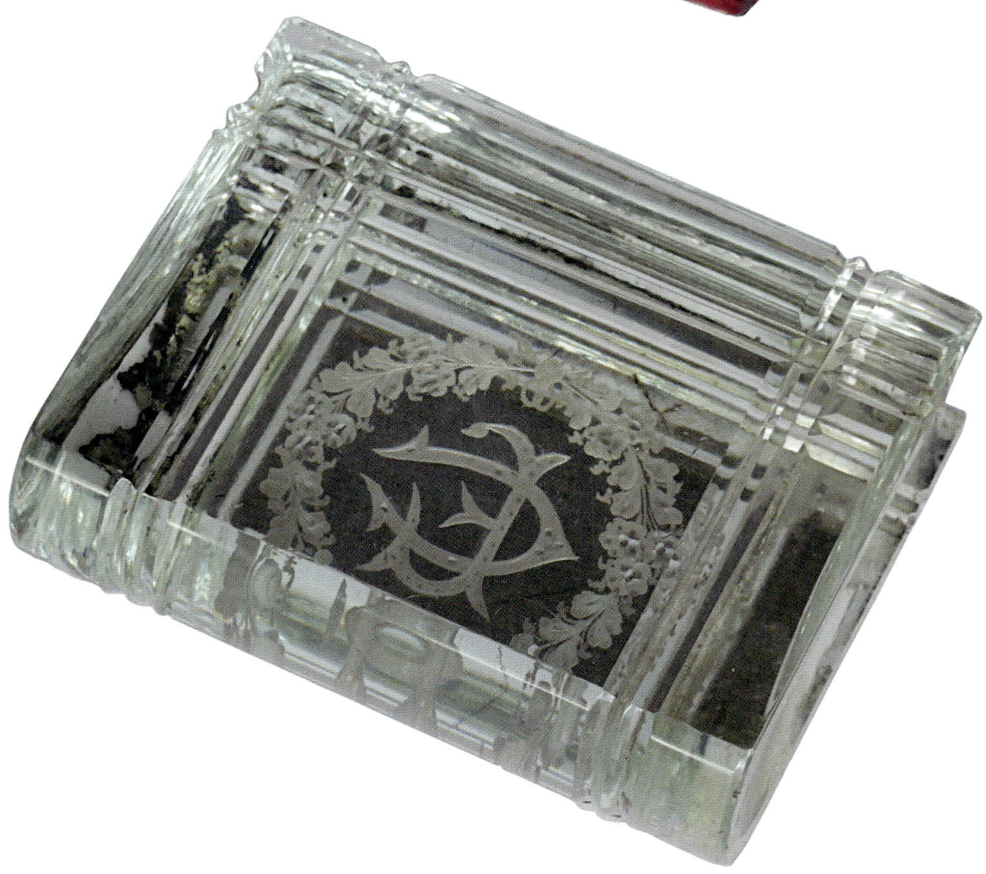

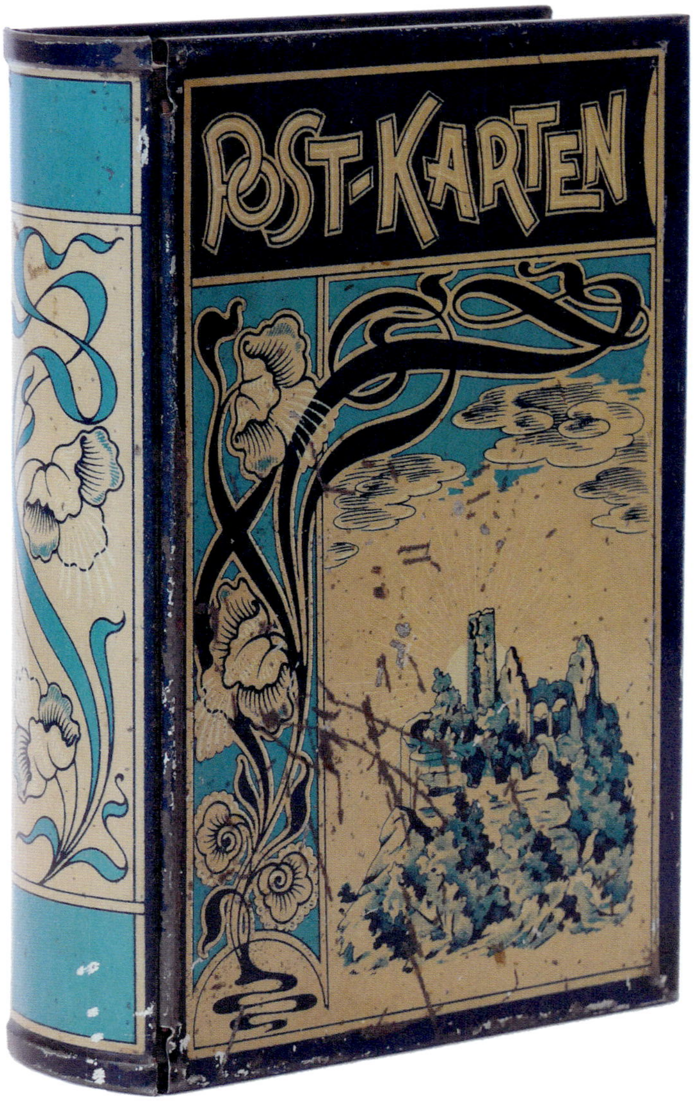

10.007
Lithografierte Jugendstil-Blechdose
für Postkarten
Lithographed tin box for postcards
Jugendstil / *Art Nouveau*
Um / *Around* 1900 | 15,8 x 11,2 x 3,9 cm

10.008
Grüsse aus der Ferne / ***Greetings from afar***
Postkarten-Sammler-Album,
lithografierte Blechdose
Album for a postcard collection,
lithographed tin box
Jugendstil / *Art Nouveau* | Um / *Around* 1900
10,7 x 31,3 x 21,3 cm

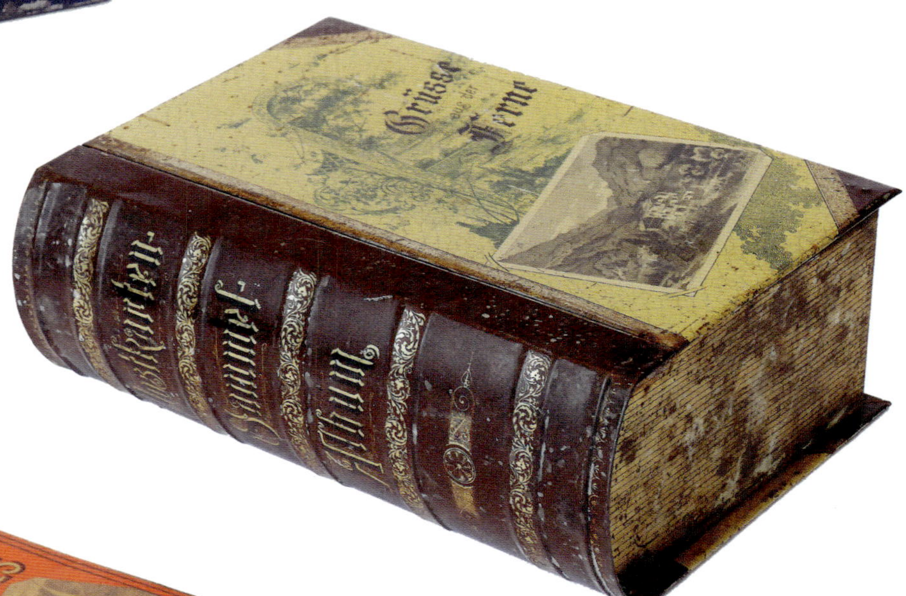

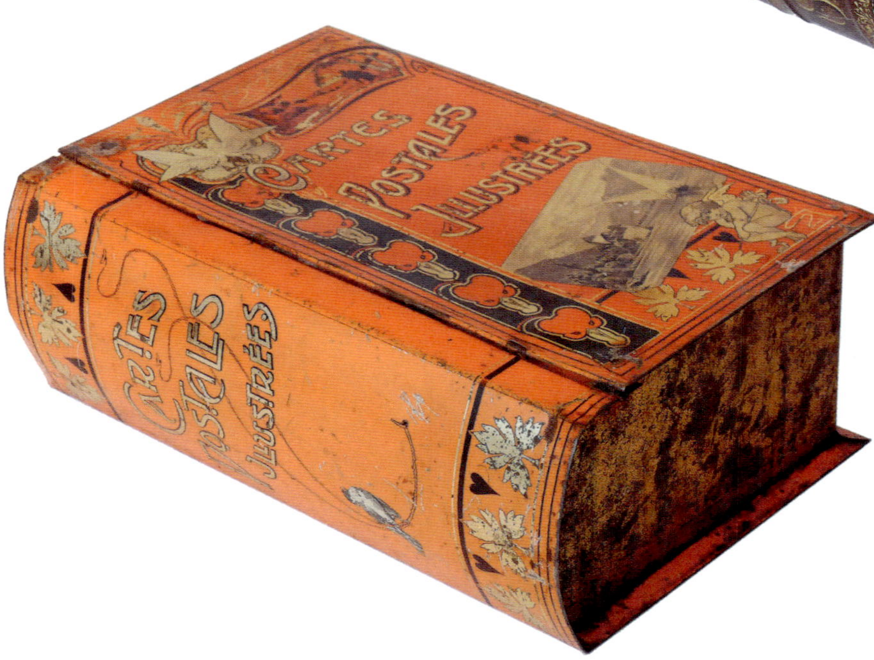

10.009
Cartes Postales Jllustrées
Lithografierte Blechdose mit Schloss Chillon
Lithographed tin box with the Chillon Castle
Jugendstil / *Art Nouveau*
Um / *Around* 1900 | 10,3 x 30,1 x 20 cm

10.010
Stereographic Library. United States, Vol. I + II, Keystone View Co.
Die 105 Stereobilder, die einen räumlichen Eindruck vermitteln, hauptsächlich Ansichten aus Amerika, werden mittels einem Schuber in die Buchkassette eingeschoben.
The 105 stereo pictures, which provide a spatial effect, mainly pictures taken in the USA, are inserted into the box by using a slipcase.
19 x 18 x 10,2 cm

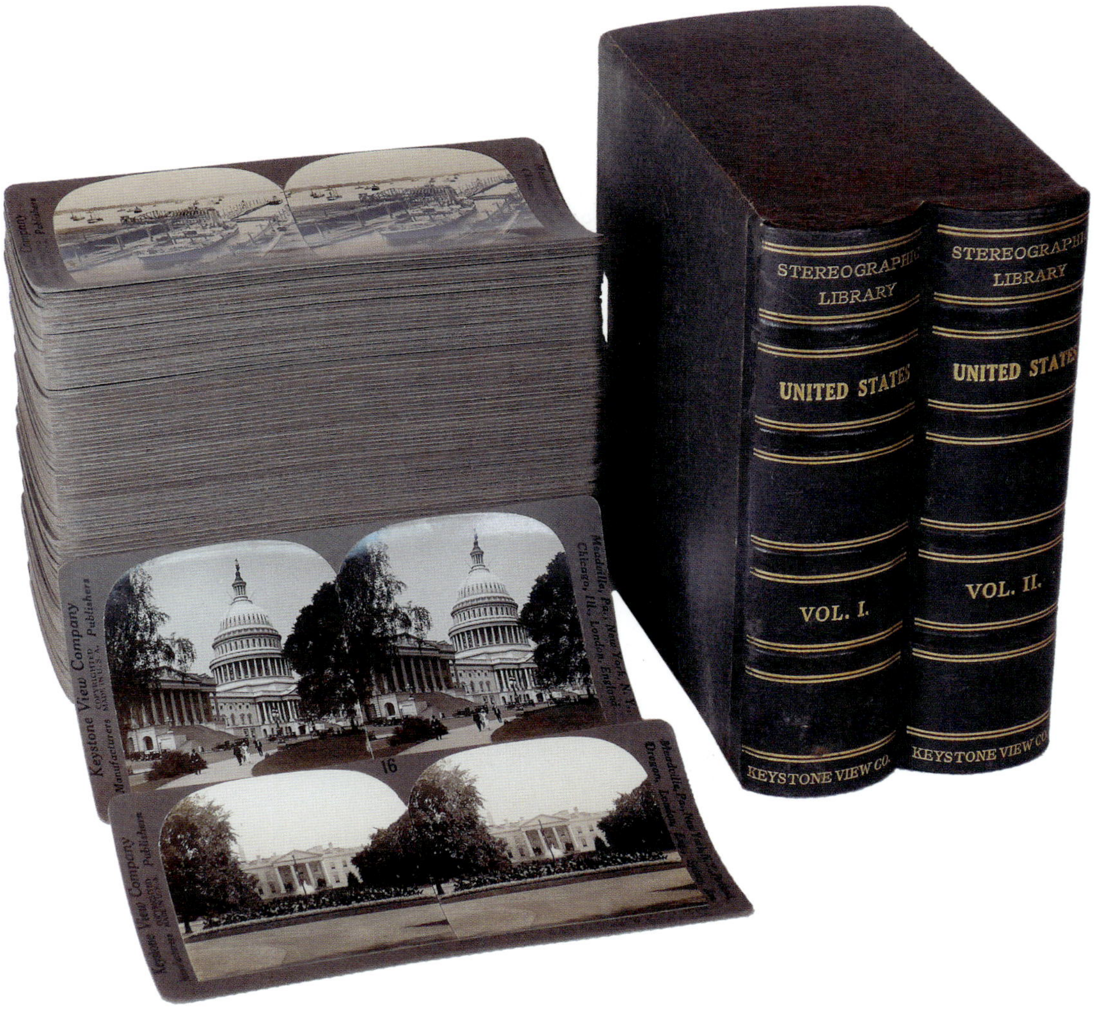

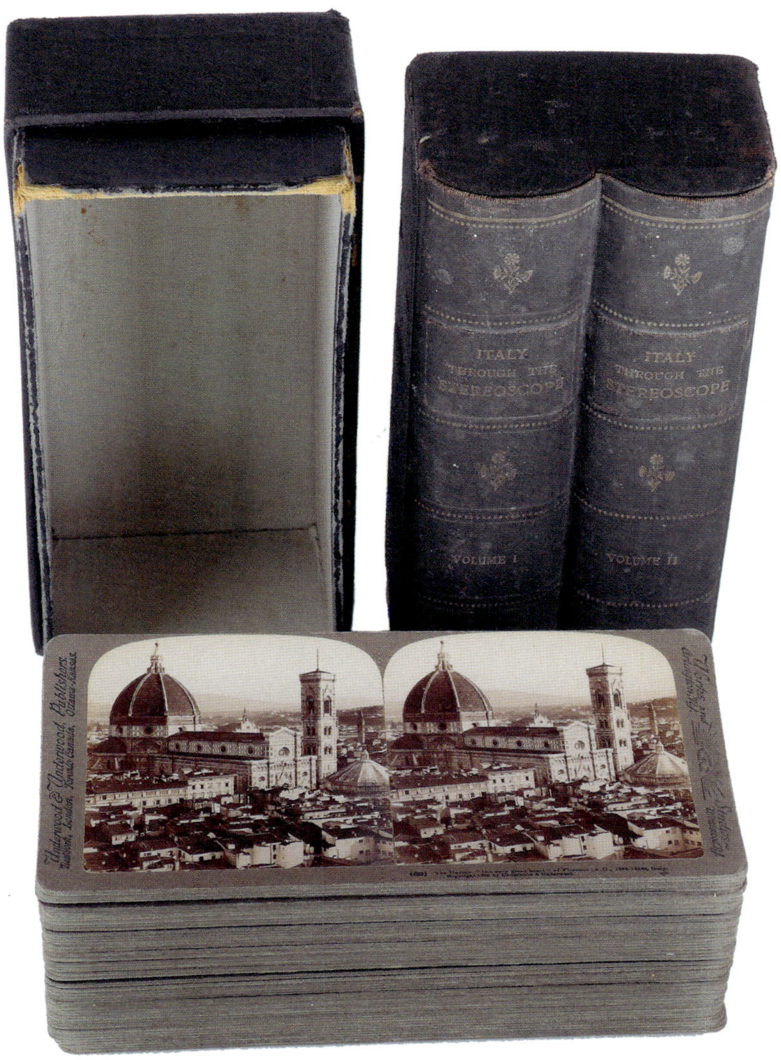

10.011
Italy Through the Stereoscope, Volume I + II
Gewebebuchkassette mit Hals, Rückenvergoldung, zwei Titelschilder, 50 Stereobilder, die einen räumlichen Eindruck vermitteln, Ansichten aus Italien
Textile box with neck, spine gilt, two labels, 50 stereo pictures giving a spatial impression, pictures from Italy
Underwood & Underwood, New York, London
Um / *Around* 1900 | 19 x 9,3 x 11,2 cm

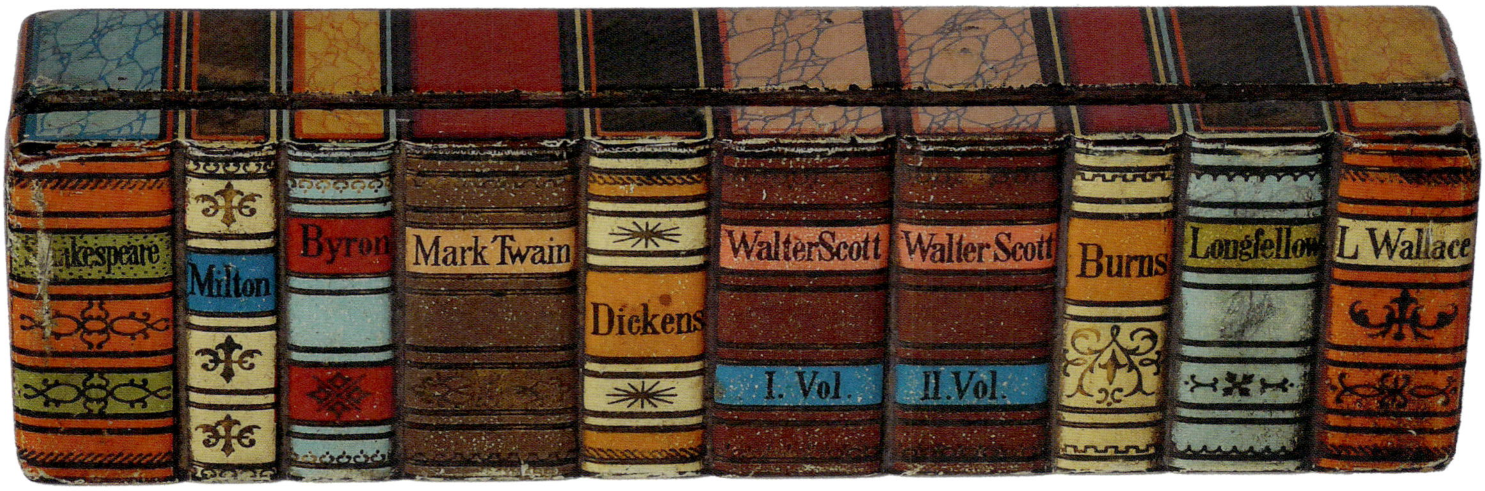

10.012
Schreibzeugschatulle aus Bakelit, farbig bedruckt, Klassiker-Titel, marmorierte Buchschnitte, innen dreiteilig
Writing tool box made of bakelite, printed in color, classic book titles, marbled edges, three compartments
Um / *Around* 1900 | 3,7 x 20,3 x 5,5 cm

10.013
Sechs Halbkartonschächtelchen auf Kunststoffstand zur Aufnahme von Kleinbüromaterial
Six semi cardboard boxes on a plastic stand for stationery
Critchley Bros LTD, England
7,1 x 9 x 4,8 cm

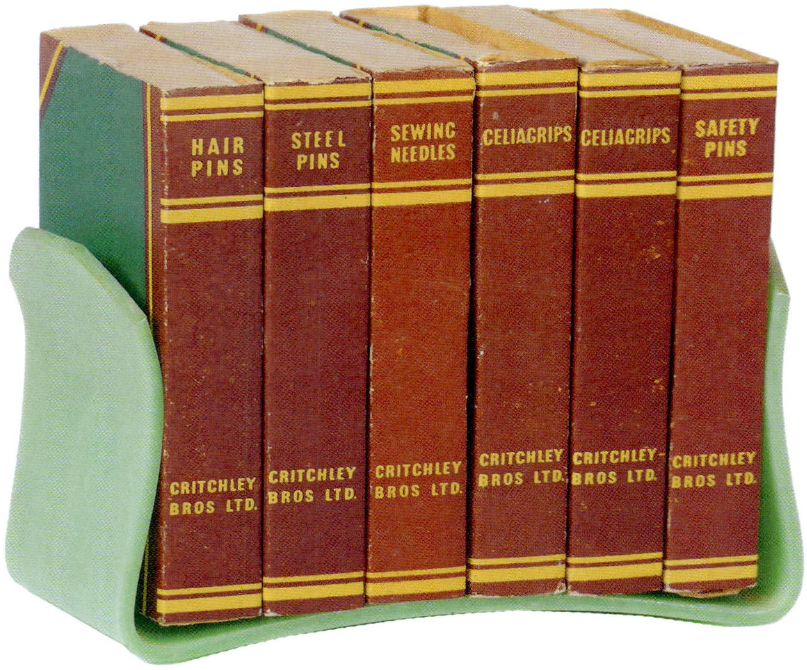

10.014
Bürobutler mit vier Kaliko-Buchschächtelchen zur Aufnahme von Kleinbüromaterial, Ablage für Schreibmaterial
Desk organizer with four calico boxes for storing small office supplies, shelf for storing stationery
Buchbinderei Bookbindery Eibenstein, Dresden, Germany | 8 x 13,7 x 7 cm

10.015
Bürobutler aus Karton mit sechs Halbkartonschächtelchen in Buchform zur Aufnahme von Kleinbüromaterial, Zugbänder
Cardboard desk organizer with a drawstring and six semi cardboard boxes to storing stationery
REG. U.S. PAT. OFF.
Um / *Around* 1940 | 5,9 x 11,3 x 5 cm

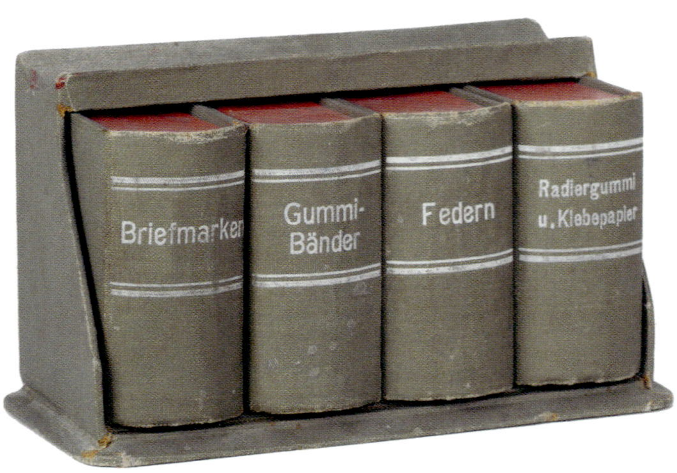

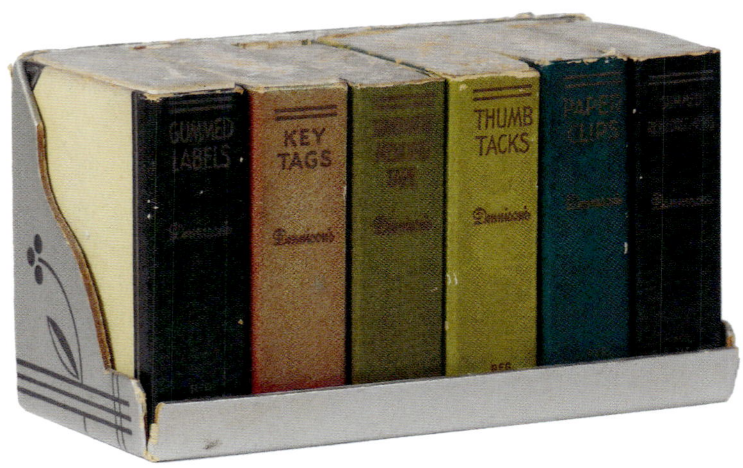

10.016
Bürobutler aus Karton mit zwölf Halbkartonschächtelchen zur Aufnahme von Kleinbüromaterial, zweistöckig, Holzimitationspapierüberzug, Zugbänder
Two-story cardboard desk organizer with a drawstring and six semi cardboard boxes to store stationery, faux wood paper cover
REG. U.S. PAT. OFF
Um / *Around* 1940 | 13,6 x 12,7 x 6 cm

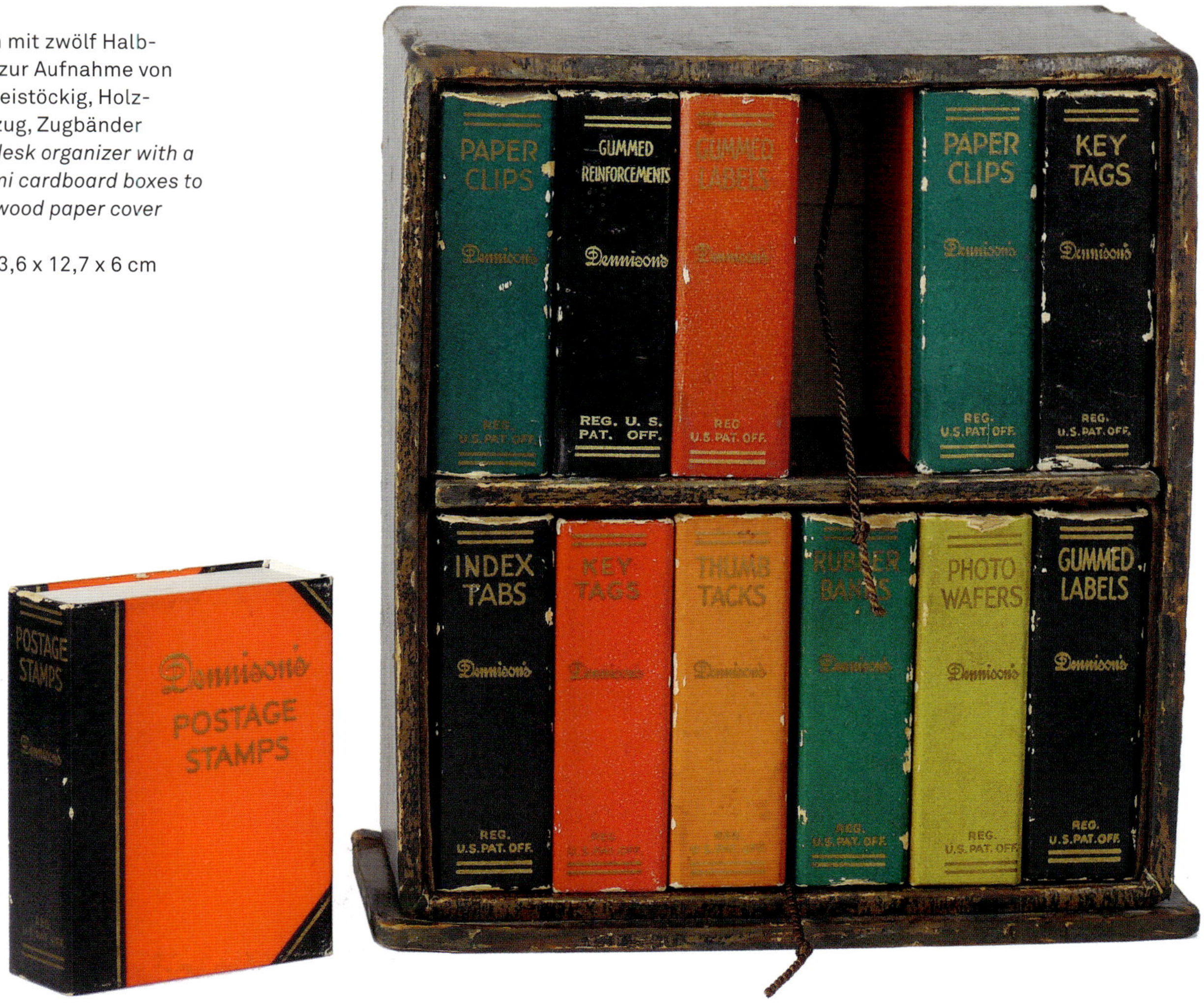

10.017
Bürobutler aus Karton mit zwölf Halbkartonschächtelchen zur Aufnahme von Kleinbüromaterial, Holzimitationspapierüberzug, Zugbänder
Cardboard desk organizer with a drawstring and six semi cardboard boxes to store small stationery, faux wood over board
Made in USA
Um / *Around* 1940 | 7,7 x 22,5 x 5,5 cm

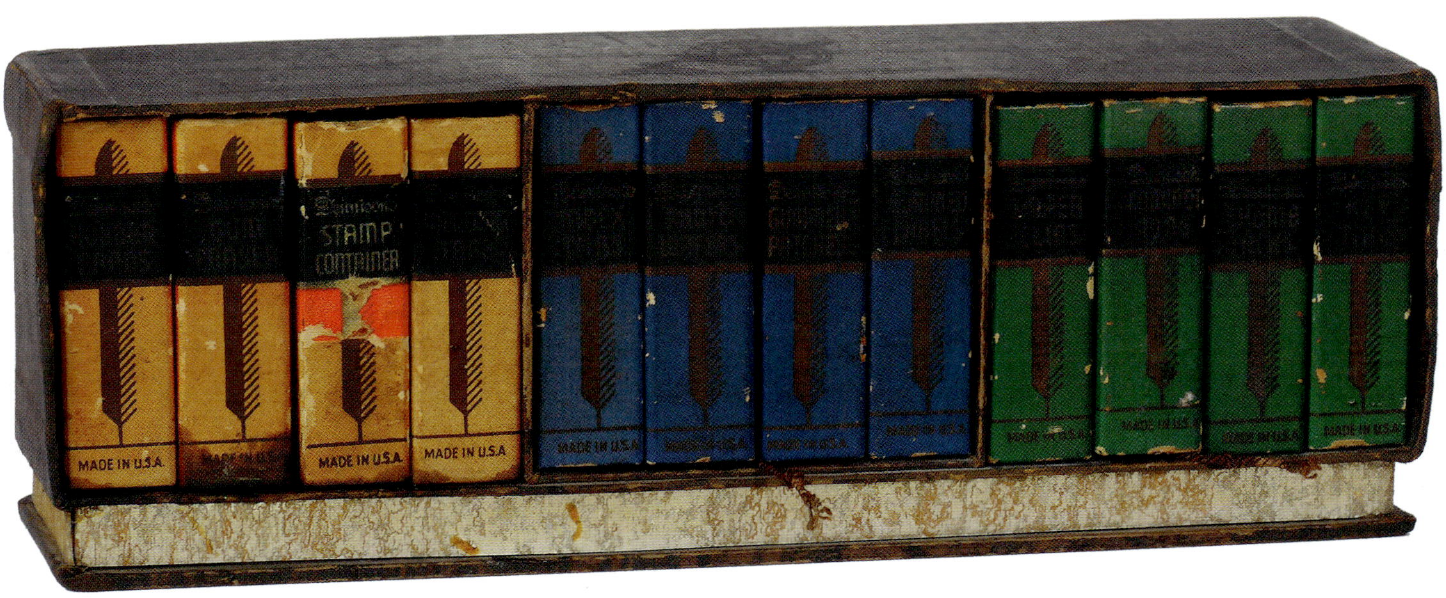

10.018
Holzkästchen mit vierundzwanzig Buchrücken auf der Tür, Stofftaschen und verschiedene Ablagefächer für Schreibzeug und Raucherutensilien (?), Kerbschnitzereien
Carved wooden box with twenty-four book spines on the door, fabric pockets and various storage compartments for pens and smoking accessories (?)
20 x 18,8 x 9 cm

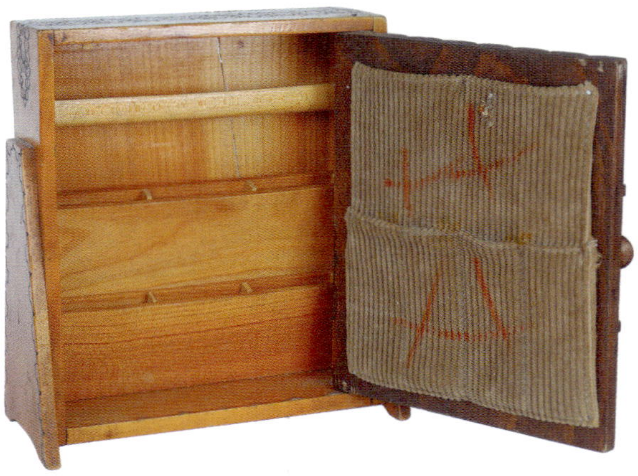

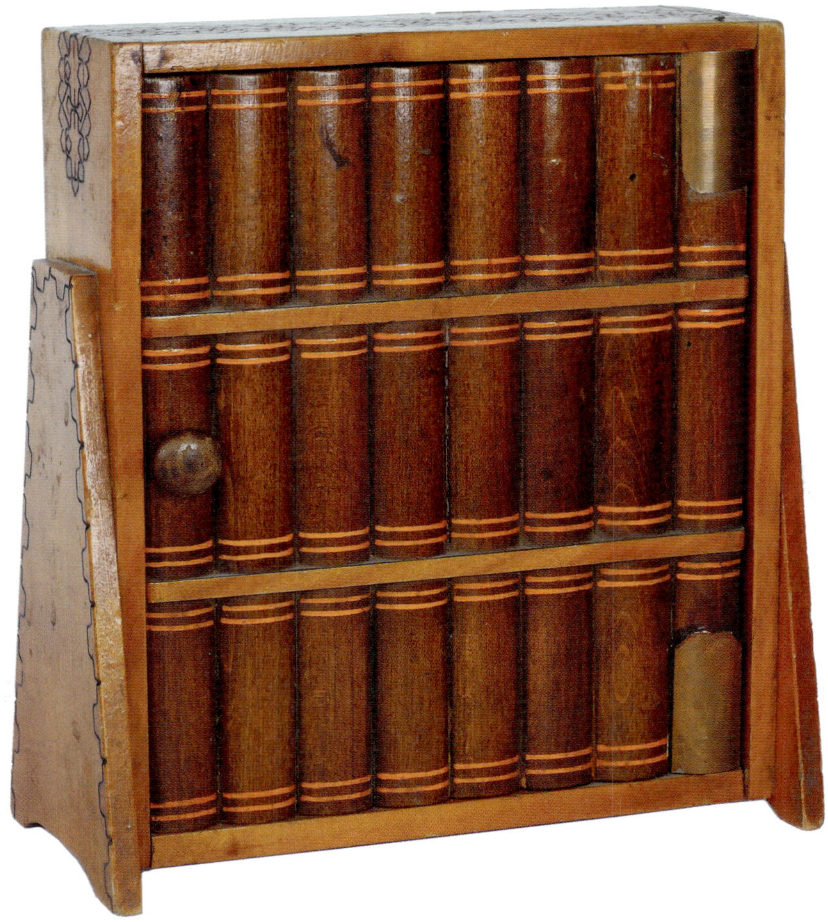

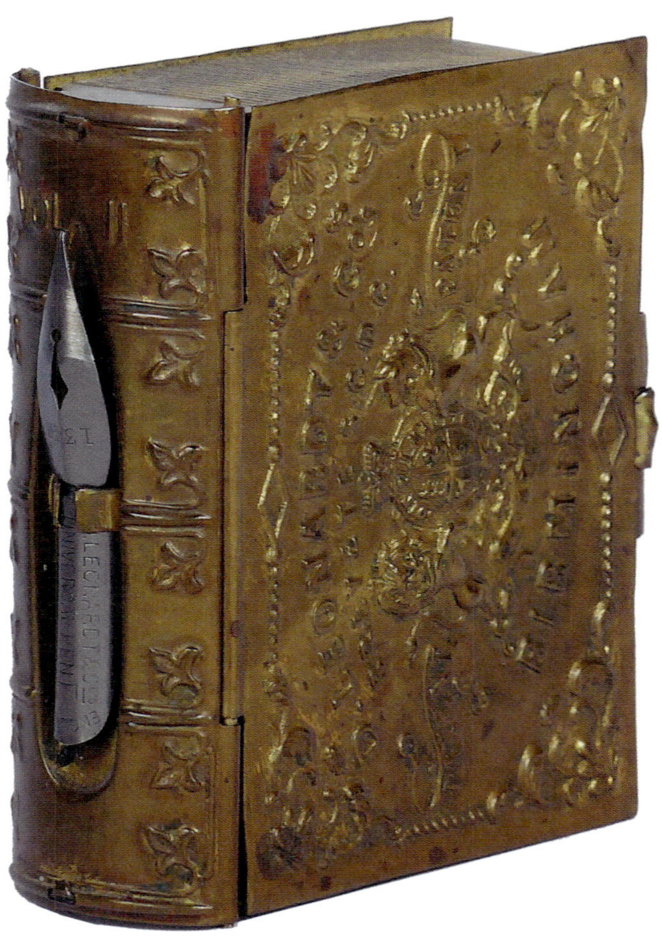

10.019
D. Leonardt & Co. Birmingham, A. Horster's Deutsche Handels Feder / ***German Trade Pen***
Messingdosen für Schreibfedern, Reliefprägung, Schließe
Brass boxes with a clasp for pens, relief embossing
Ende 19. Jh. / *Late 19th century*
2,3 x 6,7 x 5,7 cm

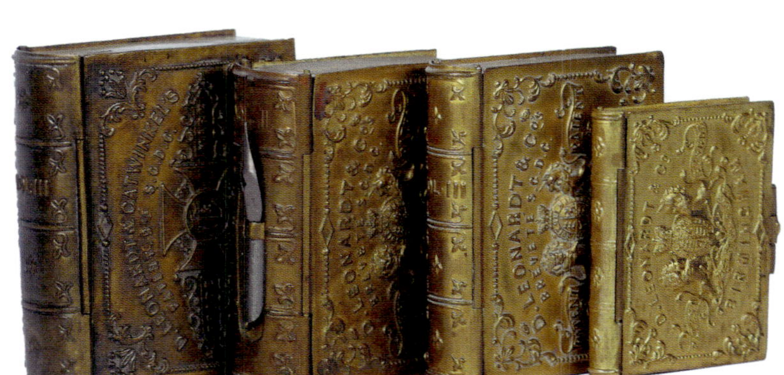

10.020

Ganzlederbox mit eingebautem Rollmeter am Kopfschnitt, Notizblock, Bleistift, Radiergummi, Spitzer, Vergoldung auf beiden Deckeln, Schließe

Full leather box with integrated ruler at the head, notepad, pencil, eraser, sharpener, gilding on the covers, clasp closure

Hersteller / *Manufacturer:* Sybille & August Wirz
Winterthur, Switzerland | 9,5 x 6,9 x 2,7 cm

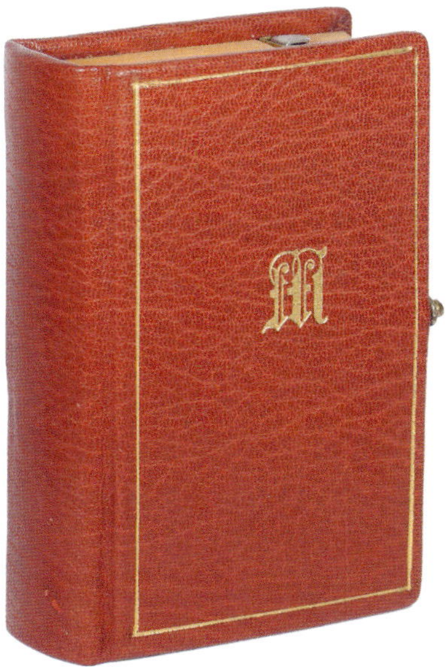

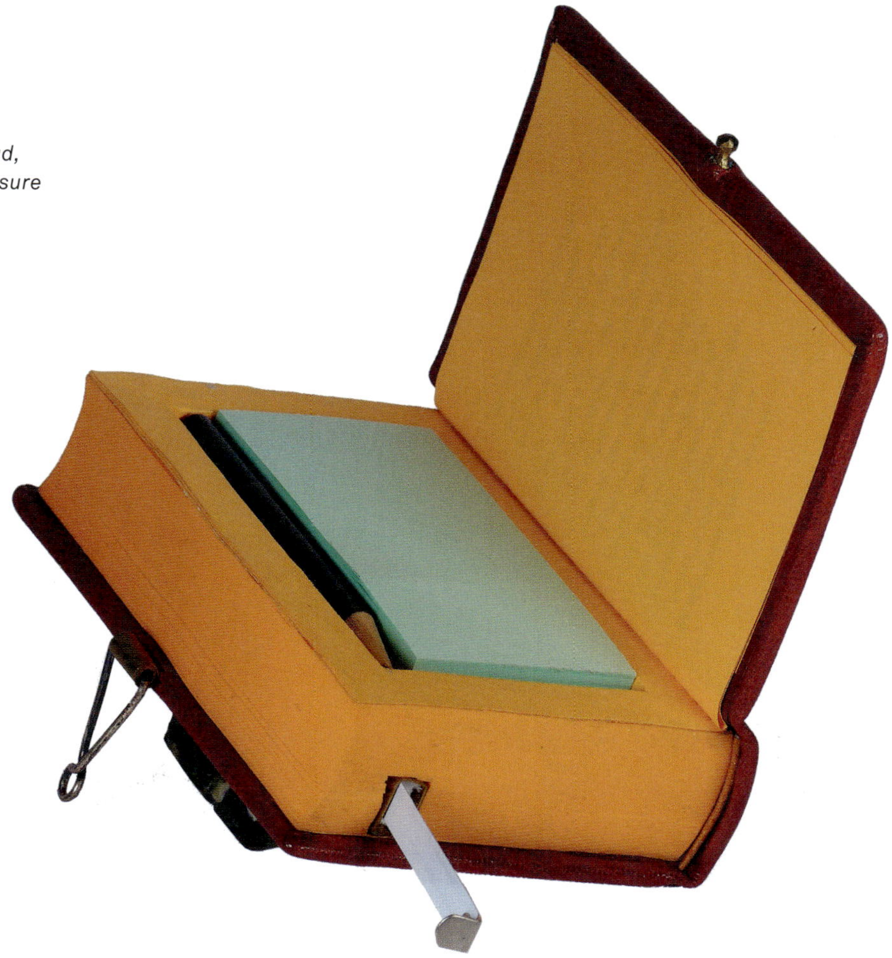

10.021

Tennyson's Works

Halblederkassette mit fünf Buchrücken, herausnehmbarer Einsatz mit drei Fächern, Vergoldung, ausgefüttert mit Spaltleder, Kammmarmorpapierüberzug

Half leather box with five book spines, removable compartments, gilding, lined with split leather, comb marbled paper-over-board

12,7 x 12,8 x 8,8 cm

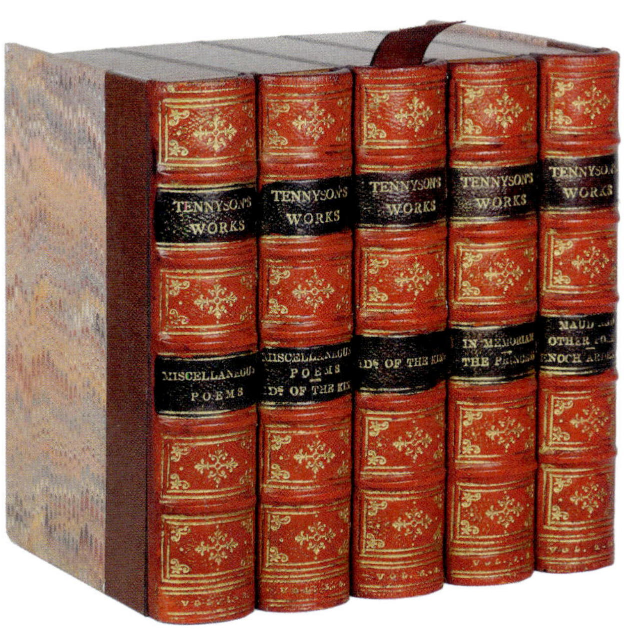

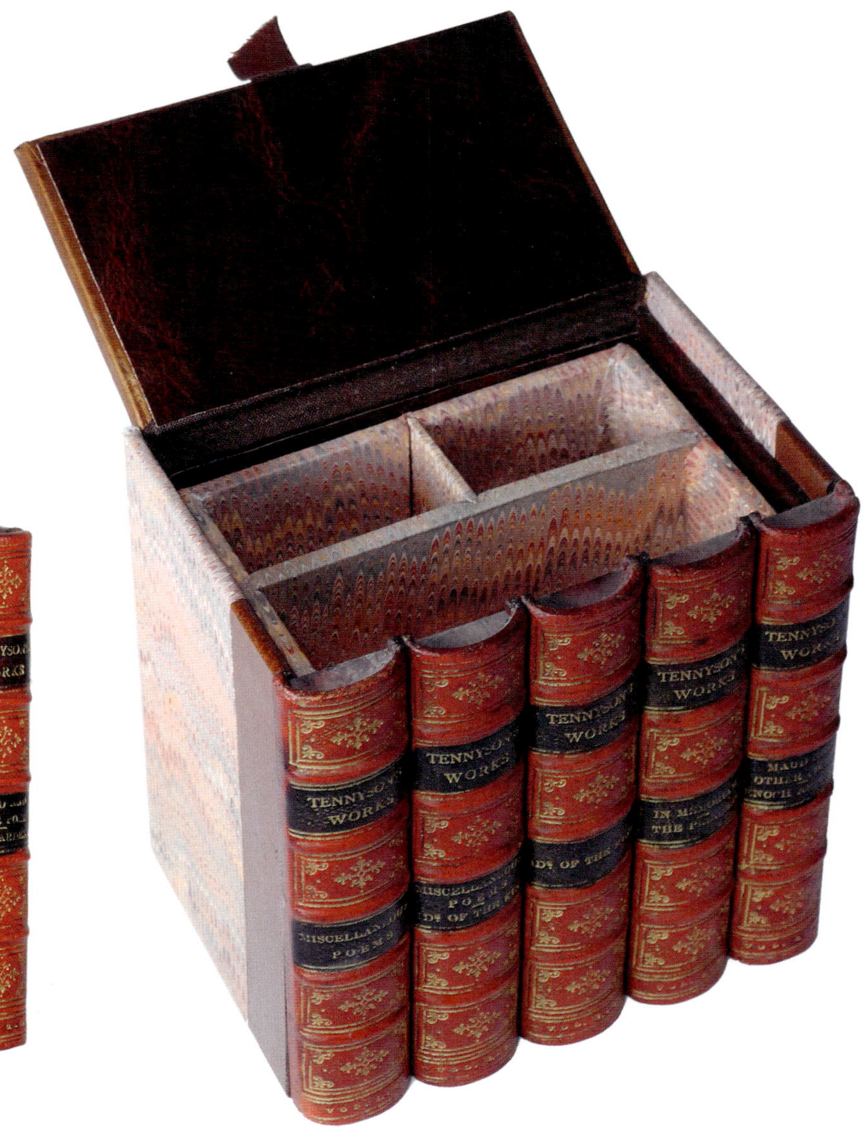

10.022
Handy Pointer, British Made
Metallbuchdose mit Bleistiftspitzer, Rückentitel, Vorderdeckelschild
Metal box with pencil sharpener, label on the spine and on the front cover
Nach / *After* 1900 | 4 x 3 x 1,5 cm

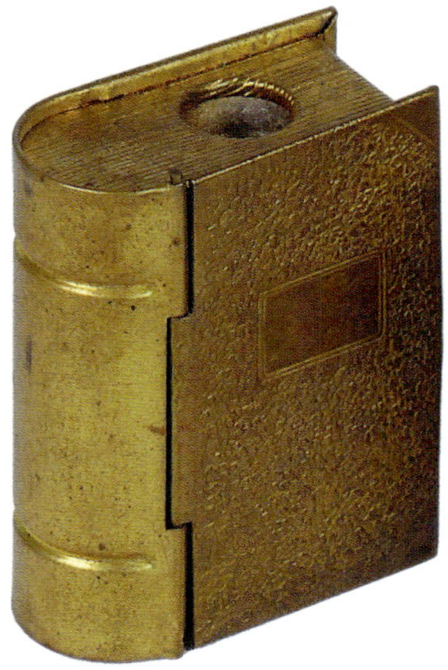

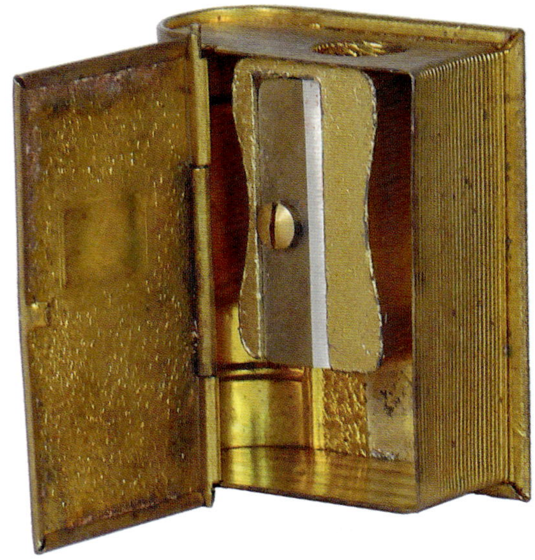

10.023
Blair Castle
Bleistiftspitzer aus Kunststoff, zweifarbig
Two-color plastic pencil sharpener
Zeitgenössisch / *Contemporary*
5 x 3,8 x 1,9 cm

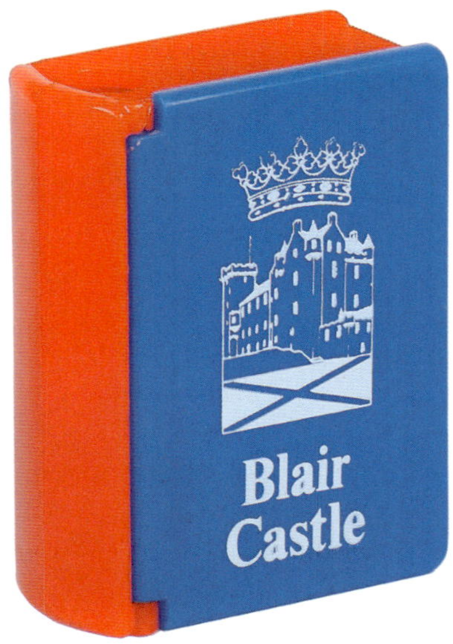

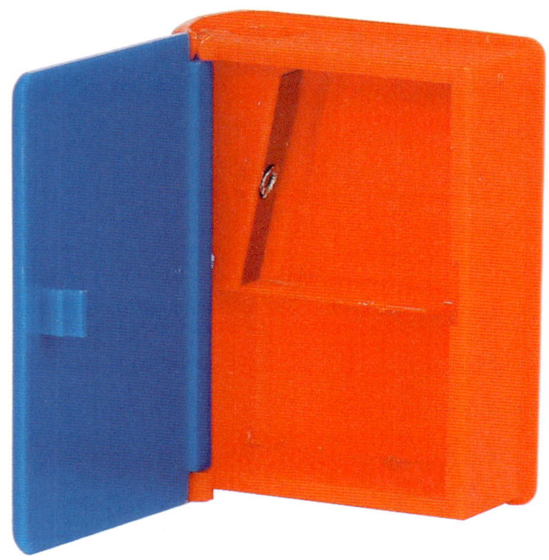

10.024
Bleistiftspitzer aus Kunststoff in der Form eines Ordners, Rückenschild
Plastic pencil sharpener in the design of a binder, with a label on the spine
Zeitgenössisch / *Contemporary*
5,2 x 3,9 x 1,7 cm

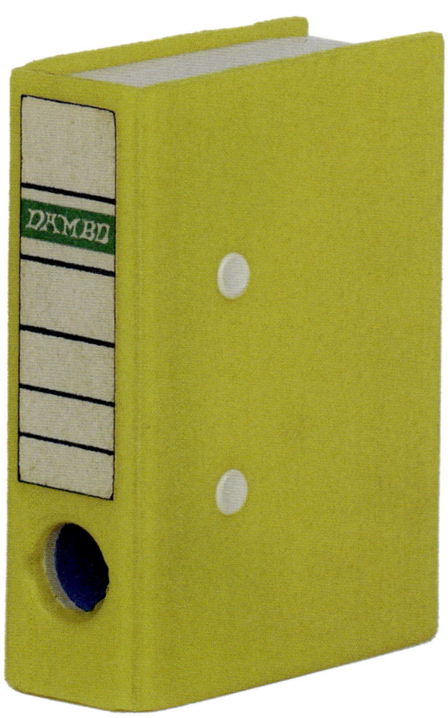

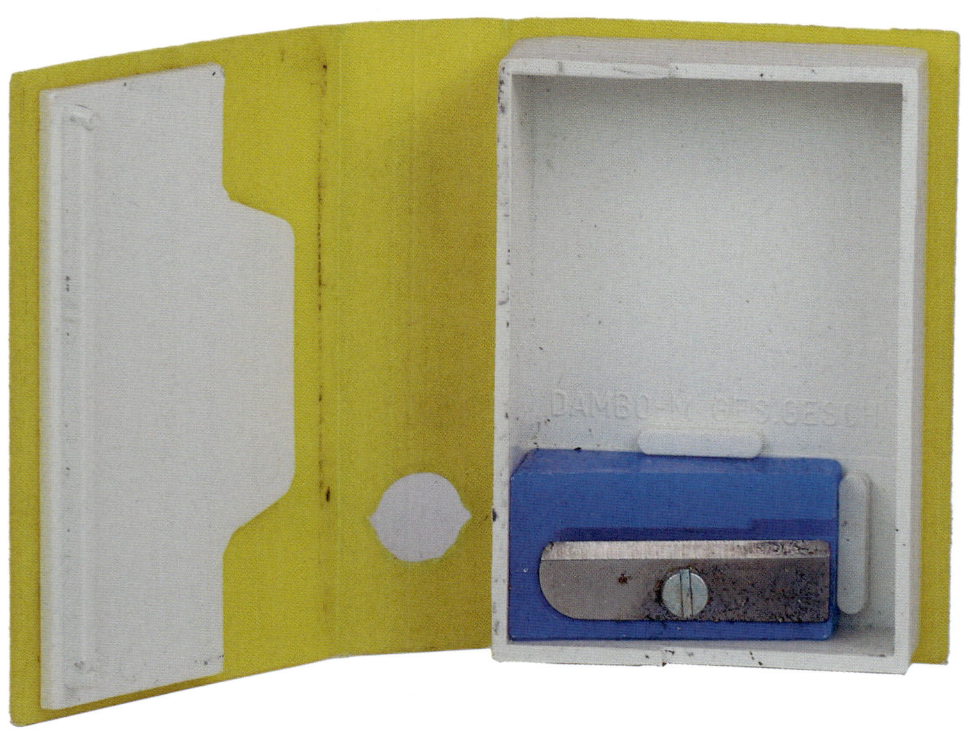

10.025
A Point to Remember
Blechdose mit Bleistiftspitzer, verschiebbarer Buchblock zum Entleeren der Späne, Rücken- und Deckelbeschriftung
Tin box with a pencil sharpener, a mobile book block for emptying the shavings, labels on the spine and cover
Made in England
Um / *Around* 1900 | 4,6 x 4 x 2,2 cm

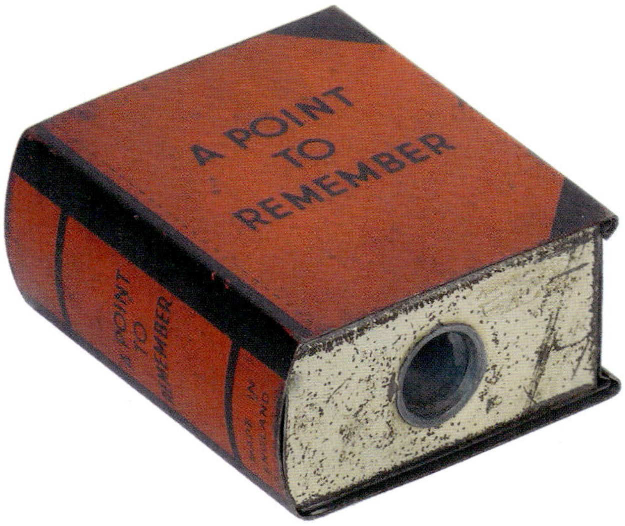

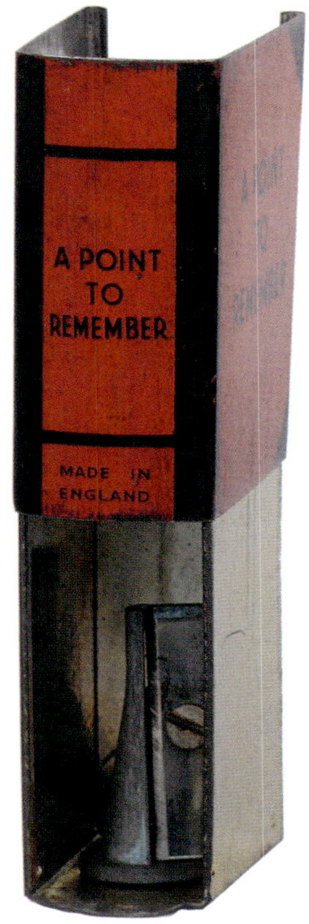

10.026
Post Office London Directory 1902. 103 D Edition. London, Kelly's Directories Limited. 182 High Holborn. W.C.
Aufklappbares Reisetintenfässchen, roter, vergoldeter Ledereinband und Supralibros
Small hinged travel inkwell, with red, gilt leather binding and supralibros
6,5 x 6 x 3,2 cm

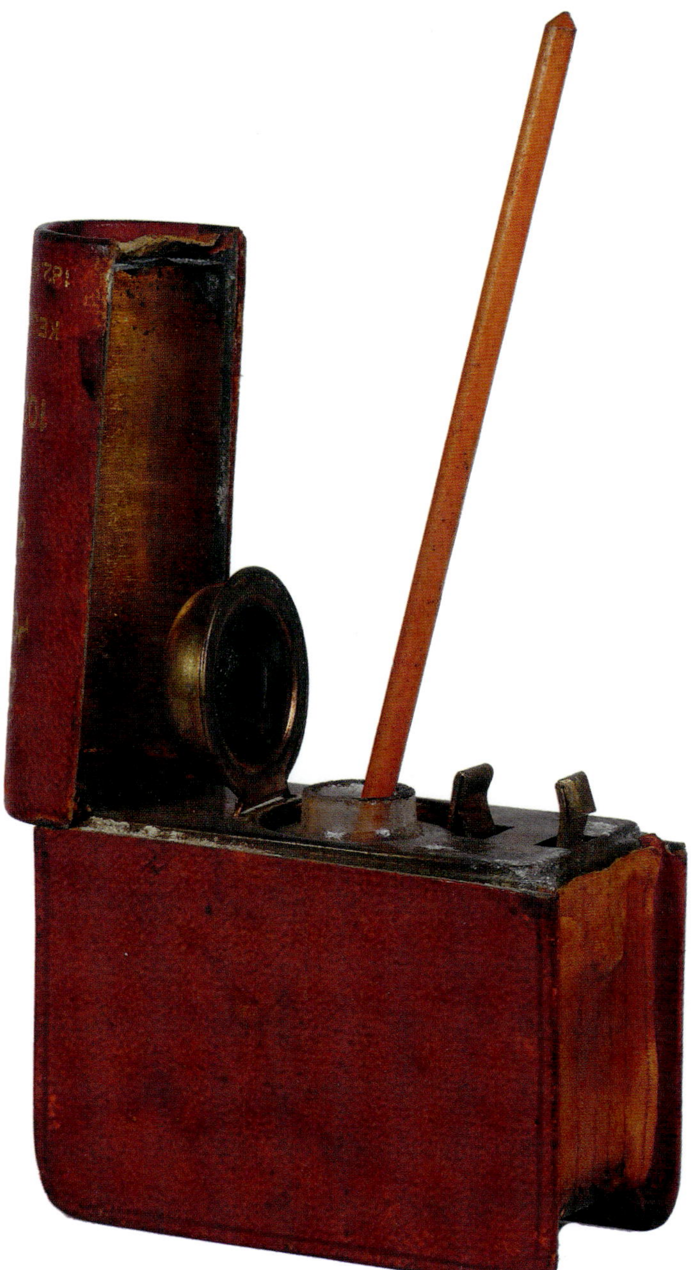

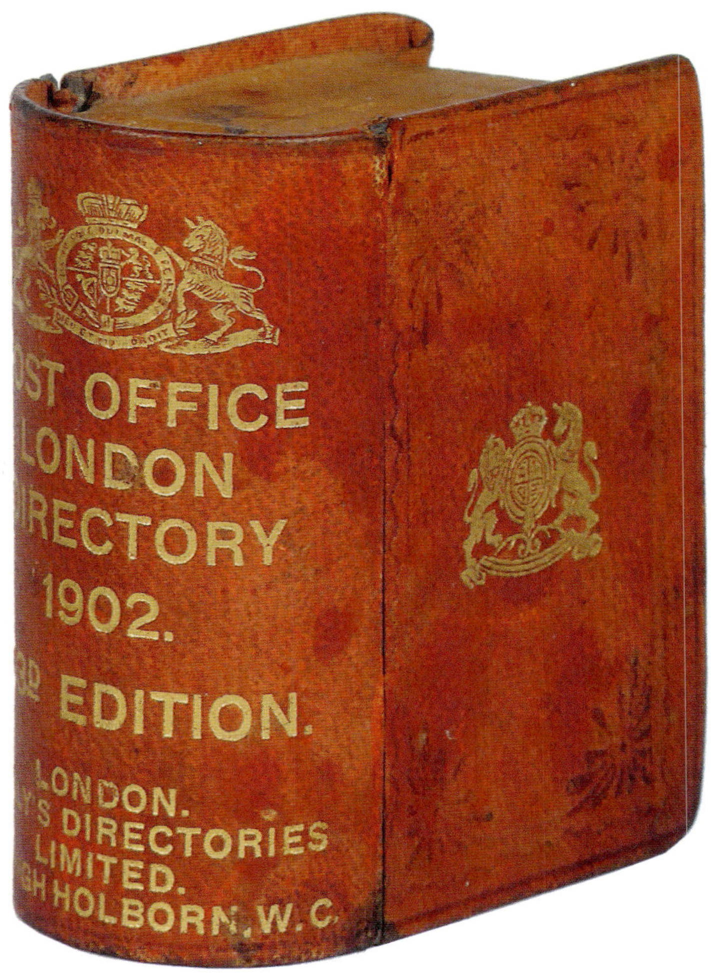

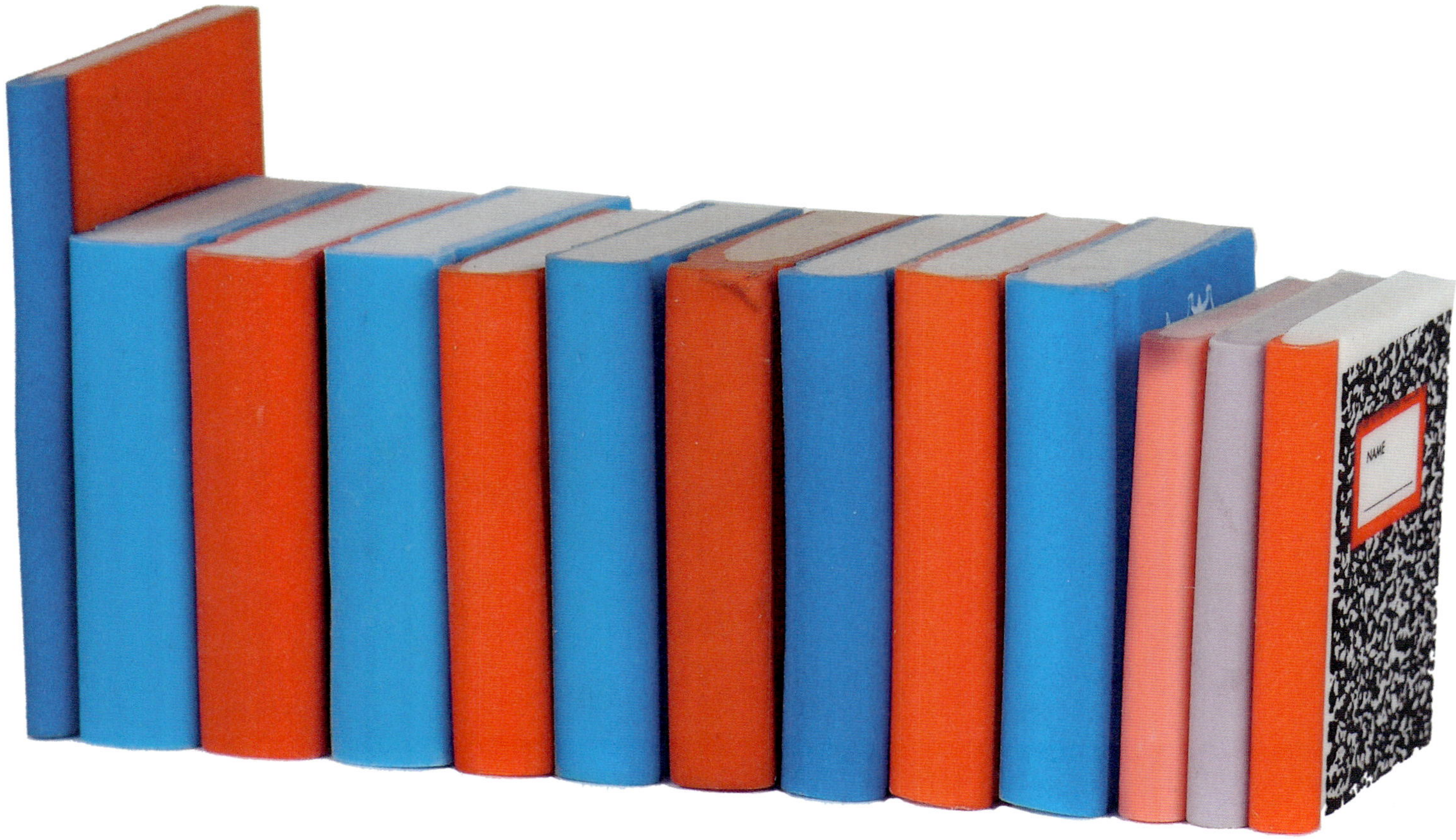

10.027
Radiergummis in Buchform verschiedener Herkunft
Erasers of different origins:
British Library, Bodleian Library, Brodie Castle, Blair Castle, Cawdor Castle, Madame Tussaud, Uppsala Domkyrka, Rothiemurchus Fish Farm
4 x 3,2 x 1 cm

10.028
Siegfried MCMXXXIX
Messing-Löschwiege mit sitzender Eule auf einem aufgeschlagenen Buch
Brass rocker blotter with an owl sitting on an open book
10 x 14,5 x 8 cm

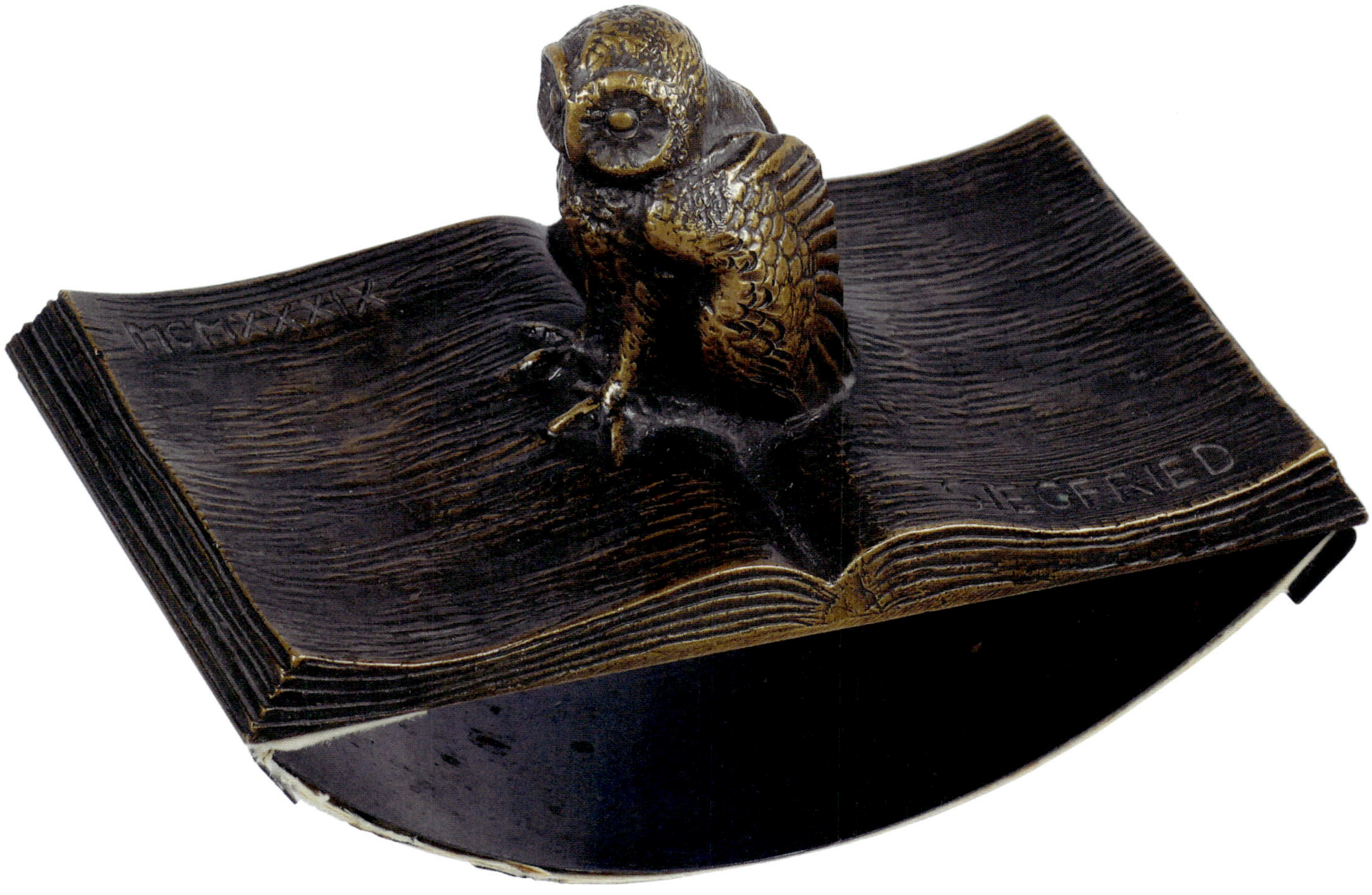

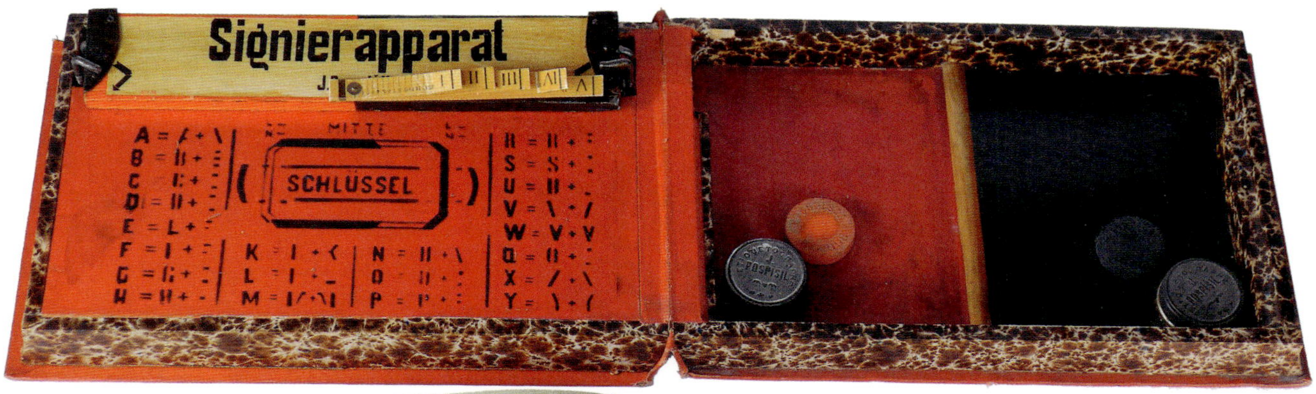

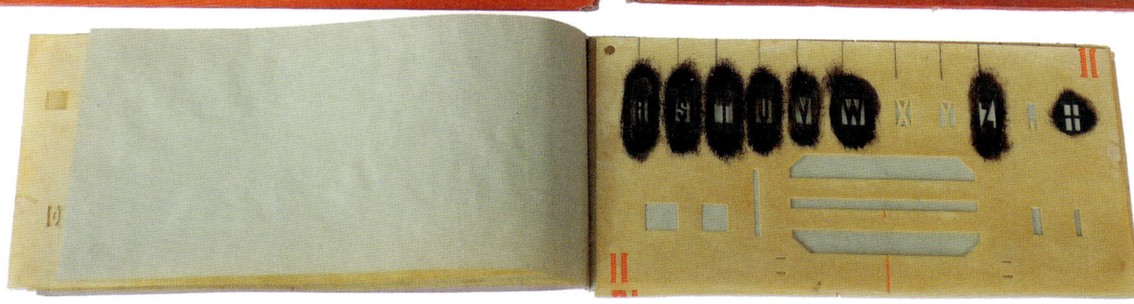

10.029
Signier-Apparat 57, J.Pospisil (1878–1935)
Signierapparat für Pharmazeuten und Apotheker. Aufklappbare Kaliko-Buchkassette, gold- und schwarzgeprägter Vorderdeckel, dreiseitiger Achatmarmorpapierschnitt. Zubehör: Alphabete, Farben, Pinsel und Gebrauchsanweisung
Signing device for pharmacists. Openable calico box, gold and black embossing on the front cover, agate marbled paper edges. Accessories: alphabets, colors, brushes and manual
Stefanau (Olmütz), Mähren, Österreich / *Austria*
6,2 x 27,1 x 17,3 cm

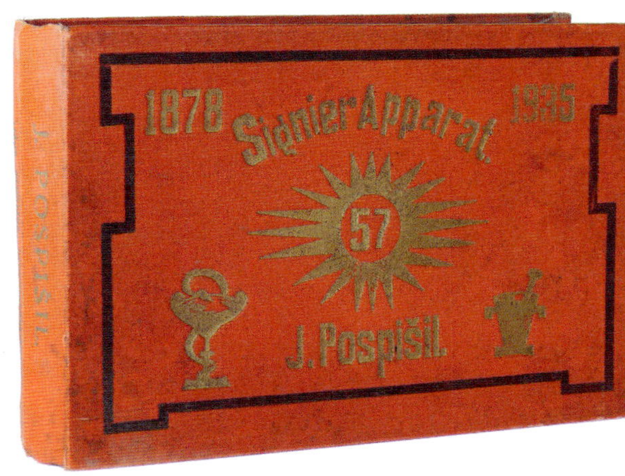

10.030
Signirapparat vom Pharmaceuten J.Pospisil
***J. Pospisil's signing device* (1878–1908)**
Signierapparat für Pharmazeuten und Apotheker. Aufklappbare Gewebe-Buchkassette, farbig bedruckt, Verschlussriegel, dreiseitiger Haarmarmorpapierschnitt, Zubehör: Alphabete, Farben und Pinsel
Signing device for pharmacists. Foldable box in fabric, printed in color, closure, marbled paper edges, accessories: alphabets, colors and brushes
Stefanau (Olmütz), Mähren, Österreich /*Moravia, Austria*
4,5 x 26,3 x 15,5 cm

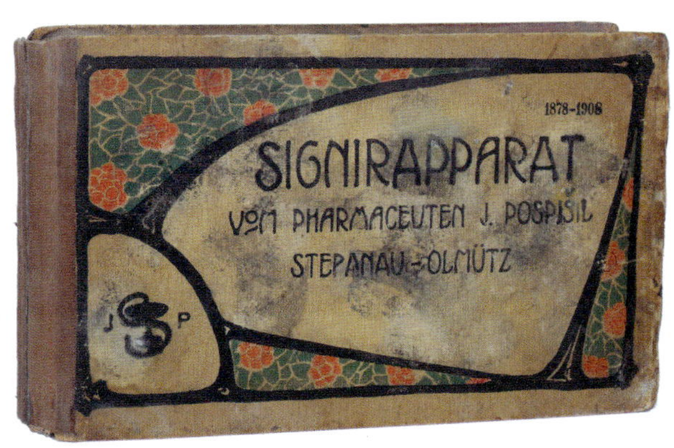

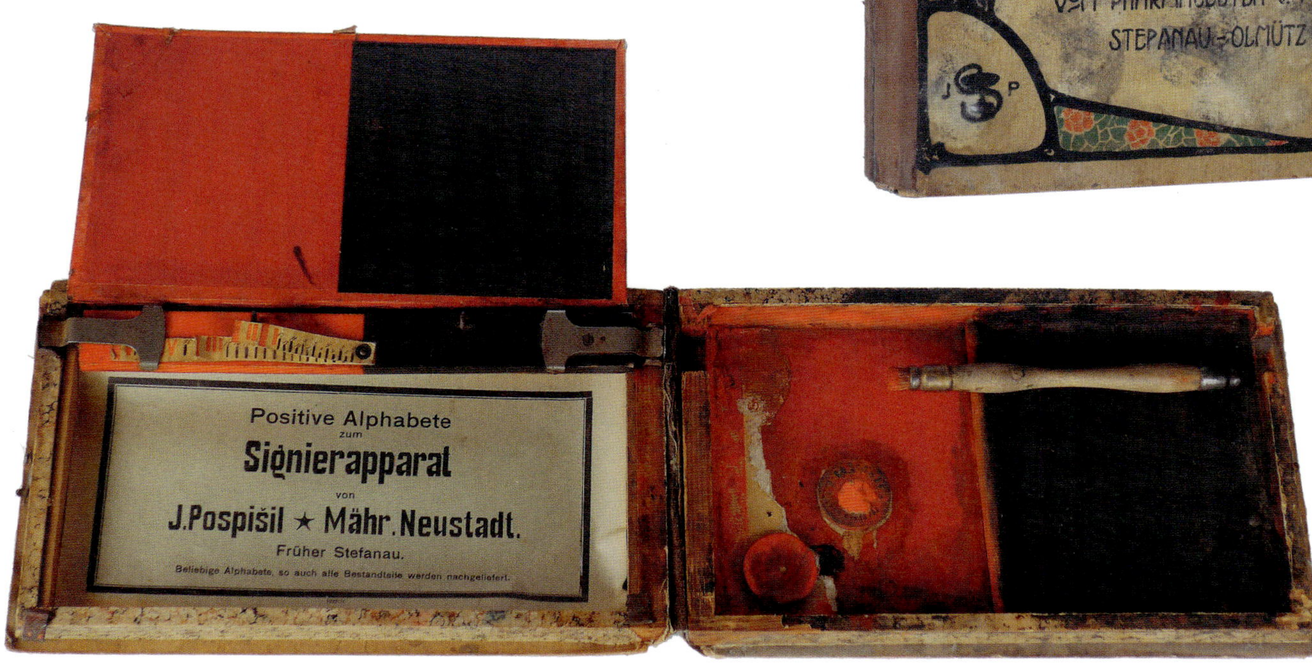

10.031
Ganzledereinband mit drei eingebundenen offenen Mäppchen, nummeriert 5–10, für Briefmarken (?), Metallschließe, Wappen aus Horn auf dem Vorderdeckel, dreiseitiger Goldschnitt
Full leather binding with three integrated open pockets, numbered 5–10, for stamps (?), metal clasp, coat of arms made of horn on the cover, all edges gilt
Um / *Around* 1900 | 1,5 x 6 x 5,1 cm

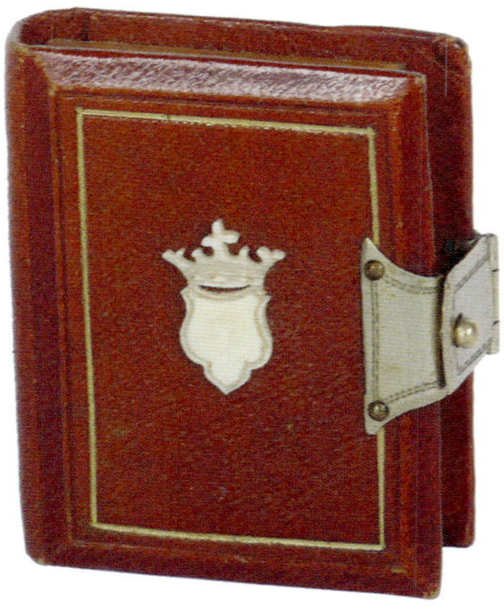

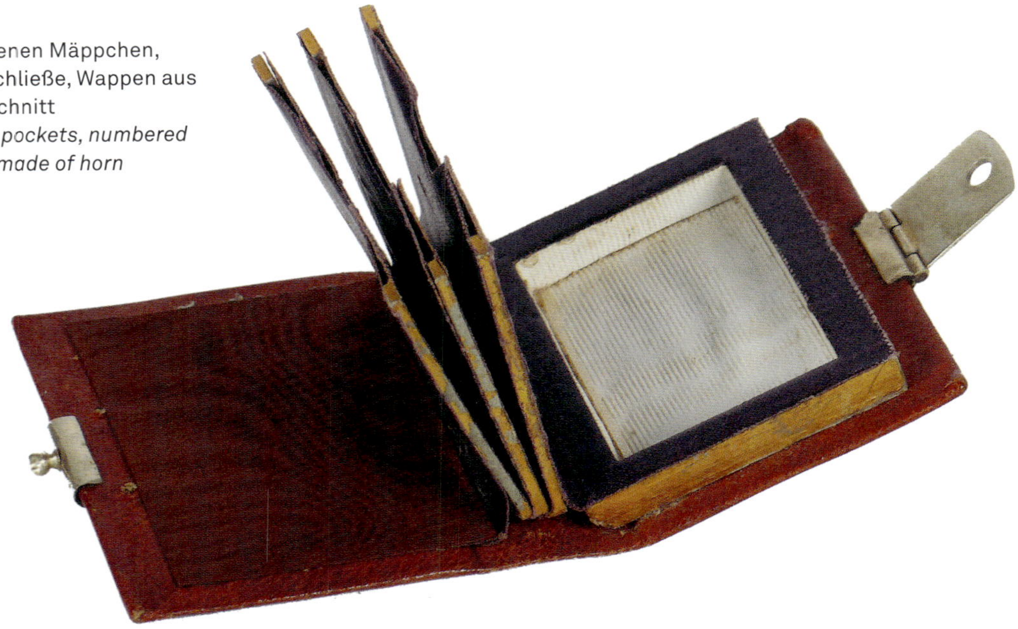

10.032
Coleman National Business College. H. Coleman Postage and Revenue Stamps.
Kunststoffdose mit schwenkbarem Metalleinsatz für Briefmarken, Griffloch, Rücken- und Deckelbeschriftung mit Porträt
Plastic box with hinged metal insert for stamps, grip hole, lettering on the spine and cover combined with a portrait
USA
Um / *Around* 1900 | 0,6 x 3,3 x 2,7 cm

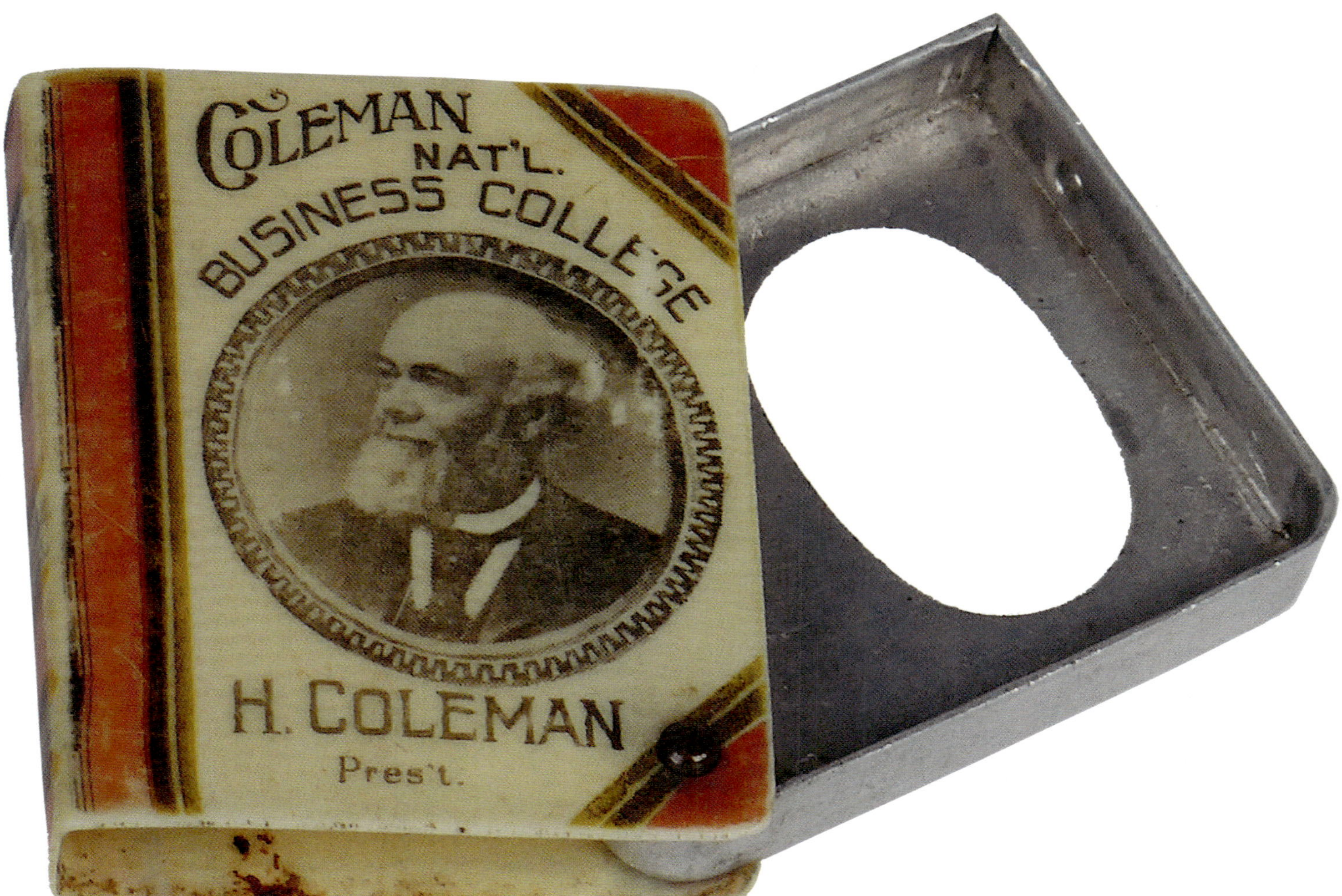

10.033
Holzdose mit geschnitztem Blumenmotiv auf dem Vorderdeckel für Briefmarken
Wooden box for stamps with carved floral design on the front lid
2,8 x 12,5 x 6,1 cm

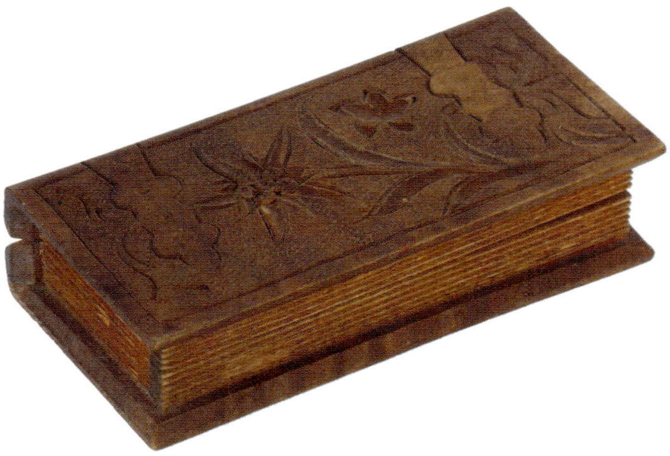

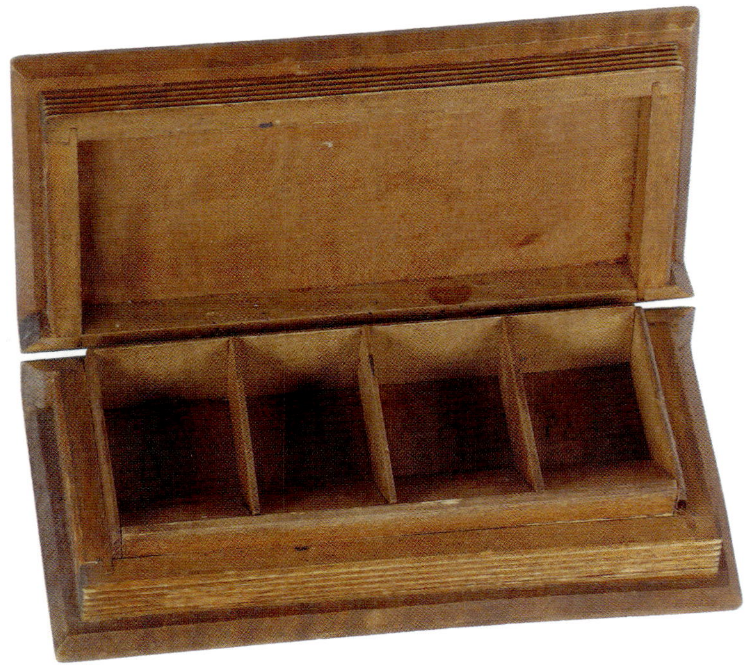

10.034
Holzdose mit geschnitztem und bemaltem Früchtemotiv auf dem Vorderdeckel für Briefmarken
Wooden box for stamps with carved and painted fruit design on the front lid
2,8 x 8,4 x 6,7 cm

10.035
Antiquité Expliquée
Holzdose mit Lederüberzug, Rückenvergoldung, abgeschrägter Innenboden, zwei Fächer für Briefmarken (?)
Wooden box covered with leather, gilt spine, sloping inner bottom, two compartments for stamps (?)
4 x 4,5 x 14,5 cm

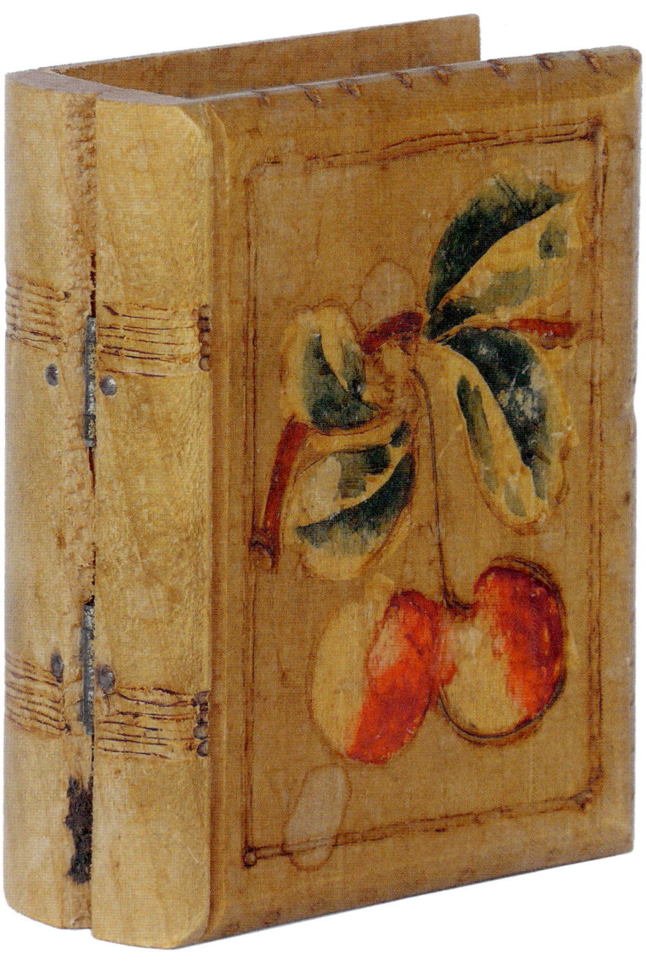

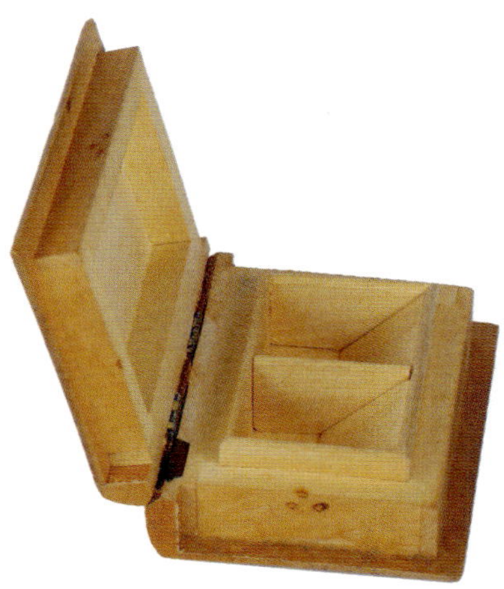

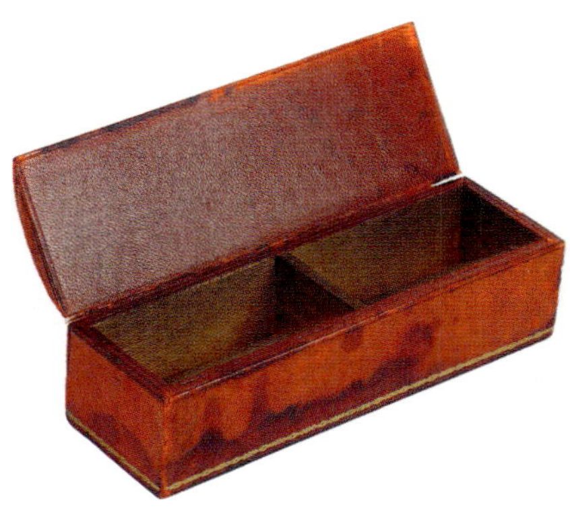

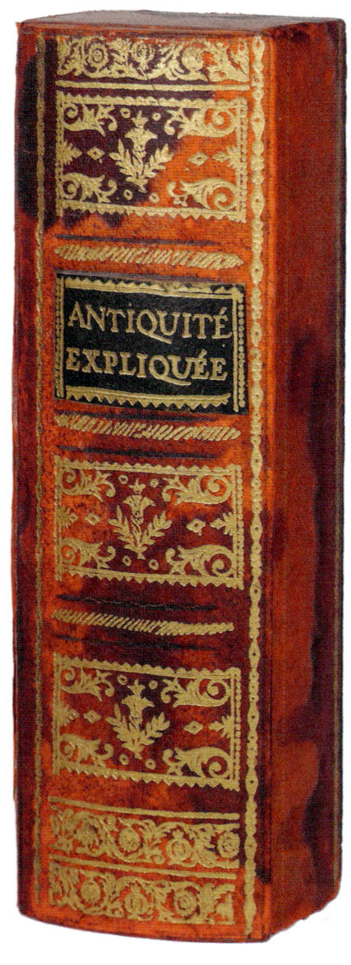

10.036
Bücherstützen aus Holz mit je zwei Büchern und zwei auffliegenden Enten aus Metall
Wooden bookends, each with two books and two flying metal ducks
16,3 x 11,2 x 11,8 cm

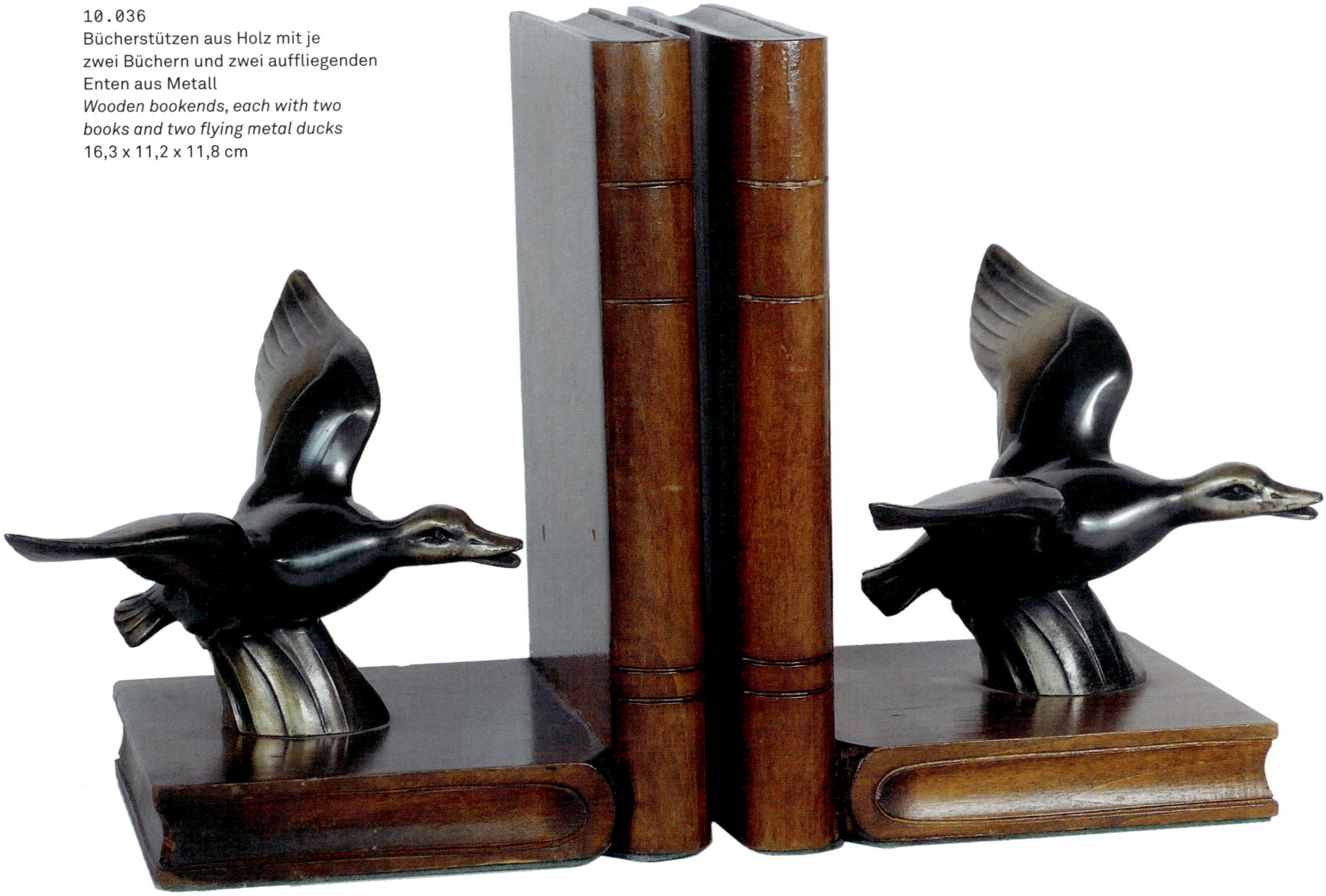

10.037
Bücherstütze aus Holz mit drei Büchern, Metallbeschläge
Wooden bookend with metal fittings and three books
14,9 x 8 x 10,6 cm

10.038
Bücherstützen aus Holz mit je einem Buch
Wooden bookends with one book each
15,9 x 11 x 10,2 cm

10.039
Bücherstützen aus Holz mit je drei Büchern, bemalt und graviert
Wooden bookends with three books each, painted and engraved
15 x 8 x 10,7 cm

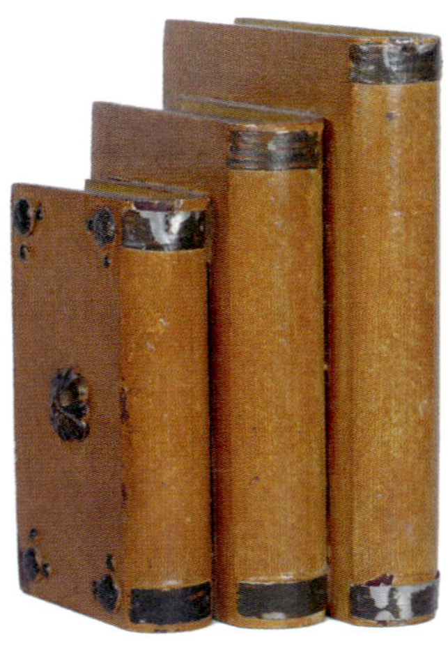

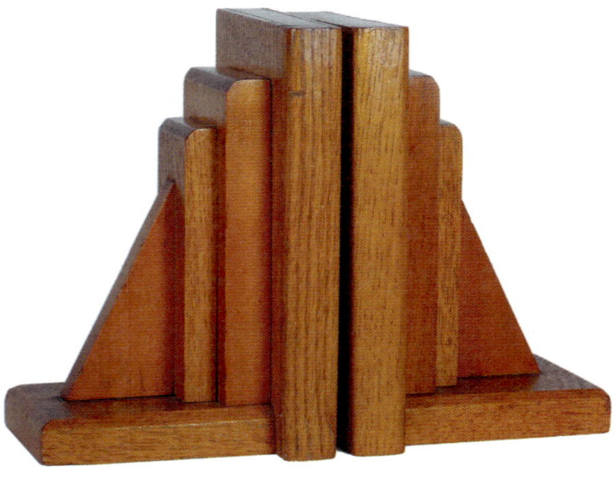

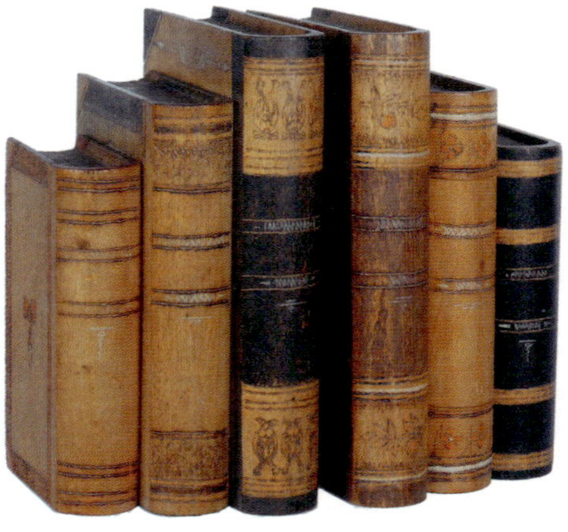

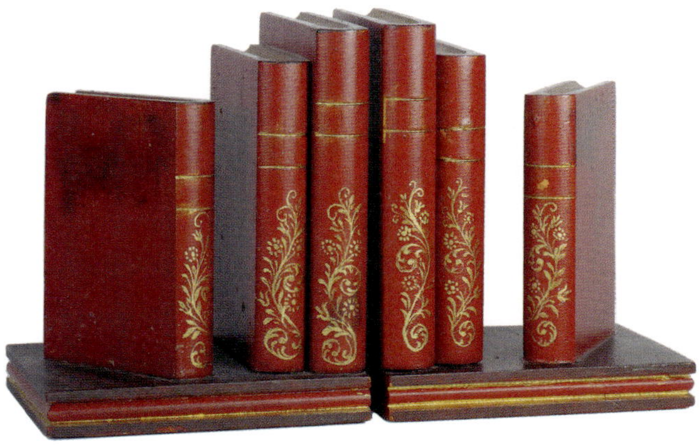

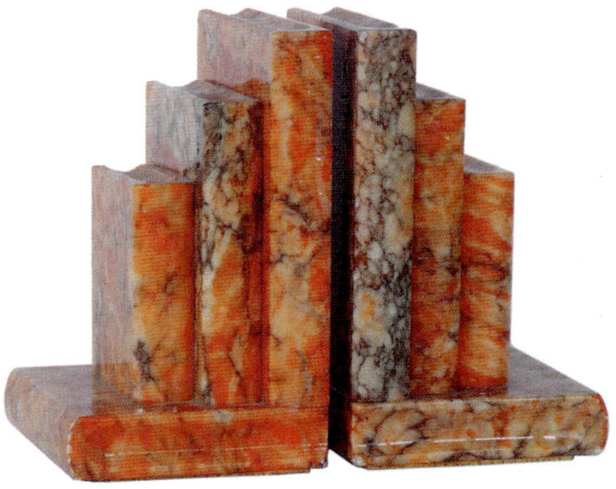

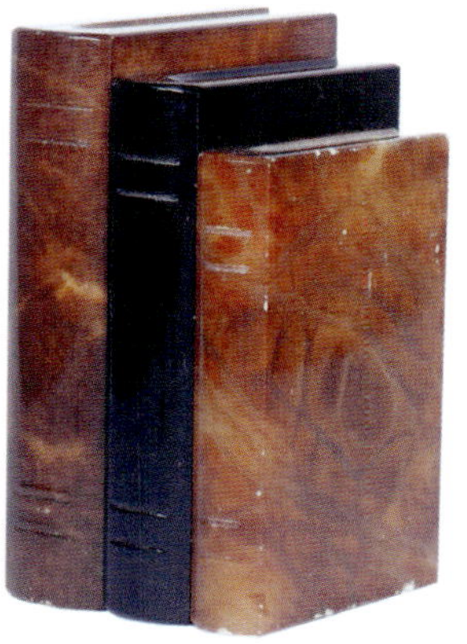

10.040
Bücherstützen aus Holz mit je
drei Büchern, bemalt und goldfarben verziert
*Wooden bookends with three books
each, painted and golden ornaments*
14,8 x 12,3 x 9,5 cm

10.041
Bücherstützen aus Marmor
mit je vier Büchern
*Marble bookends with four
books each*
12,8 x 7,5 x 7,9 cm

10.042
Bücherstütze aus Onyx
mit drei Büchern
*Onyx bookend with
three books*
13,5 x 7,5 x 10 cm

10.043
Bücherstützen aus Holz mit je zwei Büchern
und zwei geschnitzten lesenden Hunden
*Wooden bookends, each with two books and
two carved reading dogs*
13,3 x 12 x 7,3 cm

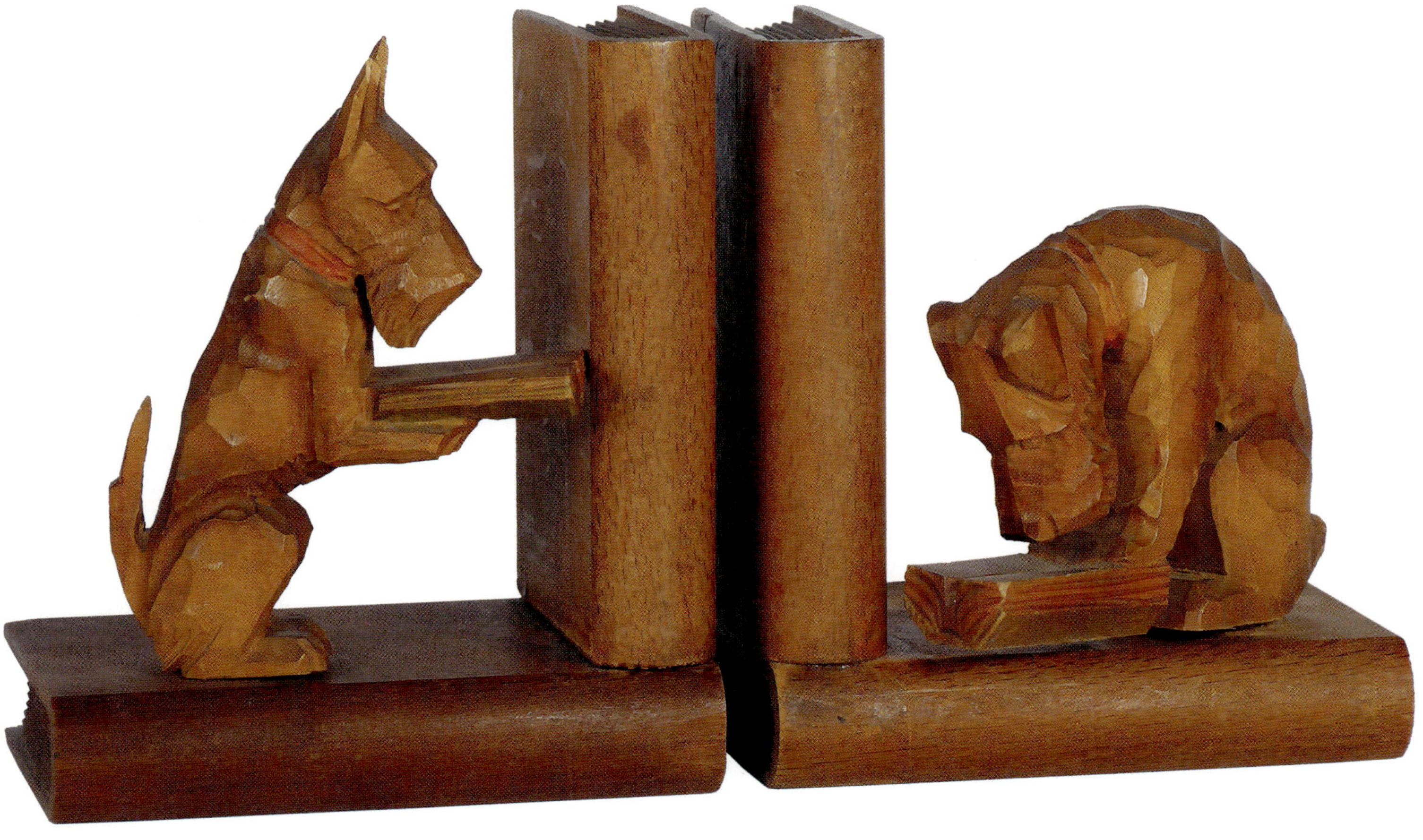

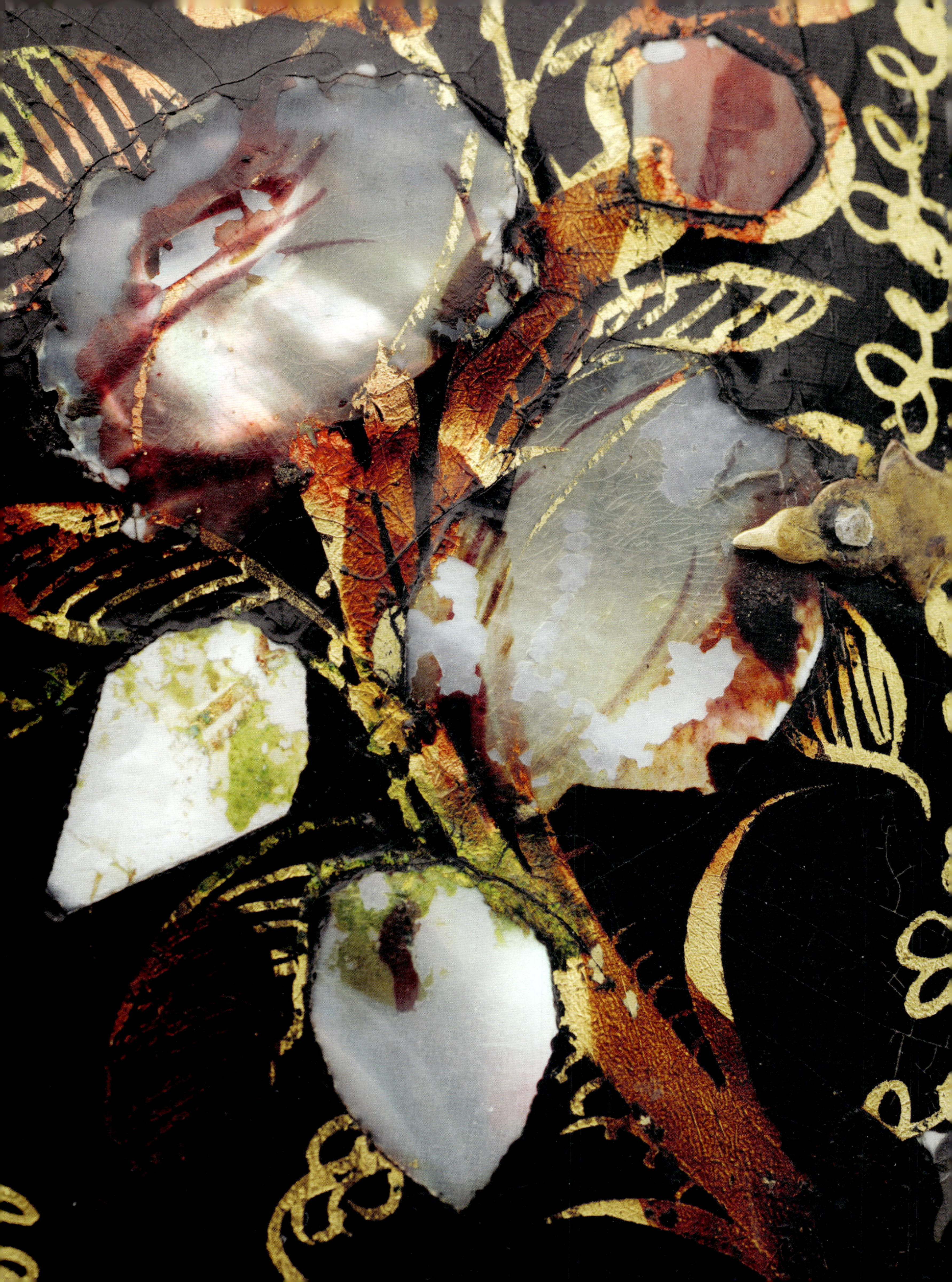

Dies & Das
Miscellaneous

Viel Glück hatte ich an einer Möbelauktion in Zürich. Man vermutet da eigentlich keine Bücher, und vor allem keine Buchattrappen-Sammler.

Zur Dekoration lag auf einem teuren Stilmöbel eine reich handvergoldete Kassette aus Ziegenleder in Buchform mit dreiseitigem Goldschnitt. Das Herbarium besteht aus 107 Pflanzenarten der Schweiz, im Zeitraum von 1849–1852.

Zum Glück waren da keine Botaniker und Buchliebhaber zugegen, sodass ich die botanische Rarität zu einem Schnäppchenpreis erwerben konnte.

I was very lucky at a furniture auction in Zurich. You wouldn't normally expect to find any books there, not to mention collectors of fake books.

An elaborate, hand-gilded box made of goatskin in the style of a book, with gilt edges on three sides, was placed on an expensive piece of period furniture. The herbarium consists of 107 Swiss plant species, dated 1849–1852.

Fortunately, there were no botanists or book-lovers present, so I was able to acquire this botanical rarity at a bargain price.

11.001
Blumenvase Delfter Keramik blau, bemalt mit Windmühlemotiv, vier erhabene Bünde, zwei Schließen
Delft blue ceramic flower vase, with an illustration of a windmill, four raised bands, two clasps
Um / *Around* 1800 | 12,6 x 9,2 x 4,7 cm

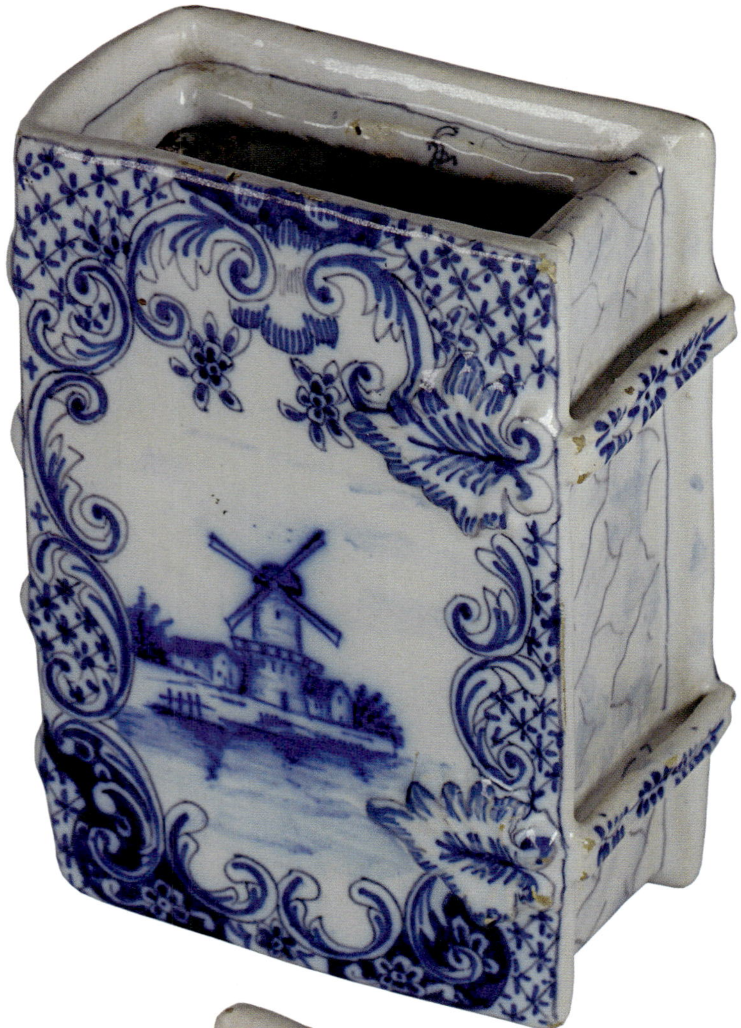

11.002
Physik. Wir wissen zwar nicht, was wir wollen aber das mit ganzer Kraft!
Physics. We do not know what we want but we want it with all our might!
Porzellan-Blumenvase
Porcelain flower vase
Funny Design
Made in West Germany
8,6 x 4,7 x 5,5 cm

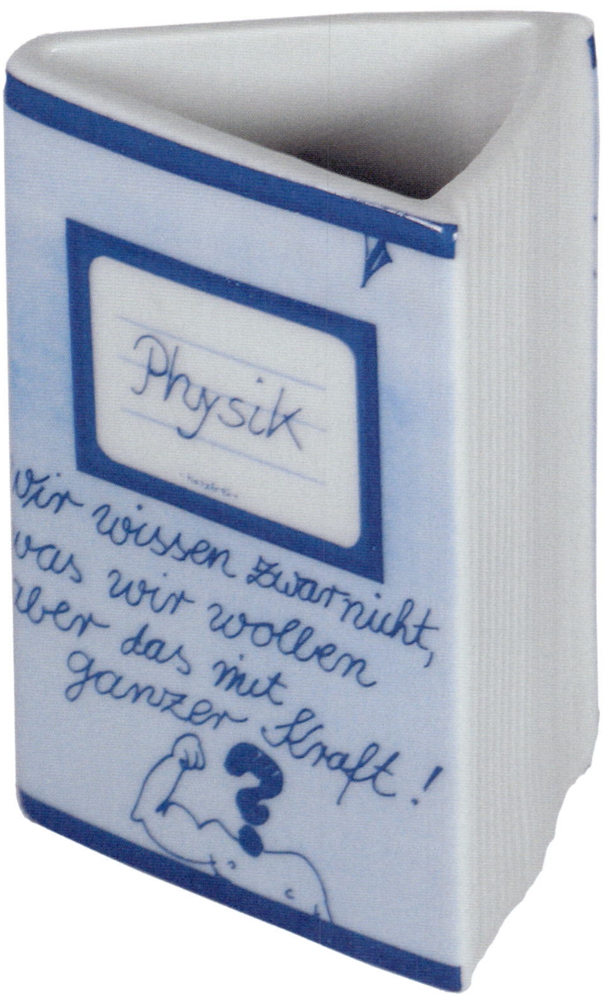

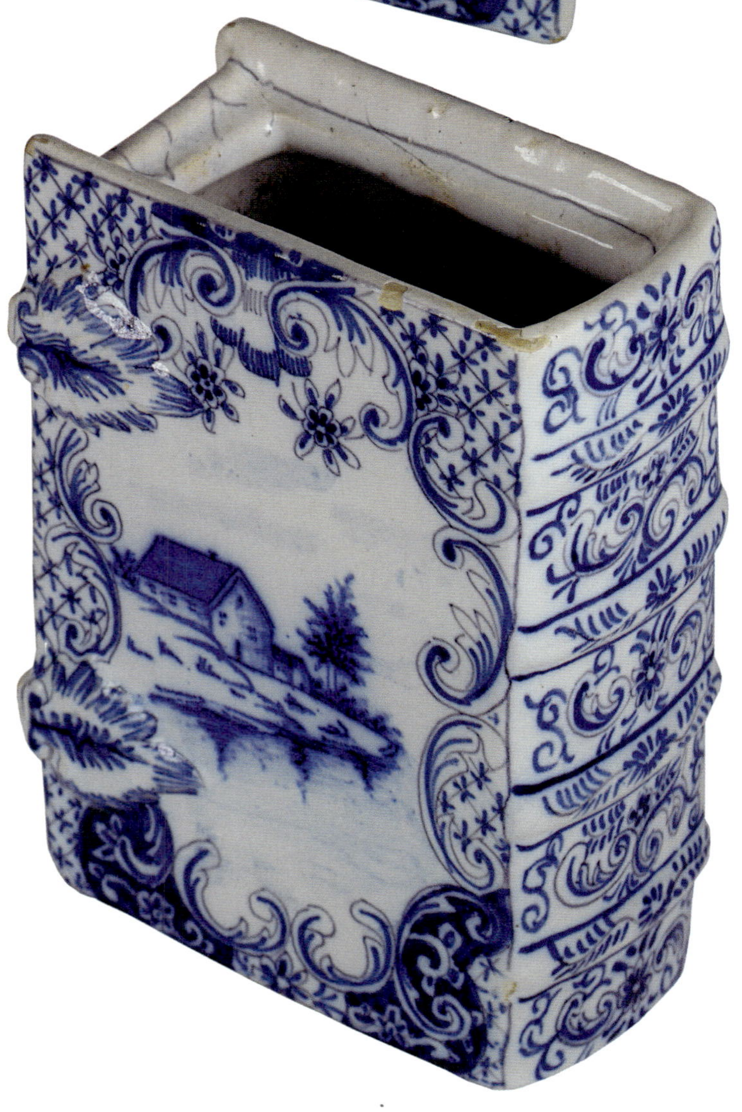

11.003
Blumenvase in der Form eines verschlissenen Buches, Blumendekor auf beiden Deckeln, Firmenstempel
Flower vase in the shape of a used book, floral design on both covers, company stamp
Stipo Dorohoi Porcelain, Rumänien / *Romania*
12,4 x 8,4 x 5 cm

11.004
Keramikblumenvase von Rabiusla Herrliberg, zwei erhabene Bünde, signiert
Ceramic flower vase by Rabiusla Herrliberg, two raised bands, signed
12,8 x 11,5 x 4,8 cm

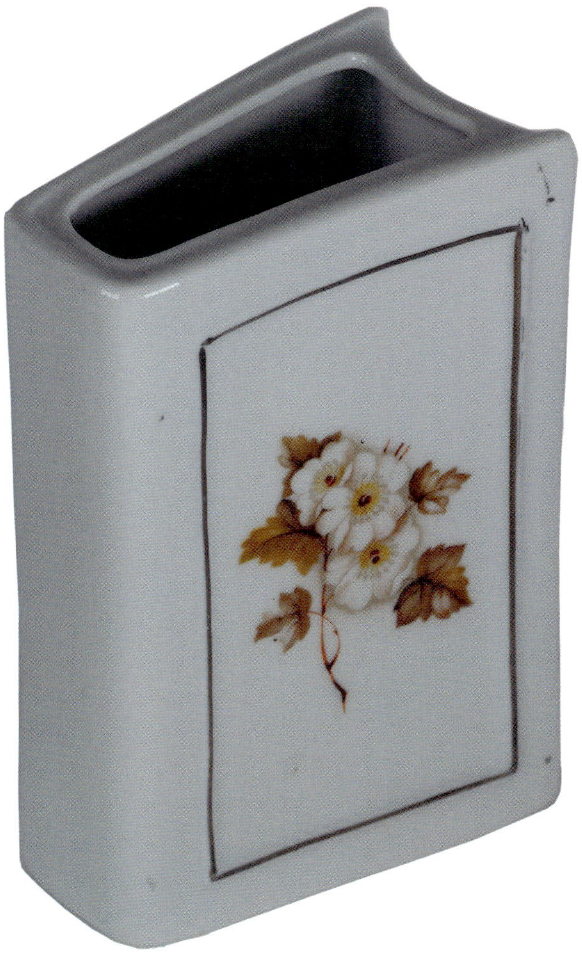

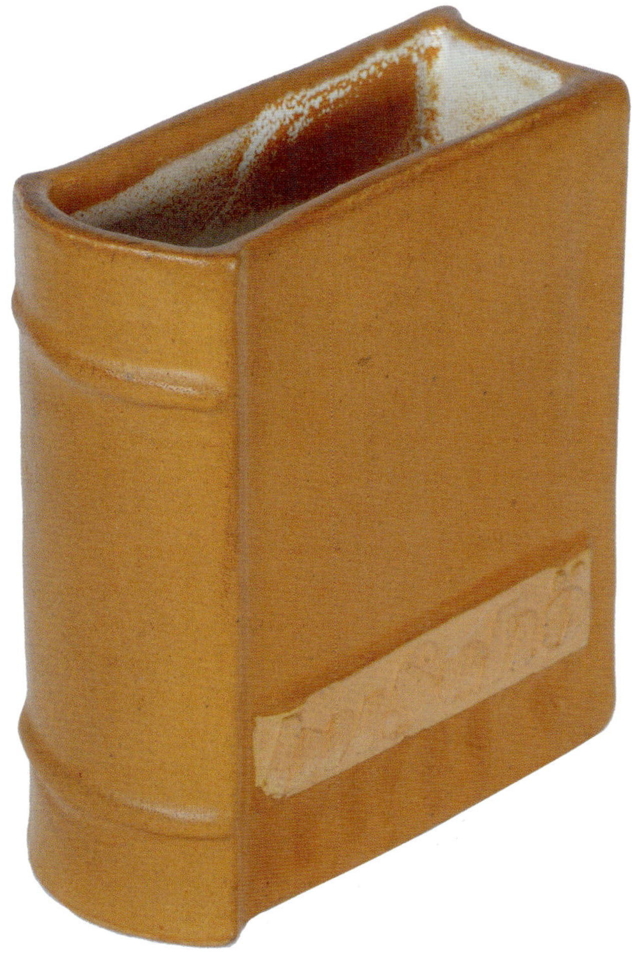

11.005
Wohl Weihwasserbehälter aus Milchglas zum Aufhängen, reliefiertes Blumensujet auf dem Vorderdeckel mit ornamentiertem Rahmen, seitliche Zierlinien
Probably a holy water container made of frosted glass to hang up, floral design in relief on the front cover with an elaborated frame, lateral decorative lines
7,2 x 8,2 x 3,1 cm

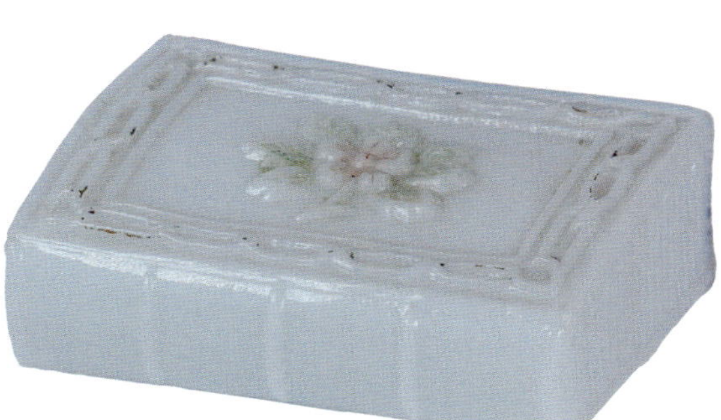

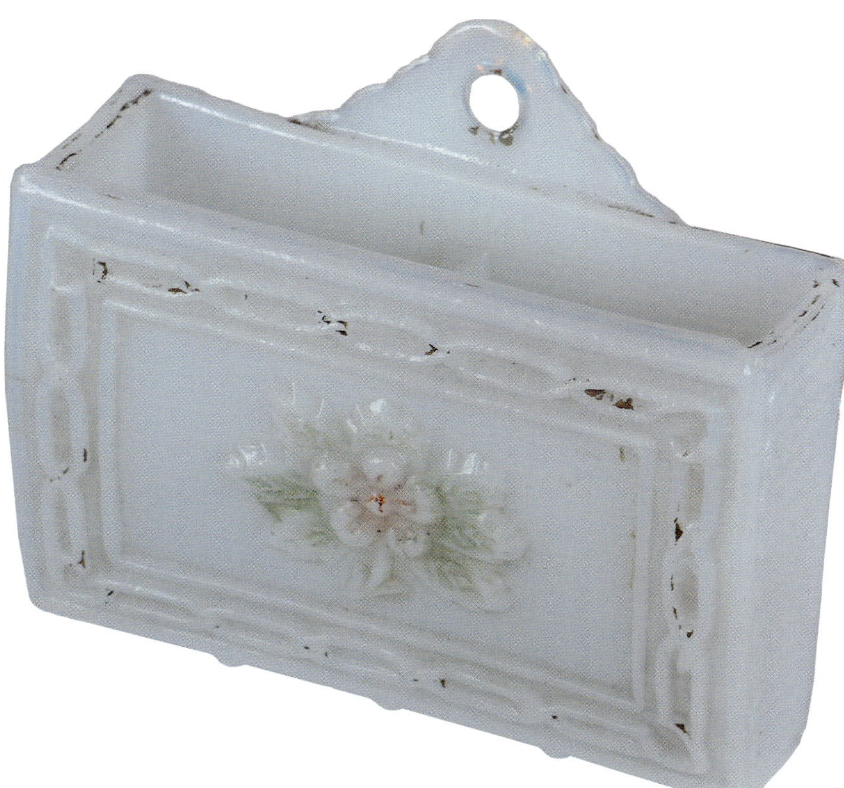

11.006
Connais-tu le pays aublemit
Keramik-Kerzenständer mit offenem Buch und Gefäß
Ceramic candle holder with an open book and a container
4,9 x 12,7 x 4 cm

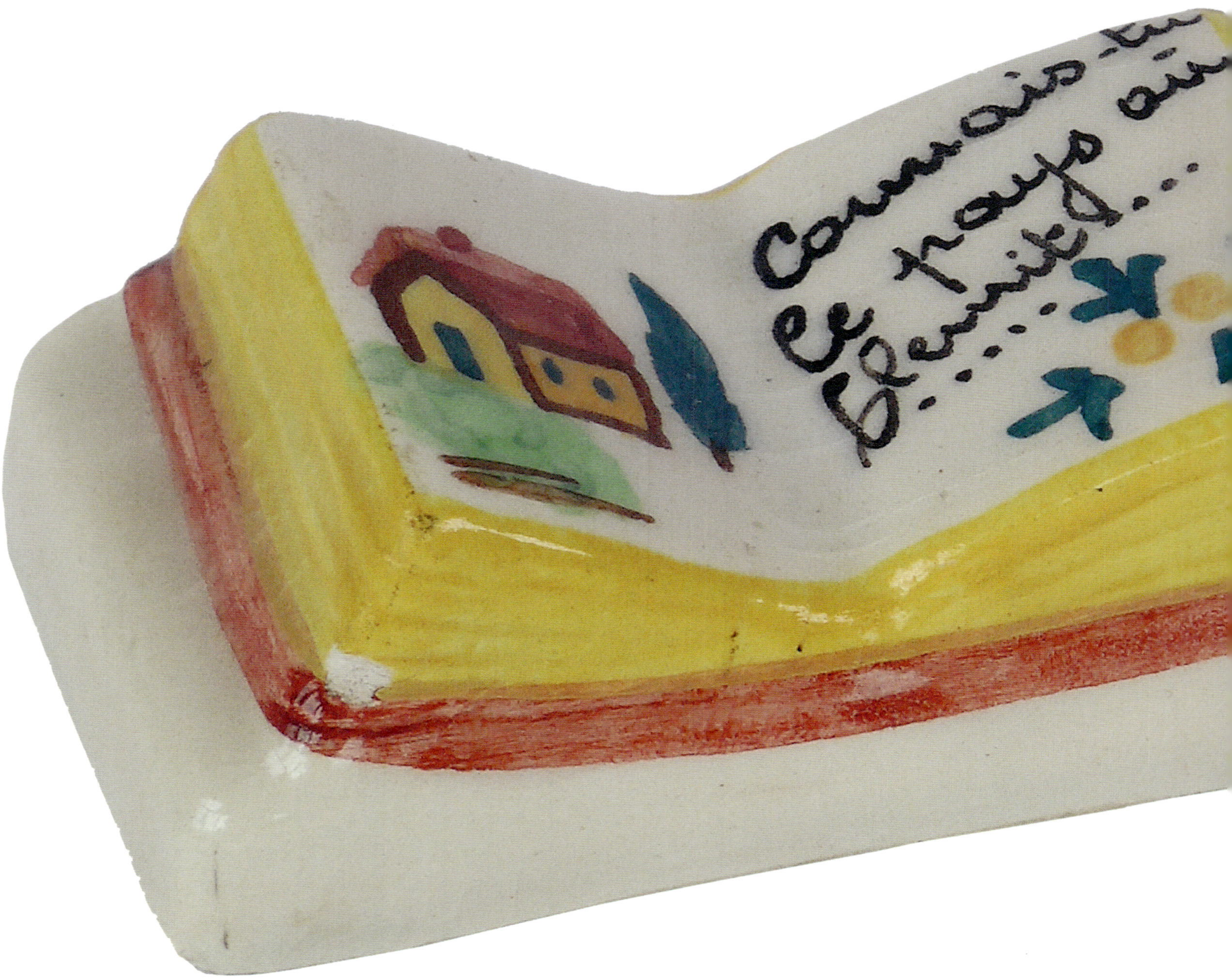

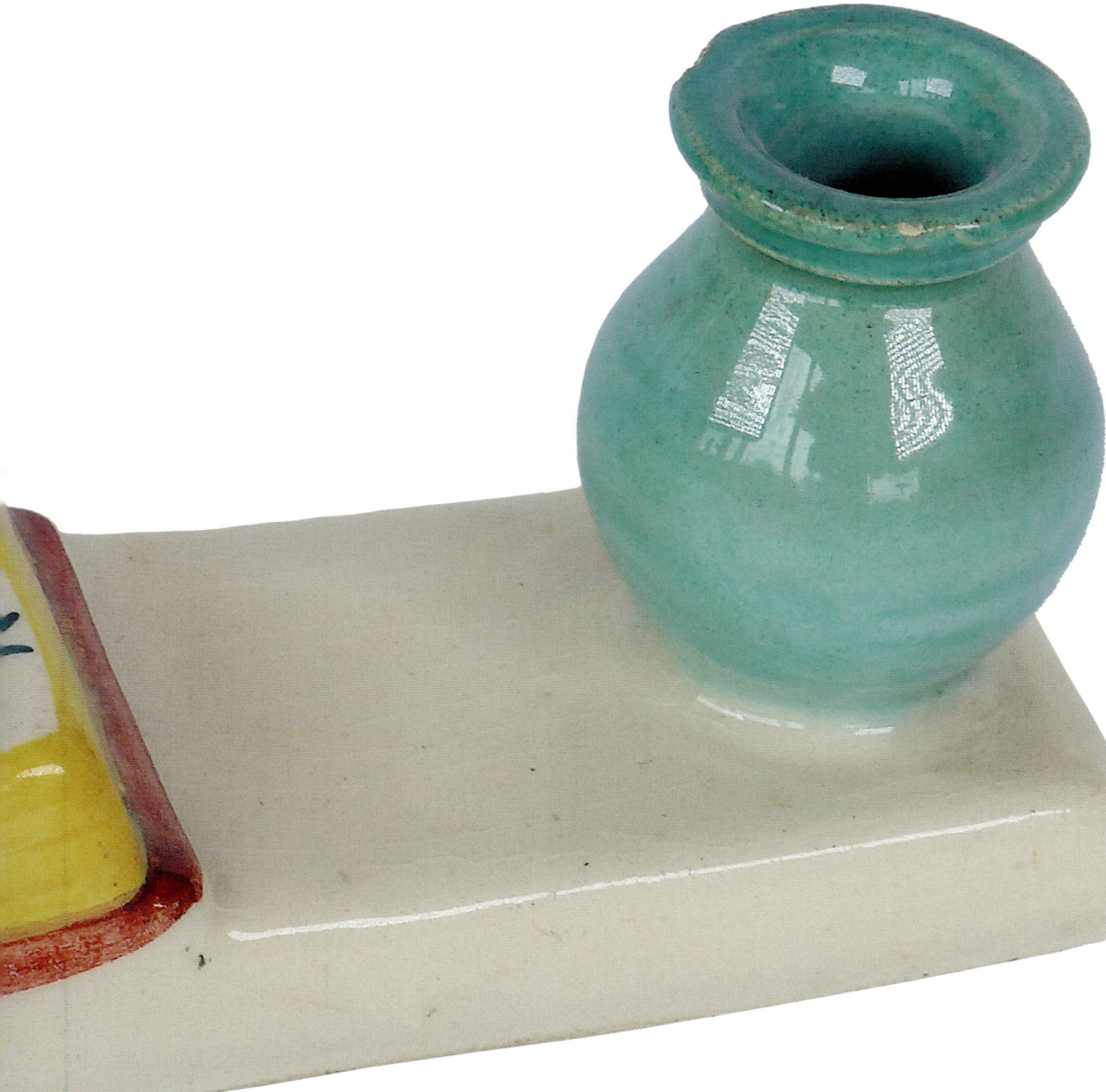

11.007
The Age of Innocence, Rob Roy. Walter Scott
Buchattrappe mit acht bemalten Buchrücken aus Holz, zwei seitliche Steller, Dekorations- und Werbeobjekt
Fake book with eight painted wooden spines, two side stands, decoration and advertising object
England | 27,8 x 39,1 x 22 cm

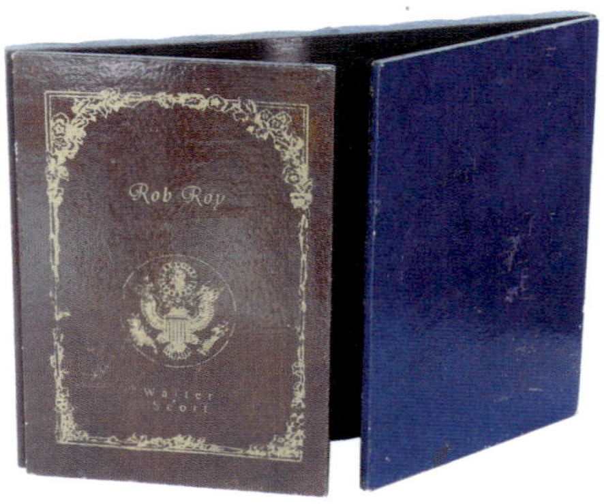

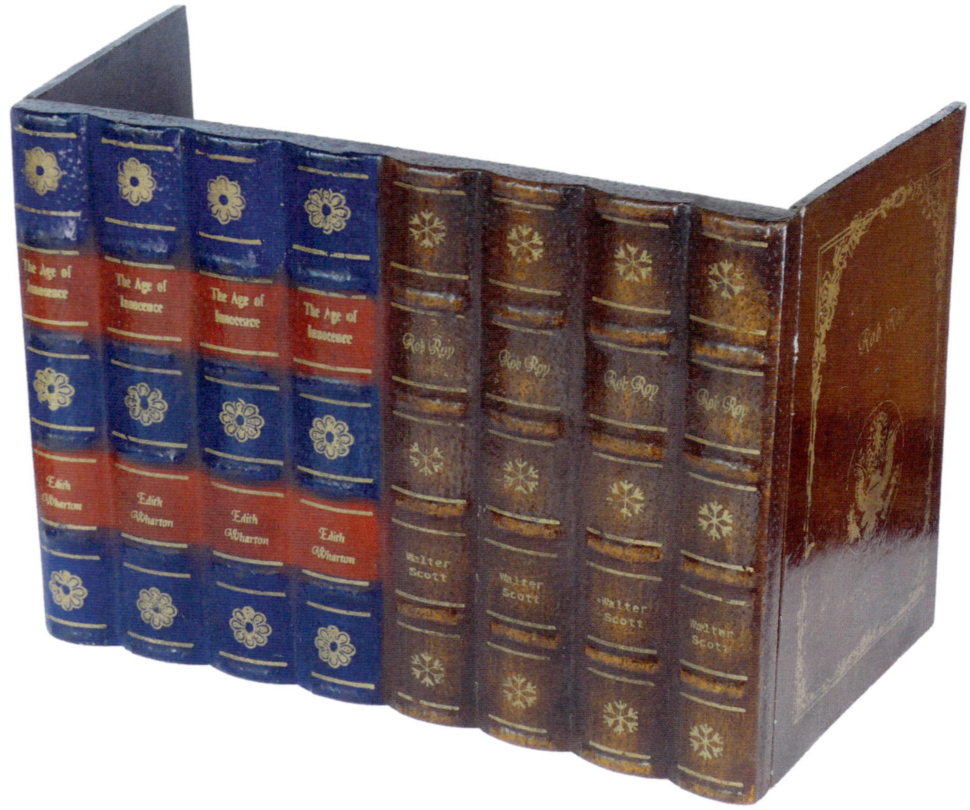

11.008
Kappstein: Goethe Werk und Welt
Goethe's Work and World
Buchattrappe aus Karton für Dekorationszwecke und Möbelhäuser, Rückenprägung
Fake book made of cardboard, used for decoration and furniture stores, embossing on the spine
19,5 x 12,2 x 3,2 cm

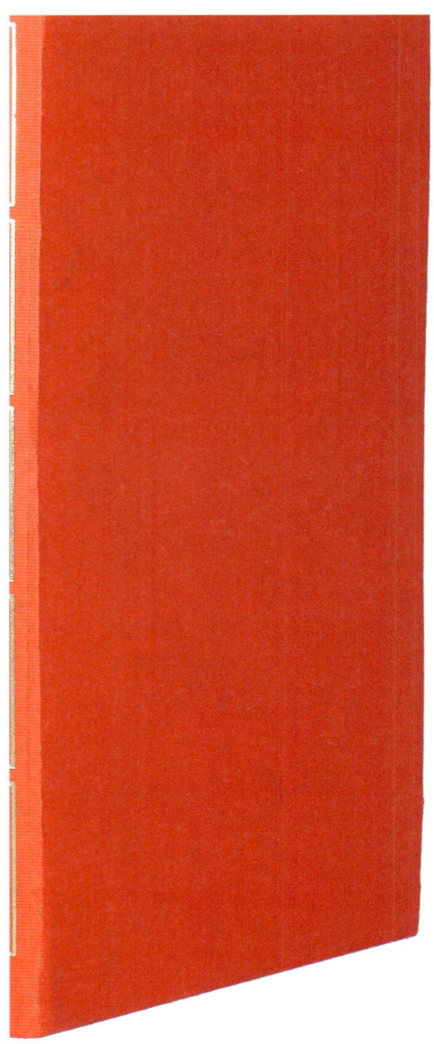

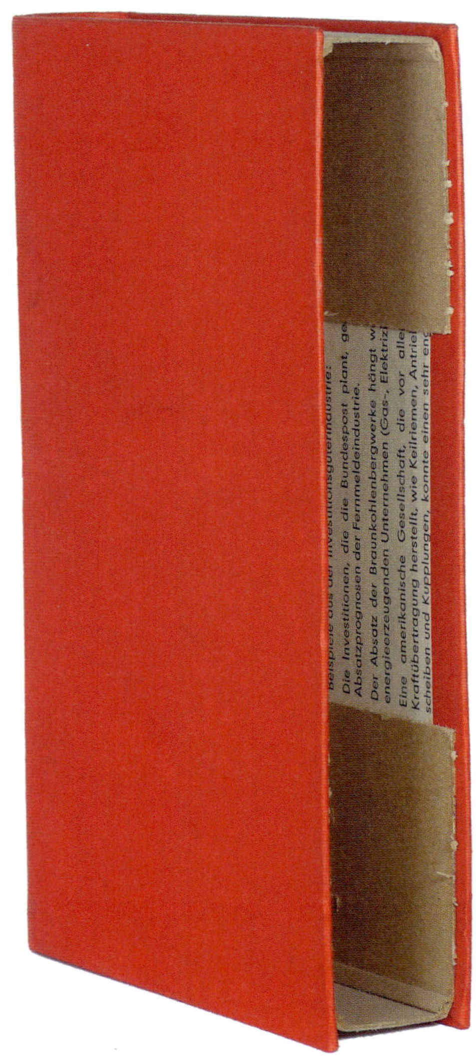

11.009
Oeuvres de la Fontaine, Volume III
Lederbuchrücken als Dekorationsobjekt, eine Scheinbibliothek vortäuschend, Rückenvergoldung
Leather book spines simulating a library, for decoration, gilt spine
18,1 x 4,4 x 1 cm

11.010
Theatr Franco, Tom. XI
Vollholz-Buchattrappe mit Lederrücken, handvergoldet, zwei Titelschilder, Vorder- und Hinterdeckel bemalt, Marmorpapierschnitt, Dekorationsobjekt
Solid wood fake book with a leather spine strip, manual gilding, with two label, painted front and back cover, marbled paper edges, for decoration
20,8 x 13,5 x 2,8 cm

11.011
Memoir de Sully, Tom. II + VII
Vollholz Buchattrappe mit Lederrücken, handvergoldet, zwei Titelschilder, Marmorpapierschnitt, Dekorationsobjekt
Solid wood fake book with leather spine, manual gilding , with two title plates, painted covers, marbled paper edges, decorative object
14,5 x 10,5 x 2,5 cm

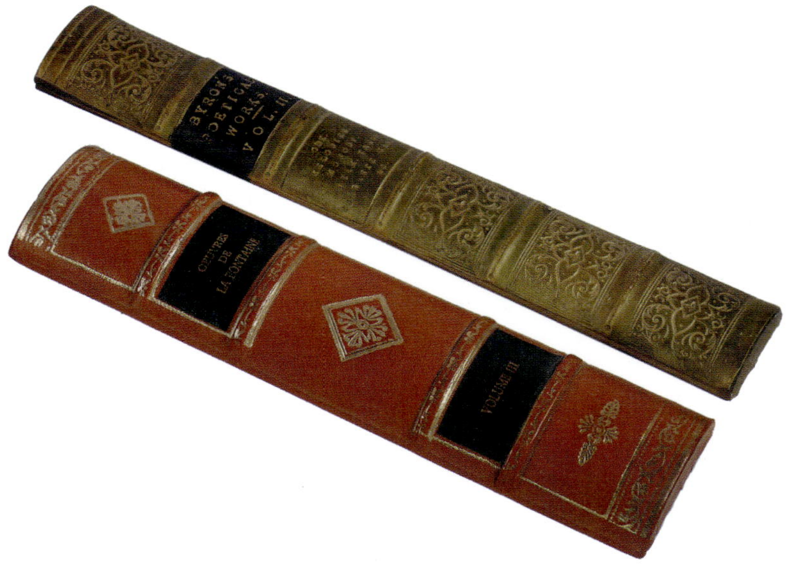

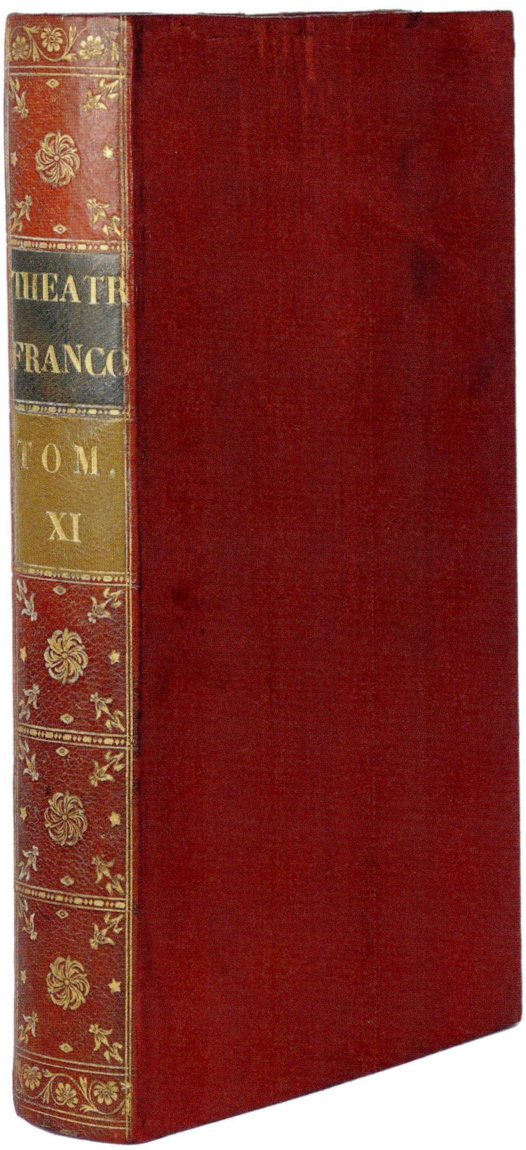

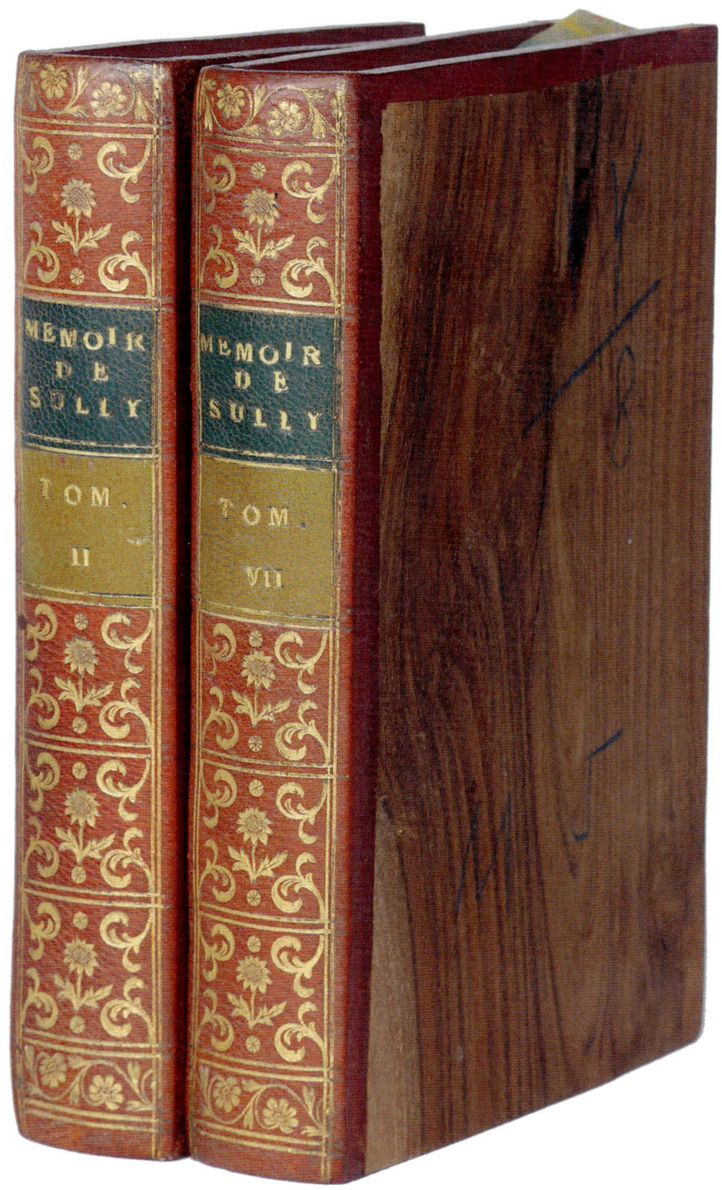

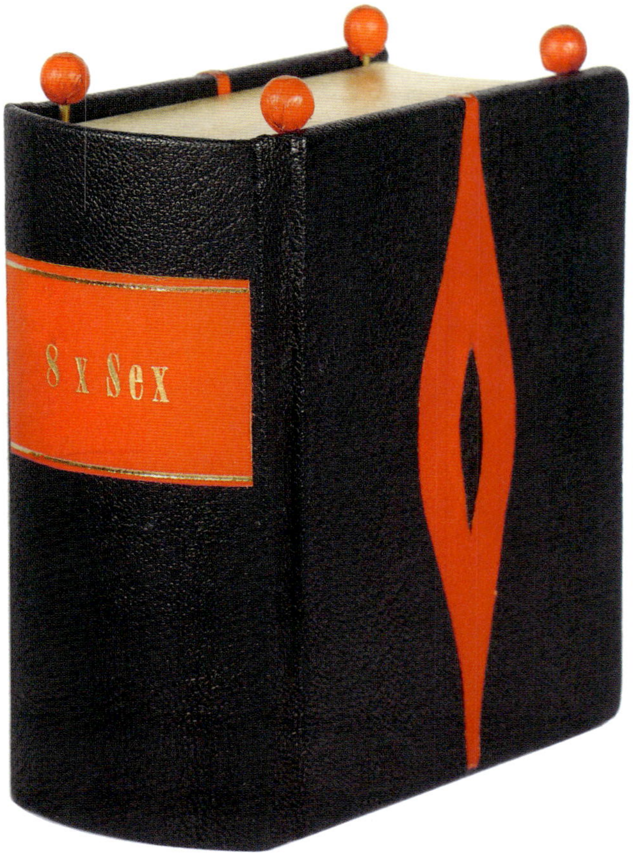

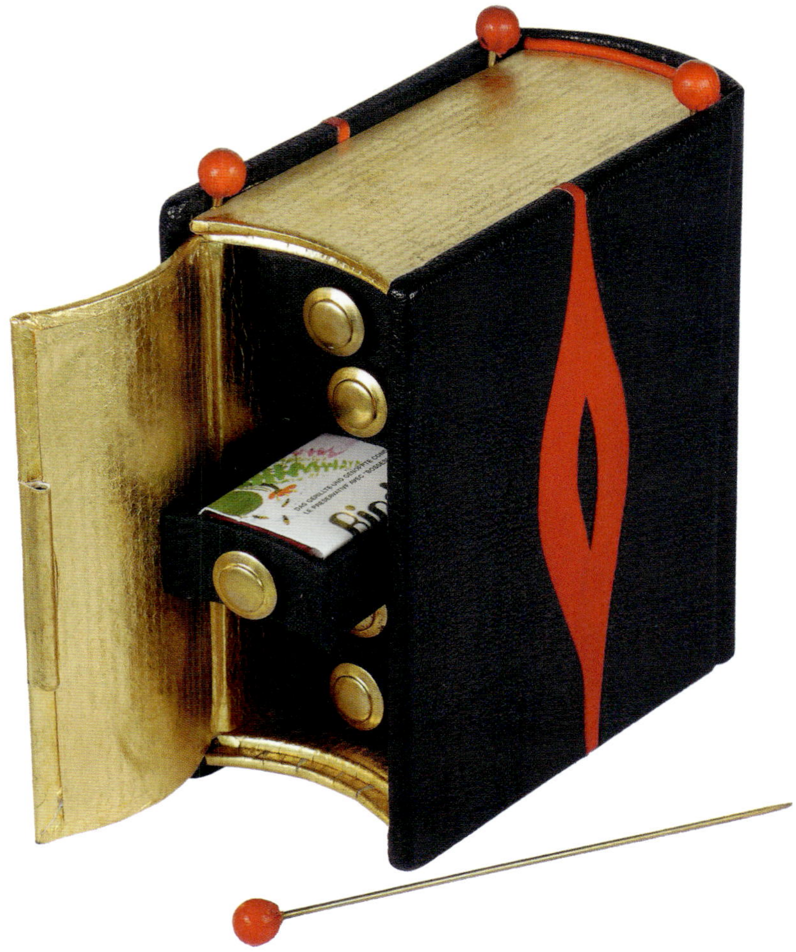

11.012
8 × Sex
Ganzlederkassette mit aufklappbarem Vorderschnitt und fünf Schubladen mit Kondomen, Rückenschild, Lederintarsien auf beiden Deckeln, Verschluss mittels eines langen Stifts, dreiseitiger Goldschnitt.
Full leather box with hinged fore edge and five drawers with condoms, label on the spine, leather inlays on both covers, closure with a long pin, all edges gilt
Hersteller / *Manufacturer*: Sybille & August Wirz Winterthur, Switzerland | 12,7 x 11,8 x 5,9 cm

11.013
Kunststoff- Streichholzschachtelhalter, beim Herausziehen vom Einschub erscheint eine erotische Szene, Reibfläche am Vorderschnitt
Plastic matchbox holder, an erotic picture appears when you pull it out of the slot, friction surface on the fore edge
2,2 x 5,2 x 4,1 cm

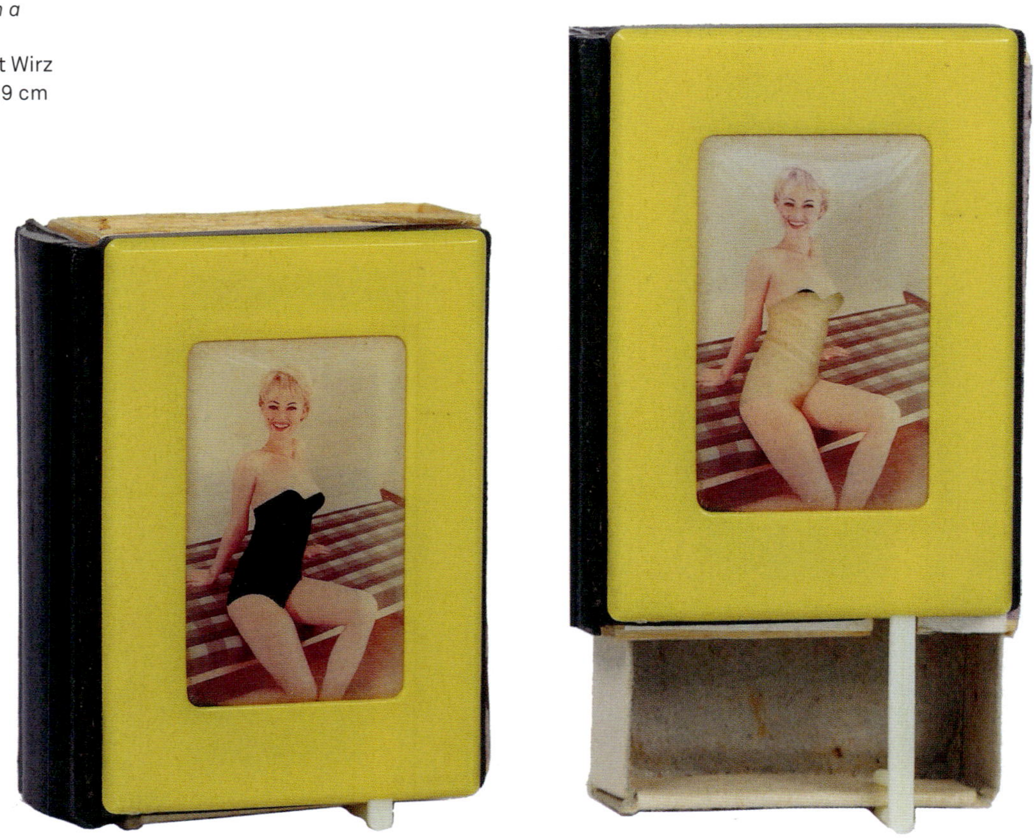

11.014
Record Shaves
Lithografierte Blechdose für die Entsorgung von gebrauchten Rasierklingen, Einwurfschlitz am Kopfschnitt, abnehmbarer Rücken
Lithographed tin box for the disposal of used razor blades, slot at the head edge, removable spine
England | Um / *Around* 1900
4,9 x 4,7 x 2,7 cm

11.015
Schnurrbartbürste aus Bakelit, aufklappbar
Hinged bakelite moustache brush
Um / *Around* 1900 | 6,4 x 2,3 x 1,2 cm

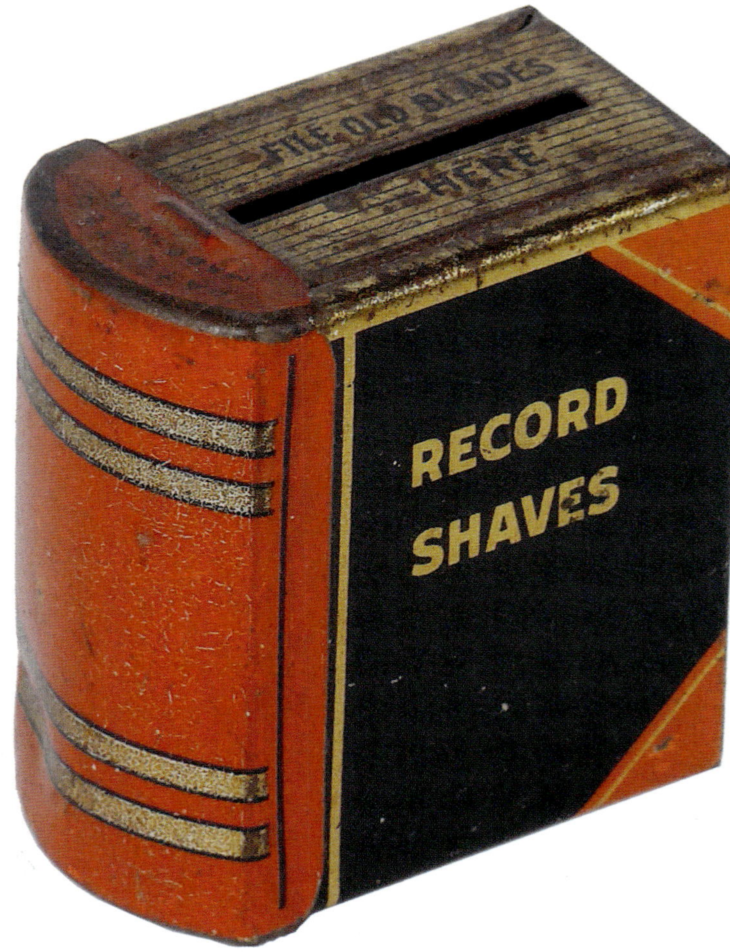

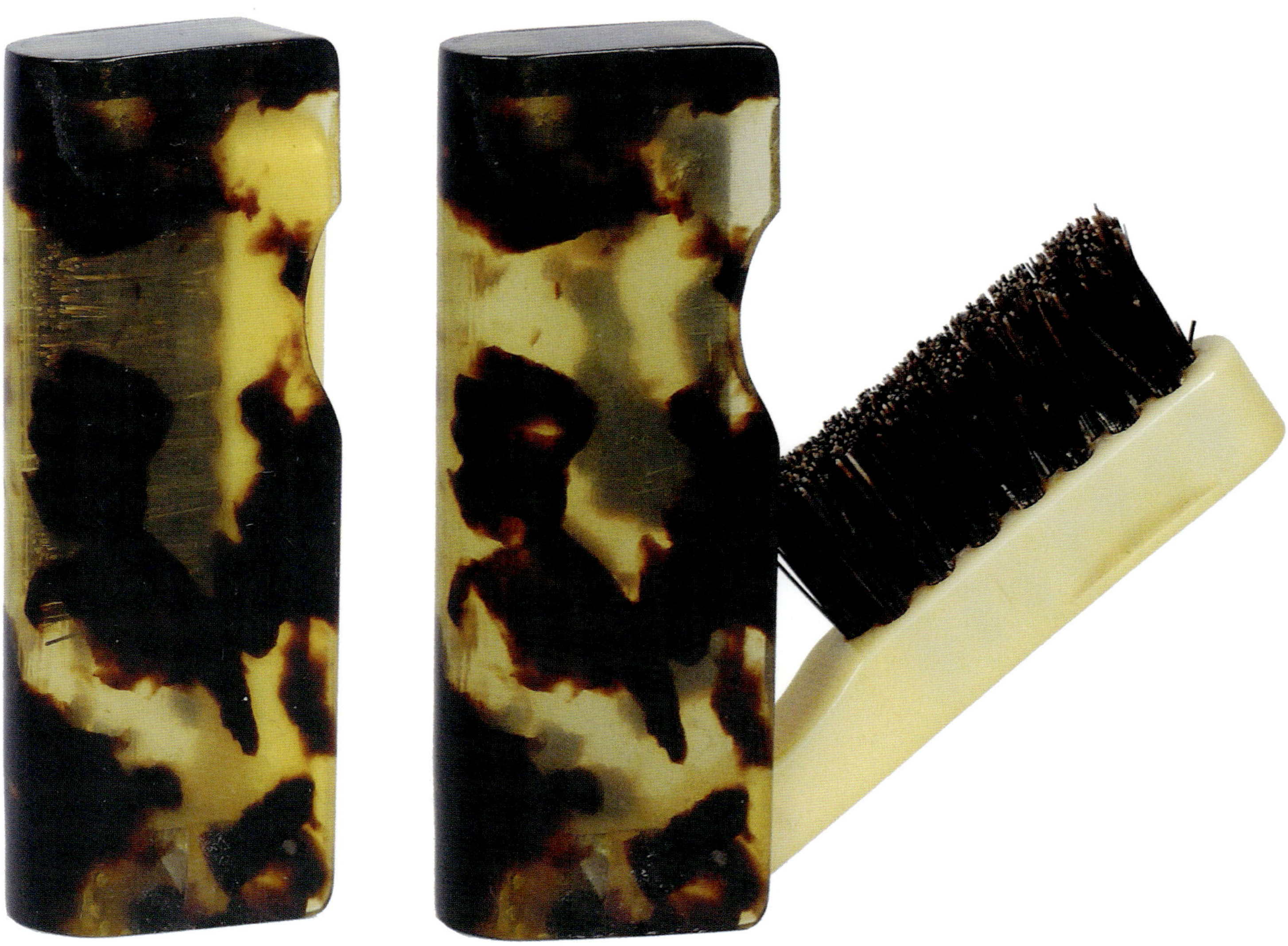

11.016
Geldbörse aus Schweinsleder,
aufklappbar, genähte Deckelkanten
Hinged wallet made of pigskin
with sewn edges on the cover
1,7 x 9,7 x 8 cm

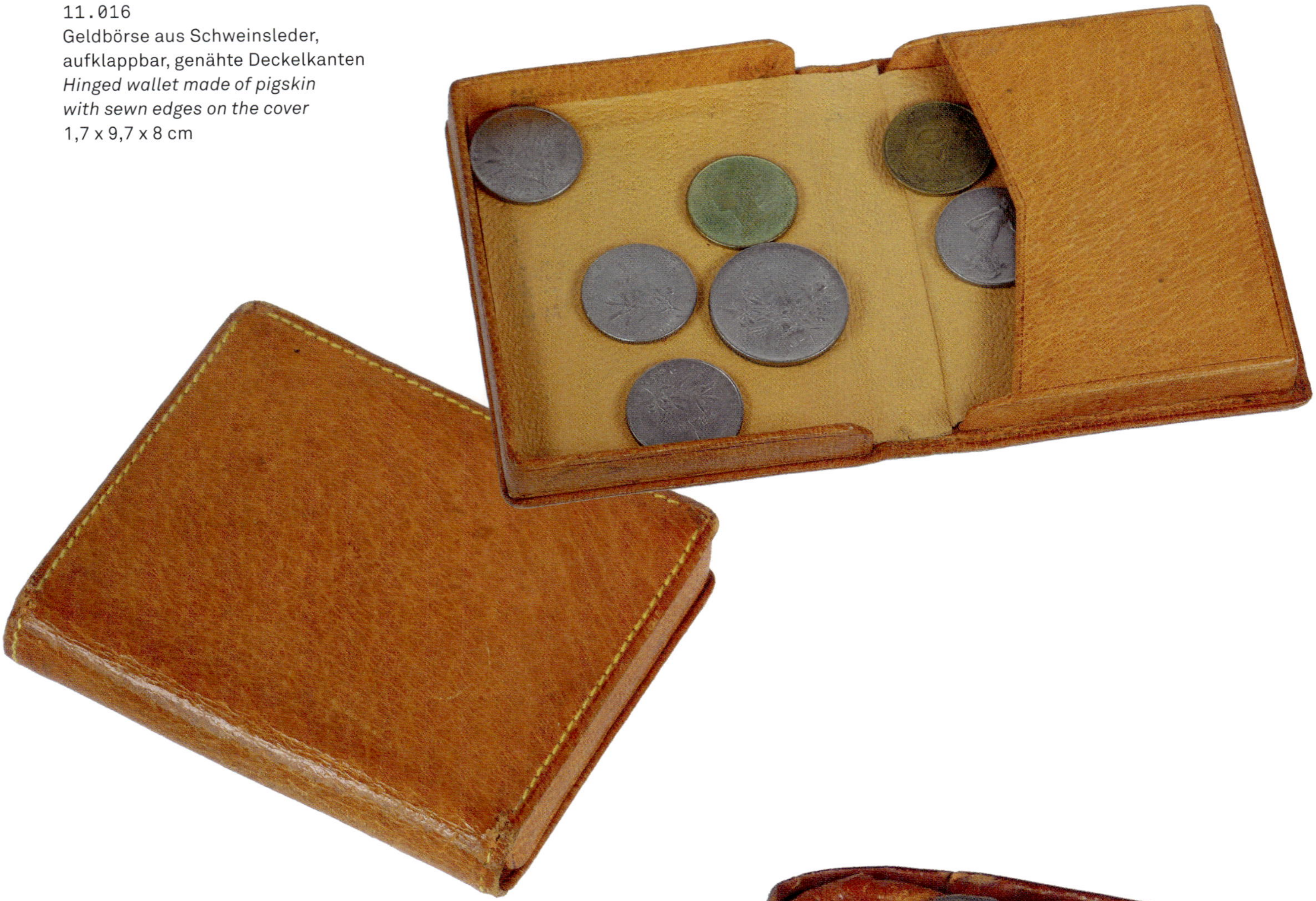

11.017
Mini Portemonnaie aus Leder,
Rücken- und Deckelvergoldung,
Klemmverschluss
Mini leather wallet with
clap closure, gilt spine and cover
Um / *Around* 1900 | 4,8 x 4,8 x 1,5 cm

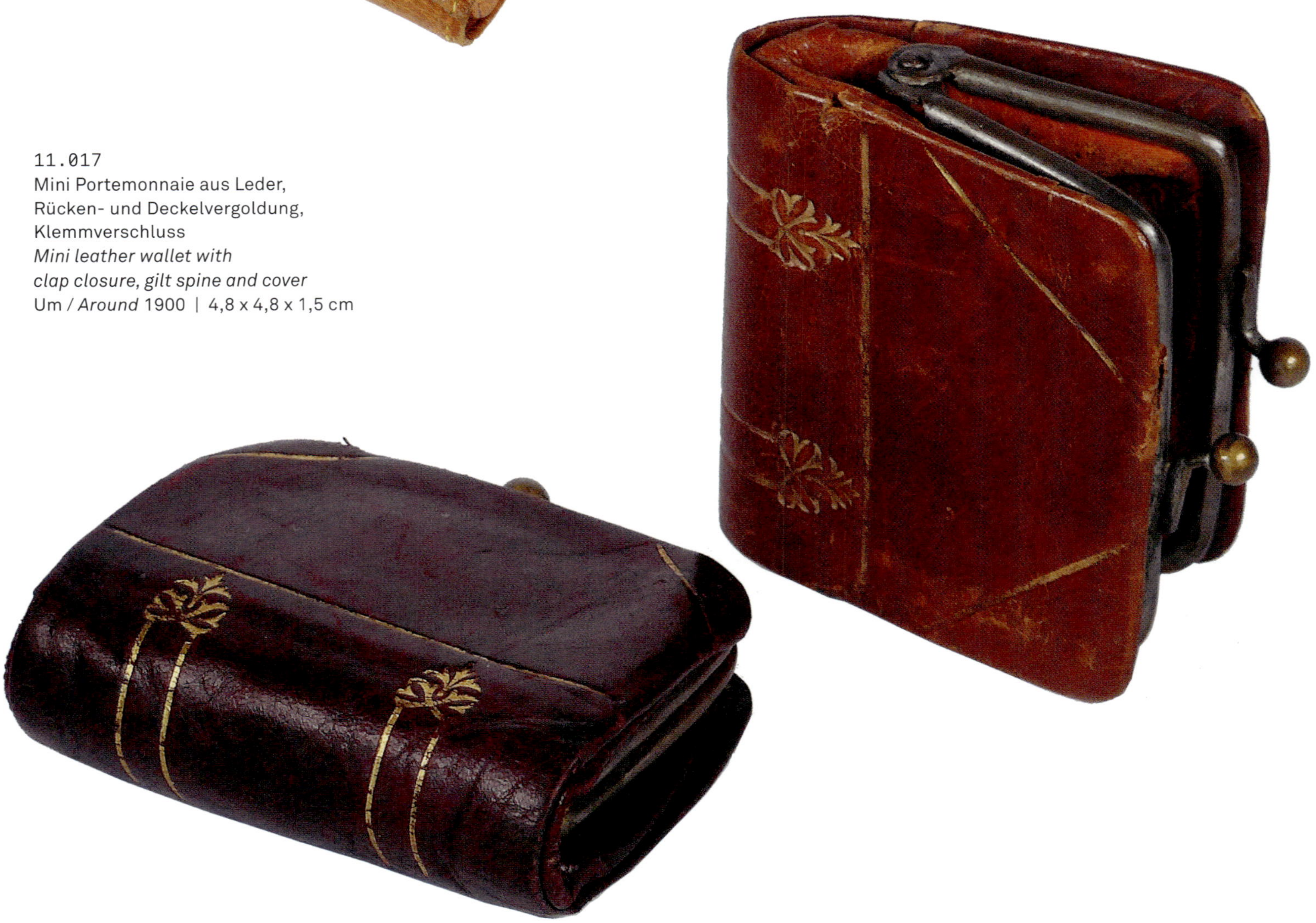

11.018

Dento

Lederbox mit Hals für die Zahnpflege-utensilien, Rückenschild, Lederintarsien, dreiseitiger Marmorabziehschnitt, ausgefüttert mit Steinmarmorpapier.

Leather box for dental care utensils, label on the spine, leather marquetry, marbled edges, lined with stone marble paper

Hersteller / *Manufacturer*: Sybille & August Wirz Winterthur, Switzerland | 10,5 x 11 x 3,7 cm

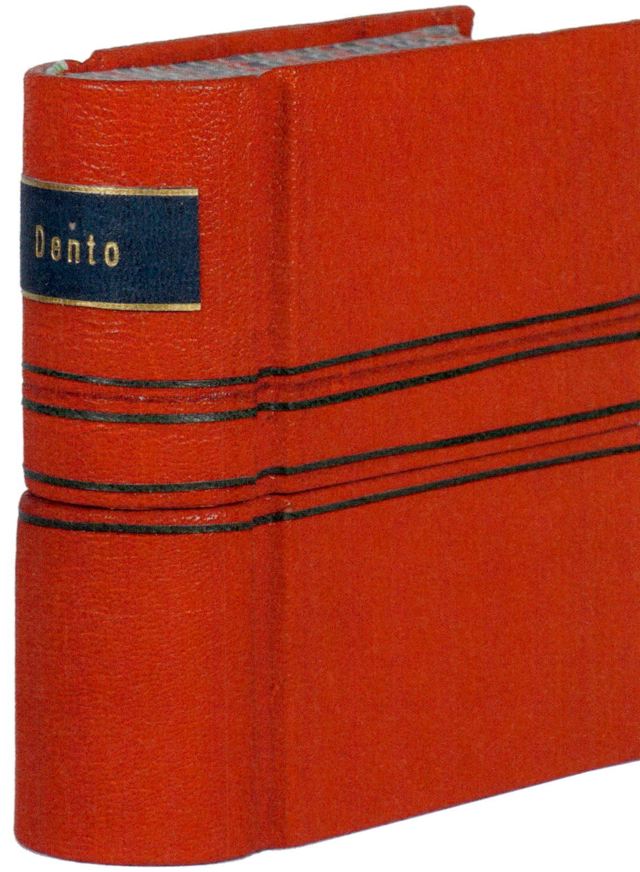

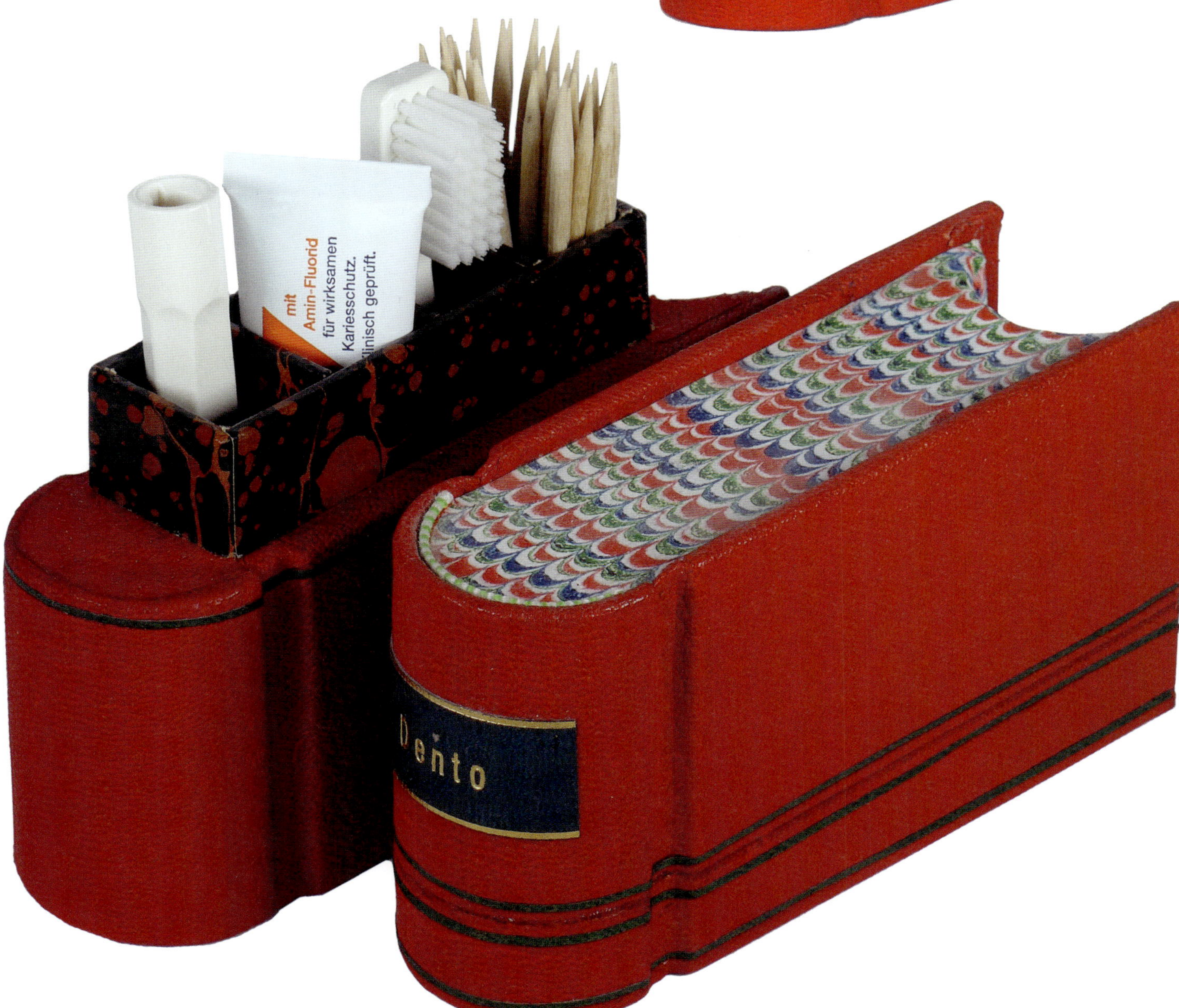

11.019
Asiatische Lackdosen mit Hals, schwarz lackiert, goldene Bemalung auf Rücken und Vorderdeckel, grauer Farbschnitt
Asian boxes with black varnish, golden decoration on the spine and the front cover, edges in grey color
3,5 x 8,7 x 6,5 cm

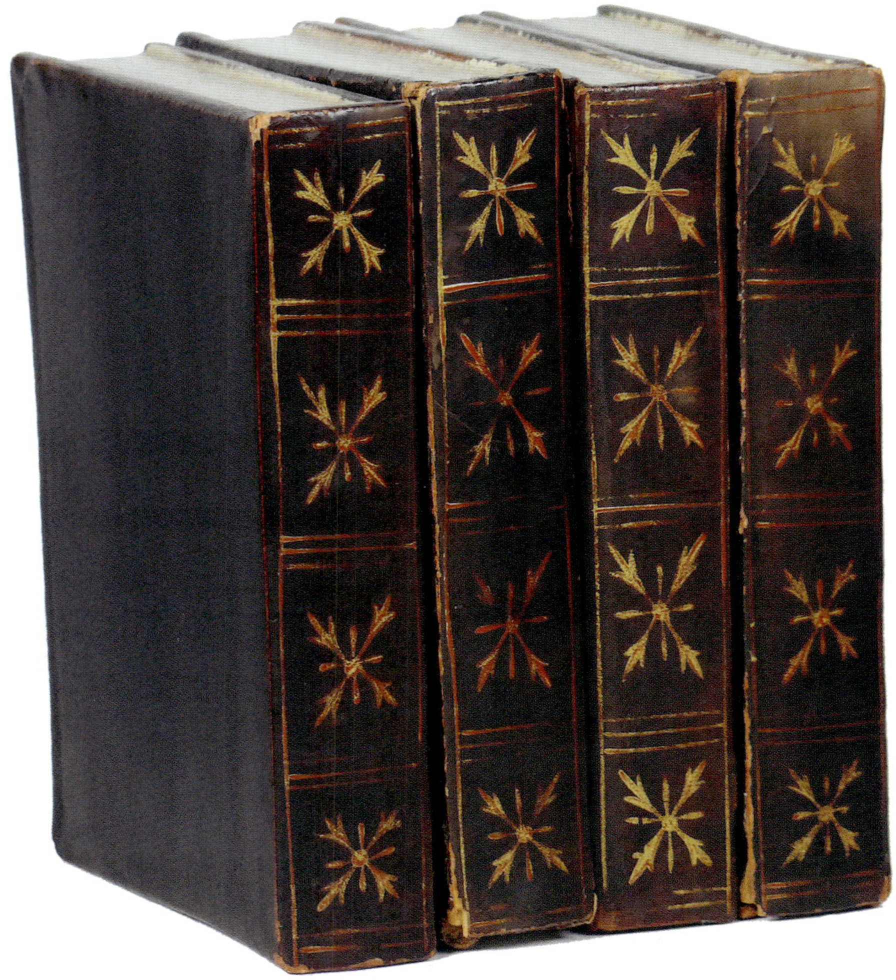

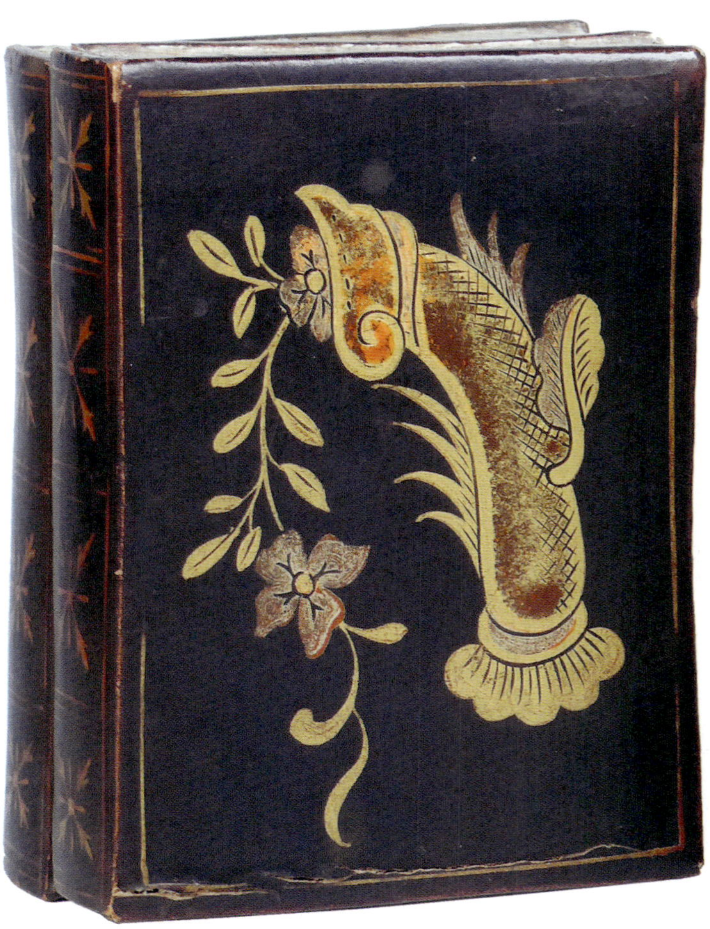

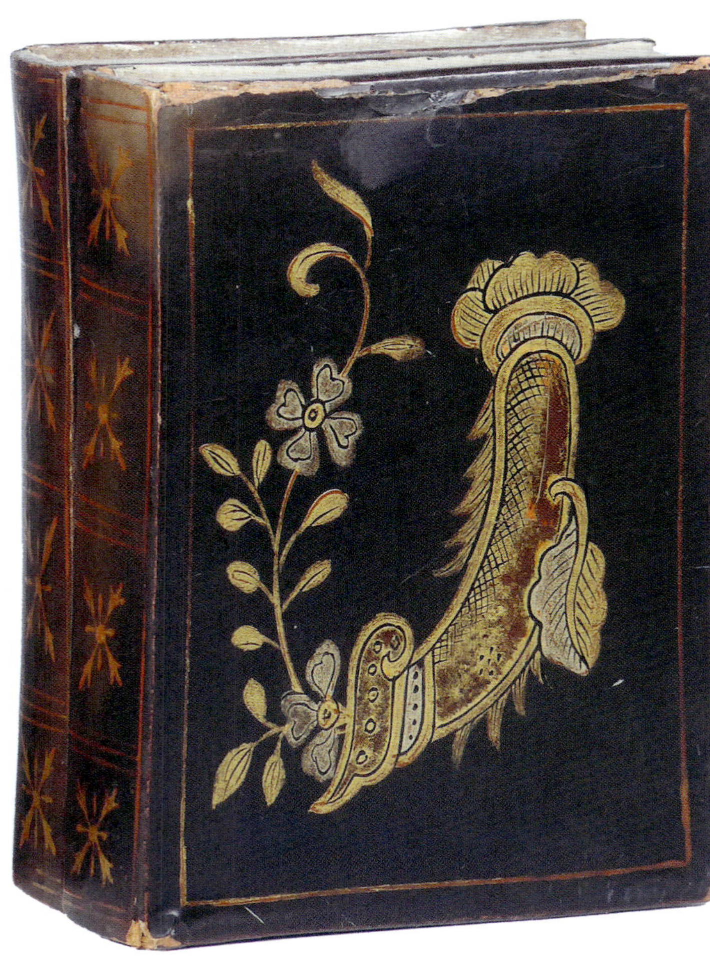

11.020
Chinesische Lackschatulle aus Holz mit gewelltem Deckel, golden und farbig bemalt mit Vögeln und Blütenzweigen, abschließbar
Chinese lacquer box made of wood with a wavy cover, painted with birds and flowering twigs in gold and color, lockable
5 x 27 x 9 cm

11.021
Chinesische Lackschatulle aus Holz, farbig und golden bemalt mit Vogel und Blütenzweigen, gravierte Metallschließe
Chinese wooden lacquer box, decorated with a bird and flowering twigs in gold and color, engraved metal clasp
5,5 x 14 x 9,7 cm

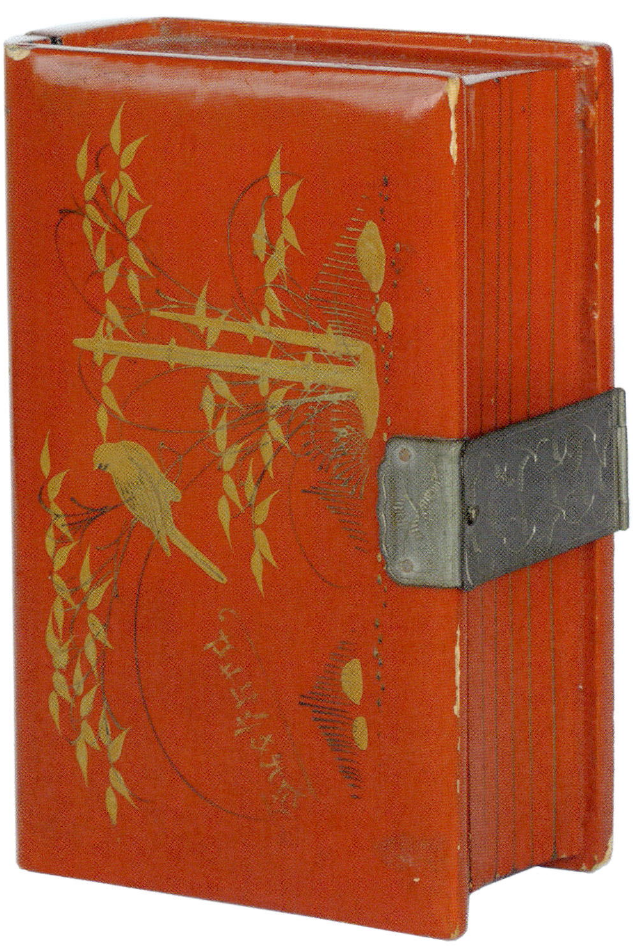

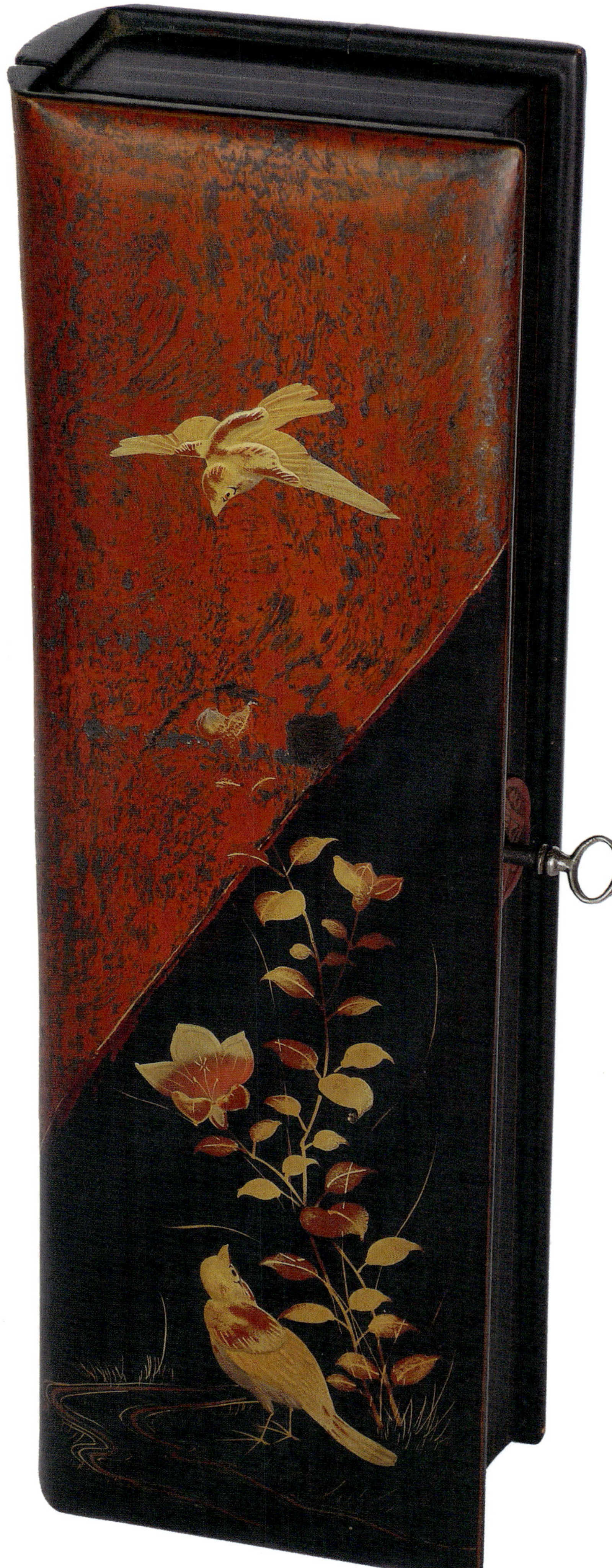

11.022
Chinesische Lackschatulle aus Holz, golden und farbig bemalt mit Vögeln und Blütenzweigen, Metallverschluss
Chinese lacquer box made of wood, decorated with birds and flowering twigs in gold and color, metal clasp
8,4 x 20,5 x 17,2 cm

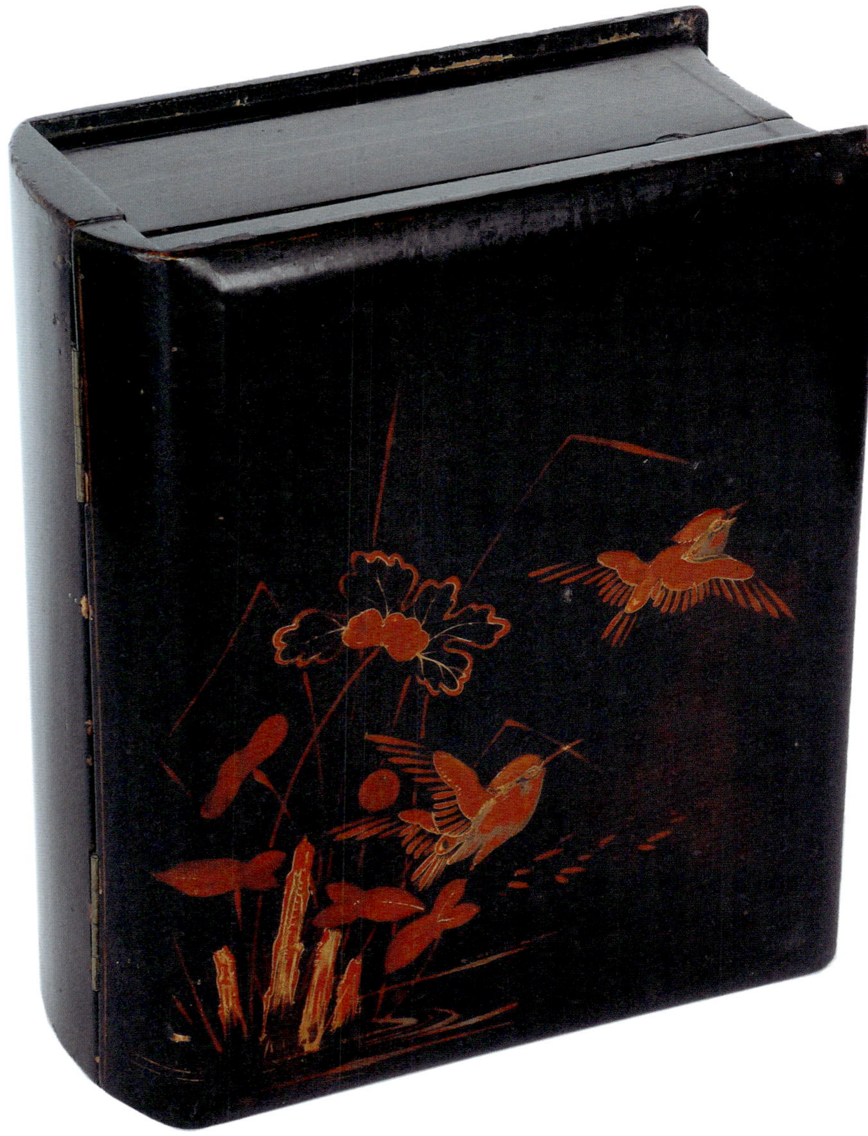

11.023
Chinesische Lackschatulle mit Hals, golden und farbig bemalt, Theaterszene mit drei Putten, dreiseitiger Goldschnitt
Chinese lacquer box with neck, painted in gold and color, theater scene with three putti, all edges gilt
18,4 x 14,2 x 6,5 cm

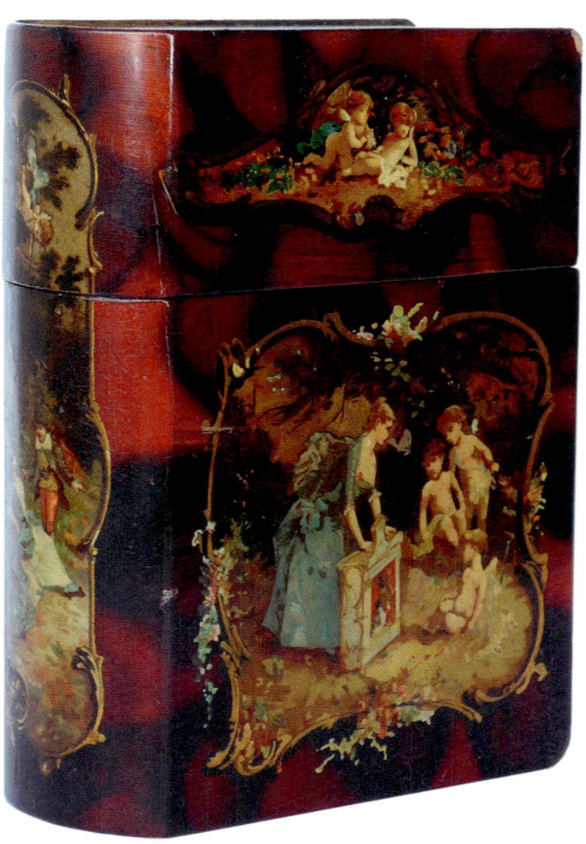

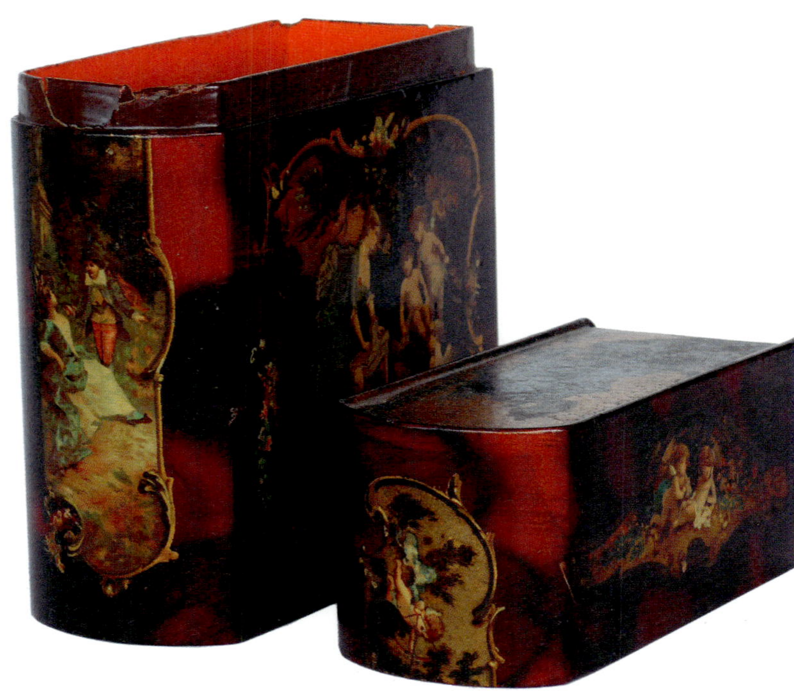

11.024
Japanische Holzschatulle mit Schublade am Fußschnitt, farbig bemalter Buchrücken und Buchschnitte, vorderer Deckel bemalt und graviert
Wooden Japanese box with drawer at the foot edge, colored book spine and edges, painted and engraved front cover
3,7 x 12 x 9,3 cm

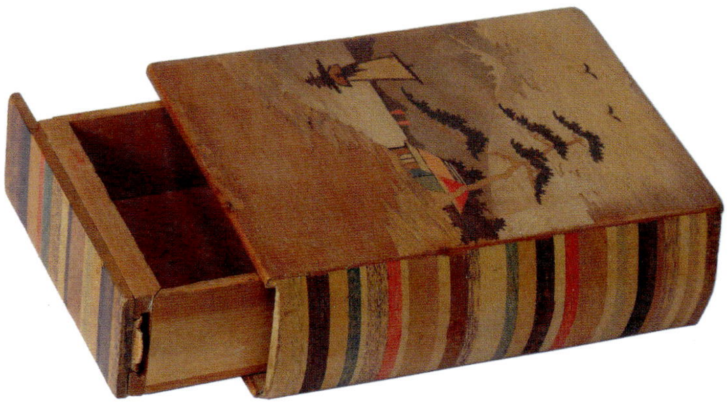

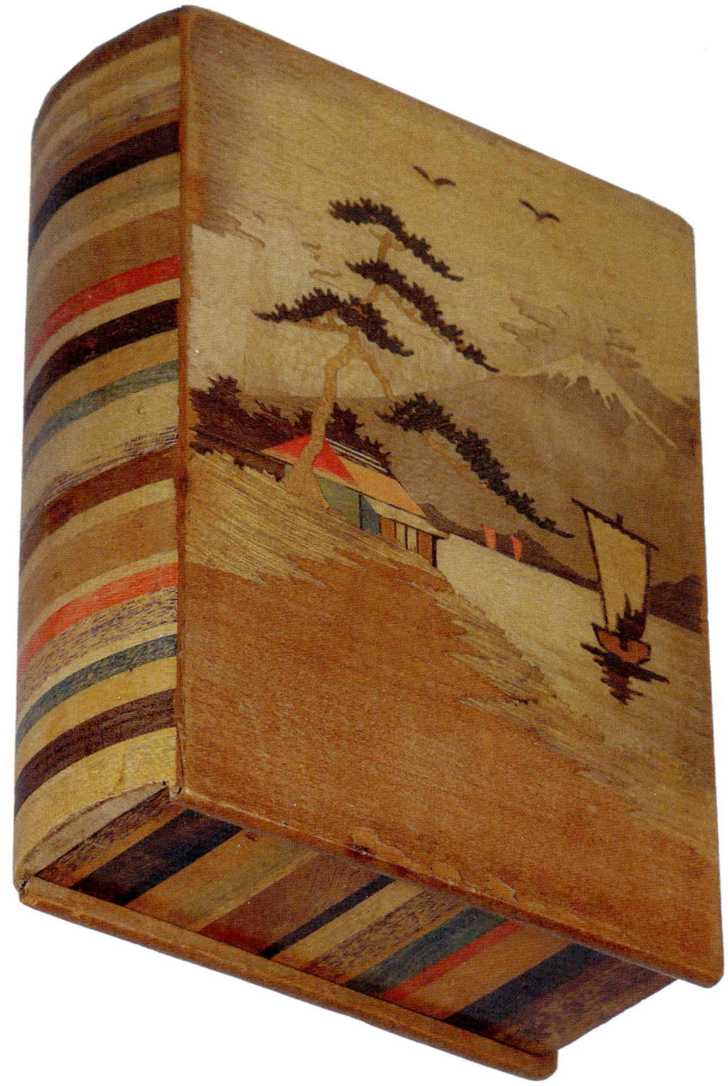

11.025
Japanische Email-Deckeldose, drei liegende Messingbücher mit Hals, Kirschblütendekor auf dem Vorderdeckel
Japanese enamel box with lid, three horizontal books of brass with neck, cherry blossoms on the front cover
Zeitgenössisch / *Contemporary*
3,5 x 6,2 x 4,4 cm

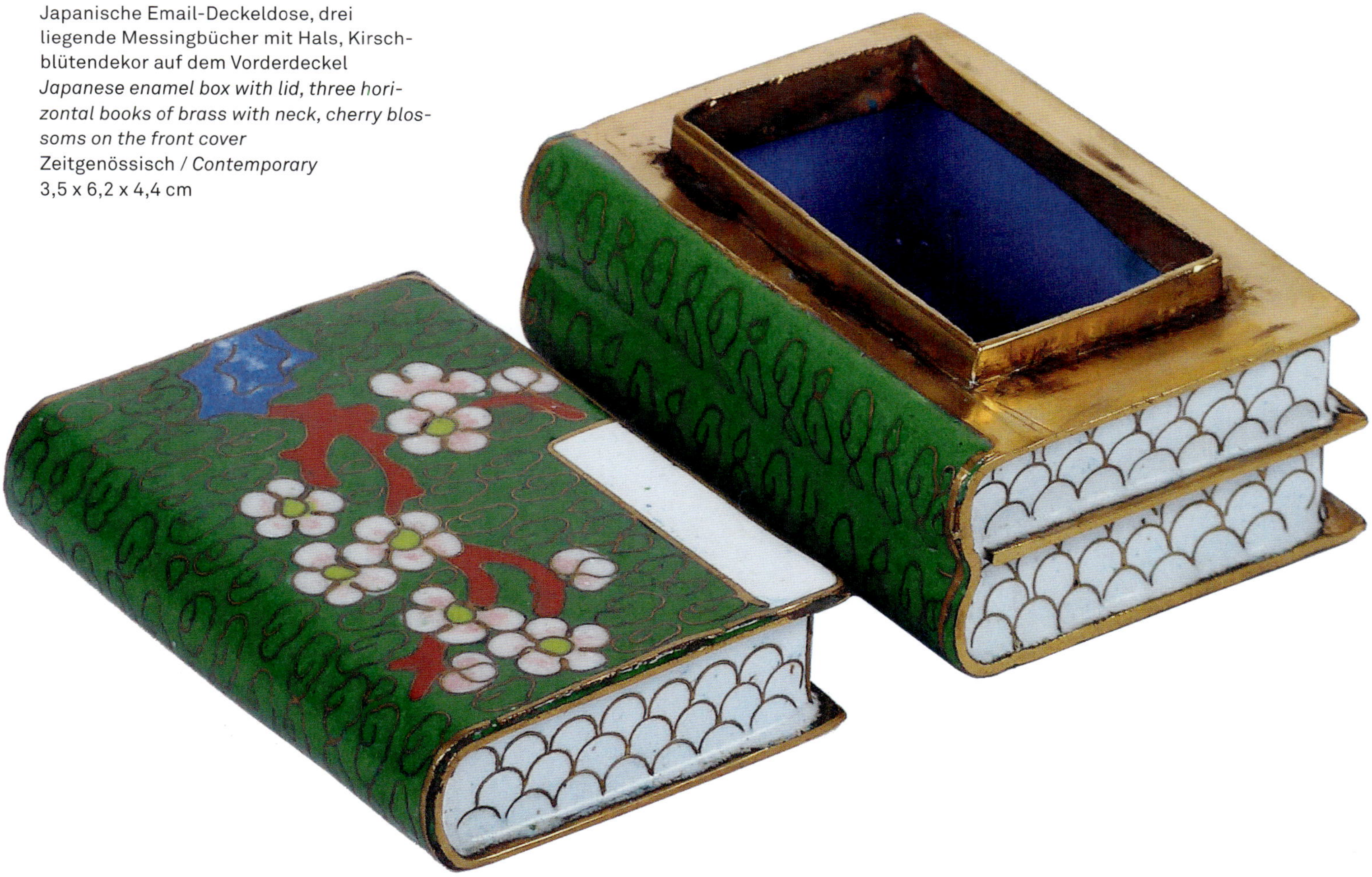

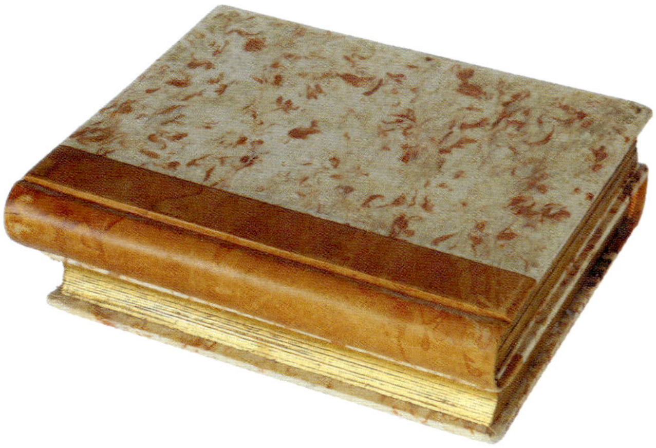

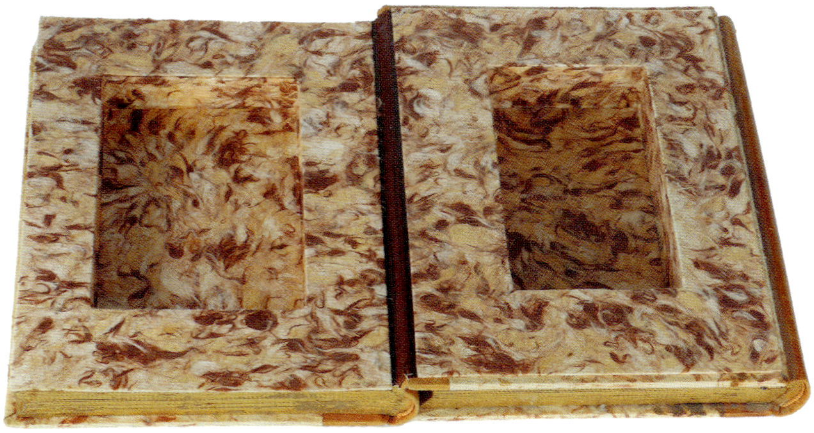

11.026
Halbleder Zwillingsbuch / ***Half leather twin book***
Zwei ausgehöhlte Bücher so verbunden, dass die Rücken einander gegenüberstehen, Überzug und Innenleben aus Japanpapier, dreiseitiger Goldschnitt
Two hollowed out books connected in such a way that the spines face each other, cover and interior made of Japanese paper, all edges gilt
8 x 25,9 x 23 cm

11.027
Ausgehöhlter brauner Ledereinband Versteck für einen Trommelrevolver, Holzdeckel, zwei Schließen, Blindendruck mit Stempel und Streicheisen, Buchschnitt und ausgefüttert mit Bouquetmarmorpapier
Hollowed out book with brown leather binding, hiding place for a revolver, wooden cover, two clasps, blind printed with stamp and prankster, book edges and lining of bouquet marbled paper
16. Jh. / *16th century* | 18 x 11,7 x 4 cm

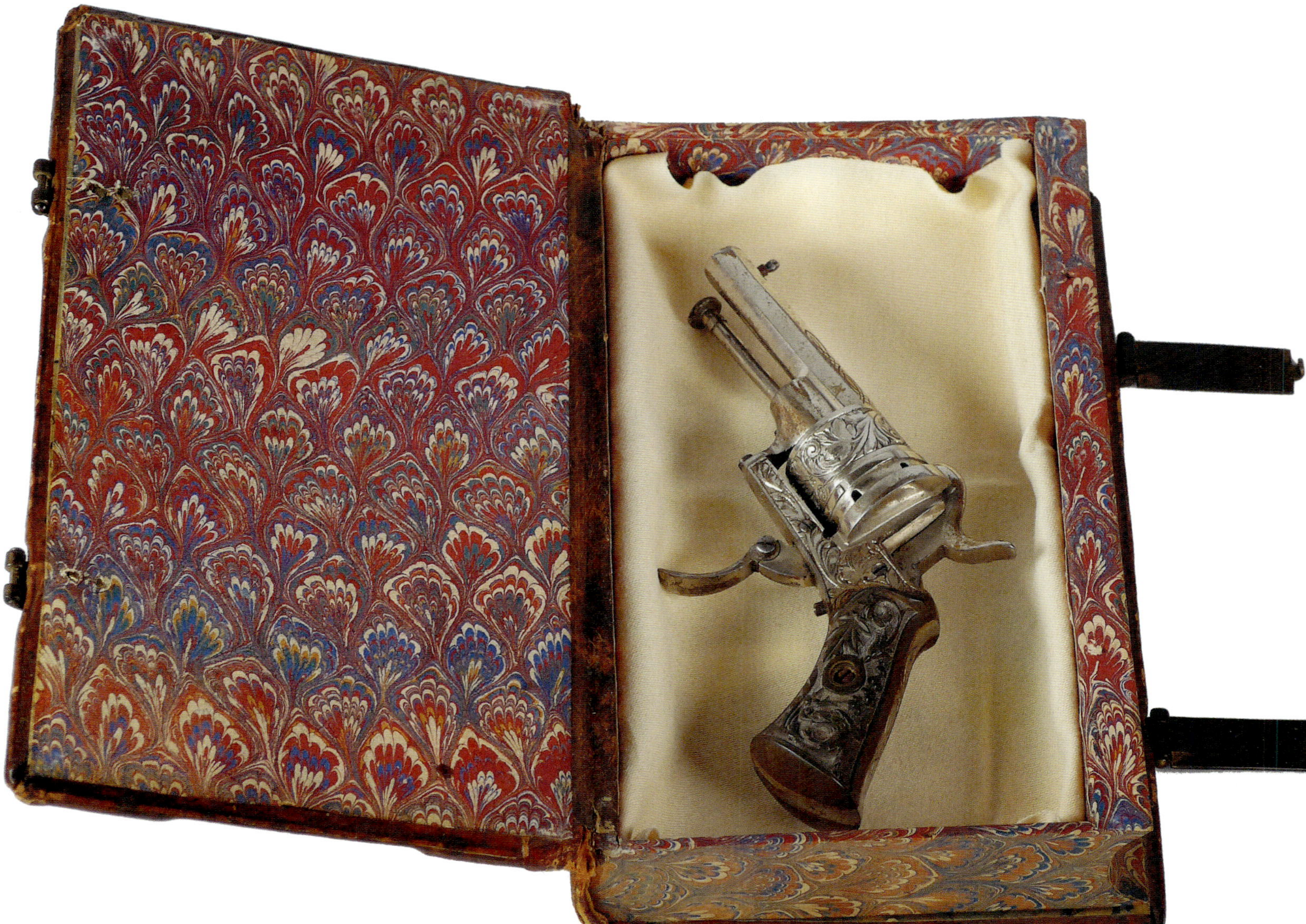

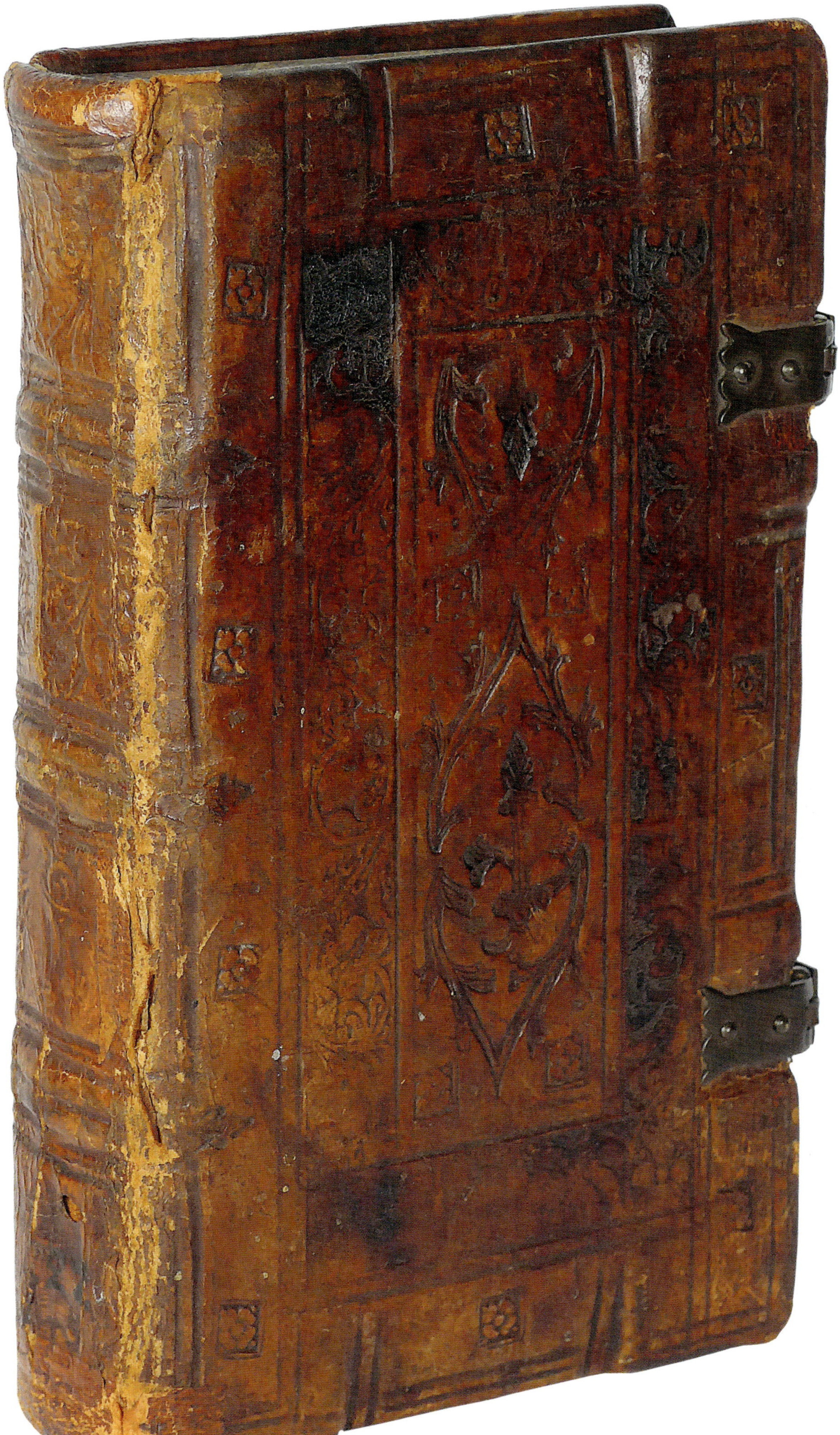

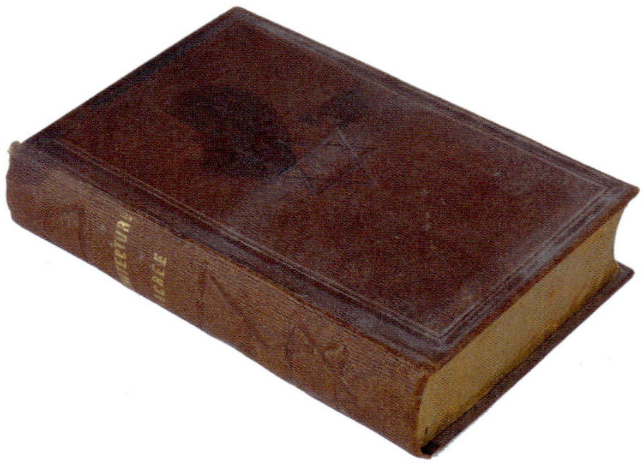

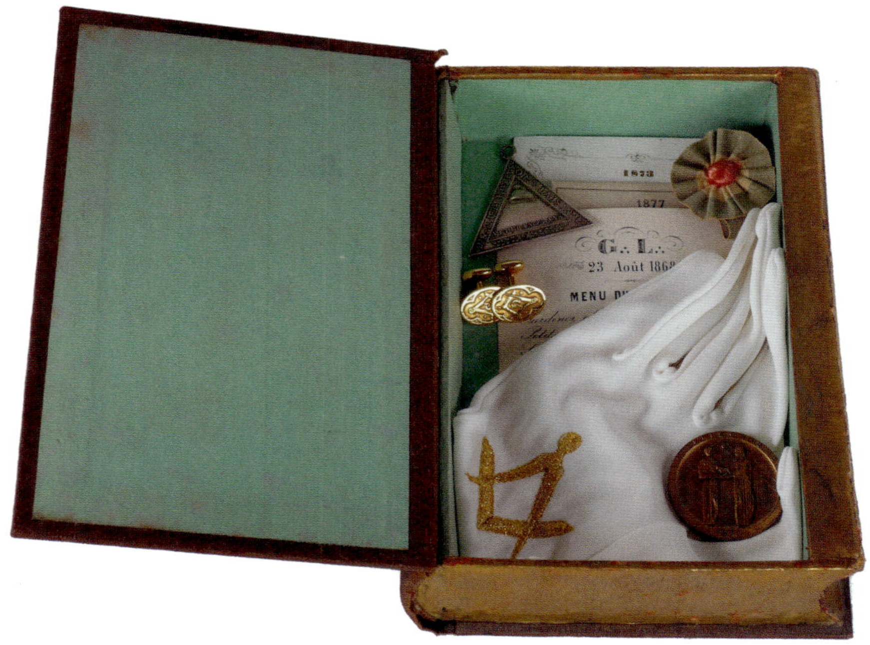

11.028
Architectural Sacree
Kaliko-Buchkassette mit geprägtem sechseckigem Hexagramm der Freimaurer auf Deckeln und Rücken, dreiseitiger Goldschnitt, Inhalt: Freimaurerhandschuh mit goldenem, gesticktem Zirkel und Winkel, Manschettenknöpfe mit Symbol, Freimaurerorden und Medaille, zwei Karten „Les Amis Fidèles" von 1873+1877, eine „Karte Menü du Banquet" von 1868
Calico box with embossed hexagram of the Freemasons on both covers and the spine, all edges gilt, contents: a Masonic glove with golden embroidered compass and angle, cufflinks with the symbol, Masonic medals, two cards "Les Amis Fidèles" from 1873 and 1877, one "Menu card Menu du Banquet" from 1868
4,5 x 20,5 x 15,1 cm

11.029
Mikro-Magie, Jaspis W.H
Ausgehöhlter Kalbsledereinband für Zauberutensilien, zwei Titelschilder, zwei Schließen, Blindstempel auf Vorderdeckel, Buchbehältnis für Zauberutensilien, Anleitungen für Zaubertricks
Hollowed calfskin book for magic items, two title labels, two clasps, blind stamp on the front cover, book box for Magic items, instructions for magicians› tricks
Um / *Around* 1940 | 38,5 x 31,1 x 8 cm

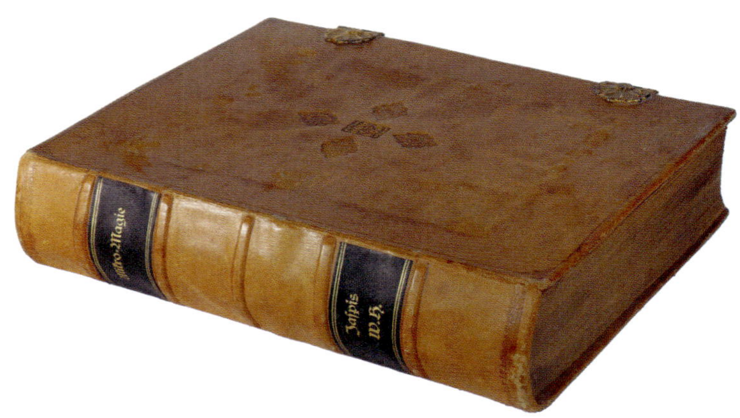

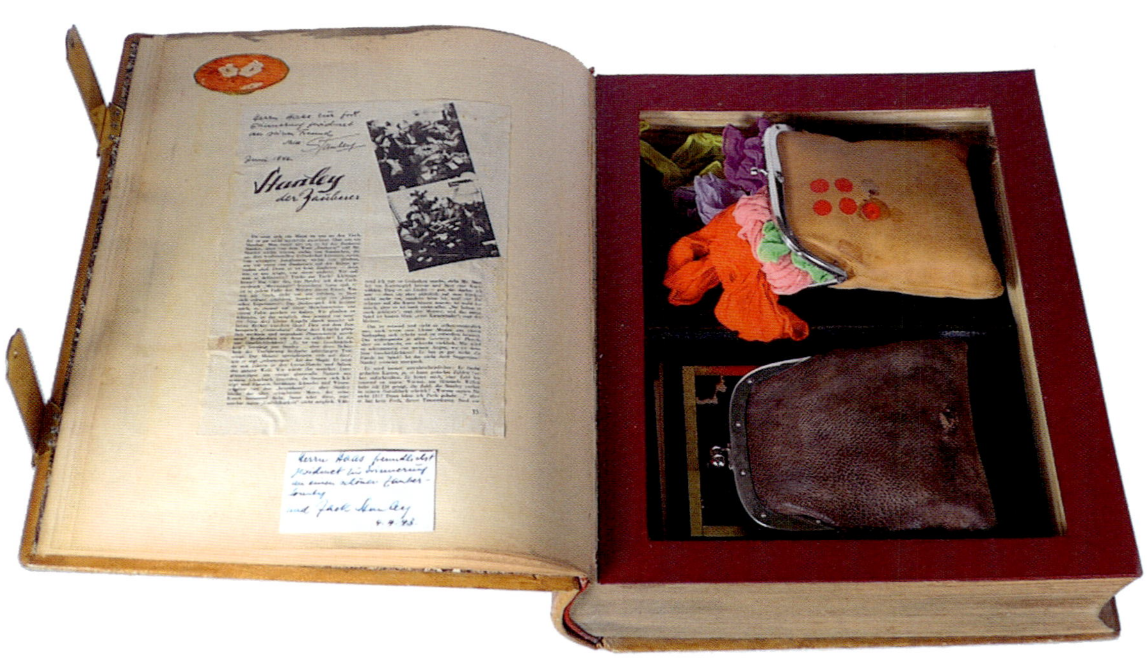

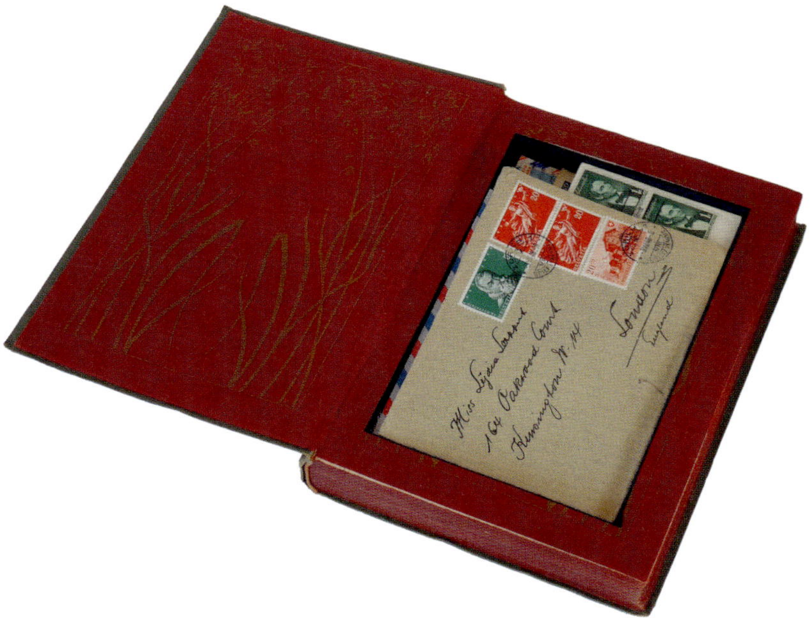

11.030
Corray, Garben und Kränze / ***Sheaves and wreaths***
Gute Kunst und Literatur für Jugend und Volk, Gesammelt von H. Corray, ausgehöhlter Buchblock für Versteck für Liebesbriefe
Fine art and good literature for the youth and the people, Collected by H. Corray, hollowed out book block used as hiding place for love letters
Verlag Edward Erwin Meyer, Aarau, Leipzig, Wien, 1912
3,5 x 25,7 x 18,8 cm

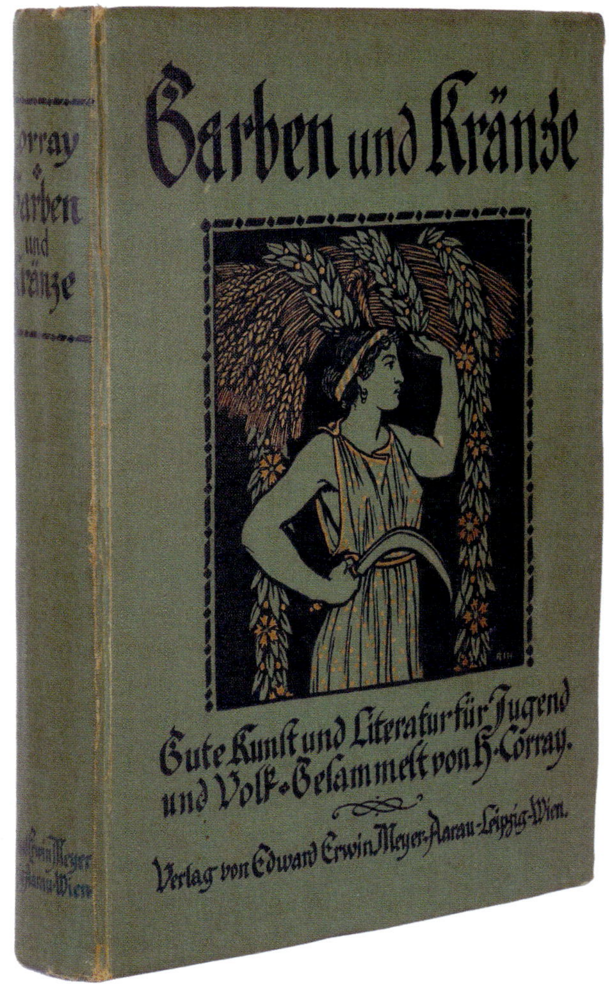

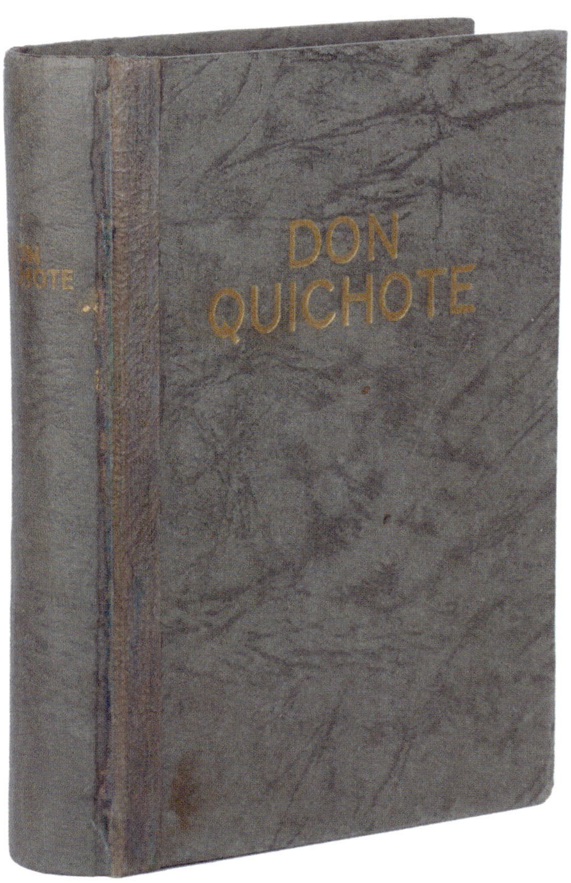

11.031
Don Quichote
Scherz- oder Juxbuch, Pappschachtel mit Papierüberzug, Rücken- und Deckeltitelprägung. Beim Öffnen springt ein Hundekopf mit Feder aus der Schachtel, dreiseitiger Goldschnitt
Book with Jokes cardboard box with paper-over-board, embossed spine and stamped title. When opening the box, a dog›s head with a feather jumps out of the box, all edges gilt
3 x 13,5 x 10,2 cm

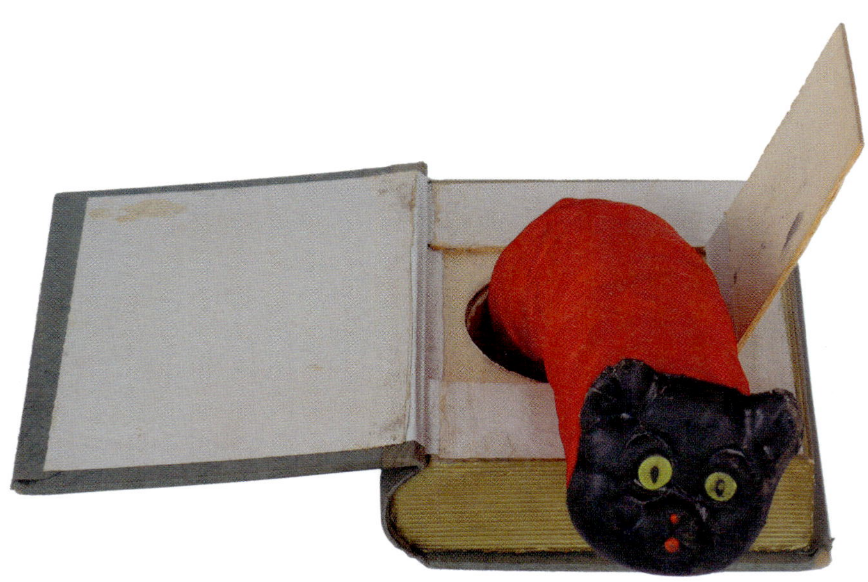

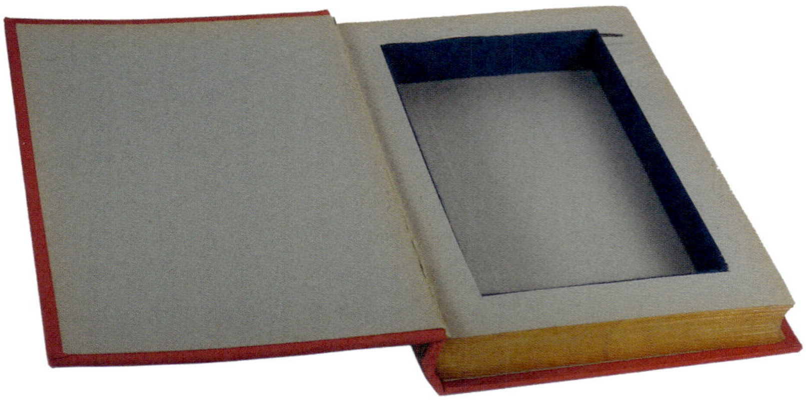

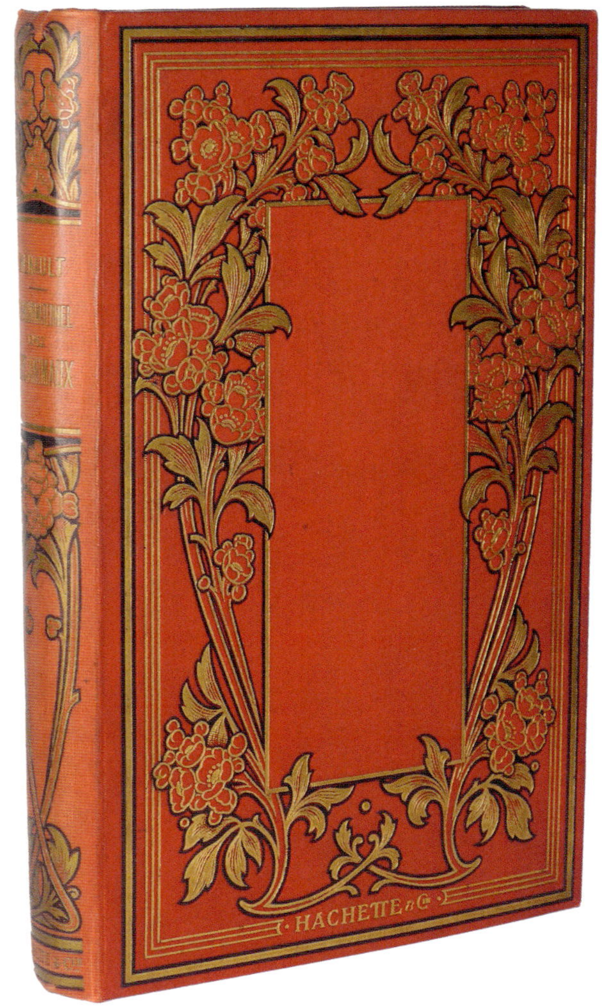

11.032
Ménault: L'amour maternel chez les animaux
Ausgehöhlter Kaliko-Jugendstileinband mit reicher Rücken- und Deckelvergoldung, dreiseitiger Goldschnitt
Hollowed calico Art Nouveau book with elaborate gilding on the spine and cover, all edges gilt
Edité par Hachette & Cie. Paris 1911
25 x 16,9 x 3 cm

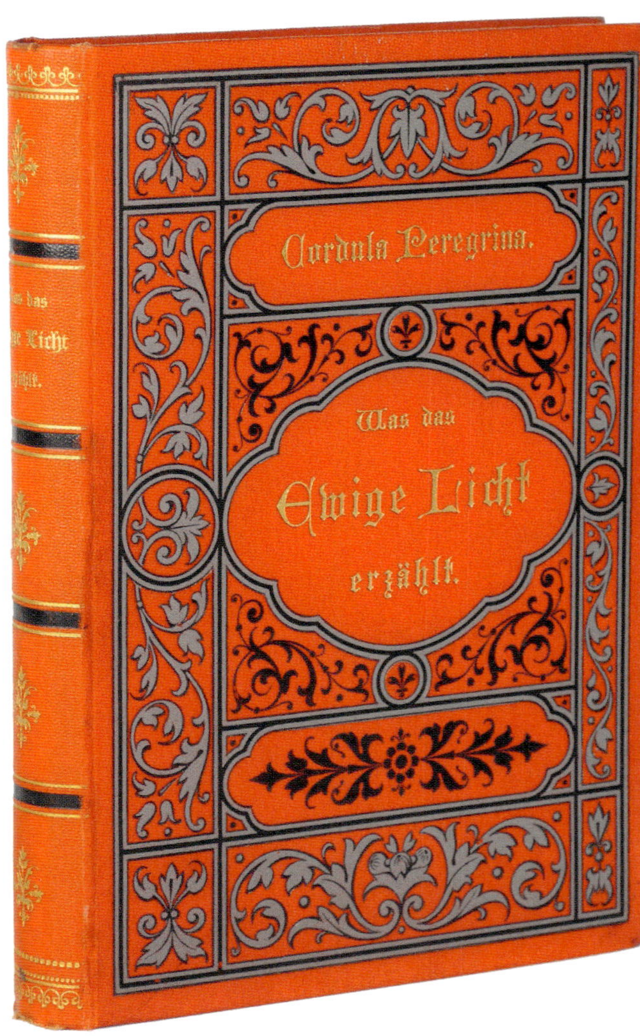

11.033
Was das Ewige Licht erzählt / *What the eternal light says*, Cardula Peregrina
Ausgehöhlter Kaliko-Einband mit Farb- und Goldprägung, ausgefüttert mit farbigem lithografiertem Buntpapier, dreiseitiger Goldschnitt
Hollowed calico book with color embossing and gold tooling, lined with lithographed colored paper, all edges gilt
2 x 16,6 x 12,1 cm

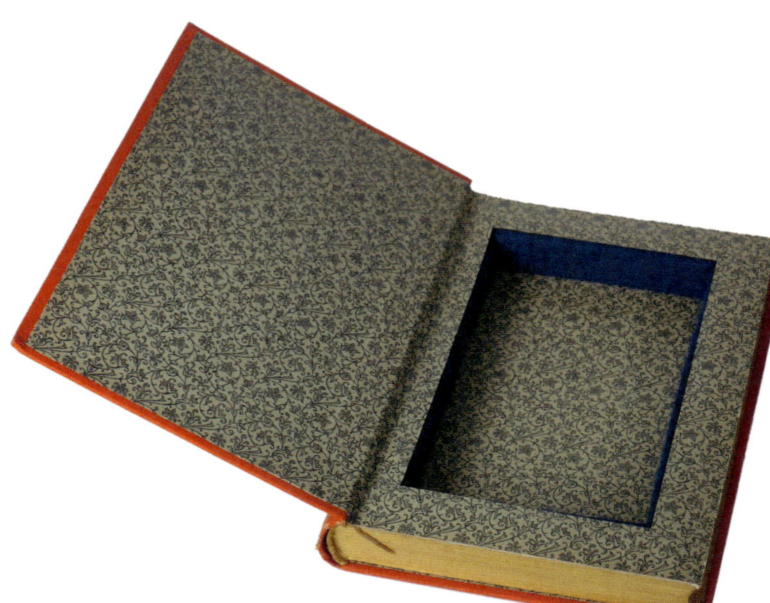

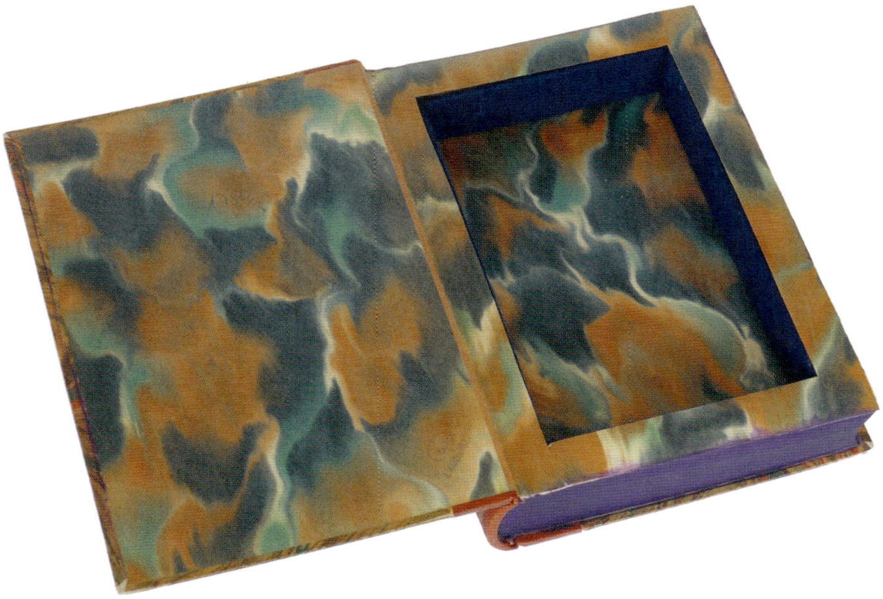

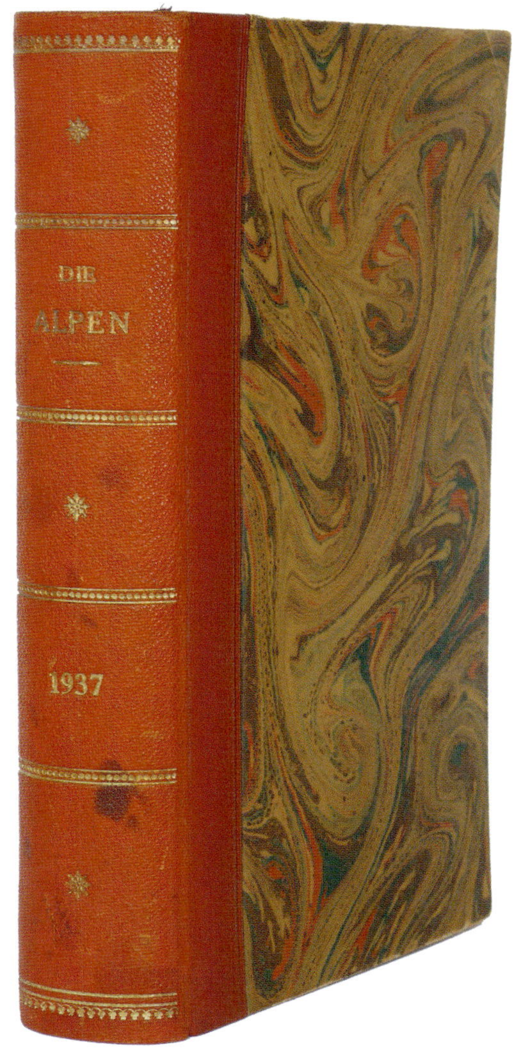

11.034
Die Alpen / ***The Alps***
Saffian-Buchkassette mit Pariser Fantasiemarmorüberzug, ausgehöhlter Buchblock, ausgefüttert mit Pariser Marmor, Handvergoldung, dreiseitiger Farbschnitt
Saffian xase with Parisian marbled cover, hollowed out book block, lined with Parisian marble, manual gilding, all edges colored
1937 | 4,7 x 25,5 x 19,1 cm

11.035
Metalldose mit zwei Federklappdeckeln für Streichhölzer und Briefmarken, farbige Kunststoffdeckel und ovale Medaillons, große Ecken, Aufhängevorrichtung mit Ring am Kopfschnitt, Reibfläche am Vorderschnitt
Metal box with two hinged spring lids for matches and stamps, colored plastic covers and oval medallions, large corners, hanging device with a ring at the head, friction surface at the fore edge
Um / *Around* 1900 | 1,2 x 4,8 x 3,5 cm

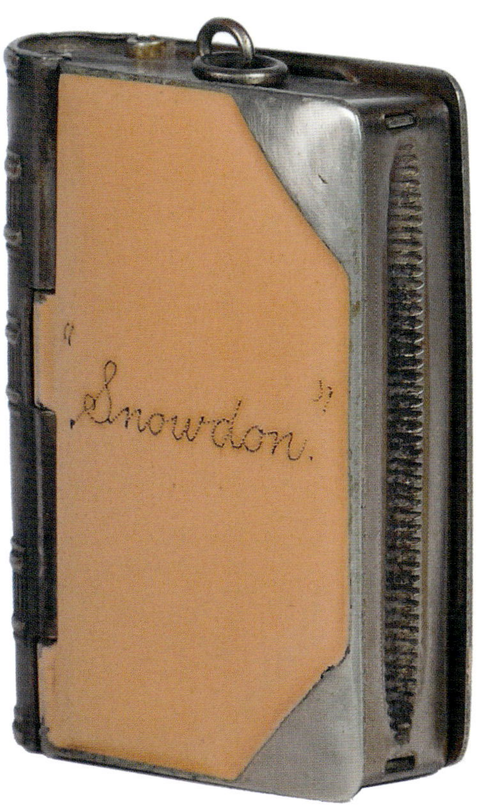

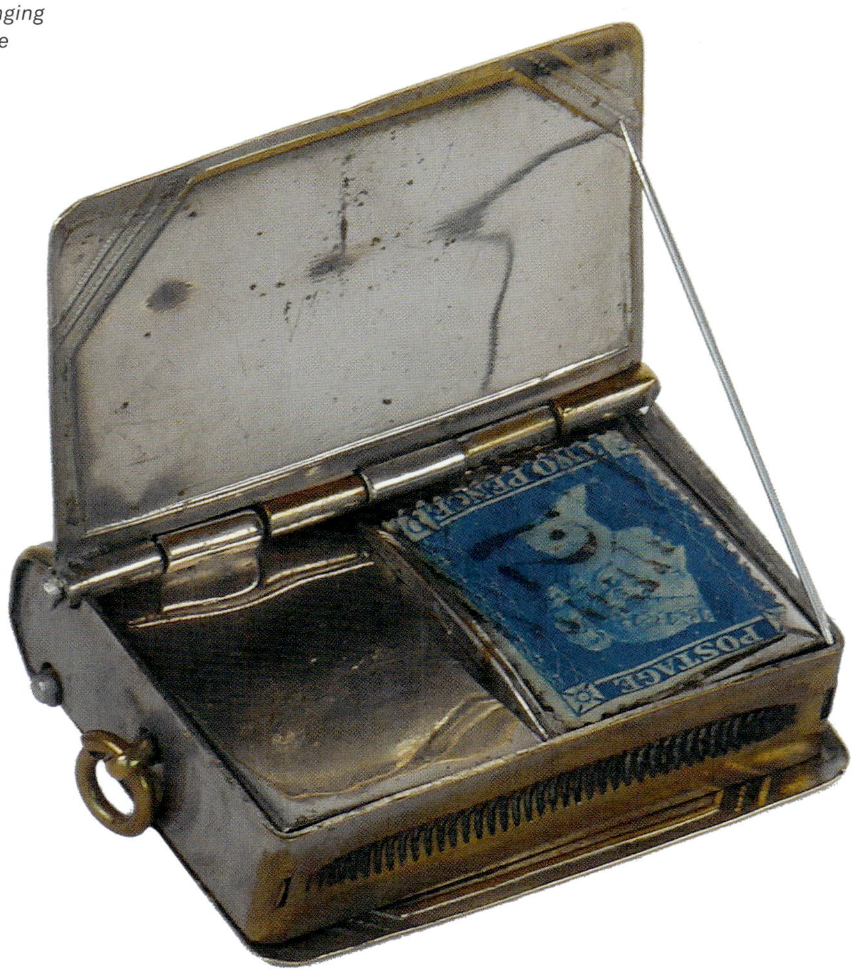

11.036
NPG Stereoskop Apparat, D.R.P. angemeldet Neue Photographische Gesellschaft, Aktiengesellschaft Steglitz-Berlin, Verlag von Stereoskop-Bildern. Lager von vielen tausend Darstellungen: Skulpturen, Landschaften, Stadtansichten aus allen Weltteilen, Genrebilder, Messingdose in Buchform aufklappbar
NPG Stereoscope, D.R.P. registered Neue Photographische Gesellschaft, Aktiengesellschaft Steglitz-Berlin, publishing house for pictures of stereoscopes. Stock of thousands of images: Sculptures, landscapes, cityscapes from all over the world, genre pictures, hinged brass box in the design of a book
Jugendstil / *Art Nouveau* | 1,9 x 14,8 x 10,2 cm

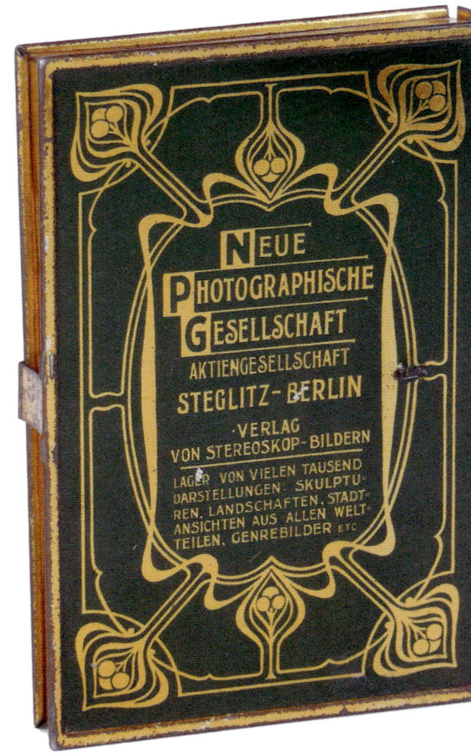

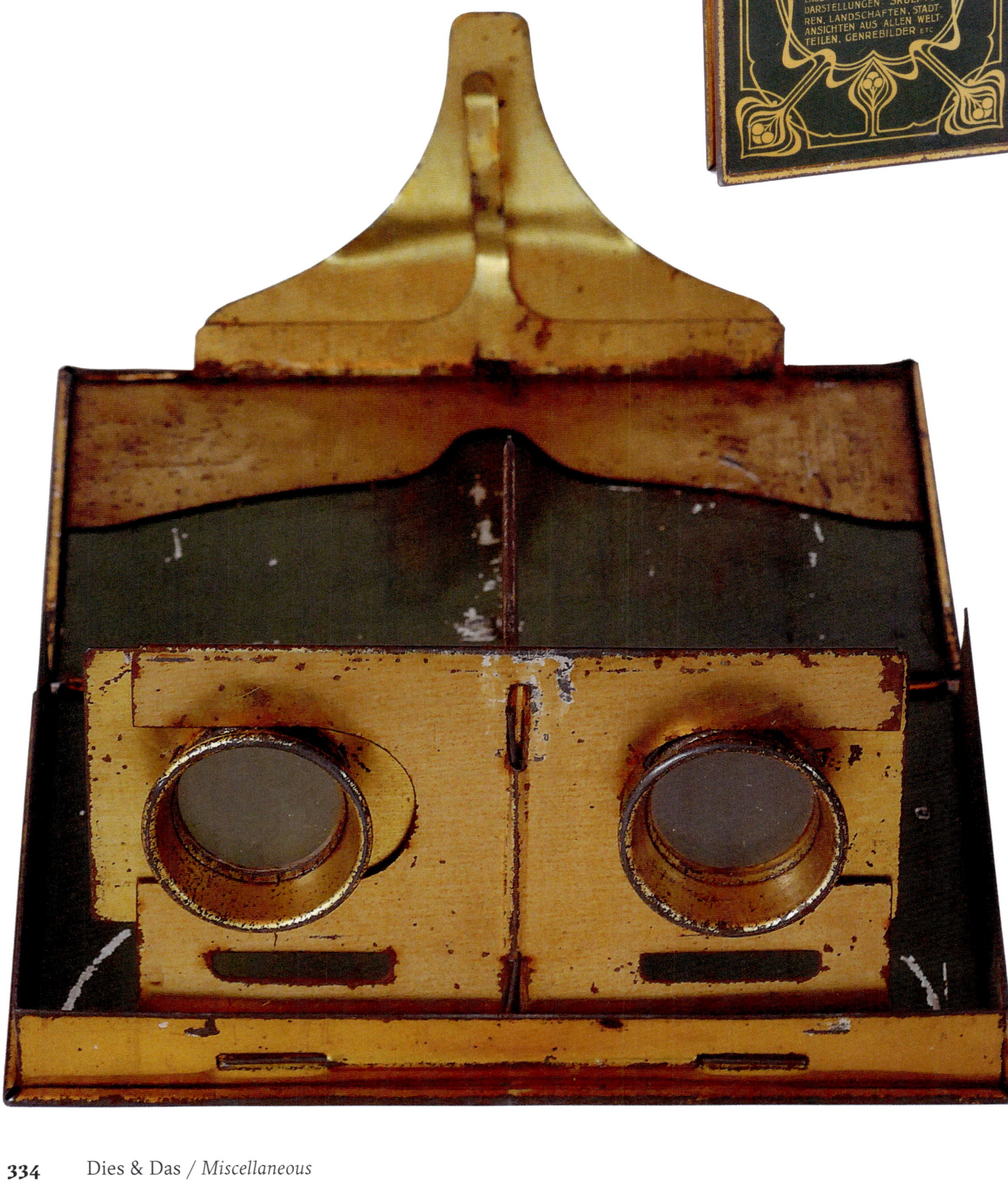

11.037

The Pocket Rotoscope, The Rotary Photographic Co. London. With 12 real photographic stereograms: Views, Statuary, Celebrities, Childern, Comic Scenes etc.

Ausfklappbare Messingdose im Taschenformat

Hinged pocket size brass box

Um / *Around* 1915 | 1,4 x 7,5 x 4,4 cm

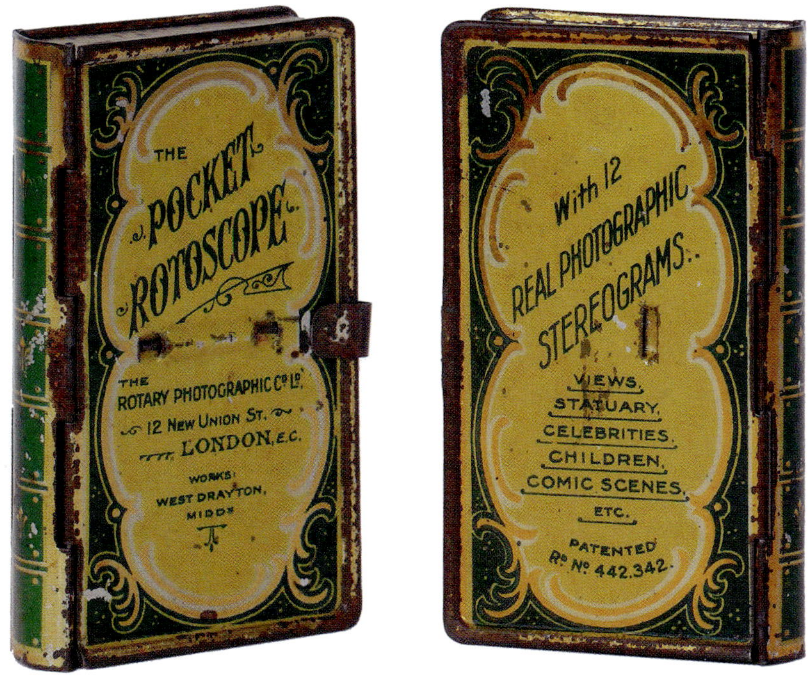

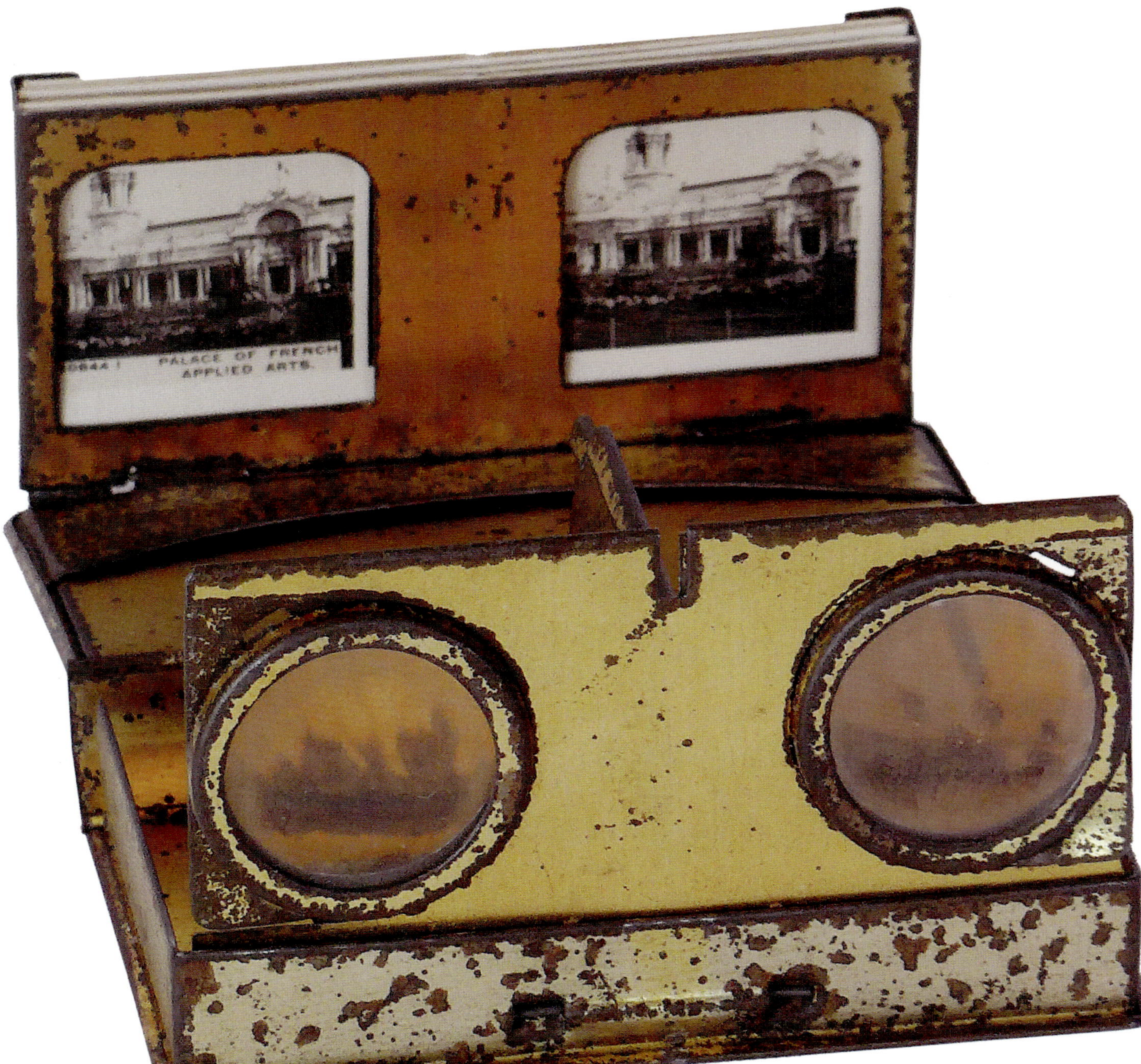

11.038

Friendships Offering

Saffian-Lederdose für eine Daguerreotypie, Rückendeckel-, Kanten- und Innenkantenvergoldung, geprägter Samtspiegel, dreiseitiger Goldschnitt, Messingschließe

Saffian leather box with brass clasp for a daguerreotype, gilt back cover and edges, embossed velvet pastedown

19. Jh. / *19th century* | 10 x 9,2 x 2,3 cm

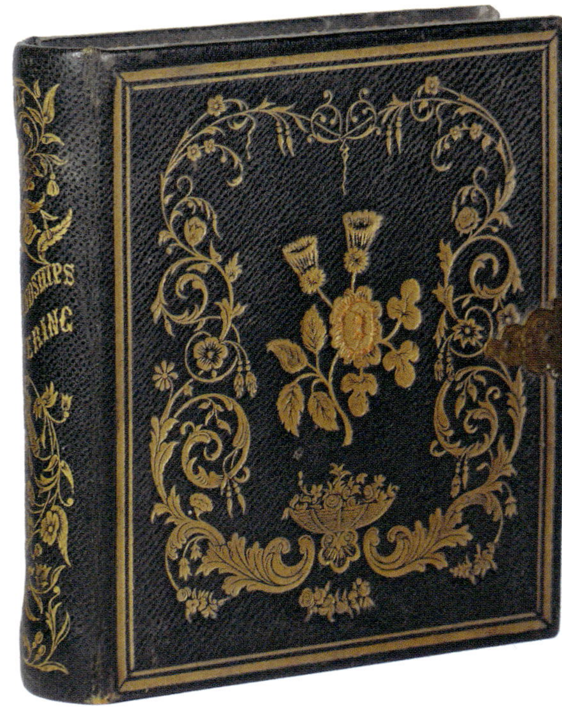

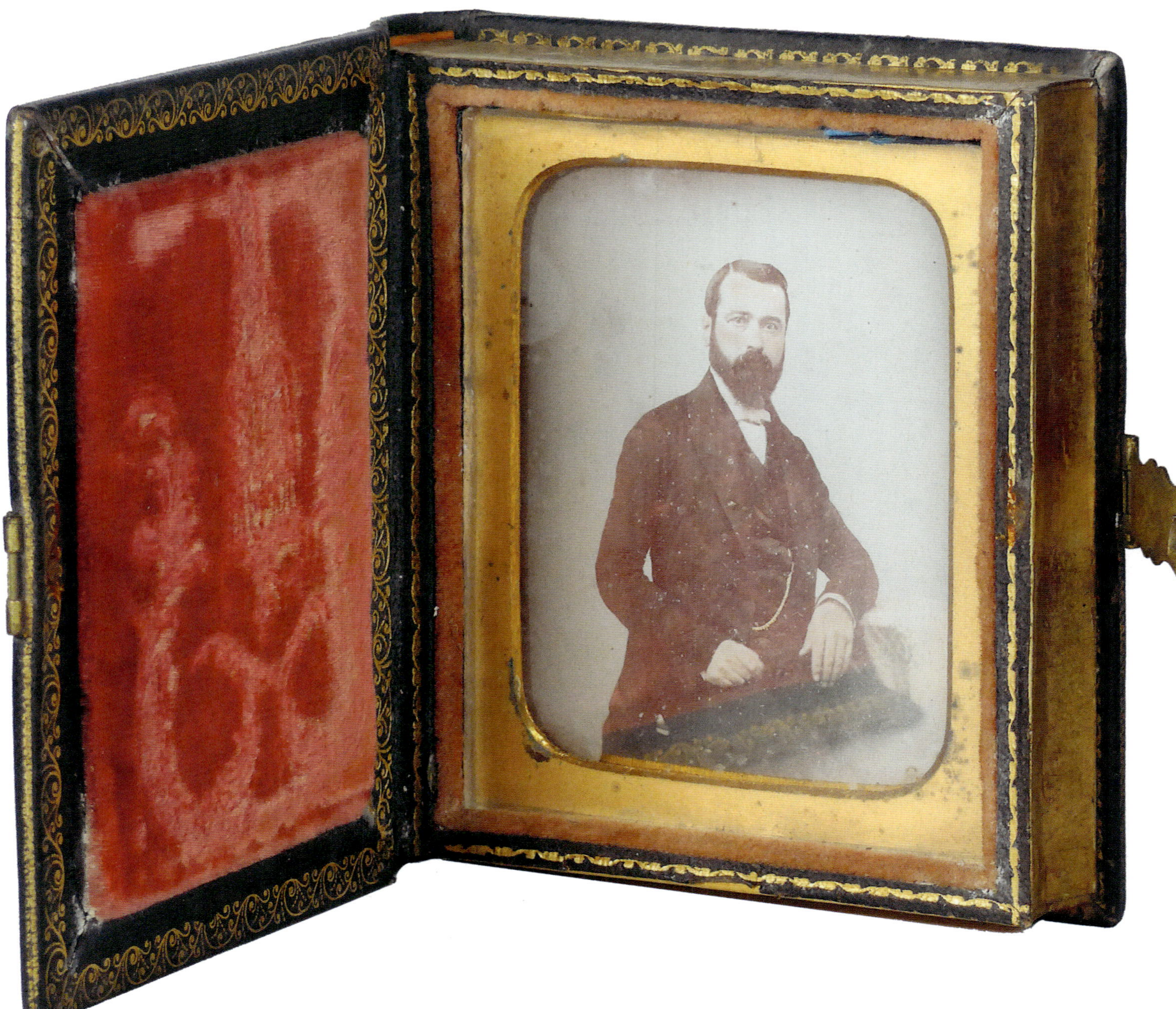

11.039
Saffian-Lederdose für eine Daguerreotypie, mit zwei Buchrücken, Gold- und Blindprägung, Samtspiegel, Messingschließe
Saffian leather box for a daguerreotype, with two spines, gold and blind tooling, velvet pastedown, brass clasp
19. Jh. / *19th century* | 7,5 x 6,6 x 1,7 cm

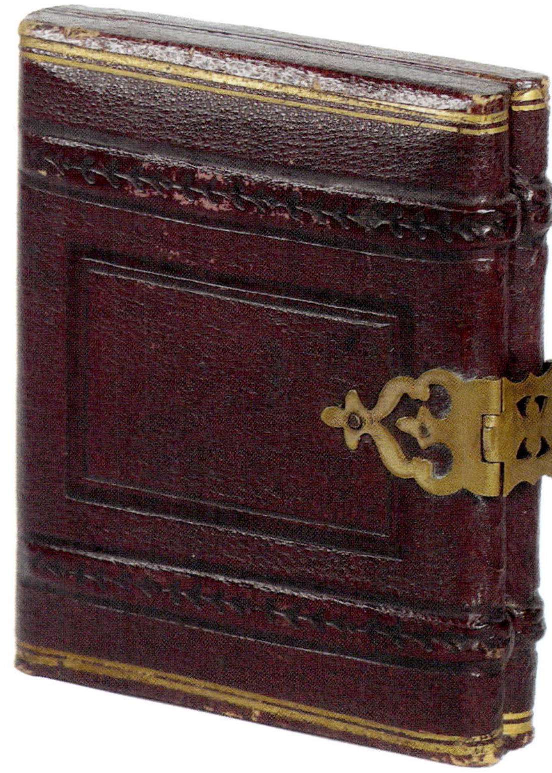

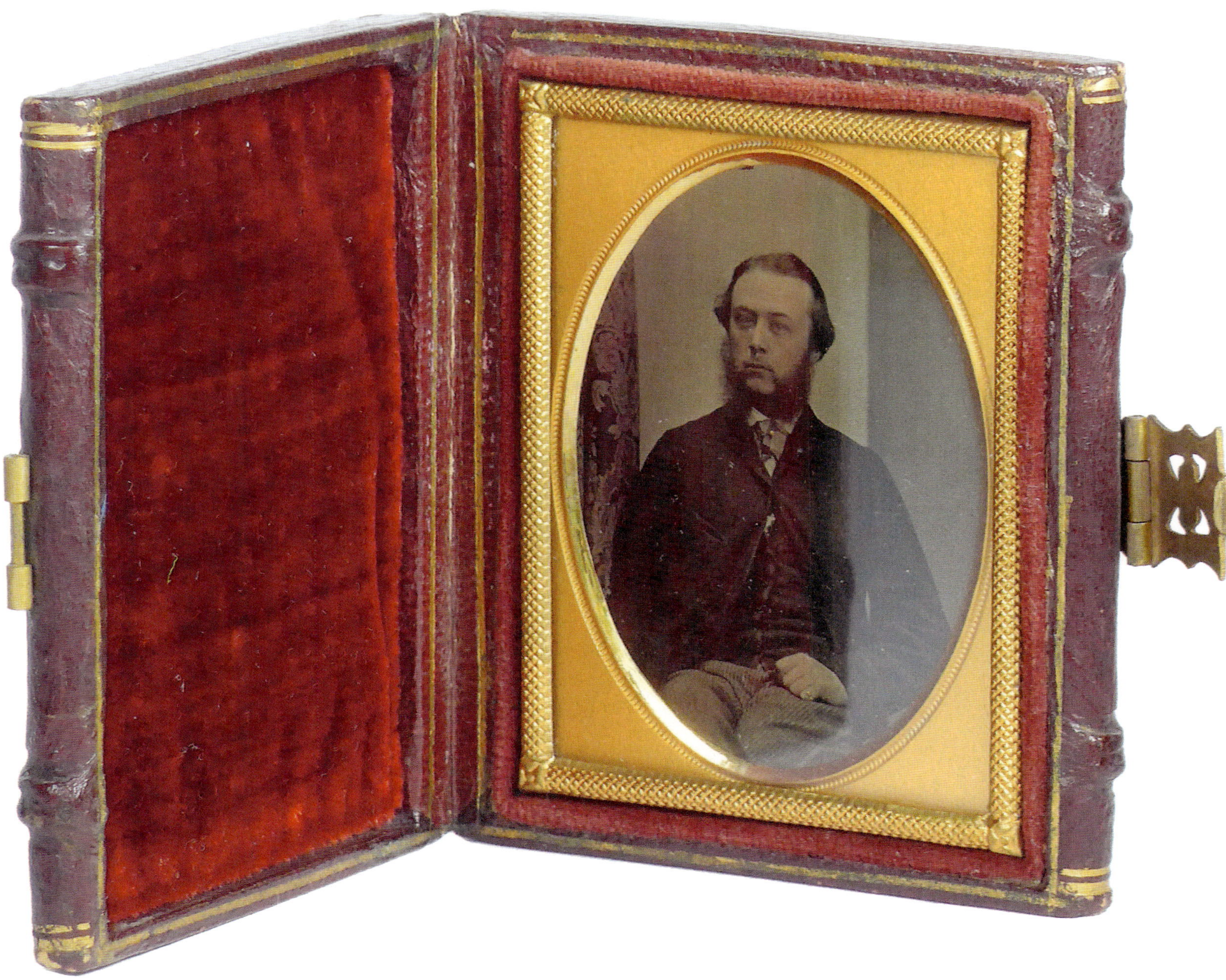

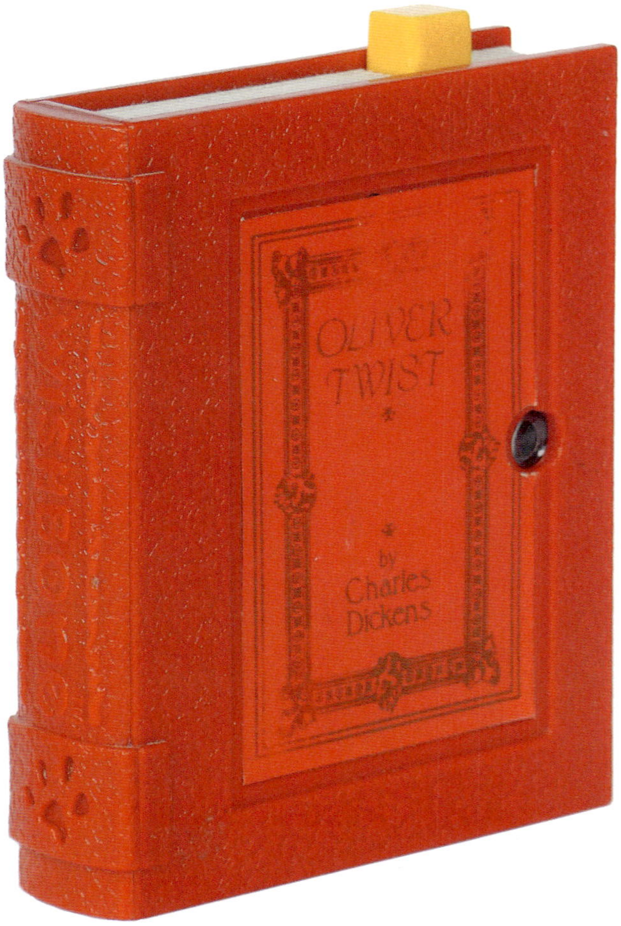

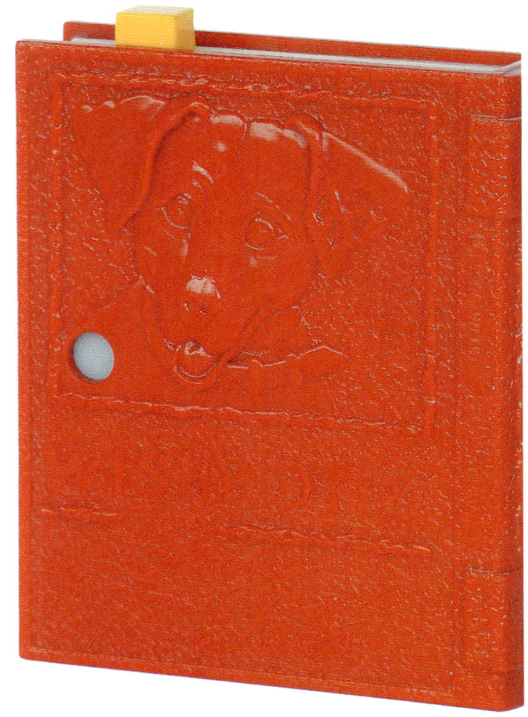

11.040
Wishbone Classic Tales
Plastiskop Gucki Bildbetrachter, verschiedene Hundebilder, Hundekopf auf der Vorderseite, Guckloch
Plastiscope Gucki viewer, several pictures of dogs, a dog's head on the front cover, peephole
9 x 7,7 x 2 cm

11.041
Ten Commandments
Kunststoffbuch mit Stanhope-Betrachtungslinse (Optical Bijou), Abbildung der Zehn Gebote, dreiseitiger Goldschnitt
Plastic book with a Stanhope lens (Optical Bijou), illustration of the Ten Commandments, all edges gilt
Um / *Around1900* | 2,9 x 2,3 x 0,8 cm

11.042
Souvenir d'Aix les Bains
Perlmuttbuch mit Stanhope-Betrachtungslinse (Optical Bijou), Abbildung des französischen Thermalbads der Belle Époque, Rücken- und Deckelgravur
Pearl cover book with a Stanhope lens (Optical Bijou), illustration of the French thermal bath of the Belle Époque, engraving on the spine and cover
1,6 x 1,3 x 0,5 cm

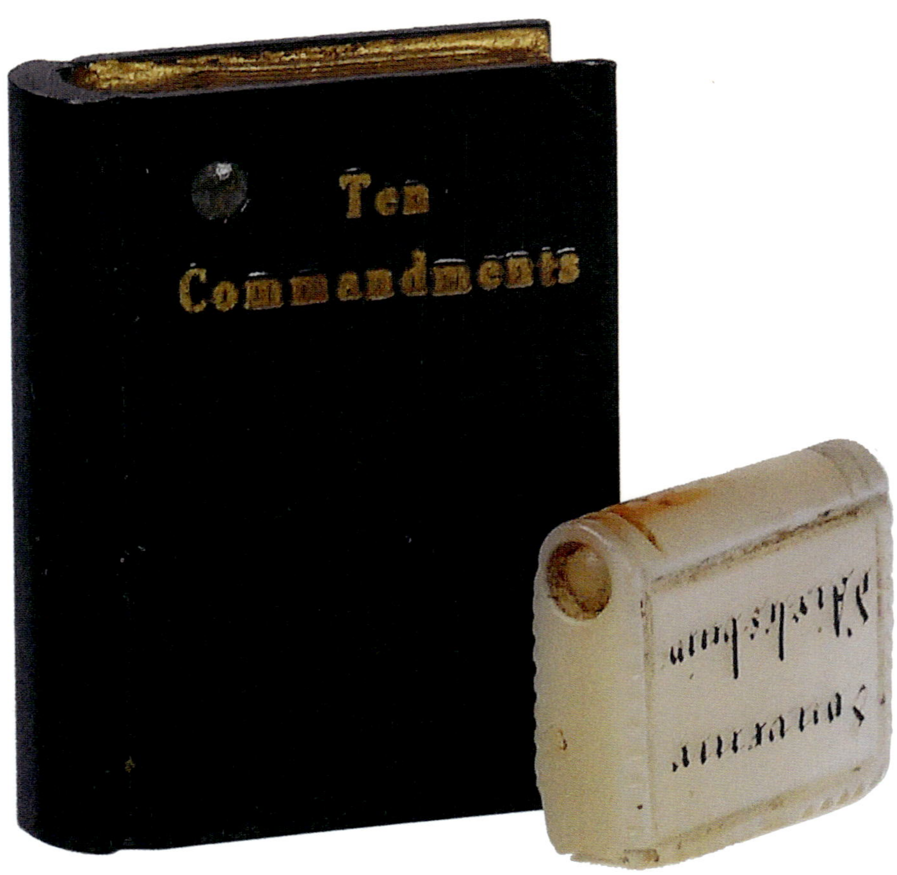

11.043
Handvergoldeter Halbledereinband mit aufgesetzten Lackdeckeln für eine Daguerreotypie, Porträt eines jungen Mannes, eingefasst mit einer Samt- und Goldbordüre, eingelegte Rose aus Perlmutt auf dem Vorderdeckel, Innenkantenvergoldung, Samtspiegel, dreiseitiger Goldschnitt, Messingschließe
Half leather book with manual gilding for a daguerreotype, with a brass buckle and applied varnished covers, portrait of a young man, edged with a velvet and golden border, front cover with a rose made with marquetry in mother-of-pearl, gold-plated inner edges, velvet pastedown, all edges gilt
19. Jh. / *19th century* | 7,7 x 7 x 1,3 cm

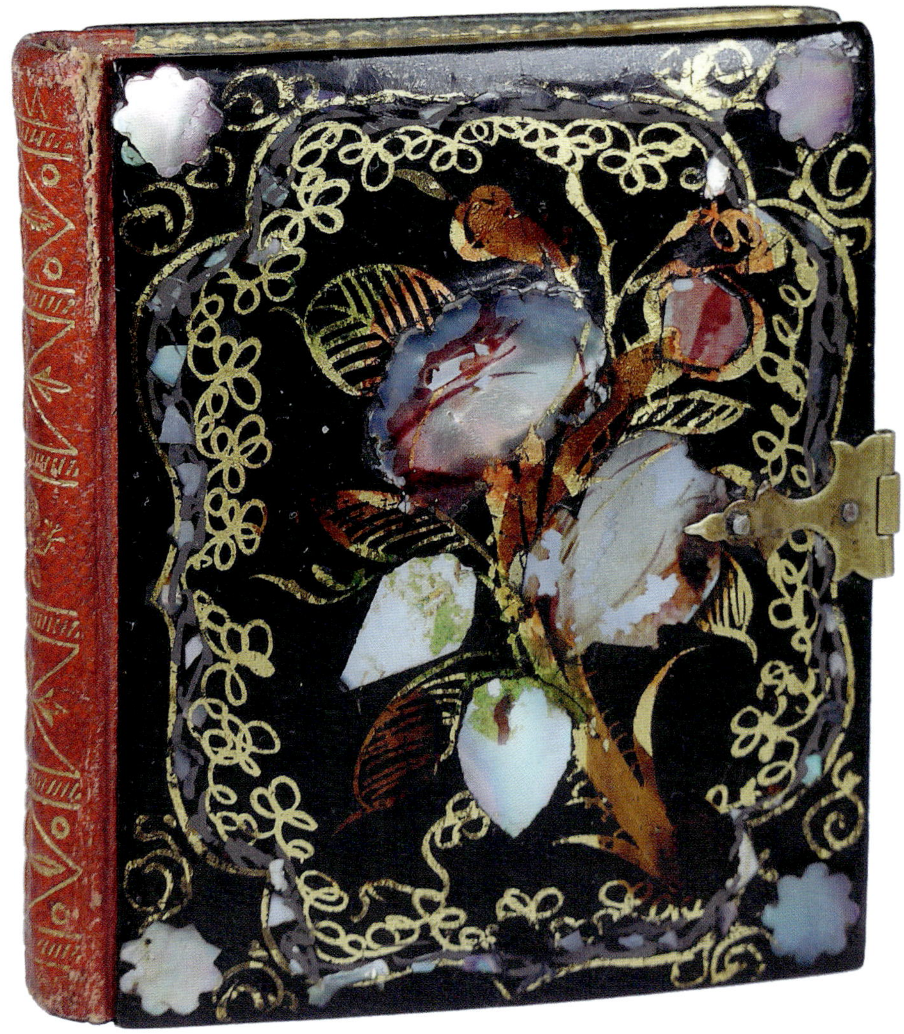

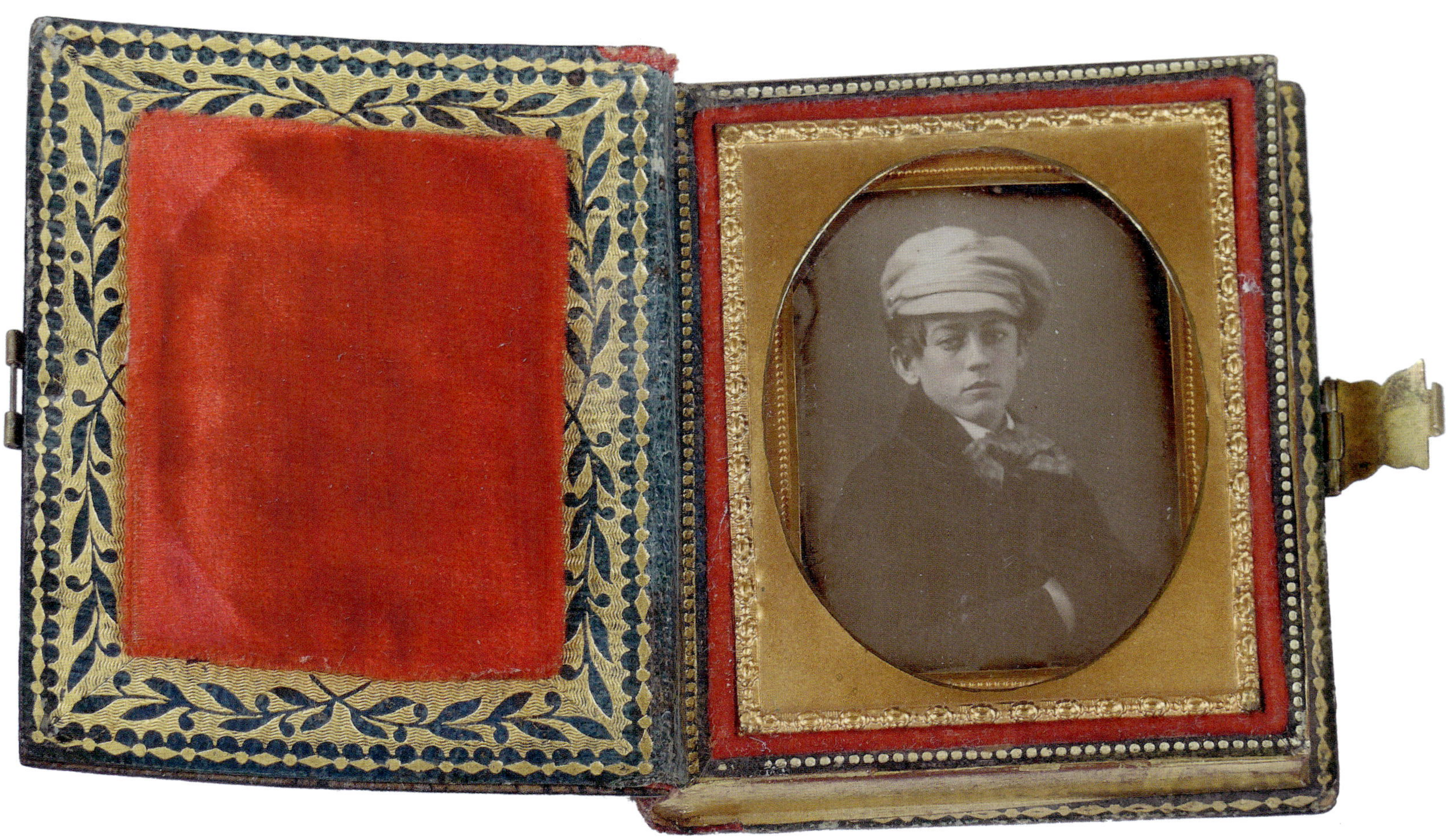

11.044
Herbarium mit 107 Pflanzenarten der Schweiz, Zeitraum von 1849–1852.
Schwarzer Safian-Einband mit reicher Goldprägung, dreiseitiger Goldschnitt, ausgefüttert mit hellgrünem Moirépapier.
107 gefalzte Blätter mit montierten Pflanzen mit Goldschnitt versehen
Book with black Saffian cover, rich gold embossing, all edges gilt, lined with light green moiré paper. 107 folded leaves with attached plants, gilt edges
19,3 x 15,6 x 6,5 cm

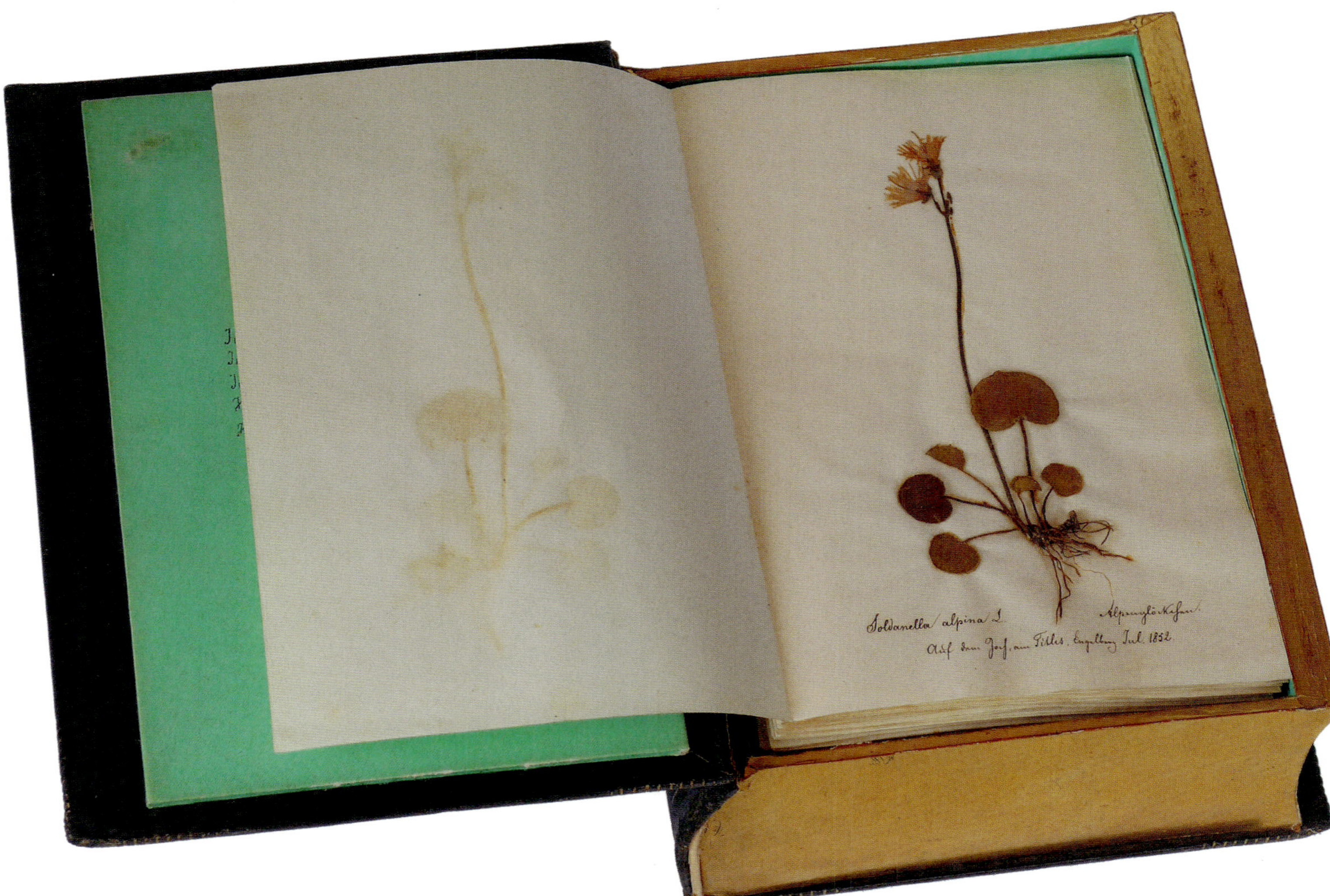

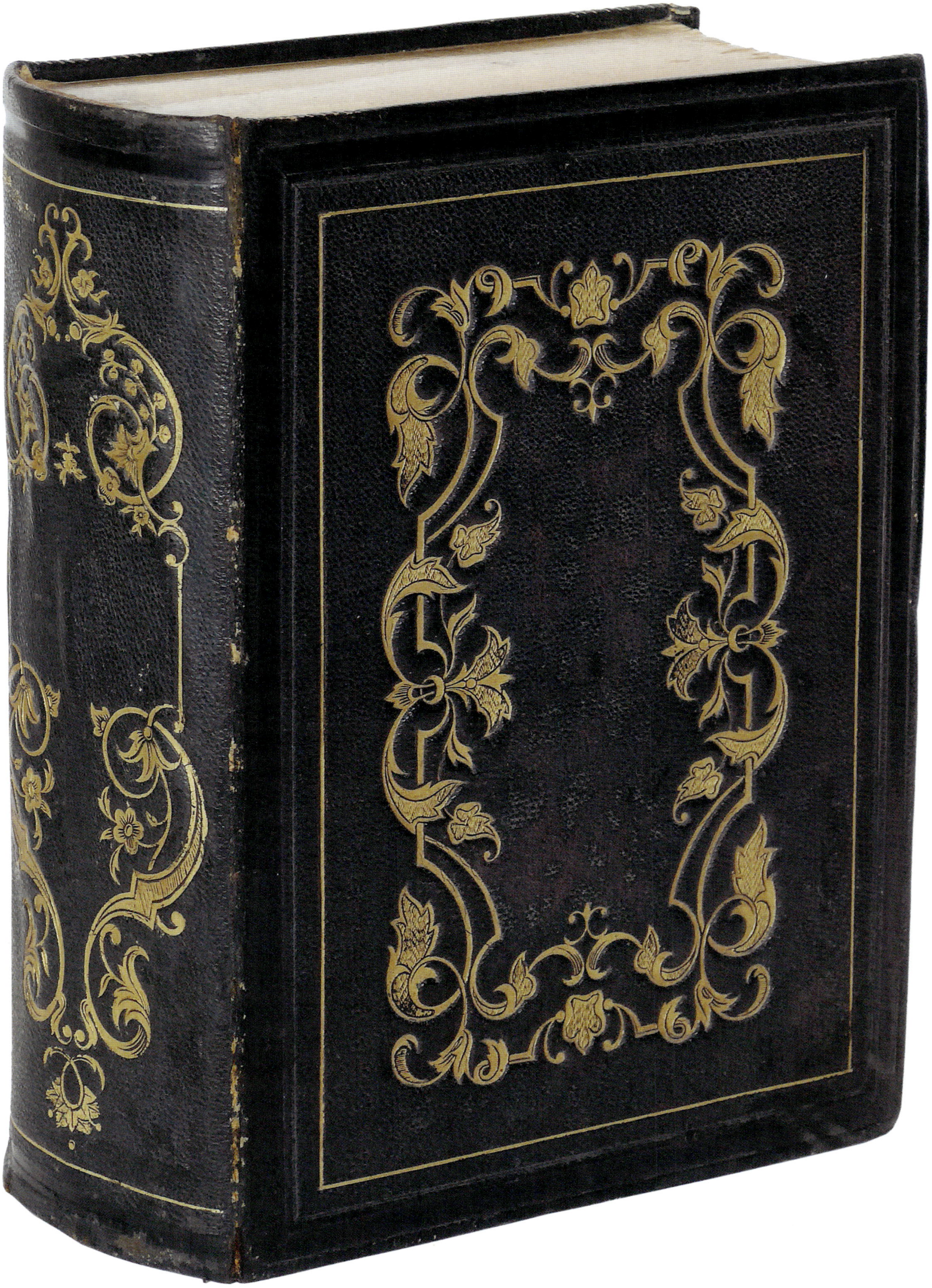

11.045
Damenhandtasche, Leder vergoldet, Messing-Mechanik, aufklappbare Fächer aus Seide, golden umrandet, Spiegel, Sicherheitskette, drei erhabene Bünde, Halteschlaufe
Ladies' handbag, gilt leather, brass mechanism, hinged silk compartments with golden edging, a mirror, security chain, three raised bands, strap
16,3 x 12,5 x 3,2 cm

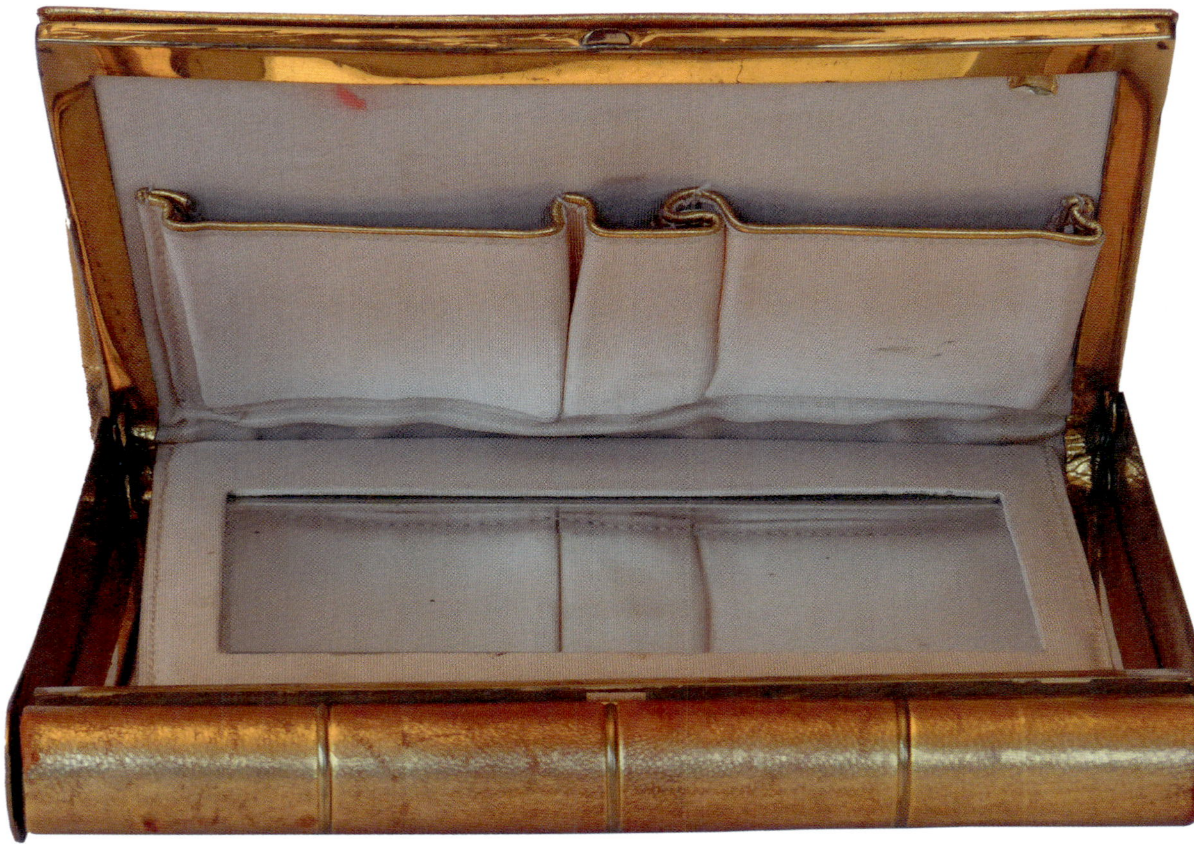

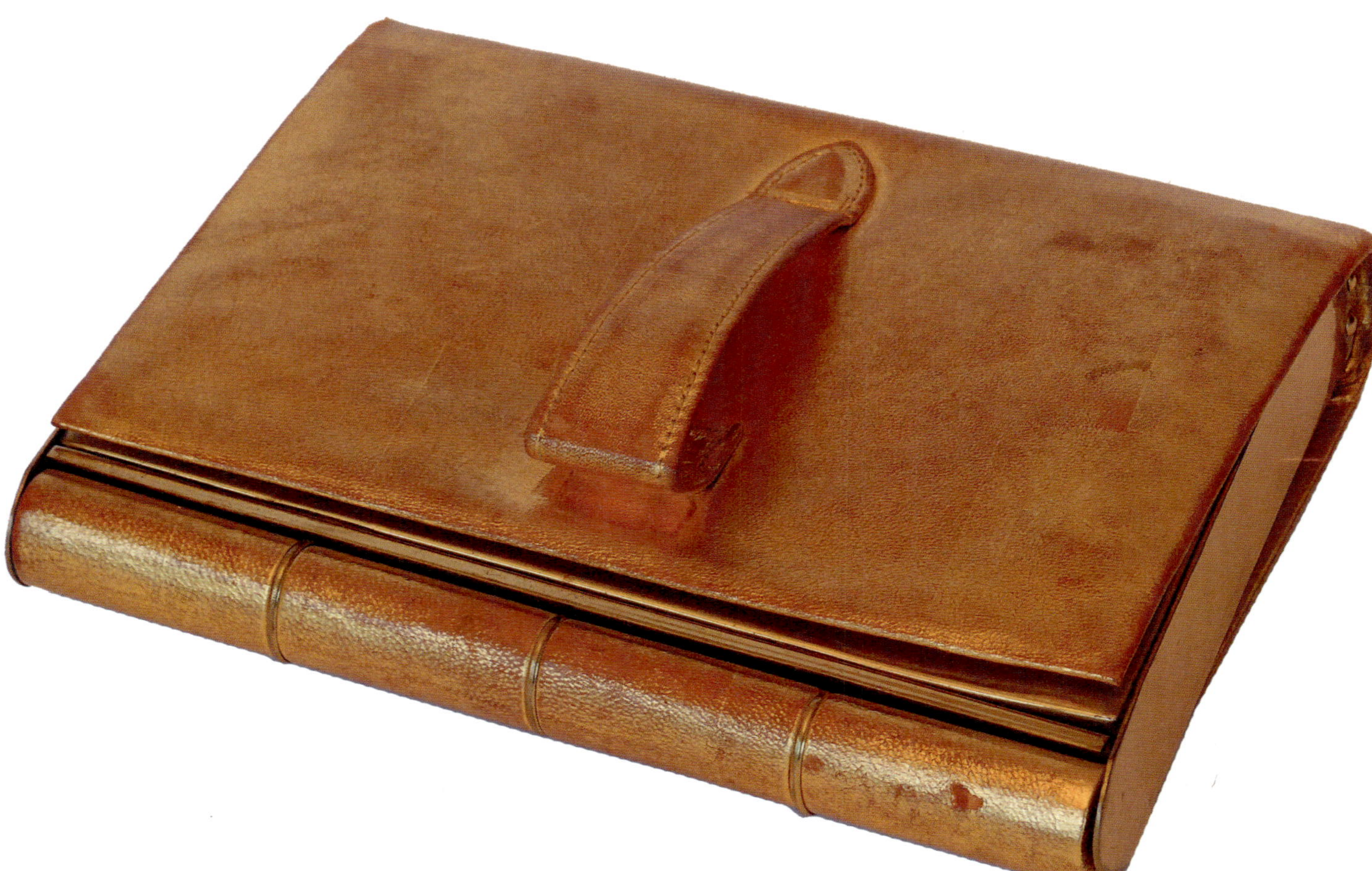

Die Schein-Bar

Fritz Franz Vogel

Man stelle sich vor, man komme in ein Herrenhaus, und der Herr gibt sich die Ehre, den Gast im Salon zu treffen. Hinter ihm die Bücherwand, er stellt sich davor und redet sich ins Zeug. Der Gast denkt, welch belesenen Gastgeber er vor sich hat, bei so vielen Ledereinbänden, fettleibigen Folianten, eng gedruckten Seiten, wundersamen Umschlägen, Schnallen und Schließen. Jedenfalls haben wir es mit einem Buchkenner zu tun, der seine Buchreihen schön ordnet und die Einbände sorgsam pflegt. Keine Unsitte ist auszumachen, bei der Bücher horizontal übereinandergestapelt oder, noch peinlicher, Bücher selbst als Bücherstützen missbraucht werden.

Doch bei zunehmendem Ablegen bürgerlicher Konvention und eskapistischer Parliererei und nachdem man über das eine und andere Buch den Kopf gereckt hat, holt der Gastgeber Cognacgläser hervor. Doch statt in den Schnapsschrank greift er wieder ins Büchergestell: John Haig „Träume" steht auf dem Rücken. Das stattliche Buch enthält zwei Gläser, ein weiteres Buch den Spiritus, ein drittes einen zweiten edlen Tropfen als Alternative. Die Auswahl an Spirituosen ist nicht klein, aber gut versteckt. Der Hausherr kennt seine „Bücher", um bei all den Ledereinbänden den richtigen Griff zu tun. Gut gereift ist der Alkohol; Bücher scheinen ihm nicht abträglich zu sein, gerade das unabsichtliche Vergessen lässt die Reife erst entfalten. In diesem Sinne ein fruchtbar symbiotisches Verhältnis, um im Verborgenen zu altern und zu reifen. Und die Zigarren, die der Besitzer aus der Bücherwand holt, sind ebenso bestens in Papierspitze verpackt, inkl. Aschenbecher. Er legt Musik auf, ebenfalls aus dem Regal, eine Kurbel für die Aufziehfeder sorgt für die notwendige Energie, um die Schallplatte in Bewegung zu setzen. Bei einem anderen Buch zieht er an einem Lesebänder und eine Musikdose erklingt. Dank des Hohlraums tönen diese Bücher gut. Falls dem perplexen Gast schlecht wird vor Überraschung, so findet sich auch Medizin, Kräuterextrakt und Arznei in Pastillen- und Fläschchenform in einem als Minibibliothek getarnten Giftschrank. Und wenn der Hausherr – ja, es ist eine männliche Leidenschaft, denn Frauen lesen Bücher eher als dass sie sie besitzen wollen! – dereinst nicht mehr will oder kann oder es anders muss als er eigentlich möchte, so erklärt er, er hätte noch eine Buchattrappe mit einer geladenen Pistole. Welches es sei, verrät er natürlich nicht; auch im Falle eines Überfalls muss zur Selbstverteidigung der Bluff 100-prozentig wirken.

Scheinbücher heißen diese Objekte, die Falsches vorspiegeln, die so tun als ob: libri simulati dank Patina. Bezeichnungen wie Fake-Bücher, Trompe-l'œil-Bände, Dummies sind gebräuchlicher. Ihr Aussehen sind Schatullen in Kästchen, Kistchen in Buchform, hochkant gesetzte Blechschachteln mit vorangegangener Biskuitsfüllung, gläserne Attrappen des gehobenen Geschmacks, mit Samt oder Marmorpapier ausgekleidete, doppelbödige, mehrfächige Kartonagen, in Kunstleder oder Efalin gebundene Behältnisse mit ergötzlichem Innenleben, Aufbewahrungsboxen mit Papierspitz, kaschierte Schatzkammern und -kästchen für Heimlichkeiten. Und ihre Funktionen sind vielfältig: Sparbüchsen und Reptilienfonds in Geldkassen, Feueranzünder und Notnähzeugs, Zigarrenkistchen und Tabatieren, Handschmeichler und Körperwärmeflaschen, Blumenvasen und Blechspieldosen, Rosenkranzdöschen und Amulettversteck, Brett- und Würfelspiele, Laternen und Gewürzstreuer, Stammbücher mit Bänderzug für Liebesbriefe und unverfängliche Buchschachteln für Pornographica, für Ringe, Revolver und Gleitmittel. Trotz dieser vielfältigen Helferchen kommt der Begriff „Scheinbuch" im Netz kaum vor. Zu schräg und unbekannt ist die bürgerliche Täuschungsabsicht.

Die Objekte des Sammlers sind also weit mehr als nur Blindbände, mit denen der Layouter Bindetechnik, Aufschlagverhalten und Haptik des Buchblocks überprüft. Solche Blindbände, Alben gleich, papierene Weißwaren, die dann später als Notizbücher verwendet werden, sind ja immer noch Bücher, wenn auch ohne Inhalt. Scheinbücher hingegen haben einen Inhalt, nur ist es eben kein Buch, kein Text, keine Abhandlung, kein Bildmaterial. Sie geben vor, Buch zu sein, sind es aber nicht. Die eigentlichen Buchfunktionen – Visualisierung, Information, Unterhaltung – werden unterlaufen. Sie kaschieren Bibliophilie, dabei spiegeln sie manisches Verstecken, die Vorspiegelung falscher Fakten, die Tarnung als gehobene Literatur oder währschafte Enzyklopädie, als unverfängliche Reiseliteratur, Libretto oder Souveniralbum. All das Profane und Unbürgerliche, das Abwegige und gesellschaftlich wenig Tolerierte verschwindet in vermeintlichen Büchern.

Über diese Art der falschen Bücher gibt es wenig Material. Es ist, als ob sich die autothematischen Bücher selbst verstecken. Wer weiß überhaupt, ob all die Büchereien und Bibliotheken, die wir ihrer Wissensschätze wegen bewundern, tatsächlich mit dem bestückt sind, was sie nach außen vorgeben? Der Illusionismus der Trompe-l'œil-Malerei ist hingegen besser aufgearbeitet. So finden sich in entsprechend Themenmonografien Abbildungen von gemalten Zettelsammlungen, Steckfächern, Quodlibets, Bücherwänden und Scheinbibliotheken, z. B. von Giuseppe Maria Crespi („Librerie", ca. 1725) oder von Winthrop Chandler („Shelf of books", 1769), abgesehen von zeitgenössischen Dekovarianten mit stupenden Fototapeten, die verschiedene bürgerliche Ordnungstemperamente befriedigen (www.hausbest.com).

Die Scheinbücher haben außerhalb des gut gepflegten Herrenhaushalts auch andere Anwendungsgebiete. In Möbelgeschäften und in Auslagen für Inneneinrichtungen simulieren solche Bücherwände in ganz profaner Art den beabsichtigten Nutzen von Gestellen und Regalen. Solche Attrappen, auf- und zusammenklappbare Buchreihen aus kaschiertem Karton, sind weitaus leichter als tatsächliche Bücher. Diese Scheinbücher, vielfach ganze Minibibliotheken, wollen ja lediglich sagen, hier stünden Bücher, wenn es denn welche zu stellen gäbe. Pro-forma-Werke von Goethe und Schiller; schnell hindrapiert, ebenso schnell weggelegt.

Darüber hinaus sind solche Fake-Bücher aber auch im modernen Zeitalter eventuell gut genug, um eine Überwachungskamera oder Wanzen in einem ausgehöhlten Buchrücken einzusetzen, um Kamingespräche zu belauschen und private Tête-à-Têtes zu voyeurisieren.

Nun denn: Wofür überhaupt die Scheinbücher? Es gibt achtbare Gründe, ein repräsentatives Büchergestell zu füllen, damit es nicht so leer aussieht.

1. Der englische Terminus „fake books for shelves" geht in diese Richtung, denn gerade im englischsprachigen Raum ist es eher Usus, sich mit derlei Schein zu zieren (vgl. ein anderes Ding des dekorativen Scheins: Kaminfeuer in allen Varianten der Künstlichkeit).

2. Wer Bücher nicht mehr beim nächsten Umzug mitschleppen will, der kauft sich vielleicht eine Attrappe. Doch scheint diese Verminderung von Gewicht kaum ein Äquivalent, die geliebten Bücher zu vermissen.

3. Nicht jeder will sich in die Karten schauen lassen, was ihn so täglich bewegt. Also täuscht er Belesenheit und Interesse an religiöser Erbauungsliteratur vor, um sich nicht als heimlicher Trinker, Pornograf oder Millionär verraten zu müssen.

4. Also bleibt die Funktion des Verstecks, die Lust an der Leichtgläubigkeit. Das Scheinbuch ist eben nicht einfach eine Buchattrappe, um den Kassenschrank zu verbergen oder das Geheimfach in der Wand zu vertuschen. Denn hinter der bibliophilen Quacksalberei verbirgt sich eine zweite Schicht: die verborgene Libido, die geheime Leidenschaft, der heimliche Genuss.

Falsche Bücher wollen in erster Linie das Auge täuschen und den Menschen überraschen, weil das Vorgestellte doch nicht das ist, was man sich vorstellt. Es ist der Wettstreit um die Deutungshoheit des Richtigen und Wahren, den Plinius in seiner Naturgeschichte anhand des Wettstreits zwischen Zeuxis und Parrhasios exemplifizierte. Während erster damit bluffte, dass Vögel zu seinen gemalten Tauben flögen, verblüffte der zweite, indem er einen Vorhang, der das vermeintlich wahre Werk verdeckte, nicht beiseite schieben konnte, weil auch dieses gemalt war, zur großen Entrüstung von Zeuxis, dem die Täuschung nicht aufgefallen war. Täuschungen, Trugbilder und Camouflagen, und das ist die Quintessenz des kunsthistorischen Paradigmas, wollen den Blick schärfen, indem dem Objektiven grundsätzlich misstraut wird, egal ob einem realitätsnah gemalten Bild oder einem falschen Buch, oder, zwischen den Zeilen, dem Inhalt, dem in einem Buch vermittelten Wissen.

Die Sammlung von Armin Müller in Winterthur ist sehr vielfältig. 1500 Objekte aus verschiedenen Zeitepochen, jedweder Couleur, Machart, Provenienz und derselben Funktion von Tarnung und Blendwerk. Dass Bücher eben nicht nur Ort des Wissens und der Lektüre sind, sondern auch die pure Funktion der Rekreation, der Unterhaltungsmathematik, der Späße, Freuden und Genüsse sein können, wird hier in extenso vor Augen geführt. Diese falschen Bücher sind bisher kaum auf dem Radar in der Bibliothekswissenschaft oder im Bereich der Sammlungskunde und Exponatik erschienen, weshalb sich diese Publikation geradezu aufdrängt. Am ehesten ist das Rubrum der Buchobjekte bewirtschaftet, das aber weniger die schelmische Buchbinderei ins Zentrum rückt als vielmehr die Rezyklierung von ausgedienten Büchern zum Kunstobjekt.

Buchrücken mit all ihren schönen Beschriftungen und Materialitäten sind Spiegel des Innenlebens und lassen an einen bestimmten Inhalt glauben, dessen Offenbarung der Ergötzung dienen kann. Wie wir hiermit wissen, ist dieser Spiegel nicht tatsachengetreu; er spielt mit vertauschten Seiten, gezinkten Karten, mit der Illusion von Werten. Er spiegelt mehr vor als er Leitmotiv für den Inhalt ist. Die falsche Fährte lässt erschaudern ob der Raffinesse der Täuschung. „Karl Knausrig: Das Sparbuch", „How to get along with yout mother-in-law", „Vom Wunder des XY", „Goethe: Werk und Welt" heißen dann die gefälschten Titel mit den imitierten Beschlägen.

Eine ganze Bücherwand kann somit eine Scheinheiligkeit sein, eine Fassade vermeintlichen literarischen Reichtums, wo in Wahrheit profane Gelüste verborgen sind. In allgemeinem Verständnis haben Bücher generell die Aura des Besseren und Höherwertigen, repräsentieren Geist und Belesenheit und fördern Macht und Ruhm. Wer Bücher sein Eigen nennt, wirkt welterfahren, aufgeschlossen und meinungstolerant. Wer eine Bibliothek besitzt, weiß, dass sie, einem Fingerabdruck gleich, einzigartig ist; sie ist das nach Außen gekehrte Psychogramm des Besitzers, aussagekräftiger als jede Psychoanalyse. Und so zeigt auch eine solche Nichtbibliothek die Matrix des Sammlers.

Heute, wo Bücherwände in Wohnungen obsolet geworden (alles lässt sich blitzschnell im Netz nachschlagen) und Fenster bis zum Boden Standard sind, wo großformatige Kunst an den tragenden Restwänden hängt und überhaupt die Bürgerlichkeit mit Spleens und Leidenschaften, ihren Männerzirkeln und Herrenabenden abhanden gekommen ist, da erübrigt sich auch der Schein falscher Bücher.

Verdacht schöpft man also kaum bei diesen Scheinbüchern, jedenfalls nicht, wenn sie in Gegenwart tatsächlicher

Bücher zu finden sind. Es braucht halt ein scharfes Auge, das richtige vom falschen Buch zu unterscheiden, hinter der Attrappe den Tresor zu entdecken. Und wenn die Gastgeber wie Spechte an die Buchrücken klopfen, weil sie den Standort ihrer falschen Bücher immer wieder verschieben, dann ist es vielleicht doch Zeit, die Rücken mit Etikettenschwindel zumindest zu verklausulieren. Die geprägten Titel heißen dann großspurig: „The age of innocence", „Investors syndicate", „Livre d'heures"..., womit Verballhornung und Parodie bereits angedeutet sind.

Der Beruf des Falschbüchermachers ist – im Gegensatz zum Kleinkriminellengewerbe des Falschmünzers oder Falschgelddruckers – noch nicht erfunden worden. Hiermit liefern wir die historisch verbürgte Anleitung für den großen innerhäuslichen Betrug, das Referenzwerk für die Irreführung des Buchbanausen, die Enzyklopädie für den Racheschwindel verhinderter Bibliothekare, falls in Zukunft ein solches Metier des schönen Scheins gefragt sein sollte. Denn der Falschbüchermacher ist nicht nur ein Kenner der historischen Materie und Materialitäten, er muss sich auch in Fertigungstechniken auskennen. Er weiß, wie Schnallen, Schließen und Klinken funktionieren und wie sich Papier zu Lederschein veredeln oder Pappe zum Folianten trimmen lässt. Er lässt Velours und Samt alt aussehen und appliziert auf Neuware eine Aura des Gebrauchs und der Vernutzung. Er zaubert auf Weißblech eine Patina und kokettiert mit vermeintlicher Nostalgie. Er weiß, wie seine Wunderkammern versiegelt und mit welchen Tricks – drehen, klicken, verschieben, klappen, gegeneinanderpressen und miteinander kombiniert etc. – sie wieder geöffnet werden können. Denn auch das gehört dazu: ein Falschbuch ist eben auch ein Geheimnis, das den Erfindergeist der Verschlusstechnik herauskitzelt, um gegebenenfalls den Finder vor rätselhafte Probleme zu stellen. Wie bei der Entdeckung von Geheimtüren in falschen Wänden und Verliesen hinter Schränken will man ja nichts kaputtmachen, sondern mit dem Staunen auch die Erkenntnis des Gebrauchs ermitteln, will Kerbungen, Gehrungen und Verzapfungen erkennen, Druckstellen abtasten, kaum sichtbare Abriebflecken untersuchen, um die raffinierte Mechanik herauszufinden, ohne die zu lösen man nicht an den verborgenen Inhalt kommt. Falsche Objekte sind Fallen für den Sehsinn, Hinterhalte der Wahrnehmung.

Ein Versteck ist nur so gut wie sein unsichtbarer Schutz. Und das ist eben die Macht von List und Täuschung, dass jemand seinem Sehen glaubt, seinen Sinneseindruck für wahr nimmt. Selbst auf den Leim zu kriechen, traut man sich am wenigsten zu. Somit sind Bücher Bücher, weil in einer Bibliothek üblicherweise Bücher stehen.

Looks like ...

Fritz Franz Vogel

Imagine entering a manor house, and the landlord is honoured to meet his guest in the parlour. He positions himself in front of a wall of books and talks. What a well-read host, the guest thinks, in front of so many leather bindings, obese folios, tightly printed pages, wondrous envelopes, buckles and clasps. In any case, I am dealing with a book connoisseur who arranges his rows of books beautifully and treats the covers carefully. There is no such bad habit as stacking books horizontally or, even more embarrassingly, misusing them as bookends.

However, after a while with leaving behind bourgeois convention and escapist chatting, and after the guest's head has risen above one book or another, the host brings out cognac glasses. But instead of the liquor cabinet, he reaches back into the bookcase and takes out another book: John Haig 'Dreams' on its back. An impressive book contains two glasses, another book the spirit, and a third a second noble drop as an alternative. The selection of spirits is not small, but well hidden. The good man knows his 'books' well in order to grip the right one among all the leather bindings. Well matured is the alcohol; books do not seem to be detrimental to its quality: it is the unintentional oblivion that finally unfolds its maturity. In that sense it is a fruitful symbiotic relationship to age and mature in secret. And the cigars that the owner fetches from the bookcase are also well packed in paper lace, including an ashtray. He puts music on, also off the shelf; a crank for the wind-up spring provides the energy that is necessary to set the record in motion. At another book he pulls a book ribbon and a music box resounds. Thanks to their cavity, these books sound good. If the perplexed guest gets sick with surprise, there is also medicine, herbal extracts and a remedy in pastille and in vial form in a poison cabinet camouflaged as a mini library. And if the landlord – yes, it is a male passion, because women would rather read books than want to own them! – he no longer wants to continue nor keep on going nor act differently more than he wants to, he explains, he still has a book dummy with a loaded pistol. Of course, he does not reveal which one it is; even in the case of a robbery, for self-defence the bluff must be 100 percent effective.

These objects are known as mock books, they pretend to be something other than books: libri simulati thanks patina. Terms such as fake books, trompe-l'œil volumes, dummies are more common. Their appearance are caskets in boxes, boxes in book form, upright set tin boxes with previous biscuit infill, glass dummies of sophisticated taste, lined with velvet or marble paper, double layered, multi-fold cardboard boxes, bound in faux leather or Efalin containers with delightful inner life, storage boxes with paper lace, laminated treasure chambers and treasure chests for secrecy. And their functions are diverse; money boxes and reptile funds in cash registers, firelighters and emergency sewing kits, cigar boxes and tobacco tins, worry stone and warm water bottles, flower vases and brass boxes, rosary boxes and amulet cache, board and dice games, lanterns and spice shakers, family register with string binding for love letters and harmless book boxes for pornographica, for rings, revolvers and lubricants. Despite these diverse little helpers, the term 'pseudo-book' hardly appears on the net. Too oblique and unknown is the bourgeois intention to deceive.

The objects of the collector are therefore much more than just dummy tapes, with which the art editor checks the binding technique, impact behaviour and haptic of the body of the book. Such dummy volumes, like albums, paper white goods, which are later used as notebooks, are still books, albeit without content. On the other hand, bogus books have content, only it is not a book, without text, essay, nor pictorial material. They claim to be a book, but they are not. The actual book functions – visualisation, information, entertainment – are subverted. They hide bibliophilia, while they reflect manic hiding, the illusion of false facts, and the camouflage as upscale literature or well-behaved encyclopædia, as harmless travel literature, libretto or souvenir album. All the profane and un-bourgeois, the outlandish and socially ineligible disappears in supposed books.

There is little material about this kind of wrong book. It's as if the auto thematic books are hiding themselves. Does anyone even know whether all the public libraries and personal libraries we admire for their treasures of knowledge are actually equipped with what they pretend to be? – The illusionism of trompe-l'œil painting, however, is better revisioned. Thus, according to theme monographs, there are illustrations of painted collections of notes, slots, quodlibets, walls of books and dummy libraries, e.g. by Giuseppe Maria Crespi ('Librerie', c. 1725) or by Winthrop Chandler ('Shelf of books', 1769), apart from contemporary deco variants with remarkable photo wallpapers that satisfy various bourgeois temperamental tastes (www.hausbest.com).

The fake books have outside the well-kept man's household other applications. In furniture stores and indoor displays, such book walls quite profanely simulate the intended use of racks and shelves. Such fictitious books, collapsible bookshelves made of laminated cardboard, are far easier than actual books. These fake books, often entire mini-libraries, just want to say that there are books here, if there were any. Pro forma works by Goethe and Schiller; quickly draped and put away in its place.

In addition, such fake books are useful in the modern age to use as surveillance cameras or bugs in a hollowed-out spine of a book, to eaves-drop fireside chats and private tête-à-têtes.

Well then: What are the fake books good for? There are honourable reasons to fill a prestigious bookshelf so it does not look so empty.

1. The English term 'fake books for shelves' goes in this direction, because it is more common in English speaking countries to adorn oneself with such appearances (cf. another example of the decorative fake: artificial chimney fires in all its variants).

2. If you do not want to carry books with you during your next move, you might buy a dummy. Yet, this reduction of weight seems barely an equivalent to missing the beloved books.

3. Some people want to keep their cards close to their chest or don't want to divulge their business. So he deceives literacy and interest in religious devotional literature to avoid revealing himself as a secret drinker, pornographer or millionaire.

4. So the function of the hiding place remains the desire for credulity. The bogus book is not just a book dummy to conceal the cash register or to cover up the secret compartment in the wall. Behind the bibliophilic quackery is hidden a second layer: the hidden libido, the secret passion, the undetected pleasure.

False books are primarily intended to deceive the eye and surprise people, because what they present is not what you imagine. It is the competition for the interpretive sovereignty of right and true, which Pliny exemplified in his natural history by means of the competition between Zeuxis and Parrhasius. While the first bluffed that birds flew to his painted pigeons, the second stunned by not being able to push aside a curtain that concealed the supposedly true work, because it too was painted, to great indignation of Zeuxis, who failed to notice the deception. Deceptions, illusions and camouflage, and that is the quintessence of the art historical paradigm, want to sharpen the view by fundamentally mistrusting the objective, be it a picture painted in a realistic way or a wrong book, or, between the lines, the content, the taught knowledge of a book.

The collection of Armin Müller in Winterthur is very diverse. 1500 objects from different eras, all couleur, style, provenance and the same function of camouflage and illusion. The fact that books are not only a place of knowledge and reading, but also the pure function of recreation, of entertainment mathematics, which can be fun, joy and pleasure, is shown here for the first time in extenso. These false books have hardly impacted in library science or in the field of collection science and exhibits, which is why this publication is almost inevitable. Most of all, the rubrum of the book objects is cultivated, which, however, focuses less on the mischievous bookbinding than on the recycling of disused books into an art object.

Book spines with all their beautiful inscriptions and materialities are mirrors of the inner life and allow belief in a certain content, the revelation of which can serve visual pleasure. As we know, this mirror is not factual; it plays with exchanged pages, marked cards, with the illusion of values. It simulates more than it is a leitmotif for the content. The wrong track makes you shudder due to the sophistication of the deception. 'Karl Knausrig: The passbook', 'How to get along with your mother-in-law', 'From the miracle of XY', 'Goethe: Work and World' are the so-called forged titles with their imitated metal fittings.

An entire wall of books can thus be hypocrisy, a facade of supposed literary wealth, where in truth profane desires are hidden. In general terms, books generally have the aura of the better and higher, represent the spirit and the reading, and promote power and fame. Those who own books are worldly, open-minded and opinion-tolerant. Anyone who owns a library knows that it is unique, like a fingerprint; it is the outwardly turned psychogram of the owner, more meaningful than any psychoanalysis. And so, even such a non-library shows the matrix of the collector.

Today, where wall-to-wall bookshelves have become obsolete (everything can be looked up on the net at lightning speed) and windows down to the ground are standard, where large-format art hangs on the supporting vestiges and altogether the bourgeoisie with spleens and passions, their men's circles and gentlemen's dinners no longer exist, so there is no need for the appearance of false books.

There is hardly any suspicion with these fake books, at least not if they can be found in the presence of actual books. It takes a keen eye to distinguish the right from the wrong, to discover the vault behind the dummy. And if the hosts knock on the spines of the books like woodpeckers, because they postpone the location of their false books again and again, then it may be time to at least convolute their book backs with misleading labels. The blind tooled titles are then pompously named: 'The age of innocence', 'Investors syndicate', 'Livre d'heures' ..., with which corruption and parody are already indicated.

The profession of the false book maker has not yet been invented – in contrast to the petty-currency printer's business. Herewith, we provide the historical, guaranteed guidance for the great domestic fraud, the reference work for the misleading book philistine, the encyclopædia for the revenge trickle of prevented librarians, if in the future such a profession of the beautiful sham should be asked. Because the false book maker is not only a connoisseur of historical matter and materialities, he must also know about manufacturing techniques. He knows how buckles, closures and pawls work and how paper refines into leather or cardboard can be trimmed to a folio. He makes velour and velvet look old and applies to virgin material an aura of the used up and destroyed. He conjures a patina on tinplate and flirts with supposed nostalgia. He knows how his 'Wunderkammern' are sealed and with which tricks – turn, click, move, fold, press against each other and combined together, etc. – they can be opened again. Because that too is part of it: a false book is also a secret that teases out the ingenuity of the closure technique, if necessary to confront the finder with enigmatic problems. As with the discovery of secret doors in false walls and dungeons behind cabinets you do not want to break anything, but also to discover with astonishment the knowledge of use, want to recognise notches, mitres and taps, scan pressure points, investigate hardly visible abrasion spots to find the sophisticated mechanics, without which one does not come to the hidden content. False objects are traps for the sense of sight, ambushes of perception.

A hiding place is only as good as its invisible protection. And that is the power of cunning and deception that someone believes he is seeing, his sense of impression taken seriously. No one can imagine being the one who falls for someone else's tricks. Thus, books are just seen as books because there are usually found in a library.

Bibliografie / *Bibliography*

Autrand, Françoise: Jean de Berry. L'art et le pouvoir, Paris 2000 (S. 308, Hôtel de Nesle; S. 435, Wohnhaus in Bourges; S. 436, Scheinbuch von 1411; S. 468–472, Büchersammlung).

Barnert, Arno: Sammelbehälter der Moderne. Buchattrappen und Scheinbücher im Deutschen Literaturarchiv Marbach. In: Jahrbuch der Deutschen Schiller-Gesellschaft, 58, 2014, S. 450–460.

Borges, Jorge Luis: Die Bibliothek von Babel. Erzählungen. Aus dem Spanischen übertragen von Karl August Horst und Curt Meyer-Clason. Mit einem Nachwort hrsg. von José A. Friedl Zapata, Stuttgart 2016 (Reclams Universal-Bibliothek, 9497), S. 53–63: Die Bibliothek von Babel.

Champeaux, Alfred de / Gauchery, Paul: Les travaux d'art exécutés pour Jean de France, duc de Berry, avec une étude biographique sur les artistes employés par ce prince, Paris 1894 (S. 136, Scheinbuch von 1411).

Chazelle, Annie / Goldman, Philippe: Bourges, une ville capitale sous Jean de Berry. In: Alain Salamagne (Hrsg.): Palais et son décor. Au temps de Jean de Berry, Tours 2010, S. 35–55 (S. 40, Rue Porte-Jaune).

Durrieu, Paul: Les Très Riches Heures de Jean de France, duc de Berry, Paris 1904 (S. 81 und 83, Scheinbuch von 1411, Wohnhaus in Bourges).

Dückers, Rob / Roelofs, Pieter (Hrsg.): The Limbourg brothers, Nijmegen masters at the French court 1400–1416, [Ghent] 2005 (S. 21–22 und 166, Scheinbuch von 1411, Wohnhaus in Bourges).

Enderli, Hans: Buntpapiere. Geschichte und Rezepte des Buntpapiers mit 205 Original-Buntpapier-Mustern. Winterthur 1971.

Feuchter-Schawelka, Anne: Carl Schildbachs „Holzbibliothek nach selbstgewähltem Plan" von 1788. Eine „Sammlung von Holzarten, so Hessenland von Natur hervorbringt". Naturkundemuseum im Ottoneum Kassel 2001.

Franklin, M.J.: Biscuit Tins 1868–1939, the art of decorative packaging. London 2001.

Grünbaum, Gabriele: Bücher, die keine sind. Kunst und Kitsch in Buchgestalt. In: Kreis Neuss – Der Oberkreisdirektor, Museum ZonsBurg Friedestrom 1988.

Guiffrey, Jules: Inventaires de Jean duc de Berry (1401–1416), publiés et annotés, 2 Bde., Paris 1894, 1896 (Bd. 1, S. XLIX–L und 265 Nr. 994, Scheinbuch von 1411).

Haemmerle, Albert: Buntpapier. Herkommen, Geschichte, Techniken, Beziehungen zur Kunst. München [2]1977.

Heckscher, William Sebastian: Reflections on seeing Holbein's portrait of Erasmus at Longford Castle. In: Essays presented to Rudolf Wittkower on his sixty-fifth birthday, Bd. 2: Essays in the history of art, London 1967, S. 128–148 (passim).

Kleinlaut, Brigitte: Ewig soll die Freundschaft blüh'n. In: Sammler-Journal, Reichertshausen, o. J., 1579–1581.

Krause, Susanne / Porck, Henk / Rinck, Julia / Schmidt, Frieder / Schrijver Ida: Buntpapier – ein Bestimmungsbuch. Hamburg 2009.

König, Eberhard: Limburg (Limbourg), Gebrüder. In: Allgemeines Künstler-Lexikon, Bd. 84, Berlin 2005, S. 460–463.

Köster, Kurt: Buchverfremdung. In: Lexikon des gesamten Buchwesens. Zweite, völlig neu bearbeitete Ausgabe, Bd. 1, Stuttgart 1987, S. 638.

Köster, Kurt: Bücher, die keine sind. Über Buchverfremdungen, besonders im 16. und 17. Jahrhundert. In: Buchhandelsgeschichte 2/4 = Börsenblatt für den Deutschen Buchhandel, Frankfurter Ausgabe, Nr. 98, 7. Dezember 1979, S. B 177–202.

Köster, Kurt: Mehrfachbände und Vexierbücher. Materialien zu Einbandkuriosa des sechzehnten und siebzehnten Jahrhunderts. In: Archiv für Geschichte des Buchwesens, 14, 1974, Sp. 1879–1936.

Köster, Kurt: Schnapsbibeln und Teufelsgebetbücher. Trinkgefäße in Buchform vom 16. bis zum 19. Jahrhundert. In: Festschrift für Wilhelm Meister zum 65. Geburtstag am 16. Mai 1974, Hamburg 1975, S. 136–150.

Köster, Kurt: Zwei fingierte Büchersammlungen des 18. Jahrhunderts. Turgots „Büchertür" in Limoges (1774). Ein Kasseler „Bücherschrank" (um 1790). In: Archiv für Geschichte des Buchwesens, 15, 1974, Sp. 963–998.

La scatola di latta tra arte e funzionalità. Collezione Blass, Zurigo. Galleria Gottardo una fondazione per la cultura della Banca del Gottardo, 28.05.–23.08.2003. Ausstellungskatalog. Mendrisio 2003.

Lehoux, Françoise: Jean de France, duc de Berri. Sa vie, son action politique (1340–1416), 4 Bde., Paris 1966-1968 (Bd. 3, 1967, S. 419–421, 508, 1.12. und spätestens vor 28.12.1410 in Bourges).

Meiss, Millard: French painting in the time of Jean de Berry. The Limbourgs and their contemporaries, 2 Bde., New York 1974 (Bd. 1, S. 69–70, 76 und 80–81, Scheinbuch von 1411, Wohnhaus in Bourges).

Michelant, Henri Victor: Inventaire des vaisselles, joyaux, tapisseries, peintures, manuscrits, etc. de Marguerite d'Autriche, régente et gouvernante des Pays-Bas, dressé en son palais de Malines le 9 juillet 1523. In: Bulletin de la Commission royale d'histoire, 3e série, 12, Bruxelles 1871, S. 5–78, 83–136 (S. 60, 77 und 100, Scheinbücher, Klappsonnenuhr).

Nyffeler, Paul: Die Blechdose, Verpackung als Kunstobjekt, Kunstobjekt als Verpackung. Schalterhalle Valiant Bank AG, Ausstellungskatalog. Bern 16.11.–10.12.2010.

Petersen, Heinz: Bucheinbände. Graz 1988.

Pfisermeiser, Ursula: Wachs, Volkskunst und Brauch. Ein Buch für Sammler und Liebhaber alter Dinge, Band 1. Nürnberg 1981.

Ribault, Jean-Yves: Enlumineurs et financiers, documents berrichons inédits sur les frères de Limbourg. In: Revue de l'art, Nr. 88, 1990, S. 48–51.

Richner, Barbara / Hauser, Janina: Die Holzbibliothek im Naturmuseum Thurgau. In: KGS Forum Nr.20/2013, 62–68.

Sitterwerk, St.Gallen: Mit/Ohne Anspruch auf Vollständigkeit – Rarität Holzbibliothek. Auswahl aus der 117-bändigen Holzbibliothek des Museums Wald und U mwelt in Ebersberg von Candid Huber, 25.01.–22.03.2015.

Tafelmeier, M. und W.: Die dreidimensionale Verführung. Reklame auf alten Blechdosen. Die bibliophilen Taschenbücher Nr. 311. Dortmund 1982.

Valéry, Paul: Mon Faust (Ebauches). In: Paul Valéry: Œuvres. Edition établie et annotée par Jean Hytier, Bd. 2, Paris 1960 (Bibliothèque de la Pléiade, 148), S. 276–403 (Zitate S. 364–366).

Weber, Bruno: Schöner Bücher Schein. Trompe-l'œil-Bücher aus einer Zürcher Privatsammlung. Text zur Ausstellung in Zürich, Zentralbibliothek, 1. November 1994 bis 31. März 1995 (Faltblatt, 10 S. nicht paginiert).

Winner, Matthias: Terminus als Rebus in Holbeins Bildnissen des Erasmus. In: Christian Müller / Stephan Kemperdick (Hrsg.): Hans Holbein d. J. Die Jahre in Basel 1515–1432, Basel und München 2006, S. 97–109, Abb. 1 (Porträt Erasmus 1523).

Autoren / *Authors*

Armin Müller (geb. 1948 in Winterthur)
Lehre als Handbuchbinder mit Berufsschule bei Richard Bretscher Winterthur. Angestellter als Buchbinder und Einrahmer in Winterthur, danach in der Zentralbibliothek Zürich, schließlich daselbst Abteilungsleiter Buchbinderei und Bestandserhaltung bis 2012. 1971 und 1975 Teilnahme am Internationalen Bucheinbandwettbewerb Prix Paul Bonet im Centro del bel libro Ascona (Bronzemedaillen für Gestaltung). Weiterbildungen am Institut für Buch- und Handschriftenrestaurierung in der Bayerischen Staatsbibliothek München. Berufsbegleitende Ausbildung zum Papier- und Buchrestaurator bei der Arbeitsgemeinschaft für Papier-Restauration Bern. Er lebt in Winterthur.

***Armin Müller** (born 1948 in Winterthur)*
Trained as a manual binder with vocational school at Richard Bretscher Winterthur. He worked as a bookbinder and framer in Winterthur, then at the Zurich Central Library, where he was head of the department of bookbinding and conservation until 2012. In 1971 and 1975 he took part in the International Bookbinding Competition Prix Paul Bonet at the Centro del bel libro Ascona (bronze medals for design). Further professional training at the Institute for Book and Manuscript Restoration at the Bavarian State Library in Munich. Further he was trained as a paper and book restorer at the Arbeitsgemeinschaft für Papier-Restauration Bern. He lives in Winterthur.

Bruno Weber (geb. 1937 in Zürich)
Dr. phil., Studium der Kunstgeschichte, Philosophie und Kirchengeschichte an der Universität Basel. 1967–2002 Leiter der Graphischen Sammlung der Zentralbibliothek Zürich. Als wissenschaftlicher Bibliothekar zahlreiche Aufsätze in Periodica und Büchern. Autor von Publikationen zur Grafik und Buchillustration, Porträt- und Landschaftskunst des 15. bis 20. Jahrhunderts, zu topografischen Ansichten und Panoramen der Schweiz, zu Zürcher Persönlichkeiten wie Salomon Gessner, Gottfried Keller und Conrad Ferdinand Meyer. Aktuar des Vereins Museen Maur seit 1992. 2002 Ehrenmitglied der Gottfried Keller-Gesellschaft. Er lebt in Ebmatingen.

***Bruno Weber** (born 1937 in Zurich)*
Dr. phil., he studied art history, philosophy and church history at the University of Basel. From 1967-2002 he was director of the Graphic Collection of the Central Library in Zurich. As a scientific librarian he has published numerous articles and books. He is the author of publications on graphic art and book illustration, on portrait and landscape art of the 15th to 20th century, on topographical views and panoramas of Switzerland, on Zurich personalities such as Salomon Gessner, Gottfried Keller and Conrad Ferdinand Meyer. Since 1992 he has been actuary of the Verein Museen Maur. In 2002 he became an honorary member of the Gottfried Keller Society. He lives in Ebmatingen.

Fritz Franz Vogel (geb. 1957 in Luzern)
Dr. phil., arbeitet seit 1992 produktiv, kooperativ und interdisziplinär in den Medien Text, Fotografie und Buch (Gestaltung, Druckvorstufe und Herausgeberschaft). Sammlungen, Forschungen, Lehrtätigkeit, Publikationen und Ausstellungen in den Bereichen inszenierte und dokumentarische Fotografie, populäres und freies Theater, Alphabete und visuelle Kommunikation, Kunst, Körperbilder und Erotica.

***Fritz Franz Vogel** (born 1957 in Lucerne)*
Dr. phil., he has been working productively, cooperatively and interdisciplinary in the fields of text, photography and books (design, pre-press and publishing) since 1992. He is a lecturer, researcher, publisher and editor. He has collected, researched, taught, published and exhibited in the fields of staged and documentary photography, popular and free theatre, alphabets and visual communication, art, body images and erotica.

Die Deutsche Nationalbibliothek verzeichnet diese Publikation in der Deutschen Nationalbibliografie; detaillierte bibliografische Daten sind im Internet über http://dnb.dnb.de abrufbar.

The Deutsche Nationalbibliothek lists this publication in the Deutsche Nationalbibliografie; detailed bibliographic data are available on the Internet at http://dnb.dnb.de

ISBN 978-3-7165-1859-5

www.benteli.ch

1. Auflage 2020
Texte: Armin Müller, Bruno Weber, Fritz Franz Vogel
Fotos und Bildlegenden: Armin Müller
Übersetzung: Andrea Buck, Diessenhofen;
Maria Neergheen, Birmingham
Korrektorat: Sandra Ellegiers, Sophie Steybe
Grafisches Konzept & Layout: Benjamin Wolbergs
Schrift: GT Sectra & Akkurat Pro
Papier: GalerieArt Volume 135 g/m²

1st edition 2020
Texts: Armin Müller, Bruno Weber
Fritz Franz Vogel
Photography and captions: Armin Müller
English translation: Andrea Buck, Diessenhofen; Maria Neergheen, Birmingham
Proofreading: Sandra Ellegiers, Sophie Steybe
Graphic concept & layout: Benjamin Wolbergs
Typeface: GT Sectra, Akkurat Pro
Paper: GalerieArt Volume 135 g/m²

Diese Publikation wurde ermöglicht dank großzügiger Unterstützung folgender Institutionen:

This publication was made possible thanks to the support of the following institutions:

Stadt Winterthur

Stadt Winterthur, Departement Kulturelles und Dienste (Schweiz)
City of Winterthur, Department of Culture and Services (Switzerland)

Ulrico Hoepli-Stiftung, Zürich
Ulrico Hoepli Foundation, Zurich